D1380207

MARKETING COMMUNICATIONS

100633203

PEARSON

At Pearson, we have a simple mission:
to help people make more of their lives through

We combine innovative learning technology with trusted
content and educational expertise to provide engaging
and effective learning experiences that serve people
wherever and whenever they are learning.

From classroom to boardroom, our curriculum materials,
digital learning tools and testing programmes help to
educate millions of people worldwide-more
than any other private enterprise.

Every day our work helps learning flourish, and wherever
learning flourishes, so do people.

To learn more please visit us at **www.pearson.com/uk**

SEVENTH EDITION

MARKETING COMMUNICATIONS

discovery, creation and conversations

CHRIS FILL AND SARAH TURNBULL

PEARSON

Harlow, England • London • New York • Boston • San Francisco • Toronto • Sydney • Auckland • Singapore • Hong Kong
Tokyo • Seoul • Taipei • New Delhi • Cape Town • São Paulo • Mexico City • Madrid • Amsterdam • Munich • Paris • Milan

00633203

658.8
8
FIL

PEARSON EDUCATION LIMITED
Edinburgh Gate
Harlow CM20 2JE
United Kingdom
Tel: +44 (0)1279 623623
Web: www.pearson.com/uk

First published under the Prentice Hall Europe imprint 1995 (print)
Fourth edition 2005 (print)
Fifth edition 2009 (print)
Sixth edition 2013 (print and electronic)
Seventh edition published 2016 (print and electronic)

© Prentice Hall Europe 1994, 1999 (print)
© Pearson Education Limited 2006, 2009 (print)
© Pearson Education Limited 2013, 2016 (print and electronic)

The rights of Chris Fill and Sarah Turnbull to be identified as authors of this work have been asserted by them in accordance with the Copyright, Designs and Patents Act 1988.

The print publication is protected by copyright. Prior to any prohibited reproduction, storage in a retrieval system, distribution or transmission in any form or by any means, electronic, mechanical, recording or otherwise, permission should be obtained from the publisher or, where applicable, a licence permitting restricted copying in the United Kingdom should be obtained from the Copyright Licensing Agency Ltd, Saffron House, 6–10 Kirby Street, London EC1N 8TS.

The ePublication is protected by copyright and must not be copied, reproduced, transferred, distributed, leased, licensed or publicly performed or used in any way except as specifically permitted in writing by the publisher, as allowed under the terms and conditions under which it was purchased, or as strictly permitted by applicable copyright law. Any unauthorised distribution or use of this text may be a direct infringement of the authors' and the publisher's rights and those responsible may be liable in law accordingly.

All trademarks used herein are the property of their respective owners. The use of any trademark in this text does not vest in the author or publisher any trademark ownership rights in such trademarks, nor does the use of such trademarks imply any affiliation with or endorsement of this book by such owners.

Pearson Education is not responsible for the content of third-party internet sites.

ISBN: 978-1-292-09261-4 (print)
      978-1-292-09383-3 (PDF)
      978-1-292-09382-6 (eText)

British Library Cataloguing-in-Publication Data
A catalogue record for the print edition is available from the British Library

Library of Congress Cataloging-in-Publication Data
A catalogue record for the print edition is available from the Library of Congress

10 9 8 7 6 5 4 3 2 1
20 19 18 17 16

Print edition typeset in 10/12pt Sabon LT Pro by 71
Printed in Slovakia by Neografia

NOTE THAT ANY PAGE CROSS REFERENCES REFER TO THE PRINT EDITION

Brief contents

For Karen ..... thank you for the music (CF)
For Simon, Daisy and Bea (ST)

Contents

Part 3 The marketing communications mix

353

Companion Website

For open-access **student resources** specifically written to complement this textbook and support your learning, please visit **www.pearsoned.co.uk/fill**

Lecturer Resources

For password-protected online resources tailored to support the use of this textbook in teaching, please visit **www.pearsoned.co.uk/fill**

Preface

This is the seventh edition of *Marketing Communications* and it marks the introduction of Dr Sarah Turnbull as my co-author. Sarah has a wealth of advertising experience from both a practical and academic perspective. She has provided a valuable new perspective and her contribution has undoubtedly enriched the book. We have made several changes which we believe enhance the book significantly. These changes are explained here in the Preface but you will be the judge of the impact of these changes.

So thank you for reading our book, and if you have any comments, observations, suggestions or opinions, please feel free to contact me through chris@chrisfill.com or Sarah through sarah.turnbull@port.ac.uk.

This book has been written to help you in four ways:

1 To understand and appreciate the variety of ways in which organisations use marketing communications.
2 To identify and understand some of the key theories and concepts associated with marketing communications.
3 To appreciate the way in which academic materials can be used to interpret practical aspects of marketing communications.
4 To develop insights into the reasoning behind the marketing communications activities used by organisations.

Marketing communications is a complex subject and draws on a variety of disciplines. This book has been written in the hope of disentangling some of the complexity so that you can enjoy the subject, be stimulated to want to know more and wish to engage further with the exciting and fast-changing world of marketing communications.

A world of marketing communications

All organisations, large and small, commercial, government, charities, educational and other not-for-profit and third-sector organisations need to communicate with a range of stakeholders. This may be in order to get materials and services to undertake their business activities or to collaborate and coordinate with others to secure suitable distribution of their goods and services. In addition, there are consumers who are free to choose among the many hundreds and thousands of product/service offerings. Marketing communications provides a core activity so that all interested parties can understand the intentions of others and appreciate the value of the goods and services offered.

The world of marketing communications is changing, and some of it is changing at an incredible speed. Technology, buyer behaviour, economic cycles, industry and organisational performance have all evolved and all impact on the way we communicate, when we communicate and how we communicate.

Many of these changes and their impact are explored in this book. It is not possible to cover them all in depth but many of the key academic and practitioner reactions to these developments are examined.

Structure

This book is structured around three parts: Introduction to marketing communications; Managing marketing communications; and The marketing communications mix.

Content

Each chapter has been updated and where appropriate includes current academic materials (ideas, arguments, models, references and papers). The fundamental principles associated with marketing communications remain.

Cases

Each chapter is introduced with a practitioner-based case study. The majority of these have been written by a client organisation or its agency. Reference to each case is made throughout the relevant chapter and questions relating to these cases can be found at the end of the chapter.

Many of these cases have been written and supplied by several communications agencies who are associated with the Institute of Practitioners in Advertising (IPA). Indeed, the IPA has again provided important support for this edition.

Viewpoints

Examples of marketing communications practice can be found as Viewpoints. There are a minimum of four Viewpoints per chapter, each illustrating particular issues or topics. For the first time we have included Viewpoints written by students from UK universities. We wish to extend this form of co-creation in the future and incorporate examples co-created by students from other countries and regions. Please contact us if you feel you would like to contribute to the next edition.

Scholars' papers

The Scholars' paper innovation has been continued and where feasible enhanced by including papers that offer divergent views. Reference to various topics such as ethics, business-to-business (B2B) communications, social media and international dimensions are embedded throughout the book.

Positioning and style

The book is positioned as an academic resource about marketing communications. The practitioner element, however, is acknowledged as an important distinguishing feature of this book (Rossiter, J.R. and Percy, L. (2013) How the roles of advertising merely appear to have changed, *International Journal of Advertising*, 32(3), 391–8) and is reinforced in this edition. The support and endorsement provided by the IPA has been continued and is appreciated.

We have continued to present a variety of perspectives and approaches, rather than portray a single view as the conventional wisdom. This enables readers to consider different views, and develop a critical understanding of the subject.

Overview of the book

This book recognises the complexity of marketing communications, it considers the strategic, tactical and operational aspects, and attempts to consider the subject from an integrative perspective. Above all else this book considers marketing communications from a contextual standpoint. This means that no one single theory is used to explain all marketing communications activities. Indeed, several theories are presented and readers are encouraged to consider multiple interpretations of marketing communications behaviour.

This book has been written from an academic perspective and seeks to provide a consistent appraisal of the ever-changing world of marketing communications. The intention is to stimulate thought and consideration about a wide range of interrelated issues, and to help achieve this aim a number of theories and models are advanced. Some of these theories reflect marketing practice, while others are offered as suggestions for moving the subject forward. Many of the theories are abstractions of actual practice, some are based on empirical research and others are pure conceptualisation. All seek to enrich the subject, but not all need carry the same weight of contribution. Readers should form their own opinions based upon their reading, experience and judgement.

Structure of the text

There are three main parts to the book:

- Part 1: Introduction to marketing communications

  This part introduces readers to the subject from a general perspective and then seeks to establish some of the key issues that are necessary in order to provide a foundation for the subject. These include communications theory, the ways in which audiences process information and make purchase decisions, and, in the final chapter in this part, ideas about how marketing communications works.

- Part 2: Managing marketing communications

  This part explores some of the managerial aspects associated with marketing communications. The core content concerns the various aspects of *strategy* and how organisations should develop their marketing communications in the light of their contextual positions. This part then considers the role and nature of objectives and positioning, before exploring some of the issues associated with the communications industry, the financial implications associated with managing marketing communications, and the issues associated with the evaluation and measurement of marketing communications. The chapter concludes with the important topic of integrated marketing communications.

- Part 3: The marketing communications mix

  The marketing communications mix material constitutes by far the largest part of the book, covering half of the book's chapters. This content is of course crucial to all courses on marketing communications. Unlike other texts the approach here emphasises the use of three components of the mix, namely the tools, content and media.

Part 1: Introduction to marketing communications

This opening part serves to establish the scope of the book and provides a brief overview of the content and style adopted throughout the rest of the text. Chapter 1 provides an introductory perspective to marketing communications and sets out some important, key concepts. Chapter 2 addresses issues concerning communications theory and in particular moves on from the simple linear interpretation of how communications work to one that recognises the influence of people, behaviour and interactional elements on the communications process. Chapter 3 is concerned with aspects of buyer behaviour, upon which marketing communications should be developed. Only by understanding the market and the target audience can appropriate objectives, strategies, promotional methods, applications and resources be determined, allocated and implemented.

The final chapter in this part introduces ideas about how marketing communications might work. Rather than suggest a single approach, five separate approaches are presented. These are the sequential buying processes, attitude change, shaping relationships, significant value, and cognitive processing.

Part 2: Managing marketing communications

Part 2 concerns a variety of managerial issues related to marketing communications. These embrace strategy, goals, industry, financial, measurement and integration issues. Chapter 5 is concerned with the nature of communications strategy and considers the interrelationship between strategy and planning. The first section of this chapter considers ideas about four distinct approaches to marketing communications strategy. The second section of the chapter introduces the marketing communications planning framework and works through the model, highlighting issues and linkages, and ends with an operational approach to devising, formulating and implementing a strategic marketing communications plan.

Chapter 6 examines the nature of objectives and positioning in marketing communications and considers both academic and practitioner (IPA) approaches to the nature of communications-based objectives.

The nature and characteristics of the UK marketing communications industry is the focus of Chapter 7. This material can be useful as it specifically examines the strategic and operational issues of communications agencies and their interaction with client organisations. This chapter also considers aspects of budgeting for marketing communications.

Chapter 8 examines the ways in which the performance of marketing communications activities can and should be evaluated.

Chapter 9 is significant because it focuses on the role marketing communications can play in the development and maintenance of product/service brands. New to this chapter are Keller's ideas about building brands. It also considers the role and issues associated with B2B branding, branding in interactive environments, employee branding and brand equity.

The final chapter in this part is about integrated marketing communications. This chapter challenges ideas about the nature and validity of the 'integrated' view of marketing communications. Five separate interpretations about what integrated marketing communications might be is presented. This is a core chapter because it bridges the contextual elements and the application of the various disciplines. The notion that integrated marketing communications (IMC) is a valid and realistic concept is explored and readers are encouraged to consider the arguments for and against this approach. Its position at the end of the management part of the book is designed to encourage readers to reflect on what should be integrated and what integration incorporates.

Part 3: The marketing communications mix

This is the biggest part in the book, and examines the various elements that constitute the marketing communications mix. There are 10 chapters in this section, configured as three sections. The first examines the tools or disciplines, the second, message content and creativity issues, and the third explores issues related to the media.

Chapter 11 is about advertising and contains three elements. The first considers the role and use of advertising, and how ideas about selling propositions and emotion can be used in advertising. Prominence is also given to the different types or forms of advertising. Time is spent exploring the way advertising might work. Here consideration is given to some of the principal models and frameworks that have been published to best explain the process by which advertising might influence audiences. The third element concerns the way in which advertising can be used strategically as part of a brand's development, and to review the significance of consumer-generated advertising.

Chapter 12 examines the role and characteristics of public relations, including a review of the various methods used in public relations, and crisis communications. The following chapter leads on naturally to explore sponsorship, while Chapter 14 examines both direct marketing and personal selling.

Chapters 15 and 16 both consider a range of disciplines. The first considers the principles and techniques of sales promotion, field marketing and brand experiences. The second explores brand placement, exhibitions, packaging and the rapidly developing area of brand licensing.

The second element in this third part of the book is the content, or the messages conveyed to, with and between audiences. This chapter examines message appeals through four broad elements. First, attention is given to the source of a message and issues relating to source credibility. Second, the role and issues associated with using spokespersons, either to be the face of a brand or to endorse it, are explored. Third, the need to balance the use of information and emotion in messages and the way messages are constructed are reviewed before finally exploring the various appeals and ways in which messages can be presented.

The second part of this chapter explores ideas associated with the nature, role and processes organisations use to manage the creative process, and the ways in which the creative process can be harnessed. Here message framing and storytelling are developed before concluding with a review of a more contemporary perspective of content generation and creativity, namely user-generated content.

The final element considers the media. Chapter 18 considers the principles and practice of media, and reference is made to both the 'Classes' and 'POEM' classifications. In addition, however, we introduce a new classification based on communications function. The conventional and traditional media labels are changed to 'linear' media. New or digital media are redefined as 'interactive' media.

Chapter 19 considers social, search and other interactive media. This chapter reflects the contemporary nature of these important and evolving topics. The final chapter in this part and the book considers ideas and theories associated with media planning and the way in which people use media.

Cases

In this edition 19 of the 20 cases are new. These have been written by a variety of people including client organisations and marketing communications agencies.

These cases either refer to broad issues concerning a particular topic, or focus on a specific issue that is included in the chapter to which the case is assigned. Some refer to several campaigns undertaken for a specific brand or company, whilst others consider a specific campaign and associated activities. All serve to introduce a particular aspect of marketing communications and should be used to frame the way readers approach the content of each chapter. There are review questions at the end of each chapter that refer directly to the introductory case.

Design features and presentation

In addition to the three-part structure of the book, there are a number of features that are intended to help readers navigate the material.

Chapter objectives

Each chapter opens with both the aims of what is to be covered and a list of learning objectives. This helps to signal the primary topics that are covered in the chapter and so guide the learning experience.

Cases

Each chapter opens with a campaign–based case study. The majority of these have been written by marketing managers at client organisations or planners at agencies. These are used either to introduce the broad flow of the chapter's material or to focus on a particular topic.

These short cases can be used in class for discussion purposes and to explore some of the salient issues raised in the chapter. Students working alone can use the cases to test their own understanding.

Visual supports

This book is produced in four colours and throughout the text there are numerous colour and black and white exhibits, figures (diagrams) and tables of information which serve to highlight, illustrate and bring life to the written word. The pictures used serve either to illustrate particular points by demonstrating theory in practice or to complement individual examples. The examples are normally highlighted in the text as Viewpoints. These examples are easily distinguishable through the colour contrasts and serve to demonstrate how a particular aspect of marketing communications has been used by an organisation in a particular context. We hope you enjoy these Viewpoints of marketing communications practice.

In this edition several Viewpoints have been contributed by students from a range of universities. We hope you like this development and perspective that students bring to the subject. Contributions from students and marketing practitioners to the next edition would be warmly welcomed.

Key points and review questions

At the end of each chapter is a section headed 'Key points', and another 'Review questions'. The key points from the chapter are presented in chronological order, and are normally in the order of the learning objectives listed at the beginning of each chapter.

Readers are advised to test their own understanding of the content of each chapter by considering some or all of the review questions. The first group of questions relate directly to the chapter's opening case study, the other questions relate to the overall material in the chapter.

Web support

Students and lecturers who adopt this text have a range of support materials and facilities to help them. Readers are invited to use the website designed for *Marketing Communications*, not only as a source of additional material but also as an interactive forum to explore and discuss marketing communications issues, academic and practitioner developments and to improve learning. The site accommodates the needs of student readers and lecturers.

Student resources

- Additional learning materials including chapters, adverts, podcasts, Viewpoints, and cases
- Annotated web links
- Full online glossary
- Multiple choice questions
- Additional cases and examples

Lecturer resources

- Instructors' Resource Guide
- PowerPoint slides for each chapter
- Annotated web links

A test bank of multiple choice questions has been developed for use by students and lecturers. In addition, there are links to a range of related sites, an online glossary and chapters from previous editions that some readers have requested be made available.

For lecturers and tutors not only is there an Instructors' Resource Guide containing a range of slides and exercises in downloadable format, but there is also a password-protected section of the companion website for their use. From this site a much larger range of PowerPoint slides, teaching schemes and case material can be downloaded.

Acknowledgements

This book could not have been written without the support of a wide range of brilliant people. Contributions range from those who provided information and permissions, to those who wrote cases, answered questions and those who tolerated our persistent nagging, sending through photographs, answering phone calls and emails, and those who simply liaised with others. Finally, there are those who have read reviewed drafts, made constructive comments and provided moral support and encouragement.

Lucy Alexander	Leeds Beckett University
Eloise Augestine	Buckinghamshire New University
Carlton Bradley	University of the West of England
Matt Buttrick	Grey
Rebecca Clay	PHD
Amanda Coleman	Greater Manchester Police
James Devon	MBA
Reece Drew	Manchester Business School
Julian Earl	Publicis
Ellie Harris	Leeds Beckett University
Hanne Haugen	Wilden Kennedy
Lisa Hides	Newcastle University
Ben Hitchcock	Everest
Jon Holden	Mondeléz International
Miquet Humphryes	Millward Brown
Jasmine Kendal	University of Huddersfield
Pavel Laczko	University of Portsmouth
Sarah Mayo	Tro
Tom Patterson	Now
Bilyana Petrova	GreenHopping
Toby Pilcher	Buckinghamshire New University
James Price	MBA
Harriet Rich	Brands2Life
Phil Springall	Kärcher
Richard Storey	M & C Saatchi
Ray Sylvester	Associate Professor at Anderson University, USA
Tarek Temrawi	Northampton University
Anne-Fay Townsend	Johnny Fearless
Rachel Walker	Grey
Jonathan Ward	Buckinghamshire New University
Pieter-Jan van Wettere	Sales Operations Manager for Lidl Belgium &Luxembourg
WPP	Press Office
Melanie Bruton	University of Huddersfield
Sarah Warwick	Ink

The list of individuals and organisations involved with this book is extensive. Our thanks are offered to all of you. We have tried to list everyone but if anyone has been omitted then we offer our sincere apologies.

Case contributors

Many people have given their time and energies either to writing or to cajoling others to write a cases and Viewpoints. The fruits of their labour are on show here and may we express our gratitude for the time and energy you all gave to write your material.

Above all perhaps are the various individuals at Pearson and their associates who have taken our manuscript, managed it and published it in this form. In particular we should like to thank Tom Hill, as the editor of this book, for his openness and support of our initiatives. In support has been Eileen Srebernik who has been actively involved with both the front and back end aspects of this project. In addition we should like to thank Tim Parker and his team for transforming the manuscript into the final product. Thank you all.

Publisher's acknowledgements

We are grateful to the following for permission to reproduce copyright material:

Figures

Figure 1.3 from Redefining the nature and format of the marketing communications mix, *The Marketing Review*, 7 (1), 45–57 (Hughes, G. and Fill, C. 2007), reproduced by permission of Westburn Publishers Ltd; Figure 1.4 from *Essentials of Marketing Communications*, Pearson Education (Fill, C. 2011) figure 1.3, p. 10, reproduced by permission of Pearson Education Ltd.; Figure 2.2 from *Essentials of Marketing Communications*, Pearson Education (Fill, Chris 2011) figure 2.2, p. 39; Figure 2.3 from *Essentials of Marketing Communications*, Pearson Education (Fill, C. 2011) figure 2.3, p. 39; Figure 2.4 from *Essentials of Marketing Communications*, Pearson Education (Fill, C. 2011) figure 2.4, p. 41; Figure 3.9 from *Essentials of Marketing Communications*, Pearson Education (Fill, C. 2011) figure 3.5, p. 72; Figure 3.10 from *Essentials of Marketing Communications*, Pearson Education (Fill, C. 2011) figure 3.6, p. 73; Figure 3.11 from *Essentials of Marketing Communications*, Pearson Education (Fill, C. 2011) figure 3.7, p. 74; Figure 4.3 adapted from Managing market relationships, *Journal of the Academy of Marketing Science*, 28(1), pp. 24–30 (Day, G. 2000), with kind permission from Springer Science+Business Media; Figure 4.5 from How advertising affects the sales of packaged goods brands, *Millward Brown* (Brown, G. 1991); Figure 4.6 from *Attitude toward the ad as a mediator of advertising effectiveness, in Advances in Consumer Research*, Association for Consumer Research (Lutz, J., Mackensie, S.B. and Belch, G.E. (Bagozzi, R.P. and Tybout, A.M. eds) 1983) pp. 532–539, Republished with permission of Association for Consumer Research. Permission conveyed through Copyright Clearance Center, Inc.; Figure 5.2 adapted from Work towards an 'Ideal Self' *Marketing*, 02/02/2011 (Edwards, H.), reproduced from Marketing with the permission of the copyright owner, Haymarket Media Group Limited; Figure 5.3 from *Essentials of Marketing Communications*, Pearson Education (Fill, C. 2011) figure 4.2, p. 99; Figure 5.4 from *Essentials of Marketing Communications*, Pearson Education (Fill, C. 2011) figure 4.3, p. 102; Figure 5.5 from *Essentials of Marketing Communications*, Pearson Education (Fill, C. 2011) figure 4.4, p. 102; Figure 6.2 from *Essentials of Marketing Communications (2011)* Pearson Education (Fill, C. 2011) figure 4.6, p. 105; Figure 6.4 from How El Al Airlines transformed its service strategy with employee participation, *Strategy & Leadership*, Strategy & Leadership, pp. 21–25 (Herstein, R. and Mitki, Y. 2008), © Emerald Group Publishing Limited, all rights reserved; Figure 7.1 from *Essentials of Marketing Communications*, Pearson Education (Fill, C. 2011) figure 7.1, p. 165; Figure 7.3 from Ad spending: growing market share, *Harvard Business Review* January/February, pp. 44–48 (Schroer, J. 1990), Reprinted by permission of Harvard Business Review. Copyright (c) 1990 by Harvard Business School Publishing Corporation; all rights reserved; Figure 7.4 from Ad spending: maintaining market share, *Harvard Business Review*, January/February, pp. 38–42 (Jones, J.P. 1990), Reprinted by permission of Harvard Business Review. Copyright (c) 1990 by Harvard Business School Publishing

Corporation; all rights reserved; Figure 8.3 from *Public Relations Theories, Practices, Critiques,* Pearson Education (Macnamara, J. 2012) p.337, reproduced with permission; Figure 8.4 from Social media measurement: it's not impossible, *Journal of Interactive Advertising,* 10(1), pp. 94–99 (Murdough, C. 2009), ISSN 1525–2019, American Academy of Advertising; Figure 9.2 from *The New Strategic Brand Management,* Kogan Page (Kapferer, J.–N. 2012) Reproduced with permission of Kogan Page in the format Book via Copyright Clearance Center; Figure 9.3 from Implication of brand identity facets on marketing communications of lifestyle magazine: case study of a swedish brand *Journal of Applied Economics and Business Research,* 4(1), pp. 23–41 (Farhana, M. 2014); Figure 9.5 from Building strong brands in a modern marketing communications environment, *Journal of Marketing Communications,* 15(2–3), April– July, 139–155 (Keller, K.L. 2009), reprinted by permission of the publisher (Taylor & Francis Ltd., http://www.tandfonline.com); Figure 9.6 adapted from Branding the business marketing offer: exploring brand attributes in business markets, *Journal of Business and Industrial Marketing,* 22(6), pp. 394–399 (Beverland, M., Napoli, J. and Yakimova, R. 2007), © Emerald Group Publishing Limited all rights reserved; Figure 9.7 from Rethinking internal communications: a stakeholder approach, *Corporate Communications: An International Journal,* 12(2), 177–98 (Welch, M. and Jackson, P.R. 2007), © Emerald Group Publishing Limited all rights reserved; Figure 10.3 from Revisiting the IMC construct: a revised definition and four pillars, *International Journal of Advertising,* 27(1), pp. 133–160 (Kliatchko, Jerry 2008), reprinted by permission of the publisher (Taylor & Francis Ltd., http://www.tandfonline.com); Figure 11.1 after *Marketing Communications: A European Perspective,* 4th ed., Pearson Education (Pelsmaker de. P., Guens, M. and Bergh, van den, J. 2010) reproduced by permission of Pearson Education Ltd.; Figure 11.4 from How advertising works: a planning model, *Journal of Advertising Research,* October, pp. 27–33 (Vaughn, R. 1980), Journal of advertising research by ADVERTISING RESEARCH FOUNDATION Reproduced with permission of Warc Ltd. in the format Book via Copyright Clearance Center; Figure 11.5 adapted from *Advertising, Communications and Promotion Management,* 2nd ed., McGraw–Hill (Rossiter, J.R. and Percy, L. 1997); Figure 11.6 from Understanding consumer conversations around ads in a Web 2.0 world, *Journal of Advertising,* 40(1), pp. 87–102, figure 5 (Campbell, C., Pitt, L.F., Parent, M., and Berthon, P.R. 2011), reprinted by permission of Taylor & Francis Ltd, http://www.tandfonline.com; Figure 12.1 from *Managing Public Relations,* Holt, Rineholt & Winston (Grunig, J. and Hunt, T. 1984) reprinted by permission of James E. Grunig; Figure 13.1 after Match game: linking sponsorship congruence with communication outcomes, *Journal of Advertising Research,* June, pp. 214–226 (Poon, D.T.Y., Prendergast, G. and West, D. 2010), Journal of advertising research by ADVERTISING RESEARCH FOUNDATION Reproduced with permission of Warc Ltd. in the format Book via Copyright Clearance Center; Figure 14.1 from *Essentials of Marketing Communications,* Pearson Education (Fill, C. 2011) figure 11.1, p. 280; Figure 14.2 from A review of social media and implications for the sales process, *Journal of Personal Selling & Sales Management,* vol. XXXII (3) (Summer), pp. 305–316 (Andzulis, J.M., Panagopoulos, N.G. and Rapp, A. 2012), reprinted by permission of the publisher (Taylor & Francis Ltd, http://www. tandfonline.com); Figure 14.3 from Proactive and reactive: drivers for key account management programmes, *European Journal of Marketing,* 43(7/8), pp. 961–984 (Brehmer, P–O. and Rehme, J. 2009), © Emerald Group Publishing Limited all rights reserved; Figure 15.5 from Is your loyalty programme really building loyalty? Why increasing emotional attachment, not just repeat buying, is key to maximizing programme success, *Journal of Targeting Measurement and Analysis for Marketing,* 12(3), pp. 231–241 (Hallberg, G. 2004), Reprinted by permission from Macmillan Publishers

Ltd; Figure 16.1 from Branded entertainment: a new advertising technique or product placement in disguise?, *Journal of Marketing Management*, 22(5–6), pp. 489–504 (Hudson, S. and Hudson, D. 2006), reprinted by permission of Taylor & Francis Ltd, www.tandf.co.uk/journals; Figure 16.2 from Understanding B2C brand alliances between manufacturers and suppliers, *Marketing Management Journal*, 18(2), pp. 32–46 (Ervelles, S., Horton, V. and Fukawa, N. 2008); Figure 17.2 from Does it pay to shock? Reactions to shocking and nonshocking advertising content among university students, *Journal of Advertising Research*, 43(3), pp. 268–281 (Dahl, D.W., Frankenberger, K.D. and Manchanda, R.V. 2003), Journal of advertising research by ADVERTISING RESEARCH FOUNDATION Reproduced with permission of Warc Ltd. in the format Book via Copyright Clearance Center; Figures 17.3, 17.4, 17.5, 17.6 after *Advertising and Promotion Management*, 2nd ed., McGraw–Hill (Rossiter, J.R. and Percy, L. 1997)

Tables

Table 2.1 from Dialogue and its role in the development of relationship specific knowledge, *Journal of Business and Industrial Marketing*, 19 (2), pp. 111–23 (Ballantyne, D. 2004), © Emerald Group Publishing Limited all rights reserved; Table 2.2 after Word of mouth effects on short–term and long–term product judgments, *Journal of Business Research*, 32(3), pp. 213–23 (Bone, P.F. 1995), copyright 1995, with permission from Elsevier; Table 2.4 from *Communications in interpersonal relationships: social penetration theory, in Interpersonal Processes: New Directions in Communications Research* Sage Publications Inc. (Taylor, D. and Altman, I. (eds M.E. Roloff and G.R. Miller) 1987) pp. 257–77, republished with permission of Sage Publications, Inc., permission conveyed through Copyright Clearance Center, Inc.; Table 3.5 adapted from Tribal mattering spaces: social–networking sites, celebrity affiliations, and tribal innovations, *Journal of Marketing Management*, 26 (3/4), March, pp. 271–89 (Hamilton, K. and Hewer, P. 2010), reprinted by permission of Taylor & Francis Ltd; Table 4.3 from *Essentials of Marketing Communications*, Pearson Education (Fill, C. 2011) table 8.1, p. 190; Table 4.5 from Toward a dialogic theory of public relations, *Public Relations Review*, 28(1), pp. 21–37 (Kent, M.L. and Taylor, M. 2002), copyright 2002, with permission from Elsevier; Table 7.1 from http://expenditurereport.warc.com/, Used with permission from WARC; Table 7.2 from Brandrepublic (2015a) Top Holding Companies, BrandRepublic, 28 March. Retrieved 27 May 2015 from http://www.brandrepublic.com/article/1339955/top–holding–companies, reproduced from Brand Republic magazine with the permission of the copyright owner, Haymarket Media Group Limited; Table 7.3 from Marriage material, *The Marketer*, September, pp. 22–23 (Sclater, I. 2006); Table 7.4 from *Agency remuneration: a best practice guide to agency search and selection*, IPA/ISBA/CIPS (IPA/ISBA/CIPS 2012); Table 7.5 from Nielsen cited by Key Note (2014), Advertising Agencies. , Copyrighted information. (c) 2014 of the Nielsen Company, licensed for use herein; Table 7.7 from How to set digital media budgets, *WARC Exclusive, www.warc.com* (Renshaw, M. 2008), Reproduced with permission from WARC; Tables 8.1, 8.9 from *How to Evaluate the Effectiveness of Communications Plans*, IPA, London (ed. Bussey, S. et al 2014) Tables replicated with the kind permission of the Institute of Practitioners in Advertising (IPA), the world's most influential professional body for advertising practitioners.; Table 8.2 from Conceptualization and measurement of multidimensionality of integrated marketing communications, *Journal of Advertising Research*, September, pp. 222–236 (Lee, D.H. and Park, C.W. 2007), Journal of advertising research by ADVERTISING RESEARCH FOUNDATION Reproduced with permission of Warc Ltd. in the format Book via Copyright Clearance Center; Table 8.3 from Turnbull, S. (2011) The creative development process within U.K. advertising agencies: an exploratory study. Unpublished PhD Thesis, University of Portsmouth. , reproduced with permission; Table 8.7 from Macnamara, J. (2014). Breaking the PR measurement and evaluation deadlock: A new approach and model. Paper presented to the AMEC International Summit on Measurement, Upping the Game', Amsterdam, 11–12 June. Retrieved from http://amecorg.com/downloads/amsterdam2014/Breaking–the–PR–Measurement–Deadlock–A–New–Approach–and–Model–Jim–Macnamara.pdf reproduced with permission; Table 8.8 adapted from The world wide web as an advertising medium: toward an understanding of conversion efficiency, *Journal of Advertising Research,* 6(1), pp. 43–53 (Berthon, P., Pitt, L. and Watson, R. 1996), Journal of advertising research by ADVERTISING RESEARCH FOUNDATION Reproduced with permission of Warc Ltd. in the format Book via Copyright Clearance Center; Table 8.11 from Buckley, E. (2013). The business return from social media. Admap. Retrieved 10 April 2015 from http://www.warc.com/Content/ContentViewer.aspx?MasterContent Ref=24ca6283–696c–4822–9dd4–dc62db9807b3&q=the+business+return+for+social +media&CID=A99742&PUB=ADMAP Admap : the journal of advertising media analysis and planning by Warc Ltd.. Reproduced with permission of Warc Ltd. in the format Book via Copyright Clearance Center; Table 9.2 from *The New Strategic Brand Management,* Kogan Page (Kapferer, J.-N. 2012) Reproduced with permission of Kogan Page in the format Book via Copyright Clearance Center; Table 9.4 from Rethinking internal communications: a stakeholder approach, *Corporate Communications: An International Journal,* 12(2), 177–98 (Welch, M. and Jackson, P.R. 2007), © Emerald Group Publishing Limited all rights reserved; Table 9.6 from Developing a new model for tracking brand equity as a measure of marketing effectiveness, *The Marketing Review,* 11(4), 323–336 (Mirzaei, Gray and Baumann 2011), Reproduced by permission of Westburn Publishers Ltd.; Table 10.4 adapted from Jenkinson, A. and Sain, B. (2004) Open planning: media neutral planning made simple, www.openplanning.org/cases/openplanning/whitepaper.pdf; Tables 10.5, 10.6 from *New Models of Marketing Effectiveness From Integration to Orchestration,* WARC (IPA 2011) Tables replicated with the kind permission of the Institute of Practitioners in Advertising (IPA), the world's most influential professional body for advertising practitioners; Table 10.7 after Performance auditing of integrated marketing communication (IMC) actions and outcomes, *Journal of Advertising,* 34(4), pp. 41–54 (Reid, M. 2005), reproduced with permission of Taylor & Francis; Table 12.3 after Toward public relations theory–based study of public diplomacy: testing the applicability of the excellence study, *Journal of Public Relations Research,* 18(4), pp. 287–312 (Yun, S.-H. 2006), reprinted by permission of Taylor & Francis Ltd.; Table 12.7 from Image repair discourse and crisis communication, *Public Relations Review,* 23(2), pp. 177–86 (Benoit, W. L. 1997), copyright 1997, with permission from Elsevier; Table 12.8 after Protecting organization reputations during a crisis: The development and application of situational crisis communication theory, *Corporate Reputation Review,* 10(3), pp. 163–176 (Coombs, W.T. 2007), Reprinted by permission from Macmillan Publishers Ltd; Tables 13.1, 13.3, 13.6 from IEG (2015) Sponsorship spending report: where the dollars are going and trends for 2015, retrieved 30 March 2015 from www.sponsorship.com/IEG/files/4e/4e525456–b2b1–4049–bd51–03d9c35ac507.pdf reproduced with permission; Table 13.5 from Changes in sponsorship value: Competencies and capabilities of successful sponsorship relationships, *Industrial Marketing Management,* 35(8), pp. 1016–1026 (Farrelly, F. Quester, P. and Burton, R. 2006), copyright 2006, with permission from Elsevier; Table 14.3 from A Review of Social Media and Implications for the Sales Process, *Journal of Personal Selling & Sales Management,* vol. XXXII, 3 (Summer), pp. 305–316 (Andzulis, J.M., Panagopoulos, N.G. and Rapp, A. 2012); Table 14.5 from From key account selling to key account management,

Journal of Marketing Practice: Applied Marketing Science, 1(1), pp. 9–21 (Millman, T. and Wilson, K. 1995), © Emerald Group Publishing Limited, all rights reserved; Table 15.1 from *Sales promotion. In The Marketing Book,* 3rd ed., Butterworth–Heinemann (Peattie, S. and Peattie, K.J. (M.J. Baker, ed.) 1994) copyright Elsevier 1994; Table 15.4 adapted from Loyalty trends for the 21st century, *Journal of Targeting Measurement and Analysis for Marketing,* 12(3), pp. 199–212 (Capizzi, M., Ferguson, R. and Cuthbertson, R. 2004); Table 15.7 adapted from Fighting for a new view of field work, *Marketing,* 9 March, pp. 29–30 (McLuhan, R. 2000), reproduced from Marketing magazine with the permission of the copyright owner, Haymarket Media Group Limited; Table 15.8 from Which way forward? *Marketing,* 13 December, p. 12 (Bashford, S. 2007), reproduced from Marketing magazine with the permission of the copyright owner, Haymarket Media Group Limited; Table 16.1 from Ray Sylvester, Buckinghamshire New University; Table 16.2 from An exploratory study of attendee activities at a business trade show, *Journal of Business & Industrial Marketing,* 25(4), pp. 241–248 (Gopalakrishna, S., Roster, C.A. and Sridhar, S. 2010), © Emerald Group Publishing Limited, all rights reserved; Table 17.4 adapted from The advertising creative process: A study of UK agencies, *Journal of Marketing Communications,* January, pp. 1–19 (Turnbull, S. and Wheeler, C. 2015), reprinted by permission of the publisher (Taylor & Francis Ltd, http://www.tandfonline.com); Table 18.5 from *Advertising Statistics Yearbook,* Advertising Association (2003) World Advertising Research Centre; Table 18.6 after What is personalization? A conceptual framework, *European Journal of Marketing,* 41(5/6), pp. 409–418 (Vesanen, J. 2007), © Emerald Group Publishing Limited, all rights reserved; Table 19.1 from Users of the world unite! The challenges and opportunities of social media, *Business Horizons,* 53, pp. 59–68 (Kaplan, A.M. and Haelein, M. 2010), copyright 2010, with permission from Elsevier; Table 19.2 after Social media? Get serious! Understanding the functional building blocks of social media, *Business Horizons,* 54(3), pp. 241–251 (Kietzmann, J.H., Hermkens, K., McCarthy, I.P. and Silvestre, B.S. 2011), copyright 2011, with permission from Elsevier; Table 20.2 adapted from *Putting the 'group' back into group support systems: some theoretical issues about dynamic processes in groups with technological enhancements. In Group Support Systems: New Perspectives, ISBN 0023606258* 1st ed., Macmillan (McGrath, J.E. and Hollingshead, A.B. (L.M. Jessup and J.S. Valacich, eds) 1993) pp. 78–79, ©1993. Reprinted and Electronically reproduced by permission of Pearson Education, Inc., New York, NY; Table 20.5 adapted from Recency planning, *Admap,* February, pp. 32–34 (Ephron, E. 1997), World Advertising Research Center; Table 20.6 adapted from Study reveals negativity towards ads, *Campaign,* 28 November, p. 8 (Beale, C. 1997), reproduced with the permission of the copyright owner, Haymarket Business Publications Limited; Table 20.7 adapted from Setting frequency levels: an art or a science?, *Marketing and Media Decisions,* 24(4), pp. 9–11 (Ostrow, J.W. 1984), The Nielsen Company

Exhibits

The publisher would like to thank the following for their kind permission to reproduce their photographs:

5 Grey Group 2011 all rights reserved. 6 Grey Group 2011 all rights reserved. 7 Grey Group 2011 all rights reserved. 15 Alamy Images: Reiner Elsen. 27 Blue Rubicon Ltd. 39 British Heart Foundation. 40 British Heart Foundation. 43 2015 Adidas. 48 Bray Leino Ltd. 59 Getty Images: David M. Benett / Getty Images for Zoella Beauty. 64 Getty Images: Buyenlarge. 72 Renault UK. 73 Renault UK. 79 DeBeers UK Ltd. 80 Freud Communications. 82 The National Trust . 103 Elia Mörling / Tribaling.com. 107 Contains public sector information licensed under the Open Government Licence

v3.0.. 115 PHD Media UK: JCDecaux (b, t). 131 2015 Arnold Worldwide . 136 Alamy Images: Heritage Image Partnership Ltd. 150–151 Alamy Images: Justin Kase z12z. 156 Getty Images: Jamie McDonald. 159 Getty Images: Dario Cantatore. 162 Copyright of Bayer AG. 182 Now. 183 Now. 204 Getty Images: Suhaimi Abdullah. 212 Hanne Haugen. 213 Hanne Haugen. 215 Specsavers Optical Group. 219 WPP plc . 224 WPP plc. 226 Getty Images: Richard Stonehouse / Stringer. 230 Getty Images: Catherine Lane. 244 Fotolia.com: Zarya Maxim. 253 Millward Brown (c)2015. 254 Millward Brown (c)2015. 259 www.storyboardace.co.uk. 264 Alamy Images: Guy Bell. 270 Corbis: Fang Zhe / Xinhua Press. 288 Colruyt Group 2013. 289 Colruyt Group 2013. 296 Created by Lowe Lintas Bangalore . 299 Rolex UK. 310 Alamy Images: image-BROKER. 316 Fotolia.com: Intheskies. 325 Jon Holden. 330 Hewlett Packard. 335 Getty Images: Anadolu Agency / Mehmet Kaman. 356 Aardman/IWM. 357 Aardman/IWM. 360 Ad(c)Amnesty International UK 2015. Illustration (c) Ben Jennings. 361 (c) Amnesty International UK 2015. 363 BuzzFeed News. 365 Hovis Ltd. 366 . 368 Almond Board of California. 370 Alamy Images: Howard Davies. 381 Peperami. 389 Rentokil Initial. 390 Rentokil Initial. 395 Alamy Images: PjrStudio. 400 Paddy Power plc. 405 Rex Shutterstock: Mikael Buck. 414 Alamy Images: epa european pressphoto agency b.v.. 423 Getty Images: Duif du Toit / Gallo Images. 424 Getty Images: Duif du Toit / Gallo Images. 434 Alamy Images: Aflo Co. Ltd. 436 Channel Four Television Corporation 2016. 437 Alamy Images: directphoto.bz. 439 Rex Shutterstock: James North / Hunter Boots. 440 MasterCard. 442 Getty Images: Andrew Yates / AFP. 451 Everest Ltd (created by MBA). 452 Everest Ltd (created by MBA): (l). 455 Alamy Images: Camera Lucida. 463 Alamy Images: David J. Green – lifestyle 2. 465 www.samaritans.org. 466 Direct Line Group. 470 Speech Processing Solutions UK Ltd. 486 TRO. 487 TRO. 496 Getty Images: Martin Poole. 500 Image courtesy of oneworld Management Company Inc. . 503 Shutterstock.com: TungCheung. 506 Budweiser. 508 Getty Images: Andersen Ross. 511 'The Boursin Sensorium, delivered by BEcause Brand Experience.'. 521 Corbis: Rune Hellestad. 525 The Kobal Collection: Summit Entertainment. 529 Stylecraftltd.co.uk. 533 Paddy Power plc. 536 Tetra Pak. 547 John Lewis. 548 John Lewis. 552 Save the Rhino International. 553 Rex Shutterstock: Tom Oldham. 558 Radiant, part of the PZ Cussons Group plc. 562 McVities. 569 McCann Australia. 578 Arla skyr. 580 Pinterest. 588 Heineken. 589 Heineken. 593 Getty Images: ChinaFotoPress. 595 Iberia. 601 British Airways. 622 Greater Manchester Police. 623 Greater Manchester Police. 632 Daxon. 633 Daxon. 637 A.P. Moller – Maersk Archives. 645 Getty Images: Alan Crowhurst. 659 Kärcher (U.K.) Ltd. 660 Kärcher (U.K.) Ltd. 665 Rex Shutterstock: Denis Jones / Associated Newspapers. 681 Shutterstock.com: Stokkete. 683 courtesy of esure group

Cover images: *Front:* Getty Images

All other images © Pearson Education

Part 1

Introduction to marketing communications

Part 1 is concerned with establishing the scope and contextual aspects of marketing communications. It provides an underpinning for the other chapters in this book.

Chapter 1 provides an introductory perspective on marketing communications and sets out some of the key concepts. From a consideration of the scope, role and tasks of marketing communications it explores ideas associated with engagement and the way the marketing communications mix is configured.

Chapter 2 explores issues concerning communications theory. In particular it examines a range of theoretical interpretations and communications that reflect developments in the media and the way marketing communications is thought to work. In addition, this chapter highlights the influence of people, their behaviour and the interactional elements within the communications process.

Chapter 3 is concerned with two main aspects of audience behaviour. The first considers traditional, academic approaches to the way audiences process marketing communications messages and the purchase decisions and behaviour that can follow. It also explores more contemporary approaches, such as those based on behavioural economics and tribal consumption.

The final chapter in this part introduces ideas about how marketing communications might work. Rather than trust a single approach, five separate approaches are presented. These reflect the diverse thinking and developing knowledge about how marketing communications might work. These five are the sequential, attitude, relationship, significant value, and cognitive processing approaches.

For readers with access to the companion website that accompanies this book, there are supplementary chapters, drawn from previous editions, available in PDF form.

Understanding how customers process information

Customer decision-making

Ethics in marketing communications

Shareholders: supply chains and inter-organisational relationships

Chapter 1

Introducing marketing communications

Marketing communications is concerned with the methods, processes, meanings, perceptions and actions that audiences (consumers and organisations) undertake with regard to the presentation, consideration and actions associated with products, services and brands.

Aims and learning objectives

The primary aim of this chapter is to introduce some of the key concepts associated with marketing communications. In addition, readers are encouraged to consider the scope and purpose of marketing communications, and to develop an appreciation of the key characteristics of the communications mix.

The learning objectives are to enable readers to:

1. understand the concept of exchange and how it impacts marketing communications;
2. discuss the scope, role and tasks of marketing communications;
3. explore ideas about how marketing communications can be used to engage audiences;
4. define marketing communications and examine ways in which the environment can influence the use of marketing communications;
5. appraise the nature and characteristics of the marketing communications mix;
6. evaluate the reasons why the configuration of the marketing communications mix varies.

Sensodyne Pronamel

Sensodyne Pronamel is a toothpaste designed to help protect against the problem of acid wear. This occurs when enamel, the toughest substance in the body, starts to soften and weaken as a result of the acids in our diet. Weakened and worn enamel can lead to thinning, yellow enamel and chipped teeth. If allowed to worsen, cracks can appear in the enamel, and there can be sensitivity pain through the exposure of underlying dentine. Enamel can't grow back – once it's gone, it's gone. Acid wear can't be fixed with fillings. Serious sufferers can require complicated and expensive dentistry such as porcelain veneers.

One in three young adults have early signs of acid wear due to acids in their diets at a time when cavities have been falling. The main reason for this increase in the prevalence of acid wear is the cultural shift to an increased consumption of healthy foods and drinks, many of which are acidic.

Since fluoride toothpaste first gained medical approval for the prevention of cavities in 1955, there have been many developments in format, taste and active ingredients, but only three distinct new categories: sensitivity (1961); gum health (1968); and whitening (1989). The launch of Sensodyne Pronamel introduced a fourth category: enamel protect.

Sensodyne Pronamel allows minerals to penetrate deep into a weakened enamel surface, strengthen it, and help prevent further enamel loss. Being a daily toothpaste, it also cleans, freshens breath and prevents cavities. As it is from Sensodyne, it also relieves sensitivity.

The launch of Sensodyne Pronamel was far from straightforward, however, as there were some serious communications challenges. These included the fact that acid wear is invisible at first so there are no visual cues for consumers. Second, dentists weren't telling their patients about acid wear, so there was no one raising awareness of the condition. In addition, people thought they were doing enough already in terms of brushing, flossing and rinsing, and no one wants to hear bad news.

To achieve the 4 per cent market share that we needed to be commercially viable, and overcome the communications hurdles, we created a two-phase launch campaign. The first was to create condition awareness and educate about the causes. The second was to establish relevancy, both in terms of helping consumers identify with the problem, and establish Pronamel as the solution.

Campaign phase 1: Condition awareness (2006–2009)

In order to protect people from acid wear, we had to let them know it existed. To achieve this we communicated directly with dentists, educating them about acid wear and Sensodyne Pronamel's unique formulation. We did this using clear, instructional leaflets and ads in dentistry industry titles, plus visits by Sensodyne representatives.

Once the ground had been prepared, we communicated with consumers to educate them about acid wear. We did not want to scare them as this could have generated cynicism, and comments such as 'Of course they say it's serious, they have a toothpaste to sell.' To establish the credibility of the condition people needed to hear real dentists (not actors) provide authoritative, expert and independent recommendations. These opinion formers never used scripts, and were not paid, so their endorsement was genuine. We enhanced credibility by inviting people

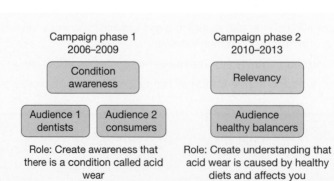

Campaign phase 1
2006–2009

Condition awareness

Audience 1 dentists   Audience 2 consumers

Role: Create awareness that there is a condition called acid wear

Campaign phase 2
2010–2013

Relevancy

Audience healthy balancers

Role: Create understanding that acid wear is caused by healthy diets and affects you

Figure 1.1   **The Structure of the Sensodyne Pronamel Campaign**

to not just take our word for it, but to ask their own dentist about it.

Early stage acid wear is difficult to show, so we created The Torch Test. It's a visually impactful demonstration of the truth that only dentists can see early signs such as translucent enamel.

We weighted the media mix towards television for several reasons. First, television gave the feel of a public health announcement. Second, its broad reach also allowed dentists to oversee consumer activity, underlining acid wear's importance to their patients.

After three years competitors began to launch their own versions, yet despite their global size, they lacked our experience in this new market. Many made mistakes on entry, such as the shock tactics used by Colgate Sensitive Enamel Protect which demonised

NEW

Five Questions To Ask Your Dentist About Acid Wear

Your teeth may look healthy

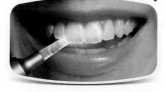
A dentist can see the early signs of Acid Wear

1 What is it?
Acid Wear is a softening and wearing away of the surface of your tooth's enamel. If you do nothing about Acid Wear it may lead to thinning, weakening and discoloration of your enamel.

2 What are the causes?
Acids that lead to Acid Wear can be found in everyday food and drink, such as fruit juices, some soft drinks, salad dressings and even wine. After contact the surface of your enamel can be softened which then makes it more vulnerable to the effects of brushing. Once you lose any enamel it's gone for good.

3 What are the effects?
At first the effects of acid wear aren't noticeable to the naked eye. But over time the signs become more visible. As the enamel thins your teeth may become dull and yellow. They could also become translucent, weaker and softer.

4 Can I stop it happening to me?
Don't worry, there's no need to avoid the food and drinks that you love. Visit your dentist for the best advice. He may tell you to think carefully about how you eat and drink. For example don't mull fruit over in your mouth; drink acidic drinks through a straw; and wait at least an hour after consuming anything acidic before brushing your teeth.

5 Can a simple thing like a toothpaste help?
Yes it can. It's important to start protecting your tooth's enamel now, because loss of enamel is irreversible. Pronamel toothpaste is specifically designed to help re-harden your tooth's softened enamel. Pronamel has low abrasivity, it's non-acidic, and contains the optimum amount of fluoride you need. Dentists recommend you brush with Pronamel twice a day to help protect against daily Acid Wear.

"I recommend Pronamel."
Dr Farda. Dentist. Budapest.

ASK YOUR DENTIST ABOUT ACID WEAR

www.pronamel.com

*Image adjusted to illustrate clinical situation

Exhibit 1.1   **Long-copy print to provide consumers hints for starting conversations with their dentist**
Source: Grey Group 2011 all rights reserved.

healthy food and drinks, literally sounding a warning siren over their images. Having been in this market a little longer, we knew this approach would lead to resistance and cynicism.

Campaign phase 2: Creating relevancy

Having established strong levels of awareness our next task was to make this knowledge relevant to consumers. Three opportunities to protect and cement Sensodyne's lead were identified.

Although awareness of acid wear was good, non-buyers of Enamel Protect toothpaste simply didn't think the condition affected them personally. We had to make it relevant. Rather than spread ourselves thin with a broad audience, a segmentation study identified a sizable group called 'healthy balancers'. They have healthy diets and lifestyles and are highly engaged in oral health. These people were not only the most at risk, but also the most likely to act.

We wanted to engage people through their love of healthy food, and this was achieved by positioning Sensodyne Pronamel as a facilitator. The brand allows them to continue to enjoy their aspirational healthy lifestyles, worry free.

Dentists were encouraged to explain to their patients how healthy diets lead to acid wear. Television remained our lead medium, but we now included real consumers (opinion leaders) in our the ads, to reinforce the news that healthy diets cause acid wear. We extended the media mix to reach healthy balancers when they were considering or consuming acidic foods or drinks. These relevant times included in and around gyms, in the aisles of acidic food and drink in supermarkets, and in the lifestyle press.

In just 7 years, the new Enamel Protect category has become a significant sector in the toothpaste market. Econometrics shows that the UK campaign contributed approximately 30 per cent to the total revenue of the Sensodyne Pronamel brand and helped launch the Enamel Protect category, worth over £32 million. The campaign required significant investment, as the total media spend (including production costs) was £9.8 million in Phase 1 and £7.2 million in Phase 2.

This case was written by Rachel Walker, Planning Director at Grey London

Questions relating to this case can be found at the end of this chapter.

Everyday acids.

Every day enamel protection.

| Exhibit 1.2 | **A Sensodyne Pronamel yoga mat** |

Source: Grey Group 2011 all rights reserved.

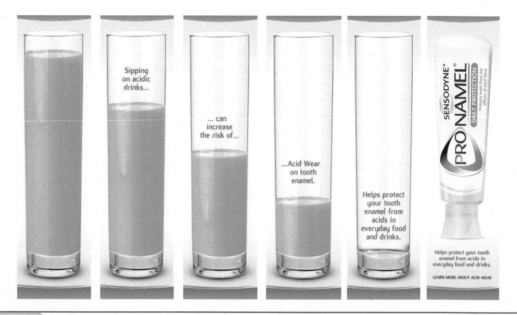

Exhibit 1.3	**Banner ad**
	Source: Grey Group 2011 all rights reserved.

Source: Grey Group 2011 all rights reserved.

Introduction

Have you ever considered how organisations use communications to reach and engage with their various audiences? Organisations such as Sensodyne, whose campaign to launch Sensodyne Pronamel, presented above, and others as diverse as Kraft Heinz company and the Wei-Chuan Food Corporation, Google and Samsung, Delta Airlines and Air China, Oxfam and Médecins Sans Frontières, and the Swedish and Singapore governments, all use marketing communications in different ways, to achieve different goals, and to pursue their marketing and business objectives. The aim of this book is to help people, just like you, to explore the various academic and practitioner views of marketing communications.

The opening sentence contains the word 'engage'. 'Engagement' refers to the nature of the communications that can occur between people, and between people and technology. There is no universally agreed definition of the term 'engagement', and it is used in many different contexts. Marketing communications is closely aligned to an educational context and Li et al. (2014) refer to three types of engagement taken from a learning perspective. These are cognitive, relational and behavioural engagement. Cognitive engagement refers to the degree to which individuals are engrossed and intellectually involved in what they are learning (messages). Relational engagement refers to the extent to which individuals feel connected with their environment, whilst behavioural engagement reflects the extent to which individuals feel involved and participate in activities.

All three of these forms of engagement are relevant to marketing communications. Here engagement refers to a range of communications events used first to expose, and then sometimes to capture the attention, captivate and then enable interaction with an audience. It is often achieved through a blend of intellectual and emotional content.

Engagement may last seconds, such as the impact of a stunning ad, the sight of a beautiful person, or the emotion brought on by a panoramic view, or what a piece of music might bring to an individual. Alternatively, engagement may be protracted and last hours, days, weeks, months or years, depending on the context and the level of enjoyment or loyalty felt towards the event, object or person.

Organisations such as Apple and Google, John Lewis and Aldi, HSBC and Santander, Haier and LG, Samsung and Sony, Ryanair and easyJet, Chanel and L'Oréal, Boeing and Airbus, Oxfam and Shelter, and Merlin and Disney all operate across different sectors, markets and countries and use a variety of marketing communications activities to engage with their various audiences. These audiences consist not only of people who buy their products and services but also of people and organisations who might be able to influence them, who might help and support them by providing, for example, labour, finance, manufacturing facilities, distribution outlets and legal advice or who are interested because of their impact on parts of society or the business sector in particular.

The organisations mentioned earlier are all well-known brand names, but there are hundreds of thousands of smaller organisations that also use marketing communications to engage their audiences. Each of these organisations, large and small, is part of a network of companies, suppliers, retailers, wholesalers, value-added resellers, distributors and other retailers, which join together, often freely, so that each can achieve its own goals.

The structure of this chapter is as follows. First there is a consideration of the ideas associated with exchange that underpin marketing principles and, of course, marketing communications. We then consider the scope, role and tasks of marketing communications, which includes defining marketing communications. This is followed by an introduction to the elements that constitute the marketing communications mix, before concluding with a view of the key differences between marketing communications used in consumer and business markets.

The concept of marketing as an exchange

The concept of exchange, according to most marketing academics and practitioners, is central to our understanding of marketing. For an exchange to take place there must be two or more parties, each of whom can offer something of value to the other and who are prepared to enter freely into the exchange process, a transaction. It is generally accepted that there are two main forms of exchange: transactional and relational (or collaborative) exchanges.

Transactional (or market) exchanges (Bagozzi, 1978; Houston and Gassenheimer, 1987) occur independently of any previous or subsequent exchanges. They have a short-term orientation and are primarily motivated by self-interest. When a consumer buys a 'meal' from a burger van they have not used before, then a market exchange can be identified. Burger and chips in exchange for money. In contrast to this, *collaborative* exchanges have a longer-term orientation and develop between parties who wish to build and maintain long-term supportive relationships (Dwyer et al., 1987). So, when someone frequents the same burger van on a regular basis, perhaps on their way home after lectures, or an evening's entertainment, increasingly relational or collaborative exchanges can be considered to be taking place.

These two types of exchange represent the extremes in a spectrum of exchange transactions. This spectrum of exchanges, as depicted in Figure 1.2, is underpinned by relational theory. This means that elements of a relationship can be observed in all exchanges

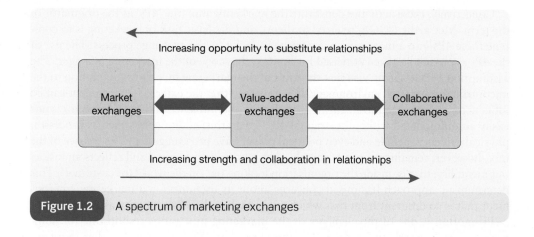

Increasing opportunity to substitute relationships

Market exchanges ⟷ Value-added exchanges ⟷ Collaborative exchanges

Increasing strength and collaboration in relationships

Figure 1.2   A spectrum of marketing exchanges

(Macneil, 1983). Relationships become stronger as the frequency of exchanges increases. As exchanges become more frequent the intensity of the relationship strengthens, so that the focus is no longer on the product or price within the exchange but on the relationship itself.

In industrial societies transactional exchanges have tended to dominate commercial transactions, although recently there has been a substantial movement towards establishing collaborative exchanges. In other words, a variety of exchanges occurs, and each organisation has a portfolio of differing types of exchange that it maintains with different customers, suppliers and other stakeholders. Communications can be considered in terms of oil in that they lubricate these exchanges and enable them to function. However, just as different types of oil are necessary to lubricate different types of equipment, so different types of communications are necessary to engage with different audiences.

Collaborative exchanges form the basis of the ideas represented in relationship marketing. Many organisations use the principles of relationship marketing manifest in the form of customer relationship marketing or loyalty marketing programmes. However, it is important to note that short-term relationships are also quite common and a necessary dimension of organisational exchange. This book is developed on the broad spectrum of relationships that organisations develop directly with other organisations and consumers, and indirectly on a consumer-to-consumer and inter-organisational basis.

Marketing communications and the process of exchange

The exchange process is developed and managed by:

- researching customer/stakeholder needs;
- identifying, selecting and targeting particular groups of customers/stakeholders who share similar discriminatory characteristics, including needs and wants;
- developing an offering that satisfies the identified needs at an acceptable price, which is available through particular sets of distribution channels;
- making the target audience aware of the existence of the offering. Where competition or other impediments to positive consumer action exist, such as lack of motivation or conviction, a promotional programme is developed and used to communicate with the targeted group.

Collectively, these activities constitute the marketing mix (the '4Ps' as the originator of the term, McCarthy (1960), referred to them), and the basic task of marketing is to combine these 4Ps into a marketing programme to facilitate the exchange process. The use of the 4Ps approach has been criticised for limiting the scope of the marketing manager. The assumption by McCarthy was that the tools of the marketing mix allow adaptation to the uncontrollable external environment. It is now seen that the external environment can be influenced and managed strategically, and the rise and influence of the service sector is not easily accommodated within the original 4Ps. To do this, additional Ps such as processes, physical evidence, people and even political power have been suggested. The essence of the mix, however, remains the same: namely, that it is product-focused and reflects an inside/out mentality; that is, inside the organisation looking out on the world (or customer). This deterministic approach has raised concerns about its usefulness in a marketing environment that is so different from that which existed when the 4Ps concept was conceived.

Promotion is one of the elements of the marketing mix and is responsible for communicating the marketing offer to the target market. While recognising that there are implicit and important communications through the other elements of the marketing mix (through a high price, for example, symbolic of high quality), it is the task of a planned and integrated set of communications activities to communicate effectively with each of an organisation's stakeholder groups.

At a fundamental level it is possible to interpret the use of marketing communications in two different ways. One of these ways concerns the attempt to develop brand values. Historically, advertising has been used to focus on establishing a set of feelings, emotions and beliefs about a brand or organisation. In this way brand communications used to help consumers think positively about a brand, helping them to remember and develop positive brand attitudes in the hope that, when they are ready to buy that type of product again, Brand x will be chosen because of the positive feelings, or absence of any serious negative feelings.

The other and perhaps more contemporary use of marketing communications is to help shape behaviour, rather than feelings. In an age where short-term results and managerial accountability are increasingly critical, investment in brands is geared to achieve a fast return on investment (ROI). This does not allow space and resources to build positive attitudes towards brands. Now the urgency is to encourage people to behave differently. This might be by driving them to a website, buying the product or making a telephone call. This behaviour change can be driven by using messages that provide audiences with a reason to act – or what is referred to as a 'call-to-action'.

So, on the one hand communications can be used to develop brand feelings and on the other to change or manage the behaviour of the target audience. These are not mutually exclusive: for example, many television advertisements are referred to as *direct-response ads* because, not only do they attempt to create brand values, but they also carry a website address, telephone number or details of a special offer (sales promotion). In other words, the two goals can be mixed into one – a hybrid approach.

The scope of marketing communications

At a basic level marketing communications, or 'promotion' as it was originally known, is used to communicate elements of an organisation's offering to a target audience. This offer might refer to a product, a service or the organisation itself as it tries to build

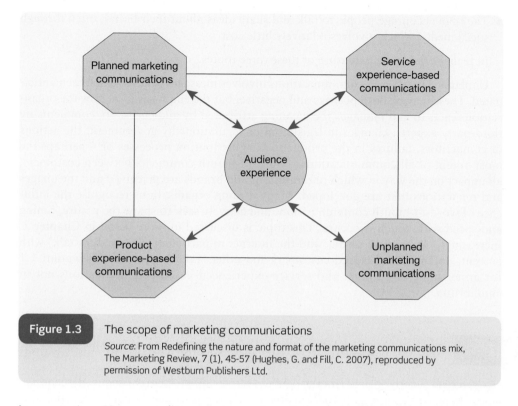

Figure 1.3   The scope of marketing communications

Source: From Redefining the nature and format of the marketing communications mix, The Marketing Review, 7 (1), 45-57 (Hughes, G. and Fill, C. 2007), reproduced by permission of Westburn Publishers Ltd.

its reputation. However, this represents a broad view of marketing communications and fails to incorporate the various issues, dimensions and elements that make up this important communications activity. Duncan and Moriarty (1997) and Gronroos (2004) suggest that in addition to these 'planned' events there are marketing communications experienced by audiences relating to both their experience from using products (how tasty is this smoothie?) and the consumption of services (just how good was the service in that hotel, restaurant or at the airport?). In addition to these there are communications arising from unplanned or unintended brand-related experiences (empty stock shelves or accidents). These dimensions of marketing communications are all represented in Figure 1.3 (Hughes and Fill, 2007).

Figure 1.3 helps demonstrate the breadth of the subject and the complexity associated with the way audiences engage with a brand. Although useful in terms of providing an overview, this framework requires elaboration in order to appreciate the detail associated with each of the elements, especially planned marketing communications. This book builds on this framework and in particular considers issues associated with both planned and unplanned aspects of marketing communications.

Planned marketing communications incorporates three key elements: tools, media and content (messages). The main communications tools are advertising, sales promotion, public relations, direct marketing, personal selling and added-value approaches such as sponsorship, exhibitions and field marketing. Content can be primarily informative or emotional but is usually a subtle blend of both dimensions, reflecting the preferences and needs of the target audience. To help get these messages through to their audiences, organisations have three main routes:

● They can pay for the use of particular media that they know their target audiences will use – for example, magazines, websites or television programmes.

● They can use their own assets to convey messages, such as their buildings, employees, vehicles and websites, which they do not have to pay to use.

● They can encourage people to talk and share ideas about their brand, often through social media, which involves relatively little cost.

In reality brands use a mixture of these three routes.

Unplanned marketing communications involves messages that have not been anticipated. These may be both positive and negative, but the emphasis is on how the organisation reacts to and manages the meaning attributed by audiences. So, comments by third-party experts, changes in legislation or regulations by government, the actions of competitors, failures in the production or distribution processes or – perhaps the most potent of all communications – word-of-mouth comments between customers, all impact on the way in which organisations and brands are perceived and the images and reputations that are developed. Many leading organisations recognise the influence of word-of-mouth communications and actively seek to shape the nature, timing and speed with which it occurs. This topic is discussed in more detail in Chapter 2. Increasingly, interactive media, and the Internet in particular, are used to 'talk' with current, potential and lapsed customers and other stakeholders. See Viewpoint 1.1 for an example of planned and service experienced-based communications not in equilibrium.

Viewpoint 1.1   The right scope for a new sports channel

In 2013 BT spent £738 million over three years for the rights to screen 38 live Premier League matches a season. BT had previously bought up the rights to show Premiership Rugby as well as many other sports. This was all part of its battle with Sky who had moved into BT's telephony and broadband domain in 2006. BT Sport represented their move into Sky's sporting territory, with a view to winning the triple-play market, namely the bundling of television, telephone and broadband.

Building awareness for the new sports channel featured the use of outdoor media across the UK. Sky used the recently retired David Beckham while BT featured Manchester United's Robin van Persie, Manchester City's Joe Hart and Tottenham's Gareth Bale. In addition BT used its 'Name that Team' competition. This required fans to locate and name the 44 sports teams hidden in visual clues in an illustration.

This activity raised interest, shaped expectations of the services to be experienced and stimulated people to become subscribers. Unfortunately some customers were disappointed that their service expectations were not realised. Some customers were confused because BT Sport was initially free on BT TV, but was subsequently encrypted. Consequently there was a surge in the number of complaints at around the time of the launch of the sports channel. In particular these related to BT TV's service issues and complaints handling. According to the media regulator Ofcom, the rate of complaints per 1,000 subscribers was more than 10 times that at Virgin and more than 20 times the rate at Sky.

BT were quick to apologise to their customers, suggesting that the high volume of interest in their services, and their attempt to support multiple TV platforms in a very short space of time were partly to blame for the issues. No doubt the intensive awareness campaign didn't help matters.

Source: Based on Adie (2013); Anon (2013); Brignall (2013); Staff (2013).

Question: How does this reflect an imbalance in the scope of BT TV's marketing communications?

Task: Find another campaign where the balance across the four scoping elements might not have been as planned.

The role of marketing communications

Organisations communicate with a variety of audiences in order to pursue their marketing and business objectives. Marketing communications can be used to engage with a variety of audiences and in such a way that meets the needs of the audience. Messages should encourage individuals to respond to the focus organisation (or product/brand). This response can be immediate through, for example, purchase behaviour or the use of customer-support lines, or it can be deferred as information is assimilated and considered for future use. Even if the information is discarded at a later date, the communications will have attracted attention and consideration of the message.

The reason to use marketing communications may vary according to the prevailing situation or context but the essential goal is to provoke an audience response. For Rossiter and Percy (2013: 392) this response is only about selling products and services. They see the role of advertising as unquestionably about selling 'more of the branded product or service, or to achieve a higher price that consumers are willing to pay than would obtain in the absence of advertising'.

To get to the point of purchase, however, several communications effects may need to have been achieved. So, the response might be geared to developing brand values, attitudes, preferences, and the positive thoughts an individual might have about a brand. This is grounded in a 'thinking and feeling orientation', a combination of both cognitive thoughts and emotional feelings about a brand.

Another type of response might be one that stimulates an audience to act in particular ways. Referred to as 'behavioural' or sometimes 'brand response', the goal is to 'encourage particular audience behaviours'. For example, these might include trying a piece of cheese in a supermarket, encouraging visits to a website, sampling a piece of music, placing orders and paying for goods and services, sharing information with a friend, registering on a network, opening letters, signing a petition or calling a number. Brands with a Facebook presence can utilise call-to-action buttons. These link to any destination on or off Facebook and include: Book Now, Contact Us, Use App, Play Game, Shop Now, Sign Up, and Watch Video. All of these are an integral part of an engagement strategy (Anon, 2014a). Figure 1.4 depicts the two key drivers of engagement.

Apart from generating cash flows, the underlying purpose of these responses can be considered to be a strategic function of developing relationships with particular audiences and/or for (re)positioning brands. For example, marketing communications at

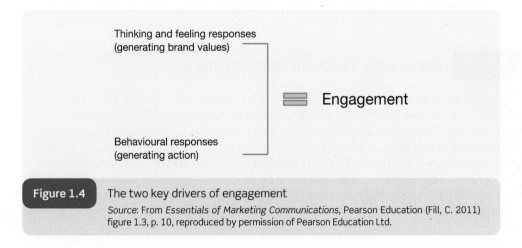

Thinking and feeling responses
(generating brand values)

Engagement

Behavioural responses
(generating action)

| Figure 1.4 | The two key drivers of engagement |

Source: From *Essentials of Marketing Communications*, Pearson Education (Fill, C. 2011) figure 1.3, p. 10, reproduced by permission of Pearson Education Ltd.

Magners, the drinks brand, used to be based on communicating product information. One campaign featured Magners set in a timeless idyll and conveyed messages about the brand being made in the dark, that the apples were soundly pressed, and that they required the pollination of 17 varieties of apple.

Willifer (2013) reports that this strategy shifted to one founded on dramatising the emotional benefits. A brand representative/narrator was depicted visiting various contemporary Irish bars, urging viewers through rhyming couplets to embrace all things 'Now'. The endline is 'Now is a good time'. The word 'Now', according to Willifer, refers to being spontaneous and embracing opportunities as they arise, going with the flow. It also means modern, not historic, with both representing the new associations audiences should make with the brand. Magners changed the way audiences engaged with the brand.

Engagement, therefore, can be considered to be a function of two forms of response. The quality of engagement cannot be determined, but it can be argued that marketing communications should be based on driving a particular type of response that captivates an individual. For example, Petplan used television to develop new brand values and then switched to behavioural advertising to drive responses to call centres and their website. This activity was supported with an online competition via Facebook, inviting pet owners to join in with the campaign and to submit a photo of their pet to form the basis of a user-generated version of the advert. Over 28,000 owners entered their pets into the Facebook competition, demonstrating not only their positive feelings towards the campaign, but also a growing affinity with the Petplan brand (see the case study at the start of Chapter 6 for more information).

Where engagement occurs, an individual might be said to have been positively captivated and, as a result, opportunities for activity should increase. Engagement acts as a bridge, a mechanism through which brands and organisations link with target audiences and through which the goals of all parties can be achieved. In other words, there is mutual value.

An extension of the engagement process can be seen in the way many brands now focus on developing customer experiences. This requires linking together the various points at which customers interact with brands so that there is consistency in their brand experiences. Today there is a multitude of media channels which represents a major challenge for those seeking to interlink their communications. For example, many retailers attempt to manage the multichannel environment but do so by treating each channel as an independent entity, a silo approach.

Some retailers have moved to a customer-centric focus and have tried to link the channels so that customer perception of the brand is less disjointed and more consistent with the desired perceptions (Patel, 2012). For example, Poletti and Viccars (2013) report that the upmarket supermarket brand Waitrose uses an iPhone app to bring together functional activities such as recipes, shopping lists and wine matching, with customer publishing and magazines, social media communities, and YouTube and TV channels, all anchored by celebrity chef ambassadors (see Viewpoint 1.2 for another example of this approach).

Viewpoint 1.2   Experience Victoria's Secret in store

In view of the growing trend towards multichannel retailing and online sales the design of Victoria's Secret's (VS) flagship store in New Bond Street, London, needed to incorporate a digital experience.

The store, set over four floors, features elaborately carved mouldings, ornate decorative painting and custom Murano glass chandeliers, all of which suggest lavishness and splendour. However, it is the use of multimedia technology that provides flexibility around this base to create memorable customer experiences throughout a visit. These experiences cannot be replicated online, but do provide consistency in every channel. By introducing multimedia to a store experience a very different level of customer engagement is developed.

The focal point is a giant two-storey HD LCD video wall, which is reflected into the mirrored hallway. The content, which is changed frequently, features live feeds to the latest fashion shows, behind-the-scenes material on the production of ads, or plays footage from the most recent Victoria's Secret Fashion Show. The result is that every visit to the store provides a fresh and unique experience.

Video walls are integrated throughout the store, for example in the cash and wrap areas, whilst a gallery of iconic photography features the Victoria's Secret Angels (models) and illuminated fragrance bars display the brand's signature scents. The use of in-store video and soundscapes helps generate energy around the store, adding to the brand experience and helping to stimulate return visits. This demonstrates how the use of an in-store digital environment can act as a key competitive advantage, in what is increasingly an experience-consuming society.

| Exhibit 1.4 | The exterior of Victoria's Secret store hides the bright, digital state of the art interior design |

Source: Alamy Images/Reiner Elsen.

In addition, VS has adopted a mobile strategy enabling users to download an app in order to access the VS catalogue, undertake quizzes and games, enable mobile chat to allow users to socialise with others, and provide a messaging feature to provide access to the brand's annual Fashion Show.

The use of multimedia technologies in this way helps customers to connect directly with a brand regardless of channel.

Source: Bergin (2012); Bohannon (2015); Patel (2012); www.fashionfoiegras.com/2012/08/first-look-victorias-secret-new-bond.html.

This Viewpoint was written by Reece Drew when he was a marketing student at Manchester Business School.

Question: To what extent are these in-store experiences a manifestation of behavioural engagement?

Task: Identify other brands that have attempted to incorporate digital technology within a retail environment. What success did they have?

Successful engagement indicates that understanding and meaning have been conveyed effectively, that the communications have value. Counting the number of likes, viewers, readers or impressions says little about the quality of the engagement and the value that it represents to individuals. At one level, engagement through one-way communications enables target audiences to understand product and service offers, to the extent that the audience is sufficiently engaged to want to enter into further communications activity. At another level, engagement through two-way or interactive communications enables information that is relationship-specific (Ballantyne, 2004) to be exchanged. The greater the frequency of information exchange, the more likely collaborative relationships will develop.

As if to emphasise the appropriateness of the term 'engagement' the concept is now being tested as an alternative measurement to impressions, clicks and page-views. Ideas of 'engaged time', the amount of time that individuals spend on a web page, is a metric being considered by several organisations. The *Financial Times* was reported to be about to start selling display ads based on how long an audience spends with its content (Anon, 2014b). A key measurement metric at *ScribbleLive* is User Engagement Minutes, or UEMs. These represent the amount of time a person spends 'engaged' with their content (Anon, 2015). All of this suggests that the primary role of marketing communications is to engage audiences.

Scholars' paper 1.1   Beware, engaging confusion

Verhoef, P.C., Reinartz, W.J. and Krafft, M. (2010) Customer engagement as a new perspective in customer management, *Journal of Service Research*, 13(3), 247–52.

As already mentioned in the text, the use of the term 'engagement' has become increasingly widespread in the marketing literature. The term is used in different ways to mean different things and this paper is a good example of the different interpretations that are available. This paper considers engagement as a behavioural manifestation towards the brand or firm, one that goes beyond transactions. The authors propose a conceptual model of the antecedents, impediments, and firm consequences of customer engagement. Readers might be interested to know that this journal published a special edition on customer engagement.

The tasks of marketing communications

Bowersox and Morash made a significant contribution in their 1989 paper when they demonstrated how marketing flows, including the information flow, can be represented as a network that has the sole purpose of satisfying customer needs and wants. Communications are important in these exchange networks as they can help achieve one of four key tasks:

● Communications can *inform* and make potential customers aware of an organisation's offering. They can also provide knowledge and understanding about a brand.

● Communications may attempt to *persuade* current and potential customers of the desirability of entering into an exchange relationship.

● Communications can also be used to *reinforce* experiences. This may take the form of *reminding* people of a need they might have or reminding them of the benefits of past transactions with a view to convincing them that they should enter into a similar exchange. In addition, it is possible to provide *reassurance* or comfort either immediately prior to an exchange or, more commonly, post-purchase. This is important, as it helps to retain current customers and improve profitability, an approach to business that is much more cost-effective than constantly striving to lure new customers.

■ Finally, marketing communications can act as a *differentiator*, particularly in markets where there is little to separate competing products and brands. Mineral water products, such as Perrier and Highland Spring, are largely similar: it is the communications surrounding the products that has created various brand images, enabling consumers to make purchasing decisions. In these cases it is the images created by marketing communications that enable people to differentiate one brand from another and position them so that consumers' purchasing confidence and positive attitudes are developed.

Therefore, communications can inform, persuade, reinforce and build images to differentiate a product or service, or to put it another way, DRIP (see Table 1.1).

At a higher level, the communications process not only supports the transaction, by informing, persuading, reinforcing or differentiating, but also offers a means of exchange itself, for example communications for entertainment, for potential solutions and concepts for education and self-esteem. Communications involve intangible benefits, such as the psychological satisfactions associated with, for example, the entertainment associated with engaging and enjoying advertisements (Schlinger, 1979) or the experiences within a sponsored part of a social network.

Communications can also be seen as a means of perpetuating and transferring values and culture to different parts of society or networks. For example, it is argued that the way women are portrayed in the media and stereotypical images of very thin or 'size zero' women are dysfunctional in that they set up inappropriate role models. The form and characteristics of the communications process adopted by some organisations (both the deliberate and the unintentional use of signs and symbols used to convey meaning) help to provide stability and continuity. Dove, for example, understood this and successfully repositioned itself based on natural beauty, using a variety of ordinary people for its communications.

Other examples of intangible satisfactions can be seen in the social and psychological transactions involved increasingly with the work of the National Health Service (NHS), charities, educational institutions and other not-for-profit organisations, such as housing associations. Not only do these organisations recognise the need to communicate with various audiences, but they also perceive value in being seen to be 'of value' to their customers. There is also evidence that some brands are trying to meet the emerging needs of some consumers who want to know the track record of manufacturers with respect to their environmental policies and actions. For example, the growth in 'Fairtrade' products, designed to provide fairer and more balanced trading arrangements with producers and growers in emerging parts of the world, persuaded Kraft that it should engage with this form of commercial activity.

Table 1.1 DRIP elements of marketing communications

Task	Sub-task	Explanation
Differentiate	Position	To make a product or service stand out in the category
Reinforce	Remind, reassure, refresh	To consolidate and strengthen previous messages and experiences
Inform	Make aware, educate	To make known and advise of availability and features
Persuade	Purchase or make further enquiry	To encourage further positive purchase-related behaviour

The notion of value can be addressed in a different way. All organisations have the opportunity to develop their communications to a point where the value of their messages represents a competitive advantage. This value can be seen in the consistency, timing, volume or expression of the message. Heinonen and Strandvik (2005) argue that there are four elements that constitute communications value. These are the message content, how the information is presented, where the communications occur and their timing: in other words, the all-important context within which a communications event occurs. These elements are embedded within marketing communications and are referred to throughout this book.

Some marketing communications activity, however, can be considered culturally dysfunctional. For example, Kemp (2014: 49) cites Green, the editor at trends consultancy LSN:Global. She believes that social media drive many users to 'want more, do more and be more'. This involves observing others, making comparisons and judgements, which can lead to personal dissatisfaction. This in turn can lead to a form of culturally induced social anxiety. It follows that brands should attempt to acknowledge people's anxieties, and then help to resolve them. Kemp cites Dawson who refers to Sainsbury's with its 'Live well for less' campaign and Aldi with its 'Like brands. Only cheaper' activity as recognition of social anxiety and good examples of empathic positioning.

Scholars' paper 1.2   Early days of marketing communications

Ray, M.L. (1973) A decision sequence analysis of developments in marketing communications, *Journal of Marketing,* 37 (January), 29–38.

This older paper has been included because it provides perspective. Much of contemporary marketing communications has a digital orientation. This paper reminds us of the evolution of marketing communications, way before digitisation. This paper could also be listed in Chapter 5, about strategy and planning, because Ray introduces a planning model in the paper, and Chapter 10 as there are embryonic ideas about integrated marketing communications as well. It may not be da Vinci but it is certainly forward thinking.

Communications can be used for additional reasons. The tasks of informing, persuading and reinforcing and differentiating are primarily activities targeted at consumers or end-users. Organisations do not exist in isolation from each other, as each one is a part of a wider system of corporate entities, where each enters into a series of exchanges to secure raw material inputs or resources and to discharge them as value-added outputs to other organisations in the network.

The exchanges that organisations enter into require the formation of relationships, however tenuous or strong. Andersson (1992) looks at the strength of the relationship between organisations in a network and refers to them as 'loose or tight couplings'. These couplings, or partnerships, are influenced by the communications that are transmitted and received. The role that organisations assume in a network and the manner in which they undertake and complete their tasks are, in part, shaped by the variety and complexity of the communications in transmission throughout the network. Issues of channel or even network control, leadership, subservience and conflict are implanted in the form and nature of the communications exchanged in any network.

Within market exchanges, communications are characterised by formality and planning. Collaborative exchanges are supported by more frequent communications activity. As Mohr and Nevin (1990) state, there is a bi directional flow to communications and an informality to the nature and timing of the information flows.

Defining marketing communications

Having considered the scope, role and tasks of marketing communications, it is now appropriate to define the topic. There is no universal definition of marketing communications and there are many interpretations of the subject. Table 1.2 depicts some of the main orientations through which marketing communications has evolved. The origin of many definitions rests with a promotional outlook where the purpose was to use communications to persuade people to buy products and services. The focus was on products, one-way communications, and the perspective was short-term. The expression 'marketing communications' emerged as a wider range of tools and media evolved and as the scope of the tasks these communications activities were expected to accomplish expanded.

In addition to awareness and persuasion, new goals such as developing understanding and preference, reminding and reassuring customers became accepted as important aspects of the communications effort. Direct marketing activities heralded a new approach as one-to-one, two-way communications began to shift the focus from mass to personal communications efforts. Now a number of definitions refer to an integrated perspective. This view has gathered momentum since the mid-1990s and is even an integral part of the marketing communications vocabulary. This topic is discussed in greater depth in Chapter 10.

However, this transition to an integrated perspective raises questions about the purpose of marketing communications. For example, should the focus extend beyond products and services; should corporate communications be integrated into the organisation's marketing communications; should the range of stakeholders move beyond customers; what does integration mean and is it achievable? With the integrative perspective, a stronger strategic and long-term orientation has developed, although the basis for many marketing communications strategies appears still to rest with a 'promotional mix' orientation.

Table 1.2 The developing orientation of marketing communications

Orientation	Explanation
Information and promotion	Communications are used to persuade people into product purchase, using mass-media communications. Emphasis on rational, product-based information.
Process and imagery	Communications are used to influence the different stages of the purchase process that customers experience. A range of tools is used. Emphasis on product imagery and emotional messages.
Integration	Communications resources are used in an efficient and effective way to enable customers to have a clear view of the brand proposition. Emphasis on strategy, media neutrality and a balance between rational and emotional communications.
Relational	Communications are used as an integral part of the different relationships that organisations share with customers. Emphasis on mutual value and meaning plus recognition of the different communications needs and processing styles of different stakeholder groups.
Experience	In some contexts communications are used to develop unique customer experiences. These involve both integration and relational elements necessary for consistency and meaning.

Some of these interpretations fail to draw out the key issue that marketing communications provides added value, through enhanced product and organisational symbolism. They also fail to recognise that it is the context within which marketing communications flows that impacts upon the meaning and interpretation given to such messages. Its ability to frame and associate offerings with different environments is powerful. Today, in an age where the word 'integration' is used to express a variety of marketing and communications-related activities, where corporate marketing is emerging as the next important development within the subject (Balmer and Gray, 2003) and where interaction is the preferred mode of communications and relationship marketing is the preferred paradigm (Gronroos, 2004), marketing communications embraces a wider remit, one that has moved beyond the product information model and now forms an integral part of an organisation's overall communications and relationship management strategy. This perspective embraces communications as a one-way, two-way, interactive and dialogic approach necessary to meet the varying needs of different audiences. The integration stage focuses on the organisation, whereas the next development may have its focus on the relationships that an organisation has with its various audiences. Above all else, marketing communications should be an audience-centred activity.

Two definitions are proposed: one short and memorable, the other deeper, more considered and involving. First, the short definition:

> *Marketing communications is an audience-centred activity, designed to engage audiences and promote conversations.*

This definition focuses marketing communications on generating engagement and conversations as outputs of the activity. The longer definition that follows has three main themes:

> *Marketing communications is a process through which organisations and audiences attempt to engage with one another. Through an understanding of an audience's preferred communications environments, participants seek to develop and present messages, before evaluating and responding. By conveying messages that are relevant and significant, participants are encouraged to offer attitudinal, emotional and behavioural responses.*

The first concerns the word *engages*. By recognising the different transactional and collaborative needs of the target audience, marketing communications can be used to engage with a variety of audiences in such a way that one-way, two-way, interactive and dialogic communications are used that meet the needs of the audience (Chapters 2 and 10). It is unrealistic to believe that all audiences always want a relationship with your organisation/brand, and, for some, one-way communications are fine. Messages, however, should encourage individual members of target audiences to respond to the focus organisation (or product/brand). This response can be immediate through, for example, purchase behaviour, use of customer carelines or use of the FAQs on a web page. Alternatively it can be deferred as information is assimilated and considered for future use. Even if the information is discarded at a later date, the communications will have attracted attention and consideration of the message.

The second theme concerns the *audiences* for, or participants in, marketing communications. Traditionally, marketing communications has been used to convey product-related information to customer-based audiences. Today, a range of stakeholders have connections and relationships of varying dimensions, and marketing communications needs to incorporate this breadth and variety. Stakeholder audiences, including customers, are all interested in a range of corporate issues, sometimes product-related and sometimes related to the policies, procedures and values of the organisation itself. Marketing communications should be an audience-centred activity and in that sense it is important that messages be based on a firm understanding of both the needs and environment of the audience. To be successful, marketing communications should be grounded in the behaviour and information-processing needs and style of the target audience. This is referred to as 'understanding the context in which the communications event is to occur'. From this base it is easier to present and position brands in order that they are perceived to be different and of value to the target audience.

The third theme from the definition concerns the *response*. This refers to the outcomes of the communications process, and can be used as a measure of whether a communications event has been successful. There are essentially two key responses, cognitive and emotional. Cognitive responses assume an audience to be active problem-solvers and that they use marketing communications to help them in their lives, in purchasing products and services and in managing organisation-related activities. For example, brands are developed partly to help consumers and partly to assist the marketing effort of the host organisation. A brand can inform consumers quickly that, among other things, 'this brand means x quality' so, through experience of similar brand purchases, consumers are assured that their risk is minimised. If the problem facing a consumer is 'which new soup to select for lunch', by choosing one from a familiar family brand the consumer is able to solve it with minimal risk and great speed. Cognitive responses assume audiences undertake rational information processing.

Emotional responses, on the other hand, assume decision-making is not made through rational, cognitive processing but as a result of emotional reaction to a communications stimulus. Hedonic consumption concerns the purchase and use of products and services to fulfil fantasies and to satisfy emotional needs. Satisfaction is based on the overall experience of consuming a product. For example, sports cars and motorbikes are not always bought because of the functionality and performance of the vehicle, but more due to the thrill of independence, power and a feeling of being both carefree and in danger. Marketing communications and content, in particular, should be developed in anticipation of an audience's cognitive or emotional response.

Marketing communications, therefore, can be considered from a number of perspectives. It is a complex activity and is used by organisations with varying degrees of sophistication and success. It is now possible, however, to clarify both the roles and the tasks of marketing communications. The role of marketing communications is to engage audiences and the tasks are to differentiate, reinforce, inform or persuade audiences to think, feel or behave in particular ways.

Scholars' paper 1.3   Consumerism and ethics in IMC

Kliatchko, J.G. (2009) The primacy of the consumer in IMC: espousing a personalist view and ethical implications, *Journal of Marketing Communications*, 15(2–3), April–July, 157–77.

Having established that marketing communications should be audience-centred, this paper by Kliatchko provides an interesting view of some of the issues about the portrayal of consumers in marketing communications, as reflected in previous studies. His focus is integrated marketing communications (Chapter 10) and concludes that consumers have invariably been treated as 'mere subjects for financial gain at any cost above all other considerations'. This paper should be read in conjunction with Richard Christy's chapter on ethics in marketing communications, which can be found on the website supporting this book (www.pearson.com).

Environmental influences

The management of marketing communications is a complex and highly uncertain activity. This is due in part to the nature of the marketing communications variables, including the influence of the environment. The environment can be considered in many different ways, but for the purposes of this opening chapter, three categories are considered: the internal, external and market environments. The constituents of each of these are set out in Figure 1.5.

Internal influences

The internal environment refers primarily to the organisation and the way it works, what its values are and how it wants to develop. Here various forces seek to influence an organisation's marketing communications. The overall strategy that an organisation adopts should have a huge impact. For example, how the organisation wishes to differentiate itself within its target markets will influence the messages and media used and, of course, the overarching positioning and reputation of the company. Brand strategies will influence such things as the way in which brands are named, the extent to which sales promotions are an integral part of the communications mix and how they are positioned. The prevailing organisational culture can also be extremely influential. A hierarchical management structure and power culture usually leads to a subservient, risk-averse culture. This can lead to communications which are largely orientated to USPs and product benefits, rather than orientated to engaging audiences emotionally.

The amount of money available to a marketing communications budget will influence the media mix or the size of the sales force used to deliver messages. Apart from the quality and motivation of the people employed, the level of preferences and marketing skills deployed can impact on the form of the messages, the choice of media, and the use of agencies and support services. Finally, the socio-political climate of the firm shapes not only who climbs the career ladder fastest, but how and to which brands scarce marketing resources are distributed.

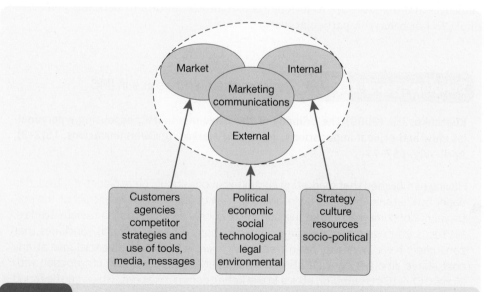

Figure 1.5   The environmental forces that shape marketing communications

Marketing communications is sometimes perceived as only dealing with communications that are external to the organisation. It should be recognised that good communications with internal stakeholders, such as employees, are also vital if, in the long term, favourable images, perceptions and attitudes are to be established successfully. Influences through the workforce and the marketing plan can be both positive and effective. For example, staff used in B&Q and Halifax advertising are intended to project internal values that should reflect positively upon the respective brands.

Market influences

Market influences are characterised by partial levels of control and typified by the impact of competitors. Competitors occupy particular positions in the market and this shapes what others claim about their own products, the media they use, the geographic coverage of the sales force and their own positioning. Intermediaries influence the nature of business-to-business marketing communications. The frequency, intensity, quality and overall willingness to share information with one another are significant forces. Of course, the various agencies an organisation uses can also be very influential, as indeed they should be. Marketing research agencies (inform about market perception, attitudes and behaviour), communications agencies (determine what is said and then design how it is said, what is communicated) and media houses (recommend media mixes and when it is said) all have considerable potential to influence marketing communications.

However, perhaps the biggest single market group consists of the organisation's customers and network of stakeholders. Their attitudes, perceptions and buying preferences and behaviours, although not directly controllable, (should) have a far-reaching influence on the marketing communications used by an organisation.

External influences

As mentioned earlier, the external group of influencers are characterised by the organisation's near lack of control. The well-known PEST framework is a useful way of considering these forces. Political forces, which can encompass both legal and ethical issues, shape their use of marketing communications through legislation, voluntary controls and individual company attitudes towards issues of right and wrong, consequences and duties and the formal and informal communications an organisation uses. Indeed, increasing attention has been placed upon ethics and corporate responsibility to the extent that in some cases a name and shame culture might be identified.

Economic forces, which include demographics, geographics and geodemographics, can determine the positioning of brands in terms of perceived value. For example, if the government raises interest rates, then consumers are more inclined not to spend money, especially on non-staple products and services. This may mean that marketing communications needs to convey stronger messages about value and to send out strident calls-to-action.

Social forces are concerned with the values, beliefs and norms that a society enshrines. Issues to do with core values within a society are often difficult to change. For example, the American gun culture or the once-prevalent me-orientation with respect to self-fulfilment set up a string of values that marketing communications can use to harness, magnify and align brands. The current social pressures with regard to obesity and healthier eating habits forced McDonald's to defend its appointment as the official restaurant partner at the London Olympics (Rowley, 2012). This and other criticism of the fast-food company influenced it to introduce new menus and healthier food options. As a result, its marketing communications has not only to inform and make audiences aware of the new menus but also to convey messages about differentiation and positioning and provide a reason to visit the restaurant (see Viewpoint 1.3).

Technological forces have had an immense impact on marketing communications. New technology continues to advance marketing communications and has already led to more personalised, targeted, customised and responsive forms of communications. What was once predominantly one-way communications, based upon a model of information provision and persuasion, have given way to a two-way model in which integration with audiences, and where sharing and reasoning behaviours are enabled by digital technology, are now used frequently with appropriate target audiences.

Legal forces may prevail in terms of trademarks and copyrights, while environmental forces might impact in terms of what can be claimed and the associated credibility and social responsibility issues.

Marketing communications has evolved in response to changing environmental conditions. For example, direct marketing is now established as a critical approach to developing relationships with buyers, both consumer and organisational. New and innovative forms of communications through social media, digital technologies such as near-field technologies, plus sponsorship, ambient media and content marketing, all suggest that effective communications require the selection and integration of an increasing variety of communications tools and media, as a response to changing environmental contexts.

Viewpoint 1.3   Coca-Cola respond to social forces

The interface between a brand and the social context within which it exists has often been ignored. However, many FMCG (fast-moving consumer goods) brands have embraced the issues and have tried to harness social forces within their propositions and positioning. With regard to the obesity crisis, for example, McDonald's introduced salads and low-calorie options.

Coca-Cola are heavily dependent on the support of the local communities and local governments. This support enables Coke to sustain their global manufacturing facilities and bottling plants, as well as backing up their local distribution networks. It was therefore imperative that the company defend their reputation and readdress their stance on the obesity issue.

In 2013 Coca-Cola's strategy involved the provision of no- or low-calorie beverages of their main brands in all their markets. They also tried to defuse the arguments that sugary drinks contribute to the global obesity epidemic, by putting the calorie counts of their drinks on their respective packaging and by distributing diet options.

In addition, the company realigned some of their sponsorship activities to focus on physical activities in each of the markets in which they operate.

Source: Boyle (2014); Warc (2013); Webb (2014).

Question: Under what circumstances might organisations be accused of responding to social forces in order to avoid accusations of unethical behaviour and to maintain commercial performance?

Task: Visit www.forbes.com/sites/larryhusten/2014/04/27/what-role-should-coca-cola-play-in-obesity-research/ and consider whether it was right to include the report authors with connections with Coca-Cola.

The marketing communications mix

In the recent past there have been several major changes in the communications environment and in the way organisations can communicate with their target audiences. Digital technology has given rise to a raft of different media at a time when people have developed a variety of new ways to spend their leisure time. These phenomena are referred to as *media* and *audience fragmentation* respectively, and organisations have developed fresh combinations of the communications mix in order to reach their audiences effectively. For example, there has been a dramatic rise in the use of direct-response media as direct marketing has become a key part of many campaigns. The Internet and digital technologies have enabled new interactive forms of communications, where receivers can be more participative and assume greater responsibility for their contribution in the communications process.

Successful marketing communications involves managing various elements according to the needs of the target audience and the goals the campaign seeks to achieve. Originally the elements that made up the marketing communications mix were just the tools or disciplines, namely advertising, sales promotions, public relations, direct marketing and personal selling. These were mixed together in various combinations and different degrees of intensity in order to attempt to communicate meaningfully with a target audience.

This mix was used at a time when brands were developed through the use of advertising to generate 'above-the-line' mass communications campaigns. The strategy was based around buying space in newspapers and magazines, or advertising time (called spots) in major television programmes that were watched by huge audiences (20+ million people). This strategy required media owners to create programmes (content) that would attract brand owners because of the huge, relatively passive audiences. By interrupting the audience's entertainment, brand owners could talk to (or at) their markets in order to sell their brands.

Since the days of just two commercial television stations there has been a proliferation of media. Although the use of television is actually increasing, audiences, especially young adults, no longer use television as their main source of information or entertainment. When considered together with falling newspaper and magazine readership, it is clear that consumers are using media for a variety of purposes. These include a need to explore and discover new activities, people, experiences and brands, to participate in events and communities, to share experiences and information, and to express themselves as individuals. This reveals that people seek active engagement with media.

We now have a huge choice of media and leisure activities, and we decide how and when to consume information and entertainment. People are motivated and able to develop their own content, be it through text, music or video, and consider topics that they can share with friends on virtual networks. Media and messages are therefore key to reach consumers today, not the tools. More direct and highly targeted, personalised communications activities using direct marketing and the other tools of the mix now predominate. This indicates that, in order to reach audiences successfully, it is necessary to combine not just the tools, but also the media and the content and messages.

So, in addition to the five principal marketing communications tools, it is necessary to add the media, or the means by which advertising and other marketing communications messages are conveyed. Tools and media should not be confused as they have different characteristics and seek to achieve different goals. Also, just in case you were thinking something is missing, the Internet is a medium, not a tool.

To complete the trilogy, messages need to be conveyed to the target audience. Increasingly referred to as content, four forms can be identified: informational, emotional,

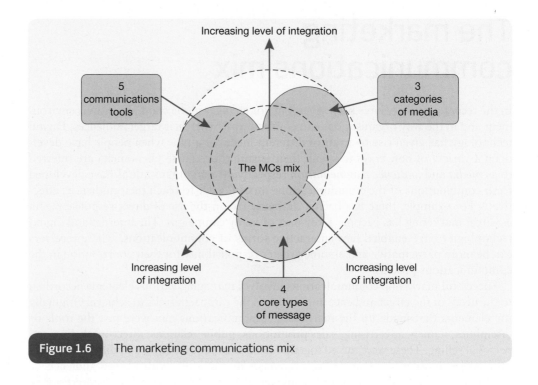

Figure 1.6   The marketing communications mix

user-generated and branded content. These are explored in Chapter 17, but Viewpoint 1.4 shows how some brands are switching from informational to emotional messages in order to connect with consumers. Previously organisations were primarily responsible for the origin and nature of the content about their brand. Today an increasing number of messages are developed by consumers, and shared with other consumers.

The marketing communications mix depicted in Figure 1.6 represents a shift in approach. Previously the mix represents an *intervention*-based approach to marketing communications, one based on seeking the attention of a customer who might not necessarily be interested, by interrupting their activities. The shift is towards *conversation*-based marketing communications, where the focus is now on communications with and between members of an audience who may even have contributed content to the campaign. This has a particular impact on direct marketing, interactive communications and, to some extent, personal selling. Figure 1.6 depicts the marketing communications mix at the core of three overlapping elements: tools, media and content. The dashed lines serve to illustrate the varying degree of integration and coordination between the three elements. The wider the circle, the higher the level of integration and the more effective the marketing communications mix.

Viewpoint 1.4   Building brands around emotion in the home

Paint brands such as Crown and Dulux are not newcomers to a marketing communications strategy based on emotional benefits. Since 77 per cent of consumers say they feel better when they decorate, Dulux try to connect with this, using an emotional approach to their communications.

However, for a large proportion of brands in the home improvement sector this approach is unusual. The primary approach has been to place undue emphasis on advertising, direct marketing and sales promotion to offer low prices, discounts and 'buy me now' offers. This behavioural approach is now giving way to advertising designed to build a brand through emotionally led messages.

For example, the furniture retailer DFS has used a formulaic approach of functionally driven advertising, conveyed through the use of minor celebrities sitting on sofas, urging viewers to get to the sale to take advantage of the low prices and extended credit facilities. However, this has changed as a more emotionally led campaign has evolved. Now, instead of prices, comfort is stressed, as children are seen playing on sofas and a slogan that says 'Making everyday more comfortable', using an updated, heart-shaped logo, appeals to the mind rather than the wallet or credit card. The 2013 Christmas ads showed Santa entering a DFS store and jotting down what's available, or working in a factory, before delivering furniture for people who ordered in time for Christmas.

In a similar way, bedroom-furniture retailers 'Dreams' and 'Harvey's' have released more emotional campaigns. Harvey's used to use their communications to push several – as many as ten – products in an ad. This is now seen as too masculine, since the decision-makers are more often than not women, who are getting more involved in home improvements anyway. One of their changes has been to develop a mobile app that lets users 'test-drive' sofas in their own homes. Dreams show people switching off their lights to go to sleep, accompanied by soothing music.

Why the change, especially in times of recession when typically price-based brands lead the way? There are several reasons put forward. First, research by Mintel reveals that over 40 per cent of consumers express more trust in retailers such as John Lewis and IKEA, who use an emotional approach. Unfortunately, less than 20 per cent of consumers trust price-focused brands. More women are getting involved in home improvements and the success of the pre-Christmas John Lewis campaigns is felt to have prompted a review of brand development in home and in marketing communications.

Source: Based on Brownsell (2012); Vizard (2013).

Question: What role do informational messages play in the market communications used in the DIY market?

Task: List the different types of key message a furniture retailer might use.

(a)

(b)

Exhibit 1.5 Traditional and emotional advertising used by DFS
(a) A traditional DFS ad where price, functionality and style are predominant;
(b) represents a more emotional approach to advertising.
Source: Blue Rubicon Ltd.

Criteria when devising a mix

Using the key characteristics it is possible to determine the significant criteria organisations should consider when selecting the elements of the marketing communications mix. These are:

- the degree of control required over the delivery of the message;
- the amount of available financial resources;
- audience size, and geographic dispersion;

- media preferences and the behaviour of the target audiences;
- the tasks to be accomplished.

It should be noted that there are other elements that can influence the configuration of the mix. These include competitive activity, media rates, internal political perspectives, agency bias, and strategy.

Control

Control over the message is necessary to ensure that the intended message is shared with and among the target audiences. Furthermore, messages must be capable of being understood in order that the receiver can act appropriately. Message control is complicated by interference or negative 'noise' that can corrupt and distort messages. Obsessive media attention to a brand in distress can lead to a freeze on all paid-for marketing communications, that is no advertising.

Advertising, sales promotions, and most paid-for media allow for a reasonable level of control over a message, from design to transmission. Interestingly, they afford only partial control or influence over the feedback associated with a message or how it is disseminated among audiences.

Control can also be an important factor when considering online and digital-based communications. For example, the ability to place banner ads, to bid for sponsored links and determine keyword rankings in search engines require control and deliberation. However, it should be noted that message control is an ambiguous term. Brand owners desire control over message placement and seeding but they also want people to talk about their brands. Here owners sacrifice control over what is said about a brand, who says it and in which context. Engagement is about provoking conversations and that implies that there is virtually no control over this aspect. Planned marketing communications carries a high level of control, while unplanned word-of-mouth conversations carry little control. See Viewpoint 1.5 for an example of controlling social media.

Viewpoint 1.5   ## Hyatt listen to social media

Like many agencies Sparks and Honey manages social-media comment on behalf of its clients. However, in addition to listening to what is being said about a brand, and scoring it on a sentiment rating scale, it also observes other hot topics, assigns each to a particular category, and uses predictive analytics to estimate the speed at which a trend might become established. This information is then used to feed clients with relevant, salient branded content.

This process also helps clients to avoid material that might damage their brand. For example, hotel group Hyatt had spent a lot of time and resources developing a content marketing strategy based on the theme 'women having it all'. This was intended to lead to a campaign targeted at career-minded women, but it was all stopped after its agency had monitored an increasing number of negative discussions about the recently published book *Lean In* written by Facebook's COO Sheryl Sandberg.

Other material identified for use by Hyatt included content on yoga and meditation, getting a good night's sleep and how travellers can benefit from the use of various digital tools.

Source: Kaye (2013).

Question: Is real control of social media possible or is it simply a matter of reducing the margins for error? Explain your reasoning.

Task: Find two examples of poor brand-based social media activity. Make notes on how these events might have been avoided.

Financial resources

Control is also a function of financial power. In other words, if an organisation is prepared to pay a third party to transmit a message, then long-term control will rest with the sponsor for as long as the financial leverage continues. However, short-term message corruption can exist if management control over the process is less than vigilant. For example, if the design of the message differs from that originally agreed, then partial control has already been lost. This can happen when the working relationship between an advertising agency and the client is less than efficient and the process for signing off work in progress fails to prevent the design and release of inappropriate creative work.

Advertising and sales promotion are tools that allow for a high level of control by the sponsor, whereas public relations, and publicity in particular, is weak in this aspect because the voluntary services of a third party are normally required for the message to be transmitted.

In business-to-business (B2B) communications the sales department often receives the bulk of the marketing budget and little is spent on research in comparison with the consumer market.

There is a great variety of media available to advertisers. Each type of medium carries a particular cost, and the financial resources of the organisation may not be available to use particular types of media, even if such use would be appropriate on other grounds.

Audience size and geographic dispersion

The size and geographic dispersion of the target audience can be a significant influence on the configuration of the communications mix. A national consumer audience can be reached effectively through tools such as advertising and sales promotion. Similarly, various specialist businesses require personal attention to explain, design, demonstrate, install and service complex equipment. In these circumstances personal selling – one-to-one contact – is of greater significance. The choice of media can enable an organisation to speak to vast national and international audiences through the Internet and satellite technology, or with single persons or small groups through personal selling and the assistance of word-of-mouth recommendation.

Media behaviour and preferences

An insight into the characteristics of the target audiences can have a very strong influence on the shape of the mix. For example, understanding the way different consumers use different media can have a considerable influence over the way a message is formulated, the media used, and the way paid media are scheduled. The McCain case study at the start of Chapter 4 shows dramatically how the location, choice and scheduling of the media were influenced by the behaviour of the target audience.

With many audiences now familiar with multiscreen and mobile usage and as interactive media have become widespread so it is necessary to use a range of media to understand the behaviour preferences of audiences in order to cut through the clutter and noise that can lead people to screen out marketing communications messages.

Communications tasks

Each element of the communications mix has strengths and weaknesses, therefore the selected mix should be based on a configuration designed to maximise the strengths and accomplish specific tasks. For example, one of the reasons direct marketing has become so successful is that it delivers a call-to-action and is therefore a very good persuasive tool as well as being good at reinforcing messages. This behavioural dimension is counter-balanced by advertising and public relations where engagement is largely based on differentiating offerings and informing audiences about key features and benefits.

Communications differences

Another way of considering these issues involves comparing the communications used to reach consumer and B2B audiences. Organisational purchases are intended for company usage, whereas products bought in a consumer context are normally intended for personal consumption. Table 1.3 and the following are intended to set out some of the more salient differences.

Message reception

The contextual conditions in which messages are received and meanings ascribed are very different. In organisational settings the context is more formal, and as the funding for a purchase is derived from company sources (as opposed to personal sources for consumer market purchases), there may be a lower orientation to price as a significant variable in the purchase decision, and more on the benefits of use in the message.

Number of decision-makers

In consumer markets a single person very often makes the decision. In organisational markets decisions are made by many people within a buying centre. This means that the

Table 1.3 Differences between consumer and business-to-business marketing

	Consumer-oriented markets	Business-to-business markets
Message reception	Informal	Formal
Number of decision-makers	Single or few	Many
Balance of the communications mix	Advertising and sales promotions dominate	Personal selling dominates
Specificity and integration	Broad use of communications mix with a move towards integrated mixes	Specific use of below-the-line tools but with a high level of integration
Variety of media	Huge assortment of media	Narrow range of media
Message content	Greater use of emotions and imagery	Greater use of rational, logic and information-based messages although there is evidence of a move towards the use of imagery
Message origin	Increasing use of user-generated content	Limited use of user-generated materials
Length of decision time	Normally short	Long and involved
Negative communications	Limited to people close to the purchaser/user	Potentially an array of people in the organisation and beyond
Target marketing and research	Great use of sophisticated targeting and communications approaches	Limited but increasing use of targeting, segmentation and community approaches
Budget allocation	Majority of budget allocated to brand management	Majority of budget allocated to sales management
Evaluation and measurement	Great variety of techniques and approaches used	Limited number of techniques and approaches used

interactions of the participants should be considered. In addition, a variety of different individuals need to be reached and influenced and this may involve the use of different media and message strategies.

The balance of the communications mix

The role of advertising and sales promotions in B2B communications is primarily to support the personal selling effort. This contrasts with the mix that predominates in consumer markets. Personal selling plays a relatively minor role and is only significant at the point of purchase in some product categories where involvement is high (cars, white goods and financial services), reflecting high levels of perceived risk. However, the high use of direct marketing in consumer markets suggests that personal communications are becoming more prevalent and in some ways increasingly similar to the overall direction of B2B communications.

Specificity and integration

B2B markets have traditionally been quite specific in terms of the tools and media used to reach audiences. While the use of advertising literature is very important, there has been a tendency to use a greater proportion of 'below-the-line' activities. This compares with consumer markets, where a greater proportion of funds are allocated to 'above-the-line' activities. It is interesting that the communications in the consumer market are moving towards a more integrated format, more similar in form to the B2B model than was previously considered appropriate. In both contexts the use of social media has become increasingly prevalent as brands seek to develop relationships with specific audiences.

Variety of media

Increasingly the role of media within the communications mix has become a critical effectiveness factor. The surge towards the incorporation of interactive media within an integrated format in order to engage and interact with consumers has recently started to be mirrored by organisations operating in the B2B market. Viewpoint 19.3 demonstrates this vividly. The range of media available for use within consumer markets far exceeds those that are available and effective within B2B markets. Although television remains a dominant medium for some major FMCG brands, the selection of the right media mix has become more complex for brands operating in consumer markets.

Content

Purchase decisions can be characterised as high involvement in many B2B contexts, so messages tend to be much more rational and information-based than in consumer markets.

Message origin

Increasingly, consumers are taking a more active role in the creation of content. Blogging, for example, is important in both consumer and business markets, but the development of user-generated content and word-of-mouth communications is a significant part of consumer-based marketing communications activities.

Length of purchase decision time

The length of time taken to reach a decision is much greater in organisational markets. This means that the intensity of any media plan can be dissipated more easily in organisational markets.

Negative communications

The number of people affected by a dissatisfied consumer, and hence negative marketing communications messages, is limited. The implications of a poor purchase decision in an organisational environment may be far-reaching, including those associated with the use of the product, the career of participants close to the locus of the decision and, depending on the size and spread, perhaps the whole organisation.

Target marketing and research

The use of target marketing processes in the consumer market is more advanced and sophisticated than in the organisational market. This impacts on the quality of the marketing communications used to reach the target audience. However, there is much evidence that B2B market organisations are becoming increasingly aware and sophisticated in their approach to segmentation techniques and processes.

Measurement and evaluation

The consumer market employs a variety of techniques to evaluate the effectiveness of communications. In the organisational market, sales volume, value, number of enquiries and market share are the predominant measures of effectiveness.

Marketing communications goals

Perhaps the most influential factors when considering the configuration of the marketing communications mix are the communications goals that the mix is intended to accomplish. Apart from financial returns, the reasons to use marketing communications can be varied and are explored in Chapter 6. However, these goals can be considered in layers and as we saw earlier the type of engagement can provide an initial indicator of the type of tools, media and messages to be used. For example, if the goal is to drive consumer brand values then the message is more likely to have significant emotional content and will not be designed to drive responses. The tools chosen are more likely to involve advertising, public relations and sponsorship, not direct marketing, sales promotions or personal selling. Paid-for online and offline media will be used to support the advertising element and earned media will be used to enhance message distribution.

Another filter might be whether the goal is to penetrate a market, and that means finding new customers, or whether retention and creating customer loyalty is the primary goal. A penetration goal leans towards informing and creating awareness and this means advertising, public relations, paid media and informing or emotional messages will be primary. If retention is the goal then a mix aimed at rewarding current customers will be preferable.

A third layer, referred to by the IPA as intermediate communications goals, involves creating awareness, consideration or preference as the focus of the activity. Again the mix should reflect these goals.

The way in which a mix is configured reflects a number of issues and contextual elements. There is no algorithm, fixed schematic or single way of creating the appropriate marketing communications mix. What we can do, however, is consolidate our understanding about the role, the tasks and the marketing communications mix. The role is to engage audiences, the tasks are to DRIP and through the selection and deployment of the elements of the mix, organisations seek to engage audiences and achieve their goals (DRIP).

There can be no doubt that there are a number of major differences between the marketing communications mixes used in consumer and organisation contexts. These reflect the nature of the environments, the tasks involved and the overall need of the recipients for particular types of information. Throughout this book, reference will be made to the characteristics, concepts and processes associated with marketing communications in each of these two main sectors.

Scholars' paper 1.4	Abandon island thinking

Gummesson, E. and Polese, F. (2009) B2B is not an island! *Journal of Business & Industrial Marketing,* 24(5/6), 337–50.

The reason for encouraging readers to see this paper is because it suggests that marketing should be considered not as just B2B or B2C, but as a joined-up part of the same marketing context and service system, one in which there is a coherent network of relationships. The authors stress the interdependency between B2B and B2C. The implications are that marketing planning should incorporate the relational patterns within a company's network and that systematic attention should be given to the customers' role in value creation and treating them as a resource and co-creator.

Key points

- There are two broad types of exchange and they can be considered to sit at either end of a spectrum of exchange transactions. At one end are transactional or market exchanges, which are characterised as one-off exchanges in which price and product are central elements. At the other end are relational or collaborative exchanges where there has been a stream of transactions and the relationship is the central element.

- Relationships become stronger as the frequency of exchanges increases. As exchanges become more frequent, the intensity of the relationship strengthens so that the focus is no longer on the product or price within the exchange but on the relationship itself.

- The scope of marketing communications embraces an audience-centred perspective of planned, unplanned, product and service experiences. The role of marketing communications is to engage audiences with a view to provoking relevant conversations. The tasks of marketing communications are based within a need to differentiate, reinforce, inform or persuade audiences to think and behave in particular ways.

- Engagement is a function of two elements. The first is the degree to which a message encourages thinking and feeling about a brand: the development of brand values. The second is about the degree to which a message stimulates behaviour or action. Engagement may last a second, a minute, an hour, a day or even longer.

- Definitions have evolved as communications have developed. Here marketing communications is defined as:

  a process through which organisations and audiences engage with one another. Through an understanding of an audience's preferred communications environments, participants seek to develop, and present messages, before evaluating and acting upon any replies. By conveying messages that are relevant and significant, participants are encouraged to offer attitudinal, emotional and behavioural responses.

- The internal, market and external environments all influence the use of marketing communications. The internal environment refers to employees, the culture, the financial resources and the marketing skills available to organisations. The market environment refers principally to the actions of competitors and the perceptions and attitudes held by customers towards an organisation or its brands.

- The external environment can be considered in terms of the PEST framework. The influence of any one of these elements on marketing communications can be significant, although the impact is usually generic and affects all organisations rather than any single brand or organisation.

- The marketing communications mix consists of various tools, media and messages that are used to reach, engage and provoke audience-centred conversations. The five tools, three categories of media and four types of message can be configured in different ways to meet the needs of target audiences.

- The way in which the marketing communications mix is configured for consumer markets is very different from the mix used for business markets. The tools, media and messages used are all different as the general contexts in which they operate require different approaches. Business markets favour personal selling: consumer markets, advertising. Both make increasing use of interactive media, and while rational messages are predominant in business markets, emotion-based messages tend to prevail in consumer markets.

Review questions

Sensodyne Pronamel case questions

1. Evaluate the main role of marketing communications in the Sensodyne Pronamel launch campaign.

2. Using the DRIP framework identify and explain the key tasks that marketing communications was required to accomplish for the successful launch of Sensodyne Pronamel.

3. Examine the main elements of the marketing communications mix that were used in this campaign.

4. Appraise the main forces in the external environment that influenced the shape, nature and characteristics of the campaign.

5. Explain how the marketing communications mix was adapted for the different audiences in the Sensodyne campaign.

General questions

1. Define marketing communications. What are the key elements in the definition?

2. Briefly compare and contrast the two main types of exchange transaction. How do communications assist the exchange process?

3. How might the contribution of the tools differ from those of the media within a marketing communications programme?

4. Discuss the way in which the elements of the mix compare across the following criteria: control, communications effectiveness and cost.

5. Evaluate the ways in which engagement might vary across campaigns.

6. Explain how marketing communications might differ within consumer and business marketing strategies.

References

Adie, N. (2013) BT apologises over issues with sports channel launch, *Cable.co.uk*, 13 December 2013, retrieved 20 December 2013 from www.cable.co.uk/news/bt-apologises-over-issues-with-sports-channel-launch-801672424/.

Andersson, P. (1992) Analysing distribution channel dynamics, *European Journal of Marketing*, 26(2), 47–68.

Anon (2013) BT launches sports TV channels in battle with Sky, 1 August 2013, retrieved 20 December 2013, from www.bbc.co.uk/news/business-23527897.

Anon (2014a) Facebook adds more features, *Warc*, retrieved 15 December from www.warc.com/LatesNews/News/EmailNews.news?ID=34024&Origin=WARCNewsEmail&CID=N34024&PUB=Warc_News&utm_source=WarcNews&utm_medium=email&utm_campaign=WarcNews20141215.

Anon, (2014b) 'Engaged time' could replace CPM, *Warc*, 14 June, retrieved 8 July 2014 from www.warc.com/LatestNews/News/EmailNews.news?ID=33140&Origin=WARCNewsEmail&CID=N33140&PUB=Warc_News&utm_source=WarcNews&utm_medium=email&utm_campaign=WarcNews20140619.

Anon (2015) How to measure success in content marketing, *ScribbleLive*, retrieved 14 February 2015 from http://media.dmnews.com/documents/105/scribblelive_whitepaper_measur_26084.pdf.

Bagozzi, R. (1978) Marketing as exchange: a theory of transactions in the market place, *American Behavioral Science*, 21(4), 257–61.

Ballantyne, D. (2004) Dialogue and its role in the development of relationship specific knowledge, *Journal of Business and Industrial Marketing*, 19(2), 114–23.

Balmer, J.M.T. and Gray, E.R. (2003) Corporate brands: what are they? What of them? *European Journal of Marketing*, 37(7/8), 972–97.

Bergin, O. (2012) Exclusive first look inside Victoria's Secret London flagship store, *Telegraph*, 28 August 2012, retrieved 22 December 2013 from http://fashion.telegraph.co.uk/article/TMG9503894/Exclusive-first-look-inside-Victorias-Secret-London-flagship-store.html.

Bohannon, C. (2015) Victoria's Secret's catalog gets a mobile boost for Valentine's Day, *Mobile Commerce Daily*, 21 January, retrieved 15 February from www.mobilecommercedaily.com/victorias-secret-enhances-catalog-merchandising-with-mobile-quiz.

Bowersox, D. and Morash, E. (1989) The integration of marketing flows in channels of distribution. *European Journal of Marketing*, 23(2), 58–67.

Boyle, S. (2014) Critics slam Coca-Cola's £20m anti-obesity 'stunt', *Daily Mail*, 26 May, retrieved 10 November 2014 from www.dailymail.co.uk/news/article-2639940/Critics-slam-Coca-Colas-20m-anti-obesity-stunt-Experts-say-firms-plan-offer-families-free-sports-sessions-attempt-distract-attention-role-health-crisis.html.

Brignall, M. (2013) BT sorry for poor TV service after launch of sports channel, *Guardian*, Friday 13 December, retrieved 19 December 2013 from www.theguardian.com/money/2013/dec/13/bt-tv-complaints-sports-launch.

Brougaletta, Y. (1985) What business-to-business advertisers can learn from consumer advertisers, *Journal of Advertising Research*, 25(3), 8–9.

Brownsell, A. (2012) Brand building comes home, *Marketing*, 21 March, 14–15.

Clark, N. (2010) Eurostar plots mag to boost customer loyalty, *Marketing*, 17 February, p. 4.

Duncan, T.R. and Moriarty, S. (1997) *Driving Brand Value*, New York: McGraw-Hill.

Dwyer, R., Schurr, P. and Oh, S. (1987) Developing buyer–seller relationships, *Journal of Marketing*, 51 (April), 11–27.

Gronroos, C. (2004) The relationship marketing process: communication, interaction, dialogue, value, *Journal of Business and Industrial Marketing*, 19(2), 99–113.

Gummesson, E. and Polese, F. (2009) B2B is not an island! *Journal of Business & Industrial Marketing*, 24(5/6), 337–50.

Heinonen, K. and Strandvik, T. (2005) Communication as a element of service value, *International Journal of Service Industry Management*, 16(2), 186–98.

Houston, F. and Gassenheimer, J. (1987) Marketing and exchange, *Journal of Marketing*, 51 (October), 13–18.

Hughes, G. and Fill, C. (2007) Redefining the nature and format of the marketing communications mix, *The Marketing Review*, 7(1), 45–57.

Kaye, K. (2013) How social data influenced Hyatt to pull part of campaign days before launch, *Adage.com*, 8 August 2013, retrieved 26 December 2013 from http://adage.com/article/datadriven-marketing/social-data-influenced-hyatt-pull-part-acampaign/243539/?utm_source=digital_email&utm_medium=newsletter&utm_campaign=adage&ttl=1376578743.

Kemp, N. (2014) Why social media is constructing a reality unworthy of your anxiety, *Marketing Magazine*, August, 49–51.

Kliatchko, J.G. (2009) The primacy of the consumer in IMC: espousing a personalist view and ethical implications, *Journal of Marketing Communications*, 15(2–3), April–July, 157–77.

Li, T., Berens, G. and Maertelaere de, M. (2013) Corporate Twitter channels: the impact of engagement and informedness on corporate reputation, *International Journal of Electronic Commerce*, 18(2), 97–125.

McCarthy, E.J. (1960) *Basic Marketing: A Managerial Approach*, Homewood, IL: Irwin.

Macneil, I.R. (1983) Values in contract: internal and external, *Northwestern Law Review*, 78(2), 340–418.

Mohr, J. and Nevin, J. (1990) Communication strategies in marketing channels, *Journal of Marketing*, 54 (October), 36–51.

Patel, D. (2012) Brands are placing multimedia at the heart of the in-store experience, 6 September 2012, retrieved 7 January 2014 from www.brandrepublic.com/opinion/1148554/Think-BR-Brands-placing-multimedia-heart-in-store-experience/?DCMP=ILC-SEARCH.

Poletti, J. and Viccars, J. (2013) Three steps to help brands connect digital content with in-store experience, *Marketing*, 22 August, retrieved 8 July 2014 from www.marketingmagazine.co.uk/article/1208216/three-steps-help-brands-connect-digital-content-in-store-experience.

Ray, M.L. (1973) A decision sequence analysis of developments in marketing communications, *Journal of Marketing*, 37 (January), 29–38.

Rossiter, J.R. and Percy, L. (2013) How the roles of advertising merely appear to have changed, *International Journal of Advertising*, 32(3), 391–8.

Rowley, T. (2012) London 2012 Olympics: McDonald's 'the wrong choice' for athletes, says Team GB sport science head, *Telegraph*, 19 July 2012, retrieved 10 November 2014 from www.telegraph.co.uk/sport/olympics/news/9412953/London-2012-Olympics-McDonalds-the-wrong-choice-for-athletes-says-Team-GB-sport-science-head.html.

Schlinger, M. (1979) A profile of responses to commercials, *Journal of Advertising Research*, 19, 37–46.

Staff (2013) BT Sport unveils 'Name that Team' competition, *The Drum*, 3 September 2013, retrieved 20 December, 2013 from www.thedrum.com/news/2013/09/03/bt-sport-unveils-name-team-competition.

Verhoef, P.C., Reinartz, W.J. and Krafft, M. (2010) Customer engagement as a new perspective in customer management, *Journal of Service Research*, 13(3), 247–52.

Vizard, S. (2013) Christmas ads: the good, the bad and the bizarre, *Marketing Week*, 13 November, retrieved 13 January 2015 from www.marketingweek.co.uk/news/christmas-ads-the-good-the-bad-and-the-bizarre/4008560.article.

Warc (2013) Coke tackles obesity issue, retrieved 19 May 2013 from www.warc.com/LatestNews/News/EmailNews.news?ID=31380&Origin=WARCNewsEmail\#FjSW7X3M6Q1WKV4J.99.

Webb, M. A. (2014) How brands get our attention, retrieved 10 November 2014 from www.ami.org.au/imis15/News_2014_July/Member_Say_How_Brands.aspx.

Willifer, M. (2013) Adwatch: Magners ad embraces emotions, *Marketing Magazine*, 17 June, retrieved 13 July 2014 from www.marketingmagazine.co.uk/article/1187655/adwatch-magners-ad-embraces-emotions.

Chapter 2
Communications: forms and conversations

Communications are concerned with receiving, interpreting and sending messages, but are essentially about sharing meaning with others. Only by using messages that reduce ambiguity, and which share meaning with audiences, can it be hoped to stimulate meaningful interaction and dialogue. To create and sustain valued conversations the support of influential others is often required. These may be people who are experts, those who share common interests, those who have relevant knowledge or people who have access to appropriate media channels.

Aims and learning objectives

The aims of this chapter are to introduce communications theory and to set it in the context of marketing communications.

The learning objectives are to enable readers to:

1. understand the linear model of communications and appreciate how the various elements link together and contribute to successful communications;
2. examine the characteristics of the influencer, interactional, relational and network forms of communications;
3. explain the influence of opinion leaders, formers and followers;
4. examine the nature and characteristics associated with word-of-mouth communications;
5. describe the processes of adoption and diffusion as related to marketing communications.

British Heart Foundation: Vinnie – stayin' alive!

In the UK, 60,000 cardiac arrests occur outside of hospital every year and only an average of 7 per cent (4,200) survive to be discharged from hospital. However, if someone can step in before emergency services arrive and perform CPR (getting the blood circulating again by performing chest compressions and rescue breaths), survival rates can double.

It is the speed of intervention that is critical. Performing CPR is about buying time and restoring oxygenated blood to the brain and heart until professional help arrives. For every minute that goes by, a victim's chance of survival drops 10 per cent.

With ambulances struggling to get through crowded road networks, and the number of people calling 999 increasing all the time, the British Heart Foundation (BHF), the UK's number one heart charity, felt compelled to mobilise the public to step in and fill the time before ambulances arrived.

Previously CPR instruction had been complex, intimidating and sparsely communicated, let alone understood. It was little wonder that there was a fear of making things worse, and that 76 per cent of people admitted a lack of confidence to perform CPR. In fact 82 per cent of adults didn't even know if CPR was the right response, and BHF research showed that 73 per cent of adults claimed they were unfamiliar with the CPR procedure.

A new simplified 'Hands-only CPR' approach had been devised, one not requiring mouth-to-mouth, or the 'kiss of life' as it was once known. The BHF saw an opportunity to create an army of knowledgeable bystanders ready to apply CPR wherever they were: a fifth emergency service.

With a tiny budget, the communications needed to accomplish four main tasks:

1. Ensure people knew *how* to perform the new technique.
2. Remove the fear and instil the confidence to act.
3. Register mass awareness of the new 'Hands-only CPR' technique at a national level.
4. Save lives.

There are five steps to the new procedure with no need for mouth-to-mouth:

1. Call 999.
2. Check the person is breathing.
3. No need for kissing.
4. Push hard and fast in the middle of the chest.
5. To the tempo of 100 BPM.

The challenge was to teach this behaviour, not just drive awareness. Previous public service communications, such as *Clunk, Click Every Trip* and *Slip! Slop! Slap,* worked because of their simplicity, and the instruction which used different 'hooks' that pulled on different senses. Many used a clear visual moment with a snappy-sounding phrase. Others offered a simple action that could easily be copied. Just as a catchy tune infiltrates your brain and doesn't leave you, we needed to create our own simple and sticky piece of communications that stepped people through the procedure.

As we began to develop the campaign we found some advice that suggested fear could be defused through the power of laughter. Could we use humour to enable our message to cut through the fear felt by our audience about cardiac arrests? Our train of thought was roughly:

Ok, we need a song and it has to be the right tempo. 100 BPM.

It needs to be something everyone knows. Disco? Yes.

Stayin' Alive! by The Bee Gees and at 100 BPM.

Who would get noticed saving a life? A celeb.

Not any celeb, a hard man . . . one famed for violence. Someone who could push hard and fast. Vinnie Jones. Doing Stayin' Alive!

We'd created a funny and memorable 'dance' that brought together five elements to maximise 'cut through':

1. A 100 BPM soundtrack with universal appeal: 'Stayin' Alive' by The Bee Gees.
2. A well-known character famous for toughness and hurting people: Vinnie Jones, football and Hollywood.
3. A sticky phrase that conveyed the key action: hard and fast.
4. A tone that would challenge traditional government first aid messaging: the comedic and the serious.
5. A script that clearly walked the five steps of hands-only CPR.

The TV buying strategy for 'Vinnie' was designed to reach 80 per cent of the population at least once. During a 4-week campaign, we ran 480 TVRs (television ratings) and 'road blocked' the nation's most popular programmes to ensure we generated maximum fame. The 'Vinnie' film became the most shared online video in launch week, with 72,601 shares across social media in the first 10 days.

We debuted the ad socially on Twitter with the hashtag '\#hardandfast', which trended organically five times on launch day. It was bolstered further with promoted tweets and 37 million impressions booked as rich display media on national sites such as Yahoo!, MSN and AOL. Public relations and social media further amplified the campaign.

We launched a how-to-do 'Hands-only CPR' app through websites such as iTunes and Google Play and sold a set of limited edition 'Vinnie' T-shirts across the BHF's 700 shops nationwide.

The 'Vinnie' campaign gained major PR coverage across the biggest online and offline national media channels including the *BBC,* the *Sun* and *Daily Mail.* The Hands-only TV ad was parodied on the biggest TV shows including *The Graham Norton Show* (BBC1), *The Alan Carr Show* (Channel 4) and *Soccer AM* (Sky Sports). Reconstructed 'Hands-only CPR' rescues were made the feature on two mainstream BBC shows. The ad was even recreated in LEGO as part of the promotion for *The LEGO Movie* where famous UK ads were spoofed and pulled together for a special ad break.

The campaign was a huge success, and by turning something that is serious and scary into something funny, we changed people's lives and behaviour. Our aim was to recruit an army of bystanders who were more likely to step in during an emergency. Post-tracking told us that we created an extra 6 million people who were now more likely to perform 'Hands-only CPR'. We know that 30 lives were saved as a direct result of people seeing the ad, due to the letters we have received.

How were these lives saved? Research indicates that the likability element of the campaign message enabled it to become easily understood and 'sticky' as it resonated with people and was passed on to others. Neuro-linguistic programming (NLP) suggests people learn in three key ways: through pictures and images (visually); through chants and rhythm (auditory); and through gestures and body movements (kinaesthetically). 'Vinnie' combined all three and it was this that helped to communicate effectively, maximise reach, and enable a mass audience to learn a new behaviour.

Exhibit 2.1	**Vinnie – Hands-Only CPR**
	Source: British Heart Foundation.

| Exhibit 2.2 | **Vinnie is now used for NHS training** |
| | *Source*: British Heart Foundation. |

This case was written by Matt Buttrick, Planning Director at Grey London

Questions relating to this case can be found at the end of this chapter.

An introduction to the process of communications

It was established in Chapter 1 that marketing communications is partly an attempt by an organisation/brand to create and sustain conversations with its various audiences. It is also necessary to encourage members of these audiences to talk amongst themselves about a brand. As communications are the process by which individuals share meaning, each participant in the communications process needs to be able to interpret the meaning embedded in the messages, and be able to respond in appropriate ways.

In the British Heart Foundation (BHF) case, or 'Vinnie' as it is generally understood, appreciating the nature and characteristics of the target audience was an important element of the BHF's successful campaign. Their campaign required that information was transmitted *to,* and then *among,* key participants. It is important, therefore, that those involved with marketing communications understand this complexity. Through knowledge and understanding of the communications process, participants are more likely to achieve their objective of sharing meaning with each member of their target audiences and so have an opportunity to enter into a sustainable dialogue.

This chapter examines several models, or forms, of the communications process. It considers the characteristics associated with word-of-mouth communications and looks at the way products and ideas are adopted by individuals and markets.

A linear model of communications

Wilbur Schramm (1955) developed what is now accepted as the basic model of mass communications, shown in Figure 2.1. The components of the linear model of communications are:

1. Source: the individual or organisation sending the message.
2. Encoding: transferring the intended message into a symbolic style that can be transmitted.
3. Signal: the transmission of the message using particular media.
4. Decoding: understanding the symbolic style of the message in order to understand the message.
5. Receiver: the individual or organisation receiving the message.
6. Feedback: the receiver's communications back to the source on receipt of the message.
7. Noise: distortion of the communications process, making it difficult for the receiver to interpret the message as intended by the source.

This is a linear model, one that emphasises the 'transmission of information, ideas, attitudes, or emotion from one person or group to another (or others), primarily through symbols' (Theodorson and Theodorson, 1969). The model and its components are straightforward, but it is the quality of the linkages between the various elements in the process that determine whether a communications event will be successful.

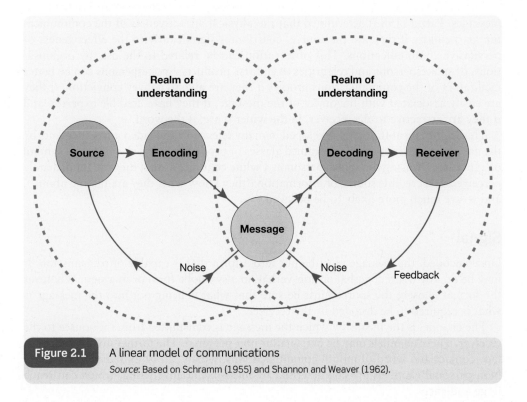

Figure 2.1 A linear model of communications
Source: Based on Schramm (1955) and Shannon and Weaver (1962).

Source/encoding

The source is an individual or organisation, which identifies a need to transmit a message. It then selects a combination of appropriate words, pictures, symbols and music to represent the message to be transmitted. This is called 'encoding'. The purpose is to create a message that is capable of being understood by the receiver. The BHF understood people's confusion and reluctance to get involved with CPR but used humour and a catchy song to encode the message sufficiently that audiences could understand (decode), learn and act on (and share) the message.

There are a number of reasons why the source/encoding link might break down. For example, the source may fail to diagnose a particular situation accurately. By not fully understanding a stakeholder's problem or level of knowledge, inappropriate information may be included in the message, which, when transmitted, may lead to misunderstanding and misinterpretation by the receiver. By failing to appreciate the level of education of the target receiver, a message might be encoded in words and symbols that are beyond the comprehension of the receiver.

Some organisations spend a great deal of time and expense on market research, trying to develop their understanding of their target audience. The source of a message is an important factor in the communications process. A receiver who perceives a source lacking conviction, authority, trust or expertise is likely to discount any message received from that source, until such time as credibility is established.

Many organisations spend a great deal of time and expense recruiting sales representatives. The risk involved in selecting the wrong people can be extremely large. Many high-tech organisations require their new sales staff to spend over a year receiving both product and sales training before allowing them to meet customers. From a customer's perspective, salespersons who display strong product knowledge skills and who are also able to empathise with the individual members of the decision-making unit are more likely to be perceived as credible. Therefore, an organisation that prepares its sales staff and presents them as knowledgeable and trustworthy is more likely to be successful in the communications process than one that does not take the same level of care.

The source is a part of the communications process, not just the generator of detached messages. Patzer (1983) determined that the physical attractiveness of the communicator, particularly if they are the source, contributes significantly to the effectiveness of persuasive communications. This observation can be related to the use, by organisations, of spokespersons and celebrities to endorse products. Spokespersons can be better facilitators of the communications process if they are able to convey conviction, if they are easily associated with the object of the message, if they have credible expertise and if they are attractive to the receiver, in the wider sense of the word.

This legitimate authority is developed in many television and video advertisements by the use of the 'white coat', black-framed glasses or product-specific clothing, as a symbol of expertise. Dressing the spokesperson in a white coat means that they are immediately perceived as a credible source of information ('they know what they are talking about'), and so are much more likely to be believed.

Signal

Once encoded, the message must be put into a form that is capable of transmission. It may be oral or written, verbal or non-verbal, in a symbolic form or in a sign. Whatever the format chosen, the source must be sure that what is being put into the message is what is required to be decoded by the receiver.

The channel is the means by which the message is transmitted from the source to the receiver. These channels may be personal or non-personal. The former involves face-to-face contact and word-of-mouth communications, which can be extremely influential. Non-personal channels are characterised by mass-media advertising, which can reach large audiences.

Information received directly from personal influence channels is generally more persuasive than information received through mass media. This may be a statement of the obvious, but the reasons for this need to be understood. First, the individual approach permits greater flexibility in the delivery of the message. The timing and power with which a message is delivered can be adjusted to suit the immediate 'selling' environment. Second, a message can be adapted to meet the needs of the customer as the sales call progresses. This flexibility is not possible with mass-media messages, as these have to be designed and produced well in advance of transmission and often without direct customer input.

Viewpoint 2.1 — Encoding ads for Chinese empathy

Adidas developed a campaign for the Beijing Olympics with the goal of overtaking the share of the Chinese market held by their arch competitor Nike. Adidas chose to promote Chinese nationalism at a time when human rights issues and environmental policies dominated the approaches used by advertisers.

The platform for the Adidas campaign was the pride the Chinese felt in winning and hosting the Games. The campaign featured Chinese athletes such as basketball player Sui Feifei and diver Hu Jia. Ads featured computer-animated Chinese fans helping Chinese athletes in their events. For example, fans were shown blocking a volleyball shot, another flicking a pass to a basketball player or helping to launch a diver. Another ad showed the Chinese women's volleyball team talking about how they overcame the huge expectations of their country to win a medal at the previous Olympic Games in Greece. Adidas even made the outfit worn by the Chinese delegation at each medal ceremony, and featured this is an ad.

Exhibit 2.3	Adidas ad used to appeal to the pride of the Chinese at hosting the 2008 Beijing Olympics

Source: 2015 Adidas.

Unlike its normal global approach to ads during major sporting events, this campaign was only shown in China. It used TV, outdoor, retail, mobile and online marketing.

Some brands occasionally misinterpret the context of their audience and develop ads whose meaning is not understood because they are decoded in a different way to that intended. As a result they are passed over or in some cases cause annoyance or generate outright indignation. Part of the reason for this is that the encoding process was misjudged and the associated marketing management processes failed.

For example, Bruce Lee fans and Chinese film-makers voiced their disapproval when Diageo resurrected the martial-arts star for a Johnnie Walker ad for their Blue Label whisky brand. The video, aimed at Chinese markets, depicted Lee being brought back to life through animation. The encoding process failed to anticipate the timing of the ad's release which coincided with the considerable commemorative activity celebrating Lee's death 40 years previously. In addition to this, using Lee in association with alcohol was misjudged because Lee never drank. The final encoding mishap concerned the actor used to represent Lee. In the ad he spoke Putonghua, a standardised form of Chinese, whereas Lee was born in Hong Kong and spoke Cantonese.

Source: Anon (2010a); Barnes (2013).

Question: Why did Adidas restrict the campaign to a China-only audience?

Task: Find two other campaigns which are anchored in a particular context.

Decoding/receiver

Decoding is the process of transforming and interpreting a message into thought. This process is influenced by the receiver's realm of understanding, which encompasses the experiences, perceptions, attitudes and values of both the source and the receiver. The more the receiver understands about the source and the greater their experience in decoding the source's messages, the more able the receiver will be to decode and attribute the intended meaning to the message.

Feedback/response

The set of reactions a receiver has after seeing, hearing or reading a message is known as the *response*. These vary from the extreme of calling an enquiry telephone number, returning or downloading a coupon or even buying the product, sending a text/email, to storing information in long-term memory for future use. Feedback is that part of the response that is sent back to the sender, and it is essential for successful communications. The need to understand not just whether the message has been received but also 'which' message has been received is vital. For example, the receiver may have decoded the message incorrectly and a completely different set of responses may have been elicited. If a suitable feedback system is not in place then the source will be unaware that the communications have been unsuccessful and is liable to continue wasting resources. This represents inefficient and ineffective marketing communications.

Scholars' paper 2.1   Mass communication – uncut

Schramm, W. (1962) Mass communication, *Annual Review of Psychology*, 13(1), 25–84.

This is a seminal paper. Schramm explores mass communications and the various elements that influence or constitute the mass communications process. This paper provides an excellent insight into the theoretical development of the topic, at which point the linear model of communications was possibly at its highest point of popularity. You will be surprised at the range of elements considered by Schramm.

The evaluation of feedback is vital if effective communications are to be developed. Only through evaluation can the success of any communications be judged. Feedback through personal selling can be instantaneous, through overt means such as questioning, raising objections or signing an order form. Other means, such as the use of gestures and body language, are less overt, and the decoding of the feedback needs to be accurate if an appropriate response is to be given. For the advertiser, the process is much more vague and prone to misinterpretation and error.

Feedback through mass-media channels is generally much more difficult to obtain, mainly because of the inherent time delay involved in the feedback process. There are some exceptions, namely the overnight ratings provided by the Broadcasters' Audience Research Board (see www.barb.co.uk) to the television contractors, but as a rule feedback is normally delayed and not as fast. Some commentators argue that the only meaningful indicator of communications success is sales. However, there are many other influences that affect the level of sales, such as price, the effect of previous communications, the recommendations of opinion leaders or friends, poor competitor actions or any number of government or regulatory developments. Except in circumstances such as direct marketing, where immediate and direct feedback can be determined, organisations should use other methods to gauge the success of their communications activities: for example, the level and quality of customer enquiries, the number and frequency of store visits, the degree of attitude change and the ability to recognise or recall an advertisement. All of these represent feedback, but, as a rough distinction, the evaluation of feedback for mass communications is much more difficult than the evaluation of interpersonal communications.

Noise

A complicating factor, which may influence the quality of the reception and the feedback, is noise. Noise, according to Mallen (1977), is 'the omission and distortion of information', and there will always be some noise present in all communications. Management's role is to ensure that levels of noise are kept to a minimum, wherever it is able to exert influence.

Noise occurs when a receiver is prevented from receiving all or part of a message in full. This may be because of either cognitive or physical factors. For example, a cognitive factor may be that the encoding of the message was inappropriate, thereby making it difficult for the receiver to decode the message. In this circumstance it is said that the realms of understanding of the source and the receiver were not matched. Another reason noise may enter the system is that the receiver may have been physically prevented from decoding the message accurately because the receiver was distracted. Examples of distraction are that the telephone rang, or someone in the room asked a question or coughed. A further reason could be that competing messages screened out the targeted message.

Some sales promotion practitioners are using the word 'noise' to refer to the ambience and publicity surrounding a particular sales promotion event. In other words, the word is being used as a positive, advantageous element in the communications process. This approach is not adopted in this text.

Realms of understanding

The concept of the 'realm of understanding' was introduced earlier. It is an important element in the communications process because it is a recognition that successful communications are more likely to be achieved if the source and the receiver understand each other, that is they share meaning. This understanding concerns attitudes, perceptions, behaviour and experience: the values of both parties to the communications process. Therefore, effective communications are more likely when there is some common ground, a realm of understanding between the source and receiver.

Some organisations, especially those in the private sector, spend a huge amount of money researching their target markets and testing their advertisements to ensure that their messages can be decoded and understood. The more organisations understand their receivers, the more confident they become in constructing and transmitting messages to them. Repetition and learning are important elements in marketing communications. Learning is a function of knowledge and the more we know, the more likely we are to understand.

Factors that influence the communications process

The linear, sequential interpretation of the communications process was developed at a time when broadcast media dominated commercial communications. It no longer provides an accurate representation of contemporary communications processes and fails to accurately represent all forms of communications. Issues concerning media and audience fragmentation, the need to consider social and relational dimensions of communications, and the impact of interactive communications has reduced the overall applicability of the linear model.

However, there are two particular influences on the communications process that need to be considered. First, the media used to convey information, and, second, the influence of people on the communications process. These are considered in turn.

The influence of the media

The dialogue that marketing communications seeks to generate with and among audiences is partially constrained by an inherent time delay based on the speed at which responses are generated by the participants in the communications process. Technology allows participants to conduct marketing-communications-based 'conversations' at electronic speeds. The essence of this speed attribute is that it allows for real-time interactively based communications, where enquiries can be responded to more or less instantly.

Digital-based technologies, and the Internet in particular, provide opportunities for interaction and dialogue with customers. With conventional (linear) media the tendency is for monologue or at best delayed and inferred interaction. One of the first points to be made about these new, media-based communications is that the context within which marketing communications occurs is redefined. Traditionally, dialogue occurs in a (relatively) familiar context, which is driven by providers who deliberately present their messages through a variety of communications devices into the environments that they expect their audiences may well pass or recognise. Providers implant their messages into the various environments frequented by their targets. Yuan et al. (1998) refer to advertising messages being 'unbundled', such as direct marketing, which has no other content, or 'bundled' and embedded with other news content such as television, radio and web pages with banner ads. Perhaps more pertinently, they refer to direct and indirect online advertising. Direct advertising is concerned with advertising messages delivered to the customer (email) while indirect advertising is concerned with messages that are made available for a customer to access at their leisure (websites).

Digital media communications tend to make providers relatively passive. Their messages are presented in an environment that requires specific equipment and actions to search them out. The roles are reversed, so that the drivers become active information seekers, represented by a target audience (members of the public and other information providers such as organisations), not just the information-providing organisations.

The influence of people

The traditional view of communications holds that the process consists essentially of one step. Information is directed and shot at prospective audiences, rather like a bullet is propelled from a gun. The decision of each member of the audience whether to act on the message is the result of a passive role or participation in the process. Organisations can communicate with different target audiences simply by varying the message and the type and frequency of channels used.

The linear model has been criticised for its oversimplification, and it certainly ignores the effect of personal influences on the communications process and potential for information deviance. To accommodate these influences two further models are introduced, the influencer model and the interactional model of communications.

The influencer model of communications

The influencer model depicts information flowing via media channels to particular types of people (opinion leaders and opinion formers) to whom other members of the audience refer for information and guidance. Through interpersonal networks, opinion leaders not only reach members of the target audience who may not have been exposed to the message, but may reinforce the impact of the message for those members who did receive the message (Figure 2.2). For example, feedback and comments from travellers on Tripadvisor.com assist others when making travel plans, and constitute opinion leadership. However, editors of travel sections in the Sunday press, television presenters of travel programmes, and professional travel bloggers fulfil the role of opinion former and can influence the decision of prospective travellers through their formalised knowledge.

Originally referred to as the 'two-step model', this approach indicates that the mass media do not have a direct and all-powerful effect over their audiences. If the primary

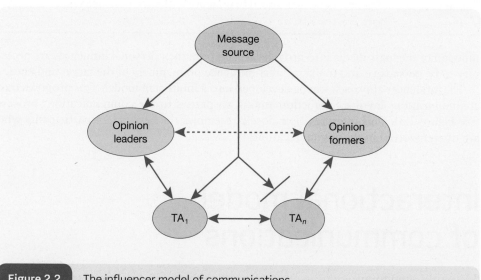

Figure 2.2	The influencer model of communications

Source: From *Essentials of Marketing Communications*, Pearson Education (Fill, C. 2011) figure 2.2, p. 39.

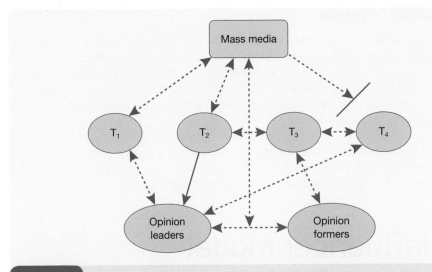

Figure 2.3	Multi-step variation of the influencer model of communications

Source: From *Essentials of Marketing Communications*, Pearson Education (Fill, C. 2011) figure 2.3, p. 39.

Exhibit 2.4	**Influencer communications to promote authentic Caribbean rum**

Source: Bray Leino Ltd.

function of the mass media is to provide information, then personal influences are necessary to be persuasive and to exert direct influence on members of the target audience.

The influencer approach can be developed into a multi-step model. This proposes that communications involve interaction among all parties to the communications process (see Figure 2.3). This interpretation closely resembles the network of participants who are often involved in the communications process.

Interactional model of communications

The models and frameworks used to explain the communications process so far should be considered as a simplification of reality and not a true reflection of communications in practice. The linear model is unidirectional, and it suggests that the receiver plays a passive role in the process. The influencer model attempts to account for an individual's participation in the communications process. These models emphasise individual behaviour but exclude any social behaviour implicit in the process.

The interactional model of communications attempts to assimilate the variety of influences acting upon the communications process. This includes the responses people give to communications received from people and machines. Increasingly communications are characterised by attributing meaning to messages that are shared, updated and a response to other messages. These 'conversations' can be termed interactional and are an integral part of society. Figure 2.4 depicts the complexity associated with these forms of communications.

Interaction is about actions that lead to a response. The development of direct marketing helped make a significant contribution to the transition from what is essentially one-way to two-way and then interactive-based communications. Digital technology has further enabled this interaction process. However, interaction alone is not a sufficient goal, simply because the content of the interaction could be about a radical disagreement of views, an exchange of opinion or a social encounter.

Ballantyne refers to two-way communications with audiences as first, as a 'with' experience, as manifest in face-to-face encounters and contact centres. Second, he distinguishes a higher order of two-way communications based on communications 'between' parties. It is this latter stage that embodies true dialogue where trust, listening and adaptive behaviour are typical. These are represented in Table 2.1. L'Oréal has gradually been adapting its strapline, 'Because I'm worth it'. In the mid-2000s this changed to 'Because you are worth it' and then in 2009 there was a further move to 'Because we're worth it' (Clark, 2012), a recognition perhaps of the word 'we' as a key to building customer relationships as it denotes stronger consumer involvement in, and satisfaction with, L'Oréal.

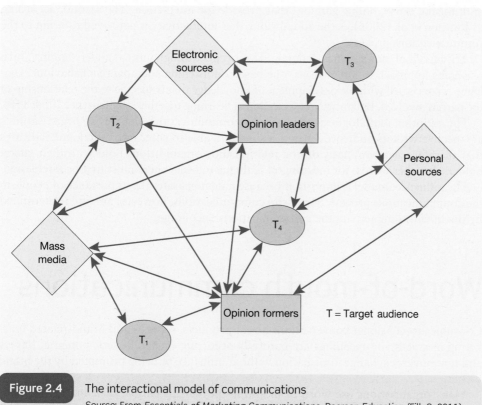

| Figure 2.4 | The interactional model of communications |

Source: From *Essentials of Marketing Communications*, Pearson Education (Fill, C. 2011) figure 2.4, p. 41.

Table 2.1 Communications matrix

Direction	Mass markets	Portfolio/mass-customised	Networks
One-way. Planned communications designed to inform and persuade. Medium to high wastage.	Communications 'to'. Planned persuasive messages aimed at securing brand awareness and loyalty; e.g. communications of USPs and ESPs.	Communications 'for'. Planned persuasive messages with augmented offerings for target markets; e.g. communicating targeted lifecycle products, guarantees, loyalty programmes.	
Two-way. Formal and informal with a view to listening and learning. Minimal wastage.		Communications 'with'. Integrated mix of planned and interactively shared knowledge; e.g. face-to-face, direct (database), contact centres, interactive B2B Internet portals.	Communications 'between'. Dialogue between participants based on trust, learning and adaptation with co-created outcomes; e.g. key account liaison, expansion of communities, staff teamwork.

Source: Ballantyne (2004).

A key question emerges: what is interaction and what are its key characteristics? If we can understand the dynamics and dimensions of interactivity then it should be possible to develop more effective marketing communications. In this context interactivity can be considered from one of two perspectives. One is the technology, tools and features (e.g. multimedia, www, online gaming) that provide for interaction. The second, according to Johnson et al. (2006), is the added value that interactivity is perceived to bring to the communications process.

Arising out of interaction is dialogue. This occurs through mutual understanding and a reasoning approach to interactions, one based on listening and adaptive behaviour. Dialogue is concerned with the development of knowledge that is specific to the relationship of the parties involved. Ballantyne refers to this as 'learning together' (Ballantyne, 2004: 119).

The adoption of dialogue as the basis for communications changes an organisation's perspective with its audiences. Being willing and able to enter into a dialogue indicates that there is a new emphasis on the relationships organisations hold with their stakeholders. In other words, for meaningful dialogue to occur there must first be interaction.

The influencer model is important because it demonstrates the importance of people in the communications process. Successful communications, however, are often determined by the level of interactivity the communications encourage.

Word-of-mouth communications

Consumer-to-consumer conversations about products, services and brand-related marketing messages and meanings are naturally occurring events. Buyers, potential buyers and non-buyers exchange information without influence or being prompted by the brand owner.

Many organisations use word of mouth as an integral part of their marketing communications and deliberately encourage people to have positive conversations about their particular brand. They do this because word-of-mouth communications (WoM) are considered to be the primary driver behind 20 to 50 per cent of all purchasing decisions

(Bughin et al., 2010). Shih et al. (2013) refer to a Nielsen survey of online consumers which found that whereas only 33 per cent of consumers trust online advertisements, 90 per cent trust recommendations from friends and 70 per cent trust eWoM (electronic WoM).

WoM communications are characterised as informal, unplanned and unsolicited conversations. These recommendations provide information and purchasing support and serve to reinforce an individual's purchasing decisions. At the heart of this approach is the source credibility that is assigned to people whose opinions are sought after and used in the purchase decision process. Those who provide information in WoM communications can be characterised as informal experts who are unbiased, trustworthy and who can be considered to be objective. Personal influence is important and can enrich the communications process. Unlike advertising, where messages are primarily linear, unidirectional and formal, WoM communications are interactive, bidirectional and more believable. Or, as Hamilton et al. (2014: 197) put it, the 'opinions of other consumers are appreciated because they are more likely to include negative information about a product or service than one could find in formal marketing communications'.

Scholars' paper 2.2 — So why am I talking about this brand?

Berger, J. and Schwartz, E.M. (2011) What drives immediate and ongoing word of mouth? *Journal of Marketing Research*, XLVIII (October), 869–80.

These researchers consider the psychological drivers of WoM and how companies can design more effective WoM marketing campaigns. Whereas most of the research in this area looks at the consequences of WoM, the focus here is on what causes WoM, how the product itself can shape what is discussed, and how WoM may vary over different time horizons. They distinguish between immediate and ongoing WoM. This paper should be considered in terms of updating Dichter's 1966 paper.

Definition and motives

Arndt (1967: 66) sets out WoM as 'an oral, person-to-person communication between a receiver and a communicator whom the receiver perceives as non-commercial, regarding a brand, product, or service'. Put in more simple terms, WoM communications concerns the sharing of an opinion among people independent from a company or its agents (Santo, 2006: 29).

Stokes and Lomax (2002) define WoM communications as 'interpersonal communication regarding products or services where the receiver regards the communicator as impartial'. This simple definition was developed from some of the more established interpretations that failed to accommodate contemporary media and the restrictions concerning the perceived independence of the communicator.

Kawakami et al. (2014: 17) define WoM as 'the exchange of information and evaluative beliefs between adopters and potential adopters regarding a product in which the communications content is not created or sponsored by the product manufacturer or related marketing organisations'. They also make the point that WoM can occur between people who know each other personally (pWoM) and between people who have never met each other in real life, which they refer to as virtual (vWoM). Weisfeld-Spolter et al. (2014) identify several different formats of eWoM, which suggests that there needs to be care when referring to eWoM.

People like to talk about their product (service) experiences for a variety of reasons that are explored in the next section. By talking with a neighbour or colleague about the good experiences associated with a holiday, for example, the first-hand 'this has

University of Ulster LIBRARY

actually happened to someone I know' effect can be instrumental in the same views being passed on to other colleagues, irrespective of their validity or the general impression people have of other holidays and destinations. Mazzarol et al. (2007) identify the 'richness of the message' and the 'strength of the implied or explicit advocacy' as important triggers for WoM. Palmer (2009) brings these together and refers to WoM as information people can trust as it comes from people just like them and it helps them make better decisions.

Helm and Schlei (1998: 42) refer to WoM as 'verbal communications (either positive or negative) between groups such as the product provider, independent experts, family, friends and the actual or personal consumer'. As discussed later, organisations use eWoM techniques in a commercial context in order to generate brand-based conversations around a point of differentiation. Where WoM used to be a one-to-one conversation, the digital influence makes this a one-to-many communications when product reviews are posted online or when blogs or videos go viral.

One important question that arises is: why do people want to discuss products or advertising messages? Bone (1995) as cited by Stokes and Lomax (2002) refers to three elements of WoM (see Table 2.2).

Dichter (1966) determined that there were four main categories of output WoM.

1. *Product involvement*

People, he found, have a high propensity to discuss matters that are either distinctly pleasurable or unpleasurable. Such discussion serves to provide an opportunity for the experience to be relived, whether it be the 'looking for' or the 'use' experience, or both. This reflects the product and service experience elements of marketing communications, identified as part of the scope of the topic, in Chapter 1.

2. *Self-involvement*

Discussion offers a means for ownership to be established and signals aspects of prestige and levels of status to the receiver. More importantly, perhaps, dissonance can be reduced as the purchaser seeks reassurance about a decision.

3. *Other involvement*

Products can assist motivations to help others and to express feelings of love, friendship and caring. These feelings can be released through a sense of sharing the variety of benefits that products can bestow.

4. *Message involvement*

The final motivation to discuss products is derived, according to Dichter, from the messages that surround the product itself, in particular the advertising messages and,

Table 2.2 Elements of word-of-mouth communications

Element of WoM		Explanation
Direction	Input WoM	Customers seeking recommendation prior to purchase
	Output WoM	Expression of feelings as a result of the purchase experience
Valence		The positive or negative feelings resulting from the experience
Volume		The number of people to which the message is conveyed

Source: After Bone (1995).

in the B2B market, seminars, exhibitions and the trade press, which provide the means to provoke conversation and so stimulate WoM recommendation.

Marketing communications can be used to stimulate conversations, by using these motivations as an anchor for messages.

People who identify very closely with a brand and who might be termed 'brand advocates' often engage in WoM communications. Advocacy can be demonstrated not only through WoM communications but also through behaviour – for example, by wearing branded clothing or using tools and equipment.

Viewpoint 2.2   GreenHopping's start through WoM

GreenHopping is an online platform that promotes the green side of European destinations and businesses. The brand presents a destination's sustainability credentials and other attributes, with a view to inspiring, engaging, and providing visitors an insightful experience and understanding. It achieves this by providing local stories, beautiful pictures, and detailed information about the various local labels and certificates. For example, it informs about how a hotel in a region can achieve eco certification, or how a restaurant can become part of the Slow food network, plus other key points related to these good practices. This enables professionals to spot opportunities to promote and assist organisations to improve and achieve their green based goals.

As a start-up company, headquartered in Brussels, the first big issue GreenHopping faced was the fact that the brand was unknown and new to the market. The major task therefore, was to inform and make professionals and potential investors aware of the new and unique brand. With limited resources, targeted paid advertising was out of the question. The GreenHopping team, all recent graduates, decided to use a word of mouth strategy instead. Although the platform was developed for the B2C market, the initial focus was on the B2B sector.

The team targeted 200 potential businesses to green map Brussels. They also contacted local influencers such as NGOs, bloggers, photographers and other professionals; some they met in person. Examples include organisations such as the Brussels Greeters, USE it maps, Slow food Brussels and others. These were selected on the basis of their sustainability and eco-tourism credentials. The team visited several marketing conferences and through personalised word of mouth communications they managed to spread the word about GreenHopping between marketers.

Professionals were presented with written articles, pictures, statements and documents about Green-Hopping's beliefs, aims and values, plus insights about specific labels and certificates. As a result they learned about the major issues that organisations and destinations faced when defining and delivering their green identity. They were also kept up to date with the latest trends in sustainability.

As a result these professionals became real supporters of the GreenHopping brand. The platform helped people to start talking to one another and to share their new knowledge. With people in Brussels talking about GreenHopping, organisations soon started to work and collaborate with the brand. Journalists began to contact the team with the result that articles started to appear in newspapers, whilst the founders were interviewed on television. From this potential partnerships for new and exciting projects began to emerge for both the B2B and B2C markets, all as a result of the WoM strategy.

This Viewpoint was contributed by Bilyana Petrova, a Digital Marketing Specialist at BGMenu, Bulgaria. Previously she studied Advertising and Marketing at Coventry University, UK.

Question: If WoM communications are so important, why are they not a core activity for all brands?

Task: When you next visit a leisure or entertainment complex, make a mental note of the ways in which the brand owner encourages visitors to talk about the complex.

These motivations to discuss products and their associative experiences vary between individuals and with the intensity of the motivation at any one particular moment. There are two main persons involved in this process of WoM communications: a sender and receiver. Research indicates that the receiver's evaluation of a message is far from stable over time and accuracy of recall decays (expectedly) through time. What this means for marketing communications is that those people who have a positive product experience, especially in the service sector, should be encouraged to talk as soon as possible after the event (Christiansen and Tax, 2000). Goldsmith and Horowitz (2006) found that risk reduction, popularity, reduced costs, access to easy information, and even inspiration from offline sources such as cinema, TV and radio were some of the primary reasons why people seek the opinions of others online.

Opinion leaders

Katz and Lazarsfeld (1955) first identified individuals who were predisposed to receiving information and then reprocessing it to influence others. Their studies of American voting and purchase behaviour led to their conclusion that those individuals who could exert such influence were more persuasive than information received directly from the mass media. These opinion leaders, according to Rogers (1962), tend 'to be of the same social class as non-leaders, but may enjoy a higher social status within the group'. Williams (1990) uses the work of Reynolds and Darden (1971) to suggest that they are more gregarious and more self-confident than non-leaders. In addition, they have a greater exposure to relevant mass media (print) and, as a result, have more knowledge/familiarity and involvement with the product class, are more innovative and more confident of their role as influencer (leader) and appear to be less dogmatic than non-leaders (Chan and Misra, 1990).

Opinion leadership can be simulated in advertising by the use of product testimonials. Using ordinary people to express positive comments about a product to each other is a very well-used advertising technique.

The importance of opinion leaders in the design and implementation of communications plans should not be underestimated. Midgley and Dowling (1993) refer to *innovator communicators*: those who are receptive to new ideas and who make innovation-based purchase decisions without reference to or from other people. However, while the importance of these individuals is not doubted, a major difficulty exists in trying to identify just who these opinion leaders and innovator communicators are. While they sometimes display some distinctive characteristics, such as reading specialist media vehicles, often being first to return coupons, enjoying attending exhibitions or just involving themselves with new, innovative techniques or products, they are by their very nature invisible outside their work, family and social groups.

Table 2.3 Characteristics associated with opinion leaders

Characteristic	Explanation
Social gregariousness	Refers to an opinion leader's level of social embeddedness because they tend to have more social ties, more friends, and more social contacts than non-leaders.
Efficacy and trust	Opinion leaders have a higher self-confidence and self-reliance than non-leaders, although it is noted that they generally have lower confidence in political systems.
Values and satisfaction	Opinion leaders are less concerned with material gain and financial success than non-leaders. They tend to exhibit higher levels of social responsibility, political tolerance, civic-mindedness, and environmental concern.

Nisbet (2005) provides a useful insight into the background of opinion leadership. He observes that opinion leadership has been previously defined as exhibiting three primary dimensions: social embeddedness (Weimann, 1994), information-giving (Rogers, 2003), and information-seeking (Keller and Berry, 2003) behaviours. Table 2.3 sets out some of the main characteristics associated with opinion leaders.

Viewpoint 2.3   Advocates, influencers and ambassadors

To assist the development of the Sensodyne Pronamel brand in Hungary, Glaxosmithcline used a word of mouth campaign. This involved the recruitment of 1,000 brand ambassadors who were required to drive conversations about the acid wear of teeth, and the Sensodyne Pronamel range. The ambassadors had to convey messages that this is a special toothpaste that helps prevent acid erosion. To do this they had to experience the product, use a starter kit to explain and pass samples on to friends, family members and acquaintances, and generate conversations about the product. Over 185,000 conversations were made during the campaign period, plus the many that happened after the campaign officially finished.

The 'I am Stela' campaign used brand advocates such as Tony Robinson, Claudia Winkleman and Sir Ranulph Fiennes. These and other celebrities openly declared on social media that 'I am Stela'. Their posts were linked to a video about Stela, a 12-year-old girl from Turkana. Her life had been changed radically following the installation of a freshwater pump funded by sales of One Water.

Carlos Soria is a Spanish mountaineer who represents many of BBVA's values: integrity, humility, the quest for excellence, commitment and cooperation. His aim at the age of 73 is to scale the 14 mountains in the world that are over 8,000 metres.

Marmite is a sticky, dark brown, yeast extract paste. It is used to spread on bread and toast, and is made from the by-products of brewing, the brewer's yeast that's been used to ferment sugars into alcohol. Not surprising then that Marmite has a strong, distinctive taste. Marmite encourage the creation of brand endorsers through an online community called the 'Mamarati'. This is a secret club for super fans, entirely fabricated through social media and given a history, identity and various rituals and traditions. Community members seeking acceptance into the Marmarati have to be inducted into the 'First Circle', read the Marmarati Oath, and take part in blindfolded tastings.

It is believed that sales of single malt whisky are driven primarily by WoM recommendations and so it is not surprising that William Grant & Sons, producer of Glenfiddich and Sailor Jerry's, decided to realign its marketing budget in order to create more content to encourage influencers to talk about the brand.

Source: Anon (2010b); Bamford (2013); Bolger (2013); Joseph (2014); Rantal (2011); www.marmite.com; www.wearesocial.net; www.bbva.com/.

Question:	What is the main difference between a brand ambassador and a celebrity endorser?
Task:	Find two examples of brand ambassadors and then make a list of the other brands they endorse. Are there any similarities across each list?

Opinion formers

Opinion formers are individuals who are able to exert personal influence because of their authority, education or status associated with the object of the communications process. Like opinion leaders, they are acknowledged and sought out by others to provide information and advice, but this is because of the formal expertise that opinion formers are adjudged to have. For example, community pharmacists are often consulted about symptoms and medicines, and film and theatre critics carry such conviction in their reviews that they can make or break a new production.

Popular television soap operas such as *General Hospital* (USA), *Alles was zählt* (Germany), *Shortland Street* (New Zealand) and *Coronation Street* (UK), all of which attract huge audiences, have been used as vehicles to draw attention to and open up debates about many controversial social issues, such as contraception, abortion, drug use and abuse, and serious illness and mental health concerns.

The influence of opinion formers can be great. For example, the editor of a journal or newspaper may be a recognised source of expertise, and any offering referred to by the editor in the media vehicle is endowed with great credibility. In this sense the editor acts as a gatekeeper, and it is the task of the marketing communicator to ensure that all relevant opinion formers are identified and sent appropriate messages.

The credibility of opinion formers is vital for communications effectiveness. If there is a suspicion or doubt about the impartiality of the opinion former, then the objectivity of their views and comments is likely to be perceived as tainted and not believed so that damage may be caused to the reputation of the brand and those involved.

Many organisations constantly lobby key members of parliament in an effort to persuade them to pursue 'favourable' policies. Opinion formers are relatively easy to identify, as they need to be seen shaping the opinion of others, usually opinion followers.

Opinion followers

The vast majority of consumers can be said to be opinion followers. The messages they receive via the mass media are tempered by the opinions of the two groups of personal influencers just discussed. Some people actively seek information from those they believe are well informed, while others prefer to use the mass media for information and guidance (Robinson, 1976). However, this should not detract from the point that, although followers, they still process information independently and use a variety of inputs when sifting information and responding to marketing stimuli.

Ethical drug manufacturers normally launch new drugs by enlisting the support of particular doctors who have specialised in the therapy area and who are recognised by other doctors as experts. These opinion formers are invited to lead symposia and associated events activity around the new product to build credibility. At the same time, public relations agencies prepare press releases with the aim that the information will be used by the mass media (opinion formers) for editorial purposes and create exposure for the product across the target audience, which, depending upon the product and/or the media vehicle, may be GPs, hospital doctors, patients or the general public. All these people, whether they be opinion leaders or formers, are active influencers or talkers (Kingdom, 1970).

Developing brands with word-of-mouth communications

So far in this section WoM communications have been examined as naturally occurring, unplanned conversations. This is not entirely correct, as many organisations deliberately attempt to reach their audiences using WoM principles. The term 'word-of-mouth marketing' (WoMM) refers to the electronic version of the spoken endorsement of a product or service, where messages are targeted at key individuals who then voluntarily pass the message to friends and colleagues. In doing so they endorse the message and provide it with a measure of credibility. WoMM is a planned, intentional attempt to influence consumer-to-consumer communications using professional marketing methods and technologies (Kozinets et al., 2010) to prompt WoM conversations (see www.womma.org).

From this it can be assumed that there are a variety of methods that organisations use to influence their audiences, all in the name of WoM. Of these, three main forms of WoM can be identified: voluntary, prompted and managed.

1. *Voluntary WoM* – can be considered to be the most natural form of interpersonal conversation, free from any external influence, coercion or intent. This still occurs among genuine opinion leaders, formers and followers for reasons considered earlier.

2. *Prompted WoM* – occurs when organisations convey information to specific opinion leaders and formers, with the intention of deliberately encouraging them to forward and share the information with their followers. The goal is to prompt conversations among followers based around the credibility bestowed on the opinion leader. This outward perspective can be counterbalanced by an inward view. For example, some organisations use various elements of social media, such as blogs, online communities and forums, to prompt consumer-to-consumer conversations and then listen, observe and revise their approaches to the market.

3. *Managed WoM* – occurs when organisations target, incentivise and reward opinion leaders for recommending their offerings to their networks of followers. In these situations opinion leaders lose their independence and objectivity within the communications process, and become paid representatives of a brand. As a result, the credibility normally attached to these influencers diminishes and the essence of freely expressed opinions about products and brands is removed.

There is evidence that organisational use of contemporary marketing communications seeks to drive voluntary conversations, stimulated by positive product and service experiences. The prompted approach is used extensively and enables organisations to retain credibility and a sense of responsibility. The organisations that exploit their audiences through managed WoM conversations are not acting illegally, but may be guilty of transgressing ethical boundaries and demonstrating disrespect for their audiences – not a position for long-term strength.

Traditionally brands were built partly through offline communications directed to opinion leaders, when they could be identified, and through opinion formers. Sporting and entertainment celebrities have been used as brand ambassadors for a long time. They are used to enable audiences to develop positive associations between the personality of the ambassador and a brand. A celebrity endorser is defined as 'any individual who enjoys public recognition and who uses this recognition on behalf of a consumer good by appearing with it in an advertisement' (McCracken, 1989: 310).

McCracken (1989) believes that celebrity endorsement works through the theory of meaning transfer. Consumers make an overall assessment of what a celebrity 'represents' to them, based on their perception and interpretation of the celebrity's identity cues. These cues relate to their behaviour, comments, ability and attributes that are of particular interest to the consumer. McCracken (1989: 315) refers to their public image as demonstrated in 'television, movies, military, athletics, and other careers'.

Jin and Phua (2014) found that celebrities who use Twitter to endorse brands are invariably perceived by their followers as fellow social media users. This helps make their endorsements more credible and trustworthy than if they had appeared in television or print advertisements. In addition, their research found that the celebrities who endorse a large number of brands through eWoM are likely to lose trust as they are perceived to be 'tweeters for hire'.

The meaning assigned to a celebrity is transferred from the celebrity endorser to the product when the two are paired in a commercial message. Gwinner and Eaton (1999) argue that, when a consumer acquires/consumes the product, the meaning is transferred to the user and the process is complete.

Scholars' paper 2.3   **Effective eWoM through bloggers**

Kozinets, R.V., de Valck, K., Wojnicki, A.C. and Wilner, S.J.S. (2010) Networked narratives: understanding word-of-mouth marketing in online communities, *Journal of Marketing*, 74 (March), 71–89.

This paper considers the use and effectiveness of word-of-mouth communications through online influencers, bloggers. The authors reveal four distinct blogger communications strategies. These are evaluation, embracing, endorsement, and explanation. Each of them is influenced by character narrative, communications forum, communal norms, and the nature of the marketing promotion. The implications for online and offline and word-of-mouth campaigns are presented.

Brand development now incorporates the use of social media, and bloggers in particular, who play an increasingly critical role in the dissemination of brand-related information. More detailed information about the use of social media can be found in Chapter 19, but here it is important to establish the way in which brands can be developed through WoM marketing communications.

Opinion formers such as journalists find or receive information about brands through press releases. They then relay the information, after editing and reformatting, to their readers and viewers through their particular media. Accordingly, brand-related information is targeted at journalists, with the intention that their messages will be forwarded to their end-user audience through media channels.

Bloggers are now an important and influential channel of communications. However, they do not share the same characteristics as journalists. For example, the number of bloggers in any one market can be counted in terms of tens of thousands of people in contrast to the relatively small, select number of opinion formers. The majority of bloggers have an informal interest in a subject, whereas opinion formers are deemed to have formal expertise. Bloggers, however, are not tied to formal processes or indeed an editor. As a result, bloggers do not have to be objective in their comments and are not constrained by any advertising messages. Most importantly, bloggers conduct conversations among themselves and their followers, whereas journalists receive little feedback (see Viewpoint 2.4 and Chapter 19).

Viewpoint 2.4   **Fashionable bloggers**

As a 15 year old, Isy Hossack developed a food-based blog, 'Top with Cinnamon', which within 2 years had attracted a following of over 300,000. Her blog is notable not only for the recipes but also for her friendly yet direct writing style, and for the quality of the photography and videos. Her influence in social media led to a publisher offering a book deal to feature her recipes, advertisers who place ads on her website attempting to reach her followers, and of course a growing array of people attracted to her recipes and food ideas.

Organisations use bloggers to reach and influence their target audiences. For example, Unilever developed a YouTube channel 'All Things Hair' to advertise their brands such as Toni & Guy, Dove and VO5. Zoella, a video blogger who has over seven million followers, is paid to develop hair styling tutorials based on trends in social media and Google data about current hair styling talking points. Unilever then enable followers to purchase the brands.

Exhibit 2.5	**Zoella – an established hair styling vblogger**
	Source: Getty Images/David M. Benett / Getty Images for Zoella Beauty.

Source: Rivalland (2014); Robinson and Malm (2015); Swift (2014).

Question: Is blogging just a means of self-expression?

Task: Find three different blogs in fashion, travel and sport. Make a list of their similarities and differences.

To conclude this section on WoM communications, three elements concerning the potential of any one WoM recommendation to change behaviour or dissuasion from doing so can be identified. According to Bughin et al. (2010) these are what is said, who says it and where it is communicated.

The primary driver is the content of a message, what is said. The message must address important product or service features. For example, in skin care, functional aspects such as packaging and ingredients create more powerful WoM communications than emotional messages about how a product makes people feel.

The second driver concerns the person sending the message. Opinion leaders or influentials embody trust and competence. As a result, they generate three times more WoM messages than non-influentials. Each leader-based message has four times more impact on a recipient's purchasing decision.

The third driver is about the environment and power with which WoM messages circulate. Compact, trust-based networks enable low reach, but messages in this type of environment have great impact, relative to those circulated through dispersed communities. This is because there is often a high correlation between people whose opinions we trust and the members of networks we most value.

Amplification

Marketing communications is about enabling relevant brand based conversations. It might be claimed that an effective communications programme should therefore be based on the number, as well as the quality, of conversations. There are several circumstances when this logic does not tie together, but in principle the volume, diversity and perhaps the dispersion of conversations can be indicative of a successful communications event.

In essence therefore, WoM communications are about amplifying a message so that it reaches as many people as possible. Today, the interaction of people through various media, and social media in particular, can lead to an exponential increase in the number of conversations. Indeed, viral marketing programmes (considered in more detail in Chapter 19) can be generated either by the judicious and deliberate seeding of content around the Internet, or spontaneously, as a result of a cultural spark. In both cases a message is amplified and reaches a much wider audience than would normally be expected.

Amplification involves both the cognitive and behavioural elements of the engagement concept. This means saving reviews about a brand, either as thoughts and feelings about a brand, or actions such as a brand trial, experience, or purchase, and then sharing it with a network of contacts, friends and family. In social media the use of sponsored stories, embedded tweets and social ads using trending content all serve to amplify messages.

The use of and measurement of both online and offline WoM communications are recognised as important although not always undertaken or prioritised as highly as they should (Leggatt, 2014). Groeger and Buttle (2014: 1186) use social networking analysis to investigate the effectiveness of eWoM. One of their findings concerns the possible overstatement of WoM conversations. They refer to standard metrics for these campaigns which assume that reach equates to the number of campaign-related conversations. They argue that this approach does not recognise that some people may be exposed multiple times to campaign-related messaging. What this means is that campaigns could be 'significantly less efficient in terms of cost-per-conversation' than is normally understood and that 'multiple exposures mean that the total number of campaign-related conversations cannot be regarded as equivalent to the number of individuals reached'.

Relational approaches to communications

The previous model accounts for social behaviour but does not account for the context within which the behaviour occurs. Communications events always occur within a context (Littlejohn, 1992) or particular set of circumstances. It is the context which not only influences the form of the communications but also affects the nature and the way the communications are received, interpreted and acted upon. There are a huge number of variables that can influence the context, including the disposition of the people involved, the physical environment, the nature of the issue, the history and associated culture, the goals of the participants and the expected repercussions of the dialogue itself.

Littlejohn identifies four main contextual levels: interpersonal, group, organisational and mass communications. These levels form part of a hierarchy whereby higher levels incorporate the lower levels but 'add something new of their own'.

The relational approach means that communications events are linked together in an organised manner, one where the events are 'punctuated' by interventions from one or more of the participants. These interventions occur whenever the participants attempt cooperation or if conflict arises.

Soldow and Thomas (1984), referring to a sales negotiation, state that a relationship develops through the form of negotiations rather than the content. An agreement is necessary about who is to control the relationship or whether there will be equality. Rothschild (1987) reports that 'sparring will continue' until agreement is reached or the negotiations are terminated. In other words, without mutual agreement over the roles of the participants, the true purpose of the interaction, to achieve an exchange, cannot be resolved.

An interesting aspect of relational communications theory is social penetration (Taylor and Altman, 1987). Through the disclosure of increasing amounts of information about themselves, partners in a relationship (personal or organisational) develop levels of intimacy, which serve to build interpersonal relationships. The relationship moves forward as partners reveal successive layers of information about each other and, as a greater amount or breadth of information is shared, confidence grows. These levels can be seen to consist of orientation, exploratory affective exchange, affective exchange and stable exchange (see Table 2.4). These layers are not uncovered in a logical, orderly sequence. It is likely that partners will return to previous levels, test the outcomes and rewards and reconsider their positions as the relationships unfold through time. This suggests that social penetration theory may lie at the foundation of the development of trust, commitment and relational exchanges between organisations.

Relationships need not be just dyadic, as the interactional approach suggests, but could be triadic or even encompass a much wider network or array of participants. Through this perspective a 'communications network' can be observed, through which information can flow. Participants engage in communications based upon their perception of the environment in which the communications occur and the way in which each participant relates to the others.

Rogers (1986) identifies a communications network as 'consisting of interconnected individuals who are linked by patterned communications flows'. This is important, as it views communications as transcending organisational boundaries. In other words, it is not only individuals within an organisation that develop patterned communications flows but also individuals across different organisations. These individuals participate with one another (possibly through exchanges) and use communications networks to achieve their agenda items.

The extent to which individuals are linked to the network is referred to as *connectedness*. The more a network is connected, the greater the likelihood that a message will be disseminated, as there are few isolated individuals. Similarly, the level of integration in a network refers to the degree to which members of the network are linked to one another. The greater the integration, the more potential channels there are for a message to be routed through.

Systems theory recognises that organisations are made of interacting units. The relational approach to communications is similar to systems theory. The various

Table 2.4 Layers of social penetration

Layer	Explanation
Orientation	The disclosure of public information only.
Exploratory affective exchange	Expansion and development of public information.
Affective exchange	Disclosure, based upon anticipated relationship rewards, of deeper feelings, values and beliefs.
Stable exchange	High level of intimacy where partners are able to predict each other's reactions with a good level of accuracy.

Source: Taylor and Altman (1987).

'criss-crossing' flows of information between reciprocating units allow individuals and groups to modify the actions of others in the 'net', and this permits the establishment of a pattern of communications (Tichy, 1979).

Scholars' paper 2.4   **Let's get relational**

Soldow, G.F. and Thomas, G.P. (1984) Relational communication: form versus content in the sales interaction, *Journal of Marketing,* **48 (Winter), 84–93.**

This was the first paper that attempted to develop ideas about face-to-face communications, which until that point had been well established. Soldow and Thomas introduced the concept of relational communications, which refers to that part of a message beyond the actual content which enables participants to negotiate their relative positions. Thus, the message sender can bid for dominance, deference, or equality. The message receiver, in turn, can accept the bid or deny it.

Network approaches to communications

The regular use of these patterned flows leads to the development of communications networks, which have been categorised as *prescribed* and *emergent* (Weick, 1987). Prescribed networks are formalised patterns of communications, very often established by senior management within an organisation or by organisational representatives when inter-organisational communications is considered. It follows that emergent networks are informal and appear as a response to the social and task-orientated needs of the participants.

The linear or one-way model of communications fails to accommodate the various complexities associated with communications. As discussed earlier, the model is too simplistic and fails to represent many aspects of communications events. Although the linear model is essentially a sequential rather than an interactional approach, it is still used and practised by many organisations. Varey (2002) refers to this as the 'Informational model' of communications and, as both Grunig (1992) and Ballantyne (2004) suggest, it is just one of a number of ways in which communications can work. Communications are an integral part of relationship marketing, and within this collaborative context, interaction and dialogue are essential factors. Varey refers to this as 'Transformational communications'.

Process of adoption

An interesting extension to the concept of opinion followers and the discussion on WoM communications is the process by which individuals become committed to the use of a new product. Rogers (1983) has identified this as the process of adoption and the stages of his innovation decision process are represented in Figure 2.5. These stages in the

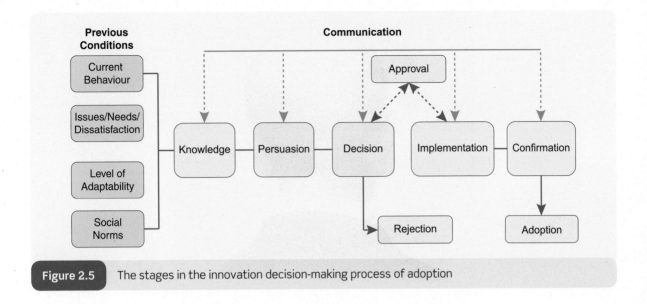

Figure 2.5   The stages in the innovation decision-making process of adoption

adoption process are sequential and are characterised by the different factors that are involved at each stage (e.g. the media used by each individual).

1. *Knowledge*

   The innovation becomes known to consumers, but they have little information and no well-founded attitudes. Information must be provided through mass media to institutions and people whom active seekers of information are likely to contact. Information for passive seekers should be supplied through the media and channels that this group habitually uses to look for other kinds of information (Windahl et al., 1992).

   Shane washes his hair regularly, but he is beginning to notice tufts of hair on his comb. He becomes aware of an advertisement for Mane in a magazine.

2. *Persuasion*

   The consumer becomes aware that the innovation may be of use in solving known and potential problems. Information from those who have experience of the product becomes very important.

   Shane notices that the makers of Mane claim that, not only does their brand reduce the amount of hair loss, but also it aids hair gain. Mane has also been recommended to him by someone he met in the pub last week. Modelling behaviour predominates.

3. *Decision*

   An attitude may develop and may be either favourable or unfavourable, but as a result a decision is reached whether to trial the offering or not. Communications need to assist this part of the process by continual prompting.

   Shane is prepared to believe (or not to believe) the messages and the claims made on behalf of Mane. He thinks that Mane is potentially a very good brand (or not). He intends trying Mane because he was given a free sample (or because it was on a special price deal).

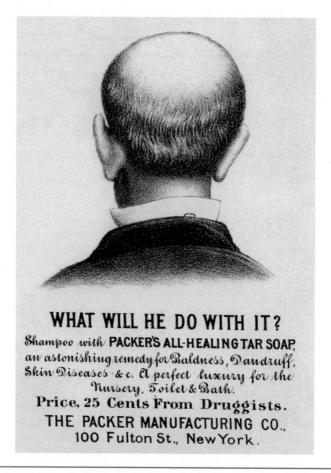

WHAT WILL HE DO WITH IT?
Shampoo with **PACKER'S ALL-HEALING TAR SOAP,**
an astonishing remedy for Baldness, Dandruff,
Skin Diseases &c. A perfect luxury for the
Nursery, Toilet & Bath.
Price, 25 Cents From Druggists.
THE PACKER MANUFACTURING CO.,
100 Fulton St., New York.

Exhibit 2.6	A Victorian trade card for Packer's All-Healing Tar Soap, a hair restorative from 1890
	Source: Getty Images/Buyenlarge.

4. *Implementation*

For the adoption to proceed in the absence of a sales promotion, buyers must know where to get it and how to use it. The product is then tested in a limited way. Communications must provide this information in order that the trial experience be developed.

Shane tries the Mane treatment.

5. *Confirmation*

The innovation is accepted or rejected on the basis of the experience during trial. Planned communications play an important role in maintaining the new behaviour by dispelling negative thoughts and positively reaffirming the original 'correct' decision. McGuire, as reported in Windahl et al. (1992), refers to this as *post-behavioural consolidation.*

It works. Shane's hair stops falling out as it used to before he tried the Mane treatment. He reads an article that reports that large numbers of people are using these types of products satisfactorily. Shane resolves to buy and use Mane in the future.

This process can be terminated at any stage and, of course, a number of competing brands may vie for consumers' attention simultaneously, so adding to the complexity and levels of noise in the process. Generally, mass communications are seen to be more effective in the earlier phases of the adoption process for products that buyers are actively interested in, while more interpersonal forms are more appropriate at the later stages, especially trial and adoption. This model assumes that the stages occur in a predictable sequence, but this clearly does not happen in all purchase activity, as some information that is to be used later in the trial stage may be omitted, which often happens when loyalty to a brand is high or where the buyer has experience in the marketplace.

Process of diffusion

The process of adoption in aggregate form, over time, is diffusion. According to Rogers (1983), diffusion is the process by which an innovation is communicated through certain channels over a period of time among the members of a social system. This is a group process and Rogers again identified five categories of adopters. Figure 2.6 shows how diffusion may be fast or slow and that there is no set speed at which the process occurs. The five categories are as follows:

1. *Innovators*

   These groups like new ideas and have a large disposable income. This means they are more likely to take risks associated with new products.

2. *Early adopters*

   Research has established that this group contains a large proportion of opinion leaders and they are, therefore, important in speeding the diffusion process. Early adopters tend to be younger than any other group and above average in education. Internet activity and use of publications are probably high as they actively seek information. A high proportion of early adopters are active bloggers. This group is important to the marketing communications process because they can determine the speed at which diffusion occurs.

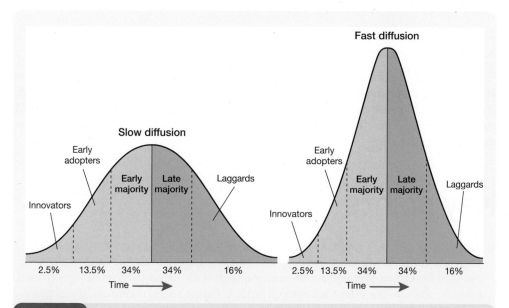

Figure 2.6   Fast and slow diffusion of an innovation

Source: From Hawkins et al. (1989) *Consumer Behavior*, 4th edition. Used with permission of the McGraw-Hill Companies.

3. *Early majority*

The early majority are usually composed of opinion followers who are a little above average in age, education, social status and income. Although not capable of substantiation, it is probable that web usage is high and they rely on informal sources of information and take fewer publications than the previous two groups.

4. *Late majority*

This group of people is sceptical of new ideas and only adopts new products because of social or economic factors. They take few publications and are below average in education, social status and income. Their web usage may be below average.

5. *Laggards*

This group of people is suspicious of all new ideas and is set in their opinions. Lowest of all the groups in terms of income, social status and education, this group takes a long time to adopt an innovation.

This framework suggests that, at the innovation stage, messages should be targeted at relatively young people in the target group, with a high level of income, education and social status. This will speed WoM recommendation and the diffusion process. Mahajan et al. (1990) observe that the personal influence of WoM communications does not work in isolation from the other communications tools and media. Early adopters are more likely to adopt an innovation in response to 'external influences' and only through time will the effect of 'internal influences' become significant. In other words, mass-media communications needs time to work before WoM communications can begin to build effectiveness. However, digital developments circumvent the need to use mass media, which means that viral communications and social networks alone can lead to substantial WoM penetration.

Gatignon and Robertson (1985) suggest that there are three elements to the diffusion process, which need to be taken into account, particularly for the fast-moving consumer goods sector:

1. The rate of diffusion or speed at which sales occur.

2. The pattern of diffusion or shape of the curve.

3. The potential penetration level or size of the market.

Care should be taken to ensure that all three of these elements are considered when attempting to understand the diffusion process. It can be concluded that if a campaign is targeted at innovators and the early majority, and is geared to stimulating WoM communications, then the diffusion process is more likely to be successful than if these elements are ignored.

Key points

- The linear or one-way communications process suggests that messages are developed by a source, encoded, transmitted, decoded and meaning applied to the message by a receiver. Noise in the system may prevent the true meaning of the messages from being conveyed, while feedback to the source is limited. The effectiveness of this communications process is determined by the strengths of the linkages between the different components.

- There are two particular influences on the communications process that need to be considered. First, the media used to convey information have fragmented drastically as a raft of new media have emerged. Second, people influence the communications process considerably, either as opinion leaders or formers or as participants in the word-of-mouth process.

- The influencer model depicts information flowing via media channels to particular types of people (opinion leaders and opinion formers; see p. 54) to whom other members of the audience refer for information and guidance. Through interpersonal networks, opinion leaders not only reach members of the target audience who may not have been exposed to the message, but may reinforce the impact of the message for those members who did receive the message.

- Increasingly communications are characterised by attributing meaning to messages that are shared, updated and a response to other messages. These 'conversations' can be termed 'interactional' and are an integral part of society. The interactional model of communications attempts to assimilate the variety of influences acting upon the communications process and account for the responses (interactions) people give to messages received from people and machines.

- Opinion leaders are members of a peer group who have informal expertise and knowledge about a specific topic. Opinion formers have formal expertise bestowed upon them by virtue of their qualifications, experience and careers. Opinion followers value and use information from these sources in their decision-making processes. Marketing communications should, therefore, target leaders and formers as they can speed the overall communications process.

- Word-of-mouth (WoM) communications are 'interpersonal communications regarding products or services where the receiver regards the communicator as impartial'. WoM is an increasingly important form of effective communications. It is relatively cost-free yet very credible, and embodies the increasingly conversational nature of marketing communications.

- The process of adoption in aggregate form, over time, is diffusion. It is a group process by which an innovation is communicated through certain channels over a period of time among the members of a social system. Five particular groups, each with distinct characteristics, can be identified.

Review questions

British Heart Foundation case questions

1. Discuss the way in which the BHF encoded their message. Could it be improved and if so how?

2. Make brief notes explaining how consumer insight assisted the development of the BHF campaign.

3. What role might opinion leaders have had in the effectiveness of the campaign?

4. How might the BHF case be interpreted through the influencer model of communications?

5. Which of the linear, influencer and interactional models best illustrates how communications worked for the BHF?

6. Discuss ways in which the BHF message might be interpreted through the process of adoption.

General questions

1. Name the elements of the linear model of communications and briefly describe the role of each element.
2. How do opinion leaders differ from opinion formers and opinion followers?
3. What are the three elements of word-of-mouth communications identified by Bone?
4. If voluntary is one form of WoM, what are the other two and how do they differ?
5. Using a product of your choice, show how the stages in the process of adoption can be depicted.

References

Anon (2010a) Decoding Adidas Beijing 2008 Olympics Games advertisement, *Galuhnadi,* 21 April, retrieved 24 August from www.scribd.com/doc/30312096/advertisements-semiotics-encoding-decoding.

Anon (2010b) Case study – Marmite, *The Marketer* (May), p. 35.

Arndt, J. (1967) Role of product-related conversations in the diffusion of a new product, *Journal of Marketing Research,* 4 (August), 291–5.

Ballantyne, D. (2004) Dialogue and its role in the development of relationship specific knowledge, *Journal of Business and Industrial Marketing,* 19(2), 114–23.

Bamford, V. (2013) Simon Pegg, Claudia Winkleman declare: 'I am Stela' as part of One Water push, *The Grocer,* 15 February 2013, retrieved 18 August 2014 from www.thegrocer.co.uk/fmcg/simon-pegg-claudia-winkleman-declare-i-am-stela/236551.article.

Barnes, R. (2013) Top 10 marketing mishaps of 2013, *Marketing Magazine,* 11 December, retrieved 5 May 2015 from www.marketingmagazine.co.uk/article/1223477/top-10-marketing-mishaps-2013.

Bolger, M. (2013) Mouthing off, *The Marketer,* November/December, 26–9.

Bone, P.F. (1995) Word of mouth effects on short-term and long term product judgments, *Journal of Business Research,* 32(3), 213–23.

Bughin, J., Doogan, J. and Vetvik, O.J. (2010) A new way to measure word-of-mouth marketing, *McKinsey Quarterly,* Issue 2.

Chan, K.K. and Misra, S. (1990) Characteristics of the opinion leader: a new dimension, *Journal of Advertising,* 19(3), 53–60.

Christiansen, T. and Tax, S.S. (2000) Measuring word of mouth: the questions of who and when, *Journal of Marketing Communications,* 6, 185–99.

Clark, N. (2012) Meet the new Type A, *Marketing,* 29 February, 28–30.

Dichter, E. (1966) How word-of-mouth advertising works, *Harvard Business Review,* 44(November/December), 147–66.

Gatignon, H. and Robertson, T. (1985) A propositional inventory for new diffusion research, *Journal of Consumer Research,* 11, 849–67.

Goldsmith, R.E. and Horowitz, D. (2006) Measuring motivations for online opinion seeking, *Journal of Interactive Advertising,* 6(2), 3–14. Retrieved 5 April 2010 from www.jiad.org/article76.

Groeger, L. and Buttle, F. (2014) Word-of-mouth marketing: towards an improved understanding of multi-generational campaign reach, *European Journal of Marketing,* 48(7/8), 1186–208.

Grunig, J. (1992) Models of public relations and communication, in *Excellence in Public Relations and Communications Management* (eds J.E. Grunig, D.M. Dozier, P. Ehling, L.A. Grunig, F.C. Repper and J. Whits), Hillsdale, NJ: Lawrence Erlbaum, 285–325.

Gwinner, K.P. and Eaton, J. (1999) Building brand image through event sponsorship: the role of image transfer, *Journal of Advertising,* 28(4), Winter, 47–57.

Hamilton, R., Vohs, K.D. and McGill, A.L. (2014) We'll be honest, this won't be the best article you'll ever read: the use of dispreferred markers in word-of-mouth communications, *Journal of Consumer Research,* 41, June, 197–212.

Hawkins, D.I., Best, R.J. and Coney, K.A. (1989) *Consumer Behavior: Implications for Marketing Strategy,* Homewood, IL: Richard D. Irwin.

Helm, S. and Schlei, J. (1998) Referral potential – potential referrals: an investigation into customers' communication in service markets, Proceedings of 27th EMAC Conference, *Marketing Research and Practice,* 41–56.

Jin, S.A.A. and Phau, J. (2014) Following celebrities' tweets about brands: the impact of Twitter-based electronic word-of-mouth on consumers' source credibility perception, buying intention, and social identification with celebrities, *Journal of Advertising,* 43(2), 181–95.

Johnson, G.J., Bruner II, G.C. and Kumar, A. (2006) Interactivity and its facets revisited, *Journal of Advertising,* 35(4), 35–52.

Joseph, S. (2014) Sailor Jerry's owner bets on organic content to 'unlock the power of recommendation, *Marketing Week,* 15 July, retrieved 14 August 2014 from www.marketingweek.co.uk/sectors/food-and-drink/news/sailor-jerrys-owner-bets-on-organic-content-to-unlock-the-power-of-recommendation/4011115.article.

Katz, E. and Lazarsfeld, P.F. (1955) *Personal Influence,* Glencoe, IL: Free Press.

Kawakami, T., Kishiya, K. and Parry, M.E. (2014) Personal word of mouth, virtual word of mouth and innovation use, *Journal of Product Innovation Management,* 30(1), 17–30.

Keller, J.A. and Berry, J.L. (2003) *The Influential: One American in Ten Tells the Other Nine How to Vote, Where to Eat, and What to Buy,* New York: Simon & Schuster.

Kingdom, J.W. (1970) Opinion leaders in the electorate, *Public Opinion Quarterly,* 34, 256–61.

Kozinets, R.V., de Valck, K., Wojnicki, A.C. and Wilner, S.J.S. (2010) Networked narratives: understanding word-of-mouth marketing in online communities, *Journal of Marketing,* 74 (March), 71–89.

Leggatt, H. (2014) Marketers struggle to measure offline word-of-mouth marketing, *BizReport: Social Marketing,* 28 April, retrieved 5 August 2014 from www.bizreport.com/2014/04/marketers-struggle-to-measure-offline-word-of-mouth-marketin.html.

Littlejohn, S.W. (1992) *Theories of Human Communication,* 4th edition, Belmont, CA: Wadsworth.

Mahajan, V., Muller, E. and Bass, F.M. (1990) New product diffusion models in marketing, *Journal of Marketing,* 54 (January), 1–26.

Mallen, B. (1977) *Principles of Marketing Channel Management,* Lexington, MA: Lexington Books.

Mazzarol, T., Sweeney, J.C. and Soutar, G.N. (2007) Conceptualising word-of-mouth activity, triggers and conditions: an exploratory study, *European Journal of Marketing,* 41(11/12), 1475–94.

McCracken, G. (1989) Who is the celebrity endorser? Cultural foundations of the endorsement process, *Journal of Consumer Research,* 16 (December), 310–21.

Midgley, D. and Dowling, G. (1993) Longitudinal study of product form innovation: the interaction between predispositions and social messages, *Journal of Consumer Research,* 19 (March), 611–25.

Nisbet, E.C. (2005) The engagement model of opinion leadership: testing validity within a European context, *International Journal of Public Opinion Research,* 18(1), 1–27.

Palmer, I. (2009) WoM is about empowering consumers in shaping your brand, *Admap,* 504, retrieved 2 June 2010 from www.warc.com/admap.

Patzer, G.L. (1983) Source credibility as a function of communicator physical attractiveness, *Journal of Business Research,* 11, 229–41.

Rantal, Z. (2011) Word-of-mouth marketing for Sensodyne Pronamel toothpaste, *Trnd,* retrieved 22 August 2014 from www.kreativ.hu/download.php?id=11083.

Reynolds, F.D. and Darden, W.R. (1971) Mutually adaptive effects of interpersonal communication, *Journal of Marketing Research,* 8 (November), 449–54.

Rivalland, M. (2014) Student blogger may be the next Nigella, *The Times,* 2 August, p. 16.

Robinson, J.P. (1976) Interpersonal influence in election campaigns: two step flow hypothesis, *Public Opinion Quarterly,* 40, 304–19.

Robinson, M. and Malm, S. (2015) The house that 7 million followers on YouTube bought, *Mail Online,* 17 February, retrieved 30 May 2015 from www.dailymail.co.uk/news/article-2957053/That-s-7-million-subscribers-buy-Blogging-sensation-Zoella-buys-1million-five-bedroom-mansion-Brighton-six-years-YouTube-diary.html.

Rogers, E.M. (1962) *Diffusion of Innovations,* 1st edition, New York: Free Press.

Rogers, E.M. (1983) *Diffusion of Innovations,* 3rd edition, New York: Free Press.

Rogers, E.M. (1986) *Communication Technology: The New Media in Society,* New York: Free Press.

Rogers, E.M. (2003) *Diffusion of Innovations,* 5th edition, New York: Free Press.

Rothschild, M. (1987) *Marketing Communications,* Lexington, MA: D.C. Heath.

Santo, B. (2006) Have you heard about word of mouth? *Multichannel Merchant,* 2(2), 28–30.

Schramm, W. (1955) How communication works, in *The Process and Effects of Mass Communications* (ed. W. Schramm), Urbana, IL: University of Illinois Press, 3–26.

Shannon, C. and Weaver, W. (1962) *The Mathematical Theory of Communication,* Urbana, IL: University of Illinois Press.

Shih, H.p., Lai, K.h. and Cheng, T.C.E. (2013) Informational and relational influences on electronic word of mouth: an empirical study of an online consumer discussion forum, *International Journal of Electronic Commerce,* 17(4), 137–65.

Soldow, G.F. and Thomas, G.P. (1984) Relational communication: form versus content in the sales interaction, *Journal of Marketing*, 48, 84–93.

Stokes, D. and Lomax, W. (2002) Taking control of word of mouth marketing: the case of an entrepreneurial hotelier, *Journal of Small Business and Enterprise Development*, 9(4), 349–57.

Swift, J. (2014) Unilever pilots multi-brand advertising with YouTube beauty channel, *Campaignlive*, retrieved 3 August 2014 from www.campaignlive.co.uk/news/1289962/Unilever-pilots-multi-brand-advertising-YouTube-beauty-channel/?DCMP=ILC-SEARCH.

Taylor, D. and Altman, I. (1987) Communication in interpersonal relationships: social penetration theory, in *Interpersonal Processes: New Directions in Communication Research* (eds M.E. Roloff and G.R. Miller), Newbury Park, CA: Sage, 257–77.

Theodorson, S.A. and Theodorson, G.R. (1969) *A Modern Dictionary of Sociology*, New York: Cromwell.

Tichy, N. (1979) Social network analysis for organisations, *Academy of Management Review*, 4, 507–19.

Varey, R. (2002) Requisite communication for positive involvement and participation: a critical communication theory perspective, *International Journal of Applied Human Resource Management*, 3(2), 20–35.

Weick, K. (1987) Prescribed and emergent networks, in *Handbook of Organisational Communication* (ed. F. Jablin), London: Sage.

Weimann, G. (1994) *The Influentials: People Who Influence People*, Albany, NY: State University of New York Press.

Weisfeld-Spolter, S., Sussan, F. and Gould, S. (2014) An integrative approach to eWOM and marketing communications, *Corporate Communications: An International Journal*, 19(3), 260–74.

Williams, K. (1990) *Behavioural Aspects of Marketing*, Oxford: Heinemann.

Windahl, S., Signitzer, B. and Olson, J.T. (1992) *Using Communication Theory*, London: Sage.

Yuan, Y., Caulkins, J.P. and Roehrig, S. (1998) The relationship between advertising and content provision on the Internet, *European Journal of Marketing*, 32(7/8), 667–87.

Chapter 3

Audience insight: information processing and behaviour

Understanding the way in which people perceive their world, the way they learn, develop attitudes and respond to marketing communications stimuli is fundamental if effective communications are to be developed. In the same way, understanding the ways in which people make decisions and the factors that impact upon the decision process can also influence the effectiveness of marketing communications.

Aims and learning objectives

The aims of this chapter are first to consider some of the ways information is processed by people and second to examine the key issues associated with purchase decision-making and their impact on marketing communications.

The learning objectives are to enable readers to:

1. appreciate the primary elements associated with information processing: perception, learning, attitudes;

2. explain how information is used by both consumers and organisations when making purchase decisions;

3. discuss ideas associated with purchase decision-making;

4. understand how perceived risk and involvement can influence the use of marketing communications;

5. suggest ways in which marketing communications can be influenced by an understanding of behavioural economics, and hedonic and tribal consumption.

The intellectual Alibi – or how the Dacia challenged conventional perceptions of value

Renault, the French car manufacturer, bought Dacia, a former state-owned Romanian car manufacturer, in 1999. Renault then relaunched the Dacia brand across Europe, as a no-frills value brand. The strategy required undercutting the competition and enabling customers on restricted budgets to buy a new car at used car prices, yet with a three-year warranty. The communications carried the message 'shockingly affordable', and positioned the Dacia as the cheapest car in the market. This approach was successful, profitable and upset the stability of the car market across Europe.

In 2012 Renault turned their attention to launching the Dacia into the UK, a market characterised by deep recession which had reshaped the car market. In a search for savings and great value, buyers preferred cars that were expensive, cheap, or second-hand. This spelt trouble for the mass-market, mid-range brands,

Joy

It doesn't need to be complicated.

Merry Christmas from Dacia.

Dacia Sandero
from **£5,995***

Dacia Duster
from **£8,995****

#SimpleJoys

Exhibit 3.1	**A Christmas press ad used to support the UK launch of the Sandero and Duster.**
	Source: Renault UK.

including Renault who languished in 18th place in the UK car sales rankings with just 1.99 per cent market share.

Renault's strategy for recovery partly rested on the value brand it already owned, and they launched the Dacia Duster in 2013 as the lowest-priced SUV in the UK market. Its price was £5,000 cheaper than its nearest rival, the Skoda Yeti. The Dacia Sandero (a five-door hatchback), at just £5,995, was the UK's cheapest new car of any kind.

The key to unlocking the UK market, however, was not going to be a low price. This is because people in the UK tend to think that the lower the price, the lower the quality, and this encourages jokes, mockery and derision. The Skoda, Lada and Trabant are all budget-priced Eastern European car brands and each had long been the butt of cruel jokes. The Dacia was to be no exception, with the presenters of the popular TV motoring show *Top Gear* already cracking jokes about the brand even before it was launched.

People have a relationship with their cars that goes beyond the purely functional. There is a sense that your car says something about you, and you are judged by it. The emotional connection people have with their cars reflects both a social and ego risk attachment. Indeed, Renault saw this as a stigma that had to be negotiated if the Dacia stood any chance of success in the UK.

The 'intellectual alibi' is a term accredited to the French psychoanalyst Clotaire Rapaille, to describe the reason people give for doing what they do. If Dacia buyers were going to find themselves the butt of jokes from the likes of *Top Gear*, then they needed a damn good, foolproof alibi to retain their dignity and their belief in having made the right choice.

Research has shown that the reasons people given for choosing a particular car are often rationalisations rather than literal truths. For example, SUV drivers often described why they really, *really* needed four-wheel drive and chunky tyres, even though they lived in a town and mainly used their car for the school-run. Rapaille commented that New York SUV drivers give 'the difficulty of parking in snow' as one of their main reasons for choice. Other drivers describe how they paid extra for a higher-range model because of certain features and buttons – and yet when probed about how often they used these features and buttons, it turned out that the answer was mostly 'seldom or never'.

Although Renault were sure that people really did want to save money, they were also aware of the strength of the emotional connection between people and their cars, and the degree to which cars were perceived to make social statements about their owners.

They knew that the launch campaign had to provide a really good intellectual alibi to make buyers feel good, not shoddy, for choosing Dacia, and to rebut the purveyors of mirth and derision.

To make buyers feel good, competitors communicated 'generosity' and packed in as many extras (e.g. body colour bumpers, electric windows with auto up and down driver controls, daytime running lights) into the price as possible. Consumers had been conditioned into thinking that value was about getting more for less. Dacia took a different path. The basic models on sale had no gadgets at all – no cup holders, no electric door mirrors, no tinted glass, no sat-nav, not even a radio. The car was stripped down to the bare essentials needed for a comfortable, safe drive from A to B.

Thus, Dacia challenged the idea that more is better and exposed the unnecessary extravagance of paying for things that were not needed. Good value would be about paying for what was really needed in a car and saving on things that weren't. Dacia targeted people who got a kick from saving money by cutting out unnecessary frills, and made them feel that they'd got absolutely everything that mattered in a car, but that they'd been clever enough to save thousands by not paying for all of the superfluous stuff that other people get sucked into by sharp-suited sales staff.

This positioned Dacia as the 'enemy of the unnecessary', and the intellectual alibi involved reframing the concept of value in the car market and to extol the virtues of having less rather than more. This translated into a campaign which said:

> Look, here's what you actually want from a car. Now, you can get all that in a car costing £30,000. Or you can get the exact same things in a car costing less than £10,000. So which would you choose? In fact, which would anyone in their right mind choose? You do the maths.

Different executions featuring the two main models (Duster and Sandero) tackled the message from different angles. Some playful, some 'straight,' some mocking other car brands' ways of doing things, some casting a Dacia eye over topical issues like the way footballers are bought and sold. But all coming back to the same point. The same alibi. You don't choose Dacia because you're hard up, or struggling, or because you can't afford a well-known brand. You choose Dacia because you're smart, because you're

Clever design
Solidly built
From only £8,995*
You do the maths

> **Exhibit 3.2** **A print ad for the Duster, presenting the intellectual alibi.....'you do the maths'**
> *Source*: Renault UK.

savvy, and because you're not taken in by the expensive hype that fools so many other people.

By the end of its first year, Dacia had sold 17,263 new cars, far surpassing its base sales volume target. Dacia UK outstripped launches in all other European countries outside of Dacia's home nation of Romania. Astonishingly, by March 2014, Dacia UK had outsold Dacia in France where sales had been buoyed by the prominence of Renault.

This case was written by Julian Earl, Planning Director at Publicis

Questions relating to this case can be found at the end of this chapter.

Introduction

People consume products and services not only because of the utilitarian value but also because of what they represent, their meaning and symbolic value. In other words, people make purchase decisions, either knowingly or subconsciously, about their identity and how they might wish to be seen. The Dacia case on the intellectual alibi illustrates this wonderfully.

Marketing communications is about managing promises: their creation, delivery and realisation. It makes sense, therefore, to understand the way buyers think and behave, in order that these promises remain realistic and effective. Understanding the ways in which buyers make decisions, the factors that impact upon the decision process and their preferred identities, can influence the effectiveness of marketing communications. In particular, it can affect message structure, content and media scheduling. In this chapter, and indeed the book, reference is made to both buyers and audiences. This is because, although all buyers constitute an audience, not all audiences are buyers.

The whole process of customer purchasing is often referred to as a journey. This encapsulates the initial stages of problem awareness, the search for solutions, decision-making and then through to post-purchase experience and reflection.

There are numerous, largely practitioner-based ideas, about what constitutes a journey. The customer decision journey was once conceptualised as a linear format, often represented by a (sales) funnel as set out in Figure 3.1 (Court et al., 2009). This approach was used to portray the way customers identified a problem, how they considered a certain set of brands, and then their systematic reduction of the number of feasible solutions until a purchase was made (McNeal, 2013).

Today, the complexity of the media landscape, the variety of buying opportunities and the huge volume of data that is available have made the linear interpretation redundant. Now a non-linear explanation, one based on a circular or even a jigsaw format, is used to express the multiplicity of paths customers use to make purchase decisions.

This complexity means that organisations have less time, fewer resources per journey format and hence less control than they thought they used to have. Court et al. (2009) argue that there are four distinct phases to the contemporary customer decision journey:

- initial consideration;
- active research and evaluation of potential purchases;
- closure through the selection and purchase of a brand;
- post-purchase, the overall experience of the brand as a solution and shaping of future purchases.

Figure 3.2 sets out the way in which these elements work together.

Most organisations attempt to isolate one key journey and from that build a business model. This is not a feasible approach and their attempt to manage the various consumer/brand touchpoints in order to improve efficiency and customer satisfaction at individual parts of the journey is equally questionable. Rawson et al. (2013: 92) believe that customer satisfaction is not a factor of these multiple, yet individual interactions, it is the 'cumulative experiences across multiple touchpoints and in multiple channels over

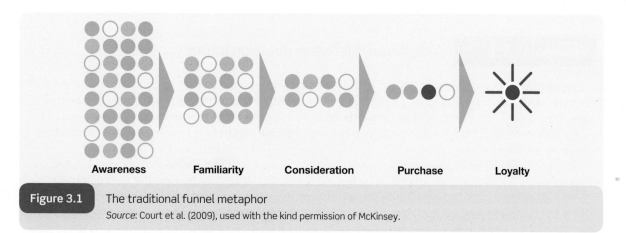

Awareness   Familiarity   Consideration   Purchase   Loyalty

Figure 3.1   The traditional funnel metaphor
Source: Court et al. (2009), used with the kind permission of McKinsey.

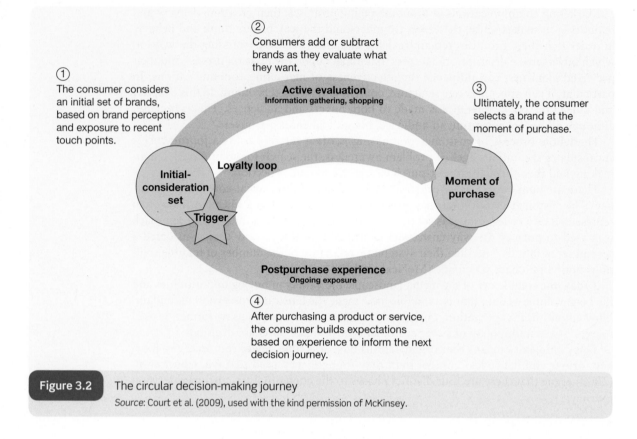

Figure 3.2   The circular decision-making journey

Source: Court et al. (2009), used with the kind permission of McKinsey.

time' that influence the overall experience and levels of customer satisfaction. Indeed, it is the sum of all the different types and forms of engagement with a brand that appears to be critical. Viewpoint 3.1 describes a journey that is nearing reality.

This chapter considers some of the key issues that impact on the use of marketing communications at various points within these customer journeys. There are three main sections. The first considers issues relating to the classical way people are thought to process information. The second embraces conventional ideas about decision-making, again based on a classical interpretation which assumes rational decision-making. The third looks at some alternative, less orthodox, approaches to understanding consumer behaviour. These assume that individuals make decisions based on incomplete information, and that their decisions are often based on heuristics and rules of thumb, are essentially irrational and founded largely on emotion.

Viewpoint 3.1   A digitised customer decision journey

Imagine that a couple have just bought their first home and are now looking to purchase a washer and a dryer. Mike and Linda start their journey by visiting several big-box retailers' websites. At one store's site, they identify three models they are interested in and save them to a 'wish list'. Because space in their starter home is limited – and because it is a relatively big purchase in their eyes – they decide they need to see the items in person.

Under an optimised cross-channel experience, the couple could find the nearest physical outlet on the retailer's website, get directions using Google Maps, and drive over to view the desired products. Even before they walk through the doors, a transmitter mounted at the retailer's entrance identifies Mike and Linda and sends a push alert to their mobile phones welcoming them and providing them with personalised offers and recommendations based on their history with the store. In this case, they receive quick links to the wish list they created, as well as updated specs and prices for the washers and dryers that they had shown interest in (captured in their click trails on the store's website). Additionally, they receive notification of a sale – '15 per cent off selected brand appliances, today only' – that applies to two of the items they had added to their wish list.

When they tap on the wish list, the app provides a store map directing Mike and Linda to the appliances section and a 'call button' to speak with an expert. They meet with the salesperson, ask some questions, take some measurements, and close in on a particular model and brand of washer and dryer. Because the store employs sophisticated tagging technologies, information about the washer and dryer has automatically been synced with other applications on the couple's mobile phones – they can scan reviews using their Consumer Reports app, text their parents for advice, ask Facebook friends to weigh in on the purchase, and compare the retailer's prices against others. Mike and Linda can also take advantage of a 'virtual designer' function on the retailer's mobile app that, with the entry of just a few key pieces of information about room size and decor, allows them to preview how the washer and dryer might look in their home.

All the input is favourable, so the couple decides to take advantage of the 15 per cent offer and buy the appliances. They use Mike's 'smartwatch' to authenticate payment, and walk out of the store with a date and time for delivery; a week later, on the designated day, they receive confirmation that a truck is in their area and that they will be texted within a half hour of arrival time – no need to cancel other plans just to wait for the washer and dryer to arrive. Three weeks after that, the couple gets a message from the retailer with offers for other appliances and home-improvement services tailored towards first-year home owners. And the cycle begins again.

Source: An extract from van Bommel et al. (2014). Used with permission from McKinsey.

Question: How might this journey change in the future?

Task: Make notes about the digital journey someone might make when shopping for food and another one for fashion clothing.

Information processing

Marketing communications is an audience-centred activity, so it is vitally important to understand the way in which people process information prior to, during and after making product/service purchase decisions. Traditionally, awareness has been considered an integral part of information processing. However, this important topic is considered as part of an organisation's objectives and positioning activities (see Chapter 6). Here three main information-processing issues are considered: perception, learning and attitudes.

Perception

Perception is concerned with how individuals see and make sense of their environment. It is about how individuals select, organise and interpret stimuli, so that they can understand their world.

Perceptual selection

The vast number of messages mentioned earlier needs to be filtered, as individuals cannot process them all. The stimuli that are selected result from the interaction of the nature of the stimulus with the expectations and the motives of the individual. Attention is an important factor in determining the outcome of this interaction: 'Attention occurs when the stimulus activates one or more sensory receptor nerves and the resulting sensations go to the brain for processing' (Hawkins et al., 1989).

The nature of the stimuli, or external factors such as the intensity and size, position, contrast, novelty, repetition and movement, are factors that have been developed and refined by marketing communicators to attract attention. Animation is used to attract attention when the product class is perceived as bland and uninteresting, such as margarine or teabags. Unexpected camera angles and the use of music can be effective methods of gaining the attention of the target audience, as used successfully in the Ibis ad, 'Everybody's Famous', supported by Martin Solveig's 'Everybody'. Sexual attraction, as promoted through perfume ads, can be a powerful means of capturing the attention of audiences and, when associated with a brand's values, can be a very effective method of getting attention.

The expectations, needs and motives of an individual, or internal factors, are equally important. Individuals see what they expect to see, and their expectations are normally based on past experience and preconditioning. From a communications perspective, the presentation of stimuli that conflict with an individual's expectations will invariably receive more attention. The attention-getting power of erotic and sexually driven advertising messages is understood and exploited. For example, jeans manufacturers such as Levis, Wranglers and Diesel often use this type of stimulus to promote their brands. However, advertising research based on recall testing often reveals that the attention-getting stimulus (e.g. the male or female) generates high recall scores, but the product or brand is very often forgotten. Looked at in terms of Schramm's model of communications (Chapter 2), the process of encoding was inaccurate, hence the inappropriate decoding.

Of particular interest is the tendency of individuals to select particular information from the environment. This process is referred to as *selective attention*. Through attention, individuals avoid contact with information that is felt to be disagreeable because it opposes strongly held beliefs and attitudes.

Individuals see what they want or need to see. If they are considering the purchase of a new car, there will be heightened awareness of car advertisements and a correspondingly lower level of awareness of unrelated stimuli. Selective attention allows individuals to expose themselves to messages that are comforting and rewarding. For example, reassurance is often required for people who have bought new cars or expensive technical equipment and who have spent a great deal of time debating and considering the purchase and its associated risk. Communications congratulating the new owner on their wise decision often accompany post-purchase literature such as warranties and service contracts. If potentially harmful messages do get through this filter system, perceptual defence mechanisms help to screen them out after exposure.

Perceptual organisation

For perception to be effective and meaningful, the vast array of selected stimuli needs to be organised. The four main ways in which sensory stimuli can be arranged are: figure–ground, grouping, closure and contour.

Figure-ground

Each individual's perception of an environment tends to consist of articles on a general background, against which certain objects are illuminated and stand proud. Williams (1981) gives the examples of trees standing out against the sky and words on a page. This has obvious implications for advertisers and the design and form of communications, especially advertisements, to draw attention to important parts of the message, most noticeably the price, logo or company/brand name.

Grouping

Objects that are close to one another tend to be grouped together and a pattern develops. Grouping can be used to encourage associations between a product and specific attributes. For example, food products that are positioned for a health market are often displayed with pictures that represent fitness and exercise, the association being that consumption of the food will lead to a lifestyle that incorporates fitness and exercise, as these are important to the target market.

Closure

When information is incomplete, individuals make sense of the data by filling in the gaps. This is often used to involve consumers in the message and so enhance selective attention. Advertisements for American Express charge cards or GM credit cards ('if invited to apply'), for example, suggest that ownership denotes membership, which represents exclusiveness and privilege.

Television advertisements that are run for 60 seconds when first launched are often cut to 30, 15 or even 7 seconds later in the burst. The purpose is two-fold: to cut costs and to keep reminding the target audience. This process of reminding is undertaken with the assistance of the audience, who recognise the commercial and mentally close the message even though the advertiser only presents the first part.

We never made it to the restaurant.
What better way to celebrate your next anniversary? A diamond is forever.

Exhibit 3.3	**De Beers Shadows**

This message draws on a grouping of the silhouetted depersonalised individuals and the ring and requires a cultural decoding of what the event represents.

Source: DeBeers UK Ltd.

Contour

Contours give objects shape and are normally formed when there is a marked change in colour or brightness. This is an important element in package design and, as the battle for shelf space in retail outlets becomes more intense, so package design has become an increasingly important aspect of attracting attention. The Coca-Cola bottle and the packaging of the Toblerone bar are two classic examples of packaging that conveys the brand.

These methods are used by individuals in an attempt to organise stimuli and simplify their meanings. They combine in an attempt to determine a pattern to the stimuli, so that they are perceived as part of a whole or larger unit. This is referred to as *gestalt psychology*.

Perceptual interpretation

Interpretation is the process by which individuals give meaning to the stimuli once they have been organised. As Cohen and Basu (1987) state, by using existing categories, meanings can be given to stimuli. These categories are determined from the individual's past experiences and they shape what the individual expects to see. These expectations, when combined with the strength and clarity of the stimulus and the motives at the time perception occurs, mould the pattern of the perceived stimuli.

The degree to which each individual's ascribed meaning, resulting from the interpretation process, is realistic is dependent upon the levels of distortion that may be present. Distortion may occur because of stereotyping: the predetermined set of images which we use to guide our expectations of events, people and situations. Another distortion factor is the halo effect that occurs when a stimulus with many attributes or dimensions is evaluated on just a single attribute or dimension. Brand extensions and family branding strategies are based on the understanding that if previous experiences with a different offering are satisfactory, then risk is reduced and an individual is more likely to buy a new offering from the same 'family'.

Marketing and perception

We have seen that individuals select and interpret particular stimuli in the context of the expectations arising from the way they classify the overall situation. The way in which individuals perceive, organise and interpret stimuli is a reflection of their past experiences and the classifications used to understand the different situations each individual frames every day. Individuals seek to provide a context within which their role becomes clearer. Shoppers expect to find products in particular situations, such as rows, shelves or display bins of similar goods. They also develop meanings and associations with some grocery products because of the utility and trust/emotional satisfaction certain pack types evoke. The likelihood that a sale will be made is improved, if the context in which a purchase transaction is undertaken does not contradict a shopper's expectations.

Marketing communications should attempt to present products (objects) in a frame or 'mental presence' (Moran, 1990) that is recognised by a buyer, such as a consumption or purchase situation. A product has a much greater chance of entering an evoked set if the situation in which it is presented is one that is expected and relevant. A new pack design, however, can provide differentiation and provoke people into reassessing their expectations about what constitutes appropriate packaging in a product category.

Javalgi et al. (1992) point out that perception is important to product evaluation and product selection. Consumers try to evaluate a product's attributes using the physical cues of taste, smell, size and shape. Sometimes no difference can be distinguished, so the consumer has to make a judgement on factors other than the physical characteristics of the product. This is the basis of branding activity, where a personality is developed for the product which enables it to be perceived differently from its competitors. The individual may also set up a separate category or evoked set in order to make sense of new stimuli or satisfactory experiences.

Exhibit 3.4	**KFC – Gender-driven advertisement**

When KFC introduced their BBQ Rancher, a range launched in response to market needs for a healthy non-fired burger, the 400-calorie, chicken-based product was communicated through two ad themes. One was aimed at men using a 'fun-loving' approach. The other was designed to appeal to women and was based on etiquette (Reynolds, 2012).

Source: Freud Communications.

Scholars' paper 3.1   Simply a cosmetic perception

Guthrie, M.F. and Kim, H.S. (2009) The relationship between consumer involvement and brand perceptions of female cosmetic consumers, *Journal of Brand Management,* **17(2), 114–33.**

Although this may not be ranked as a seminal or great paper, it is interesting because it provides an application of Kapferer and Laurent's consumer-involvement profile. It shows how segmentation can be undertaken based on consumer perceptions and from this brand communications used to develop suitable images.

The concept of positioning products in the mind of each consumer is fundamental to marketing strategy and is a topic that will be examined in greater depth in Chapter 6. Individuals carry a set of enduring perceptions or images. These relate to themselves, to products/services and to organisations. The way a brand is positioned is partly based on how people perceive the brand. For example, many consumers perceive the financial services industry negatively. Originally this was due to the inherent complexity associated with the propositions. This has been compounded by a string of banking scandals, seemingly outrageous bonus systems and the banking industry's contribution to the cause of the recession. Creating positive perceptions of a brand such as the Cooperative Bank becomes problematic when it is held up to be guilty of unethical practices, when deliberately positioned as an ethical bank.

Organisations need to monitor and adjust their identities constantly in respect of the perceptions and expectations held by other organisations in their various networks. For example, the level of channel coordination and control can be a function of the different

Viewpoint 3.2   Time spent . . . changing perceptions

Many campaigns are designed to change the way people see or perceive a brand. For example, the National Trust used marketing communications to move away from an image based on formality, a demographic rooted in middle/older age, and a brand that was way out of date. The strategy was to broaden the range of products and experiences people could have with the National Trust.

The campaign has now been running for several years and uses the strapline, 'Time well Spent'. The principle was that people should be encouraged to perceive the National Trust as an opportunity for 'simple pleasures and quality, memorable experiences at affordable rates'. This was translated into a series of outdoor ads that showed various types of people enjoying different experiences. A couple might be attempting a topiary maze, or a family might be shown sitting near a beautiful river. Radio ads featured chirping birds and the delight of children playing. Online ads included an interactive facility helping people identify their nearest National Trust property. All the ads began with the message, 'Time to . . .', which was followed by a message, such as, be together . . . see something . . . unwind . . . explore.

Since then the Trust has launched an iPhone app designed to help gardeners and day-trippers to find and explore and browse any of the 150 National Trust gardens whenever they want. In 2010 visitor numbers increased by 16 per cent and membership increased by nearly 18 per cent.

Typical of the revised orientation, in 2013 the NT launched a nationwide campaign called '50 things to do before you're 11¾'. This was designed following the publication of a report that highlighted a long-term and dramatic decline in the relationship children have with the outdoors. Typically, fewer than 10 per cent of children regularly play in wild places, 33 per cent have never climbed a tree, 10 per cent can't ride a bike; whilst three times as many are taken to hospital after falling out of bed, as from falling out

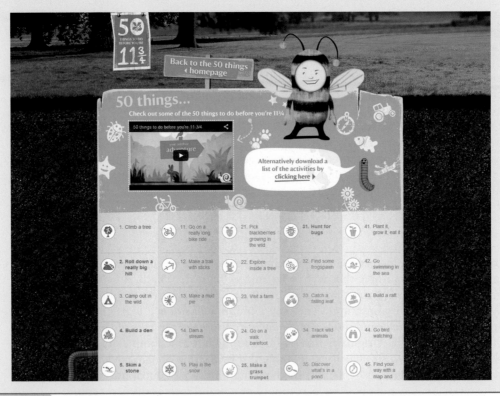

| Exhibit 3.5 | **The National Trust's '50 things to do before you're 11¾' campaign** |

Source: The National Trust

of a tree. The campaign, therefore, was designed to encourage sofa-bound, gadget-orientated children to get outside and to explore nature and the environment.

Source: Anon (2011); Eleftheriou-Smith (2011); McMeeken (2012); Staff (2013).

Question:	How might the National Trust make best use of social media?
Task:	Find a campaign where the core task appears to be to change perceptions about health issues.

perceptions of channel members. These concern the perception of the channel depth, processes of control and the roles each member is expected to fulfil. Furthermore, the perception of an organisation's product quality and its associated image (reputation) are becoming increasingly important. Both end-user buyers and channel members are attempting to ensure that the intrinsic and extrinsic cues associated with their products are appropriate signals of product quality (Moran, 1990).

Learning

There are two mainstream approaches to learning. These are behavioural and cognitive and their core characteristics are set out in Table 3.1.

Behavioural learning

The behaviourist approach to learning views the process as a function of an individual's acquisition of responses. There are three factors important to behavioural learning: association, reinforcement and motivation. However, it is the basic concept of the stimulus–response orientation that will be looked at in more detail.

It is accepted that for learning to occur all that is needed is a 'time–space proximity' between a stimulus and a response. Learning takes place through the establishment of a connection between a stimulus and a response. Marketing communications is thought to work by the simple process of people observing messages and being stimulated/motivated to respond by requesting more information or purchasing the advertised product in search of a reward. Behaviour is learned through the conditioning experience of a stimulus and response. There are two forms of conditioning: classical and operant.

Table 3.1 Types of learning

Type of learning		Explanation
Behavioural	**Classical**	Individuals learn to make associations or connections between a stimulus and their responses. Through repetition of the response (the behaviour) to the stimulus, learning occurs.
	Operant	Learning occurs as a result of an individual operating or interacting with the environment. The response of the individual is instrumental in getting a positive reinforcement (reward) or negative reinforcement (punishment). Behaviour that is rewarded or reinforced will be continued, whereas behaviour that is not rewarded will cease.
Cognitive		Assumes that individuals attempt to actively influence their immediate environment rather than be subject to it. They try to resolve problems by processing information from past experiences (memory) in order to make reasoned decisions based on judgements.

Classical conditioning

Classical conditioning assumes that learning is an associative process that occurs between a stimulus and a response, within an existing relationship. By far the best-known examples of this type of learning are the experiments undertaken by the Russian psychologist Ivan Pavlov. He noticed that dogs began to salivate at the sight of food. He stated that this was not taught, but was a reflex reaction. This relationship exists prior to any experimentation or learning. The food represents an unconditioned stimulus and the response (salivation) from the dogs is an unconditioned response.

Pavlov then paired the ringing of a bell with the presentation of food. Shortly the dogs began to salivate at the ringing of the bell. The bell became the conditioned stimulus and the salivation became the conditioned response (which was the same as the unconditioned response).

From an understanding of this work it can be determined that two factors are important for learning to occur:

- To build the association between the unconditioned and conditioned stimulus, there must be a relatively short period of time.
- The conditioning process requires that there be a relatively high frequency/repetition of the association. The more often the unconditioned and conditioned stimuli occur together, the stronger will be the association.

Classical conditioning can be observed operating in each individual's everyday life. An individual who purchases a new product because of a sales promotion may continue to buy the product even when the promotion has terminated. An association has been established between the sales promotion activity (unconditioned stimulus) and the product (conditioned stimulus). If product quality and satisfaction levels allow, long-run behaviour may develop despite the absence of the promotion. In other words, promotion need not act as a key purchase factor in the long run.

Advertisers attempt to frame the way their products/services are perceived by using images and emotions that are known to evoke positive associations and reactions from consumers. Image advertising seeks to develop the associations that individuals have when they think of a brand or an organisation, hence its reputation. Messages of this type show the object with an unconditioned stimulus that is known to evoke pleasant and favourable feelings. So, the puppet 'Aleksandr Orlov' is the face for comparethemarket.com, Gary Lineker is associated with Walker's crisps, Gisele with Pantene, Jennifer Lopez with L'Oréal, and Jeremy Lin represents Volvo. The product becomes a conditioned stimulus eliciting the same favourable response.

Operant conditioning

This type of learning, sometimes known as *instrumental conditioning*, occurs as a result of an individual operating or acting on some part of the environment. The response of the individual is instrumental in getting a positive reinforcement (reward) or negative reinforcement (punishment). Behaviour that is rewarded or reinforced will be continued, whereas behaviour that is not rewarded will cease.

B.F. Skinner was a pioneer researcher in the field of operant conditioning. His showed that rats learned to press levers in order to receive food. He went on to demonstrate that the rats learned to press the lever when a light was on (discriminative stimulus). This highlights the essential feature of this form of conditioning, that reinforcement follows a specific response.

Many organisations use reinforcement in their communications by stressing the benefits or rewards that a consumer can anticipate receiving as a result of using a product or brand. For example, airlines offer air miles, Tesco offers 'reward points' and Nectar offers a reward of money savings which 'makes the difference'. Reinforcement theories emphasise the role of external factors and exclude an individual's ability to process information internally. Learning takes place either through direct reinforcement of a particular response or through an associative conditioning process. However, operant conditioning is a mechanistic process that is not realistic, as it serves only to simplify an extremely complex process.

Cognitive learning

This approach to our understanding of learning assumes that individuals are capable of and attempt to control their immediate environments. They are seen as active participants in that they try to resolve problems by processing information that is pertinent to each situation. Central to this process is memory. Just as money can be invested in short-, medium- and long-term investment accounts, so information is memorised for different periods of time. These memories are sensory, short-term and long-term, set out in Figure 3.3.

Sensory storage refers to the period in which information is sensed for a split second. If an impression is made the information is transferred to short-term memory where it is rehearsed before transfer to long-term memory. Short-term memory lasts no longer than approximately eight seconds and a maximum of four or five items can be stored in short-term memory at any one time. Readers will probably have experienced being introduced to someone at a social event only to forget the name of the guest when they next meet them at the same event. This occurs because the name was not entered into long-term memory. Information can be stored for extended periods in long-term memory. This information is not lying dormant, however, it is constantly being reorganised and recategorised as new information is received.

There are four basic functions by which memory operates. The first is *rehearsal,* where information is repeated or related to an established category. This is necessary so that the second function, *encoding,* can take place. This involves the selection of an image to represent the perceived object. Once in long-term memory it is *categorised and stored,* the third function. *Retrieval* is the final function, a process by which information is recovered from storage.

Cognitive learning is about processing information in order that problems can be resolved. These information-handling processes can range from the simple to the complex. There are three main processes: iconic, modelling and reasoning.

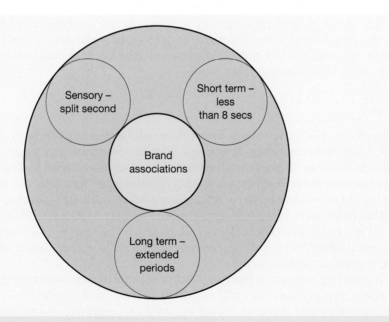

| Figure 3.3 | Memory and information storage |

Iconic rote learning involves understanding the association between two or more concepts when there is an absence of a stimulus. Learning occurs at a weak level through repetition of simple messages. Beliefs are formed about the attributes of an offering without any real understanding of the source of the information. Advertisers of certain products (low value, frequently purchased) will try to remind their target audiences repeatedly of the brand name in an attempt to help consumers learn. Through such repetition, an association with the main benefits of the product may be built, if only via the constant reminders by the spokesperson.

Learning through the *modelling* approach involves the observation and imitation of others and the associated outcomes of their behaviour. In essence, a great deal of children's early learning is developed in this way. Likewise, marketing communicators use the promise of rewards to persuade audiences to act in a particular way. By using positive images of probable rewards, buyers are encouraged to believe that they can receive the same outcome if they use the particular product. For example, clothing advertisements often depict the model receiving admiring glances from passers-by. The same admiration is the reward 'promised' to those who wear the same clothing. A similar approach was used by Kellogg's to promote its Special K breakfast cereal. The commercial depicted a (slim) mother and child playing on a beach. The message was that it is important to look after yourself and to raise your family through healthy eating, an outdoor life and exercise.

Reasoning is perhaps the most complex form of cognitive learning. Through this process, individuals need to restructure and reorganise information held in long-term memory and combine it with fresh inputs in order to generate new outputs. Financial services providers have to convey complex information, strictly bounded by the Financial Services legislation and the Financial Conduct Authority. So, brands such as Nationwide and Hiscox convey key points about simplicity and specialist services respectively, to differentiate their brands. This enables current and potential customers to process detailed information about these brands and to make judgements or reason that these brands reach acceptable (threshold) standards.

Of all the approaches to understanding how we learn, cognitive learning is the most flexible interpretation. The rational, more restricted approach of behavioural learning, where the focus is external to the individual, is without doubt a major contribution to knowledge. However, it fails to accommodate the complex internal thought processes that individuals utilise when presented with various stimuli.

It is useful to appreciate the way in which people are believed to learn and forget as there are several issues which are useful to media planners in particular. Cognitive theory has underpinned much of the research that has been undertaken to explain how marketing and communications work.

Decay

The rate at which individuals forget material assumes a pattern, as shown at Figure 3.4. Many researchers have found that information decays at a negatively decelerating rate. As much as 60 per cent of the initial yield of information from an advertisement has normally decayed within six weeks. This decay, or wear-out, can be likened to the half-life of radioactive material. It is always working, although it cannot be seen, and the impact of the advertising reduces through time. Like McGuire's (1978) retention stage in his hierarchy of effects model (see Chapter 12), the storage of information for future use is important, but with time, how powerful will the information be and what triggers are required to promote recall?

Advertising wear-out is thought to occur because of two factors. First, individuals use selective perception and mentally switch off after a critical number of exposures. Second, the monotony and irritation caused by continued exposure lead to counter-arguments to both the message and the advertisement (Petty and Cacioppo, 1979). Advertisements for alcoholic drinks such as Carlsberg and Stella Artois attempt to prevent wear-out by

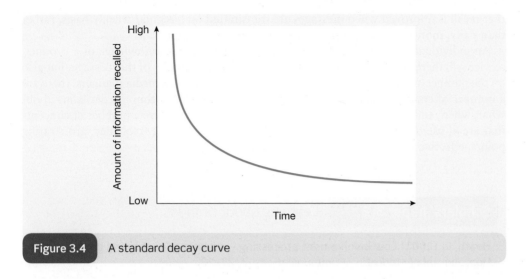

Figure 3.4	A standard decay curve

using variations on a central theme to provide consistency yet engage audiences through interest and entertainment.

Cognitive response

Learning can be visualised as following either of the curves set out in Figure 3.5. The amount learnt 'wears out' after a certain repetition level has been reached. Grass and Wallace (1969) suggest that this process of wear-out commences once a satiation point has been reached. A number of researchers (Zielske, 1959; Strong, 1977) have found

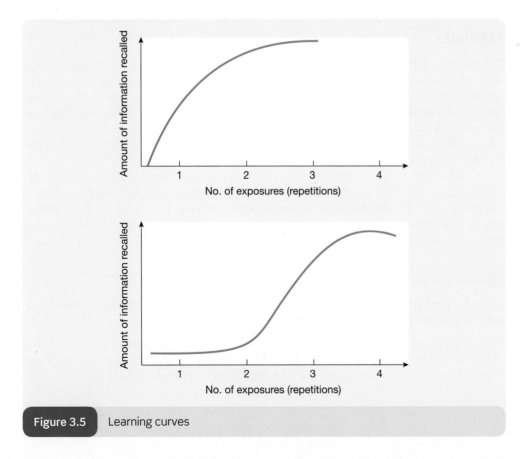

Figure 3.5	Learning curves

that recall is improved when messages are transmitted on a regular weekly basis, rather than daily, monthly or in a concentrated or dispersed format.

An individual's ability to develop and retain awareness or knowledge of a product/service will therefore be partly dependent not only on the quality of the message, but also on the number and quality of exposures to a message. To assist media planners, there are a number of concepts that need to be appreciated and used within the decisions about what, where and when a message should communicate. There are a number of concepts that are of use to media planners: these are reach and coverage, frequency, gross rating points, effective frequency, efficiency and media source effects.

Scholars' paper 3.2   Learning about brands

Heath, R. (2001) Low involvement processing – a new model of brand communication, *Journal of Marketing Communications*, 7, 27–33.

At the beginning of the noughties, Heath began publishing papers about low-involvement processing and how we learn about brands through communications. He subsequently changed the terminology to low- and high-attention theory. Since then he has published a stream of papers on this topic, one of which contradicts the traditional rational view of brand choice. Heath offers a new and different perspective on how consumers are influenced by advertising. This paper provides an insight into the literature and his thinking. It also serves to link various concepts, many of which are covered in this chapter.

Attitudes

The perceptual and learning processes usually lead to the formation of attitudes. These are predispositions, shaped through experience, to respond in an anticipated way to an object or situation. Attitudes are learned through past experiences and serve as a link between thoughts and behaviour. These experiences may relate to the product itself, to the messages transmitted by the different members of the channel network (normally mass-media communications) and to the information supplied by opinion leaders, formers and followers.

Attitudes tend to be consistent within each individual: they are clustered and very often interrelated. This categorisation leads to the formation of stereotypes, which is extremely useful for the design of messages as stereotyping allows for the transmission of a lot of information in a short time period (30 seconds) without impeding learning or the focal part of the message.

Attitude components

Attitudes are hypothetical constructs, and classical psychological theory considers attitudes to consist of three components:

1. Cognitive component (learn). This component refers to the level of knowledge and beliefs held by individuals about a product and/or the beliefs about specific attributes of the offering. This represents the learning aspect of attitude formation.

Marketing communications is used to create attention and awareness, to provide information and to help audiences learn and understand the features and benefits a particular product/service offers.

2. Affective component (feel). By referring to the feelings held about a product – good, bad, pleasant or unpleasant – an evaluation is made of the object. This is the component that is concerned with feelings, sentiments, moods and emotions about an object.

   Marketing communications is used to induce feelings about the product/service such that it becomes a preferred brand. This preference may be based on emotional attachment to a brand, conferred status through ownership, past experiences and longevity of brand usage or any one of a number of ways in which people can become emotionally involved with a brand.

3. Conative component (do). This is the action component of the attitude construct and refers to the individual's disposition or intention to behave in a certain way. Some researchers go so far as to suggest that this component refers to observable behaviour. Marketing communications, therefore, should be used to encourage audiences to do something. For example, visit a website, phone a number, take a coupon, book a visit, press red (on a remote control unit) for interactivity though digital television.

This three-component approach to attitudes, set out in Figure 3.6, is based upon attitudes towards an object, person or organisation. The sequence of attitude formation is generally considered to be learn, feel and do. However, this approach to attitude formation is limited in that the components are seen to be of equal strength. A single-component model has been developed where the attitude only consists of the individual's overall feeling towards an object. In other words, the affective component is the only significant component.

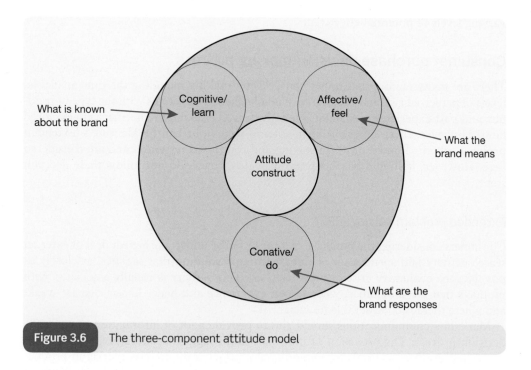

Figure 3.6　The three-component attitude model

Attitudes impact on consumer decision-making, and the objective of marketing communications is often to create a positive attitude towards a product and/or to reinforce or change existing attitudes. An individual may perceive and develop a belief that British Airways has a friendly and informal in-flight service and that the service provided by Lufthansa is cold and formal. However, both airlines are perceived to hold a number of different attributes, and each individual needs to evaluate these attributes in order that an attitude can be developed. It is necessary, therefore, to measure the strength of the beliefs held about the key attributes of different products. There are two main processes whereby beliefs can be processed and measured: compensatory and non-compensatory models.

An understanding of attitude components and the way in which particular attributes can be measured not only enables organisations to determine the attitudes held towards them and their competitors, but also empowers them to change the attitudes held by different stakeholders, if it is thought necessary.

Decision-making

Much of marketing communications activity has been orientated towards influencing decision-making processes used by customers. This requires identifying the right type of information, to be conveyed at the right time, in the appropriate format, in order to engage with the target audience.

There are two broad types of customer, consumers and organisational buyers, and each is considered to follow particular rational, sequential and logical pathways when making purchase decisions. The consumer decision-making process is depicted at Figure 3.7 and the organisational process in Figure 3.8. The consumer pathway consists of five stages, and marketing communications can impact upon any or all of these stages with varying levels of potential effectiveness.

Consumer purchase decision-making process

There are many factors that impact on decision-making including the time available, levels of perceived risk and the degree of involvement a buyer has with the type of product, and past experience – to name a few. Perceived risk and involvement are explored later. However, three types problem-solving behaviour can be identified (extended problem solving, limited problem solving and routinised response) and are considered here. However, it should be noted that in reality buyers do not follow these decision steps.

Extended problem solving (EPS)

Consumers considering the purchase of a car or house undertake a great deal of external search activity and spend a lot of time reaching a solution that satisfies, as closely as possible, the evaluative criteria previously set. This activity is usually associated with products that are unfamiliar, where direct experience and hence knowledge are weak, and where there is considerable financial risk.

Marketing communications should aim to provide a lot of information to assist the decision process. The provision of information through sales literature, such as brochures and leaflets, websites for determining product and purchase criteria in product categories where there is little experience, access to salespersons and demonstrations and advertisements, are just some of the ways in which information can be provided.

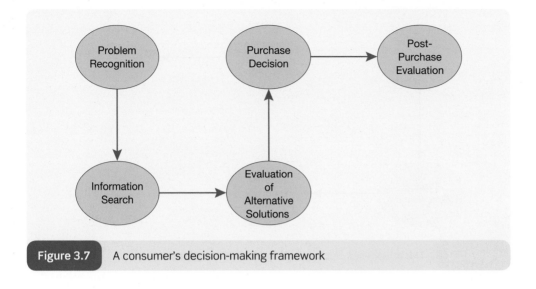

Figure 3.7   A consumer's decision-making framework

Limited problem solving (LPS)

Having experience of a product means that greater use can be made of internal, memory-based search routines and the external search can be limited to obtaining up-to-date information or to ensuring that the finer points of the decision have been investigated.

Marketing communications should attempt to provide information about any product modification or new attributes and convey messages that highlight those key attributes known to be important to buyers. By differentiating the product, marketing communications provides the buyer with a reason to select that particular product.

Routinised response behaviour (RRB)

For a great number of products the decision process will consist only of an internal search. This is primarily because the buyer has made a number of purchases and has accumulated a great deal of experience. Therefore, only an internal search is necessary, so little time or effort will be spent on external search activities. Low-value items that are frequently purchased fall into this category – for example, toothpaste, soap, tinned foods and confectionery.

Communicators should focus upon keeping the product within the evoked set or getting it into the set. Learning can be enhanced through repetition of messages, but repetition can also be used to maintain attention and awareness.

Organisational decision-making process

In much the same way organisational buying decisions can be considered in terms of processes and procedures. In order to function, organisations need to buy materials, parts, general supplies and services from a range of other organisations. Although referred to as *business-to-business marketing*, the term 'organisational marketing' is used here to reflect the wide range of organisations involved with such activities.

The term 'buyphases' was given by Robinson et al. (1967) to the several stages of the organisational buying decisions, as depicted in Figure 3.8. However, considering the buying process in terms of these neat steps is also misleading, again owing to the various forces acting on organisations.

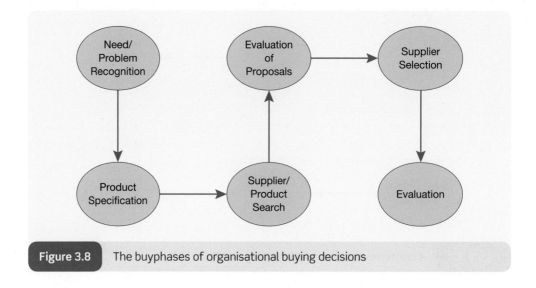

Figure 3.8   The buyphases of organisational buying decisions

Just like consumers, organisational buyers make decisions that vary with each buying situation and buyclass. Buyclasses, according to Robinson et al. (1967), comprise three types or contexts: new task, modified rebuy and straight rebuy (see Table 3.2).

Some readers may have noticed how these phases bear a strong resemblance to the extended, limited and routinised responses identified earlier with respect to the consumer market.

Organisational buying, according to Webster and Wind (1972), is 'the decision making process by which formal organisations establish the need for purchased products and services and identify, evaluate and choose among alternative brands and suppliers'. Of particular significance is the relationship that develops between organisations that enter market exchange transactions. As mentioned previously, the various networks that organisations belong to will influence the purchase decisions that other organisations in the network make. However, before exploring these issues, it is necessary to review the context in which organisational decisions are made.

One way of examining the context is to compare organisational decisions with those made in consumer markets. There are far fewer buyers in the organisational context than in the consumer market, although there can be a number of people associated with a buying decision in an organisation. Orders are invariably larger and the frequency with which they are placed is much lower. It is quite common for agreements to be made

Table 3.2 The main characteristics of the buyclasses

Buyclass	Degree of familiarity with the problem	Information requirements	Alternative solutions
New buy	The problem is fresh to the decision-makers.	A great deal of information is required.	Alternative solutions are unknown, all are considered new.
Modified rebuy	The requirement is not new but is different from previous situations.	More information is required but past experience is of use.	Buying decision needs new solutions.
Rebuy	The problem is identical to previous experiences.	Little or no information is required.	Alternative solutions not sought or required.

between organisations for the supply of materials over a number of years. Similarly, depending upon the complexity of the product (photocopying paper or a one-off satellite), the negotiation process may also take a long time.

Many of the characteristics associated with consumer decision-making processes can be observed in the organisational context. However, organisational buyers make decisions which ultimately contribute to the achievement of corporate objectives. To make the necessary decisions, a high volume of pertinent information is often required. This information needs to be relatively detailed and is normally presented in a rational and logical style. The needs of the buyers are many and complex and some may be personal. Goals, such as promotion and career advancement within the organisation, coupled with ego and employee satisfaction combine to make organisational buying an important task, one that requires professional training and the development of expertise if the role is to be performed optimally.

Reference has been made on a number of occasions to organisational buyers, as if these people are the only representatives of an organisation to be involved with the purchase decision process. This is not the case, as very often a large number of people are involved in the purchase decision. This group is referred to as either the decision-making unit (DMU) or the buying centre.

Buying centres vary in size and composition in accordance with the nature of each individual task. Webster and Wind (1972) identified a number of people who make up the buying centre.

Users are people who not only initiate the purchase process but also use the product, once it has been acquired, and evaluate its performance. *Influencers* very often help set the technical specifications for the proposed purchase and assist the evaluation of alternative offerings by potential suppliers. *Deciders* are those who make purchasing decisions. In repeat buying activities the buyer may well also be the decider. However, it is normal practice to require that expenditure decisions involving sums over a certain financial limit be authorised by other, often senior, managers. *Buyers* (purchasing managers) select suppliers and manage the process whereby the required products are procured. As identified previously, buyers may not decide which product is to be purchased but they influence the framework within which the decision is made.

Gatekeepers have the potential to control the type and flow of information to the organisation and the members of the buying centre. These gatekeepers may be technical personnel, secretaries or telephone switchboard operators.

The size and form of the buying centre is not static. It can vary according to the complexity of the product being considered and the degree of risk each decision is perceived to carry for the organisation. Different roles are required and adopted as the nature of the buying task changes with each new purchase situation (Bonoma, 1982). It is vital for seller organisations to identify members of the buying centre and to target and refine their messages to meet the needs of each member of the centre.

The task of the communications manager and the corresponding sales team is to decide which key participants have to be reached, with which type of message, at what frequency, and to what depth should contact be made. Just like individual consumers, each member of the buying centre is an active problem-solver and processes information so that personal and organisational goals are achieved.

Influences on the buying centre

Three major influences on organisational buyer behaviour can be identified as stakeholders, the organisational environment and those aspects which the individual brings to the situation, as set out in Table 3.3.

Stakeholders develop relationships between the focus organisation and other stakeholders in the network. The nature of the exchange relationship and the style of

Table 3.3 Major influences on organisational buying behaviour

Stakeholder influences	Organisational influences	Individual influences
Economic conditions	Corporate strategy	Personality
Legislation	Organisational culture and values	Age
Competitor strategies	Resources and costs	Status
Industry regulations	Purchasing policies and procedures	Reward structure and systems
Technological developments	Interpersonal relationships	
Social and cultural values		
Inter-organisational relationships		

Source: Based on Webster and Wind (1972).

communications will influence buying decisions. If the relationship between organisations is trusting, mutually supportive and based on a longer-term perspective (a relational structure) then the behaviour of the buying centre may be seen to be cooperative and constructive. If the relationship is formal, regular, unsupportive and based on short-term convenience (a market, structure-based relationship) then the purchase behaviour may be observed as courteous yet distant.

Without doubt the major determinant of the organisational environment is the cost associated with switching from one supplier to another (Bowersox and Cooper, 1992). When one organisation chooses to enter into a buying relationship with another organisation, an investment is made in time, people, assets and systems. Should the relationship with the new supplier fail to work satisfactorily, then a cost is incurred in switching to another supplier. It is these switching costs that heavily influence buying decisions. The higher the potential switching costs, the greater the loss in flexibility, and the greater the need to make the relationship appropriate at the outset.

Behaviour within the buying centre is also largely determined by the interpersonal relationships of the members of the centre. Participation in the buying centre has been shown to be highly influenced by the perceptions individuals have of the personal consequences of their contribution to each stage in the process. The more that individuals think they will be blamed for a bad decision or praised for a good one, the greater their participation, influence and visible DMU-related activity (McQuiston and Dickson, 1991). The nature and dispersal of power within the unit can influence the decisions that are made. Power is increasingly viewed from the perspective of an individual's ability to control the flow of information and the deployment of resources (Stone and Gronhaug, 1986). This approach reflects a network approach to, in this case, intra-organisational communications.

Fear and perceived risk

Of the many emotions experienced by individuals fear is an underlying driver of consumer behaviour. Fear is generated by the presence or anticipation of a specific danger or threat. So, rather than fear itself it is the threat of fear that can evoke complex psychophysiological arousal responses (LaTour and Rotfeld, 1997).

Research shows that anxiety and fear can make consumers more risk averse, and the use of scarcity appeals are less likely to be successful. Dunn and Hoegg (2014) report that fear can also motivate individuals to connect with others, as demonstrated by troops on a battlefield (Marshall, 1947), and the victims of natural disasters (Fried, 1963). By sharing experiences and affiliating with others people are effectively trying to manage the fear they perceive. Dunn and Hoegg have demonstrated that this affiliation process in the presence of a threat of fear can also enhance an emotional attachment to a brand. For example, Birkner (2014) reports that Doritos promoted old chip flavours, that were back-from-the-dead, through an online video horror game (Hotel 626). The only reference to Doritos was a small logo in the corner of the screen. Within a month all of these flavours were sold out and a further game was produced (Asylum 626).

The threat of fear induces a sense of risk or uncertainty. The concept of perceived risk, first proposed by Bauer (1960), concerns the negative and positive consequences that are perceived to arise from a purchase decision, whether that might be not to buy or to buy.

Risk is perceived because a buyer has little or no experience of the performance of the product or the decision process associated with the purchase. As Chang and Hsiao (2008) state, perceived risk includes two factors. The first can occur prior to a purchase and the second subsequent to a purchase when an individual experiences the unfavourable consequences of a purchase (Cox and Rich, 1967).

Risk is related not only to brand-based decisions but also to product categories, an especially important aspect when launching new technology products, for example. The level of risk an individual experiences varies through time, across products, and is often a reflection of an individual's propensity to manage risk. Settle and Alreck (1989) suggest that there are five main forms of risk that can be identified and Stone and Gronhaug (1993) added time as a further factor. These are set out in Table 3.4 using the purchase of a laptop to illustrate each element.

What constitutes risk is a function of the contextual characteristics of each situation, the individuals involved and the product under consideration. Indeed, it is possible to use contextual risk to frame communications when launching new products, as evidenced through the launch of Sensodyne Pronamel (Chapter 1 case), Ready Baked Jackets (Chapter 4 case), and the Kärcher window cleaning system (Chapter 20 case) (see Fill, 2015).

A major reason to use marketing communications, therefore, is to reduce levels of perceived risk. By providing extensive and relevant information a buyer's risks can be reduced substantially. Mass media, word of mouth, websites and sales representatives, for example, are popular ways to set out the likely outcomes from purchase and so reduce the levels of risk. Brand loyalty can also be instrumental in reducing risk when launching new products. The use of guarantees, third-party endorsements, money-back offers (some car manufacturers offer the opportunity to return a car within 30 days or exchange it for a different model) and trial samples (as used by many haircare products) are also well-used devices to reduce risk.

Table 3.4 Types of perceived risk

Type of perceived risk	Explanation
Performance	Will the laptop perform all the functions properly?
Financial	Can I afford that much or should I buy a less expensive version?
Physical	Is the laptop built to the required safety standards . . . will it catch fire?
Social	Will my friends and colleagues approve?
Ego	Will I feel cool about using this equipment?
Time	Can I afford the right amount of time to search for a good laptop?

Source: Derived from Settle and Alreck (1989) and Stone and Gronhaug (1993).

Many websites and direct-response magazine ads seek to reduce a number of different types of risk. Companies offering wine for direct home delivery, for example, try to reduce performance risk by providing information about each wine being offered. Financial risk is reduced by comparing the 'special' prices with those in the high street, social risk is approached by developing the brand name associations trying to improve credibility and time risk is reduced through the convenience of home delivery.

Scholars' paper 3.3   Well, it must be risky

Stone, R.N. and Gronhaug, K. (1993) Perceived risk: further considerations for the marketing discipline, *European Journal of Marketing*, 27(3), 39–50.

Readers interested in consumer behaviour and marketing communications should understand the basic principles associated with perceived risk. This is the seminal paper in this area, although the concept was introduced much earlier by Bauer. This paper provides an insight into the literature and issues associated with perceived risk and references the uncertainty experienced by consumers when making purchasing decisions.

See also: Boshoff, C., Schlechter, C. and Ward, S.-J. (2011) Consumers' perceived risks associated with purchasing on a branded website: the mediating effect of brand knowledge, *South African Journal of Business Management*, 42(1), 45–54.

Involvement theory

One of the factors thought to be key to brand choice decisions is the level of involvement a consumer has with either the product or the purchase process. Involvement is about the degree of personal relevance and risk perceived by consumers when making a particular purchase decision (Rossiter et al., 1991). This implies that the level of involvement may vary through time as each member of the target market becomes more (or less) familiar with the purchase and associated communications. At the point of decision-making, involvement is high or low, not somewhere on a sliding scale or on a continuum between two extremes.

High involvement

High involvement occurs when a consumer perceives an expected purchase that not only is of high personal relevance but also represents a high level of perceived risk. Cars, washing machines, houses and insurance policies are seen as 'big ticket' items, infrequent purchases that promote a great deal of involvement. The risk described is financial but, as we saw earlier, risk can take other forms. Therefore, the choice of perfume, suit, dress or jewellery may also represent high involvement, with social risk dominating the purchase decision. Consumers therefore devote a great deal of time to researching these intended purchases and collect as much information as possible in order to reduce, as far as possible, levels of perceived risk.

Low involvement

A low-involvement state of mind suggests that an intended purchase represents little threat or risk. Low-priced items such as washing powder, baked beans and breakfast cereals are bought frequently. Purchase and consumption experience of the product class and the brand provides purchase cues, so little information or support is required. Items such as alcoholic and soft drinks, cigarettes and chocolate are also normally seen as low involvement, but they induce a strong sense of ego risk associated with the self-gratification that is attached to the consumption of these products.

Two approaches to decision-making

From this understanding of general decision-making processes, perceived risk and involvement theory, it is possible to identify two main approaches to consumer decision-making.

High-involvement decision-making

If an individual is highly involved with the initial purchase of a product, EPS is the appropriate decision sequence, as information is considered to be processed in a rational, logical order. Individuals who are highly involved in a purchase are thought to move through the process shown in Figure 3.9. When high-involvement decision-making is present, individuals perceive a high level of risk and are concerned about the intended purchase. The essential element in this sequence is that a great deal of information is sought initially and an attitude is developed before a commitment or intention to trial is determined.

Information search is an important part of the high-involvement decision-making process. Because individuals are highly motivated, information is actively sought, processed and evaluated. Many media sources are explored, including websites, the mass media, word-of-mouth communications, and point-of-sale communications. As individuals require a lot of information, print media used to be the primary media where high involvement was identified. Today, websites are the primary source of large volumes of detailed information. Unlike print, these sites can also be updated quickly but both types enable visitors to search and process information at a speed they can control.

Viewpoint 3.3   **'Live Chat' reduces booking anxiety at Exodus**

Exodus offers adventure and alternative experience based holidays such as walking, cycling and trekking trips, cross-country skiing, and wildlife, polar and dogsledding expeditions. A typical Exodus customer is a 40-year-old city dweller with a high level of disposable income. Although they are computer literate and are totally familiar with online booking processes, committing to a once in a lifetime holiday experience can involve substantial perceived risks associated with finance, physical safety, social, ego and time associated with the decision-making and booking process. As a result of their high involvement they appreciate advice and guidance in order to follow through and invest their financial resources, time, and energy.

It was clear that website bookings needed to be improved in order to attract, engage and convert website visitors in order to boost online bookings. A 'Live Chat' facility was available 24/7, with users sending a message to invite an expert to discuss their holiday requirements. This served to improve engagement rates and facilitate the collection of pertinent customer data used to feed promotional activities.

Part of the issue, however, was that the 'Live Chat' tool was positioned at the foot of the web pages. Action was required to make visitors more aware of the 'Live Chat' tool. A pop-up, designed to invite a chat or offer a callback, was designed to get the attention of site visitors. The pop-up was triggered after a site visitor had been on the site for a minute on the home page. The timing and frequency of the pop-up varies according to the average time spent on the page. Roughly 1,500 visitors per month will engage with a Live Chat expert each month and of these 50 per cent are regarded as hot leads.

Exodus have introduced a content targeting tool to aim sales promotions and guide site traffic to particular parts of the website. Communications were targeted at either new customers with special offers or current customers with incentives to book another trip. Non-sales messages are used during periods when the use of price offers is not necessary. These are used to boost the Exodus online community and help develop user generated content and encourage customer feedback.

These changes have had a big impact on performance. Online sales have increased by 14 per cent reflecting the improvement in conversion rates; 25 per cent of online sales are now generated through Live Chat, and 75 per cent of the hot leads proceed to make a booking.

Source: Bolger (2014); www.exodus.co.uk.

Question:	To what extent is Live Chat a facility designed to overcome the impersonal nature of website technology?
Task:	Make a list of product categories where this type of facility would be inappropriate

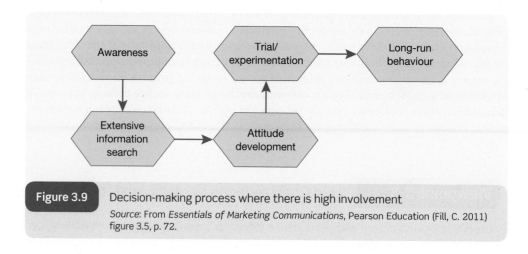

Figure 3.9	Decision-making process where there is high involvement

Source: From *Essentials of Marketing Communications*, Pearson Education (Fill, C. 2011) figure 3.5, p. 72.

Low-involvement decision-making

If an individual has little involvement with an initial purchase of a product, LPS is the appropriate decision process. Information is processed cognitively but in a passive, involuntary way. Processing occurs using right-brain thinking so information is stored as it is received, in sections, and this means that information is stored as a brand association (Heath, 2000). An advertisement for Andrex toilet tissue featuring a puppy is stored as the 'Andrex Puppy' without any overt thinking or reasoning. Because of the low personal relevance and perceived risk associated with this type of processing, message repetition is necessary to define brands and create meaningful brand associations. Individuals who have a low involvement with a purchase decision choose not to search for information and are thought to move through the process shown in Figure 3.10.

Communications can assist the development of awareness in the low-involvement decision-making process. However, as individuals assume a passive problem-solving role, messages need to be shorter than in the high-involvement process and should contain less information. Broadcast media are preferred as they complement the passive learning posture adopted by individuals. Repetition is important because receivers have little or

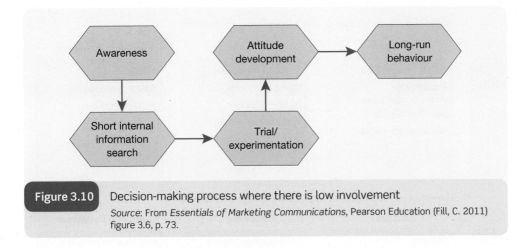

Figure 3.10 Decision-making process where there is low involvement

Source: From *Essentials of Marketing Communications*, Pearson Education (Fill, C. 2011) figure 3.6, p. 73.

no motivation to retain information, and their perceptual selection processes filter out unimportant information. Learning develops through exposure to repeated messages, but attitudes do not develop at this part of the process (Harris, 1987).

Where low involvement is present, each individual relies upon internal, rather than external, search mechanisms, often prompted by point-of-purchase displays.

Impact on communications

Involvement theory is central to our understanding of the way in which information is processed and the way in which people make decisions about product purchases. We have established in the preceding section that there are two main types of involvement, high and low. These two types lead directly to two different uses of marketing communications. In decisions where there is high involvement, attitude precedes trial behaviour. In low-involvement cases this position is reversed.

Where there is high involvement, consumers seek out information because they are concerned about the decision processes and outcomes. This can be because of the levels of uncertainty associated with the high costs of purchase and usage, inexperience of the product (category) – often due to the infrequency of purchases – the complexity of the product and doubts about its operational usefulness. Because they have these concerns, people develop an attitude prior to behaviour. Informational ads that require cognitive processing are recommended.

Where there is low involvement, consumers are content to select any one of a number of acceptable products and often rely on those that are in the individual's evoked set. Low involvement is thought to be a comfortable state, because there are too many other decisions in life to have to make decisions about each one of them, so an opportunity not to have to seek information and make other decisions is welcome. See Figure 3.11, which indicates the marketing communications strategies best suited for each level within both involvement sequences. Emotional or transformational ads are recommended.

Planning communications based on involvement are not as straightforward as the preceding material might suggest. There are various factors that might influence the outcomes. For example, some individuals who are cognitively capable of processing information may not always be able to process information in information-based ads because they are overloaded. In these circumstances they are more likely to develop positive attitudes towards affective or transformational ads. Ranjbariyan and Mahmoodi (2009) also found that people under time pressure are more prone to use transformational ads, as they will pick up visual cues to help their decision-making.

The material presented so far in this section is based on classical research, theoretical development and is supported by empirical research. However, much of the knowledge has

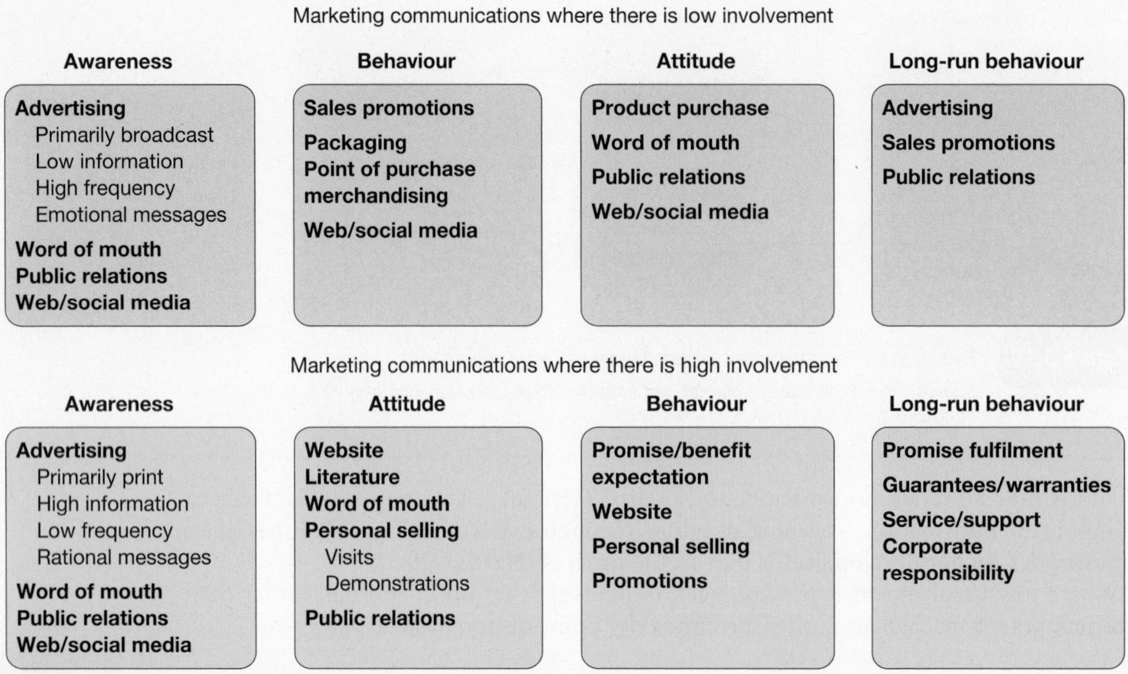

Marketing communications where there is low involvement

Awareness	Behaviour	Attitude	Long-run behaviour
Advertising Primarily broadcast Low information High frequency Emotional messages **Word of mouth** **Public relations** **Web/social media**	**Sales promotions** **Packaging** **Point of purchase merchandising** **Web/social media**	**Product purchase** **Word of mouth** **Public relations** **Web/social media**	**Advertising** **Sales promotions** **Public relations**

Marketing communications where there is high involvement

Awareness	Attitude	Behaviour	Long-run behaviour
Advertising Primarily print High information Low frequency Rational messages **Word of mouth** **Public relations** **Web/social media**	**Website** **Literature** **Word of mouth** **Personal selling** Visits Demonstrations **Public relations**	**Promise/benefit expectation** **Website** **Personal selling** **Promotions**	**Promise fulfilment** **Guarantees/warranties** **Service/support** **Corporate responsibility**

Figure 3.11 Marketing communications approaches for the two levels of involvement
Source: From *Essentials of Marketing Communications*, Pearson Education (Fill, C. 2011) figure 3.7, p. 74.

been developed in a non-digital era, and that raises questions about the depth of its validity in the contemporary world. Foley et al. (2009) undertook research that showed that people organise product categories according to the level of risk associated with brand-choice decisions and the level of reward, together with the enjoyment people derive from the decisions they make. They also found that the types of categories people organise lead to different patterns of decision-making. Four main product categories were identified:

1. *Routine.*

   In this category people perceive low risk and low reward. Brand choice decision-making is therefore characterised by inertia and decision-making is robotic.

2. *Burden.*

   People perceive high risk and low reward. Search is extensive and decision-making improved if someone can assist.

3. *Passion.*

   Risk is high and reward is high because people are emotionally engaged with these types of products and services. The symbolism and meaning attached to brands in the category is high, reflected in high ego and social risks.

4. *Entertainment.*

   People use this category where risk is low but reward can be high. This means that decision-making can be a pleasant, if brief, experience.

Each of these categories has implications for the communications strategies necessary to reach people and be effective. For example, consideration of the type of website that best suits each of these categories provides immediate insight into how having an understanding or insight into the target audience can shape marketing communications.

Other approaches

Consideration so far has been given to what might be called 'the rational and cognitive approach' to both information processing and decision-making. These are informative and enable us to build an organised understanding. Indeed, organisations often instal logical buying procedures as a means of controlling and managing the procurement process.

Many organisations recognise that the linear, logic journey that consumer decision follows is no longer relevant. As a result they now consider issues concerning customer experience, and focus on maximising engagement opportunities at particular 'touchpoints' on a consumer journey. There is a view that this approach misses the bigger picture of a consumer's overall decision journey (Rawson et al., 2013). As will be seen shortly, implicit decision-making concerns the emotional value that people attach to the various options they are faced with when making a decision. Damasio (1996) argues that when faced with time pressures or too many options, complex decisions are resolved by choosing an option that evokes the greatest number of positive emotional associations (Kent-Lemon, 2013). These implicit heuristics, it is argued, are the emotional shortcuts we use every day, when it is not possible, due to the available time or energy required, to use rational analysis.

A number of different views about consumer decision-making and behaviour have been advanced. Three are considered here. The first to be considered is called *hedonic consumption*, the second is *tribal consumption* and the third is *behavioural economics*, which, although not new, has received increased attention recently. All have implications for the way marketing communications should be used.

Hedonic consumption

There is a range of products and services that can evoke high levels of involvement based on the emotional impact that consumption provides buyers. This is referred to as 'hedonic consumption', and Hirschmann and Holbrook (1982) describe this approach as 'those facets of consumer behaviour that relate to the multisensory, fantasy and emotive aspects of one's experience with products'. With its roots partly in the motivation research and partly in the cognitive processing schools, this interpretation of consumer behaviour seeks to explain how and why buyers experience emotional responses to the act of purchase and consumption of particular products.

Historical imagery occurs when, for example, the colour of a dress, the scent of a perfume or cologne, or the aroma of a restaurant or food can trigger an individual's memory to replay an event. In contrast, *fantasy imagery* occurs when a buyer constructs an event, drawing together various colours, sounds and shapes to compose a mental experience of an event that has not occurred previously. Consumers imagine a reality in which they derive sensory pleasure. Some smokers were encouraged to imagine themselves as 'Marlboro Men': not just masculine, but as idealised cowboys (Hirschmann and Holbrook, 1982).

The advertising of fragrances and luxury brands is often based on images that encourage individuals to project themselves into a desirable or pleasurable environment or situation: for example, those which foster romantic associations. Some people form strong associations with particular fragrances and use this to develop and maintain specific images. Advertising is used to create and support these images and, in doing so, enhance the emotional benefits derived from fragrance brand associations. As Retiveau (2007) indicates, hedonics are closely related and influence the simultaneous perception of fragrances.

There are a number of challenges with this approach – namely, measurement factors of reliability and validity; nevertheless, appreciating the dreams, ideals and desires of the target audience can be an important contribution to the creation of promotional messages.

Exhibit 3.6	**Attendance at music festivals represents hedonic consumption**
	Source: Shutterstock.com/Monkey Business Images.

Tribal consumption

Another approach to understanding consumption concerns the concept of individualism and tribes. Cova (1997) identifies two schools of thought about consumption and identity. The Northern school believe that consumption enables individuals to reveal their self-identity in society. People consume as an end in itself as this allows them to *take* meaning for their lives through what they consume. Here consumption is a means of individual differentiation.

The Southern school believe that it is important to maintain a culture's social fabric. As society reconfigures itself into groups of people that, according to Maffesoli (1996), reflect primitive tribes, so the role of consumption evolves into a means of linking people to multiple communities, or tribes. Here consumption is a means of offering value to a tribe (Cooper et al., 2005).

Maffesoli (1996) considers contemporary culture to be not one based on individualism, but one defined by 'fluidity, occasional gatherings and dispersal'. This might be likened to a fragmentation of social groupings (Hamilton and Hewer, 2010) many of which are transient. According to Jenkins (2006), tribes represent a participatory culture where business and social interests and affiliations come together.

Scholars' paper 3.4   Thriving networks and tribal identities

Hamilton, K. and Hewer, P. (2010) Tribal mattering spaces: social-networking sites, celebrity affiliations, and tribal innovations, *Journal of Marketing Management*, 26(3–4), 271–89.

Further to the exploration of tribes in consumer behaviour, these authors use ideas about tribal identities and fandom to explore Web 2.0. They argue that social networks which focus on iconic celebrities provide a rich context to consider the interaction, connectivity, and creativity of the fans that populate them.

See also: Cova, B. and Cova, V. (2001) Tribal aspects of postmodern consumption research, *Journal of Consumer Behaviour*, 1(1), 67–76.

The term 'tribe' refers to communities characterised by people who share emotions, experiences, lifestyles and patterns of consumption. In order that these tribes are able to effect tribal communion (Cova et al., 2007) so that members can reaffirm their identity, various emblems, sites, recognition or support are used. Products and services are not consumed for their utility value, or for the sense of individual identification. Their consumption is considered to be important for the 'linking value' they provide within a tribal network. Tribes serve to link people who share passions and interests, examples of which, according to Hamilton and Hewer (2010), include brands such as Harley-Davidson, Saab, Star Trek and the X-Files, adrenalin activities such as skydiving, dancing, river rafting, or a variety of sports, or even sports stars and celebrities. Tribes are loosely interconnected communities (Cova and Cova, 2001) where bonding and linking represent key activities designed to retain tribal membership (see Exhibit 3.7).

Tribes proliferate on the Internet, thanks mainly to its power to aggregate communities who share similar interests. These e-tribes have the same characteristics as traditional communities: namely, shared rituals and traditions, a similar consciousness of kind, and an obligation, or sense of duty, to the community and to its individual members (Muniz and O'Guinn, 2001). Kozinets (2008) established that there were eight Es that can be associated with e-tribes. These are set out in Table 3.5.

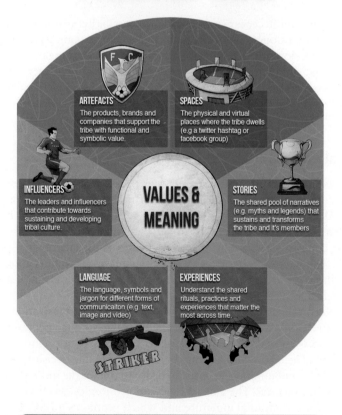

Exhibit 3.7	**The tribal map**
	Source: Elia Mörling / Tribaling.com.

Table 3.5 Eight Es of e-tribes

E reference	Explanation
Electronic	e-tribes communicate via the medium of the Internet
Enculturating	e-tribe members learn and adopt the language, practices, rituals and values of the community
Emotive	e-tribes generate a high level of emotional involvement from members
Expressive	e-tribe members engage in creative, product work
Empowered	e-tribe members gain great satisfaction from the agentic potential of their practices
Evangelical	e-tribe membership can be compared with a quasi-religious or spiritual experience
Emergent	e-tribes are self-generated, emerging on their own rather than under the control of a company
Entangled	Network boundaries overlap and merge

Source: Hamilton and Hewer's (2010) adaption of Kozinets (2008).

According to Hamilton and Hewer, this listing indicates the breadth and complexity of the virtual tribal environment and the openness and opportunities that people have to explore, work, play and become immersed and passionate about interests, which Kozinets et al. (2008) relate to the intimate feelings people experience in childhood.

The recognition and acceptance of e-tribes and tribal consumption for marketing communications practitioners is not clear cut. Indeed, some commentators warn against outright tribal intrusion and recommend activities that encourage a tribe's social and linking behaviours, simply because these are critical for members. Organisations should aim to become listeners and to work 'with' tribes by fostering conversations and enabling them to function through the provision of 'play rich mattering spaces' (Hamilton and Hewer, 2010: 285).

Behavioural economics

Just as ideas about tribal consumption are a rejection of 'rational man' perspectives, so behavioural economics is grounded in the belief that people are 'fundamentally irrational in their decision-making and motivated by unconscious cognitive biases' (Ariely, 2009). The third issue to be considered under the banner of alternative approaches to understanding consumer behaviour, therefore, concerns the emerging popularity of the concept called 'behavioural economics'. One of the interesting points about behavioural economics is that it challenges established thinking, and another is that it is not a million miles from the idea of low-attention processing.

Behavioural economics has emerged following decades of frustration with classical economic theory. Conventional economic theory suggests that people make rational choices in their decision-making and even seek to maximise their opportunities and minimise expenditure. The 'rational man' makes the best possible decisions, on the basis of maximising benefits and minimising costs, in order to obtain the most advantageous and efficient economic outcome. The classical view of economics is reflected in advertising that is essentially informational in nature and which promotes a USP. The Persil slogan 'washes whiter' typifies the traditional perspective of advertising: one core message, we are better, faster, safer or cleaner than the rest. The utilisation of behavioural economics in advertising is reflected in the use of emotional content that seeks to embrace audiences and develop brand associations.

Classical economics assumes rational decision-making and that, in general, markets and institutions are self-regulating. The collapse of the banks and much of the financial sector in 2008, however, casts serious doubt on the efficacy of this view. Behavioural economics, therefore, challenges the conventional view about the way people and organisations behave. Indeed, the central platform on which behavioural economics is constructed is behaviour. This moves advertising and marketing communications forward because the focus is no longer on attitudes, beliefs and opinions, USPs, or even on what people intend to do, but on how they behave, what they actually do.

In order to change existing behaviours, or encourage new ones, people need to be presented with a choice that makes decision-making feel effortless, even automatic, or as Gordon (2011) puts it, 'a no-brainer'. Thaler and Sunstein (2008) refer to this as 'choice architecture'. This posits that there is no neutral way to present a choice. People choose according to what is available, not what they absolutely want. What is also important is that they do not expend much energy or thought when they make a choice, and they use *heuristics* or rules of thumb to assist them. As mentioned earlier, these heuristics are thought to be rooted in emotional drivers. See Viewpoint 3.4 for some examples of BE in action.

Table 3.6 Elements of behavioural economics

BE element	Explanation
How	Helping people to make a decision by presenting easy methods can encourage action now, rather than in the future. For example, paying for tickets for a festival online is easier than being in a queue on the telephone. Schemes that require people to opt out are more likely to generate the desired behaviour, than requiring people to make the choice to opt in.
When	When required to do something disagreeable, people are more likely to delay making a decision or taking action – for example, to stop smoking, to complete an income tax return form, or start an essay.
Where	Although price and perceived value can be important, it can be location and convenience that shape a decision. Questions such as 'Do I have to go there to do this or should I do it here where it is convenient?' can often influence behaviour.
Availability	Items that appear to be scarce have a higher value than those items that are plentiful. For example, recorded music is abundant and virtually free, yet live music is relatively expensive, as it is scarce.
Price	The price of an item leads people to give it a value. So, people who pay more for a product/service often perceive increased benefit or gain. However, price needs to be contextualised and supported by other indicators of value.
Task duration	People prefer to complete parts of a task rather than try to finish in a single attempt. Therefore, the way a task is presented can influence the behaviour and the number of people completing the task. Filling in forms seems less daunting with the opportunity to save and return. Colour coding antibiotic pills might ensure more people complete the treatment and avoid repeat visits, further illness and lost days from work.

Source: Based on Gordon (2011); IPA (2010).

The idea that people follow a sequential decision-making process is a long way from the truth. Both Kooreman and Prast (2010) and Grapentine and Altman Weaver (2009) agree that people's behaviour is often not congruent with their intentions, that they are sensitive to the way choices are presented to them, and that they have limited cognitive abilities. However, not everyone agrees that BE is a good step forward. For example, Mitchell (2010) puts forward a number of doubts about the validity of the concept.

So, purchase decisions are not made deliberatively and consciously by evaluating all permutations and outcomes. Decisions are made around choices that are based on comparison, rather than absolutely. These decisions are based on what is available rather than scanning the whole market or options and, as Gordon says, in terms of 'how this makes me feel' both emotionally and instinctively, but not rationally.

One of the main areas in which behavioural economics impacts upon advertising and brand communications is choice architecture. Indeed, the Institute of Practitioners in Advertising (IPA, 2010) has embraced behavioural economics and observed its relevance to campaign planning, purchase decisions, brand experiences, how behaviour can be changed, and the way that choice works in complex situations. All of these can be reflected in the advertising and brand communications.

Viewpoint 3.4   BE drives action and behaviour

Various organisations have adopted behavioural economics, partly as a result of the IPA championing it by providing visibility, information and insight. Here are a few examples:

Fire safety – attitudes and intentions often have a very weak correlation to actual behaviour in real life. This can be seen when people say testing their smoke alarms is important, but in reality many don't actually follow through and test. As a result over 100 people die in house fires in England each year, in dwellings where there was a non-working fire alarm.

There have been many previous attitudinal campaigns designed to encourage and motivate people to test their alarms. This campaign used the ideas of behavioural economics and focused on changing behaviour by decreasing the perceived effort required to test the alarms. The campaign nudged people into testing their smoke alarms by piggy-backing on existing behaviours, namely the twice-yearly clock change.

A print campaign featured a single powerful image of a burnt clock in the context of a real home. The ad was designed to look as if it was forensic evidence retrieved from a home that had been on fire. The goal was to provide a visual stimulus between the need to change our clocks (twice a year) and the need to test smoke alarms.

Hyundai – consumer fear at the huge depreciation incurred when buying a new car prompted Hyundai into reframing the choice car buyers are faced with. Instead of shying away from the issue, Hyundai offered new car buyers a guaranteed price for their car, valid for four years after purchase. Television advertising was used to communicate the deal and so reduce perceived risk.

Transport for London (TfL) had been telling people about the advantages of cycling to work for many years, but the communications had not been very successful. So, rather than keep telling people, TfL installed a bicycle hire scheme, sponsored by Barclays, which enabled two things. First, people could hire a bike and leave it at a designated point in London, and avoid capital outlay, maintenance, and storage costs. Second, the scheme encouraged a change in behaviour because the bikes were made available, and their distinctive Barclays logo and bike stands are visible across the capital.

Cadbury's reintroduced the Wispa bar in 2007 following its axing in 2003, and the subsequent campaigns on various social network sites Bebo, Myspace and Facebook, and a stage rush by Wispa fans at

Exhibit 3.8	**Burnt clocks used in a fire safety campaign**
	Source: Contains public sector information licensed under the Open Government Licence v3.0.

Glastonbury. Instead of simply announcing its return, Cadbury's announced that Wispa would be back with a special-edition limited run. Sales went through the roof, and the Wispa bar was available on a regular basis. However, by announcing a limited run of the brand it encouraged people to think that they needed to buy a Wispa, otherwise it would be removed once again. In other words, loss aversion was used to stimulate demand.

Source: Huntley and Hoad (2014); McCormick (2011); Panlogic (2011).

Question: Choose a brand and consider ways in which the principles of behavioural economics might be utilised.

Task: Choose three product categories and make notes about the way behavioural economics might be applied to enhance communications.

Key points

- Awareness of the existence and availability of a product/service or an organisation is necessary before information can be processed and purchase behaviour expected. Much of marketing communications activity is directed towards getting the attention of the target audience.

- Awareness needs to be created, developed, refined or sustained, according to the characteristics of the market and the particular context facing an organisation (or audience) at any one point in time.

- Perception is concerned with how individuals see and make sense of their environment. The way in which individuals perceive, organise and interpret stimuli is a reflection of their past experiences and the classifications used to understand the different situations each individual frames every day.

- Marketing communications is used to position brands using a variety of stimuli so that consumers understand and recognise them.

- There are three factors important to the behavourist approach to learning: association, reinforcement and motivation. Behaviour is learned through the conditioning experience of a stimulus and response.

- Cognitive learning considers learning to be a function of an individual's attempt to control their immediate environment. Cognitive learning is about processing information in order that problems can be resolved. Central to this process is memory.

- Information-handling processes can range from the simple to the complex. There are three main processes: iconic, modelling and reasoning.

- Attitudes are predispositions, shaped through experience, to respond in an anticipated way to an object or situation. Attitudes are learned through past experiences and serve as a link between thoughts and behaviour. Attitudes tend to be consistent within each individual: they are clustered and very often interrelated. Attitudes consist of three interrelated elements: the cognitive, affective and conative, otherwise referred to as learn, feel, do.

- Marketing communications can be used to influence the attitudes held by a target market. When developing campaigns, consideration needs to be given to the current and desired attitudes to be held by the target audience. The focus of communications activities can be on whether the audience requires information (learning), an emotional disposition (feeling) or whether the audience needs to be encouraged to behave in a particular way (doing).

- Classical theory suggests that there are five stages to the general process whereby buyers make purchase decisions and implement them. These are problem recognition, information search, alternative evaluation, purchase decision and post-purchase evaluation. Organisations use marketing communications in different ways in order to influence these different stages.

- Buyers do not follow the general purchase decision sequence at all times and three types of problem-solving behaviour are experienced by consumers. These are extended problem solving, limited problem solving and routinised response. The procedure may vary depending upon the time available, levels of perceived risk and the degree of involvement a buyer has with the type of product.

- The organisational buying decision process consists of six main stages or buyphases. These are need/problem recognition, product specification, supplier and product search, the evaluation of proposals, supplier selection and evaluation.

- There are a wide variety of individuals involved in organisational purchase decisions. There are *users*, *influencers*, *deciders*, *buyers* and *gatekeepers*. All fulfil different functions, all have varying degrees of impact on purchase decisions and all require different marketing communications in order to influence their decision-making.

- Consumers and organisational buyers experience risk when making purchasing decisions. This risk is perceived and concerns the uncertainty of the proposed purchase and the outcomes that will result from a decision to purchase a product. Five types of perceived risk can be identified. These are ego, social, physical, financial and performance risks.

- Individuals and groups make purchasing decisions on behalf of organisations. Different types of risk can be experienced, relating to a range of organisational and contextual issues. Marketing communications has an important task to reduce risk for consumers and organisational buyers.

- Involvement is about the degree of personal relevance and risk perceived by individuals in a particular purchase situation. Individuals experience involvement with products or services to be purchased.

- The level of involvement may vary through time as each member of the target market becomes more (or less) familiar with the purchase and associated communications. At the point of decision-making, involvement is either high or low.

- Some products and services can evoke high levels of involvement based on the emotional impact that consumption provides the buyer. This is referred to as *hedonic consumption* and refers to behaviour that relates to the multi-sensory, fantasy and emotive aspects of an individual's experience with products. *Historical imagery* and *fantasy imagery* are two aspects of hedonic consumption.

- Tribes are loosely interconnected communities where bonding and linking represent key activities designed to retain tribal membership. Tribes serve to link people who share passions and interests and 'tribal consumption' refers to consumption of products and services, not for their utility value, or for the sense of individual identification. Their consumption is considered to be important for the 'linking value' they provide within a tribal network.

- Tribes proliferate on the Internet, thanks mainly to its power to aggregate communities who share similar interests. These e-tribes have the same characteristics as traditional communities: namely, shared rituals and traditions, a similar consciousness of kind, and an obligation, or sense of duty, to the community and to its individual members.

- Behavioural economics is grounded in the belief that people make irrational rather than rational decisions and the central platform is about actual behaviour, not attitudes or opinions. People choose according to what is available, not what they absolutely want.

Review questions

Dacia case questions

1. How might an understanding of perception have assisted Dacia's marketing communications?

2. Identify the different types of perceived risk that potential Dacia customers might have experienced. How did Dacia's communications help reduce them?

3. Explain how Dacia's marketing communications can be understood in terms of learning theory.

4. Explain how Dacia's marketing communications can be interpreted in the light of attitude theory.

5. Explain ways in which the *intellectual alibi* assisted Dacia customers in their decision-making processes.

General questions

1. Make brief notes explaining each of the following: buyclasses, buying centre, EPS, LPS and RRB.

2. Describe the high- and low-involvement decision-making processes. How do these help the practice of marketing communications?

3. Make brief notes about the characteristics of each of the attitude components and explain how marketing communications can be used to change attitudes.

4. Find examples of tribal consumption or hedonic consumption.

5. What is behavioural economics and what does it mean for marketing communications?

References

Anon (2011) Voluntary sector: the week in charities, *PR Week UK*, 4 November, retrieved 21 March 2012 from www.brandrepublic.com/features/1102013/Voluntary-Sector-Week-Charities/?DCMP=ILC-SEARCH.

Ariely, D. (2009) The end of rational economics, *Harvard Business Review,* July–August, 78–84.

Bauer, R.A. (1960) Consumer behaviour as risk taking, in *Dynamic Marketing in the Changing World,* (ed. R.S. Hancock) Chicago, IL: American Marketing Association, 389–98.

Birkner, C. (2014) Fear factor: scary situations can result in greater brand attachment, research shows, *Marketing News*, June, 98–112.

Bolger, M. (2014) Exodus's digital strategy, *The Marketer,* March, retrieved 8 June 2015 from www.themarketer.co.uk/how-to/case-studies/exodus-digital-strategy/.

Bommel van, E., Edelman, D. and Ungerman, K. (2014) Digitising the consumer decision journey, *McKinsey,* June, retrieved 14 January 2015 from www.mckinsey.com/insights/marketing_sales/digitising_the_consumer_decision_journey?cid=other-eml-nsl-mip-mck-oth-1406.

Bonoma, T.V. (1982) Major sales: who really does the buying? *Harvard Business Review,* May/June, 113.

Bowersox, D. and Cooper, M. (1992) *Strategic Marketing Channel Management,* New York: McGraw-Hill.

Chang, H.-S. and Hsiao, H.-L. (2008) Examining the casual relationship among service recovery, perceived justice, perceived risk, and customer value in the hotel industry, *The Service Industries Journal,* 28(4), May, 513–28.

Cohen, J. and Basu, K. (1987) Alternative models of categorisation, *Journal of Consumer Research*, March, 455–72.

Cooper, S., McLoughlin, D. and Keating, A. (2005) Individual and neo-tribal consumption: tales from the Simpsons of Springfield, *Journal of Consumer Behaviour,* 330–44.

Court, D., Elzinga, D., Mulder, S. and Vetvik, O.J. (2009) The consumer decision journey, *McKinsey Quarterly,* June, retrieved 15 January 2015 from www.mckinsey.com/insights/marketing_sales/the_consumer_decision_journey.

Cova, B. (1997) Community and consumption: towards a definition of the 'linking value' of product or services, *European Journal of Marketing,* 31 (May), 297–316.

Cova, B. and Cova, V. (2001) Tribal aspects of postmodern consumption research: the case of French in-line roller skaters, *Journal of Consumer Behaviour,* 1(1), 61–76.

Cova, B., Kozinets, R.V. and Shankar C.A. (2007) *Consumer Tribes,* Oxford: Butterworth-Heinemann.

Cox, D.F. and Rich, S.U. (1967) Perceived risk and consumer decision making – the case of telephone shopping, in *Consumer Behaviour,* (ed. D.F. Cox) Boston, MA: Harvard University Press.

Damasio, A.R. (1996) The somatic marker hypothesis and the possible functions of the prefrontal cortex, *Transactions of the Royal Society (London), 351*(1346), 1413–20.

Dunn, L. and Hoegg, J. (2014) The impact of fear on emotional brand attachment, *Journal of Consumer Research,* 41 (June), 152–68.

Eleftheriou-Smith, L.-M. (2011) Clare Mullin on cleaning out the cobwebs at the National Trust, *Marketing,* 24 August, retrieved 21 March from www.brandrepublic.com/features/1085979/Clare-Mullin-cleaning-cobwebs-National-Trust/?DCMP=ILC-SEARCH.

Fill, C. (2015) In with the new: what can we learn from the newcomer story? In *Advertising Works 22* (ed. L. Hawtin), IPA Effectiveness Awards 2014, London: WARC, 239–43.

Foley, C., Greene, J. and Cultra, M. (2009) Effective ads in a digital age, *Admap,* 503 (March), retrieved 2 June 2010 from www.warc.com/articlecentre.

Fried, M. (1963) 'Grieving for a Lost Home', in *The Urban Condition: People and Policy in the Metropolis* (ed. Leonard J. Duhl) New York: Basic Books, 151–71.

Gordon, W. (2011) Behavioural economics and qualitative research – a marriage made in heaven? *International Journal of Market Research,* 53(2), 171–85.

Grapentine, T.H. and Altman Weaver, D. (2009) What really affects behaviour? *Marketing Research,* 21(4), Winter, 12–17.

Grass, R.C. and Wallace, H.W. (1969) Satiation effects of TV commercials, *Journal of Advertising Research,* 9(3), 3–9.

Hamilton, K. and Hewer, P. (2010) Tribal mattering spaces: social-networking sites, celebrity affiliations, and tribal innovations, *Journal of Marketing Management,* 26(3–4), 271–89.

Harris, G. (1987) The implications of low involvement theory for advertising effectiveness, *International Journal of Advertising,* 6, 207–21.

Hawkins, D., Best, R. and Coney, K. (1989) *Consumer Behaviour,* Homewood, IL: Richard D. Irwin.

Heath, R. (2000) Low-involvement processing, *Admap,* March, 14–16.

Heath, R. (2001) Low involvement processing – a new model of brand communication, *Journal of Marketing Communications,* 7, 27–33.

Hirschmann, E.C. and Holbrook, M.B. (1982) Hedonic consumption: emerging concepts, methods and propositions, *Journal of Marketing,* 46 (Summer), 92–101.

Huntley, A. and Hoad, A. (2014) Fire safety – IPA effectiveness awards 2014, retrieved 15 January 2015 from www.ipa.co.uk/page/fire-safety-2014-ipa-effectiveness-awards-shortlist-interview\#.VLffpUesUh8.

IPA (2010) *Behaviour Economics: Red Hot or Red herring?* London: IPA.

Javalgi, R., Thomas, E. and Rao, S. (1992) US travellers' perception of selected European destinations, *European Journal of Marketing,* 26(7), 45–64.

Jenkins, H. (2006) *Fans, Bloggers and Gamers: Essays on Participatory Culture,* New York: New York University Press.

Kent-Lemon, N. (2013) Researching implicit memory: get to the truth, *Admap,* May, retrieved 16 January 215 from www.warc.com/Content/ContentViewer.aspx?ID=dd4efd93-d775-42b3-bcdb-569f914b74a7&MasterContentRef=dd4efd93-d775-42b3-bcdb-569f914b74a7&Campaign=admap_may13.

Kooreman, P. and Prast, H. (2010) What does behavioural economics mean for policy? Challenges to savings and health policies in the Netherlands, *De Economist,* 158(2), June, 101–22.

Kozinets, R.V. (2008) e-Tribes and marketing: the revolutionary implications of online communities, Seminar presented at Edinburgh University Business School, 24 November 2008.

Kozinets, R.V., Hemetsberger, A. and Schau, H.J. (2008) The wisdom of crowds: collective innovation in the age of networked marketing, *Journal of Macromarketing,* 28(4), 339–54.

LaTour, M.S.C. and Rotfeld, H.J. (1997) There are threats and (maybe) fear-caused arousal: theory and confusions of appeals to fear and fear arousal itself, *Journal of Advertising,* 26 (Autumn), 45–59.

Maffesoli, M. (1996) *The Time of Tribes,* London: Sage.

Marshall, S.L.A. (1947) *Men Against Fire,* New York: Morrow.

McCormick, A. (2011) Behavioural economics: when push comes to nudge, *Marketing,* 19 May 2011, retrieved 27 April 2012 from www.brandrepublic.com/features/1070184/Behavioural-economics-When-push-comes-nudge/?DCMP=ILC-SEARCH.

McGuire, W. (1978) An information processing model of advertising effectiveness, in *Behavioural and Management Science in Marketing* (eds H.J. Davis and A.J. Silk), New York: Ronald Press, 156–80.

McMeeken, R. (2012) A fresh start, *The Marketer,* March/April, 22–4.

McNeal, M. (2013) A never-ending journey, *Marketing Insights,* Fall, retrieved 21 August 2014 from https://www.ama.org/publications/MarketingInsights/Pages/trader-joes-retail-customer-experience-consumer-behaviour-marketing-metrics-big-data.aspx.

McQuiston, D.H. and Dickson, P.R. (1991) The effect of perceived personal consequences on participation and influence in organisational buying, *Journal of Business,* 23, 159–77.

Mitchell, A. (2010) Behavioural economics has yet to deliver on its promise, *Marketing,* 15 September, 28–9.

Moran, W. (1990) Brand preference and the perceptual frame, *Journal of Advertising Research*, October/November, 9–16.

Muniz, A.M. and O'Guinn, T.C. (2001) Brand community, *Journal of Consumer Research,* 27(4), 412–23.

Panlogic (2011) Getting people to do what you want, retrieved 4 September 2011 from www.panlogic.co.uk/downloads/Behavioural-Economics-Getting-people-to-do-what-you-want.pdf.

Petty, R.E. and Cacioppo, J.T. (1979) Effects of message repetition and position on cognitive responses, recall and persuasion, *Journal of Personality and Social Psychology,* 37 (January), 97–109.

Ranjbariyan, B. and Mahmoodi, S. (2009) The influencing factors in ad processing: cognitive vs. affective appeals, *Journal of International Marketing and Marketing Research,* 34(3), 129–40.

Rawson, A., Duncan, E. and Jones, C. (2013) The truth about customer experience, *Harvard Business Review,* September, 90–98, retrieved 21 August 2014 from http://hbr.org/2013/09/the-truth-about-customer-experience/.

Retiveau, A. (2007) The role of fragrance in personal care products, retrieved 26 October 2008 from www.sensoryspectrum.com/presentations/Fragrances.

Reynolds, J. (2012) KFC rolls out 'his and hers' ads, *Marketing,* 15 February, p. 4.

Robinson, P.J., Faris, C.W. and Wind, Y. (1967) *Industrial Buying and Creative Marketing,* Boston, MA: Allyn & Bacon.

Rossiter, J.R., Percy, L. and Donovan, R.J. (1991) A better advertising planning grid, *Journal of Advertising Research,* October/November, 11–21.

Settle, R.B. and Alreck, P. (1989) Reducing buyers' sense of risk, *Marketing Communications,* January, 34–40.

Staff (2013) National Trust: 50 things to do before you're 11¾, *PR Week,* 15 July, retrieved 19 February 2015 from www.prweek.com/article/1191017/national-trust-50-things-youre-11-3-4.

Stone, R.N. and Gronhaug, K. (1993) Perceived risk: further considerations for the marketing discipline, *European Journal of Marketing,* 27(3), 39–50.

Strong, E.C. (1977) The spacing and timing of advertising, *Journal of Advertising Research,* 17 (December), 25–31.

Thaler, R. and Sunstein, C. (2008) *Nudge: Improving Decisions About Health, Wealth and Happiness,* New York: Yale University Press.

Webster, F.E. and Wind, Y. (1972) *Organisational Buying Behaviour,* Englewood Cliffs, NJ: Prentice Hall.

Williams, K.C. (1981) *Behavioural Aspects of Marketing,* London: Heinemann.

Zielske, H.A. (1959) The remembering and forgetting of advertising, *Journal of Marketing,* 23 (January), 239–43.

Chapter 4
How marketing communications might work

Understanding how marketing communications might work with its rich mosaic of perceptions, emotions, attitudes, information and patterns of behaviour is challenging in itself. Any attempt to understand how marketing communications might work must be cautioned by an appreciation of the complexity and contradictions inherent in this complicated commercial activity.

Aims and learning objectives

The aims of this chapter are to explore some of the theoretical concepts associated with ideas about how marketing communications might work and to consider the complexities associated with understanding how clients can best use marketing communications.

The learning objectives are to enable readers to:

1. explore ideas concerning strategy, engagement and the role of marketing communications;
2. explain how marketing communications works through sequential processing;
3. understand how marketing communications can be used to influence attitudes;
4. appraise the way relationships can be shaped through the use of marketing communications;
5. consider ways in which marketing communications might develop significant value;
6. examine the role marketing communications might play in helping people process information.

McCain – Ready Baked Jackets

Jacket potatoes are traditionally cooked in an oven, for over an hour. Although the taste, aroma and crispiness is deeply satisfying, the length of time they take to cook can be an inconvenience. It is not surprising, therefore, that many consumers cook them in a microwave to speed up the process. The result is a soggy, mediocre, tasteless spud that satisfies hunger but little else. Consumers, therefore, had to either compromise on time by oven baking a potato, or compromise on taste by using a microwave.

This represented a worthy commercial challenge to McCain, whose famous 'Oven Chips' had established their brand credentials as the makers of excellent frozen potato products. After 12 months of development McCain broke the need for compromise when they developed an oven baked jacket potato that was ready in just 5 minutes. The product was a slow-cooked, fluffy jacket potato that had been baked by McCain and then frozen for consumers to be able to enjoy in just 5 minutes from the microwave.

The communications to launch the Ready Baked Jackets (RBJs) had to drive new consumers into the brand and bring consumers to the frozen aisle who were not currently buying into the frozen potato category. We also wanted to convert consumers from making their own jacket potatoes to using McCain's RBJs.

Research revealed that consumers simply didn't believe that a frozen jacket potato that was ready in just 5 minutes from the microwave would taste as good as one that was oven baked. McCain needed their communications to stimulate consumer appetites and to leverage the brand's food credentials by focusing on the delicious end product not the process. We therefore developed a piece of communications which very simply informed consumers that this new product tastes just like an oven baked jacket because that's exactly what it is. Three key reasons to believe were identified: smell/taste/fluffy texture.

Research also found that many consumers who held negative associations towards microwaved food changed their attitude once they had smelt and tasted RBJs. Statements such as 'Tastes really delicious' and 'Tastes the same as a jacket made in the oven' meant that our communications had to drive brand trial.

With this product having such a cynical audience we couldn't rely on advertising alone to tell people how great the product was. Positive mentions and comments from those who had tried the product were shown to be more motivating to the sceptics than anything advertising could deliver. The launch of RBJs therefore had to incorporate a strong word-of-mouth element.

The communications strategy was developed around these three points by matching paid, owned and earned media with the three specific communications tasks. Awareness and appetite appeal had a bias towards paid for media, while trial was matched with owned, and advocacy and conversations utilised earned media.

Awareness and appetite appeal

A heavyweight TV campaign was deployed across February 2012 driving broad awareness of the new product. We identified a time when a cynical audience would be much more open to the concept of a 5-minute jacket: when it was too late to bake one from scratch for an hour in the oven. We coined the concept of the '9 p.m. post-jacket watershed' and ensured a significant amount of TV ratings hit our audience at this time.

An extensive press and outdoor campaign delivered the mouth-watering product visuals across multiple environments to maximise appetite appeal. We also stimulated appetites when people were making their way home thinking about what to have for dinner. We incorporated over 20 large format digital screens that we switched on at 4 p.m. each evening across the campaign.

We worked with JCDecaux to create a series of ten bespoke bus stops across the UK to deliver a unique McCain Jackets experience. The comforting warmth of a jacket potato was delivered through a realistic fibreglass heated potato built into bus shelters to warm up cold hands in a freezing February. With the insight that nothing makes you salivate like the smell of a jacket potato, the product's delicious aroma was delivered by a spray of the scent of freshly baked potatoes when consumers passed the site.

Finally, we built a taste and trial driving element into the bus shelters by incorporating couponing into the six-sheets. At the press of a button consumers were able to collect a 50p-off coupon so they could try McCain Jackets for themselves. This was the first campaign of its kind in the UK.

| Exhibit 4.1 | **Six-Sheet poster with hand warming potato feature** |
Source: PHD Media UK/JCDecaux.

Driving trial

Owned media was used to drive trial once people had been made aware of the product. A 'money-back guarantee' was issued across all product packaging. This meant that potential customers could be reassured that if they weren't satisfied with the product they wouldn't have to pay.

Working alongside the deals to drive further trial was an extensive couponing campaign. During launch there were three million money-off coupons distributed across multiple channels. These coupons successfully generated 300,000 new customers.

An online display running across MSN and AOL networks drove traffic straight through to a sponsored section on MySupermarket.co.uk where consumers could purchase the product. Behaviourally targeted placements also ran on this site, activated when consumers were browsing products that are used as jacket potato toppings, such as grated cheese or baked beans. To target consumers who made jacket potatoes from scratch we ran placements across the fresh potato section within the site.

To maximise in-store sales and act as a final call to action before purchase, a geo-targeted text message campaign was activated to target shoppers as

| Exhibit 4.2 | **Outdoor media timed to meet peak time commuter rush** |
Source: PHD Media UK/JCDecaux.

they entered supermarkets. Over 300,000 texts were delivered targeting the biggest retailers nationally.

Advocacy and conversations

Foodie and convenience food sceptics, Tom Parker-Bowles (food writer for the *Daily Mail*) and Alex James (food writer for the *Sun*) turned out to be our most powerful advocates, once they had tasted the product. In addition to the national press, McCain were also able to get TV editorial, gaining further endorsement and advocacy from some of Britain's best-loved TV celebrities such as Matthew Wright on Channel 5's *The Wright Stuff*, and Holly Willoughby and Philip Schofield on ITV's *This Morning*.

RBJs passed the Good Housekeeping Institute tests, and the GHI endorsement was used across all of our communications and packaging, lending an extra layer of credibility to the product. The Facebook brand page drove awareness, over 100,000 likes and, most importantly, it started and fuelled conversations from consumers about RBJs. Positive reviews of the new product were positioned so that they were the first thing visitors to the page would see.

Results

Paid for media was so successful that we smashed our awareness target (reaching 56 per cent prompted awareness in just 6 weeks) and delivered an impressive RROI of £1.25. Paid media drove 19 per cent of all RBJs sales, double the average contribution of media expected.

McCain RBJs was the most successful FMCG (fast-moving consumer goods) launch of 2012 (Kantar Worldpanel). By December 2012 cumulative penetration had reached 15.6 per cent with the product having been bought by 4.1 million households. This beat the Year 1 target by 50 per cent.

This case was written by Rebecca Clay, Media Director at PHD

Questions relating to this case can be found at the end of this chapter.

Introduction

The McCain case describes aspects of the marketing communications used to launch a new product. A range of tools, media and messages were used within a common theme, and particular time scale, to reinforce predetermined brand messages. What may not be clear is just how these elements work together and how marketing communications might actually work. This chapter explores this topic, and introduces a number of concepts and frameworks that have contributed to our understanding. Ideas about how advertising works dominate the literature, whereas ideas about how marketing communications is thought to work appear to be of secondary importance, which is strange when so much energy is put into the idea of integrated marketing communications. It is clear that there is no single, universally agreed explanation about how marketing communications works. This chapter therefore presents a variety of explanations and interpretations about how marketing communications might work.

The strategic context

For a long time marketing communications was considered to be a purely operational issue, one which worked by delivering messages about products, to audiences who then, if the communications were effective, purchased the product. No real consideration was given to combining or synchronising the tools, reinforcing messages, understanding the target audience or keying the communications into an overall strategy.

This silo approach has changed. Propelled by the emerging focus on a wider range of stakeholders, the excitement about relationship marketing, surging developments in digital technology and media applications (Chapters 18 and 19), and questions concerning integrated marketing communications (Chapter 10), have all served to raise the profile and importance of a strategic orientation for marketing communications.

It could be argued that marketing communications works when it reflects the-corporate-level strategy and supports the marketing plan and other related activities. It does not work simply because it complements strategy, but it certainly will not work unless it does reflect an organisation's marketing and business imperatives.

Engagement and the role of marketing communications

In Chapter 1 the term 'engagement' was introduced to explain the role of marketing communications. 'Engagement', rather like 'integrated marketing communications', is a term that is used regularly and inconsistently by commentators, journalists and academics.

What can be said, however, is that for engagement to occur there must first be some attention or awareness, be that overt or at a low level of processing. Engagement can be considered to consist of two main elements: intellectual and emotional (Thomson and Hecker, 2000). The intellectual element is concerned with audiences engaging with a brand on the basis of processing rational, functional information. The emotional element is concerned with audiences engaging and aligning themselves with a brand's values on the basis of emotional and expressive information.

It follows that marketing communications should be based on the information-processing styles and needs of audiences, and their access to preferred media. Communications should reflect a suitable balance between the need for rational information to meet intellectual needs and expressive types of communications to meet emotional needs of different audiences. These ideas are important foundations and will be returned to later.

Brakus et al. (2009) refer to engagement as a form of (brand) experience. They believe engagement consists of two dimensions both evoked by brand-related stimuli, including the design, packaging, identity, communications and environment. One dimension concerns the sensations, feelings and cognitions experienced individually and subjectively as an internal response. The second concerns the behavioural responses the stimuli prompt. From this it is possible to conclude that the primary role of marketing communications is to engage audiences in one of two ways:

● To drive a response to the message itself, often reflected in building awareness, and brand associations, cultivating brand values or helping to position brands in markets, or the minds of people in target audiences.

● To drive a response to the brand itself. This might be to encourage calls to a particular number, visits to a website, shop or showroom, or participation in a game, discount scheme or other form of entertainment. These requests within a message are referred to as a *call-to-action*.

When engagement occurs an individual might be said to have been positively captivated, and as a result opportunities for further communications activity should increase. Engagement involves attention-getting and awareness but it also encompasses the decoding and processing of information at a conscious or subconscious level, so that meaning can be attributed to a message, at the appropriate time. See Viewpoint 4.1 for an example of how engagement can be generated.

Viewpoint 4.1	Using unusual animals to assist engagement

When First Direct started in 1989, it offered no branches, just 24/7, 365-day telephone banking with a high level of personal service. This challenged the established practices within the banking sector and although the model has been superseded initially by its competitors and then the Internet, First Direct's values have continued to challenge expected attitudes and beliefs.

Although most of the bank's customers are acquired through recommendation, poor recent performance led to the launch of The Unexpected Bank campaign, aimed at acquiring customers in the 25–34 age range.

The essence of the campaign was to communicate the spirit of independence and individuality that still lies at the heart of the bank's brand values. Using First Direct's brand challenger orientation, ideas about deviation emerged that led to the campaign which sought to get people to see the bank in a different, deviated way. The aim of the campaign, therefore, was to encourage people to see the bank's personality as a deviation from what might normally be expected of a bank, the unexpected element. The first phase featured an unbranded 9-second teaser, featuring three 'dubstep birds', which set up consumers to 'expect the unexpected'. This led to more than 6,000 mentions on Twitter and a video which attracted around 150,000 views on YouTube.

The next phase featured above-the-line advertising involving outdoor and a TV ad to drive engagement through awareness and a consideration of what the bank represented. The ads featured various strange and unusual members of the animal kingdom as 'spokes-creatures'. These animals fronted each piece of communications activity. For example, Barry the platypus, half bird, half mammal, who collects vinyl on Colombia Road, captured the essence of The Unexpected Bank.

In addition, behavioural engagement was sought through a series of 10-second direct response ads. Each of these offered potential new customers a £100 incentive to switch to First Direct. The campaign was so successful it had to be pulled six weeks early. This was because the new customer target had been met and, if more customers switched, First Direct felt they would not be able to sustain the required level of customer service.

'The Unexpected Bank' platform was revived in September 2014 and entitled 'little frill'. This campaign centred on the story of a frilled lizard who was frustrated by a number of poor customer service experiences, the solution to which is First Direct. Little Frill has its own Twitter account, with a bio that reads, 'Discerning pizza lover, keen runner and reptilian celebrity. Not a fan of shoddy service.'

Source: Brownsell (2013); Jack (2014); Roderick (2014).

Question: In addition to communicating their differences, how might First Direct have behaved in order to better express their 'deviant' positioning?

Task: Compare the advertising for two other banks. What, if any, are the core differences in their approach?

Successful engagement suggests that understanding and meaning have been conveyed effectively. At one level, engagement through one-way communications enables target audiences to understand, for example, product and service offers, to the extent that the audience is sufficiently engaged to want further communications. This is what advertising does well. At another level, engagement through two-way, or interactive, communications enables information that is relationship-specific (Ballantyne, 2004) to be exchanged. Advertising is not always able to generate or sustain this frequency or type of information exchange so other communications tools are often used to support these relationship needs.

The communications mix has expanded and become more complex managerially, but essentially it is capable of developing brand values, and changing behaviour through the delivery of calls-to-action. From a strategic perspective, the former is oriented to the long term and the latter to the short term. It is also apparent that the significant rise of the below-the-line tools within the mix is partly a reflection of the demise of the USP, but it is also a reflection of the increasing financial pressures experienced by organisations to improve performance and improve returns on investment.

How does marketing communications work?

The main thrust of this chapter is to consider how marketing communications works in order to achieve successful engagement. Despite years of research and speculation by a great many people, there is no single model that can be presented as the definitive way marketing communications works. However, from all the work undertaken in this area, mainly with regard to advertising, a number of views have been expressed, and the following sections attempt to present some of the more influential perspectives. For an interpretation of how advertising might work, this chapter should be read in conjunction with Chapter 11. Here five different interpretations of how marketing communications is considered to work are presented (see Figure 4.1).

For a message to be communicated effectively, it should be meaningful to the participants in the communications process. Messages need to be targeted at the right audience, be capable of gaining attention, and be understandable, relevant and acceptable. For effective communications to occur, messages should be designed that fit the context in which the messages are 'processed'. In the sections that follow, a number of different interpretations about how marketing communications works are considered, each in a different context.

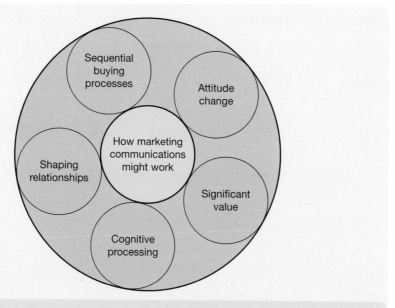

Figure 4.1   Five interpretations of how marketing communications works

HMCW Interpretation 1: Sequential models

Various models have been developed to assist our understanding of how communications tasks are segregated and organised effectively. Table 4.1 shows some of the better-known models. These models were developed primarily to explain how advertising worked. However, the principle of these hierarchical models also applies to marketing communications. The context for all of these sequential models is the general purchase process.

AIDA

Developed by Strong (1925), the AIDA model was designed to represent the stages that a salesperson must take a prospect through in the personal selling process. This model shows the prospect passing through successive stages of attention, interest, desire and action. This expression of the process was later adopted, very loosely, as the basic framework to explain how persuasive communications, and advertising in particular, was thought to work.

Hierarchy of effects models

An extension of the progressive, staged approach advocated by Strong emerged in the early 1960s. Developed most notably by Lavidge and Steiner (1961), the hierarchy of effects models represent the process by which advertising was thought to work and assume that there is a series of steps a prospect must pass through, in succession, from unawareness to actual purchase. Advertising, it is assumed, cannot induce immediate behavioural responses; rather, a series of mental effects must occur, with fulfilment at each stage necessary before progress to the next stage is possible.

The information-processing model

McGuire (1978) contends that the appropriate view of the receiver of persuasive advertising is as an information processor or cognitive problem-solver. This cognitive perspective

Table 4.1 Sequential models of marketing communications

Stage	AIDA[a]	Hierarchy of effects[b]	Information processing[c]
		Awareness	Presentation ↓
Cognitive			Attention
		↓	↓
	Attention	Knowledge	Comprehension
	↓	↓	↓
	Interest	Liking	Yielding
		↓	
Affective		Preference	
	↓	↓	↓
	Desire	Conviction	Retention
Conative	↓	↓	↓
	Action	Purchase	Behaviour

Source: [a]Strong (1925); [b]Lavidge and Steiner (1961); [c]McGuire (1978).

becomes subsumed as the stages presented reflect similarities with the other hierarchical models, except that McGuire includes a retention stage. This refers to the ability of the receiver to understand and retain information that is valid and relevant. This is important, because it recognises that marketing communications messages are designed to provide information for use by a prospective buyer when a purchase decision is to be made at some time in the future.

Difficulties with the sequential approach

For a long time the sequential approach was accepted as the model upon which advertising should be developed. However, questions arose about what actually constitute adequate levels of awareness, comprehension and conviction and how one can determine which stage the majority of the target audience has reached at any one point in time.

The model is based on a logical and sequential movement of consumers towards a purchase via specified stages. The major criticism is that it assumes that the consumer moves through the stages in a logical, rational manner: learn, then feel and then do. This is obviously not the case, as anyone who has taken a child into a sweetshop can confirm. There has been a lot of research that attempts to offer an empirical validation for some of the hierarchy propositions, the results of which are inconclusive and at times ambiguous (Barry and Howard, 1990). Among these researchers is Palda (1966), who found that the learn–feel–do sequence cannot be upheld as a reflection of general buying behaviour and provided empirical data to reject the notion of sequential models as an interpretation of the way advertising works.

The sequential approach sees attitude towards the product as a prerequisite to purchase, but there is evidence that a positive attitude is not necessarily a good predictor of purchase behaviour. Ajzen and Fishbein (1980) found that what is more relevant is the relationship between attitude change and an individual's intention to act in a particular way. Therefore, it seems reasonable to suggest that what is of potentially greater benefit is a specific measure of attitude *towards* purchasing or *intentions* to buy a specific product. Despite measurement difficulties, attitude change is considered a valid objective, particularly in high-involvement situations.

All of these models share the similar view that the purchase decision process is one in which individuals move through a series of sequential stages. Each of the stages from the different models can be grouped in such a way that they are a representation of the three attitude components, these being cognitive (learn), affective (feel) and conative (do) orientations. This could be seen to reflect the various stages in the buying process, especially those that induce high involvement in the decision process but do not reflect the reality of low-involvement decisions.

Scholars' paper 4.1   Let's do it in sequence

Lavidge, R.J. and Steiner, G.A. (1961) A model for predictive measurements of advertising effectiveness, *Journal of Marketing*, 25(6), (October), 59–62.

Published in the *Journal of Marketing* in 1961, this paper was pivotal in changing the way we considered advertising. Up until then advertising research and measurement was very much orientated to techniques and methods. This paper asked the question: what is advertising supposed to do and what function should it have?

The answer was broadly that advertising should help consumers move through the various steps in the purchasing process. Lavidge and Steiner then made the link to the attitude construct, upon which so much work has been done and from which so many ideas have subsequently emerged.

HMCW Interpretation 2: Changing attitudes

Attitude change has been regarded by many practitioners as the main way to influence audiences through marketing communications. Although it is recognised that product and service elements, pricing and channel decisions all play an important part in shaping the attitudes held, marketing communications has a pivotal role in conveying each of these aspects to the target audience and in listening to responses. Branding (Chapter 9) is a means by which attitudes can be established and maintained in a consistent way, and it is through the use of the communications mix that brand positions can be sustained. The final point that needs to be made is that there is a common thread between attributes, attitudes and positioning. Attributes provide a means of differentiation, and positions are shaped as a consequence of the attitudes that result from the way people interpret the associated marketing communications.

Environmental influences on the attitudes people hold towards particular products and services are a consequence of many factors. First, they are a reflection of the way different people interpret the marketing communications surrounding them. Second, they are an expression of their direct experience of using them and, third, they are the result of the informal messages and indirect messages received from family, friends and other highly credible sources of information. These all contribute to the way people perceive (and position) products and services and the feelings they have towards them and towards competing products. Managing brand attitudes is considered to be very important, and marketing communications can play an important part in changing or maintaining the attitudes held by a target audience. There are a number of ways in which attitude change can be implemented through marketing communications.

Influencing the components of the attitude construct

As outlined previously (Chapter 3), attitudes are made up of three components: cognitive, affective and conative. Marketing communications can be used to influence each of these elements: namely, the way people think, feel or behave towards a brand.

Cognitive component

When audiences lack information, misunderstand a brand's attributes or when their perception of a brand is inappropriate, the essential task of marketing communications is to give the audience the correct or up-to-date information. This enables perception, learning and attitude development based on clear truths. This is a rational, informational approach, one that appeals to a person's ability to rationalise and process information in a logical manner. It is, therefore, important that the level and quality of the information provided is appropriate to the intellectual capabilities of the target audience. Other tasks include showing the target audience how a brand differs from those of competitors, establishing what the added value is and suggesting who the target audience is by depicting its members in the message.

Both advertising and public relations are key tools, and the Internet, television, print are key media for delivering information and influencing the way people perceive a brand. Rather than provide information about a central or popular attribute or aspect of an offering, it is possible to direct the attention of an audience to different aspects of an object and so shape its beliefs about a brand in ways that are different to those of competitors. So, some crisp and snack food manufacturers used to communicate the importance of taste. Now in an age of chronic social obesity, many of these manufacturers have changed the salt and fat content and appeal to audiences on the basis of nutrition and health. They have changed the focus of attention from one attribute to another.

Although emotion can be used to provide information, the overriding approach is informational.

Scholars' paper 4.2   Do I really need to get your attention?

Heath, R. and Feldwick, P. (2008) 50 years using the wrong model of TV advertising, *International Journal of Market Research,* **50(1), 29–59.**

For several years Heath (and Feldwick) have challenged the dominance and pervasiveness of the information-processing approach and believe that attention is not necessary for ads to be effective. Students will find this paper helpful because it sets out the arguments and history associated with information processing. The authors argue that people can be influenced by advertising, even when they cannot recall ads. Decision-making is founded on emotions triggered through associations made at subconscious levels.

Affective component

Rational, logical information may not be enough to stimulate behaviour, in which case marketing communications can be used to convey a set of emotional values that will appeal to and, hopefully, engage a target audience.

When attitudes to a brand or product category are discovered to be either neutral or negative, it is common for brands to use an emotional rather than rational or information-based approach. This can be achieved by using messages that are unusual in style, colour and tone and, because they stand out and get noticed, they can change the way people feel and their desire to be associated with that object, brand or product category. There is often great use of visual images and the appeal is often to an individual's senses, feelings and emotional disposition. The goal is to help people feel, 'I (we) like, I (we) desire (aspire to), I (we) want or I (we) belong to' whatever is being communicated. Establishing and maintaining positive feelings towards a brand can be achieved through reinforcement and to do this it is necessary to repeat the message at suitable intervals.

Creating positive attitudes used to be the sole preserve of advertising, but today a range of tools and media can be used. For example, product placement within films and music videos helps to show how a brand fits in with a desirable set of values and lifestyles. The use of music, characters that reflect the values of either the current target audience or an aspirational group, a tone of voice, colours, images, and even brand experience, all help to create a particular emotional disposition and understanding about what the brand represents or stands for.

Perhaps above all else, the use of celebrity endorsers is one of the main ways attitudes are developed. The role for marketing communications is to stimulate desire for the object by helping to make an association (celebrity and brand) which is based on an emotional disposition towards the celebrity. This approach focuses on changing attitudes to the communications (attitudes to the ad) rather than the offering. Fashion brands are often presented using a celebrity model and little or no text. The impact is visual, inviting the reader to make positive attitudes and associations with the brand and the endorser.

Marmite uses an emotional approach based on challenging audiences to decide whether they love or hate the unique taste. The government has used a variety of approaches to change people's attitude to drink/driving, smoking, vaccinations, tax, pensions and the use of rear seat belts, to name but a few of their activities. The government will often use an information approach, but in some cases use an affective approach, based on dramatising the consequences of a particular behaviour to encourage people to change their attitudes and behaviour. The overriding strategy is therefore emotional.

Conative element

In some product categories people are said to be inert because they are comfortable with a current brand, have little reason to buy into a category, do not buy any brand or are just reluctant to change their brand. In these situations attitude change should be based on provoking behaviour. The growth and development of direct marketing, through both online and mobile-based communications, are based partly on the desire to encourage people to do something rather than undertake passive attitude change that does not necessarily result in action or a sale. Accordingly, a conative approach stimulates people to try, test, trial, visit (a showroom or website) a brand, usually free and often without overt commitment.

Sales promotion, personal selling and direct marketing are the key tools used to drive behavioural change. For example, sales promotions are geared to driving behaviour by getting people to try a brand, direct marketing seeks to encourage a response and hence engage in interaction, and salespeople will try to close a customer to get a sale. Advertising can be used to raise awareness and lead people to a store or website.

In addition to these approaches, experiential marketing has become increasingly popular, as it is believed that direct experience of touching, feeling or using a product helps establish positive values and develop commitment. For example, many car manufacturers offer opportunities to test-drive a car not only for a few hours but for several days. They have test circuits where drivers can spend time driving several different cars in the range across different terrains.

The overriding strategy in this context is to provoke customers into action. See Viewpoint 4.2.

| Viewpoint 4.2 | Chipotle change attitudes through their values |

In 1993 Steve Ellis opened the first Chipotle restaurant. Since then the Mexican-based brand has been bought and sold by McDonald's, and has consolidated its position as a fresh food, fast service brand, whose values are diametrically opposed to its larger high street competitors. Their success is mirrored in their third quarter results in 2014 which reflect revenue and strong profit growth, unlike McDonald's whose sales fell. These and other recent industry trends indicate that increasing numbers of customers are getting the message that Chipotle and other alternatives are superior to traditional fast food.

Chipotle's rivals spend, on average, 5 per cent of revenues on advertising. Chipotle spends just 1.75 per cent, with the budget split equally across local, traditional and brand-building activity. What is so distinctive about Chipotle's communications is that they are rooted in storytelling. Unlike their competitors who focus on deals, product features and their corporate brand, Chipotle's work is based around its values and mission to change the way people think about and eat fast food.

The brand launched an animated story called 'back-to-the-start' in 2011. The film tells about the way the food system has been hijacked by commercial and political interests. It depicts a farmer, perhaps Old McDonald, and the emotional journey he followed once his humane family farm was converted into a horrific factory-style farm. Eventually he sees his error and moves back towards a more sustainable farming approach. The film is supported by a haunting version of Coldplay's 'The Scientist', sung by country singer Willie Nelson. At the end of the film, people could download the song on iTunes, with the proceeds benefiting the Chipotle Cultivate Foundation. This is dedicated to creating a sustainable, healthy and equitable food future.

In 2013 Chipotle released *The Scarecrow*. This award-winning film is again an animated statement, but this time about the world of industrial food production. The film features the Crow Foods factory, whose employees are scarecrows, all of whom have lost their farm jobs and are forced into supporting the processed-food system. The film depicts the horror of factory-fed chickens and cows being pumped with additives. The animation ends with the Scarecrow breaking free to open his own fresh food restaurant and the opportunity for viewers to download a free game about farming. Moderate achievement at the game leads to a coupon for free food at Chipotle.

Source: Champagne (2013); Johnson (2014); McGrath (2014); Nudd (2013); Solomon (2014).

Question:	How does this campaign demonstrate how marketing communications can be used to change attitudes?
Task:	Make brief notes outlining other ways in which attitudes towards fast food restaurants might be changed.

HMCW Interpretation 3: Shaping relationships

So far in this chapter the way marketing communications might work has been considered in terms of progressing the buying process, and by changing or influencing attitudes. Here we explore ideas that marketing communications works by influencing relationships. To do this, we shall look first at ideas about the relationship lifecycle, and then consider how marketing communications can support an audience's preferred mode of exchange. The context for this approach is the buyer–seller relationship.

The customer relationship lifecycle

Customer relationships can be considered in terms of a series of relationship–development phases: customer acquisition, development, retention and decline. Collectively these are referred to as the *customer lifecycle*. The duration and intensity of each relationship phase in the lifecycle will inevitably vary and it should be remembered that this representation is essentially idealistic. A customer relationship cycle is represented in Figure 4.2.

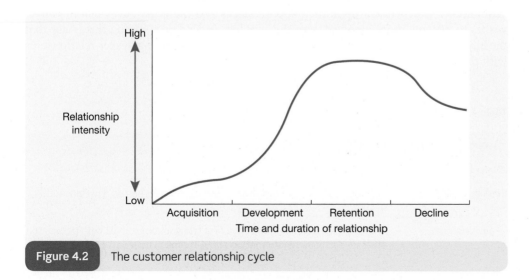

Figure 4.2	The customer relationship cycle

Marketing communications plays an important role throughout all stages of the customer lifecycle. Indeed, marketing communications should be used to engage with audiences according to each audience's relational needs, whether transactional and remote, or collaborative and close.

Customer acquisition

The acquisition phase is characterised by three main events: search, initiation and familiarisation (see Table 4.2).

The logical sequence of acquisition activities moves from search and verification through the establishment of credentials. The length of this initiation period will depend partly on the importance of the buying decision and the complexity of the products, and partly upon the nature of the introduction. If the parties are introduced by an established and trusted source, certain initiation rites can be shortened.

Once a transaction occurs, buyers and sellers start to become more familiar with each other and gradually begin to reveal more information about themselves. The seller receives payment, delivery and handling information about the buyer, and as a result is able to prepare customised outputs. The buyer is able to review the seller's products and experience the service quality of the seller.

During the acquisition phase, marketing communications needs to be geared towards creating awareness and providing access to the brand. Included within this period will be the need to help potential customers become familiar with the brand and to help them increase their understanding of the key attributes, possible benefits from use and to know how the brand is different from and represents value that is superior to the competition. Indeed, marketing communications has to work during this phase because it needs to fulfil a number of different roles and it needs to be targeted at precise audiences. Perhaps the overriding task is to create a set of brand values that are relevant and which represent significant value for the target audience. In DRIP terms, differentiation and information will be important and, in terms of the communications mix, advertising and direct marking in the B2C market and personal selling and direct marketing in the B2B market.

Customer development

The development phase is characterised by a seller attempting to reduce buyer risk and enhancing credibility. This is achieved by encouraging cross-selling. This involves a buyer consuming other products, increasing the volume of purchases, engaging buyers with other added-value services, and by varying delivery times and quantities. The buyer's acquiescence is dependent upon their specific needs and the degree to which the buyer wishes to become more involved with the supplier. Indeed, it is during this phase that the buyer is able to determine whether or not it is worth developing deeper relationships with the seller.

Table 4.2 Customer acquisition events

Acquisition event	Explanation
Search	Buyers and sellers search for a suitable pairing.
Initiation	Both parties seek out information about the other before any transaction occurs.
Familiarisation	The successful completion of the first transaction enables both parties to start revealing more information about themselves.

The main goals during the development phase are for the seller to reduce buyer-perceived risk and to enhance their own credibility. In order to reduce risk, a number of messages will need to be presented though marketing communications. The selection of these elements will depend upon the forms of risk that are present either in the market sector or within individual customers. Marketing communications needs to engage by communicating messages concerning warranties and guarantees, finance schemes, third-party endorsements and satisfied customers, independent testing and favourable product performance reports, awards and the attainment of quality standards, membership of trade associations, delighted customers, growth and market share, new products and alliances and partnerships, all of which seek to reduce risk and improve credibility.

In DRIP terms, information and persuasion will be important, and in terms of the communications mix, public relations, sales promotion and direct marking in the B2C market and personal selling, public relations and direct marketing in the B2B market.

Customer retention

The retention phase is the most profitable, where the greatest level of relationship value is experienced. The retention phase will generally last as long as both the buyer and seller are able to meet their individual and joint goals. If the relationship becomes more involved, greater levels of trust and commitment between the partners will allow for increased cross-buying and product experimentation and, for B2B relationships, joint projects and product development. However, the very essence of relationship marketing is for organisations to identify a portfolio of customers with whom they wish to develop a range of relationships. This requires the ability to measure levels of retention and also to determine when resources are to be moved from acquisition to retention and back to acquisition.

The length of the retention phase will reflect the degree to which the marketing communications is truly interactional and based on dialogue. Messages need to be relational and reinforcing. Incentive schemes are used extensively in consumer markets as a way of retaining customers and minimising customer loss (or churn, defection or attrition). They are also used to cross-sell products and services and increase a customer's commitment and involvement with the brand. Through the use of an integrated programme of communications, value can be enhanced for both parties and relational exchanges are more likely to be maintained. In business markets, personal contact and key account management are crucial to maintaining interaction, understanding and mutual support. Electronic communications have the potential to automate many routine transactions and allow for increased focus on one-to-one communications.

In DRIP terms, reinforcement and information will be important and, in terms of the communications mix, sales promotion and direct marking in the B2C market and personal selling (and key accounts), public relations and direct marketing in the B2B market.

Customer decline

Customer decline is concerned with the closure of a relationship. Termination may occur suddenly as a result of a serious problem or episode between the parties. The more likely process is that the buying organisation decides to reduce its reliance on the seller because its needs have changed, or an alternative supplier who offers superior value has been found. The buyer either formally notifies the established supplier or begins to reduce the frequency and duration of contact and moves business to other, competitive organisations.

The termination process, therefore, may be sharp and sudden, or slow and protracted. Marketing communications plays a minor role in the former but is more significant in the latter. During an extended termination, marketing communications, especially direct marketing in the form of telemarketing and email, can be used to deliver orders and profits. These forms of communications are beneficial, because they allow for continued personal messages but do not incur the heavy costs associated with field selling (B2B) or advertising (B2C).

In DRIP terms, reinforcement and persuasion will be important and, in terms of the communications mix, direct marketing in both markets and sales promotion in the B2C market will be significant.

This cycle of customer attraction (acquisition), development, retention and decline provides a customer- rather than a product-orientated approach to explaining how marketing communications might work. The car manufacturer Audi developed the Audi Customer Journey. This is used to chart the ownership cycle and then to superimpose optimised brand communications for each owner. This approach is reflected in Audi's loyalty rate, which has grown consistently since the 'Journey' was introduced.

Scholars' paper 4.3   **Relationship-based communications**

Gronroos, C. (2004) The relationship marketing process: communication, interaction, dialogue, value, *Journal of Business and Industrial Marketing,* **19(2), 99–113.**

This is a classic paper and one that all students of marketing communications should experience first-hand. Gronroos considers relationship marketing as a process and then explores ideas about planned and integrated marketing communications. He observes that, if the interaction and planned communications processes are successfully integrated and geared towards customers' value processes, a relationship dialogue may emerge. There are a large number of interesting issues in this paper.

Influencing value exchanges

In Chapter 1 the notion of transactional and collaborative exchanges was established. It is within this framework that ideas about how engagement might be established through a relationship marketing perspective are now considered.

A useful way of considering these types of exchanges is to see them at either end of a continuum, as set out in Figure 4.3. At one end of the continuum are transactional

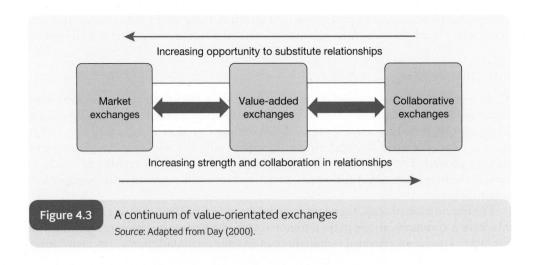

Figure 4.3   A continuum of value-orientated exchanges
Source: Adapted from Day (2000).

exchanges. These are characterised by short-term, commodity- or price-oriented exchanges, between buyers and sellers coming together for one-off exchanges independent of any other or subsequent exchanges. Both parties are motivated mainly by self-interest. Movement along the continuum represents increasingly valued relationships. Interactions between parties are closer, more frequent and stronger. The focus moves from initial attraction, to retention and to mutual understanding of each other's needs.

At the other end of the continuum is what Day (2000) refers to as *collaborative exchanges*. These are characterised by a long-term orientation, where there is complete integration of systems and processes and the relationship is motivated by partnership and mutual support. Trust and commitment underpin these relationships, and these variables become increasingly important as collaborative exchanges become established.

These two positions represent extremes. In the middle there are a range of exchanges where the interaction between customers and sellers is based around the provision and consumption of perceived value. The quality, duration and level of interdependence between buyers and sellers can vary considerably. The reasons for this variance are many and wide-ranging, but at the core are perceptions of shared values and the strength and permanence of any relationship that might exist.

Perceived value may take many forms and be rooted in a variety of attributes, combined in different ways to meet segment needs. However, the context in which an exchange occurs between a buyer and a seller provides a strong reflection of the nature of their relationship. If the exchange is focused on the product (and the price) then the exchange is considered to be essentially transactional. If the exchange is focused around the needs of customers and sellers, the exchange is considered to be collaborative. The differences between transactional and collaborative exchanges are set out in Table 4.3 and provide an important starting point in understanding the nature of relationship marketing.

Relationship marketing can be characterised by the frequency and intensity of the exchanges between buyers and sellers. As these exchanges become more frequent and more intense, so the strength of the relationship between buyer and seller improves. It is this that provided the infrastructure for a perspective on marketing which is based on relationships (Rowe and Barnes, 1998), rather than the objects of a transaction: namely, products and services. Using this relationship framework, it is possible to superimpose ways in which marketing communications might be considered to work.

Table 4.3 The characteristics of transactional and collaborative exchanges

Attribute	Transactional exchange	Collaborative exchange
Length of relationship	Short-term – abrupt end	Long-term – a continuous process
Relational expectations	Conflicts of goals, immediate payment, no future problems (there is no future)	Conflicts of interest, deferred payment, future problems expected to be overcome by joint commitment
Communications	Low frequency of communications, formal, mass-media communications	Frequent communications, informal, personal, interactive communications
Cooperation	No joint cooperation	Joint cooperative projects
Responsibilities	Distinct responsibilities, defined obligations	Shared responsibilities, shared obligations

Source: From Essentials of Marketing Communications, Pearson Education (Fill, C. 2011) table 8.1, p. 190.

Transactional exchanges, where the relationship has little value for the buyer, and possibly the seller, are best supported with communications that do not seek to build a relationship but are generally orientated towards engaging through the provision of product and price (attribute-based) information. Communications are essentially a monologue as the buyer does not wish to respond, so the one-way or linear model of communications predominates. The communications might coincide with purchase cycles but are generally infrequent and regularised. These communications are one-sided, so an asymmetric pattern of communications emerges as they are driven by the seller. In many cases the identity of the buyer is unknown, so it is not possible to personalise messages and media channels and the largely informational messages are delivered through mass-communications media. These communications are formal and direct.

Collaborative exchanges, on the other hand, reflect the strong bond that exists between a buyer and a seller. Marketing communications, therefore, should seek to engage buyers by maintaining or strengthening the relationship. This means that communications patterns are irregular, informal, frequent and indirect. This is because buyers and sellers, working collaboratively, seek to provide mutual value. It means there are frequent interactions, often through dialogue, as one party responds to the other when discussing and resolving issues and challenges. The communications flow is symmetrical, messages are indirect and personalised as the identities are known. See Figure 4.4 for a visual interpretation of this spectrum and Table 4.4 for an explanation of the terms used.

Key to these ideas is the notion of dialogue. The adoption of dialogue as the basis for communications changes an organisation's perspective of its audiences and signals a transition from transactional relationships. Being willing and able to enter into a dialogue indicates that there is a new emphasis on the relationships organisations hold with their stakeholders. Kent and Taylor (2002) argue that there are five main features of a dialogical orientation. These are presented in Table 4.5.

It can be seen in Table 4.5 that many aspects of dialogue require interaction as a precursor. In other words, for dialogue to occur there must first be interaction and it is the development and depth of the interaction that leads to meaningful dialogue.

However, a word of caution is necessary as not everyone believes relationship marketing is an outright success. For example, Rapacz et al. (2008: 22) suggest that relationship marketing has become 'stuck in a rut'. They argue that audits of the relationship marketing practices used to support many leading brands indicate that relationship marketing is not working. The goal, Rapacz et al. suggest, should be commitment to the brand rather than the relationship itself. They refer to the over-promise of one-to-one marketing, the difficulties and inefficiencies associated with databases and CRM technology, and to issues concerning loyalty programmes. The result of their critique is that they advocate

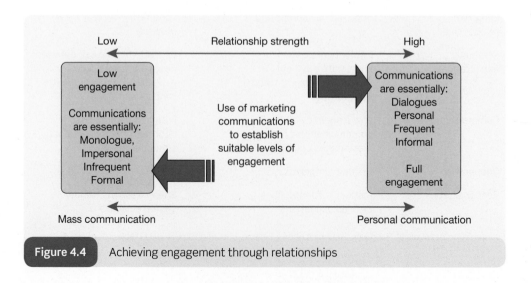

Figure 4.4   Achieving engagement through relationships

Table 4.4 Elements of relational marketing communications

Elements	Explanation	Transactional exchanges	Collaborative exchanges
Content	The extent to which the content of the message is intended to change behaviour (direct) or attitudes and beliefs (indirect)	Direct	Indirect
Formality	The extent to which communications are structured and routinised (formal) or spontaneous and irregular (informal)	Formal	Informal
Individuality	The extent to which recipients are identified by name	Impersonal	Personal
Frequency	How often do communications events occur?	Infrequent	Frequent
Audience	The size of the target audience for a communications event	Mass	Personal
Interaction	The level of feedback allowed or expected	Monologue	Dialogue

Source: Based on Mohr and Nevin (1990).

Table 4.5 The five features of a dialogical orientation

Role	Explanation
Mutuality	The recognition of the presence of organisational stakeholder relationships
Propinquity	The temporality and spontaneity of organisation–stakeholder interactions
Empathy	Support for stakeholder interests and their goals
Risk	Willingness to interact with others on their terms
Commitment	The extent to which an organisation actually interprets, listens to and practises dialogical communications

Source: Kent and Taylor (2002). Used with permission.

the use of a variety of marketing communications techniques to generate increased brand commitment. They use the Jack Daniels brand to make their point about good practice, highlighting communications that, if disciplined, entertaining, benefit-oriented and multifaceted, serve to bring greater commitment to a brand. See Exhibit 4.3.

Exhibit 4.3   **Jack Daniels uses storytelling to personalise the brand**
Source: 2015 Arnold Worldwide.

Viewpoint 4.3   Building relationships through celebrities

F*ck Cancer, a Canadian based non-profit organisation, offer their Generation Y target market the opportunity to host events in separate nightclubs in the USA and Canada. The aim is to provide community support for those who have been affected, directly or indirectly, with the disease. Entry to a venue is through a T-shirt with the company title printed on it. These are available in eight different colours, each representative of different coloured cancer ribbons.

F*ck Cancer is well known among Generation Y both for its events as well as the numerous endorsements it has received from various celebrities, including Stephen Amell, star of the CW television series, and for playing comic book superhero, the Green Arrow.

Traditionally endorsements are received in the form of celebrity event appearances or free of charge music sets from famous DJs. This digital campaign, however, featured Stephen Amell as a focus for developing relationships and to raise funds.

A significant aspect of F*ck Cancer's marketing communications strategy is the relational dimension. For instance, the collaboration with Stephen Amell resulted from F*ck Cancer asking him to help their cause after seeing a picture he had uploaded to Twitter of himself and his mother, soon after they had received news that she was in remission.

On 9 September 2014, Amell announced, through a self-taken video posted on his Facebook page, that he was crowdsourcing a print for a T-shirt which F*ck Cancer would sell via Represent, the charity retail website. Viewers were invited to suggest print ideas through his video post's thread on Facebook, and the most popular print would be used and sold to raise money for F*ck Cancer. The goal was to sell 500 T-shirts and raise US$10,000 in 3 weeks. Within 3 months, including a relaunch, over 62,000 products had been sold raising over US$1 million.

After the campaign, the company compiled a video thanking Stephen Amell for his support and contribution. In addition, they also featured several T-shirt purchasers from across the world who also thanked and commended him for his care and support.

The media have acclaimed Amell as a real-life hero for his involvement in the campaign, and celebrities such as Supernatural's Jared Padalecki and Micha Collins have spoken about Stephen Amell's influence and inspiration to their support for philanthropic activities.

This campaign developed a community's relationships by helping people share mutual experiences and understanding. With the aid of celebrity referent power, F*ck Cancer was able to engage audiences by conveying messages of empathy and trust, and show that cancer can affect anyone, regardless of age, social standing or occupation.

Source: Amell (2014a, 2014b, 2015); F*ck Cancer (2015); Dixon (2014); Greenbaum et al. (2015); Prudom (2015).

This Viewpoint was written by Tarek Temrawi when he was an Advertising student at the University of Northampton.

Question: Discuss the ways in which the F*ck Cancer campaign worked by developing relationships.

Task: Find two other campaigns in the for-profit sector and list three elements that demonstrate the development of relationships.

The notion that relationships will improve as they evolve across a continuum is not accepted by all. The expectation that relationships can be enhanced through the application of marketing programmes is not one that is always experienced in practice. For example, Palmer (2007) believes that the continuum perspective is too simplistic and unrealistic. Better to consider the prevailing contextual conditions as the key dynamics that shape relationships, which inevitably wax and wane over time.

Rao and Perry (2002), cited by Palmer, suggest that relationship development can be considered in terms of stages theory or states theory. Stages theory reflects the notion of incremental development (along the continuum), while states theory suggests that relationship development does not conform to the processional interpretation, because of the complexity and sheer unpredictability of relationship dynamics.

Palmer offers a compromise, namely a 'stages-within-a-state' interpretation. He draws on the work of Anderson and Narus (1999) and Canning and Hammer-Lloyd (2002) to make his point. There may be some validity in this view but the notion that all exchanges reflect a degree of relational commitment (Macneil, 1983) should not be ignored.

Ideas about how marketing communications works must be founded, in part, on the notion and significance of the level of interaction and dialogue that the organisation and its stakeholders desire. One-way communications, as reflected in traditional, planned, mass-media-based communications, still play a significant role, especially for audiences who prefer transactional exchanges. Two-way communications based on interaction with audiences who desire continuing contact, or dialogue for those who desire a deeper, more meaningful relationship, will form an increasingly important aspect of marketing communications strategy in the future.

HMCW Interpretation 4: Developing significant value

Marketing communications involves utilising a set of tools and media to convey messages to, with and among audiences. Depending upon the context in which a message is created, delivered and interpreted, a brand and the individual have an opportunity to interact. Marketing communications messages normally pass individuals unobserved. Those that are remembered contain particular characteristics (Brown, 1991; Fletcher, 1994). These would appear to be that the offering must be different or new, that the way the content (of a message) is executed is different or interesting, and that it proclaims something that is personally significant to the recipient in their current context.

The term 'significance' means that the content is meaningful, relevant (e.g. the individual is actually looking to buy a new car or breakfast cereals tomorrow or is planning to gather information on a new project), and is perceived to be suitably credible. These three characteristics can be tracked from the concept of ad likeability (Chapter 11), which many researchers believe is the only meaningful indicator of the effectiveness of an advertisement.

To be successful, therefore, it is necessary for marketing communications messages to:

- present an offering that is new to the receiver;
- be interesting and stimulating;
- be personally significant.

The object referred to in the first element refers to both products and services (or an offering that is substantially different from others in the category) and to organisations as brands. The net effect of all these characteristics might be that any one message may be *significantly valuable* to an individual.

Content that announces new brands or new attributes may convey information that is perceived to be significantly different. As a result, individuals may be intrigued and interested enough to want to try the brand at the next purchase opportunity. For these people there is a high level of personal relevance derived from the message, and attitude change can be induced to convince them that it is right to make a purchase. For them the message is significantly valuable and as a result may well generate a purchase decision, which will, from a market perspective, drive a discernible sales increase.

However, the vast majority of marketing communications are about offerings that are not new or that are unable to proclaim or offer anything substantially different. The content of these messages is either ignored or, if interest is aroused, certain parts of the message are filed away in memory for use at a later date. The question is: if parts are filed away, which parts are filed and why and how are they retrieved?

Marketing communications can provide a rationale or explanation for why individuals (cognitive processors) have bought a brand and why they should continue buying it. Normally, advertising alone does not persuade, it simply reminds and reassures individuals. To put it another way, individuals use advertising and public relations to remind themselves of preferred brands or to reassure themselves of their previous (and hence correct) purchase behaviour. Sales promotions, personal selling and direct marketing are then used by organisations to help consumers behave in particular ways.

Consumers, particularly in fast-moving consumer goods (FMCG) markets, practise repertoire buying based on habit, security, speed of decision-making and, to some extent, self-expression. The brands present in any single individual repertoire normally provide interest and satisfaction. Indeed, advertising needs to ensure that the brand remains in the repertoire or is sufficiently interesting to the individual that it is included in a future repertoire. Just consider the variety of messages used by mobile phone operators. These are continually updated and refreshed using particular themes, all of which are intended to be visually and cognitively engaging.

We know that messages have two main elements, an informational and an emotional component, and that each message should balance these elements according to the prevailing context of the target audience. Marketing communications that delivers significant value therefore can be considered to have either informational content or emotional content that is of value.

Significant value – informational content

Messages that consistently deliver relevant and meaningful content are considered to have a positive and cumulative influence on purchase decision-making. This understanding has given rise to the contemporary practice called '*content marketing*'. The Content Marketing Institute advises that the purpose is to attract and retain customers by consistently 'creating and curating relevant and valuable content with the intention of changing or enhancing consumer behavior' (CMI, 2015), and that its focus is on owned, not paid-for, media. Content marketing is concerned with delivering information that consistently informs and boosts an audience's knowledge. The rise in popularity of customer magazines is a reflection of the growth in content marketing (see Viewpoint 18.2 for an example of content marketing and owned media).

The importance of content in a message should not be underestimated. Content enables positioning and provides a means by which individuals perceive value. For example, Netflix used to be a platform through which people could watch television programmes and films. This model was easily imitated by others. The solution was to create original content that was only available through Netflix, such as *Orange is the New Black* and *House of Cards*. The result was that people chose Netflix over its competitors because the content represented significant value (Clark, 2015). *House of Cards* was so successful that Netflix gained two million new subscribers (Falconi, 2015). Sky pursues a similar strategy, generating original television shows, such as *Game of Thrones* and *Fortitude*, that are only available through the Sky Atlantic channel.

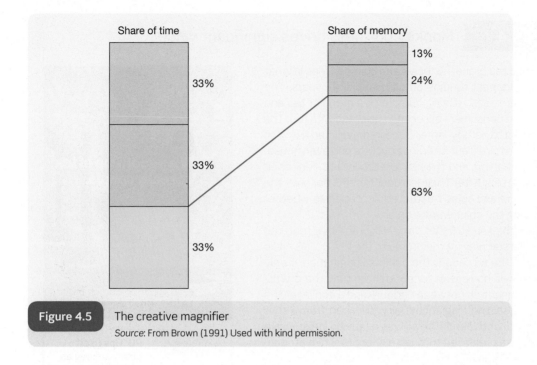

Figure 4.5   The creative magnifier

Source: From Brown (1991) Used with kind permission.

Significant value – emotional content

Messages, in particular advertising messages that are interesting, immediately relevant or interpreted as possessing a deep set of personal meanings (all subsequently referred to as 'likeable' (see Chapter 11)), are stored in long-term memory.

Research shows repeatedly that only parts of an advertisement are ever remembered – those parts that are of intrinsic value to the recipient and are sometimes referred to as 'the take-out'. Brown (1991) refers to this selectivity as the creative magnifier effect. Figure 4.5 illustrates the effect that parts of a message might have on the way a message is remembered.

The implication of this is that messages work best through the creation of emotional interest and likeable moments, from which extracts are taken by individuals and stored away in memory. However, it might also be reasonable to suggest that the other tools of the mix are also capable of enabling individuals to take extracts. For example, the size of a sales promotion offer, or the tone of a sales presentation, the professionalism of a direct mail piece or the immediacy of an online promotion might all give due reason for an individual to generate a take-out. Interest is generated through fresh, relevant ideas where the brand and the messages are linked together in a meaningful and relevant way. This in turn allows for future associations to be made, linking brands and marketing communications messages in a positive and experiential way.

Marketing communications is used to trigger emotionally based brand associations and experiences for people, not only when seated in front of a television, or with a tablet or laptop, or when reading a magazine, text or mobile messages, but also when faced with purchase decisions. Of all low-value FMCG decisions 70 per cent are said to be made at the point of purchase. All forms of marketing communications, but principally advertising, can be used to generate brand associations, which in turn are used to trigger advertising messages or, rather, 'likeable' extracts. The other tools of the mix can benefit from the prior use of advertising to create awareness so that the call-to-action brought about through below-the-line communications can occur naturally, unhindered by brand confusion or uncertainty.

Viewpoint 4.4   Monkey business drives significant value

The Brooke Bond tea brand, PG Tips, used chimpanzees in what was one of the longest running ad campaigns, 45 years. The chimpanzees were used to bring humour to a brand of tea and in doing so helped consumers associate the brand with fun. The chimps were used to parody James Bond, removal men trying to get a piano downstairs, Tour de France cyclists and even house-wives doing the ironing, and they all (pretended) to drink their favourite cup of tea. After their introduction PG became the number one brand and sales fluctuated according to whether the ads featuring the chimps were on air.

Cadbury launched an ad for its Dairy Milk brand that featured a man in a gorilla suit playing the drums to the Phil Collins hit 'In the Air Tonight'. The ad caught the public's imagination, if only because there was no reason for a gorilla to play the drums, there was no connection between Cadbury and a gorilla (at the time), and the ad said nothing about Dairy Milk apart from a shot of the brand name at the end. The ad was relatively inexpensive to produce and was released through a spoof real film produc-tion company, 'A Glass and a Half Full Productions'.

The ad featured in a pre-ad teaser campaign in television list-ings that resembled a film. The Glass and a Half Full Productions website helped to sustain dialogue with fans while 90-second spots during the Rugby World Cup and Big Brother Finals deliv-ered the ad to huge audiences.

Exhibit 4.4	**PG Tips used chimpanzees as an integral part of their advertising**

Source: Alamy Images/Heritage Image Partnership Ltd.

The ad is still regarded as a masterpiece of creativity, one that resonated with the nation. Sales rose 7 per cent by the end of October in value terms, and weekly sales were up 9 per cent year on year during the period 'gorilla' was on air. The ad generated the highest recognition scores ever recorded by Hall & Partners.

In both of these campaigns the chimps/gorilla represented significant value because they stood out from the ads and were the key elements that people remembered. The ads went viral, word-of-mouth conversations and media coverage about the chimps/gorilla soared.

Sources: Benady (2013); Blackstock (2002); Campaign (2007); Carter (2008).

Question: How should the 'Gorilla' ad be evaluated, and how would you measure its success?

Task: Gorillas feature in other ways for some other brands. Find two other campaigns that feature gorillas.

This last point is of particular importance, because advertising alone may not be suf-ficient or appropriate to trigger complete recall of brand and communications experi-ences. The brand, its packaging, sales promotion, interactive media, point of purchase, and outdoor media all have an important role to play in providing consistency and interest and prompting recall and recognition. Integrated marketing communications is important, not just for message take-out or likeable extracts, but also for triggering recall and recognition and stimulating relevant brand associations.

Content delivered through pertinent and relevant information, or as a result of what individuals take out emotionally from an advertisement, represents significant value. Marketing communications, therefore, can be considered to work by delivering either significant information or emotional take-outs that are relevant and meaningful.

HMCW Interpretation 5: Cognitive processing

Reference has already been made to whether buyers actively or passively process information. In an attempt to understand how information is used, cognitive processing tries to determine 'how external information is transformed into meanings or patterns of thought and how these meanings are combined to form judgments' (Olsen and Peter, 1987).

By assessing the thoughts (cognitive processes) that occur to people as they read, view or hear a message, an understanding of their interpretation of a message can be gained, which is useful in campaign development and evaluation (Greenwald, 1968; Wright, 1973). These thoughts are usually measured by asking consumers to write down or verbally report the thoughts they have in response to such a message. Thoughts are believed to be a reflection of the cognitive processes or responses that receivers experience and they help shape or reject communications.

Researchers have identified three types of cognitive response and have determined how these relate to attitudes and intentions. Figure 4.6 shows these three types of response,

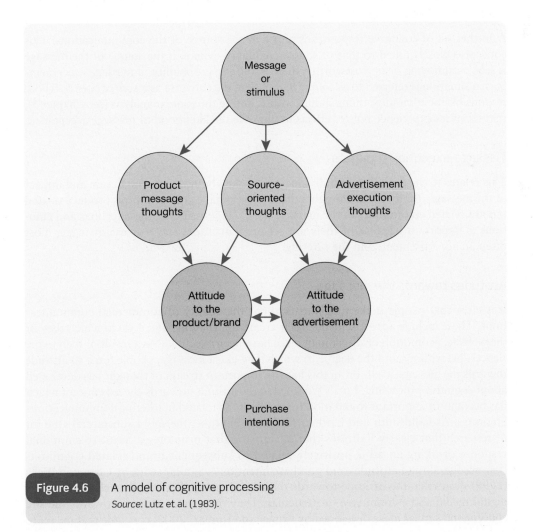

| Figure 4.6 | A model of cognitive processing |

Source: Lutz et al. (1983).

but readers should appreciate that these types are not discrete; they overlap each other and blend together, often invisibly.

Product/message thoughts

These are thoughts that are directed to the product or communications. Much attention has been focused on the thoughts that are related to the message content. Two particular types of response have been considered: counter-arguments and support arguments.

A counter-argument occurs when the receiver disagrees with the content of a message. According to Belch and Belch (2004):

> The likelihood of counter-argument is greater when the message makes claims that oppose the beliefs or perceptions held by the receiver. Not surprisingly, the greater the degree of counter-argument, the less likely the message will be accepted. Conversely, support-arguments reflect acceptance and concurrence with a message. Support-arguments, therefore, are positively related to message acceptance.

Advertisements and general communications should encourage the generation of support arguments.

Source-oriented thoughts

A further set of cognitive responses is aimed at the source of the communications. This concept is closely allied to that of source credibility, where, if the source of the message is seen as annoying or untrustworthy, there is a lower probability of message acceptance. Such a situation is referred to as *source derogation*, the converse as a *source bolster*. Those responsible for communications should ensure, during the context analysis (see Chapter 5), that receivers experience bolster effects to improve the likelihood of message acceptance.

Message-execution thoughts

This relates to the thoughts an individual may have about the overall design and impact of the message. Many of the thoughts that receivers have are not always product-related but are related emotionally to the message itself. Understanding these feelings and emotions is important because of their impact upon attitudes towards the message, most often an advertisement, and the offering.

Attitudes towards the message

It is clear that people make judgements about the quality of commercial communications. These include advertisements, their creativity, the tone and style in which they or the website, promotion or direct mail piece have been executed. As a result of their experiences, perceptions and the degree to which they like a message, people form an attitude towards the message itself. From this base an important stream of thought has developed about cognitive processing. Lutz's work led to the attitude-towards-the-ad concept which has become an important foundation for much of the related marketing communications literature. As Goldsmith and Lafferty (2002: 319) argue, there is a substantial amount of research that clearly indicates that advertising that promotes a 'positive emotional response of liking an ad is positively related to subsequent brand-related cognitions (knowledge), brand attitudes and purchase intentions'. Similar work by Chen and Wells (1999) shows that this attitude-towards-the-ad concept applies equally well with various digital media and e-commerce in particular. They refer to an attitude-towards-the-site concept and similar ideas developed by Bruner and Kumar (2000) conclude that the more a website is liked, so attitudes improve towards the brand and purchase intentions. A word of caution, however, is required. Rossiter and Percy (2013) dismiss the attitude-to-the-ad concept as an irrelevant mediator of advertising effectiveness.

Despite this view the overwhelming evidence makes it seem highly reasonable therefore to conclude that attitudes-towards-the-message (and delivery mechanism) impact on brand attitudes, which in turn influence consumers' propensity to purchase. It is also known that an increasing proportion of advertisements attempt to appeal to feelings and emotions, simply because many researchers believe that attitudes towards both the advertisement and the product should be encouraged and are positively correlated with purchase intention. Similarly, time and effort are invested in the design of sales promotion instruments, increasing attention is given to the design of packaging in terms of a pack's communications effectiveness, and care is taken about the wording in advertorials and press releases. Perhaps above all else, more and more effort is being made to research and develop websites with the goal of designing them so that they are strategically compatible, user-friendly and functional, or to put it another way – liked.

Low Attention Processing

Just as a word of caution was offered with regard to the continuum of marketing relationships, so an alternative view needs to be mentioned with regard to cognitive processing. The cognitive processing model assumes that people attend to and process information in a logical rational way. Sometimes referred to as the 'Information Processing (IP)' model, the approach assumes that messages are processed and stored in memory, and later retrieved and updated (see Chapter 3 for more information on this topic). This processing approach is related to both informational and emotional messages. The latter were considered to be a consequence of people's thoughts and that by understanding what we think then we can understand everything (Heath and Hyder, 2005). Unfortunately psychologists such as Zajonc (1980) and Damasio (2000) upset this thinking, because their research showed that this was the wrong way round and that it was feelings and emotions (affect) that shaped our thoughts, at all times. This meant that advertising might be effective through mere exposure, rather than having to attend to, and cognitively process, a message.

In 2001 Heath published his 'Low Attention Processing Model', previously referred to as the Low *Involvement* Processing Model. The core characteristics of the Low Attention Processing (LAP) Model are summarised by Heath and Hyder in Table 4.6.

Table 4.6 Core characteristics of the Low Attention Processing Model

Characteristic	Explanation
Intuitive choice	Intuitive decision-making is more common than considered choice, so emotions will be more influential.
Information acquisition	Intuitive decision-making dampens information seeking and minimises the need to attend to ads.
Passive and implicit learning	Brand information is acquired through low level of attention by passive learning and implicit learning.
Enduring associations	Associations are developed and reinforced through time and linked to the brand through passive learning. These associations can activate emotional markers, which in turn influence decision-making.
Semi-automatic	Learning occurs semi-automatically, regardless of the level of attention paid.

The prevailing view is that messages need only be seen, that is attended to, just once or twice. This is known as *high-attention processing* (HAP). What the LAP model says is that advertising can exploit low-attention processing when an individual is able to see the ad several times. The argument, based around empirical research, is that advertising messages can be processed with low attention levels. Typically people watch television passively (Krugman, 1965) and today many multitask with other media, so their attention to ads can be extremely low. As a result, people may not have any conscious recall of 'receiving' a message yet make decisions based on the emotions and the associations made at a low level of consciousness. According to Heath and Feldwick (2008), ad messages do not necessarily need to create impact and they do not need to deliver a proposition or functional benefit. What is important is that a creative 'influences emotions and brand relationships' (p. 45).

If this view is accepted then cognitive processing does not explain how marketing communications works, or at least diminishes the power of the conventional view that advertising works through information processing.

Cognitive styles

Unsurprisingly, individuals do not share the same way of processing information. Referred to as brain lateralisation theory, various studies have demonstrated that the left side of the brain tends to specialise in rational, analytic and sequential information processing. The right side specialises in visual, intuitive and simultaneous information processing (Armstrong, 1999).

The term 'cognitive styles' is given to the different ways people receive, organise and process information (Messick, 1972). In effect, 'cognitive styles', refers to the differences in the way groups of people consistently 'perceive, think, solve problems, learn, take decisions and relate to others' (Witkin et al., 1977). The dominant style is stable through time and contexts, and importantly is independent of an individual's level of intelligence (Vinitzky and Mazursky, 2011).

Understanding cognitive styles is important for many disciplines because they influence the way individuals behave. In marketing, insight into cognitive styles is important particularly for multinational organisations. This is because matching advertising formats to consumers' style (analytical versus imagery) improves advertising performance (Thompson and Hamilton, 2006). Comparative style ads were shown to be more effective when consumers used analytical processing, whereas non-comparative ads were more effective when consumers used imagery processing (Armstrong et al., 2012). For example, research cited by Cuia et al. (2013: 17) has found that that East Asians emphasise right-brain processing as more receptive to transformational or symbolic advertising. Westerners tend to emphasise left-brain processing and as a result informational advertising is more effective (Chan, 1996).

The principles of cognitive style have been distilled into a 'thinking and feeling' dimension and used to shape advertising strategy. These are explored in Chapter 11 on advertising strategy.

Conclusion

In this chapter five different interpretations about how marketing communications might work have been considered. None of them are completely wrong or completely right. Indeed, it is safe to conclude that marketing communications works in different ways in different contexts and that traces of several of these interpretations can be found in most campaigns.

For example, the sequential interpretation includes the principle of attitude change, while some would argue that cognitive processing underpins all of these approaches. Some of these approaches evolved in the pre-digital era and, therefore, it might be unsafe to suggest that they are equally applicable or relevant today. For example, it could be argued that marketing communications needs to include more emphasis on listening to audiences, customers and tribes in social networks, yet this aspect is not explicit in any of the models presented here.

Scholars' paper 4.4　　　**Modelling B2B communications**

Gilliland, D.I. and Johnston, W.J. (1997) Towards a model of marketing communications effects, *Industrial Marketing Management,* 26, 15–29.

This paper provides a useful counterbalance to the wealth of consumer-orientated papers about marketing communications. As the title describes, the authors develop a well-respected model that explains how marketing communications works in a business-to-business context.

Key points

- Marketing communications should be used to complement an organisation's marketing, business and corporate strategies. Such harmonisation serves to reinforce core messages, reflect the mission and provide a means of using resources efficiently yet at the same time to provide reinforcement for the whole business strategy.

- The primary role of marketing communications is to engage audiences by either driving a response to the message itself, or encouraging a response to the brand itself, referred to as a *call-to-action*.

- There are five main ways in which marketing communications can be considered to work. These are the sequential buying process, attitude change, shaping relationships, developing significant value, and cognitive processing.

- The sequential approach assumes that marketing communications needs to take consumers through the decision-making process in a series of logical steps.

- Attitude change has been regarded by many as the main way to influence audiences through marketing communications. Marketing communications can be used to focus one of the three elements of the attitudinal construct: that is, the cognitive, affective or conative component.

- Relationship marketing can be characterised by the frequency and intensity of the exchanges between buyers and sellers. As these exchanges become more frequent and more intense, so the strength of the relationship between a consumer and a brand improves.

- These customer relationships can be considered in terms of a series of relationship–development phases: customer acquisition, development, retention and decline. Collectively these are referred to as the *customer lifecycle*. The duration and intensity of each relationship phase in the lifecycle vary. Marketing communications works by influencing customers according to the stage they have reached in the lifecycle.

- Marketing communications is used to trigger brand associations and experiences for people.

- Those messages that are remembered contain particular characteristics. These are that the product must be different or new, that the way the message is executed is different or interesting, and that the message proclaims something that is personally significant to the individual in their current context.

- The term 'significance' means that the message is meaningful, relevant, and is perceived to be suitably credible. This is based on the concept of ad likeability, which many researchers believe is the only meaningful indicator of ad effectiveness. The net effect of all these characteristics might be that any one message may be *significantly valuable* to an individual.

- The cognitive processing model assumes that people attend to and process information in a logical rational way. Three types of cognitive response and how these relate to attitudes and intentions have been determined. These are attitudes towards the product, attitudes towards the message and attitudes towards the ad and its execution.

- There is a substantial amount of research that indicates that marketing communications (advertising) which promotes a 'positive emotional response of liking an ad is positively related to subsequent brand-related cognitions (knowledge), brand attitudes and purchase intentions'.

- Marketing communications works because liking an ad is positively related to subsequent brand-related cognitions (knowledge), brand attitudes, and purchase intentions. Attitude-towards-the-ad concept applies equally well with interactive media, e-commerce (attitude-towards-the-site), sales promotion and personal selling.

Review questions

McCain case questions

1. How does McCain use marketing communications to change attitudes towards Ready Baked Jackets?

2. To what extent is McCain's marketing communications influenced by transactional or collaborative exchange-based relationships?

3. Interpret the launch of Ready Baked Jackets in terms of the concept of significant value.

4. Discuss ways in which in which McCain seeks to engage audiences.

5. Explain how McCain's use of media might be said to complement ideas about attitude development.

General questions

1. Sketch the customer relationship lifecycle and show how marketing communications can be used to influence each of the stages.

2. Describe the creative magnifier effect. Why is it important?

3. Cognitive processing consists of three main elements. Name them.

4. Write brief notes outlining the difference between three sequential models and evaluate the ways in which they are considered to work.

5. Why might cognitive processing not be an entirely acceptable approach?

References

Ajzen, I. and Fishbein, M. (1980) *Understanding Attitudes and Predicting Social Behavior,* Englewood Cliffs, NJ: Prentice Hall.

Amell, S. (2014a) FACEBOOK!! Our campaign for Fuck Cancer is back!! Facebook, retrieved 21 December 2014 from www.facebook.com/video.php?v=76002735408253 4&set=vb.146921975393078&type=2&theatre.

Amell, S. (2014b) 17,180 Shirts Sold. Sooooo much $ raised. 18 hours left, *Fuck Cancer,* Facebook, retrieved 21 December 2014 from www.facebook.com/video.php? v=728188040599799&set=vb.146921975393078&type =2&theatre.

Amell, S. (2015) Stephen Amell Profile, Facebook, retrieved 31 March 2015 from www.facebook.com/stephenamell.

Anderson, J.C. and Narus, J.A. (1999) *Business Market Management,* Upper Saddle River, NJ: Prentice Hall.

Armstrong, S. (1999) The influence of individual cognitive style on performance in management education, in *Proceedings of the 4th Annual Conference of the European Learning Styles Information Network* (eds J. Hill, S. Armstrong, M. Graff, S. Rayner and E. Sadler-Smith), Preston: University of Central Lancashire, pp. 31–50.

Armstrong, S.J., Cools, E. and Sadler-Smith, E. (2012) Role of cognitive styles in business and management: reviewing 40 years of research, *International Journal of Management Reviews,* 14, 238–62.

Ballantyne, D. (2004) Dialogue and its role in the development of relationship specific knowledge, *Journal of Business and Industrial Marketing,* 19(2), 114–23.

Barry, T. and Howard, D.J. (1990) A review and critique of the hierarchy of effects in advertising, *International Journal of Advertising,* 9, 121–35.

Belch, G.E. and Belch, M.A. (2004) *Advertising and Promotion: An Integrated Marketing communications Perspective,* 6th edition, Homewood, IL: Richard D. Irwin.

Benady, D. (2013) What makes the perfect viral ad? *theguardian.com,* retrieved 12 August 2014 from www.theguardian.com/best-awards/what-makes-the-perfect-viral-ad-john-west-ronaldinho.

Blackstock, C. (2002) Tea party over as PG Tips chimps are given the bird, *Guardian,* 12 January, retrieved 12 February 2008 from www.monkeyworld.co.uk/press.php?ArticleID=59.

Brakus, J.J., Schmitt, B.H. and Zarantello, L. (2009) Brand experience: What is it? How is it measured? Does it affect loyalty? *Journal of Marketing,* 73(3), 52–68.

Brown, G. (1991) *How Advertising Affects the Sales of Packaged Goods Brands,* Warwick: Millward Brown.

Brownsell, A. (2013) First Direct returns to 'challenger' origins with 'unexpected bank' relaunch, *Marketing Magazine,* 22 May, retrieved 6 February 2015 from www.marketingmagazine.co.uk/article/1183334/first-direct-returns-challenger-origins-unexpected-bank-relaunch?HAYILC=RELATED.

Bruner, G.C. and Kumar, A. (2000) Web commercials and advertising hierarchy of effects, *Journal of Advertising Research,* January/April, 35–42.

Campaign (2007) Cadbury 'gorilla' wins Campaign of the Year, *Campaign,* 13 December, retrieved 16 August 2014 from www.brandrepublic.com/InDepth/Features/773064/Cadbury-gorilla-wins-Campaign-Year/.

Canning, L. and Hammer-Lloyd, S. (2002) Modeling the adaptation process in interactive business relationships, *Journal of Business & Industrial Marketing,* 17(7), 615–36.

Carter, M. (2008) Monkey business, *Independent,* 17 March, 8–9.

Champagne, C. (2013) How to make a Cannes contender: Chipotle's 'back to the start', *FastCompany,* 21 September, retrieved 8 January 2015 from www.fastcocreate.com/1680942/how-to-make-a-cannes-contender-chipotles-back-to-the-start.

Chan, D. (1996) Cognitive misfit of problem-solving style at work: a facet of person–organisation fit, *Organisational Behavior and Human Decision Processes,* 68, 194–207.

Chen, Q. and Wells, W.D. (1999) Attitude toward the site, *Journal of Advertising Research,* September/October, 27–37.

Clark, A. (2015) How to measure success in content marketing, *ScribbleLive,* retrieved 14 February 2015 from http://media.dmnews.com/documents/105/scribblelive_whitepaper_measur_26084.pdf.

CMI (2015) What is content marketing? *Content Marketing Institute,* retrieved 17 February 2015 from http://contentmarketinginstitute.com/what-is-content-marketing/.

Cuia, G., Liub, H., Yang, X. and Wang, H. (2013) Culture, cognitive style and consumer response to informational vs. transformational advertising among East Asians: evidence from the PRC, *Asia Pacific Business Review,* 19(1), 16–31.

Damasio, A.A. (2000) *The Feeling of What Happens,* London: Heinemann.

Day, G. (2000) Managing market relationships, *Journal of the Academy of Marketing Science,* 28, 1, Winter, 24–30.

Dixon, L. (2014) *It's Not Just Arrow, Stephen Amell is a True Hero!* Retrieved 29 March 2015 from http://moviepilot.com/posts/2014/11/03/it-s-not-just-arrow-stephen-amell-is-a-true-hero-2400985?lt_source=external,manual.

Falconi, J. (2015) What marketers can learn from Netflix and the wisdom of the crowd, *The Marketer*, 13 February, retrieved 17 February 2015 from http://blog.themarketer.co.uk/2015/02/what-marketers-can-learn-from-netflix-and-the-wisdom-of-the-crowd/.

Fletcher, W. (1994) The advertising high ground, *Admap*, November, 31–4.

Fuck Cancer (2015) Fuck Cancer Profile, Facebook, retrieved 23 February 2015 from www.facebook.com/fcancernow.

Gilliland, D.I. and Johnston, W.J. (1997) Towards a model of marketing communications effects, *Industrial Marketing Management*, 26, 15–29.

Goldsmith, R.E. and Lafferty, B.A. (2002) Consumer response to websites and their influence on advertising effectiveness, *Internet Research: Electronic Networking Applications and Policy*, 12(4), 318–28.

Greenbaum, J. et al. (2015) *Our Story*, retrieved 28 September 2014 from http://fcancerevents.com/about-us/.

Greenwald, A. (1968) Cognitive learning, cognitive response to persuasion and attitude change, in *Psychological Foundations of Attitudes* (eds A. Greenwald, T.C. Brook and T.W. Ostrom), New York: Academic Press, 197–215.

Gronroos, C. (2004) The relationship marketing process: communication, interaction, dialogue, value, *Journal of Business and Industrial Marketing*, 19(2), 99–113.

Heath, R. (2001) Low involvement processing – a new model of brand communication, *Journal of Marketing Communications*, 7, 27–33.

Heath, R. and Feldwick, P. (2008) 50 years using the wrong model of TV advertising, *International Journal of Market Research*, 50(1), 29–59.

Heath, R. and Hyder, P. (2005) Measuring the hidden power of emotive advertising, *International Journal of Market Research*, 47(5), 467–86.

Jack, L. (2014) First Direct launches campaign in Downton Abbey slot, *campaignlive.co.uk*, 22 September, retrieved 6 February 2015 from www.campaignlive.co.uk/news/1313274/.

Johnson, L. (2014) What marketers can learn from the fast-casual restaurant boom–Taco Bell and Chipotle's models go beyond the in-store experience, *Adweek*, 29 September, retrieved 8 January 2015 from www.adweek.com/news/advertising-branding/what-marketers-can-learn-fast-casual-restaurant-boom-160440.

Kent, M.L. and Taylor, M. (2002) Toward a dialogic theory of public relations, *Public Relations Review*, 28(1), 21–37.

Krugman, H.E. (1965) The impact of television advertising: learning without involvement, *Public Opinion Quarterly*, 29 (Fall), 349–56.

Lavidge, R.J. and Steiner, G.A. (1961) A model for predictive measurements of advertising effectiveness, *Journal of Marketing*, October, 61.

Lutz, J., Mackenzie, S.B. and Belch, G.E. (1983) Attitude toward the ad as a mediator of advertising effectiveness, *Advances in Consumer Research*, 10(1), 532–9.

Macneil, I.R. (1983) Values in contract: internal and external, *Northwestern Law Review*, 78(2), 340–418.

McGrath, M. (2014) The advertising game: how brands like Chipotle, Google and Gap rise above competitors, *Forbes*, 21 October, retrieved 8 January 2015 from www.forbes.com/sites/maggiemcgrath/2014/10/21/the-advertising-game-how-brands-like-chipotle-google-and-gap-rise-above-competitors/.

McGuire, W.J. (1978) An information processing model of advertising effectiveness, in *Behavioral and Management Science in Marketing* (eds H.L. Davis and A.J. Silk), New York: Ronald/Wiley, 156–80.

Messick, S. (1972) Beyond structure in search of functional modes of psychological process, *Psychometrica*, 37, 357–75.

Mohr, J. and Nevin, J.R. (1990) Communication strategies in marketing channels, *Journal of Marketing*, October, 36–51.

Nudd, T. (2013) Move into gaming, too, *Adweek*, 12 September, retrieved 8 January 2015 from www.adweek.com/news/advertising-branding/ad-day-chipotle-makes-magic-again-fiona-apple-and-dark-animated-film-152380.

Olsen, J.C. and Peter, J.P. (1987) *Consumer Behavior*, Homewood, IL: Irwin.

Palda, K.S. (1966) The hypothesis of a hierarchy of effects: a partial evaluation, *Journal of Marketing Research*, 3, 13–24.

Palmer, R. (2007) The transaction–relational continuum: conceptually elegant but empirically denied, *Journal of Business and Industrial Marketing*, 22(7), 439–51.

Prudom, L. (2015) 'Supernatural' Star Jared Padalecki Talks Depression and Why You Should 'Always Keep Fighting', retrieved 29 March 2015 from http://variety.com/2015/tv/people-news/jared-padalecki-always-keep-fighting-depression-suicide-twloha-1201451708.

Rao, S. and Perry, C. (2002) Thinking about relationship marketing: where are we now? *Journal of Business and Industrial Marketing*, 17(7), 598–614.

Rapacz, D., Reilly, M. and Schultz, D.E. (2008) Better branding beyond advertising, *Marketing Management,* 17(1), 25–9.

Roderick, L. (2014) Youthful banking, *The Marketer,* September/October, 24–7

Rossiter, J.R. and Percy, L. (2013) How the roles of advertising merely appear to have changed, *International Journal of Advertising,* 32(3), 391–8.

Rowe, W.G. and Barnes, J.G. (1998) Relationship marketing and sustained competitive advantage, *Journal of Market-Focused Management,* 2(3), 281–9.

Solomon, B. (2014) Chipotle continues explosive growth in the burrito bull market, *Forbes,* 20 October, retrieved 8 January 2015 from www.forbes.com/sites/briansolomon/2014/10/20/chipotle-continues-explosive-growth-in-the-burrito-bull-market/.

Strong, E.K. (1925) *The Psychology of Selling,* New York: McGraw-Hill.

Thompson, D.V. and Hamilton, R.W. (2006). The effects of information processing mode on consumers' responses to comparative advertising, *Journal of Consumer Research,* 32, 530–40.

Thomson, K. and Hecker, L.A. (2000) The business value of buy-in, in *Internal Marketing: Directions for Management* (eds R.J. Varey and B.R. Lewis), London: Routledge, 160–72.

Vinitzky, G. and Mazursky, D. (2011) The effects of cognitive thinking style and ambient scent on online consumer approach behavior, experience approach behavior, and search motivation, *Psychology & Marketing,* 28(5), 496–519.

Witkin, H.A., Moore, C.A., Goodenough, D.R. and Cox, P.W. (1977) Field dependent and field independent cognitive styles and their educational implications, *Review of Educational Research,* 47, 1–64.

Wright, P.L. (1973) The cognitive processes mediating the acceptance of advertising, *Journal of Marketing Research,* 10 (February), 53–62.

Zajonc, R.B. (1980) Feeling and thinking: preferences need no inferences, *American Psychologist,* 39, 151–75.

Part 2
Managing marketing communications

Part 2 is concerned with the management of marketing communications. The topics embrace strategy, goals and positioning, industry, evaluation and metrics, branding, and integration.

Chapter 5 is concerned with the nature of communications strategy and the interrelationship between strategies and planning. The first section of this chapter considers ideas about strategy and four distinct approaches to marketing communications strategy. The second section of the chapter works through the marketing communications planning framework (MCPF), highlighting issues and linkages; it ends with an operational approach to devising, formulating and implementing a strategic marketing communications plan.

Chapter 6 examines the nature of objectives and positioning in marketing communications and considers both academic and practitioner (IPA) approaches to the nature of communications-based objectives.

The nature and characteristics of the UK marketing communications industry is the focus of Chapter 7. This material specifically examines the strategic and operational issues of communications agencies and their interaction with client organisations, including the various budgeting and remuneration issues experienced by agencies and clients.

Chapter 8 examines the ways in which the performance of marketing communications activities can be evaluated, and highlights the criticality of metrics in marketing communications today.

Chapter 9 focuses on branding and the role, approaches and methods of marketing communications that are used to help, develop and sustain brands.

Chapter 10 is about integrated marketing communications. This chapter challenges ideas about the nature and validity of the 'integrated' view of marketing communications. Five separate interpretations about what integrated marketing communications might be are presented. This is a core chapter because it bridges the contextual elements and the application of the various disciplines.

For readers with access to the companion website that accompanies this book, there are supplementary chapters, drawn from previous editions, available in PDF form:

Marketing: relationships and communications

Employee branding

Corporate branding and communications

Financial resources for marketing communications

Chapter 5

Marketing communications: strategy and planning

Marketing communications strategy refers to a brand's thematic platform, its overall positioning, and their customers and other stakeholders preferred approach to communications. Strategy should not be confused with objectives. Tactics are concerned with the communications mix developed to deliver the strategy. Marketing communications strategies should at all times be aligned with the business and marketing strategies an organisation pursues.

Marketing communications plans are concerned with the resources associated with the delivery of ongoing programmes and campaigns designed to articulate a brand's marketing communications tactics and strategy.

Aims and learning objectives

The aims of this chapter are to develop understanding about the elements and concepts associated with marketing communications strategy and planning, and a planning framework within which to implement these strategies.

The learning objectives are to enable readers to:

1. examine the meaning of strategy within a marketing communications context;

2. evaluate positioning as an interpretation of marketing communications strategy;

3. appraise the audience interpretation of marketing communications strategy;

4. discuss the use of various platforms as an interpretation of marketing communications strategy;

5. consider the value of the configuration interpretation of marketing communications strategy;

6. present a planning framework and consider the different elements and linkages involved in the development of marketing communications plans.

The London Olympics – a strategic success

The success of any major sporting, religious or cultural event is partly dependant on the transport system and the movement of participants, organisers, suppliers, audiences and, of course, the people who live and work in the local environment. The Atlanta 1996 Olympic Games are considered as an example of poor forecasting, planning and communication, which resulted in the city grinding to an unceremonious halt. The Atlanta transport system was overcrowded, travellers queued for hours and services were heavily delayed, while some events opened to near-empty stadia. In some cases competitors were unable to reach venues in time, resulting in rescheduling and cancellations.

It was important, therefore, for the organisers of the London 2012 Olympics to avoid this type of disaster. At the time the London transport network carried over 25m journeys daily and was operating close

Exhibit 5.1   **Managing the volume and flow of people around London during the Olympic Games became a core activity for TfL**
Source: Alamy Images/Justin Kase z12z

Scholars' paper 5.1   **What is strategy?**

These are classic publications from the 'early' strategy literature and they provide an insight into some of the principal ideas and approaches.

Andrews, K. (1987) *The Concept of Corporate Strategy*, Homewood, IL: Richard D. Irwin.

Ansoff, H.I. (1965) *Corporate Strategy*, New York: McGraw-Hill.

Chaffee, E. (1985) Three models of strategy, *Academy of Management Review*, 10(1), 89–98.

Kay, J. (1993) The structure of strategy, *Business Strategy Review*, 4(2), 17–37.

Mintzberg, H. and Waters, J.A. (1985) Of strategies, deliberate and emergent, *Strategic Management Journal*, 6(3), 257–72.

This chapter begins with a contextual and audience perspective on which to build marketing communications strategy. This is used in preference to a production orientation, which is founded purely on a resource base. From this, four different interpretations of marketing communications strategy are considered. The chapter closes with an exploration of a framework within which to plan, develop and implement marketing communications strategies.

Marketing communications strategies

The strategy adopted by TfL, as outlined in the case study, to engage London travellers and prompt them to modify their own journeys for a defined period of time was a planned, and complex, activity. It involved various audiences, consumed a large amount of resources, and required several messages, media and tools which had to be sequenced to maximise effectiveness.

The prevailing approach to marketing communications strategy has traditionally been founded upon the configuration of the 'promotional' mix. Strategy was an interpretation of the tools in the mix and, hence, the resources an organisation deploys. This inside-out form of strategy is essentially resource-driven. Unfortunately this represents a production rather than a market orientation and as such is restricted and discredited. In addition, it cannot explain what it was that TfL did.

A market orientation to strategy requires a consideration of the needs of the audience first and then a determination of the various messages, media and disciplines necessary to accomplish the strategy: an outside-in approach. This approach equates more closely to that undertaken by TfL.

Many organisations do not develop and implement a communications strategy. They may develop brand strategies, advertising strategies, message strategies, and indeed some form of integrated marketing communications strategy, but there is little evidence of organisations developing overarching corporate-led communications strategies.

Undoubtedly ideas concerning communications and strategy have not always been well articulated or taught together; they are often tactical and there is certainly little agreement on what constitutes corporate communications and marketing communications strategies.

Just as general strategy has been interpreted in different ways, so there are various explanations regarding what is marketing communications strategy. Broadly marketing communications strategy concerns the overall approach used to realise marketing and communications objectives, within an audience-related context. However, this is a broad brush perspective, especially as the phrase 'overall approach' can be interpreted in different ways. Here, four main explanations are considered. They are drawn from the academic literature and practitioner experience and comment. These four are marketing communications as a position, as an audience, as a platform and as a configuration or pattern. These should not be considered to be discrete or exclusive interpretations, as aspects of each can be observed within the others. See Figure 5.1 and note that these strategic forms are loosely aligned with Mintzberg's interpretation of strategy, featured at Scholars' paper 5.1.

MC strategy interpretation 1: Positioning strategies

The process of market analysis and evaluation leading to planned strategies designed to meet prescribed and measurable goals is well established. It is argued that this enables finite resources to be used more efficiently as they can be directed towards markets that hold, potentially, greater value than other markets. This approach involves three main activities: market segmentation, target market selection, and positioning (otherwise referred to as STP).

Market segmentation is the means by which organisations define the broad context within which their strategic business units (SBUs) and products are offered. Market segmentation is the division of a mass market into identifiable and distinct groups or segments, each of which has common characteristics and needs and displays similar

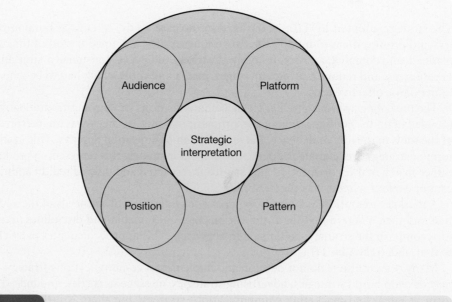

Figure 5.1   Four interpretations of marketing communications strategy

responses to marketing actions. Through this process specific target segments can be selected and marketing plans developed to satisfy the individual needs of the potential buyers in these chosen segments. The development, or rather identification, of segments can be perceived as opportunities and, as Beane and Ennis (1987) suggest, 'a company with limited resources needs to pick only the best opportunities to pursue'.

Viewpoint 5.1   Li Ning repositions against Chinese values

Li Ning is China's largest sportswear brand but its commercial success has recently been challenged. With increasingly intense competition from both international brands such as Nike and Adidas, and domestically from ANTA Sports and Peak Sport, Li Ning has reported considerable financial losses, and lost 80 per cent of its market value.

Chinese brand ANTA Sports is popular among consumers in lower tier cities such as Chengdu, Xian and Nanjing. Here there has been rapid growth in disposable income and ANTA has positioned itself as affordable and durable.

Nike, Adidas and other foreign sportswear brands have strong positions among sports-conscious consumers in the Tier 1 cities, such as Beijing, Shanghai, Guangzhou, Shenzhen. These consumers are willing to pay higher prices for equipment that is positioned on a high quality and technology platform.

Li Ning's strategy involved targeting fashionable, fast-growing areas of sport in China, such as basketball. Using Western sports stars such as NBA basketball superstar Dwayne Wade, the goal was to attract younger consumers with a mid-range pricing strategy. The danger of this approach was that older, loyal customers would feel excluded. Li Ning positioned itself as a high-quality brand, equivalent to the international brands, but did not support this with a suitable pricing strategy.

As if in recognition of this flawed strategy Li Ning shifted its positioning to one that embraced its roots in China and Chinese sports. This meant developing a different set of brand values to those introduced by the international brands. Three core values, sports legacy, Chinese health, and wisdom, were utilised. Each of these are not capable of being copied or eroded by the international competitors.

The brand's sports legacy involves associating Li Ning with what people can do with sports, which is to gain both physical and mental well-being. So, rather than using sport to win and be better than the competition, as exemplified by Nike and their 'I can do' orientation, Li Ning associates with inner and outer harmony through team sports, a 'We' orientation.

Instead of following Nike and Adidas down the technology and innovation positioning Li Ning associated itself with Chinese health, which incorporates traditional Chinese medicine, acupuncture, and an appreciation of how the body works. The advantage of this positioning is that it appeals to both the serious and fun sports enthusiast.

To differentiate Li Ning and divert attention away from the values associated with its international competitors, Li Ning taps into ancient Chinese wisdom, with China's expertise in physical training and sports performance, particularly martial arts, being emphasised.

Source: Fan and Murata (2015); Kwok (2014); Waldmeir (2011).

Question: How might this positioning affect Li Ning's competitors?

Task: Find two other sports brands and compare their approach to the Chinese market.

Exhibit 5.2	**Chinese gymnasts delivering the Li Ning salute**
	Source: Getty Images/Jamie McDonald

This process of segmentation is necessary because a single product is unlikely to meet the needs of all customers in a mass market. If it were, then a single type of toothpaste, chocolate bar or car would meet all of our needs. This is not so, and there are a host of products and brands seeking to satisfy particular buyer needs.

Having identified a market's various segments the next step is to select particular target markets. These represent the best marketing potential and, once selected, require that resources are concentrated on these and no others. Targeted segments, therefore, constitute the environment and the context for a marketing communications strategy and activities. It is the characteristics of the target segment and their perception that should shape an audience-centred marketing communications strategy. Edwards (2011) suggests that rather than refer to a *target* audience, a static interpretation of people, it is better to consider them on an emotional journey, and that we all fluctuate between four different emotional states.

The *actual* self represents who we really are on a day-to-day basis, and perhaps this is the static person that the term 'target audience' refers to. There are times, however, when we move into a *worry* state, and times when we daydream and move into a *fantasy* self. Closest to our actual self is the *idealised* self, that person we would like to be, the person we strive to become. Marketing communications, as well as other elements of the marketing strategy, can be shaped to engage people according to their perceptions of themselves and their emotional states (see Figure 5.2).

The final element in this process is *positioning*. Reference to the DRIP model emphasises the importance of differentiation and the need to communicate a brand's core point(s) of difference with its competitors (see Chapter 1). Positioning is about audiences understanding the claimed differences.

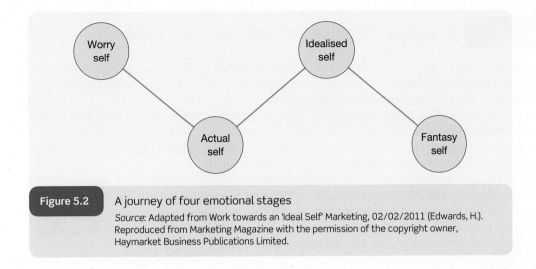

Figure 5.2   A journey of four emotional stages

Source: Adapted from Work towards an 'Ideal Self' Marketing, 02/02/2011 (Edwards, H.). Reproduced from Marketing Magazine with the permission of the copyright owner, Haymarket Business Publications Limited.

As noted in the earlier discussion about strategy, positioning is an integral concept, and for some the essence of strategy. Wind (1990) stated quite clearly that positioning is the key strategic framework for an organisation's brand-based communications, as cited by Jewell (2007). All products and all organisations have a position in the minds of audiences. The task, therefore, is to manage actively the way in which audiences perceive brands. This means that marketing communications strategy should be concerned with achieving effective and viable positions so that the target audiences understand what the brand does, what it means (to them) and can ascribe value to it. This is particularly important in markets that are very competitive and where mobility barriers (ease of entry into and exit from a market, e.g. plant and production costs) are relatively low.

Positioning is about visibility and recognition of what a product/service/organisation represents to a buyer. In markets where the intensity of rivalry and competition are increasing and buyers have greater choice, the fast identification and understanding of a product's intrinsic values become critical. Channel members have limited capacities, whether this is the level or range of stock they can carry or, for retailers, the amount of available shelf space that can be allocated. An offering with a clear identity and orientation to a particular target segment's needs not only will be stocked and purchased, but can warrant a larger margin through increased added value.

It is generally accepted that positioning is the natural conclusion to the sequence of activities that constitute a core part of strategy. Market segmentation and target marketing are prerequisites to successful positioning. Having established that marketing communications should be an audience-centred rather than product-centred activity, it can be concluded with some confidence that marketing communications strategy is essentially about positioning. For new products and services, marketing communications needs to engage target audiences so that they can understand what the brand means, how it differs from similar offerings and, as a result, position it in their minds. For the vast majority of products and services that are already established, marketing communications strategy should be concerned with either developing a strong position or repositioning it in the minds of the target audiences. Chapter 6 explores the positioning concept and the different strategies used by organisations to position their brands.

Viewpoint 5.2　　Changing the perceptions of Colombian coffee

Coffee production and exporting has always been a critical element of the Colombian economy. Formed in 1927, The National Federation of Coffee Growers of Colombia (Federacafe) is a not-for-profit cooperative business association mainly made up of small family businesses.

Much of the Colombian coffee is high-quality beans but is used by roasters primarily as part of a blended coffee formula. In the late 1950s two environmental issues struck. First, the demand for coffee from the USA began to wane, as American consumers developed a preference for Brazilian coffee. The second issue concerned international prices for coffee, which were falling.

To address this situation a brand strategy was developed. Part of this strategy required a change in the way international markets perceived Colombian coffee, and this required a strong, clear point of differentiation for the brand. The goal was to reposition Colombian coffee as a high-quality product, something that would warrant consumers and coffee roasters paying premium prices. In turn, these higher prices would enable the Colombian coffee growers to receive higher incomes.

Federacafe developed a character called Juan Valdez. He was depicted with a sombrero, leather bag, poncho and his faithful mule 'Conchita'. The character was designed to represent the thousands of coffee farmers that constitute the Colombian coffee industry, and be a means by which consumers could recognise and identify with the Colombian coffee brand. Juan Valdez was not just the face of Colombian coffee, he embodied the values of the coffee growers themselves: their pride, simplicity, dedication and knowledge.

Juan Valdez was first presented to American consumers in January 1960 through a full-page ad in the *New York Times*. His picture was accompanied by the strapline 'Colombian Coffee is drinking New York'. It was television, however, that established the character, as his task was to educate consumers about what it was that made Colombian coffee such high quality. This was achieved through a creative that showed him on his own farm, hand-picking coffee beans, with family and donkey, talking to camera and explaining how the various ingredients, such as soil components, altitude, varieties and harvesting methods, all combine to create rich flavour, contributing to the high quality of Colombian coffee. This informational message was conveyed using the Juan Valdez character in order to drive an emotional response and bond consumers with the brand. This proved highly effective to the point that consumer demand for Colombian coffee encouraged coffee roasters to included increasing amounts of Colombian coffee in their blends, before offering 100 per cent Colombian coffee.

Subsequent campaigns showed Juan Valdez demonstrating how to make coffee, and with his donkey he showed consumers where to find Colombian coffee in supermarkets. More recent campaigns have been targeted at younger adult audiences as a response to the surge in demand for coffee houses, espresso bars, and out-of-home coffee consumption, all of which attracted a new generation of younger coffee drinkers. These campaigns featured Juan Valdez experiencing various diverse extreme sports, such as surfing, snowboarding and hang-gliding. The campaign was called 'Grab Life by the Beans'.

In 2014 the brand began challenging Starbucks by opening coffee houses in Florida.

Source:　Kurata (2008); Paajanen (2012); Patton (2014); Ramirez-Vallejo (2003).

Question:	What might be the limitations of a man and a donkey when attempting to change perceptions of a country/market?
Task:	Find another example of an attempt to change perceptions of a brand based on the use of an animal.

Exhibit 5.3	**Juan Valdez – the face of Colombian coffee**
	Source: Getty Images/Dario Cantatore

MC strategy interpretation 2: Audience strategies

Consumer purchase decisions can be characterised, very generally, by a single-person buying centre, whereas organisational buying decisions can involve a large number of different people fulfilling different roles and all requiring different marketing communications messages. In addition to this there are other stakeholders who have an interest in a brand's development – for example, suppliers and the media. It follows from this that communications with these three very different audiences should be radically different, especially in terms of what, where, when and how a message is communicated. Three audience-focused marketing communications strategies emerge:

● *Pull strategies* – these are intended to influence end-user customers (consumers and B2B).

● *Push strategies* – these are intended to influence marketing (trade) channel buyers.

● *Profile strategies* – these are intended to influence a wide range of stakeholders, not just customers and intermediaries.

These are referred to as the '3Ps' of marketing communications strategy and can be considered to be generic strategies thanks to their breadth. *Push* and *pull* relate to the direction of communications in a marketing channel: pushing communications down through a marketing channel or pulling consumers/buyers into a channel via retailers, as a result of receiving communications. They do not relate to the intensity of communications and only refer to the overall approach. *Profile* refers to the presentation of an

Table 5.1 An audience interpretation of marketing communications strategy

Target audience	Message focus	Communications goal
Consumers	Product/service	Purchase
End-user B2B customers	Product/service	Purchase
Channel intermediaries	Product/service	Developing relationships and distribution network
All relevant stakeholders	The organisation	Building reputation

organisation as a whole and the reputation that it bestows on its brands. The identity is said to be 'profiled' to various other target stakeholder audiences, which may well include consumers, trade buyers, business-to-business customers and a range of other influential stakeholders. Normally, profile strategies do not contain or make reference to the specific products or services that the organisation offers. See Table 5.1 for a further explanation of each of these three dimensions.

A pull strategy

If messages designed to position a brand are to be directed at targeted, end-user customers, then the intention is invariably to generate increased levels of awareness, change and/or reinforce attitudes, reduce risk, encourage involvement and ultimately provoke a motivation within the target group. This motivation is to stimulate action so that the target audiences expect the offering to be available to them when they decide to enquire, experiment or make a repeat purchase. This approach is a *pull (positioning)* strategy and is aimed at encouraging customers to 'pull' products through the channel network (see Figure 5.3). This usually means that consumers go into retail outlets (shops) to enquire about a particular product and/or buy it, or to enter a similar transaction direct with the manufacturer or intermediary through direct mail or the Internet. B2B customers are encouraged to buy from dealers and distributors while both groups of consumers and B2B customers have opportunities to buy through direct marketing channels where there is no intermediary.

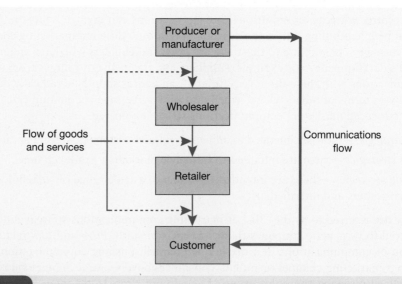

Figure 5.3   The direction of a marketing communications pull strategy

Source: From *Essentials of Marketing Communications*, Pearson Education (Fill, C. 2011) figure 4.2, p. 99.

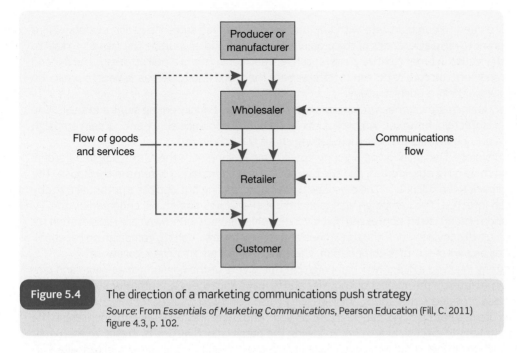

Figure 5.4	The direction of a marketing communications push strategy
	Source: From *Essentials of Marketing Communications*, Pearson Education (Fill, C. 2011) figure 4.3, p. 102.

A push strategy

A second group or type of target audience can be identified on the basis of their contribution to the marketing channel and because these organisations do not consume the products and services they buy, but add value before selling the product on to others in the demand chain. The previous strategy was targeted at customers who make purchase decisions related largely to their personal (or organisational) consumption of products and services. This second group buys products and services, performs some added-value activity and moves the product through the marketing channel network.

The 'trade' channel has received increased attention in recent years as the strategic value of intermediaries has become both more visible and questioned in the light of the Internet. As the channel networks have developed, so has their complexity, which impacts upon the marketing communications strategies and tools used to help reach marketing goals.

A push communications strategy concerns an attempt to influence other trade channel organisations and, as a result, encourage them to take stock, to allocate resources (e.g. shelf space) and to help them to become fully aware of the key attributes and benefits associated with each product with a view to adding value prior to further channel transactions. This strategy is designed to encourage resale to other members of the network and contribute to the achievement of their own objectives. This approach is known as a push strategy, as it is aimed at pushing the product down through the channel towards the end-users for consumption (see Figure 5.4).

The example set out in Viewpoint 5.3 demonstrates how push and pull strategies very often work together, because audiences are not silos. This approach is quite common in FMCG markets.

Viewpoint 5.3	Push–pull dog owners

Pharmaceutical firm Bayer market a brand called Advocate. This is designed to prevent the onset of lungworm, a potentially fatal parasitic infection in dogs. The disease is most often contracted by dogs licking or eating slugs and snails. As this is a pharmaceutical product it cannot be promoted or sold directly to the public, and has to be prescribed by vets.

Bayer therefore need to communicate with two audiences. The first audience is dog owners where the primary tasks are to raise awareness of the problem (lungworm) and encourage the owners to talk to their vet about the issues in order to have a preventative treatment. This is a pull strategy. The second audience is vets and here the core tasks are to differentiate the brand and to persuade vets to prescribe Advocate. This is essentially a push strategy.

Previous Bayer/Advocate awareness campaigns had showed dogs happily eating slugs and snails. The seriousness of the infection, however, was not understood by the audience so a new, harder campaign was required to alert dog owners and get them talking about the condition.

A TV ad was developed which showed a young boy playing Frisbee with the family dog in a garden. The dog is shown to be lying still, lifeless, and the boy calls out in alarm to his parents in the house. The dog then springs back to be full of life. The message has a happy ending but depicts a potential tragedy had the dog been infected. The campaign was launched at the Crufts dog show, endorsed by the TV personality Amanda Holden, a self-confessed dog lover. Bayer launched Houndwaves, a radio station for the event, to stimulate conversations and fun stories among dog lovers. A photo campaign on Facebook was also launched as part of a Crufts competition. This ran the line that 'I'm lungworm aware'.

The push strategy involved a direct mail campaign informing vets of the consumer campaign and preparing them for an increase in the number of enquiries and to make sure they had sufficient stock of Advocate. Vets were also provided with leaflets, point-of-sale posters, and wall displays for their waiting areas.

The campaign drove sales up by 41 per cent year on year, and there was a 78 per cent increase in the number of visits to vets to discuss lungworm. Following the press launch at Crufts, traffic to the Bayer Animal Health's website spiked at 427 per cent, whilst various social media metrics grew substantially. Perhaps not intended, but 86 per cent of vets claim that they have added lungworm to their routine check-ups.

Source: Bradley (2014); www.animalhealth.bayer.com/4910.0.html; www.lungworm.co.uk/.

Question: Discuss the notion that the depiction of a pet's death is unethical and should not be used in advertising.

Task: Develop an outline plan concerning ways in which social media could be used to extend the reach of the Advocate brand.

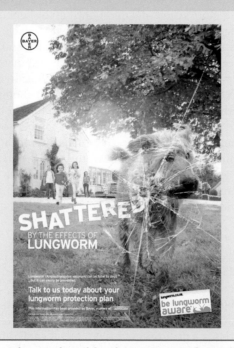

Exhibit 5.4	**Bayer's Advocate brand for the treatment of parasites**
	Source: Copyright of Bayer AG

A profile strategy

The strategies considered so far concern the need for dialogue with customer audiences (pull) and trade channel intermediaries (push). However, there is a whole range of other stakeholder audiences, many of whom need to know about and understand the organisation rather than actually purchase its products and services (see Figure 5.5). This group of stakeholders may include financial analysts, trade unions, government bodies, employees or the local community. It should be easy to understand that these different stakeholder groups can influence the organisation in different ways and, because of this, need to receive (and respond to) different types of messages. Thus, the financial analysts need to know about financial and trading performance and expectations, and the local community may be interested in employment and the impact of the organisation on the local environment, whereas the government may be interested in the way the organisation applies health and safety regulations and pays corporation, VAT and other taxes. It should also be remembered that consumers and business-to-business customers may also be more interested in the organisation itself and so help initiate an umbrella branding strategy.

Traditionally these organisation-oriented activities have been referred to as *corporate communications*, as they deal more or less exclusively with the corporate entity or organisation. Products, services and other offerings are not normally the focus of these communications. It is the organisation and its role in the context of the particular stakeholders' activities that are important. Communications used to satisfy this array of stakeholder needs and the organisation's corporate promotional goals are developed through what is referred to as a *profile strategy*, a major element of which is corporate branding.

A *profile* strategy focuses an organisation's communications upon the development of stakeholder relationships, corporate image and reputation, whether that be just internally, just externally or both. To accomplish and deliver a profile strategy, public relations, including media relations, sponsorship and corporate advertising, become the pivotal tools of the marketing communications mix.

| Figure 5.5 | The direction of a marketing communications profile strategy |

Source: From *Essentials of Marketing Communications*, Pearson Education (Fill, C. 2011) figure 4.4, p. 102.

Within each of these overall strategies, individual approaches should be formulated to reflect the needs of each particular case. So, for example, the launch of a new shampoo product will involve a push strategy to get the product on the shelves of the appropriate retailers. The strategy would be to gain retailer acceptance of the new brand and to position it as a profitable new brand to gain consumer interest. Personal selling supported by trade promotions will be the main marketing communications tool. A pull strategy to develop awareness about the brand will need to be created, accompanied by appropriate public relations work. The next step will be to create particular brand associations and thereby position the brand in the minds of the target audience. Messages may be primarily functional or expressive, but they will endeavour to convey a brand promise. This may be accompanied or followed by the use of incentives to encourage consumers to trial the product. To support the brand, care lines and a website will need to be put in place to provide credibility as well as a buyer reference point and an opportunity to interact with the brand.

The 3Ps provide a generic approach to marketing communications strategy. To provide more precision and utility it is possible to combine the positioning approach considered previously with each of these 3Ps.

Scholars' paper 5.2	The benefits of keeping the ivories clean

Haley, R.I. (1968) Benefit segmentation: a decision-oriented research tool, *Journal of Marketing,* 32 (July), 30–5.

Russell Haley's paper is a classic as it demonstrates some pioneering research through which he identifies four distinct types of customer: those who bought toothpaste for white teeth (sociables); those who wished to prevent decay (worriers); those who liked the taste and refreshment properties (sensors); and, finally, those who bought on a price basis (independents). Each of these groups has particular demographic, behaviouristic and psychographic characteristics from which different brands have developed, all of which require audience-focused brand communications.

MC strategy interpretation 3: Platform strategies

A brand's communications should express its promise, and much of this is achieved through a brand's values and differential claims. In order to maintain brand authority and legitimacy, it is critical to maintain consistency in these communications. This requires a brand to be anchored, to have a set of grounded principles through which the brand is presented at all times. This anchoring has a central role in developing the core images stakeholders have of a brand.

Many organisations, in conjunction with their agencies, determine a strategic theme or platform to anchor their brands. These platforms concern the essence of the promise a brand makes to its customers. For example, this promise may be that the brand delivers happiness (Coca-Cola), safety (Volvo – cars), whiteness (Persil – washing powder), winning mentality (Nike), extra-long life (Duracell – batteries), value (Aldi and Lidl – supermarkets), reliability (Kia – cars), adrenalin rush (Red Bull), or any number of things.

Marketing communications strategy should be developed thematically and consistently around an agreed core theme, or a platform. If stakeholders do not discern any core messages then the brand will not be positioned clearly and the resultant diffused or confused messages might lead to underperformance.

Strategy and the Institute of Practitioners in Advertising

Utilising some of the findings of the IPA's research into successful campaigns, three main platforms can be identified. These are based on an advertising-led creative platform, a brand concept or need-state platform, and platforms based on conversation and participation.

Creative platforms are strategies based on a big, core advertising-led idea that enables audiences to recognise the idea across different media and touchpoints. These campaigns might share the same 'look and feel', response mechanic, competition, brand icon across channels, or central idea that is disseminated through the most appropriate media. P&O Ferries uses a flag as its visual identity across all channels, including on-board communications, advertising and customer communications. The Hovis (bread) revival campaign, the Still Red Hot campaign by Virgin Atlantic, and the 118 118 directory service all serve to illustrate the advertising-led platform.

Brand concept platforms are characterised by their root within the brand. This means they can be communicated using a variety of different creative expressions over time, something an advertising-led idea cannot accomplish.

These types of campaigns can be disaggregated into those based on tangible product attributes and those founded on more intangible conceptual ideas. Tangible campaigns identify a specific occasion (e.g. a birthday celebration), a tightly defined target audience (e.g. first-time mothers) or a specific 'point of market entry' (e.g. a new product).

Intangible campaigns are developed from emotional concepts which allow them a high degree of creative inconsistency, are used across a range of tools and, unlike the advertising-led platforms, last a long time. Honda's 'The Power of Dreams' (2004) and Johnnie Walker's global campaign in 2009 are cited by the IPA as great examples of the use of this type of strategic platform (IPA, 2011).

Participation platforms represent a more recent strategic approach, thanks mainly to the interactive properties of digital media. This enables brands and audiences to interact, engage in dialogue, conversations and participation in a range of events, actions and communities.

This platform aims to integrate a brand into people's life patterns in a way that is significant and relevant to them. Audiences are invited to participate in a centrally driven brand idea, which is then played back through public media in order to involve others. BT (telecoms) invited audiences to suggest storylines for the relationship that was developing, and later sagging, between its ad-brand couple.

Viewpoint 5.4   Crisp user participation

The Super Bowl is more than a game of football, it is an advertising spectacular. The annual event attracts not only die hard football fans but also those drawn by the entertainment staged during time outs. The cleverly styled ads have become an integral part of the viewing experience. In 2014 over 111 million people in the USA tuned in, and that ignores the world-wide audience, to watch the NFL final and the ads that each cost approximately US$4 million for a 30-second spot. This event is seen as a fantastic vehicle to showcase brands, generate vast brand awareness and achieve a positive impact on sales.

Doritos use the opportunity to reach and influence a highly engaged audience and their brand users in 46 countries. With advertising clutter becoming more intense companies are constantly looking for innovative ways to break through the noise. In the light of the ever increasing use of digital technology and the growth of social media, Doritos decided to run a major user-generated campaign called 'Crash the Super Bowl'. Consumers are invited to make and submit an ad for the brand. In 2015, 29 semi-finalists were selected, from which a panel found the top 10, which were presented for an online vote. The winner not only has the prestige of winning but also receives a substantial money prize – US$1 million – and the opportunity to work as a creative contractor at Universal Pictures in Hollywood for a year.

Doritos also win because they optimise their interaction with amateur filmmakers through the creation of an ad, who then seek support and votes from all their contacts. This results in a highly engaged audience with plenty of brand exposure, even before the game starts. Add to this the publicity that the event and Doritos generate, the savings the brand makes in not hiring an agency, and the wealth of creative ideas that are unleashed, the end result is a resounding user-generated success. Handing all power over to consumers is a huge risk but can result in a massive pay-out and, in fact, it has proven so successful that Doritos have repeated their 'Crash the Super Bowl' campaign in subsequent years.

Source: Anon (2014a, 2014b); Baumgarten (2012); Cassinelli (2014); Faeth (2014); Jarboe (2015); Power (2014).

This Viewpoint was written by Ellie Harris when she was a Marketing and Advertising student at Leeds Beckett University.

Question:	To what extent might the co-creation theme adopted by Doritos be disadvantaged against an agency-managed campaign run by Budweiser and others?
Task:	Make notes about the social media performance of any two brands at the Super Bowl.

MC strategy interpretation 4: Configuration strategies

The configuration approach to marketing communications strategy gives emphasis to the structural aspects associated with the design of a message, and the way it is conveyed and received. This approach seeks to maximise the effectiveness of a communications activity by matching goals and resources with an audience's needs. This might involve varying the frequency with which a message is received by the target audience, continuity issues; others involve managing the formality, permanence or direction of a message. Communications strategies designed to get the attention of the audiences are commonplace, while others seek to be immersed or provide continual presence. This approach to communications strategy involves the configuration of four facets of communications: the frequency, direction, modality and content of communications (Mohr and Nevin, 1990).

Frequency

The amount of contact between members of a communications network can impact on effectiveness. Too much information (too frequent, aggregate volume or pure repetition) can overload people and have a dysfunctional effect and affect learning. Too little information can undermine the opportunities for favourable performance outcomes by failing to provide the necessary operational information, motivation and support. As a consequence, it is important to identify the current volume of information being provided and to make a judgement about the desired levels of communications and optimise learning opportunities.

Direction

This refers to the horizontal and vertical movement of communications within a network. Each network consists of people who are dependent on others, but the level of dependence will vary, so that the distribution of power and influence is unequal.

Communications can be unidirectional in that they flow in one direction only. For example, information from a major food retailer, such as Aeon in Japan, Pão de Acucar in Brazil, or Metro in Canada, to small food manufacturers might be considered to be unidirectional because the small food manufacturers perceive little reason to respond, as these supermarkets represent a source of power. Communications can also be bidirectional: that is, to and from organisations and influential opinion leaders and formers.

Modality

Modality refers to the method used to transmit information and there is a wide variety of interpretations of the methods used to convey information. Modality can be seen as communications that is formal, planned and regulated, or informal, unplanned and spontaneous, such as word-of-mouth communications and water-cooler conversations.

Content

This refers to what is said. Frazier and Summers (1984) distinguish between direct and indirect influence strategies. Direct strategies are designed to change behaviour by specific request (recommendations, promises and appeals to legal obligations). Indirect strategies attempt to change another person's beliefs and attitudes about the desirability of the intended behaviour. This may take the form of an information exchange, where the source uses discussions about general business issues to influence the attitudes of the receiver. Social networks and online communities serve to influence consumer attitudes and change behaviour.

Exchange relationship

Communications strategies work within particular contexts, often characterised by the nature of the prevailing relationships and associated exchanges, the level of trust and support experienced by those in the communications network, and aspects of power as perceived by organisations in a B2B environment.

According to Stern and El-Ansary (1988), the nature of the exchange relationship structures the way communications should be used. Collaborative exchanges have a long-term perspective and high interdependence and involve joint decision-making. By contrast, market exchanges are ad hoc and hence have a short-term orientation where interdependence is low.

Climate

Climate refers to the degree of mutual supportiveness that exists between participants. Anderson et al. (1987) used measures of trust and goal compatibility in defining communications climate.

Power

Dwyer and Walker (1981) showed that power conditions within a marketing channel can be symmetrical (with power balanced between members) or asymmetrical (with a power imbalance).

Two specific forms of communications strategy can be identified. The first is a combination referred to as a 'collaborative communications strategy' and includes higher-frequency, more bidirectional flows, informal modes and indirect content. This combination is likely to occur where there are collaborative structures, supportive climates or symmetrical power. The second combination is referred to as an 'autonomous communications strategy' and includes lower-frequency, more unidirectional communications, formal modes and direct content. This combination is likely to occur in channel conditions of market structures, unsupportive climates and asymmetrical power.

Communications strategy should, therefore, be built upon the characteristics of the situation facing each communications episode. Not all audiences share the same conditions, nor do they all possess the same degree of closeness or collaborative expectations. By considering the nature of the channel conditions and then developing communications strategies that complement them, the performance of the focus organisation and other members can be considerably improved, and conflict and tension substantially reduced.

Although the configuration approach is often associated with marketing-channel-based communications, the principles can be observed in consumer markets. Stern and El-Ansary (1992) stress consideration of information flows and movement, and, in particular, the timing and permanence of the communications flows. In addition, work by Mohr and Nevin (1990) takes into account the various facets of communications and the particular channel structures through which communications are intended to move.

| Scholars' paper 5.3 | Configuration and communications |

Mohr, J. and Nevin, J.R. (1990) Communication strategies in marketing channels, *Journal of Marketing,* **October, 36–51.**

Written at a time when there was little published material on marketing communications strategy, this paper shed new light on strategy within marketing channels. Now the contingency principles presented by Mohr and Nevin have relevance in terms of the configuration approach to marketing communications strategy. All marketing communications students should read this paper.

Planning marketing communications

The context in which a communications event occurs not only shapes what and how messages are developed and conveyed, but also influences the interpretation and meaning ascribed to communications. In other words, the goals can be missed if the marketing communications is not entirely effective. The development of marketing communications plans helps to minimise errors and provide for efficiency and effectiveness.

There are a number of contexts that influence or shape marketing communications. All marketing managers (and others) should understand these contextual elements and appreciate how they contribute and influence the development of marketing communications programmes. In addition, there are a number of other elements and activities that need to be built into a programme in order that it can be implemented. These elements concern the goals, the resources, the communications tools to be used and measures of control and evaluation. Just like the cogs in a clock, these elements need to be linked together if the plan is to work. Planning frameworks aim to bring together the various elements into a logical sequence of activities. The rationale for decisions is built on information generated at previous levels in the framework. It also provides a checklist of activities that need to be considered.

However, there needs to be a word of caution as sometimes unforeseen events can lead to serious disruption of marketing communications plans. For example, companies working in the holiday industry set out detailed marketing communications plans accounting for economic conditions and forecasts. Unfortunately these plans can be disrupted by a number of different crises, such as terrorism and outbreaks of civilian unrest or even war, extreme weather conditions such as volcanic ash clouds, hurricanes, heavy rain and snow, or health issues such as illness and disease.

To help students and managers comprehend the linkages between the elements and to understand how these different components complement each other, the rest of this chapter deals with the development of marketing communications plans. To that extent it will be of direct benefit to managers seeking to build plans for the first time or for those familiar with the activity to reconsider current practices. Second, the material should also be of direct benefit to students who are required to understand and perhaps prepare such plans as part-fulfilment of an assessment or examination in this subject area.

The marketing communications planning framework

The principal tasks facing those managing marketing communications are to decide:

- Who should receive the brand's messages.
- What is to be achieved.
- What the messages should say.
- How the messages are to be delivered.
- What actions the receivers should take.
- What image of the organisation/brand receivers are expected to retain.
- How much is to be spent establishing this new image.
- How to control the whole process once it has been implemented.
- What was achieved.

Note that more than one message is transmitted and that there is more than one target audience. This is important, as recognition of the need to communicate with multiple audiences and their different information requirements, often simultaneously, lies at the heart of marketing communications. The aim is to generate and transmit messages which present the organisations and their offerings to their various target audiences, encouraging them to enter into a dialogue. These messages must be presented consistently and they must address the points stated above. It is the skill and responsibility of the marketing communications planner to blend the communications tools and to create a mix that satisfies these elements.

The marketing communications planning framework (MCPF) (presented in Figure 5.6), represents a sequence of decisions that marketing managers undertake when preparing, implementing and evaluating communications strategies and plans. It does not mean that this sequence reflects reality; indeed, many marketing decisions are made outside any recognisable framework. However, as a means of understanding the different components, appreciating the way in which they relate to one another and bringing together various aspects for work or for answering examination questions leading to a qualification, both academic and professional, this approach has many advantages and has been used by a number of local, national and international organisations.

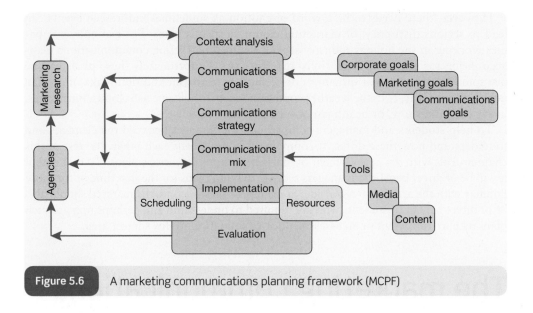

Figure 5.6   A marketing communications planning framework (MCPF)

Marketing communications activities should seek to satisfy particular objectives through the explicit and deliberate development of a communications strategy. The MCPF will be used to show, first, the key elements, second, some of the linkages and, third, the integrated approach that is considered good practice.

This framework reflects the deliberate or planned approach to strategic marketing communications. The processes associated with marketing communications, however, are not linear, as depicted in this framework, but integrative and interdependent. To that extent, this approach recognises the value of stakeholder theory and the requirement to build partnerships with buyers and other organisations networked with an organisation.

Other 'decision sequences' have been advanced, in particular one by Rothschild (1987) and another by Engel et al. (1994). One of the difficulties associated with these frameworks is that they fail to bring strategy into the development of the promotional mix. These frameworks rely on the objective and task approach, whereby plans are developed for each of the individual communications tools, and then aggregated to form strategy.

Viewpoint 5.5   Pringles plan a Chinese crunch

The snack brand Pringles had a small share of the highly competitive market in China. Additionally, their 50 per cent price premium made life even more challenging. In 2009 the product was made 'crunchier' than earlier offerings. An integrated campaign was launched aimed at promoting the functional product benefit – 'crunchiness' – fun and engaging. Following the model, the campaign consisted of the following stages:

1. Campaign responsibilities
   Agency, Grey Advertising in Hong Kong, was appointed to develop the campaign for Pringles.

2. Target audience
   This was termed Generation (G) Y – single males and females 18–24 years old. In most other markets, the target audience is primarily mothers with children.

3. Campaign objectives
   - Engage target audience.
   - Strengthen brand equity attributes (crunchiness).
   - Drive sales and profit.

4. Budget
   - Media budget was less than US$1 million.

5. Media selection and planning
   - Online videos.
   - Application game and social networking site.
   - Bulletin Board System (BBS) programme – Internet forum.
   - Flash mobbing video in Beijing – used top video-sharing sites.
   - Online press releases.
   - Instore activity.

6. Advertising development and testing
   Consumer insights were gained via visits to Gen Y homes, accompanied store visits and social interaction. This identified that Gen Y spend little time watching TV compared to online sources of entertainment. Other information was gathered from published market research, magazines, blogs and websites. Qualitative product research was carried out on the crunchiness – 'KaCha' – concept. Positive results were followed up using quantitative techniques.

7. Implementation and scheduling
   Three branded online videos were launched at the end of July 2009. Two weeks later, three unbranded videos with a twist were released.
   - Game and brand zone went live in mid-August 2009.
   - End of August – BBS programme launched.
   - Flash mobbing, one month after online videos.
   - August–September in-store activities, point of sale and tastings.

8. Campaign evaluation
   - Sales outperformed category average annualised growth.
   - Online videos achieved excellent impact on brand metrics and significantly increased all Pringles brand equity attributes (Millward Brown). Over 10 million hits in eight weeks.
   - Brand zone and application game performed much better than most site campaigns (Millward Brown).
   - Flash mobbing video generated over 1.1 million views.

Source: Based on www.warc.com/prize.

Question: Why were the media chosen by Pringles effective in this case?

Task: Prepare an outline advertising campaign plan for a consumer brand in a market of your choice.

Another framework, the SOSTAC® approach (situation, objectives, strategy, tactics, action, control), was developed by Smith (2003). This is essentially a sound system, and moves closer than most of the others to help formulate suitable marketing communications plans. However, as SOSTAC is multi-purpose and is intended for application to a variety of planning situations, there is a danger that the communications focus is lost at the situation analysis phase when used for developing marketing communications plans. This can lead to a reiteration of a SWOT (strengths, weaknesses, opportunities, threats) and/or a general marketing plan, with subsequent problems further down the line in terms of the justification and understanding of the communications strategy and mixes that need to be deployed. In addition, the SOSTAC model does not give sufficient emphasis to the need to identify and understand the characteristics of the target audience, which is so important for the development of coherent marketing communications.

The MCPF approach presented here is not intended to solve all the problems associated with the formulation of such plans, but it is sufficiently robust to meet the needs of employers and examiners, and is recommended.

Elements of the plan

Marketing communications plans should consist of the following elements. These elements are now considered in turn.

- Context analysis (developed from a communications perspective)
- Communications objectives
- Marketing communications strategy
- Coordinated communications mix (tools, media and content)
- Resources (human and financial)
- Scheduling and implementation
- Evaluation and control
- Feedback.

Context analysis

Analysing the context in which marketing communications events occur is a necessary, indeed vital, first step in the planning process. Bloxham and Sylvester (2013) stress the importance of a context analysis within a media context, and state that an understanding of the context in which media are used and messages consumed is necessary in order to optimise the impact of marketing communications. This can be seen clearly in the TfL case at the beginning of this chapter.

Bosiljevac (2015) argues that an understanding of context helps bridge the work of strategists, creatives and the media team, in order to create customer relevancy. This might be in terms of really understanding the audience and saying something insightful, or finding a point of connection that complements the audience's pattern of media usage.

The purpose of a context analysis is to understand the key market and communications drivers that are likely to influence (or are already influencing) a brand (or organisation) and either help or hinder its progress towards meeting its long-term objectives. This is different from a situation analysis, because the situation analysis considers a range of wider organisational factors, most of which are normally considered in the development of marketing plans (while the communications focus is lost). Duplication is to be avoided, as it is both inefficient and confusing.

The compilation of a context analysis (CA) is very important, as it presents information and clues about what the promotional plan needs to achieve. Information and market research data about target audiences (their needs, perception, motivation, attitudes and decision-making characteristics), the media and the people they use for information about offerings, the marketing objectives and time scales, the overall level of financial and other resources that are available, the quality and suitability of agency and other outsourced activities, and the environment in terms of societal, technological, political and economic conditions, both now and at some point in the future, all need to be considered.

Table 5.2 The main elements of the context analysis

Context element	Dimensions
The customer context	Segment characteristics
	Levels of awareness, perception and attitudes towards the brand/organisation
	Levels of involvement and types of perceived risk
	DMU characteristics and issues
	Media usage
The business context	Corporate and marketing strategy and plans
	Brand/organisation analysis
	Competitor analysis
The internal context	Financial constraints
	Organisation identity
	Culture, values and beliefs
	Marketing expertise
	Agency availability and suitability
The external context	Who are the key stakeholders and why are they important?
	What are their communications needs?
	Social, political, economic and technological restraints and opportunities

At the root of the CA is the marketing plan. This will already have been prepared and contains important information about the target segment, the business and marketing goals, competitors and the time scales in which the goals are to be achieved. The rest of the CA seeks to elaborate and build upon this information so as to provide the detail in order that the plan can be developed and justified.

The CA provides the rationale for the communications plan. It is from the CA that the marketing objectives (from the marketing plan) and the marketing communications objectives are derived. The type, form and style of the message are rooted in the characteristics of the target audience, and the media selected to convey messages will be based on the nature of the tasks, the media habits of the audience and the resources available. The main components of the CA are set out in Table 5.2.

Communications objectives

The role of communications objectives in the planning process is important for a number of reasons. First, they provide a balance to the plan and take away the sole emphasis on sales that inevitably arises. Second, they indicate positioning issues, third, they highlight the required balance of the mix, fourth, they provide time parameters for campaigns and, finally, they provide a crucial means by which particular marketing communications activities are evaluated.

Ideally, communications objectives should consist of three main elements:

1. Corporate objectives.
   These are derived from the business or marketing plan. They refer to the mission and the business area that the organisation believes it should be in.
2. Marketing objectives.

These are derived from the marketing plan and are output-oriented. Normally these can be considered as sales-related objectives, such as market share, sales revenues, volumes, ROI and profitability indicators.

3. Marketing communications objectives.

These are derived from an understanding of the current context in which a brand exists and the future context in the form of where the brand is expected to be at some point in the future. These will be presented as awareness levels, perception, comprehension/knowledge, attitudes towards and overall degree of preference for the brand. The choice of communications goal depends on the tasks that need to be accomplished. In addition, most brands need either to maintain their current brand position or to reposition themselves in the light of changing contextual conditions.

These three elements constitute the communications objectives and they all need to be set out in SMART terminology (see Chapter 6). What also emerges is a refinement of the positioning that managers see as important for success. Obviously, not all plans require express attention to positioning (e.g. government information campaigns) but most commercial and brand-oriented communications programmes need to communicate a clear position in their market. Thus, at this point the positioning intentions are developed and these will be related to the market, the customers or some other dimension. The justification for this will arise from the CA.

Marketing communications strategy

As noted earlier, the communications strategy can take many different forms, but should always be customer-, not method/media-oriented. Therefore, the strategy depends on whether the target audience is a customer segment, a distributor or dealer network or whether other stakeholders need to be reached. In addition, it is imperative that the strategy be geared to the communications needs of the target audience that is revealed during the customer and business context analyses. This will show what the task is that marketing communications needs to fulfil. Having established who the audience is, push-, pull- or profile-dominated strategies can be identified. The next step is to determine the task that needs to be accomplished. This will have been articulated previously in the marketing communications objectives, but the approach at this stage is less quantitative and softer.

The DRIP tasks of marketing communications can be used to suggest the strategy being pursued. For example, if a new brand is being launched, the first task will be to inform and differentiate the brand for members of the trade before using a pull strategy to inform and differentiate the brand for the target, end-user customers. An organisation wishing to signal a change of strategy and/or a change of name following a merger or acquisition may choose to use a profile strategy and the primary task will be to inform of the name change. An organisation experiencing declining sales may choose to remind customers of a need or it may choose to improve sales through persuasion.

Coordinated communications mix

Having formulated, stated and justified the required position, the next step is to present the basic form and style of the key message that is to be conveyed. Is there to be a lot of copy or just a little? Is there to be a rational or emotional approach or some weighting between the two? What should be the tone of the visual messages? Is there to be a media blitz? It is at this point that those responsible for the development of these plans can be imaginative and try some new ideas. Trying to tie in the message to the strategic orientation is the important part, as the advertising agency will refine and redefine the message and the positioning.

From this the communications mixes need to be considered *for each* of the strategies proposed: that is, a mix for the consumer strategy, a mix for the trade strategy and a distinct mix for the communications to reach the wider array of stakeholders.

The choice of methods should clearly state the tools and the media to be used. A short paragraph justifying the selection is very important, as the use of media in particular is to a large extent dependent upon the nature of the goals, the target audience and the resources. The key is to provide message consistency and a measure of integration.

Resources

This is a vitally important part of the plan, one that is often avoided or forgotten about. The resources necessary to support the plan need to be determined and these refer not only to the financial issues but to the quality of available marketing expertise and the time that is available to achieve the required outcomes.

Project management software such as Prince2, and Gantt charts and other planning aids, are best used to support this part of the plan. Preferably, actual costs should be assigned, although percentages can be allocated if being written for examination purposes. What is important is the relative weighting of the costs, and a recognition and understanding of the general costs associated with the proposed communications activities.

It must be understood that the overall cost of the strategy should be in proportion to the size of the client organisation, its (probable) level of profitability and the size and dynamics of the market in which it operates.

Scheduling and implementation

The next step is to schedule the deployment of the methods and the media. Events should be scheduled according to the goals and the strategic thrust. So, if it is necessary to communicate with the trade prior to a public launch, those activities tied into the push-positioning strategy should be scheduled prior to those calculated to support the pull strategy.

Similarly, if awareness is a goal then, if funds permit, it may be best to use television and posters first before sales promotions (unless sampling is used), direct marketing, point of purchase and personal selling.

Evaluation and control

Unless there is some form of evaluation, there will be no dialogue and no true marketing communications. There are numerous methods to evaluate the individual performance of the tools and the media used, and for examination purposes these should be stated. In addition, and perhaps more meaningfully, the most important measures are the communications objectives set in the first place. The success of a promotional strategy and the associated plan is the degree to which the objectives set are achieved.

Feedback

The planning process is completed when feedback is provided. Not only should information regarding the overall outcome of a campaign be considered, but so should individual aspects of the activity. For example, the performance of the individual tools used within the campaign, whether sufficient resources were invested, the appropriateness of the strategy in the first place, any problems encountered during implementation and the relative ease with which the objectives were accomplished are all aspects that need to be fed back to all internal and external parties associated with the planning process.

This feedback is vitally important because it provides information for the CA that anchors the next campaign. Information fed back in a formal and systematic manner constitutes an opportunity for organisations to learn from their previous campaign activities, a point often overlooked and neglected.

Links and essential points

It was mentioned earlier that there are a number of linkages associated with different parts of the marketing communications plan. It is important to understand the nature of these links as they represent the interconnections between different parts of the plan and the rationale for undertaking the CA in particular. The CA feeds the items shown in Table 5.3. For example, research undertaken by Interbrand for Intercontinental Hotels, to find out what influenced the brand experience of hotel guests, discovered that one of the key factors was the hotel concierge. As a result, the role of the concierge became a central element in the communications strategy, influencing the campaign goals, positioning and message strategy (Gustafson, 2007). The objectives derived from the CA feed decisions concerning strategy, tools and media, content, scheduling and evaluation.

The marketing communications strategy is derived from an overall appreciation of the needs of the target audience (and stakeholders) regarding the brand and its competitive position in the market. The communications mix is influenced by the previous elements and the budget that follows. However, the nature of the tools and the capacity and characteristics of the media influence scheduling, implementation and evaluation activities.

Table 5.3 Linkages within the MCPF

MCPF	Elements explanation
Objectives	From the marketing plan, from the customer, stakeholder network and competitor analysis and from an internal marketing review
Strategic balance between push, pull and profile	From an understanding of the brand, the needs of the target audiences, including employees and all other stakeholders, and the marketing goals
Brand positioning	From users' and non-users' perceptions, motivations, attitudes and understanding about the brand and its direct and indirect competitors
Message content and style	From an understanding about the level of involvement, perceived risk, DMU analysis, information-processing styles and the positioning intentions
Promotional stools and media	From the target audience analysis of media habits, involvement and preferences, from knowledge about product suitability and media compatibility, from a competitor analysis and from the resource analysis

Scholars' paper 5.4	Planning Renault's expansion

Caemmerer, B. (2009) The planning and implementation of integrated marketing communications, *Marketing Intelligence & Planning*, 27(4), 524–38.

Students of marketing communications should read this paper, simply because it illustrates the tasks involved in the planning and implementation of integrated marketing communications. Using a case study approach based on Renault's attempt to expand their market share in Germany, the paper considers the range of tasks involved in planning an integrated marketing communications campaign. These include the context analysis and the identification of marketing communications opportunities; choosing the right marketing communications agency; campaign development and implementation, including the selection of the marketing communications mix, creative execution and media planning; campaign evaluation; planning of follow-up campaigns; and managerial coordination between all tasks and parties involved to ensure integration of marketing communications initiatives throughout the campaign.

Key points

- There are many different views of what constitutes strategy. The planning and emergent perspectives have gained most agreement.

- Marketing communications strategy is not just about the mix, and should start with an audience-centred orientation.

- Marketing communications strategy should be concerned with the overall direction of the programme and target audiences, the fit with marketing and corporate strategy, the key message and desired positioning the brand is to occupy in the market, plus the resources necessary to deliver the position and accomplish the goals.

- There are four core ways of interpreting marketing communications strategy. These are the positioning, audience, platform and configuration approaches. Each of these emphasises particular elements and issues but they are not mutually discrete. Aspects of each can be found in the others.

- The positioning approach is derived from the STP process.

- The audience approach is referred to as the '3Ps' of marketing communications strategy.

- The platform approach can be advertising-led (around a creative idea), brand-led (around a core brand characteristic) or take the form of a participatory platform.

- The configuration approach requires managing the structural elements of an intended communications event, within the prevailing relationship, climate and power context, where appropriate.

- To manage efficiently and perhaps more effectively, marketing communications should be implemented through the use of a planning framework.

- The framework consists of a number of elements which are presented sequentially, but in reality often happen simultaneously. Key to understanding the planning framework are the linkages between the various elements.

Review questions

TfL case question

1. Explain the role strategy plays in marketing communications, using the TfL case to illustrate your points.

2. Evaluate which of the four interpretations of strategy presented in this chapter might best be used to explain the success of the TfL campaign, described at the beginning of this chapter.

3. Draw two diagrams depicting the direction of communications in both the push and the pull strategies when applied to the TfL campaign.

4. Which type of engagement best explains the TfL approach to marketing communications?

5. Identify the elements of the marketing communications mix used by TfL to implement their strategy.

General questions

1. Compare strategy with planning. In what ways might planning be the same as strategy?

2. Make notes for your friend in which you explain the differences between an advertising-led and a brand-led platform for marketing communications strategy.

3. Explain the configuration approach to marketing communications strategy.

4. Sketch the marketing communications planning framework – from memory.

5. Following on from the previous question, check your version of the MCPF with the original and then prepare some bullet-point notes, highlighting the critical linkages between the main parts of the framework.

References

Anderson, E., Lodish, L. and Weitz, B. (1987) Resource allocation behaviour in conventional channels, *Journal of Marketing Research*, February, 85–97.

Andrews, K. (1987) *The Concept of Corporate Strategy*, Homewood, IL: Richard D. Irwin.

Anon (2012) Delivering Transport for the London 2012 Games, Olympic Delivery Authority, October, retrieved from http://learninglegacy.independent.gov.uk/documents/pdfs/transport/london-2012-report-lowres-withlinks.pdf, accessed 14 April 2016

Anon (2014a) Doritos crash the Super Bowl contest: which ad will be worth $1 million? *Inquisitor*, 4 November, retrieved 27 November 2014 from www.inquisitr.com/1584150/2015-doritos-crash-the-super-bowl-mcontest-which-ad-will-be-worth-1-million/.

Anon (2014b) Crash the Super Bowl, *Doritos*, retrieved 27 November 2014 from https://crashthesuperbowl.doritos.com.

Ansoff, H.I. (1965) *Corporate Strategy*, New York: McGraw-Hill.

Baumgarten, C. (2012) 3 user-generated campaigns that got it right, *Mashable*, 26 June, retrieved 27 November

2014 from http://mashable.com/2012/06/26/user-generated-content-campaign/.

Beane, T.P. and Ennis, D.M. (1987) Market segmentation: a review, *European Journal of Marketing*, 21(5), 20–42.

Bloxham, M. and Sylvester, A.K. (2013) Media research: planning for context, *Admap*, April, retrieved 13 July 2014 from www.warc.com/Content/ContentViewer.aspx?ID=7e94ad81-00d2-4696-ab8e-e8077187bbeb&MasterContentRef=7e94ad81-00d2-4696-ab8e-e8077187bbeb&Campaign=admap_apr13&utm_campaign=admap_apr13.

Bosiljevac, J. (2015) Advertising in context: create context and relevancy, *Admap*, May.

Bradley, G. (2014) Dog days are over, *themarketer*, 1 August, retrieved 7 August from www.themarketer.co.uk/how-to/case-studies/bayer-animal-health-campaign/.

Caemmerer, B. (2009) The planning and implementation of integrated marketing communications, *Marketing Intelligence & Planning*, 27(4), 524–38.

Cassinelli, A. (2014) 10 great examples of user generated content campaigns, *Postano*, 21 April, retrieved

27 November 2014 from www.postano.com/blog/10-great-examples-of-user-generated-content-campaigns.

Chaffee, E. (1985) Three models of strategy, *Academy of Management Review,* 10(1), 89–98.

Dwyer, R. and Walker, O.C. (1981) Bargaining in an asymmetrical power structure, *Journal of Marketing,* 45 (Winter), 104–15.

Edwards, H. (2011) Work towards an 'Ideal Self', *Marketing,* 2 February, p. 21.

Engel, J.F., Warshaw, M.R. and Kinnear, T.C. (1994) *Promotional Strategy,* 8th edition, Homewood, IL: Richard D. Irwin.

Faeth, B. (2014) User-generated content: this is how you do it, *Inbound,* 2 February, retrieved 27 November 2014 from www.inboundmarketingagents.com/inbound-marketing-agents-blog/bid/334456/Doritos-Wins-the-SuperBowl-with-Perfect-Content-Marketing.

Fan, K. and Murata, P. (2015) Revitalizing a national icon, *Millward Brown,* retrieved 30 January 2015 from www.millwardbrown.com/docs/default-source/insight-documents/case-studies/Firefly_MB_Li_Ning_Case_Study_2013.pdf?sfvrsn=4.

Frazier, G.L. and Summers, J.O. (1984) Interfirm influence strategies and their application within distribution channels, *Journal of Marketing,* 48 (Summer), 43–55.

Gustafson, R. (2007) Best of all worlds, *Marketing: Brands by Design,* 14 November, 11.

Haley, R.I. (1968) Benefit segmentation: a decision-oriented research tool, *Journal of Marketing,* 32 (July), 30–5.

Hanley, C. (2012) London 2012 Travel Demand Management, Journeys, 1 November, retrieve from http://www.lta.gov.sg/ltaacademy/doc/J12%20Nov-p29Chris_London%202012%20Travel%20Demand%20Management.pdf, accessed 14 April 2016.

IPA (2011) *New Models of Marketing Effectiveness: From Integration to Orchestration,* WARC.

Jarboe, G. (2015) Doritos 'Crash the Super Bowl' video contest wins the big brand game', *Reelseo,* 5 January, retrieved 6 January 2015 from www.reelseo.com/crash-super-bowl-2015-video-contest-doritos/?utm_source=ReelSEO+Subscribers&utm_campaign=3d4bb7dae0-Daily-Email&utm_medium=email&utm_term=0_c3543eda94-3d4bb7dae0-213991241.

Jewell, R.D. (2007) Establishing effective repositioning communications in a competitive marketplace, *Journal of Marketing Communications,* 13(4), 231–41.

Kay, J. (1993) The structure of strategy, *Business Strategy Review,* 4(2), 17–37.

Kurata, P. (2008) Juan Valdez travels the world, sends profits home to Colombia, *America.gov,* 9 April, retrieved 24 May 2012 from www.america.gov/st/business-english/2008/April/20080409101828cpataruk0.7881891.html.

Kwok, D. (2014) China's Li Ning stumbles from gold medal position to no man's land *Reuters,* Monday 1 September, retrieved 31 January 2015 from www.reuters.com/article/2014/09/01/us-lining-outlook-dUSKBN0GW33B20140901.

Mintzberg, H. and Waters, J.A. (1985) Of strategies, deliberate and emergent, *Strategic Management Journal,* 6(3), 257–72.

Mohr, J. and Nevin, J.R. (1990) Communication strategies in marketing channels, *Journal of Marketing,* October, 36–51.

Paajanen, S. (2012) Who is Juan Valdez? This face has been selling Colombian coffee for over 40 years, retrieved 24 May 2012 from http://coffeetea.about.eom/cs/culture/a/juanvaldez.htm.

Patton, L. (2014) Juan Valdez goes after Starbucks with new cafes in Florida, *Bloomberg,* 21 July, retrieved 4 August 2014 from www.bloomberg.com/news/2014-07-21/juan-valdez-goes-after-starbucks-with-franchise-cafes-in-florida.html.

Power, J. (2014) Is $4m for a 30-second Super Bowl spot really worth it? In short – yes, *Marketing Magazine,* 29 January, retrieved 14 August 2014 from www.marketingmagazine.co.uk/article/1229049/4m-30-second-super-bowl-spot-really-worth-it-short--yes.

Ramirez-Vallejo, J. (2003) Colombian Coffee, *ReVista: Harvard Review of Latin America,* retrieved 24 May 2012 from www.drclas.harvard.edu/revista/articles/view/273.

Rothschild, M. (1987) *Marketing Communications,* Lexington, MA: DC Heath.

Smith, P.R. (2003) *Great Answers to Tough Marketing Questions,* 2nd edition, London: Kogan Page.

Stern, L. and El-Ansary, A.I. (1988) *Marketing Channels,* Englewood Cliffs, NJ: Prentice - Hall.

Stern, L. and El-Ansary, A.I. (1992) *Marketing Channels,* 4th edition, Englewood Cliffs, NJ: Prentice - Hall.

Storey, R. (2014) Olympic Delivery Authority / Transport for London: Securing Gold at London 2012, *Institute of Practitioners in Advertising,* retrieve from www.warc.com/Pages/Search/WordSearch.aspx?Sort=ContentDate%7c1&q=storey*+TFL, accessed 14 April 2016.

Topham, G. and Gibson, O. (2012) London 2012: campaign seeks to cut commuter numbers during Games, The Guardian, Monday 30 January, retrieve from http://www.theguardian.com/sport/2012/jan/30/london-olympics-2012-cut-commuter, accessed 14 April 2016.

Waldmeir, P. (2011) Li Ning raises concerns for Chinese brands, *FT.com,* 10 October, retrieved 31 January 2015 from www.ft.com/cms/s/0/e8a1aa66-eda3-11e0-a9a9-00144feab49a.html\#axzz3QPldxsIE.

Wind, Y.J. (1990) Positioning analysis and strategy, in *The Interface of Marketing and Strategy* (eds G. Day, B. Weitz and R. Wensley), Greenwich, CT: JAI Press, 387–412.

Chapter 6

Marketing communications: objectives and positioning

The setting of formalised marketing communications objectives is important because they provide guidance about what is to be achieved and when. These objectives form a pivotal role between the business/marketing plans and the marketing communications strategy. The way in which a product or service is perceived by buyers is the only positioning that really matters.

Aims and learning objectives

The aims of this chapter are to establish the role and characteristics of marketing communications objectives and to explore the concept of positioning.

The learning objectives are to enable readers to:

1. explore the different types of organisational objectives;
2. appreciate the relationship between corporate strategy and communications objectives;
3. determine the components of SMART-based objectives;
4. examine the differences between sales- and communications-based objectives;
5. understand the concept of positioning and the principles of perceptual mapping;
6. explain the main types of positioning strategies.

Petplan

Petplan provides specialist insurance cover for pets. At the heart of the Petplan brand is the Covered For Life® policy. This represents Petplan's hero, quality product that offers lifetime cover. Covered For Life® policyholders are far less likely to switch, and frequently they're worth more than customers buying fixed-term policies.

Following three decades of strong growth that had cemented Petplan as market leader, there were signs that the company was beginning to struggle in 2012. There were several reasons behind this.

First, the number of pets in the UK had begun to plateau and, more worrying still, the number of owners with insurance was beginning to fall. This was a clear result of the contraction of disposable incomes following the financial crisis.

Second, there had been a number of new market entrants into the category. These included the big supermarket and direct insurance brands (Tesco Bank, More Th>n, Direct Line, Sainsbury's Finance) who had all begun to offer pet insurance, at low prices, supported by their large advertising budgets. Petplan found itself drawn into this cost-driven environment, and the brand had begun to play the same low-cost game.

Third, Petplan had always relied heavily on intermediaries with 60 per cent of sales driven through vets, breeders and charities. But a new market place was emerging, one in which direct sales were growing and sales through partners declining. In addition, comparison websites were beginning to play an increasingly important role in purchasing. These sites were becoming a first port of call for consumers considering pet insurance and Petplan wasn't on them.

The shift away from intermediaries meant that Petplan needed to start communicating directly with end user consumers. But, at the beginning of 2012, Petplan's spontaneous brand awareness had slipped to fourth, behind Tesco, Direct Line and Sainsbury's.

Brand share had also stagnated and, in contrast, Tesco and More Th>n (second and third biggest brands, respectively) were gaining share, as was the smaller specialist, Animal Friends. Petplan was being squeezed at both ends and needed a strategy to regain its market leadership and financial health.

The strategy required repositioning Petplan as the consumers' premium brand of choice in the category, based on Petplan's expertise and heritage. To accomplish the strategy a clear set of business and marketing objectives were set for 2013.

Business objectives

- Drive volume into the business by increasing penetration.
- Drive value into the business by attracting higher value customers.

Marketing objectives

- Drive brand awareness levels to help combat the threat of comparison sites.
- Drive people to the brand's direct channels.
- Improve conversion rates of our direct channels.
- Justify our premium position.
- To achieve these goals we set out a six-point re-launch plan.

A new positioning

We went back to what made Petplan great in the beginning – a real knowledge and understanding of pets. The brand had an unrivalled 36 years' experience and had helped more pets through more instances of accident and illness than any other insurer. This gave us a clear sustainable competitive advantage upon which we built a new position as the 'knowledgeable experts'.

A new target

A target segment of the pet-owning population was identified as having the greatest propensity to take out Petplan's premium insurance. These were pet owners with the strongest emotional bond with their animal, who believed their pets deserved a certain quality of life. They were also the consumers most open to paying more for insurance, but didn't have a policy. We called them the 'Responsible Uninsured'. They were Petplan's heartland consumer and we knew we had to reconnect with them.

A new identity

While we now had a new positioning fit for a brand leader, it was important that Petplan began to look like one. Prior to re-launch the brand had different 'looks'

Exhibit 6.1	**Examples of Petplan's new branding and salience approach** *Source*: Now.

in different channels and a disparate collection of brand assets. In communications the brand looked and sounded like a low-cost insurer. A premium and distinctive identity for Petplan was created, the first brand toolkit was completed, and an image library compiled to ensure that all the brand's agencies could implement the look and feel effectively. By the time the brand relaunched at the beginning of 2013, over 400 pieces of collateral had been created in line with the new identity and distributed through over 16,000 touch points.

New salience-driving advertising

Advertising had to increase salience in order to drive people to us directly and bypass the aggregator sites. TV was key as it is an effective means of emotively building brands in the long-term and is also able to drive short-term responses.

The TV commercial brought to life the brand's unrivalled depth of expertise by dramatising the number and variety of pets Petplan had helped over the years. The ad featured 45 breeds of cats, dogs and rabbits that appeared on screen in quick succession,

accompanied by an updated version of 'The Major-General's Song' from *Pirates of Penzance* with the original lyrics replaced with the names of the breeds. The execution was created with high production values to bolster our premium position.

We created a *brand* version, which allowed us to take the high ground and start shifting the category dialogue away from cost, and a *direct response* version, which was shorter and featured an incentive to trigger response. The ad introduced the new endline, 'Every Pet Deserves Petplan', a line that framed our expert knowledge in a way that resonated with our target's desire to give their pets the best.

A new focus online

User experience was put at the heart of our approach. The website was totally re-designed and transactional mobile/tablet versions of the site created. The site was purposefully designed to promote Covered For Life® above fixed-term policies. This was achieved through subtle layout changes that were continually monitored and optimised.

Exhibit 6.2   **Examples of Petplan's new response and engagement communications**
Source: Now.

Drive constant response and create on-going dialogue

Our media strategy comprised three streams: salience, response and engagement.

Brand TV drove salience through focused bursts and response-driving media harvested the effects of these spikes across the year. Our response-driving media comprised: DRTV, SEO and digital advertising (with behavioural and contextual targeting).

Social and CRM built engagement with the brand, reinforcing our 'knowledgeable experts' positioning and increased the perceived value of being a Petplan customer. We targeted our CRM activity more closely, ensuring we were talking to the 'responsible uninsured', and also adding greater personal relevance to our messaging.

The results of this action plan can be considered against the objectives.

Business objectives

● Drive volume into the business by increasing penetration.

Our direct sales grew and the volume of the customer base increased by 8.7 per cent over the course of the campaign. This equates to a 5 per cent increase in penetration.

● Drive value into the business by attracting higher value customers.

Petplan's value increased 11 per cent ahead of our volume increase. This was due to the increased number of Covered For Life® sales, indicating that our communications were working to attract higher value customers as intended. Our brand share increased by an impressive 5 per cent points, reaching 29.4 per cent, up from 24.6 per cent in 2012. Over the same period we saw Tesco decline, even though they continued to outspend us.

Marketing objectives

● Drive brand awareness levels to help combat the threat of comparison sites.

Pre-campaign the brand's spontaneous awareness level stood at 15 per cent. One month into the campaign, spontaneous awareness had increased to 21 per cent and two months into the campaign to 26 per cent. Over the course of the year spontaneous awareness didn't drop back to pre-campaign levels.

● Drive people to the brand's direct channels.

Over the course of 2013 we saw call centre volumes increase significantly, 6.6 per cent on 2012 levels, but critically, we also saw sales increase. By the end of the year our call centre sales were up 8.9 per cent on 2012.

Online the results were better still. Google Trends revealed 'interest' in Petplan rising over the course of 2013 and even more gratifyingly showed the brand significantly pulling away from Tesco during the year.

● Improve conversion rates of our direct channels.

Visits to our website rose by 30.3 per cent and web sales increased by a staggering 29 per cent. More people than ever before came to us directly, and more people than ever before were purchasing from us directly.

At the time of writing Mintel predicted that the category grew by 7.5 per cent in 2013 (from £644 million to £714 million). Petplan increased its value over the same period by 11 per cent.

This case was written by Tom Patterson, a Planner at Now

Questions relating to this case can be found at the end of this chapter.

Introduction

There are many different opinions about what it is that marketing communications seeks to achieve. The conflicting views have led some practitioners and academics to polarise their thoughts about what constitutes an appropriate set of objectives. First, much effort has been spent trying to determine what 'promotion' and marketing communications activities are supposed to achieve; second, how should the success of a campaign be evaluated; and finally, how is it best to determine the degree of investment that should be made in each of the areas of the communications mix? The Petplan campaign shows that marketing communications worked to restablish and reposition the brand, and this was accomplished through the utilisation of a clear set of objectives.

The process of resolving these different demands that are placed on organisations has made the setting of 'promotional' objectives very complex and difficult. It has been termed 'a job of creating order out of chaos' (Kriegel, 1986). This perceived complexity has led a large number of managers to fail to set promotional objectives or to set the wrong ones. Many of those who do set them do so in such a way that they are inappropriate, inadequate or merely restate the marketing objectives. The most common marketing communications objectives set by managers are sales-related. These include increases in market share, return on investment, sales volume increases and improvements in the value of sales made after accounting for the rate of inflation.

Such a general perspective ignores the influence of the other elements of the marketing mix and implicitly places the entire responsibility for sales performance with communications. This is not an accurate reflection of the way in which businesses and organisations work. In addition, because sales tests are too general, they would be an insufficiently rigorous test of promotional activity and there would be no real evaluation of promotional activities. Sales volumes vary for a wide variety of reasons:

● competitors change their prices;
● buyers' needs change;

- changes in legislation may favour the strategies of particular organisations;
- favourable third-party communications become known to significant buyers;
- general economic conditions change;
- technological advances facilitate improved production processes;
- economies of scale, experience effects and, for some organisations, the opportunity to reduce costs;
- the entry and exit of different competitors.

These are a few of the many reasons why sales might increase and conversely why sales might decrease. Therefore, the notion that marketing communications is entirely responsible for the sales of an offering is clearly unacceptable, unrealistic and incorrect.

The role of objectives in corporate strategy

Objectives play an important role in the activities of individuals, social groups and organisations because:

1. They provide direction and an action focus for all those participating in the activity.
2. They provide a means by which the variety of decisions relating to an activity can be made in a consistent way.
3. They set out the time period in which the activity is to be completed.
4. They communicate the values and scope of the activity to all participants.
5. They provide a means by which the success of the activity can be evaluated.

It is generally accepted that the process of developing corporate strategy demands that a series of objectives be set at different levels within an organisation (Johnson et al., 2014; Quinn et al., 2003). This hierarchy of objectives consists of mission, strategic business unit (SBU) or business objectives, and functional objectives, such as production, finance or marketing goals.

The first level in the hierarchy (mission) requires that an overall direction be set for the organisation. If strategic decisions are made to achieve corporate objectives, both objectives and strategy are themselves constrained by an organisation's mission. Mission statements should be a vision that management has of what the organisation is trying to achieve in the long term. A mission statement outlines who the organisation is, what it does and where it is headed. A clearly developed, articulated and communicated mission statement enables an organisation to define whose needs are to be satisfied, what needs require satisfying and which products and technologies will be used to provide the desired levels of satisfaction. The mission should clearly identify the following:

- the customers/buyers to be served;
- the needs to be satisfied;
- the products and/or technologies by which these will be achieved.

In some organisations these points are explicitly documented in a mission statement. These statements often include references to the organisation's philosophy, culture, commitment to the community and employees, growth, profitability and so on, but these should not blur or distract attention from the organisation's basic mission. The words 'mission' and 'vision' are often used interchangeably, but they have separate meanings. Vision refers to the expected or desired outcome of carrying out the mission over the agreed period of time.

The mission provides a framework for the organisation's objectives, and the objectives that follow should promote and be consistent with the mission. While the word 'mission' implies a singularity of purpose, organisations have multiple objectives because of the many aspects of the organisation's performance and behaviour that contribute to the mission, and should, therefore, be explicitly identified. However, many of these objectives will conflict with each other. In retailing, for example, if an organisation chooses to open larger stores, then total annual profit should rise, but average profit per square metre will probably fall. Short-term profitability can be improved by reducing investment, but this could adversely affect long-term profitability. Organisations therefore have long-term and short-term objectives.

At the SBU level, objectives represent the translation of the mission into a form that can be understood by relevant stakeholders. These objectives are the performance requirements for the organisation or unit, which in turn are broken down into objectives or targets that each functional area must achieve, as their contribution to the unit objectives. Marketing strategies are functional strategies, as are the strategies for the finance, human resource management, production and other departments. Combine or aggregate them, and the SBU's overall target will, in reductionist theory, be achieved.

The various organisational objectives are of little use if they are not communicated to those who need to know what they are. Traditionally, such communications have focused on employees, but there is increasing recognition that the other members of the stakeholder network need to understand an organisation's purpose and objectives. The marketing objectives developed for the marketing strategy provide important information for the communications strategy. Is the objective to increase market share or to defend or maintain the current situation? Is the product new or established? Is it being modified or slowly withdrawn? The corporate image is shaped partly by the organisation's objectives and the manner in which they are communicated. All these impact on the objectives of the communications plan.

The role of brand communications objectives and plans

Many organisations, including some advertising agencies, fail to set realistic (if any) communications or campaign objectives. There are several explanations for this behaviour, but one of the common factors is that managers are unable to differentiate between the value of promotion as an expense and as an investment. However, the value of these objectives can be seen in terms of the role they play in communications planning, evaluation and brand development.

The databank created by the Institute of Practitioners in Advertising consists of data concerning over 900 successful campaigns, recorded since 1980. This clearly shows that those campaigns that set clear objectives are more successful than those that do not (Binet and Field, 2007). As a result of this data an increasing number of agencies appear to be setting a hierarchy of goals for the campaigns they develop.

The setting of marketing communications objectives is important for three main reasons. The first is that they provide *a means of communications and coordination* between groups (e.g. client and agency) working on different parts of a campaign. Performance is improved if there is common understanding about the tasks the promotional tools have to accomplish. Second, objectives constrain the number of options available to an organisation. Campaign objectives act as *a guide for decision-making* and provide a focus for decisions that follow in the process of developing communications plans. The third reason is that objectives provide *a benchmark* so that the relative success or failure of a programme can be evaluated.

There is no doubt that organisations need to be flexible, to be able to anticipate and adjust to changes in their environments. This principle applies to the setting of campaign objectives. To set one all-encompassing objective and expect it to last the year (or whatever period is allocated) is both hopeful and naive; multiple objectives are necessary.

Viewpoint 6.1   Goals galore

Different brands encounter different situations, and arising from this are a rich variety of goals.

The Shangri-La Hotels and Resorts campaign, 'It's in our nature', set a goal of achieving an extra US$90 million in room revenues, and this meant that it had to sell 10 more rooms per hotel per night.

VisitScotland attempted to inspire tourists to visit the country during winter. The campaign was designed to appeal to all of the senses, reversing preconceptions of dreariness and presenting Scotland as a romantic and exciting destination, with an emphasis on luxury.

Country Life's campaign goals were to correct the misperception that their main rival 'Anchor' was a British brand, and to enable consumers to make an informed butter choice.

China's shower gel market segment has 11 brands and 93 variants. Unilever's Dove had been dormant for five years. Its campaign aim was to challenge market leader Olay and grow market share from 2 per cent to 3.4 per cent. This meant persuading 4 million Chinese women to buy Dove Bodywash.

Minute Maid Pulpy is the biggest juice brand in China, but the challenge was to convert brand 'triers' into brand 'lovers', and to grow sales.

The campaign goal for Leeds Castle was to encourage repeat visits, particularly during the winter period, by emphasising the different events that take place at the castle all year round.

When the B2B market in Singapore started to recover, HP and Intel joined forces to accomplish two main goals. The first was to generate new business leads by an incremental positive 30 per cent over the previous year. The second was to change their image from being perceived as cold and corporate to a more personable and approachable profile. A target of a 1:3 return on investment was set.

Source: Various including *The Marketer* and www.ame.asia/winnerCategory/2011/.

Question:	If goals are designed to focus activities, are they the most important element of marketing communications or is something else more important?
Task:	Make a list of the different types of goal that might be used for marketing communications.

The academic literature suggests a combination of sales and communications objectives. Practitioners appear to use a variety of approaches and demonstrate inconsistency in their use and format. Consideration is given first to the academic interpretations before turning to the practitioner views. The content of campaign objectives has also been the subject of considerable debate. Academics refer to two distinct schools of thought: those that advocate sales-related measures as the main factors and those that advocate communications-related measures as the main orientation.

The sales school

As stated earlier, many managers see sales as the only meaningful objective for campaigns. Their view is that the only reason an organisation spends money on communications is to sell its product or service. Therefore, the only meaningful measure of the effectiveness of the spend is in the sales results.

These results can be measured in a number of different ways. Sales turnover is the first and most obvious factor, particularly in business-to-business markets. In consumer markets and the fast-moving consumer goods sector, market share movement is measured regularly and is used as a more sensitive barometer of performance. Over the longer term, return-on-investment measures are used to calculate success and failure. In some sectors the number of products sold, or volume of product shifted, relative to other periods of activity, is a common measure. There are a number of difficulties with this view. One of these has been considered earlier: that *sales result from a variety of influences*, such as the other elements in the marketing mix, competitor actions and wider environmental effects, such as the strength of a currency, changing social preferences or the level of interest rates.

A second difficulty rests with the concept of *adstock* or *carryover*. The impact of promotional' expenditure may not be immediately apparent, as the receiver may not enter the market until some later date, but the effects of the promotional programme may influence the eventual purchase decision. This means that, when measuring the effectiveness of a campaign, sales results will not always reflect its full impact.

Sales objectives do little to assist the media planner, copywriters and creative team associated with the development of the communications programme, despite their inclusion in campaign documents such as media briefs.

Sales-oriented objectives are, however, applicable in particular situations. For example, where direct action is required by the receiver in response to exposure to a message, measurement of sales is justifiable. Such an action, a behavioural response, can be solicited in direct-response advertising. This occurs where the sole communications are through a particular medium, such as television or print.

The retail sector can also use sales measures, and it has been suggested that packaged goods organisations, operating in mature markets with established pricing and distribution structures, can build a databank from which it is possible to isolate the advertising effect through sales. For example, supermarkets that have used celebrity chefs such as Jamie Oliver, Delia Smith and Nigella Lawson can monitor the stock movements of particular ingredients used in 'celebrity recipe' commercials. Not only does this enable supermarkets to evaluate the success of particular campaigns, recipes and particular celebrities, but they can also learn to anticipate demand and stock ingredients in anticipation of particular advertisements being screened. However, despite this cause-and-effect relationship, it can be argued that this may ignore the impact of changes in competitor actions and changes in the overall environment. Furthermore, the effects of the organisation's own corporate advertising, adstock effects and other family brand promotions need to be accounted for if a meaningful sales effect is to be generated.

The sales school advocate the measure on the grounds of simplicity. Any manager can utilise the tool, and senior management does not wish to be concerned with information which is complex or unfamiliar, especially when working to short lead times and accounting periods. It is a self-consistent theory, but one that may misrepresent consumer behaviour and the purchase process (perhaps unintentionally), and to that extent may result in less than optimal expenditure on marketing communications.

The communications school

There are many situations, however, where the aim of a communications campaign is to enhance the image or reputation of an organisation or product. Sales are not regarded as the only goal. Consequently, promotional efforts are seen as communications tasks, such as the creation of awareness or positive attitudes towards the organisation or product. To facilitate this process, receivers have to be given relevant information before the appropriate decision processes can develop and purchase activities become established as a long-run behaviour.

Various models have been developed to assist our understanding about how these promotional tasks are segregated and organised effectively. AIDA and other hierarchy of effects models were considered earlier at some length and need not be repeated here (see Chapter 4). However, one particular model was developed deliberately to introduce clear objectives into the advertising development process: Dagmar.

Dagmar

Russell Colley (1961) developed a model for setting advertising objectives and measuring the results. This model was entitled 'Defining Advertising Goals for Measured Advertising Results – Dagmar'. Colley's rationale for what is effectively a means of setting communications-oriented objectives was that advertising's job, purely and simply, is to communicate to a defined audience information and a frame of mind that stimulates action. Advertising succeeds or fails depending on how well it communicates the desired information and attitudes to the right people at the right time and at the right cost.

Scholars' paper 6.1	First time to set advertising goals

Colley, R. (1961) *Defining Advertising Goals for Measured Advertising Results,* New York: Association of National Advertisers.

Colley is credited with introducing the idea that good advertising practice requires setting precise advertising goals. Defining Advertising Goals for Measured Advertising Results, or DAGMAR as it inevitably became, was first published in this book. In tune with the then current practice, Colley recommended a hierarchical model of communications – one which paralleled the purchase decision process. Colley's model is significant in its focus on the setting and measurement of objectives and is not purely an examination of the communications process itself. It has also been used widely in the context of setting advertising budgets (see Chapter 7).

Colley proposed that the communications task be based on a hierarchical model of the communications process: awareness–comprehension–conviction–action (Table 6.1).

Table 6.1 A hierarchy of communications

Stage	Explanation
Awareness	Awareness of the existence of a product or brand is necessary before any purchase will be made.
Comprehension	Audiences need information and knowledge about the product and its specific attributes. Often the audiences need to be educated and shown either how to use the product or how changes (in attributes) might affect their use of the product.
Conviction	By encouraging beliefs that a product is superior to others in a category or can confer particular rewards through use, audiences can be convinced to trial the product at the next purchase opportunity.
Action	Potential buyers need help and encouragement to transfer thoughts into behaviour. Providing call-free numbers, website addresses, reply cards, coupons and salespeople helps people act upon their convictions.

Source: Based on Colley (1961).

Awareness

Awareness of the existence of a product or an organisation is necessary before purchase behaviour can be expected. Once awareness has been created in the target audience, it should not be neglected. If there is neglect, an audience may become distracted by competing messages and the level of awareness of the focus product or organisation may decline. Awareness, therefore, needs to be created, developed, refined or sustained, according to the characteristics of the market and the particular situation facing an organisation at any one point in time (see Figure 6.1).

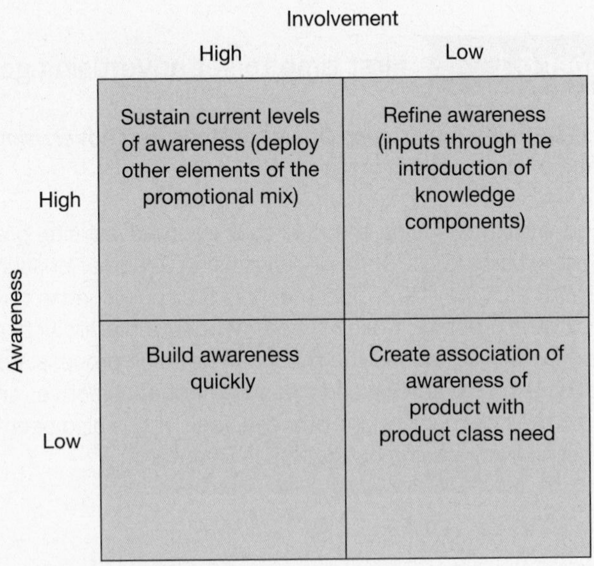

Figure 6.1   An awareness grid

In situations where the buyer experiences high involvement and is fully aware of a product's existence, attention and awareness levels need only be sustained, and efforts need to be applied to other communications tasks, which maybe best left to the other elements of the communications mix. For example, sales promotion and personal selling are more effective at informing, persuading and provoking purchase of a new car once advertising has created the necessary levels of awareness.

Where low levels of awareness are found, getting attention needs to be a prime objective so that awareness can be developed in the target audience. Where low involvement exists, the decision-making process is relatively straightforward. With levels of risk minimised, buyers with sufficient levels of awareness may be prompted into purchase with little assistance from the other elements of the mix. Recognition and recall of brand names and corporate images are felt by some (Rossiter and Percy, 1987) to be sufficient triggers to stimulate a behavioural response. The requirement in this situation would be to refine and strengthen the level of awareness in order to provoke interest and stimulate a higher level of involvement during recall or recognition.

Where low levels of awareness are matched by low involvement, the prime objective has to be to create awareness of the focus product in association with the product class. It is not surprising that organisations use awareness campaigns and invest a large proportion of their resources in establishing their brand or corporate name. Many brands seek to establish 'top of mind awareness' as one of their primary objectives for their advertising spend.

It is interesting to observe that most advertising programmes still include awareness as an objective. The logic is clear: if the ad is not seen, it is not going to be effective. However, in the light of the Low Attention Processing theory, are high-awareness goals necessary and, more important, are they a waste of financial resources? Heath (2009) and colleagues would argue that they are, but convincing a client, or agency even, that driving high levels of awareness is not necessary is going to be problematic.

Comprehension

Awareness on its own is, invariably, not enough to stimulate purchase activity. Knowledge about the product (or what the organisation does) is necessary, and this can be achieved by providing specific information about key brand attributes. These attributes and their associated benefits may be key to the buyers in the target audience or may be key because the product has been adapted or modified in some way. This means that the audiences need to be educated about the change and shown how their use of the product may be affected. For example, in attempting to persuade people to try a different brand of mineral water, it may be necessary to compare the product with other mineral water products and provide an additional usage benefit, such as environmental claims.

Conviction

Having established that a product has particular attributes that lead to benefits perceived by the target audience as important, it is then necessary to establish a sense of conviction. By creating interest and preference, buyers are moved to a position where they are convinced that one particular product in the class should be tried at the next opportunity. To do this, the audience's beliefs about the product need to be moulded, and this can be accomplished by using messages that demonstrate a product's superiority over its main rival or by emphasising the rewards conferred as a result of using the product – for example, the reward of social acceptance associated with many fragrance, fashion clothing and accessory advertisements, and the reward of self-gratification associated with many confectionery messages, such as 'Cadbury's Flake' and Terry's 'Chocolate Orange'.

High-involvement decisions are best supported with personal selling and sales promotion activities, in an attempt to gain conviction. Low-involvement decisions rely on the strength of advertising messages, packaging and sales promotion to secure conviction.

Action

A communications programme is used to encourage buyers to engage in purchase activity. Advertising can be directive and guide buyers into certain behavioural outcomes: for example, to the use of free phone numbers (0800 in the United Kingdom), direct mail activities and reply cards and coupons. However, for high-involvement decisions the most effective tool in the communications mix at this stage in the hierarchy is personal selling. Through the use of interpersonal skills, buyers are more likely to want to buy a product than if the personal prompting is absent. The use of direct marketing activities by Avon Cosmetics, Tupperware, Betterware and suppliers of life assurance and double-glazing services has been instrumental in the sales growth experienced by organisations in these markets.

Colley's dissatisfaction with the way in which advertising agencies operated led him to specify the components of a good advertising objective: 'A specific communications task to be accomplished among a defined audience to a given degree in a given period of time' (Dutka, 1995). An analysis of this statement shows that it is made up of four distinct elements:

- a need to specify the communications task;
- a need to define the audience;
- a need to state the required degree of change;
- a need to establish the time period in which the activity is to occur.

Colley's statement is very clear – it is measurable and of assistance to copywriters. Indeed, Dagmar revolutionised the approach taken by advertisers to the setting of objectives. It helped to move attention from the sales effect to the communications effect school and has led to improved planning processes, as a result partly of a better understanding of advertising and promotional goals.

Many of the difficulties associated with sequential models (as presented in Chapter 4) are also applicable to Dagmar. Additional to problems of hierarchical progression, measurement and costs are issues concerning the sales orientation, restrictions upon creativity and short-term accountability.

Sales orientation

This criticism is levelled by those who see sales as the only valid measure of effectiveness. The sole purpose of communications activities, and advertising in particular, is to generate sales. So, as the completion of communications tasks may not result in purchases, the only measure that need be undertaken is that of sales. This point has been discussed earlier and need not be reproduced here.

Restrictions upon creativity

Dagmar is criticised on the grounds that creative flair can be lost as attention passes from looking for the big idea to concentration on the numbers game, of focusing on measures of recall, attitude change and awareness. It is agreed that the creative personnel are held to be more accountable under Dagmar and this may well inhibit some of their work. Perhaps the benefits of providing direction and purpose offset the negative aspects of a slight loss in creativity.

Short-term accountability

To the above should be added the time period during which management and associated agencies are required to account for their performance. With accounting periods being reduced to as little as 12 weeks, the communications approach is impractical, for two reasons. The first is that the period is not long enough for all of the communications tasks to be progressed or completed. Sales measures present a much more readily digestible benchmark of performance.

The second concerns the unit of performance itself. With the drive to be efficient and to be able to account for every communications pound spent, managers themselves need to use measures that they can understand and that they can interpret from published data. Sales data and communications spend data are consistent measures and make no further demands on managers. Managers do not have enough time to spend analysing levels of comprehension or preference and to convert them into formats that are going to be of direct benefit to them and their organisations. Having said that, organisations that invest in a more advanced management information system will be able to take a more sophisticated view.

The approach adopted by the communications school is not universally accepted. Those who disagree argue that it is too difficult and impractical to translate a sales objective into a series of specific communications objectives. Furthermore, what actually constitutes adequate levels of awareness and comprehension and how can it be determined which stage the majority of the target audience has reached at any one point in time? Details of measurement, therefore, throw a veil over the simplicity and precision of the approach taken by the communications-orientation school.

Viewpoint 6.2   Logistical communications

Norbert Dentressangle (ND) is a French-based transport company that moved into supply chain logistics and freight following several acquisitions. It is now the second largest business of its kind in the UK, with turnover over £1 billion, the number of employees exceed 14,000, across 195 sites, and it has 3.5 million square metres of warehouse space.

Although its 1,700 eye-catching bright red trucks are quite recognisable, the scale and scope of ND was less well known. The task therefore was to reposition the brand with decision-makers across a broad range of industry sectors, as a thought leader that understands the issues faced by businesses today. In addition it was important to communicate the crucial role employees play in the success of ND. All employees are enabled to provide their clients with a high level of personal service, delivered at a local level. It was seen as important to express the expertise of ND staff and to communicate their pride in being a 'person in red'.

The solution was found through the *Daily Telegraph* and its 750,000 business section readers. A press partnership featured ND in a series of six articles under the topic 'Move your business on'. This involved the *Daily Telegraph* interviewing (and videoing) six CEOs from ND's target business sectors: automotive and industrial, construction, paper and packaging, FMCG, chemicals, retail and e-fulfilment. ND then prepared its own tailored piece to accompany and address the issues raised by the CEOs. The editorial content was supported by print ads and videos of ND experts talking about how they make a difference in their everyday working lives. Ads appeared in the main part of the *Daily Telegraph* and its business section, as well as in the online version of the newspaper. Further online ads ran with the *Financial Times* and *The Economist*. Video content appeared on ND's website and YouTube. ND employees helped choose who should represent the company in the ads, whilst the criticality of the campaign was reinforced internally through posters, coverage in the staff magazine and a behind-the-scenes video. The HR team briefed line managers across the organisation about the campaign.

The results showed in the increased quality of the website leads and an increase in invitations to tender. There was a 29 per cent increase in web traffic, 64 per cent of whom were new visitors. The LinkedIn InMail open rate rose 5 per cent higher than the platform's B2B campaign norm and there was also a 188 per cent rise in people 'considering working with' ND in future.

Since this was written ND has been taken over by XPO Logistics, a top ten global provider of transportation and logistics solutions.

Source: Gray (2013); www.norbert-dentressangle.co.uk/.

Question:	What are the strengths and weaknesses of these objectives?
Task:	Find a campaign for the not-for-profit sector and compare the objectives with those for a profit-based brand.

From a practical perspective, it should be appreciated that most successful marketing organisations do not see the sales and communications schools as mutually exclusive. They incorporate both views and weight them according to the needs of the current task, their overall experience, the culture and style of the organisation and the agencies with whom they operate.

Derivation of campaign objectives

It has been established that specific campaign objectives need to be set up if a suitable foundation is to be laid for the many communications-orientated decisions that follow. Campaign objectives are derived from understanding the overall context in which the communications will work. Comprehending the contexts of the buyer and the organisation allows the objectives of the planned communications to be identified: the *what* that is to be achieved. For example, objectives concerning the perception that different target customers have of a brand, the perception that members of a performance network have of the organisation's offerings, the reactions of key stakeholders to previous communications and the requirements of the current marketing plan all impact upon the objectives of the communications plan. Therefore, campaign objectives evolve principally from a systematic audit and analysis of the key communications contexts, and specifically from the marketing plan and stakeholder analysis.

It was established earlier that there are three main streams of objectives (see Figure 6.2). The first concerns issues relating to the buyers of the product or service

Figure 6.2	The three streams of objectives

Source: From *Essentials of Marketing Communications*, Pearson Education (Fill, C. 2011) figure 4.6, p. 105.

offered by the organisation. The second concerns issues relating to market share/sales volume, profitability and revenue. The third stream relates to the image, reputation and preferences that other stakeholders have towards the organisation.

All these objectives are derived from an analysis of the current situation. The marketing communications brief that flows from this analysis should specify the sales-related objectives to be achieved, as these can be determined from the marketing plan. Sales-related objectives might concern issues such as market share and sales volume.

Customer-related objectives concern issues such as awareness, perception, attitude, feelings and intentions towards a brand or product. The exact issue to be addressed in the plan is calculated by analysing the contextual information driven by the audit.

Issues related to the perception of the organisation are often left unattended or, worse, ignored. Research may indicate that the perception of particular stakeholders, in either the performance or the support network, does not complement the current level of corporate performance or may be misplaced or confused. Objectives will need to be established to correct or reinforce the perception held of the organisation. The degree of urgency may be directly related to the level of confusion or misunderstanding or be related to competitive or strategic actions initiated by competitors and other members of the network. Corporate strategy may have changed and, as identified earlier, any new strategy will need to be communicated to all stakeholders.

Setting realistic marketing communications objectives

Hierarchy of effects models which specify stages of development were first proposed as far back as 1898 by E. St Elmo Lewis (Barry and Howard, 1990) and similar views were expressed by Colley (Dagmar) in 1961. Yet, despite the passage of time since their publication, a large number of organisations still either fail to set any promotional objectives or confuse objectives with strategy. Organisations seeking to coordinate their

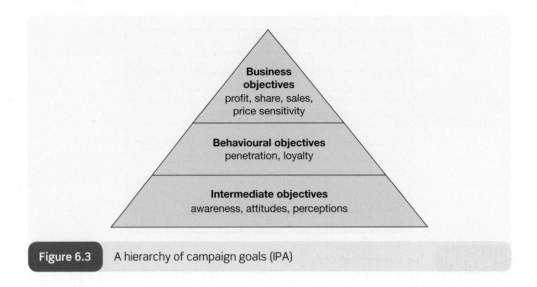

Figure 6.3   A hierarchy of campaign goals (IPA)

communications need to recognise the necessity of setting multiple objectives at different times in the campaign period and of being prepared to adjust them in the light of environmental changes. These changes may be due to ever-decreasing product lifecycles or technological developments that may give a competitor comparative advantage, and perhaps legislative developments (or the timing of management's interpretation and implementation of certain legislation) may bring about a need to reconfigure the promotional mix.

Analysis of the IPA databank mentioned earlier shows that successful campaigns are characterised not only by the use of objectives but also by the use of tiered or a hierarchy of objectives (see Figure 6.3).

Business objectives

At the top of this hierarchy are objectives that concern the business and these include profit, market share and pricing goals. Campaigns that clearly make increasing profit the ultimate objective outperform others (Binet and Field, 2007). However, only 7 per cent of the cases in the IPA databank use profit as an objective. One of the reasons for this may be the difficulties associated with defining and using suitable measures of payback, and isolating the other factors that impact on profitability. This is where the use of econometric modelling is important. One of the other business objectives recommended as a result of the analysis of the IPA databank is market share. Although sales are used as a primary goal by 62 per cent of cases, these campaigns underperform. It is market share (by value), used with profitability, that leads to the best performance outcomes. Linking market share with profitability is crucial, otherwise it is likely that share will be gained at the expense of profitability. One highly successful way of achieving this is to develop campaigns that seek to reduce price sensitivity.

Behavioural objectives

The business objectives are the primary goals. In order that these are achieved, relevant behavioural objectives need to be established. Although various required behaviours can be identified, Binet and Field (2007) reduce these to two: the acquisition of new customers (penetration) and the retention of customers (loyalty).

It is interesting that loyalty features in twice as many campaigns as an objective than penetration, yet it is those with the latter objective that are the most successful, in all categories, not just grocery and FMCG. This indicates that this objective should be used when market share is the main business objective. Note that Petplan set out to penetrate its market by acquiring new customers.

Intermediate objectives

At the third level in the hierarchy the IPA identifies factors that will influence future business performance. The IPA refers to these as *intermediate objectives,* such as awareness, beliefs and attitudes. These correspond to the communications goals considered earlier and contain many of the elements used in Dagmar. Awareness, perception, attitude and brand image goals are the more common factors to be accommodated in this part of the hierarchy. These goals are regarded as secondary as they can lead to the achievement of the behavioural goals in the future.

A large number of campaigns set awareness as the main objective, yet analysis shows that these are the least effective from a business perspective. It is suggested that their heavy usage is due to their relative ease of achievement and accountability. When there is more than one intermediate objective, such as building brand awareness and improving perceptions, then success rates improve. Also, setting out to achieve brand fame achieves very strong results. Fame is concerned with being perceived as an authority in a category, as opposed to knowledge which characterises awareness. This is best considered as a strategy and is examined in Chapter 5.

However, one interesting point emerges. The measures used to test for most communications effects are geared to reflect high-attention processing. As noted previously, the development of ideas about low-attention processing and the long-term effects of advertising suggest that further insight is required, as the impact of these objectives may be underestimated.

The issue therefore is to encourage brands to ensure not only that they use objectives, but that they also use them in a tiered format, and make profit or market share the primary, clear and overriding goal.

SMART objectives

To assist managers in their need to develop suitable objectives, regardless of source, a set of guidelines has been developed, commonly referred to as SMART objectives. This acronym stands for specific, measurable, achievable, relevant, targeted and timed.

The process of making objectives SMART requires management to consider exactly what is to be achieved, when, where and with which audience. This clarifies thinking, sorts out the logic of the proposed activities and provides a clear measure for evaluation at the end of the campaign:

- Specific – What is the actual variable that is to be influenced in the campaign? Is it awareness, perception, attitudes or some other element that is to be influenced? Whatever the variable, it must be clearly defined and must enable precise outcomes to be determined.

- Measurable – Set a measure of activity against which performance can be assessed. For example, this may be a percentage level of desired prompted awareness in the target audience.

- Achievable – Objectives need to be attainable, otherwise those responsible for their achievement will lack motivation and a desire to succeed.

- Realistic – The actions must be founded in reality and be relevant to the brand and the context in which they are set.

- Targeted and timed – Which target audience is the campaign targeted at, how precisely is the audience defined and over what period are the results to be generated?

Multiple objectives rather than a single objective should be set. The primary objectives should be business-orientated, preferably around profit. Next, the appropriate behavioural objectives need to be established. From this point communications goals should be determined. Whatever the level, the objectives should be written in SMART format.

Positioning

The final act in the target marketing process of segmentation and targeting is positioning. Following on from the identification of potential markets, determining the size and potential of market segments and selecting specific target markets, positioning is the process whereby the brand is perceived by the consumer/stakeholder to be differentiated from the competition, to occupy a particular space in the market, and will achieve the business goals. According to Kotler (2003), 'Positioning is the act of designing the company's offering and image so that they occupy a meaningful and distinct competitive position in the target customers' minds.'

Scholars' paper 6.2   Positioning is key

Ries, A. and Trout, J. (1972) The positioning era cometh, *Advertising Age*, 24 April, 35–8.

This is a classic paper that should be read by everyone associated with this subject. It was the first paper to outline the positioning concept. Ries and Trout argue that it is not what marketers do to a product itself, but how they influence the mind of a prospective customer. As the level of competition has extended so much, there is often little to choose between the actual products themselves. It should, therefore, be the role of marketing to differentiate on the basis of what customers think about them. Such differences might be real or merely perception.

This is an important aspect of the positioning concept. Positioning is not about the product but what the buyer thinks about the product or organisation. It is not the physical nature of the product that is important for positioning, but how the product is perceived that matters. This is why part of the context analysis requires a consideration of perception and attitudes and the way stakeholders see and regard brands and organisations (see Chapter 5). Of course, this may not be the same as the way brand managers intend their brands to be seen or how they believe the brand is perceived.

This audience orientation is emphasised by Blankson and Kalafatis (2007). They considered the positioning strategies of several leading credit card providers from three perspectives. These were the banks' executives, the positioning strategies that were implemented, and finally, but most important, the perception of the target audiences of the positioning strategies. In the words of the researchers: presumed practice, actual practice and perceived practice. One of the outcomes of their work was the need to manage the potential gulf that may occur when the presumed and actual positioning strategies drift away from the way audiences actually perceive the brand.

In the consumer market established brands from washing powders (Ariel, Daz, Persil) and hair shampoos (such as Wash & Go, Timotei), to cars (Peugeot, GM, Nissan) and grocery multiples (Sainsbury's, Aldi, and Maxi ICA Stormarknad) each carry communications that enable audiences to position them in their respective markets.

The positioning concept is not the sole preserve of branded or consumer-oriented offerings or indeed those of the business-to-business market. Organisations are also positioned relative to one another, mainly as a consequence of their corporate identities, whether they are deliberately managed or not. The position an organisation takes in the mind of consumers may be the only means of differentiating one product from another. King (1991) argues that, given the advancement in technology and the high level of physical and functional similarity of products in the same class, consumers' choices will be more focused on their assessment of the company they are dealing with. Therefore, it is important to position organisations as brands in the minds of actual and potential customers.

One of the crucial differences between the product and the corporate brand is that the corporate brand needs to be communicated to a large array of stakeholders, whereas the product-based brand requires a focus on a smaller range of stakeholders: in particular, the consumers and buyers in the performance network.

Whatever the position chosen, either deliberately or accidentally, it is the means by which customers understand the brand's market position, and it often provides signals to determine a brand's main competitors, or whether (as is often the case) customers fail to understand the brand or are confused about what the brand stands for.

Scholars' paper 6.3 — The benefit of positioning

Fuchs, C. and Diamantopoulos, A. (2010) Evaluating the effectiveness of brand-positioning strategies from a consumer perspective, *European Journal of Marketing*, 44(11/12), 1763–86.

This paper considers the overall effectiveness of positioning strategies. The paper provides an interesting and readable review of the positioning literature. The results of the authors' research show that the success of a brand is influenced by the type of positioning strategy used. They also find that benefit-based positioning and surrogate (user) positioning generally outperform feature-based positioning strategies along the three effectiveness dimensions.

The positioning concept

From the research data and the marketing strategy, it is necessary to formulate a positioning statement that is in tune with the promotional objectives.

One of the roles of marketing communications is to convey information so that the target audience can understand what a brand stands for and differentiate it from other competing brands. Clear, consistent positioning is an important aspect of integrated marketing communications. So, the way in which a brand is presented to its audience influences the way it is going to be perceived. Therefore, accepting that there are extraneous reasons why the perception of a brand might not be the same as that intended, it seems important that managers approach the positioning task in an attentive and considered manner.

Generally there are two main ways in which a brand can be positioned: *functional* and *expressive* (or *symbolic*) positioning. Functionally positioned brands stress the features and benefits, while expressive brands emphasise the ego, social and hedonic satisfactions that a brand can bring.

In the context of washing powder, both approaches make a promise. The functional promise embraces whiter, cleaner and brighter clothes. The emotional approach considers clothes that we are confident to hang on the washing line (for all to see), dress our children in and send to school and not feel guilty, or dress ourselves in for a social evening or to complete a major business deal (symbolic).

Viewpoint 6.3	Revlon's lovely positioning

The US cosmetics company Revlon withdrew from mainland China in 2015. One of the reasons for this move was that the market perceived the higher Revlon price brought few added benefits. Consumers could buy similar local products at a lower price. In addition to this value perception, the positioning confused customers because Revlon was available in supermarkets as well as in high-end department store beauty counters.

Revlon, however, continues to operate in Hong Kong and launched a new campaign within the brand's global platform, 'Love is On', accompanied by a new logo shortly before Valentine's Day. Rather than use the brand's logo in white text, the revised identity presents the brand name in red text, with the tagline 'Love is On'. The use of the word 'love' within the logo was designed to attract young customers who often fantasise about love and what the future might hold for them. By making the brand more approachable the positioning enables people to share stories and talk about love.

The Hong Kong campaign featured the use of video, which was distributed online and through an outdoor TV screen in Tsim Sha Tsui, near Chungking Mansions. The campaign also featured billboards and transport (buses) media.

Revlon also launched a Facebook game, in which, apart from music, the sound was muted. Users were required to guess what the female character in the video said with regard to love. Users then had to 'like' the page and share a post about the contest on Facebook. They also had to publish their post to the page and tag their significant other. The rewards for this were cash coupons and lipsticks.

The goal was to establish the Revlon Facebook page as a platform for messages of love. Revlon's previous 'Kissable' campaign required that people share kissable moments in the form of text or images. The content submitted revealed the depth of engagement experienced by users.

In New York the 'Global Love Beacon' features digital images displayed on a screen outside Times Square. Users can have their photo taken in a photo booth set up by the brand near Times Square. Alternatively, Twitter and Instagram users around the world can submit their photographs to be broadcast in New York with the hashtag LoveIsOn.

Source: Ap and Sun (2014); Elliott (2014); Lam (2015).

Question:	Is this functional or emotional positioning and why did Revlon exclude the use of terrestrial television in the Hong Kong campaign?
Task:	Make a list of the different ways in which Revlon could use the 'love' platform. What might be the disadvantages of this positioning?

EasyJet's communications at one time were almost exclusively orientated to its (low) price, a functional position. However, when this position was challenged and overtaken, the company's communications began to convey a closer association with premium carriers yet one that maintained its challenger spirit. Messaging switched to one that focused on championing the destination, selling Europe and associated experiences. This created a new long-term brand platform, 'Europe by easyJet', allowing the brand to create emotional affinity and be more aspirational in its look and feel.

This expressive positioning used an emotional brand message, one which required a different media mix. The functional position used print, outdoor and digital, whilst the expressive position required heavy use of television (Anon, 2014).

Managing positions

The development and establishment of a position is a core strategic marketing communications activity. Positioning is one of two dynamics considered within communications strategy (see Chapter 5). The first dynamic is concerned with who, in broad terms, is the target audience. End-user customers need to derive particular benefits based on perceived value from the exchange process. These benefits are very different from those that intermediaries expect to derive, or indeed any other stakeholder who does not consume the product or service. The second dynamic concerns the way in which an audience understands the offering it is experiencing either through use or through communications. The way in which people interpret messages and frame objects in their mind is concerned with positioning. Therefore, positioning is an integral part of marketing communications strategy.

In order that suitable positions be set, managers wishing to develop a position can be guided by the following process:

1. Determine the positions held by competitors. This will almost certainly require research to determine attitudes and perceptions and, possibly, the key attributes that consumers perceive as important. Use perceptual mapping.
2. From the above, it will be possible to determine which position, if any, is already held by the focus brand.
3. From the information gathered so far, will it be possible to determine a positioning strategy – that is, what is the desired position for the brand?
4. Is the strategy feasible in view of the competitors and any budgetary constraints? A long-term perspective is required, as the selected position has to be sustained.
5. Implement a programme to establish the desired position.
6. Monitor the perception held by consumers of the brand, and of their changing tastes and requirements, on a regular basis.

Perceptual mapping

In order to determine how the various offerings are perceived in a market, the key attributes that stakeholders use to perceive products in the market need to be established. A great deal of this work will have been completed as part of the research and review process prior to developing a communications plan. The next task is to determine perceptions and preferences in respect of the key attributes as perceived by buyers.

The objective of the exercise is to produce a perceptual map (brand and multidimensional maps) where the dimensions used on the two axes are the key attributes, as seen by buyers. This map represents a geometric comparison of how competing products are perceived (Sinclair and Stalling, 1990). Figure 6.4 shows that consumers considered national/international and popular/exclusive as key dimensions in the airline market. Each airline is positioned on the map according to the perception that buyers have of the strength of each attribute of each airline. By plotting the perceived positions of each brand on the map, an overall perspective of the market can be developed.

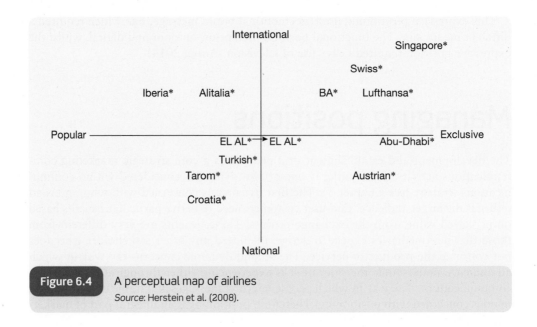

Figure 6.4 A perceptual map of airlines
Source: Herstein et al. (2008).

The closer airlines are clustered together, the greater the competition. The further apart the positions, the greater the opportunity to enter the market, as competition is less intense. From the map it can be seen that Croatia Airlines is perceived to be a strong national airline, whereas Swiss Air and Singapore Airlines are seen to be very international and exclusive. El Al was repositioned from being reasonably popular to one that was more exclusive, yet retained the same level of nationality. It may be that both Turkish and Tarom might find it less competitive if they attempted to become more popular and so provide a strong point of differentiation. However, such a move would only be endorsed if research showed that it would be acceptable to consumers, and profitable.

Substitute products are often uncovered by their closeness to each other (Day et al., 1979). It is also possible to ask buyers and other stakeholders what an ideal brand would consist of. This perfect brand can then be positioned on the map, and the closer an offering is to the ideal point, the greater its market share should be, as it is preferred over its rivals. These maps are known as *preference maps*.

By superimposing the position of an ideal brand on the map, it is possible to extend the usefulness of the tool. Perceptions of what constitutes the right amount of each key attribute can assist management in the positioning exercise. Marketing communications can, therefore, be designed to convey the required information about each attribute, thus adjusting buyers' perceptions so that they are closer to the ideal position, or to the position on the map that management wants the brand to occupy. For example, Austrian Airlines may wish to reposition by changing the perception that users have of its exclusivity and relative unpopularity. Following any necessary adjustments to the routes followed and services provided, marketing communications would emphasise the popularity and accessibility attributes and hope to move it away from its association with exclusivity.

Neal (1980) offered the following reasons why perceptual mapping is such a powerful tool for examining the position of products:

1. It develops understanding of how the relative strengths and weaknesses of different products are perceived by buyers.

2. It builds knowledge about the similarities and dissimilarities between competing products.

3. It assists the process of repositioning existing products and the positioning of new products.

4. The technique helps to track the perception that buyers have of a particular product, and assists the measurement of the effectiveness of communications programmes and marketing actions intended to change buyers' perceptions.

Perceptual mapping is an important tool in the development and tracking of marketing communications strategy. It enables brand managers to identify gaps and opportunities in the market and allows organisations to monitor the effects of past marketing communications. For example, in the early 1980s none of the available brands in the newly emerging lager market was seen as refreshing. All brands were perceived as virtually the same. Heineken saw the opportunity and seized the position for refreshment, and has been able to occupy and sustain the position ever since.

Positioning strategies

The development of positions that buyers can relate to and understand is an important and vital part of the marketing communications plan. In essence, the position adopted is a statement about what the brand is, what it stands for and the values and beliefs that customers (hopefully) will come to associate with the particular brand. The visual images or the position statement represented in the strapline may be a significant trigger that buyers use to recall images and associations of the brand.

There are a number of overall approaches to developing a position. These can be based on factors such as the market, the customer or redefining the appeal of the brand itself.

To implement these three broad approaches, various strategies have been developed. The list that follows is not intended to be comprehensive or to convey the opinion that these strategies are discrete. They are presented here as means of conveying the strategic style, but in reality a number of hybrid strategies are often used.

Product features

This is one of the easier concepts and one that is more commonly adopted. The brand is set apart from the competition on the basis of the attributes, features or benefits that the brand has relative to the competition. For example, Red Bull gives you energy; Weetabix contains all the vitamins needed each day; and Audi proclaims Vorsprung durch Technik or 'advancement through technology.'

Price/quality

This strategy is more effectively managed than others because price itself can be a strong communicator of quality. A high price denotes high quality, just as a low price can deceive buyers into thinking a product to be of low quality and poor value. Retail outlets such as Harrods and Aspreys use high prices to signal high quality and exclusivity.

At the other end of the retail spectrum, Matalan, BHS and Primark position themselves to attract those with less disposable income and to whom convenience is of greater importance. The price/quality appeal used to be best observed in Sainsbury's, 'where good food costs less' before it was changed, and with the alcoholic lager Stella Artois, which was positioned as 'refreshingly expensive'.

| Exhibit 6.3 | **A store's architecture signals the price/quality relationship** |
Source: Getty Images/Suhaimi Abdullah

Use

By informing markets of when or how a product can be used, a position can be created in the minds of the buyers. For example, Kellogg's, the breakfast cereal manufacturer, repositioned itself as a snack food provider. Its marketing strategy of moving into new markets was founded on its over-dependence on breakfast consumption. By becoming associated with snacks, not only is usage increased, but the opportunity to develop new products becomes feasible. The launch of Pop Tarts is a testimony to this strategy. Milky Way, 'the sweet you can eat between meals', informs just when it is permissible to eat chocolate, and After Eight chocolate mints clearly indicate when they should be eaten. The hair shampoo Wash & Go positions the brand as a quick and easy-to-use (convenience) product, for those whose lifestyles are full and demanding.

Product class dissociation

Some markets are essentially uninteresting, and most positions have been adopted by competitors. A strategy used by margarine manufacturers is to disassociate themselves from other margarines and associate themselves with what was commonly regarded as a superior product, butter. The moisturising bar Dove is positioned as 'not a soap'.

User

A sensible extension of the target marketing process is to position openly so that target users can be clearly identified. Flora margarine was for men, and then it became 'for all the family'. Perfumes are not just endorsed by celebrities but some celebrities launch their own perfume brands, such as Christina Aguilera, Kate Moss, David Beckham, Donald Trump, Cliff Richard and, of course, Beyoncé, Britney Spears and Paul Smith.

Some hotels position themselves as places for weekend breaks, as leisure centres or as conference centres. Revlon repositioned to appeal to a younger customer segment (see Viewpoint 6.3).

Competitor

For a long time, positioning oneself against a main competitor was regarded as dangerous and was avoided. Avis, however, performed very successfully 'trying even harder' against Hertz, the industry number one. Saab contested the 'safest car' position with Volvo; Petplan, featured in the case study opening this chapter, repositioned itself against its competitors as the 'knowledge experts' based on its unrivalled experience in the market.

Benefit

Positions can also be established by proclaiming the benefits that usage confers on those who consume. Sensodyne toothpaste appeals to all those who suffer from sensitive teeth, and a vast number of pain relief formulations claim to smooth away headaches or relieve aching limbs, sore throats or some offending part of the anatomy. Daewoo entered the UK market offering car buyers convenience by removing dealerships and the inherent difficulties associated with buying and maintaining cars.

Heritage or cultural symbol

An appeal to cultural heritage and tradition, symbolised by age, particular heraldic devices or visual cues, has been used by many organisations to convey quality, experience and knowledge. Kronenbourg 1664, 'Established since 1803', and the use of coats of arms by many universities to represent depth of experience and a sense of permanence are just some of the historical themes used to position organisations.

Whatever the position adopted by a brand or organisation, both the marketing and communications mixes must endorse and support the position so that there is consistency throughout all communications. For example, if a high-quality position is taken, such as that of the Ritz Carlton Hotel Group, then the product/service quality must be relatively high compared with competitors, the price must be correspondingly excessive and distribution synonymous with quality and exclusivity. Sales promotion activity will be minimal in order not to convey a touch of inexpensiveness, and advertising messages should be visually affluent and rich in tone and copy, with public relations and personal selling approaches transmitting high-quality, complementary cues.

The dimensions used to position brands must be relevant and important to the target audience and in the image cues used must be believable and consistently credible. Positioning strategies should be developed over the long term if they are to prove effective, although minor adaptions to the position can be carried out in order to reflect changing environmental conditions.

Repositioning

Technology continues to develop rapidly, consumer tastes and behaviours are evolving and new and substitute offerings enter the market. This dynamic perspective of markets means that the relative positions occupied by offerings in the minds of consumers will be challenged and shifted on a frequent basis. If the position adopted by an offering is strong, if it was the first to claim the position and the position is being continually reinforced with clear simple messages, then there may be little need to alter the position originally adopted.

However, there are occasions when offerings need to be repositioned in the minds of consumers/stakeholders. This may be due to market opportunities and development, mergers and acquisitions or changing buyer preferences, which may be manifested in declining sales. Research may reveal that the current position is either inappropriate or superseded by a competitor, or that attitudes have changed or preferences been surpassed; whatever the reason, repositioning is required if past success is to be maintained. However, repositioning is difficult to accomplish, often because of the entrenched perceptions and attitudes held by buyers towards brands and the vast (media) resources required to make the changes. Google began to reposition itself as a collaborative, technology brand, rather than a media company focused on aggregating and distributing content (Boyd, 2010).

Viewpoint 6.4	Morrison's reposition on price

Structural changes in the UK supermarket industry resulting from the recession and developments in consumer behaviour, have led to some operators such as Lidl and Aldi experiencing significant growth, if from a fairly small base. Their growth has been at the expense of Tesco, the market leader, who were reported to be losing one million customers a week at one point, and to some extent Sainsbury's and ASDA. All have reviewed their strategies, but Morrisons were possibly hit hardest, demonstrated by a 7.1 per cent like-for-like sales fall in the quarter ending 4 May 2014.

The impact of these changes has led all of the operators to review their strategies. Morrisons adopted a new positioning as a lower-priced retailer aimed at re-establishing themselves and their reputation as a value-led grocer with a focus on fresh food.

Their new brand positioning, 'I'm your new cheaper Morrisons', was supported by a cut in the cost of more than 1,200 items in-store and online. This strategy was communicated using a campaign that reflects the UK's love of food through a series of everyday moments: each ad shows an everyday food item that is now permanently cheaper at Morrisons, using a 'Love 'em cheaper' strapline. There were 31 different TV spots highlighting different products; it also took over the front cover wrap of the *Sun* newspaper, and used outdoor as well as in-store communications to announce the price cuts.

In addition, and as part of its Morrisons.com site, the supermarket also launched a 'Pricecuts' page designed to show how much cheaper their food is. Powered by mysupermarket.co.uk, customers can view the pricing history of an item, providing transparency and credibility for the strategy.

Source: Chapman (2014); Eleftheriou-Smith (2014); Ruddick (2014); Vizard (2014).

Question: To what extent is positioning contingent on sound segmentation?

Task: Find two other supermarkets and compare their positioning statements.

Jewell (2007) draws attention to the need to consider repositioning from a customer's perspective, something neglected in the literature. He also shows that two key tasks need to be accomplished during a repositioning exercise. First, the old positioning needs to be suppressed so that customers no longer relate to it and, second, consumers need to learn the new position. These twin tasks are complementary, as interference or rather the deliberate weakening of the old position will help strengthen acceptance of the new position.

Viewpoint 6.5	Planning the repositioning of the Fausto Puglisi brand in the UK

Fausto Puglisi is a luxury apparel brand based in Milan, Italy. The reputation of the Fausto Puglisi brand has grown enormously in recent years, partly due to the support of the celebrity market. The brand has been featured in high-fashion magazines all over the world, and praised for its eccentric, extravagant and unique designs.

Despite this success Fausto Puglisi has had difficulty in establishing itself in the UK. With its apparel being sold only in Selfridges, London, access to the wider market is not just limited but often its fashion is disregarded as being a brand which 'real people' cannot relate to and wear freely.

The brand's UK marketing strategy involves increasing distribution and repositioning the Fausto Puglisi brand as an apparel brand worn that is loved by 'real' women, not just the celebrity market.

The challenge, therefore, is to prepare a marketing communications plan that meets these goals. To do this requires utilising the marketing communications planning principles and framework (as set out in Chapter 5).

This Viewpoint and solution was written by Lisa Hides when she was a marketing student at Newcastle University.

Lisa's solution to this challenge can be seen in the resources that support this book. See www.pearson/fillturnbull.

Scholars' paper 6.4	Repositioning through interference

Jewell, R.D. (2007) Establishing effective repositioning communications in a competitive marketplace, _Journal of Marketing Communications_, 13(4), 231–41.

This paper considers positioning from a consumer's perspective, rather than through the traditional manufacturer's lens. Product positioning is important to marketers because it can influence consumers. The author proposes that successful repositioning should be based not only on the audience learning the new positioning but also on interfering with competitors' communications in order to inhibit messages about the previous positioning.

Key points

- Objectives play an important role in the activities of individuals, social groups and organisations for a variety of reasons. These include providing direction and an action focus for all those participating in the activity, a means by which the variety of decisions relating to an activity can be made in a consistent way, and they set out the time period in which the activity is to be completed. In addition, they communicate the values and scope of the activity to all participants and, finally, they provide a means by which the success of the activity can be evaluated.

- The use of objectives in the management process is vital if an organisation's desired outcomes are to be achieved. Each of the objectives, at corporate, unit and functional levels, contributes to the formulation of the communications objectives. They are all interlinked, interdependent, multiple and often conflicting.

- The various organisational objectives are of little use if they are not communicated to those who need to know what they are. Traditionally, such communications have focused on employees, but there is increasing recognition that the other members of the stakeholder network need to understand an organisation's purpose and objectives.

- The major task for communications objectives is two-fold: first, to contribute to the overall direction of the organisation by fulfilling the communications requirements of the marketing mix; second, to communicate the corporate thrust and values to various stakeholders so that they understand the organisation, can respond to its intentions and help develop appropriate relationships.

- Communications objectives are derived from an initial review of the current situation and the marketing plan requirements. They are not a replication of the marketing objectives but a distillation of the research activities that have been undertaken subsequently.

- There are three main streams of objectives. The first concerns issues relating to the buyers of the product or service offered by the organisation. The second concerns issues relating to market share/sales volume, profitability and revenue. The third stream relates to the image, reputation and preferences that other stakeholders have towards the organisation.

- The IPA has identified a hierarchy of brand communications objectives following its analysis of effective campaigns. These are business, behavioural and intermediate goals.

- Communications objectives consist of two main elements: sales-oriented and communications-oriented. A balance between the two will be determined by the situation facing the organisation, but can be a mixture of both product and corporate tasks. These objectives, once quantified, need to be ranked and weighted in order that other components of the plan can be developed.

- To assist managers in their need to develop suitable objectives, a set of guidelines has been developed, commonly referred to as SMART objectives. This acronym stands for specific, measurable, achievable, relevant, targeted and timed.

- The position adopted is a statement about what the brand is, what it stands for and the values and beliefs that customers (hopefully) will come to associate with the particular brand. Visual and text/copy images or the position statement represented in a strapline may be a significant trigger that buyers use to recall images and associations of the brand.

- There are two main ways in which a brand can be positioned: these are functional and expressive (or symbolic) positioning. Functionally positioned brands stress the features and benefits, and expressive brands emphasise the ego, social and hedonic satisfactions that can be associated with a brand.

- A perceptual map represents a geometric comparison of how competing products are perceived by customers, based on important attributes. Each product is positioned on the map according to the perception that buyers have of the strength of each attribute of each product. By plotting the perceived positions of each brand on the map, an overall perspective of the market can be developed and strategies formed to develop clearer, more rewarding positions.

- There are a number of overall approaches that can be used to develop a position. These can be based on factors such as the market, the customer or redefining the appeal of the brand itself. To implement these three broad approaches, various strategies have been developed. These include product features, price/quality, use, product class dissociation, user, competitor, benefit and heritage or use of cultural symbols.

Review questions

Petplan case questions

1. What type of objectives did Petplan set for its campaign?

2. What led Petplan to set these objectives and what was their origin?

3. What was the positioning adopted by Petplan's competitors and how did Petplan's revised position differ?

4. How did Petplan communicate its desired positioning? How could it have been improved?

5. Identify three strengths associated with the rebrand.

General questions

1. Write a brief report arguing the case both for and against the use of an increase in sales as the major objective of all promotional activities.

2. Why is positioning an important part of marketing communications? Use the Petplan case to illustrate your response.

3. What is perceptual mapping?

4. Select four print advertisements for the same product category and comment on the positions they have adopted.

5. What are the main positioning strategies?

References

Anon (2014) Grand Prix: Easyjet, Marketing Society Awards, *Marketing,* June, p. 7.

Ap, T. and Sun, C. (2014) L'Oreal brand and Revlon call time in China, *South China Morning Post,* 13 January, retrieved 9 May 2015 from www.scmp.com/business/companies/article/1404118/loreal-brand-and-revlon-call-time-china.

Barry, T. and Howard, D.J. (1990) A review and critique of the hierarchy of effects in advertising, *International Journal of Advertising,* 9, 121–35.

Binet, L. and Field, P. (2007) *Marketing in an Era of Accountability,* Henley: IPA-WARC.

Blankson, C. and Kalafatis, S.P. (2007) Positioning strategies of international and multicultural-orientated service brands, *Journal of Services Marketing,* 21(6), 435–50.

Boyd, M. (2010) Google shows adland the new tools of its trade, *Campaign,* 25 June, p. 11.

Chapman, M. (2014) Morrisons' sales plummet ahead of major 'cheaper' repositioning, *Marketing Magazine,* 8 May 2014, retrieved 13 July 2014 from www.marketingmagazine.co.uk/article/1293382/morrisons-sales-plummet-ahead-major-cheaper-repositioning.

Colley, R. (1961) *Defining Advertising Goals for Measured Advertising Results,* New York: Association of National Advertisers.

Day, G., Shocker, A.D. and Srivastava, R.K. (1979) Customer orientated approaches to identifying product markets, *Journal of Marketing,* 43(4), 8–19.

Dutka, S. (1995) *Defining Advertising Goals for Measured Advertising Results,* 2nd edition, New York: Association of National Advertisers.

Eleftheriou-Smith, L.M. (2014) Morrisons positions itself as low-priced supermarket with 'love it cheaper' strategy, *Marketing Magazine,* 2 May 2014, retrieved 13 July 2014 from www.marketingmagazine.co.uk/article/1292679/morrisons-positions-itself-low-priced-supermarket-love-cheaper-strategy.

Elliott, S. (2014) To reconnect with consumers, Revlon looks for love, *New York Times,* 16 November, retrieved 9 May 2015 from www.nytimes.com/2014/11/17/business/media/to-reconnect-with-consumers-revlon-looks-for-love.html?_r=0.

Gray, R. (2013) Mission to deliver, *The Marketer,* 1 May, retrieved 3 February 2015 from www.themarketer.co.uk/how-to/case-studies/norbert-dentressangle/.

Heath, R. (2009) Emotional engagement: how television builds big brands at low attention, *Journal of Advertising Research,* March, 62–73.

Herstein, R. and Mitki, Y. (2008) How El Al Airlines transformed its service strategy with employee participation, *Strategy & Leadership,* 36(3), 21–5.

Jewell, R.D. (2007) Establishing effective repositioning communications in a competitive marketplace, *Journal of Marketing Communications,* 13(4), 231–41.

Johnson, G., Whittingham, R., Angwin, D., Regnér, P. and Scholes, K. (2014) *Exploring Strategy,* 10th edition, Harlow: Pearson Education.

King, S. (1991) Brand building in the 1990s, *Journal of Marketing Management,* 7, 3–13.

Kotler, P. (2003) *Marketing Management: Analysis, Planning, Implementation and Control,* 11th edition, Englewood Cliffs, NJ: Prentice Hall.

Kriegel, R.A. (1986) How to choose the right communications objectives, *Business Marketing,* April, 94–106.

Lam, A. (2015) Revlon repositions brand with love, *marketing-interactive.com,* 13 February, retrieved 8 May 2015 from www.marketing-interactive.com/revlon-repositions-brand-with-love/.

Neal, W.D. (1980) Strategic product positioning: a step by step guide, *Business (USA),* May/June, 34–40.

Quinn, J.B., Mintzberg, H., James, R.M., Lampel, J.B. and Ghosal, S. (2003) *The Strategy Process,* 4th edition, New York: Prentice Hall.

Ries, A. and Trout, J. (1972) The positioning era cometh, *Advertising Age,* 24 April, 35–8.

Rossiter, J.R. and Percy, L. (1987) *Advertising and Promotion Management,* Lexington, MA: McGraw-Hill.

Ruddick, G. (2014) Tesco 'losing 1m shoppers a week' as shocking figures reveal pressure on supermarkets, *Telegraph,* 3 June, retrieved 13 July 2014 from www.telegraph.co.uk/finance/newsbysector/epic/tsco/10872572/Tesco-losing-1m-shoppers-a-week-as-shocking-figures-reveal-pressure-on-supermarkets.html.

Sinclair, S.A. and Stalling, E.C. (1990) Perceptual mapping: a tool for industrial marketing: a case study, *Journal of Business and Industrial Marketing,* 5(1), 55–65.

Vizard, S. (2014) Morrisons launches 'ambitious' campaign to shout about 'biggest ever' price cuts, *Marketing Week,* 1 May, retrieved 13 July 2014 from www.marketingweek.co.uk/sectors/retail/news/morrisons-launches-ambitious-campaign-to-shout-about-biggest-ever-price-cuts/4010350.article.

Chapter 7

The communications industry: structure, operations and finance

The communications industry has undergone significant changes over the last decade. These changes have been driven by a number of factors including the severe economic trading conditions, changing consumer behaviours, rapid developments in digital technologies as well as increased fragmentation of the media.

Managing new media landscapes and embracing new forms of communications have been challenging for the industry. This has led to the emergence of new types of agencies to service new media opportunities and communications forms, as well as restructuring the way that some agencies manage their clients' business.

Aims and learning objectives

The aim of this chapter is to explore issues relating to the communications industry, including the structure, the types of organisations involved and the operations and processes used to develop marketing communications for clients.

The learning objectives are to enable readers to:

1. understand the nature and structure of the communications industry;
2. consider the role and characteristics of the main types of organisations involved in the industry;
3. examine the principal methods and operations used within agencies to meet their clients' needs;
4. explore relationships and methods of remuneration used within the industry;
5. appraise the role of the communications budget and trends in budgeting;
6. appreciate the different techniques used to set marketing communications budgets.

The Kasiisi Project

Working as Account Director at London creative agency, Wieden+Kennedy, my job means I'm responsible for leading and developing the relationship between the agency and our clients. The lynchpin for everything and everyone, the Account Director, is part of the process from beginning to end – from planning, to creative development, production and evaluation of the creative solution, be it a TV ad, an app or an interactive experience.

Wieden+Kennedy has a long-standing relationship with The International Exchange (TIE), an organisation that combines social change with personal and professional development. TIE pairs individuals in the communications industry with projects in developing countries that need their skills.

For the project, TIE provides valuable communications expertise, which is often desperately needed, but can't be afforded. For the individual, it's an opportunity to use their expertise in a very different context, putting them on the ground where it's needed.

In 2013, I got a chance to do a TIE placement, and jumped at the opportunity. At that point in my career – having worked at Wieden+Kennedy for 4 years – it felt like the right time to try something new, independently from the support structure I usually rely on. From a personal point of view, I wanted to gain a different perspective – on myself, what I do and on the world – by spending a month in a new culture and reality.

I chose to spend my month-long placement with a small NGO in rural, western Uganda, called The Kasiisi Project. They work to improve the poor educational opportunities available to children in areas surrounding the Kibale National Forest – East Africa's largest primate habitat. Most people in this area are subsistence farmers, with many mouths to feed and little income.

Education is the best hope of breaking the cycle of poverty, but as many as 70 per cent of children don't complete primary school. Through a range of programmes, The Kasiisi Project helps children stay in school, opening up opportunities for them beyond subsistence farming, whilst instilling in them an understanding of the importance of their natural environment.

Close to 100 per cent of The Kasiisi Project's funding comes from donations from the UK and USA, but their long-term ambition is to become at least in part self-sustainable, with income-generating initiatives to support the school programmes. My brief was to create a business and communications strategy for them.

Exhibit 7.1	**Children at Kiko, one of the primary schools which The Kasiisi Project works in**
	Source: Hanne Haugen.

Exhibit 7.2 | **Kigarama School's mission statement**
Source: Hanne Haugen.

The task was in and of itself a big challenge. I'm involved in strategy development in my job, but it's not really my area. Add to that a culture I wasn't familiar with, the complexity of the issues the project works to tackle, and a board of directors that had to approve everything I did. There were also a few practical challenges. Power and Internet connections were, if not quite luxuries, then unreliable at best. Particularly during the rainy season power-outages were frequent. The heavy rain also meant that the roads – and I use the term loosely – were so bad that a journey of a few miles could easily take hours. There was a lot to contend with!

But I quickly found my feet. And I discovered that a new way of thinking was welcomed by the project. The problem wasn't a lack of understanding of the importance of communications and the need for a clear strategy – it was not having the resources to develop it. The project looked at me as providing them with valuable knowledge, which made me more confident in my skills and what I could bring to the project.

On a personal level, living and working in one of the world's poorest counties had a big impact on me and made me more conscious and interested in issues surrounding poverty – the massive challenges, but also the positive developments.

However, of all the things I took from my month in Uganda, what felt like the biggest revelation was the change in my perception of the advertising industry and the skills I've developed from being a part of it.

I've always enjoyed working in advertising and taken pride in what I do – but to some extent I've been guilty of seeing the industry as divorced from the 'real' world. The perceived wisdom in society isn't that advertising can affect change for good – probably the opposite.

It can be easy to look at what I do as tricking people into buying things they don't need. People are inherently distrustful of 'big business' – and of agencies as their henchmen. There are also misconceptions around what an agency actually does – as most people only see the output of a long process. On the surface, it might look fun and easy, but the truth is that behind every campaign, there are months, sometimes years, of hard work, sweat and tears.

What I learnt from my TIE placement is that my skills were hugely beneficial for an NGO. Budget and resource constraints require innovative approaches to solving problems. Complex problems require the ability to understand underlying issues, find the pertinent insight and drill down to a workable solution. Making sure a message is clearly articulated and heard by the right people – which is the crux of what advertising agencies do – will have a big impact on an NGO's future development, and in turn drive social change.

For The Kasiisi Project specifically, what became clear to me during my time there was that for the organisation to become self-sustainable, it needed to move from being an NGO operating within a community, to more of a community-based social enterprise. My background and experience gave me licence to present some quite challenging ideas to the board, and help them to see and appreciate that they needed to approach things differently as an organisation to communicate effectively around what they do. They needed to look outside the board – to their community – and be open to involving them in their work.

I feel fortunate to have had the opportunity to be a 'skilled' volunteer, and adding value beyond just donating my time. Through applying what I know from advertising, I was able to help the project find a focus, to think differently about their approach, and find ways of working to allow them to implement and evaluate their future efforts. I returned to London knowing

that I had achieved something, feeling proud of my job and my agency, which supported me in doing it, and excited about what the advertising industry can do.

As the trend towards brands becoming more socially responsible continues to grow, our ability as an industry to help affect social change can become a more explicit part of our purpose. The more agency people who benefit from an experience such as TIE, the more people will help make this shift happen from the inside.

This case was contributed by Hanne Haugen, former Account Director at Wieden+Kennedy

Questions relating to this case study can be found at the end of the chapter.

Introduction

The marketing communications industry consists of four principal actors or types of stakeholders. These are the media, clients, who fund the whole process, agencies, historically the most notable of which are advertising agencies, and finally the thousands of support organisations, such as production companies and fulfilment houses, that enable the whole communications process to function. At the centre of this theatre are consumers, audiences who engage with the output with varying levels of intensity and involvement.

It is the operations and relationships between these organisations and, increasingly, audiences that not only drive the industry but also form an important context within which marketing communications can be understood. Figure 7.1 sets out the main actor organisations in the industry.

Some organisations choose to manage and develop their marketing communications 'in-house' – that is, do it themselves. This may be to keep costs low or to provide a good level of control over the messages and media. While this does offer advantages, there are also a number of disadvantages of not using an outside agency. In particular the organisation is unlikely to have the same access to creative talent and range of specialist skills that an agency has. This is an important concern as creativity has a powerful impact on the effectiveness of marketing communications and there is a risk that work will be less effective. There are also benefits of economies of scale to be considered from having access to expertise when required, without having to hire the specialist staff permanently. Furthermore, managing the marketing communications activity in-house will increase the organisation's fixed costs, reduces flexibility and often introduces political dimensions that can greatly impact on the objectivity and creativity.

Specsavers is one UK brand that runs its own in-house creative department. The brand which has been producing its own advertising since 1985 argues that developing creative work in-house has a number of distinct advantages over using an agency, including brand knowledge and greater freedom to reformulate briefs (Daldry, 2015). Other brands that use in-house creatives include Jaguar and Land Rover (Degun, 2015). There are also a growing number of brands operating their own in-house media departments,

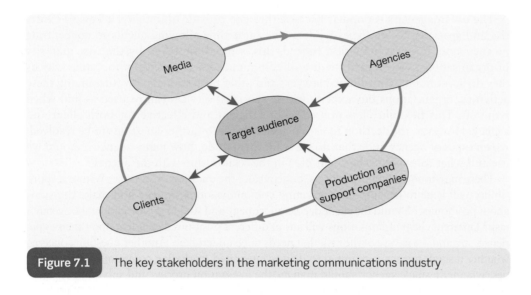

Figure 7.1	The key stakeholders in the marketing communications industry

including BT, Unilever, Procter & Gamble, GlaxoSmithKline, Reckitt Benckiser, the COI and Anheuser Busch (Media Week, 2005).

An alternative route is to use freelancers or self-employed consultants. Although each individual's skills may have been developed within a particular discipline, such as public relations or advertising, freelancers can provide flexibility and access to some experts through their network of personal contacts. However, it should be remembered that the use of freelancers and in-house facilities requires use of the client organisation's resources, if only to manage the freelancers. Crowd-sourcing, the use of the public to generate creative advertising content, is an attempt by clients to circumnavigate the agency sector in order to find new material and cut costs. This form of user-generated content is explored in more detail later in the text (Chapter 17).

Exhibit 7.3	**Specsavers operates its own in-house agency and has won awards for its creative work.**
	Source: Specsavers Optical Group.

The use of agencies is popular because they can provide objectivity, access to expertise and specialist technologies while at the same time allowing clients to concentrate on their core business activities. Indeed, this is the route taken by the vast majority of organisations, who regard the use of communications agencies in the same way as they do accountants, consultants, lawyers and other professionals. By outsourcing these activities, organisations buy experts whose specialist services can be used as and when required. This flexibility has proved to be efficient and effective for both client and agency. However, the decision to use an agency leads to further questions to be resolved: which types of agency and what do we want them to do, how many agencies should we use and what role should the client play in the relationship with the agency?

These may sound strange questions, but consider the question of strategy. Whose responsibility will it be to develop the marketing communications strategy and make decisions about positioning? Should the client decide on strategy and should this be part of the agency's task? Different client organisations will adopt different positions depending upon their experience, size and the nature of the task that needs to be undertaken. Another question concerns whether a single agency is required to deliver integrated marketing communications activities, whether a single agency should manage the integration process and sub-contract tasks to other specialist or group-based agencies (and in doing so act as lead agency) or whether a series of specialist agencies should be appointed, each reporting to the client.

Dimensions of the UK marketing communications industry

It is useful to consider the size and value of the industry by considering the sums of money spent by clients on marketing communications. Some of these figures are acknowledged to be estimates, and there is some evidence of 'double counting' (one or more sectors claiming part of the overall spend for itself). That said, however, the total spend for advertising in the UK was valued at just under £18 billion in 2015 (Warc, 2015a) (see Table 7.1).

The trend has been for increased expenditure online with advertisers moving budgets out of print (newspapers and magazines). While there has been considerable speculation that television expenditure would suffer from organisations increasing their investment

Table 7.1 Total UK advertising expenditure (£million)

Media	2005 (£m)*	2010 (£m)	2015 (£m)
Print	6797.2	4305.7	2757.7
Television	4242.9	4295.1	5003.0
Outdoor	896.8	881.0	1083.4
Radio	613.4	523.0	600.0
Cinema	157.7	184.3	215.2
Internet	1366.5	4097.1	8102.8
Total	14074.5	14286.2	17762.1

Source: http://expenditurereport.warc.com/. Used with permission from WARC.

online, the impact has not been as great as some commentators feared. In 2015, total media expenditure in the UK saw an increase over 2010 levels of spend (Warc, 2015a).

Other areas of the marketing communications mix such as sponsorship have experienced significant growth. The International Events Group (IEG) suggest that global sponsorship rights reached US$57.5 billion in 2015 (IEG, 2015). This means that since 2011 the sponsorship market has grown by nearly US$9 billion, with growth expected to continue in the future (IEG, 2015).

Publicly available figures regarding the size of the public relations, direct marketing and sales promotion industries are based on the size of the industry rather than what has been spent by each client. The global public relations (PR) industry was valued at US$13.5 billion in 2015 which saw a 7 per cent rise over the previous year value (World PR Report, 2015). The world's top 10 PR firms accounted for US$4.8 billion of the total value (World PR Report, 2015).

Although estimates vary, mainly because of problems of definition, the direct marketing industry has similarly experienced large growth, with the European industry estimated to be worth £14.2 billion (DMA, 2015).

Sales promotion is another area of the industry that is difficult to measure given that the breadth of activities attributable to sales promotion are many and varied. In 2013 the industry body, The Institute of Promotional Marketing (IPM), undertook a major research project to gain a better understanding of the size of the UK promotional marketing industry. The study identified that the total spend for the UK industry was £54.8 billion, although £40.4 billion of that value was price discounting. Despite this, the study showed that £14.4 billion was spent through agencies and on media and rewards (IPM, 2013).

Expenditure patterns do change, albeit at different rates, but, given the domination of advertising and sales promotion, the overall balance is unlikely to change dramatically in the short term. However, it is clearly important for those responsible for the future and current planning of marketing communications activities to monitor trends, particularly those in the fastest-growing sectors of the industry, in order to identify and target creative opportunities.

Having painted a picture of the size and dynamics of the industry, a word needs to be said about the consumer view of the industry. Here issues about ethics and morality surface, accompanied by a suggestion that the public view the industry with cynicism and distrust. Mitchell (2012) reports that the chief executive of the Advertising Association said that, 'Advertising is facing a problem, favourability has evaporated, the public's trust and confidence in [it] has fallen through the floor and the industry has missed a trick by failing to renegotiate its deal with society in which it operates.' He continued by commenting on the increasing media criticism and the number of people calling for more regulation.

Viewpoint 7.1   UK setting the standards for best practice

The UK advertising industry is seen to have one of the best self-regulation frameworks in the world. All advertising is governed by codes of practice that have been established to protect the consumer and ensure advertising is honest, legal, decent and truthful. These codes of practice are maintained by the Committees of Advertising Practice (CAP) and must be followed by all advertisers, media and agencies. The codes are enforced by the Advertising Standards Authority (ASA) and regulate all forms of advertising, including banner and display ads, paid-for search, company websites and networking sites such as Twitter and Facebook, commercial email and SMS text message ads, in-app ads and online behavioural advertising (OBA).

The code provides general guidance to industry about what is responsible advertising and makes it clear that all advertising must not mislead or offend. There are also codes for advertising to specific audiences such as children and special guidance on advertising within categories such as alcohol, health, motoring, gambling and financial products.

Any complaints about advertising are handled by the ASA. While some complaints such as a minor mistake on an ad are resolved with the advertiser quickly, others undergo a formal investigation by the ASA Council who will rule on the issue. They will decide if the Advertising Codes have been breached and if ads are seen to have broken the rules they are required to be changed or withdrawn.

In 2014 the ASA handled 35,000 complaints about advertising and ruled on 17,000 ads. Some of those complaints were about the advertising for Duracell Ultra Power with Duralock batteries. The ad featured a Duracell battery-powered bunny playing drums next to 12 zinc battery-powered gorillas and tells us, 'You all know Duracell lasts longer than leading zinc batteries, but exactly how much longer?' A number of complaints were made, including the challenge of whether it was fair to compare alkaline batteries with zinc batteries. The investigation resulted in the ASA asking Duracell to make the basis of comparison clearer in future ads to ensure that the presentation of comparisons was not likely to mislead consumers.

Source: Advertising Standards Authority (ASA) (2015); Campaign (2015).

Question: Why do you think the UK has a system of self-regulation? Do you think it is effective? Explain why.

Task: Visit the ASA website for yourself and look at three recent complaints that have been made about advertising in the UK. Look at the advertising and consider if you think the complaint is justified.

Some of the problems faced by the advertising/communications industry have been revealed by Gordon, cited by Mitchell (2012), as bombardment, intrusiveness, poor creativity, irrelevance and condescension. Much of this is seen to be a function of the increasing power, often afforded by technology, that consumers have experienced in recent years. It can be argued that consumers today are not so reliant on ads as they can now search, compare, contrast, ask friends and peers and use ads. According to Research Director Karen Fraser at Credos, this means that ads are not so critical in the decision-making process as they used to be (Bain, 2012).

Structure and development of the UK marketing communications industry

The structure of the industry has inevitably changed through time. Some may argue that it has not changed enough, but the shape and size of the industry have developed. Over the last 20 years the size of the industry has increased in response to changes in technology, the growth in the number of marketing communications activities and with it the real value of advertising, sales promotion, public relations and direct marketing.

The configuration of the agency services industry partly reflects the moves made by the larger agencies to consolidate their positions. They have attempted to buy either smaller, often medium-sized competitors, in an attempt to protect their market shares or provide an improved range of services for their clients, particularly in areas of digital and content.

Table 7.2 Top holding companies ranked by advertising

Rank 2014	Holding company	Billings 2014 (£m)	Key UK media assets
1	Omnicom	888.4	Abbott Mead Vickers BBDO, Adam & Eve/DDB, TBWA UK, Rapp, Proximity
2	WPP	863.6	RKCR/Y&R, CHI & Partners (49 per cent), Grey, O&M, JWT, Cheetham Bell, Wunderman, G2
3	Publicis Groupe	829.1	BBH, Leo Burnett, Publicis, Saatchi & Saatchi, Fallon, Kitcatt Nohr, Saatchi Masius
4	Interpublic	506.9	McCann Erickson, DLKW Lowe, FCB Inferno
5	Havas	192.6	Worldwide London, BETC London

Source: From Brand Republic (2015a with the permission of the copyright owner, Haymarket Media Group Limited).

This has led to an industry characterised by very large agencies, many owned by holding companies that dominate the industry landscape. Companies such as Omnicom, WPP and Publicis Groupe own some of the world's largest agency networks (see Table 7.2).

In contrast to these large agency networks there are an even greater number of very small agencies. These smaller agencies have formed as the result of people formerly employed in large agencies becoming frustrated with having to work within tight margins and increased administration, and then leaving and setting up their own fledgling businesses.

Broadly speaking, the industry consists of a few very large groups of agencies, some big agencies, a large number of very small agencies and relatively few medium-sized agencies. Although ownership has been an important factor driving industry development, the

Exhibit 7.4	**Sir Martin Sorrell is the highest-paid chief executive in the FTSE 100** The chief executive of WPP was reported to have earned £43 million in 2014 (Campaign, 2015). *Source*: WPP plc.

current preference for loose, independent networks has enabled some large organisations to offer clients an improved range of services and the small agencies a chance to work with some of the bigger accounts. Miln (2004) speculated that structural changes to the way in which clients and agencies work together would give rise to what he referred to as 'new agencies', who would provide a limited range of specific communications services, most commonly involved with thinking around the creative or media elements, but would outsource or delegate the implementation to a third-party organisation. These organisations possess the core skills associated with project management and are better placed to fulfil this specialist role. The agency will remain responsible to the client for the implementation, but would be in a better position to continue advising about the overall communications strategy and media imperatives. The extent to which this has happened is questionable, but the principles behind this thinking remain interesting, even if they require a change of cultural awareness and strategic reorientation.

The recession in 2008 heralded a major restructuring within most agencies. The goal was to lower costs and vulnerability as billings shrank. For many it was an opportunity to reshape their businesses at a time of great uncertainty and differing economic predictions. Some agencies attempted to broaden their services into new areas away from their traditional billings-based business (Beale, 2012). Clients have similarly felt the pressure of the global recession and many have evaluated their marketing costs. Proctor & Gamble (P&G), one of the world's largest advertisers, decided to cut its marketing budget by US$500 million through reducing the number of agencies it works with and production, media, public relations, packaging design and in-store marketing costs (Warc, 2015b). Other brands like Jaguar have moved more of their business in-house in an effort to cut costs in recent years (Degun, 2015).

Scholars' paper 7.1	Grandstanding Amsterdam

Röling, R.W. (2010) Small town, big campaigns: the rise and growth of an international advertising industry in Amsterdam, *Regional Studies*, 44(7), August, 829–43.

For those interested in international advertising this paper provides an interesting analysis through the use of 'four waves of advertising' from early twentieth-century Western capitalism. This analysis considers the structure of the industry and provides reasoning for the development of small, flexible, and independent international advertising agencies, especially those that use Amsterdam as a hub to create advertisements for the international market.

Agency types and structures

The marketing communications industry consists of a number of different types of organisations whose purpose is to enable clients to communicate effectively and efficiently with their target audiences. Essentially, clients appoint agencies to develop and implement campaigns on their behalf. To accomplish this, advertising agencies buy media time and space from media owners, public relations agencies place stories with the media for their clients' representation, and other agencies undertake a range of other communications activities on behalf of their clients.

Originally, advertising agencies undertook two main roles, creative message design and media planning and buying. The media component has subsequently been spun off to specialist agencies. However, the interest in and drive towards integrated marketing communications have helped agencies assume new, more independent roles in the communications industry. The development of digital media has had a profound impact on all areas of marketing communications and agencies are now being asked to provide services that meet the needs of these new media platforms. Clients want agencies to help develop blogger programmes, deliver digital content and design social media campaigns, and the industry has seen the emergence of a new wave of specialist agencies in response to this demand.

Clients will typically work with a number of different agencies, each with its own area of expertise to develop communications ideas. Having a range of agencies on their roster provides the clients with access to different specialisms and they will brief agencies together to respond to their brief with an integrated marketing communications campaign. While many clients choose to manage this process themselves, some large holding groups such as WPP have identified a need to develop a new client servicing model. This 'horizontal' service model allows agencies access to all the specialist services within the holding group with a Global Client Leader coordinating services for them (see Viewpoint 7.2).

The IPA identifies 11 main types of agency that exist: full-service or integrated agencies, creative agencies, media agencies, digital agencies, search agencies, social media agencies, direct marketing agencies, branded content agencies, experiential agencies, healthcare agencies and outdoor or out-of-home (OOH) agencies (IPA, 2015).

Full-service or integrated agencies

The full-service agency offers the full range of services that a client requires in order to advertise its products and services. Agencies such as J. Walter Thompson and Leo Burnett offer a full service consisting of strategic planning, research, creative development, production, media planning and buying, and evaluation services. Very often these are offered on a global basis, but this does not mean a full-service agency needs to be large, employing thousands of people. Some mid-size agencies employing a couple of dozen people can offer a full service. Whatever the size, some of these activities may be subcontracted, but overall responsibility rests with the full-service agency.

Creative agencies

Creative agencies provide specialist or niche services for clients such as copywriting developing creative content and other artistic services. These agencies provide clients with an alternative source of ideas, new ways of thinking about a problem, issue or product. They will develop a communications strategy for the client and generate creative ideas based on that strategy to meet the needs of the communications channel. Clients choose to use them because they either wish to use particular styles and approaches for their creative work or want to generate a raft of creative ideas.

Media agencies

Similarly, media specialists provide clients with media services expertise. These organisations deliver media strategy and consulting services for both client advertisers and agencies. Their core business, however, is focused on the planning, scheduling, buying and monitoring of a client's media schedule. Media agencies will research the target audience and match their lifestyle to their media habits, enabling them to determine the best media to use for the campaign. In addition to their access to data on media habits, a key advantage of using media specialists is that they have the capacity to buy media time and space at rates far lower than a client or advertising agency can procure them. This is because of the sheer volume of business that media specialists buy.

Two main forms of media specialist have emerged: media independents, where the organisation is owned and run free of the direction and policy requirements of a full-service agency; and media dependents, where the organisation is a subsidiary of a creative or full-service organisation. The largest media agency in the UK is MediaCom, part of the WPP Group (Brand Republic, 2015b).

Digital agencies

The development of digital media agencies is the inevitable consequence of the rapid growth of the digital media industry. The growth has come from two main areas. The first concerns the surge of online brands that hit the market full of expectation of transforming the way business is conducted. The second concerns established offline brands seeking to reach customers by adding interactive capabilities to their marketing channels.

While most agencies now offer their clients some digital capability, digital agencies specialise in their digital offering. Services range from those offering digital media planning to those offering creative services such as web design and display advertising. Digital agencies will provide search, social media, content and mobile campaigns.

Search agencies

Search agencies specialise in a range of services that help to drive traffic to an organisation's website. While the range of expertise they offer differs, most have expertise in pay-per-click advertising, search engine optimisation (SEO), as well as affiliate and social media marketing.

Social media agencies

The rise in consumers' use of social media has led to the emergence of social media agencies. These agencies provide a range of services to organisations, including community management, channel monitoring and analysis, crisis management and a range of content development including blogging content.

Direct marketing agencies

Direct marketing has become a significant and influential part of the marketing communications industry. Direct marketing and direct-response agencies create and deliver campaigns through direct mail, telemarketing or through a variety of offline and online media, which are referred to as direct-response media.

One of the distinguishing elements of a direct marketing agency is the database. These agencies maintain large databases that contain mailing lists. The data can be merged and reconstructed to reflect a client's target market. The agency helps to develop promotional materials and then implements the campaign through the data list. Direct agencies will either own or have access to a fulfilment house. These organisations fulfil customer orders – that is, process the order and take payment resulting from the direct marketing campaign, send out the ordered products and deal with after-sales services as necessary.

Branded content agencies

Branded content agencies plan and develop digital content and commercials largely for the Internet. Most offer video production for viral advertising, product videos, films and some offer app development. Most branded content agencies are keen to differentiate their services from those of traditional advertising agencies.

Experiential marketing agencies

Experiential agencies develop experiences for consumers. These experiences often come in the form of roadshows, product launches, live events, PR stunts, in-store sampling, pop-up showrooms and even guerrilla activity. We explore the nature of field marketing and brand experiences in Chapter 17.

Healthcare agencies

Healthcare agencies specialise in providing marketing communications solutions for the pharmaceutical and healthcare sector. While they offer a range of services that may be similar to other agencies such as campaign planning and development, it is their specialist knowledge of the healthcare, medical and medical device sectors that makes them attractive to clients.

Outdoor agencies/out-of-home

These agencies specialise in planning, buying, implementing and evaluating out-of-home media. What used to be classified as 'outdoor' media and included traditional billboards, tube posters, taxis and buses has now been extended to include a diverse range of ambient media under the umbrella of out-of-home. These agencies continue to find new and increasingly interactive media opportunities for clients. Many out-of-home agencies use petrol pumps, ATM machines, beer mats and increasingly, due to technological advancements, interactive screens using QR codes and live data feeds are being used.

Other communications agencies

The agencies and organisations set out so far in this chapter have their roots and core business firmly set within the advertising part of the communications industry. In addition to these there is a raft of other agencies, each specialising in a particular aspect of the marketing communications industry. So, there are agencies that provide sales promotion, public relations and sponsorship. Their structure and operations reflect the needs of their market specialism, and many are based on the principles through which the advertising agencies operate.

Viewpoint 7.2   WPP's new 'Horizontal' Service Model

WPP is the world's largest advertising and marketing services groups. With several hundred different companies operating out of more than 3,000 offices in 112 countries, WPP offers a truly global communications service. The Group employs over 190,000 people (including associates and investments) and in 2014 had revenues of £11.5 billion.

The group's major networks include some of the biggest global advertising and media agencies such as Grey, Ogilvy & Matheur, J. Walter Thompson, Y&R, Mediacom, Mindshare, MEC and Maxus. Other networks offer services in areas such as data investment management (formerly known as consumer insight or market research); public relations and public affairs; branding and identity; healthcare communications; and direct, digital, promotion and relationship marketing. In addition the Group has companies that provide specialist services such as corporate and business-to-business marketing, employer branding, event marketing, sports marketing, and media and production services.

WPP companies work with many global brands, including 344 of the Fortune Global 500, all 30 of the Dow Jones 30, and 69 of the NASDAQ 100. Many of these clients use a range of WPP's services, with over 470 of them serviced across four disciplines, and 385 work with WPP across six or more countries. This global offering and the range of communications skills provide clients with a comprehensive marketing communications service.

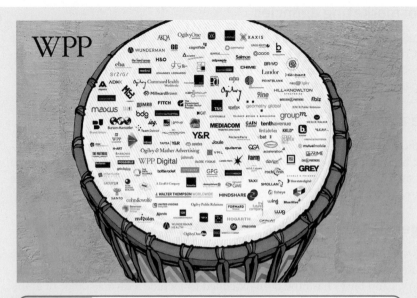

Exhibit 7.5	**WPP's palette of organisations**
	Source: WPP plc.

A key challenge for many global clients is operating consistently across markets and ensuring they max-imise effectiveness and efficiency in their marketing communications activities. In the past, many clients have appointed a lead global agency to assist with this; however, while working with one agency network may ensure that synergy and opportunities for cost efficiencies are realised, this servicing structure has not always been the most effective at allowing clients to tap into the vast range of communications ser-vices a holding group such as WPP can offer. Recognising the added value that access to all of its commu-nications companies would provide clients led WPP to pioneer a new service model for some many clients.

The 'Horizontal' WPP service model offers clients access to all of its companies, allowing them to draw on the talent across the group's vast agency networks and providing access to more than 190,000 com-munications professionals. This has created a virtual 'super agency' with clients being managed by Global Client Leaders and the support of Country Managers to coordinate services and talent in each country. In the past, agencies have been keen to promote a 'full service' offering, but this is the first service model that allows clients to access resources from different companies. A good example of how the model brings talent together from different WPP Group companies to service one account is the recent work for Al Gore's Climate Reality Project, which involved teams from Blue State Digital, The Futures Company, Glover Park Group, Grey, GroupM, Hogarth, J. Walter Thompson, Maxus, Ogilvy & Mather, PPR, VICE and Y&R.

This unique cross-group way of working has proved successful with many clients and there are over 40 Global Client Leaders servicing accounts in WPP. Clients that are taking advantage of this 'horizontal' service model include Bayer, Colgate-Palmolive, Danone, Dell, Emirates, Ford, HSBC, Janssen J&J, Kimberly-Clark, Procter & Gamble, Shell and Vodafone. WPP reports that the group is increasingly being asked to put forward 'horizontal' service teams for pitches and suggests there will be more clients serviced with this model in the future.

Source: Based on a number of sources including www.wpp.com.

Question: What do you think the main advantages are for clients having (a) Global Client Leaders and (b) Country Managers?

Task: List the challenges you think there might be for the Global Client Leaders and Country Managers.

Selecting an agency

There has been much debate in recent years about the process used by clients when selecting a new agency. One of the main concerns raised by industry bodies such as the IPA and ISBA has been the costs involved. The 'pitch' process as it is called is an expensive one for agencies, with an average of £178,000 and 99 person days being spent by agencies on pitch costs a year (ISBA, 2013). With reports that organisations are changing agencies with increasing frequency (Quebra et al., 2013), the cost for agencies is significant. Concerns about the pitch process led to industry bodies holding a 'good pitch week' and the release of a '100-day charter' in an attempt to improve the manner in which pitches are undertaken and explore new ways for organisations to select new agencies.

While the industry discussion has been centred around the pitch process, the academic literature has largely focused on the criteria used by organisations when choosing a new agency (Fam and Waller, 2008; van Rensburg et al., 2010). Studies provide evidence that creative skill, agency people, cost and experience are the key determinants of what agency an organisation selects (Turnbull and Wheeler, 2014).

The process of selecting an agency, often referred to as the pitch process, as set out below appears to be rational and relatively straightforward. The reality, however, is that the process is infused with political and personal issues, some of which can be contradictory. Logically the process commences with a *search*, undertaken to develop a long list of potential agencies. This is accomplished by referring to industry publications such as *Campaign*, visiting agency websites and often with guidance from an intermediary. In some cases personal recommendations or prior experience with an agency may help with this initial stage. As many as 10 agencies could be included at this stage, although four or eight are to be expected.

Next, the client will make a request for information (RFI) from each agency. While there are a number of different formats used for this, the IPA provides a standardised template to help organisations. In addition to requesting information from the agency, the RFI provides the agency with details about why the organisation is reviewing the agency's account, the scope of the work, geographical regions to be covered and the type of agency it is looking for. At this stage the agency can evaluate whether there is a conflict of interest with any other clients. The RFI requires the agency to respond with details of its published financial accounts, HR policies and experience on similar brands and within the sector (IPA, 2009a).

The client will then request a *credentials meeting* (creds meeting) with each of the agencies. This is a crucial stage in the process, as it is now that the agency is evaluated for its degree of fit with the client's expectations and requirements. This provides the client with an opportunity to visit the agency offices, see the resources the agency can offer, meet with key agency personnel and see examples of current creative work. Following these meetings, the organisation will then decide on a shortlist of agencies, which usually results in between three to five agencies being invited to continue to the next stage in the process: the pitch presentation.

In the PR industry agencies are selected to pitch on the basis of the quality and experience of the agency people, its image and reputation, and relationships with existing clients. In addition, Pawinska (2000) reports that the track record of the agency and the extent of its geographical coverage are also regarded as important. The same is true for other disciplines in the industry.

In advertising, those agencies that have made it to the shortlist will be given a brief by the organisation and invited to respond with a mix of strategic, creative and media recommendations, as required at a *pitch* presentation. The time given to agencies to prepare their recommendations varies and is often around 6–8 weeks, although two-week deadlines are not unknown. Often during this time the agency will arrange to meet the client for a *chemistry meeting*. This provides an opportunity for the agency both to clarify the brief and to develop the potential relationship between the agency and the client (Turnbull and Wheeler, 2015).

The pitch presentation itself is about how the agency would approach the strategic and creative issues and the account is awarded to whichever produces the most suitable proposal. Suitability is a relative term, and a range of factors need to be considered when selecting an organisation to be responsible for a large part of a brand's visibility. A strategic alliance is being formed and, therefore, a strong understanding of the strategic objectives of both parties is necessary, as is an appreciation of the structure and culture of the two organisations.

Viewpoint 7.3   Strictly pitching

Winning new business is a key focus for agencies and competition has always been fierce between rival companies pitching for accounts. The pitch presentation itself has become infamous for its drama with some agencies adding theatrical elements to the meeting to impress potential new clients and demonstrate their creativity. This has led to many pitch presentations becoming theatrical performances with clients treated to role-playing scenarios and displays to add a sense of drama to the occasion. On one occasion an agency dressed the reception area up as an airline check-in desk and the receptionists as crew to impress a prospective airline client. Another agency turned the car park into a series of rooms and led the client around the rooms, using each room to introduce a different aspect of its response to the brief.

Exhibit 7.6   *Strictly Come Dancing's* **routines were the inspiration for the agency's pitch**
Source: Getty Images/Richard Stonehouse/Stringer.

To impress *Strictly Come Dancing*, who were looking to appoint a new partner, one agency choreographed its own routine to the *Strictly Come Dancing* theme tune and had the whole agency perform the dance when the client arrived for the pitch presentation.

Agencies have been known to go to great lengths in their efforts to win new business and this may account, in part, for why agencies spend so much time and money on pitches.

Source: Robinson (2010); Swift (2015).

Question: Why do you think agencies put on such dramatic performances for new business clients?

Task: Imagine you are an agency pitching for a fashion brand client and think of some theatrical ways you could liven up the pitch presentation.

The selection process is a bringing together of two organisations whose expectations may be different but whose cooperative behaviour is essential for these expectations to have any chance of materialising. For example, agencies must have access to comprehensive and often commercially confidential data about products and markets if they are to operate efficiently. Otherwise, they cannot provide the service that is expected. However, it should be noted that pitches are not mandatory, and as Jones (2004) reports, nearly one-third of clients move their accounts without involving pitches.

The immediate selection process is finalised when terms and conditions are agreed and the winner is announced to the contestants and made public, often through press releases and the use of trade journals such as *Campaign*, *Marketing* and *Marketing Week*.

This formalised process is now being questioned as to its suitability. The arrival of new media firms and the need to find communications solutions in one rather than eight weeks have meant that new methods have had to be found. In addition, agencies felt that they had to invest a great deal in a pitch with little or no reward if the pitch failed. Their response has been to ask for payment to pitch, which has not been received well by many clients. The tension that arises is that each agency is required to generate creative ideas over which it has little control once a pitch has been lost. The pitching process also fails to give much insight into the probable working relationships and is very often led by senior managers who will not be involved in the day-to-day operations. One solution has been to invite agencies to discuss mini-briefs. These are essentially discussion topics about related issues rather than the traditional challenge about how to improve a brand's performance. Issuing the mini-brief on the day eliminates weeks of preparation and associated staff costs, and enables the client to see agency teams working together. Another approach promoted by the IPA is the use of workshops and trial projects. However, it should be noted that it is the IPA's experience that 'many successful appointments are founded on reputation, personal chemistry, credentials and references from other clients, as opposed to pitches' (IPA, 2009b: 3).

Scholars' paper 7.2 | **Selecting a new advertising agency**

Turnbull, S. and Wheeler, C. (2014) Exploring advertiser's expectations of advertising agency services, *Journal of Marketing Communications*, DOI: 10.1080/13527266.2014.920902.

The authors identify the expectations clients have of the agency at the selection stage. The study which was undertaken in the United Arab Emirates identifies that clients expect agencies to offer craft skill such as creative ability; functionality, such as geographical or media capabilities; strategic perspective and to feel an affinity towards the agency team. The authors conclude that not all expectations are made clear at the selection stage and this can be problematic once the relationship with the agency develops further. They provide recommendations for clients to adopt service level agreements (SLAs) with their agency to help make expectations more explicit.

See also: Moeran, B. (2005) Tricks of the trade: the performance and interpretation of authenticity, *Journal of Management Studies*, 42(5), 901–22.

Agency operations

Many communications agencies are generally organised on a functional basis. There have been moves to develop matrix structures utilising a customer orientation, but this is very inefficient and the low margins prohibit such luxuries. There are departments for planning, creative and media functions coordinated on behalf of the client by an account handler or executive.

The account executive fulfils a very important role, in that these people are responsible for the flow of communications between the client and the agency. The quality of the communications between the two main parties can be critical to the success of the overall campaign and to the length of the relationship between the two organisations. Acting at the boundary of the agency's operations, the account executive needs to perform several roles, from internal coordinator and negotiator to presenter (of the agency's work), conflict manager and information gatherer. Very often account executives will experience tension as they seek to achieve their clients' needs while trying to balance them with the needs of their employer and colleagues. These tensions are similar to those experienced by salespersons and need to be managed in a sensitive manner by management.

Once an account has been signed, a client brief is prepared that provides information about the client organisation (see Figure 7.2). It sets out the nature of the industry it operates in, together with data about trends, market shares, customers, competitors and the problem that the agency is required to address. This is used to inform agency personnel. In particular, the account planner will undertake research to determine market, media and audience characteristics and make proposals to the rest of the account team concerning how the client problem is to be resolved.

Briefing is a process that is common across all client–agency relationships in the communications industry. Regardless of whether working in direct marketing, sales promotion, advertising, public relations, media planning and buying or other specialist area, the brief has a special importance in making the process work and the outcomes significant. However, the importance of preparing a brief of suitable quality has for some been underestimated and studies show that client briefs are often inadequate (Koslow et al., 2006). This has led to a recent joint industry initiative to establish common working practices. The outcome of the process was a briefing template intended to be used

Project management – Provide basic project details, e.g. timescales, contacts and people, project numbers

Where are we now? – Describe current brand details, e.g. background, position, competitors, key issues

Where do we want to be? – What needs to be achieved in terms of goals, e.g. sales, market share, ROI, shareholder value, awareness, perception, etc.?

What are we doing to get there? – What is the context in terms of the marketing strategy, overall communications strategy and campaign strategy?

Who do we need to talk to? – What is understood about the audiences the communications are intended to influence?

How will we know if we have arrived? – What will be measured, by whom, how and when to determine whether the activity has been successful?

Practicalities – Budgets, timings and schedules, creative and media imperatives

Approvals – Who has the authority to sign off the brief and the agency work?

Figure 7.2   A new briefing structure

by all across the communications agencies in the industry. Eight key headings emerged from the report and these can be seen at Figure 7.2.

In addition to the role of account handler, who is often seen as the 'shepherd' within the agency (Sorrell, 2014), there is the role of the account planner. The role of the account planner has been the subject of debate (Collin, 2003; Zambarino and Goodfellow, 2003; Grant and McLeod, 2007; Mackert and Munoz, 2011; Patwardhan et al., 2011). The general conclusion of these papers is that the role of account planner, which has been evolving since the beginning of the 1960s, has changed as the communications industry has fragmented and that a new role is emerging in response to integrated marketing communications and media-neutral planning initiatives (see Chapter 9 for details about these concepts).

Scholars' paper 7.3   What do account planners do?

Haley, E., Taylor, R. and Morrison, M. (2014) How advertising creatives define excellent planning, *Journal of Current Issues & Research in Advertising*, 35(2), 167–89.

The authors provide a rich insight into the role and the value of planning within advertising agencies. Investigating the role from the perspective of creatives, the authors identify factors that are seen to make a good planner.

See also: Crosier, K., Grant, I. and Gilmore, C. (2003) Account planning in Scottish advertising agencies: a discipline in transition, *Journal of Marketing Communications*, 9(1), 1–15; Patwardhan, P., Patwardhan, H. and Vasavada-Oza, F. (2011) Diffusion of account planning in Indian ad agencies: an organisational perspective, *International Journal of Advertising*, 30(4), 665–92.

The traditional role of the account planner, which began in full-service agencies, was to understand the client's target consumers and develop strategies for the creative and media departments. As media broke away from full-service agencies, so the role of the account planner shifted to the creative aspect of the agency work. Media planners assumed the same type of work in media companies, although their work focused on planning the right media mix to reach the target audience. With the development of integrated perspectives and the move towards a broader view of a client's communications needs comes an expectation that the planning role will evolve into a strategic role. The role will be to work with a broad range of marketing disciplines (tools) and media, but not to brief creatives or media planners directly (Collin, 2003). Account planning is a strategically important activity in agencies, and a major source of power and conflict (Grant et al., 2012).

Creative teams comprise a copywriter and an art director, supported by a service team. This team is responsible for translating the proposal into an advertisement. In a full-service agency, a media brief will also be generated, informing the media planning and buying department of the media and the type of media vehicles required. However, the vast majority of media planning work is now undertaken by specialist media agencies, media independents, and these will be briefed by the client, with some support from those responsible for the creatives.

In recent years, partly as a response to the growth of new media, a raft of small entrepreneurial agencies has emerged, to exploit the new opportunities arising from the digital media. Many of these are run without the control and structures evident in large, centralised agencies. While dedicated teams might theoretically be the best way to manage a client's project, the reality in many cases is the use of project teams comprising expert individuals working on a number of projects simultaneously. This is not a new phenomenon, but as a result many people are multitasking and they assume many roles with new titles. For example, the title *Head of Content* has arisen to reflect the significance of content issues in the new media market. Project managers assume responsibility for the implementation phase and the coordination of all aspects of a client's technological facilities. In addition, there are positions such as head of marketing, mobile (increasing focus on WAP technology), production and technology. The result is no hierarchies, flat structures and flexible working practices and similar expectations.

Viewpoint 7.4   Getting an agency job

Agencies are always on the lookout for new talent. There are lots of routes into agencies and one of the most popular ways to get your foot in the door is through an agency graduate scheme. Most of the large agency networks offer such schemes and although competition to get on them is usually very high, they are an excellent way to start your career in advertising. Agencies post details of their schemes on their own websites and the Institute of Practitioners in Advertising (IPA) has a dedicated careers section which highlights schemes available.

Not all agencies run graduate schemes, but other entry-level opportunities do come up. The IPA and industry practitioner websites like Brand Republic regularly show entry-level positions available. Creative, experiential, branding and media planning, and buying agencies are often looking to recruit at this level.

Internships are another route into adland. Whilst these are usually on a short-term basis they allow an opportunity to gain experience in the business. Again these are usually posted on agency and IPA websites.

What are agencies looking for? Most want creative individuals that are passionate about the industry. Experience is always a good way to show interest and volunteering can be a good way to get relevant experience. Charities, museums and arts centres are often keen to get volunteers to help with their marketing communications activities and this can provide valuable experience.

Source: Turnbull (2013).

Exhibit 7.7   **Agencies are looking for creativity and passion**
Source: Getty Images/Catherine Lane.

Question: What sort of skills do you think agencies are looking for from entry-level recruits?

Task: Look for two examples of agencies that run entry-level recruitment schemes. Consider what skills and experience they are looking for in candidates. Which of these do you currently have on your CV? If there are gaps, consider things you could do to fill them.

Relationships

The relationships inevitably shape and influence the strategies and operations that are pursued. There are a vast number of relationships that form between various clients and agencies, disciplines and within individual organisations.

Client/agency relationships

If the briefing process provides the mechanism for the agency operations, it is the relationship between the agency and the client that very often determines the length of the contract and the strength of the solutions advanced for the client.

There are a number of client-agency relationships that have flourished over a very long period of time, and some for several decades. Sclater (2006) refers to the agency BBH, which was established in 1982. The agency started with three key clients, Audi, Levi's, and Whitbread (now InBev UK), and in all three cases they are still working together over two decades later (Sclater, 2006). Spanier (2010) also reports on examples of agencies that have retained clients over long periods of time. These include DDB who have held the Volkswagen car account for more than 25 years, JWT has had Shell as a client for approaching 50 years, Rolex for over 60 and Unilever for over 100. There are a huge number of other accounts who have excellent relationships that have lasted a long time Table 7.3 provides a snapshot of some of the longer public client-agency relationships.

However, these appear to be in the minority as industry sources suggest the average length of client-agency relationships has fallen to under 3 years (ISBA, 2013). Many relationships appear to founder as clients abandon agencies and search for better, fresher solutions, because a contract expires, the client needs change or owing to takeovers and mergers between agencies, which require that they forfeit accounts that cause a conflict of interest.

From a contextual perspective these buyer/seller relationships can be seen to follow a pattern of inception, development, maintenance and dissolution stages (Fam and Waller, 2008). During this life cycle clients and agencies enter into a series of interactions (West and Paliwoda, 1996) or exchanges through which levels of trust and commitment develop. Hakansson (1982) identified several contexts, or atmospheres, within which relationships develop. These contexts had numerous dimensions: closeness/distance, cooperation/conflict, power/dependence, trustworthiness and expectations. Therefore, the client-agency relationship should be seen in the context of the network of organisations and the

Table 7.3 Longer-lasting client-agency relationships

Agency	Clients (since)
Abbott Mead Vickers BBDO	Volvo (1985), Sainsbury's (1981), The Economist (1986), Homebase (1991), BT (1994)
Grey Advertising	GlaxoSmithKline (1955, 21 brands), Procter & Gamble (1956, 31 brands)
Lowe Worldwide	Unilever/Lever Faberge (1963), Unilever/Best Foods (1964), Stella Artois (1981), Vauxhall (1983), Johnson & Johnson (1986)
Ogilvy & Mather	Unilever (1952), Mattel (1954), Kraft Foods (1954), Nestlé (1959), American Express (1963), Ford (1975)
Saatchi & Saatchi	Carlsberg (1973), Pepsi (1981), Procter & Gamble (1983), NSPCC (1984), Toyota (1992)

Source: Adapted from Sclater (2006).

exchanges or interactions that occur in that network. It is through these interactions that the tasks that need to be accomplished are agreed, resources made available, strategies determined and goals achieved. The quality of the client-agency relationship is a function of trust, which is developed through the exchanges and which fosters confidence. Commitment is derived from a belief that the relationship is worth continuing and that maximum effort is warranted to maintain the relationship (Morgan and Hunt, 1994). The development of new forms of remuneration (see p. 267) based around payment by results also signifies a new client focus and a willingness to engage with clients and to be paid according to the success and contribution the agency can provide (Lace and Brocklehurst, 2000).

The way in which clients use multiple agencies to fulfil the whole range of communications tasks does not encourage the establishment of strong relationships nor does it help the cause of integrated marketing communications. The use of roster agencies means that marketing teams have to manage more agencies, often with reduced resources. This means that agencies get a smaller share of the available budget, which in turn does not help agencies feel comfortable (Child, 2007).

Poor relationships between agencies and clients are likely to result from a lack of trust and falling commitment. As it appears that communications are a primary element in the formation and substance of relational exchanges, clients might be advised to consider the agencies in their roster as an extended department of the core organisation and use internal marketing communications procedures to assist the development of identity and belonging.

Scholars' paper 7.4 — Client-agency battles

Gambetti, R., Biraghi, S., Schultz, D.E. and Graffigna, G. (2015) Brand wars: consumer-brand engagement beyond client–agency fights, *Journal of Strategic Marketing*, DOI: 10.1080/13527266.2014.920902.

This paper reveals the conflict that exists in the relationship between clients and agencies. The study reveals the lack of a 'relationship culture' between agency and client, with each blaming the other for inhibiting consumer-brand engagement.

See also: Zolkiewski, J., Burton, J. and Stratoudaki, S. (2008) The delicate power balance in advertising agency-client relationships: partnership or battleground? The case of the Greek advertising market, *Journal of Customer Behaviour*, 7(4), 315–32.

Agency remuneration

One factor that has a significant impact on the quality of the relationship between the parties is the remuneration the agency receives for its work. One major cause for concern and complaint among marketing managers is the uncertainty over how much their marketing communications programmes will finally cost and the complexity surrounding the remuneration system itself.

According to the IPA there are 10 different ways in which agencies can be remunerated. These are explained in Table 7.4. Of these *payment by results* (PBR) and *value-based* approaches are considered to be leading edge and the most appropriate forms of remuneration. Each of these approaches is discussed below and it should be noted that it is very rare for a single method to be used within a single contract.

Traditionally, advertising agencies were paid a commission by media owners for selling space in their publications. This commission was soon referred to as 'the line' and a

Table 7.4 The IPA's 10 forms of agency remuneration

Method	Explanation
Payment by results	PBR is based on the attainment of predetermined KPIs. Here both parties can win and results are transparent and measurable.
Value-based	Value-based approaches consider the agency's results in terms of outputs and outcomes. This can incorporate a base fee to cover the agency's cost of producing the outputs, with a mark-up, rather than discretionary bonus, based on actual performance metrics.
Retainers	A negotiated activity fee for a defined period (e.g. one year) is paid monthly in advance for agreed workloads and activities.
Project fees	Rather than an annual fee, fees are based on an individual project.
Variable fees	Fees are based on actual time spent on a client's account, paid after the activity has been incurred.
Scale fees + win bonus	Client pays a 'salary' based on sales (bonus included) or marketing budget plus a bonus if based on a marketing budget.
Consultancy and concept fees	This is a one-off fee designed to reward an agency for developing a creative concept.
Licensing fees	The client pays for concept development but at a reduced rate before paying a licence fee for the finished concept, once approved.
Output or 'off-the-shelf' rate fee	Used where the output can be readily measured and costed. Here a fixed price per unit of output is agreed, typically suited to the 'pay-per-click' approach.
Commission	A percentage (originally 15 per cent of the gross media cost within a full-service arrangement) is paid by media owners for the work placed with them by agencies on behalf of their client.

Source: IPA/ISBA/CIPS (2012).

figure of 15 per cent above the line emerged as the norm and was adjudged to be a fair reward for the efforts of the agency. However, as relationships between agencies and clients strengthened, it seemed only reasonable that the clients should feel that agencies should act for them (and in their best interests), and not for the media owners. A number of questions were raised about whether the agency was actually being rewarded for the work it did and whether it was being objective when recommending media expenditure. As media independents emerged, questions started to be asked about why media agencies received 3 per cent and the creative agency received 12 per cent.

Client discontent is not the only reason why agency remuneration by commission has been called into question, and alternatives are being considered. In times of recession marketing budgets are inevitably cut, which means less revenue for agencies. Increasing competition means lower profit margins if an agency is to retain the business, and if costs are increasing at the same time, the very survival of the agency is in question. As Snowden stated as long ago as 1993, 'Clients are demanding more for less.' She went on to say, 'It is clear to me that the agency business needs to address a number of issues; most important amongst them, how agencies get paid. It is the key to the industry's survival.' Well, changes have been made since then, but there are still various combinations of methods used to suit particular agencies, clients and projects.

During the early 1990s there was a great deal of discussion and energy directed towards non-commission payment systems. This was a direct result of the recession, in which clients cut budgets, and there was a consequent reduction in the quantity of media purchased and hence less revenue for the agencies. Fees became more popular, and some experimented with payment by results. Interestingly, as that recession died and the economy lifted, more revenue resulted in larger commission possibilities, and the death throes of the commission system were quickly replaced by its resuscitation and revival. It is likely that there will continue to be a move away from a reliance on the payment of commission as the only form of remuneration to the agency.

For many, payment by results seems a good solution. In 2009 Coca-Cola introduced a new way by which its agencies were to be remunerated. It is referred to as a *value-based compensation model* and Tylee (2010) argues that it extends the PBR model. Agencies are promised profit mark-ups of 30 per cent if specific targets are met. If they are not, then only their costs are covered. Procter & Gamble have also adopted a similar value-based reward programme and, as Williams (2010) indicates, value-based systems can involve a variety of factors, as long as they are not timesheets and hours and costs.

However, agencies have no control over the other marketing activities of the client, which might determine the degree of success of the campaign. Indeed, this raises the very thorny question of what 'success' is and how it might be measured. Despite these considerations, it appears that PBR is starting to become an established form of remuneration with over 30 per cent of client-agency contracts containing an element of PBR.

The use of bonuses is widespread but, whereas the intention is to reward excellent work, some agencies see bonuses as a means by which fees are reduced and, as some clients refuse to pay, the impact on relationships can be far from positive (Child, 2007).

Fees have been around for a long time, either in the form of retainers or on a project-by-project basis. Indeed, many agencies charge a fee for services over and above any commission earned from media owners. The big question concerns the basis for calculation of fees (and this extends to all areas of marketing communications, not just advertising), and protracted, complicated negotiations can damage client-agency relationships.

A different way of looking at this is to consider what the client thinks the agency does, and from this evaluate the outcomes from the relationship. Jensen (1995) proposed that advertising agencies should be regarded as an *ideas business* that seeks to build brands for clients. An alternative view is that agencies are *advertising factories* where the majority of the work is associated with administration, communications, coordination and general running around to ensure that the advertisement appears on the page or screen as desired.

If the 'ideas business' view is accepted, the ideas generated add value for the client, so the use the client makes of the idea should be rewarded by way of a royalty-type payment. If the 'factory concept' is adopted, then it is the resources involved in the process that need to be considered and a fee-based system is more appropriate. Both parties will actively seek to reduce costs that do not contribute to the desired outcomes. These are different approaches to remuneration and avoid the volume of media purchased as a critical and controversial area.

Budgeting for communications

One of the key questions associated with investing in marketing communications is: what is the right amount an organisation should spend on marketing communications? In addition, how should organisations divide this sum across their brands, regions, territories and various activities? These two questions underpin the setting of communications budgets and the allocation of the budget once it is agreed (Corstjens et al., 2011). According to White (2007) the answers to these questions can lead directly to operational success or failure.

The rate at which advertising and associated media costs have outstripped the retail price index in developed economies was regarded as both alarming and troublesome. This disproportionate increase in the costs of advertising served to make it less and less attractive to some clients. Larger clients became more discerning and introduced procurement specialists to overview media purchasing. Unsurprisingly, this has spurred the increased use of other tools such as brand placement, sponsorship, event marketing, direct marketing, and new media formats, especially online and interactive-based marketing communications media and, more recently, mobile communications.

Scholars' paper 7.5 — Setting the budget

West, D. and Prendergast, G.P. (2009) Advertising and promotions budgeting and the role of risk, *European Journal of Marketing*, 43(11/12), 1457–76.

The authors provide a useful insight into the budgetary methods used by industry. They find that judgemental methods tend to dominate, especially the 'what is afford-able' method. They also uncover methods such as 'objective and task', and measurement techniques such as 'return on investment' are used by a good percentage of respondents. It appears that, on average, two methods are used by managers to determine the most efficient budget.

See also: Corstjens, M., Umblijs, A. and Wang, C. (2011) The power of inertia: conservatism in marketing resource allocation, *Journal of Advertising Research*, June, 356–72; West, D., Ford, J.B. and Farris, P.W. (2014) How corporate cultures drive advertising and promotion budgets, *Journal of Advertising Research*, 54(2), 149–62.

Some advertising agencies have argued that this disproportionately high increase was necessary because of the increasing number of new products and the length of time it takes to build a brand. The biggest spending advertiser was BSkyB who invested £272 million in advertising in the UK, principally to launch its investment in BT Sports (see Viewpoint 1.1). Second was Procter & Gamble with £182 million across its product portfolio, and third was BT who spent £147 million. Most notable about these figures is that two of the top three are in the telecoms sector. See Table 7.5 which specifies all of the top 10 brands by adspend.

Large investment and commitment are required over a period of years if long-term, high-yield performance is to be achieved. Many accountants and procurement managers, however, view communications from a different perspective. For a long time their attitude has been to consider these activities, and advertising in particular, as an expense, to be set against the profits of the organisation. Many see planned marketing communications as a variable, one that can be discarded in times of recession (Whitehead, 2008).

These two broad views of advertising and of all marketing communications activities, one as an investment to be shown on the balance sheet and the other as a cost to be revealed in the profit and loss account, run consistently through discussions about how much should be allocated to advertising and other brand communications spend. For management, the four tools of the communications mix are often divided into two groups. The first contains advertising, sales promotion and public relations, while the second group contains the financial aspects that relate to personal selling.

This division reflects not only a functional approach to marketing but also the way in which, historically, the selling and marketing departments have developed. This is often observed in older, more established organisations, those that find innovation and

Table 7.5 Top 10 UK advertisers in 2013 (by value of spend)

Organisation	£million total (2013)
BSkyB	272
Procter & Gamble	182
BT	147
Unilever UK	127
Tesco	118
ASDA	104
Talk Talk	93
Virgin Media	92
Morrisons	78
Vodafone	78

Source: Nielsen, cited by Key Note (2014).

change seriously difficult and challenging. Accountability and responsibility for communications expenditure in the first group often fall to the brand or product manager. In the second group, this aspect is managed by sales managers who often, at national level, report to a sales director.

The communications costs that need to be budgeted include the following. First, there is the airtime on broadcast media or space in print media that has to be bought to carry the message to the target audience. Then there are the production costs associated with generating the message and the staff costs of all those who contribute to the design and administration of the campaign. There are agency and professional fees, marketing research and contributions to general overheads and to expenses such as cars, entertainment costs and telephones that can be directly related to particular profit centres. In addition to all of these are any direct marketing costs, for which some organisations have still to find a suitable method of cost allocation. In some cases a particular department has been created to manage all direct marketing activities, and in these cases the costs can be easily apportioned.

The budget for the sales force is not one that can be switched on and off like an electric light. Advertising budgets can be massaged and campaigns pulled at the last minute, but communications through personal selling require the establishment of a relatively high level of fixed costs. In addition to these expenses are the opportunity costs associated with the lengthy period taken to recruit, train and release suitably trained sales personnel into the competitive environment. This process can take over 15 months in some industries, especially in the fast-changing, demanding and complex information technology markets.

Strategic investment to achieve the right sales force, in terms of its size, training and maintenance, is paramount. It should be remembered, however, that managing a sales force can be rather like turning an ocean liner: any move or change in direction has to be anticipated and actioned long before the desired outcome can be accomplished. Funds need to be allocated strategically, but for most organisations a fast return on an investment should not be expected.

A variety of techniques are used to determine the correct allocation of funds to advertising, sales promotion, public relations, the field sales force and other marketing communications activities. In an era in which shareholder value is becoming increasingly prominent and a means of distinguishing between alternative strategic options, however, companies also need to consider how a brand's value might influence the budget setting.

Trends in communications expenditure

It was stated earlier that advertising expenditure in the UK rose faster for a while than consumer expenditure. While this is true, the rapid increases in advertising spend in the 1980s slowed at the beginning of the 1990s, then speeded up again as the economy recovered, only to waver again in 2001 after a buoyant previous year fuelled by the dot-com excitement. After a few years during which the advertising spend levels stabilised, only online advertising has grown substantially, in percentage terms. There has been considerable speculation that offline advertising revenues were about to plummet as organisations moved their spend online. Although many organisations have increased their online investment by some considerable amount and have reduced their offline, especially newspaper, spend, the impact has not been as great as some commentators had feared. In 2015 the total media expenditure in the United Kingdom has grown. Although some areas such as print have seen expenditure decline, the growth in internet spend has increased the overall advertising expenditure (Warc, 2015a).

The cutback in offline advertising expenditure when trading conditions tighten reflects the short-term orientation that some organisations have towards brand development or advertising. The IPA warns that budget reductions can lead to a 'loss of market share, a decline in brand image and long term sales damage', as reported by Donnelly (2008: 4). The report suggests that if a company cuts its advertising to zero it could take five years to recover, whereas a budget slashed by 50 per cent will take three years to recover.

What is also of interest is the way in which the communications mix has been changing over the past 20 years. For a long time spend on media advertising dominated the marketing budget of consumer brands. Sales promotion became a strong influence but spend on this tool stagnated, although revived as the recession took hold. Now sponsorship, direct marketing and digital activities attract the most investment. The reasons for this shift are indicative of the increasing attention and accountability that management is attaching to marketing communications. Increasingly, marketing managers are being asked to justify the amounts they invest/spend on their entire budgets, including advertising and sales promotion. Senior managers want to know the return they are getting for their communications investments, in order that they meet their business objectives and that scarce resources can be used more efficiently and effectively in the future.

It is not uncommon to find companies that are experiencing trading difficulties deciding to slash their adspend, if only on a temporary basis. Exceptions to this have been companies such as Marks & Spencer and Sainsbury's who, although experiencing difficulties, either increased or maintained their above-the-line spend and improved brand and share value. Research by Profit Impact on Market Strategy (PIMS) (Tomkins, 1999; Tylee, 1999) found that companies that maintain or even increase their adspend during a recession are likely to grow three times faster when the economy turns round than those companies that cut the adspend.

A report undertaken for the Advertising Association (2004) found that the majority of brand leaders that use advertising as a substantial proportion of the communications mix continue to dominate their markets, just as they did 30 years ago. In doing so, the report concludes, they have thwarted the challenge of own brands. In other words, advertising can protect brands, as long as the adspend is substantial.

In anticipation of the recent recession the Institute of Practitioners in Advertising (IPA) launched a book of case studies. This was sent to the CEOs of 350 FTSE companies and opinion formers such as journalists in the financial sector, fund managers and analysts. The 38 cases demonstrated how the use of advertising can improve brand value (Whitehead, 2008).

The role of the communications budget

The role of the communications budget is the same regardless of whether the organisation is a multinational trading from numerous international locations, or a small manufacturing unit on an industrial estate outside a semi-rural community. Both types of organisation want to ensure that they achieve the greatest efficiency with each euro they allocate to promotional activities. Neither can afford to be profligate with scarce resources, and each is accountable to the owners of the organisation for the decisions it makes.

There are two broad decisions that need to be addressed. The first concerns how much of the organisation's available financial resources (or relevant part) should be allocated to marketing communications over the next period. The second concerns how much of the total amount should be allocated to each of the individual disciplines of the communications mix.

Benefits of budgeting

The benefits of engaging in budgeting activities are many and varied, but in the context of marketing communications planning they can be considered as follows:

1. The process serves to focus people's attention on the costs and benefits of undertaking the planned communications activities.
2. The act of quantifying the means by which the marketing plan will be communicated to target audiences instils a management discipline necessary to ensure that the objectives of the plan are capable of being achieved. Achievement must be at a level that is acceptable and will not overstretch or embarrass the organisation.
3. The process facilitates cross-function coordination and forces managers to ensure that the planned communications are integrated and mutually supportive. The process provides a means by which campaigns can be monitored and management control asserted. This is particularly important in environments that are subject to sudden change or competitive hostility.
4. At the end of the campaign, a financial review enables management to learn from the experiences of the promotional activity in order that future communications can be made more efficient and the return on the investment improved.

The process of planning the communications budget is an important one. Certain elements of the process will have been determined during the setting of the campaign objectives. Managers will check the financial feasibility of a project prior to committing larger resources. Managers will also discuss the financial implications of the communications strategy (i.e. the push/pull positioning dimension) and those managers responsible for each of the individual tools will have estimated the costs that their contribution will involve. Senior management will have some general ideas about the level of the overall appropriation, which will inevitably be based partly upon precedent, market and competitive conditions and partly as a response to the pressures of different stakeholders, among them key members of the distribution network. Decisions now have to be made about the viability of the total plan, whether the appropriation is too large or too small and how the funds are to be allocated across the promotional tools.

Communications budgets are not formulated at a particular moment in a sequence of management activities. The financial resources of an organisation should be constantly referred to, if only to monitor current campaigns. Therefore, budgeting and the availability of financial resources are matters that managers are constantly aware of and able to tap into at all stages in the development and implementation of planned communications.

Difficulties associated with budgeting for communications

There are a number of problems associated with the establishment of a marketing communications budget. Of them all, the following appear to be the most problematic. First, it is difficult to quantify the precise amount that is necessary to complete all the required tasks. Second, communications budgets do not fit neatly with standard accounting practices. The concept of brand value is accepted increasingly as a balance sheet item, but the concept of investment in communications to create value has only recently begun to be accepted, for example by Jaguar and Nestlé. Third, the diversity of the tools and the means by which their success can be measured renders like-for-like comparisons null and void. Finally, the budget-setting process is not as clear-cut as it might at first appear.

There are four main stakeholder groups that contribute to the budget decision. These are the organisation itself, any communications agencies, the media and production or fulfilment houses whose resources will be used to carry designated messages and the target audience. It is the ability of these four main stakeholders to interact, to communicate effectively with each other and to collaborate that will impact most upon the communications budget. However, determining the 'appropriate appropriation' is a frustrating exercise for marketing managers. The allocation of scarce resources across a communications budget presents financial and political difficulties, especially where the returns are not easily identifiable. The development and significance of technology within marketing can lead to disputes concerning ownership and control of resources. For example, in many companies management and responsibility for the website rests with the IT department, which understandably takes a technological view of issues. Those in marketing, however, see the use of the website from a marketing perspective and need a budget to manage it. Tension between the two can result in different types of website design and effectiveness and this leads to different levels of customer support.

Budgeting – techniques and approaches

At a broad level there are a number of techniques used by organisations to determine the communications budget. The main models, proposed by different authors to determine the appropriation of the communications mix, are set out in Table 7.6.

Marginal analysis suffers from a number of disadvantages. First, it assumes that communications can be varied smoothly and continuously. This is not the case. Second, it assumes that communications are the only influence upon sales. As discussed previously, sales are influenced by a variety of factors, of which planned communications are but one. Controllable and uncontrollable elements in the environment influence sales. Next, no account is taken of the other costs associated indirectly with the presentation of the offering, such as those allied to distribution. Each communications thrust will often be matched, or even bettered, by the competition. Furthermore, the actions of rivals may even affect the sales performance of all products in the same category.

The competitive parity approach fails to consider the qualitative aspects of the advertising undertaken by the different players. In addition, there are a number of disadvantages with this simple technique. The first is that, whilst information is available, there is

Table 7.6 Principal budgeting methods and techniques

Budgeting technique	Explanation
Marginal analysis	Otherwise referred to as the advertising response function, this theoretical approach involves determining how many extra sales are generated from an extra unit of communications spend. A point will be reached when an extra pound/euro/dollar spent on communications will generate an equal amount (a single pound/euro/dollar's-worth) of revenue. At this point marginal revenue is equal to marginal costs, which represents the point of maximum communications expenditure and which generates maximum profit.
Arbitrary	Sometimes referred to as 'chairperson's rules', this approach is based on what the' boss' decides. Simple but inappropriate as the boss may not have a clue what the optimal figure should be and these decisions, made on-the-hoof, lack consideration of customer needs, the demands of the environment or marketing strategy, and there is an absence of any critical analysis. Unfortunately this approach is often used by many small organisations.
Inertia	This approach involves 'let's keep it the same'. Here all elements of the environment and the costs associated with the tasks facing the organisation are ignored. Not recommended.
Media multiplier	In order to maintain the same impact in the next period, this approach requires that spend be changed by the rate at which media costs have altered. This assumes all previous decisions were sound and that marketing strategies and the environment remain unchanged. This is unlikely.
Percentage of sales	Here the budget is set at a level equal to some predetermined percentage of past or expected sales. However, as advertising is intended to create demand, not be the result of past sales, then it is likely that the next period's results will be similar, all things being equal. As no consideration is given to sales potential, this technique may limit performance.
Affordable	This requires each unit of output to be allocated a proportion of all the costs associated with the value-adding activities in production, manufacturing and distribution. After making an allowance for profit, what is left is what can be afforded to be spent on communications. The affordable technique is not in the least analytical, nor does it have any market or task orientation.
Objective and task	After attempting to determine the resources required to achieve each objective, these separate costs are aggregated into an overall budget. This focuses management attention on the goals to be accomplished. On the down side, this approach does not generate realistic budgets, in the sense that the required level of resources may not be available and the opportunity costs of the resources are not usually determined.
Competitive parity	Assuming advertising is the only effective factor influencing demand and that all others are self-cancelling, some organisations deliberately spend the same amount on advertising as their competitors – competitive parity. Unfortunately, this approach fails to consider the qualitative aspects of the advertising undertaken by the different players.
Advertising-to-sales (A/S) ratio	The underlying principle of the A/S ratio is that, in each industry, it is possible to determine the average advertising spend of all the players and to compare it with the value of the market. Therefore, it is possible for each organisation to determine its own A/S ratio and compare it with the industry average.
Share of voice (SOV)	Within any market the adspend of any one advertiser can be compared with the total spend of all competitors. This is known as share of voice (SOV). This figure can be compared with the share of market (SOM) that each player holds. If these percentages are equal then there is equilibrium. Variations above and below this represent strategic intent.

a problem comparing like with like. For example, a carpet manufacturer selling a greater proportion of output into the trade will require different levels and styles of advertising and promotion from another manufacturer selling predominantly to the retail market. Furthermore, the first organisation may be diversified, perhaps importing floor tiles. The second may be operating in a totally unrelated market. Such activities make comparisons difficult to establish, and financial decisions based on such analyses are highly dubious.

The relationship between SOV (share of voice) and SOM (share of market) is recognised by a number of authors, including Broadbent (1989), Buck (2001), Field (2009), Jones (1990) and Schroer (1990). When a brand's market share is equal to its share of advertising spend, equilibrium is said to have been reached (SOV = SOM). Increasing the SOV above the point of equilibrium generally raises SOM, whilst lowering SOV reduces SOM and reaches a new point of stability.

These concepts of SOV and SOM frame an interesting perspective of competitive strategy based upon the relative weight of advertising expenditure. Schroer (1990) reports that, following extensive research on the US packaged goods market (FMCG), it is noticeable that organisations can use advertising spend to maintain equilibrium and to create disequilibrium in a market. The former is established by major brand players maintaining their market shares with little annual change to their advertising budgets. Unless a competitor is prepared to inject a considerable increase in advertising spend and so create disequilibrium, the relatively stable high spend deters new entrants and preserves the status quo. Schroer claims that, if the two market leaders maintain SOV within 10 per cent of each other, then competitive equilibrium will exist. This situation is depicted in Figure 7.3. If a market challenger launches an aggressive assault upon the leader by raising advertising spend to a point where SOV is 20–30 per cent higher than the current leader, market share will shift in favour of the challenger.

The concepts of SOV and SOM have also been used by Jones (1990) to develop a new method of budget setting. He suggests that those brands that have an SOV greater than their SOM are 'investment brands', and those that have an SOV less than or equal to their SOM are 'profit-taking brands'.

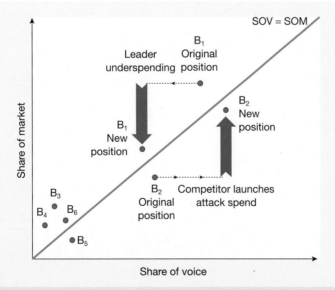

| **Figure 7.3** | Strategy to gain market share by increasing adspend |

Source: From Ad spending: growing market share, *Harvard Business Review* January/February, pp. 44–48 (Schroer, J. 1990), Reprinted by permission of *Harvard Business Review*. Copyright (c) 1990 by Harvard Business School Publishing Corporation; all rights reserved.

Using data collected from an extensive survey of 1,096 brands across 23 different countries, Jones 'calculated the difference between share of voice and share of market and averaged these differences within each family of brands' (p. 40). By representing the data diagrammatically (see Figure 7.4), Jones shows how it becomes a relatively simple task to work out the adspend that is required to achieve a particular SOM. The first task is to plot the expected (desired) market share from the horizontal axis, then move vertically to the intersection with the curve and read off the SOV figure from the vertical axis. For more insight see Scholars' paper 7.6.

Scholars' paper 7.6   **Does having a loud voice matter?**

Schroer, J. (1990) Ad spending: growing market share, *Harvard Business Review*, January/February, 44–8.

This article is based on research amongst US FMCG firms that shows how varying adspends can be used to maintain equilibrium or create disequilibrium in a market. Schroer identifies that if two market leaders maintain SOV within 10 per cent of each other, competitive equilibrium in terms of SOM will be maintained. Further, if a challenger raises SOV by 20–30 per cent more than the current market leader, this will increase SOM.

See also: Jones, J.P. (1990) Ad spending: maintaining market share, *Harvard Business Review,* January/February, 38–42; Field, P. (2009) Account planners need to care more about share of voice, *Admap,* September, 28–30.

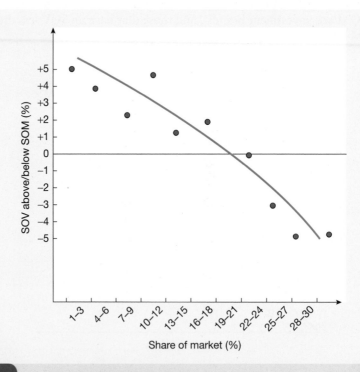

Figure 7.4   Curve comparing SOV with SOM

Source: From Ad spending: maintaining market share, *Harvard Business Review* January/February, pp. 38–42 (Jones, J.P. 1990), Reprinted by permission of *Harvard Business Review*. Copyright (c) 1990 by Harvard Business School Publishing Corporation; all rights reserved.

It is interesting to note that the SOV concept commanded a reasonable profile in the early to mid-1990s but then subsided from view. Its revival by Binet and Field (2007) when communicating with advertising practitioners is helpful and commensurate with the emerging emphasis on accountability and the use of metrics. As these authors point out, marketing success is predicated on SOV rather than size of budget. In addition, the vast proportion of budget is invested in order to maintain or slow the decline of market share, rather than grow it.

Which methods are most used?

A major question, therefore, is which of these tools are used in practice, and which ones should be used? Research in this area is relatively limited but Mitchell's (1993) study to determine the methods and criteria used by companies to determine their advertising budgets provides a starting point. He found that 40 per cent of respondents claimed to use the objective and task approach, 27 per cent used percentage of future sales (8 per cent used past sales) and 19 per cent used a variety of company-specific methods that do not fit neatly within any one item from the list presented above. Although the figures resulting from the study can only be used to indicate trends of overall preferences, another set of important factors also emerged from this study. These are the range of organisational influences that impact on individual organisations. Over half the respondents reported that the method used to set these budgets actually varied, internally, across product categories. Different methods were used for new and established products.

The criteria used by organisations to set their communications budgets are many and varied. Mitchell (1993) suggests that the criteria used could be grouped as *controllables* (41 per cent), such as financial, product, production and goals; *uncontrollables* (41 per cent), such as sales, competition, market, media and distribution; and *signals* (18 per cent), such as national activities, experience, effectiveness of expenditures and awareness. He reported that the processes used to determine the budgets were found as essentially centralised or top down (52 per cent), decentralised or bottom up (13.5 per cent) or bargaining (top down and bottom up) (21 per cent). Gullen (2003) suggests ways in which all of the techniques can be grouped, but concludes that management judgement based on weighting key criteria is required to determine the optimal budget.

West and Prendergast (2009) found that approximately 28 per cent of their respondents claimed that their firms used judgemental budgeting methods, with a similar number claiming use of the objective and task processes. Measurement-based budgeting methods were reported by 20 per cent, sales 15 per cent and competitive with roughly 8 per cent. However, their key finding was that budgeting is not about methods, measurement or analysis. The real factors that influence budgets are 'personalities, organisation, timing, planning, the nature of the market and access to data'. They identify a 'cultural code' which permeates and shapes the budgeting strategy within organisations.

Indeed, organisational culture was found to be the most important budgetary factor. Culture serves as an 'interpretive frame' through which managers act and may even influence individuals who authorise and sanction budgets. Culture, therefore, provides the decision-making frame within which budgets are developed, balanced, influenced and agreed.

The main factors associated with the determination of marketing communications (advertising) budgets are:

- organisational culture, plus strategy, direction, and values;
- the relative amount of financial resources that are available;
- competitive activities and market conditions;
- the overall level of economic confidence felt by buyers and sellers;
- the level of product/brand development and the marketing objectives.

It appears that over time a number of models and methods have been developed. A selected number, usually two, are then utilised within an organisation and its cultural framework, to reinforce the expected outcomes, rather than develop purposeful and market-orientated budgets.

Kim and Cheong (2009) have developed an approach to budgeting that is intended to improve the efficiency with which advertising budgets are determined. Referred to as data envelopment analysis (DEA), the approach is based on setting advertising budgets across different media, relative to other firms in the market. This idea was first advanced by Farrell (1957), and is based on the principle that efficiency is a function of the relationship between input and output variables. Advertising effectiveness is considered in terms of the 'spend' on six specific media (television, radio, magazines, newspapers, outdoor, and the Internet) as input variables, and revenue and brand value as two output variables. DEA complements competitive parity, and leads to benchmarking activities within the advertising budget decision process. From this these researchers believe managers can develop performance ratios such as revenue per advertising spend for each medium.

Viewpoint 7.5   Can advertising be linked to sales?

The 1985 re-launch ad for Levi's 501s shrink-to-fit jeans has been attributed for the brand's change in fortune. Facing a decline in jeans sales amongst younger target audiences, Levi's launched a TV ad to revitalise the brand. In an attempt to reposition the brand as cool, the ad was set in a 1950s, American launderette and starred actor Nick Kamen, who we see stripping off in front of onlookers to the song 'I heard it through the grapevine'. Although he strips down to his boxer shorts, the original intention was to have the actor wearing Y-fronts, but the censors prevented this and so we see him looking cool in his boxer shorts instead.

Exhibit 7.8	**Sales of Levi's 501s increased by 800%**
	Source: Fotolia.com/Zarya Maxim.

The campaign accounted for an increase of Levi's 501s sales of 800 per cent within a year. In addition, it caused a 'revolution' in the male underpants category with sales of boxer shorts increasing significantly. The effect of the ad on the male underwear market and usage was so significant that it is often referred to in articles about the history of male underwear. In the *Independent* newspaper's 'brief history of pants' it claims the ad accounts for 'causing women to rush out and stockpile boxers for their partners in the hope that their Dave would resemble the pouting model from the Levi's ad' (*Independent*, 2015).

Sources: Anon (2014); Levi's 'laundrette' (2014); Townshend (2014); Usborne et al. (2015).

Question: What other factors could account for the increase in sales of both Levi's 501s and boxer shorts? Which other brands or categories may have seen a rise in sales following the ad?

Task: Find a recent example of an advertising campaign that claims to have increased brand sales. Discuss what other factor need to be accounted for.

Budgeting for the other elements of the communications mix

The methods presented so far have concentrated on the FMCG sector. The assumption has been that only one product has been considered. In reality, a range of products will need investment for communications and the allocation decision needs to reflect the requirements of an organisation's portfolio of brands. Broadbent (1989) suggests that this situation and others (e.g. direct marketing, corporate advertising) require particular combinations of the approaches presented so far. The recommendation again is that no single method will help organisations to determine the optimal investment sum.

Sales promotion activities can be more easily costed than advertising in advance of a campaign. Judgements can be made about the expected outcomes, based upon experience, competitive conditions and the use of predictive software tools. The important variable with sales promotion concerns the redemption rate. How many of the extra pack, price deals and samples will customers demand? How much extra of a brand needs to be sold if all the costs associated with a campaign are to be covered? The production and fulfilment costs can also be determined, so in general terms a return can be calculated in advance of a sales promotion event. However, there are a large number of sales promotion activities and these will often overlap. From a management perspective the brand management system is better, since a single person is responsible for the budget, one who is able to take a wider view of the range of activities. While the objective and task approach appears to be more easily applied to this element of the mix, other methods, such as competitive parity and fixed ratios, are often used.

The costs of *public relations* activities can also be predicted with a reasonable degree of accuracy. The staffing and/or agency costs are relatively fixed and, as there are no media costs involved, the only other major factor is the associated production costs. These are the costs of the materials used to provide third parties with the opportunity to 'speak' on the organisation's behalf. As with sales promotion, if a number of public relations events have been calculated as a necessary part of the overall communications activities of the organisation, then the costs of the different tasks need to be anticipated and aggregated and a judgement made about the impact the events will make. The relative costs of achieving a similar level of impact through advertising or other elements of the mix can often be made, and a decision taken based on relative values.

It has already been stated that the costs associated with the *sales force* can be the highest of all the elements of the mix, especially in business-to-business situations. This would indicate that the greatest degree of care needs to be taken when formulating the size and deployment of the sales force. The costs associated with each activity of personal selling and the support facilities (e.g. car, expenses, training) can be calculated easily, but what is more difficult to predict is the return on the investment.

These approaches to calculating the amount that should be invested in communications activities vary in their degree of sophistication and usefulness. Of all these methods, none is the ideal answer to the question of how much should be allocated to marketing communications or, more specifically, the advertising spend. Some of the methods are too simplistic, while others are too specific to particular market conditions. For example, formulating strategy to gain market share through increasing SOV seems to ignore the dynamic nature of the markets and the fact that organisations need to satisfy a range of stakeholders and not concentrate solely on winning the greatest market share.

Setting budgets specifically across digital media has not yet been well researched. Renshaw (2008) offers advice for those with and without digital budgets. Where there is a digital budget, he advocates that 70 per cent should be allocated to 'emerged' digital media, 20 per cent to media 'going mainstream' and the remaining 10 per cent going to emerging digital media (see Table 7.7).

Organisations that do have a digital marketing budget are advised to consider a four-step process:

1. *Audiences* – what do they do, when do they do it, when and what media/content do they consume?
2. *Media* – which media type has worked in the past?
3. *Competitors* – use media that deliver results, but are there media which present opportunities for advantage?
4. *Be bold* – consider all digital opportunities, not just the Internet.

Readers may well have reached the conclusion that the most appropriate way forward for management is to consider several approaches in order to gather a ball-park figure. Such a composite approach negates some of the main drawbacks associated with particular methods. It also helps to build a picture of what is really necessary if the organisation is to communicate effectively and efficiently. West and Prendergast (2009) found that the mean number of methods used by organisations in their sample was two, indicating that organisations are not relying on a single method.

Table 7.7 Leo Burnett's recommended allocations for digital media budgets

Status of digital media	Explanation
Emerged digital media 70 per cent	These media can be optimised and will provide results. Key media include: broadband video, rich media/video-based ads and search marketing.
Going mainstream 20 per cent	These are media that are not as well proven as emerged media but which are increasingly prominent and likely to be emerged media at some point in the future. These include: mobile marketing, online social networks and specific types of gaming.
Emerging digital media 10 per cent	These media are just appearing and are not well known either by large audiences or by researchers in terms of their commercial potential and performance.

Source: Renshaw (2008). Used with permission from WARC.

Of all the methods and different approaches, the one constant factor that applies to all concerns the objectives that have been set for the campaign. Each element of the communications mix has particular tasks to accomplish and it is these objectives that drive the costs of the promotional investment. If the ultimate estimate of the communications spend is too high, then the objectives, not the methods used, need to be revised.

Key points

- The communications industry consists of a variety of very large-, medium- and small-sized agencies, with many agencies owned by large global holding companies. Technology and new media channels have had a significant influence on shaping the structure of the industry.

- In 2015 UK media expenditure grew to just under £18 billion, with internet spend seeing the largest growth (Warc, 2015). Other sectors of the industry have experienced high growth rates and are expected to continue to rise (IEG, 2015; World PR Report, 2015).

- Agencies broker or facilitate the communications needs of clients, while media houses plan, buy and monitor media purchases for their clients. Production facilitators ensure the processes work by making videos, providing fulfilment or staging events. All deliver specific value to the industry and have different roles to play.

- The IPA has identified 11 different types of agencies: full service or integrated, creative, media, digital, search, social media, direct marketing, branded content, experiential, healthcare, and outdoor or out-of-home (OOH) agencies.

- Clients use a fairly standardised process to select an agency which involves a search, request for information and a credentials meeting. Shortlisted agencies often arrange chemistry meetings with the client team and a formal pitch presentation is used to make a final decision.

- Relationships between clients and agencies are of critical importance and part of their trust and commitment is reflected in the remuneration agencies receive for their contribution. There are three keys methods: commission, payment by results and fees. These are normally combined within a contract.

- The decision to invest in marketing communications is relatively easy. The real difficulty lies in determining just how much to invest and in which tools and media. This is because the direct outcomes are intangible and often distant, as the advertising effects may be digested by potential buyers immediately but not acted upon until some point in the future.

- Setting the marketing communications budget serves to focus people's attention on the costs and benefits of undertaking planned communications activities. The act of quantifying the means by which the marketing plan will be communicated to target audiences instils a management discipline necessary to ensure that the objectives of the plan are achievable. The process facilitates cross-function coordination and forces managers to ensure that the planned communications are monitored and controlled.

- Marginal analysis provides a theoretical basis to determine the 'right' budget. However, this approach is impractical so organisations use a variety of practical approaches. These range from guesswork, a percentage of sales, what is affordable, inertia and objective and task. The last is considered to be the most appropriate.

- Within any market the adspend of any one advertiser can be compared with the total spend of all competitors. This is known as share of voice (SOV). This figure can be compared with the share of market (SOM) that each player holds. If these percentages are equal then there is equilibrium. Variations above and below this represent strategic intent.

- There are specific techniques available to determine the optimum sales force size and costs. The size of the public relations effort depends on usage, but the financial investment can be reduced to a judgement. Sales promotions and direct marketing are project-oriented and can be costed accordingly.

Review questions

The Kasiisi Project case questions

1. Why do you think Wieden+Kennedy sent Hanne to Uganda? What do you think that tells you about the advertising industry?

2. What are the advantages of taking part in such a project? Consider from both an organisational and employee perspective.

3. What challenges did Hanne face undertaking the project?

4. Consider the skills that Hanne took with her to Uganda. How do you think these helped the project?

5. Think about your own marketing communications knowledge and skills. How could these be used to help similar projects in your own country?

General questions

1. Outline the arguments for and against using an agency.

2. What factors should be taken into consideration and what procedures might be followed when selecting an agency?

3. What problems might be encountered in client-agency relationships?

4. Explain the commission payment system, and outline alternative approaches.

5. Discuss the issues that might be encountered when setting communications budgets. Explain how the notion of SOV can assist in setting adspend levels.

References

Advertising Agencies (2014) *Market Digest,* Key Note Database, retrieved 10 April 2015 from www. keynote.co.uk/market-digest/business-services/advertising-agencies.

Advertising Association (2004) *Advertising Statistics Year Book,* Henley: World Advertising Research Centre.

Anon (2014) Keep your pants on: marking 80 years of the Y-front, *ITV News,* 30 November, retrieved 27 May 2015 from www.itv.com/news/2014-11-30/keep-your-pants-on-marking-80-years-of-the-y-front/.

ASA (2015) *About ASA,* retrieved 10 May 2015 from www.asa.org.uk/About-ASA.aspx.

Bain, R. (2012) Do you want the good news or the bad news? *Research,* retrieved 9 September 2012 from www.research-live.com/features/do-you-want-its-good-news-or-the-bad-news?/4006957.article.

Beale, C. (2012) School Reports 2012: A–Z of agencies, Introduction, *Campaign,* 2 April, retrieved 3 April 2012 from www.brandrepublic.com/news/1122211/School-Reports-2012-A-Z-agencies/.

Binet, L. and Field, P. (2007) Marketing in the era of accountability, *IPA dataMine,* Henley-on-Thames: WARC.

Brand Republic (2015a) Top holding companies, *Brand Republic,* 28 March, retrieved 27 May 2015 from www.brandrepublic.com/article/1339955/top-holding-companies.

Brand Republic (2015b) Top 50 media agencies. *Brand Republic,* retrieved from www.brandrepublic.com/article/1339845/top-50-media-agencies.

Broadbent, S. (1989) *The Advertising Budget,* Henley: NTC Publications.

Buck, S. (2001) Advertising and the long-term success of the premium brand, *Advertising Association,* Henley-on-Thames: WARC.

Campaign (2015) Nobody does it better, *Campaign,* 15 May, p. 27.

Child, L. (2007) How to manage your relationship, *Marketing Agency,* December, 4–7.

Collin, W. (2003) The interface between account planning and media planning – a practitioner perspective, *Marketing Intelligence and Planning,* 21(7), 440–5.

Corstjens, M., Umblijs, A. and Wang, C. (2011) The power of inertia: conservatism in marketing resource allocation, *Journal of Advertising Research,* June, 356–72.

Crosier, K., Grant, I. and Gilmore, C. (2003) Account planning in Scottish advertising agencies: a discipline in transition, *Journal of Marketing Communications,* 9(1), 1–15.

Daldry, G. (2015) 2015: the year of the in-house agency? *Brand Republic,* 6 February, retrieved 10 May 2015 from www.campaignlive.co.uk/article/1332781/2015-year-in-house-agency\#ThJExkxrb2fr6L8m.99.

Degun, G. (2015) Land Rover to move global ad account into Spark44, *Brand Republic,* retrieved 20 May 2015 from www.brandrepublic.com/article/1340480/land-rover-move-global-ad-account-spark44.

DMA (2015) DMA and IDM merge to create new group, 21 May, *DMA,* retrieved from www.dma.org.uk/press-release/dma-and-idm-merge-to-create-new-group.

Donnelly, A. (2008) Cut spend, damage the brand, *Marketing,* 19 March, p. 4.

Fam, K.S. and Waller, D.S. (2008) Agency-client relationship factors across life-cycle stages, *Journal of Relationship Marketing,* 7(2), 217–36.

Farrell, M.J. (1957) The measurement of productive efficiency, *Journal of the Royal Statistical Society,* Series A CXX, Part 3, 253–90.

Field, P. (2009) Account planners need to care more about share of voice, *Admap,* September, 28–30.

Gambetti, R., Biraghi, S., Schultz, D.E. and Graffigna, G. (2015) Brand wars: consumer–brand engagement beyond client–agency fights, *Journal of Strategic Marketing,* DOI: 10.1080/0965254X.2015.1011199.

Grant, I. and McLeod, C. (2007) Advertising agency planning: conceptualising network relationships, *Journal of Marketing Management,* 23(5/6), 425–42.

Grant, I., McLeod, C. and Shaw, E. (2012) Conflict and advertising planning: consequences of networking for advertising planning, *European Journal of Marketing,* 46(1/2), 73–91.

Gullen, P. (2003) 5 steps to effective budget setting, *Admap,* July/August, 22–4.

Hakansson, H. (1982) *International Marketing and Purchasing of Industrial Goods: An Interaction Approach,* Chichester: Wiley.

Haley, E., Taylor, R. and Morrison, M. (2014) How advertising creatives define excellent planning, *Journal of Current Issues & Research in Advertising,* 35(2), 167–89.

IEG (2015) Sponsorship spending report: where the dollars are going and trends for 2015, retrieved 30 March 2015 from www.sponsorship.com/IEG/files/4e/4e525456-b2b1-4049-bd51-03d9c35ac507.pdf.

IPA (2009a) Request for Information (RFI) Template, *IPA,* retrieved 5 May 2015 from www.ipa.co.uk/document/request-for-information-rfi-template.

IPA (2009b) *Finding an Agency: A Best Practice Guide to Agency Search and Selection,* London: IPA.

IPA (2015) Admission. Industry Guide. *IPA,* retrieved 10 May 2015 from www.theadmission.co.uk/industry-guide.

IPA/ISBA/CIPS (2012) *Agency remuneration: a best practice guide to agency search and selection,* London: IPA/ISBA/CIPS.

IPM (2013) Director's Report and Financial Statements. *Institute of Promotional Marketing,* retrieved 10 May from www.theipm.org.uk/Uploaded/1/Documents/accounts/2013_accounts.pdf.

ISBA (2013) The good pitch: best practice for clients and agencies, retrieved 20 December 2013 from www.thegoodpitch.com/alternatives.

Jensen, B. (1995) Using agency remuneration as a strategic tool, *Admap,* January, 20–2.

Jones, J.P. (1990) Ad spending: maintaining market share, *Harvard Business Review,* January/February, 38–42.

Jones, M. (2004) 10 things agencies need to know about clients, *Admap,* 39(5), 21–3.

Kim, K. and Cheong, Y. (2009) A frontier analysis for advertising budgeting: benchmarking efficient advertisers, *Journal of Current Issues and Research in Advertising,* 31, 2 (Fall), 91–104.

Koslow, S., Sasser, S.L. and Riordan, E.A (2006) Do marketers get the advertising they need or the advertising they deserve? Agency views of how clients influence creativity, *Journal of Advertising,* 35(3), 81–101.

Lace, J.M. and Brocklehurst, D. (2000) You both win when you play the same game, *Admap,* October, 40–2.

Levi's 'launderette' (2014) *Brand Republic and Thinkbox,* 3 December, retrieved from www.brandrepublic.com/article/1323966/levis-launderette.

Mackert, M. and Munoz, I.I. (2011) Graduate Account Planning Education: insights from the classroom, *Journal of Advertising Education,* 15(2), 35–9.

Media Week (2005) Keeping your options in-house, *Media Week,* 1 February, retrieved 10 May 2015 from www.mediaweek.co.uk/article/511893/keeping-options-in-house\#AxOFltIL0Mu2icO4.99.

Miln, D. (2004) New marketing, new agency? *Admap,* 39(7), 47–8.

Mitchell, A. (2012) Face it, your consumers hate you, *Marketing,* 28 March 2012, 30–2.

Mitchell, L.A. (1993) An examination of methods of setting advertising budgets: practice and literature, *European Journal of Advertising,* 27(5), 5–21.

Moeran, B. (2005) Tricks of the trade: the performance and interpretation of authenticity. *Journal of Management Studies,* 42(5), 901–22.

Morgan, R.M. and Hunt, S.D. (1994) The commitment–trust theory of relationship marketing, *Journal of Marketing,* 58 (July), 20–38.

Patwardhan, P., Patwardhan, H. and Vasavada-Oza, F. (2011) Diffusion of account planning in Indian ad agencies: an organisational perspective, *International Journal of Advertising,* 30(4), 665–92.

Pawinska, M. (2000) The passive pitch, *PR Week,* 12 May, 14–15.

Quebra, B., Bick, G. and Abratt, R. (2013) Service quality of advertising and promotions agencies in South Africa, *Journal of Promotion Management,* 19(5), 605–28.

Renshaw, M. (2008) How to set digital media budgets, *WARC Exclusive,* retrieved 20 March 2008 from www.warc.com.

Robinson, M. (2010) The pitch, new business: a guide to life on the front-line, *IPA,* 32–5, retrieved 10 December 2014 from www.thegoodpitch.com/wp-content/uploads/2011/09/IPA_Life-on-the-front-line-Final.pdf.

Röling, R.W. (2010) Small town, big campaigns: the rise and growth of an international advertising industry in *Amsterdam, Regional Studies,* 44(7), August, 829–43.

Schroer, J. (1990) Ad spending: growing market share, *Harvard Business Review,* January/February, 44–8.

Sclater, I. (2006) Marriage material, *The Marketer,* September, 22–3.

Snowden, S. (1993) The remuneration squeeze, *Admap,* January, 26–8.

Sorrell, Sir M. (2014) Future of the agency service model, *Admap,* October, 1–3.

Spanier, G. (2010) What's the secret of a long-term relationship in advertising? *London Evening Standard,* 19 July, retrieved 8 August 2011 from www.thisislondon.co.uk.

Swift, J. (2015) BBH to scoop Strictly Come Dancing brief, *Brand Republic,* 19 March, retrieved 20 April 2015 from www.brandrepublic.com/article/1338939/bbh-scoop-strictly-dancing-brief.

Tomkins, R. (1999) If the return is right, keep spending, *Financial Times,* 19 March, p. 8.

Townshend, J. (2014) 3 great ads I had nothing to do with, *Brand Republic and Thinkbox,* 26 November, retrieved 12 May 2015 from www.brandrepublic.com/article/1323980/3-great-ads-i-nothing-with-john-townshend.

Turnbull, S. (2013) What are advertising agencies looking for? *Brand Republic,* p. 1.

Turnbull, S. and Wheeler, C. (2014) Exploring advertiser's expectations of advertising agency services, *Journal of Marketing Communications,* DOI:10.1080/13527266.2014.920902.

Turnbull, S. and Wheeler, C. (2015) The advertising creative process: a study of UK agencies, *Journal of Marketing Communications,* DOI:10.1080/13527266.2014.1000361.

Tylee, J. (1999) Survey warns against adspend cuts, *Campaign,* 12 March, p. 10.

Tylee, J. (2010) Will others follow Coke's remuneration model? *Campaign,* 19 February, p. 17.

Usborne, S., Sharpe, R. and Walker, E. (2015) A brief history of pants: why men's smalls have always been a subject of concern, *Independent,* 24 May, retrieved 27 May 2015 from www.independent.co.uk/life-style/fashion/features/a-brief-history-of-pants-why-mens-smalls-have-always-been-a-subject-of-concern-771772.html.

van Rensburg, J.M., Venter, P. and Strydom, J.W. (2010) Approaches taken by South African advertisers to select and appoint advertising agencies, *South African Business Review,* 14(4), 25–36.

Warc (2014) US Advertising/Sales Ratios, *Warc,* retrieved 10 May 2015 from www.warc.com/Pages/ForecastsAndData/AdvertisingSlesRatios.aspx.

Warc (2015a) Adspend Database. *Warc,* retrieved 10 March 2015 from www.warc.com/Pages/ForecastsAndData/InternationalDataForecast.aspx?Forecast=DatabaseAndCustomTables&isUSD=True.

Warc (2015b) P&G axes agency fees by $500m, *Warc,* retrieved 10 May 2015 from www.warc.com/Content/News/N34666_P26G_axes_agency_fees_by_24500m_.content?PUB=Warc%20News&CID=N34666&ID=025e3103-e3ab-4723-8e37-8c9f0ab6355b&q=P%26G+axes+agency+fees&qr=.

West, D. and Prendergast, G.P. (2009) Advertising and promotions budgeting and the role of risk, *European Journal of Marketing,* 43(11/12), 1457–76.

West, D.C. and Paliwoda, S.J. (1996) Advertising client–agency relationships, *European Journal of Marketing,* 30(8), 22–39.

White, R. (2007) How to use the budget better, *Admap,* July/August, 14–15.

Whitehead, J. (2008) IPA backs ads in face of downturn, *Brand Republic,* 9 January, retrieved 20 April 2015 from www.brandrepublic.com/article/775516/ipa-backs-ads-face-downturn.

Williams, T. (2010) Why agencies should call time on selling time, *Campaign,* 16 July, p. 12.

World PR Report (2015) retrieved 20 May from www.holmesreport.com/ranking-and-data/world-pr-report/analysis/executive-summary.

Zambarino, A. and Goodfellow, J. (2003) Account planning in the new marketing and communications environment (has the Stephen King challenge been met?), *Marketing Intelligence and Planning,* 21(7), 424–34.

Zolkiewski, J., Burton, J. and Stratoudaki, S. (2008) The delicate power balance in advertising agency-client relationships: partnership or battleground? The case of the Greek advertising market, *Journal of Customer Behaviour,* 7(4), 315–32.

Chapter 8

Evaluation and metrics

Evaluation is an important part of the marketing communications process. All activities need to be evaluated to understand the impact and effect that a campaign has on a target audience. There is also increasing pressure to measure the return on investment from all areas of marketing communications.

Aims and learning objectives

The aims of this chapter are to review the ways in which marketing communications activities can be evaluated.

The learning objectives are to enable readers to:

1. discuss the role of evaluation within marketing communications;
2. explore the value and methods of pre-testing and post-testing advertisements;
3. explain the main ideas behind different physiological measures of evaluation;
4. consider ways in which advertising and public relations can be evaluated;
5. examine other ways in which the effectiveness of marketing communications can be evaluated;
6. review the issues associated with measuring the fulfilment of brand promises and online and social media communications.

Millward Brown - optimising a dramatic performance

An automotive marketing team needed guidance on how their new, dramatic 60-second TV ad could be optimised before going on air. We researched it with Link™, our global copy testing tool, among 150 consumers who intended to purchase or lease a new vehicle within the next 12 months.

Engagement

The research found that for some, the story was enjoyable: 34 per cent found it very enjoyable, compared with our norm of 21 per cent. However, the ad was somewhat polarising; verbatim comments highlighted that some were not clear what was going on.

> 'It was a great story told very naturally and one which kept your mind on the story as if it were a programme or documentary. It was very well done and enjoyable.'

> 'That man was annoying and it didn't seem to make much sense.'

> 'Without the appearance of the car itself and the brand name being in the ad, it could have been for any car commercial.'

The ad drew parallels with a famous novel, which was not clear to all. As a consequence some tuned out early on, saying they didn't really get what was going on in the ad; only 50 per cent found it 'very easy' to understand, compared with our norm of 71 per cent. As a consequence, the ad's ability to break through was limited.

As well as a series of introspective closed and open questions, Link capitalises on tools developed from neuroscience. Using facial coding within Link provides a deeper understanding of what drives emotional engagement and attention, without asking questions. When people feel something they instinctively show it on their face, even if they don't know they are doing it, so facial coding provides diagnostics to help us understand and optimise consumers' emotional engagement with advertising.

In this case, facial coding revealed that the behaviour of the lead character was a turn-off for some, with overall positivity (essentially a net of smiles minus frowns and disgust) dropping early in the story, only recovering at the point when it became clear the character was the loser. This was also appreciated by those who reported they didn't understand the ad; so it was clear that the ad could work even among people who did not get the literary reference.

Branding

Branding was a challenge, with a branding score below our norms. Some viewers recognise the car's signature headlights early on, but for most that were not this familiar with the car, this cue was missed, and so for them the brand itself is not revealed until the end. Our learning over many thousands of ads suggests that branding at the end of an ad is a risky strategy. It can go one of two ways. It may make sense of everything

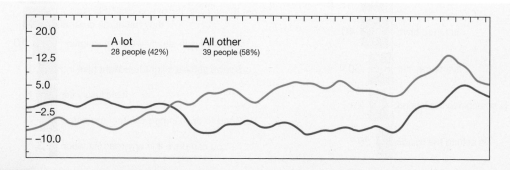

Figure 8.1 Facial coding: positive response
Source: Millward Brown © 2015.

that went before, and prompt an 'aha' moment. Then branding is strong, and there are many examples of hugely successful campaigns where branding works in this way. However, if not, the ad becomes little more than sponsored entertainment; then branding tends to be weak. In this case, the moment of branding was too brief, and not strong enough at the end of a 60-second ad. As one respondent expressed it, 'The full name of the car was only shown for such a fraction of time and at the end of the ad that it was not easy to see the name.'

We predicted that, overall, branded memorability would be slightly below average: an awareness index of 3 versus an average of 4 (broadly speaking, the awareness index is the percentage rise in ad awareness per 100 gross rating points (GRPs, see page 671). The awareness index can be viewed as the opportunity to communicate; it relates to sales effectiveness.

Communications

The ad communicated on strategy. When asked directly, both spontaneously and prompted, respondents told us that the ad communicated the functional messages that the car was reliable in bad weather, with a powerful AWD (all-wheel drive) system.

However, we also explored the intuitive associations generated by the ad. Using techniques borrowed from neuroscience, these show us the ideas or associations that viewers make most readily – and intuitively – after watching an ad, enabling us to better understand the range of ideas that will be registered by the ad. In this case, intuitively, people took away associations of power, innovation, intelligence and being progressive.

Motivation

Ads can work in a number of different ways. When they convey powerful, relevant news, they can generate a strong persuasive effect. In this case there was little in the way of news, so a strong persuasion score was not expected. However, the powerful way the car's features were demonstrated in the ad resulted in a creditable persuasion score, in line with our norms.

The cut-down solution

While the ad did successfully connect with some consumers, the ad was polarising. While understanding the literary allusions was not essential to the ad,

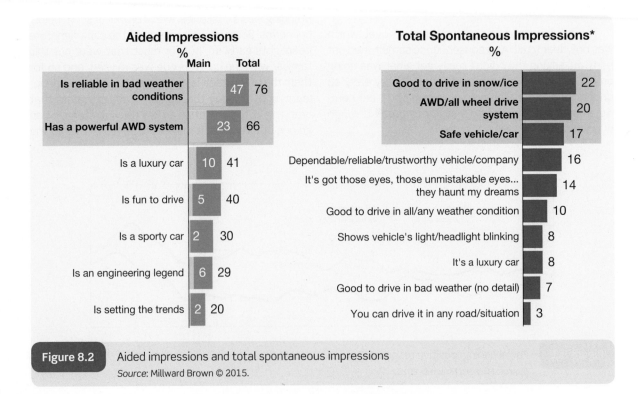

| **Figure 8.2** | Aided impressions and total spontaneous impressions |

Source: Millward Brown © 2015.

without an appreciation of them, people tended to tune out of the middle of the ad.

We considered that the 60-second ad may have been too long. Facial coding had highlighted the most engaging moments in the ad – and, crucially, which were the less engaging elements. This, along with our knowledge of successful advertising and a sensitive understanding of the flow of the ad, suggested a route to editing the ad to a 30-second version.

This case was written by Miquet Humphryes, Director, Global Corporate Marketing at Millward Brown

Questions relating to this case study can be found at the end of the chapter.

Introduction

All organisations should review and evaluate the performance of their various activities. In the Millward Brown case the key measures used to evaluate the advertising were engagement, branding, communications and motivation. This example of pre-testing a campaign highlights how important it is to ensure the message is right and that the campaign objectives are likely to be met before the ad goes to air. Many organisations do use formal mechanisms to evaluate their campaigns, but there are many others who do not review and if they do it is informal, and ad hoc.

Evaluation allows an organisation to reflect on what happened and determine whether the communications objectives have been met. It provides an opportunity to evaluate which areas of the communications had the most, and the least, impact and make decisions about future campaigns. Evaluation also allows organisations to calculate the return on investment. As there is likely to be a range of stakeholders involved in the evaluation process it is important to consider the evaluation priorities of each group (IPA, 2014). Table 8.1 highlights the possible requirements of each stakeholder.

The evaluation of planned marketing communications consists of two distinct elements. The first element is concerned with the development and testing of individual messages. The automotive ad being tested by Millward Brown in the case study provides an example of how individual messages are evaluated to ensure they meet the objectives set

Table 8.1 Stakeholder requirements

Stakeholder	Requirement
Marketing Director	Did the campaign build market share? What was the ROI?
Sales Director	Did the campaign increase sales?
Finance Director	What was the ROI?
Brand Manager	Did the campaign improve image dimensions?
Media Manager	Do we look good against our peers? Is this new channel working for us?
Communications agency	Is the campaign delivering as planned? Is the mix right?
Agency channel specialists	Is the deployment optimal?

Source: IPA (2014).

for the campaign. An advertising message has to achieve, among other things, a balance of emotion and information in order that the communications objectives and message strategy be achieved. To accomplish this, testing is required to ensure that the intended messages are encoded correctly and are capable of being decoded accurately by the target audience and the intended meaning ascribed to the message. In the Millward Brown case the pre-testing of the ad highlighted that many consumers did not decode the literary references and this resulted in audiences tuning out half way through the commercial.

The second element concerns the overall impact and effect that a campaign has on a target audience once a communications plan has been executed. This post-test factor is critical, as it will either confirm or reject management's judgement about the viability of its communications strategy. The way in which the individual components of the communications mix work together needs to be understood so that strengths can be capitalised on and developed and weaknesses negated.

Prediction and evaluation require information about options and alternatives. For example, did sales presentation approach A prove to be more effective than B and, if so, what would happen if A was used nationally? Predictably, the use of quantitative techniques is more prevalent with this set of reasons.

Millward Brown's Link™ global copy testing tool discussed in the case is just one technique used by brands to help them evaluate their advertising. This chapter considers the range of methods available to help managers evaluate their brand marketing communications. It starts with a review of the principles and need for measurement and evaluation. It then examines the traditional methods used to test and evaluate marketing communications activities. It also reviews some of the more contemporary approaches and the issues associated with the measurement and evaluation of online communications.

The role of evaluation in planned communications

The evaluation process is a key part of marketing communications. The findings and results of the evaluative process feed back into the next campaign and provide indicators and benchmarks for further campaign decisions. The primary role of evaluating the performance of a communications strategy is to ensure that the communications objectives have been met and that the strategy has been effective. The secondary role is to ensure that the strategy has been executed efficiently, and that the full potential of the individual tools and media has been extracted and that resources have been used economically.

The prevalence and acceptance of the integrated marketing communications (IMC) concept (Chapter 10) suggests that its measurement should be a central aspect when evaluating marketing communications activities. One of the predominant issues surrounding the development of IMC is the challenges and lack of empirical evidence concerning the measurement of this concept. In an attempt to resolve this, Lee and Park (2007) provide one of the first multidimensional-scaled measures of IMC. Their model is based on four key dimensions drawn from the literature. These are set out in Table 8.2.

Each of these dimensions is regarded as a separate yet integral element of IMC. Lee and Park (2007) developed an 18-item scale, derived from the literature, to measure these dimensions. The use of this approach may advance our understanding of IMC and provide a substantial basis on which IMC activities can be measured. It is interesting to note that Lee and Park (2007) see IMC as a customer-only communications activity and choose to exclude other critical stakeholders from their measurement model.

Table 8.2 Four dimensions of IMC

Dimension of IMC	Explanation
Unified communications for consistent messages and images	Activities designed to create a clear, single position, in the target market, delivering a consistent message through multiple channels.
Differentiated communications to multiple customer groups	The need to create different marketing communications campaigns (and positions) targeted at different groups (in the target market) who are at different stages of the buying process. Sequential communications models based on the hierarchy of effects or attitude construct apply.
Database-centred communications	This dimension emphasises the need to generate behavioural responses through direct marketing activities created through information collected and stored in databases.
Relationship fostering communications for existing customers	The importance of retaining customers and developing long-term relationships is a critical element of marketing communications.

Source: Lee and Park (2007). Used with permission from WARC.

Scholars' paper 8.1   **Evaluating IMC**

Ewing, M.T. (2009) Integrated marketing communications measurement and evaluation, *Journal of Marketing Communications,* **15(2–3), 103–17.**

This paper marks out the difficulties and challenges involved in measuring integrated marketing communications. Working from the base that it is consumers that determine when marketing communications is integrated, Ewing identifies and considers five areas of integrated marketing communications (IMC) measurement worthy of future research.

See also: Kerr, G. and Patti, C. (2015) Strategic IMC: from abstract concept to marketing management tool, *Journal of Marketing Communications,* 21(5),317-33; Lee, D.H. and Park, C.W. (2007) Conceptualization and measurement of multidimensionality of integrated marketing communications, *Journal of Advertising Research,* September, 222–36.

Advertising

There are numerous ways in which advertising effectiveness can be measured. Chang et al. (2010: 63) refer to 'awareness (Hansen, Olsen, and Lundsteen, 2006), brand choice (Cobb-Walgren, Ruble and Donthu, 1995), purchase likelihood (Aaker, Stayman and Hagerty, 1986), viewing time (Olney, Holbrook and Batra, 1991), brand perceptions (MacKenzie and Lutz, 1989), purchase intentions (Bellman, Schweda and Varan, 2009), memory-based tests (Brennan, Dubas and Babin, 1999) and so on'.

The techniques used to evaluate advertising are by far the most documented and, in view of the relative sizes of the communications tools, it is not surprising that slightly more time is devoted to this tool. This is not to disregard or disrespect the contribution each of the communications tools can make to an integrated campaign. Indeed, it is the collective measure of success against the goals set at the outset that is the overriding imperative for measurement, as will be seen later.

Pre-testing unfinished ads

Advertisements can be researched prior to their release (pre-test) or after they have been released (post-test). Pre-tests, sometimes referred to as *copy tests*, have traditionally attracted more attention, stimulated a greater variety of methods and generated much controversy, in comparison with post-tests.

The effectiveness of *pre-testing*, the practice of showing unfinished commercials to selected groups of the target audience with a view to refining the commercial to improve effectiveness, is still subject to debate. Turnbull and Wheeler (2015), however, identified that pre-testing is used extensively by some brands, especially fast-moving consumer goods (FMCG) brands, during the creative development process to validate the advertising creative. The study found that pre-testing creative ideas provided a means of validating the creative ideas with consumers and was also used in some instances to resolve creative disagreements between the agency and client. The study found that in some cases up to 10 different creative ideas were put into pre-testing (Turnbull and Wheeler, 2015).

The methods used to pre-test advertisements are based upon either qualitative or quantitative criteria. The most common methods used to pre-test advertisements are concept testing, focus groups, consumer juries, dummy vehicles, readability, theatre and physiological tests. Focus groups are the main qualitative method used and theatre or hall tests the main quantitative test. Each of these methods will be discussed later. Many organisations use proprietary tools such as Millward Brown's Link™ global copy testing tool which was discussed in the case study.

The primary purpose of testing advertisements during the developmental process is to ensure that the final creative work will meet the advertising objectives. Pre-testing ads at an earlier stage allows the agency and client to make changes before the costs become too high and commitment too final. Changes to an advertisement that are made too late may be resisted partly because of the sunk costs and partly because of the political consequences that 'pulling' an advertisement might have. Pre-testing, as the case described by Millward Brown highlights, also provides an opportunity to optimise ads before they go to air. The Newspaper Marketing Agency (NMA), in conjunction with Millward Brown, has pre-tested a large number of newspaper ads and has found that pre-testing newspaper ads can more than double ad recognition levels (see www.nmauk.co.uk).

Once a series of advertisements has been roughed or developed, advertisers seek reassurance and guidance regarding which of the alternatives should be developed further. Concept tests, in-depth interviews, focus groups and consumer juries can be used to determine the better of the proposed ads, by using ranking and prioritisation procedures. Of those selected, further testing can be used to reveal the extent to which the intended message is accurately decoded. As the Millward Brown case showed, pre-testing can also help refine the final TV edits. These comprehension and reaction tests are designed to prevent inappropriate advertisements reaching the finished stage.

Concept testing

The concept test is an integral part of the advertising creative development process. The purpose is to reduce the number of alternative advertising ideas, to identify and build upon the good ideas, and to reject those that are judged by the target audience not to be suitable. While many clients see this as a valuable stage in the creative process, not least because it can identify potential problems with the creative route early, not all advertising undergoes pre-testing.

Concept testing can occur very early on in the creative development process. Agencies have been known to put creative ideas into concept testing before they are shown to the client to help the agency decide which route to propose (Turnbull and Wheeler, 2015). In most cases, however, concept testing occurs after initial ideas are shown to the client and an agreed route or number of routes are then tested with the target audience.

The agency prepares scamps or a storyboard (see Table 8.3) which is essentially a rough version of the ad used to illustrate the intended artwork and the messages to be used. There are varying degrees of sophistication associated with concept testing, from the use of simple cards with no illustrations to photomatics, which are films of individual photographs shot in sequence, and livematics, which are films very close to

Table 8.3 Terminology used in creative development

Term	Meaning
Animatics	Storyboards using animated footage to illustrate the narrative of the TV commercial.
Scamps	Roughly drawn television storyboards or press ads.
Stealomatic	A compilation of video material to show the intended tone of the television advert.
Storyboards	A sequence of illustrations that show the narrative of the television commercial.

Source: Turnbull (2011).

the intended finished message. Animatics and stealomatics are also used (see Table 8.3). Some storyboards will consist of as many as 20 sketches, depicting key scenes, camera and product shots, close-ups, along with background scenery and essential props. Which type of storyboard is used depends on the size of the advertiser's budget, the completion date of the campaign and the needs of the creative team.

In the case of print ads scamps are shown to the target audience. These are roughly drawn versions of the creative idea. An inherent problem with pre-testing print or TV ads is asking consumers for feedback on unfinished ideas. As ideas are presented in a rough format there is always the danger that the concept behind the idea is not realised.

Concept testing, by definition, has to be undertaken in artificial surroundings, but the main way of eliciting the target's views is essentially qualitatively oriented, based on group discussion. This group discussion is referred to as a focus group and is a technique used by most agencies.

Exhibit 8.1	**Storyboards are roughly drawn versions of the TV ad.**
	Source: www.storyboardace.co.uk.

Focus groups

When a small number (8–10) of target consumers are brought together and invited to discuss a particular topic, a focus group is formed. By using in-depth interviewing skills a professional moderator can probe the thoughts and feelings held by the members of the group towards a product, media vehicles or advertising messages. One-way viewing rooms allow clients to observe the interaction without the focus group's behaviour being modified by external influences.

The advantage of focus groups is that they are relatively inexpensive to set up and run and they use members of the target audience. In this sense they are representative and allow true feelings and emotions to be uncovered in a way that other methods deny. They do not attempt to be quantitative and, in that sense, they lack objectivity. It is also suggested that the group dynamics may affect the responses in the 'artificial' environment. This means that there may be in-built bias to the responses and the interaction of the group members. Focus groups are very popular, but they should not be used on their own.

Consumer juries

A 'jury' of consumers, representative of the target market, is asked to judge which of a series of ideas would be their choice of a final advertisement. They are asked to rank in order of merit and provide reasons for their selections.

There are difficulties associated with ranking and prioritisation tests. First, the consumers, realising the reason for their participation, may appoint themselves as 'experts', so they lose the objectivity that this process is intended to bring. Second, the halo effect can occur, whereby an advertisement is rated excellent overall simply because one or two elements are good and the respondent overlooks the weaknesses. Finally, emotional advertisements tend to receive higher scores than informational messages, even though the latter might do better in the marketplace.

Pre-testing finished ads

When an ad is finished it can be subjected to a number of other tests before being released.

Dummy vehicles

Many of the pre-testing methods occur in an artificial environment such as a theatre, laboratory or meeting room. One way of testing, so that the reader's natural environment is used, is to produce a dummy or pretend magazine that can be consumed at home, work or wherever participants normally read magazines. Dummy magazines contain regular editorial matter with test advertisements inserted next to control advertisements. These 'pretend' magazines are distributed to a random sample of households, which are asked to consume the magazine in their normal way. Readers are encouraged to observe the editorial and at a later date they are asked questions about both the editorial and the advertisements.

The main advantage of using dummy vehicles is that the setting is natural but, as with the focus group, the main disadvantage is that respondents are aware that they are part of a test and may respond unnaturally. Research also suggests that recall may not be the best measure for low-involvement decisions or where motivation occurs through the peripheral route of the elaboration likelihood model (ELM). If awareness is required at the point of sale, then recognition may be a more reliable indicator of effectiveness than recall.

Readability tests

Flesch (1974) developed a formula to assess the ease with which print copy could be read. The test involves, among other things, determining the average number of syllables per 100 words of copy, the average length of sentence, and the percentage of personal words and sentences. By accounting for the educational level of the target audience and by comparing results with established norms, the tests suggest that comprehension is best when sentences are short, words are concrete and familiar, and personal references are used frequently.

Projective techniques

Projective techniques are used to probe the subconscious and have close associations with Freudian thinking and the motivation school advocated by Dichter (1966). Individuals or groups can be encouraged through projective techniques to express their inner thoughts and feelings about brands, products, services and organisations, among others. Four main projective techniques can be identified (see Table 8.4).

Projective techniques have been used by many leading brands to understand how their brands are perceived, to test advertising and creative ideas and to segment their markets. For example, Guinness used projective techniques to understand how to position its brand and how advertising should be used to develop the ideal position.

Theatre tests

As a way of testing finished broadcast advertisements, target consumers are invited to a theatre (laboratory or hall) to pre-view television programmes. Before the programme commences, details regarding the respondents' demographic and attitudinal details are recorded and they are asked to nominate their product preferences from a list. At the end of the viewing their evaluation of the programme is sought and they are also requested to complete their product preferences a second time.

There are a number of variations on this theme: one is to telephone the respondents a few days after the viewing to measure recall and another is to provide joysticks, push buttons and pressure pads to measure reactions throughout the viewing. The main

Table 8.4 Projective techniques

Projective technique	Explanation
Association	Free word association tests require respondents to respond with the first word that comes to mind in response to a stimulus word. Often used when naming brands.
Completion	Spontaneous sentence or story telling completion are the most used methods. Responses can be graded as approval, neutral or disapproval, enabling attitudes towards brands to be determined.
Transformation	These are also known as 'expressible' techniques and involve techniques such as psychodrawing. This requires respondents to express graphically their inner feelings about a brand or event (e.g. a shopping trip, holiday or purchase process).
Construction	This approach can involve role playing where respondents are asked to act out their feelings towards a purchase, a brand, event or organisation.

Source: Based on Robson (2002).

outcome of this process is a measure of the degree to which product preferences change as a result of exposure to the controlled viewing. This change is referred to as the persuasion shift. This approach provides for a quantitative dimension to be added to the testing process, as the scores recorded by respondents can be used to measure the effectiveness of advertisements and provide benchmarks for future testing.

It is argued that this form of testing is too artificial and that the measure of persuasion shift is too simple and unrealistic. Furthermore, some believe that many respondents know what is happening and make changes because it is expected of them in their role of respondent. Those in favour of theatre testing state that the control is sound, that the value of established norms negates any 'role play' by respondents and that the actual sales data supports the findings of the brand persuasion changes in the theatre.

This technique is used a great deal in the USA, but has had limited use in the UK. Agencies are concerned that the simplistic nature of recording scores as a means of testing advertisements ignores the complex imagery and emotional aspects of many messages. If likeability is an important aspect of eventual brand success then it is unlikely that the quantitative approach to pre-testing will contribute any worthwhile information.

Viewpoint 8.1   Pre-testing: is there a downside?

Making a decision about which creative route to use can be challenging for clients. There is often a high level of risk involved, not least of all for a client's own career. Pre-testing a creative route is seen to be one way to reduce the risk and although it doesn't provide a guarantee of success it can at least help justify the choice made (should they need to later down the line).

So what's the downside? Some creatives argue that pre-testing can limit creativity. Creativity by definition means something new and unexpected and often this can make someone feel uncomfortable. Asking the consumer to judge ideas that are new is asking them to respond to something that may make them feel uncomfortable just because it's novel. Pre-testing also relies on consumers being able to express what they are thinking and this has sometimes been known to produce inaccurate responses.

In some cases the agency and client have been known to ignore pre-testing results and go with their gut instinct that an ad will work. Heineken's iconic and highly successful 'Refreshes the parts other beers cannot reach' campaign which ran in the 1970s is a good example of this. The campaign did not perform well in pre-testing but despite this the marketing director decided to run the ad. The campaign resulted in a huge uplift in sales and the slogan quickly entered into popular culture.

There are also instances when pre-testing has been carried out and the ad performed well when researched, but when launched has had a negative response. A KFC ad, which had tested well, showing call centre operators talking with food in their mouths, received 1,671 complaints. The pre-testing was carried out with KFC's core target market, young adults and mums, who didn't have any concerns about the operators talking with their mouths full. When launched, however, it seems the rest of the market did and objected to the poor manners shown in the ad.

While pre-testing is not always able to accurately predict how an ad will perform in the market it does provide clients and agencies with some insight into how consumers will react and respond to advertising. In this sense the consumers act to validate the idea.

Source: Murphy (2005); Turnbull (2011).

Question: What are the advantages and disadvantages of pre-testing?

Task: Find an example of current advertising that some parts of the market might object to. What part of the ad do you think they would object to and how do you think the advertising would be affected if this was changed?

Physiological measures

A bank of physiological tests has been developed, partly as a response to advertisers' increasing interest in the emotional impact of advertising messages and partly because many other tests rely on the respondents' ability to interpret their reactions. Physiological tests are designed to measure the involuntary responses to stimuli that avoid the bias inherent in other tests. There are substantial costs involved with the use of these techniques, and the validity of the results is questionable. Consequently they are not used a great deal in practice, but, of them all, eye tracking is the most used and most reliable (see Table 8.5).

On the surface, pupil dilation has a number of attractions, but it is not used very much as research has shown little evidence of success. The costs are high and the low number of respondents that can be processed limits the overall effectiveness. Eye tracking can be a useful means of reviewing and amending the layout of an advertisement. Galvanic skin response is flawed because the range of reactions and emotions, the degree of learning and recall, and aspects of preference and motivation are all ignored. When these deficiencies are combined with the high costs and low numbers of respondents that can be processed, it is

Table 8.5 Physiological tests

Pupil dilation
Pupil dilation is associated with action and interest and is used to measure a respondent's reaction to a stimulus. If the pupil is constricted then interest levels are low and energy is conserved. The level of arousal is used to determine the degree of interest and preference in a particular advertisement or package design.
Eye tracking
This technique requires the use of eye movement cameras that fire an infrared beam to track the movement of the eye as it scans an advertisement. The sequence in which the advertisement is read can be determined and particular areas that do or do not attract attention can be located.
Galvanic skin response
This measures the resistance the skin offers to a small amount of current passed between two electrodes. Response to a stimulus will activate the sweat glands, which in turn will increase the resistance. Therefore the greater the level of tension induced by an advertisement, the more effective it is as a form of communication.
Tachistoscopes
These measure the ability of an advertisement to attract attention. The speed at which an advertisement is flashed in front of a respondent is gradually slowed down until a point (about 1/100 second) is reached at which the respondent is able to identify components of the message. This can be used to identify those elements that respondents see first as a picture is exposed, and so facilitates the creation of impact-based messages.
Electro-encephalographs
This involves the use of a scanner that monitors the electrical frequencies of the brain. Hemispheric lateralisation concerns the ability of the left-hand side of the brain to process rational, logical information and the right-hand side handles visual stimuli and responds more to emotional inputs. Brain activation measures the level of alpha-wave activity, which indicates the degree to which the respondent is aroused by and interested in a stimulus. Therefore, the lower the level of alpha activity, the greater the level of attention and cognitive processing. It would follow that, by measuring the alpha waves while a respondent is exposed to different advertisements, different levels of attention can be determined.

not surprising that this method of pre-testing has little value. Similarly, other physiological tests such as tachistoscopes and electro-encephalographs, although used in academic research, are not widely used by clients or agencies in the creative development process.

<table>
<tr><td>Scholars' paper 8.2</td><td>What other neuroscience techniques can we use?</td></tr>
</table>

Plassmann, H., Ambler, T., Braeutigam, S. and Kenning, P. (2007) What can advertisers learn from neuroscience? *International Journal of Advertising,* 26(2), 151–75.

This paper provides an overview of the main techniques used in functional brain imaging. The authors provide an explanation of electro-encephalography (EEG), magnetoencephalography (MEG), positron emission tomography (PET) and functional magnetic resonance imaging (fMRI), and describes what each technique measures. The advantages and disadvantages are highlighted and the use of neuroscience techniques in past advertising research discussed.

See also: Treutler, T., Levine, B. and Marci, C.D. (2010) Biometrics and multi-platform messaging: the medium matters, *Journal of Advertising Research,* 50(3), 243–9.

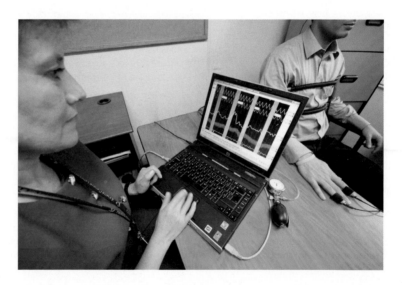

<table>
<tr><td>Exhibit 8.2</td><td>**Galvanic skin response process being used**
Source: Guy Bell/Alamy Images.</td></tr>
</table>

Post-testing

Testing advertisements that have been released is generally more time-consuming and involves greater expense than pre-testing. However, the big advantage with post-testing is that advertisements are evaluated in their proper environment, or at least the environment in which they are intended to be successful.

There are a number of methods used to evaluate the effectiveness of such advertisements, and of these inquiry, recall, recognition and sales-based tests predominate.

Inquiry tests

These tests are designed to measure the number of inquiries or direct responses stimulated by advertisements. Inquiries can take the form of returned coupons and response cards, requests for further literature or actual orders. They were originally used to test print messages, but some television advertisements now carry 0800 (free) telephone numbers. An increase in the use of direct-response media will lead to an increase in the sales and leads generated by inquiry-stimulating messages, so this type of testing will become more prevalent.

Inquiry tests can be used to test single advertisements or a campaign in which responses are accumulated. Using a split run, an advertiser can use two different advertisements and run them in the same print vehicle. This allows measurement of the attention-getting properties of alternative messages. If identical messages are run in different media then the effect of the media vehicles can be tested.

Care needs to be given to the interpretation of inquiry-based tests, as they may be misleading. An advertisement may not be effective simply because of the responses received. For example, people may respond because they have a strong need for the offering rather than the response being a reflection of the qualities of the advertisement. Likewise, other people may not respond despite the strong qualities of the advertisement, simply because they lack time, resources or need at that particular moment.

Recall tests

Recall tests are designed to assess the impression that particular advertisements have made on the memory of the target audience. Interviewers, therefore, do not use a copy of the advertisement as a stimulus, as the tests are intended to measure impressions and perception, not behaviour, opinions, attitudes or the advertising effect.

Normally, recall tests require the cooperation of several hundred respondents, all of whom were exposed to the advertisement. They are interviewed the day after an advertisement is screened, hence the reference to day-after-recall (DAR) tests. Once qualified by the interviewer, respondents are first asked if they remember a commercial for, say, air travel. If the respondent replies 'Yes, Virgin', then this is recorded as unaided recall and is regarded as a strong measure of memory. If the respondent says 'No', the interviewer might ask the question 'Did you see an advertisement for British Airways?' A positive answer to this prompt is recorded as aided recall.

These answers are then followed by questions such as, 'What did the advertisement say about British Airways?', 'What did the commercial look like?' and 'What did it remind you of?' All the answers provided to this third group of questions are written down word for word and recorded as verbatim responses.

The reliability of recall scores is generally high. This means that each time the advertisement is tested, the same score is generated. Validity refers to the relationship or correlation between recall and the sales that ultimately result from an audience exposed to a particular advertisement. The validity of recall tests is generally regarded by researchers as low.

Recall tests have a number of other difficulties associated with them. First, they can be expensive, as a lot of resources can be consumed by looking for and qualifying respondents. Second, not only is interviewing time expensive, but the score may be rejected if, on examination of the verbatim responses, it appears that the respondent was guessing.

It has been suggested by Zielske (1982) that thinking/rational messages appear to be easier to recall than emotional/feeling ones. Therefore, it seems reasonable to assume that recall scores for emotional/feeling advertisements may be lower. It is possible that programme content may influence the memory and lead to different recall scores for the same offering. The use of a preselected group of respondents may reduce the costs associated with finding a qualified group, but they may increase their attention towards the commercials in the knowledge that they will be tested the following day. This will inevitably lead to higher levels of recall than actually exist.

On-the-air tests are a derivative of recall and theatre tests. By using advertisements that are run live in a test area, it is possible to measure the impact of these test advertisements with DAR. As recall tests reflect the degree of attention and interest in the advertisement, this is a way of controlling and predicting the outcome of a campaign when it is rolled out nationally.

Recall tests are used a great deal, even though their validity is low and their costs are high. It is argued that this is because recall scores provide an acceptable means by which decisions to invest heavily in advertising programmes can be made. Agencies accumulate vast amounts of recall data that can be used as benchmarks to judge whether an advertisement generated a score that was better or less than the average for the product class or brand. Having said that, and despite their popularity, recall tests are adjudged to be poor predictors of sales (Lodish and Lubetkin, 1992).

Recognition tests

Recall tests are based upon the memory and the ability of respondents to reprocess information about an advertisement. A different way of determining advertising effectiveness is to ask respondents if they recognise an advertisement. This is the most common of the post-testing procedures for print advertisements. One of the main methods used to measure the readership of magazines is based on the frequency-of-reading and generally there are three main approaches:

- *recency* – reading any issue during the last publishing interval (e.g. within the last seven days for a weekly magazine);
- *specific issue* – reading of a specific issue of a publication;
- *frequency-of-reading* – how many issues a reader has read in a stated period (such as a month in respect of a weekly magazine).

Worldwide, the recency approach is the most widely used method in national readership surveys (www.roymorgan.com). Of the many services available, perhaps the Starch Readership Report is the best known. These recognition tests are normally conducted in the homes of approximately 200 respondents. Once it has been agreed that the respondent has previously seen a copy of the magazine, it is opened at a predetermined page and the respondent is asked, for each advertisement, 'Did you see or read any part of the advertisement?' If the answer is yes, the respondent is asked to indicate exactly which parts of the copy or layout were seen or read.

Four principal readership scores are reported: noted, seen-associated, read most and signature, as set out in Table 8.6.

The reliability of recognition tests is very high, higher than recall scores. Costs are lower, mainly because the questioning procedure is simpler and quicker. It is also possible to deconstruct an advertisement into its component parts and assess their individual effects on the reader. As with all interviewer-based research, bias is inevitable. Bias can

Table 8.6 Principal readership scores

Readership scores	Explanation
Noted	The percentage of readers who remember seeing the advertisement.
Seen-associated	The percentage of readers who recall seeing or reading any part of the advertisement identifying the offering.
Read most	The percentage of readers who report reading at least 50 per cent of the advertisement.
Signature	The percentage of readers who remember seeing the brand name or logo.

also be introduced by the respondent or the research organisation through the instructions given or through fatigue of the interviewer.

The validity of recognition test scores is said to be high, especially after a number of insertions. However, there can be a problem of false claiming, where readers claim to have seen an advertisement but, in fact, have not. This, it is suggested, is because when readers confirm they have seen an advertisement the underlying message is that they approve of and like that sort of advertisement. If they say that they have not seen an advertisement, the underlying message is that they do not usually look at that sort of advertisement. Krugman (1988) believes that readers are effectively voting on whether an advertisement is worth spending a moment of their time to look at. It might be that readers' memories are a reliable indicator of what the reader finds attractive in an advertisement and this could be a surrogate indicator for a level of likeability. This proposition has yet to be fully investigated, but it may be that the popularity of the recognition test is based on the validity rating and the approval that high scores give to advertisers.

Sales tests

If the effectiveness of advertisements could be measured by the level of sales that occurs during and after a campaign, then the usefulness of measuring sales as a testing procedure would not be in doubt. However, the practical difficulties associated with market tests are so large that these tests have little purpose. Counting the number of direct-response returns and the number of enquiries received are the only sales-based tests that have any validity.

Practitioners have been reluctant to use market-based tests because they are not only expensive to conduct but also historical by definition. Sales occur partly as a consequence of past actions, including past communications strategies, and the costs (production, agency and media) have already been sunk. There may be occasions where it makes little political and career sense to investigate an event unless it has been a success, or at the very least reached minimal acceptable expectations.

For these reasons and others, advertisers have used test markets to gauge the impact their campaigns have on representative samples of the national market.

Simulated market tests

By using control groups of matched consumers in particular geographic areas, the use of simulated test markets permits the effect of advertising on sales to be observed under controlled market conditions. These conditions are more realistic than for tests conducted within a theatre setting and are more representative of the national market than the limited in-house tests. This market representation is thought by some to provide an adequate measure of advertising effect. Other commentators, as discussed before, believe that unless advertising is the dominant element in the marketing mix, there are usually too many other factors that can affect sales. It is therefore unfair and unrealistic to place the sole responsibility for sales with advertising.

Single-source data

With the advances in technology it is now possible to correlate consumer purchases with the advertisements they have been exposed to. This is known as *single-source data* and involves the controlled transmission of advertisements to particular households whose every purchase is monitored through a scanner at supermarket checkouts. In other words, all the research data is derived from the same households.

The advent of cable television has facilitated this process. Consumers along one side of a street receive one set of control advertisements, while the others on the other side receive test advertisements. Single-source data provides exceptionally dependable results, but the technique is expensive, is inappropriate for testing single advertisements, and tends to focus on the short-term effect, failing, for example, to cope with the concept of adstock.

In the UK facilities such as Adlab and Homescan have helped advertisers assess their advertising effectiveness in terms of copy testing, weight testing and even the use of mixed media. The use of split regions can be very important, allowing comparisons to be made of different strategies.

Other methods of evaluation

There is a range of other measures that have been developed in an attempt to understand the effect of advertisements. Among these are tracking studies and financial analyses.

Tracking studies

A tracking study involves interviewing a large number of people on a regular basis, weekly or monthly, with the purpose of collecting data about buyers' perceptions of marketing communications messages – not just advertisements – and how these messages might be affecting buyers' perceptions of the brand. By measuring and evaluating the impact of a campaign when it is running, adjustments can be made quickly. The most common elements that are monitored, or tracked, are the awareness levels of an advertisement and the brand, image ratings of the brand and the focus organisation, and attributes and preferences.

Tracking studies can be undertaken on a periodic or continuous basis. The latter is more expensive, but the information generated is more complete and absorbs the effect of competitors' actions, even if the effects are difficult to disaggregate. A further form of tracking study involves monitoring the stock held by retailers. Counts are usually undertaken each month, on a pre- and post-exposure basis. This method of measuring sales is used frequently. Audited sales data, market share figures and return on investment provide other measures of advertising effectiveness.

Tracking studies are also used to measure the impact and effectiveness of online activities. These may be applied to banner ads, email campaigns and paid-for search engine placements and have for a long time been geared to measuring site visitors, clicks through or pages visited. Increasingly these studies are attending to the volume and value of traffic with regard to the behaviour undertaken by site visitors. Behaviour, or the more common term, *call-to-action*, can be considered in terms of the engagement through exchanges or transactions, the number of site or subscription registrations, the volume of downloads requested or the number of offline triggers such as 'call me buttons' that are activated.

Financial analysis

The vast amount of resources that are directed at planned communications and, in particular, advertising, requires that the organisation reviews, on a periodic basis, the amount and the manner in which its financial resources have been used. For some organisations the media spend alone constitutes one of the major items of expenditure.

Variance analysis enables a continuous picture of the spend to be developed and acts as an early warning system should unexpected levels of expenditure be incurred. In addition to this and other standard financial controls, the size of the discount obtained from media buying is becoming an important and vital part of the evaluation process.

Increasing levels of accountability and rapidly rising media costs have contributed to the development of centralised media buying. Under this arrangement, the promotion of an organisation's entire portfolio of brands, across all divisions, is contracted to a single media-buying organisation. Part of the reasoning is that the larger the account, the greater the buying power an agency has, and this in turn should lead to greater discounts and value of advertising spend.

The point is that advertising economies of scale can be obtained by those organisations that spend a large amount of their resources on the media. To accommodate this, centralised buying has developed, which in turn creates higher entry and exit barriers, not only to and from the market, but also from individual agencies.

Likeability

A major study by the American Research Foundation investigated a range of different pre-testing methods with the objective of determining which were best at predicting sales success. The unexpected outcome was that, of all the measures and tests, the most powerful predictor was likeability: 'how much I liked the advertisement'.

From a research perspective, much work has been undertaken to clarify the term 'likeability', but it certainly cannot be measured in terms of a simple Likert scale of 'I liked the advertisement a lot', 'I liked the advertisement a little', etc. The term has a much deeper meaning and is concerned with the following issues (Gordon, 1992):

> *personally meaningful, relevant, informative, true to life, believable, convincing relevant, credible, clear product advantages, product usefulness, importance to 'me'; stimulates interest or curiosity about the brand; creates warm feelings through enjoyment of the advertisement.*

The implication of these results is that post-testing should include a strong measure of how well an advertisement was liked at its deepest level of meaning.

Research by Smit et al. (2006) determined that there are four main elements associated with likeability. These are entertainment, relevance, clearness (or clarity) and pleasantness. Of these they found relevance to be the most important for changing viewers' opinions and entertainment for explaining how people process ads.

There are two main approaches to measuring likeability. One seeks to isolate what it is that viewers think and feel after seeing particular ads, that is how they feel. The other measures attitudes towards the ad itself. Essentially likeability is concerned with the affective element of the attitude construct. Indeed, some researchers argue that likeability is a suitable response to the cognitive processing school of thought where individuals are considered to be rational problem-solvers.

Marketing mix modelling

Marketing mix modelling (MMM), or econometric analysis, uses multivariate analysis to evaluate the impact of marketing communications. Using statistical analysis, MMM allows brands to isolate the effects of factors such as advertising, weather and competitive activity to quantify the effects of each on sales (IPA, 2014).

Consider, for example, an ice-cream brand that wanted to identify the effect of advertising on sales. Since there are many other factors that could account for an increase in sales, such as a rise in the temperature or a new distribution channel, it is necessary to separate the effects of the other influences in order to allow the advertising effect to be quantified.

Using MMM can assist in setting budgets and deciding when campaigns should run. For example, in the case of the ice-cream brand it can help to evaluate which season to advertise in. Analysis can also help brands to explore campaign weight, flighting, levels of coverage and frequency, and decide when diminishing returns on expenditure are likely to start (IPA, 2014).

While MMM can be a valuable tool to evaluate marketing communications it involves building econometric models using regression analysis and other sophisticated techniques. This requires specialist knowledge of statistical analysis and also requires data that is valid, since the model will only be as good as the data that went into it.

Viewpoint 8.2   Chengdu 'Pambassador'

| Exhibit 8.3 | **The Chengdu 'Pambassador' campaign included panda-themed publicity stunts around the globe** |

Source: Corbis/Fang Zhe / Xinhua Press

Chengdu is the capital of Sichuan province in western China. Despite being the fourth largest city in China, however, it only saw 1.2 million annual tourist visitors in 2011, less than 1 per cent of China's 135 million total visitors that year. To address this imbalance the city decided to run a public relations campaign to raise awareness of the city as a tourist destination and increase international visitors to Chengdu.

Research indicated that consumer perception of Chengdu was poor with many seeing the city as a rundown industrial centre. These impressions were overcome with the 'Pambassador' campaign which associated Chengdu with China's lovable giant panda. The campaign included panda-themed stunts and events, as well as a competition offering three people to become a guest panda keeper and ambassador.

In addition to key global tourist markets, the campaign wanted to engage tourists from neighbouring Asian countries such as Singapore, Hong Kong, Taiwan, Japan and Korea. A competition to find the 'Pambassadors' was launched with a host of events around the world and both traditional and social media used to promote digital content.

The results were impressive with the number of international tourists visiting Chengdu increasing by 30.3 per cent. In addition to measuring the tourism rates the campaign was evaluated by media coverage, fan engagement, awareness, action and commercial value. A variety of metrics were used:

- *Traditional media coverage:* 2,852 international media reports in 30 countries and in 13 languages. Media included the *Wall Street Journal,* US networks ABC and CBS, BBC, Global Al Jazeera, Japan's Kyoto News and CCTV China.
- *Social media coverage:* 128 million YouTube channel views on Chengdu.
- A total of 1.6 million impressions were generated across social and traditional media.

- *Creating deeper fan engagement:* 410,000 Facebook fans. Facebook PTAT (people talking about this) scores were higher than for Visit London or other tourism campaigns.

City/country Facebook page	Likes	PTAT	PTAT score
Chengdu Pambassador	406,344	117,258	29%
Australia	3,835,886	257,834	7%
Visit London	95,484	4,881	5%
New Zealand	657,435	22,349	3%

Source: Facebook (28 November 2012).

- *Driving awareness:* Research indicated awareness of Chengdu's connection to pandas increased from 19 per cent to 43 per cent in the UK, from 14 per cent to 27 per cent in the USA and from 58 per cent to 75 per cent in Singapore.
- *Translating to action:* 16,495 daily Google searches for Chengdu (representing a 54 per cent daily increase). The campaign attracted 255,000 applicants to live and work in Chengdu.
- *Estimating the commercial value to Chengdu:* The visitor increase accounted for US$161 million in tourism revenue.

Source: AMEC (2014); CNN (2012); WPP (2015).

Question: Why did 'Pambassador' use so many different metrics to measure the public relations campaign? Which metric provides the best measure of the campaign outcomes? Explain why.

Task: Visit the Chengdu Pambassador Facebook page and consider ways that you could evaluate the content.

Public relations

The objectives that are established at the beginning of a campaign must form the basis of any evaluation and testing activity. However, much of the work of public relations (PR) is continuous, and therefore measurement should not be campaign-oriented or time-restricted but undertaken on a regular, ongoing basis. PR is mainly responsible for the identity cues that are presented to the organisation's various stakeholders as part of a planned programme of communications. These cues signal the visibility and profile of the organisation and are used by stakeholders to shape the image that each has of the focus organisation.

PR is, therefore, focused on communications activities, such as awareness, but there are others such as preference, interest and conviction. Evaluation should, in the first instance, measure levels of awareness of the organisation. Attention should then focus on the levels of interest, goodwill and attitudes held towards the organisation as a result of all the planned and unplanned cues used by the organisation.

Traditionally these levels were assumed to have been generated by PR activities. The main method of measuring their contribution to the communications programme was to collect press cuttings and to record the number of mentions the organisation received in the electronic media. These were then collated in a cuttings book that would be presented to the client. While this provides a simple means of measuring media coverage it is not an effective way to evaluate the overall value of a PR campaign.

The content of the cuttings book and the recorded media mentions can be converted into a different currency. The exchange rate used is the cost of the media that would have been incurred had this volume of communications or awareness been generated by advertising activity (advertising value equivalents, or AVEs). For example, a 30-second news item about an organisation's contribution to a charity event may be exchanged for a 30-second advertisement at rate card cost. The temptation is clear, but the validity of the equation is not acceptable. By translating PR into advertising currency, the client is expected not only to understand, but also to approve of, the enhanced credibility that advertising possesses. It is not surprising that the widely held notion that PR is free advertising, has grown so substantially when practitioners use this approach.

A further refinement of the cuttings book is to analyse the material covered. The coverage may be positive or negative, approving or disapproving, so the quality of the cuttings needs to be reviewed in order that the client organisation can make an informed judgement about its next set of decisions. This survey of the material in the cuttings book is referred to as a content analysis and has traditionally been undertaken using a qualitative approach (Macnamara, 2005). Content analysis has been subject to poor interpretation and reviewer bias, however well the task was approached. Today, increasingly sophisticated software is being used to produce a wealth of quantitative data reflecting the key variables that clients want evaluated.

The 2010 Barcelona Declaration of Measurement Principles has set new standards for evaluating PR. As outlined in Viewpoint 8.3, the industry has been encouraged to move away from traditional measures such as AVEs and consider measuring the effect on outcomes rather than outputs. Among the principles is the need to measure social media communications. Macnamara (2014) suggests that a key challenge to measuring and evaluating PR comes from the range of terminology used, particularly in social media evaluation, and the inconsistency with which terms are used. To clarify the metrics used across PR and social media communications Macnamara (2014) provides definitions of outputs, outtakes and outcomes (see Table 8.7).

Table 8.7 Metrics used in public relations

Basic outputs	Outputs → outtakes	Outtakes → outcomes
Counts of press clippings	Unique visitors	Engagement
Audience	Views	Influence
Reach	Likes	Impact
Target audience reach	Followers	Awareness
Impressions	Fans	Attitudes
Opportunities to see (OTS)	Clickthroughs	Trust
Share of voice	Downloads	Loyalty
Cost per thousand (CPM)	Comments	Reputation
Hits	Tone	Relationships
Visits	Sentiment	Return on investment (ROI)

Source: Reproduced from Macnamara (2014).

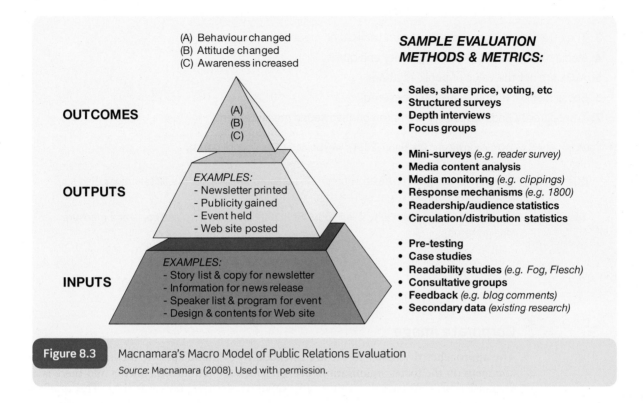

(A) Behaviour changed
(B) Attitude changed
(C) Awareness increased

OUTCOMES

(A)
(B)
(C)

OUTPUTS

EXAMPLES:
- Newsletter printed
- Publicity gained
- Event held
- Web site posted

INPUTS

EXAMPLES:
- Story list & copy for newsletter
- Information for news release
- Speaker list & program for event
- Design & contents for Web site

SAMPLE EVALUATION METHODS & METRICS:

- **Sales, share price, voting, etc**
- **Structured surveys**
- **Depth interviews**
- **Focus groups**

- **Mini-surveys** *(e.g. reader survey)*
- **Media content analysis**
- **Media monitoring** *(e.g. clippings)*
- **Response mechanisms** *(e.g. 1800)*
- **Readership/audience statistics**
- **Circulation/distribution statistics**

- **Pre-testing**
- **Case studies**
- **Readability studies** *(e.g. Fog, Flesch)*
- **Consultative groups**
- **Feedback** *(e.g. blog comments)*
- **Secondary data** *(existing research)*

Figure 8.3	Macnamara's Macro Model of Public Relations Evaluation

Source: Macnamara (2008). Used with permission.

Macnamara (2008) provides a Macro Model of Public Relations Evaluation, which breaks activity into three stages: *inputs*, *outputs* and *outcomes*. The model differentiates between each PR activity and indicates appropriate formal and informal methods of evaluation for each stage (see Figure 8.3).

Viewpoint 8.3	The Barcelona Principles

In 2010 the Barcelona Declaration of Measurement Principles was developed by the International Association for the Measurement and Evaluation of Communications (AMEC) in association with a number of industry bodies, including the Institute of Public Relations and the Public Relations Society of America. The principles represent a significant landmark in public relations measurement since they challenge the premise of using advertising value equivalents (AVEs) and false multipliers as a means of evaluating public relations outcomes. The industry has traditionally used AVEs which provide an equivalent cost of paid media and false multipliers which multiply the AVE by at least twice to provide a value on the earned media to measure public relations outcomes. The Barcelona Principles clearly state that AVEs should not be used as a measure of public relations value.

The principles also place measurement clearly at the top of the public relations agenda, with a focus being on the measurement of campaign effects rather than just outcomes. There is also an emphasis on measuring business results and a requirement that social media should be measured. The principles set the agenda for a new era in public relations measurement and accountability.

The seven Barcelona Principles are as follows:

1. Importance of goal setting and measurement
2. Measuring the effect on outcomes is preferred to measuring outputs

3. The effect on business results can and should be measured where possible

4. Media measurement requires quantity and quality

5. AVEs are not the value of public relations

6. Social media can and should be measured

7. Transparency and replicability are paramount to sound measurement

Source: AMEC (2010); Manning and Rockland (2011); Westminster City Council (2011).

Question: Why are AVEs not seen to be an appropriate measure of value for public relations? Discuss why some practitioners might still be using this method.

Task: Make a list of the reasons why it is important in public relations to set goals and measure campaign results.

Corporate image

The approaches discussed so far are intended to evaluate specific media activity and comment on the focus organisation. Press releases are fed into the media and there is a response that is measured in terms of positive or negative, for or against. This quality of information, while useful, does not assist the management of the corporate identity. To do this requires an evaluation of the position that an organisation has in the eyes of key members of the performance network. In addition, the information is not specific enough to influence the strategic direction that an organisation has or the speed at which the organisation is changing. Indeed, most organisations now experience perpetual change; stability and continuity are terms related to an environment that is unlikely to be repeated.

The evaluation of the corporate image should be a regular exercise, supported by management. There are three main aspects. First, key stakeholders (including employees, as they are an important source of communications for external stakeholders), together with members of the performance network and customers, should be questioned regarding their perceptions of the important attributes of the focus organisation and the business they are in. Second, how does the organisation perform against each of the attributes? Third, how does the organisation perform relative to its main competitors across these attributes?

The results of these perceptions can be evaluated so that corrective action can be directed at particular parts of the organisation and adjustments made to the strategies pursued at business and functional levels. For example, in the computer retailing business, prompt home delivery is a very important attribute. If company A had a rating of 90 per cent on this attribute, but company B was believed to be so good that it was rated at 95 per cent, regardless of actual performance levels, then although A was doing a superb job it would have to improve its delivery service and inform its stakeholders that it was particularly good at this part of the business.

Recruitment

Recruitment for some organisations can be a problem. In some sectors, where skills are in short supply, the best staff gravitate towards those organisations that are perceived to be better employers and provide better rewards and opportunities. Part of the task of corporate public relations (CPR) is to provide the necessary communications so that a target pool of employees is aware of the benefits of working with the focus organisation and develops a desire to work there.

Measurement of this aspect of CPR can be seductive. It is tempting just to measure the attitudes of the pool of talent prior to a campaign and then to measure it again at the end. This fails to account for the uncontrollable elements in CPR, for example the actions of others in the market, but, even if this approach is simplistic and slightly erroneous, it does focus attention on an issue. A major chemical-processing company found that it was failing to attract the necessary number of talented undergraduates, partly because the organisation was perceived as unexciting, bureaucratic and lacking career opportunities. A coordinated marketing communications campaign was targeted at university students, partly at repositioning the organisation in such a way that the students would want to work for it when they finished their degrees. The results indicated that students' approval of the company as a future employer rose substantially in the period following the campaign.

Crisis management

During periods of high environmental turbulence and instability, organisations tend to centralise their decision-making processes and their communications (Quinn and Mintzberg, 1992). When a crisis occurs, communications with stakeholders should increase to keep them informed and aware of developments. It can be observed that crises normally follow a number of phases, during which different types of information must be communicated. When the crisis is over, the organisation enters a period of feedback and development for the organisation. 'What did we do?', 'How did it happen?', 'Why did we do that?' and 'What do we need to do in the future?' are typical questions that socially aware and mature organisations, which are concerned with quality and the needs of their stakeholders, should always ask themselves.

Pearson and Mitroff (1993) report that many organisations do not expose themselves to this learning process in the fear of 'opening up old wounds'. Those organisations that do take action should communicate their actions to reassure all stakeholders that the organisation has done all it can to prevent a recurrence, or at least to minimise the impact should the origin of the crisis be outside the control of management. A further question that needs to be addressed concerns the way the organisation was perceived during the different crisis phases. Was the image consistent? Did it change, and if so why? Management may believe that it did an excellent job in crisis containment, but what really matters is what stakeholders think – it is their attitudes and opinions that matter above all else.

The objective of crisis management is to limit the effect that a crisis might have on an organisation and its stakeholders, assuming the crisis cannot be prevented. The social system in which an organisation operates means that the image held of the organisation may well change as a result of the crisis event. The image does not necessarily become negative. On the contrary, it may be that the strategic credibility of the organisation could be considerably enhanced if the crisis were managed in an open and positive way. However, it is necessary that the image that stakeholders have of an organisation should be tracked on a regular basis. This means that the image and impact of the crisis can be monitored through each of the crisis phases. Sturges et al. (1991) argue that the objective of crisis management is to influence public opinion to the point that 'post-crisis opinions of any stakeholder group are at least positive, or more positive, or not more negative than before the crisis event'. This ties in with the need to monitor corporate image on a regular basis. The management process of scanning the environment for signals of change, along with change in the attitudes and the perception held by stakeholders towards the organisation, make up a joint process that PR activities play a major role in executing.

Scholars' paper 8.3   Evaluating public relations

Macnamara, J. (2014) Breaking the PR measurement and evaluation deadlock: a new approach and model, *AMEC International Summit on Measurement, 'Upping the Game',* Amsterdam, 11-12.

This paper provides a review of public relations evaluation research. The author identifies reasons why practitioners do not undertake evaluation and presents a refined version of the author's seminal Macro Model of Public Relations Evaluation. Types of evaluation are explained including: secondary data, case studies, readability tests, media monitoring, advertising value equivalents, media content analysis, audience and reader surveys, and focus groups.

See also: Watson, T. (2012) The evolution of public relations measurement and evaluation, *Public Relations Review,* 38(3), 390–8.

Measuring the fulfilment of brand promises

Brands make promises and communicate them in one of two main ways. One is to make loud claims about the brand's attributes and the benefits these deliver to customers. This approach tends to rely on advertising and the strength of the brand to deliver the promise. The alternative is not to shout, but to whisper, and then surprise customers by exceeding their expectations when they experience the brand. This is an under-promise/over-deliver strategy, one which reduces risk and places a far greater emphasis on word-of-mouth communications and brand advocacy. This in turn can reduce an organisation's investment in advertising and lead to a redirection of communications effort and resources in order to improve the customer experience.

It follows therefore that there are measurable gaps between the image and perceptions customers have of brands and their actual experiences. Where expectations are exceeded the promise gap is said to be positive. Where customers feel disappointed through experience of a brand, a negative promise gap can be identified. These gaps are reflected in the financial performance of brands.

The Promise Index, reported by Simms (2007), found that, although 66 per cent of the brands surveyed had positive promise gaps, only 15 per cent had gaps that impacted significantly on business performance. Other research by Weber Shandwick found that the main factor for creating brand advocacy was the ability to 'surprise and delight customers'. This survey of 4,000 European consumers, reported by Simms, found that brand advocacy is five times more likely to prompt purchase than advertising.

A related metric, the Net Promoter Score (NPS), seeks to identify how likely an individual is to recommend a brand. Again, a key outcome is that brand growth is driven principally by surprising and delighting customers.

On the basis that brand advocacy is of major importance, two key marketing communications issues emerge. The first concerns how the marketing communications mix should be reformulated in order to encourage brand advocacy. It appears that advertising and mass media have an important role to play in engaging audiences to create awareness and interest. However, more emphasis needs to be given to the other tools and media in order to enhance each customer's experience of a brand beyond their expectations.

The second issue concerns identifying and communicating with passive rather than active advocates. Encouraging customers to talk about a brand means developing content that gives passive advocates a reason to talk about a brand. This means that the message component of the mix needs to be designed away from product attributes and towards stories and memorable events that can be passed on through all customer contact points. This in turn points to a greater use of PR, viral and the use of user-generated content, networks and communities, and the use of staff in creating brand experiences.

Online communications

Online research has grown as the internet population has soared and the measures used have developed through trial and experience. However, the notion that measurement of online communications is easy simply because all that is necessary is 'counting clicks' is misleading. Indeed, when speaking about marketing communications, Roisin Donnelly, UK & Ireland Corporate Marketing Director and Head of Marketing for Procter & Gamble, states that measurement is 'their biggest difficulty'. It is not an issue to measure the overall impact of a campaign but, when measuring the return generated by integrated campaigns, the contribution that word of mouth, blogging, online and PR make, for example, is extremely difficult to isolate (Lannon, 2007).

Viewpoint 8.4   The problem of ad fraud

Ad fraud has become one of the biggest challenges facing the global communications industry today. Estimated to cost brands £6.5 billion a year, ad fraud and non-human traffic (NHT) make it difficult for advertisers to accurately measure their viewability and return on investment.

A number of different types of fraud have emerged, including click fraud and impression fraud, also called botnets, and fake pre-roll. These are all forms of non-human-generated traffic which imitate views or clicks or in the case of fake pre-roll plays videos. The result is that advertisers end up paying for false ad impressions. As well as wasting advertising budgets, ad fraud makes it difficult for brands to evaluate campaign reach, frequency and GRPs.

The non-human impressions essentially contaminate the data used for measurement. Since methods such as marketing mix models and other evaluation techniques rely on the quality of the data input, if the data is flawed so is the model.

Many proprietary tools are now available that allow media buyers and sellers to measure audience delivery, viewability, engagement and geographical delivery separate from non-human traffic.

Source: ComScore (2015); Gilligan (2015); Reid (2014).

Question: Why is ad fraud problematic for the evaluation of campaign effectiveness?

Task: Consider the wider impact that ad fraud has had on the industry and suggest ways that the industry could reduce the impact of ad fraud.

Table 8.8 Criteria to assess website effectiveness

Type of visitor	Cognitive state	Management action
All surfers	Level of awareness that a site exists: aware or not aware	Provide offline and online information and directions
Those aware	Level of interest in the site: interested or not interested	Create interest and curiosity
Those interested	Known route to the site: determined or accidental	Enable greater opportunities for site hit
Determined visitors	Was the visit completed successfully? Transaction or no transaction	Encourage bookmarking and post-purchase communications to permit legitimate dialogue
Those who transacted	Will these visitors return to the site? Retained or not retained	Maintain and enhance top-of-mind site recall

Source: Adapted from Berthon et al. (1996). Used with kind permission from WARC.

Ideas and approaches towards measuring the effectiveness of banner ads and websites, in whatever shape or form, have always been a cause of controversy. The notion that click-through or dwell time represents engagement or a sign of an embryonic relationship has now been dismissed by the majority. The reasons organisations have for setting up a website are many and varied. These might be to establish a presence on the Web, to move to new methods of commercial activity, to enter new markets, to adhere to parent company demands or to supplement current distribution channels. Consequently, it is not practicable to set up a definitive checklist to use as a measure of website effectiveness, although certain principles need to be followed (see Table 8.8).

However, a core activity still persists. This is the need to develop insights and understanding about the nature and characteristics of website visitors. From this it is necessary to develop visitor profiles so that media planners can optimise banner ad placement. Many organisations use free tools such as Google Analytics and Google Trends to analyse web traffic and search volume.

Changes to the transactional aspects associated with online display ads, the emergence of demand-side platforms that aggregate data for from multiple sources, and the development of real-time bidding (see Chapter 19) have all advanced the processes and means by which this core activity is undertaken and through which online advertising is measured and interpreted.

Table 8.9 Types of attribution models

Type of attribution	Advantages	Disadvantages
Last Click	Easy to calculate and monitor	Ignores previous channels and events
Time Decay	Fairer than last click	Overnight breaks distort. Still seen as arbitrary
Efficiency Score	More objective than last click and time decay	Cannot calculate granular metrics
Statistical	Seen as best approach. Can include unconverted users	Resource intensive

Source: IPA (2014).

Attribution modelling is a current method used to evaluate digital ad placements. Also known as path to conversion analysis, this uses Ad Server or Tag Management System (TMS) data to evaluate interactions that occur online to measure the number and function of each channel (IPA, 2014). This works to attribute the channel's role within the consumer's online journey. The IPA identifies four key types of attribution models used and the advantages and disadvantages of each (see Table 8.9). The Last Click method is the easiest measure but does not take previous channels visited into account. Other methods such as Time Decay and Efficiency Score are seen to improve upon Last Click, but are seen as less robust than the Statistical method.

Mobile

Measuring mobile is challenging because much of the mobile analytics is held with the mobile platforms or applications themselves. This makes it difficult for brands to evaluate the success of their campaigns. There is, however, a large number of companies offering a range of mobile analytics and tracking tools that can help. The use of tag management solutions for example can make it easier for brands to evaluate how consumers are engaging with campaign content (MMA, 2012).

The context of how the user is interacting with the mobile device is seen to be an important analytic. Information about the location, time, proximity and mobile device allows the brand to understand where the consumers are seeing the content, at what time they are viewing it, how close they are to a kiosk or store and what device they are using. Although this information provides valuable data for brands there are also privacy issues to be considered and brands need to be sensitive of this (MMA, 2012).

The IAB provides a framework for measuring mobile engagement which identifies three categories of measurement: cognitive, behavioural and emotional (2015). The IAB framework suggests each category can be measured using specific metrics. Cognitive engagement, for example, can use metrics such as Campaign Awareness, Brand Message Recall, Attribute Recall and other measures which identify how consumers are thinking differently about the brand or message. While a number of behavioural engagement metrics are identified, including viewthroughs and location, the IAB suggests metrics such as movement (shakes or tilts) and calls are important for mobile. Metrics for emotional engagement include change in Baseline Brand Perception, Favourability and Loyalty. Additionally, physiological response can be used to measure emotional engagement (IAB, 2015).

Social media

Ideas and approaches to measuring social media activities are in their infancy (Murdough, 2009), and as such many of the tools, techniques and our understanding are evolving. An example of this development is the misplaced reliance on counting the numbers of clicks, fans and followers and using these as surrogate measures of social media activity (Owyang, 2011). What is more relevant is measuring what these fans and followers do, the outcomes of the social media activities.

For example, rather than count the number of blogs and tweets, it is thought that a measure of the level of social influence exacted is more appropriate. This is because online influence can help attract and develop brand ambassadors, and also convey an intention to interact with consumers (McCormick, 2011). The IPA (2014) highlights a number of common mistakes made by organisations when trying to measure their social media:

- vanity metrics;
- fake followers;
- the wrong number of KPIs;
- perverse incentives;
- benchmarking problems;
- attempting to replicate GRPs too closely.

Buckley (2013) argues that social media need to be measured against the business objectives set and should demonstrate a return on investment (ROI). To assist in measuring social media, Buckley (2013) suggests it is best practice to use a variety of tools to evaluate social media as each has different functions (see Table 8.10).

Table 8.10 Measurement tools for social media

Evaluation	Function	Examples
Listening and monitoring	Overview of all public-related conversation online	Radian6, Crimson Hexagon, Sysomos, Netbase, Synthesio
Third-party-owned channel performance and competitor tracking	Tracking of owned and competitor channel performance	Simply Measured, Social Bakers
Social CMS analytics	Data available through the social content management solution	Buddy Media, Hootsuite
Platform analytics	Data available through the platform	Facebook Insights, YouTube Analytics

Source: Buckley (2013).

Viewpoint 8.5   Evaluating tweets

Westminster City Council is seen to set the standard when it comes to social media evaluation. Westminster's communications and strategy team evaluate their communications activity on a daily basis. Based on a morning meeting to update the communications team on media coverage and meetings with the research team to discuss planned activity, evaluation is seen to be a key part of the communications process. In addition to the daily meetings that take place the team hold a weekly operational management meeting to evaluate ongoing communications activity and campaign outcomes.

A tweet deck is also used to provide continual monitoring of social media and team members contribute to conversations when it is seen to be appropriate.

The 'Westminster Model' suggests that to evaluate Twitter an organisation first needs to decide what the objectives are and outlines three main reasons:

- to gain a better understanding of what is happening in a particular sector or among particular groups. Evaluating who is tweeting regularly will be important.
- *Connections* – to build the number of people that follow your tweets. More importantly, to ensure that you have highly connected and influential followers. Evaluate who follows you.

● *Getting the message out* – timing and quality are key to getting a message to go far. Evaluate what messages work and which ones don't.

Westminster Council uses a number of tools to monitor and evaluate its communications and recommends a number of Twitter evaluation tools:

www.twaxxup.com

http://hashtags.org

http://tweetreach.com

http://bufferapp.com

www.klout.com

It advocates continuous monitoring of all social media sites and platforms, and suggests that evaluation should include consideration of the credibility of the author, the tone of the message, comments and debate.

Source: Cartmell (2011); Westminster City Council (2011).

Question: Why do you think Westminster City Council continuously monitors Twitter?

Task: Visit the website for two of the recommended Twitter evaluation tools mentioned above and make a list of what each tool measures. Compare and contrast each tool.

From this we should conclude that measurement should focus on the associated business outcomes arising from the deliberate use of social media. This might be related to the level of influence, leads or conversions, generating conversations and word of mouth, improving customer service and support, or stimulating ideas for brand development.

In order to be able to measure these business outcomes, it is necessary to develop a digital marketing strategy. The strategy and plan should contain the social media goals that are to be achieved (the objectives) and the ways in which performance is to be measured (the metrics), and how the data is to be collected and analysed (the tools or analytics).

The goals can vary from selling more products, and getting more traffic through the website, to increasing a fan base, reaching a specific audience, or getting established as a thought leader. Benchmarks are the quantified goals against which all metrics are measured. These might include current sales volumes or values, the number of hits in Google, various website stats or whatever is relevant to a particular type of business (Hay, 2012).

Another key part of the social media strategy is the channel mix that is to be utilised to reach and engage audiences. Where the engagement takes place is the location for the information to be collected. So, if Facebook, Twitter and a blog are the core channels, then the tools and technologies associated with these channels are going to be the most appropriate: for example, Google Analytics and Hootsuite Analytics (Reid, 2012). At the end of the process the goal is to determine the return on investment. However, as several commentators observe, it can be difficult to derive an accurate ROI in social media.

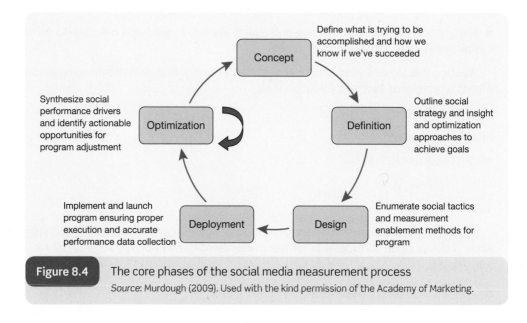

Figure 8.4 The core phases of the social media measurement process
Source: Murdough (2009). Used with the kind permission of the Academy of Marketing.

Murdough (2009) suggests that certain core phases associated with the social media measurement process can be isolated. These are set out in Figure 8.4.

Each of the phases requires a consideration of the goals and both the quantitative and qualitative measures that reveal insight and performance. As Murdough (2009: 95) states: 'Social media is unique in bringing both types of insight together to characterize performance and the value derived from social media efforts.'

Scholars' paper 8.4   **#measuring social**

DiStaso, M.W., McCorkindale, T. and Wright, D.K. (2011) How public relations executives perceive and measure the impact of social media in their organizations, *Public Relations Review*, 37(3), 325–8.

This short paper provides an interesting insight into the views of practitioners regarding the challenges of using social media. The authors explore the questions that public relations executives have about measuring social media and highlight that practitioners hold different views about what should be measured.

See also: Sharma, R., Sharma, H. and Sharma, P. (2014) Measuring the influence and intensity of customer's sentiments in Facebook and Twitter, *Journal of Psychology (JPsych)*, 1(2); Neiger, B.L., Thackeray, R., Burton, S.H., Giraud-Carrier, C.G. and Fagen, M.C. (2012) Evaluating social media's capacity to develop engaged audiences in health promotion settings: use of Twitter metrics as a case study, *Health Promotion Practice*, 14(2), 157–62.

Key points

- The evaluation of a marketing communications plan is a key part of the planning process. The evaluation provides a potentially rich source of material for the future campaigns.

- Evaluation consists of two distinct elements. The first element is concerned with the development and testing of individual messages. For example, a particular advertising campaign. The second element concerns the overall impact and effect that a campaign has on a target audience.

- Pre-testing is the practice of showing unfinished commercials to selected groups of the target audience with a view to refining the commercial to improve effectiveness. The most common methods used to pre-test advertisements are concept testing, focus groups, consumer juries, dummy vehicles, projective assessments, readability, theatre and physiological tests.

- Physiological tests are designed to measure the involuntary responses to stimuli and so avoid the bias inherent in other tests. As there are substantial costs involved with the use of such techniques they are not used a great deal in practice.

- Post-testing is the practice of evaluating ads that have been released. The most common methods are inquiry, recall, recognition and sales-based tests. The main advantage with post-testing is that advertisements are evaluated in their proper environment.

- Public relations (PR) has a number of established forms of measurement and evaluation based on quantitative and qualitative methods. While measurements such as AVEs have been widely used in the past, greater emphasis is being placed on measuring outcomes rather than just outputs.

- Tracking studies involve interviewing a large number of people on a regular basis, weekly or monthly, with the purpose of collecting data about buyers' perceptions of marketing communications messages. Perceptions, attitudes and meanings attributed to campaigns can be tracked and adjustments made to campaigns as necessary.

- Other methods of evaluation include financial analysis, likeability and media mix modelling (MMM). Using media mix modelling requires sophisticated statistical analysis.

- There are measurable gaps between the image and perceptions customers have of brands and their actual experiences. Where expectations are exceeded, the promise gap is said to be positive. Where customers feel disappointed through experience of a brand, a negative promise gap can be identified. These gaps are reflected in the financial performance of brands. The Promise Index and the Net Promoter Score (NPS) are two approaches to measuring the success of delivering brand promises.

- Online communications can be measured in a number of ways, although attribution models are commonly used. Four main types of attribution models exist: Last Click, Time Decay, Efficiency Score and Statistical.

- Social media evaluation is undertaken for a number of reasons: listening and monitoring, third-party-owned channel performance and competitor tracking, social CMS analytics and platform analytics. A range of tools are available to help with each type of evaluation.

Review questions

Millward Brown case questions

1. Why do you think the advertisement was pre-tested in the Millward Brown case?

2. What specific measures were used in the pre-testing? Why were these seen to be important?

3. What were the advantages of using pre-testing in the case?

4. What influence did the pre-testing have on the final editing of the advertisement?

5. Other than Millward Brown's Link™ copy testing tool, what other techniques could have been used to pre-test the advertisement? Would the results have been different and, if so, why?

General questions

1. Explain the difference between pre-testing and post-testing.

2. Explain why AVEs are seen to be a less effective method of measuring public relations outcomes. What other methods could be used to evaluate public relations outcomes?

3. What is the core activity of online communications? Discuss the issues associated with measuring online advertising.

4. What are the challenges with measuring social media communications? Choose two tools available for social media evaluation and visit their websites. Explain what measurements they undertake.

5. Many organisations fail to undertake suitable research to measure the success of their campaigns. Why is this and what can be done to change this situation?

References

Aaker, D.A., Stayman, D.M. and Hagerty, M.R. (1986) Warmth in advertising: measurement, impact, and sequence effects, *Journal of Consumer Research*, 12(4), 365–81.

AMEC (2010) Barcelona summit, *AMEC*, retrieved 10 April 2015 from http://amecorg.com/2010/06/knowledge-share-barcelona-summit-2010/.

AMEC (2014) Chengdu Pambassador: the cutest job in the world, *AMEC Case study*, retrieved 10 April 2015 from http://amecorg.com/case-studies/.

Bellman, S., Schweda, A. and Varan, D. (2009) A comparison of three interactive television ad formats, *Journal of Interactive Advertising*, 10(1), 14–34.

Berthon, P., Pitt, L. and Watson, R. (1996) The World Wide Web as an advertising medium: toward an understanding of conversion efficiency, *Journal of Advertising Research*, 6(1), 43–53.

Brennan, I., Dubas, K.M. and Babin, L.A. (1999) The influence of product-placement type and exposure time on product-placement recognition, *International Journal of Advertising*, 18(3), 323–38.

Buckley, E. (2013) The business return from social media, *Admap*, retrieved 10 April 2015 from www.warc.com/Content/ContentViewer.aspx?MasterContentRef=24ca6283–696c-4822-9dd4-dc62db9807b3&q=the+business+return+for+social+media&CID=A99742&PUB=ADMAP.

Cartmell, M. (2011) Westminster City Council launches evaluation guide, *PR Week*, October 27, retrieved April 10 from www.prweek.com/article/1100625/westminster-city-council-launches-evaluation-guide.

Chang, Y., Yan, J., Zhang, J. and Luo, J. (2010) Online in-game advertising effect: examining the influence of a match between games and advertising, *Journal of Interactive Advertising*, 11(1), 63–73.

CNN (2012) Cutest job in the world? Chengdu seeks panda ambassadors, *CNN*, 11 September, retrieved 10 April 2015 from http://travel.cnn.com/shanghai/life/cutest-job-world-chengdu-seek-panda-ambassadors-532161.

Cobb-Walgren, C.J., Ruble, C.A. and Donthu, N. (1995) Brand equity, brand preference, and purchase intent, *Journal of Advertising*, 24(3), 25–40.

ComScore (2015) Non-human traffic: why it matters and why you should care, *ComScore*, retrieved 1 May 2015 from www.comscore.com/Insights/Presentations-and-Whitepapers/2015/Non-Human-Traffic-Why-it-Matters-and-Why-You-Should-Care.

Dichter, E. (1966) How word-of-mouth advertising works, *Harvard Business Review*, 44 (November/December), 147–66.

DiStaso, M.W., McCorkindale, T. and Wright, D.K. (2011) How public relations executives perceive and measure the impact of social media in their organizations, *Public Relations Review*, 37(3), 325–8.

Ewing, M.T. (2009) Integrated marketing communications measurement and evaluation, *Journal of Marketing Communications,* 15(2–3), 103–17.

Flesch, R. (1974) *The Art of Readable Writing,* New York: Harper & Row.

Gilligan, J. (2015) Facing up to ad fraud: three steps to beat the bots, *Brand Republic,* 20 April, retrieved 10 April 2015 from www.brandrepublic.com/article/1343357/facing-ad-fraud-three-steps-beat-bots.

Gordon, W. (1992) Ad pre-testing's hidden maps, *Admap,* June, 23–7.

Hansen, F., Olsen, J.K. and Lundsteen, S. (2006) The effects of print vs. TV advertising, documented using short-term advertising strength (STAS) measures, *International Journal of Advertising,* 25(4), 431–46.

Hay, D. (2012) 4 simple steps to measuring social media success, *Socialmedia.biz,* retrieved 9 May 2012 from www.socialmedia.biz/2012/03/19/4-steps-to-measuring-social-media-success/.

IAB (2015). Mobile Frameworks and Definitions. IAB Website. Retrieved 7th February 2016 from http://www.iab.com/wp-content/uploads/2015/08/Engagement-Digital-Simplified-Final.pdf

IPA (2014) *How to Evaluate the Effectiveness of Communications Plans,* IPA.

Kerr, G. and Patti, C. (2015) Strategic IMC: from abstract concept to marketing management tool, *Journal of Marketing Communications,* 21(5), 317-339, 1–23.

Krugman, H.E. (1988) Point of view: limits of attention to advertising, *Journal of Advertising Research,* 38, 47–50.

Lannon, J. (2007) Marketing is the boss, *Market Leader,* 39 (Winter), retrieved 27 February 2008 from www.warc.com.

Lee, D.H. and Park, C.W. (2007) Conceptualization and measurement of multidimensionality of integrated marketing communications, *Journal of Advertising Research,* 47(3), 222–36.

Lodish, L.M. and Lubetkin, B. (1992) General truths? *Admap,* February, 9–15.

MacKenzie, S.B. and Lutz, R.J. (1989) An empirical examination of the structural antecedents of attitude toward the ad in an advertising pretesting context, *Journal of Marketing,* 53(2), 48–65.

Macnamara, J. (2005) Media content analysis: its uses, benefits and best practice methodology, *Asia Pacific Public Relations Journal,* 6(1), 1–34.

Macnamara, J.R. (2008) Research in public relations: a review of the use of evaluation and formative research, retrieved 10 April 2015 from http://195.130.87.21:8080/dspace/bitstream/123456789/233/1/Macnamara-research%20in%20public%20relations.pdf.

Macnamara, J. (2014) Breaking the PR measurement and evaluation deadlock: a new approach and model, *AMEC International Summit on Measurement 'Upping the Game',* Amsterdam, 11–12.

Manning, A. and Rockland, D.B. (2011) Understanding the Barcelona Principles, *The Public Relations Strategist,* March 21, retrieved 10 April 2015 from www.prsa.org/Intelligence/TheStrategist/Articles/view/9072/1028/Understanding_the_Barcelona_Principles\#.VW8qWM9VhBc.

McCormick, A. (2011) Online influence, *Revolution,* September, 32–3.

MMA (2012) *The MMA Primer on Mobile Analytics,* Mobile Marketing Association, retrieved 10 June 2015 from www.mmaglobal.com/whitepaper-request?filename=The-MMA-Primer-on-Mobile-Analytics.pdf.

Murdough, C. (2009) Social media measurement: it's not impossible, *Journal of Interactive Advertising,* 10(1), 94–9.

Murphy, C. (2005) Pre-testing: gut or numbers? *Brand Republic,* 15 June, retrieved 10 May 2015 from www.brandrepublic.com/article/480267/pre-testing-gut-numbers.

Neiger, B.L., Thackeray, R., Burton, S.H., Giraud-Carrier, C.G. and Fagen, M. C. (2012) Evaluating social media's capacity to develop engaged audiences in health promotion settings use of Twitter metrics as a case study, *Health Promotion Practice,* 14(2), 157–62.

Olney, T.J., Holbrook, M.B. and Batra, R. (1991) Consumer responses to advertising: the effects of ad content, emotions, and attitude toward the ad on viewing time, *Journal of Consumer Research,* 17(4), 440–53.

Owyang, J. (2011) Number of fans and followers is NOT a business metric – what you do with them is, *webstrategist.com,* retrieved 9 May 2012 from www.webstrategist.com/blog/category/social-media-measurement/.

Pearson, C.M. and Mitroff, I. (1993) From crisis prone to crisis prepared: a framework for crisis management, *Academy of Management Executive,* 7(1), 48–59.

Plassmann, H., Ambler, T., Braeutigam, S. and Kenning, P. (2007) What can advertisers learn from neuroscience? *International Journal of Advertising,* 26(2), 151–75.

Quinn, J.B. and Mintzberg, H. (1992) *The Strategy Process,* 2nd edition, Englewood Cliffs, NJ: Prentice Hall.

Reid, A. (2012) Measuring social media: a step-by-step guide for newbies, *business2communicty.com,* retrieved 9 May 2012 from www.business2community.com/social-media/measuring-social-media-a-step-by-step-guide-for-newbies-0163705.

Reid, N. (2014) Tech viewpoint on online ad fraud, *Brand Republic,* 21 August, retrieved 10 April 2015 from www.brandrepublic.com/article/1308417/tech-viewpoint-online-ad-fraud.

Robson, S. (2002) Group discussions, in *The International Handbook of Market Research Techniques* (ed. Robin Birn), London: Kogan Page.

Sharma, R., Sharma, H. and Sharma, P. (2014) Measuring the influence and intensity of customer's sentiments in Facebook and Twitter, *Journal of Psychology,* 1(2) 47–55.

Simms, J. (2007) Bridging the gap, *Marketing,* 12 December, 26–8.

Smit, E.G., van Meurs, L. and Neijens, P.C. (2006) Effects of advertising likeability: a 10-year perspective, *Journal of Advertising Research,* 46(1), 73–83.

Sturges, D.L., Carrell, B.J., Newsom, D.A. and Barrera, M. (1991) Crisis communication management: the public opinion node and its relationship to environmental nimbus, *SAM Advanced Management Journal,* Summer, 22–7.

Treutler, T., Levine, B. and Marci, C.D. (2010) Biometrics and multi-platform messaging: the medium matters, *Journal of Advertising Research,* 50(3), 243–9.

Turnbull, S. (2011) The creative development process within U.K. advertising agencies: an exploratory study, Unpublished PhD Thesis, University of Portsmouth.

Turnbull, S. and Wheeler, C. (2015) The advertising creative process: a study of UK agencies, *Journal of Marketing Communications,* DOI:10.1080/13527266.2014.1000361, 1–19.

Watson, T. (2012) The evolution of public relations measurement and evaluation, *Public Relations Review,* 38(3), 390–8.

Westminster City Council (2011) *The Westminster Model,* Westminster City Council, retrieved 10 January 2015 from www3.westminster.gov.uk/Newdocstores/publications_store/communications/evaluating_your_comms_aw_lr-1319206316.pdf.

WPP (2015) Panda: global ambassador for Chengdu, *WPP,* retrieved 10 April 2015 from www.wpp.com/govtpractice/our-work/case-studies/ogilvy-pambassador/.

Zielske, H.A. (1982) Does day-after recall penalise 'feeling' ads? *Journal of Advertising Research,* 22(1), 19–22.

Chapter 9

Branding and marketing communications

The images, associations and experiences that customers have with brands, and the brand identities that managers seek to create, need to be closely related if long-run brand purchasing behaviour is to be achieved. Marketing communications plays an integral part in the development of positive brand associations that have meaning, relevance and purpose for customers.

Aims and learning objectives

The aims of this chapter are to explore how marketing communications assists the development and maintenance of brands that engage their respective target audiences.

The learning objectives are to enable readers to:

1. explore the meaning of the brand concept through definitions;
2. understand the variety of brand characteristics;
3. evaluate the significance of associations and personalities in branding;
4. discuss the way in which marketing communications can be used to build and support brands;
5. consider the branding issues within business-to-business, employee and interactive contexts.
6. appraise the nature and characteristics of brand equity.

Branding at the Colruyt Group

The way in which an organisation structures and manages its brands not only affects its overall success but also influences the marketing communications used to support them. The development of brand portfolios is a means of gaining and protecting brand advantage. The fundamental structure of a brand portfolio consists of three main levels: the architecture, the form and the individual brand.

The Colruyt Group is the leading food retailer in Belgium, who began life as a single retail brand, but as the group grew, it became a collection of multiple retail channels and (own) brands. With their recent rapid expansion it became apparent that a managed brand portfolio, including a corporate brand, was needed to provide a hierarchy and a clear distinction between the different retail formulas and brands.

The first step in creating the portfolio was to create the Colruyt Group brand, which acts as the umbrella brand under which all the retail formulas are collected. The Colruyt Group brand acts as a purely non-commercially loaded brand. This creates a clear distinction and purpose for both the Colruyt Group brand as well as for the individual retail brands. This enabled the Colruyt Group to create a 'family of brands'.

The great benefit of creating a clear brand hierarchy is that individual brands can be clearly outlined and they can each be loaded with an individual identity and function. This helps communications in different ways. Corporate social responsibility (CSR) and employer branding is now communicated through the Colruyt Group brand, while the individual retail brands are responsible for communicating their own commercial brand identities.

This strategic development led to an evolution in product brand management. Over the years the Colruyt Group had created over 150 different 'home brands', each of which focused on a different product group. For 95 per cent of customers it was not clearly understood that these were home brands. It also meant that these brands were not able to communicate with a single voice.

The solution involved creating three different layers of retail brands, each reporting into the Colruyt Group. The first layer consisted of the established major international and national brands such as Coca-Cola. The second layer required the creation of a new brand, 'Boni Selection', which incorporated nearly 100 individual own brands. The third layer is 'Everyday', which represents the lowest-price brand. This helped to position the core message for both the home brand and the lowest-price brand. Boni Selection offers added value, whereas Everyday Selection stands for simple, low-priced products for everyday use.

The challenge lay in creating 'Boni Selection', a brand that was accessible for customers yet different enough to have a clear positioning and impact. The solution to this problem was both simple and brilliant. Instead of creating a new private label, Colruyt

Exhibit 9.1	**Colruyt Group**
	Source: Colruyt Group 2013.

Group created a 'homebrand'. In Dutch this is only a one letter difference, but one with a very different connotation. It makes the brand feel more personal and relevant to the customer and positions the brand where it needs to be, in a customer's home.

The next challenge involved informing customers that 'Boni Selection' was made up of a bundle of own brands. Market research showed that only a very few customers understood own brands, most of them considered them to be at the same level as national brands. In itself this is a great asset but not when there is a need to communicate a new brand, one which is replacing the previous group of brands.

The solution required making sure that each food group's conversion to 'Boni Selection' used messages that were clear, both in-store and on the packaging. In addition it was important that it was clear that the particular food group had switched to 'Boni Selection' and what the relevance was to the customer.

The name 'Boni Selection' refers to the early years of Colruyt and is associated with quality and customer service. Using an established name avoided the investment necessary to develop a new brand name. 'Boni Selection' had its roots in trust and quality, and so provides rich ground on which to build. 'Boni Selection' thus represents a valuable alternative to national brands and has its own personality.

The logo has a key role to play in easing a customer's shopping experience. Not only had it to be sufficiently contrasting and recognisable but it also had to avoid clashing with the different types of packaging. The logo acts as a guide throughout the store, so that the 'Boni Selection' range stands out and in doing so simplifies the customer decision-making process.

In much the same way, the packaging needed to be inviting and interesting yet at the same time be clear and convey the brand values of honesty and respect for the customer. The clear and recognisable packaging enables customers to find 'Boni Selection' easily on the shelves.

One of the next steps in this transformation was to communicate these brand layers to both internal and external stakeholders. In order to do so, ground rules needed to be established that enabled everybody to see a clear distinction in terms of what each brand stood for. This is important since certain brands will lose some authority and some will gain more responsibility than they have now. This all needed to be done without losing the overall 'group' image and connectivity.

This simplified brand architecture has helped to deliver a clear consumer message in terms of the values and benefits offered by individual brands. It has helped to create clear distinctions and to communicate individual key brand messages, in order for relevant brand stories to be effective.

This case was written by Pieter-Jan Van Wettere, former Corporate Project Manager at Colruyt Group

Questions relating to this case can be found at the end of this chapter.

Exhibit 9.2	**Boni Selection – logo and branding**
	Source: Colruyt Group 2013.

Introduction

Brands such as 'Boni Selection' mentioned in the case study are promises which frame the way they are positioned in the minds of stakeholders, and which shape their expectations. Ideally these expectations match the promises, which are realised or experienced through brand usage and performance. Brand performance can be experienced directly, perhaps through consumption, sampling, or first-hand interpretation, or indirectly, through observations and comments made by other people and the media. Successful brands deliver consistently on their promises, by meeting or exceeding expectations, and in doing so reinforce the positioning and the credibility of the promise.

Successful brands, therefore, might be considered to encapsulate three core brand elements: promises, positioning and performance. These are depicted in Figure 9.1, as the Three Brand Ps (3BPs).

Central to the interaction of these 3BPs are communications. Communications are used to make the promise known (brand awareness), to position a brand correctly (brand attitude) and to encourage and realise brand performance (brand response). Unsurprisingly, advertising has a critical role to play in building and sustaining this interaction of branding elements.

As the Colruyt case indicates, consistent brand performance, fulfilled brand promises and strong levels of customer satisfaction through time can help consumers to trust a brand. Trust, over time, leads to commitment (Morgan and Hunt, 1994) and is reflected in customers prioritising a brand within their buying repertoire for a product category. Accepting that consumers are active problem-solvers means that brands can be regarded as a way in which the amount of decision-making time and associated perceived risk can be reduced for buyers. This is because brand names provide information about content, taste, durability, quality, price and performance, without requiring a buyer to undertake time-consuming comparison tests with similar offerings or other risk-reduction approaches to purchase decisions.

In much of the literature, brands assume a myopic perspective: namely, one that is centred just on customers. In reality, brands encompass a range of stakeholders (de Lencastre and Côrte-Real, 2010) and branding should be considered not only from a managerial but also from service, relational and social perspectives (Brodie and de Chernatony, 2009).

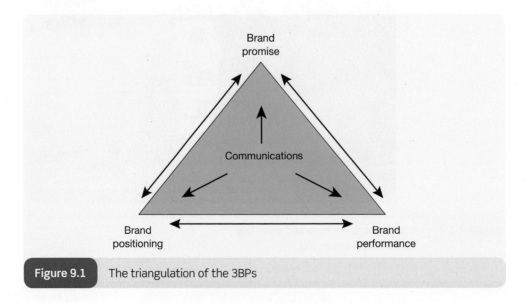

| Figure 9.1 | The triangulation of the 3BPs |

Successful brands such as 'Boni Selection' create strong, positive and lasting impressions, all of which are perceived by audiences to be of value to them personally. Individuals perceive brands without having to purchase or have direct experience of them. The elements that make up this impression are numerous, and research by de Chernatony and Dall'omo Riley (1998a) suggests that there is little close agreement on the definition of a brand. They identified 12 types of definition; among them is the visual approach adopted by Assael (1990) that a brand is the name, symbol, packaging and service reputation. The differentiation approach is typified by Kotler (2000), who argues that a brand is a name, term, sign, symbol or design or a combination of these intended to identify the goods or services of one seller or group of sellers, and to differentiate them from those of competitors. Some of the more commonly quoted definitions are presented in Table 9.1.

In recent times there have been few significant developments in how a brand is defined. There has been increasing recognition of brand co-creation, explored later, and this has evolved into ideas about brand types and typologies. For example, Muzellec et al. (2012) consider how the brand as a concept may now be detached from being merely a physical embodiment. They explore the application of branding to the fictional and computer-synthesised worlds, using examples of virtual brands from books, films, video games and other multi-user virtual environments.

In 2009 de Chernatony suggested that, from a managerial perspective, there is a 'plethora of interpretations', which can lead to brand management inefficiencies. To support his argument, he identifies a spectrum of brand interpretations, ranging from differentiation through to added value. He suggests a brand might be defined 'as a cluster of values that enables a promise to be made about a unique and welcomed experience'.

What these researchers have identified is that brands are a product of the work of managers who attempt to augment their products with values and associations that are recognised by, and are meaningful to, their customers. In other words, brands are a composite of two main logics: the first is an identity that managers wish to portray, while the second is images, construed by audiences, of the identities they perceive. The development of Web 2.0 and user-generated content in the form of blogs, wikis and social

Table 9.1 Brand definitions

Author	Brand definition
Alexander (American Marketing Association, 1960)	'A name, term, sign, symbol, or design, or a combination of them, intended to identify the goods or services of one seller or group of sellers and to differentiate them from those of competitors.'
Assael (1990)	'Name, symbol, packaging and service reputation.'
Schmitt (1999)	'A rich source of sensory, affective, and cognitive associations that result in memorable and rewarding brand experiences.'
Riezebos (2003)	'Every sign that is capable of distinguishing the goods or services of a company and that can have a certain meaning for consumers both in material and in immaterial terms.'
Keller (2008)	'Something that has actually created a certain amount of awareness, reputation, prominence . . . in the marketplace.'
American Marketing Association (2014)	'A customer experience represented by a collection of images and ideas; often, it refers to a symbol such as a name, logo, slogan, and design scheme.'
Aaker (2014)	This last definition refers to 'brand and branding': 'an organisation's promise to a customer to deliver what a brand stands for . . . in terms of functional benefits but also emotional, self-expressive and social benefits.'

networks has added a new dimension to the managerial-driven perspective of brands. Consumers are assuming a greater role in defining what a brand means to them, and now they are prone to sharing this with their friends, family and contacts rather than with the organisation itself. What this means is that brand managers have reduced levels of influence over the way their brands are perceived and this in turn impacts on the influence they have in managing brand reputation.

It is important, therefore, to recognise that both managers and customers are involved in the branding process. In the past, the emphasis and control of brands rested squarely with brand owners. Today, this influence has shifted to consumers as they redefine what brands mean to them and how they differentiate among similar offerings and associate certain attributes or feelings and emotions with particular brands. Indeed, there is now a discussion about whether brands should be considered outside the narrow marketing perspective, since they are a construct of a wider realm of influences. For those interested in these issues see Brodie and de Chernatony (2009), and for developments in managerial aspects, see de Chernatony (2009) and de Lencastre and Côrte-Real (2010).

In line with moves towards integrated marketing communications (as presented in Chapter 10), many organisations have moved the balance of their communications mix away from an emphasis on advertising (especially offline) towards other tools and media. For example, mobile phone companies have used advertising to develop brand awareness and positioning and have then used sales promotion and direct marketing activities to provide a greater focus on loyalty and reward programmes. These companies operate in a market where customer retention is a challenge. Customer loss (or churn rate) can exceed 30 per cent per annum, and there was a strong need to develop marketing and communications strategies to reduce this figure and provide for higher customer satisfaction levels and, from that, improved profitability. One solution is to use experiential-based communications – for example, sponsorship of events and festivals – to get closer to customers and drive associations that are of value to audiences. Another has been to foster brand-based relationships through social media.

Scholars' paper 9.1   Brand worlds united

Berthon, P., Pitt, L., Chakrabarti, R., Berthon, J.-P. and Simon, M. (2011) Brand worlds: from articulation to integration, *Journal of Advertising Research (Supplement)*, 51, 182–8.

There are many papers on branding, but this one looks back over the past 50 years of branding research, and provides an interesting view of how brands have evolved. The authors move from the origins of branding through mimesis, expression, and symptom to a self-organising phenomenon. They use Popper's 'Three Worlds' hypothesis (We, I and It) to show how the different streams of branding research can be integrated.

Brand characteristics

The essence of a strong brand is that it is sufficiently differentiated to the extent that it cannot be easily replicated by its competitors. This level of differentiation requires that a brand possess many distinctive characteristics and, to achieve this, it is important to understand how brands are constructed.

Brands consist of two main types of attributes: intrinsic and extrinsic. Intrinsic attributes refer to the functional characteristics of the product, such as its shape, performance and physical capacity. If any of these intrinsic attributes were changed, it would directly alter the product. Extrinsic attributes refer to those elements that are not intrinsic and, if changed, do not alter the material functioning and performance of the product itself: devices such as the brand name, marketing communications, packaging, colour, price and mechanisms that enable consumers to form associations that give meaning to the brand. Buyers often use the extrinsic attributes to help them distinguish one brand from another, because in certain categories it is virtually impossible for them to make decisions based on the intrinsic attributes alone.

Biel (1997) refers to brands being composed of a number of elements. The first refers to the functional abilities a brand claims and can deliver. The particular attributes that distinguish a brand are referred to as *brand skills*. He cites cold remedies and their skill to relieve cold symptoms, for six hours, 12 hours or all day.

The second element is the *personality* of a brand and its fundamental traits concerning lifestyle and perceived values, such as being bland, adventurous, exciting, boring or caring. Brand personification or the transformation into 'a character endowed with human-like characteristics' (Cohen, 2014) is not a new idea. It is, however, an important part of understanding how a brand might be imagined as a person and how a brand is different from other brands (people). See the section on brand associations later in this chapter for more information.

The third branding element is about building a *relationship* with individual buyers. People are said to interact with brands. A two-way relationship can be realistically developed when it is recognised that the brand must interact with the consumer just as much as the consumer must interact with the brand. Blackston (1993) argues that successful branding depends on consumers' perceptions of the attitudes held by the brand towards them as individuals. He illustrates the point with research into the credit card market, where different cards share the same demographic profile of users and the same conventional brand images. Some cards provide recognition or visibility of status, which by association are bestowed upon the owner in the form of power and authority. In this sense the card enhances the user. This contrasts with other cards, where the user may feel intimidated and excluded from the card because as a person the attitudes of the card are perceived to be remote, aloof, condescending and hard to approach. For example, respondents felt the cards were saying, 'If you don't like the conditions, go and get a different card', and 'I'm so well-known and established that I can do as I want'.

The implications for brand development and associated message strategies become clearer. In line with this thinking, Biel cites Fournier (1995), who considers brand/consumer relationships in terms of levels of intimacy, partner quality, attachment, interdependence, commitment and love.

Therefore, Biel sees brands as being made up of three elements: skills, personality and relationships. These combine to form what he regards as 'brand magic', which underpins added value.

A more recent approach to brand development work involves creating a brand experience. Tango was an early pioneer of this approach. Tango used roadshows to create indirect brand-related experiences, such as bungee jumping, trampolining and other out-of-the-norm activities. Fujifilm underpins a great deal of its UK marketing communications with events, if only because they provide opportunities to provide direct experiences, in this case of the features and benefits of Fujifilm's brand values. Their events are grouped under three main headings: exhibitions, product launches and sponsorship. The first two of these enable contact with trade customers and consumers, who can handle the products and become immersed in the brand. They can also provide direct feedback.

Kapferer (2012) refers to a brand identity prism and its six facets (see Figure 9.2). The facets to the left represent a brand's outward expression, while Kapferer argues that those to the right are incorporated within the brand, an *inner expression* or *spirit* as he refers to it. Farhana (2014) refers to the facets 'Physique' (physical attributes) and 'Personality' (human characteristics), which portray the source. The 'Reflection' (image of target audience) and 'Self-image' (how the brand is perceived by the consumers) facets characterise the receiver of brand messages. The two central elements 'Culture' (values) and 'Relationship' (the way of conduct) form a source–receiver linkage.

These facets represent the key dimensions associated with building and maintaining brand identities and are set out in Table 9.2; they are interrelated and define a brand's identity, while also representing the means by which brands can be managed, developed and even extended. All brands consist of a mixture of intrinsic and extrinsic attributes

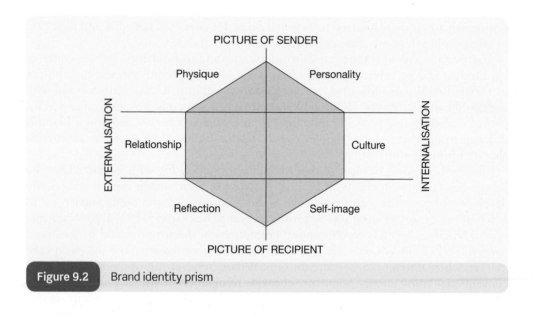

Figure 9.2   Brand identity prism

Table 9.2 Brand facets

Brand facet	Explanation
Physique	Refers to the main physical strength of the brand and its core added value. What does the brand do and what does it look like (e.g. the Coca-Cola bottle)?
Personality	Those human characteristics that best represent the identity, best understood by the use of celebrity spokespersons who provide an instant personality.
Culture	A set of values that are central to a brand's aspirational power and essential for communications and differentiation.
Relationship	A brand's relationship defines the way it behaves and acts towards others. Apple exudes friendliness, IBM orderliness and Nike provocation. Important in the service sector.
Customer reflection	Refers to the way customers see the brand . . . for old people, for sporty people, clever people, people who want to look younger. This is an outward reflection.
Self-image	Refers to how individuals feel about themselves, relative to the brand. This is an inner reflection.

Source: Adapted from Kapferer (2012). Used with permission.

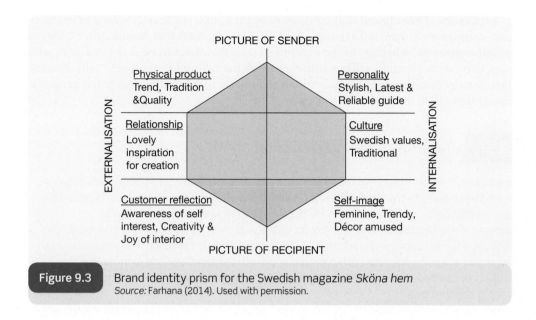

PICTURE OF SENDER

Physical product
Trend, Tradition
&Quality

Personality
Stylish, Latest &
Reliable guide

EXTERNALISATION

Relationship
Lovely
inspiration
for creation

Culture
Swedish values,
Traditional

INTERNALISATION

Customer reflection
Awareness of self
interest, Creativity &
Joy of interior

Self-image
Feminine, Trendy,
Décor amused

PICTURE OF RECIPIENT

Figure 9.3 Brand identity prism for the Swedish magazine *Sköna hem*
Source: Farhana (2014). Used with permission.

and management's task is to decide on the balance between them. Indeed, this decision lies at the heart of branding in the sense that it is the strategy and positioning that lead to strong brands.

Farhana (2014) uses Kapferer's brand prism to interpret the identity of the internationally recognised Swedish lifestyle magazine *Sköna hem*. This is reproduced in Figure 9.3.

The task of marketing communications in branding

Marketing communications plays a vital role in the development of brands and is the means by which products become brands. The way in which marketing communications is used to build brands is determined strategically by the role that the brand is expected to play in achieving an organisation's goals. de Chernatony and Dall'Olmo Riley (1998b) argue that there are several tasks that marketing communications can play in relation to brand development. For example, they suggest the task during brand extensions is to show buyers how the benefits from the established brand have been transferred or extended to the new brand.

Another task, based on the work of Ehrenberg (1974), is to remind buyers and reinforce their perceptions and in doing so defend the market. However, above all of these, marketing communications has a primary task: namely, to build associations through which consumers identify, recognise, understand, assign affection, become attached, and develop relationships with a brand. These associations can be many and varied but they are crucial to brand strength and equity.

Associations and personalities

Successful brands trigger associations in the minds of consumers, and these are not necessarily based on a function or utility. These associations enable consumers to construe an emotional connection with a particular brand. See the Tanishq example at Viewpoint 9.1.

McCracken (1986) found that consumers might search for brands with a personality that complements their self-concept. Belk (1988) suggested that brands offer a means of self-expression, whether this be in terms of who they want to be (a desired self), who they strive to be (an ideal self) or who they think they should be (an ought self). Brands, therefore, provide a means for individuals to indicate to others their preferred personality, as they relate to these 'self' concepts.

Viewpoint 9.1   Tanishq challenges cultural norms

Tanishq is a famous Indian jewellery brand owned by the Tata group. The brand is positioned with a strong appeal for women and has helped to transform the way in which jewellery is bought and sold in India. This has helped Tanishq establish a growing reputation for business ethics and product reliability.

Tanishq uses a range of media to communicate with its target audience but television and video advertising are key to making suitable brand associations. In 2013 it released a film in which it challenged many cultural norms and Indian stereotypes. The core creative approach for jewellery ads in India is either to use a romantic context or to show parents presenting jewellery as a gift to their fair-skinned daughters as part of the wedding celebrations.

In a country where remarriage is considered a taboo, and where widowed and divorced women are regarded as outcasts, the approach adopted by the Tanishq brand broke society's expectations. The film showed a confident, happy dark-skinned woman preparing for her remarriage, accompanied by her young daughter. The ad caused a sensation on social media partly because the ad depicted a dark-skinned woman achieving happiness, whereas society's expectation was that only fair-skinned girls are successful. The ad brought to everyone's attention that attitudes towards single parenting and remarriage in India are becoming increasingly accepting.

The Tanishq ad makes brand associations between the views held by those who are forward thinking and progressive and a brand that seeks to challenge established norms.

Source: Narang (2013); Timmons (2013); www.tanishq.co.in.

Question: Do you believe challenging cultural norms can benefit a brand in the long term?
Task: Find another brand that has openly challenged society's values.

Exhibit 9.3   **Tanishq's ad depicting a woman remarrying shook the established value system**
Source: Created by Lowe Lintas Bangalore.

This emotional and symbolic approach is intended to provide consumers with additional reasons to engage with a brand, beyond the normal functional characteristics a brand offers (Keller, 1998), but which are so easily copied by competitors. Aaker (1997) refers to brand personality as the set of human characteristics that consumers associate with a brand. She developed the Brand Personality Scale, which consists of five main dimensions of psychosocial meaning, which subsume 42 personality traits. The dimensions are sincerity (wholesome, honest, down-to-earth), excitement (exciting, imaginative, daring), competence (intelligent, confident), sophistication (charming, glamorous, smooth), and ruggedness (strong, masculine).

Aaker's initial research was conducted in the mid-1990s and revealed that in the USA, MTV was perceived to be best on excitement, CNN on competence, Levi's on ruggedness, Revlon on sophistication, and Campbell's on sincerity.

These psychosocial dimensions have subsequently become established as dimensions of brand personality. Aaker developed a five-point framework around these dimensions in order to provide a consistent means of measurement. The framework has been used frequently and cited many times by both academics and marketing practitioners. For example, Arora and Stoner (2009) report that various studies have found that consumers choose offerings which they feel possess personalities similar to their own personalities (Linville and Carlston, 1994; Phau and Lau, 2001). They prefer brands that project a personality that is consistent with their self-concepts. As Arora and Stoner (2009: 273) indicate, 'brand personality provides a form of identity for consumers that expresses symbolic meaning for themselves and for others'. Brand personality, therefore, can be construed as a means of creating and maintaining consumer loyalty, if only because this aspect is difficult for competitors to copy. Readers are encouraged to reconsider the ideas about tribal consumption (considered previously in Chapter 3).

Scholars' paper 9.2   **Brand relationships for everyone**

Fournier, S. (1998) Consumers and their brands: developing relationship theory in consumer research, *Journal of Consumer Research*, 24(4), 343–73.

Fournier argues that it is important to understand people's life experiences as this frames the assortment of brands and the relationships they develop with brands. She argues that meaningful consumer brand relationships are shaped not by symbolism/functional category measures, or by involvement, but through the ego significance a brand offers an individual. This much-cited paper should be read by all involved in both academic and practitioner brand management.

See also: Cohen, R.J. (2014) Brand personification: introduction and overview, *Psychology and Marketing*, 31(1), 1–30.

Ideas about brand personification are important when considering brand associations. Cohen (2014) identifies four different ways in which brand personification can be used. The first involves a brand being anthropomorphised or changed into a form with human-like characteristics. Kellogg's used 'Tony the Tiger' to represent their cereal brand Frosties. The second involves associating the brand with an object with human-like characteristics. These could be items used to illustrate brand attributes that speak to the viewer but which are not an integral part of the way the brand functions.

A third interpretation involves a real person, not an anthropomorphised animal or object, to represent or symbolise particular product benefits or values. This might be a character in an ad that depicts a service or brand attribute, but not the brand as a whole.

The fourth interpretation of 'brand personification' occurs when the brand itself is personified by the person who founded, built, owned or is known to be the dominant force in the life of the brand. This is accomplished by pairing the brand name with the brand personifier's likeness. Cohen suggests this might be a real photo, an artist's rendering, a caricature or perhaps that person's handwritten signature, or even just the person's name presented in a distinctive but consistent way (see Viewpoint 5.2, where Juan Valdez, a fictional character, became the face of the Colombian coffee market).

Brand ambassadors

Many brands appoint brand ambassadors to help audiences associate particular personality types with a brand and to assist brand positioning. Celebrities are often used to endorse brands because of their high media profile and popularity (see Chapter 2). This provides what Belch and Belch (2013) refer to as 'stopping power', or a way for an ad to stand out in a cluttered media environment and attract the attention of audiences. Belch and Belch also claim that celebrities are also used because they can positively influence the attitudes and perceptions, feelings and intentions a consumer has about a brand. In other words, celebrities impact on the consumer decision-making process.

Celebrities can be used for a campaign or a short series of ads. Others are contracted for a longer period to feature not just in ads but to represent the brand at events, across various media platforms including social media activities, and to help build relationships and open new markets. In this circumstance celebrities are referred to as the face-of-a-brand, or a brand ambassador.

| Viewpoint 9.2 | Rolex embraces brand ambassadors |

The role of brand ambassadors is to attract attention to a brand and transfer their own personal values and personality to the brand.

Rolex, the Swiss manufacturer of luxury watches, uses brand ambassadors as an integral part of its communications. Innovation and a devotion to precision engineering has helped inform its positioning and communications, which in turn enables Rolex to be associated with high prices and very high quality – a brand synonymous with prestige and affluence. Rolex is perceived to be a status item and symbolic of an individual's wealth and achievements.

A substantial part of Rolex's communications strategy is structured around arts, culture, event sponsorship and the use of brand ambassadors. Perhaps the most notable of the events they are involved with is their role as official timekeeper for the prestigious Wimbledon tennis tournament. Other events include 'The Masters' (golf), the 'Maxi Yacht Rolex Cup', the 'Rolex Grand Slam of Eventing' and the 'Hahnenkamm Race' (skiing).

People who become Rolex brand ambassadors are clear winners in their chosen field. Leaders such as Roger Federer in tennis, skiers Carlo Janka and Lindsey Vonn, Zara Phillips in equestrian, and Phil Mickelson and Luke Donald from the world of golf, are just a few who represent the Rolex brand.

Rolex advertising can be considered to be either factually product-orientated, or associative through the use of brand ambassadors and the events they sponsor. Brand ambassadors such as Ed Visteurs, a mountain climber who has conquered 14 of the world's highest peaks without the use of supplemental oxygen, provide a rich form of source credibility.

Ambassadors demonstrate qualities such as endurance and individual achievement, which Rolex hopes others will value and associate with the brand. The individual performance of a brand ambassador is associated with the functional performance of a Rolex watch. This can be observed through an ad which depicts Mercedes Gleitze, who wore a Rolex during her 10-hour swim of the English Channel in 1926 (see Exhibit 9.4). This demonstrated the world's first waterproof watch and the ad associates the functionality of resilience and durability.

Source: Eleftheriou-Smith (2012); Kats (2011); Lufft (2011); www.rolex.com.

Question: To what extent should brand ambassadors be an integral part of contemporary marketing communications?

Task: Find another example where brand ambassadors were used in a campaign, and determine any similarities or differences in their role.

Exhibit 9.4	**Rolex replicates the triumph of Mercedes Gleitze**
	Source: Rolex UK.

Brand ambassadors are used extensively in a variety of markets but they incur risk associated with an ambassador's behaviour and reputation, and the costs can be substantial. For example, Adidas quickly axed one of its global World Cup brand ambassadors, Louis Suarez, from its world-wide campaign, after the Uruguayan footballer striker bit Italy's Giorgio Chiellini during the tournament in Brazil (Joseph, 2014).

Procter & Gamble announced in 2014 that it intended to cut by 50 per cent the number of brand ambassadors. The goal was to simplify the use of ambassadors across multiple markets. With regard to its *Head and Shoulders* brand, P&G moved from using different brand ambassadors in each country to just two, Sofia Vergara and Lionel Messi, across 45 markets (Vizard, 2014a).

Delivering the brand associations

There are various strategic communications approaches to delivering brand associations. However, the initial decision to pursue one association strategy rather than another is partly a function of the size of the available financial resources. They are also partly a function of the context in which the communications are intended to work and the context in which audiences are most likely to interact with the brand and associated messages. However, as a general observation, five main ways to deliver brand associations can be identified (see Figure 9.4):

- *Above-the-line communications:* Should the budget be high, and the need for audience interaction low, then advertising will often be the main way through which brand name associations are shaped. The brand name itself will not need to be related to the function or use experience of the brand as the advertising will be used to create and maintain brand associations. Expressive propositions predominate.

- *Through-the-line communications:* Sometimes the brand strategy requires a behavioural response and so a direct marketing approach. Here some advertising is necessary but in combination with sales promotion, public relations, merchandising and online activity. A mix of functional and expressive associations can be observed.

- *Below-the-line communications:* Where resources are restricted and advertising is not an option, the brand name needs to be closely related to the function and use

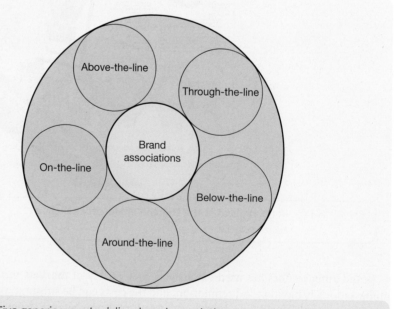

| Figure 9.4 | Five generic ways to deliver brand associations |

experience of the product. In the FMCG sector packaging should also play a significant role in building brand associations. Functional associations tend to predominate.

- *On-the-line communications:* When engagement through a behavioural approach is preferred yet the audience is large and dispersed, a combination of both offline tools and linear and interactive media is used. Initially the penetration of advertising is used to get attention. This is followed by the complementary use of social media and online communications to build relevancy and action. Functional and expressive propositions can be used (see the TfL case at the beginning of Chapter 5).

- *Around-the-line communications:* Whether resources are tight or freely available, there are circumstances when the sole use of a formal mix of brand-building tools and media is inappropriate. In these circumstances word-of-mouth communications and brand experience are sufficient to propel a brand's visibility. Expressive propositions predominate, although both approaches are possible.

Each of these is now considered in turn.

Brand delivery: *above*-the-line communications

When there are sufficient resources, and competitive conditions are intense and margins small, advertising is often the primary means to help consumers to make brand associations. In line with ideas about engagement, two main approaches can be used: a rational or an emotional approach. When a rational approach is used, the functional aspects of a brand are emphasised and the benefit to the consumer is stressed. Very often product performance is the focus of the message and a key attribute is identified and used to position the brand. Typically, unique selling propositions (USPs) were often used to draw attention to a single superior functional advantage that consumers found attractive – for example, a washing powder that washes clothes whiter, drinks that have the highest percentage of fruit juice content and paint that covers more square metres than any other paint.

Many brands now try to present two or even three brand features as the USP has lost ground. For example, when Britvic launched Juice Up into the chilled fruit juice sector to compete with Sunny Delight, it used the higher fruit juice and lower sugar attributes as the main focus of the communications strategy. The rational approach is sometimes referred to as an *informative approach* (and complements functional positioning).

When an emotional approach is used, advertising should provide emotional selling points (ESPs). These can enable consumers to make positive brand associations based on both psychological and socially acceptable meanings; a psychosocial interpretation. Product performance characteristics are dormant while consumers are encouraged to develop positive feelings towards and associations with the brand. A further goal can be to create positive attitudes towards the advertising itself, which in turn can be used to make associations with the brand. In other words, the role of likeability (discussed in Chapter 11) becomes paramount when using an emotional advertising approach. Therefore, these types of advertisements should be relevant and meaningful, credible, and of significant value to the consumer. In essence, therefore, emotional advertising is about people enjoying an advertisement (and complements expressive positioning).

Above-the-line incorporates interactive media advertising with both display and search used to develop strong positive brand associations.

Brand delivery: *through*-the-line communications

As the name suggests, through-the-line offers a blend of above- and below-the-line approaches, with direct marketing playing a strong role in the communications mix. As many brand owners have moved away from using marketing communications for brand-building purposes and then used communications to change or motivate buyer behaviour, so the development of direct marketing emerged.

Through-the-line communications involve the use of advertising to deliver a call-to-action. Often this is associated with sales promotions, events and merchandising, all of which reinforce behaviour. A variety of tools and media can be used in the name of direct marketing, usually configured to complement the business and marketing strategies. In consumer markets advertising is used to drive awareness as well as behaviour, but in business markets advertising has a relatively minor role to play, as greater emphasis is placed on email, trade shows and websites.

Brand associations in consumer markets are therefore driven by advertising, web promotions, direct mail and a functional brand name, all reinforced through brand experience and word-of-mouth communications. In business markets brand associations are normally developed through direct mail, telemarketing, personal selling, trade shows as well as the quality of the website and relationship potential. The name is not always important in terms of providing a functional association. A mix of functional and expressive associations can be observed.

Brand delivery: *below*-the-line communications

When the marketing communications budget is limited or where the target audience cannot be reached reasonably or effectively through advertising, then it is necessary to use various other communications tools to develop brand associations.

Direct marketing and public relations are important methods used to build brand values, especially when consumers experience high involvement. The Internet offers opportunities to build new dot-com brands and the financial services sector has tried to harness this method as part of a multichannel distribution policy. What appears to be important for the development of brands operating with limited resources is the brand name and the merchandising activities, of which packaging, labelling and point of purchase (POP) are crucial. In addition, as differentiation between brands becomes more difficult in terms of content and distinct symbolism, the nature of the service encounter is now recognised to have considerable impact on brand association. The development of loyalty schemes and helplines for FMCG, durable and service-based brands is a testimony to the importance of developing and maintaining positive brand associations.

The below-the-line route needs to achieve image transfer. Apart from the clarity of the brand name, which needs to describe the product functions, it is the packaging and associated labelling that shape the way a brand is perceived.

Brand delivery: *on*-the-line communications

As the multichannel environment becomes more complex and the opportunities to reach consumers become more challenging, so the need to deploy an array of tools and media becomes paramount.

If an audience is large and dispersed, and the financial resources are reasonably strong, advertising, using both linear and interactive media, can be used first to establish brand name awareness. The first phase often involves the use of emotional content delivered through conventional linear media. Sometimes interactive media are used initially to create brand presence (see Viewpoint 9.3). The second phase strengthens the association through frequency of interaction in interactive media environments. This can include games, competitions, communities and promotions that require consumers to return to the site on a reasonably frequent basis. Managed word-of-mouth communications and viral will also enable reach.

When engagement is routed through a behavioural approach, an element of direct marketing or sales promotion is used to enable responses and register consumer details by driving audiences to websites and social networks. The use of social media becomes an integral element either to enable the completion of the behavioural goals, or to maintain brand interest and frequent usage.

Although functional associations can be established in this way, expressive-based band name associations are more common (see the TfL case at the beginning of Chapter 5).

Brand delivery: *around*-the-line communications

Although not an entirely contemporary strategy, a further approach involves the development of brands without the use of formal communications tools or conventional media. The key to success is to seed the brand through word-of-mouth communications. Two of the most notable examples are Google and Hotmail. Both are global brands and both have been developed without any advertising, sales promotion or direct marketing. They have used some public relations, but their market dominance has been developed through word-of-mouth communications (often viral) and experience through usage strategies.

Communications through social media, in particular social networks, email, viral marketing, blogging and in some cases Twitter, have enabled people to pass on news and views about brands. When opinion leaders and formers are targeted with relevant and interesting brand-related material, they pass on information and views, usually with an exponential impact. Brand-based conversations among consumers enable the development of brand associations.

Brand experience has become an important factor both in marketing practice and in the marketing literature. These experiences are considered to be the 'internal responses (sensations, feelings and thoughts) and behavioural responses evoked by brand-related stimuli that are part of a brand's design and identity, packaging, communications and environments' (Brakus et al., 2009: 53).

Consumers experience brands in a number of ways, but perhaps the most common experiences occur at one of three distinct points. According to Arnould et al. (2002), cited by Brakus et al. (2009), these are when searching for brands, when they buy brands and when they consume them. Brakus et al. (2009) go on to demonstrate that brand experiences consist of four dimensions, all of which vary according to brand type and category. These are sensory, affective, intellectual and behavioural. Therefore, the sound management of these elements and dimensions can have a positive impact on developing the right brand associations.

Viewpoint 9.3   Spreading it on-the-line

The 2015 Marmite on-the-line campaign started with a 60-second digital teaser delivered through social media channels. The message warned of an imminent 'full-scale Marmageddon' ahead of the official TV launch the following week. In particular, Twitter and Facebook and YouTube were used for the teaser activity, which included an evolving and interactive social 'news feed' designed to heighten awareness of 'End Marmite Neglect'. By creating a world 'beyond' the TV commercial, the teaser and its supporting PR and social media campaign were designed to amplify the noise that accompanied the TV campaign. It also served to increase the shareability of the word-of-mouth comments. In addition the campaign served to remind audiences of the 'Love it. Hate it. Just don't forget it' strapline.

The 30-second TV spot appeared on 12 January 2015 and ran until the end of March. It was built on a spoof 'micro-documentary' approach that was designed to 'lay bare the continuing scourge of Marmite Neglect in the UK' that sees 'once beloved Marmite jars cruelly rendered to the back of kitchen cupboards'.

The campaign used a range of media, integrated and sequenced to highlight Marmite and re-establish the brand by provoking conversations both online and offline.

Source: Jenkins (2015); Millington (2015); Johnson (2014).

Question: In the light of their extensive use, to what extent are teaser campaigns likely to be successful?

Task: Identify three other brands that have used the around-the-line approach, and write brief notes explaining why they have been successful.

In addition to these five forms of brand development, there are several additional mechanisms through which brand associations can be fostered. These include: co-branding, geographical identifiers, the use of ingredient brands, support services and award symbols.

Marketing communications is the means through which products can evolve into brands. People make associations immediately they become aware of a brand name. It is the brand manager's task to ensure that the associations made are appropriate and provide a sufficient means of differentiation. By communicating the key strengths and differences of a brand, by explaining how a brand enables customers to create value for themselves, by reinforcing and providing consistency in the messages transmitted, and by enabling consumers to experience brands, a level of integration can be brought to the way a brand is perceived by the target market.

Finally in this section, the importance of branding as a part of integrated marketing communications should not be forgotten and, for this, internal brand education is crucial. The way a brand relates internally to departments and individuals and the way the brand is articulated by senior management are important parts of brand education. Brands are not just external elements – they should form part of the way in which an organisation operates, be part of its internal, cultural configuration (Marquardt et al., 2011). This is explored further in the section on employee branding later in this chapter.

Building brands with marketing communications

Having considered some of the main elements associated with the development of brands, they can now be brought together by a means provided by Keller (2009). He acknowledges the view that brands consist of both rational and emotional elements and that both need to be developed in sequence in order to create strong brand equity or value. He also recognises the importance of developing relevant brand associations.

Keller sees the brand-building processes as a series of steps within a pyramid (see Figure 9.5). The rational blocks are used to build up the left-hand side, and the blocks on the right-hand side reflect the emotional route.

There are four main steps in the brand building process:

1. *Salience or awareness:* The first building block requires that customers are helped to identify with the brand and to enable them to make associations with a specific product class or customer need.

2. *Understanding:* Customers then need to understand what the brand means and to do this links need to be established with various tangible and intangible brand associations.

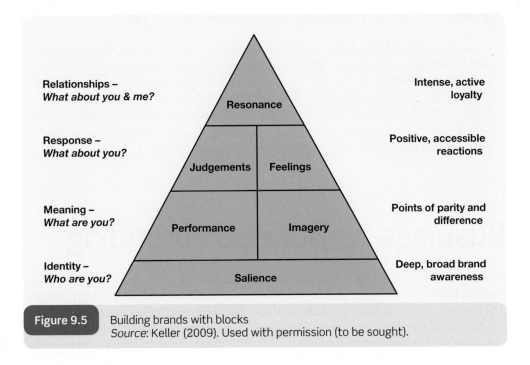

| Figure 9.5 | Building brands with blocks |

Source: Keller (2009). Used with permission (to be sought).

3. *Responses:* At this stage customers should be encouraged to provide responses in terms of their opinions and evaluations. Their feelings towards the brand reflect their emotional reaction towards the brand.

4. *Relationships:* The top of the pyramid represents the final step, the development of an active relationship between customers and the brand. This is referred to as *resonance,* which is the 'intensity or depth of the psychological bond that customers have with the brand, as well as the level of activity engendered by this loyalty' (Keller, 2009: 144).

Reaching the top of the pyramid does not end the brand development journey, as resonance itself has four dimensions: behavioural loyalty, attitudinal attachment, a sense of community or affiliation with other people about a brand, and active engagement.

Brand resonance is most likely to result when marketers create proper salience and breadth and depth of awareness. From this position 'points-of-parity and points-of-difference' (p. 143) need to be established, so that positive judgements and feelings can be made that appeal to both the head and the heart respectively.

What is clear is that Keller considers marketing communications to be an integral element in the way that the various steps and linkages within the brand development process are developed. An integrated approach to marketing communications is necessary in order that brand awareness can be created, that appropriate associations are fostered in order to link the brand image in consumers' memory; positive brand judgements or feelings are stimulated; and/or enabling a strong(er) connection between a consumer and the brand.

It is also advocated that interactive marketing communications is used as an integral brand-building component. This is because of its power and versatility across all of the building blocks of the pyramid. Readers interested in these concepts should see the paper presented at Scholars' paper 9.3.

Scholars' paper 9.3	Building brand resonance

Keller, K.L. (2009) Building strong brands in a modern marketing communications environment, *Journal of Marketing Communications,* **15(2–3), 139–55.**

This paper is a must read for all marketing students and professionals. Keller explains how brands can be developed through various building blocks which form a pyramid, at the top of which is the goal of brand resonance. Keller argues that an understanding of consumer brand knowledge structures underpins the use of marketing communications, which when integrated should enable brand resonance to be achieved.

See also: Lee, L., James, J.D. and Kim, Y.K. (2014) A reconceptualization of brand image, *International Journal of Business Administration,* 5(4), 1–11.

Business-to-business branding

Branding has been used by a number of manufacturers (e.g. Intel, Caterpillar, Cisco, DuPont, FedEx, Teflon, Nutrasweet) to achieve two particular goals. Rich (1996) reports that the first goal is to develop an identity that final end-users perceive as valuable. For example, Intel has developed its microprocessors such that PCs with the Intel brand are seen to be of high quality and credibility. This provides PC manufacturers with an added competitive advantage. The second goal is to establish a stronger relationship with the manufacturer. Nutrasweet works with food manufacturers, advising on recipes, simply because the final product is the context within which Nutrasweet will be evaluated by end-users.

A business-to-business (B2B) brand is often tied closely to the company itself, as opposed to business-to-consumer (B2C) brands, which often distance themselves from the manufacturer or company name. For example, a Rolls-Royce power turbine is branded Rolls-Royce because of the perception of tradition, high quality, performance and global reach that are associated with the Rolls-Royce name. Marketing communications should be developed so that it incorporates and perpetuates the personality of the brand. Thus, all the Rolls-Royce advertising materials should be in corporate colours and contain the logo. All copy should be in the house style and reinforce brand perceptions.

Beverland et al. (2007) offer an alternative model to Kapferer's prism (above) in order to address the needs of the business market. Their approach (see Figure 9.6), uses five main dimensions upon which business brands are built: product, service, adaptation, logistics and advice.

The researchers argue that the tangible elements (product benefits) are normally more prominent at the beginning of a business relationship. However, as the relationship develops and as the decision-making becomes increasingly complex, so there is a shift away from the tangible to the intangible aspects and abstract associations.

The use of event sponsorship, whereby an organisation provides financial support for a conference or exhibition, has become increasingly popular (Miller, 1997). Mainly because of the costs involved, event organisers have sought sponsorship aid. For sponsors, events provide a means of promoting visibility within a narrowly focused target market. In addition, they provide a means of highlighting their own particular contribution within the conference or on their exhibition stand.

The use of joint promotional activities between manufacturers and resellers will continue to be an important form of communications behaviour. The desire to build networks that provide cooperative strength and protection for participants is likely to continue. Manufacturers will use joint promotional activities as a means of forging close

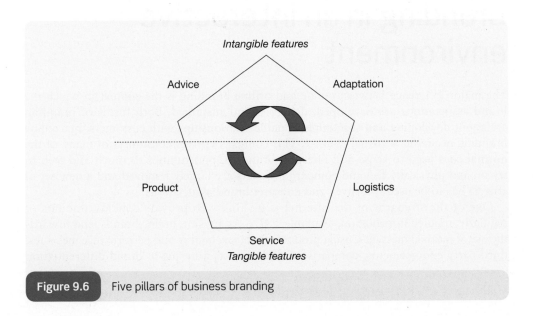

Figure 9.6   Five pillars of business branding

relationships with retailers and as a means of strengthening exit barriers (routes away from relationships).

Mudambi et al. (1997) agree that risk and performance are critical aspects in the buying decision, and that both of these are signalled by a firm's brand. In their investigation of the buying process for industrial precision bearings, they conclude that the development of relationships with individuals within supplier organisations is critical, simply because the final decision can often be a matter of 'personal preference' (Mudambi et al., 1997: 442).

Scholars' paper 9.4 — Business brands

Beverland, M., Napoli, J. and Yakimova, R. (2007) Branding the business marketing offer: exploring brand attributes in business markets, *Journal of Business and Industrial Marketing,* 22(6), 394–9.

This conceptual paper is used to develop five potential strategies for building brands in business markets. The authors refer to the business-market offer, which consists of five components that can be imitated by competitors (products, services and logistics), while two less tangible and difficult-to-imitate components (adaptation and advice) reflect the intangible capabilities of the firm.

Although not as high profile as in the consumer market, branding is a critical aspect in the B2B market. This according to Hynes (2014) is because competitive advantage and differentiation is so difficult to establish, let alone maintain. B2B products are very often bought by groups which include people who are very knowledgeable about price points, product specifications and service offerings. This is partly due to their constant monitoring of the marketplace. In these circumstances the 'brand' is the single most important differentiating factor.

Branding in an interactive environment

The major difference between online and offline branding is the context in which the brand associations are developed, delivered and sustained. Both forms of branding are about developing and sustaining valuable relationships with customers, but online branding occurs in a virtual context. This context deprives consumers of many of the normal cues used to sense and interpret brands. Opportunities to touch and feel, to try on and physically feel and compare products are largely removed and a new set of criteria has to be used to convey and interpret brand associations.

One of the strengths of the Internet is its ability to provide copious amounts of regularly updated information, available '24/7'. As a result, online brands tend towards the use of rational messages, using product attributes, quality and performance measures, third-party endorsements, comparisons and price as a means of brand differentiation and advantage. However, it should be remembered that online branding strategies are influenced by the nature of the brand itself. If the brand has a strong offline presence, then the amount of online branding work will be smaller than if it is a pure-play brand. Branding should be a part of an overall communications strategy, where online and offline work is coordinated.

In 2007–8 the online reliance on rational, informational approaches started to give way as brands became more interactive and capable of emotional engagement. Brand building, once the preserve of offline communications, is now an online expectation.

Each website provides a focus for the brand identity and it is the experience consumers have with a site that determines whether the site will be revisited. The website acts as a prime means of differentiating online brands and those that fail to develop differential advantage will probably learn that visitors are only one click away from leaving a site (Oxley and Miller, 2000). These commentators refer to a site's 'stickiness' and ability to retain visitors, which in turn can increase advertising rate card costs. However, as they point out, a long visit does not necessarily mean that the experience was beneficial, as the site may try to facilitate customer transactions quickly, or enable them to find the information they need without difficulty; in other words, reduced levels of stickiness may be appropriate in some circumstances.

All branding activities need to extend across all key consumer contact points, in both offline and online environments. Internet users generally exhibit goal-directed behaviour and experiential motivations. Goal-directed behaviour that is satisfied is more likely to make people want to return to a site. Therefore, it can be concluded (broadly) that satisfying experiential motivations makes people stay, and in so doing boosts the potency of an online brand. EasyJet built its mobile facility to provide a simple yet functional experience for its customers, as described at Viewpoint 9.4.

Viewpoint 9.4	EasyJet – punctual and very mobile

In 2010 easyJet was a struggling airline, characterised by low-tech services which contributed to a very poor record of punctuality, low profitability, a falling share price and anguish among shareholders. The founder Stelios Hajiloannou had quit the board, and was soon followed by the chairman, the finance director, and then the chief executive. Enter a new chief executive, Carolyn McCall, who proceeded to assemble a new team, including a new marketing director, Peter Duffy, in 2011.

One of the first challenges was to build a simple-to-use mobile website where customers could do all the activities performed on easyJet.com and in six languages. Mobiles are used all along the easyJet customer journey, from searching, buying, amending and ticketing right through to communications regarding any delay or disruption. Some regard the easyJet app as the fastest available to purchase a flight. It has been downloaded over 4.3 million times and over 5 per cent of revenue is now driven through mobile.

It was important to change the punctuality performance so when McCall suggested that easyJet introduce allocated seating, as 75 per cent of customers 'hated' free seating, she was met first with silence and then staff protests. This was because free seating was the fastest way to fill a plane and hence assist the punctuality goal. So, easyJet approached Formula One to learn how it managed pit stops operations in fractions of seconds. The lessons learned are regarded as one of the most successful activities easyJet has accomplished in terms of passengers and revenues.

EasyJet is now top of the punctuality charts and this was reflected in the 'Business Sense' campaign in the autumn of 2014, which was the brand's first business travel TV advertising campaign. The pan-European campaign was supported with print, outdoor and various interactive activities including social media. The campaign focused on the airline's strong punctuality record and highlighted some of the other key business travel services

The airline's success at selling an additional 500,000 seats that it added for the fourth quarter in 2014, including a record number of seats to business travellers, was directly due to the 'Business Sense' campaign.

Exhibit 9.5	**EasyJet now top of the punctuality charts**
	Source: Alamy Images/imageBROKER.

Source: Anon (2014); Hobbs (2015); Orton-Jones (2013); Vizard (2014b).

Question: If punctuality is a key success factor in the airline market, why might easyJet have not focused on the attribute previously?

Task: Find three other key success factors in the airline business and find an example of an airline that features each in its communications.

Further to previous discussion about user-generated content and who might control brands in the twenty-first century, especially within interactive media, readers are directed to Scholars' paper 9.5.

Scholars' paper 9.5	Why mash up Peppa Pig?

Wilkinson, C. and Patterson, A. (2014) Peppa Piggy in the middle of marketers and mashup makers: a netnography of absurd animation on YouTube, in *Brand Mascots* (eds S. Brown and S. Ponsonby-McCabe), London: Routledge, 123–40.

In an age of user-generated content these authors explore the motivations and brand issues associated with the various mashups that have been undertaken in the name of a popular children's cartoon character, Peppa Pig. Students wishing to delve deeper into ideas about user-generated content and branding must read this contribution as it illuminates a murky topic.

Employee branding

Berry (1980) is widely credited as the first to recognise the term 'internal marketing', in a paper that sought to distinguish between product- and service-based marketing activities.

Employees are important to external stakeholders not only because of the tangible aspects of service and production that they provide, but also because of the intangible aspects, such as attitude and the way in which the service is provided: 'How much do they really care?' Images are often based more on the intangible than the tangible aspects of employee communications. Punjaisri et al. (2009) find that employee branding influences the extent to which employees identify with, and are committed to, a brand. They also provide empirical evidence concerning the positive impact of internal communications on the alignment of employee behaviour and their consistent delivery of the brand promise.

Management, on the other hand, is responsible for the allocation of resources and the process and procedures used to create value. Its actions effectively constrain the activities of the organisation and, either consciously or unconsciously, shape the nature and form of the communications the organisation adopts. It is important, therefore, to understand how organisations can influence and affect the communications process.

The role of employees has changed. Once they could be just part of the company fulfilling their core activity, but this role has been extended so that they are now recognised as brand ambassadors (Gelb and Rangarajan, 2014). This is particularly important in service environments where employees represent an interface between an organisation's internal and external environments and where their actions can have a powerful effect in creating images among customers (Schneider and Bowen, 1985; Balmer and Wilkinson, 1991). It is evident that many people now recognise the strategic role of employees as brand ambassadors and their important contribution to brand equity (Gelb and Rangarajan, 2014). Within this context communications play a critical role (Punjaisri et al. 2009).

External communications

The quality of employees' external communications impacts on brand reputation and at one time this was closely controlled by management. Today, employees use social media so that they can have a positive influence on the perception of the organisation among key target audiences. In addition, it can be used to support thought leadership, be an advocate for brands and products, as well as the overall organisation, and can influence profitability and brand equity.

Unfortunately, the use of social media by employees can also have a negative effect. Dreher (2014) identifies three potential issues and cites Smith et al. (2010) and Agresta et al. (2010):

1. Employees are free to create and exchange content in a virtual public arena whether or not it adheres to company policies, communications strategies, or defined brand voices.

2. Once sent, employee messages are accessible to customers, regulators, journal lists and competitors, and can last a long time. The amplification and viral effects of social media extend the reach of employee messages, which can therefore potentially damage an organisation's reputation for a long time.

3. Employee social media messaging transforms the Internet into a real-time medium that can hasten decision-making. Management is required to monitor and listen 24/7 and provide considered responses in a short time span.

These three elements indicate that social media pose significant risks. These include a decline in employee productivity, inconsistent messaging, legal action, regulatory audits and fines, various types of crises, cybercrime and the loss of confidential data, plus the exposure of company secrets, and security breaches.

Social media cannot be fully regulated, nor can they be monitored, controlled, or their impact halted or messages retracted. This means that organisations effectively surrender control and must resort to a proactive approach involving coaching, training, storytelling and informal communications in order to avoid these costly and protracted consequences.

Internal communications

Research by Foreman and Money (1995) indicates that managers see the main components of internal communications falling into three broad areas: development, reward and vision for employees. These will inevitably vary in intensity on a situational basis.

All three of these components have communications as a common linkage. Employees and management (members) need to communicate with one another and with a variety of non-members, and do so through an assortment of methods. Communications with members, wherever they are located geographically, need to be undertaken for a number of reasons. These include the DRIP factors (Chapter 1), but these communications also serve the additional purposes of providing transaction efficiencies and affiliation needs (see Table 9.3).

The values transmitted to customers, suppliers and distributors through external communications need to be reinforced by the values expressed by employees, especially those who interact with these external groups. Internal marketing communications is necessary in order that internal members should be motivated and involved with the brand in such a way that they are able to present a consistent and uniform message to non-members. This is an aspect of integrated marketing communications and involves product- and organisation-centred messages. If there is a set of shared values, internal communications are said to blend and balance the external communications. This process whereby employees are encouraged to communicate with non-members so that organisations ensure that what is promised is realised by customers is referred to as 'living the brand', or 'employee branding'. Hiscock (2002) claims that employees can be segmented according to the degree and type of support they give a brand. He claims that, in the UK, 30 per cent of employees are brand neutral, 22 per cent are brand saboteurs and 48 per cent are brand champions, of whom 33 per cent would talk about the brand positively if asked, and 15 per cent do so spontaneously.

Welch and Jackson (2007) provide an interesting and helpful insight into some of the issues associated with understanding internal communications. Although they assume a stakeholder approach and refrain from considering any related marketing issues, they suggest that internal communications should be considered in terms of four dimensions: internal line management communications; internal peer communications; internal

Table 9.3 The roles of internal marketing communications

DRIP factors	To provide information
	To be persuasive
	To reinforce – reassure/remind
	To differentiate employees/groups
Transactional	To coordinate actions
	To promote the efficient use of resources
	To direct developments
Affiliation	To provide identification
	To motivate personnel
	To promote and coordinate activities with non-members

project communications; and internal corporate communications. These are intended to provide a typology of internal communications and are set out in Table 9.4.

Attention is given to the fourth dimension, internal corporate communications. Welch and Jackson believe that this refers to communications between an organisation's strategic managers and its internal stakeholders, with the purpose of promoting *commitment* to the organisation, a sense of *belonging* (to the organisation), *awareness* of its changing environment and *understanding* of its evolving goals (2007: 186). These four goals are depicted in Figure 9.7.

Table 9.4 Internal communications matrix

Dimension	Level	Direction	Participants	Content
Internal line management communications	Line managers/ supervisors	Predominantly two-way	Line managers– employees	Employees' roles; personal impact, e.g. appraisal discussions, team briefings
Internal team peer communications	Team colleagues	Two-way	Employee–employee	Team information, e.g. team task discussions
Internal project peer communications	Project group colleagues	Two-way	Employee–employee	Project information, e.g. project issues
Internal corporate communications	Strategic managers/ top management	Predominantly one-way	Strategic managers– all employees	Organisational/corporate issues, e.g. goals, objectives, new developments, activities and achievements

Source: Welch and Jackson (2007). © Emerald Group Publishing Limited. All rights reserved.

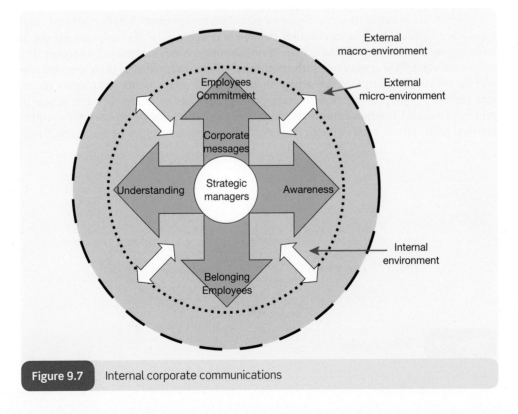

Figure 9.7   Internal corporate communications

These four goals serve to engage employees not only with their roles, tasks and jobs but also with the organisation. It is recognised that the internal environment incorporates the organisation's structure, culture, sub-cultures, processes, behaviour and leadership style and that this interacts with the external environment and provides context for the internal communications. Employees, especially 'the disgruntled within' (Grossman, 2005: 3), represent a real threat to organisations that do not make sure that external and internal messages are consistent and congruent. Just as Cubbage (2005) found, employees with sufficient information about their organisation are more likely to defend it and much less likely to spread malicious content and rumours. Some of these ideas about commitment, belonging and identity with an organisation are explored later in this chapter.

Very often employees perceive the value of internal communications in terms of the richness of information and the media used to convey it. In other words, to quote McLuhan (1964), 'the medium is the message'. White et al. (2010) interpret media richness theory in terms of the different media used to communicate with employees. Email is invariably used for short and fast updates, important information is released through printed paper, while websites are used to alert staff to fresh information but also to archive it for retrieval as necessary. Above all else, interpersonal communications are the richest and most important form of communications to employees, as this strongly influences attitudes and behaviours. This is maximised through personal contact with the CEO and other members of the dominant coalition.

Intellectual and emotional aspects

Employees are required to deliver both the functional aspects of an organisation's offering and the emotional dimensions, particularly in service environments. By attending to these twin elements it is possible that long-term relationships between sellers and buyers can develop effectively. Hardaker and Fill (2005) explore ideas concerning the notion that employees need to buy into organisational vision, goals and strategy and, as White et al. (2010: 67) confirm, 'employees want to know where their organization is headed and how they contribute to achieving the vision'.

This buy-in, or engagement, consists of two main components: intellectual and emotional (see Figure 9.8). The intellectual element is concerned with employees buying in and aligning themselves with the organisation's strategy, issues and overall direction. The emotional element is concerned with employees taking ownership of their contribution and becoming committed to the achievement of stated goals. Communications strategies should be based on the information-processing styles of employees and access to preferred media. Communications should reflect a suitable balance between the need for rational information to meet intellectual needs and expressive types of communications

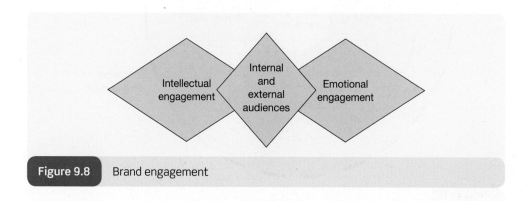

Figure 9.8   Brand engagement

to meet the emotional needs of the workforce. It follows that the better the communications, the higher the level of engagement.

The development of internal brands based around employees can be accomplished effectively and quickly by simply considering the preferred information-processing style of an internal audience. By developing messages that reflect the natural processing style and using a diversity of media that best complement the type of message and the needs of each substantial internal target audience, the communications strategy is more likely to be successful.

The key to successful employee branding hinges upon an organisation's ability to communicate desirable values and goals, as this helps employees to identify with the organisation. This in turn prompts employees to speak positively about the organisation and so influence external stakeholders.

Brand equity

The concept of brand equity has arisen from the increasing recognition that brands represent a value to both organisations and shareholders. Brands as assets can impact heavily on the financial well-being of a company. Indeed, Pirrie (2006: 40) refers to the evidence that organisations with strong brands 'consistently outperform their markets'.

According to Ehrenberg (1993), market share is the only appropriate measure of a brand's equity or value and, as a result, all other measures taken individually are of less significance, and collectively they come together as market share. However, this view excludes the composition of brands, the values that consumers place in them and the financial opportunities that arise with brand development and strength. Keller and Lehmann (2006) argue that the impact and value of brands is reflected on three levels: customer mindset, product market outcomes, and, ultimately, the stock market value of a firm. Indeed, it is this complexity that leads Mizik (2014: 691) to the conclusion that 'the need to quantify marketing's contribution to the financial bottom line is one of the great challenges facing marketing managers'.

Lasser et al. (1995) identify two main perspectives of brand equity: financial and marketing. The financial view is based on a consideration of a brand's value as a definable asset, based on the net present values of discounted future cash flows (Farquhar, 1989). The marketing perspective is grounded in the beliefs, images and core associations consumers have about particular brands. Richards (1997) argues that there are both behavioural and attitudinal elements associated with brands and recognises that these vary between groups and represent fresh segmentation and targeting opportunities.

A further component of the marketing view is the degree of loyalty or retention a brand is able to sustain. Measures of market penetration, involvement, attitudes and purchase intervals (frequency) are typical. Feldwick (1996) used a three-part definition to bring these two approaches together. He suggests brand equity is a composite of:

- *brand value*, based on a financial and accounting base;
- *brand strength*, measuring the strength of a consumer's attachment to a brand;
- *brand description*, represented by the specific attitudes customers have towards a brand.

In addition to these, Cooper and Simmons (1997) offer *brand future* as a further dimension. This is a reflection of a brand's ability to grow and remain unhindered by environmental challenges such as changing retail patterns, alterations in consumer buying methods and developments in technological and regulative fields. As if to reduce the increasing complexity of these measures, Pirrie (2006) argues that brand value needs to be based on the relationship between customer and brand owner and this has to be grounded in the value experienced by the customer, which is subsequently reflected on the company. For consumers the brand value is about 'reduction': reducing search time and costs, reducing perceived quality assurance risks, and making brand associations by reducing social and ego risks. For brand owners, the benefits are concerned with 'enablement'. Pirrie refers to enabling brand extensions, premium pricing and loyalty.

Attempts to measure brand equity by academics and practitioners have to date been varied and have lacked a high level of consensus, although the spirit and ideals behind the concept are virtually the same. Table 9.5 sets out some of the approaches developed by practitioners/consultants. Table 9.6 sets out the major academic approaches (Mirzaei et al. 2011). As a means of synthesising these approaches the following are considered the principal dimensions through which brand equity should be measured:

● *brand dominance:* a measure of its market strength and financial performance;

● *brand associations:* a measure of the beliefs held by buyers about what the brand represents;

● *brand prospects:* a measure of its capacity to grow and extend into new areas.

Brand equity is considered important because of the increasing interest in trying to measure the return on promotional investments. This in turn aids the valuation of brands for balance sheet purposes. A brand with a strong equity is more likely to be able to preserve its customer franchise and so fend off competitor attacks. Farr (2006) determined that the top brands are characterised by four factors. They are all strong in terms of innovation, great customer experience, clear values and strong sector leadership.

| Exhibit 9.6 | **Brand equity and associated factors** |

Source: Fotolia.com/Intheskies.

Table 9.5 Practitioner approaches to measuring brand equity

Source	Factors measured
David Aaker	Awareness, brand associations, perceived quality and market leadership, loyalty, market performance measures.
BrandDynamics (Millward Brown)	Brand – earnings, contribution, multiple.
Brand asset valuator (Young and Rubicam)	Strength (differentiation and relevance), stature (esteem and knowledge).
Interbrand (Omnicom)	Economic profit, the role of the brand, brand strength.
Christodoulides et al. (online brands)	Emotional connection, online experience, responsive service nature, trust and fulfilment.

Source: Adapted from Christodoulides et al. (2006); Cooper and Simmons (1997); Haigh (1997); Mirzaei et al. (2011); Pirrie (2006).

Developing brand equity is a strategy-related issue and whether a financial, marketing or twin approach is adopted, the measurement activity can help focus management activity on brand development. However, there is little agreement about what is measured and how and when it is measured. Ambler and Vakratsas (1998) argue that organisations should not seek a single set of measures simply because of the varying circumstances and contextual factors that impinge on brand performance. In reality, the measures used by most firms share many common elements.

Table 9.6 Academic approaches to measuring brand equity

Author/s	Dimensions	Perspective	Data used
Holbrook (1992)	Price premium	PMO	Price data
Kamakura and Russell (1993)	Brand intangible value and perceived quality	CMO	Scanner panel data
Simon and Sullivan (1993)	Market capitalisation	FMO	Published annual data
Park and Srinivasan (1994)	Attribute-based/non-attribute-based components (market share and price premium)	PMO	Survey/firm/ expert judgement
Yoo and Donthu (2001)	Brand awareness, brand associations, perceived quality	CMO	Customer survey
Ailawadi et al. (2003)	Revenue premium	PMO	Retail sales data
Srinivasan et al. (2005)	Awareness, attribute perception biases, and non-attribute preferences	CMO	Survey/firm/expert judgement
Pappu et al. (2005)	Brand awareness, brand associations, perceived quality, brand loyalty	CMO	Customer survey
Sriram et al. (2007)	Brand choice utility	PMO	Store-level data
Shankar et al. (2008)	Offering value, relative brand importance	CMO	Customer survey/ financial data
Buil et al. (2008)	Brand awareness, perceived quality, brand loyalty, brand associations	CMO	Customer survey

Note: CMO = Customer Mindset Outcomes, PMO = Product Market Outcomes, FMO = Financial Market Outcome.

Source: From Developing a new model for tracking brand equity as a measure of marketing effectiveness, *The Marketing Review*, 11(4), 323–336 (Mirzaei, Gray and Baumann 2011), Reproduced by permission of Westburn Publishers Ltd.

Key points

- Brands are a composite of two main constructs: (1) an identity that managers wish to portray, and (2) images, construed by audiences, of the identities they perceive, as articulated through user-generated content in the form of blogs, wikis and social networks. It is important, therefore, to recognise that both managers and customers are involved in the branding process.

- Brands consist of two main types of attributes: intrinsic and extrinsic. Intrinsic attributes refer to the functional characteristics of the product such as its shape, performance and physical capacity. If any of these intrinsic attributes were changed, it would directly alter the product. Extrinsic attributes refer to those elements that are not intrinsic and if changed do not alter the material functioning and performance of the product itself: devices such as the brand name, marketing communications, packaging, price and mechanisms which enable consumers to form associations that give meaning to the brand.

- Marketing communications can help customers make associations with brands with either a rational or an information-based approach, or alternatively with one based more on imagery and feelings. Brand associations can be developed in one of five main ways: above, through, below, on, and around-the-line.

- Employees constitute a major stakeholder group and have many roles of varying complexity. Internal marketing communications is necessary in order to drive employees' engagement so that they are motivated and aligned with the brand strategy, and able to present a consistent and uniform message to non-members.

- Employees are required to deliver both the functional aspects of an organisation's offering and the emotional dimensions, particularly in service environments.

- The major difference between online and offline branding is the context in which the brand associations are developed and sustained. Both forms of branding are about developing and sustaining valuable relationships with consumers, but online branding occurs in a virtual context. This context deprives consumers of many of the normal cues used to sense and interpret brands. Opportunities to touch and feel, to try on and physically feel and compare products are largely removed, and a new set of criteria has to be used to convey and interpret brand associations.

- Brands as assets can impact heavily on the financial well-being of a company to the extent that organisations with strong brands 'consistently outperform their markets'. There are two main ways of considering brand equity: namely, financial and marketing perspectives.

Review questions

Colruyt case questions

1. Explain the brand promise offered by Colruyt.

2. How does the Colruyt brand structure assist consumers?

3. Apply Biel's concept of 'brand magic' to the 'Boni Selection' brand.

4. Identify the main ways in which the 'Boni Selection' brand might form brand associations.

5. Explain the different ways in which marketing communications can be used to deliver brand associations. Which of these might best apply to the Colruyt Group?

General questions

1. Find three non-FMCG brands and evaluate how their brand strength has been developed without the aid of advertising. How might you improve the strength of these brands?

2. Write a short definition of internal marketing and explain how marketing communications needs to assume both internal and external perspectives.

3. What is the role of internal marketing communications?

4. How might online branding complement offline branding activities?

5. Discuss two approaches to brand equity.

References

Aaker, D. (2014) *Aaker on Branding,* New York: Morgan James.

Aaker, J. (1997) Dimensions of brand personality, *Journal of Marketing Research,* 34 (August), 347–56.

Agresta, S., Bonin, B.B. and Miletsky, J.I. (2010) *Perspectives on Social Media Marketing,* Boston, MA: Course Technology Cengage Learning.

Ailawadi, K.L., Lehmann, D.R. and Neslin, S.A. (2003) Revenue premium as an outcome measure of brand equity, *Journal of Marketing,* 67 (October), 1–17.

Alexander, R.S. (1948) Report of the Definitions Committee – American Marketing Association, *Journal of Marketing,* 13 (October), 202–10.

Ambler, T. and Vakratsas, D. (1998) Why not let the agency decide the advertising? *Market Leader,* 1 (Spring), 32–7.

American Marketing Association (1960) *Marketing Definitions: A Glossary of Marketing Terms,* Chicago, IL: American Marketing Association.

American Marketing Association (2014) *AMA Dictionary,* retrieved 29 May 2015 from www.marketingpower. com/_layouts/dictionary.aspx.

Anon (2014) EasyJet launches £8.5m business ad campaign featuring Hugh Laurie, *B2B Marketing,* 15 September, retrieved 28 January 2015 from www.b2bmarketing. net/news/archive/news-easyjet-launches-%C2%A385m-business-ad-campaign-featuring-hugh-laurie.

Arnould, E.J., Price, L.L. and Zinkhan, G.L. (2002) *Consumers,* 2nd edition, New York: McGraw-Hill.

Arora, R. and Stoner, C. (2009) A mixed method approach to understanding brand personality, *Journal of Product & Brand Management,* 18(4), 272–83.

Assael, H. (1990) *Marketing: Principles and Strategy,* Orlando, FL: Dryden Press.

Balmer, J.M.T. and Wilkinson, A. (1991) Building societies: change, strategy and corporate identity, *Journal of General Management,* 17(2), 22–33.

Belch, G.E. and Belch, M.A. (2013) A content analysis study of the use of celebrity endorsers in magazine advertising, *International Journal of Advertising,* 32(3), 369–89.

Belk, R. (1988) Possessions and the extended self, *Journal of Consumer Research,* 15, 2 (September), 139–68.

Berry, L.L. (1980) Services marketing is different, *Business,* May/June, 24–9.

Berthon, P., Pitt, L., Chakrabarti, R., Berthon J.-P. and Simon, M. (2011) Brand worlds: from articulation to integration, *Journal of Advertising Research (Supplement),* 51, 182–8.

Beverland, M., Napoli, J. and Yakimova, R. (2007) Branding the business marketing offer: exploring brand attributes in business markets, *Journal of Business and Industrial Marketing,* 22(6), 394–9.

Biel, A. (1997) Discovering brand magic: the hardness of the softer side of branding, *International Journal of Advertising*, 16, 199–210.

Blackston, M. (1993) A brand with an attitude: a suitable case for treatment, *Journal of Market Research Society*, 34(3), 231–41.

Brakus, J.J., Scmitt, B.H. and Zarantonello, L. (2009) Brand experience: what is it? How is it measured? Does it affect loyalty? *Journal of Marketing*, 73 (May), 52–68.

Brodie, R.J. and Chernatony de, L. (2009) Towards new conceptualizations of branding: theories of the middle range, *Marketing Theory*, 9(1), 95–100.

Buil, I., de Chernatony, L. and Martinez, E. (2008) A cross-national validation of the consumer-based brand equity scale, *Journal of Product and Brand Management*, 17(6), 384–92.

Chernatony de, L. (2009) Towards the holy grail of defining 'brand', *Marketing Theory*, 9(1), 101–5.

Chernatony de, L. and Dall'omo Riley, F. (1998a) Defining a brand: beyond the literature with experts' interpretations, *Journal of Marketing Management*, 14, 417–43.

Chernatony de, L. and Dall'omo Riley, F. (1998b) Expert practitioners' views on roles of brands: implications for marketing communications, *Journal of Marketing Communications*, 4, 87–100.

Christodoulides, G., de Chernatony, L., Furrer, O., Shiu, E. and Abimbola, T. (2006) Conceptualising and measuring the equity of online brands, *Journal of Marketing Management*, 22, 799–825.

Cohen, R.J. (2014) Brand personification: introduction and overview, *Psychology and Marketing*, 31(1), 1–30.

Cooper, A. and Simmons, P. (1997) Brand equity lifestage: an entrepreneurial revolution, TBWA Simmons Palmer, Unpublished working paper.

Cubbage, A.K. (2005) Inside voices, *Currents*, 31, 14–19.

Dreher, S. (2014) Social media and the world of work, *Corporate Communications: An International Journal*, 19(4), 344–356.

Ehrenberg, A.S.C. (1974) Repetitive advertising and the consumer, *Journal of Advertising Research*, 14 (April), 25–34.

Ehrenberg, A.S.C. (1993) If you are so strong why aren't you bigger? *Admap*, October, 13–14.

Eleftheriou-Smith, L.-M. (2012) Rolex, Coca-Cola and Google top consumer superbrands of 2012, *Marketing*, 27 February 2012, retrieved 4 August 2012 from www.brandrepublic.com/news/1119186.

Farhana, M. (2014) Implication of brand identity facets on marketing communications of Lifestyle magazine: case

study of a Swedish brand, *Journal of Applied Economics and Business Research*, 4(1), 23–41.

Farquahar, P. (1989) Managing brand equity, *Marketing Research*, 1(9), 24–33.

Farr, A. (2006) Soft measure, hard cash, *Admap*, November, 39–42.

Feldwick, P. (1996) What is brand equity anyway, and how do you measure it? *Journal of Market Research*, 38(2), 85–104.

Foreman, S.K. and Money, A.H. (1995) Internal marketing: concepts, measurements and application, *Journal of Marketing Management*, 11, 755–68.

Fournier, S. (1995) A consumer–brand relationship perspective on brand equity, presentation to Marketing Science Conference on Brand Equity and the Marketing Mix, Tucson, Arizona, 2–3 March, Working paper 111, 13–16.

Fournier, S. (1998) Consumers and their brands: developing relationship theory in consumer research, *Journal of Consumer Research*, 24(4), 343–73.

Gelb, B.D. and Rangarajan, D. (2014) Employee contributions to brand equity, *California Management Review*, 56(2), 95–112.

Grossman, R. (2005) Sometimes it pays to play the fool, *Business Communicator*, 6, 3.

Haigh, D. (1997) Brand valuation: the best thing to ever happen to market research. *Admap*, June, 32–5.

Hardaker, S. and Fill, C. (2005) Corporate service brands: the intellectual and emotional engagement of employees, *Corporate Reputation Review: an International Journal*, 8(1), 365–76.

Hiscock, J. (2002) The brand insiders, *Marketing*, 23 May, 24–5.

Hobbs, T. (2015) EasyJet praises business campaign for generating 'record seats', *Marketing Week*, 27 January 2015, retrieved 28 January 2015 from www.marketingweek.com/2015/01/27/easyjet-praises-business-campaign-for-generating-record-seats/?nocache=true&adfesuccess=1.

Holbrook, M.B. (1992) Product quality, attributes, and brand name as determinants of price: the case of consumer electronics, *Marketing Letter*, 3(1), 71–83.

Hynes, F. (2014) NEWS: Top 20 most valuable B2B brands in world revealed, *B2B Marketing*, 16 September, retrieved 28 September from www.b2bmarketing.net/news/archive/news-top-20-most-valuable-b2b-brands-world-revealed.

Jenkins. H. (2015) Marmite launches digital-first teaser campaign via social, *.rising*, 6 January, retrieved 7 January 2015 from www.dotrising.com/2015/01/06/marmite-launches-digital-first-teaser-campaign-via-social/.

Johnson, B. (2014) Marmite claims Brand of the Year at Marketing Week Engage Awards, *Marketing Week,* 27 June, retrieved 7 January 2015 from www.marketingweek.com/2014/06/27/marmite-claims-brand-of-the-year-at-marketing-week-engage-awards/.

Joseph, S. (2014) Six lessons from the 2014 World Cup for marketers, *Marketing Week,* 14 July, retrieved 22 September 2014 from www.marketingweek.co.uk/sectors/sport/news/six-lessons-from-the-2014-world-cup-for-marketers/4011097.articl.

Kamakura, W.A. and Russell, G.J. (1993) Measuring brand value with scanner data, International *Journal of Research in Marketing,* 10(1), 9–22.

Kapferer, J.-N. (2012) *The New Strategic Brand Management,* London: Kogan Page.

Kats, R. (2011) Rolex taps mobile to make print ad more interactive, *MobileMarketer,* retrieved 4 August 2014 from www.mobilemarketer.com/cms/news/advertising/6063.html.

Keller, K.L. (1998) *Strategic Brand Management: Building, Measuring, and Managing Brand Equity*, Upper Saddle River, NJ: Prentice Hall.

Keller, K.L. (2008) *Strategic Brand Management: Building, Measuring and Managing Brand Equity,* Englewood Cliffs, NJ: Pearson Education.

Keller, K.L. (2009) Building strong brands in a modern marketing communications environment, *Journal of Marketing Communications,* 15(2–3), 139–55.

Keller, K.L. and Lehmann, D.R. (2006) Brands and branding: research findings and future priorities, *Marketing Science,* 25(3), 740–59.

Kotler, P. (2000) *Marketing Management: The Millennium Edition,* Upper Saddle River, NJ: Prentice Hall.

Lasser, W., Mittal, B. and Sharma, A. (1995) Measuring customer based brand equity, *Journal of Consumer Marketing,* 12(4), 11–19.

Lee, L., James, J.D. and Kim, Y.K. (2014) A reconceptualization of brand image, *International Journal of Business Administration,* 5(4), 1–11.

Lencastre de, P. and Côrte-Real, A. (2010) One, two, three: a practical brand anatomy, *Brand Management,* 17(6), 399–412.

Linville, P. and Carlston, D.E. (1994) Social cognition of the self, in *Social Cognition: Impact on Social Psychology* (eds P.G. Devine, D.L. Hamilton and T.M. Ostrom), San Diego, CA: Academic Press, 143–93.

Lufft, O. (2011) Wallpaper magazine allows readers to personalise Rolex ad, *Campaignlive,* 18 May, retrieved 4 August 2014 from www.brandrepublic.com/news/1070630/Wallpaper-magazine-allows-readers-personalise-Rolex-ad/?DCMP=ILC-SEARCH.

Marquardt, A.J., Golicic, S.L. and Davis, D.F. (2011) B2B services branding in the logistics services industry, *Journal of Services Marketing,* 25(1), 47–57.

McCraken, G. (1986) Culture and consumption: a theoretical account of the structure and movement of the cultural meaning of consumer goods, *Journal of Consumer Research,* 13 (June), 71–84.

McLuhan, M. (1964) *Understanding Media: The Extensions of Man,* New York: Mentor.

Miller, R. (1997) Make an event of it, *Marketing,* 5 June, 28.

Millington, A. (2015) Marmite looks to replicate 2013 success by bringing back revamped 'End Marmite Neglect' campaign, *Marketing Week,* 6 January, retrieved 7 January 2015 from www.marketingweek.com/2015/01/06/marmite-looks-to-replicate-2013-success-by-bringing-back-revamped-end-marmite-neglect-campaign/?nocache=true&adfesuccess=1.

Mirzaei, A., Gray, D. and Baumann, C. (2011) Developing a new model for tracking brand equity as a measure of marketing effectiveness, *The Marketing Review,* 11(4), 323–36.

Mizik, N. (2014) Assessing the total financial performance impact of brand equity with limited time-series data, *Journal of Marketing Research,* LI (December), 691–706.

Morgan, R.M. and Hunt, S.D. (1994) The commitment–trust theory of relationship marketing, *Journal of Marketing,* 58 (July), 20–38.

Mudambi, S.M., Doyle, P. and Wong, V. (1997) An exploration of branding in industrial markets, *Industrial Marketing Management,* 26 (September), 433–46.

Muzellec, L., Lynn, T. and Lambkin, M. (2012) Branding in fictional and virtual environments: introducing a new conceptual domain and research agenda, *European Journal of Marketing,* 46(6), 811–26.

Narang, A. (2013) India's top five ads driving buzz are busting stereotypes while celebrating 'Indian-ness', *Marketing Magazine,* 24 December, retrieved 12 September 2015 from www.marketingmagazine.co.uk/article/1225084/indias-top-five-ads-driving-buzz-busting-stereotypes-celebrating-indian-ness.

Orton-Jones, C. (2013) Mobilising the fleet, *The Marketer,* issue 88, May/June, p 20.

Oxley, M. and Miller, J. (2000) Capturing the consumer: ensuring website stickiness, *Admap,* July/August, 21–4.

Pappu, R., Quester, P.G. and Cooksey, R.W. (2005) Consumer-based brand equity: improving the measurement – empirical evidence, *Journal of Product and Brand Management,* 14(3), 143–54.

Park, C.S. and Srinivasan, V. (1994) A survey-based method for measuring and understanding brand equity and its extendibility, *Journal of Marketing Research,* 31(2), 271–88.

Phau, I. and Lau, K.C. (2001) Brand personality and consumer self-expression: single or dual carriageway? *Journal of Brand Management,* 8(6), 428–44.

Pirrie, A. (2006) What value brands? *Admap,* October, 40–2.

Punjaisri, K., Evanschitzky, H. and Wilson, A. (2009) Internal branding: an enabler of employees' brand-supporting behaviours, *Journal of Service Management,* 20(2), 209–26.

Rich, M. (1996) Stamp of approval, *Financial Times,* 29 February, p. 9.

Richards, T. (1997) Measuring the true value of brands, *Admap,* March, 32–6.

Riezebos, R. (2003) *Brand Management: A Theoretical and Practical Approach,* Harlow: Pearson.

Schmitt, B.H. (1999) *Experiential Marketing: How to Get Customers to Sense, Feel, Think, Act, Relate to Your Company and Brands,* New York: Free Press.

Schneider, B. and Bowen, D. (1985) Employee and customer perceptions of service in banks: replication and extension, *Journal of Applied Psychology,* 70, 423–33.

Shankar, V., Azar, P. and Fuller, M. (2008) BRAN*EQT: a multicategory brand equity model and its application at Allstate, *Marketing Science,* 27(4), 567–84.

Simon, C.J. and Sullivan, M.W. (1993) The measurement and determination of brand equity: a financial approach, *Marketing Science,* 12(1), 28–52.

Smith, N., Wollan, R. and Zhou, C. (2010) *Social Media Management Handbook: Everything You Need to Know to Get Social Media Working in Your Business,* Hoboken, NJ: Wiley.

Srinivasan, V., Park, C.S. and Chang, D.R. (2005) An approach to the measurement, analysis, and prediction of brand equity and its sources, *Management Science,* 51(9), 1433–48.

Sriram, S., Balachander, S. and Kalwani, M.U. (2007) Monitoring the dynamics of brand equity using store-level data, *Journal of Marketing,* 71 (April), 61–78.

Timmons, H. (2013) This tearjerker wedding ad is a huge deal in India – it's the bride's second marriage, retrieved 3 August 2014 from http://qz.com/140858/this-tearjerker-wedding-ad-is-a-huge-deal-in-india-its-the-brides-second-marriage/.

Vizard, S. (2014a) P&G to ditch brand ambassadors in cost-cutting drive, *Marketing Week,* 5 September, retrieved 22 September from www.marketingweek.co.uk/sectors/fmcg/news/pg-to-ditch-brand-ambassadors-in-cost-cutting-drive/4011558.article.

Vizard, S. (2014b) The Marketing Society conference round-up: 5 tips on how to cope with disruption, *Marketing Week,* 27 November, retrieved 28 January 2015 from www.marketingweek.com/2014/11/27/the-marketing-society-conference-round-up-5-tips-on-how-to-cope-with-disruption/.

Welch, M. and Jackson, P.R. (2007) Rethinking internal communications: a stakeholder approach, *Corporate Communications: An International Journal,* 12(2), 177–98.

White, C., Vanc, A. and Stafford, G. (2010) Internal communications, information satisfaction, and sense of community: the effect of personal influence, *Journal of Public Relations Research,* 22(1), 65–84.

Wilkinson, C. and Patterson, A. (2014) Peppa Piggy in the middle of marketers and mashup makers: a netnography of absurd animation on YouTube, in *Brand Mascots* (eds S. Brown and S. Ponsonby-McCabe), London: Routledge, 123–40.

Yoo, B. and Donthu, N., (2001) Developing and validating a multidimensional consumer-based brand equity scale, *Journal of Business Research,* 52(1), 1–14.

Chapter 10
Integrated marketing communications

The value of integrated marketing communications (IMC) appears to be universally sup-ported by academics and practitioners. The subject, however, remains theoretically under-developed, empirically unproven and rutted with controversy and disagreement.
Is IMC just a matter of rhetoric or does it deliver enhanced engagement opportunities and cut through?

Aims and learning objectives

The aims of this chapter are to explore the nature and characteristics of integrated marketing communications and to understand the complexities associated with developing and implementing IMC.

The learning objectives are to enable readers to:

1. explore the concept of IMC;
2. explain the background and reasons for the development and interest in IMC;
3. consider which elements need to be integrated;
4. examine definitions of IMC through time;
5. analyse five different interpretations of IMC;
6. discuss the way structure influences IMC.

Oreo cookies

The Oreo cookie was baked for the first time in New York in 1912. It has become the best-selling cookie in the world, and is sold in over 100 countries. In May 2013 production of Oreo biscuits began in the UK, at the Cadbury factory at Sheffield in South Yorkshire. Oreo is a biscuit which consists of a sweet creme filling, sandwiched between two dark chocolate wafers, reflecting the high percentage of cocoa in the biscuit. Today there are numerous variations, including Double Stuf Oreos, peanut butter Oreos, mini Oreos and triple-decker Oreos, whilst green tea Oreos are popular in China.

The UK biscuit market was worth £2.4 billion in 2014 with sweet biscuits making up 60 per cent of the market value. However, the category outlook is problematic as the market is in long-term decline (−2.1 per cent MAT), struggling with a generic product offer, an ageing consumer base and following years of limited investment and innovation from the two leading manufacturers. During this time younger consumers have switched out of biscuits and into more dynamic categories such as crisps and chocolate. Price has tended to be the key battleground, with new category news limited.

Since its UK launch in 2008, Oreo has focused its strategy on two key brand issues: The first was how could we use the brand to attract younger consumers back into the category? The second was the unusual nature of the product – a black sandwich cookie, which meant it struggled for spontaneous awareness when considering biscuits (spontaneous awareness remains only 10 per cent, 7 years post launch). However, the strength of the brand and its global scale meant that prompted awareness is now as high as 90 per cent.

To address the first barrier, and bring younger consumers back to biscuits, we needed to make the messaging relevant to this audience without engaging with them through direct reference to the traditional values associated with biscuits and consumption patterns. The solution lay in breaking out of the usual 'family teatime occasion' behaviour standardised across the category, and instead to leverage a more emotional, playful style.

Initial communications centred on an eating ritual, including one ad which featured a boy demonstrating the technique to his dog. The ritual involves twisting off the chocolate outside wafers, licking the vanilla filling inside, then dunking in a glass of milk. This has become popularised as the 'twist, lick, dunk' routine, and is thought to be embraced by half of all Oreo eaters. This ritual serves to elevate the Oreo, making it more than just a biscuit, more of an eating experience, as associations with childhood and family are thought to be triggered.

Following some initial success, the brand reached out to those already engaged with the brand. They discovered the brand's playful DNA went further still, and that although 'twist, lick and dunk' was seen as a playful ritual, it didn't encompass the full possibilities of how far the brand could stretch. People already play with Oreo, for example through recipes, art and jewellery, so it was a natural step to enable play at a broader, more generic level. We tapped into this behaviour to create a campaign, stretching the brand from being a biscuit you can play with, to being a brand centred about play.

We approached this through a TV creative which was switched from showing people eating biscuits, a functional perspective, to one which showed people creating playfully with Oreos, which was colourful and had a strong visual style.

A 20-second pop art style 'Play with Oreo' spot was rolled out in the UK as part of a wider global campaign. The £1.5 million UK campaign aimed to change the tone, behaviour and mind-set of those engaged with Oreo. This was achieved by enabling a more emotional level of engagement, rather than the previous, more

Exhibit 10.1	**Oreo cookies – 'twist, lick, dunk'**
	Source: Jon Holden.

functional ritual of twist, lick and dunk. The campaign was supported by social, digital and in-store activity plus limited-edition packaging. This was followed by various stunts such as the #oreoeclipse. This featured an outdoor ad which mirrored the movement of the sky throughout the day as the total solar eclipse took place on 20 March 2015. The ad was seen in Edinburgh and London and used data from the Royal Astronomical Society and TimeAndDate.com to track movement in the sky to create a simultaneous 'Oreo eclipse' in the ad. To mark the total eclipse we also produced a translucent cover wrap on a copy of the *Sun*. The wrap was printed in black and literally 'eclipsed' the publication.

One of the outcomes was to drive conversations based on the innovativeness and high visibility of the stunt, which was seen by 15 million people. Indeed, all of Oreo's activity was followed on social media through #oreoeclipse and was supported by content across social media platforms throughout the day. This activity stimulated Vloggers to create their own interpretations of 'Play with Oreo'. The PlayWithOreo website allows consumers to upload their own playful content, whilst we encourage more playful in-store activity, closer to point of purchase in order to leverage prompted awareness. The campaign was even carried through onto the packing, generating millions of free engagement opportunities.

In addition to this change to a playful focus we changed part of our media planning. We moved to an always on strategy, meaning that instead of bursts of television activity, we levelled out our activity so that we are now on air for more weeks. This means our campaign covered a far longer period, 20 weeks instead of 12, which serves to leverage prompted awareness. We have also diverted more of our spend online. This drives a better ROI as proven by econometric modelling. Our approach to integrating our activities using a strategic 'playful' platform has proven successful. Just 12 weeks into the campaign brand sales were up 27 per cent, whilst 56 per cent of Oreo consumers are under 45 compared to 34 per cent of consumers in the total biscuits category.

This case was written by Jonathan Holden, Marketing Manager: Sweet Biscuits at Mondelēz International

Questions relating to this case can be found at the end of this chapter.

Introduction

The Oreo case describes how the brand adopted a strategic platform on which to build an integrated approach to Oreo's marketing communications. The case serves to highlight the many facets and issues associated with driving contemporary campaigns. This chapter explores the essence of IMC, its origins and the key factors that have helped shape its development.

For many years agencies and clients believed that to achieve specific communications effects *on* buyers it was necessary to use particular tools. So, for example, clients were recommended to use advertising to create awareness, sales promotions to generate immediate sales uplifts, and public relations to create interest and goodwill towards a brand. This view held that each tool has specific characteristics and particular communications abilities. As a result, clients were required to deal with a variety of functionally different and independent agencies in order to complete their communications requirements with their various audiences.

This 'specialisation' resulted in a proliferation of advertising agencies, the development of sales promotion houses and, later, the emergence of direct marketing agencies. Public relations specialists stood off from any direct association with marketing. Personal selling had already evolved as a discrete function within organisations. This approach was also legitimised by the development of trade associations and professional management groups (e.g. the Institute of Practitioners in Advertising (UK) and the Institute of Promotional Marketing) that seek to endorse, advance, protect and legitimise the actions of their professions and members. One of the outcomes of this silo perspective and functional development of the marketing communications industry has been entrenchment and an inevitable opposition to change.

Now that clients have begun to reorient their communications away from mass-media approaches to increased levels of interaction with customers, the structural inadequacies of the marketing communications industry has constrained them. IMC has emerged partially as a reaction to this structural inadequacy and the realisation by clients that their communications needs can (and should) be achieved more efficiently and effectively than previously. In other words, just as power has moved from brand manufacturers to multiple retailers and now to consumers, so power is moving from agencies to clients.

This trend away from traditional communications strategies based on mass communications, directing generalised messages to huge segmented audiences, has played a part in the development of IMC. Contemporary strategies are based more on personalised, customer-oriented and technology-driven approaches, and are often referred to as integrated marketing communications (IMC). Duncan and Everett (1993) recall that this new, largely media-oriented approach, has been referred to variously as *orchestration*, *whole egg* and *seamless communications*. More recent notions involve the explicit incorporation of corporate communications, reflected in titles such as integrated marketing and integrated communications.

It is interesting that the rapid development of direct marketing initiatives since the second half of the 1980s and the impact the Internet has made have coincided with a move towards what has become regarded as integrated marketing communications. A further significant development has been the shift in marketing philosophies, from transaction to relationship marketing.

The development of IMC

The word 'integration' has been used in various ways and it is the interpretation of the word that determines whether IMC is real, achievable or even practised. In many ways, reality suggests that the claims many organisations and the communications industry make in the name of IMC are simply a reflection of improved management and coordination of the communications tools.

Early interpretations of IMC were constructed around the idea that integration only concerned the promotional tools and media. Scholars such as Shultz et al. (1993) and Duncan and Everett (1993) led much of the IMC activity and many organisations were enthusiastic about the new ideas, driven by the desire to restructure internally, reduce costs and deliver consistent messages. Kitchen et al. (2004) refer to this as the *inside-out* approach to IMC.

The next phase was characterised by an exploration of the nature, direction and content typified by definitions that introduced management, strategy and brand development into the IMC process. Shimp (2000), among others, supported the explicit introduction of these aspects to IMC.

The next interpretation moved the IMC concept towards an audience- or customer-driven process, one that incorporates ideas concerning relationship marketing. Duncan and Mulhern (2004), cited by Reid (2005), Gronroos (2004) and Duncan (2002), have provided valuable insights into this dimension of IMC, one which Kitchen et al. (2004) refer to as the *outside-in* approach to IMC.

It should be noted that while many writers, such as Kitchen and Shultz (1997, 1998) and Duncan (2002), have written positively and consistently about IMC, other authors such as Cornelissen and Lock (2000), Percy et al. (2001) and Spotts et al. (1998), to name but a few, have been critical of the concept and have doubted the merits inherent in the concept. This dichotomy of views reveals the inherent instability of the IMC concept. Readers interested in a fuller appraisal of IMC are referred to Kitchen et al. (2004) and Cornelissen (2003).

As part of his critique Cornelissen (2003) distinguishes two different themes running through the IMC literature. The first is that IMC is regarded as a predominantly *process*-oriented concept and the second is that it is a *content*-oriented concept. These are examined in a following section.

Unsurprisingly, therefore, there is no agreement about what IMC is, what it encompasses or how it should be measured. Indeed, there is no universally agreed definition and, apart from some anecdotal comment, there is little practical evidence of the application of a strategic, customer-oriented IMC programme. There are numerous claims of IMC practice but these are little more than coordinated communications mix activities using themed messages (inside-out) (see Viewpoint 10.1). Liodice (2008), cited by Smith (2012), reports that only 25 per cent of companies give a positive rating to their IMC programmes.

IMC is a not a proven marketing theory (Cornelissen, 2003). There is no empirical evidence to support the concept, yet the ideas inherent in the overall approach hold value. Although Cornelissen refers to the IMC concept as only worthy of symbolic value, a view later refuted by Kitchen, it does appear that what is integration to one person (or agency or client) may be coordination or simply good professional practice to another.

Kliatchko and Shultz (2014: 380) found that in practice the use of IMC as a marketing framework is limited. Terms such as 'fusion marketing', 'insight-driven marketing', 'holistic marketing', 'marketing is customer experience' and 'integrated business planning' are more common.

Research into IMC practice in Asia by Kliatchko and Shultz (2014: 382) found three key features of IMC practice that were common to both agency and client respondents:

● use of multiple media in planning and delivering marketing communications messages;

● primacy of consumer understanding as the kernel of marketing communications planning and execution;

● use of proprietary frameworks or processes for IMC planning, including measurement tools, by both clients and agencies.

This is interesting because there appears to be no reference to the use of multiple tools, nor is there mention of the importance of the message within IMC.

Reasons for the developing interest in IMC

The interest in IMC has resulted from a variety of drivers. Generally they can be grouped into three main categories: those drivers (or opportunities) that are market-based, those that arise from changing communications, and those that are driven by opportunities arising from within the organisation itself. These are set out in Table 10.1.

The opportunities offered to organisations that contemplate moving to IMC are considerable and it is somewhat surprising that so few organisations have been either willing or able to embrace the approach. One of the main organisational drivers for IMC is the need to become increasingly efficient. Driving down the cost base enables managers to improve profits and levels of productivity. By seeking synergistic advantages through its communications and associated activities and by expecting managers to be able to account for the way in which they consume marketing communications resources, so IMC becomes increasingly attractive. At the same time, organisational structures are changing more frequently and the need to integrate across functional areas reflects the efficiency drive.

From a market perspective, the predominant driver is the reorientation from transaction-based marketing to relationship marketing. The extension of the brand personality concept into brand relationships (Hutton, 1996) requires a customer consideration in terms of asking not only 'What do our customers want?', but also 'What are their values, do they trust us, and are we loyal to them?' By adopting a position designed to enhance trust and commitment, an organisation's external communications need to be consistent and coordinated, if only to avoid information overload and misunderstanding.

Table 10.1 Advantages and disadvantages of IMC

Organisation-based drivers for IMC
1. Increase profits through improved efficiency
2. Drive for greater levels of accountability and responsibility within marketing
3. The emerging need to measure all activities
4. Rapid move towards cross-border marketing
5. Coordinated brand development and competitive advantage
6. Opportunities to utilise management time more productively
7. Provision of a marketing framework to guide and direct employees

Market-based drivers for IMC
8. Greater levels of audience communications literacy
9. Media costs
10. Media and audience fragmentation
11. Stakeholders' need for increasing amounts and diversity of information
12. Greater levels of message clutter
13. Competitor activity and low levels of brand differentiation
14. Move towards developing a customer relationship orientation
15. Development of networks, collaboration and alliances

Communications-based drivers for IMC
16. Technological advances (Internet, databases, big data)
17. Increased message effectiveness through consistency and reinforcement of core messages
18. More effective triggers for brand and message recall
19. More consistent and less confusing brand images
20. Need to build brand reputations and provide clear identity cues

From a communications perspective, the key driver is to provide a series of triggers by which buyers can form brand associations, understand a brand's values and consider the extent to which the brand might become or continue to be a part of their lives, however peripherally. By differentiating the marketing communications, often by providing clarity and simplicity, advantages can be attained.

An integrated approach should attempt to provide a uniform or consistent set of messages. These should be relatively easy to interpret and to assign meaning. This enables audiences to think about and perceive brands within a relational context, and so encourage behaviour as expected by the source. Those organisations that try to practise IMC understand that buyers refer to and receive messages about brands and companies from a wide range of information sources. Harnessing this knowledge is a fundamental step towards enhancing marketing communications.

Scholars' paper 10.1 — IMC – meaning and practice

Kliatchko, J.G. and Shultz, D.E. (2014) Twenty years of IMC, *International Journal of Advertising,* **33(2), 373–90.**

These two authors, both with strong associations with IMC, report on research designed to examine how clients, agencies and other senior executives use IMC and what they understand it to mean. This paper provides a useful record of the development of IMC and considers the similarities and differences between academics' and practitioners' understanding and practice of IMC.

See also: Cornelissen, J.P. (2003) Change, continuity and progress: the concept of integrated marketing communications and marketing communications practice, *Journal of Strategic Marketing*, 11(December), 217–34.

It is useful to itemise the advantages and disadvantages associated with IMC. These are set out in Table 10.2. General opinion suggests that the advantages far outweigh the disadvantages and that increasing numbers of organisations are seeking to improve their IMC resource. As stated earlier, database technology and the Internet have provided great impetus for organisations to review their communications and to implement moves to install a more integrated communications strategy.

Viewpoint 10.1 — Different claims for integration

A popular view of integration is that the goal is to bring together a wide range of disciplines, media and content. For example, when HP launched their ElitePad 900 tablet to business travellers, their press release claimed that they were using an integrated campaign that utilised advertising, experiential, PR and social channels to drive awareness.

The focal point involved two HP brand-wrapped First Great Western trains, running daily on some of the country's most popular business routes. Onboard were brand ambassadors demonstrating the tablet and offering standard class passengers the opportunity to upgrade their carriage to trial the device. These large-scale projects can be difficult to manage and maintain consistency.

Another approach is to attempt to coordinate a much smaller range of variables. For example, although the bulk of Heineken's budget is spent on TV they have developed a more targeted secondary line of communications through online marketing. This is because research has found that video on demand can add to

| Exhibit 10.2 | **HP brand-wrapped two First Great Western trains to launch the ElitePad 900 tablet**
Source: Hewlett Packard. |

the reach of TV and in doing so extend campaign messaging when television advertising is off air. In addition, it has been found that click-through rates for ads made specifically for the Web were between two and six times higher than those for ads repurposed from TV. Here Heineken's integration activity is based on developing a unified message that reflects the brand's TV messaging. This is achieved by developing more original content (video) and then actively matching their media investment with consumer behaviour.

Source: Anon (2013); Warc (2013).

> **Question:**   To what extent are these campaigns integrated? What else could have been included?
>
> **Task:**   Find another campaign and determine which elements have been integrated.

Table 10.2 Advantages and disadvantages of IMC

Advantages of IMC
Provides opportunities to cut communications costs and/or reassign budgets
Has the potential to produce synergistic and more effective communications
Can deliver competitive advantage through clearer positioning
Encourages coordinated brand development with internal and external participants
Provides for increased employee participation and motivation
Has the potential to cause management to review its communications strategy
Requires a change in culture and fosters a customer focus
Provides a benchmark for the development of communications activities
Can lead to a cut in the number of agencies supporting a brand

Disadvantages of IMC
Encourages centralisation and formal/bureaucratic procedures
Can require increased management time seeking agreement from all involved parties
Suggests uniformity and single message
Tendency to standardisation might negate or dilute creative opportunities
Global brands restricted in terms of local adaptation
Normally requires cultural change from employees and encourages resistance
Has the potential to severely damage a brand's reputation if incorrectly managed
Can lead to mediocrity as no single agency network has access to all sources of communications

What is to be integrated?

The notion that some aspects of marketing communications should be integrated begs two questions. First, what is it that needs to be integrated, and, second, what are the means by which integrated is achieved, so that it can be recognised and measured?

While the origins of IMC might be found in the prevailing structural conditions and the needs of particular industry participants, an understanding of what elements should be integrated in order to achieve IMC needs to be established.

The problem with answering this question is that unless there is an agreement about what IMC is, then identifying appropriate elements is far from easy, practical or in anyone's best interests. Figure 10.1 shows some of the elements that need integrating.

The following represents some of the fundamental elements, but readers are advised to consider some of the other issues that have been raised in this chapter before confirming their views about this stimulating yet relatively young concept.

Communications tools

One of the early and more popular views of IMC was that the messages conveyed by each of the 'promotional' tools should be harmonised in order that audiences perceive a consistent set of meanings within the messages they receive. One interpretation of this perspective is that the key visual triggers (design, colours, form and tag line) used in advertising should be replicated across the range of tools used, including POP and the sales force. At another level, integration is about bringing together the communications tools (Pitta et al., 2006). One such combination is the closer alliance of advertising with public relations. Increasing audience fragmentation means that it is more difficult to locate target audiences and communicate with them in a meaningful way. By utilising the power of public relations to get advertisements talked about, what the trade refers to as media equivalents, a form of communications consistency, or integration to some, becomes possible.

The rapid development of direct marketing approaches has helped some organisations bring together the different tools such that they undertake more precise roles and reinforce each other. For example, the use of direct mail and telemarketing to follow through on an ad campaign was commonplace. Now web-enabled communications facilitate the linking together of customer care centres and sales promotions, through database applications, so that the same core message is conveyed.

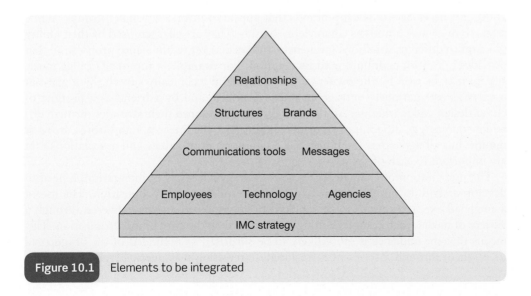

Figure 10.1   Elements to be integrated

Messages

A further interpretation, at a deeper level, is that the theme and set of core messages used in any campaign should first be determined and then deployed as an integrated whole across the communications mix (sometimes referred to as *synergy*). One of the differences is the recognition that mass-media advertising is not always the only way to launch consumer or business-to-business promotional activities, and that a consideration of the most appropriate mix of communications tools and media might be a better starting point when formulating campaigns.

Another perspective of IMC, provided by Duncan and Moriarty (1998), is that stakeholders (including customers) automatically integrate brand messages. This suggests that as long as the gaps between the different messages (in content and meaning) are acceptable, then management's task is to manage the process and seek to narrow these gaps that may be perceived.

What runs through both these approaches is the belief that above-the-line and below-the-line communications need to be moulded into one cohesive bundle, from which tools can be selected and deployed as conditions require.

Marketing mix

The elements of the marketing mix, however configured, also need to be integrated because they too communicate (Smith, 1996). The price and associated values, the product, in terms of the quality, design and tangible attributes, the manner and efficiency of the service delivery people and where and how it is made available, for example the location, website, customer contact centres, retailer/dealer reputation and overall service quality, need to be perceived by customers as a coordinated and consistent whole.

These touchpoints with brands are aspects of a consumer's brand experience and are used to develop images that through time may shape brand reputations. Traditionally the marketing mix was expected to deliver the brand proposition. Now it is expected that all these elements will be coordinated to maximise impact and enable customers to experience the brand through pre-, actual and post-product use.

Branding

Brands are themselves a form of integration. This means that organisations need to be sufficiently coordinated internally so that a brand can be perceived externally as consistent and uniform. As brands need to appeal to a number of different audiences (White, 2000) it is necessary to develop brands that appeal to diverse consumer groups. White refers to these new brands as 'chameleon' brands. They are characterised by their ability to adapt to different situations (audiences and media) yet retain a core proposition that provides a form of continuity and recognition. For example, a top-of-the-range music system may be seen by the owner as prestigious and technically superb, by a guest at a party as ostentatiously outrageous and overpriced, and by a friend as a product of clever design and marketing. All three might have developed their attitudes through different sources (e.g. different print media, exhibitions, the Internet, retail stores, word of mouth) but all agree that the brand has a common set of values and associations that are important to each of them.

The presentation of chameleon brands requires high levels of integration, a need to develop a series of innovative messages based around a core proposition. The use of a single ad execution needs to be replaced by multiple executions delivered through a variety of media, each complementing and reinforcing the core brand proposition. This means that the audience is more likely to be surprised or reminded of the brand (and its essence) through a series of refreshingly interesting messages, thereby raising the probability that 'likeability' (see Chapter 11) will be strengthened, along with the brand and all relevant associations.

Strategy

IMC is regarded by some as a means of using the communications mix in a more efficient and synergistic manner. At some level this can be true, but IMC requires a deeper understanding of how and where messages are created. At a strategic level, IMC has its roots in the overall business strategy of an organisation. Using Porter's (1980) generic strategies, if a low-cost strategy (e.g. Lidl) is being pursued, it makes sense to complement the strategy by using messages that either stress any price advantage that customers might benefit from or at least do not suggest extravagance or luxury. If using a differentiation focus strategy (e.g. Waitrose), price should not figure in any of the messages and greater emphasis should be placed on particular attributes that convey the added value and enable clear positioning. There is no right way (or formula) to establish IMC but there is a need to recognise that it has a strategic orientation and outputs.

Employees

It is generally agreed that all customer-facing employees should adopt a customer focus and 'live' the brand. While this can be achieved partially through the use of training courses and documentation, this usually requires a change of culture and that means a longer-term period of readjustment and the adoption of new techniques, procedures and ways of thinking and behaving.

Once the internal reorientation has begun (not completed), it is possible to take a message to external audiences. As long as they can see that employees are attempting to care about them as customers and do know what they are talking about in support of the products and services offered, then it is likely that customers (and other stakeholders) will be supportive. IMC should be concerned with the blend of internal and external messages so that there is clarity, consistency and reinforcement of the organisation's (or brand's) core proposition.

Technology

The use of technology, and in particular database technologies, has enabled marketing managers to have an improved view of customer behaviour, attitudes and feelings towards their brands. This has allowed more precise and insightful communications to be generated, and the subsequent feedback and measurement facilities have served to enrich the overall quality of customer communications.

The mere presence of technology, however, does not result in effective marketing communications. Technology needs to be integrated into not just the overall information systems strategy but also the marketing strategies of organisations. Technology is an enabler and to use it effectively requires integration. The effective use of technology can touch a number of areas within the IMC orbit. For example, technology can be used to develop effective websites, extranets and intranets, customer contact centres, databases, campaigns, fulfilment processes, CRM and sales force automation. If each of these applications is deployed independently of the others their impact will be limited. Developed within an integrated framework, the potential for marketing and customer service can be tremendous.

Associated with the use of technology are issues concerning the measurement and evaluation of IMC programmes. One of the criticisms of IMC is that no evaluation system has yet been proposed or implemented so that the claims made about IMC delivering superior returns can be validated (Swain, 2004).

Agencies

Reference has been made earlier to some of the structural issues involving agencies in the marketing communications industry and with the development of IMC. Agencies play a critical role in marketing communications and if IMC is to be established it cannot be accomplished without the explicit involvement of all those working on the supply side.

Questions arise concerning the level of expertise that a single agency might have access to in order to deliver IMC. For example, Virgin Media called an ad review for its £36 million budget. Virgin Media's then agency was DDB, who had only been in position for 15 months. It is suggested that the review was called because the agency had struggled to provide 'best-in-class' across the disciplines for Virgin Media's entire business. This meant that integration had not been achieved as the direct marketing aspect was maintained. It was only the creative advertising element that failed to live up to expectations (Williams, 2011).

Apart from questions concerning the range of promotional services offered by individual agencies and whether these are all delivered by a single agency or through a network of interacting agencies, two particular issues arise. The first concerns leadership and the other remuneration.

With regard to leadership, should the agency or the client lead the process of developing IMC? The consensus appears to be that this is the client's role (Swain, 2004), mainly because clients are better positioned to make integration happen across their own organisation. However, Swain then points out that there is no agreement about who in the client organisation should be responsible for implementing IMC. Indeed, Kitchen et al. (2007) confirm the reluctance of both advertising and public relations agencies to provide for integrative working practices.

A similar question concerns the implementation of integrated campaigns. Most major brands operate with several agencies, each providing different skills. These are known as 'register agencies' simply because different agencies can be brought into different campaigns to provide support when necessary. Herein lies the problem for clients implementing an integrative programme: how best to manage an integrative approach? One way is to appoint a lead agency that assumes responsibility for integration. Another way is for the client to drive the programme forward and to involve the register agencies. However, many client organisations appoint a lead agency and very often it is the generalist ad agency that is appointed.

The second issue, remuneration, is a measurement factor (Swain, 2004). A move to IMC requires a change in agency performance measures and, consequently, a change in their method of remuneration. Closer integration of agencies within an IMC process will, among other things, bring changes in structure, operations, performance measures, remuneration and new responsibilities within the client relationship.

This list of elements that need to be integrated is not exclusive. There are other influences that are particular to individual organisations that could have been included. However, consideration of these various elements suggests strongly that what is being integrated is far more than just the tools, media and messages of the communications mix. Indeed, viewed holistically, integration is a strategic concept that strikes at the heart of an organisation's marketing and business orientation.

The second question posed earlier asks how might these elements be linked together in order to drive an integrative campaign? Some might argue that the quality of an integrated campaign can be seen in the achievement of the objectives. The outcomes, however, could have been achieved without any integration so other facets need to be considered.

There are two dimensions that need to be considered. One is scheduling and the other consistency, both measured across the length or duration of the campaign.

By definition integrated campaigns consist of several tools and media. The way in which these elements of the communications mix are scheduled and the quality of the transition through the length of a campaign will impact on the quality of campaign integration. For example, the Sensodyne Pronamel campaign in Chapter 1 was in two phases. The first was designed to raise awareness of the issue of 'Acid Wear', and the second was to reveal the relevance of the issue to consumers. Across both phases dentists were involved in the campaign, either actively or passively, and this scheduling, combined with astute timing of the various components, enabled what some might argue to be an integrated campaign.

Viewpoint 10.2	Dole into banana integration

Dole is the world's largest producer of fresh fruit and vegetables, supplying over 90 countries across the globe. The fresh produce market offers little scope for differentiation, especially in terms of packaging and the products themselves. This provides supermarkets an opportunity to develop their own-brand identity in this category.

The banana sector is no exception with supermarkets dominating and rendering brand name suppliers, such as Dole, redundant. In an attempt to correct this imbalance and to establish Dole as a recognised and valued banana brand they sponsored the Tokyo Marathon campaign in 2014. Through this sponsorship Dole attempted to associate themselves with health, fitness and nutrition.

The aim of the campaign was to position Dole apart from other producers. This was achieved using an integrated marketing campaign which positioned Dole as 'The Ultimate Banana'.

The yellow banana is the perfect representation of nutrition for runners around the globe. For years, athletes have carried the fruit during training and competitions. It provides a boost of energy from carbohydrates and natural sugars found in the distinctive fruit. Naturally, Dole sponsorship involved supplying the race participants with over 91,000 bananas as a great source of energy.

A small number of runners were each provided with a special real banana that functioned as a wrist tracking tool. The banana was sliced open and an LED and a battery were inserted. The banana was then carefully closed to ensure it retained its natural form. The result was that this 'edible wearable' displayed

Exhibit 10.3	**Dole provided marathon runners with bananas for nourishment**

Source: Getty Images/Anadolu Agency/Mehmet Kaman.

useful information such as running time, distance covered, heart rate and signals about when to refuel with another banana.

In addition, 200 pre-race winners of a Facebook lottery were presented with a special banana when they finished. This banana had their finishing time, the runner's name and a congratulatory message printed in edible ink. This information was also shared with Facebook.

The campaign aimed to build brand awareness, recognition, associations with health and nutrition, and to develop relations with the public. The campaign involved a variety of marketing communications tools. These included the sponsorship itself, direct marketing of the bananas to the runners, public relations, and advertising, through traditional and digital media. The variety of media used meant that the campaign achieved wide coverage. The campaign generated the equivalent of US$1.1 million worth of media coverage, exposure of the Dole brand to over 28 million people, and resulted in 95.3 per cent of people reached having an improved perception of the Dole brand as a result of the Banana Trophy campaign.

Source: Anon (2015); Cheng (2015); Dole (2015); Polachek (2015); www.mintel.com.

This Viewpoint was written by Lucy Alexander when she was a student at Leeds Beckett University.

Questions: To what extent can the Dole banana campaign be classified as integrated communications?

Task: Find two other campaigns where novelty items featured in an integrated campaign.

We see later in this chapter that at one level integration might be considered in terms of the frequency and consistency with which logos, colours and other identification marks are used across all elements of the campaign. This provides a relatively easy means to identify and measure integration. It can be argued, however, that the mere provision of identification marks does not make for a truly integrated campaign.

Later in this chapter we consider different interpretations of IMC and each of these provide an insight into how integration occurs. The question remains, however, and one emphasised by Kliatchko and Schultz's (2014) practitioner-oriented research, how can (should) we measure IMC?

Definitions of IMC

These definitions, from Shultz et al.'s (1993) original to those used today (Table 10.3), reveal how the term has evolved. In much the same way, the very diversity of the term 'integration' has been highlighted by the Institute of Practitioners in Advertising (IPA). Their research into what is meant by integration, as practiced by clients and agencies, reveals several different interpretations, leading them to the conclusion that the term is ambiguous in practice.

For example, the IPA observes that integration can be just about channel (tools) planning, the integration of communications with brand values, the integration of data, the merging of data sources and customer understanding, the integration of offline and online media channels to achieve maximum click-throughs and sales, the facilitation of seamless working practices across internal client departments and agencies, and finding ideas that integrate into the target audience's lives.

In order to provide clarity and insight into the way integration is considered and practised, the IPA analysed over 250 cases submitted to the IPA Effectiveness Awards in the period 2000–9. The IPA searched for a common definition of integration, but it

Table 10.3 The development of IMC definitions

Author	Definition
Shultz et al. (1993)	A concept of marketing communications planning that recognises the added value of a comprehensive plan that evaluates the strategic role of a variety of communications disciplines (such as advertising, direct response, sales promotion, etc.) and combines them to provide clarity, consistency and maximum communications impact.
Duncan and Moriarty (1998)	A cross-functional process for creating and nourishing profitable relationships with customers and other stakeholders by strategically controlling or influencing all messages sent to these groups and encouraging purposeful dialogue with them.
Keller (2001)	Involves the development, implementation, and evaluation of marketing communications programmes using multiple communications options where the design and execution of any communications option reflects the nature and content of other communications options that also make up the communications programme.
Kliatchko (2008), Kliatchko et al. (2014)	An audience-driven business process of strategically managing stakeholders, content, channels, and results of brand communications programmes.

became clear that just as the academic definitions had evolved, so had working practices developed over this period.

From this review and bearing in mind that no single form of IMC can be identified, the following general definition is offered:

> *IMC can represent both a strategic and tactical approach to the planned management of an organisation's communications. IMC requires that organisations coordinate their various strategies, resources and messages in order that they enable meaningful engagement with audiences. The main purposes are to develop a clear positioning and encourage stakeholder relationships that are of mutual value.*

This definition serves to link IMC with business-level strategies and relationships. The importance of coherence within the organisation is made explicit, whether this be through systems or structural change. Implicit is the underpinning notion that IMC is necessary for the development of effective relationships and that not all relationships need be collaborative and fully relational, as so often assumed to be the case in many contemporary interpretations.

Scholars' paper 10.2   Four pillars of IMC strength

Kliatchko, J. (2008) Revisiting the IMC construct: a revised definition and four pillars, *International Journal of Advertising*, **27(1), 133–60.**

Kliatchko published this paper as an update to his 2005 paper on IMC. Here he re-examines and revises his definition of integrated marketing communications (IMC). His goal is to advance the theoretical foundations and definitional issues of IMC and to that end he introduces and examines his four pillars of IMC before exploring the interconnection between the pillars and levels of IMC.

Interpretations of IMC

The relative failure of both academics and practitioners to agree on a definition for IMC is indicative of the debate, contradiction and perhaps vagueness of the concept. It is also reflective of an emerging concept, one that has had little chance to stabilise in the context of a rapidly changing media landscape and new forms of communications. Indeed, Kliatchko and Shultz (2014) found in their survey of senior marketing practitioners in the Asia Pacific area that the term 'IMC' is hardly used. Terms such as 'integrated thinking, integrated planning, integrated marketing, full service, 360 or simply integration' are much more common (p. 380).

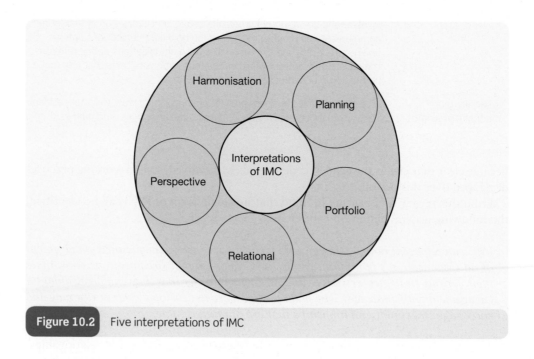

Figure 10.2	Five interpretations of IMC

Within these diverse views and perspectives of IMC, we now consider five interpretations of what IMC might be. Harmonisation, which was an early view and still practised, is considered first. We then review planning, perspective, portfolio and relational interpretations (see Figure 10.2).

Interpretation 1: IMC as harmonisation

One of the early interpretations of IMC, indeed the leading view at the time, was that integration was a function of the harmonisation of the elements of communications. This involved communicating consistent messages through all forms of relevant media to target audiences. In this view, sometimes referred to rather dismissively as 'matching luggage', harmonisation represented a largely visual interpretation of IMC.

Typically brand colours, logos and straplines had to be placed and presented in a consistent manner across all media where the target audience encountered the brand. This content view aimed to achieve a 'one voice, one look' position. Despite being perceived as an advertising-led communications programme at this stage, other disciplines were incorporated into the process, so that sales promotion, public relations, and increasingly direct marketing, all became part of the harmonised approach to IMC. Through harmonisation of all the elements of the marketing communications mix, the channels, as practitioners refer to them, represented the key integration factors. Schultz (1993: 17) refers to IMC as 'the process of developing and implementing various forms of persuasive communications programs with customers and prospects over time'. This customer-only perspective merely served to limit the scope, not only of IMC but of marketing communications as a whole.

Interestingly, this view is still prevalent today, as evidenced by some of the journalistic accounts of current campaigns. For example, TUI Travel announced that it had 'launched integrated marketing campaigns for Thomson and First Choice in the past five months (of 2012) in an effort to clarify their propositions. The £5m Thomson push promoted its "exclusive" and "tailored" offering using the strapline "Uniquely designed holidays". This was followed by a £3 million relaunch campaign for First Choice, repositioning it as "the home of all-inclusive"' (Eleftheriou-Smith, 2012).

One of the issues, however, is that harmonisation represents a resource-driven view of IMC, an inside-out approach, which by definition is not audience-centred and lacks any strategic, structural or market view. Furthermore, harmonisation fails to consider the context in which communications are to occur and remains a predominantly advertising-led activity. These issues were to be reconsidered as IMC research and practice evolved.

Interpretation 2: IMC as a plan

The media-neutral planning (MNP) approach emerged partly as a response to criticism of IMC and partly as an attempt to articulate the potential practice of IMC. For many MNP is integration under a different guise, but one of the strengths of the concept is that it focuses openly on the needs of clients and agencies. It attempts to stimulate the use of a communications mix that is driven by the needs of a target audience and not those of the communications industry. This means that, rather than keep recommending that clients use mass-media communications, which some would say has traditionally rewarded agencies through a generous commission system, a more balanced mix of tools and media should be adopted in order to be more effective and efficient.

One of the main reasons for the interest in IMC is the potential to reduce costs. The rise in some media costs, most notably television through the 1990s, the specialised and independent nature of the agency side of the industry, the proliferation of media opportunities and the splintering of audiences, and the increasing clamour for measures of return on investment in communications have led to a reappraisal of the role and nature of marketing communications and the emergence of MNP ideas.

Agencies interested in preserving margins have attempted to maintain the prominence of advertising in their media plans, but have reduced the emphasis on television advertising or have sought better deals through use of multiple television channel mixes, improved negotiation and more alliances. Some client organisations (e.g. Mondelēz International, Kellogg's, Unilever and Procter & Gamble) have moved, if unintentionally, towards a form of coordinated marketing communications activity. These organisations have reduced their reliance on above-the-line media and have attempted to move towards the use of below-and around-the-line approaches in order to reduce costs and deliver consistent messages in an attempt to cut through the increasing clutter. Ray (2002) refers to some of the problems, such as structures, areas of expertise and attitudes, faced by agencies attempting to offer a more neutral media approach for their clients.

The drive behind the development of MNP appears to be concerned more with reducing the emphasis on television advertising in media plans, rather than the formulation of distinct media plans that deliver advertising messages in the most effective way, regardless of media selection. Many of those that support media-neutral approaches are often quoted using examples that involve a mix of tools and media.

MNP recognises that mass-media advertising is not always the most appropriate way to launch or develop consumer or business-to-business promotional activities, and that a consideration of the most suitable mix of communications tools might be a better starting point when formulating campaigns. Advertising alone cannot carry the weight of a brand adequately to build and sustain the desired associations. Public relations, sales promotions and field marketing (merchandising), for example, have increasingly important roles to play in establishing and sustaining a brand. Where advertising is used, however, the changing media landscape and the increasing penetration of new technology mean that a greater use of cross-media planning approaches is likely to enhance the effectiveness of a campaign and reduce costs, especially if previous campaigns used television as the primary medium. The traditional model of media planning, whereby a primary medium and perhaps two or three secondary media are scheduled over a five-week campaign, has now to be surpassed by a more contemporary mix that uses a cross-media plan combining new and old media and that is appropriate to target audience preferences and the context of the marketing communications activities.

Therefore, it might be interpreted that media-neutral mixes represent the response of the agency side of the marketing communications industry while IMC represents the client-side approach to managing marketing communications in a more effective and strategic manner. MNP should not be about mixing tools and media but should be regarded as an integral part of IMC. However, IMC is not the same as MNP.

The development and delivery of a marketing communications programme that repeatedly delivers significant value cannot be based solely on MNP or loose notions of IMC. What is necessary is the development of a strategic marketing communications approach that delivers a total brand experience (Tobaccowala and Kugel, 2001). This requires a coordinated approach to the selection and implementation of the right tools and media that will deliver messages that are of significant value to the target audience. However, it also requires the integration of a cross-functional, multi-audience strategic approach to marketing communications – one that delivers a brand experience for the target audience.

Open planning

The MNP approach considers all media to have an equal probability of selection and those that are chosen are deemed the best vehicles to achieve the media plan's objectives. Although there are many benefits, such as changing attitudes and perhaps reducing some costs, the neutrality perspective seeks to address industry issues about the planning process and the thinking the planners undertake, rather than demonstrating direct concern with audience issues.

In an attempt to move thinking a step forward, the open-planning concept was developed by Jenkinson, who coordinated a panel of leading marketers who all wanted to simplify the MNP concept. The main goal was to reappraise the way organisations consider their processes and thinking about marketing communications activities with a view to optimising their communications potential. The MNP group argues that this requires rethinking the way communications disciplines (tools) and media are used, to develop new methods of evaluating communications activity and to accelerate the speed at which organisations are able to integrate their communications with their business and marketing strategies.

Table 10.4 Action areas within the open planning approach

Action area	Explanation
Disciplines	Any communications tool (i.e. discipline) can be used with any medium to achieve stated business and marketing objectives.
Media	Any medium can be used, by any tool (i.e. discipline), in almost all mixes. This means redefining media to mean anything that conveys a message to an audience. A salesperson becomes a medium.
Channels	Any mix of disciplines within a single medium becomes an open channel.
Process	All agencies (and others) should be involved with the thinking and planning process at the outset, to determine the message and goals before any resources are allocated (i.e. budgets).
Structure	The communications process should be driven by the communications preferences of a target audience (or community) rather than the silo structure-based functional specialisation present in much of the industry today.
Relationships	The relationship between client and agency should be open and functional. Agency remuneration should be based on the achievement of brand goals and not commission based on media choice.
Results	Defining more precise communications goals that enable a level playing field for all disciplines, media and agencies to maximise their contribution.
Tools	Use of media planning tools that embrace all touchpoints with customers.

Source: Adapted from Jenkinson and Sain (2004).

The MNP group proposed a series of new approaches based mainly on ideas concerning open thinking and planning. Open planning is concerned with eight action areas, each of which contributes to the process of MNP. These action areas are set out in Table 10.4. Readers wishing to know more should visit www.openplanning.org.uk.

Thoughts about these action areas should promote marketing communications that are audience-centred rather than reproduce the previous model that focused on the needs of the communications industry.

Interpretation 3: IMC as a perspective

Cornelissen argues that the literature indicates that there are two main interpretations of IMC: a 'content' and a 'process' perspective respectively.

The *content* perspective assumes that message consistency is the major goal in order to achieve the 'one voice, one look' position. IMC works when there is consistency throughout the various materials and messages. Interestingly, Delgado-Ballester et al. (2012) find that high levels of consistency are important when building new or unfamiliar brands, whereas moderate levels of consistency are suitable for established or familiar brands.

However, this is not a new practice, as Cornelissen points out that practitioners have been doing this long before the term 'IMC' surfaced. This view is also associated with the zero-based planning approach that holds that the choice of tools and media should be based on effectiveness criteria rather than the specialist functions for which the planners and managers are responsible. This means that the various agencies and personnel responsible for campaign design and deployment do so without prejudice or bias towards a preferred tool or media. This approach is discussed later in this chapter.

The second interpretation offered by Cornelissen is referred to as a *process* perspective. Here the emphasis is on a structural realignment of the communications disciplines within organisations, even to the point of collapsing all communications into a single department. Even if this extreme interpretation is not a valid goal for an organisation, cross-functional systems and processes are regarded as necessary to enable IMC.

The process perspective of IMC is rooted in the belief that real IMC can only be generated through an organisational structure that brings the various communications disciplines together in a single body or unit. By creating a single department out of which advertising, public relations and the other disciplines operate, cross-functional coordination between the disciplines is enabled. Some argue that the process view needs to incorporate a series of intervening stages as systems, processes and procedures are brought together incrementally to enable the cross-functionality to work.

Research suggests that organisations have made little attempt to restructure their marketing communications disciplines and that public relations and marketing remain as a clear divide. What has happened, however, is that there are much closer cross-functional relationships and systems and processes to support them. Some organisations are moving incrementally towards a process perspective on IMC.

In an attempt to develop our understanding of IMC, Lee and Park (2007) proposed a multidimensional model of IMC, based on four key dimensions. These have been drawn from the literature and, unlike Cornelissen's work, represent an attempt to measure IMC. Their four dimensions are concerned with a single message, multiple customer groups, database marketing and the need to use IMC to build customer relationships (a fuller account of these dimensions can be seen in Chapter 8).

Kliatchko (2008) suggests that IMC has several distinctive attributes and he refers to them as the 'four pillars of IMC'. These are stakeholders, content, channels and results. Figure 10.3 sets out the constituent elements within each of the pillars.

Viewpoint 10.3   Integrated savings

Ideas about IMC should not be restricted to private sector organisations. The UK government's National Savings and Investments agency, known as NS&I, is a 150-year-old organisation which serves 26 million customers and provides various types of savings and investment programmes through the postal facilities, online and by telephone, generating more than £100 billion in investments, which help to keep the Treasury financially liquid. According to Shultz, NS&I is the perfect example of IMC in practice, for three main reasons.

First, the people responsible for income generation are not part of a marketing group but are responsible for 'demand generation'. Their role is to create attractive investment products, promote them and implement them in the marketplace so that the public will invest. They have to achieve this at a cost that generates sufficient returns to meet the government funding requirements. In other words, they are responsible for both sales and 'profits'.

Second, the main focus is on forecasting, not on measuring ROI. That means that the NS&I team has to understand the marketplace, the competition and the potential returns on their efforts, and match that to the government needs in such a way that the balance of incoming and outgoing funds meets the needs of the government. In other words, they are fully accountable as an income centre for NS&I, and not, like so many marketing groups, a cost centre.

Third, unlike so many private practice organisations, the communications are not rooted in discrete, functional silos. The focus is on matching customers with products to generate returns. That means that they use a variety of tools and any resource, including people, that are available to them. There are media and promotional specialists in NS&I, but they are nomadic and are free to move around the organisation as needed. Demand generators have to build products and promote them to generate the levels of return that they have forecast. So, they use mass media, digital, promotions, public relations, direct response media, and other tools and media, in various combinations, to generate the returns they have forecast. If that means mass media, fine.

The focus on accountability and the generation of returns is a contrast to the norm of creating and sending out numerous communications through predetermined, advertising-led channels. As Shultz comments, at NS&I they build promotional programmes with returns, not awards, in mind.

Source: Shultz (2012).

Question:	Why should public service organisations attempt to develop integrated marketing communications?
Task:	Find two other public service or third sector campaigns and make notes about how they might be more integrated.

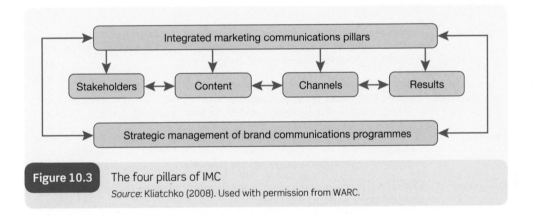

Figure 10.3   The four pillars of IMC
Source: Kliatchko (2008). Used with permission from WARC.

His argument is that these four elements can be observed at different levels of IMC and that at each level one of the elements tends to dominate.

It may be that a suitable theoretical basis upon which to develop IMC is emerging through the relationship marketing literature. We know that a relationship orientation requires a multidisciplinary approach to trigger interaction and dialogue (Gronroos, 2004). So, it may be that a deeper understanding of relational theory will help to advance the IMC concept and provide researchers with a surer footing upon which to explore the topic.

However, whether a content or process perspective is adopted, the position remains that, until there is empirical evidence to support a theoretical base upon which to build IMC strategy and operations, the phrase will probably continue to be misused, misunderstood and used in a haphazard and inconsistent way.

Interpretation 4: IMC as a portfolio

Reference was made to the IPA's research and analysis of its *Effectiveness Awards* programmes. From an investigation of the various submissions for the best integrated

Table 10.5 Four ways for integration

Form of integration	Explanation
No integration	No attempt is made to unify the tools in a consistent way.
Advertising-led integration	Based around a common creative platform.
Brand idea-led orchestration	Unification occurs around a shared brand concept or platform.
Participation-led orchestration	Characterised by a common dialogue, co-creation, experience or 'conversation' between brand and audience.

Source: IPA (2011). Used with permission from WARC.

campaign the IPA uncovered four distinct forms of integrated programmes (see Table 10.5).

Within each of these four forms of integration, the IPA observes various sub-categories. These are outlined in Table 10.6.

Table 10.6 Sub-categories of integration

Form of integration	Sub-category	Explanation
No integration	Single tool	Campaigns where there is no specific requirement to integrate other tools, media or marketing activity (such as packaging, on-pack promotions, in-store or website), into the advertising or marketing campaign.
	Pragmatically non-integrated	These campaigns use a wide variety of communications tools but there is no message integration. These campaigns tend to have no unifying concept, message or idea across any of the activities, and do not share a unifying strapline.
Advertising-led integration	Visual	These campaigns are only united by 'look and feel'. This is the so-called 'matching luggage' concept. These share the same visual identity but do not seek to integrate all campaign messages across channels.
	Promotion	Unification is achieved both visually and through a single promotional platform, competition or response mechanic.
	Icon	This refers to the use of the same brand icon across all tools and media – for example, by using the same celebrity in the store promotion, PR photo calls and events (e.g. Kerry Katona for Iceland) or by developing a specific brand persona for use in all channels (e.g. Felix for Felix Catfood).
	Idea	Here integration is achieved through one big advertising idea, which is disseminated through the most appropriate media.
Brand idea-led orchestration	Tangible	These campaigns are built on the more tangible foundations associated with a specific need-state, occasion, tightly defined target audience or a specific 'point of market entry' upon which to focus the activity and the channel orchestration.
	Intangible	Developed for higher-order, emotional engagement, these campaigns exhibit a high degree of creative inconsistency across time, while still retaining their orchestrating elements.
Participation-led orchestration		Here digital media are used to engage audiences in conversation and so improve brand and audience interaction. The goal is to integrate brands into people's lives in a way that is both relevant and valuable for the audience, rather than aiming a message out towards a target audience and hoping it will be receptive.

Source: Based on IPA (2011). Used with permission from WARC.

In many ways the revelation that there are different forms of integration should not be surprising, especially in the light of the multitude of definitions. What is interesting is the terminology used to identify the different forms. In particular attention is drawn to the use of the word 'orchestration'. This is a term identified in the very early days by academics to explain the integration concept. Here we are, roughly 20 years later, and it is practitioners who are reviving the term. Perhaps of greater interest should be what the term 'orchestration' represents. In a musical context 'to orchestrate' means to arrange or compose music to be played by an orchestra in a predetermined order. The conductor then interprets the score in order to reproduce the composer's original idea. This suggests a planned way of operating, one where there is some, but limited, flexibility. Another interpretation of the word 'orchestration' involves the organisation of an event to achieve a desired, again predetermined, effect or outcome. What is common to both of these ideas about orchestration is that there is a planned outcome. To what extent is integration more concerned with flexibility than planning, however, and what part of the difficulties associated with IMC are to be found rooted in planning and linear thinking?

Viewpoint 10.4   American Express drive participation

'Small Business Saturday' happens every year on the Saturday after Thanksgiving. It has become a regular event but the original idea behind it was a deliberate attempt by American Express to help their small-business customers boost sales.

The idea was seeded at a time when the recession was deep and when there was a groundswell towards looking after 'local' needs. For AmEx, however, the challenge lay in getting consumers and small businesses to not only participate in the programme but also help promote the idea. The answer lay in encouraging participation among various collaborative partners. These included YouTube, Foursquare and Twitter who provided free social-media support, FedEx who donated personalised signs, and business organisations from the US Chamber of Commerce to the National Federation of Independent Businesses who held events and promoted the day on their own. In addition Facebook, AmEx's agency, Crispin Porter + Bogusky, and of course consumers, shopkeepers and retail business owners.

The campaign had three core elements. The first was to enable small business owners and rally them to own the day. The second was to galvanise consumers to support the movement and to go out and shop in small business on Small Business Saturday. The third was to lobby Government officials to make it 'an official day'.

To enable small business owners and rally them to own the day, AmEx encouraged small businesses to participate with an advertising campaign which featured small business owners being urged to unite to combine forces and fight back against the mega sized retailers. In addition a communications toolkit was created for small businesses to run and promote SBS. This included a logo and simple artwork for use as in-store displays. AmEx bought advertising 'space' on Facebook then offered it free to its small business account holders. The toolkit was distributed digitally via a hub that lived online, both on Facebook and AmEx's sites.

To galvanise consumers to support the movement and to go out and shop in small businesses on Small Business Saturday, consumers needed to be made aware of and understand their role: to shop. To do this a cross-platform advertising campaign designed to position Small Business Day as a national movement was developed. The commercial depicted a cross section of shoppers making 'the pledge to shop small'. People who wanted to help their small town communities were recognised as 'Neighborhood Champions'.

AmEx built an entirely separate website at ShopSmall.com for Small Business Saturday. Here there are toolkit and social media materials for the SBS brand. AmEx built a community around Small Business

Saturday and enabled the community to do some of the work for them. This has made it easy for participants to rally around a brand that is separate from the AmEx brand itself. It is important to recognise that although AmEx have driven the movement, participants are not required to sign up to AmEx. Their CEO went on the *Today* show and said, 'I don't care how you shop, where you shop or how you pay . . . this is the day to go out and support small businesses.' American Express has developed an entire brand around Shop Small and Small Business Saturday.

The campaign has evolved and grown in strength with each year's event. Following the launch in 2010, the US Senate officially recognised the movement in 2011. In 2012, it was estimated that US$5.5 billion was spent at small independent businesses on the designated day. In 2013 over 1,450 neighborhood champions signed up to rally their communities to get involved and support small businesses. That year US$5.7 billion in sales were generated. The cause-marketing campaign won two Cannes Grand Prix awards among many other industry accolades. It is now a cultural movement that has help change the way consumers view and support small businesses.

Source: Beechler (2014); www.americanexpress.com; www.adage.com/lp/top15/#introw.

> **Question:**   How does the SBS movement reflect a participative view of IMC?
>
> **Task:**   Find two other campaigns that demonstrate participative IMC.

Interpretation 5: Relational IMC

This interpretation has emerged naturally as marketing has become more relationship-aware and, as a result, more oriented towards relational issues. Relationships are dynamic and vary in strength and intensity through time. Some are referred to as *transactional exchanges*, characterised by short-term, product- or price-oriented exchanges between buyers and sellers coming together for one-off exchanges independent of any other or subsequent exchanges. Both parties are motivated mainly by self-interest.

Other relationships are characterised by relational exchanges or what Day (2000) refers to as *collaborative exchanges*. These are characterised by a long-term orientation, where ultimately there is complete integration of systems and processes and where the relationship is motivated by partnership and mutual support. Trust and commitment underpin these relationships, and these variables become increasingly important as relational exchanges become established. IMC therefore needs to consider and adapt to these very different relational contexts. Each is considered in turn.

IMC and transactional marketing

The discussion so far has been based largely on the assumption that exchanges are (or should be) essentially collaborative in character and that customers are willing and eager to enter into a wide range of relationships. However, it appears that some, if not the majority of, exchanges are essentially transactional in character. Buyers do not always wish to enter into a deep, complex relationship with all suppliers, nor do some consumers wish to enter into a relationship with the supplier of their favourite chocolate bar, dishwasher tablets or frozen peas. As a result these convenience-based exchanges are oriented towards a value based on the product, its price and overall availability and convenience. Depending upon the product category, after-sales and service support will be important but, by definition, customers in transactional mode do not wish to enter into any serious interaction, let alone dialogue.

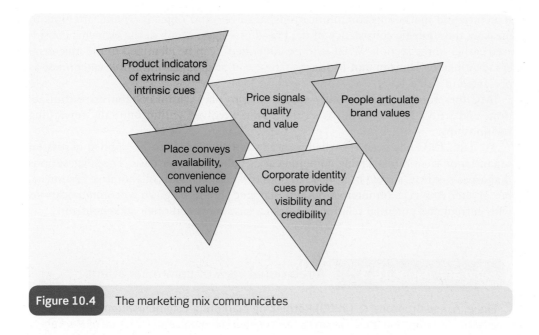

Figure 10.4 The marketing mix communicates

The target-marketing process requires the development and implementation of a distinct marketing mix to meet the requirements of selected target markets. The elements are mixed together in such a way that they should meet the needs of the target segment. Each element of the marketing mix has a variable capacity to communicate (see Figure 10.4).

Therefore, it may be that traditional forms of marketing communications are sufficient to reach transactional customers. Messages that focus mainly on attributes, features and benefits, emotional values, price and availability will continue to be valid and improved if delivered though a coordinated mix of tools and media that are customer-oriented. Using communications that contain a coordinated communications mix, which makes greater use of a range of tools and media that are neutral and seek to cut waste and improve efficiency, will be advantageous.

IMC and relationship marketing

As stated already, there is no universally agreed definition of IMC, and the development of this relatively new, embryonic concept is strewn with attempts to pin it down and label it. What can be observed, however, is that the relationship-marketing paradigm has developed at the same time as IMC and that there are areas where the two concepts intertwine and reinforce each other.

One of the difficulties associated with the IMC view, and with its half-sister, MNP, is that successful marketing communications results from an entirely planned approach. Planning is an essential aspect of managing marketing communications, but customers interact with products and services in different ways. They experience brands through their observation of others consuming them, through their own use, as well as through planned, unplanned and word-of-mouth communications. It is the totality of this communications experience that impacts on relationship development. IMC therefore has a critical role in the development of relationship marketing. This is because it is an important process, one that seeks to generate a response from customers, provoke interaction and then dialogue, which is a key characteristic of relationship marketing (Gronroos, 2004).

The Duncan and Moriarty IMC mini-audit has been designed to help assess an organisation's IMC relationship-building practices. It recognises the influence of organisational structure and marketing communications strategies and objectives, and attempts to measure the strategic consistency of the brand messages. Many of the elements considered earlier in the section 'What is to be integrated?' can be identified in the nine drivers identified by Duncan and Moriarty. These can be grouped into three categories, as presented in Table 10.7.

IMC therefore has a potentially greater role to play within collaborative transactions and with customers who wish to become involved within mutually rewarding relationships.

To date, IMC has been regarded as a concept that needs to be applied across an organisation's entire marketing communications and customer base. The suggestion is that aspects of IMC should be applied to both transactional and collaborative customers, but greater emphasis on interaction and dialogue should be given to communications with current and potential relationship-driven customers and other stakeholders.

Scholars' paper 10.3 A relational view of communications

Finne, A. and Gronroos, C. (2009) Rethinking marketing communication: from integrated marketing communication to relationship communication, *Journal of Marketing Communication*, 15(2–3), 179–95.

This paper presents a new way of considering integrated communications. In that sense it is important to appreciate the consumer-centric perspective on IMC as the principle applies equally to advertising. Much of the integration literature considers outgoing messages, whereas the authors switch the focus to consumers and the way they integrate messages.

Table 10.7 Duncan–Moriarty categories of relationship drivers

Relationship drivers	Explanation
Relationship development	Everything an organisation does and says is seen, heard and interpreted by stakeholders. The need is to provide a consistent relational focus through all messages.
Processes	The need for a process and system to provide consistent strategic positioning and in doing so help support the identity and reputation of the organisation.
Organisational	Structural and cross-functional cohesion is necessary to support internal marketing and an unbiased use of all communications resources.

Source: Derived from Reid (2005).

Structuring for IMC

Any discussion of IMC should at least acknowledge the higher-order background issue concerning integration between corporate communications and brand-based communications. It might be expected that, as responsibility for communications does, or should, rest with a single person, integration would be a natural outcome. This inevitably is not the case, often due to structural requirements. The result is that IMC becomes even harder to achieve. Separate marketing, advertising, promotion and PR budgets, combined with internal politics and personality clashes that bounce back on strategy, internal structures, which include siloed teams often accompanied by self-reinforcing functional budgets, almost inevitably lead to independent planning and action by different teams. Integration is not going to happen when the right hand may not know what the left one is doing (Benjamin, 2012).

Clients have also embraced IMC and its influence on their structures. The hierarchical structures common in many organisations in the period up to the 1970s have been subject to attack. In search of survival in recession and increasing profits and dividends in times of plenty, organisations have sought to restructure and realign themselves with their environment. Hierarchies delivered a management structure that delegated authority in compartmentalised units. The brand management system that accompanied this structural approach provided a straitjacket and gave only partial authority to incumbents. At the same time, responsibility for pricing, channel management, personal selling and public relations activities was split off and allocated to a number of others. It follows from this that the likelihood of internal integration has been hampered by the structure of the organisation and the way in which structural units have been assembled.

The restructuring process has resulted in organisations that have delayered and are leaner. This means that the gap between senior management and those within the operating core (Mintzberg et al., 2003) is smaller and now capable of sustaining viable internal communications that are truly two-way and supportive.

Scholars' paper 10.4   Small but still needs to be integrated

Gabrielli, V. and Balboni, B. (2010) SME practice towards integrated marketing communications, *Marketing Intelligence & Planning,* 28(3), 275–90.

Unlike the majority of papers about IMC, this empirical publication considers the ways in which SMEs approach marketing communications management and planning in particular. Their weakness for managing the internal processes associated with planned communications is exposed.

Increasingly, organisations are operating in overseas or cross-border markets. However, as organisations develop structurally, from international to multinational to global and transnational status, so the need to coordinate internally and to integrate internal communications becomes ever more vital to sustain IMC (Grein and Gould, 1996). Internal communications (see Chapter 9) are becoming more popular with clients (and agencies) as it is realised that employees are important contributors and invaluable spokespersons for the products they market. Internal communications can help not only to inform and remind/reassure, but also to differentiate employees in the sense that they understand the organisation's direction and purpose, appreciate what the brand values are and so identify closely with the organisation as a whole. This is a form of integration from which marketing communications can benefit.

Key points

- Integrated marketing communications (IMC) is concerned with the development, coordination and implementation of an organisation's various strategies, resources and messages.

- The role of IMC is to enable coherent and meaningful engagement with target audiences. In an age when consumers can touch brands across a range of channels it is important that each contact reinforces previous messages and facilitates the development of valued relationships.

- There has been a great deal of debate about the meaning and value of an integrated approach. Many agencies speak of integrated communications campaigns but the reality suggests different approaches, forms and interpretations. Most organisations only achieve partial or coordinated levels of communications activity.

- The interest in IMC has resulted from three main drivers. These include market-based drivers, those that arise from changing communications, and those that are driven from opportunities arising from within the organisation itself.

- A wide range of elements needs to be integrated. These include the communications tools, media and messages, plus the elements of the marketing mix, brands, strategy, employees, agencies and technology.

- Definitions of IMC have evolved from a simple coordination of the disciplines and messages perspective to one that incorporates the development of relationships and mutual value.

- There is no single agreed definition or view of IMC. The IPA observes that it is an ambiguous concept. Five interpretations of IMC can be identified. These are harmonisation, planning, perspective, portfolio and relational interpretations. Each has its own origins and theoretical grounding.

- The move away from hierarchical and highly bureaucratic organisational structures has resulted in leaner, flatter organisations. This facilitates improved internal communications which assist employee support for a brand. Horizontal reporting lines are reorganised and silo-based functions removed, along with budget processes that only serve to encourage independent behaviour and repel IMC initiatives and progression.

Review questions

Oreo cookies case questions

1. What were the reasons that led Oreo to develop an integrated approach?

2. Prepare brief notes explaining the role and contribution of any four elements within the Oreo approach to integration.

3. Consider the issues Oreo might have had to address when developing an integrated approach to their communications.

4. Which of the different interpretations of IMC best explains Oreo's approach?

5. How should Oreo measure the success of their integrated approach to communications?

General questions

1. Identify three different interpretations of IMC and make brief notes explaining the principles which underpin each of them.

2. Explain the ideas concerning media-neutral planning. What is open planning?

3. Explain how various definitions of IMC have evolved.

4. What are the structural issues that can accelerate or hinder the development of IMC?

5. Prepare the outline for an essay exploring whether IMC is a strategic approach or just a means to correct internal operational difficulties and reduce media costs.

References

Anon (2013) HP launch integrated marketing campaign, *B2B Marketing,* 5 June, retrieved 28 January 2015 from www.b2bmarketing.net/news/archive/branding-news-hp-launch-integrated-marketing-campaign.

Anon (2015) How Dole turned a banana into a trophy, *PR Week,* 12 January, retrieved 11 April from www.prweek.com/article/1328734/dole-turned-banana-trophy.

Beechler, D. (2014) 9 key marketing lessons from American Express's small business Saturday, *Salesforce Marketing Cloud,* 14 November, retrieved 20 January 2015 from www.exacttarget.com/blog/9-key-marketing-lessons-from-american-expresss-small-business-saturday/.

Benjamin, K. (2012) Insight: public relations – in-house alignment – brands find strength by uniting divisions, *Campaign Asia-Pacific,* January, retrieved 28 March 2012 from http://web.ebscohost.com/ehost/detail?vid=6&hid=11&sid=315cc079-6217-4fd6-9f0b-2d63997952bf%40sessionmgr11&bdata=JnNpdGU9ZW hvc3QtbGl2ZQ%3d%3d#db=bch&AN=70287902.

Cheng, M. (2015) Dole: the first edible wearable banana is here, because why not, *Gadgetflow,* 17 March, retrieved 11 April 2015 from http://thegadgetflow.com/blog/dole-first-edible-wearable-banana-not/.

Cornelissen, J.P. (2003) Change, continuity and progress: the concept of integrated marketing communications and marketing communications practice, *Journal of Strategic Marketing,* 11 (December), 217–34.

Cornelissen, J.P. and Lock, A.R. (2000) Theoretical concept or management fashion? Examining the significance of IMC, *Journal of Advertising Research,* 50(5), 7–15.

Day, G. (2000) Managing market relationships, *Journal of the Academy of Marketing Science,* 28(1), Winter, 24–30.

Delgado-Ballester, E., Navarro, A. and Sicilia, M. (2012) Revitalising brands through communication messages: the role of brand familiarity, *European Journal of Marketing* 46(1/2), 31–51.

Dole (2015) *Banana Trophy,* retrieved 28 March 2015 from www.spikes.asia/winners/2014/pr/.

Duncan, T. (2002) *IMC: Using Advertising and Promotion to Build Brand* (International edition), New York: McGraw-Hill.

Duncan, T. and Everett, S. (1993) Client perceptions of integrated marketing communications, *Journal of Advertising Research,* 3(3), 30–9.

Duncan, T. and Moriarty, S. (1998) A communication-based marketing model for managing relationships, *Journal of Marketing,* 62(April), 1–13.

Duncan, T. and Mulhern, F. (2004) *A White Paper on the Status, Scope and Future of IMC Programs* (from the IMC symposium by the IMC programs at Northwestern University and University of Denver), New York: McGraw-Hill.

Eleftheriou-Smith, L.-M. (2012) TUI Travel marketing director Jeremy Ellis on keeping clear of troubled rivals, *Marketing,* 23 February, retrieved 27 March from: www.brandrepublic.com/features/1118064/TUI-Travel-marketing-director-Jeremy-Ellis-keeping-clear-troubled-rivals/?DCMP=ILC-SEARCH.

Finne, A. and Gronroos, C. (2009) Rethinking marketing communication: from integrated marketing communication to relationship communication, *Journal of Marketing communications,* 15(2–3), 179–95.

Gabrielli, V. and Balboni, B. (2010) SME practice towards integrated marketing communications, *Marketing Intelligence & Planning,* 28(3), 275–90.

Grein, A.F. and Gould, S.J. (1996) Globally integrated communications, *Journal of Marketing Communications,* 2, 141–58.

Gronroos, C. (2004) The relationship marketing process: communication, interaction, dialogue, value, *Journal of Business and Industrial Marketing,* 19(2), 99–113.

Hutton, J.G. (1996) Integrated relationship-marketing communications: a key opportunity for IMC, *Journal of Marketing Communications*, 2, 191–9.

IPA (2011) *New Models of Marketing Effectiveness: From Integration to Orchestration*, WARC.

Jenkinson, A. and Sain, B. (2004) Open planning: media neutral planning made simple, retrieved 14 November 2004 from www.openplanning.org/cases/openplanning/whitepaper.pdf.

Keller, K.L. (2001) Mastering the marketing communications mix: micro and macro perspectives on integrated marketing communications programs, *Journal of Marketing Management*, 17, 819–47.

Kitchen, P.J. and Shultz, D.E. (1997) Integrated marketing communications in US advertising agencies: an exploratory study, *Journal of Advertising Research*, 37(5), 7–18.

Kitchen, P.J. and Shultz, D.E. (1998) IMC – a UK ads agency perspective, *Journal of Marketing Management*, 14(2), 465–85.

Kitchen, P., Brignell, J., Li, T. and Spickett-Jones, G. (2004) The emergence of IMC: a theoretical perspective, *Journal of Advertising Research*, 44 (March), 19–30.

Kitchen, P.J., Spickett-Jones, G. and Grimes, T. (2007) Inhibition of brand integration amid changing agency structures, *Journal of Marketing Communications*, 13(2), 149–68.

Kliatchko, J. (2008) Revisiting the IMC construct: a revised definition and four pillars, *International Journal of Advertising*, 27(1), 133–60.

Kliatchko, J.G. and Shultz, D.E. (2014) Twenty years of IMC, *International Journal of Advertising*, 33(2), 373–90.

Lee, D.H. and Park, C.W. (2007) Conceptualization and measurement of multidimensionality of integrated marketing communications, *Journal of Advertising Research*, 47(3), September, 222–36.

Liodice, B. (2008) Essentials for integrated marketing, *Advertising Age*, 72(23) p. 26.

Mintzberg, H., Lampel, J.B., Quinn, J.B. and Ghoshal, S. (2003) *The Strategy Process*, 4th edition, Englewood Cliffs, NJ: Pearson Education.

Percy, L., Rossiter, J.R. and Elliot, R. (2001) *Strategic Advertising Management*, New York: Oxford University Press.

Pitta, D.A., Weisgal, M. and Lynagh, P. (2006) Integrating exhibit marketing into integrated marketing communications, *Journal of Consumer Marketing*, 23(3), 156–66.

Polachek, E. (2015) Junk miles: Dole tests wearable banana tech in Tokyo marathon, *Competitor.com*, 23 February, retrieved 11 April 2015 from http://running.competitor.com/2015/02/video/junk-miles-dole-tests-wearable-banana-tech-tokyo-marathon_123420.

Porter, M.E. (1980) *Competitive Strategy: Techniques for Analyzing Industries and Competitors*, New York: Free Press.

Ray, A. (2002) How to adopt a neutral stance, *Marketing*, 27 June, p. 627.

Reid, M. (2005) Performance auditing of integrated marketing communications (IMC) actions and outcomes, *Journal of Advertising*, 34(4), 41–54.

Shultz, D.E. (2012) IMC: who's doing it right? *Marketing News*, 29 February, p. 14.

Shultz, D.E., Tannenbaum, S.L. and Lauterborn, R. (1993) *Integrated Marketing Communications: Putting It Together and Making It Work*, Lincolnwood, IL: NTC Business Books.

Shimp, T.A. (2000) *Advertising Promotion: Supplemental Aspects of Integrated Marketing Communications*, 5th edition, Fort Worth, TX: Dryden Press, Harcourt College Publishers.

Smith, B.G. (2012) Organic integration: the natural process underlying communication integration, *Journal of Communications Management*, 16(1), 4–19.

Smith, P. (1996) Benefits and barriers to integrated communications, *Admap*, February, 19–22.

Spotts, H.E., Lambert, D.R. and Joyce, M.L. (1998) Marketing déjà vu: the discovery of integrated marketing communications, *Journal of Marketing Education*, 20(3), 210–18.

Swain, W.N. (2004) Perceptions of IMC after a decade of development: who's at the wheel, and how can we measure success? *Journal of Advertising Research*, 44(1), March, 46–65.

Tobaccowala, R. and Kugel, C. (2001) Planning and evaluating cross-media programs, *Admap*, February, 33–6.

Warc (2013) Heineken aligns TV and web, retrieved 19 May 2013 from www.warc.com/LatestNews/News/EmailNews.news?ID=31404&Origin=WARCNewsEmail#WvzKXkGBiZ8t05AI.99.

White, R. (2000) Chameleon brands: tailoring brand messages to consumers, *Admap*, July/August, 8–40.

Williams, M. (2011) How can agencies crack the puzzle of ad integration? *campaignlive.co.uk*, 8 September, retrieved 29 March 2012 from www.brandrepublic.com/analysis/1089822/agencies-crack-puzzle-ad-integration/?DCMP=ILC-SEARCH.

Part 3

The marketing communications mix

This is the largest part in the book, configured as three sections, which looks at the various elements that constitute the marketing communications mix. The first section examines the tools or disciplines, the second, messages and creativity issues, and the third considers the media.

Chapter 11 is about advertising and considers the role, use and types of advertising. Ideas about selling propositions are explored and how emotion precedes an exploration of the way advertising might work. Here consideration is given to some of the principal models and frameworks that have been published to best explain the process by which advertising might influence audiences.

Chapter 12 examines the role and characteristics of public relations, including a review of the various methods used in public relations, and crisis communications. The following chapter leads on naturally to explore sponsorship, while Chapter 14 examines both direct marketing and personal selling.

Chapters 15 and 16 both consider a range of disciplines. The first considers the principles and techniques of sales promotion, field marketing and brand experiences. The second explores brand placement, exhibitions, packaging and the rapidly developing area of brand licensing.

Chapter 17 examines the second element of the mix, messages and creativity. Attention is first given to the message source, issues relating to source credibility, and the use of spokespersons, either as the face of a brand or as an endorser. This is followed by a review of the need to balance the use of information and emotion in messages, and the way messages are constructed, before finally exploring the various appeals and ways in which messages can be presented.

The focus then changes to explore the nature, role and processes organisations use to manage the creative process. Here ideas about message framing and storytelling are developed before concluding with a review of a more contemporary perspective of content generation and creativity – namely, user-generated content.

The third and final element consists of three chapters that explore the nature, role and issues associated with managing the media. Chapter 18 considers the principles and practice associated with the media. In particular time is spent considering the way media can best be categorised. Here we introduce the notion of linear and interactive media in order to overcome some of the current classification issues.

Chapter 19 opens with an exploration of a range of interactive advertising formats, including behavioural targeting and native advertising, before considering the characteristics of search engine marketing, social media and various other formats. The final chapter considers ideas and theories associated with media planning and the way in which people use media. In addition to the conventional planning concepts usually associated with linear media, time is spent considering how automation, and programmatic advertising in particular, impacts on the delivery of interactive media.

The tools

Content

The media

For readers with access to the companion website that accompanies this book, there are supplementary chapters, drawn from previous editions, available in PDF form.

Creativity

Multichannel campaigns: media and tools

Marketing communications across borders

Business-to-business marketing communications

Chapter 11

Advertising: role, forms and strategy

Advertising is an integral part of society and affects people in many ways: commercially, culturally and psychologically at an individual level. Indeed, advertising is a powerful force, one that can shape perceptions, feelings, emotions, attitudes, understanding and patterns of individual and group behaviour.

Advertising has been of interest to academics, researchers, authors and marketing professionals for a long time. Any attempt to understand what advertising is, how it might work and how it is developing should be tempered with an appreciation of its complexity and inherent contradictions.

Aims and learning objectives

The aims of this chapter are to explore different ideas about advertising and to consider the complexities associated with understanding how clients can best use advertising in the marketing communications mix.

The learning objectives are to enable readers to:

1. consider the role that advertising plays in influencing our thoughts and behaviour;
2. define advertising as an independent discipline;
3. examine the use of selling propositions, and the role of emotion in advertising;
4. identify different types or forms of advertising;
5. explore various models, concepts and frameworks which have been used to explain how advertising is thought to influence individuals;
6. consider ways in which advertising can be used strategically;
7. review issues associated with consumer-generated advertising.

IWM London – 'Flight of the Stories'

IWM London, part of Imperial War Museums (IWM), offers a unique social history experience to visitors with a collection of artefacts which connect us to those who have lived through modern conflicts, whether on the front line or on the home front. The museum's collections provide a rich insight into how conflicts which Britain and the Commonwealth have been involved in around the world – from the First World War to the present day – have changed people's lives.

In July 2014, to mark the start of the Centenary of the First World War, the museum opened its new First World War Galleries. In addition to 'large objects' such as the Sopwith Camel plane and the Mark V tank, the First World War Galleries include a collection of personal artefacts – often donated by individuals – such as private correspondence, clothing, and other small objects that are rich in history and emotional power.

IWM briefed its advertising agency Johnny Fearless to develop a new campaign to support the opening of the new galleries. The brief identified two main objectives: firstly, the campaign should encourage people to visit the new First World War Galleries and, secondly, it should attract new audiences to IWM London whilst not alienating its existing core. To do this required a real understanding of what sets the museum apart from other visitor attractions and the development of a creative platform that would allow the museum's unique content to be showcased in a compelling way.

First the agency Planning team set about identifying what it is that sets IWM London apart. It is the objects, the physical pieces themselves, which connect the visitor with the history and which function as witnesses to the past. Often highly personal objects – such as a camisole or a letter – these artefacts represent a unique collection. Many of them were accumulated when the First World War was still taking place; the original Imperial War Museum was established in 1917 to collect individuals' stories. This insight led the agency team to a strategic proposition of IWM London as the 'People's witness'. The agency then needed to find a creative platform that would bring the museum and its stories to life.

A Creative team consisting of an Art Director and Copywriter were given the challenge of coming up with a creative solution. When the agency's Creative Director reviewed the creative routes developed, it was clear that one stood out from all the rest. Paul Domenet, the Creative Director, wanted to ensure that the creative work itself acted as a differentiator:

> We wanted to avoid going down the usual 'mud and blood' images of the First World War. We developed a number of ideas around the brief and for me it was all about finding a creative way of bringing these unique artefacts to life. We wanted to find a creative platform that would let the artefacts speak for themselves. This led us to thinking about using quotation marks as a symbolic way of giving the objects a voice.

The idea was storyboarded and shown to the client at a Tissue session where initial ideas are presented.

Exhibit 11.1	IMW created a film to attract visitors to its new First World War Galleries

Source: © Aardman/IWM.

Exhibit 11.2	**The film shows the stories flying home**
	Source: © Aardman/IWM.

IWM recognised the strength and uniqueness of the campaign and it was agreed to take the idea forward.

For the film, the idea was simple. Fly the quotation marks – the stories – from the fields of Northern France to their spiritual home, IWM London. The next challenge was deciding how to realise the idea. The creative work had to stand apart from other museums' messaging in order to differentiate IWM London's offering.

Finding a way of bringing the idea to life with a limited production budget called for more creative thinking. The agency were convinced that animation was the route to take and they were equally certain that any animated film which touched on an event of such national significance couldn't be done without the country's most celebrated animation company, Aardman. The agency approached Aardman who were hugely supportive of what IWM was trying to achieve and generously provided support to bring the campaign to life.

Darren Dubicki, the director, arrived with a vision for the film which was inspiring but also sympathetic to the subject matter. The visual aspects of the film were to have one foot in 1914 and one in 2014. The animation was inspired by renowned First World War artists such as Paul Nash, William Orpen and Norman Wilkinson. This school of painting was paid homage to by a modern artist, Aurelien Predal, who produced frames which were mini-masterpieces in themselves. Bringing together this early twentieth century style with the very twenty-first century 3D and CGI animation gives the film its unique look and feel.

The final creative work saw Predal's art literally 'projected' onto 3D frameworks. The quotation marks take flight and make their way through one tableau after another on their trip back to Britain. To keep the film as true to its subject matter as possible, we used modern voices to speak lines from letters and diaries and stories of real people. Those who had lived and, in many cases, died on the battlefields of The Somme and Ypres and Passchendaele. One voice, that of a soldier singing 'We're here because we're here', is the actual voice from 100 years ago digitally enhanced to sound as if he were singing today. Even the sound of shelling and gunfire is from the period.

Media: Print, poster, outdoor, radio and film (online and cinema).

Results: £4.5 million of PR was generated by the film alone. In the first three months, IWM London's visitor numbers were up by 70 per cent, far exceeding their target of 30 per cent.

Of the UK's free visitor attractions, Association of Leading Visitor Attractions (ALVA) figures for 2013/2014 show that IWM London saw the most significant increase in visitor numbers across the year: almost one million visitors in just six months – a 153 per cent increase on the same period in 2013.

This case was written by Anne-Fay Townsend, former Planning Partner at Johnny Fearless

Questions relating to this case can be found at the end of the chapter.

Introduction

Advertising is considered to be a significant means of communicating with target audiences, based on its potential to influence the way people think/feel, and behave. The thinking element may be concerned with the utilitarian or aspirational benefits of product ownership, or simply a matter of memorising the brand and its features for future recall. The behavioural element may be seen in terms of buying an advertised brand, visiting a website to enquire about a product's features or even sharing brand-related ideas with a friend or colleague. In the case of IWM London advertising is considered to have had a significant influence on the number of visitors to the new galleries at the museum.

Whatever the motivation, the content and delivery of advertising messages are derived from an understanding of the variety of contexts in which the messages are to be used. For example, research might reveal a poor brand image relative to the market leader, or audiences might misunderstand when or how to use a product or service. In both cases the messages are going to be different.

This chapter explores three main advertising issues. The first is about the role and use of advertising, how ideas about selling propositions and emotion can be used in advertising, and the different types or forms of advertising that can be identified.

The second concerns the way advertising might work. Here consideration is given to some of the principal models and frameworks that have been published to best explain the process by which advertising might influence audiences.

The third concerns the way in which advertising can be used strategically as part of a brand's development, and to review the significance of consumer-generated advertising.

The role of advertising

The principal role of advertising is to engage audiences. Whether it is on an international, national, local or direct basis, advertising can engage audiences by creating awareness, changing perceptions/attitudes and building brand values, or by influencing behaviour, often through calls-to-action.

Advertising has the capacity to reach large audiences with simple messages. These messages are intended to enable individuals to comprehend what an offering is, appreciate what its primary benefit is and how this might be of value to an individual. Wherever these individuals are located, the prime goals are to build awareness of a product or an organisation in the minds of the individuals and engage them. Engagement (as explored in Chapter 1) occurs when audiences are stimulated either to think about or take action about featured products, services, brands and organisations.

Having successfully engaged an audience, advertising can be used to achieve a number of DRIP-based outcomes (as set out in Chapter 1). Advertising is excellent at differentiating and positioning brands. It can be used to reinforce brand messages by reminding, reassuring or even refreshing an individual's perception of a brand. Advertising is excellent at informing audiences, mainly by creating awareness or helping them to learn about a brand or how it works. The one part of the DRIP framework where its ability is challenged is persuasion. Advertising is not so good at provoking or changing behaviour, and a different marketing communications mix is necessary to stimulate change.

In this circumstance sales promotion, direct marketing and personal selling are going to be prominent tools in the mix.

Management's control over advertising messages is strong; indeed, of all the tools in the communications mix, advertising has the greatest level of control. The message, once generated and signed off by the client, can be transmitted in an agreed manner and style and at times that match management's requirements. This means that, should the environment change unexpectedly, advertising messages can be 'pulled' immediately. For example, in 2013 a total of 13 brands including building society Nationwide and Nissan UK pulled their advertising from Facebook after growing pressure on advertisers whose ads were appearing next to content promoting domestic violence (Kemp, 2013). The advertising was having such a negative effect on the brands with over 50,000 tweets sent about the issue that many decided to pull their ads from the social media site (Kemp, 2013).

Scholars' paper 11.1   What about ethics in advertising?

Drumwright, M.E. and Murphy, P.E. (2009) The current state of advertising ethics: industry and academic perspectives, *Journal of Advertising*, 38(1), 83–107.

The radically transformed communications industry raises the question: what is the current state of advertising ethics? The authors distinguish between ethics in messages and the industry as a whole and conduct interviews with practitioners, academics, review textbooks and the academic literature. The paper provides a useful review of the literature regarding ethics in advertising.

See also: Turnbull, S., Howe-Walsh, L. and Boulanouar, A. (2016) The advertising standardisation debate revisited: implications of Islamic ethics on standardisation/localisation of advertising in Middle East Islamic States, *Journal of Islamic Marketing*, 7(1).

Advertising costs can be considered in one of two ways. On the one hand, there are the absolute costs, which are the costs of buying the space in magazines or newspapers or the time on television, cinema or radio. These costs can be enormous, and they impact directly on cash flow. For example, the rate card cost of a full-page (colour) advertisement in the *Daily Mail* on a Thursday or Friday was £48,636 in June 2015. The national rate card cost to show an ad for a week with a blockbuster film in the UK in June 2015, through Pearl and Dean, was £36,000.

On the other hand, there are the relative costs, which are those costs incurred to reach a member of the target audience with the key message. So, if an audience is measured in hundreds of thousands, or even millions on television, the cost of the advertisement spread across each member of the target audience reduces the cost per contact significantly.

Advertising's main tasks are to build awareness and to (re)position brands, by enabling people to make appropriate brand-related associations. These associations may be based on the utility and functional value a brand represents, or on the imagery and psychological benefits that are conveyed. The regular use of advertising, in coordination with the other elements of the communications mix, can be important to the creation and maintenance of these associations and even build a brand personality.

Viewpoint 11.1   Advertising to keep the Human Rights Act

Advertising is seen as a very effective means of delivering messages for political and social causes as it offers wide reach and high coverage. The use of advertising can have a very powerful impact on audiences and often attracts additional media exposure for the organisation and the message. Amnesty International is one organisation that is well known for their use of advertising to deliver their messages and lobby governments and other organisations.

In 2015 Amnesty International ran a double-page spread in *The Times* to ask the government to keep the Human Rights Act. The crowdfunded ad was written in the style of a letter to the Lord Chancellor and Secretary of State for Justice, RT Hon Michael Gove, asking him to save the Human Rights Act. The illustration used in the ad showed the Human Rights Act being torn apart and the ad included a list of names of 1,000 people that had each paid £10 to fund it.

The use of crowdfunding for the ad is a novel way to pay for advertising and allowed the organisation to demonstrate the support they have for the campaign. Showing the names of those that have funded the ad adds to the credibility of the message. Crowdfunding also engaged audiences in the campaign before the ad ran with messages posted on social media sites to get funders to sign up.

Source: Amnesty International (2015); Facebook.com/AmnestyUK (2015); Oakes (2015).

Question: Why do you think so many people were keen to fund the ad?

Task: Find another example of a crowdfunded ad and identify why you think the advertiser chose to use crowdfunding for the campaign.

Exhibit 11.3   Amnesty International uses advertising to lobby government

Source: Ad ©Amnesty International UK 2015. Illustration © Ben Jennings.

Exhibit 11.4	**Amnesty International requested funding from supporters**
	Source: © Amnesty International UK 2015.

Advertising can be used as a mobility barrier, deterring exit from and entry to markets. Some organisations are initially attracted to a new market by the potential profits, but a key entry decision factor will be the weight of advertising, that is the investment or 'spend' necessary to generate demand and a sufficient return on the investment. Many people feel that some brands sustain their large market share by sheer weight of advertising: for example, the washing powder brands of Procter & Gamble and Unilever. In many product categories word-of-mouth communications and the use of digital technologies can stimulate strong levels of awareness. Google and Hotmail are prime examples of contemporary brands developed without the use of advertising. However, advertising, both offline and online, is still a key driver of both brand values and directing certain behaviour, most notably driving people to a website.

Advertising can create competitive advantage by providing the communications necessary for target audiences to frame a product or service. By providing a frame or the perceptual space within which to categorise a product, target audiences are enabled to position an offering relative to their other significant products much more easily. Therefore, advertising can provide the means for differentiation and sustainable competitive advantage. It should also be appreciated, however, that differentiation may be determined by the quality of the execution of the advertisements, rather than through the content of the messages. The John Lewis case study (discussed in Chapter 17) demonstrates how advertising can be used to differentiate a brand from competitors.

There has also been a shift in focus away from mass communications towards more personalised messages delivered through different, often interactive media. This shift has been demonstrated by the increased use of direct marketing and the Internet by organisations over the past 10 years. It can also be argued that the development of direct marketing is a response to some of the weaknesses, to do with cost and effectiveness of the other tools, most notably advertising.

The marketing communications mix has expanded and become a more complex concept, but essentially it is now capable of delivering two main solutions. On the one hand it can be used to develop and maintain brand values, and on the other it could be used to change behaviour through the delivery of calls-to-action. From a strategic perspective, the former is oriented to the long term and the latter to the short term.

Organisations, therefore, are faced with a dilemma. While there is the need to create brands that are perceived to be of value, there is also the need to prompt or encourage customers into purchase behaviour. To put it another way, marketing communications should be used to encourage buyers along the purchase decision path, but how should advertising be involved, what is its contribution in creating brand values, and which and how many of an organisation's other, yet scarce communications resources should be used to prompt behaviour?

Defining advertising

Definitions of advertising have always varied. Richards and Curran (2002) found differences in the way advertising was defined by authors of various textbooks. They also noted that many of the definitions used the same or similar words. These core words were *paid*, *non-personal*, *identified sponsor*, *mass media* and *persuade* or *influence*. This enabled them to propose a definition that encapsulated a general consensus around the essence of these words. They referred to this as a *current* definition:

> *Advertising is a paid, non-personal communication from an identified sponsor, using mass media to persuade or influence an audience.*

This interpretation, however, is debatable. The development of digital technology and the Internet in particular has led to a plethora of new communications techniques and approaches that raises questions about the validity of some of the words in the current definition. Is 'paid' still viable? Can some forms of advertising be unpaid? Surely the use of commercial text messaging indicates that advertising can be 'personal' and the 'mass media' label must therefore be an invalid restriction.

Using a Delphi research approach, Richards and Curran (2002) sought to develop a more contemporary definition of advertising. After much discussion and re-evaluation of the issues and wording, a consensus formed around the following *proposed* definition:

> *Advertising is a paid, mediated form of communication from an identifiable source, designed to persuade the receiver to take some action, now or in the future.*

These changes might be subtle, but they represent an important and methodical attempt to review and update the meaning of advertising. The word 'mediated' replaces the restriction of 'mass media'. 'Source' replaces 'an identified sponsor', and 'persuasion' replaces the duplication apparent in 'persuade' and 'influence'.

Since Richards and Curran (2002) published their paper, however, the media landscape has changed dramatically and new forms of advertising have emerged. Native advertising for example, which is seen to be 'a form of paid media where the ad experience follows the natural form and function of the user experience in which it is placed' (MMA, 2015: 4), has been criticised for not always being clearly 'identifiable'. As native advertising matches the design of the media format it can sometimes be difficult for consumers to differentiate between paid content and non-paid content, unless clearly indicated.

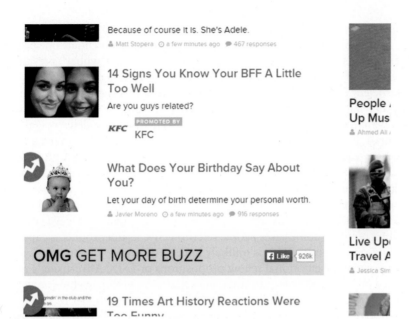

Exhibit 11.5	**Branded content in BuzzFeed**
	BuzzFeed labels all branded content with a yellow box and the words 'promoted by' written inside to make it clear to the reader that the content has been paid for.
	Source: BuzzFeed News.

Defining what is and what is not 'advertising' in online forms has created a big challenge for academics and industry. Campbell et al. (2014) highlight the problems identifying which forms of online brand-related content should be seen as advertising and propose a new categorisation to help identify different forms. See Scholars' paper 11.2 for more information.

Scholars' paper 11.2   What is advertising?

Campbell, C., Cohen, J. and Ma, J. (2014) Advertisements just aren't advertisements anymore: a new typology for evolving forms of online 'advertising', *Journal of Advertising Research*, 54(1), 7–10.

Recognising the challenges of defining online advertising the authors suggest a new typology of online brand-related content. They propose a two-dimensional categorisation which considers who created the content and whether the content or its creation was paid for.

See also: Richards, J.I. and Curran, C. M. (2002) Oracles on 'advertising': searching for a definition, *Journal of Advertising*, 31(2), 63–77.

Selling propositions

For a very long time in the advertising world, great emphasis was placed upon the use of unique selling propositions, or USPs. Advertising was thought to work most effectively when the message said something about a product that no competitor brand could offer.

For example, Olay claims its products offer 'younger looking skin'. USPs are based on product features and are related to particular attributes that differentiate one product from another, as demonstrated by many washing powders that wash 'whiter', presumably than the competition. If this uniqueness was of value to a consumer then the USP alone was thought sufficient to persuade consumers to purchase. However, as Barwise and Meehan (2009:1) point out: customers rarely buy a product because it offers something unique. What they want are better products and services, something that delivers real value.

The reign of the USP, however, was short-lived when technology enabled me-too and own-label brands to be brought to market very quickly and product lifecycles became increasingly short. The power of the USP was eroded and with it the basis of product differentiation as it was known then. In addition, the power and purpose of advertising's role to differentiate was challenged. It is interesting that many people still refer to a product and its advertising in terms of its USP. Some companies believe USP refers to a 'single' selling point. In some cases people refer to USPs, as if a product is capable of having several unique qualities. This is unlikely and is essentially a contradiction in terms.

What emerged were emotional selling propositions or ESPs. Advertising's role became more focused on developing brand values, ones that were based on emotion and imagery. This approach to communications helps build brand awareness, desire and aspirational involvement. However, it often fails to provide customers with a rationale or explicit reason to purchase, what is often referred to as a 'call-to-action'. Other tools were required to provide customers with an impetus to act and sales promotions, event marketing, road shows and, later, direct marketing evolved to fulfil this need. These tools are known collectively as *below-the-line communications tools* and their common characteristic is that they are all capable of driving action or creating behavioural change.

The use of emotion in advertising

The role of emotion in advertising is very important. For a long time advertising was thought to work by people responding to advertising in a logical, rational and cognitive manner. This indicated that people only take out the utilitarian aspect of advertising messages (cleans better, smells fresher). This is obviously not true and there is certainly a strong case for the use of emotion in advertising in order to influence and change attitudes through the affective component of the attitudinal construct (see Chapter 3).

Most advertised brands are not normally new to consumers as they have had some experience of the brand, whether that be through use or just through communications. This experience affects their interpretation of advertising as memories have already been formed. The role of feelings in the way ads work suggests a consumerist interpretation of how advertising works rather than the rational view, which is much more a researcher's interpretation (Ambler, 1998).

Viewpoint 11.2   Emotional hits

In 2014 Campaign polled readers in the industry to find out which ads they thought were the best emotional ads and released a list of the top 10 'most emotional' ads ever seen in the UK. The ads that made the top 10 were:

1. Cesar 'Journey' (2013)
2. John Lewis 'Always a woman' (2010)

3. Channel 4 'Meet the superhumans' (2012)

4. Procter & Gamble 'Best job' (2012)

5. BBC 'Perfect day' (1997)

6. Hovis 'Go on lad' (2008)

7. Oxo 'Last supper' (1999)

8. Sussex Safer Roads 'Embrace life' (2010)

9. Aviva 'Holiday packing' (2011)

10. NHS 'Rebecca' (2000)

Many of the ads which featured in the top 10 use storytelling devices to help convey the emotion. The Oxo 'Last supper' ad, for example, starred actress Lynda Bellingham who had appeared in Oxo ads for the last 16 years as the Oxo mum. The ad 'Last supper' showed the Oxo family sharing dinner for the last time and drew to an end a story that consumers had shared for nearly two decades. Hovis also used storytelling effectively to portray the emotional journey of a young boy and we share key historical moments from the UK's twentieth century as he passes through them. John Lewis's 'Always a women' ad follows a similar 'watch the child grow up' formula as the ad leads us through the life of a woman. The story of the young girl growing up, getting married and enjoying her grandchildren is supported by an emotive song track which enhances the emotional engagement.

Children often play a central role in ads to heighten the sense of emotion. As all viewers can relate to their own childhood experiences this increases an ad's emotional engagement. While Hovis uses a young boy, the NHS features a young girl called 'Rebecca'. This anti-smoking ad is a tear jerking account of how Rebecca is coping with the discovery that her Dad had lung cancer. This ad taps into parents' feeling of guilt and uses this young girl's experience to highlight the pain that smoking can bring to smokers' children.

It appears from the 2014 industry poll, however, that animals may be considered more emotionally engaging than children, since Cesar 'Journey' was voted the best emotional ad. Animals are often used in advertising to draw on viewers' heartstrings. The Cesar ad shows the close emotional bond that develops between dogs and their owners. Set in a picturesque Mediterranean village, we share the life of a widower as goes about his daily routines accompanied by his dog. The dog is with him in everything he

Exhibit 11.6	**Hovis used emotion in its campaigns**

Hovis takes an emotional route and shows the heritage of the brand through the journey of a young boy as he grows up.

Source: Hovis Ltd.

does and is even by his side when he visits his wife's grave. While dogs are seen to be 'man's best friend' Budweiser's 2015 Super Bowl commercial 'Lost dog' also chose an emotional route to show how dogs can also be a horse's best friend. The Budweiser ad shows how advertising continues to use animals to engage consumers emotionally.

Source: Anon (2015); Chase (2015); Swift (2014).

Question: Other than using children and animals, how else can advertisers make emotional associations with their audiences?

Task: Find two emotional ads. What do they have in common?

Exhibit 11.7	**Cesar's 'Journey' ad**
	This tells the story of an old man and his best friend, a Highland terrier who accompanies him everywhere, including a visit to his wife's grave. The storyline and the music combine to deliver a highly emotional ad.
	Source: © Mars, Incorporated. All Rights Reserved.

Consumers view advertising in the context of their experience of the category and memories of the brand. Aligned with this approach is the concept of likeability, where the feelings evoked by advertising trigger and shape attitudes to the brand and attitudes to the advertisement (Vakratsas and Ambler, 1999). Feelings and emotions play an important role in advertising, especially when advertising is used to build awareness levels and brand strength. The case study of John Lewis's Christmas campaign in Chapter 17 highlights the effectiveness of using emotion in advertising.

Most of the models presented later in this chapter are developed on the principle that individuals are cognitive processors and that ads are understood as a result of information processing. The best examples of these are the sequential models referred to earlier (see Chapter 4) where information is processed step by step. This view is not universally accepted. Researchers such as Krugman (1971), Ehrenberg (1974), Corke and Heath (2004), Heath and Feldwick (2008) and Heath et al. (2009) all dispute the importance of information processing, denying that attention is necessary for people to understand ads and that the creativity within an ad is more important in many circumstances than the rational message the ad purports to deliver.

Types of advertising

There are many ways of categorising advertising, but five perspectives encapsulate the variety of types available. These are the source, the message, the recipient, the media and place (see Figure 11.1).

The source or sender of a message results in different forms of advertising. Using the value chain as a frame, we can identify manufacturers, who in turn will use *manufacturing advertising* to promote their brands to end-users, and retailers who use advertising to attract consumers, *retail advertising*. On some occasions manufacturers collaborate with retailers and use *cooperative advertising*.

Outside the commercial arena, governments use *collective advertising* to communicate with nations, regions and districts, while many not-for-profit organisations use idea-based advertising. Viewpoint 11.1 provides an example of how advertising is used in a non-commercial context.

The message can provide a further way of categorising advertising. Informational advertising uses messages that predominantly provide information about product and service attributes and features. *Transformational advertising* uses messages that are essentially emotional and which have the capacity to transform the way an individual feels about a product or service. An extreme form of transformational advertising is shock advertising.

Institutional or corporate advertising is undertaken by organisations to express values, intentions, position, or other organisation-based issues. This type of advertising can also be used to build reputation, goodwill and relationships, at either a product/service or corporate level.

Theme advertising is most easily represented by ads designed for employee recruitment, or to attract people to events and entertainment venues. The origins of recruitment advertising are of course rooted in hiring help and employees in order to develop an organisation. However, more recently some employers have started to use this type of

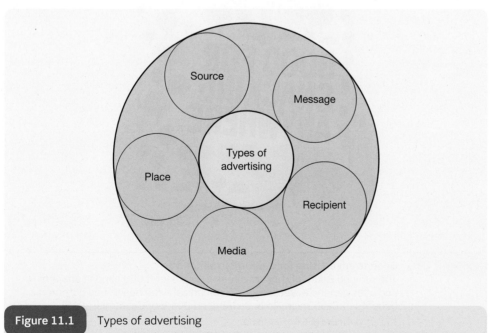

Figure 11.1	Types of advertising

Source: de Pelsmaker et al. (2010). Used with permission from Pearson Education Ltd.

advertising as a form of reputational instrument. Whether it is through broadcast, print, or online and social network media, advertising is used to influence corporate image and reputation in order to create perceptions that the organisation is a desirable place to work. This might be to sow the seeds and build relationships, in order to recruit at some point in the future, rather than now.

Generic advertising is used to promote a category of products such as dog food, New Zealand lamb or South African wine. For example, Kolsarici and Vakratsas (2010) cite Ono (1994) and Campbell's generic campaign 'Never underestimate the power of soup'. This was used to promote the general qualities of soup as a meal, and the result was increased sales for the brand.

Finally in this section, direct-response advertising is used to provoke action. Sometimes referred to as call-to-action advertising, this approach is often used to support sales promotion programmes.

The recipient of advertising messages may be *consumers (advertising)* or *businesses*. The latter can be broken down to industrial and trade advertising. The former represents advertising for products that are used within production and manufacturing processes, whereas the latter concerns products that are resold down the supply chain.

The media category refers to the type of media used to carry advertising messages. For example, *broadcast advertising* refers to the use of television and radio, *print advertising* to newspapers and magazines, *out-of-home* to billboards, posters, transport and terminal building, *digital* to Internet, mobile and online advertising. In addition, there is *ambient advertising* (petrol pump nozzles, golf holes, washrooms) and cinema advertising. Each of these media is explored in greater detail later in the text. Related to this are display

Exhibit 11.8	**Generic advertising for Californian almonds**
	The Almond Board of California represents over 6,000 almond growers and uses generic advertising to communicate the health and nutritional benefits of Californian almonds (Almond Board of California, 2015).
	Source: © Almond Board of California.

ads that are placed in media for recipients to view, consider, process and form views. These might be magazine or newspaper ads, or banners and pop-ups. Digital media enable interactivity and here both search and social media advertising have become prominent types of advertising.

Place advertising is most commonly represented by *international advertising*. Reference is normally made to *standardised advertising*, where a single message is used in all countries and regions, and to *adapted advertising* where messages and media are altered and amended to reflect local needs and customs.

Viewpoint 11.3   Using advertising to find missing people

The charity Missing People (MP) offers a lifeline to the 250,000 people who run away or go missing each year in the UK. For the families left behind, MP search and provide specialised support. This involves the provision of a free, confidential, helpline service which is available 24 hours a day, seven days a week, by phone, email, text and online.

Their work has always relied on the generosity of media owners but the long lead times of traditional low cost advertising channels, such as print or flyers, prevent MP from reacting quickly to a new search request, or stopping one when an individual is found. In order to grow the charity needed a responsive media platform that would generate appeals at a national or regional level and at the same time drive high levels of awareness for vulnerable people.

Building on US use of digital outdoor media to find escaped convicts, MP worked with the Outdoor Media Centre to develop a partnership through which unsold/spare digital advertising space could be used to find missing people. Ads for each individual missing person could be broadcast close to the location where the individual went missing. Using OpenLoop, a purpose built campaign management platform, MP could amend copy, display different copy in different cities, remove an appeal in a matter of minutes and regionalise their appeals so that multiple searches could run simultaneously and so use the available media more effectively.

The campaign was rooted in the highly flexible nature of the outdoor medium, its short lead times and controllable format, plus its ability to target key locations, such as shopping areas and transport termini. In addition to the links made to MP's Twitter and Facebook pages, audiences could donate and connect with the charity online, as well as share the campaign with friends and family.

The media laydown is always changing because it is driven by the number of appeals that are required and the level of unsold inventory in the market. This allows MP to take advantage of fluctuating markets and gain enormous exposure that would normally be unattainable for a small advertiser.

The campaign ran across digital sites with 15 different media owners, and in its first year delivered approximately 4.9 million transmissions across more than 4,000 panels and over £10 million of media value. In 2013, MP reconnected 683 missing adults and enabled 393 missing children to find a place of safety.

Source: McCarthy (2014); www.exterionmedia.com; www.missingpeople.org.uk/; www.outdoormediacentre.org.uk.

Question: How might Missing People enhance their partnership with the Outdoor Media Centre?

Task: Make a list of other charities who might benefit from liaising with a particular part of the advertising industry.

Exhibit 11.9	**A digital outdoor ad used by Missing People**
	Source: Alamy Images/Howard Davies.

Advertising models and concepts

For many years a large number of researchers have attempted to determine how advertising works. Finding a real answer would bring commercial success. We know that for
a message to be communicated successfully it should be meaningful to the recipient.
Messages need to be targeted at the right audience, be capable of gaining attention, be
understandable, relevant and acceptable.

One approach to answering this question has been to model the advertising process.
From such a model it should be possible to test the linkages and deduce how advertising
works. Unfortunately, despite the effort of many researchers over many years, no single
model has attracted widespread agreement. However, from all the work undertaken in
this area some views have been prominent. The following sections seek to present some
of these more influential perspectives.

The elaboration likelihood model

What should be clear from the preceding sections is that neither the purely cognitive nor
the purely emotional interpretation of how marketing communications works is realistic.
In effect, it is probable that both have an important part to play in the way the various
tools, and advertising in particular, work. The degree of emphasis, however, should
vary according to the context within which the marketing communications message is
expected to work.

One approach to utilise both these elements has been developed by Petty and Cacioppo
(1983). The elaboration likelihood model (ELM) has helped to explain how cognitive
processing, persuasion and attitude change occur when different levels of involvement
are present. Elaboration refers to the extent to which an individual needs to develop
and refine information necessary for decision-making to occur. If an individual has a
high level of motivation or ability to process information, elaboration is said to be high.
If an individual's motivation or ability to process information is poor, then the level

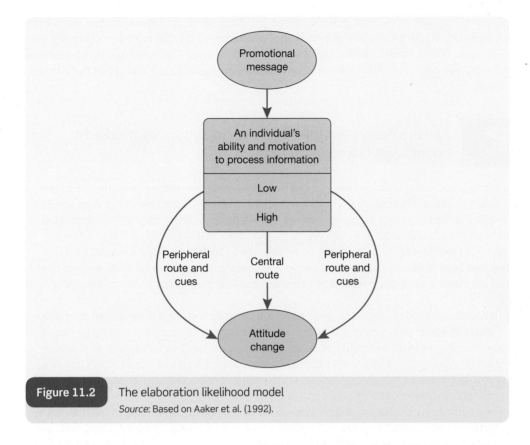

Figure 11.2	The elaboration likelihood model
	Source: Based on Aaker et al. (1992).

of elaboration is said to be low. The ELM distinguishes two main cognitive processes, as depicted in Figure 11.2.

Under the central route the receiver is viewed as very active and involved. As the level of cognitive response is high, the ability of the message (advertisement) to persuade will depend on the quality of the argument rather than executional factors. For example, the purchase of a consumer durable such as a car or washing machine normally requires a high level of involvement. Consequently, potential customers would be expected to be highly involved and willing to read brochures and information about the proposed car or washing machine prior to demonstration or purchase. Their decision to act would depend on the arguments used to justify the model as suitable for the individual. For the car purchase these might include the quiet and environmentally friendly engine, the relatively excellent fuel consumption and other safety and performance indicators, together with the comfort of the interior and the effortless driving experience. Whether the car is shown as part of a business executive's essential 'kit' or the commercial is flamboyant and rich will be immaterial for those in the central route.

Under the peripheral route, the receiver is seen to lack the ability to process information and is not likely to engage cognitive processing. Rather than thinking about and evaluating the message content, the receiver tends to rely on what have been referred to as 'peripheral cues', which may be incidental to the message content. Panasonic uses peripheral cues to attract attention to its brand. This is because most people have low levels of elaboration concerning picture technology and electronics.

In low-involvement situations, a celebrity may serve to influence attitudes positively. This is based upon the creation of favourable attitudes towards the source rather than engaging the viewer in the processing of the message content. For example, Gary Lineker has been the celebrity spokesperson used to endorse Walkers crisps for many years. Gary Lineker, former Tottenham and England football hero and now BBC sports presenter, was an important peripheral cue for Walkers crisps (more so than the nature of the product), in eventually persuading a consumer to try the brand or retaining current users. Think crisps, think Gary Lineker, think Walkers. Where high involvement is present, any celebrity endorsement is of minor significance to the quality of the message claims.

Viewpoint 11.4	'Natural' engagement in China: using social media to encourage brand involvement

The Chinese shampoo market is highly competitive and although Pantene were the market leaders they were finding it increasingly difficult to engage younger consumers. The high disposable incomes of 25–35 year old women made this target group highly attractive and Pantene were beginning to lose market share to new brands entering the market.

While their competitors were using mass media to communicate to audiences, Pantene identified that these younger consumers spent more time on social media and saw this as an opportunity to engage this target. In particular, consumers were seen to be keen to share experiences rather than have messages delivered to them.

To launch their new nature-based shampoo range Cora, which included the natural ingredient avocado, Pantene used a strategy of social engagement. To encourage consumers to share their experiences of 'nature' they set up a microblog and mobile platform which allowed opportunities for consumers to interact with each other and the brand. To start conversations, Pantene shot a series of videos with Tang Wei, a Chinese celebrity who is known for her love of nature. Consumers were encouraged to share their own experiences and comment on other postings.

The brand created a community of sharing and provided an opportunity for consumers to tell their own stories about their nature experiences. Coupons were given as rewards to those consumers who had the largest Twitter following or whose pictures were liked the most.

The campaign results were impressive. Over 2 million consumers shared their experiences on the social media platform within the first three weeks. In total 28 million retweets were generated and 87,809 watched the videos. In business terms sales increased by 30 per cent.

Source: Hsiang-yi (2012); Kumar (2013, 2014).

Question: Why do you think Pantene chose to use a Chinese celebrity in the campaign? Which route within the elaboration likelihood model (ELM) does this suggest Pantene's consumers follow when purchasing shampoo?

Task: Find three examples of shampoo advertising from a market of your choice and explain the ELM route assumed by each.

Communications strategy should be based upon the level of cognitive processing that the target audience is expected to engage in and the route taken to affect attitudinal change. If the processing level is low (low motivation and involvement), the peripheral route should dominate and emphasis needs to be placed on the way the messages are executed and on the emotions of the target audience (Heath, 2000). If the central route is expected, the content of the messages should be dominant and the executional aspects need only be adequate.

The ELM model has not been without criticism, however, and a recent review of the model by Kitchen et al. (2014) questions the validity and relevance of the model in modern communications contexts. The authors raise concerns over the model's assumptions and descriptive nature (Kitchen et al., 2014).

Scholars' paper 11.3 | **Peripheral or central thinking**

Petty, R.E. and Cacioppo, J.T. (1984) Source factors and the elaboration likelihood model of persuasion, *Advances in Consumer Research,* **11(1), 668–72.**

This is an important paper because it introduces the elaboration likelihood model. This is based on ideas about how people process ads, relative to how motivated they are to process the information. When people lack motivation and are unable to process a message, they prefer to rely on simple cues in the persuasion context, such as the expertise or attractiveness of the message source. When people are highly motivated and able to process the arguments in a message, they are interested in reviewing all the available information.

See also: Kitchen, P.J., Kerr, G., Schultz, D.E., McColl, R. and Pals, H. (2014) The elaboration likelihood model: review, critique and research agenda, *European Journal of Marketing,* 48(11/12), 2033–50.

Eclectic models of advertising

A number of new frameworks and explanations have arisen, all of which claim to reflect practice. In other words these new ideas about how advertising works are a practitioner reflection of the way advertising is considered to work, or at least used, by advertising agencies. The first to be considered here are four main advertising frameworks developed by O'Malley (1991) and Hall (1992). These reflect the idea that there are four key ways in which advertising works, depending on context and goals. This also says that different advertising works in different ways; there is no one all-embracing model. These were updated by Willie (2007) to incorporate the impact of digital media and interactivity. Figure 11.3 depicts the essence of all of these ideas. The essential point is that advertising cannot be explained by a single interpretation or model.

Each of the following sections has two components. The first refers to the original interpretation, and the second to the work of Willie and the digital element.

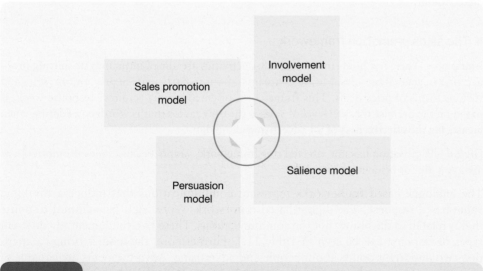

Figure 11.3 Four interpretations of how different ads work

1. The persuasion framework

Analogue – The first framework assumes advertising works rationally, and that a 'brand works harder for you'. This is based on messages that are persuasive, because they offer a rational difference, grounded in unique selling propositions (USPs). Persuasion is effected by gradually moving buyers through a number of sequential steps, as depicted through hierarchy of effects models such as AIDA.

Digital – Digitisation enables persuasion to be extended into opportunities for exploration, as individuals can now be encouraged to search, 'go to', and to find out more. Willie (2007) points out that this is still persuasion, but it occurs through guided exploration, rather than mere narration.

2. The involvement framework

Analogue – Involvement-based advertisements work by drawing the audience into the advertisement and eliciting a largely emotional form of engagement. Involvement with the brand develops because the messages convey that the 'brand means more to you'. As Willie (2007) indicates, involvement can be developed through shared values (Dove), aspirational values (American Express) or by personifying a brand, perhaps by using celebrities (Adidas).

Digital – Today digitisation develops the notion of involvement by encouraging people to play. This is about content creation and consumers controlling brands. User-generated content can be seen through ads (crowd-sourcing), blogs, wikis, videos and social networking, for example. The example of Doritos given in Viewpoint 11.4 shows how involving consumers in idea generation works.

3. The salience framework

Analogue – This interpretation is based upon the premise that advertising works by standing out, by being different from all other advertisements in the product class. The ads used by brands such as Cillit Bang, GoCompare.com, Injurylawyers4u and Sheila's Wheels were deemed by consumers to be irritating, partly because the messages make people think about the brand more frequently than they would prefer.

Digital – Contemporary interpretations of salience incorporate ideas about sharing messages about the brand either directly or virally, and getting the brand discussed, mentioned and talked about.

4. The sales promotion framework

Analogue – This view holds that advertising activities are aimed ultimately at shifting product: that is, generating sales. Messages are invitations to participate in promotions, sales and various forms of price deals. This framework, oriented mainly to direct-response work, is based on the premise that the level of sales is the only factor that is worth considering when measuring the effectiveness of an advertising campaign.

Digital – Digitisation has not affected this framework, simply because sales promotion was always a 'do' or behavioural model.

The analogue-based frameworks represent communications that induce a thinking, value-based response. The digital-based frameworks represent a behavioural response that is related to the brand, not the communications. These two fundamentally different types of response can be seen in Table 11.1. Furthermore, the models bring to attention two important points about people and advertising. Advertisements are capable of generating two very clear types of response: a response to the advertisement itself and a response to the featured brand. Both have clear roles to play in advertising strategy.

Table 11.1 Digital and analogue advertising messages

Analogue-delivered messages say	Framework	Digitally delivered messages encourage
This is the reason why this brand is different	Persuasion	People to explore a brand such as search
Imagine you are associated with the brand	Involvement	People to play and create content
Please think about this brand	Salience	People to talk and share information about a brand
Act now because you will be rewarded	Promotion	People to act now because they will be rewarded

The Strong and the Weak theories of advertising

Many of the explanations offered to date are based on the premise that advertising is a potent marketing force, one that is persuasive and which is done to people. More recent views of advertising theory question this fundamental perspective. The second group of eclectic interpretations about how advertising works concerns ideas about advertising as a force for persuasion and as a force for reminding people about brands. Prominent among these theorists are Jones, McDonald and Ehrenberg, some of whose views will now be presented. Jones (1991) presented the new views as the Strong theory of advertising and the Weak theory of advertising.

The Strong theory of advertising

All the models presented so far are assumed to work on the basis that they are capable of affecting a degree of change in the knowledge, attitudes, beliefs and, sometimes, the behaviour of audiences. Jones refers to this as the Strong theory of advertising, and it appears to have been universally adopted as a foundation for commercial activity.

According to Jones, exponents of this theory hold that advertising can persuade someone to buy a product that they have never previously purchased. Furthermore, continual long-run purchase behaviour can also be generated. Under the Strong theory, advertising is believed to be capable of increasing sales at the brand and class levels. These upward shifts are achieved through the use of manipulative and psychological techniques, which are deployed against consumers who are passive, possibly because of apathy, and are generally incapable of processing information intelligently. The most appropriate theory would appear to be the hierarchy of effects model, where sequential steps move buyers forward to a purchase, stimulated by timely and suitable promotional messages.

The Weak theory of advertising

Increasing numbers of European writers argue that the Strong theory does not reflect practice. Most notable of these writers is Ehrenberg (1988, 1997), who believes that a consumer's pattern of brand purchases is driven more by habit than by exposure to promotional messages. The framework proposed by Ehrenberg is the awareness–trial–reinforcement (ATR) framework. Awareness is required before any purchase can be made, although the elapsed time between awareness and action may be very short or very long. For the few people intrigued enough to want to try a product, a trial purchase constitutes the next phase. This may be stimulated by retail availability as much as by advertising, word-of-mouth or personal selling stimuli. Reinforcement follows to maintain awareness and provide reassurance to help the customer to repeat the pattern of thinking and behaviour and to cement the brand in the repertoire for occasional purchase activity. Advertising's role is to breed brand familiarity and identification (Ehrenberg, 1997) and is considered to be a weak force.

Following on from the original ATR model (Ehrenberg, 1974), various enhancements have been suggested. However, Ehrenberg added a further stage in 1997, referred to as the nudge.

He argues that some consumers can 'be nudged into buying the brand more frequently (still as part of their split-loyalty repertoires) or to favour it more than the other brands in their consideration sets'. Advertising need not be any different from before; it just provides more reinforcement that stimulates particular habitual buyers into more frequent selections of the brand from their repertoire.

According to the Weak theory, advertising is capable of improving people's knowledge, and so is in agreement with the Strong theory. In contrast, however, consumers are regarded as selective in determining which advertisements they observe and only perceive those that promote products that they either use or have some prior knowledge of. This means that they already have some awareness of the characteristics of the advertised product. It follows that the amount of information actually communicated is limited. Advertising, Jones continues, is not potent enough to convert people who hold reasonably strong beliefs that are counter to those portrayed in an advertisement. The time available (30 seconds in television advertising) is not enough to bring about conversion and, when combined with people's ability to switch off their cognitive involvement, means there may be no effective communications. Advertising is employed as a defence, to retain customers and to increase product or brand usage. Advertising is used to reinforce existing attitudes, not necessarily to change them drastically.

Unlike the Strong theory, this perspective accepts that, when people say that they are not influenced by advertising, they are in the main correct. It also assumes that people are not apathetic or even stupid, but capable of high levels of cognitive processing.

In summary, the Strong theory suggests that advertising can be persuasive, can generate long-run purchasing behaviour, can increase sales and regards consumers as passive. The Weak theory suggests that purchase behaviour is based on habit and that advertising can improve knowledge and reinforce existing attitudes. It views consumers as active problem-solvers.

These two perspectives serve to illustrate the dichotomy of views that has emerged about this subject. They are important because they are both right and they are both wrong. The answer to the question 'How does advertising work?' lies somewhere between the two views and is dependent upon the particular situation facing each advertiser. Where elaboration is likely to be high if advertising is to work, then it is most likely to work under the Strong theory. For example, consumer durables and financial products require that advertising urges prospective customers into some form of trial behaviour. This may be a call for more information from a sales representative or perhaps a visit to a showroom. The vast majority of product purchases, however, involve low levels of elaboration, where involvement is low and where people select, often unconsciously, brands from an evoked set.

New products require people to convert or change their purchasing patterns. It is evident that the Strong theory must prevail in these circumstances. Where products become established, their markets generally mature, so that real growth is non-existent. Under these circumstances, advertising works by protecting the consumer franchise and by allowing users to have their product choices confirmed and reinforced. The other objective of this form of advertising is to increase the rate at which customers reselect and consume products. If the Strong theory were the only acceptable approach then, theoretically, advertising would be capable of continually increasing the size of each market, until everyone had been converted. There would be no 'stationary' markets.

Considering the vast sums that are allocated to advertising budgets, not only to launch new products but also to pursue market share targets aggressively, the popularity and continued implicit acceptance of the power of advertising suggest that a large proportion of resources is wasted in the pursuit of advertising-driven brand performance. Indeed, it is noticeable that organisations have been switching resources out of advertising into digital, interactive and sales promotion activities. There are many reasons for this, but one of them concerns the failure of advertising to produce the expected levels of performance: to produce market share. The Strong theory fails to deliver the expected results, and the Weak theory does not apply to all circumstances. Reality is probably a mixture of the two.

Scholars' paper 11.4 — How does advertising really work?

Nyilasy, G. and Reid, L.N. (2009) Agency practitioner theories of how advertising works, *Journal of Advertising*, 38(3), 81–96.

This is an interesting paper because it explores how those in the industry think advertising works and helps us to understand more about the academician–practitioner gap that exists. The study suggests practitioners have their own core theories about how advertising works, which includes a two-step 'break through and engage' process and a longer term 'mutation of effects' concept. The findings also highlight the important role of emotion in advertising and the value attributed to creativity in advertising.

See also: Vakratsas, D. and Ambler, T. (1999) How advertising works: what do we really know? *Journal of Marketing*, 63(1), 26–43.

Using advertising strategically

There are many varied and conflicting ideas about the strategic use of advertising. For a long time the management of the tools of the communications mix was considered strategic. Indeed, many practitioners still believe in this approach. However, ideas concerning integrated marketing communications (see Chapter 10) and corporate identity have helped provide a fresh perspective on what constitutes advertising strategy, and issues concerning differentiation, brand values and the development of brand equity have helped establish both a strategic and a tactical or operational aspect associated with advertising.

One of the first significant attempts to formalise advertising's strategic role was developed by Vaughn when working for an advertising agency, Foote, Cone and Belding. These ideas (see below) were subsequently debated and an alternative model emerged from Rossiter and Percy. Both frameworks have been used extensively by advertising agencies, and although their influence has now subsided, the underlying variables and approach remain central to strategic advertising thought.

The FCB matrix

Vaughn (1980) developed a matrix utilising involvement and brain specialisation theories. Brain specialisation theory suggests that the left-hand side of the brain is best for handling rational, linear and cognitive thinking, whereas the right-hand side is better able to manage spatial, visual and emotional issues (the affective or feeling functions).

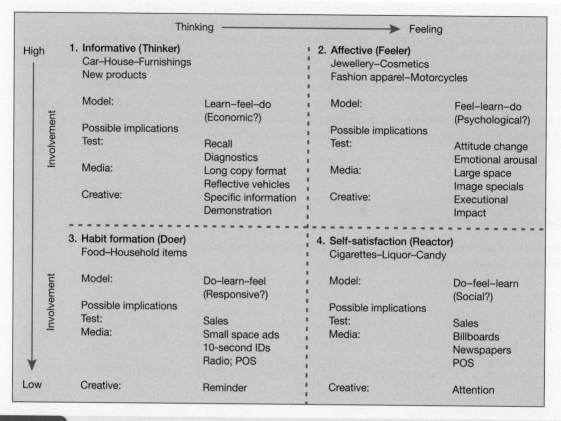

Figure 11.4	The FCB matrix

Source: Vaughn (1980). Used with kind permission from WARC.

Vaughn proposed that by combining involvement with elements of thinking and feeling, four primary advertising planning strategies can be distinguished. These are informative, affective, habitual and self-satisfaction (see Figure 11.4). According to Vaughn, the matrix is intended to be a thought provoker rather than a formula or model from which prescriptive solutions are to be identified. The FCB matrix is a useful guide to help analyse and appreciate consumer/product relationships and to develop appropriate communications strategies. The four quadrants of the grid identify particular types of decision-making and each requires different advertising approaches. Vaughn suggests that different orderings from the learn–feel–do sequence can be observed. By perceiving the different ways in which the process can be ordered, he proposed that the learn–feel–do sequence should be visualised as a continuum, a circular concept. Communications strategy would, therefore, be based on the point of entry that consumers make to the cycle.

Some offerings, generally regarded as 'habitual', may be moved to another quadrant, such as 'responsive', to develop differentiation and establish a new position for the product in the minds of consumers relative to the competition. This could be achieved by the selection of suitable media vehicles and visual images in the composition of the messages associated with an advertisement. There is little doubt that this model, or interpretation of the advertising process, has made a significant contribution to our understanding of the advertising process and has been used by a large number of advertising agencies (Joyce, 1991).

The Rossiter–Percy grid

Rossiter et al. (1991), however, disagree with some of the underpinnings of the FCB grid and offer a new one in response (revised 1997) (see Figure 11.5). They suggest that involvement is not a continuum because it is virtually impossible to decide when a person graduates from high to low involvement. They claim that the FCB grid fails to account for situations where a person moves from high to low involvement and then back to high, perhaps on a temporary basis, when a new variant is introduced to the market. Rossiter et al. regard involvement as the level of perceived risk present at the time of purchase. Consequently, it is the degree of familiarity buyers have at the time of purchase that is an important component.

A further criticism is that the FCB grid is an attitude-only model. Rossiter et al. identify the need for brand awareness to be built into such grids as a prerequisite for attitude development. However, they cite the need to differentiate different purchase situations. Some brands require awareness recall because the purchase decision is made prior to the act of purchasing. Other brands require awareness recognition at the point of purchase, where the buyer needs to be prompted into brand choice decisions. Each of these situations requires different message strategies, which are explored in Chapter 17.

The other major difference between the two grids concerns the 'think–feel' dimension. Rossiter et al. believe that a wider spectrum of motives must be incorporated, as the FCB 'think–feel' interpretation fails to accommodate differences between product category and brand purchase motivations. For example, the decision to use a product category may be based on a strictly functional and utilitarian need. The need to travel to another country often requires air transport. The choice of carrier, however, particularly over the North Atlantic, is a brand choice decision, motivated by a variety of sensory and ego-related inputs and anticipated outputs. Rossiter et al. disaggregate motives into what they refer to as *informational* and *transformational*. By detailing motives into these classifications, a more precise approach to advertising tactics can be developed. Furthermore, the confusion inherent in the FCB grid, between the think and involvement elements, is overcome.

It should be understood that these 'grids' are purely hypothetical, and there is no proof or evidence to suggest that they are accurate reflections of advertising. It is true that both

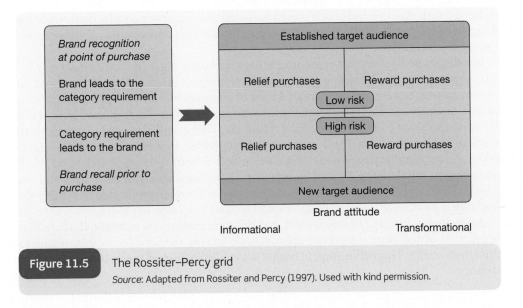

Figure 11.5   The Rossiter–Percy grid

Source: Adapted from Rossiter and Percy (1997). Used with kind permission.

models have been used as the basis for advertising strategy in many agencies, but that does not mean that they are totally reliable or, more importantly, that they have been tested empirically so that they can be used in total confidence. They are interpretations of commercial and psychological activity and have been instrumental in advancing our level of knowledge. It is in this spirit of development that these models are presented in this text.

There are parts in both of these frameworks that have a number of strong elements of truth attached to them. However, for products that are purchased on a regular basis, pull strategies should be geared to defending the rationale that current buyers use to select the brand. Heavy buyers select a particular brand more often than light users do from their repertoire. By providing a variety of consistent stimuli, and by keeping the brand alive, fresh buyers are more likely to prefer and purchase a particular brand than those that allow their brands to lose purchase currency and the triggers necessary to evoke memory impressions.

For products purchased on an irregular basis, marketing communications needs only touch the target audience on a relatively low number of occasions. Strategies need to be developed that inform and contextualise the purchase rationale for consumers. This means providing lasting impressions that enable consumers to understand the circumstances in which purchase of a particular product/brand should be made once a decision has been made to purchase from the product category. Here the priorities are to communicate messages that will encourage consumers to trust and bestow expertise on the product/brand that is offered.

Traditionally advertising has been used to develop brand identities by stimulating awareness and perception. Advertising had evolved to a point in the 1980s where the focus on developing brand identities and brand values alone was commercially insufficient for clients. The subsequent growth of direct marketing approaches and one-to-one, preferably interactive communications have become paramount. Marketing budgets have swung in sympathy, and are now very often allocated towards communications that drive a call-to-action; in particular, online communications have been taking a progressively larger share of advertising budgets since 2004. Consequently, the imperative today is about generating a behavioural rather than an attitudinal response to advertising and other marketing communications campaigns.

So, in this context, what is the role for advertising and what strategies should be used in the contemporary media landscape? One approach would be to maintain current advertising strategies on the grounds that awareness and perception are always going to be key factors. Another approach would be to call for advertising to be used solely for direct-response work. Neither of these two options seems appropriate or viable in the twenty-first century.

In an age where values and response are both necessary ingredients for effective overall communications, advertising strategy in the future will probably need to be based on emotional engagement and an increased level of integration with a range of other forms of communications. Customers will want to engage with the values offered by a brand that are significant to them individually. However, clients will also need to engage with them at a behavioural level and to encourage individuals to want to respond to advertising. Advertising strategy should therefore reflect a brand's context and be adjusted according to the required level of engagement regarding identity development and the required level of behavioural response. Advertising will no longer be able to assume the lead role in a campaign as of right and should be used according to the engagement needs of the audience, first, the brand, second, and the communications industry, third, in that order. One of the more integrative approaches concerns the need to use advertising to drive web traffic. This offline/online bridge is a critical aspect of many communications strategies.

Consumer-generated advertising

To conclude this chapter and the strategic perspective on advertising, attention needs to be given to the inexorable rise in user- or consumer-generated advertising (CGA). This is a subsection of user-generated content which, according to Stoeckl et al. (2007), cited by Campbell et al. (2011), is about circumstances where 'consumers freely choose to create and share information of value'. CGA, on the other hand, refers to specific instances where consumers create brand-focused messages with the intention of influencing others. For Campbell et al. (2011: 88) CGA is 'any publicly disseminated, consumer-generated advertising messages whose subject is a collectively recognized brand'. In other words, CGA is about ads concerning recognised brands, which are made available to the public. (UGC is considered in Chapter 17 on messages and creativity, and that material will not be repeated here.)

Much of the advertising explored in this chapter is based on the brand-to-consumer dynamic, a unidirectional interpretation, anchored in a client-agency origin. Increasingly today consumers not only reject this passive-response-based model but are now creating and distributing their own ads, very often as videos hosted on video-sharing sites such as YouTube. The growth in video is seen to be fuelling a revolution in advertising (Campbell et al., 2011).

While many brands are not comfortable with the lack of control that CGA represents and prefer to maintain a tighter control on their brand messages, others have fully embraced the phenomenon. Peperami is one brand that has taken advantage of the opportunity to encourage CGA and in 2009 ran a competition to source ideas for its TV campaign. The brand set up a special website for consumers to submit ideas for its 'Animal' character with a reward of US$10,000 for the best idea (Jones, 2009). Doritos has similarly embraced CGA with its ongoing 'Crash the Super Bowl' competition (Castillo, 2015).

From a brand's perspective there are a number of potential advantages of using CGA, including the generation of a large number of ideas at a lower cost than traditional

Exhibit 11.10   Peperami has used consumer-generated advertising
Peperami received over 1,000 responses to its advertising brief for a new advertising campaign for the brand (Jones, 2009).

Source: Peperami.

Table 11.2 Three consumer motivations to create ads

Dominant motivation	Explanation
Intrinsic enjoyment	Here people are primarily creative and enjoy the process for the satisfaction and personal reward the activity brings. They are not so interested in what becomes of their work.
Self-promotion	In this situation people generate advertising materials as a means to an end. It may be that the activity is part of the process of attracting the attention of others, possibly a potential employer.
Perception change	Rather than achieve a tangible outcome, some advertising is generated by people in order to influence the way others think or feel, intangible outcomes. The goal is to change opinions, sentiments or attitudes but for altruistic reasons rather than personally driven, career-based goals.

Source: Based on Berthon et al. (2008).

agency routes and the opportunities to generate media coverage. The reasons why consumers create and broadcast ads has been explored by Berthon et al. (2008) who identified three fundamental motivations: intrinsic enjoyment, self-promotion and perception change. These are explained in Table 11.2.

Campbell et al. (2011) explored respones to CGA and suggest these can be considered on two broad dimensions. The first dimension spans the *conceptual* – that is, curiosity in how or who created the ad – and *emotion* – how responses to the ad are driven essentially by emotion rather than reason. The second dimension concerns how a consumer's response to the ad either can be collaborative, where the viewer supports the ad's creator, or is in opposition and is hostile towards the ad, and/or its creator. From these dimensions a classic 2×2 grid can be determined identifying four response archetypes to CG ads. These are termed inquiry, laudation, debate and the flame (see Figure 11.6).

Inquiry refers to responses that say: 'That is interesting, tell me more.' Laudation is about how good the ad is thought to be, the praise viewers give it. Debate concerns the different voices and divergent views or opinions on the topic of interest. Finally, flame concerns the outpouring of emotions, the diatribe that occurs when the debate becomes enflamed and hostile.

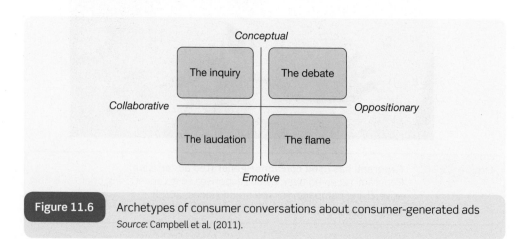

| **Figure 11.6** | Archetypes of consumer conversations about consumer-generated ads |

Source: Campbell et al. (2011).

Research by Campbell et al. (2011) identified that while viewers of CGA consider it to be a reliable source of word of mouth, most conversations driven by CGA were often not predominantly about the brand. Their study found that most conversations were around: the music in the ad, the creators of the ad, 'and larger social themes such as international justice, globalisation, poverty, and corporate social responsibility'. This could have an important bearing on advertising messages and appeals in the future, especially for functional brands.

Scholars' paper 11.5   **Let's talk about consumer-generated ads**

Campbell, C., Pitt, L.F., Parent, M. and Berthon, P.R. (2011) Understanding consumer conversations around ads in a Web 2.0 world, *Journal of Advertising*, 40(1), 87–102.

The development of consumer-generated advertising has been considerable, yet research has not been able to keep pace. This paper reports on research designed to interpret the conversations consumers have about and around consumer-generated ads. This is undertaken using the comments posted to each ad's web page. They map and interpret these conversations and then develop a typology of consumer-generated ad conversations.

See also: Lawrence, B., Fournier, S. and Brunel, F. (2013) When companies don't make the ad: a multimethod inquiry into the differential effectiveness of consumer-generated advertising, *Journal of Advertising*, 42(4), 292–307.

Key points

- The role of advertising in most marketing communications campaigns is to engage audiences and enable people to make brand-orientated associations. Engagement is enabled either by informing, changing perceptions and building brand values, or by encouraging a change in behaviour.

- A few of the established definitions have been perpetuated both by practitioners and by academics. These have generally failed to accommodate the changing media landscape and so a new definition is presented.

- Advertising is a paid, mediated form of communications from an identifiable source, designed to persuade the receiver to take some action, now or in the future.

- The idea that a product might have a unique selling proposition is in many cases totally misplaced and inaccurate. The rise of emotional selling points (ESPs) is much more realistic and practised by leading brands. This approach to communications helps build brand awareness, desire and aspirational involvement. However, it often fails to provide customers with a rationale or explicit reason to purchase, what is often referred to as a 'call-to-action'.

- The use of emotion in advertising is considered to be more important, and effective, than the use of information-based messages. Feelings and emotions play an important role in advertising, especially when advertising is used to build awareness levels and brand strength.

- There are many ways of categorising advertising, but five perspectives encapsulate the variety of types available. These are the source, the message, the recipient, the media and place.

- The elaboration likelihood model (ELM) has helped to explain how cognitive processing, persuasion and attitude change occur when different levels of involvement are present. Elaboration refers to the extent to which an individual needs to develop and refine information necessary for decision-making to occur. If an individual has a high level of motivation or ability to process information, elaboration is said to be high and central route processing is used. If an individual's motivation or ability to process information is poor, then the level of elaboration is said to be low, and peripheral processing is appropriate.

- Many of the ideas about how advertising works are a practitioner reflection of the way advertising is considered to work, or at least is used, by advertising agencies. The first to be considered here are the frameworks developed by O'Malley (1991) and Hall (1992), and later supplemented by Willie (2007). They suggest that there are four core advertising frameworks: persuasion/exploration, sales/do, salience/sharing and involvement/play.

- The Strong theory of advertising indicates that advertising is a strong influencing force and reflects the persuasion concept. The Weak theory suggests that advertising has little influence and that advertising should be regarded as a means of defending customers' purchase decisions and for protecting markets, not building them. Reality suggests that the majority of advertising cannot claim to be of significant value to most people and that the Strong and the Weak theories are equally applicable, although not at the same time nor in the same context.

- The FCB and Rossiter–Percy grids represent formalised attempts to interpret the strategic use of advertising. Intended to provide agencies with a method that might ensure consistency, meaning and value with respect to their clients' brands, these are no longer considered by agencies to be sufficiently flexible, rigorous or representative of how contemporary advertising performs. A more current perspective on advertising strategy suggests that advertising should become more engaged with the customer's experience of the brand and not be rooted just in the development of brand values.

- Consumer-generated advertising (CGA) concerns ads developed by members of the public about recognised brands. There are three fundamental motivations that consumers have for creating and broadcasting ads: intrinsic enjoyment, self-promotion and perception change. The critical issue associated with CGA concerns control and the ability of organisations to control the messages surrounding their brands.

Review questions

IWM London case questions

1. How might the elaboration likelihood model be used to interpret how IWM London advertising works?

2. Discuss whether the IWM advertising is predominantly trying to persuade audiences or designed to reinforce brand values.

3. Which of the eclectic models of advertising could be used to explain how 'Flight of the Stories' works?

4. What role does emotion play in this advertising?

5. Consider whether consumer-generated advertising would be appropriate for IWM in the future. Discuss the advantages and disadvantages of using this approach.

General questions

1. Find three different advertisements and write notes explaining how they depict the thinking and feeling aspect of advertising, and the behavioural aspect of advertising.

2. Select an organisation of your choice and find three advertisements it has used recently. Are the ads predominantly trying to persuade audiences or are they designed to reinforce brand values?

3. What are the essential differences between the involvement and salience frameworks of advertising? Find four advertisements (other than those described in this book) that are examples of these two approaches.

4. Write a short presentation explaining the differences between the Strong and Weak theories of advertising.

5. Draw the FCB grid and place on it the following product categories: shampoo, life assurance, sports cars, kitchen towels, a box of chocolates.

References

Almond Board of California (2015) *About the Almond Board*, retrieved 10 May 2015 from www.almonds.co.uk/consumers/about-almond-board.

Ambler, T. (1998) Myths about the mind: time to end some popular beliefs about how advertising works, *International Journal of Advertising*, 17, 501–9.

Amnesty International (2015) Huge response to crowdfunded newspaper ads campaign opposing repeal of Human Rights Act, *Amnesty International UK Press Releases*, 20 May, retrieved 29 May 2015 from www.amnesty.org.uk/press-releases/huge-response-crowdfunded-newspaper-ads-campaign-opposing-repeal-human-rights-act.

Anon (2015) AMVBBDO, retrieved 23 July 2015 from http://amvbbdo.com/work/campaign/cesar/love-them-back/journey.

Barwise, P. and Meehan, S. (2009) Differentiation that matters, *Market Leader*, Quarter 2, retrieved 4 May 2012 from www.warc.com.

Berthon, P.R., Pitt, L. F. and Campbell, C. (2008) 'Ad lib: when customers create the ad', *California Management Review*, 50(4), 6–30.

Campbell, C., Pitt, L.F., Parent, M. and Berthon, P.R. (2011) Understanding consumer conversations around ads in a Web 2.0 world, *Journal of Advertising*, 40(1), 87–102.

Campbell, C., Cohen, J. and Ma, J. (2014) Advertisements just aren't advertisements anymore: a new typology for evolving forms of online advertising, *Journal of Advertising Research*, 54(1), 7–10.

Castillo, M. (2015) Doritos reveals 10 'Crash the super bowl' ad finalists: which one of these will score the coveted TV spot? *Adweek*, 5 January, retrieved 23 May 2015 from www.adweek.com/news-gallery/advertising-branding/doritos-announces-10-crash-super-bowl-ad-finalists-162162.

Chase, C. (2015) Budweiser unveils the commercial that will make you cry on Super Bowl Sunday, *USA Today*, 28 January, retrieved 26 July 2015 from http://ftw.usatoday.com/2015/01/budweiser-super-bowl-commercial-clydesdales-puppy-proclaimers-500-miles.

Corke, S. and Heath, R.G. (2004) The hidden power of newspaper advertising, *Media Research Group Conference*, Madrid (November).

Drumwright, M.E. and Murphy, P.E. (2009) The current state of advertising ethics: industry and academic perspectives, *Journal of Advertising*, 38(1), 83–107.

Ehrenberg, A.S.C. (1974) Repetitive advertising and the consumer, *Journal of Advertising Research*, 14 (April), 25–34.

Ehrenberg, A.S.C. (1988) *Repeat Buying*, 2nd edition, London: Charles Griffin.

Ehrenberg, A.S.C. (1997) How do consumers come to buy a new brand? *Admap*, March, 20–4.

Facebook.com/AmnestyUK (2015) AmnestyUK page, Facebook, retrieved 29 May 2015 from www.facebook.com/AmnestyUK.

Hall, M. (1992) Using advertising frameworks, *Admap*, March, 17–21.

Heath, R. (2000) Low involvement processing – a new model of brands and advertising, *International Journal of Advertising*, 19(3), 287–98.

Heath, R. and Feldwick, P. (2008) 50 years using the wrong model of TV advertising, *International Journal of Market Research*, 50(1), 25–59.

Heath, R.G., Nairn, A.C. and Bottomley, P.A. (2009) How effective is creativity? Emotive content in TV advertising does not increase attention, *Journal of Advertising Research*, September, 450–63.

Hsiang-yi (2012) P&G launches Pantene Nature Care with '3D garden', *The China Post*, 25 September, retrieved 10 May 2015 from www.chinapost.com.tw/taiwan/business/2012/09/25/355373/PandG-launches.htm.

Jones, G. (2009) Unilever to extend crowdsourcing to other brands, *Brand Republic*, retrieved 10 April 2015 from www.brandrepublic.com/article/948330/unilever-extend-crowdsourcing-brands.

Jones, J.P. (1991) Over-promise and under-delivery, *Marketing and Research Today*, November, 195–203.

Joyce, T. (1991) Models of the advertising process, *Marketing and Research Today*, November, 205–12.

Kemp, N. (2013) Nationwide pulls Facebook advertising after consumer backlash, *Brand Republic*, 28 May, retrieved 5 December 2014 from www.brandrepublic.com/article/1183932/nationwide-pulls-facebook-advertising-consumer-backlash.

Kitchen, P.J., Kerr, G., Schultz, D.E., McColl, R. and Pals, H. (2014) The elaboration likelihood model: review, critique and research agenda, *European Journal of Marketing*, 48(11/12), 2033–50.

Kolsarici, C. and Vakratsas, D. (2010) Category versus brand-level advertising messages in a highly regulated environment, *Journal of Marketing Research*, 47(6), 1078–89.

Krugman, M.E. (1971) Brain wave measurement of media involvement, *Journal of Advertising*, 11(1), 3–9.

Kumar, P. (2013) Sharing shampoo socially, *Warc*, retrieved 10 May 2015 from www.warc.com/Content/ContentViewer.aspx?MasterContentRef=940b1be6-4c0d-450b-9cd8-85da526833fc&q=Kumar+%3apantene&CID=A100267&PUB=ADMAP.

Kumar, P. (2014) Pantene: sharing shampoo socially, *Warc*, retrieved 10 May 2015 from www.warc.com/Content/ContentViewer.aspx?MasterContentRef=8c91fc79-2018-4d7c-9ad3-da8123dde0f4&q=Kumar+%3apantene&CID=A101319&PUB=WARC-PRIZE-SOCIAL.

Lawrence, B., Fournier, S. and Brunel, F. (2013) When companies don't make the ad: a multimethod inquiry into the differential effectiveness of consumer-generated advertising, *Journal of Advertising*, 42(4), 292–307.

McCarthy, J. (2014) Digital billboards helped recover over 220 missing people in a UK scheme backed by Kate McCann, *The Drum*, 5 November, retrieved 2 June 2015 from www.exterionmedia.com/uk/who-we-are/news/digital-billboards-helped-recover-over-220-missing-people/.

MMA (2015) *The Mobile Native Ad Formats*, retrieved 20 May 2015 from www.mmaglobal.com/documents/mobile-native-ad-formatxs.

Nyilasy, G. and Reid, L.N. (2009) Agency practitioner theories of how advertising works, *Journal of Advertising*, 38(3), 81–96.

Oakes, O. (2015) Amnesty's crowdfunded newspaper ad calls on government to keep Human Rights Act, *Brand Republic*, 26 May, retrieved 27 May 2015 from www.brandrepublic.com/article/1348449/amnestys-crowdfunded-newspaper-ad-calls-government-keep-human-rights-act.

O'Malley, D. (1991) Sales without salience? *Admap*, September, 36–9.

Ono, Y. (1994) Campbell's new ads heat up soup sales, *The Wall Street Journal*, 17 March, B3.

Pelsmaker de, P., Guens, M. and Bergh, van den, J. (2010) *Marketing Communications: A European Perspective*, 4th edition, Harlow: Financial Times/Prentice Hall.

Petty, R.E. and Cacioppo, J.T. (1983) Central and peripheral routes to persuasion: application to advertising, in *Advertising and Consumer Psychology* (eds L. Percy and A. Woodside), Lexington, MA: Lexington Books, 3–23.

Petty, R.E. and Cacioppo, J.T. (1984) Source factors and the elaboration likelihood model of persuasion, *Advances in Consumer Research*, 11(1), 668–72.

Richards, J.I. and Curran, C.M. (2002) Oracles on 'advertising': searching for a definition, *Journal of Advertising*, XXXI(2), 63–77.

Rossiter, J.R., Percy, L. and Donovan, R.J. (1991) A better advertising planning grid, *Journal of Advertising Research*, October/November, 11–21.

Stoeckl, R., Rohrmeier, P. and Hess, T. (2007) Motivations to produce user generated content: differences between webloggers and videobloggers, *Twentieth Bled eConference on eMergence: Merging and Emerging Technologies, Processes, and Institutions*, Bled, Slovenia, 4–6 June.

Swift, J. (2014) Moving images: ten of the most emotional ads ever shown in the UK, *Brand Republic*, 30 January, retrieved 10 July 2015 from www.brandrepublic.com/article/1228868/moving-images-ten-emotional-ads-ever-shown-uk.

Turnbull, S., Howe-Walsh, L. and Boulanouar, A. (2016) The advertising standardisation debate revisited: implications of Islamic ethics on standardisation/localisation of advertising in Middle East Islamic State, *Journal of Islamic Marketing*, 7(1).

Vakratsas, D. and Ambler, T. (1999) How advertising works: what do we really know? *Journal of Marketing*, 63(1), 26–43.

Vaughn, R. (1980) How advertising works: a planning model, *Journal of Advertising Research*, October, 27–33.

Willie, T. (2007) New models of communication for the digital age, *Admap*, October, 487, retrieved 23 July 2010 from www.warc.com.

Chapter 12
Public relations: principles and practice

Public relations is a communications discipline used to help shape the attitudes and opinions held by an organisation's stakeholders. Through interaction and dialogue with these stakeholders an organisation seeks to adjust its own position and/or strategy.

There is an attempt therefore to identify with, and adjust an organisation's policies to, the interests of its stakeholders. To do this it formulates and executes a programme of action to develop mutual goodwill and understanding.

Aims and learning objectives

The aim of this chapter is to explore the role and characteristics of public relations in the context of profiling organisations and their products.

The learning objectives are to enable readers to:

1. explain the nature and characteristics of public relations;
2. highlight the main audiences to which public relations activities are directed;
3. discuss the role of public relations in the communications mix;
4. appreciate ways in which public relations works;
5. provide an overview of some of the main methods and approaches used by public relations;
6. examine the nature and context of crisis management.

'Pestaurant' – the world's first pop-up pest-only restaurant

Rentokil is one of the largest pest control companies in the world operating in 60 countries. The company provides services to both private and commercial clients and has been servicing the UK market for nearly 90 years.

Rentokil approached Brands2Life with the task of engaging professionals and householders with the brand. Our main objective was to deliver a creative PR campaign that would create a buzz and spark conversations, both on- and offline. The result was a creative public relations campaign that gave pest control a 'talkability' factor and became a global sensation.

Driving conversations about pest control was a challenging brief for a number of reasons. First, bugs and pests are not creatures that the public generally finds endearing. Indeed the opposite is true, with most people trying to avoid them. Second, pest control is not a topic most consumers or professionals talk about, unless they have to deal with a particular pest problem. To address this challenge we considered ways that we could engage the public with pests in a fun way. We saw that through survival programmes and celebrity TV shows, bugs had become a source of entertainment and as such had entered popular culture. TV programmes with presenters such as Ray Mears and Bear Grylls regularly featured the edible aspect of bugs and insects. TV audiences were also tuning in to shows like ITV's *I'm a Celebrity . . . Get Me Out of Here* in their millions to watch celebrities eat bugs. The UN also published a report on the value of insect protein to boost nutrition and reduce pollution providing a valuable health and sustainability angle. We saw an opportunity to capitalise on this national fascination with eating 'pests' and came up with the idea of the world's first pop-up pest-only restaurant. We presented the idea of Pestaurant to Rentokil who were equally excited about the concept and saw this as a perfect opportunity to engage audiences in 'pesty' conversations.

The first Pestaurant® appeared in London and we developed a menu to showcase Rentokil's tasty pest treats. The menu featured dishes such as sweet chilli pigeon burgers, salt and vinegar crickets, Mexican Spice Mealworms, roasted locusts and insects dipped in chocolate. Manned by Rentokil experts and chefs, the Pestaurant cooked these edible pest treats and handed them out to passers-by. We decided to enlist the support of Rentokil experts at the events to provide them with an opportunity to meet potential

Exhibit 12.1	**Grubbing around at the Pestuarant**
	Source: Rentokil Initial.

customers and share their top tips for avoiding pest problems. The one day event attracted over 3,000 visitors, many of whom were brave enough to taste the pests on offer. As well as delighting visitors to the Pestaurant, the edible pest menu caught the attention of both the national and international media.

We secured significant media coverage from the event in the UK, including 18 articles in the *Sun, Daily Mail, Guardian, Express, Metro* and *Time Out* as well as articles on BBC online. We also achieved standalone pieces in the *Evening Standard* and *Stylist,* and broadcast interviews with STV and LBC. As well as the national media, the story received international coverage including a 3-minute standalone feature on Brazilian TV and broadcast interviews on news channels in France, India, New Zealand, Singapore and the USA.

In addition to the media coverage there was considerable social buzz. On the day the campaign trended on Twitter with over 2,000 mentions, with retweets providing an estimated 58.7 million impressions. Rentokil's own website experienced a 22 per cent increase in visitors on the day of the event.

Following the initial success of the one day pop-up Pestaurant in London, we have rolled out the bug menu to a number of other UK locations, including Edinburgh and Manchester. The Pestaurant has also gone global with events in 13 different countries including Australia, Brazil, Germany, Lithuania, South Africa and the USA. This has resulted in over 13,000 people experiencing the Rentokil pop-up Pestaurant and over 1,300 pieces of media coverage.

Rentokil has now registered 'Pestaurant' as a trademark as it is seen to be a valuable asset for the brand. The success of the campaign in the UK and around the globe has led to us developing a kit to help Rentokil offices around the world to set up their own Pestaurant.

Pestaurant has proven to be a very effective campaign for our client Rentokil. It has engaged people around the globe and driven conversations in the media about the brand. The key to its success is creativity. The concept of a restaurant serving pests is undoubtedly a novel one and has excited publics. As well as delivering success for our client Rentokil, the campaign has won the agency a number of prestigious industry awards. To date Pestaurant has been awarded eight industry awards for creativity and effectiveness, making it one of the most highly acclaimed PR campaigns in recent years.

This case study was written by Harriet Rich at Brands2Life

Questions concerning this case can be found at the end of this chapter.

Exhibit 12.2   The Pestaurant
Source: Rentokil Initial.

Introduction

Rentokil clearly recognises the role that public relations can play in its communications. It used events and media coverage to create visibility and interest in the brand and through this it engaged various stakeholders. From this it was able to drive conversations, often through social media, with the result that they raised its profile and understanding about who it is and what it represents. Not only did Rentokil generate goodwill and positive feelings, but it also built relationships with critical stakeholder audiences.

Traditionally public relations has been perceived as a tool that dealt with the manner and style with which an organisation interacted with its major 'publics'. It sought to influence other organisations and individuals through public relations, projecting an identity that would affect the image that different publics held of the organisation. By spreading information and improving the levels of knowledge that people held about particular issues, an organisation sought ways to advance itself in the eyes of those it saw as influential.

This approach is reflected in the definition of public relations provided by the Institute of Public Relations: 'Public Relations practice is the planned and sustained effort to establish and maintain goodwill and mutual understanding between an organisation and its publics.' For many the core interpretation of public relations was provided by Grunig and Hunt (1984: 6), who define public relations as the 'management of communication between an organization and its publics'. Laskin (2009) refers to this work as the foundation upon which most models of public relations have been built.

Cutlip et al. (1994: 199) consider the 'essential role of public relations is to help organizations adjust and adapt to changes in their environments'. A later definition from Bruning and Ledingham (2000) suggests that public relations is the management of relationships between organisations and their stakeholders (publics). These definitions indicate the direction in which both public relations and marketing theory have moved. As Greenwood (2011) points out, public relations is about managing the interdependence of organisations and others in their environments.

Public relations has long been concerned with the development and communications of corporate and competitive strategies. The use of public relations provided visibility for Rentokil, and this in turn, allowed it to be properly identified, positioned and understood by all of its stakeholders. What some definitions do not emphasise or make apparent is that public relations should also be used by management as a means of understanding issues from a stakeholder perspective. Good relationships are developed by appreciating the views held by others and by 'putting oneself in their shoes'.

From this three major roles of public relations can be identified. The first is the traditional role of creating goodwill and stimulating interest between the organisation and its various key stakeholders. This is something that is demonstrated clearly by Rentokil. Its task is to provide a series of cues by which the stakeholders can recognise, understand and position the organisation in such a way that it builds a strong reputation. This role is closely allied to the corporate strategy and the communications of strategic intent.

The second role is to support the marketing of the organisation's products and services, and its task is to integrate with the other elements of the marketing communications mix. Public relations and advertising have complementary roles. For example, the launch of a new product commences not with advertising to build awareness in target customers but with the use of public relations to inform editors and news broadcasters that a new proposition is about to be launched. Rentokil harnessed the media really well in order to reach its key audiences. This news material can be used online at the website and through social media, within the trade and consumer press before advertising occurs and the target buyers become aware (when the news is no longer news). To some extent this role is tactical rather than strategic but, if planned, and if events are timed and coordinated with the other elements of the marketing communications mix, then public relations can help build competitive advantage.

The third role is to provide the means by which relationships can be developed. To do this, public relations has a responsibility to encourage interaction and dialogue, to provide the means through which interaction, discourse and discussion can occur, and to play a full part in the communications process and the messages that are conveyed, listened to, considered and acted upon.

By understanding these roles and using a planned approach to communications, a dialogue can be developed that is not frustrated by punctuated interruptions (anger, disbelief, ignorance and objections). Public relations should therefore be regarded as a management activity that attempts to shape the attitudes and opinions held by an organisation's stakeholders. It seeks to identify its policies with the interests of its stakeholders by formulating and executing a programme of action to develop mutual goodwill and understanding, and in turn develop relationships that are in the long-term interests of all parties.

Which publics?

The first definition of public relations quoted earlier uses, as indeed does most of the public relations industry, the word *publics*. This word is used traditionally to refer to the various organisations and groups with which an organisation interacts. So far, this text has referred to these types of organisation as *stakeholders*. 'Stakeholders' is a term used in the field of strategic management, and as public relations can be concerned with strategic issues, it could be argued that the word 'stakeholders' should be used. However, the phrase 'public relations' is so well established and culturally entrenched that a change to 'stakeholder relations' would achieve little other than confusion.

The stakeholder concept recognises that various networks of stakeholders can be identified, with each network consisting of members who are oriented towards supporting the organisation either in an indirect way or directly through the added-value processes. For the purposes of this chapter it is useful to set out who the main stakeholders are likely to be. Stakeholder groups, it should be remembered, are not static and new groups can emerge in response to changes in the environment. The main core groups, however, tend to be employees, the public, financial communities, customers through the media, and other influential organisations, and are set out in Table 12.1. These various forms of public relations are considered later in this chapter.

Table 12.1 Stakeholder audiences for public relations

Stakeholder group	Explanation
Employees	A major stakeholder group who can influence external stakeholders and influence the strength of corporate brands. This form of public relations is also referred to as internal communications or employee relations.
Financial groups	To supply analysts, shareholders and investors with current information and materials about an organisation and the markets in which it operates, organisations use investor relations.
Customers	Information is directed through the media in order to shape attitudes, perceptions and images. This form of public relations is referred to as media relations.
Organisations and communities	Organisations seek to inform significant other organisations of their strategic intentions and ways in which the objectives of both parties can be satisfied. A variety of public relations methods are used, including: public affairs directed at government and local authorities; industry relations targeted at suppliers and other trade stakeholders; and issues management designed to influence various audiences about potentially sensitive issues.

Table 12.2 Logics of historical explanation

Logic	Explanation
Functionalism	Functionalism is concerned with the different parts of a social system striving to counterbalance and adjust in order to achieve reach equilibrium. Public relations is considered to be an institutional response to muck-raking. Bernays (1928: 41) refers to 'a result of insurance scandals coincident with the muck-raking of corporate finance in the popular magazines'.
Institutionalism	The institutional perspective considers public relations to be rooted in an organisation-based, systematic, rules-and-routines approach to influencing groups through communications and persuasion. For many this was first noted when the Committee on Public Information (CPI) was formed in the USA at the outset of World War I. The committee consisted of various journalists, intellectuals, novelists and others who sought to 'unite public opinion behind the war at home and to propagandize American peace aims abroad' (Cutlip et al., 1994: 106).
Culture	This interpretation of public relations is that it was founded on meaning systems adopted from the prevailing culture. These meaning systems include cultural values, attitudes, ideas, which provide both constraints and opportunities (Geertz, 1973) for behaviour. The then new PR practitioners saw this as a natural, right, or logical approach to communication. A dominant view within the cultural movement concerns the influence of the progressive movement. 'This ideology was concerned with reform, cooperation and participation of society' (Hallahan, 2003). They believed that public policy should not be crafted by party bosses and neither should public life be dictated by business tycoons.

Source: Vos (2011).

Characteristics of public relations

Insight into the characteristics of public relations is helped by understanding its origins. There are many interpretations but Vos (2011) identifies three main theoretical perspectives, or 'logics of historical explanation' (p. 119). These are set out in Table 12.2. Each of these has fundamental flaws but they provide an interesting perspective on the roots of public relations.

There are a number of characteristics that single out this particular tool from the other disciplines in the marketing communications mix. The use of public relations does not require the purchase of airtime or space in media vehicles, such as television or magazines. The decision about whether an organisation's public relations messages are transmitted, or not, rests with those charged with managing the media resource, not the message sponsor. Those messages that are selected are perceived to be endorsements or the views of parties other than management. The outcome is that these messages usually carry greater perceived credibility than those messages transmitted through paid media, such as advertising.

Scholars' paper 12.1	Historical views of public relations

Vos, T.P. (2011) Explaining the origins of public relations: logics of historical explanation, *Journal of Public Relations Research*, 23(2), 119–40.

A contemporary paper that is useful for those interested in the academic roots of public relations. Vos considers the historical explanations underpinning the emergence of public relations as a social institution. He identifies three distinct logics of explanation: a functionalist logic, an institutional logic and a cultural logic.

The degree of trust and confidence generated by public relations singles out this tool from others in the marketing communications mix as an important means of reducing perceived risk. While credibility may be high, however, the amount of control that management is able to bring to the transmission of a public relations message is very low. For example, a press release may have been carefully prepared in-house, but as soon as it is passed to the editor of an online or offline magazine or newspaper, a possible opinion former, all control is lost. The release may be destroyed (highly probable), published as it stands (highly unlikely) or changed to fit the available space in the media vehicle (almost certain, if it is decided to use the material). This means that any changes will not have been agreed by management, so the context and style of the original message may be lost or corrupted.

The costs associated with public relations also make this an important discipline in the marketing communications mix. The absolute costs are minimal, except for those organisations that retain an agency, but even then their costs are low compared with those of advertising. The relative costs (the costs associated with reaching each member of a target audience) are also very low. The main costs associated with public relations are the time and opportunity costs associated with the preparation of press releases, videos and associated materials. If these types of activity are organised properly, many small organisations could develop and shape their visibility much more effectively and in a relatively inexpensive way.

A further characteristic of this tool is that it can be used to reach specific audiences in a way that paid media cannot. With increasing media fragmentation and finer segmentation (customisation) of markets, the use of public relations represents a cost-effective way of reaching such markets and audiences.

Digital technology has played a key role in the development and practice of public relations. Back in 2004 Gregory referred to the Internet and electronic communications as 'transforming public relations', and identified two main practitioner approaches. One refers to those who use the Internet as an extension to their established, traditional forms of communications. The second uses the Internet to develop two-way, enhanced communications. Today this demarcation is harder to observe as interactive media are woven into campaigns in order to achieve specific outcomes. There can be little doubt that digital technology has improved the transparency, speed and reach of public relations messages, while at the same time enabling more interactive communications between an organisation and its specific audiences (see Viewpoint 12.1).

Viewpoint 12.1   Taylor Swift denounces Spotify

Online streaming has become the dominant method of distributing music, with Spotify a leading platform. Although successful, Spotify has come under increasing scrutiny from many stakeholders, including Thom Yorke of Radiohead and acclaimed recording engineer Nigel Godrich. In November 2014, the popular singer–songwriter Taylor Swift removed her entire discography from Spotify, stating that the service did not 'fairly compensate the writers, producers, artists and creators'. Spotify responded with a media relations campaign, delivered mainly through social media, in an attempt to persuade her to change her mind, using the hashtag \#justsayyes. Taylor Swift has built a strong, successful brand which has a massive following. Her PR skills, based on her use of social media to create deep personal connections with fans, are widely recognised. Her decision, therefore, had a widespread influence, affecting not just Spotify's streaming figures, but also their brand reputation. Interestingly, Spotify released a statement showing Taylor Swift's streaming figures for the 30 days

▶

Exhibit 12.3	Taylor Swift has the fifth highest number of Twitter followers
	Source: Alamy Images/PjrStudio.

before she left. This revealed that 16 million of their 40 million users had streamed her songs during that period.

Social media is a major communications platform in the music industry. It is used by businesses, record labels, artists, consumers and the media, so it was important for Spotify to clarify their position on the way artists are compensated. In their press statement, they referred to how nearly 70 per cent of their revenue is fed back to the music community. They emphasised how much they valued their artists, and their right to be protected from piracy. Spotify insisted that their business plan was not designed to take revenue away from the community. In addition they tried to lure Taylor Swift back gently and with a sense of humour.

In March 2015, Taylor Swift moved to Tidal, a new streaming service set up by artists such as Jay-Z and Beyonce, which claimed to pay artists more. This was a particularly strange move after she had said that she thought Spotify felt much like a 'grand experiment'. Popular music artist Lily Allen spoke out about this issue, saying 'Spotify pay out but the artists aren't getting the money'. Many others have criticised record labels, claiming that contracts signed by the artists prevent them from gaining a fair share from the revenue received by the labels from Spotify.

This episode reflects Taylor Swift's PR skills and the thoughtful tone of Spotify's response. By not criticising the artist Spotify was able to avoid appearing like a distant and manipulative big business. Unfortunately, despite increasing numbers of subscribers, Spotify fired their PR agency in January 2015. It appears that they were not entirely happy with the agency's handling of their reputation.

Source: Fesnal (2014); Renfree (2014); Spotify (2014); Willman (2014); Wood (2015).

This Viewpoint was written by Jonathan Ward when he was a Music Performance Management student at Buckinghamshire New University.

Question:	What would Spotify hope to accomplish, through their use of public relations, in response to Taylor Swift's actions?
Task:	Find another example where public relations was used to resolve conflict.

Developments in digital media have been instrumental in assisting public relations' move from a predominantly one-way model of communications to an interactive model. In 2001 Hurme suggested that public relations practitioners could be divided into two broad groups: those that predominantly use traditional media and those that adopt online communications. Since that article was written, most practitioners have incorporated online and increasingly mobile communications, but the potential to develop true dialogue with stakeholders remains unfilled in many cases. Therefore, opportunities for online interactivity and dialogue have increased even if many websites are not designed to fulfil this requirement completely.

A framework of public relations

Communications with such a wide variety of stakeholders need to vary to reflect different environmental conditions, organisational objectives and forms of relationship. Grunig and Hunt (1984) have attempted to capture the diversity of public relations activities through a framework. They set out four models to reflect the different ways in which public relations is, in their opinion, considered to work. These models, based on their experiences as public relations practitioners, constitute a useful approach to understanding the complexity of this form of communications. The four models are set out at Figure 12.1.

	Model			
Characteristic	Press agentry/publicity	Public information	Two-way asymmetric	Two-way symmetric
Purpose	Propaganda	Dissemination of information	Scientific persuasion	Mutual understanding
Nature of communication	One way; complete truth not essential	One way; truth important	Two way; imbalanced effects	Two way; balanced effects
Communication model	Source→Rec.*	Source→Rec.*	Source⇄Rec.* Feedback	Group⇄Group
Nature of research	Little; 'counting house'	Little; readability, readership	Formative; evaluative of attitudes	Formative; evaluative of understanding
Leading historical figures	P.T. Barnum	Ivy Lee	Edward L. Bernays	Bernays, educators, professional leaders
Where practised today	Sports, theatre, product promotion	Government, not-for-profit associations, business	Competitive business, agencies	Regulated business, agencies
Estimated percentage of organisations practising today	15%	50%	20%	15%

* Receiver.

Figure 12.1 Models of public relations
Source: Grunig and Hunt (1984). Used with kind permission.

The press agentry/publicity model

The essence of this approach is that communications are used as a form of propaganda. That is, the communications flow is essentially one-way, and the content is not bound to be strictly truthful as the objective is to convince the receiver of a new idea or offering. This can be observed in the growing proliferation of media events and press releases.

The public information model

Unlike the first model, this approach seeks to disseminate truthful information. While the flow is again one-way, there is little focus on persuasion, more on the provision of information. This can best be seen through public health campaigns and government advice communications in respect of crime, education and health.

The two-way asymmetric model

Two-way communications are a major element of this model. Feedback from receivers is important, but as power is not equally distributed between the various stakeholders and the organisation, the relationship has to be regarded as asymmetric. The purpose remains to influence attitude and behaviour through persuasion.

The two-way symmetric model

This represents the most acceptable and mutually rewarding form of communications. Power is seen to be dispersed equally between the organisation and its stakeholders and the intent of the communications flow is considered to be reciprocal. The organisation and its respective publics are prepared to adjust their positions (attitudes and behaviours) in the light of the information flow. A true dialogue emerges through this interpretation, unlike any of the other three models, which see an unbalanced flow of information and expectations.

Scholars' paper 12.2   Models of public relations

Grunig, J. (1992) Models of public relations and communication, in *Excellence in Public Relations and Communications Management* (eds J.E. Grunig, D.M. Dozier, P. Ehling, L.A. Grunig, F.C. Repper and J. Whits), Hillsdale, NJ: Lawrence Erlbaum, 285-325.

Although first announced in 1976, and then published fully in 1984, this 1992 chapter is an essential work with which all serious readers of public relations should be conversant. The four primary models of public relations developed by Grunig are considered by most scholars to be the theoretical anchor for the subject.

See also: Laskin, A.V. (2009) The evolution of models of public relations: an outsider's perspective, *Journal of Communications Management*, 13(1), 37–54; Pieczka, M. (2011) Public relations as dialogic expertise? *Journal of Communications Management*, 15(2), 108–24.

Table 12.3 Dimensions of public relations

Dimension of public relations	Explanation
Direction	Refers to whether communications are one-way (disseminating) or two-way (exchange).
Purpose	Purpose refers to degree to which there are communications effects on both parties. Symmetry refers to communications effects on both sides, leading to collaboration, whereas asymmetry leads to one-sided effects and, in turn, advocacy.
Channel	Interpersonal communications refer to direct, face-to-face communications. Mediated communications are indirect and routed through the media.
Ethics	The degree to which public-relations-based communications are ethical. Grunig (1997) refers to three sub-dimensions: teleology (the consequences), disclosure (whose interests do the communications serve?) and social responsibility (who is affected?).

Source: After Yun (2006).

The Grunig model has attracted a great deal of attention and has been reviewed and appraised by a number of commentators (Miller, 1989; Laskin, 2009). As a result of this and a search for excellence in public relations, Grunig (1992) revised the model to reflect the dominance of the 'craft' and the 'professional' approaches to public relations practices. That is, those practitioners who utilise public relations merely as a tool to achieve media visibility can be regarded as 'craft'-oriented.

Those organisations whose managers seek to utilise public relations as a means of mediating their relationships with their various stakeholders are seen as 'professional' practitioners. They are considered to be using public relations as a longer-term and proactive form of planned communications. The former see public relations as an instrument, the latter as a means of conducting a dialogue.

These models are not intended to suggest that those responsible for communications should choose among them. Their use and interpretation depend upon the circumstances that prevail at any one time. Organisations use a number of these different approaches to manage the communications issues that exist between them and the variety of different stakeholder audiences with whom they interact. However, there is plenty of evidence to suggest that the press/agentry model is the one most used by practitioners and that the two-way symmetrical model is harder to observe in practice.

These models have been subjected to further investigation and Grunig (1997) concluded that these four models are not independent but coexist with one another. Therefore, it is better to characterise public relations as dimensions of communications behaviour (Yun, 2006). These dimensions are direction, purpose, channel and ethics, and are explained in Table 12.3.

Public relations and relationship management

It is important to remember that the shift to a relationship management perspective effectively alters the way public relations is perceived and practised by organisations. Kent and Taylor (2002) and Bruning and Ledingham (2000) suggest that it is the ability of organisations to encourage and practise dialogue that really enables truly symmetrical relationships to develop. What follows from this is a change in evaluation, from measuring the dissemination of messages to one that measures audience influence and behavioural and attitudinal change and, of course, relationship dynamics. Bruning and Ledingham describe this as a change from measuring outputs to one that measures outcomes.

In addition to this discernible shift in emphasis, there has been a change in the way public relations is used by organisations. Traditionally, public relations has been used as a means of managing communications between parties, whereas now communications are regarded as a means of managing relationships (Kent and Taylor, 2002). In order to use communications to develop the full potential within relationships many argue that dialogic interaction should be encouraged. There are five tenets of dialogue: mutuality, empathy, propinquity, risk and commitment (see Chapter 4). These have been offered by Kent and Taylor as the elements that may form a framework through which dialogue may be considered and developed. On a practical level, they argue that organisations should place email, web addresses, contact telephone numbers, Twitter and organisational addresses prominently in all forms of external communications, most notably advertisements and websites, to enable dialogue.

In consideration of the role of public relations, namely to build relationships that are of mutual value, Bruning et al. (2008) conclude that input, interaction and participation of key public members in the organisation–public dynamic are critically important. In other words, dialogue arising through interaction and the personalisation of communications is important for relationship development.

Objectives of public relations

As established, the main reasons for using public relations are to provide visibility for the corporate body and to support the marketing agenda at the product level. The marketing communications objectives, established earlier in the plan, will have identified issues concerning the attitudes and relationships stakeholders have with an organisation and its products. Decisions will have been made to build awareness and to change perception, preferences or attitudes. The task of public relations is to deliver a series of coordinated activities that complement the overall marketing communications strategy and which develop and enhance some of the identity cues used by stakeholders. The overall goal should be to develop the relationship that various audiences have with the organisation.

Public relations can be used to develop understanding, perceptions and positive attitudes towards the organisation. Public relations can also contribute to the marketing needs of the organisation and will therefore be focused at the product level and on consumers, seeking to change attitudes, preferences and awareness levels with respect to products and services offered. Therefore, a series of programmes is necessary – one to fulfil the corporate requirements and another to support the marketing of products and services.

Cause-related marketing

One major reason for the development of public relations and associated corporate reputation activities has been the rise in importance and use of cause-related marketing activities. This has partly been due to the increased awareness of the need to be perceived as credible, responsible and ethically sound. Developing a strong and socially oriented reputation has become a major form of differentiation for organisations operating in various markets, especially where price, quality and tangible attributes are relatively similar. Being able to present corporate brands as contributors to the wider social framework, a role beyond that of simple profit generators, has enabled many organisations to achieve stronger, more positive market positions.

Cause-related marketing is a commercial activity through which profit-oriented and not-for-profit organisations form partnerships to exploit, for mutual benefit, their association in the name of a particular cause.

Viewpoint 12.2   Paddy Power ties up with a good cause

The high street bookmaker, Paddy Power, positions itself as mischievous and irreverent in order to reach younger, 'tech-savvy' gamblers. The brand has a history of advertising that brushes with what is deemed as acceptable with several ads banned and withdrawn. Some of its outdoor work has been clever, opportunistic and witty.

In September 2013, and in collaboration with LGBT rights charity Stonewall, Paddy Power launched the 'Rainbow laces' campaign. The aim was to garner support for the movement against homophobia in football. This issue had previously not been addressed with any success and the football community appeared to be in denial. At the time there are no known openly gay footballers in either the English and Scottish professional leagues.

Statistically this was extremely improbable, and Paddy Power and Stonewall saw an opportunity to change the inertia with a joint strategy referred to as a mixture of 'Mission and Mischief'.

The 'Right Behind Gay Footballers' campaign involved sending sets of rainbow coloured football boot laces to all 92 Premier and Football League sides, plus 42 teams in the Scottish leagues, and various commentators and football pundits. They were asked to wear the laces during their next weekend game to highlight their support for the campaign and so raise awareness of the cause and provoke conversations.

To amplify the campaign, advertising, PR, digital and social media were used to generate conversations, media comment and, of course, public support. To make best use of the limited campaign funds, the £150,000 campaign activity focused on one week in September. Media partnerships were formed

| Exhibit 12.4 | **Paddy Power and the Rainbow laces campaign** |

Source: Paddy Power plc.

with *Metro*, Twitter and Talksport, and through twice daily meetings, messages were amended to reflect current events, and to ensure the campaign influenced the news agenda.

Footballers from 54 clubs wore the laces as did several football pundits. In seven days, the campaign generated 400 media stories, with a combined reach of over 500 million. These included 35 pieces of TV coverage, 161 radio items and 250 print/online stories. There were 320 million impressions on Twitter.

A year later the idea was rerun but this time the goal was to involve other brands. Two ads featured in the *Metro*: one stated 'Let's get one thing straight. We support gay players', while the other simply said 'It only takes two minutes to change the game', demonstrating a more serious position and debunking the idea that the original campaign was a stunt. Brands such as Premier Inn, who adapted their name to 'Premier Out' for the ad, Smirnoff, Icelolly and Gilbert Baker all took out advertising whilst others such as Lidl and O2 showed their support via Twitter.

Source: Joseph (2013); Lepitak (2013); Roderick (2014); Williams (2014).

Question: To what extent might greater use of spokespersons have assisted this campaign?

Task: Identify another social campaign and compare the approach with the Rainbow laces programme.

The benefits from a properly planned and constructed cause-related campaign can accrue to all participants. Cause-related marketing helps improve corporate reputation, enables product differentiation and appears to contribute to improved customer retention through enhanced sales. In essence, cause-related marketing is a means by which relationships with stakeholders can be developed. As organisations outsource an increasingly large part of their business activities and as the stakeholder networks become more complex, so the need to be perceived as (and to be) socially responsible becomes a critically important dimension of an organisation's image.

A public relations programme consists of a number of planned events and activities that seek to satisfy communications objectives. Some of the broad tools and techniques associated with public relations are considered in this chapter, but it should be noted that the list is not intended to be comprehensive.

Scholars' paper 12.3   Relationships and public relations

Bruning, S.D. and Ledingham, J.A. (2000) Perceptions of relationships and evaluations of satisfaction: an exploration of interaction, *Public Relations Review*, 26(1), 85–95.

This is a research paper based on work undertaken with a bank and the perceptions members of the public have of the various personal, professional and community relationships they have with the organisation. These perceptions are related to the respondents' evaluation of the satisfaction they have with the organisation. The paper puts relationships at the heart of public relations activities.

Public relations: methods and techniques

Public relations provides some of the intentional or deliberate cues that enable stakeholders to develop images and perceptions through which they recognise, understand, select and converse with organisations.

The range of public relations cues or methods available to organisations is immense. Different organisations use different permutations in order that they can communicate effectively with their various stakeholder audiences. For the purposes of this text, a general outline is provided of the more commonly used methods. Cues are to some extent interchangeable and can be used to build credibility or to provide visibility for an organisation. It is the skill of the public relations practitioner that determines the right blend of techniques. The various types of cue are set out in Table 12.4.

While there is general agreement on a definition, there is a lower level of consensus over what constitutes public relations. This is partly because the range of activities is diverse and categorisation problematic. The approach adopted here is that public relations consists of a range of communications activities, of which media relations, publicity and event management appear to be the main ones used by practitioners.

Table 12.4 Cues used to generate credibility and visibility

Cues to build credibility	Cues to signal visibility
Product quality	Sales literature and company publications
Customer relations	Publicity and media relations
Community involvement	Speeches and presentations
Strategic performance	Event management
Employee relations	Marketing communications/messages
Crisis management skills	Media mix
Third-party endorsement	Design (signage, logo, letterhead)
Perceived ethics and environmental awareness	Dress codes Video
Architecture and furnishing	Exhibitions/seminars; sponsorships

Media relations

Media relations consist of a range of activities designed to provide media journalists and editors with information. The intention is that they relay the information, through their media, for consumption by their audiences. The greater the coverage, the greater the awareness of the organisation, which in turn improves understanding, appreciation and eventually relationship development. Obviously, the original message may be changed and subject to information deviance as it is processed, but audiences perceive much of this information as highly credible simply because opinion formers (see Chapter 2) have bestowed their judgement on the item. Of the various forms of media relations, press releases, interviews, offering content (e.g. through press kits), press conferences and responding to media queries are, according to Waters et al. (2010), the most used.

Press releases

The press release is a common but increasingly ineffective form of media relations activity. A written report concerning a change in the organisation is sent to various media houses for inclusion in the media vehicle as an item of news. The media house may cover a national area, but very often a local house will suffice. These written statements concern developments in the organisation, such as promotions, new products, awards, prizes, new contracts and customers. The statement is deliberately short and written in such a style that it attracts the attention of the editor. Further information can be obtained if it is to be included within the next publication or news broadcast. The goal of this activity is primarily to create 'mentions' in a variety of targeted media, including other websites. This is important for establishing links and achieving higher search engine rankings. It is also important to build relationships, both with the target stakeholder groups and with journalists and others in the media.

Website hosts are able to sell advertising space and they also have opportunities to engage with public relations activities. This might lead to the conclusion that owners of websites have evolved into surrogate media owners, in the sense that they are free to publish content without recourse to the origin of the material. The problem is that the content they present (on their own behalf) has not been influenced by an independent third party, such as an opinion former, and may be no more than brochureware. The role is more complex than this, however, because websites now fulfil the role of fax machines. Previously, press releases were faxed to designated journalists. Now press releases are posted on a website and emailed as attached files to specified individuals on mailing lists. All those interested can view the files at their discretion and initiative, and then choose to enter into an interaction or even dialogue, in order to expand on the information provided. Email is regarded as essential by journalists, broadcasters and bloggers. The key difference is that, unlike the first two groups, bloggers prefer to receive attachments with full details and supplemental information (Burns, 2008).

In many ways e-newsletters and white papers are a natural extension of email communications. The differences concern content and goals. Email communications are sales-driven with product-related content. Newsletters and white papers are reputation-driven, with a diverse range of content concerning organisational and/or technical-related material. These communications can be an essential part of the 'stickiness' that good websites seek to develop. Recipients who find these communications of value either anticipate their release or return to the host's website to search in archived files for past copies and items of interest.

Most large organisations provide online newsroom facilities, but the quality of information provided has been found to be less than satisfactory. Callison (2003), cited by Waters et al. (2010), found that the average number of items available through these newsrooms was 6.5. These covered press releases, executive biographies and executive photographs. Other items found in online newsrooms included annual reports and financial data, audio and video archives, downloadable graphics, copies of executive speeches and organisational histories. What is also interesting is that only 60 per cent of organisations in a survey undertaken by Esrock and Leichty (1999) provided the names of a media contact person for follow-up questions to the news release they had made available.

Social media news releases allow photos, audio and video to be embedded and linked to blogs without virus concerns. These types of releases not only increase the possible number of people discovering the release via search engines, but also enable interaction and consumer comment.

At the beginning of this section we stated that press releases are becoming increasingly ineffective. This is because of two interrelated elements. The first concerns changes in audience behaviour and the second concerns advancements in digital technology.

As Spaeth (2014: 34) puts it so succinctly, 'people don't read, they watch'. She points out that today people tend to 'skim, view, listen, watch or visually absorb'. She refers to her finding that graduate students each watch, on average, 25 videos a day. The way ahead for organisations, especially when engaging consumers, not investors or government groups, is through video which tell stories that incorporate customers and their interaction with the organisation.

Press conferences

Press conferences are used when a major event has occurred and where a press release cannot convey the appropriate tone or detail required by the organisation. Press conferences are used regularly by politicians, and sports players and managers, but organisations in crisis (e.g. accidents and mergers) and individuals appealing for help (e.g. police requesting assistance from the public with respect to a particular incident) also use these forms of communications. The availability of press kits containing a full reproduction of any statements, photographs and relevant background information is considered important.

Interviews

Interviews with representatives of an organisation enable news and the organisation's view of an issue or event to be conveyed. These are normally disseminated through news channels and posted on websites. Associated formats include bylined articles (articles written by a member of an organisation about an issue related to the company and offered for publication), speeches, video, letters to the editor, and photographs and captions.

Media relations can be planned and controlled to the extent of what is sent to the media and when it is released. While there is no control over what is actually used, media relations allow organisations to try to convey information concerning strategic issues and to reach particular stakeholders.

The quality of the relationship between an organisation's public relations manager/ staff and the editor and journalists associated with both the press and the broadcast media dramatically affects the impact and dissemination of news and stories released by an organisation.

Publicity and events

Control over public relations events is not as strong as that for media relations. Indeed, negative publicity can be generated by other parties, which can impact badly on an organisation by raising doubts about its financial status or perhaps the quality of its products. Three main event activity areas can be distinguished: product, corporate and community events (see Exhibit 12.5 and also Chapter 16).

Media catching

Public relations is concerned with maximising opportunities to present an organisation, and its products and services, in a positive manner. One of the goals is to create 'mentions' in a variety of targeted media, including other websites, and social media such as social networks, blogs and Twitter. This is important for establishing links and achieving higher search engine rankings.

Another goal involves creating opportunities for interaction and dialogue with stakeholders – in particular, journalists. The stronger the communications tie, the more likely the relationship will grow and provide an effective means of distributing content and client materials. It is important to build relationships, both with the target stakeholder groups and with journalists and others in the media. We know that interpersonal

Exhibit 12.5	**Airbnb sailed a full-size floating house along the Thames to celebrate new rules to support home sharing in London.**

Source: Rex Shutterstock/Mikael Buck.

relationships between public relations practitioners and journalists can have a substantial influence on the effectiveness of an organisation's media relations performance (Shin and Cameron, 2003). Indeed, there is clear evidence that journalists are no longer the passive recipients of news releases and media kits from practitioners who are striving to generate publicity for their organisation. As Waters et al. (2010) indicate, journalists are using social media to get the information they need from practitioners.

As a general rule, public relations has been considered to work through the 'content throw' pattern of communications. In this approach organisations use public relations as a means of contacting journalists, broadcasters and bloggers in the hope of gaining media comment and placements to disseminate news content. A more contemporary approach is referred to as 'media catching'. Using digital media, this pattern of communications involves reversing the content throw approach. Now practitioners are being contacted by journalists and others for specific material for inclusion in stories, articles, blogs and websites where there are pressing deadlines. Rather than 'Here is a story/content please run it', media catching is about 'Do you have a story/content please?'

There are several issues arising from media catching. One of these is that strong relationships can emerge between a journalist and a public relations practitioner, which result in a better understanding of each other. For practitioners, this understanding manifests itself as an increased awareness of communications preferences and relevant media deadlines. For journalists, a stronger relationship provides an improved insight into what and how practitioners can contribute to their stories.

Back in 1998 Gray and Balmer suggested that public relations practitioners might be more successful if they used the contact methods preferred by journalists and the media. Subsequent research by Sallot and Johnson (2006) indicates practitioners had improved their performance because there was evidence that an increasing number of journalists were being asked to update their contact information and preferences.

Media and public relations

Traditionally public relations has been channelled through print and broadcast media. Editors selected and shaped the content they have received through press releases and other forms of content gathering. Developments in digital technology have impacted on public relations, however. Of these the use of social media and video have been most prominent as increasingly practitioners use interactive media to build relationships based on interaction and dialogue.

The use of social media to develop dialogic-based relationships with stakeholders is referred to by several authors including Mamic and Almaraz (2013: 854). They refer to organisations developing stakeholder conversations 'with real people inside brands, and moreover it allows businesses not only to see what people are saying about their brands in real time, but also respond to their public directly'. Engagement through social media can lead to the development of dialogic relationships which in turn can enable stakeholders to change their behaviour (Yang and Lim, 2009).

The use of video within media relations has become a crucially important form of communications with a variety of audiences. For example, video offers opportunities for interaction driven by consumer audiences contributing user-generated content. The material, often disseminated as a press release, an interview with the CEO, or a press conference with the CMO, are now commonly distributed through video. In addition there is thought-leadership content which again is often distributed through video format. These recordings are accessible on the home organisation's website, social media pages, most notably Facebook and YouTube, and other community-based pages.

It is through social media that individuals can learn about new products, consider various user reviews and post their own comments, questions and experiences regarding companies and brands. The interactional capability within digital media complements the core characteristic of public relations. Social networking sites and video-sharing platforms represent a significant opportunity for organisations to engage with their publics (Mamic and Almaraz, 2013). The extent to which they do engage successfully through social media is questionable as listening/observing the various interactions between stakeholders is said by some to be quite low.

Forms of public relations

In addition to these key activities the following are important forms of public relations:

- lobbying (out of personal selling and publicity);
- sponsorship (out of event management and advertising) (see Chapter 13);
- corporate advertising (out of corporate public relations and advertising);
- crisis management (which has developed out of issues management, a part of corporate public relations).

Lobbying

The representation of certain organisations or industries within government is an important aspect of public relations for many organisations. While legislation is being prepared, lobbyists provide a flow of information to their organisations to keep them informed about events (as a means of scanning the environment), but they also ensure that the views of the organisation are heard in order that legislation can be shaped appropriately, limiting any potential damage that new legislation might bring.

Moloney (1997) suggests that lobbying is inside public relations as it focuses on the members of an organisation who seek to persuade and negotiate with its stakeholders in government on matters of opportunity and or threat. He refers to in-house lobbyists (those members of the organisation who try to influence non-members) and hired lobbyists contracted to complete specific tasks.

His view of lobbying is that it is one of:

> *monitoring public policy-making for a group interest; building a case in favour of that interest; and putting it privately with varying degrees of pressure to public decision makers for their acceptance and support through favourable political intervention. (Moloney, 1997: 173)*

Hillman and Hitt (1999: 834) see lobbying as an element of an organisation's overall political strategy, and define it as the 'provision of information to policy makers by individuals representing the firm's interest'.

Where local authorities interpret legislation and frame the activities of their citizens and constituent organisations, the government determines legislation and controls the activities of people and organisations across markets.

This control may be direct or indirect, but the power and influence of government are such that large organisations and trade associations seek to influence the direction and strength of legislation, because any adverse laws or regulations may affect the profitability and the value of the organisation. Not surprisingly, 'firms use multiple channels of potential political influence to influence regulatory and policy outcomes' (Hill et al., 2013). The pharmaceutical industry has been actively lobbying the European Union with respect to legislation on new patent regulations and the information that must be carried in any marketing communications message. The tobacco industry is well known for its lobbying activities, as are chemical, transport and many other industries.

Although lobbying is a legitimate, interactive communications process, Bauer (2014: 64) rightly makes the point that organisations run risks concerning a 'disproportionate influence on law-making', and the moral and ethical issues that can arise from an abuse of lobbying practice. She refers to firms without a democratic mandate attempting to the influence the behaviour of policy-makers who have been elected on a democratic platform. As a result of some high-profile breaches of what might be regarded as legitimate lobbying behaviour, public scrutiny of this activity is becoming more intense. This, she argues, has led to organisations appearing to recognise the importance of ethical restraints so that relationships built on understanding and trust can evolve.

Scholars' paper 12.4   A case for ethical lobbying

Bauer, T. (2014) Responsible lobbying: a multidimensional model, *Journal of Corporate Citizenship*, 14(53), 61–76.

Following an interesting review of the literature regarding lobbying and CSR, the author highlights some of the ethical issues and then proposes a model designed to encourage practitioners to practise responsible lobbying.

Investor relations

Investor relations was once regarded as a financial function of organisations (Petersen and Martin, 1996) and, although sometimes loosely attached to public relations, it was more often conducted by the department of financial affairs (Hong and Ki, 2007). Today, the role of investor relations is seen to be of strategic importance and one which requires clarity and transparency, with communications, not finance, as a central tenant of investor relations (Laskin, 2009).

Viewpoint 12.3   Communicating with Tesco investors

Tesco, for years the golden retailer, had been confronting a number of issues including declining customer satisfaction, a shaky internal culture, increased competition from both high- and low-end retailers, and a failing reputation, not helped by the horsemeat scandal in 2013.

When CEO Philip Clarke left in September 2014 following the announcement that Tesco had misrepresented its earnings by £263 million, the crisis was gathering speed. By the end of the month the finance director and three other executives had been suspended, and Tesco became a focus for several stakeholder groups. These included the investment community, the media, the Serious Fraud Office, regulators and customers. Two months later Tesco's shareholders announced legal action to recoup lost profits.

Corporate communications at Tesco, which incorporated Media Relations (MR) and Investor Relations (IR), were all part of Corporate Affairs. The increasing pressures of this multifaceted assault on the company, and the falling share price, meant that there had be close liaison between the MR team and the IR team in order to communicate the company's financial and corporate messages. The MR team has to explain the reasoning behind the company issues and inform about what Tesco was intending to achieve, in the mid rather than the short term. This involved delivering positive stories as well as neutralising negative ones. The focus for the IR team was similar but shaped and targeted for individual and corporate investors, such as pension funds, and for the financial markets, including the buy- and sell-side analysts. Both teams needed to ensure that the tone of Tesco's messaging conveyed that it was trying to do what was best for its customers and shareholders.

Tesco appointed a new CEO, Dave Lewis, who introduced a turnaround strategy. Tight internal communications between the MR and IR were particularly important in order that shareholders were kept informed about new strategies. The teams also need to work closely when financial results were released at certain points throughout the year. At the end of the year MR help create the annual report and accounts. IR help produce the figures and arrange for them to be released to investors. At the same time MR should arrange media interviews for the chairman, CEO and FD. It is crucial that all the messaging, including what these spokespeople say, is consistent and that it concurs with the stated strategy, and information in the annual report and accounts.

In December 2014 it was announced that IR was to be moved out of Corporate Affairs and in future be located in the Finance Department, reporting to the new Finance Director. This move might reflect a less than effective working relationship within Corporate Affairs, or perhaps the severe gravity of the situation facing Tesco, and the need to work and communicate differently with shareholders.

Source: Anon (2014); Golob (2014); Harrington (2014).

Question: How might Tesco use social media to assist investor relations?

Task: Using the Web, try to identify resources that focus on investor relations.

Partly as a result of deregulation, the number of target audiences for financial services and related communications has grown. On the one hand, there are large institutional investors such as the government, multinational organisations and agencies such as stock exchanges, all of which require financially related information. On the other hand, there are increasing numbers of individual investors who wish to invest part of their savings in various funds, equities and savings plans. In addition to these there are the financial press, shareholders, investment analysts, financial advisers and fund managers. This means that communications, and the provision of timely, transparent and accurate information, should have become significant factors in the market place.

Cutlip et al. define investor relations as 'a specialized part of corporate public relations that builds and maintains mutually beneficial relationships with shareholders and others in the financial community to maximize shareholder value' (1999: 21). The UK Investor Relations Society (2009) describes investor relations as follows:

> *Investor Relations is the communication of information and insight between a company and the investment community. This process enables a full appreciation of the company's business activities, strategy and prospects and allows the market to make an informed judgement about the fair value and appropriate ownership of a company.*

Interestingly, the former stresses the maximisation of shareholder value and relationships, while the latter emphasises fair value rather than maximisation, and implicitly stresses the significance of one-way communications, which are not suitable for relationship development. In practice, the core activity of investor relations is to react to requests for information although the development and use of websites has helped to make the discipline more proactive.

If investor relations are to have an enhanced communications focus, a variety of public relations strategies are necessary to reach different target audiences. Hanrahan (1997) highlights four particular strategies: expansive, defensive, creative and adaptive.

Expansive strategies are followed during periods of growth, when the size of product portfolios increases. In this context competition can be aggressive, so it is critical that awareness, recognition and trust are developed. This can be achieved through serving on committees and public interest groups, publishing white papers, speaking at conferences, writing articles and other activities that serve to raise the profile and credibility or the organisation. Sponsorship can also be used to make associations with an event. This in turn can also be used as a way of establishing networks and leveraging goodwill.

Defensive strategies are needed in times of crisis, such as a recession, very poor trading performance, when accused of malpractice or irregular reporting or when faced by a hostile takeover bid. In these situations the timely provision of the correct information, perhaps as a separate report, is important.

Creative strategies involve the use of digital technologies to deliver the corporate identity in novel and interesting ways. This might be through the use of interviews which can be beamed across the television world instantly, if necessary, across the Internet and through Reuters and world services. With information and analysis instantly available, 24/7, the prime role of the press has shifted to one focused on the provision of comment and interpretation.

Adaptive strategies are used when an organisation experiences considerable change. Moving into new financial product and/or geographic markets, merging with another organisation or simply developing key services, all warrant strategies that are flexible and can adapt to local press and media needs. Corporate advertising, adapted for local use, has been a significant tool. Today, one of the roles of the website is to provide fast, localised information that can be targeted at particular opinion leaders and formers.

Corporate advertising

In an attempt to harness the advantages of both advertising and public relations, corporate advertising has been seen by some as a means of communicating more effectively with a range of stakeholders. The credibility of messages transmitted through public relations is high, but the control that management has over the message is limited. Advertising, however, allows management virtually total control over message dispersion, but the credibility of these messages is usually low. Corporate advertising is the combination of the best of advertising and the best of public relations.

The main purpose of corporate advertising appears to be the provision of cues by which stakeholders can identify and understand an organisation. This is achieved by presenting the personality of the organisation to a wide range of stakeholders, rather than presenting particular functions or products that the organisation markets. Schumann et al. (1991) conclude that a number of US studies indicate that the first goal of corporate advertising is to enhance the company's reputation and the second is to provide support for the promotion of products and services. There seems little reason to doubt this several decades later.

Reasons for the use of corporate advertising

The need to improve and maintain goodwill and to establish a positive reputation among an organisation's stakeholders has already been mentioned. These are tasks that need to be undertaken consistently and continuously, with the aim of building a reputational reservoir. In addition, however, there are particular occasions when organisations need to use corporate advertising. These are set out in Table 12.5.

Crisis communications

Organisational crises are low-probability, high-impact events (Pearson and Clair, 1998) that threaten the existence of an organisation. Crises can occur because of a simple or minor managerial mistake, an incorrect decision, a technology failure, or because of a seemingly distant environmental event. All organisations face the prospect of managing a crisis, indeed some commentators ominously suggest that all organisations have a crisis just around the corner (Fink, 2000).

The impact of crises is very often considered from an external perspective but crises can be of concern to specific areas such as social media environments (Pang et al., 2014), business relationships such as those with suppliers and agencies (Nätti et al., 2014), employees (Heide and Simonsson, 2014) and investors (Rytkönen et al., 2014).

Crises are emerging with greater frequency as a result of a number of factors. Table 12.6 sets out some of the main factors that give rise to crises for organisations. For example, Bailey et al. (2013) report on the growing incidence of cybercrime and the costs of recovery. They refer to the US$100,000 plus direct costs associated with investigating an incident and on remediation activities. These costs are trivial, however, compared to indirect losses incurred by investors' losing confidence as a result of the quality of response to the incident, and the multibillion-dollar loss in market capitalisation.

Figure 12.2 is used to present organisational crises in the context of two key variables. On the horizontal axis is the degree to which management has control over the origin of

Table 12.5 Reasons to use corporate advertising

Reason for use	Explanation
During change and transition	To convince stakeholders, particularly shareholders, of the value of the organisation and of the need not to accept hostile offers, before, during and after a takeover or merger.
To change a poor image	To correct any misunderstanding that stakeholders might have of an organisation. For example, financial analysts may believe that an organisation is underperforming, but reality indicates that performance is good.
Product support	To assist the launch of new products by establishing a strong, good reputational equity and so lowering costs.
Recruitment	To recruit employees by creating a positive and attractive image of the organisation.
Repositioning	To refocus the way stakeholders regard an organisation.
Advocacy	To inform stakeholders of the position or stand that an organisation has on a particular issue of social concern.

Table 12.6 Common causes of disasters

Origin of crisis	Explanation
Economic	As new economies emerge (e.g. BRIC), so many established industries in developed economies decline – for example, the UK's steel and shipbuilding industries.
Managerial	Human error and the pursuit of financial goals by some organisations give rise to the majority of disasters. For example, various banks such as RBS and the Co-operative Bank, and those organisations associated with cutting costs at the expense of safety and repair of systems.
Political	Issues concerning war, religious extremism, and terrorism have encouraged kidnapping, as well as organisations having to change the locations of their business.
Climate	The climate is changing substantially in certain parts of the world, and this has brought disaster to those who lie in the wake of natural disturbances. For example, the earthquakes in Nepal (2015), the hurricanes in 2004 that decimated the Cayman Islands and Grenada in the Caribbean.
Technology	The rate at which technology is advancing has brought about crises such as those associated with transportation systems, aircraft disasters, and cybercrime. Human error is also a significant factor, often associated with the rate of technological change. Examples include cyber-attacks on eBay and Sony.
Consumer groups	The rise of consumer groups (e.g. Amnesty International and Greenpeace) and their ability to investigate and publicise the operations and policies of organisations. For example, the campaign led by the pressure group 38 Degrees to disassociate LEGO from Shell and the latter's quest to drill for oil in the Arctic.

the crisis. Is the origin of the crisis outside management's control, such as an earthquake, or is it within its control, such as those crises associated with poor trading results? The vertical axis reflects the potential impact that a crisis might have on an organisation. All crises, by definition, have a potential to inflict damage on an organisation. However, some can be contained, perhaps on a geographic basis, whereas others have the potential to cause tremendous damage to an organisation, such as those experienced through product tampering and environmental pollution.

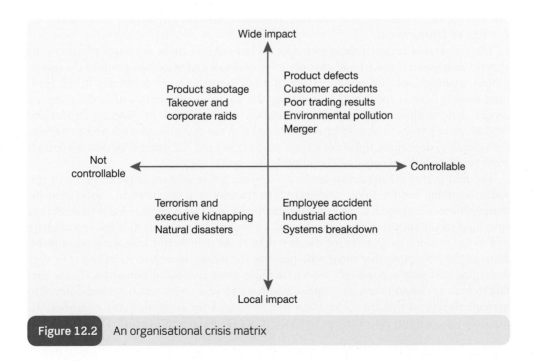

Figure 12.2 An organisational crisis matrix

The increasing occurrence of crises throughout the world has prompted many organisations to review the manner in which they anticipate managing such events, should they be implicated. It is generally assumed that those organisations that take care to plan in anticipation of disaster will experience more favourable outcomes than those that fail to plan. The extent to which this is correct is questionable.

The second reason concerns the expectations of those who design and implement crisis plans. It is one thing to design a plan; it is entirely another to implement it. Crisis planning is about putting into position those elements that can affect speedy outcomes to the disaster sequence. When a crisis strikes, it is the application of contingency-based tactics by all those concerned with the event that will determine the strength of the outcome. Spillan (2003) sought to determine whether the experience of a crisis encourages concern and attention to preventing further crisis events. This was based on the evidence of Barton (2001) and Mitroff and Anagnos (2001) that most organisations only prepare crisis management plans after suffering and then recovering from a disaster. The central issue appears to revolve around the need to assess an organisation's vulnerabilities at the earliest opportunity, before a crisis occurs (Caponigro, 2000, as cited by Spillan, 2003).

Whatever the cause, whatever the level of preparation, contemporary forms of communications including websites, social media and mobile technologies play a critical role in crisis management. News of an organisational crisis or disaster can spread around the globe instantly, whilst managers of an afflicted organisation can post up-to-date information quickly, by providing pertinent information or directing visitors to information and associated facilities.

Crisis phases

The number of phases through which a crisis passes varies according to author and the management model being proposed. For example, Penrose (2000) mentions Littlejohn's six-step model, Fink's audit, Mitroff's portfolio planning approach and Burnett's crisis classification matrix. The number of phases is also influenced by the type of crisis management an organisation uses. Essentially there are two main models, as presented in Figure 12.3: organisations that plan in order to manage crisis events and in doing so attempt to contain the impact; and then organisations that fail to plan and manage by reacting to crisis events.

The differences between these two approaches are that there are fewer phases in the shorter 'reactionary' model and that the level of detail and attention given to the anticipation, management and consideration of crisis events is more deliberate in the planning model. Time is spent here considering the sequence of events within the planning model. A three-phase (and five-episode) framework is adopted: pre-impact, impact and readjustment phases. It should be remembered that the duration of each phase can vary considerably, depending upon the nature of the crisis and the manner in which management deals with the events associated with the crisis.

The first period is referred to as the *pre-impact phase* and consists of two main episodes: scanning and planning; and event identification and preparation. Good strategic management demands that the environment be scanned on a regular basis to detect the first signs of significant change. Organisations that pick up signals that are repeated are in a better position to prepare for disaster than those that do not scan the environment. Penrose (2000) reports that those who perceive the impact of a crisis to be severe or very damaging and plan accordingly tend to achieve more successful outcomes. Those that fail to scan are often taken by surprise and have to react with less time and control to manage the events that hit them. Even if they do pick up a signal, many organisations not only ignore it but also attempt to block it out (Pearson and Mitroff, 1993). It is as if

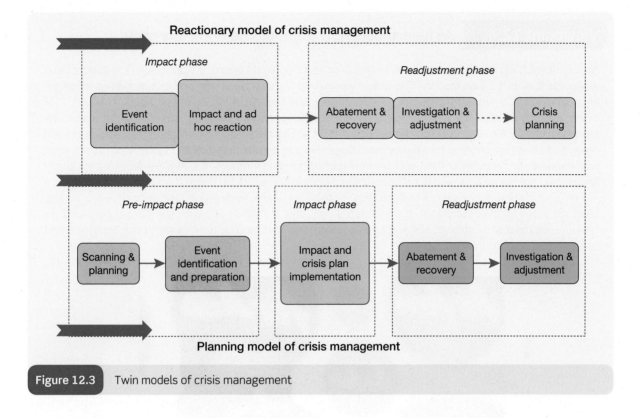

Reactionary model of crisis management

Impact phase

Event identification

Impact and ad hoc reaction

Readjustment phase

Abatement & recovery

Investigation & adjustment

Crisis planning

Pre-impact phase

Scanning & planning

Event identification and preparation

Impact phase

Impact and crisis plan implementation

Readjustment phase

Abatement & recovery

Investigation & adjustment

Planning model of crisis management

Figure 12.3   Twin models of crisis management

---

management is attempting to deny the presence of the signals in order that any stability and certainty they may have can continue.

Many of the signals detected during the pre-impact phase wither and die. Some gather strength and develop with increasing force. The next episode is characterised by the identification of events that move from possible to probable status. There is increasing activity and preparation in anticipation of the crisis, once its true nature and direction have been determined. Much of the activity should be geared to training and the preparation and deployment of crisis teams. The objective is not to prevent the crisis but to defuse it as much as possible, to inform significant stakeholders of its proximity and possible effects, and finally to manage the crisis process.

The impact phase is the period when the 'crisis breaks out' (Sturges et al., 1991). Management is tested to the limit and if a plan has been developed it is implemented with the expectation of ameliorating the damage inflicted by the crisis. One method of reducing the impact is to contain or localise the crisis. Neutralising and constraining the event can prevent it from contaminating other parts of the organisation or stakeholders. Pearson and Mitroff (1993) suggest that the containment of oil spills and the evacuation of buildings and aircraft are examples of containment and neutralisation. Through the necessity to talk to all stakeholders, management at this point will inevitably reveal its attitude towards the crisis event. Is its attitude one of genuine concern for the victims and stakeholders? Is the attitude consistent with the expectations that stakeholders have of the management team? Alternatively, is there a perception that management is making lame excuses and distancing itself from the event, and is this consistent with expectations? Readers should note that, within the reactionary model, the pre-impact and impact phases are merged into one, simply because there is little or no planning, no scanning and, by definition, no preparation in anticipation of a crisis.

Viewpoint 12.4   AirAsia shows how it should be done in a crisis

AirAsia Flight 8501 crashed into the Java Sea with 162 people on board. It was AirAsia's first ever fatal air accident in its 13-year history. The airline was saved from receivership and relaunched as a budget airline making air travel affordable for millions of people in fast-growing Southeast Asia.

Immediately on hearing the news that the flight had disappeared from radar after taking off from Surabaya in Indonesia, AirAsia's CEO Tony Fernandes was in the city meeting with families of the passengers and crew. AirAsia set up a hotline for relatives and began issuing regular updates and statements about what was known to be factually correct and avoided speculation and rumours. These were delivered in several languages. The airline arranged hotel accommodation and transport for those from outside Surabaya.

Fernandes's first actions were to apologise for the loss of life, even using Twitter to deliver a simple, clear message to express shock and sympathy: 'my only thoughts are with the passengers and my crew . . . we must stay strong'. His overt compassion was matched by his change of the airline's bright red logo to a sombre grey online.

Exhibit 12.6   **AirAsia and CEO Tony Fernandes**
Source: Alamy/epa european pressphoto agency b.v.

Fernandes subsequently issued over 20 Tweets updating his 1 million plus followers on the progress of the investigation. He emphasised that the family and friends of passengers were his principal focus to the extent that some regarded his approach as highly credible and authentic.

At news conferences he faced up to questions squarely, side-stepping speculation about the cause of the crash, which occurred during bad weather. 'I apologize profusely for what they are going through . . . I am the leader of this company. I take responsibility. That is why I am here. I am not running away from my obligations even though we don't know what's wrong. The passengers were on my aircraft, and I have to take responsibility for that.'

Source: Anon (2015); Wilson (2015); Wright (2015).

Question:	Is honesty always the right approach when the causes of a disaster are unknown?
Task:	Interpret the way AirAsia managed this crisis using the models at Figure 12.3.

The readjustment phase within the planning model consists of three main episodes. The period concerns the recovery and realignment of the organisation and its stakeholders to the new environment, once the deepest part of the crisis event has passed. The essential tasks are to ensure that the needs of key stakeholders can still be met and, if they cannot, to determine what must be done to ensure that they can be. For example, continuity of product supply is critically important. This may be achieved by servicing customers from other locations. Common characteristics of this phase are the investigations, police inquiries, public demonstrations, court cases and media probing that inevitably follow major crises and disasters. The manner in which an organisation handles this fall-out and tries to appear reasonable and consistent in its approach to such events can have a big impact on the perception that other stakeholders have of the organisation.

The rate at which organisations readjust depends partly on the strength of the image held by stakeholders prior to the crisis occurring. If the organisation had a strong reputation then the source credibility attributed to the organisation will be high. This means that messages transmitted by the organisation will be received favourably and trusted. However, if the reputation is poor, the effectiveness of any marketing communications is also going to be low. The level of source credibility held by the organisation will influence the speed with which stakeholders allow an organisation to readjust and recover after a crisis.

Benoit (1997) developed a theory concerning image restoration in the light of an organisational crisis. The theory states that there are five general approaches: denial, evade responsibility, reduce offensiveness, use corrective action and, lastly, mortification (see Table 12.7). Benoit has used these approaches to evaluate the responses given by a variety of organisations when faced by different disasters and crises.

Organisations that have not planned their management of crisis events and have survived a disaster may decide to instigate a more positive approach in order to mitigate the impact of future crisis events. This is not uncommon and crisis management planning may occur at the end of this cycle.

Table 12.7 Image restoration approaches

Damage retrieval	Explanation
Simple denial	Outright rejection that the act was caused by them or even occurred in the first place, or shifting the blame by asserting that another organisation (person) was responsible for the act.
Evasion (of responsibility)	Provocation . . . a reasonable response to a prior act.
	Defeasibility . . . the act occurred because of a lack of time or information.
	Accident . . . the act was not committed purposefully.
	Good intentions . . . the wrongful act was caused despite trying to do well.
Reducing offensiveness	This involves demonstrating that the act was of minor significance or by responding so as to reduce the impact of the accusor.
Corrective action	This may involve putting right what was damaged and taking steps to avoid a repeat occurrence.
Mortification	An apology or statement of regret for causing the act that gave offence.

Source: Benoit (1997).

Framing for crisis communications

Framing involves the selection and prominence of specific topics that are communicated and promoted through an organisation's communications processes (Romenti et al., 2014). The use of framing can shape the way stakeholders perceive an organisation and the associated crisis (see Chapter 17 for a deeper insight into the framing concept).

Crises can be categorised by type (Coombs, 2007) and the type provides the frame through which stakeholders pick up clues about how to interpret the event. Coombs identifies three main types: the extent to which the event was caused by an uncontrollable external force or agent; whether it was the result of an intentional or accidental action by the organisation; or if it was caused by human or technical error. The frame, therefore, enables stakeholders to determine the extent to which the organisation was responsible for the crisis occurring in the first place. From these three clusters of types of crisis can be identified: victim, accident and preventable clusters (see Table 12.8).

Table 12.8 Crisis types by crisis clusters

Crisis clusters	Explanation
Victim cluster	The organisation is seen as a victim of the crisis. Stakeholders attribute little responsibility to the organisation, so there is only a mild reputational threat. Common events include natural disasters, rumours, workplace violence and product tampering.
Accident cluster	The actions of the organisation leading to the crisis were minimal and the threat to reputational status is moderate. Typical events include stakeholder challenges to the operations, technical error accidents and technical errors resulting in product defect and subsequent recall.
Preventable cluster	The organisation deliberately placed people at risk, took inappropriate actions or violated regulations and in doing so caused a strong threat to the reputation. Typical events include human-error accidents and product harm/defects, deception, misconduct and actions that lead to injury.

Source: After Protecting organization reputations during a crisis: The development and application of situational crisis communication theory, *Corporate Reputation Review*, 10(3), pp. 163–176 (Coombs, W.T. 2007), Reprinted by permission from Macmillan Publishers Ltd.

Coombs (2006) claims that, in order to repair reputation, crisis response strategies are necessary to shape the perceptions of those responsible, change perceptions of the organisation and reduce the negative effects caused through the crisis event. He identifies three main forms of response based on the perceptions of those responsible for the crisis. The first are *denial strategies*, which attempt to remove connections between the organisation and the crisis. The second are *diminish strategies*, which argue that the organisation did not lack control over the crisis and that it is not as bad as is claimed by others. The third are *rebuild strategies*, which involve offering compensation or an apology to victims. Coombs develops a situational crisis communications theory which anticipates how stakeholders will perceive a crisis and how they will react to various response strategies. He argues that his approach bridges deficiencies in Benoit's image restoration theory which offers 'no conceptual links between the crisis response strategies and elements of the crisis situation' (Coombs, 2007: 171).

Finally, Kahn et al. (2013) draw attention to the need to consider the relational harm caused by crises. They consider the relational systems and propose ways in which these should be managed in order to repair the damage caused by disasters and crises. This paper is highlighted as a Scholars' paper, as it provides an interesting counter-point to the prevailing approach and literature on crisis communications.

Scholars' paper 12.4	Recovering relationships following a crisis

Kahn, W.A., Barton, M.A. and Fellows, S. (2013) Organizational crises and the disturbance of relational systems, *Academy of Management Review*, 38(3), 377–96.

The authors refer to the damage caused to relational systems that can persist once a crisis has been repaired. Referring to relational disturbances, these authors draw on family systems theory to help define the dimensions of relational systems. The paper describes the disturbances of relational systems in the context of crises and the authors develop a framework for their repair and transformation. Readers interested in crisis management and communications are advised to read this paper as it provides an interesting counter to the conventional perspective.

Key points

- Public relations is a communications discipline that can develop and maintain a portfolio of relationships with a range of key stakeholder audiences. The use of public relations does not require the purchase of airtime or space in media vehicles, such as television, third-party websites or magazines. The decision on whether an organisation's public relations messages are transmitted or not rests with those charged with managing the media resource, not the message sponsor.

- The main characteristics of public relations are that it represents a very cost-effective means of carrying messages with a high degree of credibility. However, the degree of control that management is able to exert over the transmission of messages can be limited.

- Public relations can be used to communicate with a range of publics (or stakeholders). These vary from employees (internal public relations), financial groups (financial or investor relations), customers (media relations) and *organisations and communities* (corporate public relations).

- Public relations enables organisations to position themselves and provide stakeholders with a means of identifying and understanding them. This may be accomplished inadvertently through inaction or deliberately through a planned presentation of a variety of visual cues.

- Public relations can be seen to work at a practitioner level where it is used as a tool to achieve media visibility. At a different level public relations is seen as a means of mediating the relationships organisations develop with various stakeholders. Here, public relations is perceived as a longer-term and proactive form of planned communications. In the former view, public relations is seen as an instrument, in the latter, as a means of conducting dialogue.

- Grunig and Hunt (1984) have attempted to capture the diversity of public relations activities through a framework. They set out four models to reflect the different ways in which public relations is, in their opinion, considered to work.

- There are four dimensions of communications behaviour. These dimensions are direction, purpose, channel and ethics. Using predetermined campaign objectives, ranging from publicity, through press releases, to the manner in which customers are treated and products perform, events are managed and expectations are met.

- Public relations consists of a range of communications activities, of which media relations, publicity and event management appear to be the main ones used by practitioners. However, in addition investor relations, lobbying, corporate advertising and crisis communications form an important aspect of public relations activities.

- Public relations plays an important role in preparing for and constraining the impact of a crisis and re-establishing an organisation once a crisis has passed. Crisis planning is about putting into position those elements that can affect speedy outcomes.

- Public relations has three major roles to play within the communications programme of an organisation: the development and maintenance of corporate goodwill; the continuity necessary for good product support; and, through these, the development and maintenance of suitable relationships. These roles can be accomplished more easily when public relations is integrated with the other tools and media of the communications mix.

Review questions

Pestaurant case questions

1. Using the Pestaurant case at the start of this chapter, identify the company's main stakeholders and comment on why it was important to communicate with each of them.

2. Highlight the main objectives of using public relations. How were these realised in the Pestaurant case?

3. How might the success of the public relations for Pestaurant be best evaluated?

4. Write a brief paper describing the main methods of publicity used by the Pestaurant.

5. Visit the Pestaurant site at www.rentokil.co.uk/pestaurant/ and suggest ways in which other forms of public relations might be used.

General questions

1. Define public relations and set out its principal characteristics.

2. Identify the different strategies associated with investor relations.

3. Identify the main phases associated with crisis management.

4. Suggest how the responses made by AirAsia (Viewpoint 12.4) can be interpreted through use of Benoit's 'approaches to image restoration'.

5. What roles might stakeholders adopt when a crisis occurs?

References

Anon (2014) Tesco: a tale of a comms team and an investor relations department, *MediaFirst*, 24 October, retrieved 9 February 2015 from www.mediafirst.co.uk/our-thinking/tesco-a-tale-of-a-comms-team-and-an-investor-relations-department/.

Anon (2015) Tony Fernandes: a crisis management analysis, *MediaFirst*, Tuesday 6 January, retrieved 11 February from www.mediafirst.co.uk/our-thinking/tony-fernandes-a-crisis-management-analysis/.

Bailey, T., Brandley, J. and Kaplan, J. (2013) How good is your cyberincident-response plan? McKinsey and Company, retrieved 5 November 2014 from www.mckinsey.com/Insights/Business_Technology/How_good_is_your_cyberincident_response_plan?cid=other-eml-alt-mip-mck-oth-1312.

Barton, L. (2001) *Crisis Organisations II*, Cincinnati, OH: South Western Publishing.

Bauer, T. (2014) Responsible lobbying: a multidimensional model, *Journal of Corporate Citizenship*, 14(53), 61–76.

Benoit, W. L. (1997) Image repair discourse and crisis communications, *Public Relations Review*, 23(2), 177–86.

Bernays, E. L. (1928) *Propaganda*, New York: Horace Liveright.

Bruning, S.D. and Ledingham, J.A. (2000) Perceptions of relationships and evaluations of satisfaction: an exploration of interaction, *Public Relations Review*, 26(1), 85–95.

Bruning, S.D., Dials, M. and Shirka, A. (2008) Using dialogue to build organisation–public relationships, engage publics, and positively affect organizational outcomes, *Public Relations Review*, 34, 25–31.

Burns, K.S. (2008) A historical examination of the development of social media and its application to the public relations industry. Paper presented at the International Communications Association conference, Montreal (May).

Callison, C. (2003) Media relations and the Internet: how Fortune 500 company web sites assist journalists in news gathering, *Public Relations Review*, 29, 29–41.

Caponigro, J.R. (2000) *The Crisis Counsellor: A-Step-by-Step Guide to Managing a Business Crisis*, Chicago, IL: Contemporary Books.

Coombs, W.T. (1995) Choosing the right words: the development of guidelines for selection of 'appropriate' crisis response strategies, *Management Communications Quarterly*, 8(4), 447–76.

Coombs, W.T. (2006) The protective powers of crisis response strategies: managing reputational assets during a crisis, *Journal of Promotion Management*, 12, 241–59.

Coombs, W.T. (2007) Protecting organization reputations during a crisis: the development and application of situational crisis communications theory, *Corporate Reputation Review* 10(3), 163–76.

Cutlip, S.M., Center, A.H. and Broom, G.M. (1994) *Effective Public Relations*, Englewood Cliffs, NJ: Prentice Hall.

Cutlip, S.M., Center, A.H. and Broom, G.M. (1999) *Effective Public Relations*, 8th edition, Englewood Cliffs, NJ: Prentice Hall.

Esrock, S.L. and Leichty, G.B. (1999) Corporate World Wide Web pages: serving the news media and other publics, *Journalism & Mass Communication Quarterly*, 76, 456–67.

Fesnal, E. (2014) Taylor Swift v. Spotify in the public eye, *PRSSA*, 9 November, retrieved 25 April 2015 from http://prssa.syr.edu/2014/11/09/taylor-swift-v-spotify-in-the-public-eye/.

Fink, S. (2000) *Crisis Management Planning for the Inevitable*, New York: AMACON.

Geertz, C. (1973) *The Interpretation of Cultures*, New York: Basic Books.

Golob, B. (2014) Cleanup on aisle £263m, *Communicate*, 18 December, retrieved 9 February 2015 from www.communicatemagazine.co.uk/currentissuemenu/5714-2014-12-18-13-34-33.

Gray, E.R. and Balmer, J.M.T. (1998) Managing corporate image and corporate reputation, *Long Range Planning*, 31, 695–702.

Greenwood, C.A. (2011) Evolutionary theory: the missing link for conceptualizing public relations, *Journal of Public Relations Research*, 22(4), 456–76.

Gregory, A. (2004) Scope and structure of public relations: a technology driven view, *Public Relations Review*, 30(3), 245–54.

Grunig, J. (1992) Models of public relations and communication, in *Excellence in Public Relations and Communications Management* (eds J.E. Grunig, D.M. Dozier, P. Ehling, L.A. Grunig, F.C. Repper and J. Whits), Hillsdale, NJ: Lawrence Erlbaum, 285–325.

Grunig, J.E. (1997) A situational theory of publics: conceptual history, recent challenges and new research, in *Public Relations Research: An International Perspective* (eds D. Moss, T. MacManus and D. Verčič), London: Thomson.

Grunig, J. and Hunt, T. (1984) *Managing Public Relations*, New York: Holt, Rineholt & Winston.

Hallahan, K. (2003) W.L. Mackenzie King: Rockefeller's 'other' public relations counselor in Colorado, *Public Relations Review*, 29, 401–14.

Hanrahan, G. (1997) Financial and investor relations, in P. Kitchen (ed.) *Public Relations Principles and Practice*, London: Thomson.

Harrington, J. (2014) Tesco moves investor relations function from corporate affairs to finance, *PR Week*, 2 December, retrieved 9 February 2015 from www.prweek.com/article/1324835/tesco-moves-investor-relations-function-corporate-affairs-finance.

Heide, M. and Simonsson, C. (2014) Developing internal crisis communications, *Corporate Communications: An International Journal*, 19(2), 128–46.

Hill, M.D., Kelly, G.W., Lockhart, G.B. and Ness, R.A. (2013) Determinants and effects of corporate lobbying, *Financial Management*, 42(4), 931–57.

Hillman, A.J. and Hitt, M.A. (1999) Corporate political strategy formulation: a model of approach, participation, and strategy decisions, *Academy of Management Review*, 24(4), 825–42.

Hong, Y. and Ki, E.-J. (2007) How do public relations practitioners perceive investor relations? An exploratory study, *Corporate Communications: An International Journal*, 12(2), 199–213.

Hurme, P. (2001) On-line PR: emerging organisational practice, *Corporate Communications: An International Journal*, 6(2), 71–5.

Joseph, S. (2013) Paddy Power ties with Stonewall to support gay footballers, *Marketing Week*, 16 September, retrieved 12 February 2015 from www.marketingweek.com/2013/09/16/paddy-power-ties-with-stonewall-to-support-gay-footballers/.

Kahn, W.A., Barton, M.A. and Fellows, S. (2013) Organizational crises and the disturbance of relational systems, *Academy of Management Review*, 38(3), 377–96.

Kent, M.L. and Taylor, M. (2002) Toward a dialogic theory of public relations, *Public Relations Review*, 28(1), 21–37.

Laskin, A.V. (2009) The evolution of models of public relations: an outsider's perspective, *Journal of Communication Management*, 13(1), 37–54.

Lepitak, S. (2013) PaddyPower teams with Stonewall for week-long 'Right Behind Gay Footballers' campaign, *The Drum*, 16 September, retrieved 12 February 2015 from www.thedrum.com/news/2013/09/16/paddypower-teams-stonewall-week-long-right-behind-gay-footballers-campaign.

Mamic, L.I. and Almaraz, I.A. (2013) How the larger corporations engage with stakeholders through Twitter, *International Journal of Market Research*, 55(6), 851–72.

Miller, G. (1989) Persuasion and public relations: two 'Ps' in a pod, in *Public Relations Theory* (eds C. Botan and V. Hazelton), Hillsdale, NJ: Lawrence Erlbaum.

Mitroff, I. and Anagnos, G. (2001) *Managing Crises Before They Happen*, New York: American Management Association.

Moloney, K. (1997) Government and lobbying activities, in *Public Relations: Principles and Practice* (ed. P.J. Kitchen), London: International Thomson Press.

Nätti, S., Rahkolin, S. and Saraniemi, S. (2014) Crisis communication in key account relationships, *Corporate Communications: An International Journal*, 19(3), 234–46.

Pang, A., Hassan, N.B.B.A. and Chong, A.C.Y. (2014) Negotiating crisis in the social media environment, *Corporate Communications: An International Journal*, 19(1), 96–118.

Pearson, C.M. and Clair, J.A. (1998) Reframing crisis management, *Academy of Management Review*, 23, 59–76.

Pearson, C.M. and Mitroff, I. (1993) From crisis prone to crisis prepared: a framework for crisis management, *Academy of Management Executive*, 7(1), 48–59.

Penrose, J.M. (2000) The role of perception in crisis planning, *Public Relations Review*, 26(2), 155–71.

Petersen, B.K. and Martin, H.J. (1996) CEO perception of investor relations as a public relations function: an exploratory study, *Journal of Public Relations Research*, 8(3), 173–209.

Pieczka, M. (2011) Public relations as dialogic expertise? *Journal of Communication Management*, 15(2), 108–24.

Renfree, M. (2014) 3 Things Taylor Swift does right on social media, *PRNews*, 11 July, retrieved 25 April 2015 from www.prnewsonline.com/water-cooler/2014/11/07/three-things-taylor-swift-does-right-on-social-media/.

Roderick, L. (2014) Raising the stakes, *The Marketer*, July/August, 24–7.

Romenti, S., Murtarelli, G. and Valentini, C. (2014) Organisations' conversations in social media: applying dialogue strategies in times of crises, *Corporate Communications: An International Journal*, 19(1), 10–33.

Rytkönen, S., Oy, M. and Louhiala-Salminen, L. (2014) 'Sell the sizzle' – communicating environmental, social, and governance issues to institutional investors, *Corporate Communications: An International Journal*, 19(4), 329–43.

Sallot, L.M. and Johnson, E. (2006) To contact . . . or not? Investigating journalists' assessments of public relations subsidies and contact preferences, *Public Relations Review*, 32, 83–6.

Schumann, D.W., Hathcote, J.M. and West, S. (1991) Corporate advertising in America: a review of published studies on use, measurement and effectiveness, *Journal of Advertising*, 20(3), 35–56.

Shin, J.H. and Cameron, G.T. (2003) Informal relations: a look at personal influence in media relations, *Journal of Communication Management*, 7, 239–253.

Spaeth, M. (2014) Is public relations obsolete? *ABA Bank Marketing and Sales*, September, 30–4.

Spillan, J.E. (2003) An exploratory model for evaluating crisis events and managers' concerns in non-profit organisations, *Journal of Contingencies and Crisis Management*, 11(4), 160–9.

Spotify (2014) On Taylor Swift's decision to remove her music from Spotify, *Spotify*, 3 November, retrieved 25 April 2015 from https://news.spotify.com/uk/2014/11/03/taylor-swifts-decision/.

Sturges, D.L., Carell, B.J., Newsom, D.A. and Barrera, M. (1991) Crisis communication management: the public opinion node and its relationship to environmental nimbus, *SAM Advanced Management Journal*, Summer, 22–7.

UK Investor Relations Society (2009) retrieved 23 March 2011 from www.ir-soc.org.uk/.

Vos, T.P. (2011) Explaining the origins of public relations: logics of historical explanation, *Journal of Public Relations Research*, 23(2), 119–140.

Waters, R.D., Tindall, N.T.J. and Morton, T.S. (2010) Media catching and the journalist–public relations practitioner relationship: how social media are changing the practice of media relations, *Journal of Public Relations Research*, 22(3), 241–64.

Williams, E. (2014) Ad of the week: Paddy Power rainbow laces Metro edition, *Creative Review*, 12 September, retrieved 12 February 2015 from www.creativereview.co.uk/cr-blog/2014/september/ad-of-the-week-paddy-power-rainbow-laces-metro-edition.

Willman, C. (2014) Exclusive: Taylor Swift on being pop's instantly platinum wonder . . . and why she's paddling against the streams, *Yahoo Music*, 6 November, retrieved 25 April from www.yahoo.com/music/bp/exclusive-taylor-swift-on-being-pop-s-instantly-platinum-wonder-and-why-she-s-paddling-against-the-streams-085041907.html.

Wilson, D. (2015) AirAsia CEO Tony Fernandes has given a lesson in crisis management, *PR Week*, 6 January, retrieved 11 February 2015 from www.prweek.com/article/1328007/airasia-ceo-tony-fernandes-given-lesson-crisis-management.

Wood, S.P. (2015) Spotify fires PR firm over Taylor Swift diss, *Adweek*, 28 January, retrieved 25 April 2015 from www.adweek.com/prnewser/spotify-fires-pr-firm-over-taylor-swift-diss/107905.

Wright, S. (2015) AirAsia's CEO is becoming the model for airline leaders during a crisis, *Associated Press*, 2 January, retrieved 11 February 2015 from http://skift.com/2015/01/02/airasias-ceo-is-becoming-the-model-for-airline-leaders-during-a-crisis/.

Yang, S. and Lim, J.S. (2009) The effects of blog-mediated public relations (BMPR) on relational trust, *Journal of Public Relations Research*, 21(3), 341–59.

Yun, S.-H. (2006) Toward public relations theory-based study of public diplomacy: testing the applicability of the excellence study, *Journal of Public Relations Research*, 18(4), 287–312.

Chapter 13
Sponsorship

Sponsorship has traditionally been seen as a means of supporting primary media activities and raising a brand's visibility. More recently, however, sponsorship has become a powerful marketing communications tool in its own right and sponsors are taking advantage of opportunities to leverage their partnerships for more tangible returns on their investment.

Sponsorship is being used in a more strategic manner with sponsor partners working together to develop new brands and new broadcast opportunities. In addition, sponsors are taking advantage of benefits such as stadium naming rights, team name titles and access to the sponsored organisation's database. Sponsorship has evolved into a powerful marketing communications tool and this is reflected in the steady increase in sponsorship spending globally.

Aims and learning objectives

The aims of this chapter are to introduce and examine sponsorship as an increasingly significant form of marketing communications.

The learning objectives are to enable readers to:

1. explain how sponsorship activities have developed and understand the main characteristics of these forms of communications;
2. consider reasons for the use of sponsorship and the types of objectives that might be set;
3. appraise how sponsorship might work;
4. examine some of the conceptual and theoretical aspects of sponsorship;
5. appreciate the variety and different forms of sponsorship activities;
6. understand the reasons why sponsorship has become an important part of the communications mix.

Emirates Lions

Since Emirates started in Dubai in 1985, the airline has been committed to sports sponsorship and has developed long-standing partnerships with events and teams all around the world. Today their portfolio includes some of the world's iconic sporting events and leading teams in football, cricket, sailing, horseracing, golf, tennis, motorsports and rugby. Emirates' association with these global sports has enabled the airline to connect with audiences around the world and support teams within nations that they fly to. As well as raising the awareness of the Emirates brand and helping to position Dubai as an international destination for sport, their sponsorship provides us with a way to connect with consumers across the globe.

In 2014 Emirates identified that although they had gained significant visibility in Europe and other parts of the world through their sponsorship of some of the biggest sporting events and teams, there was a need to increase the visibility of the brand in Southern Africa. This led to a search for a sporting partner in the region. Rugby seemed like an obvious choice given their previous association with the sport.

Emirates boast a strong rugby heritage with their extensive portfolio of elite rugby sponsorships. They have been the Title Sponsor of the Emirates Airline Dubai Rugby Sevens for over 20 years, helping to establish this vibrant tournament as one of the best events on the HSBC Sevens World Series circuit. They also sponsor the Emirates Airline Glasgow Sevens, the penultimate event of the annual series calendar. Emirates first sponsored the Rugby World Cup (RWC) in 2007 in France as a Tournament Sponsor, and then became a Worldwide Partner for RWC 2011 in New Zealand. They then became the first Worldwide Partner to sign an agreement for both the Rugby World Cup that was held in England in 2015 and the tournament to be held in Japan in 2019.

Emirates have partnerships with USA Rugby through sponsorship of the US Eagles mens' and womens' XVs and Sevens rugby teams. Emirates can also be found at the centre of the action at every international rugby match through their sponsorship of the International Rugby Board's (IRB) elite panel of referees – who always take to the field in their 'Fly Emirates' officials' kit.

Emirates' search for a rugby partner in Africa concluded in December 2014 when the airline signed a five-year sponsorship agreement with one of South

| Exhibit 13.1 | **Emirates signs five-year sponsorship agreement** |

Source: Getty Images/Duif du Toit/Gallo Images.

Africa's most popular and successful Super Rugby teams, the 'Lions'. From the start of the 2015 season, the 'Lions' has been known as 'Emirates Lions' and the iconic 'Fly Emirates' logo has been on players' match shirts and training jerseys.

The sponsorship agreement has also allowed Emirates to re-name Ellis Park, the scene of South Africa's famous victory in the 1995 RWC Final, as 'Emirates Airline Park'. Emirates agreed in-stadia hospitality arrangements, allowing them to provide important corporate hospitality to travel agents, cargo agents, corporate accounts and other key partners in the country and wider Southern African region.

The sponsorship has resulted in raising the visibility of the Emirates brand, not only in South Africa, where they operate scheduled services from Dubai to Cape Town, Durban and Johannesburg, but also in other key southern hemisphere markets, New Zealand and Australia, where the Super Rugby competition is played, as well as other countries that televise the matches. Emirates' sponsorship strategy is to create long-term partnerships that will not only be mutually beneficial to the airline and the sponsored organisation, but also provide a legacy for the future of the sport. Their agreement with the 'Lions' included a mutual commitment to develop grassroots rugby in both South Africa and the United Arab Emirates (UAE). Emirates saw this as a real long-term benefit of the partnership, reflecting their passion to develop sport globally.

Sources: 'Emirates becomes Lions New Title Sponsor', Long (2014), Nel (2014)

Questions relating to this case study can be found at the end of the chapter.

Exhibit 13.2	**The iconic 'Fly Emirates' logo appears on players' match shirts**
	Source: Getty Images/Duif du Toit/Gallo Images.

Introduction

Sponsorship has become an increasingly popular element of the communications mix. The sponsorship activities of global organisations like Emirates outlined in the preceding case demonstrate not only the importance to brands of being associated with a major sporting team, but also how important sponsorship is in developing international sport. In other words, sponsorship can be mutually rewarding.

Global sponsorship spending has seen a steady increase in expenditure over the last 15 years (Meenaghan et al., 2013) and current forecasts from the International Events

Table 13.1 Annual global sponsorship spend

Year	US$ billion
2011	48.6
2012	51.1
2013	53.1
2014	55.3
2015	57.5 (projected)

Source: IEG Sponsorship Spending Report (IEG, 2015).

Group (IEG) suggest that this will trend will continue with a projected US$57.5 billion to be spent on sponsorship rights globally in 2015 (IEG) (see Table 13.1).

This increase is not surprising considering the high levels of visibility that sponsorship offers and the increased opportunities for activation, especially through social media channels. According to IEG, sponsorship now accounts for an average of 23 per cent of an organisation's overall marketing budget (IEG, 2015). The report published by IEG looked at the benefits and services sponsors are looking for from their sponsorship and found that in addition to the traditional gains such as on-site signage, broadcast advertising opportunities, proprietary titles and rights to property marks and logos, sponsors are now seeking connections to personalities and talent, access to sponsored organisations' databases and mailing lists, and rights to promote co-branded products and services (IEG, 2015). These extended benefits provide new opportunities for activation for sponsors and in part explain the increase in sponsorship spending.

Sponsorship has traditionally been seen as a mix of advertising, with its capacity for high visibility, high reach and message control, and public relations with its potential for high levels of credibility and message diffusion, directed through or with a third party. So, in this sense, sponsorship lacks the harshness of advertising and the total lack of control that characterises much of the work of public relations.

While many organisations are very active in sponsoring local cultural and sporting events and teams to demonstrate their commitment to the local community, for most global companies sponsorship is now a strategic business activity that is evaluated for its effectiveness against business and brand objectives, using key performance indicators (KPIs). This reflects the increased value that is seen to be leveraged from sponsorship and the range of opportunities that partnerships with sponsored organisations can offer. Sponsorship can provide the following benefits for the sponsors:

1. To raise visibility of the organisation amongst particular audiences that each event or team attracts in order to convey simple awareness-based brand messages.

2. To suggest to the target audiences that there is an association between the sponsor and the sponsored organisation and that, by implication, this association may be of interest and/or value.

3. To allow members of the target audiences to perceive the sponsor indirectly through a third party and so mitigate any negative effects associated with traditional mass media and direct persuasion.

4. To provide sponsors with the opportunity to blend a variety of tools in the communications mix and use resources more efficiently and, arguably, more effectively.

5. To provide exclusivity to event or team in a category, hence acting as a barrier to entry to competitors.

6. To allow sponsor access to the sponsored organisation's talent and personalities, for marketing purposes.

7. To provide access to tickets and hospitality at events for sponsors to entertain clients and prospects.

8. To provide opportunities to both sponsor and sponsored organisation to develop co-branded products or services.

9. To allow an organisation to access the sponsored organisation's database.

From this it is possible to define sponsorship as a commercial activity in which one party permits another an opportunity to exploit an association with a target audience in return for funds, services or resources. It also highlights the mutual benefits that can be gained from partnerships.

It is necessary to clarify the distinction between sponsorship and charitable donations. The latter are intended to change attitudes and project a caring identity, with the main returns from the exercise being directed to society or the beneficiaries. The beneficiaries have almost total control over the way in which funds are used. When funds are channelled through sponsorship the recipient has to attend to the needs of the sponsor by allowing it access to the commercial associations that are to be exploited, partly because they have a legal arrangement, but also to ensure that the exchange becomes relational and longer-term; in other words, there is repeat purchase (investment) activity. The other major difference is that the benefits of the exchange are intended to accrue to the participants, not society at large. Although some sponsorships such as the Emirates Lions partnership shown in the case demonstrate how sponsors and sponsored organisations are working together to develop sports globally.

Normally sponsorship involves two parties, the sponsor and the sponsored organisation. The degree of fit between these two parties partly determines the relative effectiveness of the relationship (Poon and Prendergast, 2006). The degree of fit, or product relevance, as proposed by McDonald (1991) and cited by Poon and Prendergast, can be considered in terms of two main dimensions. Function-based similarity occurs when the product is used in the event being sponsored. For example, function-based similarity occurs when a piano manufacturer such as Bösendorfer sponsors a Viennese piano recital. The second dimension concerns image-based similarities, which reflects the image of the sponsor in the event. Here Airbus's sponsorship of a major technical or even artistic exhibition serves to bestow prestige on all parties. Poon et al. (2010) identify two levels (high and low) of functional and image-based congruence, before offering a four-quadrant classification (see Figure 13.1).

To illustrate how this works, these authors give as an example an airline's sponsorship of environmental activities. This, they say, is low in both functional and image congruence and there is no clear link to the airline's function or image other than to rectify the situation. The airline has a limited travel scheme, called 'Miles for Kids in Need'. This gives assistance to children who are seriously ill and in need of emergency medical treatment. This equates to high functional congruence but low image congruence (F-MATCH). Low functional congruence with high image congruence (I-MATCH) occurs with the airline's sponsorship of a variety of cultural events. The final quadrant (MATCH) occurs through the airline's travel sponsorship of a symphony orchestra, as this generates both high functional and image congruence.

Coppetti et al. (2009) emphasise the value of congruence but also demonstrate that even when there is a lack of fit, the effectiveness of the sponsorship can be enhanced by

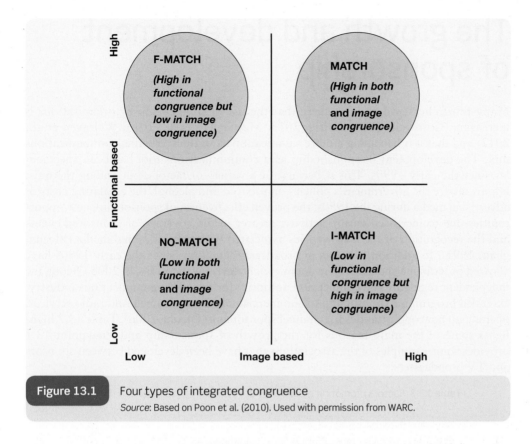

Figure 13.1   Four types of integrated congruence
Source: Based on Poon et al. (2010). Used with permission from WARC.

involving the audience in what they refer to as 'attractive sponsor activities'. This suggests that by building in experiences for the audience and encouraging its participation, and by using advertising before and after the sponsorship event, such integration can serve to increase the value of the communications programme.

Scholars' paper 13.1	Matching sponsorship opportunities

Poon, D.T.Y., Prendergast, G. and West, D. (2010) Match game: linking sponsorship congruence with communication outcomes, *Journal of Advertising Research*, 4(80), 214–26.

Building on the 2006 paper by Poon and Prendergast, these authors seek to develop the debate about the importance of congruence between a sponsor and the event being sponsored. Their research into the subject found no evidence of interaction effects between functional and image congruence. They determined that sponsorships involving low functional and low image congruence did as little to create favourable communications outcomes as if there were no sponsorship. This is an important paper for those requiring an in-depth understanding of sponsorship.

See also: Han, S., Choi, J., Kim, H., Davis, J. A. and Lee, K. Y. (2013) The effectiveness of image congruence and the moderating effects of sponsor motive and cheering event fit in sponsorship, *International Journal of Advertising*, 32(2), 301–17.

The growth and development of sponsorship

Many researchers and authors agree that the use of sponsorship by organisations is increasing (Cornwell, 2008; Letizia, 2013; Meenaghan et al., 2013; Walraven et al., 2012) and that it is becoming a more significant part of the marketing communications mix. The development of sponsorship as a communications tool has been spectacular since the early 1990s. This is because of a variety of factors, but among the most important are the government's policies on tobacco and alcohol, the escalating costs of advertising media during the 1990s, the proven effectiveness of sponsorship, new opportunities due to increased leisure activity, greater media coverage of sponsored events and the recognition of the inefficiencies associated with the traditional media (Meenaghan, 1991). In addition, changes in broadcast regulations since the early 1990s have allowed programme sponsorship in commercial television and radio. In 2006 Ofcom, the independent regulator and competition authority for the UK communications industry, extended programme sponsorship to commercial television channels and radio services, opening up new opportunities for channel sponsorship (Ofcom, 2006). Table 13.2 highlights some of the main reasons for the growth of sponsorship and Viewpoint 13.1 provides some examples of the associations that have been developed between sponsors and TV broadcasters.

Table 13.2 Factors promoting growth and development of sponsorship

Increased media coverage of events

Relaxation of government and industry regulations

Increased incidence of sponsorship event supply (and demand)

Relationship orientation and association between sponsorship participants

Positive attitude change towards sponsorship by senior management

Awareness and drive towards integrated marketing communications

Increasing rate of other media costs

Need to develop softer brand associations and to reach niche audiences

Increased opportunities to activate social media engagement

Viewpoint 13.1   Broadcast sponsorship

Broadcast sponsorships are an increasingly popular form of sponsorship. Although a relatively new form of sponsorship in the UK, broadcast sponsorship has traditionally been used to build an affinity between the brand and the audience. More recently, however, broadcast sponsors are leveraging partnerships with broadcasters to gain product placement, develop co-branded products and to activate social media engagement. The following examples are just some of the associations that have been developed between sponsors and TV broadcasters:

Nikon: Hollyoaks

Sony: Disney Channel

TRESemmé: Britain & Ireland's Next Top Model

Iceland: I'm A Celebrity . . . Get Me Out Of Here!

TalkTalk: X Factor

Morrisons: Britain's Got Talent

Samsung: Channel 4, More 4 and UKTV's Good Food shows

Question:	If affinity is a key aspect of broadcast sponsorship, why do you think the sponsors chose to partner with the programmes or channels they did?
Task:	Find a brand that has a broadcast sponsorship and evaluate the benefits to the organisation for the sponsorship.

Sponsorship, a part of public relations, should be used as an element of an integrated approach to an organisation's communications. In other words, sponsorship needs to be harnessed strategically. For example, many companies and brands originating in the Middle East, South-East Asia and the Pacific regions have used sponsorship as a means of overseas market entry in order to develop name or brand awareness. Panasonic, JVC and Daihatsu have used this approach, as indeed many companies are now doing in an attempt to become established in the BRIC countries.

Sponsorship objectives

Any organisation developing a sponsorship strategy should always include well-defined objectives and where the sponsorship allows the sponsor to connect with a range of stakeholder groups, according to Meenaghan et al. (2013), specific objectives need to be set for each group. Table 13.3 shows the importance of different objectives for sponsors.

There are both primary and secondary objectives associated with using sponsorship. The primary reasons are to build awareness, to develop relationships, possibly through loyalty, to improve perception (image) held of a brand or organisation. Secondary reasons are more contentious, but generally they can be seen to be to attract new users, to support dealers and other intermediaries, and to act as a form of staff motivation and morale building.

Sponsorship is normally regarded as a communications tool used to reach external stakeholders. However, if chosen appropriately, sponsorship can also be used effectively to reach internal audiences (Khan and Stanton, 2010).

According to Harverson (1998), one of the main reasons IT companies sponsor sports events is that this form of involvement provides opportunities to 'showcase' their products and technologies, in context. Through application in an appropriate working environment, the efficacy of a sponsor's products can be demonstrated. The relationship between sports organisers and IT companies becomes reciprocal as the organisers of sports events need technology in order for the events to run. Corporate hospitality opportunities are often taken in addition to the brand exposure that the media coverage provides. EDS claims that it uses sponsorship to reach two main audiences, customers (and potential customers) and potential future employees.

A further important characteristic concerns the impact of repeat attendance on brand image. Work by Lacey et al. (2007) found that a car manufacturer's image improved

Table 13.3 Importance of objectives when evaluating sponsorship properties

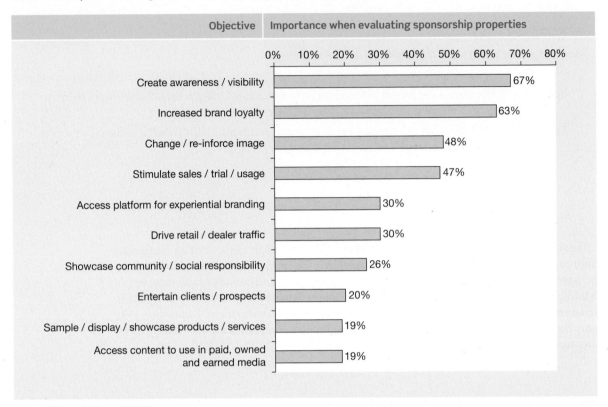

Source: IEG Special Report (2015).

modestly by sponsoring a sporting event. However, through repeat attendance, positive opinion scores towards the sponsor improved. The obvious implication for marketing is that it is important to attract attendees back to sporting events.

Following on from this is the issue of whether sponsorship is being used to support a product or the organisation. Corporate sponsorships, according to Thwaites (1994), are intended to focus on developing community involvement, public awareness, image, goodwill and staff relations. Product or brand-based sponsorship activity is aimed at developing media coverage, sales leads, sales/market share, target market awareness and guest hospitality. What is important is that sponsorship is not a tool that can be effective in a standalone capacity. The full potential of this tool is only realised when it is integrated with some (or all) of the other tools of the communications mix. As Tripodi (2001) comments, the implementation of integrated marketing communications is further encouraged and supported when sponsorship is an integral part of the mix in order to maximise the full impact of this communications tool.

How sponsorship might work

Interpretations of how sponsorship might work are varied, and research limited. However, assuming a cognitive orientation, sponsorship works through associations that consumers make with a brand. These associations will be an accumulation of previous advertising and other communications activities, and the event being supported. In addition, people make a judgement based on the fit between the event and sponsorship such that the greater the degree of compatibility, the more readily acceptable the sponsorship will be. Poon and Prendergast (2006) argue that sponsorship outcomes can best be understood in terms of the attitude construct and cite product quality, attitude to the brand and purchase intention as representative of the cognition, affection and conation components.

If a behaviourist orientation is used to explain how sponsorship works, then sponsorship should be perceived as reinforcement of previous brand experiences. An event generates rewards by reminding individuals of pleasurable brand experiences. However, this assumes that individuals have previous brand experience, and fails to explain adequately how sponsorship works when launching new products.

For many organisations sponsorship plays a supporting or secondary role in the communications mix. This is largely because the communications impact of sponsorship is limited, as sponsorship only reinforces previously held corporate (or product) images (positive or negative) rather than changing them (Javalgi et al., 1994). It is also suggested that the only significant relationship between sponsorship and corporate image occurs where there has been direct experience of the brand. This in turn raises questions about whether sponsorship should be used to influence the image of the product category and its main brands in order to be of any worthwhile effect (Pope and Voges, 1999).

As Dolphin (2003) suggests, the range of activities, events, goals and the variety of ways in which it is used by organisations suggests that it is not entirely clear how sponsorship might best be used to help an organisation achieve its business goals. It is used to shape and assist corporate image, develop name association and awareness, drive product sales, build brands, help with recruitment, defend against hostile competitors and as a means of developing and providing opportunities for corporate hospitality. However, the primary goal for its use will generally reflect the context within which it is used. In situations where transactional exchanges are predominant within the target audience, broad-based sponsorship activities are likely to be preferred. In contexts where the target audience is relatively small or geographically discrete and where relational exchanges are preferred or sought, then relationship development sponsorship activities are more likely to be successful.

Scholars' paper 13.2   What's it all about?

Meenaghan, T. (1991) The role of sponsorship in the marketing communications mix, *International Journal of Advertising*, 10(1), 35–47.

This is a classic paper written by one of the early leading researchers and authors about sponsorship. This paper sets out some of the initial perspectives on sponsorship and is recommended.

See also: Nickell, D., Cornwell, T.B. and Johnston, W.J. (2011) Sponsorship-linked marketing: a set of research propositions, *Journal of Business & Industrial Marketing*, 26(8), 577–89.

Theoretical aspects of sponsorship

The limited amount of theoretical research into sponsorship suggests that the role of sponsorship within the marketing communications mix has not yet been fully understood. Problems associated with goals, tools and measurement methods and approaches have hindered both academics and practitioners. However, two developments have helped resolve some of these dilemmas. First, the development of relationship marketing and an acknowledgement that there are different audiences, each with different relationship needs, has helped understanding about which types of sponsorship should be used with which type of audience. Second, our understanding of the nature and role of integrated marketing communications within relationship marketing has helped focus thinking about the way in which sponsorship might contribute to the overall communications process.

Relationship marketing is concerned with the concept of mutual value rather than the mere provision of goods and services (Gummesson, 1996) and is therefore compatible in many ways with the characteristics and range of benefits, both expected and realised, associated with sponsorship (Farrelly et al., 2003). Sponsorship represents a form of collaborative communications, in the sense that two (or more) parties work together in order that one is enabled to reach the other's audience. Issues regarding the relationship between the parties involved will impact on the success of a sponsorship arrangement and any successive arrangements. As Farrelly et al. quite rightly point out, further work concerning the key drivers of sponsorship and relationship marketing is required as sponsorship matures as an increasingly potent form of marketing communications.

Olkkonen (2001) adopted a similar approach as he considered sponsorship within interactional relationships and ultimately a network approach. The network approach considers the range of relationships that impact on organisations within markets and, therefore, considers non-buyers and other organisations – indeed, all who are indirectly related to the exchange process. This approach moves beyond the simple dyadic process adopted by the interaction interpretation. Some scholars have advanced a broad conceptual model within which to consider inter-organisational networks (Hakansson and Snehota, 1995, cited by Olkkonen). These are actors, activities and resources and are set out in Table 13.4.

A relationship consists of activity links based on organisations working together. Some of the activities will use particular resources in different configurations and differing levels of intensity. These activities will impact on other organisations and affect the way they use resources.

Table 13.4 Basic variables underpinning inter-organisational networks

Network variable	Explanation
Actors	These are organisations and individuals who are interconnected; they control the other two variables.
Activities	Activities are created through the use of resources, and complex activity chains arise with different organisations (actors) contributing in different ways.
Resources	There are many different types of resource that can be combined in different ways to create new resources. The relationships that organisations develop create resource ties and these ties become shaped and adapted as the relationship develops.

Source: Based on Olkkonen (2001).

In addition, organisations try to develop their attractiveness to other organisations in order to access other resources and networks. This is referred to as network identity and is a base for determining an organisation's value as a network partner. Sponsorship, therefore, can be seen as a function of an organisation's value to others in a network. The sponsored and the sponsor are key actors in sponsorship networks but agencies, event organisers, media networks and consultancies are also players, each of whom will be connected (networked) with the sponsor and sponsored.

Sponsorship has, traditionally, lacked a strong theoretical base, relying on managerial cause-and-effect explanations and loose marketing communications mix interpretations. The network approach may not be the main answer, but it does advance our thought, knowledge and research opportunities with respect to this subject.

One concept that has been established in the literature concerns emotional intensity. This concerns the audience's attention, and associated cognitive orientation, towards the stimulus that is provoking the emotion (Bal et al., 2007). So, if the event becomes dramatic and highly engaging, it is probable that attention will be diverted from the sponsors and any information they might provide (e.g. ads). What this means is that a strongly emotional event (sport, exhibition, programme, film) is likely to reduce the awareness scores associated with the sponsor.

Research by Farrelly et al. (2006), undertaken to better understand how value is perceived by parties to sponsorship agreements, has identified three key marketing competences necessary for the maintenance of successful sponsorship relationships. These are: reciprocal commitment, building capabilities and collaborative capabilities. These are set out in Table 13.5.

Table 13.5 Sponsorship relationship capabilities

Competence	Explanation
Reciprocal commitment	This is demonstrated by the reaction that one party makes to any additional investment in the sponsorship by the other. Sponsors expect the sponsee to reciprocate the investments (e.g. advertising) that the sponsor makes in the relationship. The greater the reciprocity, the greater the commitment.
Building capabilities	Sponsorship is increasingly perceived to be of value in terms of strategic branding rather than mere exposure. To what extent, therefore, do the parties link their sponsorship to broader marketing objectives?
Collaborative capabilities	This concerns the extent to which the sponsee is proactive within the relationship and sets out the ways in which the relationship and the sponsor's brand will be developed in the future. In effect, this is about collaboration.

Source: Farrelly et al. (2006).

Types of sponsorship

It is possible to identify particular areas within which sponsorship has been used. These areas are sports, broadcast, the arts and others that encompass activities such as wildlife/conservation and education. Of all of these, sport has attracted most attention and sponsorship money.

Sports sponsorship

Sports activities have been very attractive to sponsors, partly because of the high media coverage they attract. Sport is the leading type of sponsorship, mainly for the following reasons:

● Sport has the propensity to attract large audiences, not only at each event but, more importantly, through the media that attach themselves to these activities.

- Sport provides a simplistic measure of segmentation, so that as audiences fragment generally, sport provides an opportunity to identify and reach often large numbers of people who share particular characteristics.
- Visibility opportunities for the sponsor are high in a number of sporting events because of the duration of each event (e.g. the Olympics or the FIFA World Cup).

In football, Barclaycard's sponsorship of the Premier League and Coca-Cola's sponsorship of the Championship have been motivated partly by the attraction of large and specific target audiences with whom a degree of fit is considered to exist. The constant media attention enables the sponsors' names to be disseminated to distant audiences, many of them overseas. Marshall and Cook (1992) found that event sponsorship (e.g. the Olympics or the Ideal Home Exhibition) is the most popular form of sponsorship activity undertaken by organisations. This was followed by team, league and individual support.

Vodafone sponsored Manchester United in order to boost global awareness. Next, the company bought Mannesman and found it then sponsored Benfica, Porto, Olympiakos and teams in La Liga in Spain and the Bundesliga in Germany. Rationalisation was necessary and, still wanting to maintain an association with football, it then became a Champions League sponsor (Murphy, 2007). AIG became United's next shirt sponsor in an attempt to fuel AIG's expansion out of North America and reach new markets, principally Asia, where a high percentage of the target market are football (and Manchester United) fans. AIG terminated its involvement when the global financial crisis struck in 2008.

Golf has attracted a great deal of sponsorship money, mainly because it has a global upmarket appeal and generates good television and press coverage. Golf clubs are also well suited for corporate entertainment and offer the chance of playing as well as watching. The World Golf Championships are seen as golf's most prestigious global competition, a series of events sanctioned by all six of the six major golf tours (the PGA TOUR, European Tour, Japan Golf Tour, PGA Tour of Australasia, Southern Africa Tour and the Asian Tour). Collectively these form the International Federation of PGA Tours, which is supported financially by a few umbrella sponsors. At the time of writing, they

Exhibit 13.3   **Qatar Airways supports a range of international sports events and teams, such as FC Barcelona, and sees sponsorship as a valuable marketing tool to increase its brand visibility.**

Source: Alamy Images/Aflo Co.Ltd.

were Bridgestone and Cadillac and HSBC. The official sponsors of these events, a second level of sponsorship, are Rolex (WGC, 2015).

Toyota used to support the World Matchplay Championship at Wentworth each year because the tournament fitted into a much wider promotion programme. Toyota dealers sponsored competitions at their local courses, with qualifiers going through to a final at Wentworth. The winner of that played in the pro-am before the World Matchplay. Toyota incorporated the tournament into a range of incentive and promotional programmes and flew in top distributors and fleet customers from around the world. In addition, the environment was used to build customer relationships. This championship is now supported by HSBC.

Broadcast sponsorship

Broadcast sponsorship has seen significant growth in the UK since the late 1990s when broadcast regulations were relaxed. Before this time, the visibility that each sponsor was allowed was strictly controlled, being restricted to certain times: before, during the break and after each programme with the credits. This was changed so that, while sponsors are not allowed to influence the content or scheduling of a programme so as to affect the editorial independence and responsibility of the broadcaster, it is now permissible to allow the sponsor's product to be seen along with the sponsor's name in bumper credits and to allow greater flexibility in terms of the use of straplines. There is a requirement on the broadcaster to ensure that the sponsored credit is depicted in such a way that it cannot be mistaken as a spot advertisement.

Masthead programming, where the publisher of a magazine such as *Amateur Photographer* sponsors a programme in a related area, such as Photography for Beginners, is generally not permitted, although the regulations surrounding this type of activity are being relaxed. There are a number of reasons why broadcast sponsorship is appealing. First, it allows clients to avoid the clutter associated with spot advertising. In that sense it creates a space, or mini-world, in which the sponsor can create awareness and provide brand identity cues unhindered by other brands. Second, it represents a cost-effective medium when compared with spot advertising. Although the cost of broadcast sponsorship has increased as the value of this type of medium has appreciated, it does not command the high rates required for spot advertising. Third, the use of credits around a programme offers opportunities for the target audience to make associations between the sponsor and the programme. Rimmel London's sponsorship of Channel 4's Made in Chelsea provides a good example of how an association works well in broadcast sponsorship (see Exhibit 13.4).

For sponsorship to work well there needs to be a linkage between the product and the programme. Links that are spurious, illogical or inappropriate are very often rejected by viewers. For example, a branded soft drink might work well with a youth-oriented programme, but a financial services brand supporting a sports programme or film series would not have a strong or logical linkage. Viewpoint 13.1 highlights some of the broadcast partnerships that have taken place in recent years. Di Falco (2012) suggests that organisations that get the most out of their sponsorship are those that integrate their brands with the editorial environment of the programme. He cites Schwarzkopf LIVE Colour XXL's sponsorship of *Big Brother* on Channel 5 as a good example of this. As well as being the broadcast sponsor for the show, XXL was placed in the bathroom in the Big Brother House allowing housemates the opportunity to use the product. Housemates tried the products and walked around the Big Brother House with their newly dyed hair, which made great entertainment.

The line between product placement, brand entertainment and programme sponsorship has become increasingly blurred. However, programme sponsorship is not a replacement for advertising. The argument that sponsorship is not a part of advertising is clearly demonstrated by the point that many sponsors continue with their spot advertising when running major sponsorships.

Exhibit 13.4	**Rimmel London sponsors *Made In Chelsea***
	Series 9 of *Made in Chelsea* was sponsored by Rimmel London.
	Source: Channel Four Television Corporation 2016.

Arts sponsorship

Arts sponsorship, according to Thorncroft (1996), began as a philanthropic exercise, with business giving something back to the community. It was a means of developing an organisation's image and was used extensively by tobacco companies as they attempted to reach their customer base. It then began to be appreciated for its corporate hospitality opportunities: a cheaper, more civilised alternative to sports sponsorship, and one that appealed more to women.

Organisations such as Coutts, the exclusive London bank, can trace their sponsorship of the arts back to 1744 (Chapman, 2012). The bank currently sponsors exhibitions at The National Portrait Gallery, a number of productions at the Royal Opera House and is principal sponsor of the Royal Court (Coutts, 2015).

Many organisations sponsor the arts as a means of enhancing their corporate status and of clarifying their identity. Another important reason organisations use sponsorship is to establish and maintain favourable contacts with key business people, often at board level, together with other significant public figures. Through related corporate hospitality, companies can reach substantial numbers of their targeted key people.

MasterCard has a range of arts sponsorships, including its partnership with the Society of London Theatre and the Olivier awards (MasterCard, 2015). As well as being the headline sponsor of the awards, MasterCard supports the MasterCard Best New Musical award. This extends its sponsorship involvement of London's West End LIVE, which is an annual event showcasing London's top West End shows and performances from the Royal Opera House Chorus and the English National Opera (WestendLive, 2015). MasterCard's support for the arts links to the brand's Price-less London initiative, bringing unique theatre and entertainment experiences to customers.

The sponsorship of the arts has moved from being a means of supporting the community to a sophisticated means of targeting and positioning brands. Sponsorship, once part of corporate public relations, is now a significant aspect of marketing public relations. Viewpoint 13.2 sets out how luxury brand Louis Vuitton has sponsored the arts. The brand has become regarded as inventors of 'the art of travel', and has worked with painters, photographers, designers and other craftsworkers to maintain strong links with the art world.

Viewpoint 13.2   Louis Vuitton partners with Japanese artist

Louis Vuitton has a long association with the arts and since the company was founded in 1854 it has collaborated with numerous artists around the world. For example, in the 1980s the brand collaborated with painters such as César, Sol LeWitt and Olivier Debré and since then Artistic Director Marc Jacobs has developed partnerships with some of the world's most renowned contemporary artists.

In 2012 Louis Vuitton teamed up with famous Japanese artist Yayoi Kusama in one of the biggest exchanges between the art and fashion world in recent times. Sponsoring a travelling exhibition of the artist's work that visited Museo Nacional Centro de Arte Reina Sofia, Madrid; Centre Pompidou, Paris; London's Tate Modern and New York's Whitney Museum of American Art, the collaboration between Louis Vuitton and Yayoi Kusama was one of the largest the art world has ever seen.

Kusama is famous for her use of dense patterns of nets and polka dots which have become her signature. To coincide with her exhibitions, she collaborated with Louis Vuitton to develop a collection inspired by her art.

In addition to sponsoring exhibitions of the artist's work in Madrid, Paris, London and New York, Louis Vuitton set up a concept boutique in London's Selfridges store. The in-store display together with a take-over of 24 of the Oxford Street store's windows exhibited a capsule collection designed by Louis Vuitton in collaboration with Yayoi Kusama. The range included handbags, travel bags, shoes, accessories and ready-to-wear clothing, all featuring Kusama's signature designs.

In support of Kusama's London exhibition, Louis Vuitton sponsored a programme of activity for younger audiences at the Tate Modern, and to announce the release of the new collection decorated the exterior of the Paris flagship store with Kusama's signature dot pattern, which was widely photographed and shared on social media.

The Kusama exhibition is not the first collaboration Louis Vuitton has had with a Japanese artist. In 2008, Louis Vuitton sponsored an exhibition of Takashi Murakami's work in The Brooklyn Museum in New York. On this occasion the collaboration included a store within the museum to sell the collection of bags and products designed by Louis Vuitton and the artist.

Source: Tate Modern (2012); Whitney Museum of American Art (2012).

Question: To what extent do you think Louis Vuitton and Yayoi Kusama make compatible partners? Explain why.

Task: Find three other examples of fashion brands that sponsor the arts.

Exhibit 13.5	**Louis Vuitton's Kusama-inspired boutique**
	Source: Alamy Images/directphoto.bz.

To support its global brand HSBC run a 'Cultural Exchange programme'. This aims to improve 'understanding and interaction among cultures around the world through the exploration of culture in all its varied forms – including fine art, cuisine, music, language and literature' (HSBC, 2011). In 2008 the bank supported cultural events in China, in 2009 it backed various Indian cultural initiatives and in 2010 it supported 'Festival Brazil'. This event was focused on exhibitions and various artistic performances by Brazilian artists in London. HSBC also supports events in South America, the Middle East, South-East Asia and the USA. The bank has co-partnered with the *Financial Times* and the Economist Intelligence Unit to advise companies thinking of exporting and setting up in Brazil (Brownsell, 2010). HSBC believes sponsorship to be an investment for its business growth, and an opportunity to connect and build relationships with people in the local communities that it serves.

Scholars' paper 13.3	Sports sponsorships

Walraven, M., Koning, R.H. and van Bottenburg, M. (2012) The effects of sports sponsorship: a review and research agenda, *The Marketing Review*, 12(1), 17–38.

The paper provides a good overview of the literature on sponsorship effects and develops a framework to help explain sponsorship outcomes. In addition to providing a good review of current research, the article suggest areas for future research.

See also: Jensen, J.A. and Cobbs, J. (2014) Analyzing return-on-investment in sponsorship: modeling brand exposure, price and ROI in Formula One automotive competition, *Journal of Advertising Research*, 54(4), 435–47; Edwards, M.R. (2015) The Olympic effect: employee reactions to their employer's sponsorship of a high-profile global sporting event, *Human Resource Management*, DOI: 10.1002/hrm.21702.

Other forms of sponsorship

The sponsorship of causes is growing with sponsors keen to support their local communities or causes that are of interest to them and their audiences. Such sponsorship offers organisations an opportunity to enter into dialogue with audiences around causes that are seen to be mutually important. In March 2012 a Climate Week was held, with many leading companies supporting the cause. Companies such as Aviva, RBS, EDF Energy and Kellogg's sought to demonstrate what actions they are taking with regard to climate change as well as assist other organisations to become involved.

Festivals, fairs and annual events are another type of sponsorship category. In particular, festivals have attracted sponsors who are keen to connect with Millennials. McCormack (2015) suggests that brands like Hunter, who set up a welly-exchange at Glastonbury in 2013, are amongst those who are getting the most out of their festival sponsorship. The brand offered festival-goers a new pair of its orange Hunter Headliner Boots in exchange for their old shoes and resulted in its giving away over 3,000 pairs of wellies. This fun give-away was amplified through social media as festival-goers took pictures of their new boots and shared these across social media platforms. McCormack (2015) also cites Mulberry's sponsorship at the Wilderness festival as an example of good practice and describes how the luxury handbag brand set up a craft workshop at the festival to showcase the craftwork behind their bags. The 'Mulberry loves craft' tent allowed festival-goers to meet the craftsworkers who make the Bayswater bag and interact with bag designers such as Cara Delevingne. They were also given the opportunity of customising and monogramming their own leather bracelets, which was shared across social media by festival-goers.

Exhibit 13.6	**Hunter boots exchange at Glastonbury Festival**
	Festival-goers at Glastonbury were offered a new pair of orange Hunter Headliner Boots in exchange for their old shoes.

Source: Rex Shutterstock/James North/Hunter Boots.

Some brands use sponsorship to own particular space. For example, Benjamin (2011) points out that Orange has owned cinema Wednesdays for some time and now Thursdays, through which it can reward customers. Sponsoring physical spaces and modes of transport has also been popular with sponsors in recent years. Recent examples include Coca-Cola's sponsorship of London landmark The London Eye (Bold, 2015), which saw Europe's tallest Ferris wheel lit up in red. In 2015 Santander spent £43.75 million on its sponsorship deal for Boris bikes, which have been re-named 'Santander cycles' (Ghosh, 2015). More ambitiously, Emirates sponsored the entire London Transport cable car across the River Thames. As well as the naming rights to the cable car itself the deal included the sponsorship of two new stations, Emirates Greenwich Peninsula and Emirates Royal Docks, which were added to the London tube map (Reynolds, 2011).

Sponsored content is a fast-growing area of sponsorship. Viewpoint 13.3 illustrates how MasterCard sponsored The Brits Vevo channel and provides a good example of how brands are using sponsored content to connect with audiences. As well as in music, brands have sponsored content in sports channels. Kia Motor's sponsorship of the Ashes content on TalkSport shows how brands are able to engage with sports fans (Nias, 2013). Kia's multi-platform sponsorship agreement covered all the content for the 2013 Ashes series between England and Australia cricket teams, including interviews, score updates, on-air editorial, as well as outside broadcasts from the Kia Oval. The deal included Kia branding running across the Talksport.co.uk site and on all cricket coverage in the site's sister publication, *Sport* magazine, for the duration of the Ashes series, as well as Kia-branded features and a competition on TalkSport's Drive Time show (Nias, 2013). The partnership between Kia and TalkSport is just one of many sports content sponsorships that have taken place over the last few years and shows how brands are using this form of sponsorship to engage audiences in conversations around specific sports and sporting events.

The majority of sponsorships, regardless of type, are not the sole promotional activity undertaken by the sponsors. They may be secondary and used to support above-the-line work or they may be used as the primary form of communications but supported by a range of off-screen activities, such as sales promotions and (in particular) competitions. For example, Sony Pictures developed a programme to encourage school pupils to be innovative and to develop their interest in science. It uses an unbranded animated film, *Cloudy with a Chance of Meatballs*, to provide a context for activities, quizzes and competitions (Thomas, 2009). More of a partnership than a straight sponsorship, the relationship furthers Sony's positioning as an innovator.

Viewpoint 13.3   MasterCard sponsors The Brits Awards content on Vevo

MasterCard have been the headline sponsor of The Brit Awards, which celebrates British and international music talent, for the last 17 years. In 2012, MasterCard extended their association with the event to sponsor The Brit Awards ceremony coverage on The Brits Vevo channel. Vevo, the online music video platform, was appointed as the first online video partner for the awards event and MasterCard sponsored the channel.

The Brits Vevo channel hosted nomination videos from the 2012 event, as well as live coverage of the awards ceremony and performances. The channel also ran additional content such as interviews filmed with artists backstage. MasterCard's sponsorship of the online platform allowed the brand to extend their association with the event and provided a further opportunity to engage with Brit fans during the ceremony.

The MasterCard/Brits Vevo Channel association is just one of many online sponsorships that have been developed in recent years and provides a good example of how brands are using online sponsorship to amplify their sponsorship message. The growth in online channels provides increased opportunities for brands to engage with audiences in different platforms and many brands are choosing sponsorship over banner ads as they are seen to be more effective in building relationships with consumers. Online

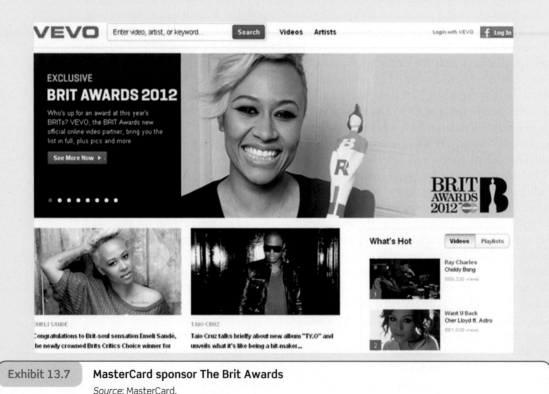

Exhibit 13.7   **MasterCard sponsor The Brit Awards**
Source: MasterCard.

sponsorship also provides increased opportunities to activate social media engagement and can play a central role in the marketing communications campaign.

For online sponsorships to work well it is important that the brand owner and the media owner work collaboratively to create content that will provide a better experience for the audiences. In cases where the brand owner has more knowledge or experience of the content, such as in the case of MasterCard, with their long relationship with The Brits, their input can be valuable in editorial decisions. With online channels likely to increase in the future, brands are increasingly seeking online channel partners that will allow them to activate sponsorships and engage with audiences in different platforms.

Source: McCabe (2012), MasterCard (2015).

> Question: Why do you think MasterCard sponsored The Brits Vevo channel?
>
> Task: Go to the Vevo website and see what other brands sponsor their channels. Find one channel that is not sponsored and suggest a brand that would make a suitable sponsor.

This section would not be complete without mention of the phenomenon called 'ambush marketing'. This occurs when an organisation deliberately seeks an association with a particular event but does so without paying advertising or sponsorship fees. Such hijacking is undertaken to get free publicity by communicating the brand, unofficially, in places where spectators, cameras or reporters are present, will see it, and pass on the message. The purpose therefore is to influence the audience to the extent that people believe the ambusher is legitimate. Several studies have explored the nature of ambush marketing activity, including Chadwick and Burton (2011) who identify 11 different types of ambush marketing. According to the authors, ambush marketing allows an organisation to capitalise on the visibility and goodwill of being associated with an event or property without any official connection.

At the 2010 World Cup in South Africa, 36 orange-clad women were ejected from the Netherlands versus Denmark game. They were accused of participation in an unofficial campaign to promote the Dutch brewery, Bavaria. Anheuser Busch's Budweiser was the official beer for the tournament. There had been a similar incident at the 2006 World Cup finals in Germany. On that occasion, the football governing body FIFA ordered that a number of Dutch men take off orange lederhosen which bore the name 'Bavaria' (Anon, 2010). Viewpoint 13.4 provides an example of how Mr Mozzarella 'ambushed' a UK by-election.

Viewpoint 13.4   Mr Mozzarella ambushes a by-election

In 2012, JUST-EAT, the online marketplace for home delivery, staged a creative ambush marketing campaign that saw Italian takeaway chef Mr Mozzarella, from an invented 'Don't Cook Party', stand for election at the Corby Parliamentary by-election. This was a high-profile by-election with all major political parties fighting hard to win the Parliamentary seat and therefore it was certain to receive significant media coverage. Such guaranteed media attention provided a perfect opportunity for JUST-EAT to ambush the event and gain high visibility for their brand both locally and nationally.

Although by-elections in Britain are well known for attracting eccentric independent candidates, JUST-EAT was the first brand to create a political party to stand for election. In doing so, the company was sure to attract increased media interest.

Mr Mozzarella's 'Don't Cook Party' launched an anti-cooking 'manifesto' claiming that too many people were cooking for themselves and wasting time. His single-issue campaign he argued was to free people from the tyranny of cooking every day. He also claimed his campaign supported British takeaway chefs who were angry that Britain's publics were cooking for themselves and taking trade from takeaway businesses.

The 'Don't Cook Party's' campaign included a number of media stunts including Mr Mozzarella taking a jet-pack ride 25 feet over Corby, dressed in chef's whites and holding an oversized ladle. The chef also took a tuk-tuk tour around the streets of the town with balloon artists, face painters and cheerleaders in tow to launch his campaign. Mr Mozzarella set up his own Twitter page to activate social media engagement in the campaign and share his campaign activities.

Although Mr Mozzarella only gained 73 votes from the Corby residents in the by-election, he raised the visibility of the brand significantly. As well as significant media coverage, he secured a photo opportunity with Nigel Farage (UKIP Leader) and a train-ride home with Labour leader Ed Milliband (former Labour Party Leader). Political commentators during the campaign mentioned Mr Mozzarella and more importantly the sales for JUST-EAT in the area during the period increased by 28 per cent (in comparison to the 3 per cent growth seen in towns with historically comparative order profiles).

The JUST-EAT campaign provides a good example of how when planned and executed with creativity an ambush campaign can be highly effective in gaining high visibility for a brand.

Source: JUST-EAT (2013); Parkinson (2013).

Question: How ethical is it for JUST-EAT to use this type of marketing?

Task: Search the Internet to find examples of ambush marketing at sporting events such as European Football Championships and the Olympic Games in 2012. Consider the ethical issues associated with this.

Exhibit 13.8   **Mr Mozzarella 'ambushed' a UK by-election**
Source: Getty Images/Andrew Yates/AFP.

The role of sponsorship in the communications mix

Whether sponsorship is a part of advertising, sales promotion or public relations has long been a source of debate. It is perhaps more natural and comfortable to align sponsorship with advertising. Since awareness is regarded as the principal objective of using sponsorship, advertising is a more complementary and accommodating part of the mix. Sales promotion from the sponsor's position is harder to justify, although from the perspective of the sponsored the value-added characteristic is interesting. The more traditional home for sponsorship is public relations (Witcher et al., 1991). The sponsored, such as a football team, a racing car manufacturer or a theatre group, may be adjudged to perform the role of opinion former. Indirectly, therefore, messages are conveyed to the target audience with the support of significant participants who endorse and support the sponsor. This is akin to public relations activities.

Hastings (1984) contests that advertising messages can be manipulated and adapted to changing circumstances much more easily than those associated with sponsorship. He suggests that the audience characteristics of advertising and sponsorship are very different. For advertising there are viewers and non-viewers. For sponsorship there are three groups of people that can be identified. First, there are those who are directly involved with the sponsor or the event, the active participants. The second is a much larger group, consisting of those who attend sponsored events, and these are referred to as personal spectators. The third group is normally the largest, comprising all those who are involved with the event through various media channels; these are regarded as media followers.

Exploratory research undertaken by Hoek et al. (1997) suggests that sponsorship is better able to generate awareness and a wider set of product-related attributes than advertising when dealing with non-users of a product, rather than users. There appears to be no discernible difference between the impact that these two promotional tools have on users.

Scholars' paper 13.4   **Activating social media**

Meenaghan, T., McLoughlin, D. and McCormack, A. (2013) New challenges in sponsorship evaluation actors, new media, and the context of praxis, *Psychology & Marketing*, 30(5), 444–60.

This paper looks at the changes that are taking place in sponsorship and the challenges of increased use of social media to activate sponsorships. Although the authors recognise social media's ability to connect with sponsorship audiences, they also discuss the issues that arise when it comes to sponsorship evaluation.

See also: Cornwall, T.B. (2008) State of art and science in sponsorship-linked marketing, *Journal of Advertising*, 37(3), 41–55.

Hoek et al. claim that sponsorship and advertising can be considered to work in approximately the same way if the ATR (attention, trial, reinforcement) model developed by Ehrenberg (1974) is adopted (Chapter 11). Through the ATR model, purchase behaviour and beliefs are considered to be reinforced by advertising rather than new behaviour patterns being established. Advertising offers a means by which buyers can meaningfully defend their purchase patterns. Hoek et al. regard this approach as reasonably analogous to sponsorship. Sponsorship can create awareness and is more likely to confirm past behaviour than prompt new purchase behaviour. The implication, they conclude, is that, while awareness levels can be improved with sponsorship, other communications tools are required to impact upon product experimentation or purchase intentions. Indeed, Smoliannov and Aiyeku (2009) make the point that integrated TV and major event sponsorship appear to work by influencing markets through TV audiences.

It was suggested earlier in this chapter that one of the opportunities that sponsorship offers is the ability to suggest that there is an association between the sponsored and the sponsor which may be of value to the message recipient. This implies that there is an indirect form of influence through sponsorship. This is supported by Crimmins and Horn (1996), who argue that the persuasive impact of sponsorship is determined in terms of the strength of links that are generated between the brand and the event that is sponsored.

These authors claim that sponsorship can have a persuasive impact and that the degree of impact that a sponsorship might bring is as follows:

$$\begin{array}{c} Persuasive \\ impact \end{array} = \begin{array}{c} strength \\ of\ link \end{array} \times \begin{array}{c} duration \\ of\ the\ link \end{array} \times \left\{ \begin{array}{c} gratitude\ felt \\ due\ to\ the\ link \end{array} + \begin{array}{c} perceptual\ change \\ due\ to\ the\ link \end{array} \right\}$$

The *strength* of the link between the brand and the event is an outcome of the degree to which advertising is used to communicate the sponsorship itself. Sponsors that failed to invest in advertising during the Olympic Games have been shown to be far less successful in building a link with the event than those who chose to invest.

The *duration* of the link is also important. Research based on the Olympic Games shows that those sponsors who undertook integrated marketing communications long before the event itself were far more successful than those who had not. The use of mass-media advertising to communicate the involvement of the sponsor, the use of event graphics and logos on packaging, and the creative use of promotional tie-ins and in-store, event-related merchandising, facilitated the long-term linkage with the sponsorship and added value to the campaign.

Gratitude exists if consumers realise that there is a link between a brand and an event. For example, 60 per cent of US adults said that they 'try to buy a company's product if they support the Olympics'. They also stated that 'I feel I am contributing to the Olympics by buying the brands of Olympic sponsors.'

Perceptual change occurs as a result of consumers being able to understand the relationship (meaning) between a brand and an event. The sponsor needs to make this clear, as passive consumers may need the links laid out before them. The link between a swimwear brand and the Olympics may be obvious, but it is not always the case. Crimmins and Horn (1996) describe how Visa's 15 per cent perceived superiority advantage over MasterCard was stretched to 30 per cent during the 1992 Olympics and then settled at 20 per cent ahead one month after the Games had finished. The perceptual change was achieved through the messages that informed audiences that Visa was the one card that was accepted for the Olympic Games; American Express and MasterCard were not accepted.

This research, while based only upon a single event, indicates that sponsorship may bring advantages if care is taken to invest in communications long before and during the event to communicate the meaning between the brand and the event, which will leverage gratitude from a grateful audience. Similarly, Olson and Thjømøe (2009) found that combining television advertising increases the effectiveness of a sponsorship activity. Nickell et al. (2011) go further and argue that leveraging sponsorships – that is, using other marketing communications activities to realise the full potential of the investment – is absolutely necessary.

Activating sponsorship through other forms of communications is therefore seen to be a key to the success of any sponsorship. A recent study by IEG suggests that nine out

Table 13.6 Channels used by sponsors to leverage sponsorships

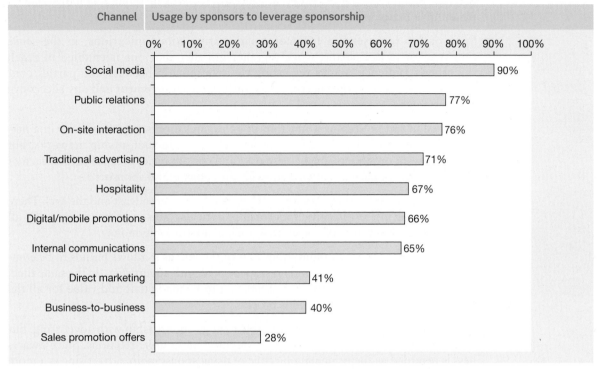

Channel	Usage by sponsors to leverage sponsorship
Social media	90%
Public relations	77%
On-site interaction	76%
Traditional advertising	71%
Hospitality	67%
Digital/mobile promotions	66%
Internal communications	65%
Direct marketing	41%
Business-to-business	40%
Sales promotion offers	28%

Source: IEG Special Report (IEG, 2015).

of ten sponsors include social media in their leveraging mix with other forms of communications such as public relations, on-site interaction and traditional advertising also being seen to be highly important (IEG, 2015) (see Table 13.6).

Key points

- Sponsorship permits one party an opportunity to exploit an association with a target audience of another organisation, in return for funds, services or resources.

- Sponsorship suggests to target audiences that there is an association between the sponsor and the sponsored organisation and that by implication this association may be of interest and/or value.

- Some organisations use sponsorship, particularly sports activities, as a means of reaching wider target audiences. Sponsorship can provide exposure to particular audiences that each event attracts in order to convey simple, awareness-based brand messages. In particular, sponsorship is an effective way to prepare markets for the arrival of new brands.

- Sponsorship works through associations that consumers make with a brand (which will be an accumulation of previous advertising and other promotional activities) and the event being supported. In addition, people make a judgement based upon the fit between the event and sponsorship in such a way that the greater the degree of compatibility, the more readily acceptable the sponsorship will be.

- An alternative view holds that a sponsorship can be perceived as a reinforcement of previous brand experiences. An event generates rewards by reminding individuals of pleasurable brand experiences.

- Sponsorship represents a form of collaborative communications, in the sense that two (or more) parties work together in order that one is enabled to reach the other's audience. Issues regarding the relationship between the parties concerned will impact on the success of a sponsorship arrangement and any successive arrangements.

- Sponsorship can be seen as a function of an organisation's value to others in a network. The sponsored and the sponsor are key actors in sponsorship networks, but agencies, event organisers, media networks and consultancies are also actors, each of whom will be connected (networked) with the sponsor and sponsored.

- Sponsorship is used in three key areas. These are sports, broadcast and the arts. There is also growing interest in cause sponsorship, festivals, fairs and annual events. Of all of these, sport has attracted most attention and sponsorship money.

- Sponsorship has become an important part of the mix as it allows brands to be communicated without the clutter and noise associated with advertising. At the same time, sponsorship enables associations and linkages to be made that add value for all the participants in the communications process.

- It is perhaps more natural and comfortable to align sponsorship with advertising, but it has also been associated with sales promotion and public relations. Since awareness is regarded as the principal objective of using sponsorship, advertising is a more complementary and accommodating part of the mix.

Review questions

Emirates Lions case questions

1. Why do you think Emirates sponsor so many international sporting events and teams?

2. List five reasons why you think Emirates chose to sponsor Emirates Lions.

3. Why do you think Emirates secured stadium naming rights within the sponsorship?

4. Explain how Emirates could evaluate the return on their investment in sponsorship.

5. How could Emirates use their sponsorship to activate social media?

General questions

1. To what extent is sponsorship more a leap of faith than a calculated marketing investment?

2. If the objective of using sponsorship is to build awareness (among other things), then there is little point in using advertising. Discuss this view.

3. Why is sport more heavily sponsored than the arts or television programmes?

4. Choose eight sporting events and name the main sponsors. Why do you think they have maintained their associations with the events?

5. Explain the role of sponsorship within the marketing communications mix.

References

Anon (2010) World Cup 2010: Women arrested over 'ambush marketing' freed on bail, *Guardian,* Wednesday 16 June, retrieved 7 November 2011 from www.guardian.co.uk/football/2010/jun/16/fifa-world-cup-ambush-marketing.

Bal, C., Quester, P. G. and Boucher, S. (2007) *Admap,* 486 (September), 51–2.

Benjamin, K. (2011) Sponsorship still a hot property, *Marketing,* 5 October, 25–7.

Bold, B. (2015) What do people think of Coca-Cola's sponsorship of The London Eye? *Brand Republic,* retrieved 15 March 2015 from www.brandrepublic.com/article/1330961/watch-people-think-coca-colas-sponsorship-london-eye.

Brownsell, A. (2010) HSBC launches Brazilian cultural sponsorship programme, *Marketing,* 16 June.

Chadwick, S. and Burton, N. (2011) The evolving sophistication of ambush marketing: a typology of strategies, *Thunderbird International Business Review,* 53(6), 709–719.

Chapman, M. (2012) The craft of arts sponsorships, *Brand Republic,* retrieved 17 February 2015 from www.brandrepublic.com/article/1134174/craft-arts-sponsorships.

Coppetti, C., Wentzel, D., Tomczak, T. and Henke, S. (2009) Improving incongruent sponsorships through articulation of the sponsorship and audience participation, *Journal of Marketing Communications,* 15(1), 17–34.

Cornwell, T.B. (2008) State of the art and science in sponsorship-linked marketing, *Journal of Advertising,* 37(3), 41–55.

Coutts (2015) The Arts, retrieved 17 February 2015 from www.coutts.com/about-us/sponsorship/coutts-and-the-arts/.

Crimmins, J. and Horn, M. (1996) Sponsorship: from management ego trip to marketing success, *Journal of Advertising Research,* July/August, 11–21.

Di Falco, A. (2012) Double standards – how should brands tackle media sponsorships? *Brand Republic,* 18 October, retrieved 17 February 2015 from www.brandrepublic.com/article/1155306/double-standards--brands-tackle-media-sponsorships.

Dolphin, R.R. (2003) Sponsorship: perspectives on its strategic role, *Corporate Communications: An International Journal,* 8(3), 173–86.

Edwards, M.R. (2015) The Olympic effect: employee reactions to their employer's sponsorship of a high-profile global sporting event, *Human Resource Management,* DOI: 10.1002/hrm.21702.

Ehrenberg, A.S.C. (1974) Repetitive advertising and the consumer, *Journal of Advertising Research,* 14 (April), 25–34.

Emirates Becomes Lions New Title Sponsor (2014) Emirates Group, 11 November, retrieved 1 November 2015 from http://www.theemiratesgroup.com/english/news-events/news-events.aspx

Farrelly, F., Quester, P. and Mavondo, F. (2003) Collaborative communication in sponsor relations, *Corporate Communications: An International Journal,* 8(2), 128–38.

Farrelly, F., Quester, P. and Burton, R. (2006) Changes in sponsorship value: competencies and capabilities of successful sponsorship relationships, *Industrial Marketing Management,* 35(8), November, 1016–26.

Ghosh, S. (2015) Boris bikes rebranded 'Santander Cycles' in £44m deal. *Brand Republic,* retrieved 15 March 2015 from www.brandrepublic.com/article/1336019/boris-bikes-rebranded-santander-cycles-44m-deal.

Gladdis, S. (2014) Leverage broadcast sponsorship, *Admap,* November, 36–7, retrieved 15 March 2015 from www.warc.com/Pages/Taxonomy/Results.aspx?SubjectRef=113&Filter=All.

Gummesson, E. (1996) Relationship marketing and imaginary organisations: a synthesis, *European Journal of Marketing,* 30(2), 31–45.

Hakansson, H. and Snehota, I. (1995) *Developing Relationships in Business Networks,* London: Routledge.

Han, S., Choi, J., Kim, H., Davis, J.A. and Lee, K.Y. (2013) The effectiveness of image congruence and the moderating effects of sponsor motive and cheering event fit in sponsorship, *International Journal of Advertising,* 32(2), 301–17.

Harverson, P. (1998) Why IT companies take the risk, *Financial Times,* 2 June, p. 12.

Hastings, G. (1984) Sponsorship works differently from advertising, *International Journal of Advertising,* 3, 171–6.

Hoek, J., Gendall, P., Jeffcoat, M. and Orsman, D. (1997) Sponsorship and advertising: a comparison of their effects, *Journal of Marketing Communications,* 3, 21–32.

HSBC (2011) Cultural sponsorship, retrieved 7 November 2011 from www.hsbc.com/1/2/about/sponsorship.

IEG (2015) Sponsorship spending report: where the dollars are going and trends for 2015, retrieved 30 March 2015 from www.sponsorship.com/IEG/files/4e/4e525456-b2b1-4049-bd51-03d9c35ac507.pdf.

Javalgi, R.G., Traylor, M.B., Gross, A.C. and Lampman, E. (1994) Awareness of sponsorship and corporate image: an empirical investigation, *Journal of Advertising*, 24 (June), 1–12.

Jensen, J.A. and Cobbs, J. (2014) Analyzing return-on-investment in sponsorship: modeling brand exposure, price and ROI in Formula One automotive competition, *Journal of Advertising Research*, 54(4), 435–47.

JUST-EAT (2013) How JUST EAT hijacked the Corby Parliamentary by-election – November 2012: press highlights, retrieved 10 March 2015 from www.just-eat.com/how-just-eat-hijacked-the-corby-parliamentary-by-election-november-2012-press-highlights/.

Khan, A. M. and Stanton, J. (2010) A model of sponsorship effects on the sponsor's employees, *Journal of Promotion Management*, 16, 1–2.

Lacey, R., Sneath, J.Z., Finney, R.Z. and Close, A.G. (2007) The impact of repeat attendance on event sponsorship effects, *Journal of Marketing Communications*, 13(4), 243–55.

Letizia, J. (2013) Sports sponsorship, *WARC*, retrieved 10 February 2015 from www.warc.com/Content/ContentViewer.aspx?MasterContentRef=0fd0b679-5d8d-4673-a225-b1f2843696fb&q=Letizia&CID=A99020&PUB=ARF-KNOWLEDGE.

Long, M. (2014) Ellis Park renamed as Emirates lands major Lions deal, *SportsPro*, 11 December, retrieved 1 November 2015 from http://www.sportspromedia.com/news/ellis_park_renamed_as_emirates_lands_major_lions_deal.

Marshall, D.W. and Cook, G. (1992) The corporate (sports) sponsor, *International Journal of Advertising*, 11, 307–24.

MasterCard (2015) The BRIT Awards, *MasterCard Website*, retrieved 18 January 2015 from www.mastercard.co.uk/brit-awards.html.

McCabe, M. (2012) MasterCard sponsors The Brits content on Vevo, *Brand Republic*, 13 January, retrieved 10 December 2014 from www.brandrepublic.com/article/1111999/mastercard-sponsors-brits-content-vevo.

McCormack, G. (2015) Unpredictable brands are the headline act for festival sponsorship, *Brand Republic*, 19 January, retrieved 15 March 2015 from www.brandrepublic.com/article/1329801/unpredictable-brands-headline-act-festival-sponsorship.

McDonald, C. (1991) Sponsorship and the image of the sponsor, *European Journal of Marketing*, 25(11), 31–8.

Meenaghan, T. (1991) The role of sponsorship in the marketing communications mix, *International Journal of Advertising*, 10, 35–47.

Meenaghan, T., McLoughlin, D. and McCormack, A. (2013) New challenges in sponsorship evaluation actors, new media, and the context of praxis, *Psychology & Marketing*, 30(5), 444–60.

Murphy, D. (2007) Lost in the crowd, *Marketing*, 29 August, 36–7.

Nel, B. (2014) Emirates set to sponsor Lions. *SuperSport*, 10 December, retrieved 1 November, 2015 from http://www.supersport.com/rugby/sa-rugby/news/141210/Emirates_set_to_sponsor_Lions.

Nias, S. (2013) Kia to sponsor Ashes content on TalkSport, *Brand Republic*, 19 June, retrieved 7 March 2015 from www.brandrepublic.com/article/1187021/kia-sponsor-ashes-content-talksport.

Nickell, D., Cornwell, T.B. and Johnston, W.J. (2011) Sponsorship-linked marketing: a set of research propositions, *Journal of Business & Industrial Marketing*, 26(8), 577–89.

Ofcom (2006) Ofcom consults on the use of sponsorship in commercial television, retrieved 3 April 2015 from http://media.ofcom.org.uk/news/2006/ofcom-consults-on-the-use-of-sponsorship-in-commercial-television/.

Olkkonen, R. (2001) Case study: the network approach to international sport sponsorship arrangement, *Journal of Business & Industrial Marketing*, 16(4), 309–29.

Olson, E.L. and Thjømøe, H.M. (2009) Sponsorship effect metric: assessing the financial value of sponsoring by comparisons to television advertising, *Journal of the Academy of Marketing Science*, 37, 504–15.

Parkinson, J. (2013) Mr Mozzarella's anti-cooking by-election campaign gets £72,000, *BBC News*, retrieved 17 March from www.bbc.co.uk/news/uk-politics-21521130.

Poon, D.T.Y. and Prendergast, G. (2006) A new framework for evaluating sponsorship opportunities, *International Journal of Advertising*, 25(4), 471–87.

Poon, D.T.Y., Prendergast, G. and West, D. (2010) Match game: linking sponsorship congruence with communication outcomes, *Journal of Advertising Research*, 4(80), 214–26.

Pope, N.K.L. and Voges, K.E. (1999) Sponsorship and image: a replication and extension, *Journal of Marketing Communications*, 5, 17–28.

Reynolds, J. (2011) Mayor Johnson to announce Emirates as cable car sponsor. *Brand Republic*, retrieved 15 March 2015 from www.brandrepublic.com/article/1097675/mayor-johnson-announce-emirates-cable-car-sponsor.

Smolianov, P. and Aiyeku, J.F. (2009) Corporate marketing objectives and evaluation measures of integrated television advertising and sports event sponsorships, *Journal of Promotion Management,* 15(1–2), 74–89.

Tate Modern (2012) Yayoi Kusama press release, retrieved 15 February 2015 from www.tate.org.uk/about/press-office/press-releases/yayoi-kusama.

Thomas, J. (2009) Sony Pictures in school science tie, *Marketing,* 23 September, p. 10.

Thorncroft, A. (1996) Business arts sponsorship: arts face a harsh set of realities, *Financial Times,* 4 July, p. 1.

Thwaites, D. (1994) Corporate sponsorship by the financial services industry, *Journal of Marketing Management,* 10, 743–63.

Tripodi, J.A. (2001) Sponsorship: a confirmed weapon in the promotional armoury, *International Journal of Sports Marketing and Sponsorship,* 3(1), 1–20.

Walraven, M., Koning, R.H. and van Bottenburg, B. (2012) The effects of sports sponsorship: a review and research agenda, *The Marketing Review,* 12(1), 17–38.

WestendLive (2015) Event information, retrieved 19 February 2015 from www.westendlive.co.uk/.

WGC (2011) Sponsors: World Gold Championships, retrieved 7 November 2011 from www.worldgolf championships.com/wgc/sponsors/index.html.

Whitney Museum of American Art (2012) Career retrospective of Yayoi Kusama to open at the Whitney, retrieved 15 February from http://whitney.org/file_columns/0003/2161/kusama_press_release_final.pdf.

Witcher, B., Craigen, G., Culligan, D. and Harvey, A. (1991) The links between objectives and functions in organisational sponsorship, *International Journal of Advertising,* 10, 13–33.

Chapter 14

Direct marketing and personal selling

Direct marketing is a strategy used to create a personal and intermediary-free dialogue with customers. This should be a measurable activity and it is very often media-based, used with a view to creating and sustaining a mutually rewarding relationship.

Personal selling involves a face-to-face dialogue between two persons or by one person and a group. Message flexibility is an important attribute, as is the immediate feedback that often flows from use of this promotional tool.

Aims and objectives

The aims of this chapter are to first consider the characteristics of direct marketing and second to explore some of the principal issues and concepts associated with personal selling.

The learning objectives are to enable readers to:

1. define direct marketing and set out its key characteristics;
2. describe the different methods used to implement direct marketing;
3. explain the significance of the database and Big Data in direct marketing and consider different direct-response media;
4. identify the different types, roles and tasks of personal selling;
5. discuss the role and evolution of social media within personal selling;
6. consider the characteristics of strategic account management.

Everest – growing the number of appointments through marginal gain

Everest sell windows, doors and conservatories. The only way to buy an Everest window is to set up an appointment with an Everest consultant who will come to your home, take measurements for what's needed, and give you a quote based on what you want.

Our marketing therefore is geared to generating appointments. We had 102,000 core appointments (windows and doors) in 2010, but this slipped back to c.91,000 in 2011, and the run rate for 2012 was 25 per cent behind this. Everest needed to take action.

Much of Everest's success had been based on the slogan, 'Fit the Best – fit Everest'. The phrase reflected our market leadership and our technically superior products. Unfortunately our product leadership was being eroded, as our competitors' offerings improved. Safestyle and Anglian had moved to a discount strategy, both offering 50 per cent off.

We saw three tasks:

1. Halt the decline in core appointments.
2. Get the brand back to 100,000 core appointments a year.
3. Put the business on an upward trajectory of growth.

We could not achieve these goals by reverting to our being the 'best' positioning. We needed a new approach and this was discovered through Dave Brailsford (the GB cycling Performance Director) and the way in which he prepared his team for the Olympics. His approach was rooted in his own-phrase 'the aggregation of marginal gains'.

> The whole principle came from the idea that if you broke down everything you could think of that goes into riding a bike, and then improved it by 1%, you will get a significant increase when you put them all together. (Dave Brailsford)

We believed we could achieve our goals and earn the growth we needed through doing lots of little things a little bit better, finding our '1 per cents' and exploiting them. In addition, we believed it would make the ideal platform for long-term growth. So, rather than search for a magical shortcut to be 'the best', we began by doing lots of things a bit 'better'.

The first search for a 1 per cent saving concerned our use of TV to generate appointments. The company, and indeed most competitors, used a 'burst' approach, concentrating the spend in January, which

Up to 50% off selected windows and doors - ends 27.11.12

Exhibit 14.1   Television was an integral element in driving appointments
Appointments increased as a result of spreading the television spend across the year.
Source: Everest Ltd (created by MBA).

Exhibit 14.2   **Two different door-drops were used to target different audiences**
    Source: Everest Ltd (created by MBA).

historically is the business's best month. Recent research on the conservatory decision-making journey found that a third of buyers take over a year to decide, but that once they have set their mind on something they move quickly. All the time we weren't on air, we were missing out on reaching people ready to buy.

Media analysis suggested that we switch to an 'always on' approach, by flattening our TV activity across the year. This enabled us to reach more people at the right time and improve the efficiency and effectiveness of the spend. Our econometric model shows that challenging the 'January rule' earned us 1,000 (2 per cent) incremental appointments between July and December 2012.

To meet the challenge of the discounters we needed value-building messaging. The first phase of TV creative set the offer against the emotional end-benefit (e.g. a cosier home or jealous neighbours); aiming to lift the story out of the discount war that was raging around us, and remind people of the roles these products play that are often taken for granted. The second phase of the TV creative then connected a rational benefit to the emotional

benefit, taking viewers up-close and inside the products to show what makes Everest better. This set us up to dispel the perception that all windows and doors are the same whilst weaving the offer even deeper into the fabric of the narrative. Using emotional and rational benefits against our competitors' 50 per cent off offer earned us an extra 3,077 (5 per cent) appointments.

Another area in which we searched for a 1 per cent improvement concerned the direct channels. Strategic analysis indicated that we could take spend out of channels that weren't performing well, such as door-drops and cold direct mail work, and move it into those that were, such as highly targeted magazine inserts, DRTV and pay-per-click ads.

We also redirected investment into pay-per-click ads as we could run tests and get almost instant feedback. We were able to increase our spend in pay-per-click by £600,000, and although it lifted its cost-per-appointment from £70 to £107, it still remained by far our most efficient channel. We were also able to move £270,000 into magazine inserts and only increase its cost-per-appointment by £9 (from £218 to £227).

All these little efficiency improvements made from a simple redistribution of spend meant we generated more appointments for the same amount of money. Our econometric model shows that between July and December 2012 it all added up to 1,500 (3 per cent) additional appointments.

For the next 6 months we looked for 1 per cents in what was working. We started to top up our TV spend, month by month, setting an acceptable cost-per-appointment increase limit of 20 per cent (which would take it up to £274). By the end of the 6-month period (from January to July 2013) we had spent 60 per cent more than we did in the same period the year before, with our cost-per-appointment only going up to £264 (14 per cent up).

Another gain was found by reviewing our door-drop material. We designed a new broadsheet format which was considerably cheaper than the old C5 envelope we had been using. In fact, between January and July 2013 we reduced the cost of door-drop by 29 per cent, driving its cost-per-appointment down from £479 to £320.

Rather than obsessing about being the highest ranked brand in organic search for 'double glazing', which was becoming increasingly inefficient, we made the decision to let it go. This freed up budget to re-invest in more efficient search terms.

The website was originally designed to get someone ready to buy to contact us. What it did not do was help those thinking about buying or those worried about making a bad decision. Using ideas of behavioural economics we shifted our thinking online from 'selling' to 'helping people buy'. This required us to:

- establish a new measurement framework that would help us set the right performance goals;
- deepen the journeys people took within the website, navigating the right way from the kernel of an idea about their home to finding the perfect product for it;
- restructure the products to help users find what they're looking for with the least number of clicks.
- refocus the site to address the questions and concerns people have with compelling content and proof at key moments to reduce any perceived risk.

The primary goal was to move overall online conversion from visit to appointment. The conversion rate rose immediately on launch by 10 per cent. The increase in conversion was responsible for an additional 2,607 (5 per cent) appointments.

By the end of 2012 our search for 1 per cent improvements had reversed the downward trend in appointments. Core appointments reached 86,300 and in 2013 we hit 99,000.

This case was written by Ben Hitchcock, Marketing Director of Everest, and James Price, Senior Account Planner, and James Devon, Planning Director, both at MBA

Questions concerning this case can be found at the end of this chapter.

Introduction

The Everest case demonstrates the variety of activities associated with direct marketing. It also shows how these are geared to driving appointments in order that consultants can meet potential customers and engage through personal selling. This chapter explores both direct marketing and personal selling, topics that complement each other in that they are both characterised by their personal and relatively transparent direct nature.

Direct marketing is a term used to refer to all media activities that generate a series of communications and responses with an existing or potential customer, as observed at Everest. Direct marketing is mainly concerned with the management of customer behaviour and is used to complement the strengths and weaknesses of the other communications disciplines. To put this another way, advertising and public relations provide information and develop brand values, but sales promotion, direct marketing and personal selling drive response, most notably behaviour. Both direct marketing and personal selling have the potential to engage customers directly, explicitly and provide both an intellectual and emotional basis upon which interaction and dialogue can be developed.

The role of direct marketing

Direct marketing is concerned with the management of customer behaviour and is used to complement the strengths and weaknesses of the other communications disciplines. To put it another way, advertising and public relations provide information and develop brand values, but sales promotion and direct marketing drive response, most notably behaviour.

Direct marketing is a tool of marketing communications used to create and sustain personal and intermediary-free communications with customers, potential customers and other significant stakeholders. As seen in the Everest case this is a media-based activity and offers great scope for the collection and utilisation of pertinent and measurable data. There are a number of important issues associated with this definition. The first is that the activity should be measurable. That is, any response(s) must be associated with a particular individual, a particular media activity and a particular outcome, such as a sale or enquiry for further information. The second issue concerns the rewards that each party perceives through participation in the communications episode. Each customer receives a variety of tangible and intangible satisfactions. These include shopping convenience, time utility and the satisfaction and trust that can develop between customers and a provider of quality products and services when the customers realise and appreciate the personal attention they appear to be receiving.

Direct marketers derive benefits associated with precision target marketing and minimised waste, increased profits and the opportunities to provide established customers with other related products, without the huge costs of continually having to find new customers. Everest uses direct marketing strategically, as it represents Everest's overall approach to the market. There are no channel intermediaries, at least from the initial communications, it reduces costs, and improves the quality and speed of service for customers. In addition to Everest, companies such as First Direct, Churchill and the pioneer, Direct Line, have all used direct marking to secure strong positions in the UK market.

Viewpoint 14.1   Driving behaviour through direct marketing

Direct marketing, in all of its different formats, is used by a great many organisations, some to a greater extent than others.

Kingdom of Sports is one of Germany's biggest gym networks, and in order to penetrate the market and reach some of the 58 per cent of Germans who are said to be overweight, they turned to direct mail. What was clever was that the messaging was printed on special paper (a paper–polyester mix) that made it impossible to tear or rip. The challenge was to rip the mailer and win a year's free subscription. All of those who tried, failed, but they all received a month's free introductory membership.

In contrast, The National Trust used direct marketing to help secure funding for the acquisition of a stretch of coast on the Llŷn Peninsula in North West Wales. Using direct mail, the campaign directed people to a bespoke microsite which contained information about the ecological importance, the threats facing the peninsula and an opportunity to make donations.

See also the BHF case (Chapter 2) and the TfL case (Chapter 5), both excellent examples of direct marketing. Financial services companies such as Santander, Axa, Aviva, Barclays and Direct Line all use direct marketing as a core element of their communications programmes. LoveFilm, the video rental company, charities such as Barnardos and Oxfam, and numerous B2B companies all invest heavily in direct marketing.

Exhibit 14.3	**The Llŷn Peninsula in North Wales**
	The National Trust used direct marking to drive donations to help fund the purchase of part of the coastline in the Llŷn Peninsula.
	Source: Alamy Images/Camera Lucida.

Source: Anon (2014a); Fernandez (2010).

Question: If an organisation does not want to compete using advertising or direct marketing, what other methods could it use?

Task: Find two examples of companies using direct marketing and list the tools and media used.

Underpinning the direct marketing approach are the principles of trust and commitment, just as they support the validity of the other communications mix tools. If a meaningful relationship is to be developed over the long term and direct marketing is an instrumental part of the interaction, then the promises that the parties make to develop commitment and stability are of immense importance (Ganesan, 1994).

Types of direct brand

Direct marketing is assumed to refer to direct communications mix activity, but this is only part of the marketing picture. Using direct-response media in this way is an increasingly common activity used to augment the communications activities surrounding a brand and to provide a new dimension to the context in which brands are perceived. However, direct marketing can be used by organisations in a number of different ways, very often reflecting the business strategy of the organisation. Four types can be identified and they should not be regarded as hierarchical, in the sense that there has to be progression from one type to another. They are reflections of the way different organisations use direct marketing and the degree to which the tool is used strategically.

Type 1: complementary tool

At this level, direct-response media are used to complement the other communications mix activities used to support a brand. Their main use is to generate leads and to some extent awareness, information and reinforcement. For example, financial services companies, tour operators and travel agents use DRTV to stimulate enquiries, loans and bookings, respectively.

Type 2: primary differentiator

Rather than be one of a number of communications mix tools, at this level direct-response media are the primary forms of communications. They are used to provide a distinct point of differentiation from competitor offerings. They are the principal forms of communications. In addition to the Type 1 advantages they are used to cut costs, avoid the use of intermediaries and reach finely targeted audiences (e.g. book, music and wine clubs).

Type 3: sales channel

A third use for direct marketing, and telemarketing in particular, concerns its use as a means of developing greater efficiency and as a means of augmenting current services. By utilising direct marketing as a sales tool, multiple sales channels can be used to meet the needs of different customer segments and so release resources to be deployed elsewhere and more effectively.

Type 4: brand vehicle

At this final level, brands are developed to exploit market space opportunities. The strategic element is most clearly evident at this level. Indeed, the entire organisation and its culture are normally oriented to the development of customer relationships through direct marketing activities. Prime examples are Lastminute.com and Amazon.

The growth of direct marketing

There can be little doubt that, of all the tools in the marketing communications mix, direct marketing has experienced the most growth in the last 15 years. The reasons for this growth are many and varied, but there have been three essential drivers behind the surge in direct marketing: technological advances; changing buyer lifestyles and expectations; and organisational expectations (see Figure 14.1). These forces for change demonstrate quite dramatically how a change in context can impact on marketing communications.

Growth driver 1: technology

Rapid advances in technology have heralded the arrival of new sources and forms of information. Technology has enabled the collection, storage and analysis of customer data to become relatively simple, cost-effective and straightforward. Furthermore, the management of this information is increasingly available to small businesses as well as the major blue chip multinational organisations. Computing and data storage costs have

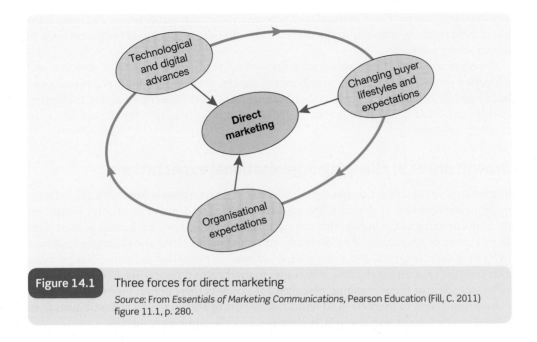

Figure 14.1	Three forces for direct marketing

Source: From *Essentials of Marketing Communications*, Pearson Education (Fill, C. 2011) figure 11.1, p. 280.

plummeted, while there has been a correspondingly enormous increase in the power that technology can deliver.

The technological surge has in turn stimulated three major developments. The first concerns the ability to capture information, the second to process and analyse it, and the third to represent part or all of the information as forms of communications to stimulate interaction and perhaps dialogue to collect further information. For example, some organisations are incorporating quick response (QR) codes and image recognition technologies to make a bridge between offline and online using smartphones. Millward (2014) refers to a shopping mall in Singapore which used four life-size QR mascots, designed as shopping bags with large QR codes on them, encouraging shoppers to scan the code to enter a contest and to register a 'like' for the mall's Facebook page. Over 50 per cent of those who scanned the code became new Facebook fans of the mall. He also refers to a bar in Tokyo where orders can be taken using QR codes, and subway posters in South Korea, China and Singapore adorned with images of grocery products and QR codes, which people can use to fill up a virtual shopping basket and pay for electronically.

Growth driver 2: changing market context

The lifestyles of people in industrialised economies, in particular, have evolved and will continue to do so. Generally, the brash phase of *selfishness* in the 1980s gave way to a more caring, society-oriented *selflessness* in the 1990s. The first decade of the twenty-first century reverted to a more *self-oriented* lifestyle, reflected in short-term brand purchase behaviour and self-centred brand values and society behaviour. The second decade has seen further change as the global economy stumbled into a major recession. Some brands have struggled to work with the various forces acting on societies, such as those for environmental care, responsible food production, healthy eating, and the continual expectation that people should seek relationships and even minor celebrity status through social media. The values that are deemed appropriate appear confused as witnessed by various celebrity misbehaviours, the continuing MPs' expenses scandals, and the plummeting reputations of various established brands such as banks, supermarkets and technology companies. This destabilisation does not help people to see clearly their role within a society and has not helped brands to interact with their audiences in any meaningful way. The continual shift towards audience fragmentation and associated buyer behaviours is reflected in the diverse ways that the media enable organisations to contact their audiences.

Direct marketing offers a solution to this splintering and micro market scenario and addresses some of the changing needs of customers, such as personalised, permission-based and informed communications. Management also benefits as direct marketing enables improved speed of response, lower waste, and justification for the use and allocation of resources.

Growth driver 3: changing organisational expectations

Organisations can expect to continue experiencing performance pressures. These vary from the expectations of shareholders who are expected to demand short-term returns on their investments, to the impact this can have on managers. They are having to cope with an increasing cost base caused by demands within the supply chain and claims on resources by developing economies, and a downward pressure on prices due to intense competition. This pressure on margins requires new routes to markets to reduce costs. Direct marketing addresses some of these changing management needs as there are no intermediary costs, there is fast access to markets (and withdrawal) plus opportunities to respond quickly to market developments and also justify their use and allocation of resources.

The impact of these drivers can be seen within the emergence of ideas about integrated marketing communications and an overall emphasis on relationship marketing principles. The enhanced ability of organisations to collect, store and manage customer lifestyle and transactional data, to generate personalised communications and their general enthusiasm for retention and loyalty schemes have combined to provide a huge movement towards an increased use of direct and interactive marketing initiatives.

Scholars' paper 14.1   **The evolution of direct marketing**

Scovotti, C. and Spiller, L.D. (2006) Revisiting the conceptual definition of direct marketing: perspectives from practitioners and scholars, *The Marketing Management Journal,* **16(2), 188–202.**

Readers wishing to know more about the development of direct marketing will find this paper interesting and helpful. The authors review the literature, albeit up to 2005, and point out the contradictions, issues and anomalies.

The role of data

Data has become a significant asset or, as Newman (2014) refers to it, the 'new oil' of the information age. Central to successful direct marketing and CRM (customer relationship marketing) activities has been the database. A database is a collection of files held on a computer that contain data that can be related to other data and which can reproduce information in a variety of formats. Normally the data consists of information collected about prospects and customers that are used to determine appropriate segments and target markets, and to record responses to communications conveyed by the organisation.

Databases therefore have a storage, sorting and administrative role designed to assist direct and personalised communications. The stored information is gathered from transactions undertaken and information provided by customers. This is insufficient on its own and a further layering of data is required. The recency/frequency/monetary (RFM) model provided a base upon which lifestyle data, often bought in from an agency list, was used to further refine the information held and which enabled more effective targeting and communications.

It should be noted that databases often store data in a highly structured format. Kuechler observed, in 2007, that data was beginning to be stored as streams of data gathered from a variety of sources. These include audio, video, organisational documents and web pages, email, customer comments, plus the major Internet platforms such as Facebook, Amazon, Twitter, Google, Apple and others. From these sources a more unstructured format has evolved.

Much of this sophisticated information has arisen through what is referred to as 'Big Data'. The dominant Internet platforms referred to earlier accumulate vast amounts of information on consumers, including purchases, interests, activities and overall behaviour. When this information is merged with privately held data, Big Data is the result. Nunan and Di Domenico (2014) consider the impact of Big Data through three perspectives. These are the:

- technological issues associated with storing, securing and analysing the vast and increasing volumes of data being gathered by organisations, and also including new types of database and 'cloud' storage, which enable innovative forms of analysis;
- added commercial value offered through the generation of more effective consumer insights;
- societal influences such as privacy, freedom of speech, regulation, and suitable guidelines for the ethical commercial use of this data.

It is through the use of data that relationships with participants can be tracked, analysed and developed. Very importantly, data has been used not only to identify strategically important customers and segments, but also to ascertain opportunities to cross-sell products (Kamakura et al., 2003).

However, the merging of data generated through transactions with attitudinal and lifestyle data poses problems. In essence, data paints a picture of what has been achieved – it describes behaviour. What it does not do is explain why the behaviour occurred. It may be possible to track back through a campaign to examine the inputs, isolate variables and make a judgement, but the problem remains that the data itself, what has been collected, does not provide insight into what underpins the behaviour.

Permission marketing

There are a number of tensions associated with the use of databases and Big Data. These tensions can be related to concerns about privacy and the need to communicate sensitively with audiences who experience varying needs for privacy (Dolnicar and Jordan, 2007). For example, customers have varying tolerances regarding the level of privacy that a database can exploit. These tolerances or thresholds (Goodwin, 1991) vary according to the nature of the information itself, how it was collected and even who collected it.

The information on a database very often exists simply because a customer entered into a transaction. The business entity that received the information as part of a transaction has a duty to acknowledge the confidential nature of the information and the context in which it was collected before selling the details to a third party or exploiting the information to the detriment of the individual who provided it in the first place. Breaking privacy codes and making unauthorised disclosures of personal details lays open the tenuous relationship an organisation thinks it has with its 'loyal' customers. These tensions have given rise to regulations requiring customers to provide organisations with their express permission to use their personal data in particular ways.

It is commonly agreed that Godin (1999) is the pioneer of permission marketing (PM) (Krishnamurthy, 2001; Gomez and Hlavinka, 2007) and that the aim of PM is to 'initiate, sustain and develop a dialogue with customers, building trust and over time lifting the levels of permission, making it a more valuable asset' (Kent and Brandal, 2003: 491). To put it another way, PM is about 'getting the okay from individuals to market to them' (Smith, 2004: 52).

PM occurs when consumers give their explicit permission for marketers to send them various types of promotional messages (Krishnamurthy, 2001). Essentially customers authorise a marketer to transmit marketing messages in certain 'interest' categories. This is usually obtained when customers register to enter a website or complete a survey indicating their interests when registering for a service. Marketers are then able to target messages more closely with the interests and needs of their registered customers. Definitions of PM vary according to the focus of the researchers, but they range from education, trust and share of wallet to enticement and clutter.

Customers benefit from using PM through:

- a reduction in search costs and clutter;
- better organisation of the information search processes;
- improved message relevance through personalisation, customisation and recognition.

For organisations the benefits of using PM are related to:

- improved segmentation and targeting precision, the acquisition of new customers, an increase of sales and the development of long-term, loyal customers;
- flexibility, resulting in improved interactivity, lower sales costs, enhanced direct communications with customers and increased profitability.

Direct-response media

The choice of media for direct marketing can be very different from those selected for general advertising purposes. The main reason for using direct-response media is that direct contact is made with prospects and customers in order that a direct response is solicited and a dialogue stimulated or maintained. In reality, as demonstrated by Everest, a wide variety of media can be used, including the provision of a telephone number, website address or response card.

Previously, broadcast media such as television and radio were the champions of the general advertiser. Now their adoption by direct marketers has changed the way these media operate. In terms of engagement (explored in Chapter 1), the broadcast format generated engagement through thinking and feeling. Their use as a direct-response instrument changes the engagement to a behavioural orientation.

Direct mail, telemarketing and door-to-door activities are the main offline forms of direct-response media, as they allow more personal, direct and evaluative means of reaching precisely targeted customers. Internet-based direct work encompasses email, mobile and affiliate marketing as forms of direct linking.

Direct mail

Direct mail refers to personally addressed advertising that is delivered through the postal system. It can be personalised and targeted with great accuracy, and its results are capable of precise measurement.

The generation of enquiries and leads together with the intention of building a personal relationship with customers are the most important factors contributing to the growth of direct mail. Management should decide whether to target direct mail at current customers with the intention of building loyalty and retention rates, or whether it should chase new customers. The decision, acquisition or retention, should be part of the marketing plan but often this aspect of direct marketing lacks clarity, resulting in wastage and inefficiency. Direct mail can be expensive; it should, therefore, be used selectively and for purposes other than creating awareness.

Organisations in the financial services sector have been heavy users of this medium and the financial health of the sector is dependent to a large extent on some of the major financial services companies maintaining their spend on direct mail (see Viewpoint 14.2). An increasing number of other organisations, however, are experimenting with this approach, as they try to improve the effectiveness of their investment in the communications mix and seek to reduce television advertising costs.

Viewpoint 14.2   Folding videos help open boutiques

State Street is a global business founded on providing a variety of investment servicing functions for the world's larger financial asset managers. This allows asset managers to focus on their core business. During the recovery from the recent recession State Street identified an opportunity to help smaller European 'boutique' asset managers, those in the UK, Germany, Switzerland, France, The Netherlands and Nordics, who manage between US$1 billion and US$50 billion assets. Although a new mid-office, end-to-end solution was developed the real challenge lay in getting in front of the key decision makers of each of the target boutiques.

Research into the challenges and opportunities faced by these asset managers was commissioned. The results were used to develop a thought leadership report entitled *Empowering Boutiques: The Rise of the Specialist Asset Manager*.

A short, impactful, 'teaser' video was created which highlighted some of the headline research results. This was embedded in a video direct mail and sent to 88 boutique asset managers. The goal was to demonstrate that State Street understood their challenges and that they had a tailored solution.

The mailing piece was an A5 single-fold in which a 3-minute video was embedded. The video centred on the asset manager's challenges, and included a clear call to action to 'Talk to Us'. The clever part was that the video played automatically when the fold was opened.

In addition State Street used public relations and media outreach which resulted in over 25 pieces of press coverage. Social media (Twitter and LinkedIn) was also incorporated to encourage digital downloads of the VISION paper. The EIU research was also turned into an infographic, which was given to journalists to use in their coverage.

The campaign drove a 44 per cent meeting rate and generated three new clients (at the time the case was written).

Source: Anon (2013); State Street (2012).

Question: To what extent was the folding video or State Street's credibility the deciding factor in the success of this campaign?

Task: Find two other campaigns in which video was a core element.

Telemarketing

The prime qualities of the telephone are that it provides for interaction, is flexible and permits immediate feedback and the opportunity to overcome objections, all within the same communications event. Other dimensions of telemarketing include the development and maintenance of customer goodwill, allied to which is the increasing need to provide high levels of customer service. Telemarketing also allows organisations to undertake marketing research which is both highly measurable and accountable in that the effectiveness can be verified continuously and call rates, contacts reached and the number and quality of positive and negative responses are easily recorded and monitored.

Growth in telemarketing activity in the business-to-business (B2B) sector has been largely at the expense of personal selling. The objectives have been to reduce costs and to utilise the expensive sales force and its skills to build on the openings and leads created by telemarketing and other lead generation activities. Some of the advantages of using the telephone as part of the media mix are that it allows for interaction between participants, enables immediate feedback and it sets up opportunities to overcome objections, all within the same communications event when both the sender and the receiver are geographically distant.

All of these activities can be executed by personal selling, but the speed, cost, accuracy and consistency of the information solicited through personal visits can often be improved upon by telemarketing. The complexity of the product will influence the degree to which this medium can be used successfully. However, if properly trained professional telemarketers are used, the sales results, if measured on a call basis, can outperform those produced by personal selling.

Contact centres use a variety of digital applications with the prime goals of reducing costs, improving efficiency and improving the client's reputation through quality of customer interaction. Automatic call distribution systems, call recording systems, computer–telephone integration, customer interaction management, predictive diallers and interactive voice response systems are just some of the ways in which technology is used in these environments.

Viewpoint 14.3 Keeping calls appropriate

The use of telemarketing within an integrated approach to marketing communications requires that all elements be fully involved, highlighting the need for a shared and complete campaign brief. It can also demonstrate the extent to which an organisation's internal structures and processes are harmonised.

Take for example the case of a New Zealand-based credit card brand. Having researched its database, analysed the market and allocated sufficient budget, the brand developed a retention strategy. Part of this involved the launch of a new, innovative and seemingly attractive loyalty programme. This went well and tracking data showed that direct mail awareness was very high but research revealed that brand consideration among current users was declining. Further qualitative-based investigation found that customers had been subject to persistent, irritating and invasive telemarketing which was geared to pushing other services, including cards, travel insurance and other financial services. The impact was to diminish the customer experience.

One significant issue associated with telemarketing has been the use of unsolicited calls related to PPI (payment protection insurance) and accident claims. In addition, the use of so called 'silent' calls has also caused widespread alarm. These occur when incoming calls are picked up but there is no response or message as the computer is unable to allocate the call to an operator.

In these circumstances the law is regarded to have been too open and is currently being revised to stamp out what some regard as unethical practices. For example, in 2013 Tetrus Telecoms was fined £300,000 for bombarding people with texts about PPI and accident claims. On appeal this decision was overturned as the Tribunal concluded that the unwanted messages did not meet the legal requirements of causing significant harm, despite being generated on an 'industrial scale'.

Exhibit 14.4	**The PPI scandal has resulted in a huge business anchored around telemarketing**
	Source: Alamy Images/David J.Green-lifestyle 2.

The government has subsequently set out to lower the burden of proof in order to protect consumers, as well as the telemarketing industry, from the scourge of nuisance calls.

Source: Anon (2015); Joseph (2014).

Question: What would you recommend organisations do to ensure their use of telemarketing is both brand and societally appropriate?

Task: Select an online newspaper, and list the number of articles featuring problematic telemarketing over a period of two years. What are the differences and similarities associated with these reports?

Operator contact with customers can be also be supported by technology. Computer-assisted telephone interviewing (CATI) can provide varying degrees of technical support. The degree to which this is used depends on the task, the product and the nature of the target audience. The behaviour of call centre employees, however much they are regulated or controlled by various software applications, is a function of service quality, as perceived by callers. Referred to as customer-orientation behaviours (COBs), Rafaeli et al. (2008) identify five COBs that are related to service quality:

- anticipating customer requests;
- offering explanations and justifications;
- educating customers;
- providing emotional support;
- offering personalised information.

When these five COBs are used by call centre employees, customers perceive a high level of service quality. The implication of this, as pointed out by the researchers, is that as call centre managers invariably seek to minimise call length in order to reduce costs and increase the number of transactions, their actions appear to endanger service quality.

Scholars' paper 14.2   Call or go online?

Rhee, E. (2010) Multi-channel management in direct marketing retailing: traditional call center versus Internet channel, *Database Marketing & Customer Strategy Management*, 17(2), 70–7.

This paper addresses issues associated with the impact on telemarketing following the rise of the Internet channel. The author looks at the benefits consumers perceive in using different channels. The research suggests that the Internet channel is helpful for purchases when there is low perceived risk and high experience and familiarity with the purchase. However, the call centre channel is helpful when there is high perceived risk and low experience and familiarity with the purchase.

Carelines

Another reason to use telemarketing concerns the role which carelines can play within consumer/brand relationships. Manufacturers use contact centres to enable customers to:

- complain about a product performance and related experiences;
- seek product-related advice;
- make suggestions regarding product or packaging development;
- comment about an action or development concerning the brand as a whole.

What binds these together is the potential all of these people have for repurchasing the brand, even those who complain bitterly about product performance and experience. If these people have their complaints dealt with properly then there is a reasonable probability that they will repurchase.

The majority of careline calls are not about complaints but seek advice or help about products. Food manufacturers can provide cooking and recipe advice, cosmetic and toiletries companies can provide healthcare advice and application guidelines, while white goods and service-based organisations can provide technical and operational support.

Carelines are essentially a post-purchase support mechanism that facilities market feedback and intelligence gathering. They can warn of imminent problems (product defects), provide ideas for new products or variants and of course provide a valuable method to reassure customers and improve customer retention levels. Call operators, or agents as many of them are now being called, have to handle calls from a variety of sources, such as the Web, email, interactive TV and mobile devices, and it is appreciated that many are more effective if they have direct product experience. Instant messaging channels enable online shoppers to ask questions that are routed to a call centre for response.

While the Internet has provided further growth opportunities, it has also taken on a number of the tasks currently the preserve of telemarketing bureaux. Websites enable product information and certain support advice to be accessed without the call centre costs and focus attention on other matters that are of concern to the customer. Chat room discussions, collaborative browsing and real-time text conversations are options to help care for customers. However, it is probably the one-to-one telephone dialogue between customer and agent that will continue to provide satisfaction and benefits for both parties.

Inserts

Inserts are media materials that are placed in magazines or direct mail letters. These not only provide factual information about the product or service but also enable the recipient to respond to the request of the direct marketer. This request might be to place an order or post back a card for more information, such as a brochure.

Inserts have become more popular, but their cost is substantially higher than a four-colour magazine ad in which the insert is carried. Their popularity is based on their effectiveness as a lead generator, and new methods of delivering inserts to the home will become important to direct mailing houses in the future. Other vehicles, such as packages rather than letter mail, will become important.

Print

There are two main forms of direct-response advertising through the printed media: first, catalogues and, second, magazines and newspapers.

Catalogues mailed direct to consumers have been an established method of selling products for a long time. Mail order organisations for a range of products from clothing and music to gardening and cosmetics continue to exploit this form of direct marketing. The size of each catalogue and the range of products included have been slimmed down so that mini-catalogues are popular.

Business-to-business marketers also use this medium, and organisations such as Dell and IBM now use online and offline catalogues, partly to save costs and partly to free valuable sales personnel so that they can concentrate their time selling into larger accounts. Direct-response advertising through the press is similar to general press advertising except that the advertiser provides a mechanism for the reader to take further action. The mechanism may be a telephone number (call free) or a coupon or cut-out reply slip requesting further information. Dell transformed its marketing strategy to one that is based around building customised products for both consumers and business customers. Consumer direct print ads which offer an incentive are designed explicitly to drive customers to the Dell website, where transactions are completed without reference to retailers, dealers or other intermediaries.

Exhibit 14.5   **Direct-response print ad from The Samaritans**
Source: www.samaritans.org.

Door-to-door

This delivery method can be much cheaper than direct mail as there are no postage charges to be accounted for. However, if the costs are much lower, so are the response rates. Responses are lower because door-to-door drops cannot be personally addressed, as can direct mail, even though the content and quality can be controlled in the same way.

Avon (Cosmetics) and Betterware are traditionally recognised as professional practitioners of door-to-door direct marketing. Other organisations, such as the utility companies (gas, electricity and water), and the domestic cleaning company, Molly Maid, are using door-to-door to create higher levels of market penetration.

Radio and television

Of the two main forms discussed earlier, radio and television, the former is often used as a support medium for other advertising, usually by providing enquiry numbers and website addresses. Television has greater potential because it can provide the important visual dimension. The original DRTV model involved generating response to 0800 numbers and a call to immediate action.

Now that consumers practise multiscreening, the model has moved to one that harnesses brand search activity through mobile devices, which in turn drives spontaneous purchases. Instead of a phone number this activity is stimulated through the use of compelling content that consumers want to share. These links boost natural search rankings.

Direct Line, originally a motor insurance organisation, has been at the vanguard in its use of DRTV not only to launch but also to propel the phenomenal growth of a range of related products. For a long time the red ringing phone symbolised their call to action. Now, it uses content to raise awareness and stimulate action. For example, Direct Line Pet Insurance invited people to upload videos of their pets 'dancing'. The activity saw the brand's Google rankings soar (Benady, 2014) (see Exhibit 14.6).

 direct line   Pet Step Winners

---

Exhibit 14.6   **A winning pet in the Direct Line Pet Insurance 'Pet Step' dance competition, designed to stimulate engagement through sharing content**
Source: Direct Line Group.

Interactive media

The explosion of activity around interactive media, and social media and email communications in particular, has been quite astonishing in recent years and now represents a major new form of interactive marketing communications. All of these challenge the scope and perception of the activities embraced under the term 'direct marketing'. Originally direct marketing was about direct mail and telemarketing. In a multiscreen and multichannel environment most marketing communications channels have the potential to reach customers and prospects directly. Some would argue that nearly all marketing communications is now conducted on a direct basis.

Data-driven ad targeting using on-demand and subscription television, the scope of social media and social networks, brands such as Shazam that enable instant response regardless of location or context, plus expanded online marketing such as email, have, according to Parsons (2013), contributed to a redefinition of what direct marketing is. Data-driven, one-to-one marketing is everywhere. (For more information on interactive marketing communications see Chapter 19.)

Personal selling

The traditional image of personal selling is one that embraces the hard sell, with a brash and persistent salesperson delivering a volley of unrelenting, persuasive messages at a confused and reluctant consumer. Fortunately this image has receded as the professionalism and breadth of personal selling has become more widely recognised and as the role of personal selling becomes even more important in the communications mix.

Personal selling activities can be observed at various stages in the buying process of both the consumer and B2B markets. This is because the potency of personal communications is very high, and messages can be adapted on the spot to meet the requirements of both parties. This flexibility, as we shall see later, enables objections to be overcome, information to be provided in the context of the buyer's environment, and the conviction and power of demonstration to be brought to the buyer when the buyer requests it.

Personal selling is different from other forms of communications in that the transmitted messages represent, mainly, dyadic communications. This means that there are two persons involved in the communications process. Feedback and evaluation of transmitted messages are possible, more or less instantaneously, so that these personal selling messages can be tailored and be made much more personal than any of the other methods of communications. It should be noted, however, that as Serviere-Munoz and Mallin (2013) point out, personal selling has long been subject to criticism due to its vulnerability to exploitation and unethical practices.

Using the spectrum of activities identified by the hierarchy of effects, we can see that personal selling is close enough to the prospective buyer to induce a change in behaviour. That is, it is close enough to overcome objections, to provide information quickly and to respond to the prospects' overall needs, all in the context of the transaction, and to encourage them directly to place orders.

The tasks of personal selling

The generic tasks to be undertaken by the sales force have been changing because the environment in which organisations operate is shifting dramatically. These changes, in particular those associated with the development and implementation of new technologies, have had repercussions on the activities of the sales force and are discussed later in this chapter.

The tasks of those who undertake personal selling vary from organisation to organisation and in accord with the type of selling activities on which they focus. It is normally assumed that they collect and bring into the organisation orders from customers wishing to purchase products and services. In this sense the order aspect of the personal selling tool can be seen as one of four order-related tasks:

1. *Order takers* are salespersons to whom customers are drawn at the place of supply. Reception clerks at hotels and ticket desk personnel at theatres and cinemas typify this role.

2. *Order getters* are sales personnel who operate away from the organisation and who attempt to gain orders, largely through the provision of information, the use of demonstration techniques and services, and the art of persuasion.

3. *Order collectors* are those who attempt to gather orders without physically meeting their customers. This is completed electronically or over the telephone. The growth of telemarketing operations was discussed earlier in this chapter but the time saved by both the buyer and the seller using the telephone to gather repeat and low-value orders frees valuable sales personnel to seek new customers and build relationships with current customers.

4. *Order supporters* are all those people who are secondary salespersons in that they are involved with the order once it has been secured, or are involved with the act of ordering, usually by supplying information. Order processing or financial advice services typify this role. In truly customer-oriented organisations all customer-facing employees will be an order supporter.

However, this perspective of personal selling is narrow because it fails to set out the broader range of activities that a sales force can be required to undertake. Salespeople do more than get or take orders. The tasks listed in Table 14.1 provide direction and purpose, and also help to establish the criteria by which the performance of members of the personal selling unit can be evaluated. The organisation should decide which tasks it expects its representatives to undertake.

It is argued that the personal selling process should be seen as something beyond simply as a series of buyer–seller interactions (Shannahan et al., 2013). By understanding the personal selling process as an interpretation system comprising individuals whose goal is to reduce uncertainty with respect to the activities within the selling process, a wider, more relational perspective can be appreciated.

Personal selling is the most expensive element of the communications mix and it is generally agreed that personal selling is most effective at the later stages of the hierarchy of effects or buying process, rather than at the earlier stage of awareness building.

Table 14.1 Tasks of personal selling

Prospecting	Finding new customers
Communicating	Informing various stakeholders and feeding back information about the market
Selling	The art of leading a prospect to a successful close
Information gathering	Reporting information about the market and reporting on individual activities
Servicing	Consulting, arranging, counselling, fixing and solving a multitude of customer 'problems'
Allocating	Placing scarce products and resources at times of shortage
Shaping	Building and sustaining relationships with customers and other stakeholders

Therefore, each organisation should determine the precise role the sales force is to play within the communications mix.

The role of personal selling

Personal selling is often referred to as interpersonal communications and from this perspective Reid et al. (2002) determined three major sales behaviours, namely getting, giving and using information:

- Getting information refers to sales behaviours aimed at information acquisition, for example gathering information about customers, markets and competitors.

- Giving information refers to the dissemination of information to customers and other stakeholders, for example sales presentations and seminar meetings designed to provide information about products and an organisation's capabilities and reputation.

- Using information refers to the salesperson's use of information to help solve a customer's problem. Associated with this is the process of gaining buyer commitment through the generation of information (Thayer, 1968, cited by Reid et al., 2002).

These last authors suggest that the using information dynamic appears to be constant across all types of purchase situations. However, as the complexity of a purchase situation increases so the amount of giving information behaviours decline and getting information behaviours increase. This finding supports the need for salespeople to be able to recognise particular situations in the buying process and then to adapt their behaviour to meet a buyer's contextual needs.

However, salespeople undertake numerous tasks in association with communications activities. Guenzi (2002) determined that some sales activities are generic simply because they are performed by most salespeople across a large number of industries. These generic activities are selling, customer relationship management and communicating to customers. Other activities such as market analysis, pre-sales services and the transfer of information about competitors to the organisation are industry-specific. Interestingly he found that information-gathering activities are more likely to be undertaken by organisations operating in consumer markets than in B2B, possibly a reflection of the strength of the market orientation in both arenas.

The role of personal selling is largely one of representation. In B2B markets sales personnel operate at the boundary of the organisation. They provide the link between the needs of their own organisation and the needs of their customers. This linkage, or boundary spanning role, is absolutely vital, for a number of reasons that will be discussed shortly, but without personal selling, communications with other organisations would occur through electronic or print media and would foster discrete closed systems. Representation in this sense therefore refers to face-to-face encounters between people from different organisations.

Many authors consider the development, organisation and completion of a sale in a market exchange-based transaction to be the key part of the role of personal selling. Sales personnel provide a source of information for buyers so that they can make the right purchase decisions. In that sense they provide a good level of credibility, but they are also perceived, understandably, as biased. The degree of expertise held by the salesperson may be high, but the degree of perceived trustworthiness will vary, especially during the formative period of the relationship, unless other transactions with the selling organisation have been satisfactory. Hamwi et al. (2013) found that a buyer's commitment to and trust in a salesperson increase when the expected number of sales calls, as perceived by the buyer, is met. This improves the relational dimension and length of a buyer–seller relationship.

As the costs associated with personal selling are high, it is vital that sales personnel are used effectively. To that end, some organisations are employing other methods to decrease the time that the sales force spends on administration, travel and office work and to maximise the time spent in front of customers, where its specific selling skills can be used.

The amount of control that can be exercised over the delivery of the messages through the sales force depends upon a number of factors. Essentially, the level of control must be regarded as low, because each salesperson has the freedom to adapt messages to meet changing circumstances as negotiations proceed. In practice, however, the professionalism and training that many members of the sales force receive and the increasing accent on measuring levels of customer satisfaction mean that the degree of control over the message can be regarded, in most circumstances, as very good, although it can never, for example, be as high as that of advertising.

This flexibility is framed within the context of the product strategy. Decisions that impact upon strategy are not allowed. There is freedom to adapt the manner in which products are presented, but there is no freedom for the sales representatives to decide the priority of the products to be detailed.

Viewpoint 14.4   Using technology to help sales teams

The importance of the role of digital technology within sales force operations is clearly understood. Indeed, numerous applications and ideas have been utilised to create time and client opportunities, improve efficiencies, and to assist with performance evaluation.

The Philips Lighting sales force in the USA contains nearly 150 account representatives. They serve at both a regional and national level and make an average of three to four customer calls each day. As per standard practice, they are required to update the CRM system following each call.

As many representatives would agree, this type of activity consumes valuable time. It needs to be fitted in around travelling and involves unpacking a laptop and finding a suitable Internet connection. The result is often inaccurate or late data entry and valuable time that could have been spent in front of clients, lost.

An initial solution was a CRM system with an integrated transcription service. This involved dictation to a dedicated number, however, which was then retrieved by transcriptionists who entered the information into the CRM system. This was not ideal as the reports often took days to appear on the CRM system and when they did they were often littered with typos, errors and did little to help sales analytics and reporting.

This was resolved through the adoption of voice technology from Philips Speech Processing Solutions. Information can now be input into the CRM system either through the dial-in number, through a

Exhibit 14.7   **Philips Lighting sales team used their own speech processing solutions to improve the efficiency of their reporting process**
Source: Speech Processing Solutions UK Ltd.

Philips digital hand-held voice recorder with editing functionality or with the Philips dictation recorder smartphone app.

Once a report has been recorded, the file is transmitted to a professional transcriptionist who enters it into the CRM system. An automated email confirmation is used to alert the sales reps when the audio file is received, and within a day they also receive an email, with their transcribed notes. The digital dictation and cloud-based recording storage and transcription solution is not only faster than typing, but it has also led to higher-quality, more actionable sales data.

As a result the use of voice technology rather than typing has enabled each account representative to save at least an hour per day. This is equivalent to the team saving 2,500 hours each month. In addition, around 13,200 records per month are now more rapidly updated, with better client data that helps create new sales opportunities.

Source: Anon (2014b).

Question: Why should organisations maintain an employed, and expensive, sales force when they can rent a sales force at any time?

Task: Make a list of the different ways digital technology might assist the management of sales teams.

Scholars' paper 14.3   Ethical issues in personal selling

Serviere-Munoz, L. and Mallin, M.L. (2013) How do unethical salespeople sleep at night? The role of neutralizations in the justification of unethical sales intentions, *Journal of Personal Selling & Sales Management*, XXXIII(3), 289–306.

As the title suggests, this paper provides an interesting review of some of the ethical issues involved in personal selling and in particular considers the ethical intentions of salespeople.

Readers interested in ethics within a marketing communications context are directed to the dedicated chapter on this topic which is available at the online resource that supports this book.

When personal selling should be a major part of the communications mix

In view of the role and the advantages and disadvantages of personal selling, when should it be a major part of the communications mix? Table 14.2 indicates some key factors using advertising as a comparison.

The following is not an exhaustive list, but is presented as a means of considering some of the important issues: complexity, network factors, buyer significance and communications effectiveness.

Table 14.2 When selling is a major element of the communications mix

	Advertising relatively important	Personal selling relatively important
Number of customers	Large	Small
Buyers' information needs	Low	High
Size and importance of purchase	Small	Large
Post-purchase service required	Little	A lot
Product complexity	Low	High
Distribution strategy	Pull	Push
Pricing policy	Set	Negotiate
Web-enabled communications and exchanges	High	Low
Resources available for promotion	Many	Few

Source: Adapted from Cravens (1987).

Complexity

Personal selling is very important when there is a medium to high level of relationship complexity. Such complexity may be associated either with the physical characteristics of the product, such as computer software design, or with the environment in which the negotiations are taking place. For example, decisions related to the installation of products designed to automate an assembly line may well be a sensitive issue. This may be due to management's attitude towards the operators currently undertaking the work that the automation is expected to replace.

When the complexity of the offering is high, advertising and public relations cannot always convey benefits in the same way as personal selling. Personal selling allows the product to be demonstrated so that buyers can see and, if necessary, touch and taste it for themselves. Personal selling also allows explanations to be made about particular points that are of concern to the buyer or about the environment in which the buyer wishes to use the product.

Buyer significance

The significance of the product to the buyers in the target market is a very important factor in the decision on whether to use personal selling. Significance can be measured as a form of risk, and risk is associated with benefits and costs.

The absolute cost to the buyer will vary from organisation to organisation and from consumer to consumer. The significance of the purchase of an extra photocopier for a major multinational organisation may be low, but for a new start-up organisation or for an established organisation experiencing a dramatic turnaround, an extra photocopying machine may be highly significant and subject to high levels of resistance by a number of different internal stakeholders.

Communications effectiveness

There may be a number of ways to satisfy the communications objectives of a campaign, other than by using personal selling. Each of the other communications tools has strengths and weaknesses; consequently differing mixes provide different benefits. Have they all been considered?

One of the main reasons for using personal selling occurs when advertising alone, or any other medium, provides insufficient communications. The main reason for this inadequacy surfaces when advertising media cannot provide buyers with the information they require to make their decision. For example, someone buying a new car may well observe and read various magazine and newspaper advertisements through which an emotional disposition towards a brand might be created. Then people go online and look at detailed information and comparison tests. The decision to buy, however, requires information and data upon which a balanced decision can be made. The rationality and emotional elements are brought together through experience of the car, through a test drive perhaps.

The decision to buy a car normally evokes high involvement, therefore car manu-facturers try to provide a rich balance of emotional and factual information in their literature. From this perspective buyers seek further information at the website and seek experience and reassurance at a dealership. Car buyers sign orders with the presence and encouragement of salespersons. Very few cars are bought on a mail order basis, although some, mainly used cars, are bought online.

Personal selling provides a number of characteristics that make it more effective than the other elements of the mix. As discussed, in B2B marketing the complexity of many products requires salespeople to be able to discuss with clients their specific needs; in other words, to be able to talk in the customer's own language, to build source cred-ibility through expertise and hopefully trustworthiness, and build a relationship that corresponds with the psychographic profile of each member of the decision-making unit (DMU). In this case, mass communications would be inappropriate.

Channel network factors

When the number of members in a network is limited, the use of a sales force is advis-able, as advertising is inefficient. Furthermore, the opportunity to build a close collabora-tive relationship with members may enable the development of a sustainable competitive advantage.

There are two further factors that influence the decision to use personal selling as part of the communications mix. When the customer base is small and dispersed across a wide geographic area it makes economic sense to use salespersons, as advertising in this situation is inadequate and ineffective.

Personal selling is the most expensive element of the communications mix. It may be that other elements of the mix may provide a more cost-effective way of delivering the message.

The role of social media in personal selling

One way in which the high costs of personal selling can be moderated is by incorporating interactive media, and social media in particular. Figure 14.2 demonstrates how social media have evolved within personal selling.

There is general agreement that a salesperson's selling behaviours are important when building a buyer's trust. There are ramifications in terms of longer-term sales perfor-mance and customer loyalty. This means that the development of relationship marketing

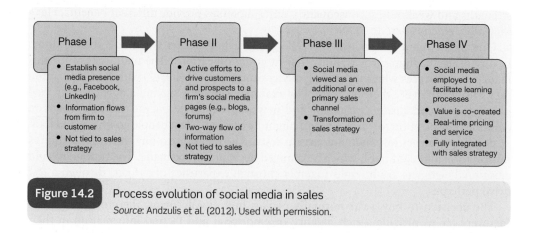

Figure 14.2   Process evolution of social media in sales

Source: Andzulis et al. (2012). Used with permission.

skills through the use of a customer-oriented selling approach by salespeople is critical if sales performance and customer loyalty targets are to be achieved (Chakrabarty et al., 2013).

One of the key points that Andzulis et al. (2012) make is that social media have a distinct role to play within each step of the sales process. These steps, or sales interactions, from understanding the customer, the approach, needs discovery, presentation, close and follow-up, require a particular set of skills and abilities. The implications for each of these stages in the selling process are set out in Table 14.3.

To fully investigate these ideas interested readers are directed to Scholars' paper 14.4 and to access the paper in their own time.

Table 14.3 Potential role of social media in the sales process

Step in the Sales Process/ Behaviors	Role of Social Media	Social Media Categories*
Understanding the Customer		1/2/4
Knowledge gathering	Creating/joining/participating in field-specific LinkedIn groups.	
Prospecting	Monitoring comments to understand how message is perceived, or what other information is wanted (Johnson & Johnson).	
Lead generation	Company product blogs with active comment monitoring and question feedback. Allowing open membership to generate future client list.	
Determining communication styles	Establishing a Twitter presence.	
Identifying risks/buying situation	Monitoring comments to understand attitudes toward purchasing and buying preferences.	
Approaching the Customer	Posting news stories on Facebook.	4
Establishing credibility	Facebook promotions inviting participation in new product testing (Chick-fil-A), or sharing stories about community involvement and fun activities that build brand.	

Continued

Step in the Sales Process/ Behaviors	Role of Social Media	Social Media Categories*
Gaining attention	LinkedIn surveys and polls to generate industry discussion about relevant topics.	
Rapport building	Tweeting about conferences/results/innovation.	
Needs Discovery	Tweeting to solicit customer/competitor feedback.	1/2/4
Questioning	Creating an app to solicit customer product and service ideas (My Starbucks Idea).	
Listening	Generating blog posts designed specifically to ignite conversation or debate.	
Understanding motives	Asking Facebook fans to vote in polls or comment on proposed changes to products, services, or logos.	
Presentation	Chatter to collaborate with customers on proposals and campaigns.	1/2/3/4
Demonstrating value propositions	Sharing success stories via Facebook.	
Prescribing a solution	YouTube channel to provide information to customers.	
Using visual aids/ demonstrations	Tweeting about price specials, coupons, loyalty rewards, or contests.	
Close	Facebook or Twitter to drive clients to sales channels. Chatter to work one-on-one to resolve deal inhibitors. Blogs or LinkedIn to address issues raised by competitors or unhappy clients.	4
Asking for the sale	Tweets to VIP clientele to sell special concert or sports event seating.	
Overcoming objections	Sharing success stories via LinkedIn or Facebook posts.	
Negotiation	Blogs to address issues raised about products or services. Facebook posts to ask for donations.	
Service and Follow-Up	Following customers on Twitter. Mining their fans and followers for prospects.	1/2/3/4
Communication	Tweets to announce sales goals, product success, new products. Facebook promotions and rewards for referring friends or asking them to like/follow your posts.	
Gaining referrals	LinkedIn and Facebook to ask for referrals.	
Determining future sales opportunities	Tweeting to communicate success stories.	

*Categories stem from the typology developed by Kaplan and Haenlein (2010): 1 = Collaborative projects: Collaborative projects enable the joint and simultaneous creation of content by many end users. 2 = Blogs: Blogs are special types of Web sites that usually display date-stamped entries in reverse chronological order. 3 = Content communities: The main objective of content communities is the sharing of media content between users. 4 = Social networking sites: Social networking sites are applications that enable users to connect by creating personal information profiles, inviting friends and colleagues to have access to those profiles, and sending e-mails and instant messages between each other. 5 = Virtual game worlds: Virtual worlds are platforms that replicate a three-dimensional environment in which users can appear in the form of personalized avatars and interact with each other as they would in real life. 6 = Virtual social worlds: The second group of virtual worlds, often referred to as virtual social worlds, allows inhabitants to choose their behavior more freely and essentially live a virtual life similar to their real life.

Source: Andzulis et al. (2012). Used with permission.

Scholars' paper 14.4 | The role of social media in the sales process

Andzulis, J.M., Panagopoulos, N.G. and Rapp, A. (2012) A review of social media and implications for the sales process, *Journal of Personal Selling & Sales Management*, XXXII(3), 305–16.

This paper, despite being written in 2010/11 before publication in 2012, provides an interesting and very readable review of the role of social media in the sales force and the sales process. The authors provide definitions of social media and consider the role and importance of social media in business.

Strategic account management

One of the major issues concerning the development and maintenance of inter-organisational relationships is the method by which very important and/or valuable customers are managed. Two main forms are considered here in turn, key account management and the emerging global account management disciplines.

Key account management

The increasing complexity of both markets and products, combined with the trends towards purchasing centralisation and industrial concentration, mean that a small number of significant accounts have become essential for the survival of many organisations. The growth in the significance of key account management (KAM) is expected to continue and one of the results will be the change in expectations of buyers and sellers, in particular the demand for higher levels of expertise, integration and professionalism of sales forces.

It has long been recognised that particular customer accounts represent an important, often large, proportion of turnover. Such accounts have been referred to variously as national accounts, house accounts, major accounts and key accounts. Millman and Wilson (1995) argue that the first three are sales-oriented, tend to the short term and are often only driven by sales management needs. However, Ojasalo (2001) sees little difference in the terminology KAM, national account marketing (NAM) and strategic account management (SAM).

Key accounts may be of different sizes in comparison to the focus organisation, but what delineates them from other types of 'account' is that they are strategically important. Key accounts are customers who, in a B2B market, are willing to enter into collaborative exchanges and who are strategically important to the focus organisation.

There are two primary issues that arise. The first is that both parties perceive relational exchanges as a necessary component and that the relationship is long term. The second aspect refers to the strategic issue. The key account is strategically important because it might offer opportunities for entry to new markets, represent access to other key organisations or resources, or provide symbolic value in terms of influence, power and stature.

The importance of the long-term relationship as a prime element of key account identification raises questions about how they are developed, what resources are required to manage and sustain them, and what long-term success and effectiveness results from identifying them.

In many ways KAM programmes are a means to reduce the various complexities and uncertainties that arise from the external and internal forces acting on both the selling and buying organisations. Brehmer and Rehme (2009) deduce that KAM-oriented complexity can be considered across two dimensions. The first is structural complexity, which is concerned with the number, location and geographical dispersion of a customer's units. The second is operational complexity, and concern here is focused on the variety of product lines, services, systems, fulfilment facilities and commercial solutions.

There are three forms of uncertainties experienced by buyers according to Håkansson et al. (1977). These are *need uncertainty*, which concerns levels of demand, and whether increased interaction might increase or decrease the level of uncertainty. *Market uncertainty* concerns suppliers and perceptions of instability and the assumptions upon which decisions are made. The third element is *transaction uncertainty*, which is related to the physical transfer of products from supplier to buyer.

A primary goal of KAM programmes should therefore be one of reducing a buyer's uncertainties by coordinating an offer according to the prevailing complexities. To do this Brehmer and Rehme (2009) formulate a grid which they refer to as the 'Sales complexity management matrix' (see Figure 14.3).

By focusing on the operational and structural complexities experienced by organisations, KAM programmes can be formulated to meet the coordination needs of buyers.

In order for these coordination activities to be designed and implemented a decision about who in the organisation should be responsible for these key accounts needs to be made. Generally speaking, there are three main responses: to assign sales executives, to create a key account division or to create a key account sales force (see Table 14.4).

The assignment of sales executives to these important accounts is common in smaller organisations. Those organisations that have the resources are able to incorporate the services of senior executives, who assume this role and bring to it the flexibility and responsive service that are required as the account grows in stature. They can make decisions about stock, price, distribution and levels of customisation.

These accounts may be major or national accounts, as very often their strategic significance is not recognised. There is a tendency for these accounts to receive a disproportionate level of attention, as the executives responsible for these major customers lose sight of their own organisation's marketing strategy.

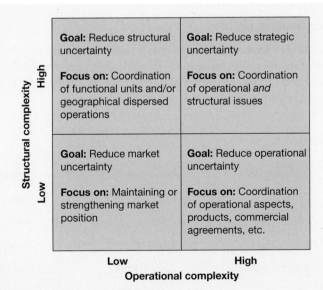

Figure 14.3   The sales complexity management matrix
Source: Brehmer and Rehme (2009). Used with permission.

Table 14.4 Three ways of managing key accounts

KAM management	Explanation
Assigning sales executives	Common in smaller organisations that do not have large resources. Normally undertaken by senior executives who have the flexibility and can provide the responsive service often required. They can make decisions about stock, price, distribution and levels of customisation. There is a tendency for key accounts to receive a disproportionate level of attention, as the executives responsible for these major customers lose sight of their own organisation's marketing strategy.
Creating a key account division	The main advantage of this approach is that it offers close integration of production, finance, marketing and sales. The main disadvantage is that resources are duplicated and the organisation can become very inefficient. It is also a high-risk strategy, as the entire division is dependent upon a few customers.
Creating a key account sales force	This is adopted by organisations that want to differentiate through service and they use their most experienced and able salespersons and provide them with a career channel. Administratively, this structure is inefficient, as there is a level of duplication similar to that found in the customer-type structure discussed earlier. Furthermore, commission payable on these accounts is often a source of discontent, both for those within the key account sales force and for those aspiring to join the select group.

A further way of managing these accounts is to create a key account division. The main advantage of this approach is that it offers close integration of production, finance, marketing and sales. The main disadvantage is that resources are duplicated and the organisation can become very inefficient. It is also a high-risk strategy as the entire division is dependent upon a few customers.

Should a key account sales force be preferred then issues concerning the management of this resource arise. Key account managers require particular skills, as, indeed, do the executives themselves.

Key account relationship cycles

A number of researchers have attempted to gain a greater understanding of KAM by considering the development cycles through which relationships move. Millman and Wilson offer the work of Ford (1980), Dwyer et al. (1987) and Wotruba (1991) as examples of such development cycles (see Table 14.5).

Table 14.5 Comparison of relational models

Ford (1980), Dwyer et al. (1987)	Wotruba (1991)	Millman and Wilson (1995)	McDonald (2000)
Pre-relationship awareness	Provider	Pre-KAM	Exploratory
Early stage exploration	Persuader	Early KAM	Basic
Development stage expansion	Prospector	Mid-KAM	Cooperative
Long-term stage commitment	Problem solver	Partnership KAM	Interdependent
Final stage institutionalisation	Procreator	Synergistic KAM	Integrated
		Uncoupling KAM	Disintegrated

Source: Updated from Millman and Wilson (1995). Used with kind permission of Emerald Group Publishing Limited.

Millman and Wilson have attempted to build on the work of the others (included in Table 14.5) and have formulated a model that incorporates their own research as well as that established in the literature. McDonald (2000) has since elaborated on their framework, providing further insight and explanation.

The cycle develops with the *exploratory KAM* level, where the main task is to identify those accounts that have key account potential, and those that do not, in order that resources can be allocated efficiently. Both organisations are considering each other: the buyer in terms of the supplier's offer in terms of its ability to match the buyer's own requirements; and the seller in terms of the buyer providing sufficient volumes, value and financial suitability.

The next level is *basic KAM*, where both organisations enter into a transactional period, essentially testing each other as potential long-term partners. Some relationships may stabilise at this level while others may develop as a result of the seller seeking and gaining tentative agreement with prospective accounts about whether they would become 'preferred accounts'.

At the *cooperative KAM* level, more people from both organisations are involved in communications. At the basic KAM level, both parties understand each other and, through experience, the selling company has established its credentials with the buying organisation. At this next level, opportunities to add value to the relationship are considered. This could be encouraged by increasing the range of products and services transacted, thereby involving more people in the relationship.

At the *interdependent KAM* level of a relationship both organisations recognise the importance of the other to their operations, with the supplier either first-choice, or only, supplier. Retraction from the relationship is now problematic as 'inertia and strategic suitability', as McDonald phrases it, holds the partners together.

Integrated KAM is achieved when the two organisations view the relationship as consisting of one entity where they create synergistic value in the marketplace. Joint problem solving and the sharing of sensitive information are strong characteristics of the relationship and withdrawal by either party can be traumatic at a personal level for the participants involved, let alone at the organisational level.

The final level is *disintegrating KAM*. This can occur at any time for a variety of reasons, ranging from company takeover to the introduction of new technology. The relationship may return to another, lower level and new terms of business are established. The termination, or readjustment, of the relationship need not be seen as a negative factor as both parties may decide that the relationship holds no further value.

McDonald develops Millman and Wilson's model by moving away from a purely sequential framework. He suggests that organisations may stabilise or enter the model at any level; indeed, he states that organisations might readjust to a lower level. The time between phases will vary according to the nature and circumstances of the parties involved. The labels provided by McDonald reflect the relationship status of both parties rather than of the selling company (e.g. prospective) or buying company (e.g. preferred supplier). While the Millman and Wilson and McDonald interpretations of the KAM relationship cycle provide insight they are both primarily dyadic perspectives. They neglect to consider the influence of significant others, in particular those other network member organisations that provide context and interaction in particular networks and that do influence the actions of organisations and those key individuals who are strategic decision-makers.

Some final aspects of KAM

In mature and competitive markets, where there is little differentiation between the products, service may be the only source of sustainable competitive advantage. KAM allows senior sales executives to build a strong relationship with each of their customers, thereby providing a very high level of service and strong point of differentiation.

In order to accomplish such strong relationships, however, it is critical that suppliers strengthen their overall orientation towards the target key account. Tzempelikosa and Gounaris (2013) argue that this also implies that suppliers should monitor their internal processes and behaviours in order to improve KAM relationships.

The development and management of key accounts is complex and evolving. Key account relationships are rarely static and should be rooted within corporate strategy, if only because of the implications for resources, which customers seek as a result of partnering in this way (Spencer, 1999). Key account relationships can generate positive financial value but not without considerable management effort (Kalwani and Narayanas, 1995; Ryals and Holt, 2007). Consideration of customer profitability appears to be the foundation for successful key account relationships.

Global account management

The development of KAM approaches highlighted the strategic importance that some customers represent to organisations. KAM represents an attempt to meet the needs of these customers in a customised and personal way. However, there are many organisations whose customers are located in many different countries, regions and even on different continents, and the management of their needs demands different skills and resources from those adopted for KAM. The management of these customers is referred to as global account management (GAM) and in many ways is evidence of a new strategic approach to business development and marketing management in B2B organisations.

Understanding the nature of GAM is helped by Hennessey and Jeannet (2003: 1), who provide a useful definition:

Global accounts are large companies that operate in multiple countries, often on two or more continents, are strategically important to the supplier and have some form of coordinated purchasing across different countries.

One of the characteristics of global accounts is that their decision-making units are influenced through inputs from various geographical locations. Wilson et al. (2000) highlight the important characteristics associated with the strategic coordination associated with GAM. To them, a strategic global account is characterised as representing a major part of a supplier's corporate objectives and where the account expects the supplier to offer an integrated global product service offering.

Scholars' paper 14.5   Looking after the global accounts

Capon, N. and Senn, C. (2010) Global customer management programs: how to make them really work, *California Management Review*, 52(2), 32–55.

This paper considers the issues and characteristics associated with successful global account management programmes. The authors track the transformation from what was regarded as low-level purchasing, and is now high-status procurement. This involves the use of greater intellectual capital and sophisticated systems and processes that are designed to improve performance. They model the process and advise on the best approach from a managerial perspective.

It would therefore be a mistake to think that KAM and GAM are the same. Indeed, Birkinshaw (2003) makes the point that global and key accounts are not identical. He argues that the roots of GAM are to be found in supply chain management, unlike KAM, which has been influenced by the sales management perspective. Hennessey and Jeannet (2003) believe that national account managers are relationship managers, whereas global account managers have a greater focus on strategic issues and coordination of personnel in different countries. Millman and Wilson (1998) refer to the importance and significance of cultural diversity and organisational issues when adopting a GAM programme.

Wilson et al. (2000) consider how global account programmes can be delivered. They identified the need for three main global competences:

- a coordinated, globally competent supply chain;
- management of the interaction process *within* the supplying company, particularly the information and communications flows;
- the establishment of a forum, with the customer, of a collaborative design process.

This suggests that relationship management skills, in particular the use of interaction and collaboration to develop dialogue, are critical factors associated with GAM. Wilson et al. (2000) identify many competences that are necessary for GAM to be successful, ranging from strong communications and relationship management skills through cultural empathy and business and financial acumen. However, they make the point that global account managers need strong political skills, especially in view of the fact that they often operate without direct authority, particularly with regard to resources and processes. They refer to this role as 'political entrepreneur'.

Understanding the nature of GAM, its management and indeed associated research are at an early stage as the discipline is very young. Early work in the area suggests that there is no fixed strategic model that represents GAM, if only because GAM needs to be flexible and dynamic as engagement with key global customers evolves.

Key points

- Direct marketing is a tool of marketing communications used to create and sustain personal and intermediary-free communications with customers, potential customers and other significant stakeholders.

- It is concerned with the management of customer behaviour and is used to complement the strengths and weaknesses of the other communications disciplines.

- Four main forms of direct marketing can be identified: as a complementary tool, a primary differentiator, as a sales channel and as a brand vehicle.

- There have been three essential drivers behind the surge in direct marketing: technological advances; changing buyer lifestyles and expectations; and organisational expectations.

- Databases and Big Data play a central role as storage, sorting and administrative devices to assist strategy formulation, cross-selling, plus direct and personalised communications.

- Permission marketing (PM) occurs when consumers give their explicit permission for marketers to send them various types of promotional messages.

- Direct mail, telemarketing and door-to-door activities are the main offline forms of direct-response media, as they allow more personal, direct and evaluative means of reaching precisely targeted customers. Internet and online-based direct work encompasses email, video, mobile and affiliate marketing as forms of direct linking.

- Personal selling activities can be observed at various stages in the buying process of both the consumer and business-to-business (B2B) markets.

- Personal selling can be considered in terms of four different tasks: order takers, order getters, order collectors and order supporters.

- Some of the issues associated with the deployment of personal selling include: complexity, network factors, buyer significance and communications effectiveness.

- Key account management (KAM) programmes are a means of reducing the various complexities and uncertainties that arise from the external and internal forces that act on both selling and buying organisations.

- The key account relationship cycle encompasses: exploratory KAM, basic KAM, cooperative KAM, interdependent KAM and integrated KAM.

Review questions

Everest case questions

1. Identify the key success factors underpinning the Everest campaign featured at the beginning of this chapter.

2. Explain how the use of rational and emotional benefits in their advertising helps Everest in their direct marketing.

3. Identify the different types of direct marketing used by Everest.

4. Why does direct mail continue to have a strong role to play in the direct marketing activities of Everest?

5. Why might Everest be concerned about permission marketing?

General questions

1. Write brief notes explaining the reasons why usage of direct marketing has grown in recent years.

2. Which industries might use personal selling as a primary element of their marketing communications mix?

3. What are the different types of personal selling and what are the tasks that salespeople are normally expected to accomplish?

4. Describe the role of personal selling and identify the main difference between house or major accounts, key accounts and global account management.

5. Explain the concept of key account relationship cycles using the McDonald (2000) framework.

References

Andzulis, J.M., Panagopoulos, N.G. and Rapp, A. (2012) A review of social media and implications for the sales process, *Journal of Personal Selling & Sales Management*, XXXII(3), 305–16.

Anon (2013) B2B AWARDS: State Street, 27 September 2013, retrieved 10 January 2015 from www.b2bmarketing.net/resources/awards-2013-category-2-state-street.

Anon (2014a) Power paper – how simple mailing drove brilliant response, *IPC*, January, retrieved 10 February 2015 from www.ipc.be/en/Reports%20library/Publications/Case-studies/DIRECT%20MAIL_Case_19_Power_Paper.

Anon (2014b) Case study: Philips Lighting sales team saves 2,500 hours per month, *B2BMarketing*, 23 October, retrieved 24 March 2015 from www.b2bmarketing.net/knowledgebank/crm-marketing/case-studies/case-study-philips-lighting-sales-team-saves-2500-hours-mon.

Anon (2015) Knowledge point: using direct marketing to build brand values, *Millward Brown*, retrieved 23 March 2015 from www.millwardbrown.com/docs/default-source/insight-documents/knowledge-points/MillwardBrown_KnowledgePoint_DirectMarketing.pdf.

Benady, D. (2014) Mastering the 'dark art' of direct response 2.0, *Campaign*, 6 March, retrieved 31 May 2015 from www.campaignlive.co.uk/news/1283202/.

Birkinshaw, J.M. (2003) *The Blackwell Handbook of Global Management*, Boston, MA: Blackwell.

Brehmer, P.O. and Rehme, J. (2009) Proactive and reactive: drivers for key account management programmes, *European Journal of Marketing*, 43(7/8), 961–84.

Capon, N. and Senn, C. (2010) Global customer management programs: how to make them really work, *California Management Review*, 52(2), 32–55.

Chakrabarty, S., Brown, G. and Widing II, R.E. (2013) Distinguishing between the roles of customer-oriented selling and adaptive selling in managing dysfunctional conflict in buyer–seller relationships, *Journal of Personal Selling & Sales Management*, XXXIII(3), 245–60.

Cravens, D.W. (1987) *Strategic Marketing*, Homewood, IL: Irwin.

Dolnicar, S. and Jordaan, Y. (2007) A market-orientated approach to responsibly managing information privacy concerns in direct marketing, *Journal of Advertising*, 36(2), 123–49.

Dwyer, F.R., Shurr, P.H. and Oh, S. (1987) Developing buyer–seller relationships, *Journal of Marketing*, 51(2), 11–28.

Fernandez, J. (2010) National Trust uses DM for Welsh coastline appeal, *Marketing Week*, 10 August, retrieved 12 August 2010 from www.marketingweek.co.uk/sectors/not-for-profit/national-trust-uses-dm-for-welsh-coastline-appeal/3016859.article.

Ford, I.D. (1980) The development of buyer–seller relationships in industrial markets, *European Journal of Marketing*, 14(5/6), 339–53.

Ganesan, S. (1994) Determinants of long-term orientation in buyer–seller relationships, *Journal of Marketing*, 58 (April), 1–19.

Godin, S. (1999) Permission Marketing: Turning Strangers into Friends, and Friends into Customers, New York: Simon & Schuster.

Gomez, L. and Hlavinka, K. (2007) The total package: loyalty marketing in the world of consumer packaged goods (CPG), *Journal of Consumer Marketing*, 24(1), 48–56.

Goodwin, C. (1991) Privacy: recognition of a consumer right, *Journal of Public Policy and Marketing*, 10(1), 149–66.

Guenzi, P. (2002) Sales force activities and customer trust, *Journal of Marketing Management*, 18, 749–78.

Håkansson, H., Johansson, J. and Wootz, B. (1977) Influence tactics in buyer-seller processes, *Journal of Marketing Management*, 5(6), 319–32.

Hamwi, G.A., Rutherford, B.N., Barksdale, Jr H.C. and Johnson, J.T. (2013) Ideal versus actual number of sales calls: an application of disconfirmation theory, *Journal of Personal Selling & Sales Management*, XXXIII(3), 307–18.

Hennessey, D.H. and Jeannet, J.-P. (2003) *Global Account Management: Creating Value*, Chichester: Wiley.

Joseph, S. (2014) Government pushes for simpler rules to swiftly punish nuisance marketers, *Marketing Week*, 27 October, retrieved 23 March 2015 from www.marketingweek.com/2014/10/27/government-pushes-for-simpler-rules-to-swiftly-punish-nuisance-marketers/.

Kalwani, M.U. and Narayanas, N. (1995) Long-term manufacturer-supplier relationships: do they pay off supplier firms? *Journal of Marketing*, 59(1), 1–16.

Kamakura, W.A., Wedel, M., de Rosa, F. and Mazzon, J.A. (2003) Cross-selling through database marketing: a mixed factor analyzer for data augmentation and prediction, *International Journal of Research in Marketing,* 20(1), 45–65.

Kaplan, A. and Haenlein, M. (2010) Users of the world, unite! The challenges and opportunities of social media, *Business Horizons,* 53(1), 59–68.

Kent, R. and Brandal, H. (2003) Improving email response in a permission marketing context, *International Journal of Market Research,* 45(4), 489–503.

Krishnamurthy, S. (2001) A comprehensive analysis of permission marketing, *Journal of Computer-Mediated Communications,* 6(2), retrieved 8 March 2008 from www.jcmc.indiana.edu/vol6/issue2/krishnamurthy.html.

Kuechler, W. (2007) Business applications of unstructured text, *Communications of the ACM,* 50(10), 86–93.

McDonald, M. (2000) Key account management: a domain review, *Marketing Review,* 1, 15–34.

Millman, T. and Wilson, K. (1995) From key account selling to key account management, *Journal of Marketing Practice: Applied Marketing Science,* 1(1), 9–21.

Millman, T. and Wilson, K. (1998) Global account management: reconciling organisational complexity and cultural diversity, in *The 14th Annual Industrial Marketing and Purchasing (IMP) Group Conference,* Turku School of Economics and Business Administration.

Millward, S. (2014) 7 awesome QR code marketing campaigns, *TechinAsia,* 19 July, retrieved 8 January 2015 from www.techinasia.com/7-awesome-qr-code-marketing-campaigns/.

Newman, N. (2014) How big data enables economic harm to consumers, especially to low-income and other vulnerable sectors of the population, *Journal of Internet Law,* 18(6), 11–23.

Nunan, D. and Di Domenico, M.L. (2013) Market research and the ethics of big data, *International Journal of Market Research,* 55(4), 505–20.

Ojasalo, J. (2001) Key account management at company and individual levels in business-to-business relationships, *Journal of Business and Industrial Marketing,* 16(3), 199–220.

Parsons, R. (2013) Is it time to rebrand direct marketing? *Marketing Week,* 12 August, retrieved 22 January 2015 from www.marketingweek.com/2013/08/12/is-it-time-to-rebrand-direct-marketing-2/.

Rafaeli, A., Ziklik, L. and Doucet, L. (2008) The impact of call center employees' customer orientation behaviors on service quality, *Journal of Service Research,* 10(3), 239–55.

Reid, A., Pullins, E.B. and Plank, R.E. (2002) The impact of purchase situation on sales-person communication behaviors in business markets, *Industrial Marketing Management,* 31(3), 205–13.

Rhee, E. (2010) Multi-channel management in direct marketing retailing: traditional call center versus Internet channel, *Database Marketing & Customer Strategy Management,* 17(2), 70–7.

Ryals, L.J. and Holt, S. (2007) Creating and capturing value in KAM relationships, *Journal of Strategic Marketing,* 15 (December), 403–20.

Scovotti, C. and Spiller, L.D. (2006) Revisiting the conceptual definition of direct marketing: perspectives from practitioners and scholars, *The Marketing Management Journal,* 16(2), 188–202.

Serviere-Munoz, L. and Mallin, M.L. (2013) How do unethical salespeople sleep at night? The role of neutralizations in the justification of unethical sales intentions, *Journal of Personal Selling & Sales Management,* XXXIII(3), 289–306.

Shannahan, R.J., Bush, A.J., Moncrief, W.C. and Shannahan, K.L.J. (2013) Making sense of the customer's role in the personal selling process: a theory of organizing and sensemaking perspective, *Journal of Personal Selling & Sales Management,* XXXIII(3), 261–75.

Smith, J.W. (2004) Permission is not enough: empowerment and reciprocity must be included, too, *Marketing Management,* 13(3), 52.

Spencer, R. (1999) Key accounts: effectively managing strategic complexity, *Journal of Business and Industrial Marketing,* 14(4), 291–310.

State Street (2012) Empowering boutiques, October, retrieved 10 January 2015 from www.statestreet.com/wps/wcm/connect/7e0bf8804cb867e9882bfc0e57cceb49/1214347_VF_Boutiques_FNL.pdf?MOD=AJPERES&CONVERT_TO=url&CACHEID=7e0bf8804cb867e9882bfc0e57cceb49.

Thayer, L. (1968) *Communication and Communication Systems,* Homewood, IL: Irwin.

Tzempelikosa, N. and Gounaris, S. (2013) Approaching key account management from a long-term perspective, *Journal of Strategic Marketing,* 21(2), 179–98.

Wilson, K., Croom, S., Millman, T. and Weilbaker, D.C. (2000) *Global Account Management Study Report,* Southampton: The Sales Research Trust.

Wotruba, T.R. (1991) The evolution of personal selling, *Journal of Personal Selling and Sales Management,* 11(3), 1–12.

Chapter 15

Sales promotion, field marketing and brand experience

By adding value to an offer and hoping to bring forward future sales, sales promotion techniques can be a source of advantage, one that has a short, rather than a long-run, orientation.

The way brands are presented and displayed, including packaging and in-store shelf management, can influence customer perception, sales volumes and market share. A key aspect of marketing communications, therefore, especially in grocery markets, is field marketing, which includes merchandising.

Enabling consumers to experience brands is often necessary to support sales promotions, as well as to help a brand cut through the clutter of competitive and distracting messages.

Aims and learning objectives

The aims of this chapter are to consider the role and techniques of sales promotion and field marketing and to appraise their contributions to the marketing communications mix.

The learning objectives are to enable readers to:

1. understand the value and the role of sales promotions;
2. discuss the ways in which sales promotion is thought to work;
3. evaluate the merits of loyalty and retention programmes;
4. explain the different sales promotion methods and techniques;
5. explore ideas associated with field marketing and related activities.
6. describe the principles associated with brand experience.

Lucozade Sport Conditions Zone

Since 2013, the UK Sports drinks category has started to grow. This has been driven predominantly by Lucozade Sport, which is the clear market leader in the Sports drink category with 67 per cent market share. Powerade is its nearest competitor.

The 2014 FIFA World Cup finals gave Lucozade Sport the perfect platform to communicate to its target audience in an innovative, immersive and credible way.

TRO and the integrated agency team were set the challenge of making Lucozade Sport 'the most talked about sports drink' during the football World Cup. With no sponsorship rights, the mission was to leverage cultural and sporting momentum, and to drive 'talkability' of the tournament. The key objective of the campaign was to create a World Cup-relevant experiential event with science at the heart, bringing to life the claim that Lucozade Sport 'Enhances Hydration, Fuels Performance'.

In order to address the target audience of 'driven winner' sports participants, Lucozade Sports team of agencies delivered a fully integrated campaign. At its heart was an experiential marketing, devised to create dynamic and credible content. The idea and execution had to be bold and relevant to gain cut-through, at a time when many brands would be competing for share of voice, and, crucially, to resonate with the target audience.

With the 2014 World Cup being hosted in Brazil, and England's opening game taking place in Manaus – with average conditions of 32°C and 76 per cent humidity – Lucozade Sport had the unique opportunity to drive the conversation around the importance of fuel and hydration.

TRO, a leading experiential marketing agency, created the 'Lucozade Sport Conditions Zone' – a bespoke, state-of-the-art immersive experience in London's Canary Wharf – offering grassroots footballers the chance to play 5-a-side football in the same extreme conditions as England's opening World Cup game in Manaus, Brazil.

The agency team were confident the extreme conditions would be high on the media agenda, so they replicated those conditions by designing and building a venue with the 'wow' factor for all consumers and media who attended. The Conditions Zone was situated in Canary Wharf for three weeks throughout June 2014, and received over 4,000 visitors. The bespoke structure housed a heated football pitch in an enclosed space (maintained at 32°C and 76 per cent humidity), and included a registration area, changing rooms, science lab and media hub (in a cooled environment).

Buzz and excitement for the Conditions Zone and Lucozade Sport was created through a multichannel integrated communications strategy that used all channels to deliver effectiveness at grassroots, social, digital and traditional media, PR as well as paid for media. From the pre-launch activity through to media launch day, the Conditions Zone developed a huge momentum of its own.

Exhibit 15.1   **The Lucozade Conditions Zone**
Source: TRO Group.

Footballing legends and Lucozade Sport brand ambassadors Steven Gerrard, Alan Shearer, John Barnes and Steve McManaman were used to help raise awareness of the event and the campaign. Steven Gerrard featured in a pre-promotional video distributed virally. Alan Shearer was the main spokesperson available for media interviews on the launch day. He also played in an exhibition match for the press with John Barnes and Steve McManaman.

Interested players were encouraged to register via a microsite which included a thorough screening and medical questionnaire. Due to the success of the pre-promotion, all the player spots were booked out within two days.

Content generated from the launch day and experience itself gained traction through both paid and earned media. Social amplification touch points were built seamlessly into the experience to ensure optimum user-generated content.

The Conditions Zone involved a 2.5-hour experience with education around Lucozade Sport's hydration properties at its core, hosted by an MSc qualified Sport Scientist.

Before playing, participants entered The Laboratory to have their key statistics recorded (resting heart rate, core body temperature and weight) and a urine test to ensure satisfactory hydration levels. Players were fitted with STATSport kit, used by the England Football Team, to monitor heart rates and track distance covered via GPS. Then the Sports Scientist took players through a presentation educating them on the science behind fuel and hydration.

The FA regulations-sized 3G 5-a-side pitch was housed within a heat and humidity-controlled chamber – and dramatically brought-to-life the Manaus conditions. A 50-minute match ensued with key stats delivered in real-time and displayed on screens throughout. Chilled bottles of Lucozade Sport were provided, and players were encouraged to hydrate and measure how much they drank.

Post-match players went into The Comparison Zone where they were weighed to ascertain how much sweat they had lost – in some cases up to 2 litres! NFC (Near Field Communications) throughout the experience ensured everything integrated seamlessly with Facebook and allowed players to compare and share their statistics. On leaving the experience each player was given Lucozade Sport to ensure they continued to rehydrate on their journey home.

If penetration is driven by fame, the Conditions Zone delivered in spades. The Conditions Zone created massive excitement amongst the media with broadcast coverage on *Good Morning Britain*, *ITV News*, BBC Radio 5 Live, *Sky Sunrise* and a 5-minute segment on *BBC Breakfast*. In total, it received 114 pieces of UK media coverage, including every national newspaper, generating 30 million+ PR reach. Social activity generated 7.5 million in additional reach and over 32 million impressions. Places at the Conditions Zone sold out in just two days with over 3,300 individuals registered to play, including media. Online content engaged the nation, delivering over 1.75 million views; 80 per cent of participants agreed that 'Lucozade Sport helped me to perform at my best',

Exhibit 15.2   **A typical piece of PR for Lucozade Sport following the launch of the Conditions Zone**
Source: TRO Group.

while 71 per cent of participants said the experience increased their likelihood to purchase Lucozade Sport products in the next 3 months. The campaign helped Lucozade achieve a record summer contributing to a 12 per cent rise in sales.

The Lucozade Sport Conditions Zone was created to dramatise the extreme conditions that England faced at the World Cup. It gave Lucozade Sport a credible and relevant story to talk about during a time when many other brands were competing for share of voice.

This case was written by Sarah Mayo, Brand and Business Development Director at TRO

Questions relating to this case can be found at the end of the chapter.

Introduction

The association that Lucozade forged with the 2014 football World Cup, described in the preceding case, shows how the brand has immersed itself with both the media and its target audience. This was achieved without overt advertising or blatant offers, but through the players' experience at the Conditions Zone. This brand experience approach has become a popular way of developing brands, and their relationships with customers, and is explored later in this chapter.

Lucozade also uses sales promotion. The main task of sales promotion is to encourage the target audience to behave in a particular way, often to buy a product. Advertising, on the other hand, is usually geared towards developing market awareness. These two tools set out to accomplish tasks at each end of the attitudinal spectrum: the conative and cognitive elements respectively. Just as advertising is used to work over the long term, sales promotion can achieve upward shifts in sales in the short term.

Sales promotion offers buyers additional value, as an inducement to generate an immediate sale. These inducements can be targeted at consumers, distributors, agents and members of the sales force. A whole range of network members can benefit from the use of sales promotion.

This tool is traditionally referred to as a form of below-the-line communications because, unlike advertising, there are no commission payments from media owners with this form of communications. The costs are borne directly by the organisation initiating the activity, which in most cases is a manufacturer, producer or service provider.

The second part of this chapter considers another below-the-line approach, field marketing. This has emerged out of what was formally referred to as merchandising but now encompasses a wider range of activities, one of which is experiential marketing, again a growing and important aspect of marketing communications for several product categories.

Understanding the value of sales promotions

There are many sales promotion techniques, but they all offer a direct inducement or an incentive to encourage receivers of these promotional messages to buy a product/service sooner rather than later. The inducement (e.g. price deals, coupons, premiums) is presented as an added value to the basic offering, one that is intended to encourage buyers to act 'now' rather than later. Sales promotion, therefore, is principally a means to accelerate sales. The acceleration represents the shortened period of time in which the transaction is completed relative to the time that would have elapsed had there not been a promotion. This action does not mean that an extra sale has been achieved, just that a potential future exchange is confirmed and transacted upon now.

Sales promotions consist of a wide range of tools and methods. These instruments are considered in more detail later in this chapter, but consideration of what constitutes sales promotion methods is important. In many cases, price is the determinant variable and can be used to distinguish between instruments. Sales promotions are often perceived purely as a price discounting mechanism through price deals and the use of coupons. This is not the whole picture, however, as there are many other ways in which incentives can be offered to buyers.

Reference has already been made to the idea that sales promotions are a way of providing value, and it is this value orientation that should be used when considering the nature and essential characteristics of sales promotions. Peattie and Peattie (1994) established a useful way of discriminating between price and non-price sales promotion instruments. These are set out in Table 15.1 where reference is made to sales promotions that are value-increasing and sales promotions that are value-adding.

This demarcation is important because a large amount of research into sales promotion has been based on value-increasing approaches, most notably price deals and coupons (Gupta, 1988; Blattberg and Neslin, 1990; Krishna and Zhang, 1999). This tends to distort the way sales promotions are perceived and has led to some generalisations about the overall impact of this promotional discipline. There is a large range of other sales promotion instruments which add value, enhance the offering and provide opportunities to drive longer-term benefits (see Table 15.2). According to Gilbert and Jackaria (2002), however, research into these was limited, and it appears that little has changed since then.

As a result of this diversity of sales promotion instruments it should be no surprise to learn that they are used for a wide range of reasons. Sales promotions can be targeted, with considerable precision, at particular audiences and there are three broad audiences at whom sales promotions can be targeted: consumers, members of the distribution or channel network, and the sales forces of both manufacturers and resellers. It should be remembered that the accuracy of these promotional tools means that many sub-groups within these broad groups can be reached quickly and accurately. However, sales promotion campaigns can backfire. When KFC offered a downloadable coupon that was endorsed by Oprah Winfrey, franchises could not keep pace with demand, especially as KFC had not placed any control on or limit to the number of coupons that could be downloaded.

The reasons why organisations use sales promotions are set out in Table 15.3.

Table 15.1 A value orientation of sales promotions

Value element	Explanation
Value-increasing	Value is increased by offering changes to the product quantity/quality or by lowering the price. Generally used and perceived as effective over the short term.
Value-adding	Value is added by offering something to augment the fundamental product/price offering. Premiums (gifts), information or opportunities can be offered as extras and the benefits realised over different periods of time: delayed (postal premiums), accumulated (loyalty programmes) or instant (scratch and win competitions). These have the potential to add value over the longer term.

Source: Peattie and Peattie (1994).

Table 15.2 A typology of sales promotion

Value-increasing (alters price/quantity or price/quality equation)	Value-adding (offers 'something extra' while leaving core product and price unchanged)
Discount pricing	Samples
Money-off coupons	Special features (limited editions)
Payment terms (e.g. interest-free credit)	Valued packaging
Refunds	Product trial
Guarantees	In-pack gifts
Multipack or multi-buys	In-mail gifts
Quantity increases	Piggy-back gifts
Group buying	Gift coupons
Buybacks	Information (e.g. brochure, catalogue)
	Clubs or loyalty programmes
	Competitions/prize draws

Table 15.3 Reasons for the use of sales promotions

Reason	Explanation
Reach new customers	They are useful in securing trials for new products and in defending shelf space against anticipated and existing competition.
Reduce distributor risk	The funds that manufacturers dedicate to them lower the distributor's risk in stocking new brands.
Reward behaviour	They can provide rewards for previous purchase behaviour.
Retention	They can provide interest and attract potential customers and in doing so encourage them to provide personal details for further communications activity.
Add value	They can encourage sampling and repeat purchase behaviour by providing extra value (superior to competitors' brands) and a reason to purchase.
Induce action	They can instil a sense of urgency among consumers to buy while a deal is available. They add excitement and interest at the point of purchase to the merchandising of mature and mundane products.
Preserve cash flow	Since sales promotion costs are incurred on a pay-as-you-go basis, they can spell survival for smaller, regional brands that cannot afford big advertising programmes.
Improve efficiency	They allow manufacturers to use idle capacity and to adjust to demand and supply imbalances or softness in raw material prices and other input costs, while maintaining the same list prices.
Integration	They can provide a means of linking together other tools of the promotional mix.
Assist segmentation	They allow manufacturers to price-discriminate among consumer segments that vary in price sensitivity. Most manufacturers believe that a high-list, high-deal policy is more profitable than offering a single price to all consumers. A portion of sales promotion expenditures, therefore, consists of reductions in list prices that are set for the least price-sensitive segment of the market.

As if in an attempt to categorise and manage this list, Lee (2002) suggests that the main reasons for the use of sales promotions can be reduced to four:

- as a reaction to competitor activities;
- as a form of inertia – this is what we have always done;
- as a way of meeting short-term sales objectives;
- as a way of meeting long-term objectives.

The first three are used widely and Lee comments that many brand owners use sales promotions as a panic measure when competitors threaten to lure customers away. Cutting prices is undoubtedly a way of prompting a short-term sales response but it can also undermine a longer-term brand strategy.

Viewpoint 15.1　　Gaming for a better seat

When Air France launched their new Business Cabins in their Boeing 777 fleet on flights out of Singapore, Tokyo, Shanghai and Jakarta to Paris, they needed to create awareness and motivate word of mouth about the facilities. These include a fully flat bed, direct access to aisle, and multi-purpose area (desk, restaurant table, bed) offering even greater privacy.

To achieve this Air France used a mobile game, which enabled travellers to compete for an instant upgrade on flights to Paris. Travellers waiting at the boarding gates at Singapore's Changi Airport and Japan's Kansai Airport in Osaka were given tablets to take part in a game called 'Cloud Slicer'. This involved swiping the screen to cut up clouds.

The top scorers were immediately upgraded to the new Business class cabin, and received their new boarding pass from the pilot. Runners-up won seats in Premium Economy. The campaign was later extended so that all Air France passengers flying from China, Hong Kong, Singapore, Indonesia or Japan could compete against each other, and the best monthly scorers in each country had the chance to be upgraded on their next flight to Paris.

Source: Air France (2015); Anon (2015a).

Question:	Why did Air France use a game to run the promotion when the winners were invariably not part of the target segment?
Task:	What game might you use to support a sales promotion for a travel company?

Not too many years ago sales promotions were regarded as a key way of developing sales, particularly in the grocery market. The use of sales promotions, however, has stagnated and in particular the use of on-pack promotions, bonus packs, competitions and price deals has failed to maintain the growth of previous years. Reasons for the decline include changing consumer behaviour, the rise of new interactive media and a distinct lack of innovation in the industry. Another important factor has been the expectations and drive of resellers, and the main supermarket chains in particular. They desire sales promotion programmes that are exclusive to them as this is seen as a major way of developing their retail brands. Supermarkets have effectively become media owners as their store space represents an opportunity for brand owners to promote their brands. On-pack promotions for individual stores are often too expensive and uneconomic so this form of promotion has suffered a great deal. Therefore, any form of sales promotion activity within their environments should be exclusive and tied into their brand.

The use of interactive media and the integration of sales promotion within other campaigns has been successful. SMS, email, viral campaigns, apps and the Internet are being used increasingly to drive sales by providing a 'call-to-action', for a long time the province of sales promotion activities. Mobile technology has also enabled the delivery of eCoupons within particular geographic areas, such as shopping centres and malls.

Although the overall use of certain sales promotion methods such as coupons has declined, sales promotion activities in the form of temporary price reductions (TPRs) have become the 'dominant marketing instrument of consumer packaged goods manufacturers and retailers' (Guyt and Gijsbrechts, 2014: 753). These researchers claim that price cuts supported by feature advertising are very effective. In the UK, supermarkets negotiate a price discount with suppliers, over and above the contracted price. This enables the supermarkets to offer a lower price for their customers. The additional earnings derived from the gap between a supplier's original and promotional costs are referred to as 'commercial income'. It was the accounting procedures associated with these sums that led Tesco to announce that it had overstated its profits for three years from 2011, and which led to negative media comment and reputational damage.

The role of sales promotion

The role of sales promotion has changed significantly over recent years. At one time, when the largest proportion of communications budgets was normally allocated to advertising, the role of sales promotion was essentially behavioural, that is selling. Now, at a time when advertising is not always the dominant discipline, the role of sales promotion has become oriented towards engagement. This can be achieved through adding value to a brand as well as still selling product. In situations where sales promotion has assumed the focus of the communications spend, for reasons that are set out below, the role is also to help integrate aspects of a campaign. This is particularly evident in consumer markets that are mature, have reached a level of stagnation, and where price and promotion work are the few ways of inducing brand-switching behaviour.

Short termism

The short-term financial focus of many developed economies has garnered a managerial climate, one that is geared to short-term performance and evaluation, over periods as short as 12 weeks. To accomplish this, communications tools are required that work quickly and impact directly upon sales. Many see this as leading to an erosion of the brand franchise.

Managerial accountability

Following on from the previous reason is the increased pressure on marketing managers to be accountable for their communications expenditure. The results of sales promotion activities are more easily justified and understood than those associated with advertising. The number of coupons returned for redemption and the number of bonus packs purchased can be calculated quickly and easily, with little room for error or misjudgement. Advertising, however, cannot be so easily measured in either the short or the long term. The impact of this is that managers can relate the promotional expenditure to the bottom line much more comfortably with sales promotion than with advertising.

Brand performance

Technological advances have enabled retailers to track brand performance more effectively. This in turn means that manufacturers can be drawn into agreements that promulgate in-store promotional activity at the expense of other more traditional forms of mass-media promotion. Developments in technology have facilitated tighter buying, delivery, stock control and tracking of merchandise, meaning that brand managers can be held responsible much more quickly for below-par performance.

Brand expansion

As brand quality continues to improve and as brands proliferate on the shelves of increasingly larger supermarkets, so the number of decisions that a consumer has to make also increases. Faced with multiple-brand decisions and a reduced amount of time to complete the shopping expedition, the tension associated with the shopping experience has increased considerably over the last decade.

Promotions make decision-making easier for consumers: they simplify a potentially difficult process. Thus, as brand choice increases, so the level of shopping convenience falls. The conflict this causes can be resolved by the astute use of sales promotions. Some feel that the cognitive shopper selects brands that offer increased value, which makes decision-making easier and improves the level of convenience associated with the shopping experience. However, should there be promotions on two offerings from an individual's repertoire then the decision-making is not necessarily made easier.

Competition for shelf space

The continuing growth in the number of brands launched and the fragmentation of consumer markets mean that retailers have to be encouraged to make shelf space available. Sales promotions have helped manufacturers win valuable shelf space and assist retailers to attract increased levels of store traffic and higher utilisation of limited resources, but this approach is not always viable today.

The credibility of this promotional tool is low, as it is obvious to the receiver what the intention is of using sales promotion messages. However, because of the prominent and pervasive nature of the tool, consumers and members of the trade understand and largely accept the direct sales approach. Sales promotion is not a tool that hides its intentions, nor does it attempt to be devious (which is not allowed, by regulation).

The absolute costs of sales promotion are low, but the real costs need to be evaluated once a campaign has finished and all redemptions received and satisfied. The relative costs can be high, as not only do the costs of the premium or price discount need to be determined, but also the associated costs of additional transportation, lost profit, storage and additional time spent organising and administering a sales promotion campaign need to be accounted for.

In its favour, sales promotion allows for a high degree of control. Management is able to decide just when and where a sales promotion will occur and also estimate the sales effect. Sales promotions can be turned on and off quickly and adjusted to changed market conditions.

The intended message is invariably the one that is received, as there is relatively little scope for it to be corrupted or damaged in transmission. However, this view needs to be tempered by some of the problems companies have experienced by not thinking through the sales promotion exercise in the first place, only to find themselves exposed to exploitation and financial embarrassment.

Scholars' paper 15.1	Promotions and the double jeopardy

Ehrenberg, A.S.C., Goodhardt, G.J. and Barwise, T.P. (1990) Double jeopardy revisited, *Journal of Marketing*, 54 (July), 82–91.

The double jeopardy phenomenon is well established. This paper, written by a distinguished array of authors, is used to explain and describe the wide range of empirical evidence for the existence of double jeopardy, the various theories that account for its occurrence, the issues and practical implications.

See also: Jones, P.J. (1990) The double jeopardy of sales promotions, *Harvard Business Review*, September/October, 145–52.

Sales promotion plans: the objectives

The objectives of using this tool are sales-oriented and geared to stimulating buyers either to use a product for the first time or to encourage use on a routine basis.

One objective of sales promotion activity is to prompt buyers into action, to initiate a series of behaviours that result in long-run purchase activity. These actions can be seen to occur in the conative stage of the attitudinal set. They reflect high or low involvement, and indicate whether cognitive processing and persuasion occur via the central or peripheral routes of the ELM (see Chapter 11). If the marketing objectives include the introduction of a new product or intention to enter a new market, then the key objective associated with low-involvement decisions and peripheral route processing is to stimulate trial use as soon as possible. When high-involvement decisions and central route processing are present, then sales promotions need to be withheld until a suitable level of attitudinal development has been undertaken by public relations and advertising activities.

If a product is established in a market, then a key objective should be to use sales promotions to stimulate an increase in the number of purchases made by current customers and to attract users from competing products (see Figure 15.1). The objectives, therefore, are either to increase consumption for established products or to stimulate trial by encouraging new buyers to use a product. Once this has been agreed, the desired trial and usage levels need to be determined for each of the target audiences. Before discussing these aspects, it is necessary first to review the manner in which sales promotions are thought to influence the behaviour of individuals.

	Involvement	
	High	Low
New product or market	Withhold sales promotion	Use sales promotion to stimulate trial
Established product or market	Non-loyals – use for switching Loyals – use carefully	Non-loyals – use sales promotions to attract for trial Loyals – use sales promotion to reward for increased usage

Figure 15.1   A sales promotion objectives grid

An overview of how sales promotions work

If the overriding objectives of sales promotions are to accelerate or bring forward future sales, the implication is that a behavioural change is required by the receiver for the sales promotion to be effective. The establishment of new behaviour patterns is the preferred outcome. If sales promotions are to work over the longer term, that is to bring about repeat purchase behaviour, then the new behaviour patterns need to be learned and adopted on a permanent basis.

This is a complex task, and is referred to by behaviourists as shaping. The behaviourists' view is advocated by Rothschild and Gaidis (1981). They suggest that by breaking the overall task into its constituent parts a series of smaller sequential tasks can be learned. When the successive actions are aggregated the new desired pattern of behaviour emerges. This view emphasises the impact of external stimuli in changing people's behaviour.

The cognitive view of the way sales promotions operate is based on the belief that consumers internally process relevant information about a sales promotion, including those of past experiences, and make a reasoned decision in the light of the goals and objectives that individuals set for themselves.

The ELM suggests that individuals using the peripheral route will only consider simplistic cues, such as display boards and price reduction signs. Individuals using the central route of the ELM have a higher need for information and will develop promotional signals to evaluate the value represented by the relative price and the salient attributes of the promoted product, before making a decision (Inman et al., 1990).

Related to this approach are ideas about how price promotions work. The use of these is widespread as it is regarded as the optimal way of generating short-term sales increases. It has been assumed that it works because it discourages purchase processing deliberation. This is because paying a lower price removes the need for additional thought or consideration of any other purchase-related factors (Aydinli et al., 2014). Consumer purchase decisions are made through the assimilation of two types of thinking. The first is automatic and loaded with emotions and feelings. The second is deliberate and controlled, dominated by access to memory and previously stored experiences and information. Aydinli et al. (2014) suggest that the switch from the former to the latter is triggered by the need for decision-making accuracy in order to avoid the risks and consequences arising from a poor decision. They argue that price promotions can trigger this switch.

An alternative view considers the role of information processing and the mental budgets people make when shopping. This involves the psychological allocation of money to different account categories, such as food, clothing, drink and entertainment, in a person's mind. Once each mental budget is exhausted consumers resist further spending in that category. However, there are opportunities to trade off an under spend in one category to support additional purchases in another.

Research also shows that consumers use mental budgeting processes for grocery shopping trips. These are expectations based on experiences developed through previous shopping excursions. From these experiences Stilley et al. (2010a) suggest that consumers allocate an itemised portion of their mental budget for planned, anticipated brand or category purchases. Consumers also allocate a proportion of their mental budget for in-store, unplanned decisions, as if they are preparing to take advantage of store suggestions and promotional offers. Of the many issues that arise one concerns what shoppers do with what might be saved from both the planned and unplanned mental budgets and whether this influences their purchasing activities and willingness to take advantage of sales promotions.

Reinforcing work by Heilman et al. (2002), Stilley et al. (2010b) agree that savings derived from the planned mental list 'only increases spending on unplanned items

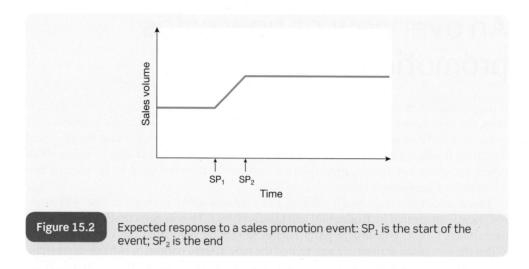

Figure 15.2   Expected response to a sales promotion event: SP_1 is the start of the event; SP_2 is the end

after in-store slack is depleted'. Another finding is that some promotions can encourage unplanned purchases, but savings from other promotions are just taken into the in-store slack. Stilley et al. (2010b) suggest that there are benefits for retailers arising from an understanding of mental budgets. For example, store layout should incorporate the placement of displays of full-price, high-margin unplanned items early in the path a customer takes around a store. Other low-margin unplanned promotional items should be placed later in the store path.

The main difference between the views of the behaviourists and those of the cognitive school of thought is that the former stress the impact of externally generated stimuli, whereas the latter emphasise the complexity of internal information processing.

The increasing proportion of budgets being allocated to sales promotions, and temporary price reductions (TPRs) in particular, has prompted concern about the costs and overall impact of these activities. It might be reasonable to expect that the sales curve following a price-based promotion would look like that depicted in Figure 15.2. There is

Exhibit 15.3   **Temporary price reductions, such as this 70% discount, serve to shift stock and promote cash flow**
Source: Getty Images/Martin Poole.

plenty of evidence that sales volumes can be increased following use of a TPR (Ehrenberg, 2000). However, a long-term upward shift in demand is unrealistic, particularly in mature markets. Extra stock is being transferred to consumers, and therefore they have more than they require for a normal purchase cycle. Ehrenberg suggests that most people who use TPRs are actually infrequent purchasers of a given category. Research suggests that these types of promotion do not attract new buyers.

Scholars' paper 15.2   **Mental adjustments to promotional spending**

Stilley, K.M., Inman, J.J. and Wakefield, K.L. (2010b) Spending on the fly: mental budgets, promotions, and spending behavior, *Journal of Marketing*, 74(3), 34–47.

The authors develop ideas about how shoppers leave room in their mental budgets when in-store, to make unplanned purchases. They explore how the impact of promotions depends on whether a person in-store considers using any slack remaining in their mental budget. The results indicate that promotions on unplanned grocery items generate incremental spending, which increases with income but only when the item is purchased after the in-store slack is exceeded.

See also: Datta, H., Foubert, B. and van Heerde, H.J. (2015) The challenge of retaining customers acquired with free trials, *Journal of Marketing Research*, LII (April), 217–34.

The graph shown in Figure 15.3 is more likely to occur with sales volume falling in the period when buyers are loaded with stock and temporarily removed from the market. However, Dawes (2004) found that there were as many buyers in a market in the period following a promotion as there were when the TPR was running.

Promotional activity does not take place in a vacuum with new products: competitors will be attracted and some customers lost to competitive offerings; in mature markets, non-loyals will take advantage of a sales promotion and then revert to competitors' sales promotions when they re-enter the market. So, the third scenario is shown in Figure 15.4. The result is that overall demand for a brand *may* be reduced owing to the combined effects of competitive promotional activity. However, Dawes found that price promotions have a neutral impact on a brand, with the benefits of volume increases being countered by the consequent fall in profitability. It may be, therefore, that the second scenario is the more accurate interpretation.

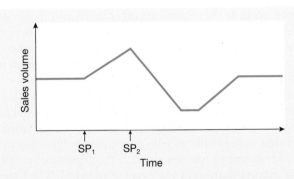

Figure 15.3   Realistic response to a sales promotion event

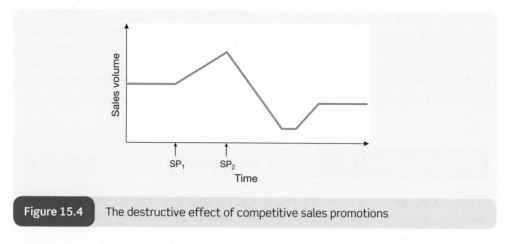

Figure 15.4   The destructive effect of competitive sales promotions

Sales promotions incur a large number of hidden costs. It was stated earlier that the cost of a sales promotion is thought to be relatively low but, as Buzzell et al. (1990) and others have demonstrated, there are a host of other indirect costs that must be considered. Manufacturers, for example, use promotional deals to induce resellers to buy stock at a promotional price, in addition to their normal buying requirements. The additional stock is then held for resale at a later date, at regular retail prices. The effect of this forward buying on the costs of the reseller can be enormous. Buzzell et al. point out that the promotional stock attracts higher interest charges, storage costs, expenses associated with the transfer of stock to different geographical areas of the organisation and the costs associated with keeping normal and promotional stock separate. When these are added to the manufacturer's forward buying costs it is probable, they conclude, that the costs outweigh the benefits of the sales promotion exercise.

As if to demonstrate this point, sales promotions, and BOGOFs ('buy one, get one free') in particular, are used by supermarkets and brand owners because they can change consumer purchasing patterns and can drive consumers to try a new product. Indeed, Simms (2007) reports that they are just as effective as television advertising in encouraging trial. There are, however, several problems with BOGOFs. According to Binet, cited by Simms, 84 per cent of trade promotions are unprofitable. This year's volumes get added into next year's targets, so manufacturers chase increased volumes as average prices fall, with the net effect of diluting profits.

Promotions give a brand presence through extra facings, but they also incur difficulties for retailers. This is because of the impact promotions can have on the relatively stable logistics associated with normal trading patterns. The capacity that stores and lorries have is finite and known. Goods are moved from warehouses, with lorries to stores whose sales performance is known. If a promotion is added to this mix these logistics patterns are thrown into temporary chaos as both the stores and the transportation create room for the promotion at the expense of other items and higher margins.

These activities suggest that the relationship between the members of the network is market-oriented rather than relational. However, many of these extra costs are unknown, and the resellers are unaware of the costs they are absorbing as a result of the deal. In the future, resellers and manufacturers should work together on such promotions and attempt to uncover all the costs involved to ensure that the exercise is successful for both parties.

Not only the short-term costs associated with a sales promotion but also the long-term costs must be evaluated. Jones (1990) refers to this as the double jeopardy of sales promotions. He argues that manufacturers who participate extensively in short-term sales promotions, mainly for defensive reasons, do so at the expense of profit. The generation of sales volume and market share is at the expense of profit. The long-term effects are equally revealing. As the vast majority of sales promotions are TPRs, the opportunity to build a consumer franchise, where the objective is the development of brand identity and loyalty, is negated. Evidence shows that as soon as a sales promotion is switched off, so any increased sales are also terminated until the next promotion. The retaliatory effect that TPRs have on competitors does nothing to stabilise what Jones calls volatile demand, where the only outcome, for some products, is decline and obscurity.

Sales promotions can lead consumers to depend on the presence of a promotion before committing to a purchase. If the preferred product does not carry a coupon, premium or TPR, then they may switch to a competitor's product that does offer some element of increased value. A related issue concerns the speed at which sales promotions are reduced following the introduction of a new product. If the incentives are removed too quickly, it is probable that consumers will have been unable to build a relationship with the product. If the incentives are sustained for too long, then it is possible that consumers have only identified a product by the value of the incentive, not the value of the product itself. The process by which a sales promotion is removed from a product is referred to as fading, and its rate can be crucial to the successful outcome of a product launch and a sales promotion activity.

The use of free-trial offers is common among many service companies, such as video streaming services (Netflix). These are used to encourage risk-free trial before signing up as a paid-for customer. Research by Datta et al. (2015) found that the higher churn rate associated with free-trial customers makes them worth nearly 60 per cent less than regular customers. Free-trial customers have underdeveloped relationships with the firm, and are more uncertain about the service benefits. This, according to the researchers, makes them more likely to rely on marketing communications and their own usage behaviour when deciding whether to retain the service. This indicates that compared with regular customers, free-trial customers are considerably more responsive to direct marketing, advertising, flat-rate usage and pay-per-use usage. Direct marketing and advertising are more appropriate disciplines to reach free-trial customers. Companies should therefore remind free-trial customers about their usage rates, especially when they are high, as this should encourage them to retain the service.

Retention programmes

Despite questions about the use of sales promotions to build loyalty, the growth of retention programmes has been a significant promotional development in recent years, as demonstrated by the Tesco and Nectar programmes. The growth of retention, or loyalty, schemes has been encouraged by the widespread use of swipe cards. Users are rewarded with points each time a purchase is made. This is referred to as a 'points accrual programme', whereby loyal users are able to build up the necessary points, which are stored (often) on a card, and 'cashed in' at a later date for gifts or merchandise. The benefit for the company supporting the scheme is that the promised rewards motivate customers to accrue more points and in doing so increase their switching costs, effectively locking them into the loyalty programme and preventing them from moving to a competitor brand. Smart cards, which have a small microprocessor embedded, can record enormous amounts of information, which is updated each time a purchase is made. However, some people have so many cards that a large number of loyalty cards are never used, or even scrapped.

Not only have loyalty schemes for frequent flyers been very successful, but the cards are also used to track individual travellers. Airlines are able to offer cardholders particular services, such as special airport lounges and magazines. Through its links to a database, the card also enables a traveller's favourite seat and dietary requirements to be offered. In addition, the regular accumulation of air miles fosters continuity, and hence loyalty, through which business travellers can reward themselves with leisure travel.

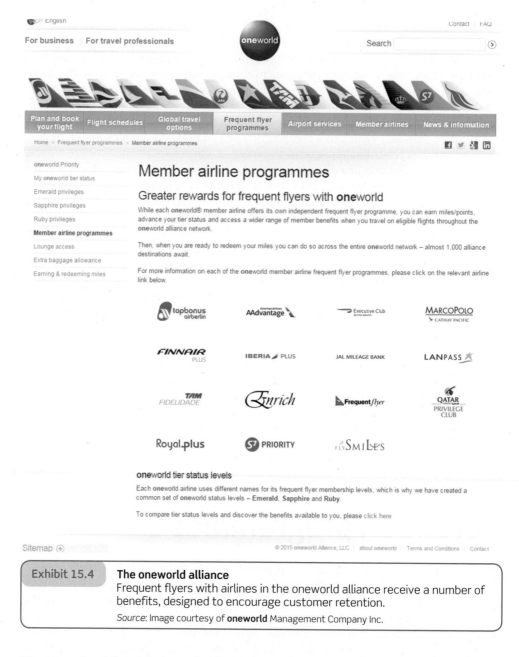

Exhibit 15.4

The oneworld alliance
Frequent flyers with airlines in the oneworld alliance receive a number of benefits, designed to encourage customer retention.
Source: Image courtesy of **oneworld** Management Company Inc.

However, the airlines' desire to develop relationships with their customers might not be fully reciprocated as many customers seek only convenience. See Exhibit 15.4.

Perhaps the attention given to loyalty and retention issues is misplaced because marketing is concerned with customer management, and that involves the identification, anticipation and satisfaction of customer needs. If these needs are being met properly it might be reasonable to expect that customers would return anyway, reducing the need for overt 'loyalty' programmes. The withdrawal by Debenhams from the Nectar scheme in 2008 was made in order to better reward store-card holders, at a time when the trading environment was getting tighter. There is an argument that these schemes are important not because of the loyalty aspect, but because the programme allows for the collection of up-to-date customer information and then the use of the data to make savings in the supply chain.

There has been a proliferation of loyalty cards, reflecting the increased emphasis on keeping customers rather than constantly finding new ones, and there is evidence that sales lift by about 2 or 3 per cent when a loyalty scheme is launched. Indeed, Diaa (2014) reports that retailers in and around Abu Dhabi have been experiencing difficulties attracting customers due precisely to the increase in loyalty programmes.

It is interesting to note that there is little evidence to support the notion that sales promotions, and in particular the use of premiums, are capable of encouraging loyalty, whether that be defined as behavioural and/or attitudinal. Loyalty schemes do enable organisations to monitor and manage stock, use direct marketing to cross- and up-sell customers, and manage their portfolio in order to consolidate/increase customer spending in a store. Whether loyalty is being developed by encouraging buyers to make repeat purchases, or whether the schemes are merely sales promotion techniques that encourage extended and consistent purchasing patterns, is debatable. Customer retention is a major issue and a lot of emphasis, possibly misplaced, has been given to loyalty schemes as a means of achieving retention targets.

There are views that loyalty schemes not only are misguided but have cost industry a huge amount of money. Hastings and Price (2004), for example, have expressed strong views about the notion and viability of so-called loyalty and points-based schemes. They claim that loyalty schemes are misunderstood for two main reasons. First, there is the assumption that loyalty can be bought when, like love, true loyalty can only be given. Second, there is an assumption that points-based schemes can be profit centres.

A major study involving in excess of 600,000 in-depth consumer interviews identified different levels of loyalty and concluded that significant financial returns were only gained only when the highest level of loyalty was achieved (Hallberg, 2004). These levels of loyalty are set out in Figure 15.5. Hallberg refers to the impact of emotional loyalty, a non-purchase measurement of attachment to a brand:

- At the 'no presence' level consumers are unaware of a brand and so there is no emotional loyalty.
- At the 'presence' level there is awareness but emotional loyalty is minimal.
- At the 'relevance and performance' level consumers begin to feel that the brand is acceptable in terms of meeting their needs.
- At the 'advantage' level consumers should feel that the brand is superior with regard to a particular attribute.
- At the 'bonding' level emotional loyalty is at its highest because consumers feel the brand has several unique properties. They love the brand.

Loyalty schemes are exponentially effective when consumers reach the bonding stage. Although sales generally increase the further up the pyramid consumers move, it is only at the 'bonding' stage that sales start to reflect the emotional attachment people feel towards the brand.

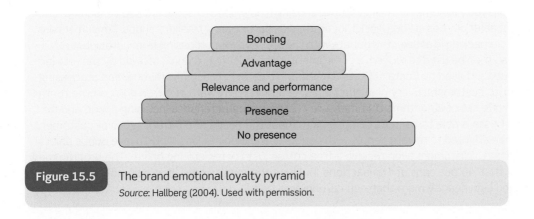

Figure 15.5 The brand emotional loyalty pyramid
Source: Hallberg (2004). Used with permission.

Table 15.4 Five loyalty trends

Trend	Explanation
Ubiquity	Loyalty programmes have proliferated in most mature markets and many members have little interest in them other than the functionality of points collection. Managers are trying to reduce communications costs by moving the scheme online but also need to be innovative.
Coalition	Schemes run by a number of different organisations in order to share costs, information and branding (e.g. Nectar) appear to be the dominant structure industry model.
Imagination	Opportunities to exploit technologies and niche markets will depend on creativity and imagination in order to get customer data to feed into the loyalty system. Employ IST imaginatively.
Wow	To overcome consumer lethargy and boredom with loyalty schemes, many rewards in future will be experiential, emotional, unique in an attempt to appeal to life stage and aspirational lifestyle goals – wow them. Differentiate to stand out.
Analysis	To be competitive the use of customer data analytics and business intelligence is becoming critical, if only to feed CRM programmes. Collect and analyse customer information effectively.

Source: Adapted from Capizzi et al. (2004).

There is a proliferation of loyalty programmes to the extent that Capizzi et al. (2004) suggest that the market is mature. They also argue that five clear trends within the loyalty market can be identified (see Table 15.4).

These trends suggest that successful sales promotion schemes are those that enable members to perceive significant value associated with their continued association with a scheme. That value will be driven by schemes run by groups of complementary brands, which use technology to understand customer dynamics and communications that complement their preferred values. The medium-term goal might be that these schemes should reflect customers' different relationship needs and recognise the different loyalty levels desired by different people. Viewpoint 15.2 offers some loyalty programmes, each of which operates under different guidelines.

Viewpoint 15.2   Different ways to generate loyalty

There is a wide range of formats used to support customer loyalty programmes. These include apps, rewards, partnerships, rebates, affinity and alliances. For example, in Hong Kong, Sodacard wanted to help retailers provide a loyalty scheme for their customers. Using a downloaded Sodacard app consumers can scan QR codes on tablet devices in Soda kiosks, located inside participating retailers' shops. Consumers are awarded points for checking in at selected outlets with the app, and for purchasing from participant retailers. The points can then be used to redeem a complimentary product (e.g. a drink) offered by the retailer.

The Coffee Club card used by Costa collects demographic data, contact information, and purchasing information from its customers. Every nine purchases results in the reward of a free drink on the tenth order. Using a unique set of algorithms that measure customer characteristics including spend and frequency of visits, Costa is able to tailor its campaigns to meet the needs of different types of customer. The scheme can be adapted to reward people with double or triple points, or simply to give bonus points on certain purchases. Customers even receive a free coffee just for registering online. The programme is so successful that 40 per cent of transactions involves the loyalty card. It is also noticeable that cardholders spend significantly more than non-cardholders.

Pacific Coffee has coffee shops located throughout China, Hong Kong, Singapore, Macau and Malaysia. It previously used a loyalty scheme based on paper cards and the accumulation of stamps issued when purchasing coffee. On achieving a certain number of stamps it was possible to redeem them for coffee. The Perfect Cup Card is activated when customers pay HK$200 up front and points are accumulated through purchase. Customers can also register online to keep track of their accumulated points in addition to receiving news and special offers. The collected points can be used to redeem rewards at partnering outlets such as IL COLPO GROUP, Café Salon and Playtimes. As a result, Pacific Coffee can now access huge volumes of data that allows customer orders to be converted into small data packets which are transmitted to the company's main network.

Source: Cross (2013); Lau (2013); Ong (2014).

Question: How significant are these retention schemes for low-value products, from both a consumer and brand perspective?

Task: Identify the different levels of emotional loyalty that customers might realistically reach within these schemes.

Exhibit 15.5	**Pacific Coffee**
	Pacific Coffee was inspired by the coffee culture of Seattle, where coffee houses were community hubs.
	Source: Shutterstock.com/TungCheung.

Sales promotions: methods and techniques

As established earlier, sales promotions seek to offer buyers additional value, as an inducement to generate an immediate sale. These inducements can be targeted at consumers, distributors, agents and members of the sales force. A whole range of network members can benefit from the use of sales promotion.

The range and variety of techniques that are used to add value and induce a sale sooner rather than later mean that different techniques work in different ways to achieve varying objectives. Here, consideration is given to the range of tasks that need to be accomplished among two key audiences: resellers and consumers.

The range of techniques and methods used to add value to offerings is enormous but there are growing doubts about the effectiveness and profitability associated with some sales promotions. Sales promotions used by manufacturers to communicate with resellers are aimed at encouraging resellers either to try new products or to purchase more of the ones they currently stock. To do this, trade allowances, in various guises, are the principal means.

The majority of sales promotions are those used by manufacturers to influence consumers. Again, the main tasks are to encourage trial or increase product purchase. A range of techniques, from sampling and coupons to premiums, contests and sweepstakes, are all used with varying levels of success, but there has been a distinct shift away from traditional promotional instruments to the use of interactive media in order to reflect consumers' preferences and media behaviour.

The following two tables set out information about key sales promotion techniques used between manufacturers and their intermediary partners, and with consumers. It should also be appreciated that sales promotions are used by retailers to influence consumers and between manufacturers and dealer sales force teams, although these are not itemised here. Table 15.5 depicts information about the audiences and reasons for using sales promotions. Table 15.6 provides information about the various sales promotion methods and techniques.

Group-buying agents such as Groupon, Wahanda and LivingSocial have spearheaded the rise of this form of discounting. Clark (2010) refers to Groupon as the leading provider, which originated in Chicago, where coupon use is a natural part of everyday buying, unlike the UK and Europe, where coupon usage is a minority activity and often favoured by deal chasers. Groupon has 53.2 million users, of which approximately 5 million are in the UK (Wood, 2014).

Table 15.5 Principal audiences and sales promotion goals

Audience	Objectives	Explanation	Methods
Manufacturers to resellers	For new products: *Sampling and trial*	For new products it is important to create adequate channels of distribution in anticipation of consumer demand. The task of marketing communications is to encourage resellers to distribute a new product and to establish trial behaviour.	Allowances: *Buying Count and recount Buy back Advertising*
	For established products: *Usage*	One of the key objectives of manufacturers is to motivate distributors to allocate increased shelf space to a product thereby (possibly) reducing the amount of shelf space allocated to competitors. The task of marketing communications, therefore, is to encourage resellers to buy and display increased amounts of the manufacturer's products and establish greater usage.	Dealer contests Dealer conventions and meetings Training and support
Manufacturers to consumers	For new users: *Stimulate trial*	Before customers buy a product they need to test or trial the product. Through the use of coupons, sampling and other techniques (see below), sales promotions have become an important element in the new product launch and introduction processes.	Sampling Coupons Price offs Bonus packs Refunds and rebates
	For established customers: *Increase product usage*	In mature markets customers need to be encouraged to keep buying a product. This can be achieved by attracting users from competitive brands, by converting non-users and by developing new uses.	Premiums Contests and sweepstakes

Table 15.6 Principal audiences and sales promotion methods

Audience	Method	Explanation
Manufacturers to resellers	**Advertising allowance**	A percentage allowance is given against a reseller's purchases during a specified campaign period. Instead of providing an allowance against product purchases, an allowance can be provided against the cost of an advertisement or campaign.
	Buying allowance	In return for specific orders between certain dates, a reseller will be entitled to a refund or allowance of x per cent off the regular case or carton price.
	Count and recount	Manufacturers may require resellers to clear old stock before a new or modified product is introduced. One way this can be achieved is to encourage resellers to move stock out of storage and into the store. The count and recount method provides an allowance for each case shifted into the store during a specified period of time.
	Buy back	Purchases made after the count and recount scheme (up to a maximum of the count and recount) are entitled to an allowance to encourage stores to replenish their stocks (with the manufacturer's product and not that of a competitor).
	Dealer contests	Used to hold a reseller's attention by focusing them on a manufacturer's products, not a competitor's.
	Dealer conventions and meetings	These enable informal interaction between a manufacturer and its resellers and can aid the development and continuance of good relations between the two parties.
	Training and support	This is an important communications function, especially when products are complex or subject to rapid change, as in IT markets. This can build stronger relationships and manufacturers have greater control over the messages that the resellers transmit.
Manufacturers to consumers	**Sampling**	Although very expensive, sampling is an effective way of getting people to try a product. Trial-size versions of the actual product are given away free. Sampling can also take the form of demonstrations, trial-size packs that have to be purchased or free use for a certain period of time.
	Coupons	These are vouchers or certificates that entitle consumers to a price reduction on a particular product. The value of the reduction or discount is set and the coupon must be presented at purchase.
	Price offs	These are a direct reduction in the purchase price, with the offer clearly labelled on the package or point of purchase display.
	Bonus packs	These offer more product for the regular pack price, typically a 2 for 1 offer. They provide direct impact at the point of purchase and represent extra value.
	Refunds and rebates	Used to invite consumers to send in a proof of purchase and in return receive a cash refund.
	Premiums	Items of merchandise that are offered free or at a low cost in return for product purchase.
	Contests and sweepstakes	A contest is a customer competition based on skill or ability. Entry requires a proof of purchase and winners are judged against a set of predetermined criteria. A sweepstake determines winners by chance and proof of purchase is not required. There is no judging and winners are drawn at random.

Viewpoint 15.3   Promotions galore

Promotions can be used in business to incentivise and motivate employees. Wickes used gift cards to help staff improve their own homes. The card enables an employer to position themselves as considerate and aware of an employee's life outside of work. The card also contributes to a reward system when average pay increases were supressed following the recession.

Budweiser's Dream Goal competition involved amateur footballers submitting videos of their 'dream goals', with a view to winning a major prize. The promotion worked in collaboration with Sky Sports and associated football pundits, plus TalkSPORT, The LAD Bible, The SPORT Bible, Buzzfeed and Grass Root Goals. The promotion featured an on-pack 'scan to win' mechanism, which via the Bud app offered the kit needed to video people's efforts. Consumers had to download the app, purchase a pack and scan the on-pack code to reveal their prizes.

Meerkat Movies, a promotion offered by Comparethemarket.com, offered cinema tickets on a two for one basis, valid every Tuesday or Wednesday for a year. Developed in partnership with Cinema First, whose primary role is to persuade people to go to the cinema, Comparethemarket.com saw the opportunity to reward their existing customers and attract new ones. The deal applied to existing customers and people who subsequently bought a product through Comparethemarket.com.

Source: Anon (2015b, 2015c); Degun (2015).

Question:	Why are many promotions developed and implemented by several stakeholders?
Task:	What would be your dream promotion and which celebrity or organisation would you choose to feature in it?

Exhibit 15.6	**Budweiser's Dream Goal competition** *Source*: Budweiser.

Whatever the promotion used, measurement and evaluation should be an integral part of the campaign. Measurement can be undertaken through a registration process, perhaps to claim a free gift.

Field marketing

Field marketing is a relatively new sector of the industry, one which seeks to provide support for the sales force and merchandising personnel together with data collection and research facilities for clients. The sector started as a way of ensuring that products were accessible in retail outlets (McLuhan, 2007). The core function is merchandising and shelf-positioning skills, and as McLuhan reports, 'at least 4 per cent of an FMCG's product's sales depend on getting this right; the rate is higher for other product types' (p. 9).

Although this element remains important, field marketing has evolved so that it now encompasses ways in which people can experience a brand. This reflects an overall shift in marketing communications from one based largely on developing brand values through an emotional proposition to one that emphasises changes in behaviour and calls-to-action.

The Field Marketing Council (FMC) states that the sector is about the use of people to communicate sales and marketing messages. This is quite an open remit and reflects the wide range of activities that practitioners within the area have recently encompassed. At a basic level, field marketing is concerned with getting free samples of a product into the hands of potential customers. At another level, field marketing is about creating an interaction between the brand and a new customer. At yet another level, it is about creating a personal and memorable brand experience for potential customers. The key to field marketing is the flexibility of services provided to clients. Sales forces can be hired on short-term contracts and promotional teams can be contracted to launch new products, provide samples (both in-store and door-to-door) and undertake a range of other activities that are not part of an organisation's normal promotion activities.

The decision about whether to own or to hire a sales force has to be based on a variety of criteria, such as the degree of control required over not only the salesperson, but also the message to be transmitted. A further criterion is flexibility. Ruckert et al. (1985) identified that in environments subject to rapid change, which brings uncertainty (e.g. because of shortening product lifecycles or major technological developments), the ability to adjust quickly the number of representatives in a distribution channel can be of considerable strategic importance. A further criterion is cost; for some the large fixed costs associated with a sales force can be avoided by using a commission-only team of representatives.

A large number of organisations choose to have their own sales force, but of these many use the services of a manufacturer's agent to supplement their activities. A number of pharmaceutical manufacturers use independent sales forces to supplement the activities of their own sales teams.

Range of FM activities

Table 15.7 sets out the range of activities undertaken in the name of field marketing (FM). To some extent it consists of tasks pulled from some of the five main promotional tools, repackaged and presented under a more contemporary title; for example, door-to-door and sales activities from personal selling, merchandising from both personal

Exhibit 15.7	**Merchandising lies at the heart of field marketing**
	Source: Budweiser.Getty Images/Andersen Ross.

selling and sales promotion, sampling (which is a straight sales promotion task) and event marketing from public relations. Field marketing is a response to market needs and is a development practitioners have pioneered to fulfil a range of customer needs that presumably had not been adequately satisfied.

Perhaps merchandising lies at the root of field marketing. This is concerned with the presentation and display of products in-store, in order to maximise impact, attention and 'pick-up' opportunities. Referred to as point-of-sale (POS), these activities occur where a decision to purchase is made – normally this will be in the aisles.

Table 15.7 Essential features of field marketing activities

Core activities	Essential features
Sales	Provides sales force personnel on either a temporary or a permanent basis. This is for business-to-business and direct to the public.
Merchandising	Generates awareness and brand visibility through point-of-purchase placement, in-store staff training, product displays and leaflets.
Sampling	Mainly to the public at shopping centres and station concourses but also for business-to-business purposes.
Auditing	Used for checking stock availability, pricing and positioning.
Mystery shopping	Provides feedback on the level and quality of service offered by retail- and services-based staff.
Event marketing	Used to create drama and to focus attention at sports events, open-air concerts and festivals. Essentially theatrical or entertainment-based.
Door-to-door (home calls)	A form of selling where relatively uncomplex products and services can be sold through home visits.

Source: Adapted from McLuhan (2000). Reproduced from Marketing magazine with the permission of the copyright owner, Haymarket Business Publications Limited.

POS is essentially about persuasion. This might be about using sampling to encourage customers to switch brands, or as Hilpern (2011) suggests it can be concerned with convincing customers that they should buy the brand they were originally intending to purchase, a defensive orientation. Apart from aligning product labels, maximising shelf space usage for a brand and using shelf signage (barkers) effectively, a variety of new techniques are either being tested or in use. For example, Lynx Excite has used a push button on the barker that releases a spray; Tesco use iPhone applications to allow shoppers to add to their virtual baskets by using a handset barcode scanner; and many retailers are experimenting with 3D signage (Hilpern, 2011).

Of central interest in merchandising is how and where products should be allocated within a scarce resource, namely the capacity and location of shelf space. Academics are attracted by the theoretical, problem-solving and statistical issues, whilst practitioners, retailers, seek increased efficiency and profitability.

There has been extensive research most of which concludes that the location of a product on a shelf has no major effect on the sales of a product (Russell and Urban, 2010). However, research by Drèze et al. (1994), cited by Russell and Urban, found that the 'vertical and horizontal positioning on the shelves for a number of (product) categories, led to an average difference in sales of 59 per cent from the worst to the best position on the shelves. They also found that half of the categories had increased sales on the end of the display, while the other half favored the center.'

Field marketing can take place virtually anywhere, but common locations are in shopping centres and supermarkets where footfall is greatest. Typically these events require agency staff to dress up in an eye-catching way in order to form associations between the clothing and the brand (e.g. dressed in Mexican ponchos and sombreros to give out free samples of Pot Noodle in a supermarket). It is regarded as a cost-effective way of demonstrating a product, getting stand-out and creating opportunities for customers to trial a product with minimum risk. Field marketing is also used to sell relatively complex products where a degree of explanation is required (e.g. computers, broadband, TV and related products, or mobile phones).

One of the reasons field marketing can take place at any location is due to digital technology. The use of apps and cloud technology in particular are helping to change the way in which the business works. Originally field marketing was about stock control and shelf positioning. These are essentially low-level jobs. The use of technology now allows field force agents to engage with in-store employees and this is enabled by real-time data and analysis. Through cloud technologies data can be accessed on demand. Without the need to manage hardware and software, field agents can present training materials, web-based instruction tools, the latest product information, and even use tablets to present data about sales of brands in similar stores (Ryan, 2012). The use of real-time sales data allows for the identification of stores that show stock irregularities. Staff can then be sent out to the stores and locations where a problem needs to be fixed.

The second development, the use of apps (with tablets and smartphones), helps agents check that stores are stocking and presenting brands in the right way. Now they are able to photograph merchandising on shelves and record data. So, although field marketing is a more sophisticated business than it was originally, the operating margins have become much tighter, in turn generating a need to find alternative high-margin activities.

One way around this margin issue is to reduce costs, and the use of apps is a route forward some agencies are pursuing. So, rather than give a smartphone and an app to a paid agent, the new approach is to encourage the public to go into stores and get them to take pictures of stock and record simple information about the way products are displayed. They then upload the data for analysis by brand owners, and get paid a small fee for their time and contribution. In a sense this is a variant on crowd-sourcing and has raised alarm bells within the industry. Issues about consistency, coverage and ethics are voiced by those against this development. For field marketing agencies and their clients, costs are halved.

So far the Field Agent app has been downloaded to over 10,000 smartphones in the UK, and according to Benady (2011) has approximately 1,000 regular users. The app enables brands to upload tasks, for example to check 100 Waitrose stores to see whether a particular item is being displayed correctly or that a promotion is well positioned. The task is then distributed to all users of the app who are near the target stores. This is based on information provided by the iPhones' geolocation technology. The offer could be £4–£6 to anyone who goes to the store, takes a picture of the promotional display and answers a few simple questions, such as how many products are on the shelf. Feedback can be received within minutes of a job being sent out (Benady, 2011).

Scholars' paper 15.3   Give me the right space please

Russell, R.A. and Urban, T.L. (2010) The location and allocation of products and product families on retail shelves, *Annals of Operations Research,* **179(1), 131–47.**

As the title of the publication suggests, there is some complex maths in this paper. However, do not be put off by this as the paper provides some interesting insights into the shelf space allocation issue, and a rare literature review on the subject.

Brand experience and events

A key aspect of field marketing concerns the growing interest in what is referred to as experiential marketing or brand experience. Many in the industry see their role as delivering brand experience opportunities for their clients' customers. Others argue that brand experience occurs through various interactions with a brand, namely purchasing, consumption and consideration. However, the term 'brand experience' appears to be owned by those in the field marketing industry and has evolved through the development of both sampling and event/roadshow activities. Unsurprisingly therefore, mystery shopping has developed as an important aspect of field marketing. Used increasingly by service-based operations, such as airlines, travel agents, restaurants and hotels, the intention is to understand how a customer experiences the service or purchase encounter and then feed the information into training and service improvements.

Whether the brand experience industry lies inside or outside of field marketing is not particularly critical. What differentiates the experiential aspect from other FM activities, however, is that it requires very precise targeting, and it is more emotionally and

Table 15.8 Two aspects of field marketing

Element	Explanation
Field marketing	The use of promotional staff in a marketing campaign to boost sales of a brand. Typically the field force will distribute product samples and carry out non-brand-related tasks that must be in place to maximise sales, such as compliance, auditing and merchandising.
Experiential marketing	The creation is a campaign delivered face-to-face, that engages the target audience in the brand through stimulation of some or all of the senses. This technique strives to forge a deeper connection with individuals and convey a sense of the brand's values.

Source: Bashford (2007). Reproduced from Marketing magazine with the permission of the copyright owner, Haymarket Business Publications Limited.

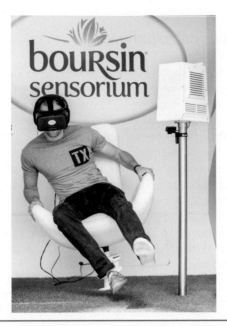

Exhibit 15.8	**Boursin gives consumers a more sensory experience of its products**
	Source: www.highlighterpr.co.uk.

physically engaging than sampling and many events or roadshows, which in turn, Bashford (2004) claims, can lead to stronger (positive) memories. She quotes Paul Ephremsen, a leading industry practitioner who says that field marketing is 'all about the numbers and not the interaction, and is driven by cost per sample' whereas brand experience is about 'creating an emotional bond between the brand and the consumer'.

The debate about what constitutes field marketing and experiential marketing is explored by Bashford (2007). She provides two definitions, set out in Table 15.8.

One of the essential tasks of field marketing is to continue to make brand signals available to consumers so that they can make the necessary brand associations that they have developed through advertising, brand and category experience. It is a matter of keeping brand values alive at the point of purchase (Kemp, 2000). Field marketing has undoubtedly expanded its role in recent years and in doing so has begun to establish itself as a core marketing support activity. Indeed, Moyies (2000) claims that field marketing should be cross-fertilised with direct marketing and sales promotion, and in doing so would not only benefit clients but also enhance the credibility of the industry.

Associated with this experience element is the growing use of events as a form of marketing communications, as demonstrated through the Lucozade example at the beginning of this chapter. Events are a part of several aspects of marketing communications, including brand experience considered here but also product and corporate branding, and sponsorship (Chapter 13). However, a deeper insight into the nature and characteristics of events can be found in Chapter 16 (www.marketing-interactive.com/fernandes-reaches-customers-personal-notes/), which incorporates a section about exhibitions and trade shows.

Finally, some consumers experience brands in unexpected ways. Through increasingly open communications, typically Twitter and social networks, some companies can sense moods, intentions, desires and consumer frustrations and intervene to help people with personalised gifts or solutions. These activities are known as 'random acts of kindness' and can result in positive word of mouth and improvements to brand image. For example, when the owner of a toy company saw on Facebook that a child's birthday present had been lost in the post he sent her a toy bunny, free of charge, and a note that said 'Sorry Royal Mail let you down, hopefully this will put a smile on your little girl's face' (Behrman, 2012) (see Viewpoint 15.4 where ideas about unwanted music experiences are explored).

Viewpoint 15.4　Evolving musical experiences

The recorded music industry is constantly evolving with new technology bringing new opportunities and experiences. From the elaborate artwork on vinyl sleeves, to the portability of the tape cassette, the increased durability of CDs and the ability to copy them, to the anytime ease of digital downloads, a consumer's relationship with their music has certainly changed over the past 40 years. With so many free options it appears streaming is becoming the preferred music format choice. Here consumers do not own a copy of the music so how does it impact their music and brand experiences?

In November 2014 Taylor Swift and her record label Big Machine decided to remove her entire library from all streaming platforms with 'freemium' accounts. Their argument was that those listening free were undermining the fans opting to buy her music. Swift's album '1989', released a month previously, sold over 1.28 million copies in the first week (the highest in over a decade). This coupled with the removal of her music from platforms such as Spotify caused her YouTube activity to double in less than a week. Swift has made the point in a number of interviews that music should be valued and valuable things should be paid for. Keeping up with the constant technology change is Thom Yorke, lead singer from English rock band Radiohead, and in September 2014 he showed everyone why. His second solo album 'Tomorrow's Modern Boxes' was initially released exclusively to download through BitTorrent. This not only attracted people through an alternative way of accessing music but by charging only $6 for the BitTorrent it was nearly half the price of a conventional album, resulting in over one million downloads in the first week. In the same month as Yorke's BitTorrent release, the Irish super-group U2 agreed with computing giant Apple Inc. to give away their thirteenth studio album for free to anyone with an iTunes account. A problem arose when the album appeared on over 500 million people's accounts without even a chance for the account holder to voice whether or not they wanted it there. Social media sites filled with negative comments pressuring Apple to release an application to remove the freebee. The following month, lead singer Bono issued an apology.

This begs the question about why there was so much anger towards the band for giving away their art. Indeed, this suggests that as the album was free it affected people's perception of value and their experience of the brands, U2 and Apple.

Sources:　Anon (2014); Battersby (2015); Booth (2014); Hernandez (2014); Malt (2014); Sherwin (2014).

This Viewpoint was written by Toby Pilcher when he was a postgraduate student at Buckinghamshire New University.

Question:	As customers take more control of how they consume music, how might the music industry boost customers' music experience, without selling itself short?
Task:	Find another example of a music artist who challenged industry norms. Did their action have a lasting effect on music experiences?

Other examples include sending restaurant vouchers to customers picked at random, upgrading to next day free delivery, sending out personalised key rings and including free gifts with an order. A Scottish brewery might give away a box of beer one day, and then give someone £200-worth of shares in the company through its fan investor scheme. For a few months, staff at airline KLM selected eight Twitter followers who were feeling low or in need of a break, and gave them a free return flight to Amsterdam. The campaign resulted in an increase of 784 followers for KLM's UK Twitter feed.

Scholars' paper 15.4	Never mind the product, feel the experience

Chang, T.-Y. and Horng, S.-C. (2010) Conceptualizing and measuring experience quality: the customer's perspective, *The Service Industries Journal,* 30(14), 2401-19.

More people are becoming aware of the importance and significance of experiences within marketing. These are characterised as satisfying customers' psychic or personal needs. These authors propose that experiences are considered as distinct economic offerings that are different from goods and services, to the extent that the focus of the economy has been transferred to experience. The number of papers on 'experience quality' is small so this research paper makes an important contribution to this growing field. This paper provides an insight into the literature and the authors also provide a definition of experience quality.

Key points

- Sales promotions offer a direct inducement or an incentive to encourage audiences to buy a product/service sooner rather than later. The inducement (e.g. price deals, coupons, premiums) is presented as an added value to the basic product, one that is intended to encourage buyers to act 'now' rather than later.

- The role of sales promotion is to engage audiences and to motivate them so that they are persuaded to behave now rather than at a later stage.

- The objective of sales promotion is to stimulate action. This can be to initiate a series of behaviours that result in long-run purchase activity, but the goal of sales promotion is to drive short-term shifts in sales. These actions can be seen to occur in the conative stage of the attitudinal set.

- The cognitive view of the way sales promotions operate is based on the belief that consumers internally process relevant information about a sales promotion, including those of past experiences, and make a reasoned decision in the light of the goals and objectives that individuals set for themselves.

- The behaviourists' view is that when the various actions that are embedded within a sales promotion activity are aggregated, a new desired pattern of behaviour emerges.

- Many organisations have developed schemes designed to retain customers based on the notion that they, the customers, are loyal. This brings into debate the notion of what is loyalty. In many ways these schemes are a function of customer convenience and all that they achieve is sufficient leverage to hold onto a customer a fraction longer than might have been possible in the absence of the scheme.

- The range of techniques and methods used to add value to offerings is enormous and runs from sampling and coupons to premiums, contests and sweepstakes, all used with varying levels of success. However, there has been a distinct shift away from traditional promotional instruments to the use of digital media in order to reflect consumers' preferences and media behaviour.

- Field marketing is a relatively new sector and seeks to provide support for the sales force and merchandising personnel along with data collection and research facilities. A key aspect of field marketing concerns the growing interest in what is referred to as experiential marketing or brand experience.

- What differentiates the experiential aspect from other FM activities is that it requires precise targeting and it is more emotionally and physically engaging than sampling, roadshows, and many events.

Review questions

Lucozade case questions

1. What might have been the motivation for Lucozade to use brand experience?
2. List the sales promotion methods that Lucozade might use.
3. How might the content generated from the Lucozade experience have gained traction through both paid and earned media?
4. Explain the term 'random acts of kindness' and suggest ways in which Lucozade might use this approach.
5. Write a brief note explaining how shaping works in the context of the Lucozade brand.

General questions

1. List the main sales promotion methods.
2. Identify the major differences between the behavioural and the cognitive explanations of how sales promotions work.
3. Write brief notes outlining some of the issues associated with loyalty programmes and customer retention initiatives.
4. Name five core activities associated with field marketing and explain their essential features.
5. Find three brand experience events and make notes of the main points of similarity.

References

Air France (2015) The upgrade challenge: new cabins launch in Asia, retrieved 23 January 2015 from www.youtube.com/watch?v=RA1qRlUynGg&feature=youtu.be.

Anon (2014) Thom Yorke's *Tomorrow's Modern Boxes* tops 1 million downloads in first week via BitTorrent, *Fact*, September, retrieved 29 April 2015 from www.factmag.com/2014/09/27/thom-yorkes-tomorrows-modern-boxes-tops-100k-downloads-in-first-24-hours-via-bittorrent/.

Anon (2015a) Air France launches 'The Upgrade Challenge' in Asian market, *Promotional Marketing*, 23 January, retrieved 23 January 2015 from www.promomarketing.info/digital/air-france-launches-the-upgrade-challenge-in-asian/21303.

Anon (2015b) Wickes for Business launches gift cards for staff reward, *Promotional Marketing*, 31 March, retrieved 1 April 2015 from www.promomarketing.info/b2b/wickes-for-business-launches-gift-cards-for-staff-/21619.

Anon (2015c) Budweiser launches 'Dream Goal' football campaign, *Promotional Marketing*, Tuesday 24 March, retrieved 1 April from www.promomarketing.info/shopper/budweiser-launches-dream-goal-football-campaign/21597.

Aydinli, A., Bertini, M. and Lambrecht, A. (2014) Price promotion for emotional impact, *Journal of Marketing*, 78 (July), 80–96.

Bashford, S. (2004) Field marketing: the great divide? *Event,* 8 September, retrieved 14 October from www.brandrepublic.com/news.

Bashford, S. (2007) Which way forward? *Marketing,* 13 December, 12.

Battersby, M. (2015) Thom Yorke's reported £13 million BitTorrent success is 'totally and utterly false', *Independent,* 7 January, retrieved 29 April 2015 from www.independent.co.uk/arts-entertainment/music/features/thom-yorkes-reported-13-million-bittorrent-success-is-totally-and-utterly-false-9962395.html.

Behrman, D. (2012) Work: better business: acts of kindness, *Guardian,* 13 April, 2.

Benady, D. (2011) Field marketing: your brand in their hands, *Marketing,* 9 November 2011, retrieved 17 February 2012 from www.brandrepublic.com/features/1102824/Field-marketing-brand-hands/?DCMP=ILC-SEARCH.

Blattberg, R.C. and Neslin, S.A. (1990) *Sales Promotion: Concepts, Methods and Strategies,* Englewood Cliffs, NJ: Prentice Hall.

Booth, R. (2014) U2's Bono issues apology for automatic Apple iTunes album download, *Guardian,* 15 October, retrieved 29 April 2015 from www.theguardian.com/music/2014/oct/15/u2-bono-issues-apology-for-apple-itunes-album-download.

Buzzell, R.D., Quelch, J.A. and Salmon, W.J. (1990) The costly bargain of trade promotion, *Harvard Business Review,* March/April, 141–9.

Capizzi, M., Ferguson, R. and Cuthbertson, R. (2004) Loyalty trends for the 21st century, *Journal of Targeting Measurement and Analysis for Marketing,* 12(3), 199–212.

Chang, T.-Y. and Horng, S.-C. (2010) Conceptualizing and measuring experience quality: the customer's perspective, *The Service Industries Journal,* 30(14), 2401–19.

Clark, N. (2010) The power of the crowd, *MarketingMagazine,* 24 August, retrieved 18 October 2011 from www.brandrepublic.com/features/1023618/power-crowd/?DCMP=ILC-SEARCH.

Cross, J. (2013) Top 10 UK loyalty programmes, *Slideshare,* 31 July, retrieved 13 February 2015 from www.slideshare.net/jaseKent/booktop10ukloyaltyprogrammesthewisemarket.

Datta, H., Foubert, B. and van Heerde, H.J. (2015) The challenge of retaining customers acquired with free trials, *Journal of Marketing Research,* LII (April), 217–34.

Dawes, J. (2004) Assessing the impact of a very successful price promotion on brand, category and competitor sales, *Journal of Product and Brand Management,* 13(5), 303–14.

Degun, G. (2015) Comparethemarket.com offers two for one cinema tickets with Meerkat Movies, *Campaign,* 20 March, retrieved 1 April 2015 from www.campaignlive.co.uk/article/1339267/comparethemarketcom-offers-two-one-cinema-tickets-meerkat-movies#uPElFB58ECkr6Ljw.99.

Diaa, S. (2014) Loyalty programmes challenge retailers in attracting customers, gulfnews.com, 18 October, retrieved 13 February 2015 from http://gulfnews.com/business/retail/loyalty-programmes-challenge-retailers-in-attracting-customers-1.1400510.

Drèze, X., Hoch, S.J. and Purk, M.E. (1994) Shelf management and space elasticity, *Journal of Retailing,* 70(4), 301–26.

Ehrenberg, A.S.C. (2000) Repeat buying: facts, theory and application, *Journal of Empirical Generalizations in Marketing Science,* 5, 392–770.

Ehrenberg, A.S.C., Goodhardt, G.J. and Barwise, T. P. (1990) Double jeopardy revisited, *Journal of Marketing,* 54 (July), 82–91.

Gilbert, D.C. and Jackaria, N. (2002) The efficacy of sales promotions in UK supermarkets: a consumer view, *International Journal of Retail and Distribution Management,* 30(6), 325–32.

Gupta, S. (1998) Impact of sales promotions on when, what and how much we buy, *Journal of Marketing Research,* 25(4), 342–55.

Guyt, J.Y. and Gijsbrechts, E. (2014) Take turns or march in sync? The impact of the National Brand promotion calendar on manufacturer and retailer performance, *Journal of Marketing Research,* LI (December), 753–72.

Hallberg, G. (2004) Is your loyalty programme really building loyalty? Why increasing emotional attachment, not just repeat buying, is key to maximizing programme success, *Journal of Targeting Measurement and Analysis for Marketing,* 12(3), 231–41.

Hastings, S. and Price, M. (2004) Money can't buy me loyalty, *Admap,* 39(2), 29–31.

Heilman, M.C., Nakamoto, K. and Rao, A.G. (2002) Pleasant surprises: consumer response to unexpected in-store coupons, *Journal of Marketing Research,* 34 (May), 242–52.

Hernandez, B.A. (2014) Taylor Swift's YouTube views doubled after pulling music from Spotify, *Mashable,* 21 November, retrieved 19 April 2015 from http://mashable.com/2014/11/20/taylor-swift-spotify-youtube/.

Hilpern, K. (2011) Persuasion, *The Marketer,* May, 28–32.

Inman, J., McAlister, L. and Hoyer, D.W. (1990) Promotion signal: proxy for a price cut? *Journal of Consumer Research,* 17 (June), 74–81.

Jones, P.J. (1990) The double jeopardy of sales promotions, *Harvard Business Review,* September/October, 145–52.

Kemp, G. (2000) Elastic brands, *Marketing Business,* October, 40–1.

Krishna, A. and Zhang, Z.J. (1999) Short or long duration coupons: the effect of the expiration date on the probability of coupon promotions. *Management Science*, 45(8), 1041–57.

Lau, A. (2013) SodaCard allows retailers to convert walk-in customers through mobile loyalty platform, *ClickZ*, 14 May, retrieved 13 February 2015 from www.clickz.com/clickz/column/2284012/sodacard-allows-retailers-to-convert-walkin-customers-through-mobile-loyalty-platform.

Lee, C.H. (2002) Sales promotions as strategic communications: the case of Singapore, *Journal of Product and Brand Management*, 11(2), 103–14.

Malt, A. (2014) Taylor Swift refuses to let you listen to her music on Spotify and now expects you to buy concert tickets too, *CompleteMusicUpdate*, 4 November, retrieved 29 April 2015 from www.completemusicupdate.com/article/taylor-swift-refuses-to-let-you-listen-to-her-music-on-spotify-and-now-expects-you-to-buy-concert-tickets-too/.

McLuhan, R. (2000) Fighting for a new view of field work, *Marketing*, 9 March, 29–30.

McLuhan, R. (2007) Face value, *Marketing*, 13 December, 9–10.

Moyies, J. (2000) A healthier specimen, *Admap*, June, 39–42.

Ong, M. (2014) Top 15 loyalty programmes in Greater China, *Terrapin*, September, retrieved 13 February 2015 from www.terrapinn.com/template/Live/PDF/Download-eBook-Top-15-loyalty-programme/6513/13386/ZWJvb2stMTUtbG95YWx0eS1wcm9ncmFtbWVzL WdyZWF0ZXJjaGluYS5wZGY=.

Peattie, S. and Peattie, K.J. (1994) Sales promotion, in *The Marketing Book* (ed. M.J. Baker), 3rd edition, London: Butterworth-Heinemann.

Rothschild, M.L. and Gaidis, W.C. (1981) Behavioural learning theory: its relevance to marketing and promotions, *Journal of Marketing Research*, 45(2), 70–8.

Ruckert, R.W., Walker, O.C. and Roering, K.J. (1985) The organisation of marketing activities: a contingency theory of structure and performance, *Journal of Marketing*, Winter, 13–25.

Russell, R.A. and Urban, T.L. (2010) The location and allocation of products and product families on retail shelves, *Annals of Operations Research*, 179(1), 131–47.

Ryan, M (2012) Forward thinking essays 2012: access all areas, *Marketing*, retrieved 17 February 2012 from www.brandrepublic.com/promotional_feature/1112655/Forward-Thinking-Essays-2012-Access-areas-Martin-Ryan-CPM-UK/?DCMP=ILC-SEARCH.

Sherwin, A. (2014) Free U2 album: how the most generous giveaway in music history turned PR disaster, *Independent*, 19 September, retrieved 29 April 2015 from www.independent.co.uk/arts-entertainment/music/features/free-u2-album-how-the-most-generous-giveaway-in-music-history-turned-into-a-pr-disaster-9745028.html.

Simms, J. (2007) Scant value in BOGOFS, *Marketing*, 7 November, 18.

Stilley, K.M., Inman, J.J. and Wakefield, K.L. (2010a) Planning to make unplanned purchases? The role of in-store slack in budget deviation, *Journal of Consumer Research*, 37(2), 264–78.

Stilley, K.M., Inman, J.J. and Wakefield, K.L. (2010b) Spending on the fly: mental budgets, promotions, and spending behavior, *Journal of Marketing*, 74(3), 34–47.

Wood, Z. (2014) Groupon revamps UK deals site in bid to become retail marketplace, *Guardian*, 19 August, retrieved 1 April 2015 from www.theguardian.com/technology/2014/aug/19/groupon-revamps-uk-site-bid-to-beomce-retail-marketplace.

Chapter 16

Brand placement, exhibitions, packaging and licensing

Brand placement enables brands to be seen in context and used by appropriate role models in order to help form effective brand associations. Exhibitions can be a significant part of a consumer marketing communications mix, while trade shows are a major part of the way B2B marketing is conducted. Packaging is always an important factor in the way consumer goods, which generally evoke low involvement, are presented. Licensing, a means of using another party's assets, has become a more common activity in the twenty-first century.

Aims and learning objectives

The aims of this chapter are to consider a range of marketing communications activities that have no specific designation, yet which can make a major contribution to a marketing communications campaign. These activities are applied to both the B2B and B2C markets.

The learning objectives are to enable readers to:

1. understand the concept and issues associated with brand placement;
2. explore the differences and significance of exhibitions and trade shows;
3. consider the main advantages and disadvantages of using exhibitions as part of the communications mix;
4. examine the role and key characteristics of packaging as a form of marketing communications;
5. describe the principles and issues associated with licensing.

Beyoncé – how brand licensing influences popular music acts

The rise in popularity of popular music in the post-Second World War era led to a demand to discover a stream of music acts. Rock 'n' roll, rhythm & blues, soul and country were among some of the popular genres that were arguably at the vanguard of this revolution. They were the result of a fusion of previously separate music cultures. This phenomenon of popular genres created a pool of popular music stars, including Elvis Presley, Chuck Berry and The Beatles. The music artist or pop star was born.

Just as most products at the time were developed, produced and distributed by a company that managed and controlled the majority of the value chain activities, so the popular music industry grew through a similar managerial approach. Organisations called 'record labels' controlled the manufacture and delivery of music products to the marketplace. Music acts did not possess music recording facilities, nor could they could manufacture or distribute music products. As a result they had no option other than to sign with a record company.

Record labels identified creative ideas and artists, bought the rights to fund, record, manufacture and promote popular music products, in return for a financial return. Marketing communications, such as live music, radio, TV promotion, plus public relations were used to create demand. During the pre-millennial period (1950 to 1999) record labels manufactured and distributed the physical recorded music, first through vinyl and later through cassette tapes and CD formats. Record labels dominated this period and music acts such as The Beatles, The Rolling Stones and Diana Ross were dependent on their contracted record labels – Parlophone Records, Decca and Motown, respectively.

Record labels would use their research and development facilities to identify commercially viable music acts. The department responsible for this activity was known as 'Artist and repertoire' (A&R), and became the priority of record labels seeking to produce and market the most profitable roster of music acts.

Record labels were authorised to record, manufacture and distribute physical music products related to a music act's brand. Income came from the copyright ownership of the song and from the manufacturing margins accrued through music product sales. Not surprisingly, some music acts broke away from their contracted record labels and formed their own companies. For example, The Beatles formed Apple Corps in an attempt to secure a greater influence over their work, and used Capital Records to undertake the distribution element, whilst EMI retained copyrights. The Rolling Stones also undertook a similar move.

Historically, the song was often owned or partially owned by the record label because it financed music act recording. A music act would normally receive an advance payment when signing with a record label. This would be recouped by the label upon successful promotion of a music act's brand through music product sales. This meant that the 'productising' of music acts often enabled record labels to control the promotion and own the major part of income generation of a music act. Such relationships meant that music acts could find themselves with limited control of their brand. Good examples of this can be seen with both Prince and George Michael, who both challenged their record label's control and ownership of their commercial brand identity.

Therefore, throughout the pre-millennial period music acts were very much dependent upon record labels to record, market and distribute their music if they wanted to reach a global audience and sell millions of albums (Figure 16.1).

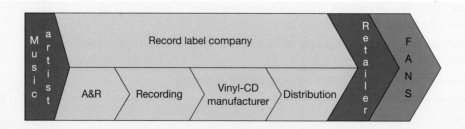

Figure 16.1   The typical distribution of products in the pre-millennial era

The changing value of the music act and the nature of the music product

The turn of the century has seen the erosion of the record labels' dominant position. It has been challenged by technology and the subsequent digitalisation of recorded music. The nature of the music product has been extended and changed to encompass digital (non-physical) music products.

Now it is possible for music acts to control the production of their music and to distribute their products directly to consumers, independently. In addition, many consumers have changed their purchasing behaviour by preferring digital (streaming/downloading) rather than owning a physical music product. Music fans can now acquire music more cheaply through digital music product and streaming sites such as iTunes and Spotify. As a result, the recorded music industry has seen significant reductions in profit margins.

The digital revolution has seen major changes in the way a music act can develop creativity and share their brand value. Record labels, now commonly known as 'entertainment companies', have sought new ways to generate income. What is commonly referred to as the '360-degree deal' is an attempt by the entertainment (record) companies to develop an extended portfolio of income opportunities from the whole realm of commercial music brand activities. Accordingly, they have moved from their traditional pre-millennial business of control of singular rights (recorded music) to the management and control of multiple (music brand) rights.

These multiple rights deals seek to obtain a significant interest and income from a music act's concerts, merchandising, TV licensing, films, games and direct sales from an artist's websites. These multiple rights deals can provide immediate returns for an entertainment/record label to offset the lucrative advance established artists can command. As the value of 'physical product' recordings has declined so much, entertainment/record labels must seek new forms of income.

Today's increasing social media network, particularly among the young, has created a global audience obsessed not only with the music of music stars, but also with a seemingly insatiable appetite for all sorts of information about their private lives and lifestyles. Subsequently, the social media-literate fan base has created a new demand for an act's music brand beyond the traditional recorded music product. Paradoxically, while the commercial value of the physical music product has gone down, the commercial value of the music act's brand has gone up.

A music act's brand is a strategic combination of cultural messages that provide meaning and connection for and among an audience. In today's social media age a music brand cannot hide from an increasingly inquisitive public. Consistent messages (good or bad) will largely represent the expectations people have when engaging with an act. Reputation is one of the most important elements in building and developing a music brand, as it represents the relationship and current market value of a music act.

Because of the change in the traditional distribution of income, the evolution of the music brand is now pivotal to an act's commercial success. The focus upon a multiple income profile that is generated from the music brand can be seen throughout the music industry today (Figure 16.2). An act can now be seen as possessing a portfolio of music brand products and/or services. This portfolio is normally made possible through several levels of brand licensing:

- the music brand (live and recorded);
- the extended brand licensing (i.e. fashion);
- the brand partnership (i.e. endorsements).

Several high-profile, 360-degree deals have been brokered between music acts and music entertainment companies. Robbie Williams signed a deal with EMI in 2002 for a reputed £80 million, while Madonna received £120 million for a deal with Live Nation in 2007.

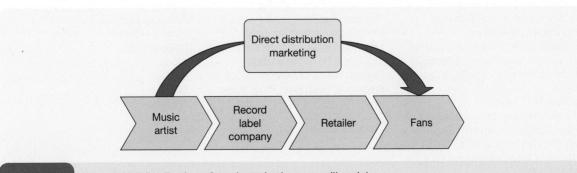

Figure 16.2   The digital distribution of products in the new millennial era

A year later Jay-Z was said to have received a deal that would see him accrue up to £150 million over 10 years. Beyoncé's portfolio provides an interesting example of how brand licensing is fundamental to both her income stream and that of her entertainment company (Table 16.1).

Summary

The music artist of the pre-millennial period (1950–99) had a predominant reliance upon income accrued from the record company which controlled manufacturing, distribution, retail placement and sale of physical music recording formats (vinyl, tape, CD).

The digital revolution of the new millennium (2000 onwards), however, has changed the nature and realm of music consumption. In 2012 the record industry body, the British Phonographic Industry (BPI), announced that income from UK digital music sales overtook that of physical music recordings for the first time. The growth is welcome but digital music income is proportionately much less than physical formats. However, technology has also greatly extended the placement and value of the music act into multiple (potential income-generating) channels. The music act is now a music brand portfolio, redefining the way in which fans can engage with the multiple representations of a music act.

Source: Various including Graham et al. (2004) and Leeds (2007).

This case was written by Ray Sylvester, Associate Professor at Anderson University, USA

Questions relating to this case can be found at the end of the chapter.

Table 16.1 The Beyoncé Knowles brand

The Music Act: Beyoncé Giselle Knowles		
Private self	**Physical self**	**Professional self**
Born Houston, Texas, USA Child prodigy Father was salesman and mother hair salon owner Suffered and overcame depression Married to Jay-Z Mother to Blue Ivy (7/1/12) Philanthropist Politics: Democrat (supported Barack Obama) Supports same-sex marriage	34 years old Female African American Voluptuous (Bootylicious) Young, sexy and street savvy fashion style	One of the best-selling artists of all-time Since 1997: Singer, songwriter, dancer Actress, choreographer, fashion designer, model, entrepreneur RIAA: top-certified artist of the 2000s Billboard: top radio, female and artist of the millennium First billion-dollar couple (with Jay-Z) in the music industry (2013) Forbes No.1 Celebrity 100 Earnings List (2014)
The music brand	**Music brand portfolio** **The extended brand**	**The brand partnership**
118 million records sold world-wide 6 Destiny's Child albums: Destiny's Child, Destiny Fulfilled, The Writing's on the Wall, Survivor, 8 Days of Christmas, Love Songs 5 Solo albums: Dangerously in Love, B'Day, I am Sash Fierce, 4, Beyoncé Numerous duets: Lady Gaga, Shakira, Jay-Z 20 Grammy awards 5 headline tours: Dangerously in Love Tour (2003), The Beyoncé Experience (2007), I am . . . World Tour (2009–10), The Mrs Carter Show World Tour (2013–14)	Tidal music streaming 11 TV and films: *Carmen*; *Goldmember*; *The Fighting Temptations*; *The Pink Panther*; *Dreamgirls*; *Cadillac Records*; *Obsessed*; *Wow, Wow, Wubbzy!: Wub Idol*; *Life is But a Dream*; *Epic* Fashion: House of Dereon Fragrance: Heat, Heat Rush, Pulse	Pepsi Emporio Armani L'Oréal American Express Tommy Hilfiger Nintendo DS Vizio H&M C&A Topshop

Source: © Ray Sylvester (2014).

Exhibit 16.1   **Beyoncé**
Source: Corbis/Rune Hellestad.

Introduction

Most of the tools presented so far are regarded as the primary instruments of the marketing communications mix. In order to provide a difference, however, and to cut through the noise of competing brands, it is necessary to provide additional resources and, preferably, integrated communications, right up to the point when customers make decisions. This chapter considers several other important means of communicating with both customers and distributors: brand placement, exhibitions and trade shows, packaging and licensing.

'Brand placement' enables a brand to be observed in a more natural environment than if viewed on a shelf, online or in a shop window. Unsurprisingly, this part of marketing communications is growing and provides income for film producers, authenticity for brand managers and relief from advertising for consumers.

Exhibitions enable customers to become familiar with new developments, new products, services and leading-edge brands. Very often these customers will be opinion leaders and will use word-of-mouth communications to convey their feelings and product experiences to others. In the B2B market, exhibitions and trade shows are very often an integral and important component in the communications mix. Meeting friends, customers, suppliers, competitors and prospective customers is an important sociological and ritualistic event in the communications calendar for many companies. In the consumer sector, and in particular the FMCG market, it is important to provide a point of difference and offer continuity for those people who make the brand choice decisions at the point of purchase.

In addition, the way products are packaged not only influences brand perception but can also be an integral part of the customer purchasing process. Packaging moves with a brand back into the home and can be present while a brand is consumed. This provides a constant visibility and reinforcement of the brand, something other forms of communications cannot do.

Brand licensing has become an important element in the way the music industry markets and communicates with stakeholders. Licensing is a commercial arrangement whereby one party, who holds certain property rights or a trademark, grants permission to particular others – a manufacturing company, for example – to allow them the right to carry the designated logo or trademark. Some might see this as a variant of brand extension, but licensing has become a significant communications activity in its own right.

Brand placement

One way of overcoming the irritation factor associated with advertisements screened in cinemas prior to a film showing is to incorporate a product within the film that is shown. This practice is now referred to as brand placement, although it originated as *product* placement. The change is a recognition that it is not products that are placed within the media, but brands with identities and associated brand meanings and messages (Kandhadai and Saxena, 2014).

Chen and Haley (2014: 286) use the following definition: the 'intentional, paid inclusion of products, services, brands, or/and brand identifiers into media content'. Kandhadai and Saxena (2014: 241) define it in terms of identities, as 'the paid inclusion of communicative brand identities, via management of intensities, in the creative content of any media, and is an audience-driven strategic communication process, managed by stakeholders for a desired outcome'.

In addition to brand associations and related identities and images, placements can also carry social information. Homer (2009: 22), for example, claims that 'brand placements have been shown to be more effective when the featured brand is paired with a character who displays one or more desirable traits' (Karrh, 1998).

A wide variety of products can be placed in this way, including drinks (both soft and alcoholic), confectionery, newspapers, cars, airlines, perfume and even holiday destinations and sports equipment. However, the development of brand placement has inevitably led to new formats and fresh approaches, some of which only serve to muddy the waters.

Hudson and Hudson (2006) set out the development of brand placement. Early forms of placement concerned brand owners making deals with film producers and film stars openly to endorse a brand. The brand owner would fund props and facilities for the film in return for spoken and visual endorsement. Some of the first television programmes were named after the brands that sponsored them, for example *The Colgate Comedy Hour* and the *Kraft Television Theatre* (Hudson and Hudson, 2006).

The establishment of brand placement agencies in the 1980s helped formalise the process and removed much of the barter and haggling that had typified arrangements. The turning point occurred when the film *ET* depicted an alien being lured by Reese's

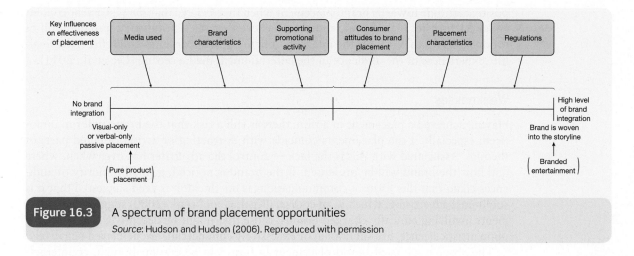

Figure 16.3   A spectrum of brand placement opportunities
Source: Hudson and Hudson (2006). Reproduced with permission

Pieces. Hershey, the manufacturer, saw sales rise over 60 per cent following the release of the film, and since then brand placement has grown year on year.

Two distinct forms of placement-related activity have emerged, partly as a result of the proliferation of the media, the consequential surge in the production of entertainment programmes and the media industries' need to generate income streams. Rather than place a brand within a film, television or radio programme where it assumes a passive role, hoping to get noticed, a new approach sees whole entertainment programmes built around a single brand. In contrast to the passivity of brand placement, here a brand is actively woven into the theme or the plot of the programme. This latter approach has been labelled 'branded entertainment'. Hudson and Hudson (2006) depict this as a continuum (represented in Figure 16.3).

Hackley and Tiwsakul (2006) suggest the term 'entertainment marketing'. They believe this reflects the diversity of ways in which brands are inserted into entertainment vehicles. This perspective subsumes brand placement and incorporates celebrity endorsement and sponsorship, elements discussed elsewhere in this book.

Characteristics of brand placement

Strengths

By presenting a brand as an integral part of a film, not only is it possible to build awareness, but source credibility can be improved significantly and brand images reinforced. The audience is assisted to identify and associate itself with the environment depicted in the film or with the celebrity who is using the brand.

Levels of impact can be very high, as cinema audiences are very attentive to large-screen presentations. Rates of exposure can be high, particularly now that cinema films and television shows are released through video outlets, various new regional cable and television organisations, and streaming providers such as Netflix, Amazon Instant Video and Now TV. Brand placement is often used as an integral part of an international marketing strategy. This is because, as McKechnie and Zhou (2003) observe, films are often produced for and play to audiences across cultures. However, it should be recognised that this approach constitutes a standardised marketing strategy, since it is difficult to customise across cultures because media content and placed brands are identical (Nelson and Devanathan, 2006).

Perhaps the major advantage is that the majority of audiences, worldwide, appear to approve of this form of marketing communications, if only because it is unobtrusive and integral to the film (Nebenzahl and Secunda, 1993). Audiences appear to have a positive attitude towards brand placement when they believe that the placement content enhances realism. In addition, audiences believe that the naturalistic representation of products serves to reinforce the integrity of fictionalised storylines and reflects the 'real-life' experiences of the audience in the entertainment media setting (Lee et al., 2011).

Weaknesses

Having achieved a placement in a film, there is still a risk that the brand will run unnoticed, especially if the placements coincide with distracting or action-oriented parts of the film. Associated with this is the lack of control the advertiser has over when, where and how the brand will be presented. If the brand is noticed, a small minority of audiences claim that this form of communications is unethical; it is even suggested that it is subliminal advertising, which is, of course, illegal. Gould et al. (2000) suggest that placements involving ethically charged brands, those that might be deceptive, that encroach upon artistic licence, are subliminal or excessively commercial, are perceived negatively.

The absolute costs of brand placement in films can be extremely high, counteracting the low relative costs or cost per contact. The final major drawback of this form of communications concerns its inability to provide explanation, detail, or indeed any substantive information about the brand. The brand is seen in use and, it is hoped, associated with an event, person(s) or objects that provide a source of pleasure, inspiration or aspiration for an individual viewer.

Brand placement is not confined to cinema films. Music videos, television plays, dramas and soap operas can also use this method to present advertisers' brands. The novel *The Sweetest Taboo*, written by novelist Carole Matthews, includes frequent references to various Ford cars, which is not surprising as Ford paid her to mention their cars in her work (Plaut, 2004). Pervan and Martin (2002) found that brand placement in television soaps was an effective communications activity. They also concluded that the way a product is used in the soap (i.e. positive and negative outcomes) may well have important implications for the attitudes held towards these products. In addition, they suggested that organisations should study the consumption imagery associated with placed brands as this might yield significant information about the way in which these products are actually consumed.

Brand placement is also used in radio. Van Reijmersdal (2011) found that placements on radio are perceived not only to be liked more than ads, but also as more credible than ads. This, in turn, affects brand recall positively. Thanks to the credibility issue, it is contended that brand placement receives more attention from listeners and so has a higher chance of being processed and recalled than commercials.

Brand placement is not confined to offline communications. For example, the growing popularity of social gaming, such as Mafia Wars, which are run on social network platforms, has also attracted an increasing number of placements (Chen and Haley, 2014). The toothpaste brand Pearl Drops was written into the plotline and integrated into the social network Bebo's interactive drama called *Sofia's Diary*, a teen-targeted programme.

Viewpoint 16.1   And these brands were placed in . . .

The James Bond films have used brand placement since the use of Red Stripe in the first film in 1962. In the 1997 Bond film *Tomorrow Never Dies*, US$100 million was contributed through brand placement in which BMW played a significant role. A range of brands such as Coke, Omega, Sony, Avon Heineken, and Virgin Atlantic all contributed placements to *Quantum of Solace* (2008). It is estimated that Heineken paid around US$45 million for placements in *Skyfall*, a third of the film's budget.

In the vampire-passion film series, *Twilight*, the lead character drove a Volvo, and sales of the S30 model rose following the release of the first *Twilight* film. Volvo saw the logic and credibility of the Swedish author, and reference to Volvo in the novels, as an opportunity to develop their involvement in the films. Volvo formulated an integrated, digital-based communications strategy, with brand placement as a pivotal element in the communications mix.

For the film *New Moon*, a website was developed that offered fans an opportunity to attend the premiere, meet the cast and win the car. Following the film's release, many parents took their children to Volvo car showrooms to have their photographs taken next to the Twilight car. In addition to media relations activities, Volvo then released TV and cinema ads which featured clips from *Eclipse* as well as flashes of the XC60. Viewers were driven to the website to play a game using the XC60 to navigate around the town of Forks, featured in the film.

Television programmes also use brand placement. For example, contestants in the TV game show *Deal or No Deal* had their mugs digitally enhanced with the PG Tips logo. The popular TV soap *Neighbours* incorporated the Aldi logo (in post-production) on the door of a taxi.

Placement activities are not confined to film or television. The short novel *The Vanishing Game* was written by William Boyd, an established author, following a commission from Land Rover. They suggested that he should mention the Defender brand in his novel but granted him total liberty over the storyline. Boyd says he gave the brand an inherent presence in the story, referring to the vehicle's various attributes to characterise its involvement, namely that it is strong, solid, reliable and ready to function.

| Exhibit 16.2 | Volvo placement in the film *The Twilight Saga: New Moon* |

Source: The Kobal Collection/Summit Entertainment.

Source: Based on Burgess (2014); Felix and Stampler (2012); Fry (2010).

| **Question:** | Consider the view that, if brand placement is a natural extension of conventional advertising campaigns, then it is a sensible, ethical and effective approach to marketing communications. |
| **Task:** | Choose two films and count the number of brand placements. |

Placement issues

The nature of a placement and the impact it has on the audience appear to be affected by a number of variables. Important issues concern: the nature of the placement (Sung et al., 2009) and its association with the storyline; whether the actors use the brand or if it remains a background object; whether the brand fits the plot; the degree to which the brand is prominently displayed; the medium used (de Gregorio and Sung, 2010); and the amount of time that the brand is actually exposed.

For example, research by Kamleitner and Jyote (2013) into the relative effectiveness of different types of placement in films found that those involving character–product interaction (where a character in a film has some physical interaction with a branded product) generate far stronger and more positive attitude changes in comparison to static placements where there is similar visual prominence.

Research into brand placement appears to have focused on three main issues concerning consumer opinion. Lee et al. (2011b) refer to the perceived realism, ethicality and influence of a brand placement. There is strong agreement that placements:

- can enhance the realism of film and TV content (Nebenzahl and Secunda, 1993; Gupta et al., 2000);
- have the potential to reinforce the integrity of a film and help viewers to become absorbed within the storyline (DeLorme and Reid, 1999);
- are perceived to be ethical, even if they are considered to be advertisements in disguise (Sung and de Gregorio, 2008).

Karrh et al. (2003) refer to the relative lack of control that marketers have over placement activities, but confirm that in comparison to advertising equivalents, brand placement can have a far greater impact on audiences and in most cases at a fraction of the cost of a 30-second advertisement.

Cultural background and ethical disposition can influence an audience's perception of brand placements (Nelson and Devanathan, 2006) whilst Russell and Belch (2005) refer to difficulties relating to the way the value of a placement is perceived. Chen and Haley (2014) reinforce the point that the meanings attributed by consumers to brand placements are determined contextually, the same way as advertising (Hirschman and Thompson, 1997). The message and the medium within brand placements combine to deliver intertextual brand image/meaning.

There is a view, held by creative and media agencies, that the 'number of seconds on screen' is a valid measurement of effectiveness. Many do not agree and prefer to consider the context of the placement and the level of continuity within a defined communications strategy as more meaningful measures.

Brand placement can take varying forms but two main forms are considered in the literature: subtle versus prominent type of placements, or *implicit* and *explicit* brand placements (D'Astous and Séguin, 1999). The premise is that prominent/explicit placements are more persuasive (in terms of attitude change) than subtle/implicit placements, owing to their attention-getting power. However, prominence raises issues about distraction, irritation and perceptions about self-serving that can inhibit persuasion. Research indicates that brand placement can impact on attitudes through mere exposure (Hang, 2012). Homer (2009) found that attitudes decrease with prominent/explicit placements and are maintained where the placement is subtle/implicit.

Following research by Smit et al. (2009) into how brand placement is used in the Netherlands, their results revealed that a quarter of Dutch television contained a mixture of brand sponsorship announcements, commercials and brand placement programmes. They also found that approximately 10 per cent of programmes, excluding sports, news, foreign movies and foreign soap operas, included brand placements. They also found that 'of these the most popular genres for brand placement were human interest programmes, soap operas, games and quiz shows'. The researchers report that 'brands were portrayed visually and prominently, were visible for a relatively long period of time and were often connected to the plot'.

Practitioners perceive brand placement and brand-integrated programmes as the future of television advertising. Sponsors are enthusiastic about brand-integrating programmes simply because they see this format as more effective than a traditional 30-second commercial.

Brand placement is normally undertaken through specialised agencies and by dedicated professionals. Some practitioners believe that the emergence of these placement agencies might eventually weaken the position of advertising agencies.

The use of brand placement as a part of an international marketing strategy has several advantages. However, as Lee et al. (2011b) suggest, local contextual elements such as the cultural environment, legal conditions, media infrastructure, plus public sentiment, all need to be considered when using brand placement on a global basis. They also warn that technologically sophisticated audiences are increasingly watching a range of content (soap operas, sitcoms and news programmes) via podcasts, mobile television (i.e. digital multimedia broadcasting) and interactive television (i.e. Internet protocol television) (Kwak et al., 2009). It is therefore important to understand the way consumers use television (active, passive and multitasking behaviours) and the impact this might have on the effectiveness of brand placement in different cultural contexts.

Scholars' paper 16.1   Defining brand placement

Kandhadai, R. and Saxena, R. (2014) Brand placement: new perspectives and a comprehensive definition, *The Marketing Review,* **14(3), 231–44.**

In recognition of the recent surge in interest and use of brand placement, these authors provide a useful review of the brand placement literature. One of the outcomes is the proposal for a new definition of brand placement.

See also: Lee, T., Sung, Y. and Choi, S.M. (2011b) Young adults' responses to product placement in movies and television shows: a comparative study of the United States and South Korea, *International Journal of Advertising,* 30(3), 479–507.

Trade shows and exhibitions

Trade shows and exhibitions fulfil a role for customers by enabling them to become familiar with new developments, new products and leading-edge brands. Very often these customers will be opinion leaders and will use word-of-mouth communications to convey their feelings and both product and exhibition experiences to others. The role of trade fairs is to enable manufacturers, suppliers and distributors to meet at a designated location. As these are drawn from a particular industry or related industries, the purpose is to exchange information about products and services and to build relationships. These events normally exclude consumers. Exhibitions are attended by consumers.

In the B2B market, trade shows are very often an integral and important component in the communications mix. Meeting friends, customers, suppliers, competitors and prospective customers is an important sociological and ritualistic event in the communications calendar for many companies. In the consumer sector, exhibitions provide a point of difference and offer continuity for those people who make the brand choice decisions at the point of purchase.

The idea of many suppliers joining together at a particular location to set out their products and services so that customers may meet, make comparisons and place orders is far from new. Indeed, not only does this form of promotional activity stretch back many centuries, but it has also been used to explain the way the Internet works (Bertheron et al., 1996).

At a basic level, trade shows can be oriented for industrial users and exhibitions for consumers and the content or purpose might be to consider general or specialised products/markets. According to Boukersi (2000), consumer-oriented general exhibitions tend to be larger and last longer than the more specialised industrial shows, and it is clear that this more highly segmented and focused approach is proving more successful, as evidenced by the increasing number of these types of exhibitions.

Reasons to use exhibitions

There are many reasons to use exhibitions, but the primary ones appear not to be 'to make sales' or 'because the competition is there' but because these events provide opportunities to meet potential and established customers and to create and sustain a series of relational exchanges. Li (2007), cited by Geigenmüller (2010), stresses that the impact of trade shows on the development of valuable, long-term buyer–seller relationships is important.

The main aims are, therefore, to develop long-term partnerships with customers, to build upon or develop the corporate identity and to gather up-to-date market intelligence (Shipley and Wong, 1993) and to exchange information about products, services and corporate developments. This implies that exhibitions should not be used as isolated events, but that they should be integrated into a series of activities, which serve to develop and sustain buyer relationships.

Costs can be reduced by using private exhibitions. The increased flexibility allows organisations to produce mini or private exhibitions for their clients at local venues (e.g. hotels). This can mean lower costs for the exhibitor and reduced time away from their businesses for those attending. The communications 'noise' and distraction associated with the larger public events can also be avoided by these private showings.

Viewpoint 16.2   Exhibiting with Stylecraft

Stylecraft, based in Yorkshire in the UK, are an established family-run business with a rich heritage in the textile trade. They provide high-quality, hand knitting yarns, and patterns that reflect the latest fashion trends.

Their target audience is women 35–65+ who craft, and they supply over 1,000 shops in the UK and export to many countries around the world. Their traditional forms of marketing communications include print, using advertisements in hobby magazines, to showcase products and competitions; direct mail, through post cards, brochures and letters sent to a direct target market; broadcast, with mentions of Stylecraft products on BBC's *This Morning*; and referral communications, which is otherwise known as 'word-of-mouth'. They have also recently reached into the digital world of marketing running social media platforms and e-campaigns alongside one another but, while they did attend some exhibitions, exhibition work was for some time not considered an effective form of communications.

Their decision to attend particular exhibitions was based on the vast number of opportunities that exhibitions present. These include the global promotion of the business and product, the local and international networking opportunities and the chance to enhance existing networks, and the chance to create new clients and customers through data capture techniques, running competitions and giveaways as an excellent way to capture data from potential customers and expand a database. It was also an opportunity to present the brand to the consumer directly, rather than through the prism of the retailers. A key part of exhibitions is to do extensive planning prior to the event, making sure to utilise all the available space and to follow up on any leads or data that is captured after the exhibition has taken place, as this will help to enhance new and existing relationships.

From May 2013 to May 2014 Stylecraft weren't involved with any type of exhibition or data capture and in 12 months saw a 30 per cent rise in social media engagement.

From May 2014 to March 2015 Stylecraft were involved in two B2B trade shows in Europe , to enhance export prospects, and one B2C exhibition at London's Alexandra Palace. During this time they saw a rise of over 500 per cent in social media engagement. E-campaign sign-ups rose from 4,000 to 9,000+ as competitions were held on the stand to capture data from interested customers and expand the brand's community. In addition, Stylecraft have seen a rise in sales each month since they did follow-up campaigns after the exhibitions to keep new customers engaged.

This Viewpoint was written by Melanie Bruton when she was studying Advertising and Marketing Communications at the University of Huddersfield.

Question: How would you use marketing communications to attract visitors to an exhibition at which Stylecraft were planning to attend?

Task: Make a list of the 10 critical activities associated with organising a trade show.

Exhibit 16.3 **Stylecraft started to attend more exhibitions and trade shows and saw their business grow**
Source: Stylecraft Ltd.co.uk.

Characteristics of exhibitions and trade fairs

The main reasons for attending exhibitions and trade fairs are that they enable organisations to meet customers (and potential customers) in an agreeable environment – one where both have independently volunteered their time to attend in order to place/take orders, to generate leads and to gather market information. The reasons for attending exhibitions are set out in Table 16.2.

From this it is possible to distinguish the following strengths and weaknesses of using exhibitions as part of the marketing communications programme.

Table 16.2 Reasons exhibitors choose to attend exhibitions

To meet existing customers
To take orders/make sales
To get leads and meet prospective new customers
To meet lapsed customers
To meet prospective members of the existing or new marketing channels
To provide market research opportunities and to collect marketing data

Strengths

The costs associated with exhibitions, if controlled properly, can mean that this is an effective and efficient means of communicating with customers. The costs per inquiry need to be calculated, but care needs to be taken over who is classified as an inquirer, as the quality of the audience varies considerably. Costs per order taken are usually the prime means of evaluating the success of an exhibition. This can paint a false picture, as the true success can never really be determined in terms of orders because of the variety of other factors that impinge upon the placement and timing of orders.

Products can be launched at exhibitions and, when integrated with a good PR campaign, a powerful impact can be made. This can also be used to reinforce corporate identity. Exhibitions are an important means of gaining information about competitors, buyers and technical and political developments in the market, and they often serve to facilitate the recruitment process. Above all else, exhibitions provide an opportunity to meet customers on relatively neutral ground and, through personal interaction, develop relationships. Products can be demonstrated, prices agreed, technical problems discussed and trust and credibility enhanced.

Weaknesses

One of the main drawbacks associated with exhibition work is the vast and disproportionate amount of management time that can be tied up with the planning and implementation of exhibitions. However, good planning is essential if the full potential benefits of exhibition work are to be realised.

Taking members of the sales force 'off the road' can also incur large costs. Depending on the nature of the business, these opportunity costs can soar. Some pharmaceutical organisations estimate that it can cost approximately £5,000 per person per week to divert salespeople in this way.

The expected visitor profile must be analysed in order that the number of quality buyers visiting an exhibition can be determined. The variety of visitors attending an exhibition can be misleading, as the vast majority may not be serious buyers or, indeed, may not be directly related to the industry or the market in question. Research by Gopalakrishna et al. (2010) has found that approximately 40 per cent of first-time exhibitors, spanning a range of industries, do not return to the same show the following year. As Gopalakrishna et al. (2010) point out, a growing concern for managers is the ability to reach relevant decision-makers. The researchers' response was to attempt an understanding of attendee behaviour, as this would help trade show organisers segment their audiences. From their research data they determined a typology of business show visitors. These are depicted in Table 16.3.

Exhibitions as a form of marketing communications

As a form of marketing communications, exhibitions enable products to be promoted, they can build brands and they can be an effective means of demonstrating

Table 16.3 A typology of trade show visitors

Segment name	Key characteristics
The basic shopper (40%)	Basic shoppers make about 7 'serious' visits to booths, 75% are planned, and 70% of visits are made to standalone booths which are accessible on all four sides.
The enthusiast (17%)	Enthusiasts make an average of 24 visits while at the trade show, more than three times that of the basic shopper; 80% of their visits are planned and they prefer to be 'where the action is'.
The niche shopper (17%)	The niche shopper makes an average of 9.2 visits, which is greater than the basic shopper but lower than the enthusiast. The key characteristic of this type of shopper is that 40% of their serious visits are made to small-sized booths. The niche shopper prefers to work with specialty exhibitors who do not have a big presence at the show.
The brand shopper (17%)	Brand shoppers make about 10 serious visits and show the highest preference for large booths. They are the most thorough in planning which booths to attend, reflecting their need to plan and make their visit to the show as efficient as possible.
The apathetic shopper (11%)	Only 33% of the apathetic shoppers' booth visits are planned. They also prefer booths that are open on three sides, and which have a wide selection of products. The suggestion is that apathetic shoppers might represent 'newcomers' or attendees who are unfamiliar with the trade show.

Source: Based on Gopalakrishna et al. (2010). © Emerald Group Publishing Limited. All rights reserved.

products and building industry-wide credibility in a relatively short period of time. Attendance at exhibitions may also be regarded from a political standpoint, in that non-attendance by competitors may be taken as an opportunity by attendees to suggest weaknesses.

In the B2B sector new products and services are often introduced at trade shows, especially if there are to be public relations activities and events that can be spun off the launch. In other words, exhibitions are not activities independent of the other communications tools. Exhibitions, if used effectively, can be part of an integrated communications campaign.

Advertising prior to, during and after a trade show can be dovetailed with public relations, sponsorship and personal selling. Sales promotions can also be incorporated through competitions among customers prior to the show to raise awareness, generate interest and to suggest customer involvement. Competitions during a show can be focused on the sales force to motivate and stimulate commercial activity and among visitors to generate interest in the stand, raise brand name awareness, encourage focus on particular products (new, revised or revolutionary) and generate sales leads and enquiries.

Perhaps above all else, trades shows and exhibitions play a major role in the development of relationships.

Multimedia and trade shows

In many ways the use of a website as brochureware represented a first attempt at an online exhibition. In these situations, commercial organisations provided opportunities for people who physically could not get to see a product to gain some appreciation of its size, configuration and capability (through text).

Online trade shows are web-based platforms giving manufacturers, suppliers and distributors an opportunity to exchange information, virtually. This facilitates speed, convenience and control of cost factors that influence small and medium-sized organisations. As noted by Geigenmüller (2010), online show visitors can call on virtual halls and booths to obtain information about a firm's products and its services. Interaction between buyers and sellers occurs through chat rooms or video conferences, and forums. Online diaries or blogs are also used to discuss issues or leave messages for other participants.

However, the development of multimedia technologies has given not only commercial but also not-for-profit organisations the opportunity to showcase their wares on a global basis. One type of organisation to explore the use of this technology has been museums and art collections (static exhibits). Dumitrescu et al. (2014) argue that virtual exhibitions are currently used as an extension to physical exhibitions. Their capacity to engage visitors with multiple forms of multimedia content, regardless of location, suggests that virtual exhibitions will become the established format.

The use of multimedia technologies enables audiences across the world to access these collections and with the use of audio, video clips and streaming video, in addition to pictures and extensive text, these exhibitions can be brought to life, visited repeatedly, focus given to particular exhibits, materials updated quickly and unobtrusively, and links made to other similar facilities (Foo, 2008). Referred to as virtual exhibitions, the key difference with previous brochureware-type facilities is the feeling of virtual reality, the sense that a digital visitor is actually in the exhibition, even though seated several thousand miles away.

The use of e-commerce and digital media in the management and presentation of exhibitions is increasing. It is unlikely that online exhibitions will ever replace the offline, real-world version, if only because of the need to form relationships and to network with industry members, to touch and feel products, and to sense the atmosphere and vitality that exhibitions generate. However, there is huge scope to develop specialised exhibitions, and to develop online showcases that incorporate exhibits (products and services) from a variety of geographically dispersed locations.

Marketing management of exhibitions

Good management of exhibitions represents some key aspects of marketing communications in general. Successful events are driven by planning that takes place prior to the exhibition, with communications inviting a range of stakeholders, not just customers, in advance of the exhibition event. Stands should be designed to deliver key messages and press releases and press information packs should be prepared and distributed appropriately.

During the event itself staff should be well briefed, trained and knowledgeable about their role in terms of the brand and in the exhibition process. After the exhibition it is vital to follow up on contacts made and discussions or negotiations that have been held. In other words, the exhibition itself is a planned marketing communications activity, one where activities need to be planned prior to, during and after the event. What is key is that these activities are coordinated, themed and supported by brand-oriented staff.

Above all else, exhibitions are an important way of building relationships and signalling corporate identity. Trade shows are an important means of providing corporate hospitality and showing gratitude to all an organisation's customers, but in particular to its key account customers and others of strategic interest. Positive relationships with customers, competitors and suppliers are often reinforced through face-to-face dialogue that happens both formally in the exhibition hall and informally through the variety of social activities that surround and support these events.

Hospitality and events

As mentioned in the previous chapter, event management is closely connected with brand experience, public relations, sponsorship and branding. It is considered here as an adjunct to the experiences associated with attending exhibitions or trade shows. Prospective purchasers visit a designated area or location where, unlike an exhibition, a single brand is available to be tried, sampled and experienced or just enjoyed as an unobtrusive support. One example is Virgin Media's V-Festival of music.

Product events

Product-oriented events are normally focused on increasing sales. Cookery demonstrations, celebrities autographing their books and the opening of a new store by the CEO or local MP are events aimed at generating attention, interest and sales of a particular product. Alternatively, events are designed to attract the attention of the media and, through stories and articles presented in the news, are able to reach a wide audience. See Exhibit 16.4 for an eye-catching example.

Corporate events

Events designed to develop the corporate body are often held by an organisation with a view to providing some entertainment. These can generate considerable local media coverage, which in turn facilitates awareness, goodwill and interest. For example, events such as open days, factory visits and donations of products to local events can be very beneficial.

| Exhibit 16.4 | **Paddy Power give the Uffington white horse a jockey** |

The public's attention was drawn to the annual Cheltenham Festival, a major horse racing event, by a 200ft wide and 110ft-tall jockey, depicted riding the 3,000-year-old chalk hillside engraving of a horse, known as the Uffington White H orse, in O xfordshire. S ponsored by the betting firm P addy P ower, the temporary jockey was created out of lightweight canvas, took six hours at night to be pinned to the ground with tent pegs, five feet from the famous chalk stallion. N ews coverage of the stunt was extensive.

McGrath (2012); The Sun (2012); www.youtube.com/watch?v=b8p4HQGX gak.

Source: Paddy Power plc.

Community events

These are activities that contribute to the life of the local community. Sponsoring local fun runs and children's play areas, making contributions to local community centres and the disabled are typical activities. The organisation attempts to become more involved with the local community as a good employer and good member of the community. This helps to develop goodwill and awareness in the community.

The choice of events an organisation becomes involved with is critical. The events should have a theme and be chosen to satisfy objectives established earlier in the communications plan.

Scholars' paper 16.2   **What is it with trade fairs?**

Yuksel, U. and Voola, R. (2010) Travel trade shows: exploratory study of exhibitors' perceptions, *Journal of Business & Industrial Marketing*, 25(4), 293–300.

This paper provides an insight into the motivations people and organisations have for participating in international trade shows. It also considers perceptions of effectiveness and the challenges faced by exhibiting firms. For exhibitors attendance is an effective and efficient way of presenting products/services and a good way of improving relationships with customers.

Packaging

Packaging has long been considered a means of protecting and preserving products during transit and while they remain in store or on the shelf prior to purchase and consumption. As Stewart (1995) aptly suggests, the function of packaging is to 'preserve product integrity'. In this sense, packaging can be regarded as an element of product strategy. To a certain extent this is still true; however, technology has progressed considerably and, with consumer choice continually widening, packaging has become a means by which buyers, particularly in consumer markets, can make significant brand choice decisions. Indeed, Wells et al. (2007) found that 73 per cent of people regard packaging as a significant contributor to their supermarket purchase decisions. Research by Silayoi and Speece (2007) found that the way Asian consumers perceive the convenience of a package can be the most important factor in the decision-making process for some segments. To that extent, because packaging can be used to convey persuasive information and be part of the decision-making process, yet still protect the contents, it is an important means of marketing communications in particular markets, such as FMCG.

Low-involvement decision-making often requires peripheral cues to stimulate buyers into action. It has already been noted that decisions made at the point of purchase, especially those in the FMCG sector, often require buyers to build awareness through recognition. The design of packages and wrappers is important, as continuity of design, combined with the power to attract and hold the attention of prospective buyers, is a vital part of point-of-purchase activity. The degree of importance that manufacturers place upon packaging and design can be seen in the increasing frequency with which brands seek legal redress when they feel their brand (packaging) has been copied (Satomura et al., 2014).

Although it is agreed that packaging can provide a strong point of differentiation, one that is increasingly recognised by food manufacturers and producers (Wells et al., 2007), the implementation of suitable packaging for different consumers is far from satisfactory. Sudbury-Riley (2014) found that packaging is regarded in many organisations as a technically based task, one where the goal is to develop particular functional specifications. Her research into the perceptions and experiences of packaging by senior citizens reveals that in addition to problems associated with wastage and mess, some forms of packaging were perceived to be 'difficult, time-consuming and frustrating' (p. 673). Part of her conclusion is that this serves to demonstrate that too few organisations appear to adopt a user-led orientation into the design of packaging and that this represents a major opportunity for companies. See Viewpoint 16.3 for a view of some of Tetra Pak's work with products for the disabled.

The communications dimensions of packaging

There are a number of dimensions that can affect the power and utility of a package. Colour is influential, as the context of the product class can frame the purchase situation for a buyer. This means that colours should be appropriate to the product class, to the brand and to the prevailing culture if marketing overseas. For example, red is used to stimulate the appetite, white to symbolise purity and cleanliness, blue to signal freshness, and green is increasingly being used to denote an environmental orientation and natural ingredients. From a cultural aspect, colours can be a problem. In China red is used to depict happiness, in Germany bright bold colours are regarded as appropriate for baby products, whereas in the UK pastel shades are more acceptable.

The shape of the packaging can be a strong form of persuasion. Verebelyi (2000) suggests that this influence may be due to the decorative impact of some brands. Various domestic cleaning products have packages with a twist in the neck, or a trigger action, facilitating directable and easier application.

The shape may also provide information about how to open and use the product, while some packages can be used for other purposes after the product has been consumed. For example, some jars can be reused as food containers, thereby providing a means of continual communications for the original brand in the home. Packaging can also be used as a means of brand identification, as a cue by which buyers recognise and differentiate a brand. The supreme example of this is the Coca-Cola contour bottle, with its unique shape and immediate power for brand recognition at the point of purchase.

Viewpoint 16.3   Making packaging work harder

Product innovation is important for both packaging manufacturers such as Tetra Pak, and consumer brands such as Coca-Cola.

To supersede the use of cans, glass jars or pouches, to store vegetables, beans, tomatoes, pet food, soups and sauces, Tetra Pak developed Tetra Recart®, a retortable carton package. This means that food content is sterilised inside the sealed package by applying heat and it can stay fresh for up to 24 months. Some of the benefits of these cartons for consumers are that they are easy to open, store and recycle, and for the retailers they occupy up to 40 per cent less shelf space than a round container. They are also more efficient to handle and transport due to the square shape and lighter weight. Tetra Pak also developed in 2013:

- HeliCap – a one-step screw cap designed to provide a good grip with a clearly visible tamper evidence ring.
- DreamCap – an ergonomically designed closure for on-the-go consumption.

Tetra Pak work with the Swedish Rheumatism Association (SRA) who certified five packages in 2013 for their ease of use. The SRA certifies products that are easy to open, close and use, and which recognise

| Exhibit 16.5 | **Tetra Pak's innovative packaging** |
| | *Source*: Tetra Pak. |

the specific needs of people with disabilities, particularly those with impaired hand strength, the elderly, and people with rheumatism-related diseases.

Packaging and the contour shaped bottle has been an integral part of the Coke brand for many years and is one of the main ways in which it engages consumers. When sales started to decline in Australia, however, Coke found a solution to reengage with the Millennials, a core consumer group. It took the risky approach of replacing its traditional branding with a customised approach that used Australia's most popular Teen first names. So, instead of asking for a 'Coke' the order was for a 'Mike', 'Dave' or 'Suzy.' Sales rebounded and the success of this customised packaging approach was then replicated in over 30 countries.

Source: www.tetrapak.com..

Question: To what extent is packaging an important element in the positioning process?

Task: Find a product positioned for the take-home market and make notes about the marketing communications used. Are the communications effective?

Package size is important, as different target markets may consume varying amounts of product. Toothpaste is available in large-size family tubes and in smaller containers for those households that do not use so much. However, the size of a package can also be an important perceptual stimulus. Research by Raghubir and Krishna (1999) found that the height of a container was an important variable that consumers used to make judgements about the volume of the container.

However, Folkes and Matta (2004) counter this by referring to *Gestalt* theory, which is concerned with holistic perspectives. They say that consumers use multiple dimensions to make judgements about objects (packages). Their research suggests that there is a relationship between the attractiveness of a package and the volume of the package. As a broad generalisation, the greater the attractiveness, the greater is the perceived volume. The implications of this insight have been implicitly known by marketing management for years, judging by the effort that is given to create attractive packaging and shelf stand-out.

In certain markets packaging can be strategically important as it can affect positioning. Ampuero and Vial (2006) identify colour, typography, graphical forms and images as the key packaging variables from a design perspective. They then consider how these combine to produce optimum positioning conditions. They conclude that cold, dark-coloured packaging, which shows the product, is perceived to be associated with products that are elegant and expensive. The packaging for products targeted at customers for whom a low price is important should be light-coloured and show illustrations of people.

In an attempt to create unity across its portfolio Coca-Cola announced that it was going to bring all Coke variants, classic Coke, Diet Coke, Coke Zero and Coke Life, under one master brand marketing banner. This had packaging implications in terms of how the variants were perceived and understood. Each variant continued to have a distinct colour, red, black, silver and green respectively, but the on-pack branding was made uniform, whilst the 'Cola-Cola' trademark was made larger and more visible. Text was also added to the front of Coke Zero, Coke Life and Diet Coke to enable consumers to better understand the range of products and their distinctive attributes (Spary, 2015).

Washing and dishwasher powder manufacturers now provide plastic refill packs that are designed to provoke brand loyalty. These packs are cheaper than the original pack, partly because some of the packaging expense has been reduced as the customer has been introduced to the product at an earlier time. Purchase of the refill pack is dependent on product quality and customer satisfaction and, as long as the brand name is prominent for identification and reminder purposes, the decision to select the refill is quicker, as most of the risk (financial, physical and social) has been removed through previous satisfactory usage.

All packages have to carry information concerning the ingredients, nutritional values and safety requirements, including sell-by and use-by dates. Eco-labels appear to generate positive reactions from consumers, particularly when there is low involvement. Research by Atkinson and Rosenthal (2014) indicates that the addition of eco-labels is likely to drive positive attitudes among consumers about both the product and the source. Traffic light colour-coded nutrition labels are used to signal that a food contains low, medium, or high amounts of particular negative contents/nutrients. The intention is to communicate that the product can therefore be consumed regularly (green), most of the time (amber), or only occasionally (red) (Koenigstorfer et al., 2014).

Non-food packages must also attempt to be sales agents and provide all the information that a prospective buyer might need, while at the same time providing conviction that this product is the correct one to purchase. Labelling of products offers opportunities to manufacturers to harmonise the in-store presentation of their products in such a way that buyers from different countries can still identify the brand and remain brand loyal.

Packages carry tangible and intangible messages. The psychological impact that packages can have should not be underestimated. They convey information about the product, but they also say something about its quality and how it differs from competitive offerings. In some cases, where there is little to differentiate products, buyers may use the packaging on its own for decision-making purposes.

Gordon and Valentine (1996) argue that the market, competitive and associated products, provide a context within which a brand's packaging communicates. This is achieved by using packaging that conforms to a design code that has been established for the category, and permits consumers to identify quickly the range of brands in the product field. However, it does not necessarily allow for the identification of individual brands. They make the important point that it is this process that allows own-label brands to become part of a category without the support of advertising to establish credibility.

Packaging has been termed passive and active (Southgate, 1994). Passive packaging relies on vast amounts of advertising to infuse the design to create interest (e.g. Heinz). This is similar to the above-the-line approach to branding. Active packaging is more demonstrative and tends to work with the other marketing and communications elements. Connolly and Davison (1996) cite Tango as an example of this type of packaging.

Scholars' paper 16.3 — Does packaging go with sponsorship?

Woodside, F. and Summers, J. (2011) Sponsorship leveraged packaging: an exploratory study in FMCG, *Journal of Marketing Communications*, 17(2), 87–105.

Integrated marketing communications often refers to the impact of a range of tools or media. Within the mix there are a number of pairs of tools that can work as primary/secondary drivers. This paper considers how consumers respond to sponsorship-leveraged packaging (SLP). This involves depicting the sponsored property's image, logos or symbols on the sponsoring brand's packaging (e.g. Weetabix sponsorship of Kids Triathlon). The paper contains useful insights into the relevant literature and associated theory.

Licensing

An increasingly important, yet expensive approach is to license a cartoon character, for example from *The Simpsons*, *Rugrats* or *South Park*, or a cyber-person such as Lara Croft who was used by Lucozade. These characters are then used strategically to build brands in order to attract the attention of children and provide the parental agreement necessary for a purchase to be made.

Licensing is not an option open to all organisations, yet of many of those who are able to utilise it, an increasing number are integrating this approach into their communications activities. Spurred by the surge in the numbers of digital characters and digital games, online and mobile games such as Angry Birds, Talking Friends, Moshi Monsters and MovieStarPlanet have, according to Macintosh (2012), not only attracted millions of players worldwide, in just a few years, but have also expanded into toys, clothing, TV shows, magazines and computer games.

According to Kwon et al. (2008), licensing is a commercial arrangement whereby a licensor, the party that holds the property rights or trademark, grants permission to others, called licensees, such as manufacturing companies, permitting them to manufacture products carrying the licensor's logo or trademark. Another simpler view is that a brand owner (licensor) grants a brand user (licensee) the right to use the brand in association with a defined product or service, for a specific period of time, and within defined terms, areas and territories, in return for the payment of a specific licence fee, royalty, or some such combination of financial rewards (Keller, 2003). Both interpretations are essentially the same, although the second might be closer to considering licensing as a form of brand extension (Weidmann and Ludwig, 2008). This is because the process of extension shifts the brand into a new, albeit slightly dissimilar, marketing context.

This practitioners' interpretation from Brand Licensing Europe (2012) states that:

it is the process of leasing a legally protected (that is, trademarked or copyrighted) entity – a name, likeness, logo, trademark, graphic design, slogan, signature, character, or a combination of several of these elements. The entity, known as the property or intellectual property, is then used in conjunction with a product. Many major companies and the media consider licensing a significant marketing tool.

Licensing is a form of brand alliance, of which there are many types. These are presented in Figure 16.4. Readers interested in brand alliances should read the paper by Ervelles et al. (2008).

A licensed product carries two different brand names or logos simultaneously. These are the brands of the licensor and the licensee. Park et al. (1996) refer to these as a *modifier*, such as a manufacturer's brand, and a *header*, the licensee's brand, such as the name or logo of a sports team. Kwon et al. (2008) cite as an example the licensing agreement between Ohio State University (OSU) and Nike over the OSU's Buckeyes' sweatshirt. Here Nike is the modifier and the header is OSU Buckeyes.

Licensing can benefit business in a number of ways. According to Weidmann and Ludwig (2008), licensing can:

- expand a product portfolio;
- increase the number of revenue streams;
- increase awareness – especially important when incorporated within an international marketing strategy;
- build brand equity;
- stimulate customer brand loyalty;
- develop partnerships with retailers;
- develop brand positioning.

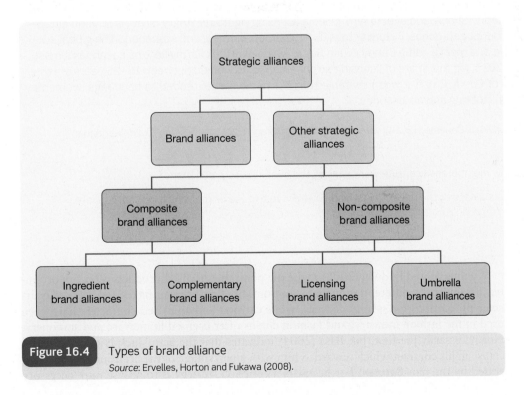

| Figure 16.4 | Types of brand alliance |

Source: Ervelles, Horton and Fukawa (2008).

Licensing enables brands to move into new businesses and markets without the major investment necessary for new manufacturing processes, machinery or facilities. Well-run licensing programmes are characterised by licensor's control over the brand image and how it is portrayed. This is achieved through an effective approvals process and other contractual obligations. The rewards of additional revenue (royalties) and profit are also accompanied by exposure in fresh media channels or even supermarket aisles (www.brandlicensing.eu).

Viewpoint 16.4	Getting the brand extended through licensing

Brands have used licensing to extend their reach and attract new customers. Jaguar have over 60 licences in operation worldwide. Harley-Davidson use a strategic licensing programme with over 100 licensees in 30 product categories worldwide. Vision-Ease, a manufacturer of optical lenses, licensed-in the Coppertone brand from Schering Plough enabling Vision-Ease to create a new premium segment of the polarised lens category.

Kodak went bankrupt in 2012, stopped making digital cameras and focused on printing-related equipment and technology markets. At the same time the company started to use its iconic name as part of a major brand licensing business. This alone was worth around US$51 million, in just a 3-month period in 2014. Traditionally Kodak's licensing arrangements have been based on a one-off, upfront payment. This is now changing to one that is based on revenue-sharing.

For example, Seedonk Inc., a video monitoring technology company, licensed the Kodak name for use with its new Baby Monitoring System, partly because the brand evokes family values. In 2013, Sakar International launched a line of Kodak camera and photo accessories whilst JK Imaging secured the rights to use the Kodak name with their digital camera. The Bullitt Group, based in the UK, make consumer electronics under the brand names of other companies, and in 2015 they launched a tablet computer and an Android smartphone under the Kodak name.

Licensing characters and content out of digital games and applications is popular and profitable, one which is replacing television and cartoon characters. The huge success of Angry Birds has led to multiple extensions, animation shorts and even a film. In India licensing rights for Angry Birds have been established over 14 product categories, including toys, board games, clothing and stationery. The global success of the online and mobile game Candy Crush Saga, which overtook Farmville 2 as Facebook's most popular game in 2013, led to a spate of licensing arrangements. As women between 18–25 years are the main consumers of Candy Crush, it was inevitable that the name was extended to handbags, women's footwear, fashion clothing and accessories.

Source: Bhushan (2014); Daneman (2014); www.beanstalk.com/brands/brand-extension-examples/jaguar/.

Question: How might brand licensing work against the best interests of a brand?

Task: Make a note of the markets in which you believe the use of licensing is not appropriate.

Weidmann and Ludwig (2008) make the point that licensed products offer opportunities for improved differentiation and stand-out. Breakfast cereals have used licensed character promotions for several decades, while cartoon and animated characters have been used in the fashion industry, and fashion chains offer licensed homeware and stationery. Not necessarily the first, but Bass (2004) indicates that the actor Jack Nicholson had a clause in his contract which rewarded him with a percentage of the licensing revenue generated by the film *Batman*. For licensors a common strategy is to license into 'accessory categories'. This occurs when the extension is something that accompanies consumption of the core product. Bass suggests that the strong emotional loyalty or bonding generated by a confectionery brand such as Kit Kat could lead into a Kit Kat mug, teaspoon, kettle and teapot.

However, although brand licensing appears to be well established and accepted, there are certain risks associated with this marketing communications activity. For example, product failure, poor quality or just a failure to reach expectations can reflect poorly on the licensor and the brand as a whole. In an age where conversations are a potent form of communications, product reviews, customer feedback as well as media comment and word-of-mouth communications can all have a negative impact on a brand. Mattell's experience of poor product quality, and associated health risks when some of its Fisher-Price toys were discovered to be coated with a potentially toxic, lead-based paint, led to a massive product recall and consequential negative conversations (Edwards, 2010). These products, made under licence in China, serve to warn of the issues at stake.

Scholars' paper 16.4   OK, so what exactly is a brand alliance?

Ervelles, S., Horton, V. and Fukawa, N. (2008) Understanding B2C brand alliances between manufacturers and suppliers, *Marketing Management Journal*, 18(2), 32–46.

The reason for singling out this paper is that the term 'brand alliance' has become increasing prevalent in the literature yet it remains fluid, loose and, at times, unclear. When trying to understand brand licensing it is helpful if the broader context of 'brand alliance' is clarified. This paper provides a useful clarification of this term and presents a typology of the common types of brand alliances in B2C markets. The differences between strategic alliances and brand alliances, and between brand alliances and co-branding, are established before there is an evaluation of composite brand alliances, including ingredient, umbrella, licensing, and complementary brand alliances.

Key points

- Brand placement is the inclusion of products and services in films (or media) for deliberate promotional exposure, often, but not always, in return for an agreed financial sum.

- It is regarded by some as a form of sales promotion, by others as sponsorship, but the most common linkage is with advertising, because the 'advertiser' pays a third party for the opportunity to present the product in their channel.

- There are distinct forms of placement. One involves the passive placement of a brand within the media; the other sees whole entertainment programmes built around a single brand, one where the placement is actively woven into the theme or the plot of the programme. This is known as 'branded entertainment'.

- The main reasons for attending exhibitions (consumer shows) and trade fairs (B2B shows) are that it enables organisations to: meet customers (and potential customers) in an agreeable environment, one where both have independently volunteered their time to attend; place/take orders; generate leads; and gather market information.

- As a form of marketing communications, exhibitions enable products to be promoted, they can build brands and they can be an effective means of demonstrating products and building industry-wide credibility in a relatively short period of time.

- Positive relationships with customers, competitors and suppliers are often reinforced through face-to-face dialogue that happens both formally in the exhibition hall and informally through the variety of social activities that surround and support these events.

- Packages carry tangible and intangible messages and packaging has become a means by which buyers, particularly in consumer markets, can make significant brand choice decisions. Packaging conveys information about the product, but it also makes a statement about the quality of the product and how it differs from competitive offerings.

- Packaging has become a means by which buyers, particularly in consumer markets, can make significant brand choice decisions and constitutes more than a means of preserving product integrity.

- Licensing is a commercial arrangement where a brand owner (licensor) grants a brand user (licensee) the right to use the brand in association with a defined product or service, for a specific period of time, and within defined terms, areas and territories, in return for the payment of a specific licence fee, royalty, or some such combination of financial rewards.

- A licensed product carries two different brand names or logos simultaneously. These are the brands of the licensor and the licensee.

- Licensing enables brands to move into new businesses and markets without the major investment necessary for new manufacturing processes, machinery or facilities.

- Well-run licensing programmes are characterised by the licensor's control over the brand image and how it is portrayed. This is achieved through an effective approvals process and other contractual obligations. The rewards of additional revenue (royalties) and profit are also accompanied by exposure in fresh media channels or even supermarket aisles.

Review questions

Beyoncé music licensing case questions

1. What might be the goals associated with licensing arrangements in the music industry?

2. Make notes about the ideal context for the use of licensing.

3. Find three examples of brand licensing in the food industry.

4. What opportunities are there for music within brand placement?

5. To what extent might individual music artists encourage licensing?

General questions

1. Identify two strengths and two weaknesses of brand placement. Identify four examples of brand placement and evaluate their effectiveness.

2. Evaluate the differences between consumer- and business-oriented trade shows.

3. As sales manager for a company making plastic mouldings for use in the manufacture of consumer durables, set out the reasons for and against attendance at trade shows and exhibitions.

4. Find three brands where the shape of a package is an integral part of the product.

5. What is the difference between active and passive packaging?

References

Advertising Association (2008) *Advertising Statistics YearBook 2008*, Henley on Thames: Advertising Association.

Ampuero, O. and Vial, N. (2006) Consumer perceptions of product packaging, *Journal of Consumer Marketing*, 23(2), 100–12.

Atkinson, L. and Rosenthal, S. (2014) Signaling the green sell: the influence of eco-label source, argument specificity, and product involvement on consumer trust, *Journal of Advertising*, 43(1), 33–45.

Bass, A. (2004) Licensed extensions – stretching to communicate, *Brand Management*, 12(1), 31–38.

Bertheron, P., Pitt, L.F. and Watson, R.T. (1996) The World Wide Web as an advertising medium, *Journal of Advertising Research*, 6(1), 43–54.

Bhushan, R. (2014) Candy Crush to launch designer clothes, handbags: inks licensing deal with Dream Theatre, *The Economic Times*, 5 December 2014, retrieved 28 December 2014 from http://economictimes.indiatimes.com/industry/services/retail/candy-crush-to-launch-designer-clothes-handbags-inks-licensing-deal-with-dream-theatre/articleshow/45379133.cms.

Boukersi, L. (2000) The role of trade fairs and exhibitions in international marketing communications, in *The Handbook of International Marketing Communications* (ed. S. Moyne), London: Blackwell, 117–35.

Brand Licensing Europe (2012) What is licensing?, retrieved 9 September 2012 from www.brandlicensing.eu/licensees-and-manufacturers-2/.

Burgess, K. (2014) Bond author drives into literary storm, *The Times*, 15 November, p. 11.

Chen, H. and Haley, E. (2014) Product placement in social games: consumer experiences in China, *Journal of Advertising*, 43(3), 286–95.

Connolly, A. and Davison, L. (1996) How does design affect decisions at point of sale? *Journal of Brand Management*, 4(2), 100–7.

Dan, A. (2014) Just how does Coca-Cola reinvent itself in a changed world? *Forbes*, 7 October, retrieved 21 December 2014 from www.forbes.com/sites/avidan/2013/10/07/just-how-does-coca-cola-reinvent-itself-in-a-changed-world/.

Daneman, M. (2014) Kodak brand is returning to store shelves, *USA Today*, 26 December 2014, retrieved 28 December 2014, from www.usatoday.com/story/tech/2014/12/26/kodak-branding/20910231/.

D'Astous, A. and Séguin, N. (1999) Consumer reactions to product placement strategies in television sponsorship, *European Journal of Marketing*, 33(9/10), 896–910.

DeLorme, D.E. and Reid, L.N. (1999) Moviegoers' experiences and interpretation of brands in films revisited, *Journal of Advertising*, 28(2), 71–95.

Dumitrescu, G., Lepadatu, C. and Ciurea, C. (2014) Creating virtual exhibitions for educational and cultural development, *Informatica Economică*, 18(1), 102–10.

Edwards, H. (2010) The supply-chain reaction, *Marketing*, 19 May, retrieved 1 March 2012 from www.brandrepublic.com/opinion/1003783/Helen-Edwards-Branding-supply-chain-reaction/?DCMP=ILC-SEARCH.

Ervelles, S., Horton, V. and Fukawa, N. (2008) Understanding B2C brand alliances between manufacturers and suppliers, *Marketing Management Journal*, 18(2), 32–46.

Felix, S. and Stampler, L. (2012) The evolution of James Bond movie product placement, *Business Insider*, 21 October, retrieved 21 December 2014 from www.businessinsider.com/heres-how-james-bonds-relationship-with-product-placement-has-changed-2012-10?op=1&IR=T.

Folkes, V. and Matta, S. (2004) The effect of package shape on consumers' judgments of product volume: attention as a mental contaminant, *Journal of Consumer Research*, 31(2), 390–402.

Foo, S. (2008) Online virtual exhibitions: concepts and design considerations, *Journal of Library and Information Technology*, 28(4), July, 22–34.

Fry, A. (2010) Cashing in on the Twilight phenomenon, *Marketing*, 21 July, 30–31.

Geigenmüller, A. (2010) The role of virtual trade fairs in relationship value creation, *Journal of Business and Industrial Marketing*, 25(4), 284–92.

Gopalakrishna, S., Roster, C.A. and Sridhar, S. (2010) An exploratory study of attendee activities at a business trade show, *Journal of Business & Industrial Marketing*, 25(4), 241–48.

Gordon, W. and Valentine, V. (1996) Buying the brand at point of choice, *Journal of Brand Management*, 4(1), 35–44.

Gould, S.J., Gupta, P.B. and Grabner-Kräuter, S. (2000) Product placements in movies: a cross-cultural analysis of Austrian, French, and American consumers' attitudes toward this emerging international promotional medium, *Journal of Advertising*, 29(4), 41–58.

Gregorio, F. de and Sung, Y.J. (2010) The influence of consumer socialization variables on attitude toward product placement, *Journal of Advertising*, 39(1), 85–99.

Gupta, P.B., Balasubramanian, S.K. and Klassen, M.L. (2000) Viewers' evaluations of product placements in movies: policy issues and managerial implications, *Journal of Current Issues and Research in Advertising*, 22(2), 41–52.

Hackley, C. and Tiwsakul, R. (2006) Entertainment marketing and experiential consumption, *Journal of Marketing Communications*, 12(1), 63–75.

Hang, H. (2012) The implicit influence of bimodal brand placement on children, *International Journal of Advertising*, 31(3), 465–84.

Hirschman, E.C. and Thompson, C.J. (1997) Why media matter: toward a richer understanding of consumers' relationships with advertising and mass media, *Journal of Advertising*, 26(1), 43–60.

Homer, P. (2009) Product placements: the impact of placement type and repetition on attitude, *Journal of Advertising*, 38(3), 21–31.

Hudson, S. and Hudson, D. (2006) Branded entertainment: a new advertising technique or product placement in disguise? *Journal of Marketing Management*, 22(5–6), 489–504.

Kamleitner, B. and Jyote, A.K. (2013) How using versus showing interaction between characters and products boosts product placement effectiveness, *International Journal of Advertising*, 32(4), 633–53.

Kandhadai, R. and Saxena, R. (2014) Brand placement: new perspectives and a comprehensive definition, *The Marketing Review*, 14(3), 231–44.

Karrh, J.A. (1998) Brand placement: impression management predictions of audience impact, PhD dissertation, College of Journalism and Communications, University of Florida, Gainesville.

Karrh, J.A., McKee, K.B., Britain, K. and Pardun, C.J. (2003) Practitioners' evolving views of product placement effectiveness, *Journal of Advertising Research*, 43(2), 138–50.

Keller, K.L. (2003) *Strategic Brand Management: Building, measuring and managing brand equity*, 2nd edition, Upper Saddle River, NJ: Pearson Education.

Koenigstorfer, J., Groeppel-Klein, A., and Kamm, F. (2014) Healthful food decision making in response to traffic light color-coded nutrition labeling, *Journal of Public Policy & Marketing*, 33(1), 65–77.

Kwak, H., Andras, T.L. and Zinkhan, G.M. (2009) Advertising to active viewers: consumer attitudes in the US and South Korea, *International Journal of Advertising*, 28(1), 49–75.

Kwon, H.H., Kim, H. and Mondello, M. (2008) Does a manufacturer matter in cobranding? The influence of a manufacturer brand on sport team licensed apparel, *Sport Marketing Quarterly*, 17, 163–72.

Lee, T., Sung, Y. and Choi, S.M. (2011a) Young adults' responses to product placement in movies and television shows: a comparative study of the United States and South Korea, *International Journal of Advertising*, 30(3), 479–507.

Lee, T., Sung, Y. and de Gregorio, F. (2011b) Cross-cultural challenges in product placement, *Marketing Intelligence & Planning*, 29(4), 366–84.

Li, L.Y. (2007) Marketing resources and performance of exhibitor firms in trade shows: a contingent resource perspective, *Industrial Marketing Management*, 36, 360–70.

MacIntosh, E. (2012) Exploring licensing's new gaming frontier, *Marketing*, 10 February.

McKechnie, S.A. and Zhou, J. (2003) Product placement in movies: a comparison of Chinese and American consumers' attitudes, *International Journal of Advertising*, 22(3), 349–74.

Nebenzahl, I.D. and Secunda, E. (1993) Consumer attitudes toward product placement in movies, *International Journal of Advertising*, 12, 1–11.

Nelson, M.R. and Devanathan, N. (2006) Brand placements Bollywood style, *Journal of Consumer Behaviour*, 5(3), 211–21.

Park, C., Jun, W.S.Y. and Shocker, A.D. (1996) Composite branding alliances: an investigation of extension and feedback effects, *Journal of Marketing Research*, 33(4), 453–66.

Pervan, S.J. and Martin, B.A.S. (2002) Product placement in US and New Zealand television soap operas: an exploratory study, *Journal of Marketing Communications*, 8, 101–13.

Plaut, M. (2004) Ford advertises the literary way, *BBC News/Business*, retrieved 20 March 2008 from http://news.bbc.co.uk/1/hi/business/3522635.stm.

Raghubir, P. and Krishna, A. (1999) Vital dimensions in volume perception: can the eye fool the stomach? *Journal of Marketing Research*, 36 (August), 313–26.

Reijmersdal, E.A. van (2011) Mixing advertising and editorial content in radio programmes: appreciation and recall of brand placements versus commercials, *International Journal of Advertising*, 30(3), 425–46.

Russell, C.A. and Belch, M. (2005) A managerial investigation into the product placement industry, *Journal of Advertising Research*, 45(1), 73–92.

Satomura, T., Wedel, M. and Pieters, R. (2014) Copy alert: a method and metric to detect visual copycat brands, *Journal of Marketing Research*, LI (February), 1–13.

Shipley, D. and Wong, K.S. (1993) Exhibiting strategy and implementation, *International Journal of Advertising*, 12(2), 117–30.

Silayoi, P. and Speece, M. (2007) The importance of packaging attributes: a conjoint analysis approach, *European Journal of Marketing*, 41(11/12), 1495–517.

Smit, E., Reijmersdal, E. van and Neijens, P. (2009) Today's practice of brand placement and the industry behind it, *International Journal of Advertising*, 28(5), 761–82.

Southgate, P. (1994) *Total Branding by Design*, London: Kogan Page.

Spary, S. (2015) Coca-Cola unveils major redesign as it shifts from brand-specific ads, *Brand Republic*, 5 March, retrieved 3 April 2015 from www.brandrepublic.com/article/1336737/coca-cola-unveils-major-redesign-shifts-brand-specific-ads.

Stewart, B. (1995) *Packaging as an Effective Marketing Tool*, Surrey: Pira International.

Sudbury-Riley, L. (2014) Unwrapping senior consumers' packaging experiences, *Marketing Intelligence & Planning*, 32(6), 666–86.

Sung, Y. and de Gregorio, F. (2008) Brand new world: a comparison of consumers' attitudes toward brand placement in film, television shows, songs and video games, *Journal of Promotion Management*, 14(1/2), 85–101.

Sung, Y., Gregorio de, F. and Jung, J. (2009) Non-student consumer attitudes towards product placement: implications for public policy and advertisers, *International Journal of Advertising*, 28(2), 257–85.

Verebelyi, N. (2000) The power of the pack, *Marketing*, 27 April, 37.

Weidmann, K.-P. and Ludwig, D. (2008) How risky are brand licensing strategies in view of customer perceptions and reactions? *Journal of General Management*, 33(3), 31–52.

Wells, L.E., Farley, H. and Armstrong, G.A. (2007) The importance of packaging design for own-label food brands, *International Journal of Retail and Distribution Management*, 36(9), 677–90.

Chapter 17
Messages and creativity

The message an organisation conveys is a critical aspect of marketing communications. This means consideration must be given to what organisations say, how they say it and the meaning people are expected to ascribe to these messages. Ensuring that the right balance of information and emotion is achieved and that the presentation of the message is appropriate for the target audience is important. Above all, messages must be creative if they are to get attention from the audiences or publics they are trying to engage.

Aims and learning objectives

The aims of this chapter are to consider some of the ways in which marketing communications messages can be presented.

The learning objectives are to enable readers to:

1. consider the importance and characteristics of source credibility;
2. explain the different ways messages can be constructed;
3. examine the various ways in which advertising appeals can be presented;
4. describe how informational and transformational motives can be used as tactical tools in a communications plan;
5. explore the role of creativity and how the creative process is managed;
6. understand how message framing, storytelling and user-generated content are used in marketing communications.

John Lewis - 'Monty's Christmas'

Founded in 1864, John Lewis are the UK's largest department store retailer, with 31 department stores, 10 home shops and an established online business. With a vast range of products on sale, from tights to home insurance, the chain's target market is broad.

In 2009 the British economy was in recession, unemployment had risen and consumer spending was falling. John Lewis found their sales were in decline and realised they needed to take action. Although before 2009 little advertising had been done by the retailer apart from supporting new store openings, John Lewis recognised that advertising had the power to influence consumers and could help in increasing consumer spending and attract new customers. They approached their agency with a brief to re-engage customers with the brand and drive greater brand loyalty.

Research showed John Lewis that emotional affinity was a key driver of customer loyalty and this made the communications strategy clear. They realised very early on in the process that they needed to engage consumers emotionally with the brand. With Christmas approaching, which is a key trading period for retailers in the UK with consumers buying gifts for family and friends, this was the time to put their new strategy to the test. In the past most retailers have used their advertising to showcase their range of gifts, with advertising acting like 'video catalogues',

and merchandise displayed in a Christmas setting. They realised that to grow their share of this seasonal spend their message needed to stand out from their competitors and engage consumers differently.

In 2009, they launched their first Christmas ad in what has become an iconic series of emotionally led campaigns for John Lewis. Based on a new positioning strategy of 'thoughtful giving', the first Christmas ad, called 'Remember the Feeling', ran in the UK. It was the start of a longer-term drive to engage consumers with the brand on an emotional level.

The first Christmas campaign was a huge success. As well as improving brand perception, the campaign delivered increased penetration, frequency and spend for the retailer, which directly contributed towards sales and profitability. They showed that they were able to activate emotional engagement with the brand through advertising. Since the first Christmas ad for John Lewis ran in 2009 the retailer has continued with the strategy of 'thoughtful giving' as a campaign.

In 2014, John Lewis created an ad called 'Monty's Christmas', a powerful story of friendship, love and compassion, which continued their strategy of engaging consumers on an emotional level. The story tells the tale of a young boy called Sam and his Adélie penguin friend, Monty.

Exhibit 17.1   **Monty the Adélie penguin, star of the Christmas campaign**
Source: John Lewis.

The plot develops as we see Monty and Sam spending their time together; they play hide-and-seek, football and go to the park together. The ad draws on childhood memories of games played and the cartoons enjoyed like Pingu: devices used to summon memories of when they too were young. As the story of this childhood friendship continues, Sam begins to notice that Monty is sad and realises that he is longing for a companion. The defining moment of the story comes on Christmas morning when Sam reveals his present for Monty, a female penguin companion called Mabel. This creates a memorable moment in the story that touched audiences on an emotional level and holds true to the brand's positioning of 'thoughtful giving'.

The idea of using a story about thoughtful giving was derived from consumer insight. Focus group research had identified how stories about finding gifts for someone you love resonated with the target audience. This insight was used to develop a creative platform about giving that was seen to be authentic and tapped into consumers' emotions. The use of storytelling is an effective creative technique used to engage audiences. Individuals are able to identify with the characters and this encourages them to want to become part of the story. Using a theme within a story that focusses on the search for love and friendship is one that most humans can relate to and allows audiences to connect with the ad emotionally. Music was used to provide a powerful emotional backdrop to the ad, with the ad set to the track of 'Real Love', a track originally written and recorded by John Lennon and re-recorded by Tom Odell.

Prior to broadcasting the ad, John Lewis ran a teaser campaign using #MontyThePenguin on digital outdoor advertising sites and on Channel 4 to build a sense of anticipation. The 120-second video ad was launched on John Lewis's social media channels on 6 November 2014 and within 24 hours it had received 7 million views. The first ad aired on TV the following day during the first advert break in Gogglebox on Channel 4. By the end of the first week the ad had received over 16 million views on social media and 'Monty' had become the most searched for term on the John Lewis website.

Previous Christmas campaigns have identified the importance of social engagement for John Lewis and this strategy was continued for 'Monty's Christmas'. Consumers were encouraged to join the Monty conversation through Twitter and Monty provided regular updates on his Christmas planning through Tweets. It did not take long for Monty to become part of the national conversation and Monty was being talked about in the media. Radio stations interviewed experts about Adélie penguins and the campaign was discussed on national TV channels. Monty had entered popular culture with magazine cartoonists using parodies of the advertising. Within days parodies appeared on YouTube, many featuring celebrities. Even some Christmas pantomimes included topical Monty jokes.

Exhibit 17.2	**A female penguin companion called Mabel is Sam's thoughtful Christmas gift to Monty**
	Source: John Lewis.

The campaign message was amplified beyond the TV campaign using interactive experiential marketing. In partnership with Samsung, John Lewis created an in-store space called Monty's Den, which used a series of technology-firsts to harness the power of children's imagination. This included 'Monty's Magical Toy Machine', which enabled children to bring their favourite toys to life through innovative Microsoft technology, and 'Monty's Goggles', which used Google Cardboard to allow children to enter a 360° virtual world and interact with Sam and Monty. Children were also able to create their very own Monty Christmas card on the Samsung Galaxy Tab S.

John Lewis also developed a range of merchandise inspired by Monty and Mabel that was available in-store over the Christmas period. This further extended the campaign in-store, providing a reminder of the campaign message. As well as Monty and Mabel clothing and plush toys, John Lewis commissioned a children's book called *Monty's Christmas*. Proceeds of the book went to Barnardo's, John Lewis's 150th anniversary charity, further extending the campaign message of 'thoughtful giving'.

Following the first week of the launch, John Lewis ran three shorter versions of the ad over the following six weeks leading up to Christmas. The media strategy aimed to optimise the emotional strategy of the campaign through TV buying that focussed on emotional programming. Media targeted shows such as *X Factor* which were seen to have higher levels of emotional engagement by audiences and were seen to generate higher levels of conversations on social media platforms.

The cost of the overall campaign was £7 million, with a budget of £1 million spent on production. The success of the campaign is reflected in John Lewis's trading results with the retailer enjoying one of the most successful Christmas trading periods in their 150-year history. Pre-Christmas sales were 5.8 per cent higher than the previous year. The campaign demonstrated the power of emotion in creativity and the commercial value that can be gained from emotional advertising.

This case was contributed by XXXX who is XXXX at adam&eveDDB

Questions relating to this case study can be found at the end of the chapter.

Introduction

Developing the right messages for the right audience is one of the biggest challenges for brands. The message that is created must engage with the target audience and stand out from competitors and other communications messages if it is to be effective. This means that the message appeal needs to be carefully considered and the organisation and its agency must work together to develop messages that are creative. This chapter considers the variety and forms of the different appeals and the importance of creativity.

The John Lewis campaign described above illustrates how an emotional appeal has been used to build brand loyalty and demonstrates the power that emotion can bring to communications messages. In addition to resonating with target audiences, breaking away from traditional retail category formats means that the message stands out from others. Being novel and yet appropriate to the target audience is a key aspect of advertising creativity.

This chapter explores four key elements that need to be considered in message appeals and creativity. First, attention is given to the source of a message and issues relating to source credibility. This includes the advantages and disadvantages of using a spokesperson. Second, consideration is given to how messages are constructed and the balance in the use of information and emotion in messages. Third, the chapter explores the various appeals and ways in which messages can be presented and framed, including storytelling. Lastly, consideration is given to creativity: the impact it can have on the effectiveness of a campaign and the management of the creative process.

Message source

Messages are perceived in many different ways and are influenced by a variety of factors. A critical determinant, however, concerns the credibility that is attributed to the source of the message itself. Kelman (1961) believed that the source of a message has three particular characteristics. These are: the level of perceived credibility as seen in terms of perceived objectivity and expertise; the degree to which the source is regarded as attractive and message recipients are motivated to develop a similar association or position; and the degree of power that the source is believed to possess. This is manifested in the ability of the source to reward or punish message receivers. The two former characteristics are evident in various forms of marketing communications, but the latter is directly observable in personal selling situations, and perhaps in the use of sales promotions.

Following this work on source characteristics, three key components of source credibility can be distinguished:

● What is the level of perceived expertise (how much relevant knowledge is the source thought to hold)?

● What are the personal motives the source is believed to possess (what is the reason for the source to be involved)?

● What degree of trust can be placed in what the source says or does on behalf of the endorsement?

No matter what the level of expertise, if the level of trust is questionable, credibility will be adversely affected.

Scholars' paper 17.1   **The credibility of source credibility**

Kelman, H.C. (1961) Process of opinion change, *Public Opinion Quarterly,* **25 (Spring), 57–78.**

This is a seminal paper in this subject and all students of marketing communications should be familiar with it. Kelman suggested that successful communications emanate from sources that are credible, attractive and powerful. Subsequently, there has been much research into the impact and effect of source credibility in different situations and on different subjects. The prevailing view remains that people think more about messages from sources that they consider to be highly credible, than those from low-credibility sources.

See also: Halonen-Knight, E. and Hurmerinta, L. (2010) Who endorses whom? Meanings transfer in celebrity endorsement, *Journal of Product & Brand Management,* 19(6), 452–60; Hollensen, S. and Schimmelpfennig, C. (2013) Selection of celebrity endorsers: a case approach to developing an endorser selection process model, *Marketing Intelligence & Planning,* 31(1), 88–102.

Establishing credibility

Credibility can be established in a number of ways. One simple approach is to list or display the key attributes of the organisation or the product and then signal trustworthiness through the use of third-party endorsements and the comments of satisfied users.

A more complex approach is to use referrals, suggestions and association. Trustworthiness and expertise are the two principal elements of source credibility. One way of developing trust is to use spokespersons to speak on behalf of the sponsor of an advertisement and, in effect, provide a testimonial for the product in question. Credibility, therefore, can be established by the initiator of the advertisement or by a spokesperson used by the initiator to convey the message.

Effectively, consumers trade off the validity of claims made by brands against the perceived trustworthiness (and expertise) of the individuals or organisations who deliver the message. The result is that a claim may have reduced impact if either of these two components is doubtful or not capable of verification but, if repeated enough times, will enable audiences to accept that the products are very effective and of sufficiently high performance for them to try.

Credibility established by the initiator

The credibility of the organisation initiating the communications process is important. An organisation should seek to enhance its reputation with its various stakeholders at every opportunity.

However, organisational credibility is derived from the image, which in turn is a composite of many perceptions. Past decisions, current strategy and performance indicators, the level of perceived service and the type of performance of network members (e.g. high-quality retail outlets) all influence the perception of an organisation and the level of credibility that follows.

The need to establish high levels of credibility allows organisations to divert advertising spend away from a focus on brands to one that focuses on the organisation. Corporate advertising seeks to adjust organisation image and to build reputation.

Viewpoint 17.1	Reverse credibility to Save the Rhino

Rhino poaching has escalated in recent years. Estimates from Save the Rhino International suggest the rate of rhino deaths may overtake the rate of births in 2015/16, potentially leading to extinction of all five species of rhinos.

Charities keen to stop the demand for rhino horn in Asia are targeting businessmen who buy rhino horn products for colleagues as part of the corporate gifting culture.

Launched on World Rhino Day, 22 September 2014, the 'Chi' campaign was an attempt to reduce the demand for rhino horn products in Vietnam using behavioural change practices. The 'Chi' campaign was a collaboration between TRAFFIC (a wildlife trade monitoring network) and Save the Rhino, and funded by the UK government. The campaign was developed by PSI (a global marketing organisation).

Research indicated that the presence of a conservation charity logo reduced the credibility of the promotional material in the eyes of the target audience, Vietnamese urban males aged 30–55. Additionally, the presence of rhinos on promotional material evoked the opposite of the response desired – it amplified the attraction of owning rhino horn products.

A new approach to gaining source credibility was needed. In Vietnamese culture, 'Chi' is the word termed to a natural energy said to come from within. 'Chi', often translated as 'will', is an old Vietnamese belief that the campaign creators felt would strike a chord with their Vietnamese target audience. The outcome was a campaign that does not use charity logos or images of rhinos. Instead, the 'chi' campaign focuses on the emotional motivations that lead the user group to use rhino horn, such as peer approval, success and health. This plays on Kelman's theory, as source attractiveness is increased when the audience can relate to the character disseminating the message. The idea communicated is that success,

> **Exhibit 17.3**   **The 'Chi' campaign was an attempt to reduce the demand for ivory products in Vietnam**
> *Source*: Save the Rhino International.

masculinity and good luck flow from an individual's internal strength of character and refutes the view that these traits come from a piece of horn.

Source: IFAW (2014); Save the Rhino International (2014); TRAFFIC (2014); WildAid (2014).

This Viewpoint was written by Carlton Brady when he was a postgraduate marketing student at the University of the West of England.

Question:	What role did source credibility play in the case of the 'Chi' campaign?
Task:	Find an animal welfare campaign that has used advertising and evaluate how they have used source credibility within their message.

Credibility established by a spokesperson

People who deliver the message are often regarded as the source, when in reality they are only the messenger. These people carry the message and represent the true source or initiator of the message (e.g. manufacturer or retailer). Consequently, the testimonial they transmit must be credible. There are four main types of spokesperson: the expert, the celebrity, the chief executive officer and the consumer.

The expert has been used many times and was particularly popular when television advertising first established itself in the 1950s and 1960s. Experts are quickly recognisable because they either wear white coats, and round glasses, or dress and act like 'mad professors'. Through the use of symbolism, stereotypes and identification, these characters (and indeed others) can be established very quickly in the minds of receivers and a frame of reference generated that does not question the authenticity of the message being transmitted by such a person. Experts can also be users of products – for example, professional photographers endorsing cameras, professional hairdressers endorsing shampoos and professional golfers endorsing golf equipment.

Entertainment and sporting celebrities are being used increasingly, not only to provide credibility for a range (e.g. Nicole Kidman for Etihad, Gary Lineker for Walkers), but also to grab the attention of people in markets where motivation to decide between competitive products may be low. The celebrity enables the message to stand out among the clutter and noise that typify many markets. However, celebrities often demand high costs to appear in campaigns. For example, Nicole Kidman was paid £2 million to appear in Chanel's 2004 No5 TV commercial (Anon, 2015).

There are some potential problems that advertisers need to be aware of when considering the use of celebrities. First, does the celebrity fit the image of the brand and will the celebrity be acceptable to the target audience? Consideration also needs to be given to the longer-term relationship between the celebrity and the brand. Should the lifestyle of the celebrity change, what impact will this change have on the target audiences and their attitude towards the brand? Yin (2008) suggests that brand owners should use proprietary agency tools and focus groups to ensure that the celebrity's personality fits the brand.

Research companies can measure the power of celebrities. Millward Brown's *Cebra Score* (celebrity + brand), for example, enables brands to research beyond just how well known a celebrity is or 'Familiarity' and measures factors such as 'Affinity' or how well they are liked and 'Marketability' and 'Entertainment', which indicate how much the celebrity is talked about online and offline (Cobra, 2010). They provide an overall FAME rating that allows brands to determine the celebrity's attractiveness for a brand. Additional commissioned research is then needed to determine if the brand and celebrity would make a good partnership. Halonen-Knight and Hurmerinta (2010), highlighted in Scholars' papers 17.1, argue that celebrity endorsement needs to be seen as a brand alliance with celebrities selected and managed in a similar manner to any other brand alliance partnership.

Exhibit 17.4	Sir Richard Branson and Steven Fry appear in an ad for Virgin Media

The ad, which aims to highlight the speed and function of Virgin Media's TiVo service, allows Sir Richard Branson to play himself in a light-hearted cameo role alongside celebrity actor Steven Fry. This is not the first time Virgin Media's CEO has appeared in the brand's advertising. He has previously had background parts in ads alongside sports personality Usain Bolt and celebrity actor David Tennant.

Source: Rex Shutterstock/Tom Oldham.

The second problem concerns the impact that the celebrity makes relative to the brand. There is a danger that those receiving the message remember the celebrity but not the brand that is the focus of the advertising spend. The *celebrity* becomes the hero, rather than the product being advertised.

Brownsell (2009) discusses the problems that can occur when the celebrity is also the CEO of the company. Apple's Steve Jobs provided a good example of the impact that transition in company leadership can have on a brand. Despite the potential issues associated with CEO celebrity endorsement, many heads of organisations have relished the chance to front their brands. One of the more prominent CEOs in the UK is Sir Richard Branson, who has fronted campaigns for a number of brands within the Virgin portfolio including Virgin Media and Virgin financial products.

When using consumers as the spokesperson to endorse products, the audience is being asked to identify with a 'typical consumer'. The identification of similar lifestyles, interests and opinions allows for better reception and understanding of the message. Consumers are often depicted testing similar products, such as margarine and butter. The Pepsi Challenge required consumers to select Pepsi from Coca-Cola through blind taste tests. Showing someone using the product, someone who is similar to the receiver, means that the source is perceived as credible and the potential for successful persuasion is considerably enhanced.

Sleeper effects

The assumption so far has been that high credibility enhances the probability of persuasion and successful communications. This is true when the receiver's initial position is opposite to that contained in the message. When the receiver's position is favourable to the message, a moderate level of credibility may be more appropriate.

Whether source credibility is high, medium or low is of little consequence, according to some researchers (Hannah and Sternthal, 1984). The impact of the source is believed to dissipate after approximately six weeks and only the content of the message is thought to dominate the receiver's attention. This sleeper effect (Hovland et al., 1949) has not been proved empirically, but the implication is that the persuasiveness of a message can increase over time. Furthermore, advertisers using highly credible sources need to repeat the message on a regular basis, in order that the required level of effectiveness and persuasion be maintained (Schiffman and Kanuk, 1991).

Structural elements in a message

An important part of any message strategy is a consideration of the best way of communicating the core message or proposition. This needs to be accomplished by structuring messages carefully to avoid encouraging objections and opposing points of view. The following are regarded as some of the important structural features that can shape the pattern of a message.

Message balance

It is evident from previous discussions that the effectiveness of any single message is dependent on a variety of factors. From a receiver's perspective, two elements appear to be significant: first, the amount and quality of the information that is communicated and, second, the overall judgement that each individual makes about the way a message is communicated.

This suggests that the style of a message should reflect a balance between the need for information and the need for pleasure or enjoyment in consuming the message. Figure 17.1 presents the two main forms of appeal. Messages can be product-oriented and rational or customer-oriented and based on feelings and emotions. For example, John Lewis, featured in the case study, originally used a product-orientated information base for its ads, but then changed to one which was customer-orientated and heavily emotional.

It is clear that when dealing with high-involvement decisions, where persuasion occurs through a central processing route, the emphasis of the message should be on the information content, in particular the key attributes and the associated benefits. This style is often factual and product-oriented. If a product evokes low-involvement decision-making, then the message should concentrate on the images that are created within the mind of the message recipient. This style seeks to elicit an emotional response from receivers. Obviously, there are many situations where both rational and emotional messages are needed by buyers in order to make purchasing decisions.

Conclusion drawing

Should the message draw a firm conclusion for an audience or should people be allowed to draw their own conclusions from the content? Explicit conclusions are more easily understood and stand a better chance of being effective (Kardes, 1988). However, it is the nature of the issue, the particular situation and the composition of the target audience that influence the effectiveness of conclusion drawing (Hovland and Mandell, 1952). Whether or not a conclusion should be drawn for the receiver depends upon the following:

1. The complexity of the issue. Healthcare products, central heating systems and personal finance services, for example, can be complex, and in the case of some members of the target audience their cognitive ability, experience and motivation may not be sufficient for them to draw their own conclusions. The complexity of the product requires that messages must draw conclusions for them. It should also be remembered that even highly informed and motivated audiences may require assistance if the product or issue is relatively new.

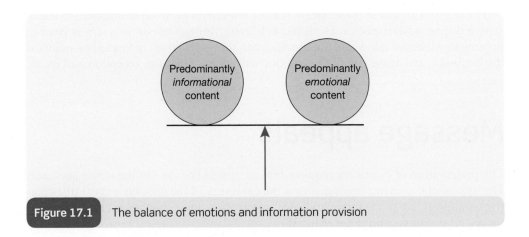

| Figure 17.1 | The balance of emotions and information provision |

2. The level of education possessed by the receiver. Better-educated audiences prefer to draw their own conclusions, whereas less-well-educated audiences may need the conclusion drawn for them because they may not be able to make the inference from the message.

3. Whether immediate action is required. If urgent action is required by the receiver, then a conclusion should be drawn very clearly. Political parties can be observed to use this strategy immediately before an election.

4. The level of involvement. High involvement usually means that receivers prefer to make up their own minds and may reject or resent any attempt to have the conclusion drawn for them (Arora, 1985).

One- and two-sided messages

This concerns how the case (or justification) for an issue is presented. One approach is to present the case for and against an issue – a two-sided message. Alternatively just the case in favour of an issue can be presented – a one-sided message. Research indicates that one-sided messages are more effective when receivers favour the opinion offered in the message and when the receivers are less-well-educated.

Two-sided messages, where both the good and the bad points of an issue are presented, are more effective when the receiver's initial opinion is opposite to that presented in the message and when they are well-educated. Credibility is improved by understanding the audience's position and then fashioning the presentation of the message. Faison (1961) found that two-sided messages tend to produce more positive perceptions of a source than one-sided messages.

Order of presentation

Further questions regarding the development of message strategy concern the order in which important points are presented. Messages that present the strongest points at the beginning use what is referred to as the *primacy* effect. The decision to place the main points at the beginning depends on whether the audience has a low or high level of involvement. A low level may require an attention-getting message component at the beginning. Similarly, if the target has an opinion opposite to that contained in the message, a weak point may lead to a high level of counter-argument.

A decision to place the strongest points at the end of the message assumes that the *recency* effect will bring about greater levels of persuasion. This is appropriate when the receiver agrees with the position adopted by the source or has a high positive level of involvement.

The order of argument presentation is more relevant in personal selling than in television or display advertisements. However, as learning through television is largely passive, because involvement is low and interest minimal, the presentation of key selling points at the beginning and at the end of the message will enhance message reception and recall.

Message appeals

The presentation of a message requires that an appeal be made to the target audience. The appeal is important, because unless the execution of the message appeal (the creative) is appropriate to the target audience's perception and expectations, the chances of successful communications are reduced.

There are two main factors associated with the presentation. Is the message to be dominated by the need to transmit product-oriented information or is there a need to transmit a message that appeals predominantly to the emotional senses of the receiver? The main choice of presentation style, therefore, concerns the degree of factual information transmitted in a message against the level of imagery thought necessary to make sufficient impact for the message to command attention and then be processed. There are numerous presentational or executional techniques, but the following are some of the more commonly used appeals.

Information-based appeals

Information or rational appeals can be presented through four main types of appeal. These are factual, slice-of-life, demonstration and comparative appeals.

Factual

Sometimes referred to as the 'hard sell', the dominant objective of these appeals is to provide, often detailed, information. This type of appeal is commonly associated with high-involvement decisions where receivers are sufficiently motivated and able to process information. Persuasion, according to the ELM, is undertaken through the central processing route. This means that ads should be rational and contain logically reasoned arguments and information in order that receivers are able to complete their decision-making processes.

Slice of life

As noted earlier, the establishment of credibility is vital if any message is to be accepted and processed. One of the ways in which this can be achieved is to present the message in such a way that the receiver can identify immediately with the scenario being presented. This process of creating similarity is used a great deal in advertising and is referred to as slice-of-life advertising. For example, many washing powder advertisers use a routine that depicts two ordinary women (assumed to be similar to the target receiver), invariably in a kitchen or garden, discussing the poor results achieved by one of their washing powders. Following the advice of one of the women, the stubborn stains are seen to be overcome by the focus brand.

On successful decoding of this message the overall effect of this appeal is for the receiver to conclude the following: that person is like me; I have had the same problem as that person; they are satisfied using brand X, therefore I, too, will use brand X. This technique is simple, well-tried, well-liked and successful, despite its sexist overtones. It is also interesting to note that a number of surveys have found that a majority of women feel that advertisers use inappropriate stereotyping to portray female roles, these being predominantly housewife and mother roles.

Demonstration

A similar technique is to present the problem to the audience as a demonstration. The focus brand is depicted as instrumental in the resolution of a problem. Headache remedies, floor cleaners and tyre commercials have traditionally demonstrated the pain, the dirt and the danger respectively, and then shown how the focus brand relieves the pain (Panadol) or removes the stubborn dirt (Flash or Cillit Bang). Whether the execution is believable is a function of the credibility and the degree of life-like dialogue or copy that is used.

Viewpoint 17.2   Radiant takes product demonstration to the extreme

Product demonstration is not an unusual route for laundry detergent brands to choose and has been a tried and tested style of advertising for many brands in this category over the years. In 2014 Australian brand Radiant decided to take this style of advertising to a new level. To launch their new range of products containing a breakthrough 'Colour Guard' technology designed to keep clothes looking 'newer for longer' they ran an extreme product demonstration campaign called 'Radiant Return'.

The integrated campaign was focussed around a series of Web films that tested the product's claims that it can keep clothes looking newer for longer. The idea behind the films was based on buying clothes in retail stores, wearing them in some extreme conditions, washing them in Radiant and then attempting to return them to the stores.

This product testing was unlike anything that had been seen in laundry detergent ads before with clothes being put into some extreme conditions. The films shot the clothes being worn whilst playing paintball, catching pigs, being rugby tackled in mud, having a ketchup fight, gutting fish, potting, painting, washing dogs and quad biking. This presented a real test for a product claiming to keep clothes looking like new.

Exhibit 17.5	Australian brand Radiant used a demonstration route

Source: Radiant, part of the PZ Cussons Group plc.

After the tests were complete clothes were seen to be washed with Radiant in normal conditions and then using hidden cameras each film captured the moment when the garments were returned to the shop for a refund. Out of the 14 garments purchased, 13 were successfully returned (one item was torn by a spiky fish when filming). The films capture the surprise on the faces of the shop owners when they are shown the video footage of what their clothes have encountered before being returned looking like new.

The online films were supported by digital media, public relations, a social seeding strategy, outdoor and television. The campaign highlights that product demonstration is still an effective route for brands to choose and how if used creatively it can help to activate social media and support other marketing communications tools.

Source: About Radiant (2015); AdNews (2014); DDB Melbourne (2015).

Question: How does Radiant's advertising differ to other product demonstration advertising in the laundry detergent category, and what were the risks associated with taking this route?

Task: Find examples of other product demonstration ads and discuss why you think this type of appeal has been chosen for the brand.

Comparative advertising

Comparative advertising is a popular means of positioning brands. Messages are based on a comparison with either a main competitor brand or all competing brands, with the aim of establishing and maintaining superiority. The comparison may centre on one or two key attributes and can be a good way of entering new markets. Entrants keen to establish a presence in a market have little to lose by comparing themselves with market leaders. However, market leaders have a great deal to lose and little to gain by comparing themselves with minor competitors.

Emotions- and feelings-based appeals

Appeals based on logic and reasons are necessary in particular situations, especially where there is high involvement. As products become similar, however, and as consumers become more aware of what is available in the category, so the need to differentiate becomes more important. Increasing numbers of advertisers are using messages that seek to appeal to the target's emotions and feelings, a 'soft sell'. Cars, toothpaste, toilet tissue and mineral water often use emotion-based messages to differentiate their products' position.

There are a number of appeals that can be used to elicit an emotional response from an individual receiver. Of the many techniques available, the main ones that can be observed to be used most are fear, humour, shock, animation, sex, music and fantasy and surrealism.

Fear

Fear is used in one of two ways. The first type demonstrates the negative aspects or physical dangers associated with a particular behaviour or improper product usage. Drink driving, life assurance and toothpaste advertising typify this form of appeal.

The second approach is the threat of social rejection or disapproval if the brand is not used. This type of fear is used frequently in advertisements for such products as anti-dandruff shampoos and deodorants and is used to support consumers' needs for social acceptance and approval.

Fear appeals need to be constrained, if only to avoid being categorised as outrageous and socially unacceptable. There is a great deal of evidence that fear can facilitate attention and interest in a message and even motivate an individual to take a particular course of action: for example, to stop smoking. Fear appeals are persuasive, according to Schiffman and Kanuk (1991), when low to moderate levels of fear are induced. Ray and Wilkie (1970), however, show that, should the level of fear rise too much, inhibiting effects may prevent the desired action occurring. This inhibition is caused by the individual choosing to screen out, through perceptive selection, messages that conflict with current behaviour. The outcome may be that individuals deny the existence of a problem, claim there is no proof or say that it will not happen to them.

Humour

Humour has been a popular appeal used in advertising for over a hundred years (Weinberger et al., 2015). The use of humour as an emotional appeal is attractive because it can attract attention, stimulate interest and foster a positive mood. This can occur because there is less effort involved with peripheral rather than central cognitive processing, and this helps to mood-protect. In other words, the positive mood state is more likely to be maintained if cognitive effort is avoided. Organisations like 118 118 have used humour to help convey the essence of their brand and to help differentiate it from competitors.

Organisations need to consider a number of factors before taking a humorous route with their advertising. First, it is important to ensure that the humour does not distract from the message itself. If the execution of the ad is too humorous then there is the risk that the message will be lost. Second, it is important to consider the geographies where the advertising will run. Since humour is seen to be culturally bound it can be difficult to determine whether target audiences in different countries will find the advertising humorous. What can be funny in one country may be offensive in another. While pretesting advertising in each country may help to determine how messages are received, choosing a humorous route for a global campaign may be a risky choice. There have been numerous academic studies undertaken on humour in international advertising. Scholars' paper 17.2 contrasts the use of humour in three countries.

Zhang and Zinkhan (2006) found that humour is more effective when there is low rather than high involvement. They also consider whether the media used also influence the impact of humour. For example, television and radio demand less effort to process messages compared with print work. The choice of media used to deliver humorous content can therefore be critical.

Another form of humour used in advertising is parody. Vanden Bergh et al. (2011) identify parodic advertising as a route that mimics other advertising or cultural work. This style of appeal takes another brand's advertising or other creative work and re-presents it in a humorous manner. It is a popular form of appeal on social media and is widely shared on social media platforms.

Scholars' paper 17.2   Does humour work for global brands?

Laroche, M., Vinhal Nepomuceno, M., Huang, L. and Richard, M.-O. (2011) What's so funny? The use of humor in magazine advertising in the United States, China and France, *Journal of Advertising Research*, 51(2), 404–16.

Humour is a common basis for advertising message appeals and this is an interesting paper not least because of the countries included in the study. Does humour work differently across different continents and cultures? The authors use a content analysis method to examine how widely humour is used and its use in advertising different types of product. They compare its use in luxury goods and personal consumer products, including automobiles. Humour was found to be used most widely in general in the USA and most commonly used in automobile advertising in China. They identify similar levels of the use of humour in advertising luxuries in China and France.

See also: Brown, M.R., Bhadury, R.K. and Pope, N.K.L. (2010) The impact of comedic violence on viral advertising effectiveness, *Journal of Advertising*, 39(1), 49–65.

Shock

Some advertisers use appeals that are intended to shock their target audiences. This is called shock advertising, which, according to Venkat and Abi-Hanna (1995), 'is generally regarded as one that deliberately, rather than inadvertently, startles and offends its audience'.

Dahl et al. (2003) suggest that shock advertising by definition is unexpected and audiences are surprised by the messages because they do not conform to social norms or their expectations. They argue that audiences are offended because there is 'norm violation, encompassing transgressions of law or custom (e.g. indecent sexual references, obscenity), breaches of a moral or social code (e.g. profanity, vulgarity), or things that outrage the moral or physical senses', for example gratuitous violence and disgusting images (p. 268). The clothing company French Connection's use of the FCUK slogan and the various Benetton campaigns depicting a variety of incongruous situations (e.g. a priest and a nun kissing and a man dying of AIDS) are examples of norm violation. Shock advertising is not only used by commercial organisations such as Diesel, Egg and Sony Entertainment but also used by not-for-profit organisations such as the government (anti-smoking, anti-drink-driving), charities (child abuse), climate change (Greenpeace) and human rights campaigners (Amnesty International).

The main reason for using a shock advertising strategy is that it is a good way to secure an audience's attention and achieve a longer-lasting impact than through traditional messages and attention-getting devices. The surprise element of these advertisements secures attention, which is followed by an attempt to work out why an individual has been surprised. This usually takes the form of cognitive engagement and message elaboration in order that the message be understood. Through this process a shocking message can be retained and behaviour influenced. This process is depicted in Figure 17.2.

Shocking ads also benefit from word-of-mouth communications as these messages provoke advertisement-related conversations (Dichter, 1966). These can be distributed orally or digitally as virals. The credibility of word-of-mouth communications impacts on others who, if they have not been exposed to the original message, often seek out the message through curiosity. Associated with this pass-along impact is the generation of controversy, which can lead to additional publicity for an organisation and its advertisements. This 'free' publicity, although invariably negative, is considered to be desirable as it leads to increased brand awareness without further exposure and associated costs. This in turn can give the organisation further opportunities to provide more information about the advertising campaign and generate additional media comment.

The use of shock tactics has spread to viral marketing (a topic discussed in more detail in Chapter 19). Virals delivered through email communications have an advantage over paid-for advertising because consumers perceive advertising as an attempt to sell

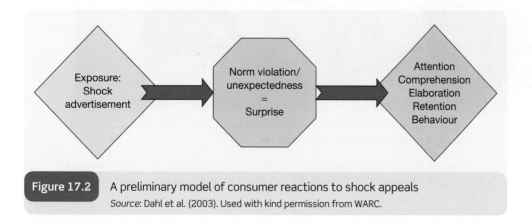

Figure 17.2   A preliminary model of consumer reactions to shock appeals
Source: Dahl et al. (2003). Used with kind permission from WARC.

a product, whereas virals are perceived as fun, can be opened and viewed (repeatedly) at consumer-determined times. Furthermore, virals are not subject to the same regulations that govern advertising, opening opportunities to convey controversial material. For example, a Volkswagen viral showed a suicide bomber exploding a device inside a car but the vehicle remained in one piece ('small but tough'). Another for Ford Ka showed a cat being decapitated by the sunroof. As Bewick (2006) suggests, joking about terrorism and pets is a sure-fire way of generating shock, and with that comes publicity.

Animation

Animation techniques have advanced considerably in recent years, particularly with the use of CGI, and there have been an increasing number of animated campaigns. In particular, there has been a noticeable rise in the number of CGI animal ads with campaigns like Muller Rice's 'Rice Rice Baby', O2's 'Be More Dog' and Three's 'danceponydance' ad (Bold, 2014). The John Lewis campaign set out at the beginning of this chapter highlights how brands are using CGI to deliver emotional messages. In many cases the main reason for using animation is that potentially boring and low-interest/involvement products can be made visually interesting and provide a means of gaining attention.

Animation also provides an opportunity for brands to differentiate themselves from competitors and develop a distinctive feel for the campaign. The animated Twinings' 'Gets You Back To You' campaign provides an example of how a brand has used animation to achieve this. The use of illustration in the Twinings' campaign was also seen to allow target audiences to project themselves into the storyline, which would have been more difficult to achieve using photography or filming (Brazier, 2011).

Sexual innuendo and the use of sex as a means of promoting products and services are both common and controversial. Using sex as an appeal in messages is excellent for gaining the attention of buyers. Research shows, however, that it often achieves little

| Exhibit 17.6 | **McVities has used animated kittens in its 'cute' ad** |

MvVities is just one of a number of brands that have used animation to include animals in their advertising. Using live animals in advertising has always been seen as difficult and CGI has encouraged creatives to consider featuring animals.

Source: McVities.

else, particularly when the product is unrelated (Paek and Nelson, 2007). Therefore, sex appeals normally work well for products such as perfume, clothing and jewellery but provide for poor effectiveness when the product is unrelated, such as cars, photocopiers and furniture. Reichert et al. (2012) identified that low-involvement products in particular use sex as an attention-getting cue and the product categories with the highest sexual content were health/ hygiene, beauty, drugs/medicine and clothing.

The degree to which sex-based advertising appeals work or are seen to be acceptable should also be considered a function of culture. For example, the use of sex appeals in Chinese society has increased in recent years as people have become more tolerant about the subject of sex. However, a study by Cui and Yang (2009) found that, despite this increasing openness, Chinese consumers remain 'cautious about embracing sex appeals in advertising' (p. 242).

Other studies have identified that although sex is an effective appeal it does not 'sell' more than any other type of appeal and that as long as the advertising is pleasant, other appeal styles such as humour are just as effective (Das et al., 2015).

The use of sex in advertising messages is mainly restricted to getting the attention of the audience and, in some circumstances, sustaining interest. It can be used openly, as in various lingerie, fragrance and perfume advertisements, such as WonderBra and Gucci, raunchily as in King of Shaves and sensually as with Lexus, surprisingly.

Music

Music can create a mood for the advertising and differentiate the message. Binet et al. (2013) suggest that the most popular and effective advertising over the last decade has included music, which can facilitate brand and message recall, improve attitudes towards the brand and can influence purchase intention. Many brands are using music to help connect with audiences emotionally. The music used in 'Monty's Christmas', the John Lewis commercial discussed at the start of this chapter, illustrates how music can help to enhance the emotional impact of the message.

Music can provide continuity between a series of advertisements and can also be a good peripheral cue. A jingle, melody or tune, if repeated sufficiently, can become associated with the advertisement or brand. This means there is potential for the campaign life to be extended beyond the advertising.

Some luxury and executive cars are advertised using commanding background music to create an aura of power, prestige and affluence, which is combined with strong visual images in order that an association be made between the car and the environment in which it is positioned. There is a contextual juxtaposition between the car and the environment presented. Readers may notice a semblance of classical conditioning, where the music acts as an unconditioned stimulus. Foxall and Goldsmith (1994) suggest that the stimulus elicits the unconditioned emotional responses that may lead to the purchase of the advertised product.

Fantasy and surrealism

The use of fantasy and surrealism in advertising has grown, partly as a result of the increased clutter and legal constraints imposed on some product classes. In fantasy appeals, associations with certain images and symbols allow advertisers to focus attention on products. The receiver can engage in the distraction offered and become involved with the execution of the advertisement. If this is a rewarding experience it may be possible to affect the receiver's attitudes peripherally. Readers may notice that this links to the earlier discussion on 'liking the advertisement'.

Finally, an interesting contribution to the discussion of message appeals has been made by Lannon (1992). She reports that consumers' expectations of advertisements can be interpreted on the one hand as either literal or stylish and on the other as serious or entertaining, according to the tone of voice. This approach vindicates the view that consumers are active problem-solvers and willing and able to decode increasingly complex messages. They can become involved with the execution of the advertisement and the product attributes. The degree of involvement (she argues implicitly) is a function of the motivation each individual has at any one moment when exposed to a particular message.

Advertisers can challenge individuals by presenting questions and visual stimuli that demand attention and cognitive response. Guinness challenged consumers to decode a series of advertisements that were unlike all previous Guinness advertisements and, indeed, all messages in the product class. The celebrity chosen was dressed completely in black, which contrasted with his blond hair, and he was shown in various time periods, past and future, and environments that receivers did not expect. He was intended to represent the personification of the drink and symbolised the individual nature of the product. Audiences were puzzled by the presentation and many rejected the challenge of interpretation. 'Surfer' and 'Bet on Black' are more recent Guinness campaigns that seek to convey the importance and necessity to wait (for the drink to be poured properly). To accomplish this, they portray a variety of situations in which patience results in achievement.

When individuals respond positively to a challenge, the advertiser can either provide closure (an answer) or, through surreal appeals, leave the receivers to answer the questions themselves in the context in which they perceive the message. One way of achieving this challenging position is to use an appeal that cognitively disorients the receiver (Parker and Churchill, 1986). If receivers are led to ask the question 'What is going on here?' their involvement in the message is likely to be very high. Benetton consistently raises questions through its advertising. By presenting a series of messages that are socially disorienting, and for many disconcerting, Benetton continually presents a challenge that moves away from involving individuals in an approach where salience and 'standing out' predominate. This high-risk strategy, with a risk of rejection, has prevailed for a number of years.

The surrealist approach does not provide or allow for closure. The conformist approach, by contrast, does require closure in order to avoid any possible counter-arguing and message rejection. Parker and Churchill argue that, when questions are left unanswered, receivers can become involved in both the product and the execution of the advertisement. Indeed, most advertisements contain a measure of rational and emotional elements. A blend of the two elements is necessary and the right mixture is dependent upon the perceived risk and motivation that the target audience has at any one particular moment.

Most message appeals should balance the informative and emotional dimensions. Furthermore, message quality is of paramount importance. Buzzell (1964) reported that, 'Advertising message quality is more important than the level of advertising expenditure' (p. 30). Adams and Henderson Blair (1992) confirm that the weight of advertising is relatively unimportant, and that the quality of the appeal is the dominant factor. However, the correct blend of informative and emotional elements in any appeal is paramount for persuasive effectiveness.

An alternative approach is to use the soft-sell, hard-sell demarcation, well established in the academic and practitioner worlds of advertising. A soft-sell appeal is designed to provoke an affective or feelings response from the receiver of the message, one in which human emotions are emphasised. These types of appeal tend to be subtle and indirect, and an image or atmosphere may be conveyed (Okazaki et al., 2010).

A hard-sell appeal is one in which the objective is to induce receivers to think in rational terms about the message. These appeals tend to be direct, emphasising a sales orientation, and often specify the brand name and product recommendations. Factual information, including numerous product (pack) shots, emphasises specific differentiating product features or some other dimension relevant to consumers. These two broad types of appeal are underpinned by three dimensions. These are feeling versus thinking, implicit versus explicit, and image versus fact.

Okazaki et al. (2010) believe that soft-sell appeals lead to more positive attitudes to the ad and to increased ad believability. This suggests that soft-sell appeals can strengthen purchase intentions. Hard-sell advertising appeals can also strengthen purchase intention. However, this is not accomplished directly through the creation of a favourable attitude, but through the formulation of convincing ad content.

Copycat messaging

There are certain occasions where the appeal used by a follower brand can be judged to mimic that of the brand leader. Brands use this if they wish to attack the brand leader in the category to reduce the potency of the competitor's marketing communications. Bowery (2007) refers to Matalan's use of four models that aped Marks & Spencer's iconic campaign based around Twiggy and three other models. Matalan did not reinforce its approach with a subsequent high-profile campaign, but M&S has continued the message strategy to considerable effect.

Advertising tactics

The main creative elements of a message need to be brought together in order for an advertising plan to have substance. The processes used to develop message appeals need to be open but systematic.

The level of involvement and combination of the rational/emotional dimensions that receivers bring to their decision-making processes are the core concepts to be considered when creating an advertising message. Rossiter and Percy (1997) devised a deductive framework that involves the disaggregation of the emotional (feel) dimension to a greater degree than that proposed by Vaughn (1980) (see Chapter 11 for details). They claim that there are two broad types of motive that drive attitudes towards purchase behaviour. These are informational and transformational motives and are now considered in turn.

Informational motives

Individuals have a need for information to counter negative concerns about a purchase decision. These informational motives, set out in Table 17.1, are said to be negatively charged feelings. They can become positively charged, or the level of concern can be reduced considerably, by the acquisition of relevant information.

Transformational motives

Promises to enhance or to improve the user of a brand are referred to as transformational motives. These are related to the user's feelings and are capable of transforming a user's emotional state, hence they are positively charged. Three main transformational motives have been distinguished by Rossiter et al. (1991), presented in Table 17.2. Various emotional states can be associated with each of these motives, and they should be used to portray an emotion that is appropriate to the needs of the target audience.

For example, Cancer Research UK changed the approach it used to communicate with donors. For a while, the campaigns used to convey messages about family loss and in that sense adopted a negative approach. The charity then adopted an 'All Clear' campaign.

Table 17.1 Informational motives

Motive	Possible emotional state
Problem removal	Anger–relief
Problem avoidance	Fear–relaxation
Incomplete satisfaction	Disappointment–optimism
Mixed approach–avoidance	Guilt–peace of mind
Normal depletion	Mild annoyance–convenience

This conveyed messages about people diagnosed with cancer and their improved chances of recovery due to the benefits of the research. For many people this is low involvement with transformational motives. This means that the use of an emotional-based claim in the message is important. The happy ending, based on people surviving, achieves this while the endline uses a voice-over that requests a donation so that the words 'all clear' can be heard by more people in the future.

One of the key communications objectives, identified earlier, is the need to create or improve levels of awareness regarding the product or organisation. This is achieved by determining whether awareness is required at the point of purchase or prior to purchase. Brand recognition (at the point of purchase) requires an emphasis upon visual stimuli, the package and the brand name, whereas brand recall (prior to purchase) requires an emphasis on a limited number of peripheral cues. These may be particular copy lines, the use of music or colours for continuity and attention-grabbing, frequent use of the brand name in the context of the category need, or perhaps the use of strange or unexpected presentation formats.

Advertising tactics can be determined by the particular combination of involvement and motives that exist at a particular time within the target audience. If a high-involvement

Table 17.2 Transformational motives

Motive	Possible emotional state
Sensory gratification	Dull–elated
Intellectual stimulation	Bored–excited
Social approval	Apprehensive–flattered

Option 1: An emotional claim

Correct emotional portrayal very important when brand is introduced

Getting the target to like the advertisement is not important

Option 2: A rational claim

If the target's initial attitude to the brand is favourable, then make benefit claims clear

If they are against the brand, use a refutational approach

If there is a clear brand leader, use a comparative approach

Figure 17.3	Message tactics where there is high involvement and informational motives

Source: After Rossiter and Percy (1997). Used with kind permission.

Option 1: An emotional claim

Use emotion in the context of the prevailing lifestyle groups

Identification with the product is as important as liking the advertisement

Option 2: A rational claim

Include information as well

Overstate the benefits but do not understate them

Use repetition for reinforcement

Figure 17.4	Message tactics where there is high involvement and transformational motives

Source: After Rossiter and Percy (1997). Used with kind permission.

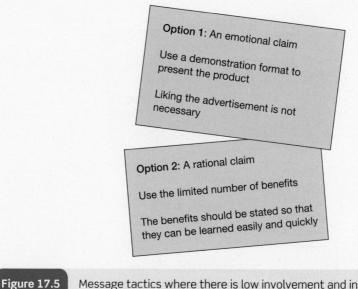

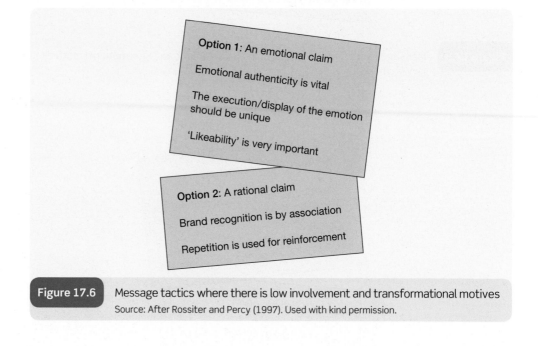

Figure 17.5 Message tactics where there is low involvement and informational motives
Source: After Rossiter and Percy (1997). Used with kind permission.

Figure 17.6 Message tactics where there is low involvement and transformational motives
Source: After Rossiter and Percy (1997). Used with kind permission.

decision process is determined, with people using a central processing route, then the types of tactics shown in Figures 17.3 and 17.4 are recommended (Rossiter and Percy, 1997). If a low-involvement decision process is determined, with the target audience using a peripheral processing route, then the types of tactics shown in Figures 17.5 and 17.6 are recommended.

The Rossiter–Percy approach provides for a range of advertising tactics that are oriented to the conditions that are determined by the interplay of the level of involvement and the type of dominant motivation. These conditions may only exist within a member of the target audience for a certain period. Consequently, they may change and the advertising tactics may also have to change to meet the new conditions. There are two main points that emerge from the work of Rossiter and Percy (1997). The first is that all messages should be designed to carry both rational, logical information and emotional stimuli, but in varying degrees and forms. Second, low-involvement conditions require the use of just one or two benefits in a message, whereas high-involvement conditions can sustain a number of different benefit claims. This is because persuasion through the central processing route is characterised by an evaluation of the alternatives within any one product category.

Viewpoint 17.3   Unlocking the power of guilt

V/Line is Australia's largest regional public transport operator with a rail network serving Melbourne and regional areas. Research identified that one of the main reasons for consumers to take a trip on V/Line trains from Melbourne to regional Victoria was to visit family and friends. The research highlighted that the Visiting Friends and Relatives (VFR) market accounted for 39 per cent of all trips taken, compared to 30 per cent for work and only 18 per cent for leisure and tourism.

Using this consumer insight and identifying an opportunity to grow this market segment, the company created 'The Guilt Trip', a pre-paid V/Line train ticket for those living in the Metropolitan areas. The concept of The Guilt Trip was to encourage more Melbourne residents that had moved from regional Victoria to return home for a trip to visit their loved ones. Those living in the regional towns were encouraged to buy tickets for their loved ones in the city and using a humorous tone-of-voice message encouraged them to get their loved ones to visit them at home. The campaign drew on the sense of obligation consumers had to visit their friends and family and used the power of guilt to deliver the message.

The integrated campaign used a range of communications tools and platforms to drive awareness. Public relations was used to launch the campaign and this was supported by outdoor, press and radio advertising. The campaign also featured a series of online films starring a fictional Guilt Trip Advisor, Louise. Social media was used to encourage consumers to share the message and Guilt Trip handbooks were used to drive consumers to a dedicated website that allowed them to buy Guilt Trip train tickets.

Does guilt work? V/Line saw a 15 per cent increase in off-peak sales, with an extra 123,000 tickets bought. Guilt Trips generated A$4 million in additional revenue, exceeding the company's KPI by 167 per cent.

Source: McCann (2015); V/Line (2013, 2014).

Exhibit 17.7   **Press and outdoor were used in the campaign**

Source: McCann Australia.

Question:	Consider which type of motive was used to drive purchase behaviour in the case of The Guilt Trip. Decide between informational and transformational motives. Explain why.
Task:	Select a British train service, visit their website and determine whether they use informational or transformational messages. Justify your response.

Creativity

Having considered the different appeal styles available to advertisers, another important element of any marketing communications campaign is creativity. Creativity is seen to increase the effectiveness of a campaign by up to 10 times (Priest, 2014). Chapter 7 highlighted the importance for advertising agencies to be creative and how much this is valued by clients when selecting an agency.

While creativity is an important feature of any marketing communications activity there is no universally agreed definition of what advertising creativity is. Early holistic ideas about creativity considered it to be about a violation of expectations, often expressed through contradictory ideas (Blasko and Mokwa, 1986; Reid and Rotfeld, 1976). These views have given way to a general agreement that creativity in advertising has two main characteristics. The first is that creative ads are divergent, or highly unique or novel, and, second, relevant or meaningful (Smith et al., 2007).

Ang et al. (2007) conceptualises advertising creativity in three dimensions: novelty, meaningfulness and connectedness. They concluded that many ads that scored high on recall and attitude towards the advertisement had also recorded high scores on each of these three dimensions of creativity.

Heath et al. (2009) believe that creativity in contemporary branded advertising involves a variety of elements. These include characters (who express mild emotion: e.g. love, irritation, excitement, boredom, curiosity, amusement), situations (that are considered humorous, poignant or dramatic), visuals (that are elegant or attractive, beautifully shot footage with high production values), and background music (that is pleasant, uplifting or evocative).

Smith and Yang (2004) refer to two key components of advertising creativity: divergence and relevance. They contest that a creative ad uses a divergent appeal (unexpected and unusual, such as fear or humour) to deliver a relevant core message about the brand (such as an attribute or benefit), yet still allows the audience to interpret and assign

Table 17.3 Interpretations of the dimensions of creativity

Dimension	Explanation
Divergence	
Originality	Ads that contain elements that are rare, surprising, or move away from the obvious and commonplace.
Flexibility	Ads that contain different ideas or switch from one perspective to another.
Elaboration	Ads that contain unexpected details or finish and extend basic ideas so they become more intricate, complicated, or sophisticated.
Synthesis	Ads that combine, connect, or blend normally unrelated objects or ideas.
Artistic value	Ads that contain artistic verbal impressions or attractive colours or shapes.
Relevance	
Ad-to-consumer relevance	Refers to situations where the ad contains execution elements that are meaningful to consumers. For example, using Beatles music in an ad could create a meaningful link to baby boomers, thereby making the ad relevant to them.
Brand-to-consumer relevance	Refers to situations where the advertised brand (or product category) is relevant to potential buyers. For example, the advertisement could show the brand being used in circumstances familiar to the consumer.

Source: Derived from Smith et al. (2008).

meaning to the message within the linkage between the fear or humour and the product. Ideas about divergence and relevance have several interpretations and these are represented in Table 17.3, drawn from Smith et al. (2008).

Creativity and attention

Creativity in advertising is considered to be important because of the common belief that creativity is an effective way of getting people to attend to an ad (Rossiter and Percy, 1998; Yang and Smith, 2009). Kover's (1995) research around the impact of emotive content and attention led to the identification of two attention-getting strategies: forcing and subversion. Forcing strategies involve the use of surprising, irrelevant or perhaps mildly shocking content. He gives as an example the famous Apple ad shown during the 1984 Super Bowl. This strategy is not used so much today.

Subversion strategies require an ad to seduce an audience, to slip by it as if unnoticed. Kover uses the words charming and seductive to describe this sort of creativity and refers to ads by O2, Honda and M&S Food campaigns as examples of this approach.

Much research into creativity in advertising is concerned with what is referred to as 'attention effects'. This is related to the links between increased attention to an ad, heightened motivation to process the message, and the depth of processing that follows (Smith and Yang, 2004). Here, as Baack et al. (2008) comment, the amount of attention paid to advertisements is a function of the amount of cognitive capacity allocated to a task. Only when consumers focus more attention on the advertisement itself, rather than divide their attention among multiple tasks, do higher levels of processing occur. The greater the originality or divergence and personal relevance a creative ad displays, the greater the attention it attracts, which leads to a greater depth of message processing. What follows from this are higher recall and recognition scores.

Scholars' paper 17.3   Is it art or advertising?

Hetsroni, A. and Tukachinsky, R.H. (2005) The use of fine art in advertising: a survey of creatives and content analysis of advertisements, *Journal of Current Issues and Research in Advertising,* **27(1), 93–107.**

A slightly different paper, in that the managerial thrust is avoided. Here the authors examine the use of fine art (paintings and sculptures) in advertising, using content analysis of print advertisements, and a survey of advertising creatives. The findings are that ads which show art tend to use a soft-sell approach and promote prestigious goods with some over-representation of cultural establishments, cosmetics, fashion apparel and furniture. The predominant artistic style in these ads is Renaissance. The representation of modern art is significantly lower, and non-Western art is largely absent.

See also: Nyilasy, G. and Reid, L.N. (2009) Agency practitioners' meta-theories of advertising, *International Journal of Advertising,* 28(4), 639–68; El-Murad, J. and West, D. (2004) The definition and measurement of creativity: what do we know? *Journal of Advertising Research,* 44(2), 188–201; Heath, R.G., Nairn, A.C. and Bottomley, P.A. (2009) How effective is creativity? Emotive content in TV advertising does not increase attention, *Journal of Advertising Research,* 49(4), 450–63.

However, Yang and Smith (2009) and Heath et al. (2009) question the proposition that creativity works by increasing attention. They all agree that some attention is necessary, but it is not the direction of attention, but the level of attention, that is important. Yang and Smith had inconclusive results from their research, yet Heath (2010) found that creativity does not increase attention; if anything, it decreases it. This might raise an argument that it would be better to use force-based strategies. However, as Binet and Field (2007) found, emotion-based ads are more successful than information-led campaigns. The conclusion, therefore, is that creative ads enable open-minded message processing, which in turn can increase a willingness to view an ad again.

The importance of context

According to Kim et al. (2010), it is crucial that creative advertising has a product-relevant or audience-relevant context if it is to be effective. This contrasts with fine art where creativity is not bounded by this type of contextual constraint or the setting of objectives by one party, as its goal is to please or stimulate the viewer's senses.

Kim et al. (2010) argue that it is the surrounding culture that influences advertisers, ad creators, and consumers when determining what constitutes the contextual component of advertising creativity. They offer the research findings of Koslow et al. (2003: 94) who found that 'creatives perceive advertisements to be more appropriate if the ads are artistic, whereas account executives perceive advertisements to be more appropriate if the ads are strategic'.

Interpretations of what constitutes advertising creativity, therefore, vary depending on the viewer's context. This may be relative to role (a client striving to meet market share targets), culture (the societal values and norms of behaviour) or perspective (media commentator or blogger).

Culture is a critical component of international advertising effectiveness as it influences how consumers in different countries and regions perceive advertising. In Asian countries, for example, collectivistic values such as sharing, trustworthiness and sincerity are a key aspect of their advertising. In contrast, American and European cultures are more individual and the advertising stresses individualistic appeals, such as 'the one for you', and 'you have the right to be you'. This can lead to different interpretations or forms of originality in advertising. For example, in Asian advertising there is an absence of what Westerners refer to as the 'big idea', when referring to creativity, and a much stronger focus on making the brand and the message socially appropriate (Han and Shavitt, 1994).

The creative process

The creative process has been studied in a variety of contexts outside advertising (Amabile, 1996), but there have been only a limited number of studies undertaken in an advertising context. Among those there have been a number of studies on idea generation (Stuhlfaut and Vanden Bergh, 2014), agency decision-making systems (Na et al., 2009), and the stages that take occur between the agency and the client (Hill and Johnson, 2004).

One of the few studies that have been undertaken within advertising agencies themselves has been Turnbull and Wheeler's (2015) study of the advertising creative process within advertising agencies. The study explores the stages that occur from when the client first mentions the need for advertising to the agency, up to the moment when the concepts are approved and ready to go into production. They offer a seven-step model of the advertising creative process (see Table 17.4).

Table 17.4 The advertising creative process

Stage	Process
Stage one	Task identification
Stage two	Agreement of task objectives
Stage three	Ideation
Stage four	Response
Stage five	Validation – internal review (Agency Creative Director and WIP meetings)
Stage six	External review (Client Tissue Sessions and consumer qual and quant pre-testing).
Stage seven	Decision

Source: Adapted from Turnbull and Wheeler (2015).

These researchers found that agencies customise the advertising creative process to meet the needs of the advertising task. In cases where the advertising brief has a limited response time, agencies were found to set up 'drive-by' briefs which allowed the entire agency to think about creative ideas rather than just a selected creative team. The study also found that in cases where the creative was for a new business client, agencies held Chemistry Meetings, and set up a War Room within the agency, to manage the process of creative development.

As with any professional service, the level of interaction between client and provider plays an important role in the output of the service. The relationship between the client and advertising agency is seen to influence the creative output (Koslow et al., 2006). There is a need not only for the client and agency to share information but for the client to provide information that can assist the development of creative advertising. The quality of the communications brief given to the agency is seen to influence greatly the creative output (Koslow et al., 2006; Sutherland et al., 2004). Despite this there is substantial anecdotal and some empirical evidence to indicate that as many as 40 per cent of clients fail to give agencies sufficient information (Helgesen, 1994) and that some clients do not provide a creative brief at all (Rossiter, 2008).

There are many other possible influences on the creative process. One major factor concerns the prevailing regulations and industry standards about what is acceptable behaviour. The amount of risk the client is prepared to take (El-Murad and West, 2004), access to consumer research and sufficient development time are seen to be important factors in determining the level of creative output (Koslow et al., 2006).

Scholars' paper 17.4　How agencies manage the creative process

Turnbull, S. and Wheeler, C. (2015) The advertising creative process: a study of UK agencies, *Journal of Marketing Communications*, DOI 10.1080/13527266.2014.1000361.

The process of developing creative work can be complex and challenging. The authors explore the stages used in UK advertising agencies when developing new creatives. Interviews with advertising account managers in London agencies provide a rare insight into the world of advertising agency creative development. The study highlights the extensive pre-testing that takes within the process and identifies the importance of stages such as Tissue Sessions, Chemistry Meetings and the setting up of War Rooms.

See also: Windels, K. and Stuhlfaut, M.W. (2014) Confined creativity: the influence of creative code intensity on risk taking in advertising agencies, *Journal of Current Issues & Research in Advertising*, 35(2), 147–66.

The creative code

We have seen that there are many internal and external influences on the creative process and, indeed, individual stakeholders can have varying levels of impact on the development of creative advertising. Stuhlfaut (2011) refers to clients, agency managers, media specialists and account planners, as well as market conditions, which have all been shown to have varying levels of influence on the creative process and its outputs.

The development of advertising materials and associated processes, however, occurs within organisations and is therefore embedded within the prevailing organisational context and culture. This embraces the organisational climate, leadership style, the available mix of skills/resources, and structure and systems.

Stuhlfaut (2011) refers to organisational culture as a learned system of meaning, which is shared among participants. People use an implicit framework of language, behaviour and symbols to communicate these meanings and provide a common bond within their community. Organisations such as advertising agencies, and all those working within creative departments, work within, and are constrained by, this framework of organisational culture.

We know that individuals tend to identify with their (employer's) organisation and, to a greater or lesser extent, align themselves with the organisation's values. It is not unrealistic to expect that creatives would choose to use methods, styles, techniques and strategies that fit with the perceived values, and which serve to constrain the range of creative outcomes and outputs. For new creatives, therefore, it is important to learn and understand the values, as this will influence what they do, how they do it, and how creative success is determined (Stuhlfaut, 2011).

Another way of considering these issues is to ask: do the creatives have the right skills and an appropriate amount of development time, and is the budget sufficient? Although the larger advertising budgets might attract better agency service, the budget itself does not appear to be a significant factor in shaping creative advertising output (Koslow et al., 2006).

Another way of reviewing creativity is to consider how all of these influences compete and result in considerations of power over a campaign. As Hackley and Kover (2007: 65) observe, this usually means that creatives 'operate in a climate of latent or actual conflict'. With political power resting with clients and account managers, creatives, Hackley and Kover report, have to use cunning strategies to get their work accepted.

It is against this background that Stuhlfaut (2011) offers an interesting concept which he refers to as the 'creative code'. Citing Goodenough (1981: 52), the code shapes the development of advertisements which are regarded as cultural artefacts or 'material manifestations of what is learned'. Through this process a sub-cultural creative code is understood and made available to others. Just as organisation theory suggests that people make mental maps of their experiences in order to help them behave appropriately (Weick, 1979), so a creative code serves to direct or limit what internal and external stakeholders believe an acceptable creative might be. However, this raises questions about whether a weak culture and code serves to encourage greater creativity because there are fewer constraints. To what extent does a creative code influence the creative process, and how might an agency or client influence the creative code, in order to achieve particular types of output?

Message framing

The principle of building a border around an idea or story, and then presenting a contained and managed view of an issue, is well known and practised regularly by politicians, and advertising and public relations professionals. Known as *framing*, the concept has roots in communications studies, psychology and sociology. As with a number of concepts, there is little agreement on what framing is and, as Tsai (2007) indicates, it is controversial and empirically unproven. However, of the many definitions Dan and Ihlen (2011) cite Entman's (1993: 52) as one definition quoted more often than others. To frame is to:

> select some aspects of a perceived reality and make them more salient in a communicating context, in such a way as to promote a particular problem definition, causal interpretation, moral evaluation, and/or treatment recommendation.

By cropping and framing an item any distracting or contradictory elements are removed and focus can be given to the interpretation intended by the source. Gamson and Modigliani (1989) indicate that those who use framing to influence public opinion often compete with each other to frame the issues of interest. The goal of these *framing contests* (Pan and Kosicki, 2001) is to get, first, the media to adopt that particular frame and then the audience.

The framing principle is used in advertising to present predetermined brand elements. Competitors frame their messages and stories in order that their brands stand out, have clarity and focus, and be positioned distinctly and clearly.

Message framing works on the hedonic principles of our motivation to seek happiness and to avoid pain. So, messages can be framed either to focus a recipient's attention on positive outcomes (happiness) or to take them away from the possible negative outcomes (pain). For example, a positively framed message might be a yogurt that is presented as 'contains real fruit' or a car as 'a stylish design'. Conversely, messages could be presented as 'contains only 5 per cent fat' and 'low carbon emissions'; these are regarded as negatively framed. According to Buda (2003), negative framing gets more attention and information is processed more intensely than positively framed messages.

Many practitioners work on the basis that positive are better than negative messages, whereas others believe negative framing promotes deeper thinking and consideration. However, there is little empirical evidence to support any of these views. Therefore,

Table 17.5 Factors associated with message framing

Factor	Range	Explanation	Positive message framing	Negative message framing
Self-construal	Independent	Individuals (the self) seek to distinguish themselves from others. These individuals respond best to positive framing.	Independent	
	Interdependent	Individuals (the self) try not to distinguish themselves from others. These individuals respond best to negative framing.		Interdependent
Consumer involvement	High/low	Refers to the extent to which personal relevance and perceived risk influence decision-making within a product category. When high, negative framing is preferred; when low, positive framing is preferred.	Low	High
Product knowledge	High/low	Product knowledge consists of two elements: behavioural (usage) experience and mental (search, exposure and information). Message framing is more suitable where product knowledge is low.	Low	Low

Source: Based on Tsai (2007).

in an attempt to understand when it is better to use positive or negative framing, Tsai argues that it is necessary to develop a holistic understanding of the target audience. This involves considering three factors: self-construal; consumer involvement; and product knowledge. These are explained in Table 17.5.

Tsai believes that these three factors moderate an individual's response when they are exposed to positively or negatively framed brand messages. In turn, these influence the three main dimensions of a brand's communications. These are generally accepted by researchers such as Mackenzie and Lutz (1989) and Lafferty et al. (2002) to be attitude to the ad, attitude to the brand and purchase intention. Tsai develops a conceptual model to demonstrate this, through which he argues brand communications persuasiveness is moderated by these three factors.

His research concludes that positive message framing should be used under the following conditions:

Independent self-construal × low consumer involvement × low product knowledge

Negative framing should be used in the case of:

Interdependent self-construal × high consumer involvement × low product knowledge

While message framing may provide a strategic approach to the way in which messages should be presented, it is also necessary to consider how the detail of a message should be included in order to maximise effectiveness. Consideration is now given to the balance of information and emotion in a message, the structure in terms of how an argument should be presented and the actual appeal, whether it is based on information or emotion.

Storytelling

Stories are considered to be an integral part of the way we lead our lives. This is because they enable us to make sense of our perceived world and our role within it, the events that we encounter, and meaning we derive from our relationships and social activities (Merchant et al., 2010). In many ways stories enable us to frame core messages. Stories are embedded in music, novels, fairytales, films, news, religion, politics and plays. They are the foundation of word-of-mouth communications and a significant dimension of brands and the advertising used to support them, yet they are often an understated aspect of marketing communications.

The versatility of storytelling is recalled by Barker and Gower (2010). They believe that in addition to helping to sell products (Wylie, 1998), storytelling is used by organisations for communications (Jones and LeBaron, 2002), to introduce and manage change (Boje, 1991), for leadership (Marshall and Adamic, 2010), organisational learning (Lämsä and Sintonen, 2006), and even design management (DeLarge, 2004). Woodside et al. (2008) refer to the use of storytelling through blogs, suggesting it may be a more effective way of driving purchase intentions than traditional websites.

Stories work because they fit or match the way people think and retrieve information from memory. McKee and Fryer (2003) argue that stories are effective at persuasion because they involve people emotionally.

Stories consist of a theme and a plot, the latter conveying the former. Papadatos (2006) refers to themes within stories, and identifies three main elements: hardship, reciprocity and a defining moment. Each story has a sequence of events, or plot. The normal sequence starts with anticipation, and then progresses through a crisis, getting help, and then achieving a goal. See Table 17.6 for more information about these elements.

Table 17.6 Elements of storytelling

	Element	Explanation
Theme	Hardship	In order to overcome obstacles perseverance and determination in the face of these difficulties and hardship are critical so that the end product has a sense of being earned.
	Reciprocity	An appreciation that there is a fair or equal exchange, that the give and take of life is present.
	Defining moments	Human experience is punctuated with moments that stand out, or even change lives, and these are the moments that are remembered and treasured.
	Anticipation	Stories begin with a sense of hope for the future – a new job, home, baby, activity, all of which represent anticipation about the future.
Plot	Crisis	The feeling of anticipation is often followed by a negative, an unanticipated event or crisis that disrupts the path to the future.
	Help along the way	The crisis is mediated by the arrival of unexpected help. This might be in the form of advice from a new person or organisation, a tip from a friend or information from a specialist such as a mentor, an experienced teacher, protector, or trusty sage. As a result, there is a period of hard work and endurance.
	The goal is achieved	Following much discomfort and many obstacles, stories conclude with the goal accomplished and, for many, muted celebration.

Source: Based on Papadatos (2006).

Stories are used to frame our understanding and to encourage individuals to want to become a part of the story itself and to identify with a brand and/or its characters. Strong brands are built around a core theme or platform from which a series of linked stories can be developed. Cordiner (2009) refers to brands having a moral premise (platform): Honda's power of dreams, and Starbucks' 'third space' about having somewhere for each of us between work and home. He suggests that the television programme *The Wire* has a platform based on broken America. The platform for Harley Davidson is to empower individuals to be free from the 'prison of suburban life'. Virgin's platform is to challenge the establishment, and Google's is to set information free and connect people.

Stories can be understood in terms of four main categories. These are:

- *Myths and origins* can be used to recall how a company started and what its principles are, but very often the focus is on how it overcame early difficulties and achieved success. The current values can often be seen embedded in these stories. For example, the founders of HP started the company in a garage. As the company grew, so a stream of stories centred on the garage developed. These referred to the roots of the company, and became a central and controlling element in the culture of the company.

- *Corporate prophecies* are predictions about an organisation's future, which are often based on past stories or stories about other organisations.

- *Hero stories* recall people from the organisation who confronted and overcame a dilemma. The story provides a set of behaviours and values to be copied by others, especially during periods of crisis. These stories help people establish priorities and make decisions. This is a common approach as used by US Airways, with respect to its pilot C.B. Sullenberger, who landed his airliner safely on the Hudson River in January 2009. He became the hero of 'the miracle on the Hudson'.

- *Archived narratives are an organisation's collection* of stories which trace its history and development. With organisations changing names, being merged, bought out and reconstituted, there is an increasing need to access key stories from the past in order to provide a sense of history.

Viewpoint 17.4   'The messenger' tells a story

Arla® skyr's 2015 TV ad, 'the messenger', created to launch Arla® skyr Yogurt in the UK, uses storytelling as a device to engage target audiences emotionally with the brand. Set in the 1960s, the ad tells the story of a young Icelandic boy who delivers telephone messages from the one village telephone to his local community. Audiences share in the joy and disappointment of the messages that he delivers and witness the efforts he makes to ensure that each of the village folk gets their message. All the time the young messenger is given the strength from Arla® skyr Yogurt.

Exhibit 17.8   **The messenger in the Arla® skyr Yogurt ad**
Source: Arla skyr.

The ad draws on many traditional narrative devices used in storytelling. The young messenger provides us with a hero for the story, living up to our expectations of all good heroes by overcoming the hardship he is confronted with. We see him climbing mountains, escaping geysers and battling snowstorms, determined to deliver his message despite the difficulties that face him. Finally the boy's goal is achieved and the villager gets the message. The TV ad uses a simple plot which tells the story of a hero who conquers all to achieve his goal in the face of adversity. Drawing on audiences' childhood memories of narratives from fairytales and myths, the ad provides a familiar plot that audiences can easily relate to.

Storytelling is an effective technique for brands to deliver their own story and encourages audiences to build associations between the hero and the brand. In this case the story allows the brand to suggest that the hero draws his strength from Arla® skyr Yogurt and sits well with the brand's Icelandic heritage and Icelanders' reputation for courage.

The TV ad is part of a multichannel campaign and the story continues through outdoor and a series of documentary films about tough Icelanders who, like the messenger in the TV plot, have grown up on Arla® skyr Yogurt.

Source: Oster (2015); Wieden + Kennedy (2015).

Question: What elements of storytelling can you identify in the Arla® skyr TV ad? Consider why Arla® skyr decided to use a storytelling approach for the launch of the new product.

Task: Find another example of storytelling in advertising and explain what elements of storytelling are used.

User-generated content (UGC)

So far in this chapter attention has been given to the issues associated with organisation-driven creativity. However, it is important to consider the increasing numbers of messages that are developed and communicated by ordinary individuals, just like you and us. Not only are these used to communicate with organisations of all types and sizes but they are also shared with peers, family, friends and others in communities such as social networks and specialist interest online communities (e.g. reunion and family history sites). This is referred to as *user-generated content* (UGC) and it can be seen in action at YouTube, Flickr, Twitter, DIGG, Vine, Pinterest and in all the millions of blogs and vlogs.

UGC can be considered to be all of the ways in which people make use of social media (Kaplan and Haenlein, 2010) and describes the various forms of media content that are publicly available and created by end-users. According to Christodoulides et al. (2011), one interpretation of UGC requires that three core conditions need to be met. First, the content needs to be published either on a publicly accessible website or on a social networking site accessible to a selected group of people. Second, the material needs to show some creative effort and, finally, it has to have been created outside of professional routines and practices.

Discussion boards and online forums can only work through consumer participation and UGC. One of the more common forms of UGC is blogging. This involves individuals, sometimes in the name of organisations, but more often as independent consumers, posting information about topics of personal interest. Sometimes these people develop opinion leader status and organisations feed them information about the launch of new brands, so that they pass on the information to opinion followers.

Social networks thrive on the shared views, opinions and beliefs, often brand-related, of networked friends. YouTube, Vine and Flickr provide opportunities for consumers to share video and photos respectively, with all material posted by users. Users post their content and respond to the work of others, often by rating the quality or entertainment value of content posted by others. Exhibit 17.9 highlights the increasing popularity of Pinterest, which allows consumers to share images of the things they like and create their own boards.

Although people understand the rules and norms associated with communicating across peer groups and social networks, organisations have yet to master these new environments. Firms are not able to use traditional forms of free communications with as much credibility and authority as individuals regularly do within these contexts. One of the reasons for this is the democratisation of the media and the language codes that have emerged. A simple example is SMS texting. Although used by millions every day to great effect, mobile communications and text messaging are only now becoming commercially prominent, mainly as a result of smartphone technology.

Muñiz and Schau (2007) refer to what they call 'vigilante marketing'. In these circumstances, consumers create self-generated advertising content to promote brands with which they have a strong affiliation. They refer to a brand community site based on the Apple Newton. This was an early PDA launched in 1993 and discontinued by Apple in 1998 as Palm Pilot undercut the Newton on price and exceeded it on quality, size and overall value. Many users at the time blamed Apple for poor communications and not explaining the Newton accurately enough to attract more customers. Roughly 3,000–4,000 Newton users still participate in online forums. They create what the authors label as *brand artefacts*, some of which closely resemble ads, all for a brand that ceased production nearly a decade earlier. Their actions serve to maintain a brand that has a special meaning for them.

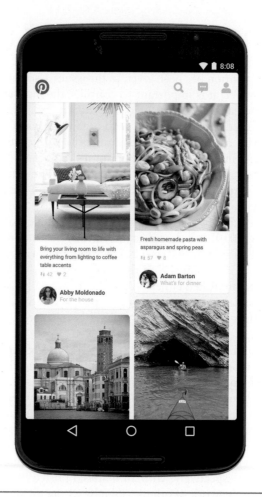

| Exhibit 17.9 | **Pinterest allows consumers to share creative images** |

Pinterest was founded in 2010 and is a popular website that allows consumers to upload and save images called pins. Users can browse content from other users on the site to create their personalised pinboards.

Source: Pinterest.

Sourcing content

UGC can be derived through one of three main processes:

- *Crowd-sourcing* – Organisations can prompt the public into action, via the web community, to develop specific types of content and materials. Where organisations deliberately invite the entire web community to suggest material that can be used commercially, in return for a reward, the term *crowd-sourcing* is used. In this circumstance the crowd may consist of amateurs or businesses. The difference between crowd-sourcing and outsourcing is that the latter is directed at a predetermined, specific organisation.

- *Open-source materials* – The public may take the initiative themselves and communicate with a specific organisation or industry. Where a group of people voluntarily offer ideas and materials, without invitation, prompting or seeking a reward from an organisation, the term *open-source materials* is used.

- *Friendsourcing* – the public may exchange information and ideas amongst themselves, without any direct communications with an organisation or brand owner. This occurs when friends and families communicate and share ideas and materials among themselves, for their own enjoyment, bonding and enrichment.

Some marketers are using the increasing occurrence of UGC as an opportunity to listen to and observe consumers and to find out what meanings they attribute to products, brands and company actions. Some companies invite consumers to offer content (ads): crow-dsourcing. Unilever dissolved its 16-year-old relationship with its ad agency Lowe London, in order to embark on a crowd-sourcing strategy. Focusing on the Peperami brand, Unilever searched for material to support a TV and print campaign. The result was 1,185 ideas, and the winner won £6,000 (Charles, 2009).

Ideas about co-creation and collaboration now pervade marketing communications. There is an increasing role for messages to be shared with audiences (as noted in reference to communications in Chapter 2), not sent to or at them (Earls, 2010). Understanding the relationships audiences prefer with product categories and brands enables the identification of opportunities to share and collaborate.

Key points

- Source credibility consists of three key elements: the level of perceived expertise; the personal motives the source is believed to possess; and the degree of trust that can be placed in what the source says or does on behalf of the endorsement.

- A spokesperson can provide credibility and four main types of spokesperson are identified: the expert, the celebrity, the chief executive officer and the consumer.

- Arguments for a brand or issue can be presented for and against an issue – a two-sided message. Alternatively just the case in favour of an issue can be presented – a one-sided message. Credibility is improved by understanding the audience's position and then fashioning the presentation of the message.

- Messages that present the strongest points at the beginning use the primacy effect. Placing the strongest points at the end of the message assumes that the recency effect will bring about greater levels of persuasion. This is appropriate when the receiver agrees with the position adopted by the source or has a high positive level of involvement.

- Messages can use informational/rational or emotional appeals. Information or rational appeals use factual, slice-of-life, demonstration and comparative style. Emotional appeals use fear, humour, animation, sex, music, fantasy and surrealism.

- There are two broad types of motive that drive attitudes towards purchase behaviour. These are informational and transformational motives. Individuals have a need for information to counter negative concerns about a purchase decision. These informational motives are said to be negatively charged feelings. They can become positively charged, or the level of concern can be reduced considerably, by the acquisition of relevant information.

- Promises to enhance or to improve a brand are referred to as transformational motives. These are related to the user's feelings and are capable of transforming a user's emotional state, hence they are positively charged.

- Creativity in advertising is considered to be an effective way of getting people to attend to an ad. This can lead to improved motivation to process a message, and from this higher recall and recognition scores can develop.

- Creativity in advertising has two main characteristics: first, ads are divergent, or highly unique or novel; and second, they are relevant or meaningful to the audience. The higher the originality or divergence and the more personally relevant, the greater the attention the ad attracts.

- The creative process in advertising agencies is seen to progress through a number of stages which include internal and external review meetings such as Tissue Sessions, Chemistry Meetings and can involve setting up War Rooms and undertaking consumer research.

- Agencies, and all those working within creative departments, work within and are constrained by the prevailing organisational culture. Stuhlfaut (2011) identifies the existence of a creative code which shapes the development of advertisements.

- Framing is concerned with the selection of particular elements in order to restrict and focus the way people perceive a problem, brand, issue or communications event.

- People use storytelling to help make sense of their lives and the events that they encounter and to derive meaning from their relationships and social activities. Stories consist of themes (hardship, reciprocity and a defining moment) and plots (a sequence of events; anticipation, crisis, getting help, and achieving a goal).

- User-generated content (UGC) considers how messages are developed by consumers. UGC has three primary characteristics: the content needs to be published either on a publicly accessible website or on a social networking site accessible to a selected group of people; the material needs to demonstrate some creative effort; and it has to have been created outside of professional routines and practices.

Review questions

John Lewis case questions

1. Why was an emotional appeal used by John Lewis in its Christmas advertising campaign? Explain why you think an information-based appeal was not used.

2. Which elements in 'Monty's Christmas' help to develop the emotional appeal?

3. Watch 'Monty's Christmas' for yourself and identify the elements of storytelling which are evident in the TV ad. List three other recent ads that use storytelling.

4. Discuss why you think 'Monty's Christmas' is seen to be a creative ad. Evaluate the ad against the terms 'divergence' and 'relevance'.

5. Find examples of advertising from three other retailers and decide whether they have used an emotional-based appeal or an information-based appeal.

General questions

1. Why is source credibility seen as important? Find examples of each type of spokesperson.

2. Explain the difference between informational and transformational motivations.

3. What do forcing and subversion mean in the context of creativity? Find a current example of each approach.

4. Outline the principles associated with framing. How does this concept assist those responsible for marketing communications?

5. Using different media, find three examples of user-generated content.

References

About Radiant (2015) *Radiant Return FAQ,* retrieved 10 May 2015 from http://radiantlaundry.com.au/about. php.

Adams, A.J. and Henderson Blair, M. (1992) Persuasive advertising and sales accountability, *Journal of Advertising Research,* 32(2), 20–5.

AdNews (2014) Buy it. Wear it. Wash it. Return it, *AdNews.* 10 June, retrieved 10 May 2015 from www.adnews.com. au/campaigns/buy-it-wear-it-wash-it-return-it.

Amabile, T.M. (1996) *Creativity in Context,* Boulder, CO Westview Press.

Ang, S.H., Lee, Y.H. and Leong, S.M. (2007) The ad creativity cube: conceptualization and initial validation, *Journal of the Academy of Marketing Science,* 35(2), 220–32.

Anon (2015) No 132: the world's most expensive TV commercial, *Campaign,* 15 May, p. 13.

Arora, R. (1985) Consumer involvement: what it offers to advertising strategy, *International Journal of Advertising,* 4, 119–30.

Baack, D.W., Wilson, R.T. and Till, B.D. (2008) Creativity and memory effects: recall, recognition, and an exploration of nontraditional media, *Journal of Advertising,* 37(4), 85–94.

Barker, R.T. and Gower, K. (2010) Strategic application of storytelling in organizations toward effective communication in a diverse world, *Journal of Business Communication,* 47(3), 295–312.

Bewick, M. (2006) Pushing the boundaries, *The Marketer,* September, p. 25.

Binet, L. and Field, P. (2007) *Marketing in the Era of Accountability,* Henley-on-Thames: Institute of Practitioners in Advertising/WARC.

Binet, L., Müllensiefen, D. and, Edwards, P. (2013) The power of music, *Admap,* October, 10–13.

Blasko, V.J. and Mokwa, M.P. (1986) Creativity in advertising: a Janusian perspective, *Journal of Advertising,* 15(4), 43–50.

Boje, D.M. (1991) The storytelling organization: a study of story performance in an office-supply firm, *Administrative Science Quarterly,* March, 106–26.

Bold, B. (2014) The best (and the worst) CGI animals in ads, *Brand Republic,* retrieved 21 February 2015 from www.brandrepublic.com/article/1325008/best-and-worst-cgi-animals-ads.

Bowery, J. (2007) Haven't I seen you before? *Marketing,* 6 June, p. 17.

Brazier, P. (2011) Behind the scenes making of the Twinings advert 2011, *YouTube* retrieved July 2014 from www. youtube.com/watch?v=rZq-jWGLkoM

Brown, M.R., Bhadury, R.K. and Pope, N.K.L. (2010) The impact of comedic violence on viral advertising effectiveness, *Journal of Advertising,* 39(1), 49–65.

Brownsell, A. (2009) When personalities become bigger than their brands, *Brand Republic,* retrieved 10 January 2015 from www.brandrepublic.com/article/872886/when-personalities-become-bigger-brands.

Buda, R. (2003) The interactive effect of message framing, presentation order, and source credibility on recruitment practices, *International Journal of Management,* 20(2), 156–63.

Buzzell, R. (1964) Predicting short-term changes in market share as a function of advertising strategy, *Journal of Marketing Research,* 1(3), 27–31.

Charles, G. (2009) Peperami ad will be test case for crowd-sourcing, *Marketing,* 4 November, p. 2.

Christodoulides, G., Jevons, C. and Blackshaw, P. (2011) The voice of the consumer speaks forcefully in brand identity: user-generated content forces smart marketers to listen, *Journal of Advertising Research,* Supplement, March, 101–8.

Cobra Study (2010) Millward Brown adds marketability measure to celebrity and brand research, WPP website, retrieved 2 April 2015 from www.wpp.com/wpp/press/2010/oct/18/millward-brown-adds-marketability-measure-to-celebrity/.

Cordiner, R. (2009) Set free your core narrative: the brand as storyteller, *Admap,* October, retrieved 8 July 2010 from www.warc.com.

Cui, G. and Yang, X. (2009) Responses of Chinese consumers to sex appeals in international advertising: a test of congruency theory, *Journal of Global Marketing,* 22, 229–45.

Dahl, D.W., Frankenberger, K.D. and Manchanda, R.V. (2003) Does it pay to shock? Reactions to shocking and nonshocking advertising content among university students, *Journal of Advertising Research,* 43(3), 268–81.

Dan, V. and Ihlen, Ø. (2011) Framing expertise: a cross-cultural analysis of success in framing contests, *Journal of Communications Management,* 15(4), 368–88.

Das, E., Galekh, M. and Vonkeman, C. (2015) Is sexy better than funny? Disentangling the persuasive effects of pleasure and arousal across sex and humour appeals, *International Journal of Advertising,* 34(3), 406–420.

DDB Melbourne (2015) Radiant return, 13 March, DDB Melbourne, retrieved 10 April 2015 from http://ddbmelbourne.com/2015/03/13/radiant-return/.

DeLarge, C.A. (2004) Storytelling as a critical success factor in design processes and outcomes, *Design Management Review*, 15(3), 76–81.

Dichter, E. (1966) How word-of-mouth advertising works, *Harvard Business Review*, 44 (November/December), 147–66.

Earls, M. (2010) The wisdom of crowds, *Admap*, May, retrieved 10 May 2010 from www.warc.com/.

El-Murad, J. and West, D.C. (2004) The definition and measurement of creativity: what do we know? *Journal of Advertising Research*, 44(2), 188–201.

Entman, R.M. (1993) Framing: toward clarification of a fractured paradigm, *Journal of Communications*, 43(4), 51–8.

Faison, E.W. (1961) Effectiveness of one-sided and two-sided mass communications in advertising, *Public Opinion Quarterly*, 25 (Autumn), 468–9.

Foxall, G.R. and Goldsmith, R.E. (1994) *Consumer Psychology for Marketing*, London: Routledge.

Gamson, W.A. and Modigliani, A. (1989) Media discourse and public opinion on nuclear power: a constructionist approach, *American Journal of Sociology*, 95, 1–37.

Goodenough, W.H. (1981) *Culture, Language, and Society*, Menlo Park, CA: Benjamin/Cummings.

Hackley, C. and Kover, A.J. (2007) The trouble with creatives: negotiating creative identity in advertising agencies, *International Journal of Advertising*, 26(1), 63–78.

Halonen-Knight, E. and Hurmerinta, L. (2010) Who endorses whom? Meanings transfer in celebrity endorsement, *Journal of Product & Brand Management*, 19(6), 452–60.

Han, S.P. and Shavitt, S. (1994) Persuasion and culture: advertising appeals in individualistic and collectivistic societies, *Journal of Experimental Social Psychology*, 30(4), 326–50.

Hannah, D.B. and Sternthal, B. (1984) Detecting and explaining the sleeper effect, *Journal of Consumer Research*, 11 (September), 632–42.

Heath, R.G. (2010) Creativity in TV ads does not increase attention, *Admap*, January, retrieved 23 October 2011 from www.warc.com.

Heath, R.G., Nairn, A.C. and Bottomley, P.A. (2009) How effective is creativity? Emotive content in TV advertising does not increase attention, *Journal of Advertising Research*, September, 450–63.

Helgesen, T. (1994) Advertising awards and advertising agency performance criteria, *Journal of Advertising Research*, 34(July/August), 43–53.

Hetsroni, A. and Tukachinsky, R.H. (2005) The use of fine art in advertising: a survey of creatives and content analysis of advertisements, *Journal of Current Issues and Research in Advertising*, 27(1), 93–107.

Hill, R. and Johnson, L.W. (2004) Understanding creative service: a qualitative study of the advertising problem delineation, communication and response (APDCR) process, *International Journal of Advertising*, 23(3), 285–307.

Hollensen, S. and Schimmelpfennig, C. (2013) Selection of celebrity endorsers: a case approach to developing an endorser selection process model, *Marketing Intelligence & Planning*, 31(1), 88–102.

Hovland, C.I. and Mandell, W. (1952) An experimental comparison of conclusion drawing by the communicator and by the audience, *Journal of Abnormal and Social Psychology*, 47 (July), 581–8.

Hovland, C.I., Lumsdaine, A. and Sheffield, F.D. (1949) *Experiments on Mass Communications*, New York: Wiley.

IFAW (2014) With a new year comes a new campaign, retrieved 28 November 2014 from www.ifaw.org/united-states/news/new-year-china-comes-new-campaign.

Jones, S.E. and LeBaron, C.D. (2002) Research on the relationship between verbal and nonverbal communication: emerging integrations, *Journal of Communication*, 52(3), 499–521.

Kaplan, A.M. and Haenlein, M. (2010) Users of the world, unite! The challenges and opportunities of Social Media, *Business Horizons*, 53(1), 59–68.

Kardes, F.R. (1988) Spontaneous inference processes in advertising: the effects of conclusion omission and involvement on persuasion, *Journal of Consumer Research*, 15 (September), 225–33.

Kelman, H. (1961) Processes of opinion change, *Public Opinion Quarterly*, 25 (Spring), 57–78.

Kim, B.H., Han, S. and Yoon, S. (2010) Advertising creativity in Korea: scale development and validation, *Journal of Advertising*, 39(2), 93–108.

Koslow, S., Sasser, S.L. and Riordan, E.A. (2003) What is creative to whom and why? Perceptions in advertising agencies, *Journal of Advertising Research*, 43 (March), 96–110.

Koslow, S., Sasser, S.L. and Riordan, E.A. (2006) Do marketers get the advertising they need or the advertising they deserve? *Journal of Advertising*, 35(3), 81–101.

Kover, A.J. (1995) Copywriters' implicit theories of communication: an exploration, *Journal of Consumer Research,* 21(4), 596–611.

Lafferty, B.A., Goldsmith, R.E. and Newell, S.J. (2002) The dual credibility model: the influence of corporate and endorser credibility on attitudes and purchase intentions, *Journal of Marketing Theory and Practice,* 10(3), 1–12.

Lämsä, A.M. and Sintonen, T. (2006) A narrative approach for organizational learning in a diverse organisation, *Journal of Workplace Learning,* 18(2), 106–20.

Lannon, J. (1992) Asking the right questions – what do people do with advertising? *Admap,* March, 11–16.

Laroche, M., Vinhal Nepomuceno, M., Huang, L. and Richard, M.-O. (2011) What's so funny? The use of humor in magazine advertising in the United States, China and France, *Journal of Advertising Research,* 51(2), 404–16.

MacKenzie, S.B. and Lutz, R.L. (1989) An empirical examination of the structural antecedents of attitude toward the ad in an advertising pretesting context, *Journal of Marketing,* 53, 48–65.

Marshall, J. and Adamic, M. (2010) The story is the message: shaping corporate culture, *Journal of Business Strategy,* 31(2), 18–23.

McCann (2015) V/Line guilt trips, retrieved from http://mccann.com.au/project/guilt-trips/.

McKee, R. and Fryer, B. (2003) Storytelling that moves people, *Harvard Business Review,* 81(6), 51–5.

Merchant, A., Ford, J.B. and Sargeant, A. (2010) Charitable organizations' storytelling influence on donors' emotions and intentions, *Journal of Business Research,* 63(7), 754–62.

Muñiz, Jr, A.M. and Schau, H.J. (2007) Vigilante marketing and consumer-created communications, *Journal of Advertising,* 36(3), 35–50.

Na, W., Marshall, R. and Woodside, A. G. (2009) Decision system analysis of advertising agency decisions, *Qualitative Market Research: An International Journal,* 12(2), 153–70.

Nyilasy, G. and Reid, L.N. (2009) Agency practitioners' meta-theories of advertising, *International Journal of Advertising,* 28(4), 639–68.

Okazaki, S., Mueller, B. and Taylor, C.R. (2010) Measuring soft-sell versus hard-sell advertising appeals, *Journal of Advertising,* 39(2), 5–20.

Oster, E. (2015) W+K London tell story of 'The Messenger' for Arla Skyr, *Adweek,* 17 April, retrieved 10 May 2015 from www.adweek.com/agencyspy/wk-london-tell-story-of-the-messenger-for-arla-skyr/84742.

Paek, H.-J. and Nelson, M.R. (2007) A cross-cultural and cross media comparison of female nudity in advertising, *Journal of Promotion Management,* 13(1/2), 145–67.

Pan, Z. and Kosicki, G. (2001) Framing as a strategic action in public deliberation, in *Framing Public Life: Perspectives on Media and Our Understanding of the Social World* (eds S.D. Reese, O.H. Gandy and A.E. Grant), Mahwah, NJ: Lawrence Erlbaum, 35–65.

Papadatos, C. (2006) The art of storytelling: how loyalty marketers can build emotional connections to their brands, *Journal of Consumer Marketing,* 23(7), 382–4.

Parker, R. and Churchill, L. (1986) Positioning by opening the consumer's mind, *International Journal of Advertising,* 5, 1–13.

Priest, I. (2014) Client-agency relationship: seven principles for better commercial creativity, *Market Leader,* Quarter 3, retrieved 10 December 2014 from www.warc.com/Content/ContentViewer.aspx?MasterContentRef=7654819d-4ed7-47f7-9323-f039e5cc8ec4&q=priest&CID=A102137&PUB=MKT.

Ray, M.L. and Wilkie, W.L. (1970) Fear: the potential of an appeal neglected by marketing, *Journal of Marketing,* 34 (January), 54–62.

Reichert, T., Childers, C.C. and Reid, L.N. (2012) How sex in advertising varies by product category: an analysis of three decades of visual sexual imagery in magazine advertising. *Journal of Current Issues & Research in Advertising,* 33(1), 1–19.

Reid, L.N. and Rotfeld, H.J. (1976) Toward an associative model of advertising creativity, *Journal of Advertising,* 5(4), 24–9.

Rossiter, J.R. (2008) Envisioning the future of advertising creativity research: alternative perspectives, defining the necessary components of creative, effective ads, *Journal of Advertising,* 37(4), 139–44.

Rossiter, J.R. and Percy, L. (1997) *Advertising and Promotion Management,* 2nd edition, New York: McGraw-Hill.

Rossiter, J. and Percy, L. (1998) *Advertising, Communications, and Promotion Management,* Singapore: McGraw Hill, International Editions.

Rossiter, J.R., Percy, L. and Donovan, R.J. (1991) A better advertising planning grid, *Journal of Advertising Research,* October/November, 11–21.

Save the Rhino International (2014) Poaching: the statistics, retrieved 24 November 2014 from: www.savetherhino.org/rhino_info/poaching_statistics.

Schiffman, L.G. and Kanuk, L. (1991) *Consumer Behavior,* 4th edition, Englewood Cliffs, NJ: Prentice Hall.

Smith, R.E. and Yang, X. (2004) Toward a general theory of creativity in advertising: the role of divergence, *Marketing Theory,* 4(1/2), 31–58.

Smith, R.E., MacKenzie, S.B., Yang, X., Buchholz, L.M. and Darley, W.K. (2007) Modelling the determinants and effects of creativity in advertising, *Marketing Science*, 26(6), 819–833.

Smith, R.E., Chen, J. and Yang, X. (2008) The impact of advertising creativity on the hierarchy of effects, *Journal of Advertising*, 37(4), 47–61.

Stuhlfaut, M. (2011) The creative code: an organisational influence on the creative process in advertising, *International Journal of Advertising*, 30(2), 283–304.

Stuhlfaut, M.W. and Vanden Bergh, B.G. (2014) Creativity is . . . : a metaphoric model of the creative thought process, *Journal of Marketing Communications*, 20(6), 383–96.

Sutherland, J., Duke, L. and Abernethy, A. (2004) A model of marketing information flow: what creatives obtain and want to know from clients, *Journal of Advertising*, 33(4), 39–52.

TRAFFIC (2014) Innovative campaign promotes success from within, retrieved 24 November 2014 from www.traffic.org/home/2014/9/22/innovative-campaign-promotes-success-from-within.html.

Tsai, S.-P. (2007) Message framing strategy for brand communication, *Journal of Advertising Research*, 47(3), 364–77.

Turnbull, S. and Wheeler, C. (2015) The advertising creative process: a study of UK agencies, *Journal of Marketing Communications*, DOI: 10.1080/13527266.2014.1000361.

Vanden Bergh, B.G., Lee, M.. Quilliam, E.T. and Hove, T. (2011) The multidimensional nature and brand impact of user-generated advertising parodies in social media, *International Journal of Advertising*, 30(1), 103–31.

Vaughn, R. (1980) How advertising works: a planning model, *Journal of Advertising Research*, 20(5), 27–33.

Venkat, R. and Abi-Hanna, N. (1995) Effectiveness of visually shocking advertisements: is it context dependent? *Administrative Science Association of Canada Proceedings*, 16(3), 139–46.

V/Line (2013) *Annual Report (2011–2012)*, retrieved 19 May 2015 from www.vline.com.au.

V/Line (2014) *Annual Report 2012–13*, retrieved 19 May 2015 from www.vline.com.au/pdf/publications/annualreports/AnnualReport12-13.pdf.

Weick, K.E. (1979) *The Social Psychology of Organizing*, Reading, MA: Addison-Wesley.

Weinberger, M.G., Gulas, C.S. and Weinberger, M.F. (2015) Looking in through outdoor: a socio-cultural and historical perspective on the evolution of advertising humour, *International Journal of Advertising*, (ahead-of-print), 1–2.

Wieden + Kennedy (2015) Arla and W+K bring Skyr to British shores, 20 April, retrieved 15 May 2015 from http://wklondon.com/news/all_clients/all_years/P0/new-arla-skyr-campaign.

WildAid (2014) China's top business leaders say no to ivory, retrieved 24 November 2014 from www.wildaid.org/news/china%E2%80%99s-top-business-leaders-say-no-ivory.

Windels, K. and Stuhlfaut, M.W. (2014) Confined creativity: the influence of creative code intensity on risk taking in advertising agencies, *Journal of Current Issues & Research in Advertising*, 35(2), 147–66.

Woodside, A.G., Sood, S. and Miller, K.E. (2008) When consumers and brands talk: storytelling theory and research in psychology and marketing, *Psychology and Marketing*, 25(2), 97–145.

Wylie, A. (1998) Story telling: a powerful form of communication, *Communication World*, 15, 30–3.

Yang, X. and Smith, R.E. (2009) Beyond attention effects: modelling the persuasive and emotional effects of advertising creativity, *Marketing Science*, 28, 935–49.

Yin, S. (2008) All about . . . celebrity endorsements, *Brand Republic*, retrieved 12 February 2015 from www.brandrepublic.com/article/789570/about-celebrity-endorsements.

Zhang, Y. and Zinkhan, G.M. (2006) Responses to humorous ads: does audience involvement matter? *Journal of Advertising*, 35(4), 113–27.

Chapter 18

Media – principles and practice

The selection and use of particular media is necessary in order to engage particular groups of consumers and organisations, and to enable conversations with and among audiences. The array of available media is continually growing but each has its characteristics that impact on the quality, effectiveness and the meaning attributed to a message by an audience.

Aims and learning objectives

The aim of this chapter is to identify and explore the principal characteristics of the main types of media. This will assist understanding of the management processes by which media are selected and scheduled to deliver messages and influence audiences.

The learning objectives are to enable readers to:

1. appreciate the three main ways in which media can be classified;
2. understand the differences between linear and interactive media;
3. describe the trends and primary characteristics of each type of linear media;
4. evaluate the different characteristics associated with interactive media, and comprehend what interactive media enable people to do;
5. explain the issues associated with multichannel campaigns and explore the role of media within a retailing context;
6. consider the dynamics associated with direct-response media.

Foster's – 'Good Call'

In 2010 the UK beer market was led by Carling, with Carlsberg second placed. Foster's had fallen back having become complacent and lost both its wit and charm. Its link to Australia, established through several campaigns, had faltered with Carling having a far stronger preference and a stronger campaign.

In order to address this situation a strategy to drive growth of the core lager business was developed. This involved re-connecting the target 18–24 year old male tribal drinkers, the heartland Foster's audience, with their Aussie cousins with whom the brand had lost touch.

The resultant 'Good Call' campaign ran for 6 years and featured the characters Brad and Dan who drove the experience of drinking a can of Fosters. These agony uncles headed a call centre and humorously advised men, from their pub beach hut, on their relationship problems, using their tongue-in-cheek, Aussie 'no worries' approach to guide UK male drinkers. Each call that Brad and Dan took involved small crises for their UK callers. Brad and Dan, however, smoothed everything over with ease as they dispensed advice with a white beach in front of them and sipping Fosters beer as they answered calls. The 'Good Call' campaign was refreshed regularly as new problems were presented for Brad and Dan to solve. This campaign consistency helped to create 'memory structure', so that hard-wired associations triggered brand recall.

A number of brand properties were created and amplified:

- Australian beach setting with the Foster's hut.
- Brad and Dan characters.
- Narrative structure of each commercial: phone call from UK (e.g. 'Steve from Southend'); Brad and Dan answer in the Aussie beach hut, 'G'day'; they offer a solution.
- 'Good Call' endline.
- Style of humour and jokes.

Although the campaign was TV led, the integrated approach involved other media. These included print, digital, media partnerships and sponsorship. Although the campaign was dominated by TV, outdoor media was used by converting some 6-sheets and telephone booths into mini beach huts. The interactive 6 Sheets placed in core drinking centres were used to reach the target audience.

In addition there was a 'Good Call Centre' digital campaign, based around a microsite. This could be used to help a 'mate in a state' about 'girl trouble'. These included, for example, problems associated with dress sense, suitable manners and personal hygiene. Brad and Dan, assisted by the Good Call Centre girls, would create responses through a personalised video message, which could be shared through social networks. The digital campaign also served to amplify some of the

| Exhibit 18.1 | **Brad and Dan give advice to UK male drinkers** |

Source: Heineken.

brand properties, and reinforced the brand's memory structure. Despite some accusations of casual sexism the media used helped the ads cut through competitive beer messages and differentiate the brand.

Tracking studies demonstrated how effective the Foster's work was at creating memory structure. The slogan, 'Good Call', and the Brad and Dan characters were the strongest performing brand properties in the UK beer market, with 70 per cent of people able to recall the brand when seeing the brand property for a split second.

Brad and Dan were also used to launch two range extensions: Radler, a lager and cloudy lemonade, and Gold, a premium 4.8 per cent lager. These new products reinforced the brand's key properties and helped avoid the brand fragmentation that could happen had there been separate campaigns. The 'Summer of Good Calls' served as an umbrella concept for several promotional items, leveraging the Aussie beach properties with ideas such as a Cooler Box.

The 'Good Call' campaign, with its variety of laddish executions, drove nearly 70 per cent of Foster's sales growth in the three years to September 2013. Each £1 invested in advertising drove £32 extra sales revenue. This moved Foster's from third to first place for both sales value and volume among lagers sold in the UK 'off-trade' (retail) sector. This growth was achieved in spite of a decline in the total volume of standard lager sold off-trade in the UK. What was also remarkable was that Foster's maintained its premium pricing, despite the fact that its share of advertising spend in the lager market did not rise.

The beer industry has often been accused of discriminating against female audiences. As a part of this debate the 'Good Call' campaign drew a steady stream of critical comments. This is particularly interesting as the number of female beer drinkers in the UK has doubled to over 1.3 million, and that women make up 31 per cent of weekly beer drinkers.

So, despite the commercial success of this campaign, it was not surprising that the chief executive of SABMiller, who own Foster's, announced in May 2015 that the 'Good Call' campaign was to end. He referred to the need to move on from themes that are dismissive and insulting to women. He added that Peroni has 'moved away from the lager lout . . . and that beer now has associations with fashion, art and design. The world has moved on from lads telling jokes on a Saturday and high-volume consumption. Beer is now drunk by women and men together.'

This case was written using a variety of sources including: Anon (2010); Bold (2014); Clements (2015); O'Connor (2015); Sweney (2015); Taylor (2014); www.creativebrief.com/agency/work/.

Questions relating to this case can be found at the end of this chapter.

Exhibit 18.2	**The idea that Brad and Dan provide expert advice was extended to the launch of the brand extension Radler**

Source: Heineken.

Introduction

The media constitute the third element of the marketing communications mix. The primary role of the media is to convey planned and unplanned messages to, from and among audiences. Just as Expedia used a range of media in the 'Travel Yourself Interesting' campaign, it was the configuration of the media mix that helped the campaign goals be achieved.

The range and variety of media available to organisations have been expanding rapidly. Media once referred to just newspapers, radio, television and film. Today the conception of what constitutes media is much broader, and as Sundar and Limpero (2013: 505) state, this reflects 'a plethora of devices (smart phones, robots) to channels (Internet, cable) to venues on those channels (social networking sites, home shopping network) and/or devices (smartphone apps), affording users the ability to not only interact with these 'media' (human-computer interaction) but also interact through them to communicate with other users (computer-mediated communications)'.

Attempts to classify them as simply *traditional* and *new*, or *conventional* and *digital*, are misplaced because they are too broad, vague and misleading. What constitutes new and old depends largely on arbitrary timelines and, in any case, digital media are used within traditional formats.

A more meaningful classification is to consider the media in terms of their physicality or location (see Figure 18.1). Here 'broadcast' and 'outdoor' describe what these media are and how they work. An alternative approach is to consider the media in terms of their origin or ownership. Here media owned by others are segregated from media that the clients own themselves.

A third type of classification, one based on their communications function, is examined and used as the foundation for exploring media in the remaining part of this and subsequent chapters.

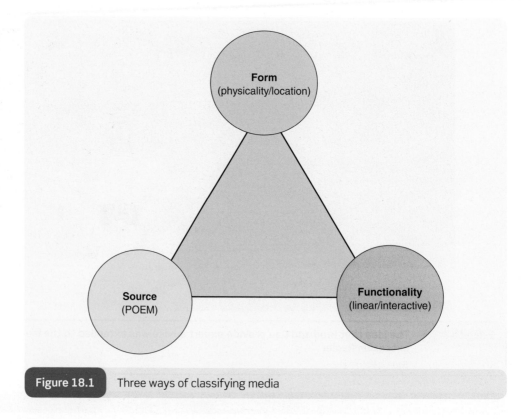

Figure 18.1   Three ways of classifying media

Media classification – by form

When classifying media in terms of their form, six main *classes* can be identified. These are broadcast, print, outdoor, digital, in-store and other media classes. Within each of these classes there are particular *types* of media. For example, within the broadcast class there are television and radio, and within the print class there are newspapers and magazines.

Within each type of media there are a huge number of different media *vehicles* that can be selected to carry an advertiser's message. For example, within UK television there are the terrestrial networks (Independent Television Network, Channel 4 and Channel 5) and the satellite (BSkyB) and cable (e.g. Virgin Media) networks. In print, there are consumer and business-oriented magazines, and the number of specialist magazines is expanding rapidly. These specialist magazines are targeted at particular activity and interest groups, such as *Amateur Photographer*, *Golf World* and the infamous *Plumbing Monthly*! This provides opportunities for advertisers to send messages to well-defined homogeneous groups, which improves effectiveness and reduces wastage in the communications spend. Table 18.1 sets out the three forms of media – classes, types and vehicles – with a few examples.

Table 18.1 Summary chart of the main forms of media by form

Class	Type	Vehicles
Broadcast	Television Radio	*Coronation Street*, *X Factor* *Capital Xtra*
Print	Newspapers Magazines: consumer business	*Sunday Times, Daily Mirror, Daily Telegraph* *Cosmopolitan, Woman, Plumbing News, The Grocer*
Out-of-home	Billboards Street furniture Transit	96-, 48- and 6-sheet Adshel Underground stations, airport buildings, taxis, hot-air balloons
Interactive media	Internet Social media Search	Websites, email, apps, RSS, intranets Networks, communities, blogs Organic, sponsored links
In-store	Point-of-purchase Packaging	Bins, signs and displays The Coca-Cola contour bottle
Other	Cinema Exhibitions and events	Pearl & Dean Ideal Home, The Motor Show
	Product placement Ambient Guerrilla	Films, TV, books Litter bins, golf tees, petrol pumps, washrooms Flyposting

Media classification – by source

The traditional demarcation regards media in terms of purely paid-for channels, used to support conventional, linear-based advertising. The second classification of the media, by source, was presented earlier (see Chapter 1). Popularly known as POEM, which stands for paid-for, owned and earned media, this classification reflects a practitioner's interpretation of the media (see Table 18.2).

Table 18.2 POEM – a classification of the media by source

Type of media		Explanation
P	Paid-for	Advertising traditionally requires that media time and space are rented from a media owner, in order to convey messages and reach target audiences. The selection of the media mix is planned, predetermined and measured in terms of probable size of audience, costs and scheduling.
O	Owned	Organisations have a range of assets that they can use to convey messages to audiences, and through which they can develop conversations. Ownership means that there are no rental costs as with paid-for media. For example, a brand name or product display on a building, a telephone number or URL on a vehicle, or the use of the company website and its links to other sites, do not incur usage fees.
E	Earned	Earned media refers to comments and conversations, both offline and online, in social media, in the news, or through face-to-face communications, about a brand or organisation. These comments can be negative or positive but the media carrying them are diverse and can be referred to as 'unplanned', although many campaigns seek to stimulate strong word-of-mouth communications through earned media.

POEM assumes that media are not just about paid-for media but media that embrace all items that can be used to convey brand-orientated messages, regardless of whether a payment is necessary. With the digital explosion, reconfiguration of the media landscape and changing consumer behaviours, POEM reflects the increasing scope of contemporary media and the range of media opportunities to engage audiences.

Whatever the classification it is important that media are considered to be more than just a technological platform. Each medium generates its own individual sets of meanings and, as Gould and Gupta (2006) indicate, it is through these that consumers forge associations by interpreting and reacting to the content that the medium delivers. Chen and Haley (2014) argue and reinforce the research of Hirschman and Thompson (1997) that the relationships consumers have with the media are a fundamental element through which the perceived meaning of commercial messages is derived.

Viewpoint 18.1   Apple use poetry on their owned media

The design of Apple's retail stores has been a deliberate and integral part of their overall brand identity. With 35 to 40 stores being opened every year each of Apple's retail outlets has a crucial role to play in the way the brand is identified, distinguished and its values reinforced.

In 2015 the West Lake Apple Store was opened in Hangzhou, the capital of Zhejiang Province in eastern China, situated on West Lake. The contemporary steel-and-glass exterior was draped by a simple yet elegant mural depicting a 2,000-year-old poem. Written in traditional Chinese characters the ancient text provides a stunning visual impact when set against the crisp, clean modern lines of the building.

The poem, called 'Praising West Lake in the Rain', was written a very long time ago, and refers to the consistent beauty of West Lake's glistening water.

Source: Gianatasio (2015).

Question: Why do you think brands generally only use signage and tend to ignore the communications value inherent in store design?

Task: Find three other stores that are used as an integral part of an owned media strategy.

Exhibit 18.3   **Apple's West Lake store in Hangzhou**
Source: Getty Images/ChinaFotoPress.

Scholars' paper 18.1   **Engaging television**

Heath, R. (2009) Emotional engagement: how television builds big brands at low attention, *Journal of Advertising Research*, 29(1), 62–73.

This paper is principally concerned with engagement and the way in which television can build brands through low attention. An interesting and thought-provoking article and one which those interested in advertising and media should read.

Media classification – by function

Another way of classifying the media is to adopt the principles of communications theory. By incorporating the principal functionality offered by individual media, and relating this to the forms embedded within communications theory, so more meaningful classifications emerge.

The reason for looking at a different approach is to provide more helpful terminology, one that overcomes the ubiquity and senseless use of the word 'digital'. As Goodwin (2014) so aptly puts it, 'technically a TV spot is digital advertising, as is a video pre-roll, interactive bus stop poster and print ad in the Wired iPad app, but a YouTube channel, tweet, Facebook page, website, viral film or an app are all not digital advertising. Now to draw the line between these outputs is absurd.'

Early theories about communications refer to a linear, mass-media interpretation, where the primary media were essentially broadcast and print. These were used to deliver messages to audiences and communications were considered to happen as a series of stages (source, encoding, decoding and receiver). Contemporary communications models embrace the responses, relationships and interaction that occur between participants. Sundar and Bellur (2011) refer to the gratifications that users experience from media usage, one of which is interactivity. From this two main classifications can be identified. The first is 'linear', which reflects media that are characterised by monologic, one-way communications. The second is 'interactive', which reflects media that, to varying levels, enable response, participation and interaction which can lead to dialogue.

Using this understanding we refer to 'linear' media and 'interactive' media to structure our exploration of this element of the mix.

Linear media

This part of the chapter explores the main types of linear media. These include broadcast, print, outdoor, in-store, cinema and ambient.

Print media

Newspapers and magazines are the two main types of print media. They attract advertisers for a variety of reasons, but the most important is that print media are very effective at delivering a message to a target audience.

However, an increasing number of people do not read newspapers and press advertising spend is declining as budgets are shifted to other media, most notably the Internet. In 2014, *Mail Online* attracted 193 million monthly unique browsers across its international network. The *Guardian*'s website is accessed by over 100 million monthly browsers and is now considered to be the third-biggest news brand in the world (Bale, 2015).

People who do use printed media tend to have consistent reading habits and buy or borrow the same media vehicles regularly. For example, most people read the same type of newspaper(s) each day and their regular choice of magazine reflects either their business or leisure interests, which are normally quite stable. This means that advertisers, through marketing research, are able to build a database of the main characteristics (a profile) of their readers. This in turn allows advertisers to buy space in those media vehicles that will be read by the sort of people they think will benefit from their product or service.

The printed word provides advertisers with the opportunity to explain their message in a way that most other media cannot. Such explanations can be in the form of either a picture or a photograph, perhaps demonstrating how a product is to be used. Alternatively, the written word can be used to argue why a product should be used and detail the advantages and benefits that consumption will provide the user. In reality, advertisers use a combination of these two forms of communications.

Print media are most suitable for messages designed when high involvement is present in the target market. These readers not only control the pace at which they read a magazine or newspaper, but also expend effort to read advertisements because they care about particular issues. Where elaboration is high and the central processing route is preferred, messages that provide a large amount of information are best presented in the printed form.

Customer magazines differ from consumer magazines because they are sent to customers direct, often without charge, and contain highly targeted and significant branded content. These have made a big impact in recent years and, partly because of high production values, have become a significant aspect of many direct marketing activities. This medium is very popular with the retail sector, with most of the supermarkets offering their own magazine and brands such as John Lewis and Harrods. Red Bull publishes *The Red Bulletin*, a magazine that gives customers another opportunity to identify themselves and bond with the brand. See Viewpoint 18.2 for another example of customer magazines.

Viewpoint 18.2   Ink media is flying high

Ink Global produces 36 inflight magazines in 17 languages, for 34 airlines including easyjet, American Airlines, Scoot, Jet2.com and United. Ink reaches 677 million passengers a year with over 100 media products.

Ink's business model is based on segmenting the passenger market using the unique anonymous data to which Ink's clients give it access. The data for each passenger concerning their gender, age, origination and destination airports, class of travel, frequent-flyer status, and travel dates and patterns, is used to generate inflight magazines and associated merchandise. This enables Ink to offer targeted advertising not only in the inflight magazines but also on customers' essential travel documents, including booking confirmations, itineraries, and print-at-home boarding passes. Ink's in-flight media starts from the moment an online reservation is made and can embrace car-park offers, vouchers to be redeemed at airport shops, and even destination entertainment attractions.

The success of inflight magazines is attributed partly to the context in which this type of media is consumed. At 35,000 ft, readers are captive and relaxed to the extent that their relationship with media is more intimate and less rushed than usual. Each magazine has its own dedicated editorial and

Exhibit 18.4	**Travel document advertising**
	Source: Iberia.

sales teams, content is not shared and all material is totally customised for each individual magazine. The capture of the American Airlines account, who for 40 years had produced all of its media in-house, enabled Ink to relaunch its three inflight titles. These include *American Way*, which alone has an annual readership of 193 million.

Germanwings, a subsidiary of Lufthansa, has 20 million passengers and operates 90 planes. To complement its growth Ink created a premium look and feel for its *GW* magazine. Each edition now includes high-quality editorial features and A-list celebrity interviews with stars such as Bruce Springsteen, Adele, Beyoncé and Anthony Hopkins. High-value international brands such as Bose, Hilton, O2, Rosetta Stone and New Balance were attracted to the magazine and the result was a 300 per cent increase in revenue in just the first 6 months.

Ink also makes travel apps for iOS and Android platforms. Ink has redesigned Iberia's Ronda and Excelente titles in a digital format. United's magazine *Hemispheres* is now available as a pdf-style tablet app, whilst its 30-year old signature feature, 'Three Perfect Days', has been reconfigured as a mobile app for sight-seeing.

To complement its high-value positioning, Ink organises leading conferences, exhibitions and events which focus on how airlines can enhance passenger experience, improve operations on the ground and in the air, and increase revenues.

Source: Burrell (2014); Halleck (2014); Shadbolt (2015); www.ink-global.com/.

Question: Which other media might Ink utilise for its travel market customers?

Task: Go to www.ink-global.com/ and determine Ink's competitive strengths.

Sales of magazines in pure hardcopy print format are falling. The magazine sector is in transition as digital formats are evolving. Publishers are having to innovate and develop their titles as media brands and extend reader relationships across mobile, tablet and the Web. Customer magazines and campaigns which integrate a variety of media, perhaps with social networks, microblogging, QR codes and augmented reality, reflect some of the ways publishers are changing their approach to reaching and engaging their audiences.

Scholars' paper 18.2   Newspaper as media efficacy

Danaher, P. and Rossiter, J. (2011) Comparing perceptions of marketing communication channels, *European Journal of Marketing*, 45(1/2), 6–42.

Danaher and Rossiter's research demonstrates that clutter in newspapers is less bothersome to newspaper readers than clutter in other media. Their research concluded that print ads in newspapers are less intrusive than other forms of media (such as the 'interruptive' quality of radio and TV) and that consumers who read newspapers feel that engagement with the traditional print medium is a good use of their time.

Broadcast media

There are two main forms of broadcast media: television and radio. Advertisers use this class of media because they can reach mass audiences with their messages at a relatively low cost per target reached.

Approximately 99 per cent of the population in the United Kingdom, and most developed economies, have access to a television and a similar number have a radio. The majority of viewers use television passively, as a form of entertainment. However, new technological applications have the potential to change this, so that television could be used proactively for a range of services, such as banking and shopping. Radio demands active participation, and can reach people who are out of the home environment.

Broadcast media allow advertisers to add visual and/or sound dimensions to their messages. The opportunity to demonstrate or to show the benefits or results that a particular product can bring gives life and energy to an advertiser's message. Television uses image, sound and movement, whereas radio can only use its audio capacity to convey meaning, but it does stimulate a listener's imagination and thus can involve audiences in a message. Both media have the potential to tell stories and to appeal to people's emotions. These are dimensions that print media find difficulty in achieving effectively within the time allocations that advertisers can afford.

Advertising messages transmitted through the broadcast media use a small period of time, called 'spots', normally 60, 30, 20 or 10 seconds, that are bought from the owners of the medium. Research by Southgate (2014) helps understanding about how to utilise the length of different lengths of video/film ads. These are summarised in Table 18.3.

The cost of the different time spots varies throughout a single transmission day and with the popularity of individual programmes. The more listeners or viewers a programme attracts, the greater the price charged for a slice of time to transmit an advertising message. Costs also vary according to region, the length of the commercial, the time of day it is screened, the programming environment, the time of year, the target audience and volume of view.

Table 18.3 When to use different ad lengths

Length of ad	Suited for
6-second spots	These micro-videos or 'vines' are considered best for the delivery of simple, explicit and authentic messages. Good for use within social networks. The ad should involve the brand as part of the story.
15-second spots	Suitable for stretching TV budgets, for simple messages or reinforcing more complex messages from longer executions, where these are well established and the shorter ad will trigger memories of the full creative.
30-second spots	Best for more complex messages, including new product launches, a new campaign or after a brand has been out of the spotlight for a long time.
60-second spots	These should seek to tell complex brand stories which engage viewers emotionally. This requires a high degree of involvement whilst the ad generates event status.
60 seconds to 5 minutes	This type of long-form format, typically found on YouTube and other video platforms, is ideal for fans who are immersed in a brand and its entertainment. The inspirational content should be regarded as a reward for advocates and other brand-loyal customers.

Source: Based on Southgate (2014).

The time-based costs for television can be extremely large. For example, the UK rate card cost of a nationwide 30-second spot in the middle of a popular soap is approximately £60,000, but this large, single cost needs to be put in perspective. The actual cost of reaching individual members of the target audience is quite low, simply because all the costs associated with the production of the message and the purchase of time to transmit the message can be spread across a mass of individuals.

The costs associated with radio transmissions are relatively low when compared with television. This reflects the lack of prestige that radio has and the pervasiveness of television. People are normally unable, and usually unwilling, to become actively involved with broadcast advertising messages. They cannot control the pace at which they consume advertising messages and as time is expensive and short, so advertisers do not have the opportunity to present detailed information. The result is that this medium is most suitable for messages where there is low involvement. Where the need for elaboration is low and the peripheral processing route is preferred, messages transmitted through electronic media should seek to draw attention, create awareness and improve levels of interest.

As the television and radio industries become increasingly fragmented, reaching particular market segments has become more challenging, as the target audience is often dispersed across other media. This means that the potential effectiveness of advertising through these media decreases. These media can reach large consumer audiences, but there is often considerable wastage and inefficiency. The result is that advertisers are moving their advertising spend, most notably to online and mobile media. It should be noted, however, that TV, according to Thinkbox (2014), contributed the greatest amount of profit for businesses, with an average return of £1.79 for every £1 invested during 2011–14. The analysis of over 4,500 campaigns led the researchers to suggest that finance and retail brands should ideally allocate 60 per cent of their advertising budgets to TV and a higher percentage for FMCG brands. In essence the role of television is changing, especially among younger age groups. Television is now perceived to be good at brand awareness and engagement, but it needs to be complemented with other media, and in particular social media and online video, in order to drive subsequent reach, frequency and content.

In 2014 television advertising spend was £4,911 million and radio advertising attracted £593 million (AA/WARC, 2015).

Outdoor media

Outdoor media (sometimes referred to as out-of-home) consist of three main formats: street furniture (such as bus shelters); billboards (consisting primarily of 96-, 48- and 6-sheet poster sites); and transit (which covers the underground/metro, lorries, buses and taxis). The range of outdoor media encompasses a large number of different formats, each characterised by two elements. First, they can be observed at locations away from home. Second, they are normally used to support messages that are transmitted through primary media: broadcast and print. Outdoor can therefore be seen as secondary but important support media for a complementary and effective communications mix.

Other reasons for the use of outdoor expenditure are that it can reinforce messages transmitted through primary media, act as a substitute medium when primary media are unavailable (e.g. tobacco organisations deprived of access to television and radio) and provide novelty and interest (electronic, inflatable and three-dimensional billboards), which can help avoid the clutter caused by the volume of advertising activity.

One of the common strands that bind these diverse media together is that they are all used to reach consumers who are themselves in transit, moving from one place to another, even if this is a shopping trip, going to/from work or taking a holiday. Advertising through television, radio, magazines, newspapers and cinema involves interrupting or accompanying editorial, informational or entertainment material. This is not the case with outdoor media.

According to Fitch (2007) the use of outdoor media must take into account the following variables: 'the length of the ad exposure (viewer "dwell time" in relation to the ad), the ad's intrusiveness on the surrounding environment, and the likely mood and mindset of the consumers who will encounter the ad'. It is the interaction of these variables that shapes each individual's experience of outdoor media and hence the effectiveness of these communications.

Media spend on outdoor advertising in 2014 was £1,019 million or approximately 5.5 per cent of total advertising expenditure (AA/WARC, 2015).

Billboards and street furniture

These are static displays and, as with out-of-home media generally, are unable to convey a great deal of information in the short period of time available in which people can attend to the messages. However, advances in technology permit precise targeting of poster campaigns on a national, regional or individual audience basis, or by their proximity to specific outlets, such as banks, CTNs (confectioner, tobacconist and newsagent) and off-licences.

There are three key developments in the industry that concern the replacement of the traditional bucket-and-paste production process. The first is the use of biodegradable one-sheet posters. The second concerns the use of high-definition (HD) billboards, which are glue-less vinyl posters that can be clipped in and out of a frame, reused and eventually recycled. The third concerns the increasing use of digital boards and the scope for interactivity and improved measurement. Outdoor was used to make McCain's 'Happy Days' campaign synonymous with the brand. A triple national campaign was run across multiple formats, including 4,100 national bus supersides, 6,050 roadside 6-sheets and 1,666 conurbation 48-sheets. Other, more iconic premium digital sites were used to elevate the McCain brand across key UK cities. Other digital formats were strategically used to target key consumption, for example chips between 4 and 7 p.m., roasties on Fridays in anticipation of the Sunday roast.

Transit

The names, signs and symbols that are painted on the sides of lorries and taxis can best represent transit or transport advertising. These moving posters, which travel around the country, serve to communicate names of organisations and products to all those who are in the vicinity of the vehicle. Indeed, transport advertising includes all those vehicles that are used for commercial purposes. In addition to lorries and taxis, transit media include buses, the Underground and Metro (trains, escalators and walkways), aeroplanes, blimps and balloons, ferries and trains, plus the terminals and buildings associated with the means of transport, such as airports and railway stations.

Research has shown that transit and, in particular, taxi advertising have very good reach and that their main role should be as a support medium (Veloutsou and O'Donnell, 2005). Messages can be presented as inside cards, where the messages are exposed to those using the vehicle. An example of this would be the small advertising messages displayed on the curvature of the roof of London Underground trains. Outside cards are those that are displayed on the exterior of taxis, buses and other commercial vehicles. For example, by adding taxi advertising to its media mix, Powwownow could reach global professionals and decision-makers potentially in every London street, and even in places where advertising was not otherwise present. Quidco incorporated 300 London SuperSide taxis into its campaign to spread its 'Get paid to shop' message amongst busy Londoners (OOH, 2015).

The difference between outdoor and transport media is arbitrary, although the former are media static and the latter are media mobile.

Scholars' paper 18.3   Outdoor works

Meurs, L. van and Aristoff, M. (2009) Split-second recognition: what makes outdoor advertising work? *Journal of Advertising Research*, 49(1), 82–92.

There are few papers on outdoor advertising so this one is recommended not only for its content but also for its scarcity. The paper considers the format and content of outdoor advertising and how the format affects the speed of brand recognition, and how it enhances appeal of the product. The research indicates how consumers process outdoor advertising posters in real life within a split second, and how content and format are variables in this process.

See also: Taylor, C.R., Franke, G.R. and Bang, H.-K. (2006) Use and effectiveness of billboards: perspectives from selective-perception theory and retail-gravity models, *Journal of Advertising*, 35(4), 21–34.

Viewpoint 18.3   Look-up now . . . it's British Airways!

In 2014 British Airways launched a digital billboard campaign called the 'Magic of Flying'. Designed to remind customers of the magic and experience of flying, as seen through a child's eyes, and highlight the breadth of its destinations, the campaign also served to drive people to the BA 'Look Up'-branded site. 'Look up' also lived as a hashtag (#LookUp).

Digital billboards in Chiswick and Piccadilly, underneath the flight path into Heathrow, featured young children who would stand up, walk across the screen and point to the sky in the direction of a passing British Airways aircraft. These actions encouraged onlookers to also look up and spot the passing aircraft, whilst a message on the board presented the flight number and the city from which the flight had originated.

The system worked using custom built surveillance technology. Using antennae on the roof of a building near each board, data from the transponders of all British Airways aircraft within 200 kilometres was used to feed information into an application that identified the flight and relevant city which was then served on the billboard. Using a 'trigger zone' as a trip wire, the system determined when a plane should instigate a message, and even considered the height of any cloud in the area to calculate whether the plane could actually be seen.

For the campaign to work the BA ads had to interrupt the normal presentation of other ads on the billboards, and cut in whenever a BA aircraft was passing. This necessitated an original type of media planning arrangement, if only to ensure that BA only paid for each activation of the ad, rather than a full-time booking.

In addition to a campaign that won a series of awards in various categories, the results revealed that traffic to BA.com increased by 75,000+ unique visits, drove over 1 million YouTube views, and became the most talked about piece of airline advertising in the year.

Source: Fera (2014); Klaassen (2014); Williams (2014).

Question:	To what extent is this type of interactive billboard more effective than the conventional, static outdoor facilities?
Task:	Find a similar outdoor billboard where there is interaction with the immediate environment, and not with the public.

Exhibit 18.5	**British Airways' digital billboard campaign – the 'Magic of Flying'**
	Source: British Airways.

In-store media

As an increasing number of brand choice decisions are made during the shopping experience, advertisers have become aware of the need to provide suitable in-store communications. The primary objective of using in-store media is to direct the attention of shoppers and to stimulate them to make purchases. The content of messages can be easily controlled by either the retailer or the manufacturer. In addition, the timing and the exact placement of in-store messages can be equally well controlled.

As mentioned previously, both retailers and manufacturers make use of in-store media although, of the two main forms (point-of-purchase displays and packaging), retailers control the point-of-purchase displays and manufacturers the packaging. Increasingly, there is recognition of the huge potential of retail stores becoming an integrated media centre, with retailers selling and managing media space and time. Attention is given here to in-store media and the retail media format (while a consideration of packaging issues can be found in Chapter 16).

Point-of-purchase (POP)

There are a number of POP techniques, but the most used are window displays, floor and wall racks to display merchandise, posters and information cards, plus counter and checkout displays. The most obvious display a manufacturer has at the point of purchase is the packaging used to wrap and protect the product until it is ready for consumption.

Supermarket trolleys with a video screen attached have been trialled by a number of stores. As soon as the trolley passes a particular infrared beam a short video is activated, promoting brands available in the immediate vicinity of the shopper. Other advances include electronic overhead signs, in-store videos at selected sites around the store and coupons for certain competitive products dispensed at the checkout once the purchased items have been scanned. Indirect messages can also play a role in in-store communications: for example, fresh bread smells can be circulated from the supermarket bakery at the furthest side of the store to the entrance area, enticing customers further into the supermarket. Some aroma systems allow for the smell to be restricted to just 45 cm (18 inches) of the display.

End-of-row bins and cards displaying special offers are POP media that aim to stimulate impulse buying. With over 75 per cent of supermarket buying decisions made in store, a greater percentage of communications budgets will be allocated to POP items.

Retail media centres

Traditionally, retailers allow their stores to be used in a variety of ways by a variety of organisations to communicate messages to their audiences. These audiences are jointly owned, not necessarily in equal proportion, by the branded food manufacturers that use stores for distribution purposes, and the retailers that try to build footfall or store traffic through retail branding approaches. As a result, the management of the media opportunities and the messages that are communicated is uncoordinated, inconsistent and the media potential, to a large extent, ignored. In the past, retailers will have argued that their core business rests with retailing, not selling and managing media. However, the media world has developed considerably in recent years, often in tandem with developments in technology. For a long time, retailers have built databases using customer information and developed sales promotion-based loyalty programmes as a result.

Cinema

The overall growth in cinema attendances in the past 10 years can be attributed to many factors, including bad summer weather and the increase in the number of multiplex cinemas (multiple screens at each site). Advertisers have consistently increased the adspend in this medium, especially as research shows that cinema audiences remember more detail than television audiences and, since they are a captive audience, there are no distractions. In 2014, cinema advertising attracted £202 million, or 1.1 per cent of the total UK advertising spend.

The Cinema Advertising Association claims that cinema users are light TV viewers so this enables brands to reach a unique audience. With an average of 10 new films being released each week, a broad swathe of the population become potential cinema visitors.

Advertising messages transmitted in a cinema have all the advantages of television-based messages. Audio and visual dimensions combine to provide high impact. However, the audience is more attentive because the main film has yet to be shown and there are fewer distractions or noise in the communications system. The implication is that cinema advertising has greater power than television advertisements. This power can be used to heighten levels of attention and, as the screen images are larger than life and because they appear in a darkened room that is largely unfamiliar to the audience, the potential to communicate effectively with the target audience is strong.

Ambient media

Ambient media are a fairly recent innovation and represent a non-traditional alternative to outdoor media. Ambient media are regarded as out-of-home media that fail to fit

Table 18.4 Ambient media categories

Ambient category	Explanation
Standard posters	Washrooms, shopping trolleys, phone boxes
Distribution	Tickets, receipts, carrier bags
Digital	Video screens, projections, LED screens
Sponsorships	Playgrounds, golf holes, petrol pump nozzles
Mobile posters	Lorries, barges, sandwich boards
Aerials	Balloons, blimps, towed banners

Source: Advertising Association (2003) Advertising Statistics Yearbook. Used by permission of WARC.

any of the established categories. Ambient media can be classified according to a variety of factors (see Table 18.4). Of these, standard posters account for the vast majority of ambient activity (59 per cent) with distribution accounting for 24 per cent and the four remaining categories just 17 per cent.

Guerrilla tactics

Guerrilla media tactics are an attempt to gain short-term visibility and impact in markets where the conventional media, normally linear, are cluttered and the life of the offering is very short.

Traditionally, flyposting was the main method, practised most often by the music business. Now the term refers to a range of activities that derive their power and visibility from being outside the jurisdiction of the paid-for media. Sabotage is a stronger interpretation, as the tactics require the hijacking of conventional media events.

Interactive media

Interactivity in marketing communications is enabled by three main digital technologies: the Internet, mobile and database technologies. From these a stream of interactive media provides various benefits for both organisations and consumers.

This section defines interactive media, identifies the various forms of interactive media, and concludes with a consideration of the benefits these bring to people and organisations.

So, what are interactive media?

Earlier in this chapter we introduced the notion that media can be classified as either linear or interactive. We have explained the characteristics of linear media and now we turn our attention to understanding interactive media.

The term 'multimedia' originated in the analogue era and was used to explain any presentation of information or material that used two or more media. Unsurprisingly the term migrated into the digital arena and was generally assumed to refer to the integration of text, audio and images in order to enhance the user interface with computer-based applications. As a result the 'streaming' of video and 'audio over the Internet' typify what is meant by the phrase multimedia applications.

England and Finney (2011) refer to the various terms that were used to highlight changes in the development of digital technology. The issue associated with the term 'digital media' is that it is too general, and the term 'new' media is made redundant very quickly as innovations are announced on a regular basis. What binds certain media together is their functionality, namely their interactive capability. The term 'interactive media' highlights media that differentiate them from older style (linear) media (England and Finney, 2011). The term refers to media that provide interactive properties that are accessible across a variety of delivery channels or 'platforms'.

Interactive media are defined as:

> *the integration of digital media including combinations of electronic text, graphics, moving images, and sound, into a structured digital computerised environment that allows people to interact with the data for appropriate purposes. (England and Finney, 2011)*

Core technologies

There are three evolving core technologies that support interactive media. These are the Internet, databases and Big Data, and mobile.

The Internet provides a wide variety of activities, including electronic mail, global information access and retrieval systems, discussion groups, multiplayer games and file transfer facilities, all of which have not only helped to transform the way we manage marketing communications, but also impacted on business strategy, marketing channel structures, inter-organisational relationships and the configuration of the marketing communications mix.

The Internet is an important way of providing product and service information and can enable organisations to provide frequent and intensive levels of customer support. With it come doubts about its ability to deliver competitive advantage and whether it could offer suitable levels of privacy, security and measures of advertising effectiveness.

Mobile phone technologies have advanced considerably and have enjoyed huge commercial success. Wireless application protocol, or WAP, phones possess the usual email and text information services, but they also have an Internet browser facility. As a result, messages can be not only location-, but also time-specific.

A marketing database is a collection of records that can be related to one another in multiple ways and from which information, usually customer-related, can be obtained in a variety of formats. This can be analysed to determine appropriate segments and target markets and used to stimulate and record individual responses to marketing communications. It, therefore, plays a role as a storage, sorting and administrative device to assist direct, personalised communications.

When customer-related transactional and response data are combined with additional information from external sources, such as a list broker, the database can become a potent source for marketing communications activities. Indeed, the increasing sophistication of information retrieval from databases and Big Data enables much more effective targeting and communications. For more information about Big Data see Chapter 14.

Characteristics of interactive media

Arising from these core technologies are interactive media which have some distinguishing characteristics, and which influence the way marketing communications is used by organisations and consumers. From a user perspective, these characteristics include speed and efficiency, interactivity, independence, personalisation, and enhanced relationships.

Speed

Interactive media enable marketing communications to be conducted at much faster – indeed, electronic – speeds. This impact is manifest in direct communications with end-users and in the production process itself. Draft documents, film and video clips, contracts, address lists and research and feedback reports, to name but a few, can all now be transmitted and shared electronically, saving processing time and reducing the elapsed production time necessary to create and implement marketing communications activities and events.

Efficiency

Efficiency is a broad term used to encompass a wide array of issues. New technology helps organisations to target their messages accurately to discrete groups or audiences. Indeed, one-to-one marketing is possible and, when compared with linear media and broad audiences, it is clear that interactive media offer huge opportunities for narrowcasting and reduced communications waste. Rather than shower audiences with messages that some of them do not wish to receive, direct marketing should, theoretically, enable each message to be received by all who are favourably disposed to the communications.

This principle of narrowcasting applies equally well to communications costs. Moving away from mass media to direct marketing and one-to-one communications reduces the absolute costs associated with campaigns. The relative costs may be higher, but these richer communications facilitate interactive opportunities with a greater percentage of the target audience than previously experienced in the mass broadcast era.

A further type of efficiency can be seen in terms of the accuracy and precision of the messages that are delivered. Marketing communications delivers product information, specifications and service details, contracts, designs, drawings and development briefs when customising to meet customer needs. The use of digital technology can help organisations provide customers with precise information and reduce opportunities for information deviance.

Interactivity

Back in 1995 Deighton and Grayson speculated correctly about the impact of the move towards digital-based marketing communications and how electronic dialogue would make marketing communications more conversational. Well, the conversational movement has gained considerable impetus and it is now a central marketing communications activity for many organisations. What enables these conversations is the interactive capacity within digital media.

Interactivity is a key characteristic of contemporary marketing communications. It is crucial because it signifies the available functionality, the ability of all participants in a communications network to respond to messages, often in real time. It is also key because it indicates that this type of communications environment is open – that is, more democratic than linear media. The latter tend to be one-sided and driven primarily by organisations and the satisfaction of their more overt needs. The word 'interactivity' suggests that all parties to a communications event are legitimately enabled to communicate. Finally, the word 'interactive' is used to cover a wide spectrum of electronic environments, one that is not limited or defined by the Internet. For example, mobile communications do not operate online, yet can be used to reach people digitally wherever they are, and have the potential to engage them interactively. Personal selling incorporates interactive behaviours.

Two researchers based in Zagreb, Vlasic and Kesic (2007), considered the various interpretations of interactivity. At a simple level they found that it is about the interchanging roles of senders and receivers within a communications event. However, this view casts little light on the depth and significance of the topic. They cite Hoey (1998) who, among others, sees it as direct communications without timespace constraints.

Some authors stress the measurability element (Morowitz and Schmittlein, 1998), while others focus on the communications and information control perspective (Liu and Shrum, 2005; Lockenby, 2005) and the influence the communications bestow on parties to the communications process. Vlasic and Kesic (2007: 111) deduce that interactivity brings benefits concerning 'convenience, diversity, relationship and intellectual challenges alongside the very important aspect of control of communications and relationships'.

Considering these perspectives, it can be concluded that interactive media concern processes through which individuals and organisations attempt to engage others with messages that are delivered primarily, but not exclusively, through electronic channels, and which offer all parties an opportunity to respond. Interaction can occur through the same or a different channel from that used to convey the previous message. However, the purpose is to build and sustain relationships that are based on mutual satisfaction, achieved through the exchange of information, goods or services that are of value to those involved.

Perhaps the strongest characteristic of interactive media is that they enable communications to move from one-way and two-way models to one where communications flow in real time. Interactivity normally precedes the establishment of dialogue between participants in the communications process. This, in turn, enables all participants to contribute to the content that is used in the communications process. This is referred to as *user-generated content*, as demonstrated by people uploading videos to YouTube, contributing to blogs, tweeting or even emailing comments to the presenters of television news programmes. For example, the theme park Thorpe Park encourages visitors to post their own images of their visit on Instagram (#ThorpePark) and then celebrate the best each week. These images can be reused if posted with the hashtag (Gray, 2015).

This form of interactivity symbolises a shift in the way in which marketing communications has developed, especially in an online environment. So, when the maintenance of 'relationships' is a central marketing activity it is possible to conclude that interactive marketing communications has an important role to play.

In addition to the Internet, technological advances have enabled a range of other interactive communications opportunities. These include television: one of the biggest factors accelerating the use of digital television is the variety of entertainment possibilities that the Internet can provide. The development of iPlayers and time-shifted recording facilities have helped shape consumer behaviour and the consumption of television programmes. This is now evolving as people are increasingly downloading or streaming their entertainment, and consuming it at times and places convenient to them. Other areas include home shopping, financial services, entertainment, education, fashion, and of course mobile and the ability to reach individuals with personalised messages when they are in the proximity of a store, or when passing an outdoor poster site.

This technology and the contemporary communications infrastructure offer increasing numbers of people the opportunity to experience interactive marketing communications. This may impact on their expectations and bring changes to the way in which people lead their lives, including their purchase decision behaviour and their associated values and responsibilities.

Independence

Digital technologies now support a range of mobile devices. These include smartphones, pads, readers, tablets and wearables such as Google Glass and Apple Watch. The prevailing usage is built around short message services (SMSs), multimedia messaging services (MMSs – which combine text with simple graphics and sound), wireless application protocol (WAP), mobile Internet and WAP push services, and full multimedia, third-generation (3G and 4G) services for both product promotion and entertainment purposes.

Mobile marketing communications, to give it its full title, involves the delivery of direct marketing messages to mobile devices using wireless technologies, which enable people to be independent of fixed or permanent computing facilities. Independence is also enabled by people having increasing levels of control over when, where and how they are reached through marketing communications.

The delivery of personalised and pertinent information plus inducements and promotional offers in order to encourage specific purchase behaviour can have greater impact. Truong and Simmons (2010) refer to studies that have shown that mobile advertising can improve attitudes and recall; result in higher levels of consumer acceptance and responsiveness (Barwise and Strong, 2002); and increase purchase intentions for mobile services (Nysveen et al., 2005).

Apart from the sheer volume of users, there are several reasons why the use of mobile communications has grown in recent years:

- *Interactivity*: the use of SMS, for example, provides recipients with the opportunity to respond directly to incoming requests. Simple yes/no answers are quick and easy to execute while opportunities to encourage interaction with brands exist 24/7, whether that be in- or out-of-home.

- *Smartphone technologies*: the recent developments in smartphone technologies have spurred a huge growth in usage. Among these are downloadable apps, which provide particular functionality or entertainment.

- *Personalisation*: mobile communications can enable messages that are customised to the personal needs of users. This means information can be highly targeted and contain relevant information.

- *Ubiquity*: the portability of mobiles means that it is possible to reach users at virtually any location, at any time and send them location-specific information. For example, Meat Pack, a Guatemalan footwear retailer, used GPS to signal when users of its smartphone app visited a competitor's store. It immediately offered a 99 per cent discount but this decreased by 1 per cent every second until the customer reached the Meat Pack store. The record is 87 per cent (Manning, 2014)!

- *Integration*: the effectiveness of mobile communications is optimised when they are used as a part of an integrated communications campaign.

- *Accountability*: the volume and nature of SMS responses can be measured, which is important from an investment perspective. In addition, it is possible to measure the contribution that different media make to drive responses. This in turn helps organisations to optimise their offline media spend and pursue integrated communications.

- *Cultural expectations*: as the number of mobile phones in circulation reaches saturation point, and as technology develops, enabling more efficient communications, so peer-group pressure and the entertainment industry encourage use of mobile phones. For example, presenters of television and radio programmes encourage their audiences to engage with them through text and mobile facilities in response to news items, quizzes and general topics of current interest. For many these forms of communications and involvement have become a normal element of their leisure and entertainment expectations.

The key attributes of mobile communications are that they are a personal, independent channel, one which enables direct, targeted and interactive communications which can occur at any time and any place. SMS communications have underpinned this growth and are used not just for brand awareness-based advertising, but also as an effective way of delivering sales promotions, such as announcing special offers and 'text and win' events. See Viewpoint 18.4 for examples of how mobile communications are being used by some global brands.

Viewpoint 18.4   Mobile and moving forward

Brands that for many years relied on linear media, typically TV, are now allocating more of their marketing communications budgets to mobile channels. By 2020 it is predicted that over 90 per cent of the global population over 6 years old will own a mobile phone. Responding to this change many companies are beginning to make increased use of mobile communications.

In 2014 Coca-Cola Australia shifted the majority of their US$10 million advertising budget to innovative digital channels in order to appeal to younger audiences. In addition to Coca-Cola's use of outdoor media, their interactive advertising campaign demonstrated some innovative ideas. For example, they turned some bus stops in Sydney and Melbourne into coke dispensers. The company also utilised digital signage which was powered by 'hidden' content that people could discover using their smartphones. The company used signage in shopping malls, which after being photographed, turned into a game that could be played on a user's smartphone.

Focusing on mobile channels enabled Coca-Cola to use behavioural targeting in their digital campaigns. The company targeted people based on their interest in music, fashion and gaming. The 'hidden' content was personalised and tailored around each user's interests. This offered a high level of engagement and interaction with the target audience, something that cannot be achieved by using linear media channels.

Heineken identified opportunities to personalise and deliver content through mobile channels. In their 2014 Desperados (beer with tequila) campaign the company shifted all of their budget to mobile channels after seeing awareness increase from virtually nothing to 23 per cent across five US states in less than 3 months. The justification for using mobile as the primary medium was the nature of the Desperados audience: very outgoing and energetic, people who enjoy an active nightlife.

McDonald's was one of the first companies to adopt a mobile marketing strategy and, in Japan, the majority of McDonald's 2014 digital budget was spent on mobile channels. McDonald's uses its mobile application to distribute weekly offers to its customers in Japan. This strategy based on sales promotions, however, can in the long run erode a company's profitability.

McDonald's also utilises NFC (near field communications) technology in its restaurants. App users can redeem coupons which benefits McDonald's because not only can it measure the success of campaigns through this channel, but it can also get a better understanding of customers' behaviour, which in turn enables McDonald's to deliver more personalised, targeted communications.

Source: Anon (2014a, 2014b); Marsh and Leong (2014); Warc (2014); Whiteside (2014).

This Viewpoint was written by Pavel Laczko when he was a research student at the University of Portsmouth.

Question: Why has advertising through mobile devices yet to be profitable?

Task: Find two mobile ads from the same category. Which do you believe is more effective and why?

The potential to develop mobile communications is enormous, simply because the channel can deliver direct marketing messages related to advertising, sales promotion and public relations to individuals, regardless of location. These messages can be used to develop brand awareness, support product launches, incentivise customers through competitions and promotions, and promote trade and distributor involvement, as well as provide branded entertainment. However, as with email, it is also important to consider the potential privacy concerns of customers, especially as the receipt of unwanted messages (i.e. spam) may well increase.

QR codes demonstrate the richness of interactivity through mobile technology. By taking a picture of a QR code with a camera phone with a built-in QR code reader, consumers can access further brand-related material that is linked to the code. Ralph Lauren took over the 15 window displays that front the Harrods store in London to launch its womenswear range. The window displays included QR stickers which shoppers scanned or tapped with their smartphones to access the extra content. This included an interactive map that guided shoppers around the Harrods range. In addition, it enabled people passing the shop to buy direct from their smartphones when the store was shut (Vizard, 2014).

An emerging technology, likely to change a raft of behaviours, is called near field communications (NFC). NFC involves a small chip that is being embedded in smartphones, and is now in most new credit cards. By presenting a phone to an advert, or signage that has an NFC symbol, information is automatically transferred to the phone. The applications are numerous, including access facilities (turnstiles at stations, offices and stadia), paying for car parking, getting information through ads (events, hotels, taxis), making credit card payments for store purchases, logging into computers and security systems, travel ticket payments, and even the exchange of business cards by touching phones.

Personalisation

Interactive media have empowered organisations to personalise messages and communicate with consumers on a one-to-one basis, and on a scale that is commercially viable. This has driven the dramatic development of direct marketing, reshaped the basis on which organisations target and segment markets, stimulated interaction and dialogue, brought about a raft of new strategies and challenged the conventional approach to mass marketing and branding techniques.

As with all forms of communications, the successful use of email requires an understanding of the recipient's behaviour. Email communications enable a high degree of personalisation, and in order to personalise messages it is necessary to understand the attitudinal and behavioural characteristics of each email audience.

It is important to understand the email behaviour of different audiences. This is because this knowledge can influence the degree of personalisation that is given to email communications, and website welcome messages. However, email communications that are based on an understanding of an audience's email behaviour should influence message content, the time when it should be sent and, most important, the keys to encouraging recipients to open the email and not delete it. These keys are the 'header' of the email, which contains the subject matter, and the 'from' address, which signifies whether the sender is known and, hence, strongly determines whether the email is perceived positively at the outset. If it is, then there is a stronger chance that the email will be opened and, therefore, a greater opportunity for response and interactivity.

Many people, however, now expect a high level of personalisation and virtual recognition as opportunities arising through 'personalisation' reach beyond email communications. Personalisation is a sensitive area, often twinned with privacy issues. Indeed, there appears to be little agreement about what constitutes personalisation and to that end Vesanen (2007) identifies five types of personalisation. These are shown in Table 18.5.

Personalisation should be an integral aspect of relationship marketing, especially in B2B markets. The degree of personalisation will inevitably vary over the customer lifecycle and become more intimate as a relationship matures.

Table 18.5 Types of personalisation

Type of personalisation	Segment marketing	Adaptive	Cosmetic	Transparent	Collaborative
Typical actor	Reader's Digest	Yahoo.com	Google.com	Amazon.com	Hairdresser
Approach	To match customer preferences better than with mass-marketing	To let customers choose from different options	The organisation changes the package of standard good	The organisation changes the content of a good with a standard look	The organisation and customer are together building the product
Occasion	Little customer knowledge, cheap	A lot of choices to choose from	Customer sacrifice is due to presentation	Customer contacts are repetitive	Determining either/or choices
Source of information	Purchase-/demographic information	Direct choice by customer	Purchase-/demographic-/behavioural information	Purchase-/demographic-/behavioural information	Direct interaction
Level of interaction	None	High	Low	Low	High
Variation of product	Possibly	No	No	Yes	Likely

Source: Based on Vesanen (2007). © Emerald Group Publishing Limited. All rights reserved.

Scholars' paper 18.4   Strategic issues arising from intrusion

Truong, Y. and Simmons, G. (2010) Perceived intrusiveness in digital advertising: strategic marketing implications, *Journal of Strategic Marketing*, 18(3), 239–56.

Following the increasing amount of advertising on digital media, concern has started to be expressed about negative consumer perceptions concerning its intrusiveness. This may be a challenge to the claimed added value of this medium over traditional media. From this the authors explore the strategic marketing issues that have arisen and, among other things, confirm previous findings that pushed Internet and mobile digital advertisements are seen as intrusive.

Enhanced relationships

Digital technology is used by organisations to gather and use information about customers in order to better meet their needs. Through the use of a database and interactive media, organisations now seek to develop longer-term relationships with customers, with programmes and strategies that are dubiously termed 'customer loyalty schemes'. While there may be doubt about the term 'loyalty', and the effectiveness of campaigns designed to increase loyalty (Binet and Field, 2007), there can be no doubt that digital media have helped develop new forms of sales promotion and have influenced customer relationships. What should also be clear is that the existence of IST in an organisation or relationship is no guarantee that additional value will be created (Ryssel et al., 2004).

Some customer-service interface functions have been replaced with technology in the name of greater efficiency, cost savings and improved service. Financial services organisations are able to inform customers of their bank balances automatically without human intervention. Meyronin (2004: 222) refers to this as an 'infomediation' strategy and suggests that this neglect of the human interaction in the creation of joint value in service environments may be detrimental.

The rapid development of social media, and social networks in particular, has added a new dimension to the way brands and their customers interact and the way in which brand-based relationships are fashioned. Indeed Fournier and Avery (2011: 194) refer to open-source branding, which involves 'participatory, collaborative, and socially-linked behaviors whereby consumers serve as creators and disseminators of branded content'. However, according to Mamic and Almaraz (2013) not all organisations fully embrace social media, and Twitter in particular, with a view to building relationships with stakeholders. Their research found that many organisations are not using the interactivity potential to build social network communities.

Relationships with intermediaries have also been affected by new technology. The development of e-commerce has given rise to channel strategies that either result in channel functions and, hence, members being discarded, or give rise to opportunities for new functions and members. These processes, disintermediation and reintermediation respectively, are both dynamic and potentially destabilising for organisations and their channel partners.

Multichannel campaigns

In addition to these characteristics is the strategic opportunity to use multiple media channels to reach audiences. Database-generated telemarketing, direct mail, email and online and mobile channels now complement field marketing, personal, retail and catalogue selling, and have allowed organisations to determine which customers prefer which channels, and which are the most profitable.

This in turn enables organisations to allocate resources far more effectively and to spread the customer base upon which profits are developed. A multichannel strategy should accommodate customers' channel preferences, their usage patterns, needs, price sensitivities and preferred point of product and service access. So, as Stone and Shan (2002) put it, the goal is to manage each channel profitably while optimising the attributes of each channel so that they deliver value for each type of customer.

Multichannel strategies have added new marketing opportunities, and enabled audiences to access products and services in ways that best meet their own lifestyle and behavioural needs. For organisations this has reduced message wastage, used media more efficiently and, in doing so, reduced costs and improved communications effectiveness.

Research undertaken by the IPA indicates that adults consume a portfolio of media that embraces 10–15 television channels, 10–15 websites and a similar number of magazines. This does not account for a wealth of other media such as radio and cinema. In addition, people are consuming media through time and place shifting and using their portfolio of media in an integrated format (Binet and Field, 2007).

Their analysis also found that when advertising is coupled with sponsorship or public relations the strongest measures of effectiveness, in terms of communications goals, was achieved. What is also clear is that multichannel campaigns are more effective than single-channel activity.

Of course, the possible number of channel combinations is huge and too numerous for each to be considered here. However, the research revealed that the use of three advertising media is optimal, although for large brands this might need to be increased. Integrated multimedia campaigns have been shown by the IPA to be more effective and efficient than single-channel campaigns (Binet and Field, 2007).

In 2011, the IPA's analysis of the most successful campaigns during the period 2004 to 2010 supports the findings of Binet and Field (2007) concerning the optimum number of channels. To achieve business goals (profit, market share, etc.), diminishing returns set in once the number of advertising media used reaches three. When interactive and web channels, plus direct marketing, sales promotion and public relations, are included in the mix, there does not appear to be a limit, apart from budget, to achieve both business and communications effects.

Broadbent (2011) considered these outcomes and suggests two reasons to explain why campaigns using many channels are less likely to be effective. The first is that the evidence indicates that brands that under spend in a channel, relative to their market share, struggle to grow. The second concerns the extent to which multichannel campaigns have integrated content. Broadbent explains that many campaigns run with seven channels and each requires content. The way each is produced, who produces it and under what brief and guidance vary considerably and consequently it is really hard to integrate the content of a three-channel campaign, let alone seven.

Retailing in a multichannel environment

Retailers are faced with particular problems that concern the amount of property/freehold they possess and the emerging patterns of consumer shopping behaviour in the light of multichannel opportunities. The Arcadia Group (which owns Dorothy Perkins, Miss Selfridge, Wallis, Topshop, etc.) made a significant attempt to make its own name synonymous with online shopping through the development of Zoom, an online shopping mall. Some people might think that retailers should dispose of their fixed assets and move into the Internet or perhaps reconfigure their store layouts. In most cases, the optimum solution is to develop a multichannel solution whereby a range of media and experiences is offered to consumers. So, some prefer online, some the high street, some mobile, others will use television, and some will prefer catalogue shopping. Most use a combination of two or more channels.

'Showrooming' concerns the use of smartphones when visiting a store to compare prices, and then leaving the store empty handed to buy online. This was considered to be a major threat to high street retailers, who responded with various tactics that included providing shoppers with their own in-store free wifi to drive them to their own websites. In addition, retailers have exploited the skills and knowledge of their sales staff, used the store for the pick-up of online orders, provided smartphone discounts to prod showroomers to buy in-store (Alder, 2014) and used networks such as Snapchat to engage consumers around the store and the brand (Emig, 2015).

Retailers have also developed 'reverse showrooming', or 'webrooming'. This involves consumers researching products online, but then physically visiting a bricks-and-mortar store to complete the purchase (Alder, 2014). Although not new, this approach is now actively utilised by retailers to drive revenue.

Most consumers use a mix of these various approaches, dependent on category and need. What is good is that this approach puts customers' needs first by determining their preferred channels.

What may happen is that shopping activities become divided into categories that reflect particular channel options. Routine, unexciting purchases may be consigned to online and interactive channels, and the more explorative, stimulating and perhaps socially important purchases are prioritised for physical shopping expeditions. Many stores have recognised the need to adapt and provide more value (than a current product focus). Related benefits and enhanced services are important as they help differentiation and attract customers. For example, the bookstore Waterstones provides coffee bars and comfortable seating, an environment in which customers are encouraged to relax and consider their possible purchases. Larger stores and mainstream brands may need to establish themselves as 'destination' stores where the attraction for consumers is bounded by excitement, entertainment and a brand experience. In some destination stores it is possible to test products in simulated but related environments. For example, people can attend cookery classes in supermarkets or test drive a range of cars in the countryside.

In the USA these types of store are now relatively common, and experience shows that high street shopping is not about to die, but take a revised shape, form and role. Mercedes has a café on the Champs-Elysées in Paris, but its role is to remind, differentiate and bring the brand into people's consciousness away from the traditional frame of reference. There is no persuasion, as cars cannot be bought, or sold, but the brand is reinforced.

Scholars' paper 18.5   **Multichannel communications**

Godfrey, A., Seiders, K. and Voss, G.B. (2011) Enough is enough! The fine line in executing multichannel relational communications, *Journal of Marketing*, 75 (July), 94–109.

Increasingly organisations are developing their relationships with customers across a range of channels. This involves the use of personalised messages and constitutes multichannel relational communications. These authors provide some interesting insights into this strategy, and consider three key drivers of relational communications effectiveness: volume of communications, mix of communications channels, and alignment of those channels with customers' preferences. From their research they argue that reciprocity explains response to lower levels of communications, and reactance explains response to higher levels of communications.

Some of the more prominent interactive media are set out in Figure 18.2. The limited amount of space in this book precludes a detailed examination of each of these types of interactive media. Some are explored in Chapter 19 and a description of each can be found in the online resources that support this book.

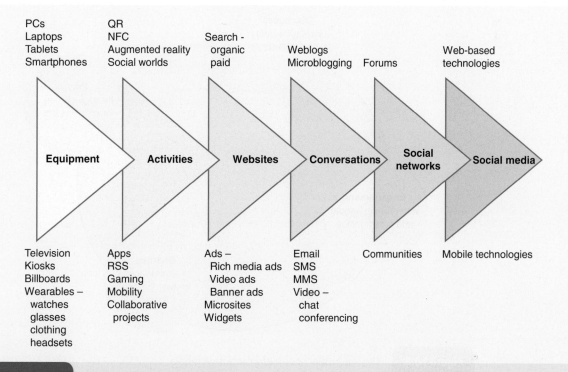

Figure 18.2   A range of interactive media

What interactive media enable users to do

Having considered what interactive media are, and what their characteristics are, we turn our attention to some of the benefits and opportunities interactive media offer and the ways in which they influence marketing communications. As noted earlier, interactive media enable users to fulfil an increasing variety of activities that encompass their work, home and leisure environments. Interactive media enable people to explore and discover new things, to play and be entertained, to share with like-minded tribes and communities, and to engage in order to do things and shape their behaviour (see Figure 18.3).

- *Discovery* – By enabling exploration people can search and find information about a wealth of subjects. Whereas linear media deliver pre-structured information in a 'tell' format, interactive media enable information mining, development and richness through interrogation (interaction) to answer specific questions on a personal basis. Search, websites and online chat facilities are at the heart of the discovery mode but email, social media, kiosks, video conferencing, augmented reality and RSS also embody this approach.

- *Play* – People use interactive media as entertainment. Interactive television and online and video gaming are obvious examples, but at a deeper level people are entertained through the interaction experienced when involved when creating (user-generated) content, blogging, visiting online communities and forums, creating and uploading videos, streaming music and film, and engaging others through social networks. Brands attempt to communicate their messages either through or by associating themselves with these play environments, with varying levels of success and at the same time risking the trust and reputation that may have been developed.

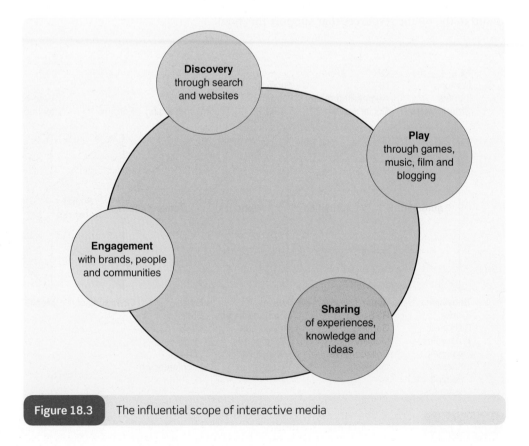

| **Figure 18.3** | The influential scope of interactive media |

- *Sharing* – Opportunities to share ideas, thoughts, memories and knowledge have been enhanced considerably. Offline word-of-mouth communications are now complemented by online, viral communications. Organisations actively encourage people to share their brand-related experiences either through social media such as networks, blogs or communities, or, alternatively, directly to them as user feedback. Marketing communications is designed to encourage people to participate and share their experiences.

- *Engagement* – Interactive media have had a profound impact on the way people and organisations engage with one another. On the one hand, interactive media enable people to develop their understanding and knowledge about brands and how they work through the provision and depth of information that can be accessed. On the other, behaviour is influenced, through prompts to interrogate a website, to provide personal information, to submit and upload content and often through direct marketing and sales promotions.

Direct-response media

This chapter would not be complete without reference to direct-response media. The principal use of the media is to convey one of two types of message: one is oriented towards the development of brands and attitudes; the other is aimed at provoking a physical (and mental) response. It follows that attitude and response-based communications require different media.

Linear media (television, print or radio), previously used just to develop brands and attitudes, are now used as a mechanism or device to provoke a response, through which consumers/buyers can follow up a message, enter into an immediate dialogue and either request further information or purchase goods. The main difference with interactive media is the time delay or response pause between receiving a message and acting on it. Through direct-response mechanisms, the response may be delayed for as long as it takes to make a telephone call, press a button or fill out a reply coupon. However, the response pause and the use of a separate form of communications highlight the essential differences.

Estimates vary, but eMarketer reports that nearly 70 per cent of all UK advertisements in 2014 carried a telephone number, web address or direct-response mechanism (Aimia, 2015). Direct-response television (DRTV) is attractive to those promoting service-based offerings and increasingly travel brands and some FMCG brands are using it. One key benefit is that advertisers can gather rich personal information for the database and subsequent sales promotion and mailing and communications purposes. Direct-response advertising revenue in the UK was £1,835 million in 2015, a decline of 1 per cent on the previous year (AA/WARC, 2015).

One aspect that is crucial to the success of a direct-response campaign is not the number of responses but the conversion of leads into sales. This means that the infrastructure to support these promotional activities must be thought through and put in place, otherwise the work and resources put into the visible level will be wasted if customers are unable to get the information they require. The provision of the infrastructure alone is not sufficient – the totality of the campaign should support the brand. Indeed, this is a chance to extend brand opportunities and provide increased brand experiences.

Key differences between linear and interactive media

Having considered the characteristics of both linear and interactive media we now compare them. The contrast is interesting, as set out in Table 18.6. Space (or time) within linear media is limited and costs rise as demand for the limited space/time increases. In interactive media, especially the Internet, space is unlimited, so absolute costs remain

Table 18.6 Comparison of linear and interactive media

Linear media	Interactive media
One-to-many	One-to-one and many-to-many
Monologue format	Dialogic format
Active provision Interruptive	Passive provision Lifestyle compatible
Mass marketing	Individualised marketing
Branding	Information
Segmentation	Communities
Impersonal	Personal
Infrequent	Frequent

very low and static, while relative costs plummet as more users participate. Another aspect concerns the focus of an advertising message. Traditionally, advertisers tend to emphasise the emotional rather than information aspect, particularly within low-involvement categories. Interactive media allow focus on the provision of information, so the emotional aspect of advertising messages tends to have a lower significance. As branding is becoming a more important aspect of Internet activity, so there will be a greater use of emotions, especially when the goal is to keep people at a website, rather than just driving them to it.

Apart from the obvious factor that interactive media, and the Internet in particular, provide interactive opportunities that linear media cannot provide, it is important to remember that opportunities-to-see are generally driven by customers rather than by an advertiser interrupting viewing or reading activities. People drive interactions at a speed that is convenient to them; they are not driven by others.

Management control over Internet-based marketing communications is relatively high, as not only are there greater opportunities to control the position and placement of advertisements, promotions and press releases, but it is also possible to change the content of these activities much more quickly than is possible with linear media. The goals outlined above indicate the framework within which advertising needs to be managed.

As mentioned earlier, interactive media are superior at providing rational, product-based information, whereas linear media are much better at conveying emotional brand values. The former have a dominant cognition orientation and the latter an emotional one. There are other differences, but the predominant message is that these types of media are, to a large extent, complementary, suggesting that they should be used together, not one independently of the other.

To conclude this chapter it is worth trying to keep all of these developments in perspective. The digital technologies, applications and interactive media considered here constitute a dynamic environment. Continual change characterises the industry and helps to reshape the form and structure of digital-based marketing communications. The changes experienced so far, from 'fixed to mobile, limited media to rich media, limited interaction to real time interaction' (England and Finney, 2011), are only steps in the development of digital technology and interactive media. Linear media still fulfil an important role in many campaigns, as witnessed by the amount and proportion of budget still spent on television by clients. Linear and interactive media should be considered and used as complementary channels.

Key points

- There are three main ways of classifying the media: form, source, and function of a media vehicle.

- Media classified according to their functionality refer to media that only enable one-way communications – linear media. Media that enable two-way or interactive communications are referred to as interactive media.

- The rich array of characteristics that each type of medium possesses serve to engage audiences in different ways. These represent opportunities for organisations to make sure they use the right media to deliver against different goals.

- The principal use of the media is to convey one of two types of message: one is oriented towards the development of brands and attitudes; the other is aimed at provoking a physical (and mental) response. It follows that attitude- and response-based communications require different media.

- There is a growing body of evidence that shows that the effectiveness of the media increases considerably when media are used in combination. The use of multichannel campaigns has been spurred by interactive media, and research which indicates that adults consume a portfolio of media that embraces 10–15 television channels, 10–15 websites and a similar number of magazines.

- People are consuming media through time and place shifting, and using their portfolio of media in an integrated format.

Review questions

Foster's case questions

1. Use the Foster's case to explain the differences between media classes, types and vehicles.

2. How might Foster's use of the media be interpreted through the use of POEM?

3. Explain the differences between linear and interactive media, making reference to the Foster's 'Good Call' case.

4. Which of the four activities that interactive media enable people to achieve might have enabled the 'Good Call' campaign?

5. Discuss the ways in which interactivity is demonstrated through the Foster's campaign.

General questions

1. What are the reasons that explain the growth in mobile communications from a marketing perspective?

2. Discuss the view that outdoor media are the last true broadcast media.

3. What are the three core technologies that underpin the use of interactive media?

4. Under which circumstances should cinema be used as the primary medium?

5. What are the characteristics of a multichannel campaign and what is considered to be the optimal number of channels?

References

AA/WARC (2015) Drive to digital sends UK advertising to its highest growth for four years, 21 April, retrieved 23 April 2015 from www.adassoc.org.uk/news/drive-to-digital-sends-uk-advertising-to-its-highest-growth-for-four-years/.

Advertising Association (2003) *Advertising Statistics Year Book,* Henley: NTC. Also at www.adassoc.org.uk/inform/.

Aimia (2015) Emotional engagement in a short-term world, *Marketing,* May, p. 23.

Alder, E. (2014) Reverse showrooming: bricks-and-mortar retailers fight back, *Business Insider,* 13 July, retrieved 28 January 2015 from www.businessinsider.com/reverse-showrooming-bricks-and-mortar-retailers-fight-back-2-2014-2?IR=T.

Anon (2010) Fosters beer advert reflects Aussie mentality, *Market Drayton Advertiser,* 2 November, retrieved 27 July 2015 from www.marketdraytonadvertiser.com/2010/11/02/fosters-beer-advert-reflects-aussie-mentality/.

Anon (2014a) Coke looks to innovate in Australia, *Warc,* 5 November, retrieved 28 November 2014 from www.warc.com/LatestNews/News/EmailNews.news?ID=33831&Origin=WARCNewsEmail&CID=N33831&PUB=Warc_News&utm_source=WarcNews&utm_medium=email&utm_campaign=WarcNews20141105.

Anon (2014b) Maturing digital to pass TV by 2016, *WARC News,* 5 November, retrieved 6 November from www.warc.com/Content/News/N33832_Maturing_digital_to_pass_TV_by_2016.content?PUB=Warc%20News&CID=N33832&ID=a950e99b-4515-4061-8a9d-78b4acec284f&q=Maturing+digital+to&qr=.

Bale, Z. (2015) The year ahead for press, *Campaign,* 14 January, retrieved 11 February 2015 from www.campaignlive.co.uk/news/1328159/the-year-ahead-press/.

Barwise, P. and Strong, C. (2002) Permission-based mobile advertising, *Journal of Interactive Marketing,* 16(1), 14–24.

Binet, L. and Field, P. (2007) *Marketing in an Era of Accountability,* Henley: IPA-WARC.

Bold, B. (2014) Foster's 'Good Call' ad campaign wins IPA Effectiveness Grand Prix, *Marketing,* 27 October, retrieved 2 June 2015 from www.marketingmagazine.co.uk/article/1319038/fosters-good-call-ad-campaign-wins-ipa-effectiveness-grand-prix.

Broadbent, T. (2011) Channel planning: effectiveness lies in channel integration, *Admap* (January), retrieved 17 May from www.warc.com/Content/ContentViewer.aspx?MasterContentRef=fbf731f8-4087-449f-a232-0f69f2863b17&q=direct+marketing.

Burrell, I. (2014) Ink global has used savvy marketing and a globe-trotting readership to take over the world's skies, *Independent,* 20 October, 36–7.

Chen, H. and Haley, E. (2014) Product placement in social games: consumer experiences in China, *Journal of Advertising,* 43(3), 286–295.

Clements, A. (2015) Foster's axes Aussie pals Brad and Dan after best-ever beer ad campaign, *Express,* 19 May, retrieved 27 July 2015 from www.express.co.uk/finance/city/577533/Foster-s-axes-Aussie-pals-Brad-and-Dan-after-best-ever-beer-ad-campaign.

Danaher, P. and Rossiter, J. (2011) Comparing perceptions of marketing communications channels, *European Journal of Marketing,* 45(1/2), 6–42.

Deighton, J. and Grayson, K. (1995) Marketing and seduction: building exchange relationships by managing social consensus, *Journal of Consumer Research,* 21(4), 660–76.

Emig, J. (2015) How Snapchat can help retailers kill 'showrooming', *Adage,* 14 January, retrieved 28 January 2015 from http://adage.com/article/digitalnext/snapchat-retailers-kill-showrooming/296593/.

England, E. and Finney, A. (2011) Interactive media – what's that? Who's involved? *ATSF White Paper – Interactive Media UK,* retrieved 27 October 2014 from www.atsf.co.uk/atsf/interactive_media.pdf.

Fitch, D. (2007) Outdoor advertising, retrieved 20 January 2008 from www.millwardbrown.com/Sites/MillwardBrown/Content/News/EPerspectiveArticles.aspx?id=%2f200711010001.

Fournier, S. and Avery, J. (2011) The uninvited brand, *Business Horizons,* 54(3), May, 193–207.

Gianatasio, D. (2015) Apple's new China store has one hell of a beautiful facade and a great story to tell, *Adweek,* 23 January, retrieved 23 January 2015 from www.adweek.com/adfreak/apples-new-china-store-has-one-hell-beautiful-facade-and-great-story-tell-162488.

Godfrey, A., Seiders, K. and Voss, G.B. (2011) Enough is enough! The fine line in executing multichannel relational communications, *Journal of Marketing,* 75 (July), 94–109.

Goodwin, T. (2014) Is vagueness killing advertising? *Adweek,* 30 November, retrieved 23 January 2015 from www.adweek.com/news/advertising-branding/vagueness-killing-advertising-161638.

Gould, S.J. and Gupta, P.B. (2006) Come on down: how consumers view game shows and products placed in them, *Journal of Advertising,* 35(1), 65–81.

Gray, R. (2015) The long haul, *The Marketer,* January/February, 28–31.

Halleck, T. (2014) American Airlines hires Ink Global to relaunch 'American Way', In-Flight Magazines, *International Business Times*, 19 August, retrieved 2 February 2015 from www.ibtimes.com/american-airlines-hires-ink-global-relaunch-american-way-flight-magazines-1662756.

Heath, R. (2009) Emotional engagement: how television builds big brands at low attention, *Journal of Advertising Research*, 29(1), 62–73.

Hirschman, E.C. and Thompson, C.J. (1997) Why media matter: toward a richer understanding of consumers' relationships with advertising and mass media, *Journal of Advertising*, 26(1), 43–60.

Hoey, C. (1998) Maximizing the effectiveness of web based marketing communications, *Marketing Intelligence and Planning*, 16(1), 31–7.

Liu, Y. and Shrum, L.J. (2005) Rethinking interactivity, in *Advertising, Promotion and New Media* (eds M.R. Stafford and R.J. Faber), New York: M.E. Sharpe, 103–24.

Lockenby, J.D. (2005) The interaction of traditional and new media, in *Advertising, Promotion and New Media* (eds M.R. Stafford and R.J. Faber), New York: M.E. Sharpe, 13.

Mamic, L.I. and Almaraz, I.A. (2013) How the larger corporations engage with stakeholders through Twitter, *International Journal of Market Research*, 55(6), 851–872.

Manning, J. (2014) Retail 2.0, *The Marketer*, March/April, 32–5.

Marsh, C. and Leong, M. (2014) Kazasu: product preference, *Warc Prize for Asian Strategy*, retrieved 15 November from www.warc.com/Content/ContentViewer.aspx?MasterContentRef=ff8db6b9-ea4c-4f8c-b9d6-9870467bc972&q=Product+preference%2c&CID=A102340&PUB=WARC-PRIZE-ASIA.

Meurs, L. van and Aristoff, M. (2009) Split-second recognition: what makes outdoor advertising work? *Journal of Advertising Research*, 49(1), 82–92.

Meyronin, B. (2004) ICT: the creation of value and differentiation in services, *Managing Service Quality*, 14(2/3), 216–25.

Morowitz, V.G. and Schmittlein, D.C. (1998) Testing new direct marketing offerings: the interplay of management judgement and statistical models, *Management Science*, 44(5), 610–28.

Nysveen, H., Pedersen, P.E. and Thorbjørnsen, H. (2005) Intentions to use mobile services: antecedents and cross-service comparisons, *Journal of the Academy of Marketing Science*, 33, 330–46.

O'Connor, R. (2015) Fosters boss blames 'sexist and insulting' adverts for putting women off beer, *Independent*, 14 May, retrieved 27 July 2015 from www.independent.co.uk/life-style/food-and-drink/news/fosters-boss-blames-sexist-and-insulting-adverts-for-putting-women-off-beer-10250099.html.

OOH (2015) Case Studies, *Outdoor Media Centre*, retrieved 15 May 2015 from www.outdoormediacentre.org.uk/advertising_facts/factsAndFigures/Case_Studies.

Ryssel, R., Ritter, T. and Gemunden, H.G. (2004) The impact of information technology deployment on trust, commitment and value creation in business relationships, *Journal of Business and Industrial Marketing*, 19(3), 197–207.

Sender, T. (2014) *Fashion Online – UK*, London: Mintel.

Shadbolt, P. (2015) Inflight empire: how Ink Global is cornering airline magazine market, *CNN*, 29 January, retrieved 2 February 2015 from http://edition.cnn.com/2015/01/28/travel/ink-inflight-empire/.

Southgate, D. (2014) The agony of choice, *Contagious.com*, 20 October, retrieved 2 February 2015 from www.contagious.com/blogs/news-and-views/15676936-the-agony-of-choice.

Stone, M. and Shan, P. (2002) Transforming the bank branch experience for customers, *What's New in Marketing*, 10 (September), retrieved 23 August 2004 from www.wnim.com/archive/.

Sundar, S.S. and Bellur, S. (2011) Concept explication in the Internet age: the case of interactivity, in *Sourcebook for Political Communication Research: Methods, measures, and analytical techniques* (eds E.P. Bucy and R.L. Holbert), New York: Routledge, 485–500.

Sundar, S.S. and Limperos, A.M. (2013) Uses and Grats 2.0: new gratifications for new media, *Journal of Broadcasting and Electronic Media*, 57(4), 504–52.

Sweney, M. (2015) Foster's to end Brad and Dan ads in move away from 'laddish' campaigns, *Guardian*, 15 May, retrieved 2 June 2015 from www.theguardian.com/media/2015/may/15/fosters-to-end-brad-and-dan-ads-in-move-away-from-laddish-campaigns.

Taylor, C.R., Franke, G.R. and Bang, H.-K. (2006) Use and effectiveness of billboards: perspectives from selective-perception theory and retail-gravity models, *Journal of Advertising*, 35(4), 21–34.

Taylor, D. (2014) Foster's fresh consistency delivers rocket-fuelled ROI, *The BrandGymBlog*, retrieved 27 July from http://wheresthesausage.typepad.com/my_weblog/2014/10/httpwwwcampaignlivecouknews1319038fosters-good-call-ad-campaign-wins-ipa-effectiveness-grand-prixhayilcrelated.html.

Thinkbox (2014) Research–Payback 4: pathways to profit, retrieved 22 May 2015 from www.thinkbox.tv/research/payback-4-pathways-to-profit/.

Truong, Y. and Simmons, G. (2010) Perceived intrusiveness in digital advertising: strategic marketing implications, *Journal of Strategic Marketing*, 18(3), 239–56.

Veloutsou, C. and O'Donnell, C. (2005) Exploring the effectiveness of taxis as an advertising medium, *International Journal of Advertising*, 24(2), 217–39.

Vesanen, J. (2007) What is personalization? A conceptual framework, *European Journal of Marketing*, 41(5/6), 409–18.

Vizard, S. (2014) Ralph Lauren makes Harrods window displays shoppable, *Marketing Week*, 30 October, retrieved 15 April 2015 from www.marketingweek.com/2014/10/30/ralph-lauren-makes-harrods-window-displays-shoppable/.

Vlasic, G. and Kesic, T. (2007) Analysis of customers' attitudes toward interactivity and relationship personalization as contemporary developments in interactive marketing communications, *Journal of Marketing Communications*, 13(2), 109–29.

Whiteside, S. (2014) Heineken USA's mobile marketing mandate: Stop the thumb, *Advertising Week*, October, retrieved 15 November from www.warc.com/Content/ContentViewer.aspx?MasterContentRef=d1436108-e768-45c9-81d7-45e599dc85b2&q=Heineken&CID=A103152&PUB=EVENT-REPORTS.

Chapter 19

Social, search and other interactive media

The significant changes in consumer behaviour, technology, media usage and digital formats experienced in recent years require organisations to find and adopt very different marketing (communications) strategies from the tried and trusted formulae used previously. Interactive media, which include search and social media, represent a democratisation of the media landscape as new forms of interactive communications, relationships and behaviour emerge.

Aims and learning objectives

The aims of this chapter are to explore ways in which interactive media are used in advertising, search marketing, social media, and other ways of types of communications.

The learning objectives are to enable readers to:

1. understand how advertising can be used in an interactive context;

2. evaluate search engine marketing and distinguish the main features of both pay-per-click and search engine optimisation;

3. explore the characteristics and value of marketing communications through social media;

4. explain how social networks can be used in marketing communications;

5. understand and identify the characteristics associated with viral marketing, web logs and microblogging, podcasting, and online communities;

6. discuss the features of email marketing communications and understand how the use of SMS, apps, widgets, affiliate marketing and augmented reality can enhance marketing communications.

Greater Manchester Police

In 2010 the Greater Manchester Police took a leap into what was then the unknown. Our first social media strategy was developed which took the organisation into a whole new world. We went from being an organisation that broadcast information to one trying to engage in meaningful conversations. For the second largest police force in England this was a major change but one that we had the support of the Chief Constable to achieve.

Strategy

Our first social media strategy had used 'buzz' monitoring to find out what people were saying about Greater Manchester Police (GMP) and where they were saying it. Using this alongside the organisational objectives we could see where the effort was needed. The strategy focused on three things:

- using interesting content to engage with people through the main social networks;
- putting social media into the hands of frontline officers and staff;
- maximising the opportunities to provide real operational benefits.

Engaging content

One thing we and other police forces have, is lots of information, advice, education and news. It all adds up to lots of interesting and engaging content that we can use to encourage people to get involved in conversations. The focus has been on using four main networks to reach people: Twitter, Facebook, Flickr and YouTube.

Our aim has been to provide as much access to the organisation and to see behind the scenes as possible. There are regular webcasts, twitterchats and 'ride-alongs' on operations and video giving people the chance to ask questions and give people access to all areas to their police service. Alongside this, all campaigns and initiatives have a strong social media presence, which has included using a spoof website as a police hotel for criminals at Christmas, and developing an interactive scenario to give people the opportunity of being a police officer investigating a case (Your Call). People are also given the chance to become community reporters and spend a shift with officers and put out the details of what they experience on social media.

It is not just something for campaigns, every day we look for what we can do to keep people speaking to us. If they speak to the police they are likely to be helping us to target criminals and keep communities safe.

Social media for the frontline

We have a network of officers and staff who provide updates on a daily basis for people living in local communities. They are given training and support in both the policy and the principles by the communications

Exhibit 19.1   **GMP officers are actively involved in social media**
Source: Greater Manchester Police.

team, and then have the responsibility for using social media to get in touch with people. Hundreds of officers and staff have been provided with the training. It means more information is now being published by GMP than at any time in its history.

Officers know the strategy and plan, are given the technical know-how about the networks and are allowed to develop their own personality and style. We allow this individuality so that we can meet the differing requirements of different communities.

Operational benefits

The key to our social media development is that it has real operational benefits. Time and resources will not be invested if there is nothing gained. Evaluation of the more than 100 social media accounts is carried out by the communications team on a quarterly basis. This detailed report considers levels of engagement, reach and the quality of the conversations. It ranks each of our accounts with clear recommendations for improvements as well as sharing details of what has worked well.

Some of the benefits we have cannot be measured in statistics and these are our success stories. Among them are the wanted offenders that are found through Facebook appeals, saving officer time and money. People have provided us with information about drug dealing, wanted people, antisocial behaviour and criminal activity all through social media. Sometimes this is through direct messages to protect their anonymity. The end result has been criminals put before the courts and missing people found. This could not have been achieved without people feeling comfortable talking to officers through social media. At the heart is ensuring trust and honesty to build the confidence of local people.

Integration

Social media has provided us in Greater Manchester Police with new channels where information and news can be shared directly with service users. Alongside robust media relations the developments we have made have maximised sharing and engagement with our very limited financial investment. It is an approach that has encouraged innovation and creativity, as well as empowering frontline staff to become frontline communicators. The outcome has been more information shared, greater access to officers and staff, and tangible operational results to tackle crime in communities.

Exhibit 19.2   **An example of GMP's Twitter feed**

Source: Greater Manchester Police.

Case study

Officers in Rochdale had a wanted offender, a prolific burglar, who they had been looking for. He was on recall to prison, which meant that once he was located he would be sent straight to jail. The local policing team had spent a considerable amount of time trying to find him. They then decided to post his photograph and details on their local Facebook page hoping that someone locally would help them find him.

Within a few hours there were a number of comments from local residents but among them was an unexpected one. The man taunted officers by posting 'catch me if you can' in a message under the wanted image of him. Little did he expect local people were helping and very quickly provided details that led to his location and swift return to prison. It took less than 12 hours for him to be found and back behind bars, which was a great result and saved lots of officer time. Officers had the last laugh as they were able to update their Facebook friends with the successful outcome adding 'go directly to jail, do not pass go, do not collect £200'.

This case was written by Amanda Coleman, Head of Corporate Communications at Greater Manchester Police

Questions relating to this case can be found at the end of this chapter.

Introduction

The communications landscape today is more open and democratic than it has ever been. Democratisation is enabled through interactivity, and the inherent transparency (Fournier and Avery, 2011), as a wide spectrum of electronic facilities enables all parties to participate in a communications episode. As the Greater Manchester Police case demonstrates, the use of social media affords public and private sector organisations huge opportunities to interact with their stakeholders.

Interactivity represents a shift in communications format, a move from a one-way model to one that is literally 'interactive'. Interactivity normally precedes the establishment of dialogue between participants in a communications process. This in turn enables all participants to contribute to the content that is used in the activity. This is referred to as *user-generated-content*, as demonstrated by people uploading videos to YouTube, emailing comments to radio and television programmes, or submitting ads to the Doritos Super Bowl competition. This represents a significant shift in the way in which marketing communications has developed. If the maintenance of 'relationships' is a central marketing activity, then interactive communications have an important role to play in these relationships.

This chapter builds on the introduction to the media in Chapter 18, and considers a variety of interactive media, and their role within marketing communications. We start with a consideration of interactive media advertising, including banners, behavioural targeting, pop-ups and other interactive advertising formats. This is followed by a consideration of search engine marketing and two advertising approaches, organic and sponsored links.

The third main section explores social media, and in particular social networks, viral marketing, blogging, including microblogging (Twitter), and online communities. The chapter concludes with an exploration of email, SMS, apps, widgets, affiliates and augmented reality.

Interactive media advertising

Interactive media advertising embraces ads that are bought and placed on websites where it is thought that members of the target market will pass, be prompted to click on the ad, and be transported to the advertiser's own designated site. So, in addition to the normal engagement elements, these ads serve to redirect people by interrupting their goal-directed browsing behaviour – ironically, a criticism often levelled at television advertising.

Just like linear media ads, interactive media ads are used to achieve one of two main tasks:

● to create brand awareness and make a favourable impression such that the reader develops a positive image of the brand;

● to provoke behaviour. This is direct-response advertising, and it is used to provide readers with a call-to-action. This may be in the form of a click-through to the advertiser's destination site, a video, to a purchase or phone call.

The vast majority of interactive ads are direct-response, making use of the two-way capacity to provide immediate measurement of the relative success of each campaign. For many brands, offline communications are used to create brand images while interactive media ads are used to generate a call-to-action. Figure 19.1 depicts the interactive media ad formats discussed below.

The most common forms of ads are referred to as 'banner ads', but as technology and marketing knowledge have improved, so more sophisticated versions of the banner ad have evolved. Some of these are outlined below.

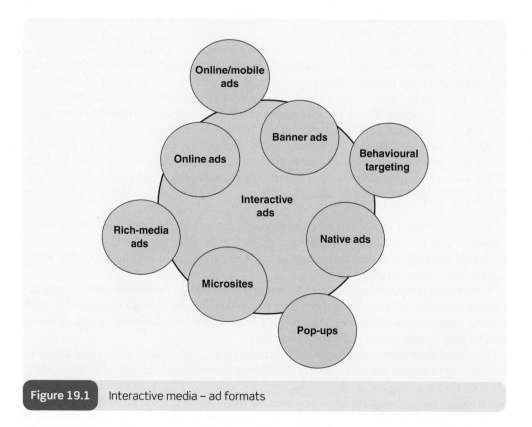

| **Figure 19.1** | Interactive media – ad formats |

Banner ads

Referred to generically as *display advertising*, these are the dominant form of paid-for online advertising. Although effective as a standalone ad, banner ads are linked through to an advertiser's chosen destination and therefore act as a gateway to other websites. Banner ads are linked to keywords submitted by a searcher into a search engine. The ad should therefore be strategically positioned to catch the optimum, or even greatest, traffic flow. Banners are said to signpost, whereas media-rich content, explored later, provides action. These allow for a depth of material and online transactions. Increasing numbers of these ads incorporate Flash, rich media, multipurpose units and skyscrapers (very tall banner ads) as these formats generate better recall scores than the standard banners.

Instead of transferring visitors to an orthodox website, banner ads can also be used to transfer visitors to a games or a competition site. These provide entertainment, seek to develop user involvement and can act as an incentive to return to the site at a later date. In addition, data about the user can be captured in order to refine future marketing offers. These ads can be saved for later use and are, therefore, more adaptable and convenient than interstitial ads (ones that pop up as users move between websites) and cannot be controlled by the user. Banner ads can also be used to transfer users to an interactive microsite.

The aim of banner ads is to attract attention and stimulate interest, but the problem is that click-through rates are very low, and have fallen for desktops to 0.1 per cent (0.35 mobile) and for video ads to 4.35 per cent for desktops (11.8 mobile) (Osman, 2014). These figures explain why advertisers have moved their adspend away from banners to video ads and other formats.

Action, that is click-through, might be driven by the way an ad has been designed and executed. This is based on the work of Lutz et al. (1983) who investigated attitude change and the way people engage cognitively with ads. Dichter (1966) also found that people's predisposition to engage with word-of-mouth communications could be stimulated by the executional qualities of an ad.

Click-through rates can be improved when online ads are integrated with a sales promotion device that is designed to reward the behaviour. Special offers, competitions and other incentives can increase rates by as much as 10 per cent. Another way of improving click-through is to consider not only the design and attractiveness of the ad, but also its placement and timing. This is because audience volumes and composition vary throughout any month or day period (Chaffey et al., 2006).

Banners have declined in importance to the extent that they are not well regarded, either by customers or clients, and many commentators regard online display to be dead. What is interesting, however, is that spend on online display is rising and, according to Wang et al. (2013), banners continue to be one of the leading web-based advertising formats.

The resolution of this apparent contradiction appears to rest with three main developments. The first concerns retargeting, which occurs when ads are placed within the browsing patterns of target audiences. Banners are thought to be more effective when used within a retargeting programme.

The second development concerns integration. According to Warner (2011), by integrating banners into social and mobile strategies and by rewarding customers through loyalty programmes when they engage with these richer ads, banners have a renewed role to play within digital marketing strategies.

The third development refers to the placing of these ads. Rather than place them on various sites that the target audiences are known to frequent, it is better to place them on sites that are relevant to the product/service offering. This is known as 'contextual advertising' and is based on ideas practised in linear media, most notably newspapers, magazines and television. Chun et al. (2013) report that web-based contextual advertising can increase brand recognition, and foster positive attitudes towards the ad and the advertised brand.

Behavioural targeting

A more recent development is behavioural targeting. This approach involves the use of information about an individual's web-browsing behaviour in order to display ads that are relevant and of particular interest to the user. To achieve this, cookies and other tracking technology are necessary to capture a user's history of online behaviour (Chen and Stallaert, 2014).

Advertisers enter an auction in order to win the opportunity to present their ad to particular users and to select a particular creative that best complements the characteristics of the web page user and the brand. This process, to implement behavioural targeting, is programmatic advertising, which has impacted on media planning (explored in Chapter 20).

Trying to determine the optimum context for presenting behavioural ads is also less of an issue than with display advertising. For example, travel brands might previously have targeted ads specifically to travel sites, but with behavioural targeting ads can be presented on various websites that are specific to a user's online browsing interests. However, ensuring that ads only appear on sites that match both campaign and brand goals is an issue which threatens *brand reputation*. This highlights an important issue. Display ads incur waste as a percentage of the ads are seen by people who are not part of the target audience. Behaviour targeting only delivers messages to people who have expressed recent interest in the category or the brand. As a result, behavioural targeting carries a cost premium as there is little wastage.

Of major concern is the intrusion and abuse of an individual's privacy that behavioural targeting represents. With so much data being collected, often without consumer consent or knowledge, this approach to advertising has caused substantial unrest and the introduction of regulations designed to empower users. This is often shaped in the form of an opt-in notice regarding the use of cookies. However, with the developing raft of tracking technologies (Chen and Stallaert, 2014) these controls are far from fit for purpose.

Many brands use behavioural advertising for direct-response-based advertising, but it is beginning to be extended to brand campaigns. However, it would be wrong to think that behavioural targeting is going to become the only media buying system and completely remove the block buying of thousands of placements and reservation of media space. It is much more likely that a tiered system will evolve with behavioural targeting providing a premium service and reservation buying continuing to offer value to particular clients.

Scholars' paper 19.1   It's new, it's behavioural targeting

Chen, J. and Stallaert, J. (2014) An economic analysis of online advertising using behavioral targeting, *MIS Quarterly*, 38(2), 429–49.

In one of the few papers on behavioural targeting, the authors provide a useful insight into this new and controversial form of advertising. They identify two effects associated with behavioural targeting: a competitive effect and a propensity effect. The relative strength of the two effects determines whether the publisher's revenue is positively or negatively affected.

Native advertising

Native advertising refers to ads that follows the form, function and sometimes the context of the host provided they have social relevance (Norman, 2015). He demonstrates that Twitter, LinkedIn Sponsored Updates, Facebook News Feed and Buzzfeed, plus other 'in-stream' ads, are examples of what constitutes 'native advertising'. In the same way ads from golf equipment manufacturers within golf magazines, fashion and beauty ads in *Cosmopolitan* or *Vogue* and car ads in automotive magazines all represent native advertising.

The native advertising format has grown significantly, partly because, like behavioural ads, native ads can be bought through programmatic processes (as explained in Chapter 20), and partly because of the surge in mobile usage. They are often but erroneously compared with content marketing (as explored in Chapter 4). The Mobile Marketing Association (MMA) identifies that there are various types of native advertising, ranging from search advertising (the earliest form of native) and in-stream advertising, to in-game native formats and others. It also states that there are several native ad formats specific to the mobile channel. These are in-feed social, in-feed content, in-feed content, in-map, in-game, paid search, recommendation widgets and custom (MMA, 2015).

Pop-ups

Also known as *transitional online ads*, pop-ups appear in separate browser windows, when web pages are being loaded or closed. Originally they were intended to appear as a relief to the boredom that can set in when downloading files took a long time.

In that sense, they were regarded as supportive communications. However, as broadband speeds and computer technology have accelerated, and 'waiting' times minimised, pop-ups are now generally regarded as an irritation.

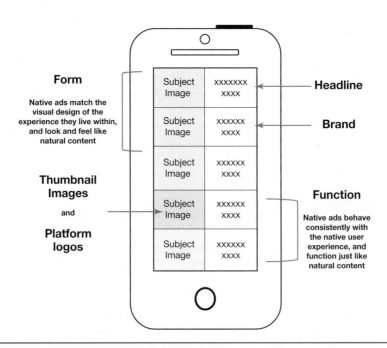

Exhibit 19.3	**The form and nature of native advertising**
	Source: Based on images developed by the MMA

Research by McCoy et al. (2007) was aimed at understanding the impact and intrusiveness of online ads. Their results showed that these types of ads, especially pop-ups, are perceived to be annoying and more intrusive than display ads. What is more, they impeded recall of both the website and the ad.

Microsites

This type of site is normally product- or promotion-specific, and is often run as a joint promotion with other advertisers. Creating a separate site avoids the difficulty of directing traffic to either of the joint partners' sites. Microsites are much less expensive to set up than traditional sites and are particularly adept at building awareness, as click-throughs to microsites are higher than through just banners.

Rich-media ads

The essential difference between regular and rich-media banner ads is that the latter allow for significantly more detailed and enhanced messages to be accessed by the target audience. Rich-media ads closely resemble offline ads and this helps to move online ads from a largely informational perspective to one that is much more emotional. This suggests that rich media are more likely to deliver stronger branding messages than in the past, which of course would negate the behavioural advantage inherent in this interactive environment.

Streaming video and other more visitor-engaging material, such as Flash and Shockwave, provide depth and interest for users. It is accepted that media-rich banner ads are highly effective, if only because the medium is said to be the message.

Online video

Online video advertising has grown enormously, partly because it can be used in a number of different ways apart from simply showing ads at the beginning or end of programmes. Online video content normally plays in an unstoppable loop, so the ads are unavoidable. In addition, advertisers will be able to place ads within video streams, another reason preventing users from avoiding them. Also, video ads can be embedded within web pages and online articles, relating closely to the site content. To date, many online ads are directly derived from television ads, but the 30-second format is not appropriate for the online environment. This means specific content for online ads needs to be developed.

One particular genre are minifilms, or microfilm advertising. Chen and Lee (2014: 292) refer to these as 'short film-like streaming advertisements produced by marketers with brand messages embedded into storylines. Minifilms have become particularly popular among advertisers in Chinese-speaking areas (primarily in China and Taiwan)', particularly as they can be easily distributed as viral advertising.

Vine, a free mobile application, allows users to share 6-second looped videos shot with a mobile phone camera. Vine dominates the video-sharing market on Twitter, partly because the app allows the users to create 'mini ads' at little cost. Vines appeal because consumers' have short attention spans, and they can provide a snapshot of a brand in a humorous and personal way (Jones, 2013).

Online gaming

The development of game technology has prompted enormous growth in the numbers of consumers who play online games. This in turn has attracted advertisers. According to Chang et al. (2010), the advergaming industry appears to have started in the late 1980s, when Sega Games put up Marlboro billboards in its racing games (Chambers, 2006). It should be noted that there are two forms of game-based advertising.

In-game advertising (IGA)

Yang et al. (2006: 63) refer to in-game advertising (IGA) as 'the placement of brands in games (usually in the form of billboards, posters, or sponsor signage in sports and racing games)'.

In many ways this resembles the model through which brand placement is considered to work. However, as Cauberghe and de Pelsmacker (2010) point out, the interactive context of in-game brand placements can evoke cognitively involving experiences for players. This is something which the static nature of traditional product placements in television programmes and films cannot achieve.

Chang et al. (2010) conclude that the effectiveness of in-game advertising is improved when two main elements are attended to. First, the advertising needs to be integrated into the game. They found that the sense of realism felt by players is not disturbed or can even be improved when the advertising is an integral part the game. The second element concerns the selection of an appropriate game in which the advertising is to be placed. By selecting a game with attributes that are similar to those of the advertised brand, such as sports brands with sports-based games, the media vehicle, the game, can enhance advertising effects.

Advergaming

Cauberghe and de Pelsmacker (2010: 5) distinguish advergaming on the basis that 'the game is specially made to promote the brand'. These games tend to be relatively simple in design, with few rules and are easy to play. This is mainly because advergames are distributed across different platforms, such as websites, viral marketing, mobiles and commercials on interactive digital television.

Mainstream advertising works partly on the principle of association, and IGA works on there being a positive association between an advertiser and the game. Lewis and Porter (2010) report that when there is a large incompatibility between the advertising and a game, perceptions of the realism of the game are reduced and the level of annoyance felt by players increases.

Chang et al. (2010) conclude that to be successful it is important to integrate the advertising closely into a game. This means embedding it as an integral part of the activity, not at the periphery or as an add-on. This helps to enhance the sense of realism for players.

They also recommend that it is important to select an appropriate game as the advertising vehicle. Player annoyance can be reduced if there is a close alignment between the game's attributes and those of the brand being advertised.

In much the same way, each player has a psychological profile. So those playing sports games are more predisposed to sports brands being integrated into the game.

Cauberghe and de Pelsmacker's (2010) research results are interesting because they find that brand prominence affects recall. Prominence in an advergame refers to the extent to which a brand is an integral and dynamic part of the game. Brands that are placed prominently in a game are likely to benefit from a player's focus on the interactive content and consequent intensive processing of ads. The result is higher brand recall (Schneider and Cornwell, 2005). This works for products that evoke both high and low involvement.

Various theories have been put forward concerning the number of times an offline or traditional ad should be repeated in order for learning to occur. Cauberghe and de Pelsmacker found repetition not to be a recall factor in an advergaming environment. Their research found that 'playing the game several times had no positive influence on brand recall, but impacted the development of brand attitudes negatively'. Again this is a function of the intensity of cognitive processing associated with gaming. The researchers' recommendation is that advertisers should work with more complex advergames.

Search engine marketing

Websites need visitors and the higher the number of visitors, the more effective the website is likely to be. Many people know of a particular site and simply type in the address or use a bookmark to access it. However, the majority of people arrive at sites following a search using particular keywords and phrases to locate products, services, news, entertainment and the information they need. We do this through search engines, and the results of each search are displayed in rank order. It is understandable, therefore, that those ranked highest in the results lists are visited more often than those in lower positions.

Consequently, from a marketing perspective it is important to undertake marketing activities to attain the highest possible ranking position, and this is referred to as search engine marketing (SEM). Zenetti et al. (2014: 7) report this to be the main way firms acquire customers through Internet marketing as it enables them to reach 'consumers directly as they search for information, products, or services online'.

There are two main search engine marketing techniques: search engine optimisation (SEO) and pay-per-click (PPC), and ideally both should be used together.

Search engine optimisation

Search engine optimisation (SEO), or *organic search* as it used to be called, is a process used to win a high-ranking page position on major search engines and directories. To achieve top-ranking positions, or least a first-page listing, it is necessary to design web pages using appropriate keywords, links with other quality websites, use inputs from social media and ensure the content is high quality. This enables search engines to match closely a searcher's keywords/phrases with the content of registered web pages.

Each search engine, such as Google and Bing in the West, Yandex in Russia, Daum and Naver in Korea, and Baidu in China, uses an algorithm to compare the content of relevant site pages with the keywords/phrases used to initiate a search (Jerath et al., 2014). Search engines use robotic electronic spiders to crawl around registered sites and from this to compile an index of the words they find, placed there by the designer of each website. When a search is activated, it is the database housing these keyword/phrases that is searched, not the millions of World Wide Web pages.

Once registered, a high ranking used to be best achieved by attaining a match between the search words/phrases entered by the searcher and the words/phrases and content on the pages stored in the index. Achieving a good match could be helped by understanding, if not anticipating, the words and phrases that are likely to be used by individual searchers. Through web analytics, the study of website visitors' behaviour, it is possible to analyse the search terms used by current visitors.

For some time designers believed that 'keyword density' was important. This refers to the number of times a keyword is repeated in the text of a web page. Another key factor was thought to be the number of inbound links from what are regarded as good-quality sites. The greater the number of quality links, the higher the ranking was likely to be. These approaches are now regarded as ineffective with the emphasis now placed on key phrases, overall content and social media.

The use of keywords in the *title tag* of a web page and the meta tags is still important. These signify the content and describe what searchers will find when they click on the site. These tags are embedded by web page designers and read by some search engine spiders. When keywords and phrases used by searchers match those in these tags, it is likely that the site will have a reasonable ranking.

In 2013, and in the name of user security, Google started to encrypt all of its searches (La Fond, 2015). This means that Google no longer delivers keyword data to websites, which means that website performance can no longer be measured on keyword performance and associated metrics. Whilst the use of keyword-rich content that matches what users are searching for is an important website design factor, now the process works by looking at longer words, phrases or questions, not just keywords. This means that it is fresh, high-quality relevant content that counts.

In addition to this the Google algorithm (called Hummingbird) now incorporates data from Google Plus and Google Authorship, indicating that social media and the production of quality content are now regarded as the most important features within search (Manning, 2014). Note that this encryption only applies to Google, and that the search engines responsible for the other 40 per cent of traffic still provide keyword statistics.

It is not surprising that an airline such as easyJet, which sells more than 98 per cent of its seats via the www.easyjet.com website, uses search engine optimisation to drive traffic to its websites across Europe. It is vital that 'easyJet' appears when the search phrases associated with the discount airlines business are used and content is revised on a daily basis.

Viewpoint 19.1   Daxon fashion a move to interactive media

Daxon is an over-50s fashion brand originating from France, who pride themselves on designing figure flattering and stylish womenswear. Daxon, who began trading in the UK in 1997, compete with brands such as JD Williams, FiftyPlus and Marisota. Due to the overcrowding in this sector it is essential for brands to keep up-to-date with the latest trends, style movements and opinions regarding their target market.

Traditionally within the over-50s fashion market, brands see the majority of their demand generated through offline marketing communications, mainly in the form of catalogues, brochures and leaflets. In the UK and France this is still Daxon's main form of communications. Since crossing the border Daxon UK have seen a steady increase in the numbers and frequency with which their customers, the majority in their 50s and 60s, purchase fashion through online channels. This has resulted in an almost 40 per cent reduction in the number of offline marketing campaigns top customers receive each fashion season, down from 26 to 16.

Exhibit 19.4	Daxon store or media image
	Source: Daxon.

In 2009, less than 10 per cent of Daxon's orders were placed online, in 2014 it had more than doubled to over 20 per cent. The brand's growth in online activity is reflected in the wider market. Mintel's Senior Consumer Analyst, Tamara Sender, reports that in a study on 'Online Fashion', 34 per cent of the 45–54s thought that shopping online for clothes had become more convenient and that they rarely go in store to purchase anymore.

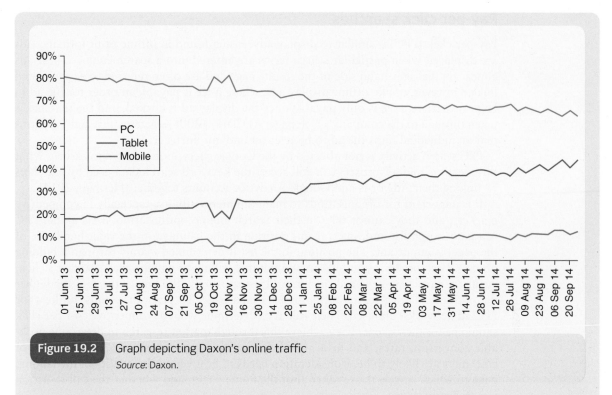

Figure 19.2   Graph depicting Daxon's online traffic
Source: Daxon.

Through analysis and understanding of the over-50s fashion market, Daxon UK re-evaluated their digital communications. Now they use email-based campaigns and interact daily with customers through social media using competitions and weekly trivia questions. This was a big step for the brand, as engagement through email and social media now represents an essential part of Daxon's marketing communications with their customers.

From this increase in online traffic, Daxon have also noticed that almost a third of these customers were viewing their website through mobile/tablet devices. Internal research revealed that the increase in traffic generated through tablets more than offset the decline in desktop traffic (see Figure 19.2). If this behavioural trend continues then tablet usage is predicted to exceed desktop in the next 18 months.

In 2014 Daxon's website wasn't optimised across all channels. In order to deal with the anticipated increase in traffic and engage with both Android and Apple devices, a more responsive website was planned for 2015. It was expected that this would make browsing their website through these devices much easier, which in turn should enhance the shopping experience, and improve Daxon's overall performance.

Source: Sender (2014); internal sources at Daxon UK.

This Viewpoint was written by Jasmine Kendal when she was a student studying Advertising and Marketing Communications at the University of Huddersfield.

Question: Discuss ways in which Daxon should develop their interactive media mix.

Task: Find another independent fashion retailer and list the media they use to reach their customers.

Pay-per-click searches

Pay-per-click (PPC) is similar to display advertising found in offline print formats. Ads are displayed when particular search terms are entered into a search engine. These ads appear on the right-hand side of the results page and are often referred to as sponsored links. However, unlike offline display ads, where a fee is payable in order for the ad to be printed, here a fee is only payable once the display ad is clicked, and the searcher is taken through to the company's web page. As Clarke (2008) suggests, this action affirms that an individual finds the ad to be relevant and not intrusive.

PPC search activity is not affected by the Google encryption referred to earlier. What this means is that advertisers can still access the keyword search data used by searchers by linking their Adwords and Google Analytics accounts together (Herman, 2014).

It is important for organisations to maintain high visibility, especially in competitive markets, and they cannot rely on their search engine optimisation skills alone. PPC is a paid search list and, once again, position in the listings (on the right-hand side of the page) is important. The position in the list is determined mainly through a bidding process. Each organisation bids an amount it is willing to pay for each searcher's click, against a particular keyword or phrase. Unsurprisingly, the higher the bid, the higher the position where a search result appears on a page. To place these bids, brokers (or PPC ad networks) are used. Their role is to determine what a competitive cost per click should be for their client. They achieve this through market research to determine probable conversion rates, and from this deduce what the purchase and lifetime value of customers are likely to be. Consideration needs to be given to the quality of the landing page to which searchers are taken (not the home page), and whether the call-to-action is sufficiently strong.

Research has found that the popularity of a keyword can also be a determining factor in search behaviour. Jerath et al. (2014) found that there was a higher proportion of sponsored clicks for less popular keywords. They also found that those consumers experiencing high involvement tend to use more clicks per search (than low-involvement consumers) and click more frequently on sponsored links. Low-involvement consumers appear to search for more popular keywords than high-involvement consumers.

Search engine marketing is important if only because of the relative ineffectiveness of other online marketing activities. The goal of SEM is to drive traffic to websites, and ranking on the search results page is achieved in two fundamentally different ways. In SEO ranking searches are based on content while the PPC approach relies entirely on price as a ranking mechanism. Of these two main approaches, research indicates that the PPC model attracts far more investment (by advertisers) than the SEO model. This indicates that paid ads or sponsored links have low credibility and do not carry high levels of trust. Added to this is the overwhelming research that shows that SEO is more effective in terms of recall and driving site traffic (Jansen and Molina, 2006). Kimberley (2010), however, reports that research undertaken by IAB has found that brands are failing to exploit the potential offered by SEM, although that has probably changed in the intervening years.

Social media

Social media embrace a range of applications, all of which incorporate a form of word-of-mouth communications. Kietzmann et al. (2011: 1) state that 'Social media employ mobile and web-based technologies to create highly interactive platforms via which individuals and communities share, co-create, discuss, and modify user-generated content.'

Table 19.1 A classification of social media

		Social presence/media richness		
		Low	Medium	High
Level of self-presentation/self-disclosure	High	Blogs	Social networking sites (e.g. Facebook)	Virtual social worlds (e.g. Second Life)
	Low	Collaborative projects (e.g. Wikipedia)	Content communities (e.g. YouTube)	Virtual game worlds (e.g. World of Warcraft)

Source: Kaplan and Haenlein (2010). Used with permission.

The impact of personal influences on the offline communications process can often be important if communications are to be successful. Online personal influencers such as opinion leaders and opinion formers, often bloggers, are equally important. Organisations target these individuals with messages, knowing that they will be disseminated to a wider audience. Recommendations to provide information and to support and reinforce purchasing decisions are an integral part of this word-of-mouth process.

The role of opinion formers is much diminished within an interactive media context, especially with digital natives, and the predominant 18–25-year-old user group. For them expert opinion, as represented by opinion formers, is rejected in favour of peer-group recommendation (opinion leaders).

The terms 'social media' and 'social networks' have become increasingly prevalent. Although similar, they do not mean the same, yet are often used interchangeably, and mistakenly. Kaplan and Haenlein (2010: 61) define social media as 'a group of Internet based applications that build on the ideological and technological foundations of Web 2.0 and that allow the creation and exchange of user generated content'. In order to understand the range of social media, they develop a classification scheme. To do this, they identify two key elements of social media: first, social presence/media richness and, second, social processes in the form of self-presentation/self-disclosure. Within these parameters they classify core aspects of social media. Table 19.1 shows this classification.

Table 19.2 The building blocks of social media

Building blocks	Explanation
Identity	The extent to which users reveal their identities in a social media setting. This can include disclosing information such as name, age, gender, profession, location, and also information that portrays users in certain ways.
Conversations	The enormous number and diversity of social media conversations leads to format and protocol implications for firms that seek to host or track these conversations. Differences in the frequency and content of a conversation can have major implications for how firms monitor and make sense of the 'conversation velocity' – that is, the rate and direction of change in a conversation.
Sharing	Social media users exchange, distribute and receive content. Firms wishing to engage with social media need to evaluate what objects of sociality their users have in common as, without these objects, a sharing network will be primarily about connections between people but without anything connecting them together.

Continued

Building blocks	Explanation
Presence	The extent to which users can know if other users are accessible. It includes knowing where others are, in the virtual world and/or in the real world, and whether they are available. If users prefer to engage in real time, the social media platform should offer a presence or status line indicator, along with a suitable mechanism through which these users can contact each other and interact.
Relationships	This about the associations users have that lead them to converse, share objects of sociality, meet up, or simply just list each other as a friend or fan. The way users are connected can determine the characteristics of information exchange. Some relationships are fairly formal, regulated and structured (LinkedIn), while others can be informal, unregulated and without structure (Skype).
Reputation	The extent to which users are able to identify the status of others, and themselves, in a social media context. Reputation can be a matter of trust, but this can be based on the number of endorsements from others (LinkedIn), content voting (YouTube) or aggregators (Twitter).
Groups	Users can form communities and sub-communities and so the more 'social' a network becomes, the larger the potential groups (of friends, followers and contacts) become. Organisations should be prepared to help users manage their groups.

Source: Based on Kietzmann et al. (2011).

In other words, *social media* refer to a broad range of web-based applications, and social networking sites are just one of the many applications that are available. Others include web logs, content communities (e.g. YouTube), collaborative projects (e.g. Wikipedia), virtual game worlds (e.g. World of Warcraft) and virtual social worlds (e.g. Second Life).

The role and presence that an organisation seeks to adopt in social media is critical. Kietzmann et al. (2011: 242) refer to a 'rich and diverse ecology of social media sites, which vary in terms of their scope and functionality'. This diversity has posed problems for organisations as they attempt to adapt and implement digital strategies, in an environment where their level of control and influence is much reduced. Kietzmann et al. (2011) developed a framework consisting of seven building blocks. These refer to identity, conversations, sharing, presence, relationships, reputation and groups. These blocks are constructs designed to enable insight into the different levels of social media functionality which in turn, they argue, can help organisations develop more effective configurations and use of social media (see Table 19.2).

Having identified the building blocks, Kietzmann et al. (2011) recommend that organisations develop strategies to monitor, understand and respond to different social media activities. They suggest a framework, called the '4Cs':

1. *Cognise*.

Each organisation should try to recognise and understand its social media landscape.

2. *Congruity*.

Each organisation should develop strategies that match the different social media functionalities and their goals.

3. *Curate*.

Each organisation should develop a policy about who should listen to conversations on a social media platform and when.

4. *Chase.*

Each organisation should undertake environmental scanning to understand the speed of conversations and the information flows that could affect the organisation and the market.

As if to confirm the importance of a well-considered digital strategy, Truong and Simmons (2010: 250) report research that finds that the use of inappropriate and intrusive pushed web-based advertising and mobile digital formats 'can lead to a negative impact upon brand equity'. Mark de Leeuw, cited by Gray (2015), speculates that as Facebook develops its advertising platform so many consumers will look for different networks.

Seven main elements of social media are considered here: social networks, viral marketing, podcasts, web logs (or blogs), microblogging and online communities.

Viewpoint 19.2   Maersk Line gets seriously social

As part of the Maersk Group, a collection of shipping and energy companies, Maersk Line is the world's largest container shipping company with 17 per cent market share, over 36,000 employees and 619 container vessels.

Maersk Line's remarkable social media presence has evolved through two main periods. The first period of development, 2011-2013, occurred when B2B social media activity was under-utilised in the shipping industry. Maersk Line's rapid development of social media was regarded as revolutionary and helped differentiate Maersk Line from its competitors and other companies. At the start the primary goal was to use social media to get close to the customers. The secondary goals were to get better press coverage, higher levels of employee engagement, and improved brand awareness. To achieve this four areas were highlighted for emphasis: communications, customer service, sales, and internal usage. After a few standard posts on Facebook the potential of sharing Maersk Line's digital archive of 14,000 photos of ships, seascapes and ports was spotted. These images were posted online under different categories:

| Exhibit 19.5 | **Part of Maersk's photos used to build its social media strategy** |

Source: A.P Moller - Maersk Archives.

Vessels, Containers, Terminals, and History; and true stories were added to enrich the material. This was received enthusiastically by followers, including seafarers, customers and many Maersk employees, all posting their own material. In the first 11 months, Maersk Line attracted more than 400,000 people to its Facebook page.

The company developed its own social media hub called Maersk Line Social in order to have a place to post more extensive stories, a place where it could have more control over social media. These followers were more hardcore and comments were very specific. The medium also allowed the company to post instantaneous information and news. At this time Maersk Line operated through 10 different social media platforms: Facebook, Twitter, Google+, LinkedIn, Instagram, Vimeo, Flickr, Pinterest, Tumblr, and Instagram.

The second main period of Maersk Line's social media presence began in 2014 and is characterised by the strategic use of social media. Previously the goal had been to drive awareness and engagement and this was often measured through 'likes' and numbers of followers. In the second period social media has become an integral part of the company's business and marketing strategies. As a result core activities now involve both talking and listening through social media, and by harnessing social media activity with the different stages of the sales funnel. Today Maersk Line's social media activity is measured through KPIs. For example, previously performance was measured through the number of 'followers', now it is the number of leads generated that is a critical measure of performance. The number of platforms used by Maersk Line has been rationalised. Today its core platforms are Facebook, Instagram, LinkedIn, YouTube, and Twitter. At a general level, Facebook is used to engage with followers in a very visual and conversational way. Twitter is used as a news outlet, and LinkedIn, the company's most important corporate platform, is used to reach over 125,000 customers.

Source: Katona and Sarvary (2014); Rapaport (2015); www.maerskline.com.

> **Question:**   If Maersk can develop this level of social media activity, what prevents other B2B firms following a similar strategy?
>
> **Task:**   Apply Kietzmann et al.'s (2011) 4Cs framework to the Maersk Line case.

There are several commentators, authors and journalists who believe the influence of social media within brand communications to be overstated. Social media enable conversation and self-expression, but to date there is little evidence that social media can provide a brand with any significant leverage. The reasoning here relates to the reach and influence of television compared to the reach and influence of Facebook and Twitter-based brand followers. The death of television as an advertising medium has been predicted too frequently and erroneously, as the statistics reveal that the number of hours people watch television has stayed the same for each of the five years to 2014. Mark Ritson argues that the number of customers a brand has dwarfs those who are 'followers', especially those followers who have engaged with the brand in the last seven days. The relative impact of a brand tweet, even if amplified through retweeting, has therefore minor economic and communicative significance compared to the power of television and radio (Joy, 2015).

As if to endorse and extend Ritson's views, the notion that social media analytics are based on measuring the performance of posts and tweets, Lumb (2015) reports that there is a growing body of opinion that believes that it is the performance of the followers, not the content, that matters. For example, he refers to 'SocialRank', which measures followers by several metrics to determine usefulness, of which there are two central metrics. The first is the Most Valuable Follower, which ranks followers by influence, and, second, Best Follower, which balances Most Valuable with the most engaged. This enables the identification of the Most Valuable Follower in Manchester, Minnesota or Melbourne prior to an event. Alternatively the system can be used to contact and reward the 10 most engaged followers who have a keyword in their Twitter bio that corresponds with a brand's core activity.

Scholars' paper 19.2   So, what are social media?

Kaplan, A.M. and Haelein, M. (2010) Users of the world unite! The challenges and opportunities of social media, *Business Horizons*, 53(1), 59-68.

This paper is important because it attempts to clarify what social media might be. The authors describe the concept of social media, and then present a classification of social media which groups applications as collaborative projects, blogs, content communities, social networking sites, virtual game worlds and virtual social worlds. They conclude with 10 pieces of advice for companies wishing to utilise social media.

See also: Fournier, S. and Avery, J. (2011) The uninvited brand, *Business Horizons*, 54(3), 193–207.

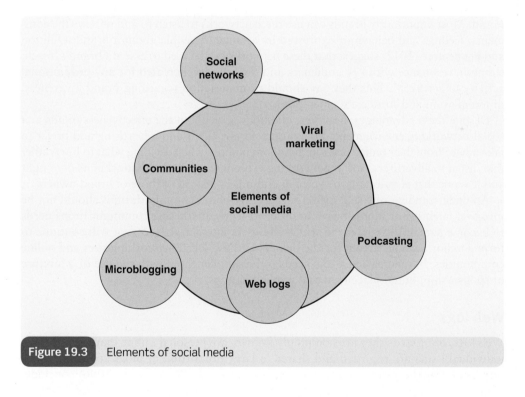

Figure 19.3   Elements of social media

Figure 19.3 shows the main elements of social media that are explored.

Social networks

Social networks are communities of people using the Internet to share lifestyle and experiences. The Greater Manchester Police case that opens this chapter demonstrates that participants in these networks not only share information and experiences, but can also use the interactive capacity to build new relationships. The critical aspect of social networks is that most of the content is user-generated and this means users own, control and develop content according to their needs, not those of a third party.

Social networks enable people to share experiences. Typical sites include Google+, LinkedIn, Qzone, Sina Weibo, YouTube, Tumblr and, of course, Facebook, which has been the largest Western network in recent years with 1.35 billion active users in 2014 (Anon, 2014). These sites provide certain segments of the population, mainly the 16–25-year-old group, with an opportunity to reach their friends, generate new ones and share experiences, information and insights, electronically. Participants take on different roles and are not equally active. For example, Li and Bernhoff (2008), cited by Quinton and Fennemore (2012), classified users according to one of six levels of network participation. In ascending order of activity these are Inactives, Spectators, Joiners, Collectors, Critics and Creators. The greatest volume of contribution, that is regular reading, writing, posting contributions and voicing opinions, is made by the last two groups, who make up 33 per cent of all subscribers.

The relative immaturity of the social networking arena and the way in which content is developed raise challenges about how organisations can best use social networks as part of their marketing communications to reach their target audiences. Creating fan pages and groups are established approaches. Unlike groups, fan pages are visible to unregistered people and are indexed, which helps improve reputation. Groups, on the other hand, facilitate viral marketing and are better at involving people and stimulating behaviour.

Social networks are a means by which organisations can assess the health of their brand. Most importantly brands can use these networks to listen to and observe the comments, feelings and behaviour expressed by a range of people about a brand. Quinton and Fennemore (2012) suggest that these networks can be used to assess a brand's 'reach, strength, resonance with key audiences and the buzz level created for any promotional activity undertaken'. This they say should prompt action regarding brand awareness, differentiation and strategic segmentation.

Despite these advantages, however, questions arise about the effectiveness of ads in a social networking environment. Many users do not like brand advertising and prefer to take advice from their online peers in these communities when deciding what to buy, rather than listen to advertisers. Social networking is becoming a media channel in its own right and it is one that is reflecting the voice of consumers instead of those of brand owners.

An understanding of social media reveals that brand communications should not be invasive, intrusive or interruptive. In order to work, marketing communications needs to become part of the context in which site users interact. Advertising will continue to form a major revenue stream for the owners of these social networking sites and online communities, but increasingly this needs to be supplemented with the use of a mixture of sponsorship, brand placement and public relations.

Web logs

Web logs, or *blogs* as they are commonly known, are personal online diaries. Although individual issues are recorded and shared, a large proportion of blogs concern organisations and public issues, and they are virtually free. As Wood et al. (2006) conclude, blogging represents a simple, straightforward way of creating a web presence.

Even if the quality and content of blogs vary considerably, their popularity has grown enormously. The informality of blogs enables information to be communicated in a much more relaxed manner than most other forms of marketing communications. This is typified by the use of podcasting and the downloading of blogs to be 'consumed' at a later, more convenient time or while multitasking. Blogs represent user-generated content and are often a key indicator of the presence of an opinion leader or former.

Blogs can be understood using a number of criteria, other than the basic consumer or corporate demarcation. Typically, the content and the type of media are the main criteria. A blog can be categorised by its content or the general material with which it is concerned. The breadth of content is only limited by the imagination, but some of the more mainstream blogs tend to cover topics such as sport, travel, music, film, fashion and politics. Blogs can also be categorised according to the type of media. For example, 'vlogs' contain video collections, whereas a 'photoblog' is a collection of photos and a 'sketchblog' contains sketches.

Nardi et al. (2004), as cited by Jansen et al. (2009), found five reasons why people choose to blog:

- documenting their lives;
- providing commentary and opinions;
- expressing deeply held emotions;
- articulating ideas through writing;
- forming and maintaining communities.

These appear to be a list of outward-facing reasons. What is not mentioned here are inner-directed reasons, such as the need for feedback, or psychological issues relating to the need for self-esteem, reassurance and reinforcement of an individual's identity.

Business-related or corporate blogs represent huge potential as a form of marketing communications for organisations. This is because blogs reflect the attitudes of the author, and these attitudes can influence others. As consumers write about their experiences with brands, opportunities exist for organisations to identify emerging trends, needs and preferences, and also to understand how brands are perceived. Blogs provide brands with a potent advertising platform, because, as Segev et al. (2014) point out, they enable contextual advertising. This occurs where advertised objects are relevant to the theme of the blog (context), which in turn are read by consumers who are interested in the content available on the platform.

Organisations can set up *external* corporate blogs to communicate with customers, channel partners and other stakeholders. Many major organisations use external blogs to provide information about company issues and other organisations use blogs to launch brands or attend to customer issues. The other form of corporate blog is the *internal* blog. Here the focus is on enabling employees to write about and discuss corporate policies, issues and developments. Some organisations encourage interaction between their employees and customers and the general public. Although problems can arise through inappropriate comments and observations, blogging is an informal communications device that can serve to counter the formality often associated with planned marketing communications.

Scholars' paper 19.3   Magazines or blogs to build a brand?

Colliander, J. and Dahlén, M. (2011) Following the fashionable friend: the power of social media, *Journal of Advertising Research,* 51(1), 313–20.

Social media and blogs in particular have become extremely fashionable, especially among writers, readers and, increasingly, marketers. The authors demonstrate the importance of social media and of building brand relationships. They achieve this by showing how the writer–brand relationship and the credibility a writer is perceived to have affect readers' perceptions of brand publicity on blogs. The research is anchored in measuring brand publicity through blogs and online magazines. They find that blogs generate higher brand attitudes and purchase intentions.

Therefore, enabling people to blog, perhaps by creating dedicated web space, facilitates interaction and communications through people with similar interests. There is also an added attraction in that communities of bloggers can attract advertisers and form valuable revenue streams. Blogs can be used by organisations as a form of public relations in order to communicate with a range of stakeholders. For example, a blog on an intranet can be used to support internal communications, on an extranet to support distributors and on the Internet to reach and influence consumers.

Microblogging

Microblogging or *nanoblogging*, as it is sometimes referred to, is a short-format version of blogging. It is a form of eWoM (electronic word of mouth) and uses web social communications services (Jansen et al., 2009) of which Twitter, which appeared in 2006, is probably the best known. A microblog, or tweet, consists of a short comment, a post of 140 characters, which is shared with a network of followers. This makes production and consumption relatively easy in comparison to blogs.

These posts can be distributed though instant messages, email, mobile phones and tablets, or the Web. Therefore, as Jansen et al. put it, people can share brand-related thoughts at any time, and more or less anywhere, with people who are connected via the Web, smartphone, tablet, or IM and email, on an unprecedented scale.

Wood and Burkhalter (2014) indicate that Twitter is used by consumers for a variety of reasons. These include informing family, friends and contacts about what they are doing or thinking, crowd-sourcing, and sharing and forwarding information and news articles to others. At a deeper level ideas about self-expression, personal identity, and a need to participate and to be seen and heard, can be added. They suggest that Twitter is used by organisations to target audiences efficiently, to collect market intelligence in real time, and to provide customer service. To this might be added ideas about engaging audiences, establishing a digital credibility and fostering relationships.

We know that WoM has a particularly significant impact on purchasing decisions, but eWoM can take place close to or even during a purchase process. Although eWoM may be less personal than face-to-face WoM, it has substantially greater reach and has greater credibility because it is in print and accessible by others (Hennig-Thurau et al., 2004). The implication of this is that microblogging offers huge potential to marketers, recognised when Twitter announced that it was to allow advertising on its site. However, these are not conventional adverts. These ads are tweets, and are an integral part of the conversations, referred to as 'Promoted tweets'. These messages, limited to 140 characters, appear at the top of the page when a user has searched for that word, and only show up in search results (Steele, 2010).

Viewpoint 19.3   Twittering brands

The way in which Twitter is used by people and brands varies but most strive to accumulate as many followers as possible. For example, Maersk Line, featured in Viewpoint 19.2, had 81,000 followers in 2013, which at the time was a large number for many B2B companies. Consumer brands such as 'Whole Foods Market' have 2.9 million Twitter followers, Zappos, 2.6 million followers, and Best Buy, 276,000 followers. Twitter is used by Maersk Line as a news outlet, the Whole Foods Market use it to find out what their customers prefer to read and watch, to invite their customers to events and to recommend new food podcasts. In essence, Twitter is used by company brands to provide news, customer insight and customer service.

▶

There are several celebrities who have considerably more followers than major brands. At the beginning of 2015 Katy Perry had over 62 million, Taylor Swift, 49 million and the footballer Cristiano Ronaldo, 32 million Twitter followers. The first to reach 1 million was the actor Ashton Kutcher. He challenged CNN to a race to see who would be the first to attract 1 million followers, and won.

The celebrity actor Charlie Sheen signed up to Twitter in March 2011. When he posted his first Tweet he embedded a picture of himself holding a bottle of chocolate milk from Broguiere's Dairy, and his friend Bree Olson was pictured holding a fruit smoothie from the Naked Juice Company. Both the brands were unaware of this unplanned and uncompensated endorsement. Both brands experienced considerable media attention and Broguiere's Dairy, a relatively small family-run business, reported that it generated some new business from the post. Within 25 hours and 17 minutes, Charlie Sheen set the then Guinness World Record for 'Fastest Time to Reach 1 Million Followers'. It was this event that led Sheen to develop his digital popularity by endorsing products on Twitter for a fee. Today some brands can pay celebrities up to US$100,000 in return for posts, with fees negotiable based on the number of followers. However, it is generally accepted that the number of fake followers, those bought in batches as spam numbers, can constitute up to 50 per cent of the claimed number. If these are stripped out, as Instagram did in 2014, the number of followers can fall drastically, which in turn can impact celebrity earnings.

Celebrities tend to use Twitter to build awareness, to remain relevant to their fans by providing news and insights about themselves, and to build their image and relationships, all with a view to driving income and sustaining their careers.

Although companies have fewer followers than many celebrities it should be noted that brands often have multiple Twitter accounts, reflecting different goals, product lines and markets.

Source: Wood and Burkhalter (2014); www.gizmodo.com; www.socialbakers.com.

> **Question:**   In which circumstances might brands concentrate on Twitter rather than any other media?
>
> **Task:**   Find three brands that use celebrities who tweet about the brand.

There are four main ways in which brands can use microblogging. These are set out in Table 19.3.

One of the advantages of Twitter, and the following/followed scenario that it provides, is that participants are enabled to 'follow one another's content without reciprocal

Table 19.3 Four ways to use Twitter in marketing communications

Twitter format	Explanation
Company organic	A brand to consumer message, at no cost, encouraging consumers to follow it on twitter.
Company paid	Known as a 'promoted tweet', a company pays to have a tweet inserted in a consumer's twitter feed. Normally these are targeted at people who do not currently follow the brand on twitter. Promoted tweets are charged on a cost per engagement event or a cost per thousand impressions model. In the case of twitter, engagement refers to clicks, favourites, retweets and @replies.
Celebrity paid	Sometimes referred to as a 'sponsored tweet', this approach involves a brand paying a celebrity to tweet on its behalf. Through the use of hashtags at the end of a tweet (the symbol # followed by the name of a group) the message discloses that the message is an ad. Each sponsored tweet can cost tens of thousands of dollars.
Celebrity organic	This involves a celebrity tweeting about a brand voluntarily and without compensation. Although this incurs no cost to the brand there is low control and high risk as the brand has no influence over the association with the celebrity tweeter, the content and the timing of these tweets.

Source: Based on Wood and Burkhalter (2014).

obligation'. Fans are free to send a celebrity they are following a personal message, yet the targeted celebrity has no way of preventing the fan having access to their personal page or site, nor is the celebrity required to respond. In the absence of a response, the fans, therefore, may never know if their message has been read or whether their messages might have been blocked by the celebrity (Stever and Lawson, 2013).

Twitter provides organisations with a platform on which to engage audiences and through interaction prompt dialogue. This is possible because Twitter gives users the opportunity to interact through response to others, and make the communications roles interchangeable (Mamic and Almaraz, 2013).

Scholars' paper 19.4   Twittering success

Wood, N.T. and Burkhalter, J.N. (2014) Tweet this, not that: a comparison between brand promotions in microblogging environments using celebrity and company-generated tweets, *Journal of Marketing Communications*, 20(1–2), 129–46.

As the use of Twitter increases, this paper provides an insight into the ways in which Twitter can be used in marketing communications. This paper provides good background information about social media and Twitter, and the results of its research indicate that celebrities in a social media context may be influential in drawing attention to unfamiliar brands.

Viral marketing

Viral marketing involves the use of email to convey messages to a small part of a target audience where the content is sufficiently informative, humorous, interesting or persuasive that the receiver feels emotionally compelled to send it on to a friend or acquaintance.

The term 'viral marketing' was developed by a venture capital company, Draper Fisher Juvertson (Juvertson and Draper, 1997). The term was used to describe the Hotmail email service, one of the first free email address services offered to the general public and one that has grown enormously. According to Juvertson (2000: 12), they defined the term simply as 'network-enhanced word-of-mouth'. However, although the literature contains a variety of terminology used to explain what viral marketing is, for example stealth marketing (Kaikati and Kaikati, 2004), *interactive marketing* (Blattberg and Deighton, 1991) and *referral marketing* (De Bruyn and Lilien, 2004), *viral marketing (communications)* is the term used here.

Viral advertising has been defined as 'a persuasive message distributed by an advertiser through an unpaid channel among peers on interactive digital platforms' (Eckler and Rodgers, 2010). It is argued that these messages are usually seeded through the Internet, are often distributed through independent third-party sites, are usually personal, more credible than traditional advertising, and humour is almost invariably employed in executions (Porter and Golan, 2006).

Kirby, a leading viral marketing consultant, agrees, indicating that there are three key elements associated with viral marketing (2003):

- *content*, which he refers to as the 'viral agent', is the quality of the creative material and whether it is communicated as text, image or video;
- *seeding*, which requires identifying websites or people to send email in order to kick-start the virus;

• *tracking*, or monitoring, the impact of the virus and in doing so providing feedback and a means of assessing the return on the investment.

There is no doubt that viral marketing is difficult to control and can be very unpredictable, yet despite these characteristics, organisations are incorporating this approach within their marketing communications in order to reach their target audiences. Increasingly organisations are using word-of-mouth communications to generate conversations before the official (re)launch of a brand. The key reasons for this approach are that it helps identify interested communities and consumer groups and it also encourages feedback, in a similar way to test marketing.

Viewpoint 19.4   Iced water buckets go viral

The 'Ice Bucket Challenge' became a viral sensation in 2014 raising awareness about amyotrophic lateral sclerosis (ALS) disease. In addition the challenge raised millions of dollars for the charity, either through one off donations or the many people who signed up to donate regularly as a result of the awareness generated by the campaign.

The stunt involved people making a video of themselves as they dumped a bucket of iced water on their heads. They then challenged friends and celebrities to do the stunt within 24 hours or donate US$100 to ALS. The video was then posted on various social media sites. Celebrities such as Mark Zuckerberg, David Beckham, Will Smith, Robert Downey Jr, Justin Timberlake, Gary Lineker and Bill Gates all took part. Homer Simpson nominated his neighbour Ned Flanders, friend Lenny and the businessman Donald Trump to also do the challenge, before hilariously pouring a small glass of cold water over his head. Homer then receives a downpour of . . . well this one needs to be watched.

The impact of the viral stunt can be seen in several ways. First the volume of views on YouTube surpassed 23.1 million views in August 2014, after users had uploaded over 16,000 'Ice Bucket Challenge' videos in just a 30-day period in July/August.

Second, copycat challenges were generated for other charities such as Macmillan and the Motor Neurone Disease Association (MDNA). It is alleged that many participants have no idea what the ice bucket

Exhibit 19.6   **Celebrities take on the iced water bucket challenge**
Source: Getty Images/Alan Crowhurst.

challenge was about, for them it was just entertainment. This permits other charities an opportunity to hijack the idea. In addition to this some brands, such as Old Spice, allowed themselves to become involved. Isaiah Mustafa, the contemporary face and body of Old Spice, took on the challenge but could not complete the challenge because his 'perfectly toned man muscles violently reject cold water', as demonstrated by a 'force-field' special effect in the film. After several failed attempts the brand's towel-clad muscle man pledged to donate US$1,000. This ad generated a lot of social media activity and also encouraged many more people to get involved, especially as 'one' of his nominations was every man named John Johnson.

The third perspective concerns the amount of money raised for charity. ALS raised over US$113 million, whilst in the UK, Macmillan raised over £3 million, and MDNA raised almost £3.2 million from 622,000 donors.

Source: Kimberley (2014); On (2014); Steel (2014); Vizard (2014).

Question: To what extent is viral just shared entertainment, and nothing more profound?

Task: Find two viral campaigns that do not seek to entertain viewers with humour-based content.

Podcasting

Podcasting emerged as a major new form of communications in 2005 and has grown significantly since then. This is mainly because of the huge growth in the adoption of MP3 players and the desire for fresh, up-to-date or different content.

Podcasting is a process whereby audio and video content is delivered over the Internet to iPods, MP3 players and computers, on demand. A podcast is a collection of files located at a feed address, which people can subscribe to by submitting the address to an aggregator. When new content becomes available it is automatically downloaded using an aggregator or feed reader which recognises feed formats such as RSS.

In many ways podcasting is similar to radio broadcasts, yet there are a couple of major differences. First, podcast material is pre-recorded and time-shifted so that material can be listened to at a user's convenience – that is, on demand. The second difference is that listeners can take the material they have chosen to listen to, and play it at times and locations that are convenient to them. They can listen to the content as many times as they wish simply because the audio files can be retained.

Podcasting is relatively inexpensive and simple to execute. It opens up publishing to a host of new people, organisations as well as individuals, and it represents a new media channel for audio content. Users have control over what they listen to, when they listen to it and how many times they listen to the content.

Online communities

Armstrong and Hagel (1996) were two of the first researchers to propose the benefits of virtual communities. They also saw that the development of these communities is one of the key elements that differentiate interactive from traditional media. Communities of people who share a common interest(s), who interact, share information, develop understanding and build relationships, all add value, in varying degrees, through their contribution to others involved with the website. In a sense, user groups and special interest groups are similar facilities, but the key with all these variations is the opportunity to share information electronically, often in real time.

Table 19.4 Four types of virtual community

Type of community	Explanation
Purpose	People who are attempting to achieve the same goal or who are experiencing a similar process.
Position	People who are experiencing particular circumstances. These might be associated with life-stage issues (the elderly, the young), health issues or perhaps career development opportunities.
Interest	People who share a hobby, pastime or who are passionately involved with, for example, sport, music, dance, family ancestry, jigsaws, wine, gardening, film, etc.
Profession	People involved with the provision of B2B services. Often created by publishers, these portals provide information about jobs, company news, industry issues and trading facilities, for example auctions.

Chaffey et al. (2006) refer to Durlacher (1999), who argues that there are four main types of community, defined by their purpose, position, interest and profession, as set out in Table 19.4.

Communities can be characterised by several determining elements. Muniz and O'Guinn (2001) identify three core components:

- consciousness of kind: an intrinsic connection that members feel towards one another;
- the presence of shared rituals and traditions that perpetuate the community's history, culture and consciousness;
- a sense of moral responsibility, duty or obligation to the community as a whole and its individual members.

Within these online or virtual communities five particular characteristics can be identified. The first concerns the model of communications, which is essentially visitor-to-visitor and in some cases customer-to-customer. Second, communities create an identity that arises from each individual's involvement and sense of membership and belonging. The more frequent and intense the interaction, the stronger the identity the participants feel with the community.

Third, relationships, even close friendships, develop among members, which in turn can facilitate mutual help and support. The fourth characteristic concerns the language that the community adopts. Very often specialised languages or codes of (electronic) behaviour emerge that have particular meaning to members. The fifth and final characteristic refers to the methods used to regulate and control the behaviour and operations of the community. Self-regulation is important in order to establish acceptable modes of conduct and interaction among the membership.

The role that members assume within these communities and the degree to which they participate also vary. There are members who attend but contribute little, those who create topics, lead discussions, those who summarise and those who perform brokerage or intermediary roles among other members. Edwards (2011) refers to the '1-9-90 rule'. This suggests that 1 per cent of any community are drivers, those who create large amounts of activity. Next, 9 per cent are influencers. These are people who either formally or informally edit, shape, modify and fashion content. The remaining 90 per cent read, observe and consider the community's content; they lurk around the community rather than participate in it. The implication for marketers is that key messages need to reach the drivers and influencers: 10 per cent of the audience.

According to Jepsen (2006) the number of consumers undertaking product information search within virtual communities can be expected to develop simply because the

Table 19.5 Segments in virtual communities

Community segment	Explanation
Insiders	Insiders have strong social ties to other members of the community and consumption and participation is central to their self-image.
Devotees	Devotees participate because of their strong ties and identification with the product.
Minglers	Minglers are tied to some other members but do not have strong associations with the community as a whole or the product.
Tourists	Tourists do not have ties to the product or other members and are transient through the community.

Source: Based on Kozinets (1999).

number of experienced Internet users will grow. The provision and form of online communities will inevitably develop and frameworks will emerge in order that understanding about the way they operate (effectively) is disseminated. Szmigin and Reppel (2004) have offered their customer bonding triangle framework, which is built on interactivity, technical infrastructure and service value elements. It is argued by the authors of this framework that it is the fit between the elements that determines the level of bonding between community members. Further work is required in this area, but this framework provides an interesting conceptualisation of the elements that characterise this approach.

The knowledge held in virtual communities can be expected to be of significant value when searching for product information. In 1999 Kozinets presented four segments related to virtual communities, based around two dimensions. These are presented in Table 19.5.

Jepsen speculates that information provided by the virtual community may be sufficiently strong for insiders that it replaces information from offline sources. This is probably not the case for any of the other three segments.

As a final comment, how should marketers manage all of this activity? Well, apart from developing an integrated approach to marketing communications, strategy and tactics, organisations should learn to listen to social media rather than invade and interrupt them. Coca-Cola has developed a 4Rs model to assist the approach to this important issue. The 4Rs are regarded as pillars of the company's social media strategy: reviewing, responding, recording and redirecting.

Fawkes (2010) explains that conversations around the various Coke brands are tracked by specialist service companies. This review provides insight into the nature of the conversations and the overall sentiment being expressed about the brands. The response is enabled in two ways. Subject matter experts from a variety of departments inside the organisation respond to the specific or unusual queries and questions. A 'blog squad' of social media power users deal with the more general and orthodox questions posed by individuals.

The recording element refers to the development of blogs, podcasts and video material designed to entertain the audiences with compelling content. The redirecting pillar concerns the way Coca-Cola enables people to find and connect with the content that it creates. This is achieved by interconnecting links through Google, Facebook and other major interfaces and search engines, through to MyCokeRewards (see also www.coca-cola.com).

Any discussion of social media and branding should consider the important point made by Fournier and Avery (2011: 193), namely that 'the Web was created not to sell branded products, but to link people together in collective conversational webs'.

At a time when interruptive offline advertising was increasingly more expensive and evaded by consumers at every reasonable opportunity, social media represented an opportunity to lower costs and improve returns. It was first thought that by simply

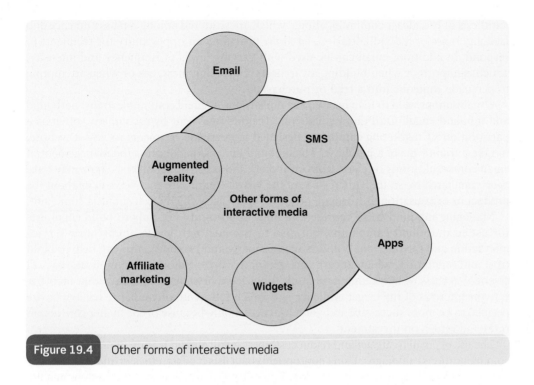

Figure 19.4   Other forms of interactive media

switching budget from offline to online all would be fine. Unfortunately fine it was not, and it is now recognised that brands have struggled to make a significant and harmonious presence in social media. The reality is that the 'technology that was supposed to empower marketers has empowered consumers instead' (p. 193).

Scholars' paper 19.5   **Looking into virtual communities**

Willi, C.H., Melewar, T.C. and Broderick, A.J. (2013) Virtual brand-communities using blogs as communication platforms and their impact on the two-step communication process: a research agenda, *The Marketing Review,* **13(2), 103–23.**

This easy-to-read paper provides excellent coverage of a range of related issues, including blogs, interactive platforms, opinion leadership, the process of adoption, social identity theory and different types of virtual community.

The final part of this chapter considers other forms of interactive media, represented in Figure 19.4.

Other forms of interactive media

Email marketing

There are two key characteristics associated with email communications. First, they can be directed at clearly defined target groups and individuals. Second, email messages can be personalised and refined to meet the needs of individuals. In this sense email is the antithesis of broadcast communications, which are scattered among a mass audience and lack any sense of individualisation, let alone providing an opportunity for recipients to respond. In addition, email can be used with varying levels of frequency and intensity, which is important when building awareness, reinforcing messages or when attempting to persuade someone into a trial or purchase.

Organisations need to manage two key dimensions of email communications: outbound and inbound email. Outbound email concerns messages sent by a company, often as a part of a direct marketing campaign, designed to persuade recipients to visit a website, to take a trial or make a purchase. The inbound dimension concerns the management of email communications received from customers and other stakeholders. These may have been stimulated by an individual's use of the website, exposure to a news item about the product or organisation, or through product experience, which often entails a complaint.

Managing inbound email represents a huge opportunity not only to build email lists for use in outbound campaigns, but also to provide high levels of customer service interaction and satisfaction. If undertaken properly and promptly, this can help to build trust and reputation, which in turn can stimulate word-of-mouth communications – all essential aspects of marketing communications. Activity-triggered emails that incorporate the interests of the target audience and which follow up on audience behaviour are deemed to be more successful and good practice, if only because of the higher conversion rates and return on investment.

The use of email to attract and retain customers is still a main feature of many marketing communications campaigns. Using appropriate email lists is a fast, efficient and effective way to communicate regularly with a market. Email-based marketing communications enables organisations to send a variety of messages concerning public-relations-based announcements, newsletters and sales promotions, to distribute online catalogues and to start and manage permission-based contact lists. Many organisations build their own lists using data collected from their CRM system. By acquiring email responses and other contact mechanisms, addresses and contact details can be captured for the database and then accessed by all customer support staff. The use of email to attract and retain customers has become a main feature of many organisations' marketing communications campaigns. Indeed, email can be used to deliver messages at all points in the customer relationship lifecycle.

Short message service (SMS)

Although different in format, short message service (SMS), or 'texting', can be regarded as an extension of email communications. SMS is a non-intrusive but timely way of delivering information and, as Doyle (2003) points out, the global system for mobile communications (GSM) has become a standard protocol, so that users can send and receive information across geographic boundaries. Apart from pure text, other simple applications consist of games, email notifications, and information-delivery services such as sports and stock market updates.

Yaobin et al. (2010) undertook a study into the reasons why consumers use SMS. The research was based in China, where SMS is used extensively, and the results highlighted three main reasons for use. These concern the perceived utilitarian value of SMS, the level of intrinsic enjoyment and the satisfaction derived from the involvement in communications. The third reason was the relatively low costs of use.

For some time organisations were relatively slow at adopting SMS despite the low costs and high level of user control (target, content and time). However, as organisations recognise these benefits, so SMS has become an integral part of the media mix for many organisations.

Marketers, however, also need to consider the potential concerns of consumers, most notably security and privacy. Just as with email, there is the potential for unwanted messages (i.e. spam) and Internet service providers (ISPs) need to manage the increasing numbers of

Table 19.6 Categories of apps

Type of community	Explanation
Campaign-based	Apps which have high brand-value content but little everyday utility. This means they will attract attention in the short term but will not serve to retain users.
Popular gimmick	Apps characterised by low brand value, which are not very useful. Their value lies in supporting short-term campaigns or events, but they can become obsolete when the campaign finishes. Often good for entertainment purposes, but once seen there is little value in repeating.
Straight utilities	Apps that serve as everyday tools. For example, location finders, currency converters, and recipe and menu directories can be useful but competition is high and stand-out opportunities are rare.
Branded utilities	Apps which are both useful and develop the brand promise. These are considered to be the most powerful types of mobile apps, simply because engagement occurs through the functionality which is tied to the essential value of the brand.

Source: Based on Goddard (2010).

unsolicited messages through improved security systems as SMS becomes more widespread. Given that most consumers pay for SMS functionality, marketers should realise that invading personal privacy greatly reduces the potential value and effectiveness of SMS.

Apps

An app is a mobile application, a piece of software that is downloaded and runs on mobile devices such as smartphones and tablets. Apps enable users to do all sorts of things, from finding a cinema, taxi or restaurant, to reading news, updating a grocery list, or remembering where a car is parked.

From a marketing communications perspective, apps enable a brand to be connected with users as they move around. Some apps can become an integral part of a user's life, some can strengthen brand awareness, and others offer opportunities for more frequent interaction and brand engagement. Apps, however, represent an additional channel and, apart from costs, questions arise about ad effectiveness in a multichannel environment. Xu et al. (2014) find that the use of an app can help sustain awareness in a crowded multichannel context. They also suggest that apps and mobile websites may need to have different digital media strategies if a brand is to gain any significant benefits from having to operate with multiple platforms.

Unsurprisingly, people prefer free apps, which is significant in terms of the limited opportunities brands have to recover the substantial costs necessary to develop a mainstream app. Goddard (2010) suggests that apps can be categorised into four types. These are campaign-based, popular gimmick, straight utility and branded utility (see Table 19.6).

Apps enable brands such as Chanel, Ford, Pepsi, Visa, Lynx and many others to provide users with branded content, as Yuill (2010) suggests, anywhere, at any time, to suit the user.

Affiliate marketing

Associated with the concepts of communities and networks, affiliate marketing has become an essential aspect of online marketing communications and ecommerce. Affiliate schemes are based on a network of websites on which ads or text links are placed.

Table 19.7 Fraudulent affiliate marketing practices

Type of fraud	Explanation
Adware	Software which sees a user's activity and redirects them through an affiliate's marketing link.
Cookie stuffing	Pages designed to repeatedly attract traffic to particular merchants. If a user makes a purchase from that merchant within a predetermined time, often 7–30 days, the affiliate is credited.
Typostuffing	The registration of domain names that are misspellings of merchants' domain names. When a user misspells a merchant's domain name in the way that the affiliate anticipated, the user is redirected to the affiliate's site.
Loyalty software	The placement of 'loyalty' software on a user's computer to remind them about possible rebates, points or other benefits from purchasing through certain merchants. When a user requests a merchant's site directly the loyalty software automatically sends them through an affiliate's link.

Source: Based on Edelman and Brandi (2015).

Those who click on them are taken directly to the host site. If this results in a sale, only then will the affiliate receive a commission, or payment for the ad.

Cookies contain information generated by a web server and stored in a user's computer. These provide fast access to a site and are used to track, monitor and record transactions and pay commission plus any agreed charges. As with many online marketing schemes, management can be undertaken in-house or outsourced. If the latter approach is adopted then many of the relationship issues discussed earlier need to be considered and managed.

Amazon is probably one of the best examples of affiliate marketing schemes. Amazon has thousands of affiliates who all drive visitors to the Amazon website. If a product is sold to the visitor as a result of the click-through, then the affiliate is rewarded with a commission payment. Affiliate schemes are popular because they are low-cost operations, paid on a results-only basis and generating very favourable returns on investment.

Affiliate marketing is, however, open to abuse. Edelman and Brandi (2015) refer to particular types of fraud that some affiliates have commonly undertaken. These are set out in Table 19.7.

Augmented reality

Glasses Direct enables customers to see, online, how they look with different frames. The 'online mirror' technologies behind this facility are referred to as augmented reality (AR). By mixing the real world with digitally generated information or images, AR opens opportunities for both business- and consumer-orientated interactive communications (Clewson, 2009).

It should be noted that AR and virtual reality technologies deliver different effects. Virtual reality systems replace the real world with a simulated environment, whereas AR systems 'overlay computer-generated visual, audio, and haptic signals onto real-world properties in real time' (Roesner et al., 2014: 88).

AR, therefore, allows people to see what they look like in different clothes, without having to get changed into them and, with developments in mobile technology, without a change of location.

AR-based technologies are still developing, but they are increasingly used in mobile applications in connection with location facilities. For example, they can be used as virtual wardrobes, shop fronts, store layouts and as a means of locating shops, tube stations, restaurants, pubs and theatres with a mobile phone. Land Rover has used AR to replicate the showroom experience on people's phones, whilst Fiat and Ford have used the technique to launch new models (Hobbs, 2015).

AR, however, also raises issues concerning privacy and security, particularly in a multichannel environment (Roesner et al., 2014).

Key points

- Social media embrace a range of Internet-based applications, all of which are characterised by two key elements. These are social presence/media richness, and, second, social processes in the form of self-presentation/self-disclosure.

- Social networks are about people using the Internet to share lifestyle and experiences. Participants in these networks also use the interactive capacity to build relationships. The critical aspect of social networks is that the content is user-generated and this means users own, control and develop content according to their needs, not those of a third party.

- The relative immaturity of the social networking arena and the way in which content is developed raise challenges about how organisations can best use social networks as part of their marketing communications to reach their target audiences.

- Viral marketing involves the use of email to convey messages to a small part of a target audience where the content is sufficiently humorous, interesting or persuasive that the receiver feels emotionally compelled to send it on to a friend or acquaintance.

- Blogs are personal online diaries. Business-related or corporate blogs represent huge potential as a form of marketing communications for organisations. This is because blogs reflect the attitudes of the author, and these attitudes can influence others. Micro-blogging is a short-format version of blogging and Twitter is probably the best known.

- Podcasting is a process whereby audio and video content is delivered over the Internet to iPods, MP3 players and computers, on demand. A podcast is a collection of files located at a feed address, which people can subscribe to by submitting the address to an aggregator.

- Online communities are people who share a common interest(s), who interact, share information, develop understanding and build relationships.

- The goal of search engine marketing (SEM) is to drive traffic to websites, and ranking on the search-results page is achieved in two fundamentally different ways. In SEO ranking, searches are based on content, while the PPC approach relies entirely on price as a ranking mechanism.

- Email-based marketing communications enables organisations to send a variety of messages concerning public-relations-based announcements, newsletters and sales promotions, to distribute online catalogues and to start and manage permission-based contact lists.

- An app is a piece of software that is downloaded and runs on mobile devices such as smartphones and tablets. Apps enable a brand to be connected with users as they move around. Some apps can strengthen brand awareness, and others offer opportunities for more frequent interaction and brand engagement.

- Affiliate marketing schemes are based on a network of websites on which advertisements or text links are placed. People who click on them are taken directly to the host site. If this results in a sale, only then will the affiliate receive a commission, or payment for an ad.

Review questions

Greater Manchester Police (GMP) case questions

1. Discuss ways in which brands might imitate GMP's use of social media to engage their target audiences.

2. Appraise the concept of word-of-mouth communications and consider their use within GMP's use of social networks.

3. Make brief notes concerning the ways in which GMP might extend their use of social networks.

4. How might GMP use SMS to improve operational efficiencies?

5. To what extent might the principles of behavioural targeting be used within GMP and other public sector organisations?

General questions

1. Explain the basic principles of search engine marketing.

2. Describe the way in which both search engine optimisation and pay-per-click systems operate.

3. Write a report examining the use of email as a form of marketing communications. Find examples to support the points you make.

4. Goddard (2010) suggests that apps can be categorised into four types. What are they and how are they different?

5. What is a cookie and why are they important to affiliate marketing?

References

Anon (2014) Tumblr is fastest-growing social site, *Warc*, 1 December, retrieved 1 December 2014 from www. warc.com/Latesnews/News/EmailNews.news?ID=33 952&Origin=WARCNewsEmail&CID=N33952& PUB=Warc_News&utm_source=WarcNews&utm_ medium=email&utm_campaign=WarcNews20141201.

Armstrong, A. and Hagel III, J. (1996) The real value of on-line communities, *Harvard Business Review*, 74(3), 134–41.

Blattberg, R.C. and Deighton, J. (1991) Interactive marketing: exploiting the age of addressability, *Sloan Management Review*, 33(1), 5–14.

Cauberghe, V. and de Pelsmacker, P. (2010) Advergames: the impact of brand prominence and game repetition on brand responses, *Journal of Advertising*, 39(1), 5–18.

Chaffey, D., Ellis-Chadwick, F., Johnston, K. and Meyer, R. (2006) *Internet Marketing*, 3rd edition, Harlow: Pearson.

Chambers, J. (2006) The sponsored avatar: examining the present reality and future possibilities of advertising in digital games, retrieved 16 May 2011 from http://ir.lib. sfu.ca/retrieve/1630/8878e0c3d9c0a0bc67670b8d9a0f. doc.

Chang, Y., Yan, J., Zhang, J. and Luo, J. (2010) Online in-game advertising effect: examining the influence of a match between games and advertising, *Journal of Interactive Advertising*, 11(1), 63–73.

Chen, T. and Lee, H.M. (2014) Why do we share? The impact of viral videos dramatized to sell, *Journal of Advertising Research*, 54(3), 292–303.

Chen, J. and Stallaert, J. (2014) An economic analysis of online advertising using behavioral targeting, *MIS Quarterly,* 38(2), 429–49.

Chun, K.Y., Song, J.H., Hollenbeck, C.R. and Lee, J.H. (2013) Are contextual advertisements effective? *International Journal of Advertising,* 33(2), 351–71.

Clarke III, I. (2008) Emerging value propositions for m-commerce, *Journal of Business Strategies,* 25(2), 41–58.

Clewson, T. (2009) Don't believe the hype, *Revolution,* December, 44–7.

Colliander, J. and Dahlén, M. (2011) Following the fashionable friend: the power of social media, *Journal of Advertising Research,* 51(1), 313–20.

De Bruyn, A. and Lilien, G.L. (2004) A multi-stage model of word-of-mouth through electronic referrals, *eBusiness Research Centre Working Paper,* February.

Dichter, E. (1966) How word-of-mouth advertising works, *Harvard Business Review,* 44 (November/December), 147–66.

Doyle, S. (2003) The big advantage of short messaging, retrieved 16 May from www.sas.com/news.

Durlacher (1999) UK on-line community, *Durlacher Quarterly Internet Report,* Q3, 7–11, London.

Eckler, R. and Rodgers, S. (2010) Viral advertising: a conceptualization. Paper presented at the Annual Meeting of the *Association for Education in Journalism and Mass Communication,* Denver, CO.

Edelman, B. and Brandi, W. (2015) Risk, information, and incentives in online affiliate marketing, *Journal of Marketing Research,* LII (February), 1–12

Edwards, J. (2011) Influencer metrics are getting a Klout, *B2B Marketing,* November/December, p. 14.

Fawkes, F. (2010) Coca-Cola's approach to social media, *FSFK,* May 17, retrieved 9 June 2010 from www.psfk.com/2010/05/brand-news-coca-cola%E2%80%99s-approach-to-social-media.html.

Fournier, S. and Avery, J. (2011) The uninvited brand, *Business Horizons,* 54, 193–207.

Goddard, M. (2010) Sizing up a proposed app, *ABA Bank Marketing,* 42(4), 20–23.

Gray, R. (2015) The long haul, *The Marketer,* January/February, 2–31.

Hennig-Thurau, T., Gwinner, K.P., Walsh, G. and Gremler, D.D. (2004) Electronic word-of-mouth via consumer-opinion platforms: what motivates consumers to articulate themselves on the internet? *Journal of Interactive Marketing,* 18(1), 38–52.

Herman, D. (2014) What Google search encryption means for webmasters, *PB&J Interactive,* 10 January, retrieved 27 January 2015 from http://pbjinteractive.com/what-google-search-encryption-means-for-webmasters/.

Hobbs, T. (2015)' Augmented reality can replace the showroom' says Land Rover marketing chief, *Marketing Week,* 2 February, retrieved 3 February 2015 from www.marketingweek.com/2015/02/02/augmented-reality-can-replace-showroom-says-land-rover/.

Jansen, B.J. and Molina, P.R. (2006) The effectiveness of web search engines for retrieving relevant e-commerce links, *Information Processing and Management,* 42(4), July, 1075–98.

Jansen, B.J., Zhang, M., Sobel, K. and Chowdury, A. (2009) Twitter power: tweets as electronic word of mouth, *Journal of the American Society for Information Science and Technology,* 60(11), 2169–88.

Jepsen, A.L. (2006) Information search in virtual communities: is it replacing use of offline communication? *Journal of Marketing Communications,* 12(4), 247–61.

Jerath, K., Ma, L. and Park, Y.H. (2014) Consumer click behavior at a search engine: the role of keyword popularity, *Journal of Marketing Research,* LI (August), 480–6

Jones, C. (2013) How to market your business with vine videos, *QuickBooks,* 30 May, retrieved 15 May 2015 from http://quickbooks.intuit.com/r/marketing/how-to-market-your-business-with-vine-videos/.

Joy, S. (2015) Why social media is mostly a waste of time for marketers: Mark Ritson presentation, *Marketing Week,* 14 January, retrieved 16 February 2015 from www.marketingweek.com/2015/01/14/why-social-media-is-mostly-a-waste-of-time-for-marketers-mark-ritson-presentation/.

Juvertson, S. (2000) *What is Viral Marketing?* Draper Fisher Juvertson website, retrieved 12 March 2006 from www.dfj.com/cgi-bin/artman/publish/printer_steve_may00.shtml.

Juvertson, S. and Draper, T. (1997) *Viral marketing,* Draper Fisher Juvertson website, Retrieved 12 March 2006 from www.dfj.com/cgi-bin/artman/publish/printer_steve_tim_may97.html.

Kaikati, A.M. and Kaikati, J.G. (2004) Stealth marketing: how to reach consumers surreptitiously, *California Management Review,* 46(4), 6–22.

Katona, Z. and Sarvary, M. (2014) Maersk Line: B2B social media – it's communication, not marketing, *California Management Review,* 56(3), Spring, 42–156.

Kaplan, A.M. and Haelein, M. (2010) Users of the world unite! The challenges and opportunities of social media, *Business Horizons,* 53, 59–68.

Kietzmann, J.H., Hermkens, K., McCarthy, I.P. and Silvestre, B.S. (2011) Social media? Get serious! Understanding the functional building blocks of social media, *Business Horizons,* 54(3), 241–51.

Kimberley, S. (2010) Search marketing fails to deliver full potential, *Marketing,* 30 June, p. 7.

Kimberley, S. (2014) Campaign viral chart: Simpson's ice bucket challenge reigns, *campaignlive.co.uk,* 5 September, retrieved 9 January 2014 from www.campaignlive.co.uk/article/1310896/campaign-viral-chart-simpsons-ice-bucket-challenge-reigns.

Kirby, J. (2003) The message should be used as a means to an end, rather than just an end in itself, *VM-People,* 16 October, retrieved 31 August 2007 from www.vm-people.de/en/vmknowledge/interviews/interviews_detail.php?id=15.

Kozinets, R.V. (1999) E-tribalized marketing: the strategic implications of virtual communities on consumption, *European Management Journal,* 17(3), 252–64.

La Fond, P. (2015) Google's 'keyword not provided', *MyInternetScout,* retrieved 27 January 2015 from http://myinternetscout.com/internet-marketing-fundamentals/wordpressinfo/googles-keyword-not-provided/.

Lewis, B. and Porter, L. (2010) In-game advertising effects: examining player perceptions of advertising schema congruity in a massively multiplayer online role-playing game, *Journal of Interactive Advertising,* 10(2), 46–60.

Li, C. and Bernhoff J. (2008) *Groundswell: Winning in a World Transformed by Social Technologies,* Boston, MA: Harvard Business Press.

Lumb, D. (2015) Most valuable followers: how SocialRank wants your brand to get closer to its audience, *Fast Company,* 22 April, retrieved 23 April 2015 from www.fastcompany.com/3045199/tech-forecast/most-valuable-followers-how-socialrank-wants-your-brand-to-get-closer-to-its-a.

Lutz, J., Mackenzie, S.B. and Belch, G.E. (1983) Attitude toward the ad as a mediator of advertising effectiveness, *Advances in Consumer Research,* X. Ann Arbor, MI: Association for Consumer Research.

Mamic, L.I. and Almaraz, I.A. (2013) How the larger corporations engage with stakeholders through Twitter, *International Journal of Market Research,* 55(6), 851–72.

Manning, J. (2014) The new SEO, *The Marketer,* July/August, 33–6.

McCoy, S., Everard, A., Polak, P. and Galletta, D.F. (2007) The effects of online advertising, *Communications of the ACM,* 50, 3 (May), 84–8.

MMA (2015) The mobile native ad formats, *Mobile Marketing Association,* retrieved 1 June 2015 from www.mmaglobal.com/files/documents/the_mobile_native_formats_final.pdf.

Muniz Jr, A.M. and O'Guinn, T.C. (2001) Brand community, *Journal of Consumer Research,* 27(4), 412–32.

Nardi, B.A., Schiano, D.J., Gumbrecht, M. and Swartz, L. (2004) Why we blog, *Communications of the ACM,* 47(12), 41–6.

Norman, R. (2015) Interaction – 2015, *GroupM,* retrieved 11 April 2015 from www.groupm.com/sites/default/files/extra-files/GroupM_Interaction_January2015.pdf.

On, B. (2014) Viral review: Old Spice does ice bucket challenge with a twist, *Marketing magazine,* 29 August, retrieved 9 January 2015 from www.marketingmagazine.co.uk/article/1309996/viral-review-old-spice-does-ice-bucket-challenge-twist.

Osman, B. (2014) Digital advertising: click-through rates, *Coull,* 14 February, retrieved 29 January 2015 from http://coull.com/our-blog/digital-advertising-click-through-rates.

Porter, L. and Golan, G.J. (2006) From subservient chickens to brawny men: a comparison of viral advertising to television advertising, *Journal of Interactive Advertising,* 6(2), 30–8.

Quinton, S. and Fennemore, P. (2012) Missing a strategic marketing trick? The use of online social networks by UK charities, *International Journal for Nonprofit Voluntary Sector Marketing,* 18 (February), 36–51.

Rapaport, D. (2015) Telephone interview and written materials, 12 October.

Roesner, F., Kohno, T. and Molna, D. (2014) Security and privacy for augmented reality systems, *Communications of the ACM,* 57(4), 88–96.

Schneider, L.P. and Cornwell, B.B. (2005) Cashing in crashes via brand placement in computer games, *International Journal of Advertising,* 24(3), 321–43.

Segev, S., Wang, W. and Fernandes, J. (2014) The effects of ad-context congruency on responses to advertising in blogs, *International Journal of Advertising,* 33(1), 17–36.

Sender, T. (2014) *Fashion Online – UK,* London: Mintel.

Steel, E. (2014) 'Ice bucket challenge' has raised millions for ALS Association, *New York Times,* 17 August, retrieved 9 January 2015 from www.nytimes.com/2014/08/18/business/ice-bucket-challenge-has-raised-millions-for-als-association.html?_r=0.

Steele, F. (2010) Twitter unveils advert tweets in bid for profits, *Times Online,* 13 April, retrieved 13 April from http://business.timesonline.co.uk/tol/business/industry_sectors/media/article7095914.ece.

Stever, G.S. and Lawson, K. (2013) Twitter as parasocial interaction, *North American Journal of Psychology,* 15(2), 339–54.

Szmigin, I. and Reppel, A.E. (2004) Internet community bonding: the case of macnews.de, *European Journal of Marketing,* 38(5/6), 626–40.

Truong, Y. and Simmons, G. (2010) Perceived intrusiveness in digital advertising: strategic marketing implications, *Journal of Strategic Marketing,* 18(3), 239–56.

Vizard, S. (2014) The ice bucket challenge: one-hit wonder or the future of fundraising? *Marketing Week,* 29 August, retrieved 9 January 2015 from www.marketingweek.com/2014/08/29/the-ice-bucket-challenge-one-hit-wonder-or-the-future-of-fundraising/.

Wang, K.Y., Shih, E. and Peracchio, L.A. (2013) How banner ads can be effective, *International Journal of Advertising,* 32(1), 121–41.

Warner (2011) Display is dead, *Revolution,* May, 20–5.

Willi, C.H., Melewar, T.C. and Broderick, A.J. (2013) Virtual brand-communities using blogs as communication platforms and their impact on the two-step communication process: a research agenda, *The Marketing Review,* 13(2), 103–23.

Wood, N.T. and Burkhalter, J.N. (2014) Tweet this, not that: a comparison between brand promotions in microblogging environments using celebrity and company-generated tweets, *Journal of Marketing Communications,* 20(1–2), 129–46.

Wood, W., Behling, R. and Haugen, S. (2006) Blogs and business: opportunities and headaches, *Issues in Information Systems,* VII(2), 312–16.

Xu, J., Forman, C., Kim, J.B. and Ittersum, K. van (2014) News media channels: complements or substitutes? Evidence from mobile phone usage, *Journal of Marketing,* 78 (July), 97–112.

Yang, M., Roskos-Ewoldsen, D.R., Dinu, L. and Arpen, L.M. (2006) The effectiveness of in-game advertising: comparing college students' explicit and implicit memory for brand names, *Journal of Advertising,* 35(4), 143–52.

Yaobin, L., Deng, Z. and Bin, W. (2010) Exploring factors affecting Chinese consumers' usage of short message service for personal communication, *Information Systems Journal,* 20(2), 183–208.

Yuill, M. (2009) Smartphones and app stores driving mobile media, *Admap,* 503 (March), retrieved 2 June 2010 from www.warc.com/articlecenter/.

Zenetti, G., Bijmolt, T.H.A., Leeflang, P.S.H. and Klapper, D. (2014) Search engine advertising effectiveness in a multimedia campaign, *International Journal of Electronic Commerce,* 18(3), 7–38.

Chapter 20

Media planning: reaching audiences

Media planning is essentially a selection and scheduling exercise. The selection concerns the choice of media vehicles to carry messages on behalf of the advertiser. With media fragmentation, audiences are switching between media with greater regularity, which impacts on media scheduling. Decisions regarding the number of occasions, timing and duration that a message is exposed, in the selected vehicles, to the target audience have become increasingly critical.

In addition, ideas about owned and earned media, and social media and search in particular, have changed the way media are understood by marketers and used by consumers. This impacts on the way in which media selection has changed and how it should be managed.

Aims and learning objectives

The aims of this chapter are to introduce the fundamental elements of media planning, and to set out some of the issues facing media planners.

The learning objectives are to enable readers to:

1. explain the principles associated with media planning and highlight the impact of media and audience fragmentation;

2. evaluate the various theories concerning different media and related switching behaviours;

3. examine the key concepts used in linear media selection: reach and cover, frequency, duplication, rating points and CPT;

4. appreciate the concept of repetition and the debate concerning effective frequency and recency planning;

5. discuss planning issues related to interactive media and scheduling;

6. introduce media source effects as an important factor in media selection, placement and timing.

Kärcher: Window Vac

Kärcher is a family-owned company that operates worldwide. Business success has been built on the manufacture and sales of specialised cleaning machinery. Of these, high-pressure washers have made a significant contribution, accounting for 87 per cent of Kärcher's UK Home and Garden turnover in 2011. A combination of high product quality and consistently favourable product reviews supported this success, one reflected in our strong 62.3 per cent market share (value) in 2011. This has also enabled Kärcher to develop strong and positive relationships with the trade, one based on high levels of trust. However, the heavy reliance on pressure washers, sales that are highly seasonal, and the prospect of longer hotter summers with the accompanying threat of hosepipe bans, drove Kärcher UK to introduce its latest cleaning innovation, the Window Vac. This was designed to make streak-free window cleaning, effortless.

Following a launch in France and Germany it was decided to launch the Window Vac in the UK. Consumer awareness of the Kärcher brand in the UK is not as high as in France and Germany, and the initial reaction of the trade to the Window Vac was sceptical – until they had seen it operating, when their attitude changed dramatically. This indicated that we needed our launch communications to engage audiences in order to build awareness of the Window Vac, clarify what it offered in terms of effectiveness and ease of use, and then propel consumer behaviour in order to help achieve the sales target of 300,000 units in the first year.

The target audience was female ABC1C2 30+ and the high visual impact of the message meant that TV had to be the primary media. The target audience was known to prefer classic light television, their viewing focused around soaps, dramas, popular comedy, crime and documentaries at peak-time. With a media budget of less than £1 millon it was crucial to get the right media vehicles.

It was also important to get the right timing for the launch campaign. People are motivated to start cleaning their windows in the Spring, especially when the clocks move forward to British Summer Time and the additional hour of daylight highlights streaky windows. So Kärcher UK decided to constrain the use of TV to a 4-week period from 26 March 2012. We used a 30-second ad appearing in peak programming from Wednesday to Sunday each week.

This timing coincided with the increased traffic experienced by our key retailers, of which B&Q, Homebase and Argos are critical partners. To support the TV campaign, press, radio, online and VOD were used to provide more information and increase OTS. Press was highly targeted via niche magazines and was supported by digital advertising. Radio was timed to reach consumers in their cars or at the weekend, when they

Exhibit 20.1   **A scene from the Kärcher television ad**
Source: Kärcher (U.K.) Ltd.

Kärcher WV comms	2012										2013									
	Mar	Apr	May	Jun	Jul	Aug	Sep	Oct	Nov	Dec	Jan	Feb	Mar	Apr	May	Jun	Jul	Aug	Sep	Oct
TV																				
VOD																				
Digital																				
Press																				
Outdoor																				
Radio																				

Figure 20.1   Kärcher Window Vac media laydown 2012 and 2013

were most likely to be visiting outlets which stocked Window Vac. In-store displays and demonstrations were also important.

This first TV burst of 308 TVRs was seen by 75 per cent of the target on average four times, three of these within the first two weeks of airtime. Crucial to maximising visibility was the time of day and position in both programme and break. Rather than dissipate the limited budget across a number of small audiences to make it work harder, the majority of activity ran in early and late peak using shows which were likely to attract large audiences. Spots were secured in programme centre breaks and first, second or last position in break.

As soon as TV went on air in March 2012 sales responded straight away. From selling an average of 1,600 units per week, Kärcher sold an average of 17,300 per week over the 10 weeks on air. This was equivalent to a weekly turnover of £865,000 at RSP. An entire year's target of 300,000 units was exceeded within 3 months of the campaign going on air.

Exhibit 20.2   Window Vac on its cardboard fixture in a retail store
Source: Kärcher (U.K.) Ltd.

The initial econometric analysis revealed that:

- TV not only worked extremely well but with very long-lasting effects – once TV came off air, its effect only decayed at 2 per cent per week;

- the north of the country responded even more strongly than the south in terms of the proportion of households buying;

- radio had very limited effects – a more visual medium was needed to get Window Vac's raison d'être and fantastic performance across;

- in-store demos (the experiential bit) did work well (as a short-term sales boost).

Kärcher UK then spent a further £549,000 with a second burst of TV in September 2012. This campaign was restricted to TV, and the ad was cut from 30 to 20 seconds. Again, sales responded immediately, and two further bursts of TV in April and September the following year were implemented. This totalled an overall investment of £2,713,490 across all media, which included TV, radio, VOD, press and digital. From launch to October 2013, 830,000 Window Vac units were sold, over 80 per cent of these directly attributable to the campaign.

The media campaign, most particularly the TV element, played a significant part in the success of Window Vac's launch, accounting for 35 per cent of total sales. Taking 2012 and 2013 together, the Window Vac campaign produced a revenue ROI of £20.60 for every £1 invested.

This case study was written by Phil Springall, Marketing Manager for Kärcher UK

Questions relating to this case can be found at the end of this chapter.

Introduction

The Kärcher case demonstrates how devising an optimum mix of media channels for the delivery of a message to a target audience is an integral part of effective marketing communications. Media (or channel) planning is normally undertaken by specialists, either as part of a full-service advertising agency or as a media independent whose primary function is to buy airtime or space from media owners (e.g. television contractors or magazine publishers) on behalf of their clients, the advertisers. This traditional role has evolved and many media independents now provide consultancy services, particularly at the strategic level, plus planning and media research and auditing services.

Media departments are responsible for two main functions. These are to 'plan' and to 'buy' time and space in appropriate media vehicles. There is a third task – to monitor a media schedule once it has been bought – but this is a function of buying. Traditionally planners define the target audience and then choose the best type of media to reach the audience. Buyers choose programmes, frequencies, spots and distribution, and assemble a multichannel schedule.

This chapter is concerned with the various issues associated with the selection, optimisation and scheduling of media. However, ideas about what constitutes media have changed considerably in recent years and the prevalence of interactive media and the importance of owned and earned media are reshaping media planning. Much of the first part of this chapter is concerned with the management of linear media. Issues relating to the incorporation and management of interactive media are considered later in this chapter.

The increasingly rich array of media opportunities begs many questions but of these one should ask whether advertisers need to concentrate on linear or interactive media formats? The answer to this question, according to Dahlen and Edenius (2007), appears to be that advertisers can improve communications effectiveness by placing ads in both linear and interactive advertising media.

Clutter

Before we explore media planning it is helpful to consider the context in which it occurs. Primarily the environment in which media vehicles are selected for a campaign is cluttered with a proliferation of different media and ad formats. This clutter, which according to Hammer et al. (2009: 159) is 'at an all-time high', affects the choices that consumers make, the placements of ads, and the potency of ads to cut through the clutter and engage the intended audience.

Ha and McCann (2008) see clutter as the 'high degree of intrusiveness and high frequency of advertising in an editorial vehicle'. The issue for clients is that although people might see more ads, it is believed that clutter reduces the effectiveness of advertising, if only because audiences attempt to avoid it.

Hammer et al. (2009) found that advertising avoidance behaviours are the same where clutter is both low and high. People exposed to more clutter do see more advertising, but they remember less of it. When there is less clutter, audiences remember a greater proportion of the ads they were exposed to. However, it does not improve people's ability to identify a brand. Furthermore, there does not appear to be any proportional changes to these effects, so that reducing clutter by 50 per cent does not double the number of ads recalled. This means that reducing the number of ads carried in a media vehicle is not necessarily going to result in a higher level of recall. Advertisers can improve effectiveness in high-clutter contexts by ensuring their ads are likeable. Using a strong creative and emphatic branding might increase cut-through, enabling higher brand recall scores.

Although clutter refers to the level of advertising within a media vehicle, it is partly a function of the increasing number of ad formats. These are increasing because of technological developments and advertisers are using them because of the difficulty they have not only reaching but also engaging people with traditional media-based campaigns (Pelsmaker and Neijens, 2009).

Media planning and the media mix

As mentioned earlier, media planning is essentially a selection and scheduling exercise. Traditionally media planning was concerned with the selection of paid media vehicles to carry a message on behalf of an advertiser. Indeed, many of the concepts referred to later have their origins in linear, paid-for media.

Scheduling refers to the number of occasions, timing and duration that a message is exposed, in the selected vehicles, to the target audience. Kärcher had identified its target audience and understood that TV was going to be the primary media. Kärcher's crucial decision was to decide when to start the campaign, how long it should run, and which programmes it was to be scheduled against in order to reach the audience.

There are several factors, however, that complicate these seemingly straightforward tasks. First, the variety of available media is huge and increasing rapidly. This proliferation of the media is referred to as *media fragmentation*. Although consumers benefit from a wider choice, advertisers and media owners are faced with smaller audiences, resulting in the former seeking cost efficiencies and the latter using differentiation approaches. One of the efficiency strategies used by advertisers is called audience targeting. These seek to match the profile of the product/brand user to that of the media vehicle (Nelson-Field and Riebe, 2011).

Second, the characteristics of the target audience are changing equally quickly. This is referred to as *audience fragmentation*. Both these fragmentation issues are discussed later in this chapter. The job of the media planner is complicated by one further element: money. Clients have restricted financial resources and require their media planners to create schedules that deliver their messages not only effectively but also efficiently, which means within the parameters of the available budget.

The task of a media planner, therefore, is to deliver advertising messages through a selection of media that matches the viewing, reading, listening or search habits of the largest possible number of people in the target audience, at the lowest possible cost. In order for these tasks to be accomplished, three sets of decisions need to be made about the choice of media, vehicles and schedules.

Decisions about the choice of media are complex. While choosing a single one is reasonably straightforward, choosing media in combination and attempting to generate synergistic effects is far from easy. Advances in technology have made media planning a much faster, more accurate process, one that is now more flexible and capable of adjusting to fast-changing market conditions.

One of the key tasks of the media planner, therefore, is to decide which combination of vehicles should be selected to carry the message to the target audience. In addition, McLuhan (1966) said that 'the medium is the message': that is, the choice of medium (or vehicle) says something about the brand and the message it is carrying. He went on to say that 'the medium is the *massage*, as each medium massages the recipient in different ways and so contributes to learning in different ways'. For example, Krugman (1965) hypothesised that television advertising washes over individuals. He said that viewers, rather than participating actively with television advertisements, allow learning to occur passively. In contrast, magazine advertising requires active participation if learning is to occur. Today, online and interactive advertising actively promotes involvement and participation.

Table 20.1 A summary of media characteristics

Type of paid media	Strengths	Weaknesses
Interactive Media	High level of interaction Immediate response possible Tight targeting Low absolute and relative costs Flexible and easy to update Measurable	Segment-specific Slow development of infrastructure High user set-up costs Transaction security issues Privacy issues
Print Newspapers	Wide reach High coverage Low costs Very flexible Short lead times Speed of consumption controlled by reader	Short lifespan Advertisements get little exposure Relatively poor reproduction, gives poor impact Low attention-getting properties
Magazines	High-quality reproduction that allows high impact Specific and specialised target audiences High readership levels Longevity High levels of information can be delivered	Long lead times Visual dimension only Slow build-up of impact Moderate costs

Continued

Type of paid media	Strengths	Weaknesses
Television	Flexible format, uses sight, movement and sound High prestige High reach Mass coverage Low relative cost, so very efficient	High level of repetition necessary Short message life High absolute costs Clutter Increasing level of fragmentation (potentially)
Radio	Selective audience, e.g. local Low costs (absolute, relative and production) Flexible Can involve listeners	Lacks impact Audio dimension only Difficult to get audience attention Low prestige
Outdoor	High reach High frequency Low relative costs Good coverage as a support medium Location-oriented	Poor image (but improving) Long production time Difficult to measure
Transport	High length of exposure Low costs Local orientation	Poor coverage Segment-specific (travellers) Clutter

The various media depicted in Table 20.1 have wide-ranging characteristics. These, and the characteristics of the target audience, should be considered when deciding on the optimal media mix. It should be clear that simply deciding on which media to use is fraught with difficulties, let alone deciding on the optimal combination – how much of each medium should be used, before even considering the cost implications. Viewpoint 20.1 demonstrates how the media mix has evolved within the music industry.

Viewpoint 20.1   Evolving mixes within the music industry

Music artists and their record labels use a variety of media to reach their audiences. Live music has always been popular and in the 1940s and 1950s and print media was prominent. Using local, regional and national advertising in newspapers and specialist magazines, plus the use of posters and billboards, big bands and music artists were able to publicise their events. Radio also enabled fans to listen to their favourite music from home.

Broadcast media became the dominant format in the 1960s and 1970s. First, commercial radio (pirate) stations such as Radio Luxembourg enabled people to listen to popular music. But, as BBC Radio 1 became established and as television ownership increased, so programmes such as *Top of the Pops* and *Ready, Steady, Go* provided additional, important routes to mass audiences for bands such as the Beatles and Fleetwood Mac, and artists such as Bob Dylan, Dionne Warwick and Cher.

Underground genres such as Punk, most notably the Sex Pistols, and New Romantic artists, used broadcast and print media, but they also developed the use of outdoor media. They used posters as a low-key and cost-effective way of targeting audiences for promotional gigs and acoustic nights. Visual art was a key medium within the subculture, and extremely important for marketing the punk aesthetic. At this time retail record shops were an important in-store medium. These featured highly visual, vinyl record covers. These provided important packaging services but they were also regarded as an important medium for helping to differentiate artists and provide added value.

Exhibit 20.3   **Radio Caroline, an offshore pirate radio station**
Source: Rex Shutterstock/Denis Jones/Associated Newspapers.

The rise of the digital era and the CD meant that fans could now listen to their favourite artists on the go. The MP3 download meant that music could be downloaded anywhere, any time. Other forms of both indoor and outdoor communications include the use of guerilla marketing. Used by artists and companies with low funds, they use a mix of graffiti, stickers, flash mobs and publicity stunts to make their product and services stand out.

Nowadays, there is a multitude of media channels available to artists. Print, broadcast, especially TV music video channels, and digital through social media, and specific music websites, provide a rich array for audiences to access music. YouTube, for example, offers an unlimited amount of music videos, a large proportion of which are posted by fans.

The latest addition to the media mix are streaming services. With a connection through social networks, these services allow people to see what music their friends, family and colleagues are listening to. Streaming services such as Spotify and Pandora have dramatically changed the way music is consumed. Streaming has also reduced the rate of illegal downloads.

The evolution of the media mix has increased the reach and frequency with which audiences can be entertained by their preferred music artists. Fans can now control and access their preferred music whenever they like. They can share it globally, 24/7. Gone are the days when access to music was controlled by those who owned particular media, and with it the days when tight planning was possible across the whole media mix.

Source: Anon (2015); Mansfield (2012); Poynor (2012); Sylvester (2013).

This Viewpoint was written by Eloise Augustine when she was a student at Buckinghamshire New University.

Question: Why is the media mix harder to plan and implement today?

Task: Select an album or gig/tour of a preferred music artist and list the media used to promote the artist.

Media switching behaviour

Even before the arrival of interactive media, researchers had recognised that different media have different capabilities and that media were not completely interchangeable. In other words, different tasks can be accomplished more effectively using particular media. This implies that there is a spectrum of media depending on the content they carry.

Increasingly people use multiple media, sometimes in a near simultaneous format but more often in a sequential manner. Understanding the reasons why particular media are chosen in any one communications context is important for advertisers, but so far there is no single complete theory that explains media choice (George et al., 2013).

Daft and Lengel (1984) were the first to propose that this content issue concerned the richness of the information conveyed through each medium. As a result, the tasks facing managers should be considered according to the degree of fit with the most appropriate media based on the richness of the information. Communications media help resolve ambiguity and facilitate understanding in different ways and to different degrees. They established that there were four main criteria that determined what level of richness a medium possessed:

- the availability of instant feedback;
- the capacity to transmit multiple cues;
- the use of natural language;
- the degree of personal focus.

Media richness theory (MRT) holds that there is a hierarchy or spectrum of media ranging from personal or face-to-face encounters as the richest media through to single sheets of text-based information as lean media at the other end. Rich media facilitate feedback, dialogue iteration and an expression of personal cues such as tone of voice, body language and eye contact that, in turn, help establish a personal connection. In descending order of richness the other media are telephone, email, letter, note, memo, special report, fliers and bulletins. At this end of the richness scale numeric and formal written communications are slow, often visually limited and impersonal.

MRT suggests that rich media reduce ambiguity more effectively than others, but are more resource-intensive than lean media. If rich media allow for more complex and difficult communications, then lean media are more cost-effective for simple or routine communications. McGrath and Hollingshead (1993) developed a matrix

Table 20.2 A media richness grid

	Computer text systems	Audio systems	Video systems	Face-to-face communications
Generating ideas and plans	Good fit	Marginal fit: medium too resource-intense	Poor fit: medium too resource-intense	Poor fit: medium too resource-intense
Choosing correct answer: intellectual tasks	Marginal fit: medium too constrained	Good fit	Good fit	Poor fit: medium too resource-intense
Choosing preferred answer: judgement tasks	Poor fit: medium too constrained	Good fit	Good fit	Marginal fit: medium too resource-intense
Negotiating conflicts of interest	Poor fit: medium too constrained	Poor fit: medium too constrained	Marginal fit: medium too constrained	Good fit

Source: Adapted from McGrath and Hollingshead (1993).

showing the levels of richness required to perform certain tasks successfully and efficiently. Their media richness grid identifies the level of fit between the information richness requirements of the tasks and the information richness capacity of the media (see Table 20.2).

Social influence theory (SIT) was developed by Fulk et al. (1990). This is intended to complement MRT as it also assumes that the relatively objective features of media do influence how individuals perceive and use media. However, these researchers argue that SIT has a strong social orientation because different media properties (such as ability to transmit richness) are subjective and are influenced by attitudes, statements and the behaviour of others. This approach recognises that members of groups influence other people in terms of their perceptions of different media. The main difference between MRT and SIT is that MRT identifies rich media as inefficient for simple or routine communications whereas SIT suggests rich media can be just as appropriate for simple messages as they are for ambiguous communications.

A third approach, the technology acceptance model (TAM), relates to the utility and convenience a medium offers. The perceived usefulness and perceived ease of use are regarded as the main issues that are considered when selecting media (King and Xia, 1997). Perceived usefulness refers to the user's subjective assessment that using a specific computer application will improve their job performance. Perceived ease of use addresses the degree to which a user expects the identified application to be free of effort.

Scholars' paper 20.1   Understanding media choice

George, J.F., Carlson, J.R. and Valacich, J.S. (2013) Media selection as a strategic component of communication, *MIS Quarterly*, 37(4), 1233–51.

In an attempt to better understand how people make decisions about the media they use, these researchers investigate how communications strategies and media characteristics affect choice. The paper provides a useful consideration of the issues relating to media selection and explores several interesting theories including media synchronicity theory.

Table 20.3 Factors influencing the choice of technology

Factor	Explanation
Experience and familiarity	With virtual operations, the amount of experience using a particular interactive medium.
Permanence	The degree to which users need an historical record of team interactions or decisions.
Symbolic meaning	The subjective meanings attached to the use of a particular medium.
Time constraints	The amount of time available to the user to use a medium in order to execute their tasks.
Access to technology and/or support	The number of and access to available media influences media choice.

Source: Duarte and Snyder (2001).

Influential factors for media selection

In addition to these richness, social and utility issues of media selection, other factors are also important. Duarte and Snyder (2001) propose a list of factors influencing technology selection (see Table 20.3).

Switching behaviour

It is clear that different media have different properties and that people switch between media according to their tasks, social environment, familiarity and access to different media. What is important, therefore, is to understand switching behaviour and the decision-making process that people use. Decisions are made through *rational* and *systematic* processes or alternatively there are unaccountable factors that 'bound' decision-making. The classic, eight-stage rational–linear decision-making model (situation analysis, objectives setting, through to choosing and evaluating alternatives, making the decisions, evaluation and consequences) is well known and its criticisms well documented. Simon (1972, 1987) showed that people make decisions within 'bounded rationality', performing limited searches and accepting the first acceptable alternative, what is regarded as 'satisficing behaviour'.

Srinavasan (1996) developed a satisfaction–loyalty curve whereby an individual's level of satisfaction is the biggest determinant of their switching behaviour. As their satisfaction increases, so does loyalty, and the reverse is equally true. For each person there is a point at which decreasing satisfaction intersects with the decreasing loyalty levels. This is the point at which switching occurs and the current brand is abandoned in favour of another.

Keaveney (1995) distinguishes between involuntary, simple and complex switching behaviours. Involuntary switching may be due to factors beyond an individual consumer's control (e.g. business liquidated), whereas simple switching is characterised by individual events where consumers can identify a single incident or factor causing the switch: for example, a price change. Complex switching behaviour occurs when a customer's loyalty has decreased due to a variety of factors, which might include core product failure, price changes and poor service. It should be noted that switching is very often a routine behaviour influenced by the expectations of the context in which the media decision is made. For example, when sending text-based documents to team members, most people would select email and use file attachments.

Table 20.4 Reasons for moving to richer or leaner media

Movement	Reasons
Towards a richer medium	Message complexity
	Increased comfort
	Time pressure
	Timely discussion required
	Need to rest from computer-based medium
Towards a leaner medium	Desire for written record
	Reducing cost
	Convenience (of being asynchronous or distant)
	Share individual written work (attachment)
	External pressure or requirement

As a final comment on media switching behaviour, it is useful to return to MRT and to consider the reasons why individuals move towards rich or lean media. These are set out in Table 20.4. Therefore, movement between media is based on a range of criteria and will vary according to the context and individual skills and preferences.

Vehicle selection

In addition to using their owned media, organisations need to use media that are owned by others in order to convey their messages effectively. These paid-for media have particular characteristics and ability to deliver rich or lean content. The discussion now moves on to consider different paid-for media and the ways in which organisations develop a media mix to meet their communications needs.

Increasingly, organisations are required to prove how advertising adds value to the bottom line. While this is not a new question, it is one that is being asked more often and in such a way that answers are required. As advertisers attempt to demonstrate effectiveness, contribution and return on investment, senior managers are increasingly haunted

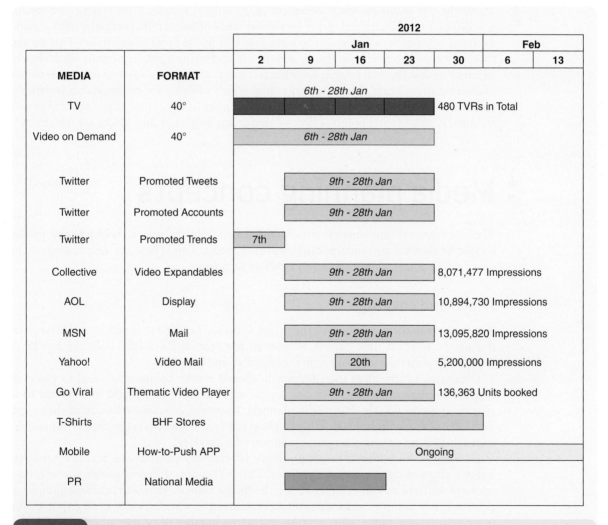

Figure 20.2 Overall activity used by the British Heart Foundation in the Vinnie campaign (see the case study at the start of Chapter 2)

by questions concerning the choice of media, how much should be spent on message delivery and how financial resources are to be allocated in a multichannel environment.

Management's attention towards media decision-making has increased as the media have become more visible and significantly more important. Companies such as Kärcher, BT, IKEA and ScottishPower need to use media strategically in order that they reach the right audience, in the right context, at the right time and at an acceptable cost. For example, the Kärcher media laydown presented in the case study at the beginning of this chapter shows that the media used, and their timing, were crucial to the success of the campaign. Similarly the media scheduling shown in Figure 20.2 for the BHF's Vinnie campaign (presented at the beginning of Chapter 2) shows how media can be used to build engagement to achieve specific goals.

To help organisations achieve these goals a variety of approaches have been adopted. This division provides objectivity, reduces partisan approaches and can deliver more effective media plans. Cost per response is certainly one way of measuring effectiveness, but the communications impact, or share of mind, is also important. There has also been a move away from volume of media to one where media decisions are made by looking at media in the context of the brand's total communications.

A further problem facing clients and media agencies concerns the quality of the integrated media experience. For a long time, some organisations in the UK have used above-the-line media to reach audiences of 20 million people. With fragmented media it is difficult to generate consistent levels and types of impact. Increasingly, media management is being outsourced so there are fewer in-house areas of expertise. This means that, to forge appropriate solutions, advertisers and media agencies need to work closely together so that the relationship becomes so close that it acts more as an extension to the marketing department. Decisions regarding which vehicles are to carry an advertiser's message depend on an understanding of a number of concepts: reach and coverage, frequency, gross rating points, effective frequency, efficiency and media source effects.

Media planning concepts

There are several fundamental concepts that underpin the way in which linear media should be selected and incorporated within a media plan. These are reach, frequency, gross rating points, duplication and effective frequency.

Reach and coverage

Reach refers to the percentage of the target audience exposed to a message at least once during the relevant time period. Where 80 per cent of the target audience has been exposed to a message, the figure is expressed as an '80 reach'.

Coverage, a term often used for reach, should not be confused or used in place of reach. Coverage refers to the size of a potential audience that might be exposed to a particular media vehicle. For media planners, therefore, coverage (the size of the target audience) is very important. Reach will always be lower than coverage, as it is impossible to reach 100 per cent of a target population (the universe).

Building reach within a target audience is relatively easy, as the planner needs to select a range of different media vehicles. This will enable different people in the target audience to have an opportunity to see the media vehicle. However, there will come a point when it becomes more difficult to reach people who have not been exposed. As more vehicles are added, so repetition levels (the number of people who have seen the advertisement more than once) also increase.

Frequency

Frequency refers to the number of times a member of the target audience is exposed to a media vehicle (not the advertisement) during the relevant time period. It has been stated that targets must be exposed to the media vehicle, but to say that a target has seen an advertisement simply because they have been exposed to the vehicle is incorrect. For example, certain viewers hop around the channels as a commercial break starts. This has been referred to as 'channel grazing' by Lloyd and Clancy (1991). Individuals have different capacities to learn and to forget, and how much of a magazine does a reader have to consume to be counted as having read an advertisement? These questions are still largely unanswered, so media planners have adopted an easier and more consistent measure – opportunities to see (OTS).

This is an important point. The stated frequency level in any media plan will always be greater than the advertisement exposure rate. The term 'OTS' is used to express the reach of a media vehicle rather than the actual exposure of an advertisement. However, a high OTS could be generated by one of two different events. First, a large number of the target audience are exposed once (high reach) or, second, a small number are exposed several times (high frequency).

This then raises the first major issue. As all campaigns are restricted by time and budget limitations, advertisers have to trade off reach against frequency. It is impossible to maximise both elements within a fixed budget and set period of time.

To launch a new product, it has been established that a wide number of people within the target audience need to become aware of the product's existence and its salient attributes or benefits. This means that reach is important but, as an increasing number of people become aware, so more of them become exposed a second, third or fourth time, perhaps to different vehicles. At the outset, frequency is low and reach high, but as a campaign progresses so reach slows and frequency develops. Reach and frequency are inversely related within any period of time, and media planners must know the objective of a campaign: is it to build reach or develop frequency?

Scholars' paper 20.2   **Digital says no to reach and frequency**

Cheong, Y., De Gregorio, F. and Kim, K. (2011) The power of reach and frequency in the age of digital advertising: offline and online media demand different metrics, *Journal of Advertising Research*, 50(4), 403–15.

This empirical paper explored the use of reach and frequency concepts. The findings are that the concepts are still used to evaluate offline media schedules. However, the use and practicality in online contexts is more limited, with agencies using qualitative and cost-based measures.

Gross rating point

To decide whether reach or frequency is the focus of the campaign objective, a more precise understanding of the levels of reach and frequency is required. The term *gross rating point* (or broadly in television a TVR) is used to express the relationship between these two concepts. GRPs are a measure of the total number of exposures (OTS) generated within a particular period of time. The calculation itself is simply reach × frequency:

$$\text{reach} \times \text{frequency} = \text{gross rating point}$$

Media plans are often determined on the number of GRPs generated during a certain time period. For example, the objective for a media plan could be to achieve 450 GRPs in a burst (usually four or five weeks). However, as suggested earlier, caution is required when interpreting a GRP, because 450 GRPs may be the result of 18 message exposures to just 25 per cent of the target market. It could also be an average of nine exposures to 50 per cent of the target market.

Rating points are used by all media as a measurement tool, although they were originally devised for use with broadcast audiences. GRPs are based on the total target audience (e.g. all women aged 18–34, or all adults) that might be reached, but a media planner needs to know, quite rightly, how many GRPs are required to achieve a particular level of effective reach and what levels of frequency are really required to develop effective learning or awareness in the target audience. In other words, how can the effectiveness of a media plan be improved?

Viewpoint 20.2   Media mix transparency at Anglian

The formulation and delivery of the right media mix has been a challenge for many organisations. Anglian, the home improvement company, experimented with various combinations of media to determine which configuration of the media mix works best for them.

Anglian's traditional mix includes press, radio, DRTV, direct mail and door drops. With a campaign to promote its replacement windows, the company experimented with different combinations of three of these media.

Unsurprisingly they found that direct mail works best when implemented at the end of a television campaign, as awareness levels have been raised. Television worked best when used with press and door drops and direct mail worked best with current customers. As a result of the experiments, radio was removed from the Anglian's media mix.

Anglian also reviewed the effectiveness of their website. One of their goals was to increase the number of leads generated from their paid search activities. Analysis found that there was an unusually high bounce rate (66 per cent) from the page visitors first encounter when clicking through from another site or sponsored link. This page is known as the landing page and bounce refers to a failure to click through the site from the landing page. It was found that the page did not contain the information or even products that visitors were looking for, despite clicking on a link that suggested a match.

Changes were made to the information provided about the products, prices and images were included, and they tested changes to the title to the form used by prospects when responding to 'Get a free quote' and 'Get a call back' to see which one worked best. Online price discounts, price-matching promises and pick & mix sale offers were all incorporated.

One of the results of this landing page work was that the 'Get a call back' invitation generated a 108 per cent increase in conversions.

Source: Anon (2009); Benjamin (2009).

Question: Why do you think Anglian did not incorporate the website in their experiment to determine the optimum media mix?

Task: Go to the Anglian website www.anglianhome.co.uk and make a list of the ways they prompt people into further action.

Homer (2009) reports that media and audience fragmentation has resulted in lower ratings across media. Referring to Ephron (2003), to achieve the same impact as in 1980 it now requires 100 spots instead of 10 to drive 100 ratings. This has led advertisers to increase their frequency of advertising, which effectively is an increase in repetition. However, although research shows that a low to moderate increase in repetition does enhance persuasion, at high levels, wear-out and tedium occur, which leads to a decline in a liking of that particular stimulus (Batra and Ray, 1986).

Effective frequency

There are a number of reasons why considering the effectiveness of a media plan has become more important in recent years. First, there is the combination of media and audience fragmentation plus increasing media costs. Second, there is short-termism, increased managerial accountability and intensifying competition. This last point about competition refers to the media planning industry itself and the restructuring and concentration of media buying points (centralisation) in response to clients' globalisation strategies and their need for more cost-effective ways of buying media.

Frequency refers to the number of times members of the target audience are exposed to the vehicle. It says nothing about the quality of the exposures and whether any impact was made. Effective frequency refers to the number of times an individual needs to be exposed to an advertisement before the communications are effective. Being exposed once or possibly twice is unlikely to affect the disposition of the receiver. But the big question facing media planners is: how many times should a message be repeated for effective learning to occur? The level of effective frequency is generally unknown, but there has been some general agreement following work by Krugman (1972) that, for an advertisement to be effective (to make an impact), a target should have at least three OTS, the three-hit theory. The first exposure provokes a 'What is this?' reaction, the second reaction is 'What does this mean to me?' The reaction to the third is 'Oh, I remember' (du Plessis, 1998). The three-exposure theory is based on messages that first provide understanding, second, provide recognition and, third, actually stimulate action. More than 10 exposures is regarded as an ineffective plan and hence a waste of resources.

Determining the average frequency partially solves the problem. This is the number of times a target reached by the schedule is exposed to the vehicle over a particular period of time. For example, a schedule may generate the following:

10 per cent of the audience is reached ten times ($10 \times 10 = 100$)

25 per cent of the audience is reached seven times ($25 \times 7 = 175$)

65 per cent of the audience is reached once ($65 \times 1 = 65$)

Total $= 340$ exposures

Average frequency $= 340/100 = 3.4$

This figure of average frequency is misleading because different groups of people have been reached with varying levels of frequency. In the example above, an average frequency of 3.4 is achieved but 65 per cent of the audience is reached only once. This means that the average frequency, in this example, may lead to an audience being underexposed.

Members of the target audience do not buy and read just one magazine or watch a single television programme. Consumer media habits are complex, although distinct patterns can be observed, but it is likely that a certain percentage of the target audience will

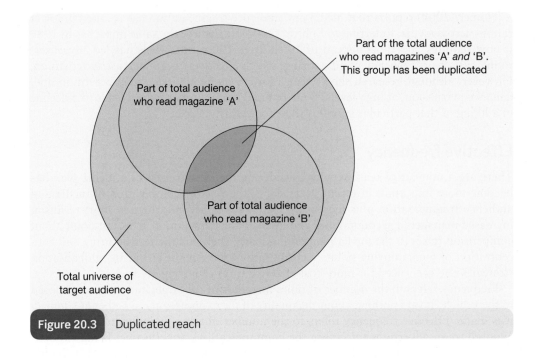

Figure 20.3   Duplicated reach

be exposed to an advertisement if it is placed in two or more media vehicles. Those who are exposed once constitute unduplicated reach. Those who are exposed to two or more of the advertisements are said to have been duplicated. Such overlapping of exposure, shown in Figure 20.3, is referred to as duplicated reach.

Duplication provides an indication of the levels of frequency likely in a particular media schedule. Duplication also increases costs, so if the objective of the plan is unduplicated reach, duplication brings waste and inefficiency. So media plans need to specify levels of duplicated and unduplicated reach.

Nevertheless, it is generally agreed that a certain level of GRPs is necessary for awareness to be achieved. It is also accepted that increased GRPs are necessary for other communications effects to be achieved. These levels of GRPs are referred to as *weights*, and the weight of a campaign reflects the objectives of the campaign. For example, a burst designed to achieve 85 per cent coverage with eight OTS would make a 680 rating, which is considered to be heavy. Such high ratings are often associated with car launches and, for example, products that are market leaders in their class, such as Nescafé or Pantene. An average rating would be one set to achieve a 400 rating, through 80 per cent coverage and five OTS over the length of a five-week period.

Our understanding about how learning works can assist the quest for effective frequency levels. The amount of learning in individuals increases up to a certain point, after which further exposure to material adds little to our overall level of knowledge. The same applies to the frequency level and the weightings applied to exposures.

Coverage and reach figures only show the numbers of people who are exposed to the vehicle. Effective reach measures those that are aware of the message. This ties in with the previous discussion on effective frequency levels. Essentially, media planners recognise that effective advertising requires that, in addition to the other aspects of advertising planning, a single transmission (reach) of an advertisement will be unproductive (Krugman, 1975; Naples, 1979). A minimum of two exposures and a reach threshold of 45 per cent of the target audience are required for reach to be regarded as effective (Murray and Jenkins, 1992).

Recency planning

A relatively new perspective to counter the effective frequency model emerged from the USA. This is known as *recency planning*, developed at a time when the weak theory of advertising started to gain greater acknowledgement as the most acceptable general interpretation of how advertising works. There is also a growing general acceptance that advertising is not the all-powerful communications tool it was once thought to be, and that the timing and presentation of advertising messages need to be reconsidered in the light of the way advertising is currently thought to work.

If it is accepted that consumer decision-making is more heavily influenced by 'running out' of particular products (opening empty fridges and store cupboards), than by exposure to advertising messages that are repeated remorselessly, then it follows that advertising needs to be directed at those people who are actually in the market and prepared to buy (Ephron, 1997).

As many fast-moving consumer goods products are purchased each week, Jones (1995) argues that a single exposure to an advertising message in the week before a purchase is to be made is more important than adding further messages, thereby increasing frequency. Recency planning considers reach to be more important than frequency.

The goal of this new approach is to reach those few consumers who are ready to buy (in the market). To do this the strategy requires reaching as many consumers as possible in as many weeks as possible (as far as the budget will extend). This requires a lower weekly weight and an extended number of weeks for a campaign. Advertising budgets are not cut; the fund is simply spread over a greater period of time. According to Ephron, this approach is quite different from effective frequency models and quite revolutionary (see Table 20.5).

This approach has been greeted with a number of objections. It has not been universally accepted, nor has it been widely implemented in the UK market. Gallucci (1997), among others, rejected the notion of recency planning because effectiveness will vary by brand, category and campaign. He claims that reaching 35 per cent of the Indonesian cola market once a week will not bring about the same result as reaching 65 per cent four times a week.

The development of banner advertising on the Internet raises interesting questions concerning effective frequency in new media. Is the frequency rate different and, if so, how many times is exposure required in order to be effective? Research into this area is in its infancy and no single, accepted body of knowledge exists. Broussard (2000) reports that, in a limited study concerning the comparison of a direct-response and a branding-based campaign on the Internet, the lowest cost per lead in the direct-response campaign

Table 20.5 The differences between effective frequency and recency planning

Recency planning model	Effective frequency model
Reach goal	Frequency goal
Continuity	Burst
One-week planning cycle	Four-week planning cycle
Lowest cost per reach point	Lowest cost per thousand
Low ratings	High ratings

Source: Adapted from Ephron (1997). Used by permission of WARC.

was achieved with low frequency levels. Results from the branding campaign suggest that up to seven exposures were necessary to improve brand awareness and knowledge of product attributes.

The debate concerning the development of recency planning and effective frequency will continue. What might be instrumental to the outcome of the debate will be a better understanding of how advertising works and the way buyers use advertising messages that are relevant to them.

Media usage and attitudes

A large number of people have a negative attitude towards advertising, and TV ads in particular. Advertising is regarded as both intrusive and pervasive. Beale (1997) developed a four-part typology of personality types based upon respondents' overall attitudes towards advertising (see Table 20.6). Through an understanding of the different characteristics, it is possible to make better (more informed) decisions about the most appropriate media channels to reach target audiences.

It is common for advertisers and media planners to discuss target markets in the context of heavy, medium, light and non-users of a product. In much the same way media planning considers the usage levels of viewers and readers. So, television audiences can be categorised as heavy, medium and light users based on the amount of time they spend watching television. One of the implications of this approach is that if light users consume so little television, then perhaps it is not worthwhile trying to communicate with them and resources should be directed to the medium and heavy user groups. The other side of the argument is that light users are very specific in the programmes that they watch, therefore it should be possible to target messages at them and a heavy number of GRPs should be used. However, questions still remain about the number of ratings necessary for effective reach in each of these categories.

Ostrow (1981) was the first to question how many rating points should be purchased. He said that, rather than use average frequency, a decision should be made about the minimum level of frequency necessary to achieve the objectives and then maximise reach at that level. Ostrow (1984) suggested that consideration of the issues set out in Table 20.7 would also assist.

The traditional approach of using television to reach target audiences to build awareness is still strong (Nelson-Field and Riebe, 2011). For example, Procter & Gamble, Unilever, Nestlé, Kellogg's and BT all spend in excess of 70 per cent of their budgets on television advertising. However, many major advertisers have moved

Table 20.6 Advertising attitudes for media determination

Cynics (22 per cent)	Enthusiasts (35 per cent)
This group perceives advertising as a crude sales tool. They are resentful and hostile to advertisements, although they are more likely to respond to advertisements placed in relevant media.	Enthusiasts like to get involved with advertising and creativity is perceived as an important part of the process. Apart from newspapers, which are regarded as boring, most types of media are acceptable.
Ambivalents (22 per cent)	**Acquiescents (21 per cent)**
While creativity is seen as superfluous and irrelevant, ambivalents are more disposed to information-based messages or those that promise cost savings. The best advertisements are those that use media that reinforce the message.	As the name suggests, this group of people has a reluctant approach to advertising. This means that they see advertising as unavoidable and an inevitable part of their world. Therefore, they are open to influence through a variety of media.

Source: Adapted from Beale (1997). Reproduced with the permission of the copyright owner, Haymarket Business Publications Limited.

Table 20.7 Issues to be considered when setting frequency levels

Issues	Low frequency	High frequency
Marketing issues		
Newness of the brand	Established	New
Market share	High	Low
Brand loyalty	Higher	Lower
Purchase and usage cycle times	Long	Short
Message issues Complexity	Simple	Complex
Uniqueness	More	Less
Image versus product sell	Product sell	Image
Message variation	Single message	Multiple messages
Media plan issues Clutter	Less	More
Editorial atmosphere	Appropriate	Not appropriate
Attentiveness of the media in the plan	Holds	Fails to hold
Number of media in the plan	Less	More

Source: Adapted from Setting frequency levels: an art or a science?, Marketing and Media Decisions, 24(4), pp. 9–11 (Ostrow, J.W. 1984), The Nielsen Company.

from a dominant above-the-line approach to one that embraces the dominance of linear media to drive reach, but also incorporates interactive media to reach smaller, niche audiences, and so increase frequency. These media are sometimes referred to as 'targeted media' (Gates-Sumner, 2014) with online video, mobile, gaming and social media sites prominent.

Efficiency

All promotional campaigns are constrained by a budget. Therefore a trade-off is required between the need to reach as many members of the target audience as possible (create awareness) and the need to repeat the message to achieve effective learning in the target audience. The decision about whether to emphasise reach or frequency is assisted by a consideration of the costs involved in each proposed schedule or media plan.

There are two main types of cost. The first of these is the *absolute cost*. This is the cost of the space or time required for the message to be transmitted. For example, the cost of a full-page, single-insertion, black and white advertisement, booked for a firm date in the *Sunday Times*, is £46,220 (January, 2016). Cash flow is affected by absolute costs.

In order that an effective comparison be made between media plans the *relative costs* of the schedules need to be understood. Relative costs are the costs incurred in making contact with each member of the target audience.

Traditionally, the magazine industry has based its calculations on the cost per thousand people reached (CPT). The original term derived from the print industry is CPM, where the 'M' refers to the Roman symbol for thousand. This term still has limited use but the more common term is CPT: CPT = space costs (absolute) × 1,000/circulation. The newspaper industry has used the milline rate, which is the cost per line of space per million circulation.

Broadcast audiences are measured by programme ratings (USA), and television audiences in the UK are measured by television ratings or TVRs. They are essentially the same in that they represent the percentage of television households that are tuned to a specific programme. The TVR is determined as follows:

$$TVR = \text{number of target TV households tuned into a programme}$$

$$\times \text{ } 100/\text{total number of target TV households}$$

A single TVR, therefore, represents 1 per cent of all the television households in a particular area that are tuned into a specific programme.

A further approach to measuring broadcast audiences uses the share of televisions that are tuned into a specific programme. This is compared with the total number of televisions that are actually switched on at that moment. This is expressed as a percentage and should be greater than the TVR. Share, therefore, reveals how well a programme is perceived by the available audience, not the potential audience. The question of how to measure relative costs in the broadcast industry has been answered by the use of the rating point or TVR. Cost per TVR is determined as follows:

$$\text{Cost per TVR} = \text{time costs(absolute costs)/TVR}$$

Intra-industry comparison of relative costs is made possible by using these formulae. Media plans that only involve broadcast or only use magazine vehicles can be evaluated to determine levels of efficiency. However, members of the target audience do not have discrete viewing habits; they have, as we saw earlier, complex media consumption patterns that involve exposure to a mix of media classes and vehicles. Advertisers respond to this mixture by placing advertisements in a variety of media, but have no way of comparing the relative costs on an inter-industry basis. In other words, the efficiency of using a *News at Ten* television slot cannot be compared with an insertion in *The Economist*. Attempts are being made to provide cross-industry media comparisons, but as yet no one formula has been provided that satisfies all demands. The television and newspaper industries, by using CPT in combination with costs per unit of time and space respectively, have attempted to forge a bridge that may be of use to their customers.

Finally, some comment on the concept of CPT is necessary, as there has been speculation about its validity as a comparative tool. There are a number of shortcomings associated with the use of CPT. For example, because each media class possesses particular characteristics, direct comparisons based on CPT alone are dangerous. The levels of wastage incurred in a plan, such as reaching people who are not targets or by measuring OTS for the vehicle and not the advertisement, may lead to an overestimate of the efficiency that a plan offers.

Similarly, the circulation of a magazine is not a true representation of the number of people who read or have an opportunity to see. Therefore, CPT may underestimate the efficiency unless the calculation can be adjusted to account for the extra or pass-along readership that occurs in reality. Having made these points, media buyers in the UK continue to use CPT and cost per rating point (CPRP) as a means of planning and buying time and space.

Target audiences and television programmes are priced according to the ratings they individually generate. The ratings affect the cost of buying a spot. The higher the rating, the higher the price will therefore be to place advertisements in the magazine or television programme.

Scholars' paper 20.3 | **Media planning for radio**

Pelsmacker, P. de, Geuens, M. and Vermeir, I. (2004) The importance of media planning, ad likeability and brand position for ad and brand recognition in radio spots, *International Journal of Market Research,* **46, Quarter 4, 465–78.**

These authors consider a range of issues associated with radio advertising in Belgium. The paper is welcome not only because it considers radio, which is often overlooked, but also because it explores media planning issues in the light of ad likeability. Among other things, they find that radio campaigns are more effective if the other instruments of the marketing mix are used to build a strong position for the brand and that likeable ads enhance the effectiveness of radio advertising.

Media buying: the block plan and automation

The prevailing media buying system involves the purchase of placements in blocks of thousands or millions of impressions in anticipation of market demand. These blocks are based on placement (of ads) within content. It is a hands-on process involving phone calls, discussions about the nature of the target audience and negotiating a price. This works but there is waste and inefficiency. According to Smith (cited by Warc, 2013a) the existing process for buying TV ads is described as 'labour intensive, very complicated, expensive, and challenging and not very user friendly'.

The block plan

The media planning concepts referred to in this chapter (reach, frequency, etc.) evolved to manage linear media. This interruption model has been the traditional way for linear media usage. This is predicated on the idea that the media manage audiences, influence what they see, when they see it and shape the pattern of their media behaviour. Advertisers therefore interrupted the audiences' viewing or reading to deliver product messages, for which, according to the advertiser's segmentation analysis, they were suitable recipients.

The planning approach for linear media has been based on the development of what is known as the 'block plan'. In this approach the goal was to place messages in locations where the 'target' audience was most likely to notice and be receptive to them. This required the construction of a complex, coloured spreadsheet containing the detail of reach, frequency, costs and timing (Morris, 2011). The block plan accounted for the use of paid media, that is space and time rented from media owners.

Technological advances, however, have brought about huge changes in the types of available media and the way in which people now use media. People use linear media for information and entertainment. Now they are active participants as interactivity enables user-generated content through search, downloading, sharing, publication and involvement in virtual communities. Advertisers should not try to interrupt participants but to listen and facilitate interaction. People use media to discover new things, to play and be entertained, to share with like-minded tribes and communities, and to engage and express themselves. Most people consume a mixture of linear and interactive media, with particular audiences skewed more to one rather than the other. So, although the selection of a media mix is complicated by the variety, there is also an unanswered question about how advertising in one channel influences sales in another channel (Dinner et al., 2014).

The argument that linear media advertising is in permanent decline is a fallacy, proved by the continuing investment by a huge range of brands in television advertising. There has certainly been a readjustment of media budgets to reflect contemporary media usage, but the new is not going to wipe out the old.

The early years of online and interactive media saw attempts to use the established methods of measurement and evaluation. However, it became clear that these methods were not entirely suitable, simply because interactive media are used differently. Instead of measuring how often a message is delivered or the share of audience reached with a message, it becomes more important to measure consumers' expectations and their interaction with brands. Put another way, these might be considered as dwell time (the amount of time consumers spend with a brand), dwell quality (a consumer's perceived richness resulting from brand interaction) and dwell insight (what motivates a consumer to spend time with a brand).

What does this mean for the block plan? It means that paid media now need to be augmented with earned and owned media. This means using media that work continually, not just at particular campaign points or bursts of six weeks. With communications continually switched 'on', all the paid, owned and earned media need to be interlinked, or integrated. It is often the case that the role of paid media changes from one of leading communications activities to one that supplements the entire media activity designed to reflect an audience's relationship, levels of advocacy and journey with a brand. A block plan cannot reflect this and although it continues to have a presence within agencies as a support for paid media activities, it is not the bedrock of media planning that it used to be.

Automation – programmatic

The development and use of automated media buying platforms was initially focused on online display ads, but this has been extended into TV and linear media, plus video, and mobile. This growth is due to the time and resources that can be saved, the reduction in human error and waste, and the improved targeting and facility to run campaigns across a greater number of media (see Viewpoint 20.3).

Apart from these efficiency gains, the growth of automated media buying for linear media is likely to impact on media planners as there is less hands-on activity, and a need for increased strategic and advisory roles.

Programmatic advertising in the UK was worth over £1 billion in 2014, according to IAB, cited by Gray (2015), and 30 per cent of this was spent on mobile. Programmatic involves the automation of large sections of the media planning and buying and selling process and it also impacts on the creative element that is presented. Norman (2015: 8) refers to programmatic trading in the context of reserve, auction and real-time markets. He states that the automation of both the buy-side and sell-side serves to link inventory supply and demand: 'Trades are executed subject to demand and yield optimization rules set by the two parties.'

Instead of buying programmes, programmatic is about buying audiences, wherever they appear. A variation of programmatic is real-time bidding (RTB), the auction dimension. This allows advertisers to buy on an impression-by-impression basis and to target specific online audiences on web pages as they browse. RTB also reduces operational issues associated with invoicing individual campaigns and tagging buying space when buying from several hundred companies.

Viewpoint 20.3   Brands start to automate the ad buying

Brands have been cautious about their investment in programmatic. For example, B&Q increased its investment in programmatic in 2014 as a form of direct response activity. That was extended in 2015 to brand awareness. B&Q used online programmatic display advertising for its kitchen campaign and has seen an increase in perception change and purchase consideration, as well as a 50 per cent reduction in cost per lead (CPL) in less than a year.

O2 was also cautious as it introduced programmatic display advertising across several campaigns. At the mental health charity Mind, however, the majority of their advertising is programmatic. They say this is because it can eliminate wastage and allows them to buy online advertising that reaches the right audience, at the right time, in the right environment and at the right price. For example, when the media feature mental health issues, Mind add this into their programmatic campaign in order to be visible in the same places where these conversations are occurring.

Exhibit 20.4	**Programmatic TV ad buying**
	Source: Shutterstock.com/Stokkete.

Heineken USA now spends 10 per cent of its ad budget on programmatic channels. In 2014 the company allocated 25 per cent of its ad spending to digital media for its portfolio of brands. This was up 20 per cent on the previous year. It spent 10 per cent of that budget on programmatic channels, or Web-based tools and software that should help Heineken buy ads more efficiently and better measure their effectiveness.

Brands such as Allianz, mobile operator 3, and Sky have been testing it with a view to cutting waste and reducing their cost per acquisition. RTB enables them to test and evaluate their creatives more frequently and at a lower cost.

One of the first signs of programmatic TV advertising involved the agency Interpublic, when they collaborated with broadcasters in New York to develop an automated TV ad buying system. The system was designed to enable a media buyer to see the available stock at each TV or radio outlet and to select ad placements based on data that the ad buyer has on its customers and their media habits. Unlike the automated buying systems used for interactive display ads, which work on an auction format, the TV system was expected to continue with media companies controlling the price of their ads.

Source: Shields (2015); Smith (2015); WARC (2013b).

Question: Why might brands be wary of programmatic advertising?

Task: Choose a category (e.g. haircare, fast food, cars) and find out the extent to which brands used programmatic ads last year, compared with the previous year.

The decision to place online ads is complicated not just by deciding which of the various formats should be used, but also where, when and how the ads need to be placed. The huge number of options includes portals, social media and community sites, plus search engines, online magazines, and shopping comparison sites.

The cross-media mix

Advertisers selecting media across the linear and interactive spectrum face a complex decision. Cross-media campaigns seek to maximise sales effectiveness yet research by Taylor et al. (2013) shows that although both online and television advertising can drive sales among those who are reached, they found no evidence of cross-media synergy effects. What they found was that a 'mixed-media campaign could well be successful if it broadens reach cost effectively but still may not generate additional sales synergies' (p. 209).

As technology advances and the number of interactive media increases, how should management develop its media mix so that it remains current yet meets consumers changing media behaviours? Any change to an established media mix can be risky and making a judgement about different options and permutations consumes resources. Using ideas advanced at Coca-Cola for managing content, Southgate and Svendsen (2015) propose the use of the 70/20/10 formula.

The 70 per cent zone requires that budget is used to support a mix of low-risk, safe, established media. These are likely to involve a proven mix of media channels, which will vary across categories and countries. So, a new service brand in Japan might use TV, event sponsorship, mobile display and QR codes, whereas a brand in a considered purchase category in Germany could well use a mix of print, sports sponsorship, online search and online display (Southgate and Svendsen, 2015).

The 20 per cent of the budget should be allocated to using innovative, yet low-risk media. This should include the adoption of media that are known to be effective, but the risk involves increasing the amount allocated. Another approach might be to adopt a channel that was experimented with previously, or where there is little research evidence to support the initiative. For many this could include social media where questions about what the return on investment should be, or what is the right content, remain unanswered for many organisations. It might involve branching out within a familiar channel. For example, sponsoring a music festival for the first time when you have previously been known for associations with sport.

Southgate and Svendsen (2015) argue that the 10 per cent zone is for pure experimentation with new and emerging channels. Typically mobile, apps, QR codes and Pinterest pages would fall into this zone, at the time of writing, but whatever the media activity it should always complement brand and campaign objectives. The goal is to use deliberately allocated time and money to experiment with and increase knowledge about unknown, new and ground-breaking media. It could be that media in this zone transfer next year to the 20 per cent zone. See Viewpoint 20.4 for an example of this approach.

Viewpoint 20.4   Sheilas' Wheels reveal use of the formula

The 70/20/10 media formula can be observed in practice with Sheilas' Wheels. This is a UK insurance brand targeted at women. When its car insurance offering was first launched in 2005, 30 per cent of its TV budget was invested in sponsoring television drama. In particular Living TV's drama strand placed the brand next to shows such as *Charmed*, *CSI* and *Grey's Anatomy*. The deal covered 15 hours of drama every week and the success of this work led to sponsorship of *Loose Women* on ITV.

Exhibit 20.5	**Sheilas' Wheels**
	Source: Courtesy of esure group.

At the time most of its competitors were clearly focused, almost exclusively, on TV spot advertising. Television sponsorship was therefore considered to be highly innovative. Sheilas' Wheels reached 75 per cent awareness within three months, and bettered its internal sales targets by 65 per cent during the first year. Sheilas' Wheels built on this success by increasing its use of sponsorship. In 2008 when the company launched its home insurance offering, it made sponsorship its largest media platform and invested £10 million in one of the UK's biggest television sponsorships, namely the ITV National Weather broadcast.

In the space of just a few years sponsorship became an established, low-risk and important 70 per cent activity for the brand.

Source: Southgate and Svendsen (2015); www.getmemedia.com/.

Question: Discuss ways in which the allocation of media using this type of formula might be both positive and disadvantageous.

Task: In a country of your choice, find two other examples where insurance brands appear to have concentrated their media spend.

Scholars' paper 20.4 | **Cross-media synergies**

Assael, H. (2010) From silos to synergy: a fifty-year review of cross-media research shows synergy has yet to achieve its full potential, *Journal of Advertising Research,* **27(4), 63–9.**

An important paper for all of those interested in cross-media activities, including its evolution, measurement, form, research and in particular the synergies that might be generated. The paper even touches on IMC.

See also: Taylor, J., Kennedy, R., Mcdonald, C., Larguinat, L., El Ouarzazi, Y. and Haddad, N. (2013) Is the multi-platform whole more powerful than its separate parts? *Journal of Advertising Research,* 53(2), 200–11.

Media source effects

Media planning is not a purely quantitative exercise. The richness of a media plan can be seen when there is evidence that qualitative elements of the media vehicles have been accommodated. The selection of vehicles needs to be based on a vehicle's environment and the way it can affect message perception and decoding.

An advertisement placed in one vehicle, such as *Cosmopolitan*, may have a different impact on an identical audience to that obtained if the same advertisement was placed in *Options*. This differential level of 'power of impact' can be caused by a number of source factors, of which a vehicle's atmosphere, technical and reproduction characteristics, and the associated audience and product characteristics are prime. These are considered in Table 20.8.

Scheduling

The way a media mix is scheduled needs to account for three elements: the objectives, purchasing cycles and level of involvement.

Effective scheduling seeks to achieve the media objectives at the lowest possible cost. If the advertising objectives are basically short term, then the placements should be concentrated over a short period of time. Conversely, if awareness is to be built over a longer term, perhaps building a new brand, then the frequency of the placements need not be so intensive and can be spread over a period so that learning can occur incrementally.

The optimum number of exposures within a purchasing cycle is thought to be between three and ten, in the packaged goods category. The longer the cycle, the less the frequency required.

If the objective of the plan is to create awareness, then when there is high involvement, few repetitions will be required compared with low-involvement decisions. This is because people who are highly involved actively seek information and need little assistance to digest relevant information. Likewise, where there is low involvement, attitudes develop from use of the product, so frequency is important to maintain awareness and to prompt trial.

Timing of placements

The timing of placements is dependent on a number of factors. One of the overriding constraints is the size of the media budget and the impact that certain placement patterns can bring to an organisation's cash flow. Putting cost to one side, many researchers

Table 20.8 Media source effects

Qualitative element		Explanation
Vehicle atmosphere	Editorial tone	The editorial views or the overall tone of the material might clash or be incompatible with a client's message.
	Vehicle expertise	Websites, magazines and journals often reflect a level of expertise and represent source credibility. These can be seen to be important sources of credible information, are more relaxed and open to persuasion.
	Vehicle prestige	Vehicle prestige can be important where vehicle status is important.
Technical and reproduction characteristics	Technical factors	The impact of a message can be influenced by the way colour, movement or sound is utilised.
	Exposure opportunities	Each vehicle has several time slots or spaces that provide opportunities for increased exposure (e.g. the back pages of magazines or facing matter often command premium advertising rates).
	Perception opportunities	The use of strong attention-grabbing elements such as loud or distinctive music or controversial headlines can help audiences perceive a message among their other activities.
Audience/product characteristics	Audience/vehicle fit	The media plan should provide the best match between the target market and the audience reached by the vehicles in the media schedule.
	Nature of the product	Expose audiences to a message at times that coincide with their preferred viewing/reading patterns.
	Vehicle mood effects	An audience's emotional status during a film or television programme (e.g. tense, relaxed, involved, anxious) can influence message perception.

have identified and labelled different scheduling patterns. There are many approaches to scheduling but continuity, flighting and pulsing as set out in Figure 20.4 represent the main approaches.

Key points

- Media planning is concerned with the selection and scheduling of media vehicles designed to carry an advertiser's message.
- The variety of media is rapidly increasing and is referred to as 'media fragmentation'. This makes the media planner's task increasingly complicated because the size of audience available to each medium reduces, making the number of media required to reach a target market increasingly large.

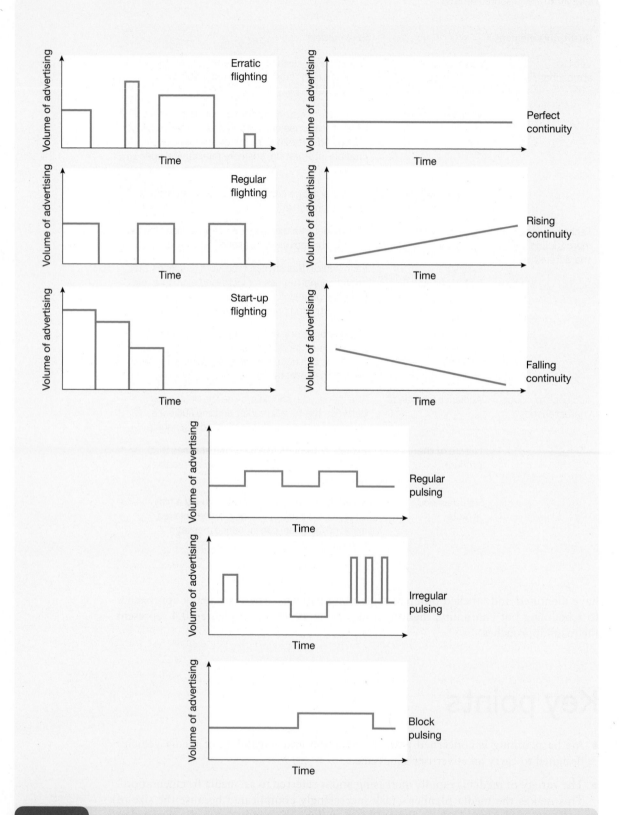

Figure 20.4   Flighting patterns

- Media richness theory (MRT) holds that there is a hierarchy of media ranging from the richest media such as personal or face-to-face encounters through to lean media typified by single sheets of text-based information.

- Social influence theory (SIT) complements MRT as it also assumes that the relatively objective features of media do influence how individuals perceive and use them. The technology acceptance model (TAM) relates to the perceived usefulness and perceived ease of use as the main issues that are considered when selecting media.

- There are several fundamental concepts that underpin the way in which media should be selected and included in a media plan. These concepts refer to the percentage of the target audiences reached, the number of times they receive a message, the number of media they are exposed to and various measures associated with the efficiency with which media deliver messages.

- The greater the number of exposures, the more likely an individual is to learn about the message content. The question is how many times should a message be repeated for effective learning to occur (i.e. what is the effective frequency)?

- Recency planning is a reach-based model and argues that a single exposure to an advertising message in the week before a purchase is more important than adding further messages, thus increasing frequency. Recency planning considers reach to be more important than frequency.

- The efficiency of a schedule refers to the costs involved in delivering messages. There are two main types of cost. The first of these is the *absolute cost*, which is the cost of the space or time required for the message to be transmitted. The second concerns the costs incurred in making contact with each member of the target audience. These are referred to as the *relative costs* and are used to compare different media schedules.

- The magazine industry uses calculations based on the cost per thousand people reached (CPT). Broadcast audiences are measured by television ratings or TVRs. These represent the percentage of television households that are tuned to a specific programme.

- The scheduling of a media plan seeks to establish when the messages are transmitted in order that the media objectives be achieved at the lowest possible cost. Various factors affect the schedule: the campaign objectives; the purchasing cycle; the level of involvement; and the characteristics of the target audiences and their preferred programmes. The selection of compatible 'spots' is likely to improve message delivery considerably.

- Developing a block plan to manage the media mix is only applicable to managing paid media. The incorporation of social media and search render the block plan redundant.

- Different media impact on audiences in different ways because of three main factors. These are the *vehicle atmosphere* – editorial tone, vehicle expertise, vehicle prestige; their *technical and reproduction characteristics* – technical factors, exposure opportunities, perception opportunities; and finally their *audience and product characteristics* – audience/vehicle fit, nature of the product.

Review questions

Kärcher case questions

1. Identify the key contextual elements facing Kärcher's media selection decisions.

2. What were the main media planning tasks facing Kärcher and how did they overcome them?

3. Was reach or frequency the primary goal of the Kärcher media strategy?

4. How might planning for interactive media differ from that for linear media? What were the roles of these two media formats in the Kärcher campaign?

5. How might an understanding of media source effects influence the use of media in the Kärcher campaign?

General questions

1. Explain the concept of effective frequency and why frequency levels are so important.

2. Compare media richness theory, social influence theory and the technology adoption model.

3. If the rate at which information decays within individuals is known, then the task of the media planner is simply to place messages at suitable intervals in the path of decay. Discuss.

4. Why might reach and frequency be inappropriate when developing media plans today?

5. What is the block plan and why is it of less use today than it used to be?

References

Anon (2009) Latitude: Anglian, *Revolution; Success Stories 2009*, December 4–5.

Anon (2015) *The Sex Pistols – No Fun*, Issue 18, retrieved 3 May 2015 from www.punk77.co.uk/groups/sex.htm.

Assael, H. (2010) From silos to synergy: a fifty-year review of cross-media research shows synergy has yet to achieve its full potential, *Journal of Advertising Research*, 27(4), 63–9.

Batra, R. and Ray, M.L. (1986) Affective responses mediating acceptance of advertising, *Journal of Consumer Research*, 13 (September), 234–49.

Beale, C. (1997) Study reveals negativity towards ads, *Campaign*, 28 November, 8.

Benjamin, K. (2009) Harmonising mail with other media, *Marketing*, 14 October, 15–17.

Broussard, G. (2000) How advertising frequency can work to build online effectiveness, *International Journal of Market Research*, 42(4), 439–57.

Cheong, Y., De Gregorio, F. and Kim, K. (2011) The power of reach and frequency in the age of digital advertising: offline and online media demand different metrics, *Journal of Advertising Research*, 50(4), 403–15.

Daft, R.L. and Lengel, R.H. (1984) Information richness: a new approach to managerial behavior and organizational design, in *Research in Organizational Behavior*, 6 (eds L.L. Cummings and B.M. Straw), Homewood, IL: JAI Press, 191–233.

Dahlen, M. and Edenius, M. (2007) When is advertising advertising? Comparing responses to non-traditional and traditional advertising media, *Journal of Current Issues and Research in Advertising*, 29(1), 33–42.

Dinner, I.M., Heerde, H.J. van and Neslin, S.A. (2014) Driving online and offline sales: The cross-channel effects of traditional, online display, and paid search advertising, *Journal of Marketing Research*, 51(5), 527–45.

Duarte, D.L. and Snyder, N.T. (2001) *Mastering Virtual Team*, 2nd edition, San Francisco, CA: Jossey-Bass.

Ephron, E. (1997) Recency planning, *Admap*, February, 32–4.

Ephron, E. (2003) The paradox of product placement, *Mediaweek*, 2 June, 20.

Fulk, J., Schmitz, J.A. and Steinfield, C.W. (1990) A social influence model of technology use, in *Organizations and Communication Technology* (eds J. Fulk and C. Steinfield), Newbury Park, CA: Sage.

Gallucci, P. (1997) There are no absolutes in media planning, *Admap,* July/August, 39–43.

Gates-Sumner, L. (2014) Sharpening the arrow: the value of modern targeting approaches, *Millward Brown,* retrieved 14 November 2014 from www.millwardbrown.com/global-navigation/insights/insights/page/5.

George, J.F., Carlson, J.R. and Valacich, J.S. (2013) Media selection as a strategic component of communication, *MIS Quarterly,* 37(4), 233–51.

Gray, R. (2015) Robotic precision, *The Marketer,* May/June, 34–7.

Ha, L. and McCann, K. (2008) An integrated model of advertising clutter in offline and online media, *International Journal of Advertising,* 27(4), 569–92

Hammer, P., Riebe, E. and Kennedy, R. (2009) How clutter affects advertising effectiveness, *Journal of Advertising Research,* 49(2), 159–63

Homer, P. (2009) Product placements: the impact of placement type and repetition on attitude, *Journal of Advertising,* 38(3), 21–31.

Jones, P. (1995) *When Ads Work: New Proof that Advertising Triggers Sales,* New York: Simon & Schuster, Free Press/Lexington Books.

Keaveney, S.M. (1995) Consumer switching behavior in service industries: an exploratory study, *Journal of Marketing,* 59(2), 71–82.

King, R.C. and Xia, W. (1997) Media appropriateness: effects of experience on communication media choice, *Decision Sciences,* 28(4), 877–909.

Krugman, H.E. (1965) The impact of television advertising: learning without involvement, *Public Opinion Quarterly,* 29 (Fall), 349–56.

Krugman, H.E. (1972) How potent is TV advertising? Cited in du Plessis (1998).

Krugman, H.E. (1975) What makes advertising effective? *Harvard Business Review,* 53(2), 96–103.

Lloyd, D.W. and Clancy, K.J. (1991) CPMs versus CPMis: implications for media planning, *Journal of Advertising Research,* 31(4), 34–44.

Longhurst, P. (2006) Budgeting for online: is it any different? *Admap,* November, 36–7.

Mansfield, B. (2013) Elvis Presley tops list of digitally streamed artists, *USA Today,* 3 October, retrieved 3 May 2015 from www.usatoday.com/story/life/music/2013/10/03/elvis-presley-tops-digitally-streamed-artists-soundexchange/2909811/.

McGrath, J.E. and Hollingshead, A.B. (1993) Putting the 'group' back into group support systems: some theoretical issues about dynamic processes in groups with technological enhancements, in *Group Support Systems: New Perspectives* (eds L.M. Jessup and J.S. Valacich, New York: Macmillan, 78–9.

McLuhan, M. (1966) *Understanding Media: The Extensions of Man,* New York: McGraw-Hill.

Morris, R. (2011) The modern media mix, *Campaignlive,* 8 July 2011, retrieved 23 April 2012 from www.brandrepublic.com/features/1079039/Modern-Media-mix/?DCMP=ILC-SEARCH.

Murray, G.B. and Jenkins, J.R.G. (1992) The concept of effective reach in advertising. *Journal of Advertising Research,* 32(3), May/June, 34–42.

Naples, M.J. (1979) *Effective Frequency: The Relationship Between Frequency and Advertising Effectiveness,* New York: Association of National Advertisers.

Nelson-Field, K. and Riebe, E. (2011) The impact of media fragmentation on audience targeting: An empirical generalisation approach, *Journal of Marketing Communications,* 17(1), 51–67.

Norman, R. (2015) Interaction – 2015, *GroupM,* retrieved 11 April from www.groupm.com/sites/default/files/extra-files/GroupM_Interaction_January2015.pdf.

Ostrow, J.W. (1981) What level of frequency? *Advertising Age,* November, 13–18.

Ostrow, J.W. (1984) Setting frequency levels: an art or a science? *Marketing and Media Decisions,* 24(4), 9–11.

Pelsmacker, P. de and Neijens, P.C. (2009) Call for papers – Journal of Marketing Communications – special issue on new advertising formats, *Journal of Marketing Communications,* 15(2–3), 205–6.

Pelsmacker, P. de Geuens, M. and Vermeir, I. (2004) The importance of media planning, ad likeability and brand position for ad and brand recognition in radio spots, *International Journal of Market Research,* 46, Quarter 4, 465–78.

Plessis, E. du (1998) Memory and likeability: keys to understanding ad effects, *Admap,* July/August, 42–6.

Poynor, R. (2012) *The Art of Punk and the Punk Aesthetic, The Design Observer Group,* 14 October, retrieved 3 May 2015 from http://designobserver.com/feature/the-art-of-punk-and-the-punk-aesthetic/36708.

Shields, M. (2015) Heineken partners with TubeMogul, now spends 10% of ad budget via programmatic channels, *The Wall Street Journal,* 3 February, retrieved 17 March from http://blogs.wsj.com/cmo/2015/02/03/heineken-partners-with-tubemogul-now-spends-10-of-ad-budget-via-programmatic-channels/.

Simon, H. (1972) Theories of bounded rationality, in *Decision and Organisation* (eds C.B. McGuire and R. Radner), London: North-Holland, 161–76.

Simon, H. (1987) Bounded rationality, in *The New Palgrave* (eds J. Eatwell, M. Milgate and P. Newman), London: Macmillan.

Smith, N. (2015) What's next for programmatic advertising? *Marketing Week,* 25 February, retrieved 17 March 2015 from www.marketingweek.com/2015/02/25/whats-next-for-programmatic-advertising/.

Southgate, D. and Svendsen, J. (2015) Changing channels with confidence: a structure for innovation, *Millward Brown,* retrieved 30 January 2015 from www.millwardbrown.com/Insights/Point-of-View/Changing_Channels_with_Confidence/default.aspx.

Srinivasan, M. (1996) New insights into switching behaviour: marketers can now put a numerical value on loyalty, *Marketing Research,* 8(3), 26–34.

Sylvester, R. (2013) Brand you, in C.F. Radbill, *Introduction to the Music Industry: An Entrepeneurial Approach,* New York: Routledge.

Taylor, J., Kennedy, R., Mcdonald, C., Larguinat, L., El Ouarzazi, Y. and Haddad, N. (2013) Is the multi-platform whole more powerful than its separate parts? *Journal of Advertising Research,* 53(2), 200–11.

Warc (2013a) Automated TV buying moves closer, retrieved 14 November 2014 from www.warc.com/LatestNews/News/Automated_TV_buying_moves_closer.news?ID=31820.

Warc (2013b) Media planners take new role, 8 April 2013, retrieved 14 November 2014 from www.warc.com/Latestnews/News/EmailNews.news?ID=31234&Origin=WARCNewsEmail.

Author index

Subject index